T0211067

Lecture Notes in Artificial Intelligence 10395

Subseries of Lecture Notes in Computer Science

More information about this series at http://www.springer.com/series/1244

Leonardo de Moura (Ed.)

Automated Deduction – CADE 26

26th International Conference on Automated Deduction
Gothenburg, Sweden, August 6–11, 2017
Proceedings

 Springer

Editor
Leonardo de Moura
Microsoft Research
Redmond, WA
USA

ISSN 0302-9743   ISSN 1611-3349 (electronic)
Lecture Notes in Artificial Intelligence
ISBN 978-3-319-63045-8   ISBN 978-3-319-63046-5 (eBook)
DOI 10.1007/978-3-319-63046-5

Library of Congress Control Number: 2017946063

LNCS Sublibrary: SL7 – Artificial Intelligence

Printed on acid-free paper

This Springer imprint is published by Springer Nature
The registered company is Springer International Publishing AG
The registered company address is: Gewerbestrasse 11, 6330 Cham, Switzerland

Preface

This volume contains the papers presented at the 26th International Conference on Automated Deduction (CADE 26), held between August 6 and August 11, 2017 in Gothenburg, Sweden. CADE is the major forum for the presentation of research in all aspects of automated deduction.

The Program Committee decided to accept 26 regular papers and 5 system descriptions from a total of 69 submissions. Each submission was reviewed by at least 3 Program Committee members and external reviewers. We would like to thank all the members of the Program Committee for their careful and thoughtful deliberations. Many thanks to Andrei Voronkov for providing the EasyChair system greatly facilitated the reviewing process, the electronic Program Committee meeting, and the preparation of the proceedings. In addition to the contributed papers, the program included three invited lectures by Philippa Gardner, Grant Passmore, and June Andronick. We thank the invited speakers not only for their presentations, but also for contributing full papers to the proceedings.

In addition, a diverse range of affiliated events took place. Five workshops:

- ARCADE: Automated Reasoning: Challenges, Applications, Directions, Exemplary Achievements
- PCR 2017: Workshop on Parallel Constraint Reasoning
- ThEdu 2017: Theorem Prover Components for Educational Software
- HCVS: Horn Clauses for Verification and Synthesis
- Vampire 2017: The 4th Vampire Workshop

One tutorial:

- Certified Functional (Co)programming with Isabelle/HOL

The CADE ATP System Competition (CASC) was also held. All this help to make the conference a success.

During the conference, the Herbrand Award for Distinguished Contributions to Automated Reasoning was presented to Lawrence Paulson for his pioneering contributions to automation in proof assistants and the foundations of formal security protocol verification as well as his impressive formalizations of deep mathematical theories. The Selection Committee for the Herbrand Award consisted of the CADE 26 Program Committee members, the trustees of CADE Inc., and the Herbrand Award winners of the last ten years. The Herbrand Award ceremony and the acceptance speech by Lawrence Paulson were part of the conference program.

Many people helped to make CADE 26 a success. We are very grateful to Wolfgang Ahrendt and Moa Johansson (CADE general chairs), Magnus Myreen (publicity chair) and Anneli Andersson for the tremendous effort they devoted to the organization of the conference. We also like to thank Philipp Ruemmer (workshop chair), all the individual workshop organizers, and tutorial speakers. Last but not least, we thank all authors who submitted papers to CADE 26 and all conference participants.

June 2017   Leonardo de Moura

Organization

Program Committee

Clark Barrett	Stanford University, USA
Christoph Benzmüller	Freie Universität Berlin, Germany
Nikolaj Bjorner	Microsoft Research
Jasmin Christian Blanchette	Inria Nancy and LORIA, France
Maria Paola Bonacina	Università degli Studi di Verona, Italy
Leonardo de Moura	Microsoft Research
Hans De Nivelle	Institute of Computer Science, University of Wroclaw, Poland
Stephanie Delaune	CNRS, IRISA, France
Gilles Dowek	Inria and ENS Paris-Saclay, France
Amy Felty	University of Ottawa, Canada
Silvio Ghilardi	Università degli Studi di Milano, Italy
Marijn Heule	The University of Texas at Austin, USA
Reiner Hähnle	Technical University of Darmstadt, Germany
Moa Johansson	Chalmers Tekniska Högskola, Sweden
Dejan Jovanović	SRI International, USA
Deepak Kapur	University of New Mexico, USA
Konstantin Korovin	Manchester University, UK
Laura Kovacs	Vienna University of Technology, Austria
Christopher Lynch	Clarkson University, USA
Assia Mahboubi	Inria, France
Aart Middeldorp	University of Innsbruck, Austria
Dale Miller	Inria and LIX/Ecole Polytechnique, France
Albert Oliveras	Technical University of Catalonia, Spain
Lawrence Paulson	University of Cambridge, UK
Ruzica Piskac	Yale University, USA
Philipp Ruemmer	Uppsala University, Sweden
Renate A. Schmidt	University of Manchester, UK
Stephan Schulz	DHBW Stuttgart, Germany
Roberto Sebastiani	DISI, University of Trento, Italy
Viorica Sofronie-Stokkermans	University of Koblenz-Landau, Germany
Geoff Sutcliffe	University of Miami, USA
Cesare Tinelli	University of Iowa, USA
Ashish Tiwari	SRI International, USA
Andrei Voronkov	University of Manchester, UK
Christoph Weidenbach	Max Planck Institute for Informatics, Germany
Freek Wiedijk	Radboud University Nijmegen, The Netherlands

Additional Reviewers

Alagi, Gábor
Aravantinos, Vincent
Audemard, Gilles
Avanzini, Martin
Bansal, Kshitij
Berdine, Josh
Bertrand, Nathalie
Beyersdorff, Olaf
Blanco, Roberto
Brotherston, James
Bubel, Richard
Carette, Jacques
Chaudhuri, Kaustuv
Claus, Maximilian
Dinsdale-Young, Thomas W.
Echenim, Mnacho
Escobar, Santiago
Felgenhauer, Bertram
Flores-Montoya, Antonio
Frumin, Daniil
Färber, Michael
Gianola, Alessandro
Graham-Lengrand, Stéphane
Griggio, Alberto
Gurfinkel, Arie
Hladik, Jan
Hojjat, Hossein
Huisman, Marieke
Hustadt, Ullrich
Höfner, Peter
Kaliszyk, Cezary
Katz, Guy
Kiesl, Benjamin
Kohlhase, Michael
Kop, Cynthia
Letz, Reinhold

Lobo Valbuena, Irene
Lonsing, Florian
Magron, Victor
McMillan, Ken
Nakazawa, Koji
Narboux, Julien
Noetzli, Andres
Passmore, Grant
Popescu, Andrei
Pratt-Hartmann, Ian
Reger, Giles
Reis, Giselle
Reynolds, Andrew
Rodríguez Carbonell, Enric
Rossi, Matteo
Schlatte, Rudolf
Schürmann, Carsten
Sighireanu, Mihaela
Sinz, Carsten
Smallbone, Nicholas
Steen, Alexander
Sturm, Thomas
Suda, Martin
Syeda, Hira
Teucke, Andreas
Thiemann, René
Tourret, Sophie
Trentin, Patrick
Van Oostrom, Vincent
Veanes, Margus
Voigt, Marco
Wand, Daniel
Wisniewski, Max
Xue, Anton
Zeljic, Aleksandar

Contents

Reasoning About Concurrency in High-Assurance, High-Performance Software Systems

June Andronick[✉]

Data61, CSIRO (formerly NICTA) and UNSW, Sydney, Australia
june.andronick@data61.csiro.au

Abstract. We describe our work in the Trustworthy Systems group at Data61 (formerly NICTA) in reasoning about concurrency in high-assurance, high-performance software systems, in which concurrency may come from three different sources: multiple cores, interrupts and application-level interleaving.

1 Formal Verification – Mentality Shift

Recent years have seen a shift in the perception of formal software verification in the academic community and, to some more emerging extent, in the industrial community. The strength of a mathematical proof to guarantee the correctness, security and safety of programs deployed in high-assurance systems has made its way from utopia to reality, and the absence of such strong evidence will hopefully soon be considered negligence for critical systems.

This shift was possible thanks to highly successful verified artifacts, such as the CompCert compiler [16] and the seL4 operating system (OS) kernel [14,15]. A remaining grand challenge in formal software verification is *concurrency reasoning*, much harder than sequential reasoning because of the explosion of the number of interleaved executions that need to be considered.

Concurrency in software systems can have three different sources: multiple cores, interrupts and application-level interleaving. In this paper we first briefly explain these kinds of concurrency and their challenges, and we then describe our recent and current work in providing concurrency reasoning framework and verifying concurrent software systems in these three areas.

2 Software Systems and Concurrency – Background

Multicore platforms provide a computing power boost that is hard to resist for a very competitive software system market, even for high-security solutions. Code execution can be parallelised on different cores, and the challenge, for implementation as well as verification, is to ensure safe sharing between cores. This can be done using locking mechanisms: a core can access shared data only after acquiring a lock guaranteeing that no other core is manipulating the data

© Springer International Publishing AG 2017
L. de Moura (Ed.): CADE 2017, LNAI 10395, pp. 1–7, 2017.
DOI: 10.1007/978-3-319-63046-5_1

at the same time. This effectively eliminates concurrency, but has a performance impact and bears liveness risks (e.g. potential for deadlocks). Another option is to let cores access shared data without any locking, relying on more indirect arguments that the resulting race conditions are still safe. This requires much more careful reasoning.

Interrupts introduce a different kind of concurrency, where interleaving is *controlled* in the sense that the only thing that truly happens in parallel with code execution is the occurrence of interrupts (i.e. a flag's being set in hardware). The code being executed can still be stopped at any time, and control switched to handler code that will service the interrupt; but the execution of the handler code is then sequential until the return from interrupt (except when nested interrupts are supported, in which case further interleaving is allowed). Handler code and "normal" code may share data (e.g. the list of runnable threads), whose access needs to be carefully designed. Once again, there is a radical way of ensuring safe sharing: manually switching off interrupts during manipulation of data shared with handlers. However, that has a performance and latency impact.

Application-level, or user-level, concurrency is another form of controlled concurrency. In an OS-based system, the OS kernel provides hardware abstraction primitives, such as threads, to applications. Threads run concurrently in the sense that the OS kernel will simulate parallel execution through scheduling and time sharing between threads. For better latency, threads are often preemptible by the kernel: their execution can be paused at any time by the kernel, their execution context saved, and execution switched to another thread. Safe memory sharing between threads can also be handled via locking mechanisms, where more feature-rich sychronisation mechanisms can be provided by the kernel.

For all these types of concurrency, the general trend on the reasoning and verification side is to aim for limiting the concurrency as much as possible: local operations can be parallelised, but sharing should be done only when mutual exclusion can be guaranteed (by locking or other indirect arguments). This approach is the basis of many existing verification frameworks and verified systems (e.g. [8,9,11,18]).

However, on the implementation side, the trend goes for more racing to improve performance: some systems need to run with interrupts enabled as much as possible, or to run some critical code unlocked. We are targeting such real-world systems, where the possible races need to be proven not to violate the desired properties for the system.

3   Interrupt-Induced Concurrency

Our work on reasoning about interrupt-induced concurrency is initially motivated by the verification of eChronos [2], a small embedded real-time operating system in commercial use in medical devices. In an eChronos-based system, the kernel runs with interrupts enabled, even during scheduling operations, to be able to satisfy stringent latency requirements. The formal verification of eChronos' correctness and key properties thus required a reasoning framework for controlled concurrency that describes interleaving between "normal" code (application code and kernel code) and interrupt-handler code. We want such a framework to support potentially racy sharing between handlers and normal code, rather than having to bear the cost of interrupt disabling to ensure safe sharing.

We developed a simple, yet scalable framework for such controlled interleaving and have used it to define a high-level model of eChronos scheduling behavior [7]. We then proved its main scheduling property: that the running task is always the highest-priority runnable task [6]. Our framework is embedded in Isabelle/HOL [17] and the verification relies on the automation of modern theorem provers to automatically discharge most of the generated proof obligations. Our models and proofs are available online [1].

Our modelling framework builds on foundational methods for fine-grained concurrency, with support for explicit concurrency control and the composition of multiple, independently proven invariants. The foundational method is Owicki-Gries [19], a simple extension on Hoare logic with parallel composition, *await* statements for synchronisation, and rules to reason about such programs by inserting assertions, proving their (local) correctness sequentially as in Hoare logic, and then proving that they are not interfered with by any other statement in parallel.

We model an interruptible software system as a parallel composition of its code with code from a number of interrupt handlers. We also model the hardware mechanisms that switch execution to handlers and that return from interrupts, via the scheduler. Such parallel composition allows more interleaving than can happen in reality – for instance it allows the execution of the handler code suddenly to jump back to executing application code at any time. We therefore then restrict the interleaving by a control mechanism, that we call *await painting*: every instruction is guarded by a condition, which by default enforces sequential execution, but is relaxed for all hardware mechanisms that do allow interleaving, such as taking an interrupt or returning from one.

For the verification, the main property of interest in an invariant, which, as most invariants, rely on a number of helper invariants. To make the verification scalable, we have a compositionality theorem allowing the proof of helper lemmas independently, with separate Owicki-Gries assertions, after which those invariants can be assumed when proving further invariants. We have also developed proof-engineering techniques to address scalability issues in the verification of the generated proof obligations. These techniques range from subgoal deduplicating and caching, to exploiting Isabelle's parallelisation and powerful simplifier.

With this framework, we proved eChronos' main scheduling property with a single tactic application. This proof is about a high-level model of eChronos and the obvious missing piece is the link to the implementation.

To bridge the gap to the implementation, we have developed a verification framework for concurrent C-like programs, called COMPLX [3], available online [10]. The COMPLX language builds on SIMPL [22], a generic imperative, sequential language embedded in Isabelle/HOL. SIMPL allows formal reasoning about sequential C programs via the translation of C programs into SIMPL by the C-to-Isabelle translation [24]. It has been used for the verification of seL4: the C-level formal specification of seL4 is in SIMPL, inside Isabelle/HOL. COMPLX extends SIMPL with parallel composition and await statements, and we developed a logic for Owicki-Gries reasoning as well as its compositional counter-part Rely-Guarantee reasoning [13]. Using this framework to extend the eChronos verification to the implementation and to full functional correctness is future work. We are also planning to use it in our ongoing verification of the multicore version of seL4.

4   Multicore Concurrency

The seL4 microkernel is a landmark in software verification [14,15]. It is the world's "most verified" OS kernel, while also being the world's fastest operating system designed for security/safety. It has formal, mechanically checked theorems for functional correctness, binary verification, integrity- and information-flow security, and verified system initialisation. It has seen 3rd-party use, demonstrated in automotive, aviation, space, military, data distribution, IoT, component OS, and military/intelligence. It is also the only verified kernel that has been maintained, extended with new features and ported to new platforms over a number of years. A direct implication is a very large (and evolving) proof stack (0.74M lines of specifications and proofs). One of the remaining challenges is to extend the formal verification, so far for unicore platforms, to multicore.

A multicore version of seL4 has been developed following a (mostly – as we will explain shortly) big-lock kernel approach. The idea of a big-lock kernel allows us to run kernel-based systems on multicore machines, where the user code can make use of the multicore computation power, while parallelism during kernel calls is reduced by a so called "big lock" around all kernel executions. Recent work in our group [20] indicates that this coarse-grained locking approach, at least for a well-designed microkernel with short system calls, can have less overhead than a fine-grained locking approach on modern hardware, and performs indistinguishably from fine-grained locking in macro-benchmarks on processors with up to 8 cores. The reason is that the time spent inside a fast microkernel using big lock is comparable to the time spent in fine-grained locks in monolithic kernels like Linux. Fine-grained locking is traditionally used for scalable multicore implementations, but comes with considerable complexity. Since the big-lock approach implies a drastic reduction in interleaving, it makes real-world verification of multicore kernels feasible.

The challenges in verifying this multicore seL4 are manifold. Firstly, the kernel is only *mostly* locked when executed. Some kernel code executes outside of the lock, for performance reasons and to deal with unavoidable hardware-software sharing. Indeed some hardware registers that are shared between cores are accessed by critical code in kernel calls, such as the deletion of a thread from another core. These operations cannot be locked and need careful design and reasoning to avoid data corruption. To start addressing this, we have performed a formal proof that the validity of such critical registers is always preserved.

This involves proving the correctness of the complex OS design for deletion on multicore. This proof is done on a very high-level model of interleaving (reusing the verification framework from our eChronos verification). It still needs to be connected to more concrete models of seL4, but it already identifies the guarantees that need to be provided by each core for the safe execution of the other cores.

The second challenge is to identify correctly the shared state between cores. This can be shared state between user code on one core and kernel code on another core, or shared state between two instances of kernel execution (at least one unlocked). There exists an earlier formal argument for an experimental multicore version of seL4 that lifts large parts of the sequential functional correctness proof to the multicore version [23]. This version relies on an informal identification of the shared state between the kernel and the user components (and very limited code outside the lock), and an informal argument that this shared state does not interfere (and therefore cannot invalidate) the kernel's (sequential) correctness result.

In our current work, we are aiming for a more foundational verification, and support for kernel-to-kernel interaction. We want to model all possible interference, then exclude the impossible ones *by proof* and finally show that the remaining ones do not violate the kernel invariants and properties. In particular we want, at the bottom level, to model explicitly the parallel composition of cores, with a framework like COMPLX (with potentially further work to port the guarantees to binary and to weak memory). This raises the question of bridging the gap, through refinement, between the high-level model of multicore seL4, a functional specification of seL4 and the lowest implementation level.

This leads to the remaining challenge, which is to leverage the existing large proof stack, whose complexity reflects the complexity of a high-performance, non-modular microkernel. This is ongoing work. We are aiming for an approach that will preserve as much as possible the sequential specifications and the corresponding refinement theorems.

5   User-Level Concurrency

Our vision for proving security for entire large systems [4,12,21] is to build them on a trustworthy foundation like seL4 and then to leverage its isolation properties in a way that the applications can be componentised into trusted- and untrusted components, avoiding in particular having to verify any of the untrusted components, thanks to the kernel's integrity and confidentiality enforcement.

We have previously built [5] an initial prototype framework that provides, for such microkernel-based, componentised systems, and for any targeted system invariant, a list of proof obligations. Once proved by the user of the framework, these theorems will imply that the invariant is preserved at the source code level of the whole system. We have already demonstrated this approach on a simplistic system with two components: a small trusted component with write access to a critical memory area, and one potentially very large untrusted component with only read access to the same region and otherwise isolated. We were able to prove properties about the memory content without any proof about the untrusted components, relying only on seL4's integrity enforcement.

This approach however suffered from strong limitations in terms of scalability and the kind of properties supported (they needed to rely solely on integrity enforcement). This piece of work was prior to the more foundational treatment of concurrency we developed more recently for the ongoing verification of eChronos and multicore seL4. Our current aim is to incorporate the possibility of user-level reasoning in the modelling and refinement framework currently developed for the multicore seL4, with proper explicit modelling of user-to-user interactions and the specification of rely- and guarantee conditions.

6   Conclusion

Tackling the formal verification of concurrent high-performance software systems is both challenging due to the combined complexity of high-performance and concurrency, and indispensable to keep such systems real-world relevant. We have presented challenges, progress made, and future work in building reasoning frameworks that can support such scale and complexity, and their application to the verification of real-world operating systems such as eChronos and seL4.

Acknowledgements. The author would like to thank the people that have worked on the research presented in this paper: Sidney Amani, Maksym Bortin, Gerwin Klein, Corey Lewis, Daniel Matichuk, Carroll Morgan, Christine Rizkallah, and Joseph Tuong. The author also thanks Carroll Morgan, Gerwin Klein and Gernot Heiser for their feedback on drafts of this paper.

Parts of the work presented are supported by the Air Force Office of Scientific Research, Asian Office of Aerospace Research and Development (AOARD) and U.S. Army International Technology Center - Pacific under grant FA2386-15-1-4055. Other parts have been supported by AOARD grants FA2386-12-1-4022 and FA2386-10-1-4105.

References

1. eChronos model and proofs. https://github.com/echronos/echronos-proofs
2. The eChronos OS. http://echronos.systems
3. Amani, S., Andronick, J., Bortin, M., Lewis, C., Christine, R., Tuong, J.: Complx: a verification framework for concurrent imperative programs. In: Bertot, Y., Vafeiadis, V. (eds.) CPP, pp. 138–150. ACM, Paris (2017)
4. Andronick, J., Greenaway, D., Elphinstone, K.: Towards proving security in the presence of large untrusted components. In: Huuck, R., Klein, G., Schlich, B. (eds.) SSV, p. 9. USENIX, Vancouver (2010)
5. Andronick, J., Klein, G.: Formal system verification - extension 2, final report AOARD #FA2386-12-1-4022. Technical report, NICTA, Sydney, Australia, August 2012

6. Andronick, J., Lewis, C., Matichuk, D., Morgan, C., Rizkallah, C.: Proof of OS scheduling behavior in the presence of interrupt-induced concurrency. In: Blanchette, J.C., Merz, S. (eds.) ITP 2016. LNCS, vol. 9807, pp. 52–68. Springer, Cham (2016). doi:10.1007/978-3-319-43144-4_4
7. Andronick, J., Lewis, C., Morgan, C.: Controlled Owicki-gries concurrency: reasoning about the preemptible eChronos embedded operating system. In: van Glabbeek, R.J., Groote, J.F., Höfner, P. (eds.) Workshop on Models for Formal Analysis of Real Systems (MARS 2015), pp. 10–24, Suva, Fiji, November 2015
8. Appel, A.W.: Verified software toolchain. In: Barthe, G. (ed.) ESOP 2011. LNCS, vol. 6602, pp. 1–17. Springer, Heidelberg (2011). doi:10.1007/978-3-642-19718-5_1
9. Chen, H., Wu, X.N., Shao, Z., Lockerman, J., Gu, R.: Toward compositional verification of interruptible OS kernels and device drivers. In: Proceedings of the 37th ACM SIGPLAN Conference on Programming Language Design and Implementation, PLDI 2016, pp. 431–447. ACM, New York (2016)
10. COMPLX entry in the Archive of Formal Proofs. https://www.isa-afp.org/entries/Complx.shtml
11. Gu, R., Shao, Z., Chen, H., Wu, X.N., Kim, J., Sjöberg, V., Costanzo, D.: CertiKOS: an extensible architecture for building certified concurrent OS kernels. In: OSDI, November 2016
12. Heiser, G., Andronick, J., Elphinstone, K., Klein, G., Kuz, I., Ryzhyk, L.: The road to trustworthy systems. In: ACMSTC, pp. 3–10. ACM, October 2010
13. Jones, C.B.: Tentative steps towards a development method for interfering programs. Trans. Program. Lang. Syst. 5(4), 596–619 (1983)
14. Klein, G., Andronick, J., Elphinstone, K., Heiser, G., Cock, D., Derrin, P., Elkaduwe, D., Engelhardt, K., Kolanski, R., Norrish, M., Sewell, T., Tuch, H., Winwood, S.: seL4: formal verification of an operating-system kernel. CACM 53(6), 107–115 (2010)
15. Klein, G., Andronick, J., Elphinstone, K., Murray, T., Sewell, T., Kolanski, R., Heiser, G.: Comprehensive formal verification of an OS microkernel. Trans. Comput. Syst. 32(1), 2:1–2:70 (2014)
16. Leroy, X.: Formal certification of a compiler back-end, or: programming a compiler with a proof assistant. In: Morrisett, J.G., Jones, S.L.P. (eds.) 33rd POPL, pp. 42–54. ACM, Charleston (2006)
17. Nipkow, T., Wenzel, M., Paulson, L.C. (eds.): Isabelle/HOL. LNCS, vol. 2283. Springer, Heidelberg (2002). doi:10.1007/3-540-45949-9
18. OHearn, P.W.: Resources, concurrency, and local reasoning. Theor. Comput. Sci. 375(1–3), 271–307 (2007)
19. Owicki, S., Gries, D.: An axiomatic proof technique for parallel programs. Acta Informatica 6, 319–340 (1976)
20. Peters, S., Danis, A., Elphinstone, K., Heiser, G.: For a microkernel, a big lock is fine. In: APSys, Tokyo, JP, July 2015
21. Potts, D., Bourquin, R., Andresen, L., Andronick, J., Klein, G., Heiser, G.: Mathematically verified software kernels: raising the bar for high assurance implementations. Technical report, NICTA, Sydney, Australia, July 2014
22. Schirmer, N.: Verification of sequential imperative programs in Isabelle/HOL. Ph.D. thesis, Technische Universität München (2006)
23. von Tessin, M.: The clustered multikernel: an approach to formal verification of multiprocessor operating-system kernels. Ph.D. thesis, School Comp. Sci. & Engin., UNSW, Sydney, Australia, December 2013
24. Tuch, H., Klein, G., Norrish, M.: Types, bytes, and separation logic. In: Hofmann, M., Felleisen, M. (eds.) POPL, pp. 97–108. ACM, Nice (2007)

Towards Logic-Based Verification
of JavaScript Programs

José Fragoso Santos[1], Philippa Gardner[1], Petar Maksimović[1,2(✉)],
and Daiva Naudžiūnienė[1]

[1] Imperial College London, London, UK
p.maksimovic@imperial.ac.uk
[2] Mathematical Institute of the Serbian Academy of Sciences and Arts,
Belgrade, Serbia

Abstract. In this position paper, we argue for what we believe is a correct pathway to achieving scalable symbolic verification of JavaScript based on separation logic. We highlight the difficulties imposed by the language, the current state-of-the-art in the literature, and the sequence of steps that needs to be taken. We briefly describe JaVerT, our semi-automatic toolchain for JavaScript verification.

1 Introduction

JavaScript is one of the most widespread languages for Web programming today: it is the de facto language for client-side Web applications; it is used for server-side scripting via Node.js; and it is even run on small embedded devices with limited memory. Standardised by the ECMAScript committee and natively supported by all major browsers, JavaScript is a complex and evolving language.

The ubiquitous use of JavaScript, especially in security-critical contexts, mandates a high level of trust in the written code. However, the dynamic nature of JavaScript, coupled with its intricate semantics, makes the understanding and development of correct JavaScript code notoriously difficult. It is because of this complexity that JavaScript developers still have very little tool support for catching errors early in development, contrasted with the abundance of tools (such as IDEs and specialised static analysis tools) available for more traditional languages, such as C and Java. The transfer of analysis techniques to the domain of JavaScript is known to be a challenging task.

In this position paper, we argue for what we believe is a correct pathway to achieving scalable, logic-based symbolic verification of JavaScript, highlighting the difficulties imposed by the language, the current state-of-the-art in the literature, and the sequence of steps that needs to be taken. Using our approach, we illustrate how to give functionally correct specifications of JavaScript programs, written in a separation logic for JavaScript. We aim to have such specifications be as agnostic as possible to the internals of JavaScript and provide an interface that gives meaningful feedback to the developer. We give a brief description of JaVerT, our semi-automatic toolchain for JavaScript verification.

© Springer International Publishing AG 2017
L. de Moura (Ed.): CADE 2017, LNAI 10395, pp. 8–25, 2017.
DOI: 10.1007/978-3-319-63046-5_2

2 Motivation

We illustrate the complexity of JavaScript by appealing to a JavaScript priority queue library, which uses an implementation based on singly-linked node lists. It is a variation on a Node.js priority queue library that uses doubly linked lists [18], simplified for exposition. We use this example to showcase the intricacies of JavaScript semantics as well as some of the major challenges that need to be addressed before JavaScript programs can be verified.

```
1  /* @id PQLib */
2  var PriorityQueue = (function () {
3    var counter = 0;
4
5    /* @id Node */
6    var Node = function (pri, val) {
7      this.pri = pri;
8      this.val = val;
9      this.next = null;
10     counter++;
11   }
12
13   /* @id insert */
14   Node.prototype.insert =
15   function (nl) {
16     if (nl === null) {
17       return this
18     }
19     if (this.pri >= nl.pri) {
20       this.next = nl;
21       return this
22     }
23     var tmp = this.insert (nl.next);
24     nl.next = tmp;
25     return nl
26   }
27
28   /* @id PQ */
29   var PQ = function () {
30     this._head = null
31   };

32   /* @id enqueue */
33   PQ.prototype.enqueue =
34   function(pri, val) {
35     if (counter > 42) {
36       throw new Error()
37     }
38     var n = new Node(pri, val);
39     this._head = n.insert(this._head);
40   };
41
42   /* @id dequeue */
43   PQ.prototype.dequeue =
44   function () {
45     if (this._head === null) {
46       throw new Error()
47     }
48     var first = this._head;
49     this._head = this._head.next;
50     counter--;
51     return {pri: first.pri,
52       val: first.val};
53   };
54
55   return PQ;
56 })();
57
58 var q = new PriorityQueue();
59 q.enqueue(1, "last");
60 q.enqueue(3, "bar");
61 q.enqueue(2, "foo");
62 var r = q.dequeue();
```

Fig. 1. A simple JavaScript priority queue library (lines 1–56) and client (lines 58–62). For verification purposes, each function literal is annotated with a unique identifier.

2.1 A Priority Queue Library

In Fig. 1, we present the priority queue library (lines 1–56) together with a simple client program (lines 58–62). The priority queue is implemented as an object with property _head pointing to a singly-linked list of node objects, ordered in descending order of priority. A new priority queue object is constructed using the PQ function (lines 28–31), which declares that property _head has value null, that is, that the queue is initially empty. The enqueue and dequeue functions (lines 32–53) provide the functionality to enqueue and dequeue nodes of the queue. These functions should be accessible by all priority queue objects. This is accomplished by following the standard JavaScript prototype inheritance paradigm, which, in this case, means storing these two functions within the object PQ.prototype.

The enqueue function constructs a new node object, and then adds it to the node list in the appropriate place given by its priority. A node object is constructed using the Node function (lines 5–11) which declares three properties, a priority, a value and a pointer to the next node in the node list, and increments the variable counter, which keeps track of how many nodes were created (lines 3,10) by the library. We limit the number of nodes that a library can create (lines 35–37) to illustrate scoping further. The node object is then inserted into the node list using the insert function (lines 13–26) which, again using prototype inheritance, is a property of Node.prototype and is accessible by all node objects.

Let us now show how the example actually works. Our first step is to initialise the priority queue library in lines 1–50. This involves: **(1)** setting up the functionalities of node objects (lines 5–26); **(2)** setting up the functionalities of priority queue objects (lines 28–53); and **(3)** providing the interface from the priority queue library to the client (line 55). At this point, the client can construct a new, empty priority queue, by calling **new** PriorityQueue(), and enqueue and dequeue nodes of the queue, by calling the enqueue and dequeue functions.

We demonstrate how this library can be used via a small client program (lines 58–62). Line 58 constructs an empty queue, identified by the variable q. In doing so, the node counter associated with q is set to zero, as no nodes have yet been created (line 3). Lines 59–62 call the enqueue and dequeue functions, for adding and removing elements from the queue. For example, the command statement q.enqueue(1,"last") in line 59 inserts a new node with priority 1 and value "last" into the (at this point empty) queue q. To do so, it first checks if the node limit has been reached and, since the value of the node counter is zero, it proceeds. Next, it uses the Node function to construct a new node object (line 38), say n, with the given priority (pri=1), value (val="last"), and a pointer to the next node (initially next = null). Finally, it then calls n.insert(this._head) (line 39), which inserts n into the existing node list at this._head, returns the head of the new node list and stores it in this._head. In this case, since we are inserting the node n into an empty queue, this head of the new node list will be n. The statements q.enqueue(3, "bar") and q.enqueue(2, "foo") behave in a similar way. After their execution, we have a queue containing three elements and the node counter is equal to 3. Finally, the statement **var** r = q.dequeue( ) removes the first element from the queue by swinging the _head pointer to the second element of the node list, decreases the node counter to 2, creates a new object containing the priority property with value 3 and the value property with value "bar", and returns the address of this new object.

Ideally, it should be possible to abstract the details of Node so that the client works with the functionalities of the priority queue. In Java, it is possible to define a Node constructor and its associated functionalities to be private. In JavaScript, there is no native mechanism that provides encapsulation. Instead, the standard approach to establish some form of encapsulation is to use function closures. For example, the call of the function Node inside the body of enqueue (line 38) refers to the variable Node declared in the enclosing scope. This makes it impossible for the clients of the library to see the Node function and use it directly.

However, they still can access and modify constructed nodes and Node.prototype through the _head property of the queue, breaking encapsulation. Our goal is to provide specifications of the queue library functions that ensure functionally correct behaviour and behavioural properties of encapsulation.

2.2 The Complexity of JavaScript

JavaScript is a highly dynamic language, featuring a number of non-standard concepts and behaviours. In this section, we describe the JavaScript initial heap and elaborate on the challenges that need to be addressed for tractable JavaScript verification to be possible.

Initial Heap. Before the execution of any JavaScript program, an *initial heap* has to be established. It contains the *global object*, which holds all global variables such as PriorityQueue, q and r from the example. It also contains the functions of all JavaScript built-in libraries, widely used by developers: for example, Object, Function and Error. In the example, the Error built-in function is used to construct a new error object when trying to dequeue an empty queue (line 36).

Internal Functions. In the ECMAScript standard, the semantics of JavaScript is described operationally, that is, the behaviour of each JavaScript expression and statement is broken down into a number of steps. These steps heavily rely on a wide variety of *internal functions*, which capture the fundamental inner workings of the language; most notably, object property management (e.g. creation (DefineOwnProperty), lookup (GetValue), mutation (PutValue) and deletion (Delete)) and type conversions (e.g. ToString and ToNumber).

To better understand the extent of the use of the internal functions, consider the JavaScript assignment o["foo"] = 42. According to its definition in the standard, it calls the internal functions five times: GetValue thrice, and ToString and PutValue once. This, however, is only at top-level: GetValue, in turn, calls Get, which calls GetProperty, which calls GetOwnProperty and possibly itself recursively; PutValue calls Put, which calls CanPut and DefineOwnProperty, which calls GetOwnProperty. In the end, a simple JavaScript assignment will make more than ten and, in some cases, even more than twenty calls to various internal functions. The more complex a JavaScript command is, the greater the number of the internal functions that it calls. Therefore, in order to be able to reason about JavaScript programs, one first has to tackle the internal functions. This brings us to the following challenge:

Challenge: To reason robustly and abstractly about the JavaScript internal functions.

JavaScript Objects. Objects in JavaScript differ C++ and Java objects in several defining ways. First, JavaScript objects are *extensible*, that is, properties can be added and removed from an object after creation. Second, property access in JavaScript is *dynamic*; we cannot guarantee statically which property of the object will be accessed. Third, JavaScript objects have two types of properties: *internal* and *named*.

Internal properties are hidden from the user, but are critical for the mechanisms underlying JavaScript, such as prototype inheritance. To illustrate, standard objects have three internal properties: @proto, @class, and @extensible. For example, all node objects constructed using the Node function have prototype Node.prototype, class "Object", and are extensible. JavaScript objects constructed by some of the built-in libraries can have additional internal properties. For example, a String object, associated with a string literal, has properties that represent the characters of that literal.

Named properties, which correspond to standard fields of C++ and Java objects, are associated not with values, but instead with *property descriptors*, which are lists of *attributes* that describe the ways in which a property can be accessed or modified. Depending on the attributes they contain, named properties can either be *data properties* or *accessor properties*. Here, we focus on data properties, which have the following attributes: *value*, holding the actual value of the property; *writable*, describing if the value can be changed; *configurable*, allowing property deletion and any change to non-value attributes; and *enumerable*, stating if a property may be used in a for−in enumeration. The values of these attributes depend on how the property is created. For example, if a property of an object is created using a property accessor (for example, this.pri = pri), then by default it is writable, configurable and enumerable. On the other hand, if a property is declared as a variable, then by default it is not configurable (for example, q in the global object).

Additionally, certain JavaScript commands and functions, such as for−in or Object.keys, traverse over all enumerable properties of an object. As JavaScript objects are extensible, these properties need not be known statically. Also, the for−in loop may modify the object over which it is traversing. This behaviour is difficult to capture and further illustrates the dynamic nature of JavaScript.

In summary, JavaScript objects have an additional, highly non-trivial layer of complexity related to object property management with respect to objects in C++ or Java. Furthermore, this complexity cannot be captured natively by the existing tools for verifying C++ or Java programs (see Sect. 3.2 for a more detailed discussion). This constitutes an important challenge:

Challenge: To reason about extensible objects, dynamic property access, property descriptors, and property traversal.

Fig. 2. The prototype chain of Node objects.

Prototype-based inheritance. JavaScript models inheritance through prototype chains. To look up the value of a property of an object, we first check the object itself. If the property is not there, we walk along the prototype chain, following the @proto internal properties, checking for the property at each object. In our example, all node objects constructed using the enqueue function (line 38) have a prototype chain like the one given in Fig. 2. There, the lookup of property val starting from object n only needs to check n. The lookup of property insert starting from n first checks n, which does not have the property, then checks Node.Prototype, which does. In general, prototype chains can be of arbitrary length, typically finishing at Object.prototype, but they cannot be circular. Moreover, prototype chain traversal is additionally complicated in the presence of String objects, which have properties that do not exist in the heap.

Prototype chain traversal is one of the fundamental building blocks of the JavaScript language and is prominently featured in the behaviour of almost every JavaScript command. This brings us to our next challenge:

Challenge: To reason about prototype chains of arbitrary complexity.

Functions, Function objects. Functions are also stored in the JavaScript heap as objects. Each function object has three specific internal properties: **(1)** @code, storing the code of the original function; **(2)** @scope, storing a representation of the scope in which the function was defined; and **(3)** prototype, storing the prototype of those objects created using that function as the constructor. For example, Node.prototype is the prototype of all node objects constructed using the Node function, and is the place to find the insert function.

There are two main challenges related to reasoning about function objects. The first involves the interaction between function objects and scoping, which we address in the following paragraph. The second has to do with higher-order functions. Namely, JavaScript has full support for higher-order functions, meaning that a function can take another function as an argument, or that a function can return another function as a result. This behaviour is not easily captured, particularly in a program logic setting, but is often used in practice and verification of JavaScript programs should ultimately be able to tackle it.

Challenge: To reason about higher-order functions of arbitrary complexity.

Scoping, Function Closures. In JavaScript, scope is modelled using environment records (ERs). An ER is an internal object, created upon the invocation of a function, that maps the variables declared in the body of that function and its formal parameters to their respective values. Variables are resolved with respect to a list of ER locations, called a *scope chain*. In the non-strict mode of JavaScript, standard JavaScript objects can also be part of a scope chain. In strict mode, the only JavaScript object that can be part of a scope chain is the global object, which is treated as the ER of the global code. Since functions in JavaScript can be nested (e.g. Node, enqueue, dequeue) and can also be returned as outcomes of other functions (e.g. the PQ function is returned by PQLib), it is possible to create complex relationships between scope chains of various functions.

We discuss scoping through the `enqueue` function, which uses five variables in its body: `pri`, `val`, `n`, `Node`, and `counter`. The scope chain of `enqueue` contains the ERs corresponding to `enqueue`, `PQLib`, and global code. As `pri` and `val` are formal parameters and `n` is a local variable of `enqueue`, they are stored in the ER of `enqueue`. However, `Node` and `counter` are not declared in `enqueue` and are not its formal parameters, so we have to look for them in the rest of the scope chain associated with `enqueue`, and we find them in the ER corresponding to `PQLib`. This means that when we reason about `enqueue`, we need to capture not only its ER, but also a part of the ER of `PQLib`. We should also note that while the value of `Node` is static, the value of `counter` is changed both by `Node` and by `dequeue`, and that this change is visible by all of the functions of the library. Overall, the interaction of scope chains in JavaScript is very intricate, especially in the presence of multiple function closures. Therefore, our next challenge is:

Challenge: To reason about scope chains and function closures of arbitrary complexity.

2.3   Specification of JavaScript libraries

There are two requirements necessary for the correct functioning of the priority queue library. First, the intention of the library developer is that all node objects constructed using the `Node` function should have access to the function `insert`. This means that the node objects themselves must not have the property `"insert"`. Second, we must always be able to construct a `Node` object. This means, due to the semantics of JavaScript, that `Node.Prototype` and `Object.Prototype` must not have properties `"pri"`, `"val"` and `"next"`, used in the node constructor, declared as non-writable. We call these two requirements *prototype safety*. We aim to provide a library specification for the priority queue that ensures prototype safety, and believe that we have identified a desired pattern of library behaviour suitable for JavaScript data structure libraries developed for Node.js.

Challenge: To provide specifications of JavaScript libraries that ensure prototype safety.

Hiding JavaScript internals. Our priority queue example illustrates some of the complexities of JavaScript: extensible objects, prototype-based inheritance, functions, scoping, and function closures. There is, in addition, much complexity that is not exposed to the JavaScript developer: for example, property descriptors, internal functions, as well as implicit type coercions, where values of one type are coerced at runtime to values of another type in order to delay error reporting. We would like to provide specifications that are as opaque as possible to such hidden features: since the code does not expose them, the specification should not expose them either. However, all of these features have to be taken into account when verifying that a program satisfies a specification. One solution is to provide abstractions that hide these internal details from view.

Challenge: To create abstractions that hide the internals of JavaScript as much as possible and allow the developer to write specifications in the style of C++ and Java specifications.

3   A Pathway to JavaScript Verification

Logic-based symbolic verification has recently become tractable for C and Java, with compositional techniques that scale and properly engineered tools applied to real-world code: for example, Infer, Facebook's tool based on separation logic for reasoning about for C, C++, Objective-C and Java [6]; Java Pathfinder, a model checking tool for Java bytecode programs [27]; CBMC, a bounded model checker for C, currently being adapted to Java at Amazon [20]; and WALA's analysis for Java using the Rosette symbolic analyser [12].

There has been little work on logic-based symbolic verification for JavaScript. As far as we are aware, the only relevant work is KJS [8, 22], a tested executable semantics of JavaScript in the $\mathbb{K}$ framework [24] which is equipped with a symbolic execution engine. The aim of K is to provide a unified environment for analysing programming languages such as C, Java and JavaScript. Specifications are written in the reachability logic of $\mathbb{K}$, and the authors use KJS to specify operations on data structures, such as lists, binary search trees (BSTs) and AVL trees, and to verify the correctness of several sorting algorithms. This work does not address many of the challenges that laid out in the previous section. For example, it does not provide a general, abstract way of reasoning about prototype chains, scope chains, or function closures; the concrete shape of a prototype chain or a scope chain always needs to be known. It does not provide JavaScript-specific abstractions, so the specifications are cumbersome and reveal all JavaScript internals. The internal functions are always executed in full. More generally, function specifications are often not given, so the symbolic execution cannot jump over function calls but executes the bodies instead. This diminishes the scalability of KJS. We argue that a more JavaScript-specific approach is needed in order to make JavaScript verification tractable.

3.1   Choosing the Battleground

We believe that separation logic has much to offer JavaScript, since it provides a natural way of reasoning modularly about the JavaScript heap. Gardner, Smith and Maffeis developed a sound separation logic for a small fragment of JavaScript with many syntactic and semantic simplifications [13]. Their goal was to demonstrate that separation logic can be used to reason about the variable store emulated in the JavaScript heap. This approach is not extensible to the entire language. For example, consider the general assignment e1 = e2, where e1 and e2 are arbitrary JavaScript expressions. Under the hood, this assignment evaluates these two expressions and calls the `GetValue` and `PutValue` internal functions. The evaluation of each expression, as well as each of these two internal functions has tens of cases, so combining these case together would result in hundreds of axioms for the JavaScript assignment alone. Such a logic would be extremely difficult to prove sound, let alone automate. In order to reason about JavaScript, we need to move to a simple intermediate representation.

Working directly with JavaScript is not tractable for verification based on program logics. We need a simple intermediate representation.

3.2   Moving to a Simpler World

Our conclusion that some sort of an intermediate representation (IR) is neces-
sary for JavaScript verification is not surprising. Most analysis tools, both for
JavaScript [1,14,17,19,23,26] and other languages [2,3,6,7,9,12,15], use an IR.
The next step is to understand what the desired features of an IR for logic-based
JavaScript verification are. We believe that the following criteria need to be met.

1. **Expressiveness.** JavaScript is a highly dynamic language, with extensible
   objects, dynamic field access, and dynamic function calls. These features create an additional level of complexity for JavaScript when compared to other
   object-oriented languages such as C++ and Java. They should be supported
   natively by the IR.
2. **Simple control flow.** JavaScript has complicated control flow constructs: for
   example, `for-in`, which iterates on the fields of an object; `try-catch-finally`
   for handling exceptions; and the breaking out of loops to arbitrary labelled
   points in the code. Logic-based symbolic verification tools today typically
   work on IRs with simple control flow. In particular, many of the separation-
   logic tools for analysing C, C++, and Java use goto-based IRs: for example,
   [2,3,6,7,9,15]. This suggests that our IR for JavaScript should be based on
   simple low-level control flow constructs.

One option is to use an IR that has already been developed for analysing
JavaScript code. We can broadly divide these IRs into two categories: (1) those
that work for analyses that are syntax-directed, following the abstract syntax
tree (AST) of the program, such as λ_{JS} [14], S5 [23], and notJS [19]; and (2) those
that aim at analyses based on the control-flow graph of the program, such as
JSIR [21], WALA [12,26] and the IR of TAJS [1,17]. The IRs in (1) are normally well-suited for high-level analysis, such as type-checking and type inference
[14,23], whereas those belonging to (2) are generally the target of separation-
logic-based tools, such as Smallfoot [2], Slayer [3], JStar [9], VeriFast [15], Abduc-
tor [7], and Infer [6], as well as tools for tractable symbolic evaluation such as
CBMC [20] and Klee [5].

We believe that an IR for JavaScript verification should belong to (2). The
JSIR [21] and WALA [12,26] IRs both capture the dynamic features of JavaScript
and provide low-level control flow constructs. However, neither JSIR nor WALA
have associated compilers. In addition, they do not provide reference implementations of the JavaScript internal functions and built-in libraries, which makes it
very difficult for us to assess their usability. TAJS [1,17] does include a compiler,
originally for ECMAScript 3 (ES3) but now extended with partial models of the
ES5 standard library, the HTML DOM, and the browser API. As TAJS is used
for type analysis and abstract interpretation, its IR is more high-level than those
typically used for logic-based symbolic verification. In addition, we believe that
the aim for verification should be at least ECMAScript 5 (ES5) [10], which is
substantially different from ES3 and essentially provides the core language for
the more recent ES6 and ES7.

Another option is to consider using or adapting an IR supported by an existing separation-logic-based tool [2,3,6,7,9,15], where we would have to provide the compiler from JavaScript, but the analysis for the IR could be reused. There are two problems worth mentioning with this approach. First, these tools all target static languages that do not support extensible objects or dynamic function calls. Hence, JavaScript objects could not be directly encoded using the built-in constructs of these languages. Consequently, at the logical level, one would need to use custom abstractions to reason about JavaScript objects and their associated operations, effectively losing most of the native reasoning features of the tool in question. Second, any program logic for JavaScript needs to take into account the JavaScript binary and unary operators, such as `toInt32` [10], and it is not clear that these operators would be expressible using the assertion languages of existing tools. This brings us to the following conclusion:

JavaScript requires a dedicated low-level control-flow-based IR for verification: the simpler the IR, the better.

We have developed a simple JavaScript IR for our verification toolchain, called JSIL. It comprises only the most basic control flow commands (unconditional and conditional gotos), the object management commands needed to support extensible objects and dynamic field access, and top-level procedures. In the following section, we use JSIL to discuss what it means to design and trust the compilation and verification process. However, the methodology and principles that we lay out are general and apply to any verification IR for JavaScript.

3.3   Trusted Compilation of JavaScript

The development of an appropriate IR is tightly connected with the development of the compiler from JavaScript to the IR, which brings up two challenges that need to be addressed:

1. The compilation has to capture all of the behaviours and corner cases of the JavaScript semantics, and must come with strong guarantees of correctness.
2. The reasoning at JavaScript level has to be strongly connected with the reasoning at the IR level; we refer to this as logic-preserving compilation.

To answer these two challenges, we unpack what it means to show that a compiler can be trusted.

– **Correctness by design.** This approach assesses the compiler by looking at the structure of the compiler code and at examples of compiled code. It is greatly simplified by using semantics-driven compilation, where the compiler and the compiled code follow the steps of the JavaScript English standard line-by-line as much as possible. This approach is feasible, because the JavaScript standard is given operationally, in an almost pseudo-code format. Given the complexity of JavaScript, this approach, albeit quite informal in nature, can give some confidence, particularly to the compiler developer, when it comes to compiler correctness. Ultimately, however, it is not formal enough to be sufficient on its own.

– **Correctness by testing.** JavaScript is a real-world language that comes with an official test suite, the ECMAScript Test262 [11]. Although Test262 is known not to be comprehensive, it features over 20,000 tests that extensively test most of the JavaScript behaviour. Correctly compiled JavaScript code should pass all of the appropriate tests.
– **Semantics-preserving compilation.** This correctness condition for the compiler is standard in compiler literature. It requires formalising the semantics and memory model of JavaScript, formalising the semantics and memory model of IR, giving a correspondence between the two memory models, and, with this correspondence, proving that the semantics of the JavaScript and compiled IR code match. For real-world languages, either a pen-and-paper proof is given for a representative fragment or a mechanised proof is given, in a proof assistant such as Coq, for the entire language.
– **Logic-preserving compilation.** This correctness condition for the compiler is not commonly emphasised in the analysis literature. It assumes semantic-preserving compilation and additionally requires: giving a strong correspondence between JavaScript and IR assertions; relating the semantics of JavaScript triples with the semantics of the IR triples; and proving a soundness result for the IR proof rules. In this way, one can formally lift IR verification to JavaScript verification.

What follows is an insight into our design process for JSIL and JS-2-JSIL, and the main lessons that we have learnt from it. We knew we wanted to achieve logic-preserving compilation, using a separation logic for reasoning about heap manipulation. From the start, a fundamental decision was to make the JavaScript and JSIL memory models as close to each other as possible. In the end, the only difference is the modelling of scope chains. We also chose to design JS-2-JSIL so that the compiled code follows the ECMAScript standard line-by-line, which meant that the choices for JSIL were quite apparent. This approach proved to be important for JS-2-JSIL. It leverages on the operational aspect of the standard, making the inspection and debugging of compiled code considerably easier.

Semantics-driven compilation is greatly beneficial.

We believe that testing is an indispensable part of establishing compiler correctness for real-world languages such as JavaScript. Regardless of how precise proof of correctness may be, there still is plenty of room for discrepancies to arise: for example, the implementation of the compiler might inadvertently deviate from its formalisation; or the formalised JavaScript semantics might deviate from the standard. For us, it was testing that guided our debugging process; without it, we would not be able to claim correctness of JS-2-JSIL.

Extensive testing of the compiled code is essential.

When writing a language compiler, one might claim that correctness-by-design and correctness-by-testing are sufficient: there is a clear design structure to the compiler that can be checked by looking at the code and by testing.

This is not enough when using the compiler for logic-based verification. In this case, we require logic-preserving compilation which formally connects JavaScript verification with JSIL verification. Logic-preserving compilation depends on semantic-preserving compilation, which is difficult to prove for such a complex language as JavaScript. We give a pen-and-paper proof correctness proof for a representative fragment of the language. We have given thought to providing a Coq proof of correctness, leveraging on our previous JSCert mechanised specification of JavaScript [4]. However, the process of formalising JSIL and JS-2-JSIL, and then proving the correctness is beyond our manpower. In contrast, the proof that the compiler is logic preserving is comparatively straightforward due to the simple correspondence between the JavaScript and JSIL memory models. Moreover, we noticed that the complexity of our proofs is strongly related to the complexity of this correspondence.

Semantic- and logic-preserving compilation is essential for verification. A simple correspondence between JavaScript and IR heaps is essential for containing the complexity of any correctness proofs.

3.4   Tackling the Javascript Internal Functions

The internal functions are described in the standard only in terms of pseudo-code and not JavaScript. They must, therefore, be implemented directly in the IR. With these implementations, we have identified two options on how to use them in verification.

- **Inlining.** The entire body of an internal function is inlined every time the function is supposed to be called in the compiled code.
- **Axiomatic specification.** Internal functions are treated as procedures of the IR and, as such, are fully axiomatically specified. Calls to internal functions are treated as standard procedure calls of the IR.

We do not believe that inlining is a viable option. Given the sheer number of calls to the internal functions and their intertwined nature, the size of the compiled code would quickly spiral out of control. We would also entirely lose the visual correspondence between the compiled code and the standard. Moreover, the bulk of verification time would be spent inside this code and the overall verification process would be very slow.

With axiomatic specifications, on the other hand, the calls to internal functions are featured in the compiled code as procedure calls to their IR implementations. In that sense, the compiled code reflects the English standard. During verification, the only check that has to be made is that the current symbolic state entails a precondition of the specification, which is both at a higher level of abstraction as well as faster than running the body of the function every time.

Axiomatic specifications of the internal functions are essential for tractable JavaScript verification.

Creating axiomatic specifications does not come without its challenges. The definitions of the internal functions are often intertwined, making it difficult to fully grasp the control flow and allowed behaviours. Specifying such dependencies axiomatically involves the joining of the specifications of all nested function calls at the top level, which results in numerous branchings. Also, some of the internal functions feature higher-order and, although it is possible to add higher-order reasoning to separation logic [25], the soundness result is known to be difficult. We believe that the resulting specifications, however, will be much more readable than the operational definitions of the standard. We also hope that they can also be easily reused for other types of analyses, by leveraging on executable code created from the axiomatic specifications.

3.5   JavaScript Verification Toolchain

We are currently developing a JavaScript verification toolchain (JaVerT), which targets the strict mode of the ES5 standard. It requires the JavaScript code to be annotated with assertions written in our assertion language for JavaScript (JS Logic). These annotations comprise specifications (the pre- and postconditions) for functions and global code, together with loop invariants and unfold/fold instructions for any user-defined predicates, such as a predicate for describing priority queues. JaVerT also features a number of built-in predicates that provide abstractions for the key concepts of JavaScript; in particular, for prototype inheritance, scoping, function objects and function closures. Such predicates enable the developer to move away from the complexity of the JavaScript semantics and write specifications in a logically clear and concise manner.

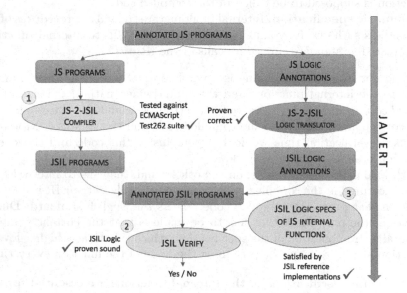

Fig. 3. JaVerT: JavaScript Verification Toolchain

Figure 3 presents the architecture of JaVerT, which rests on an infrastructure that consists of three components: **(1)** JS-2-JSIL, our semantics-preserving[1] and logic-preserving compiler from JavaScript to JSIL which has been tested using the official Test262 test suite, passing all the appropriate tests; **(2)** JSIL Verify, our semi-automatic tool for JSIL verification, based on a sound program logic for JSIL (JSIL Logic); and **(3)** our JSIL Logic axiomatic specifications of the JavaScript internal functions, which have been verified using JSIL Verify against their corresponding JSIL implementations.

Given a JavaScript program annotated with JS Logic specifications, JaVerT uses our JS-2-JSIL compiler to translate it to JSIL and the JS-2-JSIL logic translator to translate JS Logic annotations to JSIL Logic. The resulting annotated JSIL program is then automatically verified by JSIL Verify, taking advantage of our specifications of the JavaScript internal functions.

Thus far, we have used JaVerT to specify and verify a variety of heap-manipulating programs, including operations on lists (e.g. insertion sort), priority queues and BSTs, as well as a number of small JavaScript programs that showcase our treatment of prototype chains, scoping, and function closures. All examples can be found online at [16] and are continually being updated.

4   Specifying the Priority Queue Library

We illustrate JaVerT specifications by specifying the enqueue and dequeue methods of the priority queue library, given in Fig. 1. We show how these specifications are used to verify the client program given in lines 58–62 of the example.

In order to specify enqueue and dequeue, we first need to have a predicate Queue, describing a priority queue, and the predicate QueueProto, describing the priority queue prototype. The predicate Queue(lq, qp, np, pri_q, len) describes a priority queue at location lq, whose prototype is qp, whose nodes have node prototype np, whose maximum priority is pri_q, and which contains len nodes. The predicate QueueProto(qp, np, c) describes a priority queue prototype at location qp for those priority queues built from node objects whose node prototype is np. The parameter c records the value of the variable counter of the example (line 3), and holds the total number of existing node objects.

These two abstractions, which we will not unfold in detail here, capture, among others, the resource associated with the Node, insert, enqueue, and dequeue function objects, as well as the resource corresponding to the function closures of enqueue and dequeue: in particular, for enqueue, we need the variable property Node from the ER of PQLib; and, for dequeue, we need the variable resource counter from that same ER. They also capture the resources necessary to express prototype safety for both Node and PQ, which we describe using a technique from [13] for reasoning about the absence of properties in an object. We explicitly require the insert property of node object n, and the pri, val, and next properties of Node.prototype and Object.prototype not to be in the heap,

---

[1] The formal result that the compiler is semantics-preserving has been done for a fragment of the language.

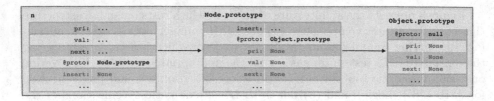

Fig. 4. Prototype safety for Node objects

as illustrated in Fig. 4 by the properties in red with value `None`. Note that the `Queue` and `QueueProto` predicates do not expose the internals of JavaScript, such as property descriptors and scope chains. Moreover, they do not expose functions not accessible to the client, such as the `Node` function. They do expose `Node.prototype` via the `np` parameter, but this is expected since the client can access it through the `_head` property of a queue.

The following specification of `enqueue` states that it should be executed on a priority queue of arbitrary length `len`, that the total number of existing nodes `c` needs to be not greater than 42, and that it receives two arguments `pri` and `val` with `pri` of type `Num`. The postcondition states that `enqueue` returns a priority queue with `len + 1` nodes and maximum priority `max(pri_q, pri)`, and that the total number of nodes has increased by one. Due to space requirements, we omit the specification of `enqueue` corresponding to the error case in which the total number of existing nodes is greater than 42.

$$\left\{ \begin{array}{c} \texttt{Queue(this, qp, np, pri\_q, len) * QueueProto(qp, np, c) *} \\ \texttt{types(pri: Num) * c <= 42} \end{array} \right\}$$
$$\texttt{enqueue(pri, val)}$$
$$\left\{ \texttt{Queue(ret, qp, np, max(pri\_q, pri), len+1) * QueueProto(qp, np, c+1)} \right\}$$

The following specification of `dequeue` states that it should be executed on a priority queue with length `len` greater than 0 and maximum priority `pri_q`. The postcondition states that, afterwards, the length of the queue has decreased by one, its priority has not increased, and the overall total number of nodes has decreased by one. The function also returns a standard object with two fields, `pri` with value `pri_q` and `val` with value `#val` which is existentially quantified. We prefix existentially quantified variables with a '`#`'. In the postcondition, the `standardObject` and `dataField` abstractions hide the internal properties and property descriptors of JavaScript objects. Again, due to space requirements, we omit the specification of `dequeue` where the queue from which we are dequeueing is empty and an error is thrown.

$$\left\{ \texttt{Queue(this, qp, np, pri\_q, len) * QueueProto(qp, np, c) * len > 0} \right\}$$
$$\texttt{dequeue()}$$
$$\left\{ \begin{array}{c} \texttt{Queue(this, qp, np, pri', len-1) * QueueProto(qp, np, c-1) * pri' <= pri\_q *} \\ \texttt{standardObject(ret) * dataField(ret, "pri", pri\_q) * dataField(ret, "val", \#val)} \end{array} \right\}$$

Given the specifications of `enqueue` and `dequeue`, we can verify the client program in lines 59–62. We show a proof sketch below, where we use the assertion scope(x: v) to state that variable x has value v in the current scope. Starting from an empty queue with maximum priority 0, we create three nodes, obtaining a queue with three nodes and maximum priority 3. Then, we dequeue the head of the queue (which we can do, as we know that the queue has 3 nodes), obtaining a queue with 2 nodes and existentially quantified priority #pri not greater than 3. Moreover, in the end, the variable r is bound to an object with two fields: pri, with value 3; and val, with value #val which is existentially quantified.

```
{ scope(q: qv) * Queue(qv, qp, np, 0, 0) * QueueProto(qp, np, 0) * scope(r: undefined) }
                q.enqueue(1, "last"); q.enqueue(3, "bar"); q.enqueue(2, "foo")
{ scope(q: qv) * Queue(qv, qp, np, 3, 3) * QueueProto(qp, np, 3) * scope(r: undefined) }
                var r = q.dequeue()
{     scope(q: qv) * Queue(qv, qp, np, #pri, 2) * QueueProto(qp, np, 2) * #pri <= 3 *     }
{ scope(r: #r) * standardObject(#r) * dataField(#r, "pri", 3) * dataField(#r, "val", #val) }
```

These specifications show that it is possible to successfully abstract over JavaScript internals, allowing both the library developer and the client developer to write specifications that are as free as possible from JavaScript-specific clutter.

4.1 Discussion

We conclude with a brief discussion of two important aspects of specifying JavaScript libraries: capturing prototype safety; and enforcing encapsulation. The situation for prototype safety is straightforward. It is not possible to verify a specification of client code if it compromises prototype safety. The situation for encapsulation is more subtle. In the example, a client can break encapsulation by modifying node objects or Node.prototype. There are ways of breaking encapsulation that we could choose to allow. The client could, for instance, add more functionalities to Node.prototype or add more properties to node objects, and this would not break the existing functionalities. However, there are ways of breaking encapsulation that we should certainly disallow. The client could, for instance, change the values of the pri, val, or next properties of a node object, or change the implementation of the insert function in Node.prototype. One way to ensure full encapsulation would be to keep the Queue and QueueProto predicates opaque to the client code. Hence, in order to be successfully verified, client code can only interact with a priority queue via its established interface, that being the enqueue and dequeue methods. By keeping library predicates opaque, we make sure that client code cannot break the existing abstractions.

Acknowledgments. Fragoso Santos, Gardner, and Maksimović were supported by the EPSRC Programme Grant REMS: Rigorous Engineering for Mainstream Systems (EP/K008528/1), and the Department of Computing in Imperial College London. Naudžiūnienė was supported by an EPSRC DTA award. Maksimović was also partially supported by the Serbian Ministry of Education and Science through the Mathematical Institute of Serbian Academy of Sciences and Arts, projects ON174026 and III44006.

References

1. Andreasen, E., Møller, A.: Determinacy in static analysis for jQuery. In: OOPSLA (2014)
2. Berdine, J., Calcagno, C., O'Hearn, P.W.: Smallfoot: Modular automatic assertion checking with separation logic. In: Boer, F.S., Bonsangue, M.M., Graf, S., Roever, W.-P. (eds.) FMCO 2005. LNCS, vol. 4111, pp. 115–137. Springer, Heidelberg (2006). doi:10.1007/11804192_6
3. Berdine, J., Cook, B., Ishtiaq, S.: Slayer: Memory safety for systems-level code. In: Gopalakrishnan, G., Qadeer, S. (eds.) CAV 2011. LNCS, vol. 6806, pp. 178–183. Springer, Heidelberg (2011). doi:10.1007/978-3-642-22110-1_15
4. Bodin, M., Charguéraud, A., Filaretti, D., Gardner, P., Maffeis, S., Naudziuniene, D., Schmitt, A., Smith, G.: A trusted mechanised JavaScript specification. In: Proceedings of the 41st ACM SIGPLAN-SIGACT Symposium on Principles of Programming Languages, POPL 2014, pp. 87–100. ACM Press (2014)
5. Cadar, C., Dunbar, D., Engler, D.R.: KLEE: unassisted and automatic generation of high-coverage tests for complex systems programs. In: Draves, R., van Renesse, R. (eds.) 8th USENIX Symposium on Operating Systems Design and Implementation, OSDI 2008, 8–10 December 2008, San Diego, California, USA, Proceedings, pp. 209–224. USENIX Association (2008)
6. Calcagno, C., Distefano, D., Dubreil, J., Gabi, D., Hooimeijer, P., Luca, M., O'Hearn, P., Papakonstantinou, I., Purbrick, J., Rodriguez, D.: Moving fast with software verification. In: Havelund, K., Holzmann, G., Joshi, R. (eds.) NFM 2015. LNCS, vol. 9058, pp. 3–11. Springer, Cham (2015). doi:10.1007/978-3-319-17524-9_1
7. Calcagno, C., Distefano, D., O'Hearn, P., Yang, H.: Compositional shape analysis by means of bi-abduction. In: POPL (2009)
8. Ştefănescu, A., Park, D., Yuwen, S., Li, Y., Roşu, G.: Semantics-based program verifiers for all languages. In: Proceedings of the 31th Conference on Object-Oriented Programming, Systems, Languages, and Applications (OOPSLA 2016), pp. 74–91. ACM, November 2016
9. Distefano, D., Parkinson, M.: jStar: towards practical verification for Java. In: OOPSLA (2008)
10. ECMAScript Committee. The 5th edn. of the ECMAScript Language Specification. Technical report, ECMA (2011)
11. ECMAScript Committee. Test262 test suite (2017). https://github.com/tc39/test262
12. Fink, S., Dolby, J.: WALA – The T.J. Watson Libraries for Analysis (2015). http://wala.sourceforge.net/
13. Gardner, P., Maffeis, S., Smith, G.: Towards a program logic for JavaScript. In: Proceedings of the 40th ACM SIGPLAN-SIGACT Symposium on Principles of Programming Languages, POPL 2013, pp. 31–44. ACM Press (2012)
14. Guha, A., Saftoiu, C., Krishnamurthi, S.: The essence of JavaScript. In: D'Hondt, T. (ed.) ECOOP 2010. LNCS, vol. 6183, pp. 126–150. Springer, Heidelberg (2010). doi:10.1007/978-3-642-14107-2_7
15. Jacobs, B., Smans, J., Philippaerts, P., Vogels, F., Penninckx, W., Piessens, F.: VeriFast: a powerful, sound, predictable, fast verifier for C and java. In: Bobaru, M., Havelund, K., Holzmann, G.J., Joshi, R. (eds.) NFM 2011. LNCS, vol. 6617, pp. 41–55. Springer, Heidelberg (2011). doi:10.1007/978-3-642-20398-5_4
16. JaVerT Team. Javert (2017). http://goo.gl/au69SV

17. Jensen, S.H., Møller, A., Thiemann, P.: Type analysis for JavaScript. In: Palsberg, J., Su, Z. (eds.) SAS 2009. LNCS, vol. 5673, pp. 238–255. Springer, Heidelberg (2009). doi:10.1007/978-3-642-03237-0_17
18. Jones, J.: Priority queue data structure (2016). https://github.com/jasonsjones/queue-pri
19. Kashyap, V., Dewey, K., Kuefner, E.A., Wagner, J., Gibbons, K., Sarracino, J., Wiedermann, B., Hardekopf, B.: JSAI: a static analysis platform for JavaScript. In: FSE, pp. 121–132 (2014)
20. Kroening, D., Tautschnig, M.: CBMC – C bounded model checker. In: Ábrahám, E., Havelund, K. (eds.) TACAS 2014. LNCS, vol. 8413, pp. 389–391. Springer, Heidelberg (2014). doi:10.1007/978-3-642-54862-8_26
21. Livshits, B.: JSIR, an intermediate representation for JavaScript analysis (2014). http://too4words.github.io/jsir/
22. Park, D., Stefănescu, A., Roşu, G.: KJS: a complete formal semantics of JavaScript. In: Proceedings of the 36th ACM SIGPLAN Conference on Programming Language Design and Implementation, PLDI 2015, New York, USA, pp. 346–356. ACM (2015)
23. Politz, J.G., Carroll, M.J., Lerner, B.S., Pombrio, J., Krishnamurthi, S.: A tested semantics for getters, setters, and eval in JavaScript. In: Proceedings of the 8th Symposium on Dynamic Languages (2012)
24. Roşu, G., Şerbănuţă, T.F.: An overview of the K semantic framework. J. Logic Algebraic Program. 79(6), 397–434 (2010)
25. Schwinghammer, J., Birkedal, L., Reus, B., Yang, H.: Nested hoare triples and frame rules for higher-order store. Logical Methods Comput. Sci. 7(3), 1–42 (2011)
26. Sridharan, M., Dolby, J., Chandra, S., Schäfer, M., Tip, F.: Correlation tracking for points-to analysis of JavaScript. In: Noble, J. (ed.) ECOOP 2012. LNCS, vol. 7313, pp. 435–458. Springer, Heidelberg (2012). doi:10.1007/978-3-642-31057-7_20
27. Visser, W., Păsăreanu, C.S., Khurshid, S.: Test input generation with java pathfinder. In: Proceedings of the 2004 ACM SIGSOFT International Symposium on Software Testing and Analysis, ISSTA 2004, New York, USA, pp. 97–107. ACM (2004)

Formal Verification of Financial Algorithms

Grant Olney Passmore[1,2]([⊠]) and Denis Ignatovich[1]

[1] Aesthetic Integration, Ltd., London, UK
{grant,denis}@aestheticintegration.com
[2] Clare Hall, University of Cambridge, Cambridge, UK

Abstract. Many deep issues plaguing today's financial markets are symptoms of a fundamental problem: The complexity of algorithms underlying modern finance has significantly outpaced the power of traditional tools used to design and regulate them. At Aesthetic Integration, we have pioneered the use of formal verification for analysing the safety and fairness of financial algorithms. With a focus on financial infrastructure (e.g., the matching logics of exchanges and dark pools and FIX connectivity between trading systems), we describe the landscape, and illustrate our Imandra formal verification system on a number of real-world examples. We sketch many open problems and future directions along the way.

1 Introduction

The algorithms running modern financial markets are highly nontrivial engineering artefacts processing tremendous volumes of data at lightning speed. These algorithms must operate in a dynamic environment, adapt to ever-changing client demands and abide by numerous regulatory and internal controls. Despite this complexity, trading system operators must demonstrate to their clients and regulators that the underlying algorithms are compliant with numerous regulatory directives, and ensure that they in fact perform as described in disclosures and marketing materials.

As with other safety-critical industries, the complexity of financial algorithms has reached a point such that traditional (pre-formal) design, QA and regulation techniques are wildly insufficient. The state-spaces of the systems are simply too large, the corner cases too subtle and numerous to be managed by hand. From dark pool matching logics to blockchain smart contracts, recent catastrophic failures make it clear that formal verification is necessary to properly design, implement and regulate these critical systems that run our global economies.

The goal of this paper is two-fold: (1) To describe the landscape of financial algorithms to the formal verification community, making the verification opportunities and challenges concrete and accessible. Through the presentation of real-world verification efforts undertaken at Aesthetic Integration, we aim to help the practitioner develop useful intuitions and analogies with other more familiar verification endeavours (e.g., hardware verification). (2) To convince the reader that the complexity of financial algorithms has reached a point such that

© Springer International Publishing AG 2017
L. de Moura (Ed.): CADE 2017, LNAI 10395, pp. 26–41, 2017.
DOI: 10.1007/978-3-319-63046-5_3

the use of formal verification is no longer optional. It is critical that formal verification becomes a required part of financial practice and regulation. The more this topic can become a mainstream focus for the verification community, the more rapidly we shall be able to effect this important change.

1.1 Overview

We begin in Sect. 2 with what we call *The Stack of Financial Algorithms*. This gives an overall structure to the landscape of financial algorithms, arranging them in a hierarchy of increasing abstraction and dependence on lower subsystems. We summarise salient features of key levels of the stack and briefly describe their respective verification challenges.

In Sect. 3, we discuss our Imandra formal verification system and describe some of its features uniquely suited to financial algorithm verification.

In Sect. 4, we focus upon the lowest level of the stack: Verifying regulatory properties of trading venues. We present examples drawn from real-world case studies: The analysis of the order priority logic of the UBS ATS dark pool, and the analysis of the order pricing logic of a public exchange.

In Sect. 5, we focus on the "glue" that holds the stack together: Connectivity logic, e.g., the FIX (Financial Information eXchange) protocol layer that facilitates communication between trading systems. This is an area that benefits greatly from formal specification, verification and model-based testing.

In Sect. 6, we consider the verification of other types of financial algorithms, from blockchain smart contracts to market making algorithms. We touch on our Imandra model of the Ethereum Virtual Machine (EVM) and discuss how it can be used to analyse smart contracts. We consider ascending the stack further and discuss the financial mathematics that must be formalised in order to do so. We argue for the need for *new* financial mathematics that properly takes into account the complex discrete behaviour of venue matching logics and other subsystems low in the stack.

Finally, we conclude with some hopes for the future.

2   The Stack of Financial Algorithms

It is natural to view financial algorithms as arranged in a stack. From the verification perspective, there is a strong analogy between our stack given in Fig. 1 and verified towers of computing systems such as the CLI Stack [2]. In general, we find the most complex critical infrastructure at low levels of the stack. This infrastructure, including the algorithms running public exchanges such as New York Stock Exchange, is shared and relied upon by market participants. As we proceed up to higher levels, we find increasingly proprietary systems which rely upon abstractions of those systems that came below.

Fundamentally, one cannot properly reason about the possible behaviours of a system higher in the stack (e.g., an "execution algo") unless one has verified the relevant properties of the supporting subsystems that ultimately will be

Fig. 1. The stack of financial algorithms

executing its intentions (e.g., a "venue"). In fact, we view the *matching logics* of venues as providing an Instruction Set Architecture (ISA) for the markets, in much the same way that a microprocessor design provides an ISA relied upon by higher-level compilers, operating systems and user-mode programs. As we ascend the stack, the algorithms involved may utilise more abstractions and higher mathematics, but ultimately their intentions (e.g., "send a MARKET order to NASDAQ to buy 10000 shares of Google") will be executed by systems lower in the stack, finally resulting in trade(s) at a collection of venues.

2.1 Venues

At the base of the stack, we have trading venues. These systems, such as New York Stock Exchange, London Stock Exchange, NASDAQ, a *multilateral trading facility* (MTF) or a *dark pool* inside of a bank, maintain *order books* and facilitate trades between clients.

Their functionality is high frequency and nonlinear with complex discrete dynamics: At each time-step, the order book they maintain for a given security is sorted with respect to an order priority criteria, and in one common mode of operation (*continuous trading*), the top eligible *bid* (buy) and *offer* (sell) orders are *matched*, potentially resulting in a *fill* (trade) at a price determined as a function of the *order types* of the bid and offer and current market conditions.

The discrete behaviour of modern trading venues is staggering in its complexity. They support a plethora of order types, transition between different *modes* of operation based upon volatility triggers and times of day, and must abide by client and jurisdiction specific constraints. Complex fairness and safety regulations govern the behaviours of these systems [7–9,19].

Venues are an ideal target for formal verification. Indeed, if venues are not safe, fair and correct, e.g., if one can exploit flaws in the venue matching logic to jump the queue and have their orders unfairly prioritised over others, then "all bets are off" as one ascends the stack to more complex algorithms. We shall describe the verification of trading venue matching logics in Sect. 4.

2.2 Smart Order Routers

Modern markets are fragmented. The same financial instrument is often traded on many different venues. The price and quantity available on different venues may vary. Smart Order Routers (SORs) are systems which track the states of a collection of venues, and attempt to decompose and route orders to venues in the "best" possible way. SORs must satisfy many regulatory controls. For example, the US Securities and Exchange Commission (SEC) Regulation NMS requires order routing to abide by strict *best execution* requirements [18].

2.3 Execution Algorithms

Execution algorithms (or "algos") typically operate on a "higher level" than SORs and encode strategies for market participation on a lower time frequency. Their objectives vary between following precise client instructions on an "agency" basis whereby the client bears ultimate execution risk and cost, to those operating on a "principal" basis such as automated market-making or inventory optimisation strategies. These algorithms, often designed by "quants" (e.g., physicists who have turned their attention to the markets), are typically closely guarded IP of financial institutions. The mathematics behind them may run the gamut of "financial mathematics," involving heavy use of statistics, machine learning, stochastic calculus, nonlinear optimisation, Monte Carlo methods and so on.

From a regulatory perspective, one must ensure many invariants. For example, an algo should not encode strategies for "spoofing" or unlawful market manipulation. Modern formal verification may be directly brought to bear on key safety and fairness criteria (e.g., for algos structured with discrete *risk gates* and *circuit breakers*). For other analyses, new methods and formalised financial mathematics are necessary. We discuss this more in Sect. 6.3.

2.4 Ascending the Stack

As we ascend the stack, we encounter many more kinds of algorithms. For example, derivatives and other structured products may be represented as algorithms [17]. There is a growing community built around trying to represent financial instruments and other legal contracts as so-called *smart contracts*, making them amenable to formal analysis and perhaps executing them autonomously on distributed ledger ("blockchain") technology like Ethereum [3]. We discuss the formal verification of smart contracts in Sect. 6.1. Similarly, the connectivity protocol layers facilitating communication between different trading systems may be very complex, with numerous regulatory and compliance requirements. We discuss connectivity in Sect. 5.

3   Introduction to Imandra

Imandra is our formal verification system designed specifically to meet the needs of financial algorithm verification and analysis. Imandra is both a programming language in which algorithms may be expressed and executed, and a reasoning engine with which properties of these algorithms may be proved, refuted and described. Programs and their properties are written in the Imandra Modelling Language (IML), a functionally pure subset of OCaml [12]. Imandra's logic is built around an executable operational semantics for IML. At the lowest level, a user interacts with Imandra via a textual toplevel read-eval-print loop, similar to OCaml's, but instrumented with additional verification features. Higher-level graphical interfaces and DSLs empower stakeholders of varying levels of technicality to converge around precise formal models, using them as the basis for design, testing, compliance and documentation generation (cf. Sect. 5). In many ways, the core of Imandra can be seen as an adaptation of ideas of ACL2 [11] from Common Lisp to OCaml, extended with first-class counterexamples, state-space decompositions and automation (e.g., specialised nonlinear decision procedures) supporting financial algorithm analysis.

Let us discuss a few features of Imandra which we find especially useful.

3.1   Computing with Counterexamples

When Imandra refutes a conjecture through the construction of a counterexample, that counterexample is reflected into the system (as a valid OCaml value) and may be computed with like any other. Imandra's reasoning engine is tailored towards the construction of counterexamples, with nonlinear and model-building SMT-based decision procedures integrated with its simplifier, induction and recursion-unrolling techniques [4,14,16]. In our experience, this unified computational environment for computing with formal models, verifying them and investigating their counterexamples is crucial for efficiently debugging regulatory violations of trading systems, where counterexamples exhibiting unlawful behaviour may consist of long sequences of FIX messages. This idea is so deeply embedded in the design of the system, and subtle flaws in trading systems so common, that we often view Imandra as an environment for "computing with counterexamples." A small example is given in Fig. 2.

3.2   Principal Region Decompositions

Imandra has a first-class notion of state-space decompositions which we call *principal region decompositions*. These allow one to compute a symbolic representation of the possible unique behaviours of a program subject to a given query constraint. For example: "Compute all regions of the venue state-space in which the price of the next trade will be the venue's reference price," or "Compute all regions of the state-space that will cause the venue to transition into volatility auction." These region descriptions are subject to a given *basis*, a collection of

```
# verify rank_antisym (x,y) =
    order_higher_ranked_long (x,y)
    ==>
    not (order_higher_ranked_long (y,x));;

Counterexample:

  { x = { order_id = 8;
          order_type = Market;
          order_qty = 9;
          hidden_liquidity = true;
          max_visible_qty = 10;
          display_qty = 11;
          replenish_qty = 6;
          order_price = 25.0;
          order_time = 0;
          order_src = { client_id = 7;
                        client_group = G_MM;
                        client_will_trade_against = []; };
          order_attr = Normal; };
    y = { order_id = 2;
          order_type = Market;
          order_qty = 3;
          hidden_liquidity = true;
          max_visible_qty = 4;
          display_qty = 5;
          replenish_qty = 6;
          order_price = 25.0;
          order_time = 7719;
          order_src = { client_id = 1;
                        client_group = G_MM;
                        client_will_trade_against = []; };
          order_attr = Normal; }; }

# CX.x;;
- : order =
{order_id = 8; order_type = Market; order_qty = 9;
 hidden_liquidity = true; max_visible_qty = 10;
 display_qty = 11; replenish_qty = 6; order_price = 25.;
 order_time = 0;
 order_src = {client_id = 7; client_group = G_MM;
              client_will_trade_against = []};
 order_attr = Normal}
# CX.y.order_type;;
- : order_type = Market
# order_higher_ranked_long (CX.x,CX.y);;
- : bool = true
# order_higher_ranked_long (CX.y,CX.x);;
- : bool = true
# verify rank_antisym_refined (x,y) =
    x.order_type <> y.order_type
    && order_higher_ranked_long (x,y)
    && not (x.hidden_liquidity || y.hidden_liquidity)
    ==>
    not (order_higher_ranked_long (y,x));;
thm rank_antisym_refined = <proved>
```

Fig. 2. Computing with counterexamples in Imandra

functions whose definitions will not be expanded and may carry lemmata expos-
ing facts about their behaviour. We compute these decompositions through a
special form of symbolic execution. Decompositions play a key role in how we
generate certified documentation and high-coverage test suites (cf. Sect. 4). We
often represent them as interactive hierarchical voronoi diagrams (cf. Fig. 3).

Fig. 3. A principal region decomposition of a venue pricing function

3.3   Staged Symbolic Execution

In Imandra, we typically model trading systems in the Boyer-Moore style of machine operational semantics [2,11]. That is, we define a `state` record type representing "all data" available to the system at any discrete time step, a `one_step : state -> state` function which executes a step of the machine, and a (clocked) recursive `run` function which iterates `one_step` until completion. Inductive properties are proved for `one_step` and then lifted to `run`. Imandra supports *staged symbolic execution* [6,11]. We usually stage the toplevel `run` function of a model, so that its recursive definition will not be unrolled unless its arguments are maximally simplified. Let us examine this modelling paradigm in practice.

4   Verifying Trading Venue Matching Logics

In this section, we examine the formal verification of a trading venue's matching logic[1]. We assume the reader has read Sect. 2.1.

4.1   A Primer on Market Microstructure

Venues maintain sorted order books (e.g., lists of buy and sell orders for a given stock), process incoming messages and execute and report on trades[2]. Modern venues support many complex order types. The simplest order type is a Market order. A Market order is of the form: "Buy (or sell) 100 shares of Microsoft at any price." Market orders are the most aggressive kind of orders. They are risky as the market can easily move against you, and there is nothing in your order to protect you. Limit orders add in a level of protection. A typical Limit order is of the form: "Buy (or sell) 100 shares of Microsoft at at most (or at least) $70/share." In a dark pool (e.g., a venue inside of a bank), orders may be *pegged* to the National Best Bid/Offer (NBBO), a representation of market conditions with accompanying regulations to ensure clients are filled at fair prices. So-called Iceberg orders may possess *hidden liquidity*. Then there are Stop-Loss orders, Stop-Limit orders, Conditional Indications (CIs), Quotes, Hide-Not-Slide orders, Retail IOCs, ... Each order type may have wildly different discrete behaviour than the next, and may even differ between venues (e.g., order X at venue V may not behave the same as order X at venue V' at 3 pm on Wednesdays).

Nevertheless, venues must abide by strict regulatory constraints and provide correct descriptions of their matching logics to clients and regulators. Regulators are tasked with ensuring these systems satisfy regulations. Clients are tasked with ensuring they understand the implications of the orders they submit. Currently, these disclosures describing how venues work are made in prose documents, often hundreds of pages long. Imagine trying to build a skyscraper, not with a mathematically analysable precise blueprint, but with the design described in hundreds of pages of prose. This is clearly insufficient as the basis of safe and fair markets.

Thus, a major thrust of our work has been to build tools for financial institutions and regulators to precisely specify the behaviours of their systems and equip them with the power of formal verification to inspect them. We refer to this as the *Precise Specification Standard* and have outlined its many benefits to the US Securities and Exchange Commission [10].

4.2   Venue Verification Goals

At AI, we have built libraries of formal encodings of regulatory directives with corresponding verification automation. For dark pools, a small subset includes:

---

[1] More details and case studies may be found in AI technical whitepapers [7–9].
[2] Harris's *Trading and Exchanges: Market Microstructure for Practitioners* provides an excellent introduction [5].

- Baseline:
  - No fills outside NBBO
  - Operator system halt ceases trading
  - Orders entered into the book must have valid prices, rejected otherwise
  - Orders entered into the book must have valid quantities (including minimum quantity), rejected otherwise
- Fairness and Priority:
  - Isolation of client information on effects of pricing and fills: client ID does not play role in determining fill price
  - No sub-penny pricing: prices only in exchange increments are accepted
  - Verification of prioritisation stability and fairness: No sequence of events can cause an order to unfairly jump the queue (price/time priority)
- Resilience/Market Volatility:
  - Effective execution following halt recovery
  - In crossed markets, no trading takes place
  - In locked markets, orders are matched
- Order Types and Pricing:
  - Orders cannot get filled for more than order quantity
  - Orders cannot get filled for less than minimum quantity
  - Fills cannot happen outside the limit prices; proper sliding and rounding
  - FOK orders cannot be partially filled: either fully filled or rejected

Violations often arise with subtle, unforeseen interactions between order types. With formal verification, we can symbolically analyse the entire state space and eliminate potential exploits. Below, we shall see how rather innocuous looking order priority logic can in fact be gamed.

4.3   UBS ATS and Transitivity of Order Ranking

Let us analyse the order priority logic of a dark pool. We base this analysis on UBS's June 1st, 2015 SEC filing (Form ATS) [7]. This work contributed to AI winning first place in the UBS Future of Finance Challenge (out of 620 companies from 52 countries).

In January of 2015, UBS was fined \$14.4M for regulatory violations of UBS ATS. In particular, UBS ATS allowed sub-penny orders and supported undisclosed crossing constraints. The investigation took place over many years, with much of the SEC's work involving analysing post-trade data.

At AI, we set out to show how formal verification could be applied to find and eliminate these issues at the design stage, before the dark pool violated regulations. In the process, Imandra found a much more fundamental flaw in the way UBS's dark pool design prioritised orders in its book: The ranking function used to prioritise orders was not *transitive*. If one then sorts the book using it, the lack of transitivity may be exploited to allow unfair behaviour. To show this, Imandra synthesised three orders and concrete market conditions illustrating the violation.

Rank Transitivity. A detailed account of the priority logic, including definitions of the order types and market condition logic may be found in AI's *Case Study: 2015 SEC Fine Against UBS ATS* [7]. Imandra formalisations of the effective pricing and final ranking logic are given in Figs. 4 and 5.
A few points of note:

1. The `order_higher_ranked` function is used to sort the order book and determine which orders are next eligible to trade.
2. The `effective_price` function takes into account order *pegging* and current market conditions (NBBO).
3. The `ci` function checks whether or not an order is a Conditional Indication.
4. The `less_agg` function determines the "least aggressive" of two prices on the same side of the book.

```
let effective_price (side, o, mkt) =
  let mkt_a = if side = Buy then mkt.nbo else mkt.nbb in
  let mkt_b = if side = Buy then mkt.nbb else mkt.nbo in
  let pegged_price = match o.peg with
    | Far -> less_agg (side, o.price, mkt_a)
    | Mid -> less_agg (side, o.price, mid_point mkt)
    | Near -> less_agg (side, o.price, mkt_b)
    | No_peg -> o.price in
  let nbbo_capped_limit =
    if side = Buy then less_agg (Buy, o.price, mkt.nbo)
    else less_agg (Sell, o.price, mkt.nbb) in
  match o.order_type with
    | Limit          -> nbbo_capped_limit
    | Market         -> mkt_a
    | Pegged         -> pegged_price
    | Pegged_CI      -> pegged_price
    | Limit_CI       -> nbbo_capped_limit
    | Firm_up_pegged -> pegged_price
    | Firm_up_limit  -> nbbo_capped_limit
```

Fig. 4. Effective pricing

With the formal model in hand, we can now pose a query to Imandra:

```
verify rank_transitivity (side, o1, o2, o3, mkt) =
  order_higher_ranked (side, o1, o2, mkt)
  && order_higher_ranked (side, o2, o3, mkt)
  ==>
  order_higher_ranked (side, o1, o3, mkt)
```

Imandra returns with a counterexample (we elide many components):

```
o1 = { peg = Near;          o2 = { peg = Near;             o3 = { peg = Near;
       order_type = Pegged;        order_type = Pegged_CI;        order_type = Pegged_CI;
       qty = 1797;                 qty = 2439;                    qty = 2438;
       price = 10.0;               price = 13.1;                  price = 10.5;
       time = 8857;                time = 8857;                   time = 8856;
       ...                         ...                            ...

}                           }                              }
```

An iterative process of studying the counterexample, fixing flaws in the design and verifying the result may then ensue [7–9].

```
let order_higher_ranked (side, o1, o2, mkt) =
  let ot1 = o1.order_type in
  let ot2 = o2.order_type in
  let p_price1 = effective_price (side, o1, mkt) in
  let p_price2 = effective_price (side, o2, mkt) in
  let wins_price =
    if side = Buy then
      if p_price1 > p_price2 then 1
      else if p_price1 = p_price2 then 0
      else −1
    else if p_price1 < p_price2 then 1
    else if p_price1 = p_price2 then 0
    else −1 in
  let wins_time =
    if o1.time < o2.time then 1
    else if o1.time = o2.time then 0 else −1 in
  let wins_qty =
    if o1.qty > o2.qty then 1
    else if o2.qty = o1.qty then 0 else −1 in
  if wins_price = 1 then true
  else if wins_price = −1 then false
  else if ci(ot1) && ci(ot2) then
    if wins_qty = 0 then wins_time = 1 else
    if wins_qty = 1 then true else false
  else if wins_time = 1 then true
  else if wins_time = −1 then false
  else if not (ci (ot1)) then true
  else o1.qty > o2.qty
```

Fig. 5. Order ranking logic

Beyond Order Priority. Once the order priority logic is bullet-proof, we may turn our attention to verifying global properties of the venue design. For example, though the venue must have access to the *source* of an order (e.g., so as to abide by client-specific crossing constraints and communicate fills and order updates), it must never be the case that the matching logic disadvantages one class of clients over another when it comes to pricing or priority.

This non-interference property can be verified for a match_price : state -> price function (cf. Fig. 6), lifted to one_step : state -> state and finally proved by induction for run [9].

```
verify match_price_ignores_order_src (s, s', b1, s1, b2, s2) =
  orders_same_except_source (b1, b2)
    && orders_same_except_source (s1, s2)
    && states_same_except_order_book (s, s')
    && sides_correspond(tl s.order_book.buys, tl s'.order_book.buys)
    && sides_correspond(tl s.order_book.sells, tl s'.order_book.sells)
    && best_buy s = Some b1
    && best_sell s = Some s1
    && best_buy s' = Some b2
    && best_sell s' = Some s2
    ==>
  match_price s = match_price s'
```

Fig. 6. Verifying that customer data does not interfere with pricing

The final verified design can then be used in production, as the basis for QA via model-based testing and the generation of high-coverage test suites, as a live market monitor to ensure conformance to the specification, to generate (interactive, queryable) documentation and disclosures and explore improvements (e.g., the addition of new order types) together with their regulatory ramifications.

5 Verifying Trading System Connectivity

Trading systems do not exist in isolation. A typical SOR may connect with tens or even hundreds of venues. The FIX protocol is often used to facilitate this communication.

FIX is an evolving global standard which gives users (i.e., trading system operators) much freedom in the precise (customised) version of the protocol that they support. These firms typically provide *FIX specs* to their clients, detailing their precise subset and customisations of the protocol. FIX specifications are complex documents, often written in hundreds of pages of prose, similar in complexity to venue matching logic disclosures. Consider the task of an SOR developer connecting to two-hundred different venues, each with their own complex FIX spec which may change multiple times a year. From design and testing to compliance sign-off, enormous resources are spent on these connectivity tasks.

Formal FIX specs are clearly needed. Once we have precise specs, we can utilise formal verification to analyse their consistency, perform model-based testing, generate certified documentation, create simulation environments and automate many tasks around connectivity compliance.

We have introduced this functionality with our FIX DSL and Imandra Markets ecosystem. FIX DSL is a high-level language designed for building formal FIX specs. FIX DSL compiles its models into IML and Imandra can then be used to power deep analyses. Imandra Markets is a cloud-based collaborative ecosystem for financial institutions to develop and share formal FIX specs with one another. Armed with these specs, Imandra verifies key properties, creates high-coverage test suites, simulators and certified documentation, and eliminates many expensive and error-prone aspects of compliance and client onboarding.

As part of this effort, we have formalised the FIX protocol in Imandra and verified an executable FIX administrative engine[3]. We hope this project will be the beginning of an industry-wide effort to mathematically formalise the rules and algorithms that run the financial markets.

FIX Engine Verification Example. Consider the following quote from Volume 2 of the FIX 4.4 specification:

> When either end of a FIX connection has not sent any data for
> [HeartBtInt] seconds, it will transmit a Heartbeat message.

---

[3] We have released our verified FIX engine under an Apache 2.0 license. See http:// fix.readme.io for documentation and http://github.com/AestheticIntegration/ fix-engine for the code.

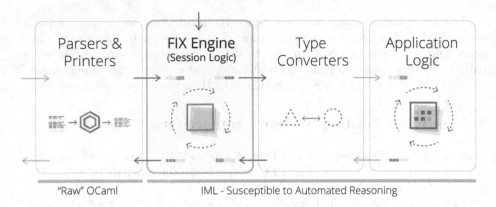

"Raw" OCaml   IML - Susceptible to Automated Reasoning

Fig. 7. Structure of our FIX engine + FIX application models

One way to formalise this statement is to create two verification goals:

1. Every outbound message will result in a properly updated `last_time_data_sent` field.
2. Every time update will result in a check as to whether a `Heartbeat` should be transmitted.

```
verify last_time_data_sent_gets_updated (engine : fix_engine_state) =
  let engine' = one_step (engine) in
  engine.outgoing_fix_msg = None && engine'.outgoing_fix_msg <> None
  ==>
  engine'.last_time_data_sent = engine'.curr_time

verify heartbeat_sent_if_no_data_received (engine : fix_engine_state) =
  let engine' = one_step (engine) in
  engine.fe_curr_mode = ActiveSession
  && is_int_message_valid (engine)
  && is_state_valid (engine)
  && time_update_received (engine.incoming_int_msg,
                           engine.last_time_data_sent,
                           engine.heartbeat_interval)
  ==>
  outbound_msg_heartbeat (engine'.outgoing_fix_msg)
```

Fig. 8. Verifying a heartbeat property of the FIX engine

We present Imandra encodings of these `one_step` progress properties in Fig. 8.

6   Ascending the Stack

Thus far, we have presented work on the verification of critical financial infrastructure. In this section, we shall consider other classes of financial algorithms.

6.1   Ethereum Virtual Machine

Ethereum is popular blockchain platform for developing and executing smart contracts [3]. Ethereum has a stack-based virtual machine (EVM), and contract code is ultimately compiled into EVM bytecode. A non-mechanised semantics for EVM bytecode was given in the so-called Ethereum "yellow paper" [20]. In 2015, we began building an executable Imandra formal model of the EVM. In June 2016, a major flaw in an Ethereum smart contract was exploited, resulting in tens of millions of dollars of losses for investors. This so-called "DAO fiasco" has made the need for formal verification utterly apparent to the smart contract community. In October, 2016 we released our formal EVM model open source[4]. Armed with this formal model, Imandra can analyse Ethereum bytecode, be used to prove theorems about its possible behaviours, perform region decompositions and symbolic executions and "lift" the bytecode into logic [15]. There is now a growing community of verification enthusiasts and practitioners in the blockchain space, with EVM bytecode analysis taking place at least in Isabelle/HOL and Coq. New smart contract platforms are being developed, with a focus towards "verifiability" at the forefront. This is often manifested through a push for applicative (i.e., functionally pure) contract specification languages. We are working on Imandra-based tools and APIs for the smart contract and blockchain communities.

6.2   Derivatives and Structured Products

Derivatives and structured products may be represented as algorithms. For example, the French company LexiFi has developed a DSL on top of OCaml (MLFi) for describing, pricing and managing the lifecycle of these artefacts [17]. Integrated with Bloomberg products, these tools are widely used. While there is no formal verification involved, we find this mainstream uptake of algorithmically described financial contracts encouraging. There are many exciting potential applications of formal verification in this space. Interesting work on formal variants of LexiFi's approach have been undertaken [1]. We see great potential for this area, especially at the portfolio level.

6.3   Formalised (New) Financial Mathematics

As we continue up the stack and consider applying verification to new classes of financial algorithms and models, we are faced with a major challenge: Much of the "financial mathematics" involved in the design and analysis of these algorithms has not yet been formalised in a proof assistant.

With Larry Paulson, we have developed a plan for the formalisation of some of this material in Isabelle/HOL. It runs the gamut from real analysis to martingales, Wiener processes, stochastic calculus and PDEs. We aim to support

---

[4] The model may be found in our Imandra Contracts Community Models repository at http://github.com/AestheticIntegration/contracts.

this work through funded PhD studentships, collaboration on formalisation and automatic proof procedures, and the contribution of real-world Imandra models of the underlying market microstructure [13].

Indeed, we believe strongly that fundamentally *new* financial mathematics must be developed that takes into account the precise discrete behaviour of the underlying software systems (venues, SORs, etc.). The stochastic and continuous models typically used by financial economists abstract away so many important details of the underlying systems, and for good reason: Before we had formal models of the financial infrastructure, it was hardly possible to do better. But as the actual precise discrete logic governing the markets becomes increasingly available and amenable to formal verification, new powerful analytical tools will make it possible to reason "closer to the metal," with financial economic models that are far more faithful to reality.

7 Conclusion

We have argued that formal verification is necessary to ensure the safety, fairness and proper regulation of modern financial markets. From dark pool matching logics to FIX connectivity and formalised financial mathematics, we have presented our views on the verification opportunities and challenges. For some classes of systems, especially infrastructure components low in the stack, there is a strong analogy with other verification endeavours and much overlap in techniques. For others, new methods are needed.

It is a most exciting time to be working in formal verification, ripe for fundamental breakthroughs. We hope that ten years from now, formal verification is as common in finance as it is in microprocessor design. Perhaps the verification practitioner of the future will be as familiar with verifying matching logics as they are with verifying compilers.

Acknowledgements. We thank our incredible team at Aesthetic Integration. Without them, much of this work would not have been accomplished. In particular, Konstantin Kanishev, Ewen Maclean, Sergey Grigorchuk and Matt Bray have been crucially involved in the design and implementation of the Imandra FIX DSL and its surrounding verification infrastructure. Elijah Kagan's unique design perspective has helped us communicate our ideas much more effectively and enjoyably than we would have been able to otherwise.

Finally, we thank Jeremy Avigad, Bob Boyer, Gerry Dunning, Paul Jackson, J Moore, Leo de Moura, Larry Paulson, John Detrixhe of Bloomberg, Philip Stafford of the Financial Times, Jim Northey of the FIX Trading Community and Austin Gerig of the US Securities and Exchange Commission for their encouragement, useful discussions and advice.

References

1. Bahr, P., Berthold, J., Elsman, M.: Certified symbolic management of financial multi-party contracts. In: 20th ACM SIGPLAN International Conference on Functional Programming, ICFP 2015, pp. 315–327 (2015)
2. Bevier, W.R., Hunt, W.A., Moore, J.S., Young, W.D.: Special issue on system verification. J. Autom. Reasoning **5**(4), 409–530 (1989)
3. Buterin, V.: Ethereum: a next-generation smart contract and decentralized application platform (2014). https://github.com/ethereum/wiki/wiki/White-Paper
4. De Moura, L., Bjørner, N.: Satisfiability modulo theories: introduction and applications. Commun. ACM **54**(9), 69–77 (2011)
5. Harris, L.: Trading and Exchanges: Market Microstructure for Practitioners. Oxford University Press, Oxford (2002)
6. Hunt Jr., W.A., Krug, R.B., Moore, J.: Integrating nonlinear arithmetic into ACL2. In: Fifth International Workshop on the ACL2 Theorem Prover and Its Applications (2004)
7. Ignatovich, D.A., Passmore, G.O.: Case Study: 2015 SEC Fine Against UBS ATS. Aesthetic Integration, Ltd., Technical Whitepaper (2015)
8. Ignatovich, D.A., Passmore, G.O.: Creating Safe and Fair Markets. Aesthetic Integration, Ltd., Technical Whitepaper (2015)
9. Ignatovich, D.A., Passmore, G.O.: Transparent Order Priority and Pricing. Aesthetic Integration, Ltd., Technical Whitepaper (2015)
10. Ignatovich, D.A., Passmore, G.O.: Comment on SEC Reg ATS-N: The Precise Specification Standard, February 2016. https://www.sec.gov/comments/s7-23-15/s72315-24.pdf
11. Kaufmann, M., Moore, J.S., Manolios, P.: Computer-Aided Reasoning: An Approach. Kluwer Academic Publishers, Norwell (2000)
12. Leroy, X., Doligez, D., Frisch, A., Garrigue, J., Rémy, D., Vouillon, J.: The OCaml system (release 4.04): Documentation and user's manual. INRIA (2017)
13. Li, W., Passmore, G.O., Paulson, L.C.: Deciding Univariate Polynomial Problems Using Untrusted Certificates in Isabelle/HOL. J. Autom. Reasoning (2017)
14. Moura, L., Passmore, G.O.: The strategy challenge in SMT solving. In: Bonacina, M.P., Stickel, M.E. (eds.) Automated Reasoning and Mathematics. LNCS, vol. 7788, pp. 15–44. Springer, Heidelberg (2013). doi:10.1007/978-3-642-36675-8_2
15. Myreen, M.O.: Formal verification of machine-code programs. Ph.D. thesis, University of Cambridge (2009)
16. Passmore, G.O.: Combined decision procedures for nonlinear arithmetics, real and complex. Ph.D. thesis, University of Edinburgh (2011)
17. Peyton Jones, S., Eber, J.M., Seward, J.: Composing contracts: an adventure in financial engineering (functional pearl). SIGPLAN Not. **35**(9), 280–292 (2000). http://doi.acm.org/10.1145/357766.351267
18. US Securities and Exchange Commission: Regulation National Market System (Reg NMS) (2005). https://www.sec.gov/rules/final/34-51808.pdf
19. US Securities and Exchange Commission: Regulation Alternative Trading Systems (Reg ATS) (2015). https://www.sec.gov/rules/proposed/2015/34-76474.pdf
20. Wood, G.: Ethereum: a secure decentralised generalised transaction ledger (2014). http://gavwood.com/paper.pdf

Satisfiability Modulo Theories and Assignments

Maria Paola Bonacina[1]($\boxtimes$), Stéphane Graham-Lengrand[2,3],
and Natarajan Shankar[2]

[1] Università degli Studi di Verona, Verona, Italy
`mariapaola.bonacina@univr.it`
[2] SRI International, Menlo Park, USA
`graham-lengrand@lix.polytechnique.fr, shankar@csl.sri.com`
[3] CNRS - INRIA - École Polytechnique, Palaiseau, France

Abstract. The CDCL procedure for SAT is the archetype of *conflict-driven* procedures for satisfiability of quantifier-free problems in a single theory. In this paper we lift CDCL to CDSAT (*Conflict-Driven Satisfiability*), a system for conflict-driven reasoning in combinations of disjoint theories. CDSAT combines *theory modules* that interact through a global *trail* representing a candidate model by Boolean and first-order assignments. CDSAT generalizes to generic theory combinations the *model-constructing satisfiability calculus* (MCSAT) introduced by de Moura and Jovanović. Furthermore, CDSAT generalizes the *equality sharing* (Nelson-Oppen) approach to theory combination, by allowing theories to share equality information both explicitly through equalities and disequalities, and implicitly through assignments. We identify sufficient conditions for the *soundness*, *completeness*, and *termination* of CDSAT.

Keywords: Theory combination · Conflict-driven decision procedures · Model building · Satisfiability modulo assignment

1 Introduction

A growing trend in automated deduction is the generalization of *conflict-driven reasoning* from propositional to first-order logic (cf. [2] for a brief coeval survey). For propositional satisfiability (SAT), the conflict-driven clause learning (CDCL) procedure works by guessing assignments to variables, propagating their consequences through clauses, and learning new clauses, or lemmas, when assignments lead to conflicts [14]. The conflict-driven paradigm has been extended to decide the $\mathcal{T}$-satisfiability of sets of literals when $\mathcal{T}$ is one of several fragments of arithmetic [4,7,10–12,15,17,18]. Key features of such *conflict-driven $\mathcal{T}$-satisfiability procedures* are the use of assignments to first-order variables and the explanation of conflicts with lemmas, which may contain atoms that are not in the input. We illustrate these features by an example. Consider the following set of literals, which is unsatisfiable in Linear Rational Arithmetic (LRA):

$$R = \{l_0 : (-2 \cdot x - y < 0), \quad l_1 : (x + y < 0), \quad l_2 : (x < -1)\}.$$

© Springer International Publishing AG 2017
L. de Moura (Ed.): CADE 2017, LNAI 10395, pp. 42–59, 2017.
DOI: 10.1007/978-3-319-63046-5_4

A conflict-driven LRA-satisfiability procedure attempts to build a model by guessing a value for one of the variables, say $y \leftarrow 0$. This lets l_0 yield the lower bound $x > 0$. Given the upper bound l_2, the space of possible values for x is empty, revealing that the guess and the constraints are in conflict. The procedure explains the conflict by the *new atom* $l_3 : (-y < -2)$, the linear combination of l_0 and l_2 that eliminates x. This excludes not only $y \leftarrow 0$, but also all assignments $y \leftarrow c$ where $c \leq 2$. Suppose the procedure retracts the assignment $y \leftarrow 0$ and tries $y \leftarrow 4$. This lets l_1 yield the upper bound $x < -4$, and l_0 the lower bound $x > -2$. The procedure explains this conflict by the new atom $l_4 : (y < 0)$, the linear combination of l_0 and l_1 that eliminates x. As l_4 is violated by the assignment $y \leftarrow 4$, the procedure retracts $y \leftarrow 4$. Then no assignment to y can satisfy both l_3 and l_4. This third conflict is explained by the linear combination of l_3 and l_4 that eliminates y, namely $0 < -2$, which is also a new atom. Since this consequence of the original problem is a contradiction, the procedure returns unsatisfiable.

Applications typically require deciding the satisfiability of arbitrary quantifier-free formulae, or, equivalently, sets of ground clauses, in a combination T of theories $T_1, \ldots, T_n$. The DPLL(T) approach [1,13] combines a CDCL-based SAT-solver with a T-satisfiability procedure, obtained from T_i-satisfiability procedures by the *equality sharing* method [16], assuming that the theories T_i are *disjoint* and *stably infinite*: they do not share symbols other than equality and admit countably infinite models. The T_i-satisfiability procedures are combined as black-boxes that only propagate equalities between shared variables. DPLL(T) uses their combination as a black-box that only detects T-conflicts and propagates T-lemmas, while the SAT-solver tries assignments and builds a candidate model. If conflict-driven T_i-satisfiability procedures were integrated in this manner, the combination would not be conflict-driven. To make it conflict-driven, the T_i-satisfiability procedures need to cooperate to build a model, sharing assignments and exporting lemmas to explain conflicts, possibly using new atoms.

MCSAT, for *Model-Constructing Satisfiability*, is a paradigm for integrating a CDCL-based SAT-solver with a conflict-driven T-satisfiability procedure [5]. MCSAT uses first-order assignments on a par with Boolean ones, coordinates the conflict explanation mechanisms at the Boolean and theory levels in a unified manner, and incorporates the capability of creating new atoms. MCSAT lifted CDCL to SMT in the sense of *satisfiability modulo a single theory T*, which was instantiated to the theory of bit-vectors [19] and to non-linear integer arithmetic [8]. A version of MCSAT was also given for the specific combination of LRA and Equality with Uninterpreted Function symbols (EUF) [9], but the conflict-driven combination of a generic range of theories remained an open problem.

In this paper we generalize *conflict-driven reasoning* to generic combinations of disjoint theories, solving the problem of combining multiple conflict-driven T_i-satisfiability procedures into a conflict-driven T-satisfiability procedure. We introduce a new method for theory combination, called CDSAT for *Conflict-Driven Satisfiability*. For example, it decides the satisfiability of problems in the combination of LRA, EUF and the theory of arrays, such as

$$P = \{f(\mathsf{select}(\mathsf{store}(a, i, v), j)) \simeq w, \ f(u) \simeq w{-}2, \ i \simeq j, \ u \simeq v\}.$$

CDSAT treats propositional and theory reasoning uniformly: formulae are terms of sort prop (for proposition); propositional logic is one of the theories $T_1, \ldots, T_n$; and CDCL is one of the T_i-satisfiability procedures to be combined. With formulae reduced to terms, *assignments* become the data manipulated by inferences. CDSAT combines T_i-inference systems, called *theory modules* [6], rather than T_i-satisfiability procedure. Ideally, a T_i-satisfiability procedure, like any reasoning procedure, is defined by an inference system and a search plan. Since all conflict-driven procedures have the same conflict-driven search plan, what needs to be combined are the inference systems, while the common conflict-driven control is factored out and handled centrally by CDSAT. We prove that CDSAT is *sound*, *complete*, and *terminating*, identifying the sufficient conditions that theories and theory modules need to fulfill for these properties to hold.

We believe that the abstraction of viewing combination of theories as combination of inference systems, rather than procedures, allows us to bring simplicity and elegance to theory combination. A T_i-satisfiability procedure that is not conflict-driven can still be integrated in CDSAT by treating it as a theory module whose only inference rule invokes the T_i-satisfiability procedure to detect the T_i-unsatisfiability of a set of assignments. Therefore CDSAT subsumes both MCSAT and equality sharing. CDSAT reduces to MCSAT, if there are only propositional logic with CDCL and another theory T with a conflict-driven T-satisfiability procedure. CDSAT reduces to equality sharing, if none of the theories has a conflict-driven T-satisfiability procedure.

2   Preliminaries

We assume the basic definitions of multi-sorted first-order logic. A *signature* $\Sigma = (S, F)$ consists of a set S of *sorts*, including prop, and a set F of *symbols*, including a collection $\simeq_S$ of equality symbols $\simeq_s : (s \times s) \rightarrow$ prop for every $s \in S$. Sorts can be omitted when clear from context. The other symbols in F may be constant, function, and predicate symbols, as well as logical connectives such as $\wedge$, $\vee$, and $\neg$. Given a class $\mathcal{V} = (\mathcal{V}^s)_{s \in S}$ of sets of sorted variables, $\Sigma[\mathcal{V}]$-*terms* are defined as usual, and formulae are terms of sort prop. We use l for formulae and t and u for terms of any sort. Formulae in the standard sense are obtained as the closure of our formulae under quantifiers and logical connectives; Σ-*sentences* are those with no free variables.

A $\Sigma[\mathcal{V}]$-*interpretation* $\mathcal{M}$ interprets each sort s in S as a non-empty set $s^{\mathcal{M}}$ with prop$^{\mathcal{M}} = \{$true, false$\}$; each symbol $f : (s_1 \times \cdots \times s_m) \rightarrow s$ in F as a function $f^{\mathcal{M}} : s_1^{\mathcal{M}} \times \cdots \times s_m^{\mathcal{M}} \rightarrow s^{\mathcal{M}}$ with $\simeq_s^{\mathcal{M}}$ returning true if and only if its arguments are identical; and each variable $v \in \mathcal{V}^s$ as an element $v^{\mathcal{M}} \in s^{\mathcal{M}}$. The interpretation $\mathcal{M}(t)$ of a $\Sigma[\mathcal{V}]$-term t is defined as usual. $\Sigma[\emptyset]$-interpretations, known as Σ-*structures*, suffice for Σ-sentences.

A *theory* T on signature Σ is defined axiomatically as a set of Σ-sentences, called its *axioms*, or model-theoretically as the class of Σ-structures, called T-*models*, that satisfy the axioms of T. A $T[\mathcal{V}]$-*model* is any $\Sigma[\mathcal{V}]$-interpretation whose underlying Σ-structure is a T-model.

Let $\mathcal{T}_1, \ldots, \mathcal{T}_n$ be *disjoint* theories with signatures $\Sigma_1{=}(S_1, F_1), \ldots,$ $\Sigma_n{=}(S_n, F_n)$: they do not share symbols other than equality, but can share sorts, meaning that $F_i \cap F_j = (\simeq_{S_i \cap S_j})$ for $i \neq j$. Let $\mathcal{T}_\infty$ be their union, with signature $\Sigma_\infty{=}(S_\infty, F_\infty)$ for $S_\infty{=}\bigcup_{k=1}^n S_k$ and $F_\infty{=}\bigcup_{k=1}^n F_k$, and axiomatization given by the union of those of $\mathcal{T}_1, \ldots, \mathcal{T}_n$. We fix a global collection of variables $\mathcal{V}_\infty = (\mathcal{V}_\infty^s)_{s \in S_\infty}$, use *variables* for variables in $\mathcal{V}_\infty$, and *terms* for $\Sigma_\infty[\mathcal{V}_\infty]$-terms.

Example 1. Problem P from Sect. 1 is written in the signatures

$$\Sigma_{\mathsf{LRA}} = (\{\mathsf{prop}, \mathsf{Q}\}, \ \simeq_{\{\mathsf{prop}, \mathsf{Q}\}} \cup \ \{0, 1 : \mathsf{Q}, \ +: \mathsf{Q} \times \mathsf{Q} \to \mathsf{Q}\} \cup \{q \cdot : \mathsf{Q} \to \mathsf{Q} \mid q \in \mathbb{Q}\})$$
$$\Sigma_{\mathsf{EUF}} = (\{\mathsf{prop}, \mathsf{Q}, V\}, \ \simeq_{\{\mathsf{prop}, \mathsf{Q}, V\}} \cup \ \{f : V \to \mathsf{Q}\})$$
$$\Sigma_{\mathsf{Arr}} = (\{\mathsf{prop}, V, I, A\}, \ \simeq_{\{\mathsf{prop}, V, I, A\}} \cup \{\mathsf{select} : A \times I \to V, \ \mathsf{store} : A \times I \times V \to A\})$$

where Q and $\mathbb{Q}$ are the sort and the set of the rationals, $q \cdot$ is scalar multiplication, and A, I, and V are the sorts of arrays, indices, and values.

3   Assignments and Theory Modules

CDSAT solves $\mathcal{T}_\infty$-satisfiability problems presented as *assignments* of values to terms. For example, a set of formulae $\{l_1, \ldots, l_m\}$ is represented as the assignment $\{l_1 \leftarrow \mathsf{true}, \ldots, l_m \leftarrow \mathsf{true}\}$. The input assignment may contain terms of any sort. Assignments are *public*, meaning visible to all $\mathcal{T}_k$-inference systems.

3.1   Assignments

We need to identify the language of values that the system can assign to terms, besides true and false. Assignable values are not necessarily in the theories' signatures (e.g., consider $x \leftarrow \sqrt{2}$ for the sort of the reals). Therefore, we introduce for each theory $\mathcal{T}_k$, $1 \leq k \leq n$, a *conservative extension* $\mathcal{T}_k^+$ with signature $\Sigma_k^+ = (S_k, F_k^+)$, where F_k^+ is the extension of F_k with a possibly empty set of *new* constant symbols called $\mathcal{T}_k^+$-*values*. An extension is *conservative* if any $\mathcal{T}_k^+$-unsatisfiable set of $\Sigma_k[\mathcal{V}]$-formulae is also $\mathcal{T}_k$-unsatisfiable. This ensures that reasoning in the extension does not change the problem: if CDSAT discovers $\mathcal{T}_k^+$-unsatisfiability, the problem is $\mathcal{T}_k$-unsatisfiable; if the problem is $\mathcal{T}_k$-satisfiable, there is a $\mathcal{T}_k^+$-model that CDSAT can build. A sort $s \in S_k$ with at least one $\mathcal{T}_k^+$-value is called $\mathcal{T}_k$-*public*, as a term of sort s may be assigned a $\mathcal{T}_k^+$-value. A sort s may be $\mathcal{T}_i$-public and $\mathcal{T}_j$-public for $i \neq j$. We stipulate that sort prop is $\mathcal{T}_k$-public for all k, with $\mathcal{T}_k^+$-values true and false, which are valid and unsatisfiable, respectively, in $\mathcal{T}_k^+$. We use $\mathfrak{b}$ for true or false. We assume that the extended theories are still disjoint except for the two Boolean values true and false.

Example 2. Let RA be the theory of real arithmetic with sorts $\{\mathsf{R}, \mathsf{prop}\}$ and symbols $\simeq_{\{\mathsf{R}, \mathsf{prop}\}} \cup \{0, 1 : \mathsf{R}; \ +, -, \cdot : \mathsf{R} \times \mathsf{R} \to \mathsf{R}\}$. RA^+ adds a new constant for every real number, so R is RA-public. The axioms of RA^+ are the formulae that hold in the standard model of the reals interpreting every RA^+-value as itself.

Extending the signature with names that denote all individuals in the domain of a $\mathcal{T}_k$-model is a standard move in automated reasoning, where models need to be built out of syntax, and especially when $\mathcal{T}_k$ has an "intended model" as in arithmetic. In such cases a $\mathcal{T}_k^+$-value is both the domain element and the constant symbol that names it.

Definition 1 (Assignment). *Given a theory $\mathcal{T}$ with extension $\mathcal{T}^+$, a $\mathcal{T}$-assignment is a set of pairs $t \leftarrow c$, where t is a term and c is a $\mathcal{T}^+$-value of the same sort. Term t and all its subterms are said to* occur *in the assignment. An assignment is* plausible *if it does not contain both $l \leftarrow$ true and $l \leftarrow$ false for any formula l.*

For example, $\{x \leftarrow \sqrt{2},\ x + y \leftarrow \sqrt{3}\}$ and $\{f(x) \leftarrow \sqrt{2},\ (1 \cdot x \simeq x) \leftarrow \text{true}\}$ are RA-assignments. If for all pairs $t \leftarrow c$ the sort of t and c is s, the $\mathcal{T}$-assignment is *of sort s*, and if $s = \text{prop}$ it is *Boolean*. A *first-order* $\mathcal{T}$-assignment is a $\mathcal{T}$-assignment that is not Boolean. We use J for generic $\mathcal{T}$-assignments, A for singleton ones, and L for Boolean singletons. We abbreviate $l \leftarrow$ true as l, $l \leftarrow$ false as $\bar{l}$, and $t \simeq_s u \leftarrow$ false as $t \not\simeq_s u$. The *flip* $\bar{L}$ of L assigns to the same formula the opposite Boolean value. The union of $\mathcal{T}_1^+, \ldots, \mathcal{T}_n^+$ is an extension $\mathcal{T}_\infty^+$ of $\mathcal{T}_\infty$, with signature $\Sigma_\infty^+ = (S_\infty, F_\infty^+)$ for $F_\infty^+ = \bigcup_{k=1}^n F_k^+$. We use H for $\mathcal{T}_\infty$-assignments, called *assignments* for short. Plausibility does not forbid an assignment $\{t \leftarrow 3.1, u \leftarrow 5.4, t \leftarrow \text{red}, u \leftarrow \text{blue}\}$, where the first two pairs are $\mathcal{T}_1$-assignments and the last two are $\mathcal{T}_2$-assignments; the sort of t and u is both $\mathcal{T}_1$-public and $\mathcal{T}_2$-public. When building a model from this assignment, 3.5 will be identified with red and 5.4 with blue.

Definition 2 (Theory view). *Let $\mathcal{T}$ and S be either $\mathcal{T}_\infty$ and S_∞, or $\mathcal{T}_k$ and S_k for $1 \leq k \leq n$. The $\mathcal{T}$-view of an assignment H is the $\mathcal{T}$-assignment $H_{\mathcal{T}} =$*

$$\{t \leftarrow c \quad \mid\ t \leftarrow c \text{ is a } \mathcal{T} - \text{assignment in } H\}\ \cup$$
$$\bigcup_{k=1}^n (\{t_1 \simeq_s t_2 \mid\ t_1 \leftarrow c, t_2 \leftarrow c \text{ are } \mathcal{T}_k - \text{assignments in } H \text{ of sort } s \in S \backslash \{\text{prop}\}\}\ \cup$$
$$\{t_1 \not\simeq_s t_2 \mid\ t_1 \leftarrow c_1, t_2 \leftarrow c_2 \text{ are } \mathcal{T}_k - \text{assignments in } H \text{ of sort } s \in S \backslash \{\text{prop}\},\ c_1 \neq c_2\}).$$

$H_{\mathcal{T}}$ contains the $\mathcal{T}$-assignments of H, plus all equalities and disequalities induced by the $\mathcal{T}_k$-assignments in H, $1 \leq k \leq n$. We introduce next *theory modules*, the abstract counterpart of theory solvers or theory plugins [9].

$$t_1 \leftarrow c_1, t_2 \leftarrow c_2 \vdash t_1 \simeq_s t_2 \text{ if } c_1 \text{ and } c_2 \text{ are the same } \mathcal{T}^+\text{-value of sort } s$$
$$t_1 \leftarrow c_1, t_2 \leftarrow c_2 \vdash t_1 \not\simeq_s t_2 \text{ if } c_1 \text{ and } c_2 \text{ are distinct } \mathcal{T}^+\text{-values of sort } s$$
$$\vdash t_1 \simeq_s t_1$$
$$t_1 \simeq_s t_2 \vdash t_2 \simeq_s t_1$$
$$t_1 \simeq_s t_2, t_2 \simeq_s t_3 \vdash t_1 \simeq_s t_3$$

Fig. 1. Equality inference rules: t_1, t_2, and t_3 are terms of sort s

3.2 Theory Modules

A *theory module* $\mathcal{I}$ for theory $\mathcal{T}$ is an inference system whose inferences, called $\mathcal{I}$-*inferences* and written $J \vdash_{\mathcal{I}} L$, derive a singleton Boolean assignment L from a $\mathcal{T}$-assignment J. Since all theories include equality, all theory modules include the *equality inference rules* of Fig. 1. The following inferences are $\mathcal{I}_{\mathsf{RA}}$-inferences:

$$(x \leftarrow \sqrt{2}), (y \leftarrow \sqrt{2}) \vdash_{\mathcal{I}_{\mathsf{RA}}} (x \cdot y \simeq 1{+}1)$$
$$(y \leftarrow \sqrt{2}), (x \leftarrow \sqrt{2}) \vdash_{\mathcal{I}_{\mathsf{RA}}} (y \simeq x)$$
$$(y \leftarrow \sqrt{2}), (x \leftarrow \sqrt{3}) \vdash_{\mathcal{I}_{\mathsf{RA}}} (y \not\simeq x)$$

$\mathcal{I}$-inferences only derive Boolean assignments because CDSAT does not justify first-order assignments by inferences, not even when a first-order assignment is forced by others (e.g., $y \leftarrow 2$ by $x \leftarrow 1$ and $(x{+}y) \leftarrow 3$). We assume we have theory modules $\mathcal{I}_1, \ldots, \mathcal{I}_n$ for $\mathcal{T}_1, \ldots, \mathcal{T}_n$. We now define acceptability and relevance.

Definition 3 (Acceptability). *Given $\mathcal{T}_k$-assignments $t \leftarrow \mathfrak{c}$ and J, $t \leftarrow \mathfrak{c}$ is acceptable for J and $\mathcal{I}_k$, if (i) J does not assign a value to t and (ii) either $t \leftarrow \mathfrak{c}$ is Boolean or there are no $\mathcal{I}_k$-inferences $J', (t \leftarrow \mathfrak{c}) \vdash_{\mathcal{I}_k} L$ with $J', \overline{L} \subseteq J$.*

When adding $t \leftarrow \mathfrak{c}$ to J, acceptability prevents repetitions (cf. Condition (i)) and contradictions: if $t \leftarrow \mathfrak{c}$ is Boolean, its flip should not be in J, preserving plausibility (cf. Condition (i)); if $t \leftarrow \mathfrak{c}$ is first-order, and therefore has no flip, so that plausibility does not apply, acceptability ensures that none of the consequences one inference step away has its flip in J (cf. Condition (ii)).

Definition 4 (Relevance). *A term is $\mathcal{T}_k$-relevant for an assignment H, if either (i) it occurs in H and has a $\mathcal{T}_k$-public sort, or (ii) it is an equality $t_1 \simeq_s t_2$ whose terms t_1 and t_2 occur in H and whose sort $s \in S_k$ is not $\mathcal{T}_k$-public.*

Relevance organizes the division of labor among modules. For instance in the assignment $\{x \leftarrow \sqrt{5}, f(x) \leftarrow \sqrt{2}, f(y) \leftarrow \sqrt{3}\}$, x and y of sort R are RA-relevant, not EUF-relevant, assuming R is not EUF-public, while $x \simeq_{\mathsf{R}} y$ is EUF-relevant, not RA-relevant. Each theory has a mechanism to fix and communicate equalities between terms of a known sort, such as x and y: EUF does it by assigning a truth-value to $x \simeq_{\mathsf{R}} y$; RA does it by assigning values to x and y.

4 Examples of Theory Modules

In this section we give theory modules for several theories. We may use $\bot$ to stand for the assignment $(x \simeq_{\mathsf{prop}} x) \leftarrow \mathsf{false}$ for an arbitrary variable x. For brevity, we omit equality symbols from signatures and equality inference from modules.

4.1 A Module for Propositional Logic

Σ_{Bool} has only the sort prop and the symbols $\neg : \mathsf{prop} \to \mathsf{prop}$, and $\vee, \wedge : (\mathsf{prop} \times \mathsf{prop}) \to \mathsf{prop}$. Let Bool^+ be the trivial extension with only $\{\mathsf{true}, \mathsf{false}\}$ as Bool^+-values. $\mathcal{I}_{\mathsf{Bool}}$ features an *evaluation* inference rule that derives the truth value $\mathfrak{b}$ of formula l, given truth values $\mathfrak{b}_1, \ldots, \mathfrak{b}_m$ of subformulae $l_1, \ldots, l_m$, and then, from left to right, two rules for negation, two rules for conjunction elimination, and two rules for unit propagation:

$$l_1 \leftarrow \mathfrak{b}_1, \ldots, l_m \leftarrow \mathfrak{b}_m \vdash_{\mathsf{Bool}} l \leftarrow \mathfrak{b}$$

$$\frac{}{\neg l \vdash_{\mathsf{Bool}} \bar{l}} \qquad \frac{}{l_1 \vee \cdots \vee l_m \vdash_{\mathsf{Bool}} \bar{l}_i} \qquad \frac{}{l_1 \vee \cdots \vee l_m, \{\bar{l}_j \mid j \neq i\} \vdash_{\mathsf{Bool}} l_i}$$

$$\frac{}{\neg \bar{l} \vdash_{\mathsf{Bool}} l} \qquad \frac{}{l_1 \wedge \cdots \wedge l_m \vdash_{\mathsf{Bool}} l_i} \qquad \frac{}{l_1 \wedge \cdots \wedge l_m, \{l_j \mid j \neq i\} \vdash_{\mathsf{Bool}} \bar{l}_i}$$

where $1 \leq j, i \leq m$, and, for the first rule, l must be in the closure of $l_1, \ldots, l_m$ with respect to the Σ_{Bool}-connectives. Although the evaluation rule alone is sufficient for completeness (cf. Sect. 6.3), the other six rules, including in particular unit propagation as in CDCL, are obviously desirable.

4.2 A Theory Module for LRA

Let Σ_{LRA} be as in Example 1 and LRA^+ be the extension that adds a constant $\tilde{q}$ and the axiom $\tilde{q} \simeq_{\mathsf{Q}} q \cdot 1$ for each rational number $q \in \mathbb{Q}$. Here too, the first rule of $\mathcal{I}_{\mathsf{LRA}}$ is an *evaluation* inference rule that derives the value $\mathfrak{b}$ of formula l, given values $\tilde{q}_1, \ldots, \tilde{q}_m$ of subterms $t_1, \ldots, t_m$ of sort Q:

Evaluation	$t_1 \leftarrow \tilde{q}_1, \ldots, t_m \leftarrow \tilde{q}_m \vdash_{\mathsf{LRA}} l \leftarrow \mathfrak{b}$
Positivization	$\dfrac{t_1 < t_2 \vdash_{\mathsf{LRA}} t_2 \leq t_1}{t_1 \leq t_2 \vdash_{\mathsf{LRA}} t_2 < t_1}$
Equality elimination	$t_1 \simeq_{\mathsf{Q}} t_2 \vdash_{\mathsf{LRA}} t_i \leq t_j$ with $\{i, j\} = \{1, 2\}$
Disequality elimination	$(t_1 \leq x), (x \leq t_2), (t_1 \simeq_{\mathsf{Q}} t_0), (t_2 \simeq_{\mathsf{Q}} t_0), (x \not\simeq_{\mathsf{Q}} t_0) \vdash_{\mathsf{LRA}} \bot$
Fourier-Motzkin resolution	$(t_1 \lessdot_1 x), (x \lessdot_2 t_2) \vdash_{\mathsf{LRA}} (t_1 \lessdot_3 t_2)$

where t_0, t_1, t_2, and x are terms of sort Q; x is a Σ_{LRA}-*variable* that is not free in t_0, t_1, t_2 (cf. Sect. 6); $\lessdot_1, \lessdot_2, \lessdot_3 \in \{<, \leq\}$ and $\lessdot_3$ is $<$ if and only if either $\lessdot_1$ or $\lessdot_2$ is $<$. For the first rule, l must be a formula whose normal form is in the closure of $t_1, \ldots, t_m$ with respect to the symbols of F_{LRA}. For example, $w - 2 \simeq_{\mathsf{Q}} w$ can be normalized to $-2 \simeq_{\mathsf{Q}} 0$ and evaluates to false. In the last two rules, each formula l appearing on the left stands for any formula that can be normalized to l. For instance, Fourier-Motzkin (FM) resolution applies to $y - x < 2 \cdot y$ and $2 \cdot x < 3$ yielding $-y < \frac{3}{2}$. The three linear combinations of constraints in the solution of problem R in Sect. 1 are instances of FM resolution, as a linear combination $e_1 + z < c_1$, $e_2 - z < c_2 \vdash e_1 + e_2 < c_1 + c_2$ is expressed as an FM resolution $e_2 - c_2 < z$, $z < c_1 - e_1 \vdash_{\mathsf{LRA}} e_2 - c_2 < c_1 - e_1$.

4.3 A Theory Module for EUF

For a signature $\Sigma_{\mathsf{EUF}} = (S, \simeq_S \cup F)$, $\mathcal{I}_{\mathsf{EUF}}$ may include

$$(t_i \simeq u_i)_{i=1 \ldots m}, f(t_1, \ldots, t_m) \not\simeq f(u_1, \ldots, u_m) \vdash_{\mathsf{EUF}} \bot$$

$$(t_i \simeq u_i)_{i=1 \ldots m} \vdash_{\mathsf{EUF}} f(t_1, \ldots, t_m) \simeq f(u_1, \ldots, u_m)$$

$$(t_i \simeq u_i)_{i=1 \ldots m, i \neq j}, f(t_1, \ldots, t_m) \not\simeq f(u_1, \ldots, u_m) \vdash_{\mathsf{EUF}} t_j \not\simeq u_j$$

for all symbols $f \in F$. The first rule alone is sufficient for completeness: it captures a lazy approach that does not propagate anything before equalities between existing terms are found to be in contradiction with a congruence axiom [9]. The other two rules can be used directly for eager congruence propagation. Since $\mathcal{I}_{\mathsf{EUF}}$ does not use first-order assignments, no sort needs to be EUF-public, and the only assignments assign truth values to equalities. Alternatively, one may make the sorts in S EUF-public, with a countably infinite collection of EUF^+-values in each sort and no axioms about them. Equality inferences can employ assignments of EUF^+-values to determine whether terms are equal, using EUF^+-values as identifiers for equivalence classes of terms. For example, assume that c_1, c_2, and c_3 are distinct EUF^+-values. The assignment $\{x \leftarrow c_1, y \leftarrow c_1, f(x) \leftarrow c_2\}$ places x and y in the equivalence class c_1, and $f(x)$ in class c_2. If $f(y) \leftarrow c_3$ is added to the assignment, two equality inferences and an application of the first rule of $\mathcal{I}_{\mathsf{EUF}}$ expose a conflict in the above-mentioned lazy style.

4.4   A Theory Module for Arrays

The array sort constructor builds from an *index sort* I and a *value sort* V the sort $I {\Rightarrow} V$ of arrays with indices in I and values in V. Consider a signature $\Sigma_{\mathsf{Arr}} = (S, F)$, where S is the free closure of a set of basic sorts with respect to the array sort constructor, and F is

$$\begin{aligned}
&\{\mathsf{select}_{I \Rightarrow V} : (I {\Rightarrow} V) \times I \to V && \mid (I {\Rightarrow} V) \in S\} \\
\cup\, &\{\mathsf{store}_{I \Rightarrow V} \;: (I {\Rightarrow} V) \times I \times V \to (I {\Rightarrow} V) \mid (I {\Rightarrow} V) \in S\} \\
\cup\, &\{\mathsf{diff}_{I \Rightarrow V} \;: (I {\Rightarrow} V) \times (I {\Rightarrow} V) \to I \quad \mid (I {\Rightarrow} V) \in S\},
\end{aligned}$$

where $\mathsf{diff}_{I \Rightarrow V}$ is the Skolem function symbol that arises from clausifying the extensionality axiom for array sort $I {\Rightarrow} V$. For brevity, subscripts are omitted, $\mathsf{select}(a, i)$ is written as $a[i]$, and $\mathsf{store}(a, i, v)$ as $a[i]{:=}v$. Module $\mathcal{I}_{\mathsf{Arr}}$ features the following rules, where a, b, c, d are variables of any $I {\Rightarrow} V$ sort, u, v are variables of sort V, and i, j, k of sort I:

$$\begin{aligned}
a \simeq b, \; i \simeq j, \; a[i] \not\simeq b[j] \;\; &\vdash_{\mathsf{Arr}} \bot \\
a \simeq b, \; i \simeq j, \; u \simeq v, \; (a[i]{:=}u) \not\simeq (b[j]{:=}v) \;\; &\vdash_{\mathsf{Arr}} \bot \\
b \simeq (a[i]{:=}u), \; i \simeq j, \; b[j] \not\simeq u \;\; &\vdash_{\mathsf{Arr}} \bot \\
b \simeq (a[i]{:=}u), \; i \not\simeq j, \; j \simeq k, \; a[j] \not\simeq b[k] \;\; &\vdash_{\mathsf{Arr}} \bot \\
a \not\simeq b \;\; &\vdash_{\mathsf{Arr}} a[\mathsf{diff}(a,b)] \not\simeq b[\mathsf{diff}(a,b)] \\
a \simeq c, \; b \simeq d, \; \mathsf{diff}(a,b) \not\simeq \mathsf{diff}(c,d) \;\; &\vdash_{\mathsf{Arr}} \bot
\end{aligned}$$

The first two inference rules capture the congruence axioms for select and store. The third and fourth rules correspond to the read-over-write axioms. The fifth rule corresponds to the clausal form of the extensionality axiom; it is the only rule that can produce new terms. The last rule states the congruence axiom for diff. These rules are triggered by the truth-values of equalities. As with $\mathcal{I}_{\mathsf{EUF}}$, in order to determine whether equalities hold, one has the option of declaring all sorts to be Arr-public, with infinitely many Arr^+-values used as identifiers of equivalence classes. One can also add rules for eager propagations of equalities.

4.5   Generic Theory Modules for Equality Sharing

Assume $\mathcal{T}$ is a stably infinite theory with signature $\Sigma = (S, F)$ and equipped with a $\mathcal{T}$-satisfiability procedure. Its inference module $\mathcal{I}_{\mathcal{T}}$ comprises the rule

$$l_1 \leftarrow \mathfrak{b}_1, \ldots, l_m \leftarrow \mathfrak{b}_m \vdash_{\mathcal{T}} \bot$$

that fires when the conjunction of the literals corresponding to the Boolean assignments on the left is $\mathcal{T}$-unsatisfiable. Unlike the previous ones, this module is coarse-grained, in the sense that a single application of its inference rule requires the execution of a $\mathcal{T}$-satisfiability procedure. As with EUF and Arr, one has the option of declaring non-Boolean sorts $\mathcal{T}$-public to determine equalities. If the $\mathcal{T}$-satisfiability procedure can produce *unsatisfiable cores*, we can restrict the above rule so that the assignment on the left is an unsatisfiable core. This provides a more precise conflict resolution mechanism, which leads us to Sect. 5.

5   The CDSAT Inference System

In this section we present CDSAT and exemplify its features by applying it to problems R and P in the introduction. A CDSAT derivation transforms a state consisting of a *trail* Γ. A *trail* is a sequence of distinct singleton assignments that are either *justified assignments*, denoted $_H\vdash A$, or *decisions*, denoted $_?A$. The justification H in $_H\vdash A$ is a set of singleton assignments that appear before A in the trail. For instance, a theory inference $J \vdash_{\mathcal{I}_k} L$ for some k, $1 \leq k \leq n$, can justify adding $_J\vdash L$ to the trail. A decision is written $_?A$ because it is generally a guess. A trail can be used as an assignment by ignoring order and justifications.

Phase 1			
id	trail items	just	lev
0	$-2 \cdot x - y < 0$	{}	0
1	$x + y < 0$	{}	0
2	$x < -1$	{}	0
3	$y \leftarrow 0$		1
4	$-y < -2$	$\{0, 2\}$	0
conflict E^1: $\{3, 4\}$			1

Phase 2			
id	trail items	just	lev
0	$-2 \cdot x - y < 0$	{}	0
1	$x + y < 0$	{}	0
2	$x < -1$	{}	0
3	$-y < -2$	$\{0, 2\}$	0
4	$y \leftarrow 4$		1
5	$y < 0$	$\{0, 1\}$	0
conflict E^2: $\{4, 5\}$			1

Phase 3			
id	trail items	just	lev
0	$-2 \cdot x - y < 0$	{}	0
1	$x + y < 0$	{}	0
2	$x < -1$	{}	0
3	$-y < -2$	$\{0, 2\}$	0
4	$y < 0$	$\{0, 1\}$	0
5	$0 < -2$	$\{3, 4\}$	0
conflict E^3: $\{5\}$			0

Fig. 2. CDSAT derivation in one theory (LRA)

The evolution of the trail for problem R is described in three successive phases in Fig. 2. The input is shown above the horizontal line of Phase 1. In each proceeding phase, the assignments above the horizontal line are those inherited from the previous phase. Assignments are numbered in chronological order, and their numbers, shown in the first column, are used as identifiers. For every justified assignment, the justification is shown as a set of identifiers in the third column. In the sequel, A_n^m is the assignment with identifier n in phase m. For example, the justification of A_4^1 is $\{0, 2\}$, because A_4^1 is derived by the FM resolution rule of $\mathcal{I}_{\mathsf{LRA}}$ from A_0^1 and A_2^1. The last column shows the *level* of A as defined next.

Definition 5 (Level). *Given a trail Γ with assignments $A_0, \ldots, A_m$,*

$$\mathsf{level}_\Gamma(A_i) = \begin{cases} 1 + max\{\mathsf{level}_\Gamma(A_j) \mid j < i\} & \text{if } A_i \text{ is a decision,} \\ \mathsf{level}_\Gamma(H) & \text{if } A_i \text{ has justification } H; \end{cases}$$

Given a $\mathcal{T}_\infty$-assignment $H \subseteq \Gamma$,

$$\mathsf{level}_\Gamma(H) = \begin{cases} 0 & \text{if } H = \emptyset, \\ max\{\mathsf{level}_\Gamma(A) \mid A \in H\} & \text{otherwise.} \end{cases}$$

The restriction of a trail Γ to its elements of level at most m is written $\Gamma^{\leq m}$.

SEARCH RULES

Decide	$\Gamma \longrightarrow \Gamma, {}_?A$	if A is a $\mathcal{T}_k$-assignment for a $\mathcal{T}_k$-relevant term of Γ that is acceptable for $\Gamma_{\mathcal{T}_k}$ and $\mathcal{I}_k$, with $1 \leq k \leq n$

The next three rules share the conditions:
$J \subseteq \Gamma$, $(J \vdash_{\mathcal{I}_k} L)$, and $L \notin \Gamma$, for some k, $1 \leq k \leq n$.

Deduce	$\Gamma \longrightarrow \Gamma, {}_{J\vdash}L$	if $\overline{L} \notin \Gamma$, and L is of the form $l \leftarrow \mathfrak{b}$ for some $l \in \mathcal{B}$
Fail	$\Gamma \longrightarrow$ unsat	if $\overline{L} \in \Gamma$ and $\mathsf{level}_\Gamma(J, \overline{L}) = 0$
ConflictSolve	$\Gamma \longrightarrow \Gamma'$	if $\overline{L} \in \Gamma$, $\mathsf{level}_\Gamma(J, \overline{L}) > 0$, and $\langle \Gamma; J, \overline{L} \rangle \Longrightarrow^* \Gamma'$

CONFLICT RESOLUTION RULES

Undo		
$\langle \Gamma; E, A \rangle$	$\Longrightarrow \Gamma^{\leq m-1}$	if A is a first-order decision of level $m > \mathsf{level}_\Gamma(E)$
Backjump		
$\langle \Gamma; E, L \rangle$	$\Longrightarrow \Gamma^{\leq m}, {}_{E\vdash}\overline{L}$	if $\mathsf{level}_\Gamma(L) > m$, where $m = \mathsf{level}_\Gamma(E)$
Resolve		
$\langle \Gamma; E, A \rangle$	$\Longrightarrow \langle \Gamma; E \cup H \rangle$	if $_{H\vdash}A$ is in Γ and H does not contain a first-order decision whose level is $\mathsf{level}_\Gamma(E, A)$
UndoDecide		
$\langle \Gamma; E, L, L' \rangle$	$\Longrightarrow \Gamma^{\leq m-1}, {}_?\overline{L}$	if $_{H\vdash}L$ and $_{H'\vdash}L'$ are in Γ and $H \cap H'$ contains a first-order decision of level $m = \mathsf{level}_\Gamma(E, L, L')$

Fig. 3. The CDSAT inference system

The rules of the CDSAT inference system, given in Fig. 3, comprise *search rules*, whose application is denoted by $\longrightarrow$, and *conflict resolution rules*, whose application is denoted by $\Longrightarrow$, with transitive closure $\Longrightarrow^*$. The system is parameterized by a set $\mathcal{B}$ of terms, called *global basis*, used to limit the range of terms that CDSAT may generate, in order to ensure termination (cf. Sect. 6.2). The global basis is fixed throughout a CDSAT derivation but depends on the input problem. We describe next the CDSAT rules, beginning with the search rules.

The Decide rule extends a trail Γ with a theory assignment A without justifying it by a theory inference: it is a decision. A assigns a value to a relevant term, and is acceptable for the theory view of the trail and the theory module (cf. Definitions 2, 3 and 4). In Fig. 2, y is the relevant term in A_3^1 and A_4^2.

The Deduce rule extends a trail Γ with an assignment L justified by a theory inference $J \vdash_{\mathcal{I}_k} L$. In Fig. 2, Deduce infers A_4^1 from $\{A_0^1, A_2^1\}$, A_5^2 from $\{A_0^2, A_1^2\}$, and A_5^3 from $\{A_3^3, A_4^3\}$, by using the FM resolution rule of $\mathcal{I}_{\mathsf{LRA}}$.

Rules Fail and ConflictSolve apply to a trail Γ that is conflicting because a theory inference $J \vdash_{\mathcal{I}_k} L$ contradicts an assignment $\overline{L}$ already present in Γ. The set $J \cup \{\overline{L}\}$ is the *conflict*. Its level is denoted $\mathsf{level}_\Gamma(J, \overline{L})$. If it is 0, rule Fail returns unsat (e.g., E^3 in Fig. 2). If it is greater than 0 (e.g., E^1 and E^2 in Fig. 2), rule ConflictSolve triggers a series of conflict resolution steps transforming Γ into a trail Γ' where the conflict is solved. In all three conflicts in Fig. 2, the inferences that expose the conflict are applications of the evaluation rule of $\mathcal{I}_{\mathsf{LRA}}$: $y{\leftarrow}0 \vdash \overline{-y < -2}$ for E^1, $y{\leftarrow}4 \vdash \overline{y < 0}$ for E^2, and $\emptyset \vdash \overline{0 < -2}$ for E^3.

Phase 1

id	trail items	just	lev
0	$f((a[i]{:=}v)[j]) \simeq w$	{}	0
1	$w{-}2 \simeq f(u)$	{}	0
2	$i \simeq j$	{}	0
3	$u \simeq v$	{}	0
4	$u{\leftarrow}c$		1
5	$v{\leftarrow}c$		2
6	$(a[i]{:=}v)[j]{\leftarrow}c$		3
7	$w{\leftarrow}0$		4
8	$f((a[i]{:=}v)[j]){\leftarrow}0$		5
9	$f(u){\leftarrow}{-}2$		6
10	$u \simeq (a[i]{:=}v)[j]$	{4,6}	3
11	$f(u) \not\simeq f((a[i]{:=}v)[j])$	{8,9}	6
	conflict E^1: {10,11}		6

Phase 2

id	trail items	just	lev
0	$f((a[i]{:=}v)[j]) \simeq w$	{}	0
1	$w{-}2 \simeq f(u)$	{}	0
2	$i \simeq j$	{}	0
3	$u \simeq v$	{}	0
4	$u{\leftarrow}c$		1
5	$v{\leftarrow}c$		2
6	$(a[i]{:=}v)[j]{\leftarrow}c$		3
7	$u \simeq (a[i]{:=}v)[j]$	{4,6}	3
8	$f(u) \simeq f((a[i]{:=}v)[j])$	{7}	3
9	$f(u) \simeq w$	{0,8}	3
10	$w{-}2 \simeq w$	{1,9}	3
	conflict E_1^2: {10}		3
	conflict E_2^2: {1,9}		3
	conflict E_3^2: {0,1,8}		3
	conflict E_4^2: {0,1,7}		3

Phase 3

id	trail items	just	lev
0	$f((a[i]{:=}v)[j]) \simeq w$	{}	0
1	$w{-}2 \simeq f(u)$	{}	0
2	$i \simeq j$	{}	0
3	$u \simeq v$	{}	0
4	$u \not\simeq (a[i]{:=}v)[j]$	{0,1}	0
5	$u{\leftarrow}c$		1
6	$v{\leftarrow}c$		2
7	$(a[i]{:=}v)[j]{\leftarrow}\mathfrak{d}$		3
8	$v \not\simeq (a[i]{:=}v)[j]$	{6,7}	3
	conflict E^3: {2,8}		3

Phase 4

id	trail items	just	lev
0	$f((a[i]{:=}v)[j]) \simeq w$	{}	0
1	$w{-}2 \simeq f(u)$	{}	0
2	$i \simeq j$	{}	0
3	$u \simeq v$	{}	0
4	$u \not\simeq (a[i]{:=}v)[j]$	{0,1}	0
5	$v \simeq (a[i]{:=}v)[j]$	{2}	0
	conflict E^4: {3,4,5}		0

Fig. 4. CDSAT derivation in three theories (LRA, EUF, and Arr)

We now describe the conflict resolution rules, referring to Figs. 2 and 4 for their application to problems R and P, respectively. Conflict resolution rules operate on pairs $\langle \Gamma; E \rangle$, where Γ is a trail and E is a set of assignments in Γ termed *conflict*. If the conflict contains a first-order decision A, whose level n is greater than that of the rest of the conflict, rule Undo removes A and all assignments of level greater than or equal to n. In Fig. 2, rule Undo solves conflicts E^1 and E^2.

The Backjump rule is similar in that the conflict contains an assignment whose level is greater than that of all others. Backjump applies if this assignment is a Boolean assignment L; its flip $\overline{L}$ is justified by the rest of the conflict E. Therefore we backjump to the level of E, and add $_E\vdash\overline{L}$ to the trail. Assignment $\overline{L}$ is a Unique Implication Point [14]. We see an application of this rule in Fig. 4. Phase 1 starts with a series of decisions, from A_4^1 through A_9^1, where c is an Arr^+-value of sort V, and A_5^1 is the only acceptable choice given A_3^1 and A_4^1. Then Deduce generates A_{10}^1 and A_{11}^1 by equality inferences (cf. Fig. 1), and ConflictSolve applies, as $E^1 \vdash_{\mathcal{I}_{EUF}} \bot$ by the first inference rule of $\mathcal{I}_{EUF}$. Rule Undo does not apply to E^1, because E^1 does not contain first-order decisions, but rule Backjump does apply, with A_{11}^1 playing the role of L. CDSAT jumps back to level 3, the level of A_{10}^1, and places $\overline{A_{11}^1}$ on the trail with justification A_{10}^1, named A_7^2 in Phase 2. Deduce places A_9^2 and A_{10}^2 on the trail by transitivity of equality (cf. Fig. 1). ConflictSolve applies as $\emptyset \vdash_{LRA} w-2 \not\simeq w$.

The Resolve rule unfolds a conflict by replacing an assignment A in the conflict with its justification H, provided H does not introduce a first-order decision of the same level as that of the conflict. Starting from E_1^2 in Fig. 4, three Resolve steps yield conflict E_4^2. Resolve does not apply to A_7^2 because its justification contains A_6^2. Backjump solves E_4^2 by jumping back to level 0 and flipping A_7^2 into A_4^3. Then CDSAT guesses A_5^3 through A_7^3, where A_6^3 is forced by A_3^3 and A_5^3. For A_7^3, another Arr^+-value $\mathfrak{d}$ of sort V is used, since A_4^3 and A_5^3 prevent assigning c to $(a[i]:=v)[j]$. Deduce generates A_8^3 by an equality inference, and conflict E^3 arises as $(i \simeq j), (v \not\simeq (a[i]:=v)[j]) \vdash_{Arr} \bot$. Backjump solves E^3 by jumping back to level 0 and flipping A_5^3 into A_5^4. The final conflict E^4 violates transitivity of equality, and because E^4 is at level 0, rule Fail closes the derivation.

The UndoDecide rule corresponds to T-*backjump-decide* [5] and *semantic split* [9]. It applies when the conflict contains two assignments L and L' whose justifications include a first-order decision of maximal level in the conflict. Rule Resolve is barred from replacing L or L' by their justification, so the only way to solve the conflict is to trade the first-order decision for a Boolean decision on the flip of L or L'. In Fig. 5, conflict E_4 is solved by UndoDecide, as both A_3^1 and A_4^1 are justified by the first-order decision A_2^1. UndoDecide arbitrarily chooses to flip A_3^1, and then values can be found for variables without raising a conflict: the problem is satisfiable.

Phase 1			
id	trail items	just	lev
0	$(x>1) \vee (y<0)$	$\{\}$	0
1	$(x<-1) \vee (y>0)$	$\{\}$	0
2	$x \leftarrow 0$		1
3	$\overline{x>1}$	$\{2\}$	1
4	$\overline{x<-1}$	$\{2\}$	1
5	$y<0$	$\{0,3\}$	1
6	$y>0$	$\{1,4\}$	1
7	$0<0$	$\{5,6\}$	1
conflict E_1: $\{7\}$			1
conflict E_2: $\{5,6\}$			1
conflict E_3: $\{0,3,6\}$			1
conflict E_4: $\{0,1,3,4\}$			1

Phase 2			
id	trail items	just	lev
0	$(x>1) \vee (y<0)$	$\{\}$	0
1	$(x<-1) \vee (y>0)$	$\{\}$	0
2	$x>1$		1
3	$x \leftarrow 2$		2
4	$\overline{x<-1}$	$\{3\}$	2
5	$y>0$	$\{1,4\}$	2
6	$y \leftarrow 1$		3
7	$\overline{y<0}$	$\{6\}$	3

Fig. 5. CDSAT derivation in two theories (Bool and LRA)

6   Soundness, Termination, and Completeness of CDSAT

In this section we establish *soundness*, *termination*, and *completeness* of CDSAT. The proofs of these theorems can be found in the technical report [3]. The key point is to reduce such global properties to theory-local requirements for the theory modules involved in the combination. In other words, we need to discover sufficient conditions whose fulfillment by all theory modules $\mathcal{I}_1, \ldots, \mathcal{I}_n$ ensures soundness, termination, and completeness of the combined system.

This reduction raises the issue of how to handle the fact that assignments contain symbols unknown to a theory. For the combination of theory modules to be truly *modular*, $\mathcal{I}_k$ treats as a variable any subterm whose root is a symbol foreign to $\mathcal{T}_k$. Formally, if $\Sigma = (S, F)$ is a signature included in Σ_∞, the *free Σ-variables* $\mathsf{fv}_\Sigma(t)$ of a term t are the *maximal* subterms of t, in the *subterm ordering* $\lhd$, whose root is not in F. For a set X of terms, $\mathsf{fv}_\Sigma(X) = \{u \mid u \in \mathsf{fv}_\Sigma(t), t \in X\}$, and for an assignment H, $\mathsf{fv}_\Sigma(H) = \{u \mid u \in \mathsf{fv}_\Sigma(t), t \leftarrow \mathfrak{c} \in H\}$. For problem P in Sect. 1, signatures $\Sigma_{\mathsf{LRA}}, \Sigma_{\mathsf{EUF}}, \Sigma_{\mathsf{Arr}}$ of Example 1 define for instance:

$$\mathsf{fv}_{\Sigma_{\mathsf{LRA}}}(P) = \quad \{f(\mathsf{select}(\mathsf{store}(a, i, v), j)), \ w, \ f(u), \ i \simeq j, \ u \simeq v\}$$
$$\mathsf{fv}_{\Sigma_{\mathsf{EUF}}}(P) = \quad \{\mathsf{select}(\mathsf{store}(a, i, v), j), \ w, \ u, \ w{-}2, \ i \simeq j, \ v\}$$
$$\mathsf{fv}_{\Sigma_{\mathsf{Arr}}}(P) = \{f(\mathsf{select}(\mathsf{store}(a, i, v))j) \simeq w, \ f(u) \simeq w{-}2, \ i, \ j, \ u, \ v\}$$

In the next two definitions, $\mathcal{T}$ and Σ stand for either $\mathcal{T}_\infty$ and Σ_∞ or $\mathcal{T}_k$ and Σ_k, $1 \leq k \leq n$. The identification of sufficient conditions for soundness and completeness and their proofs demand that we relate the assignments manipulated by CDSAT to models. This is the purpose of the notion of *endorsement*:

Definition 6 (Endorsement). *A $\mathcal{T}^+[\mathcal{V}]$-model $\mathcal{M}$ endorses a $\mathcal{T}$-assignment J, such that $\mathsf{fv}_\Sigma(J) \subseteq \mathcal{V}$, if for all $t \leftarrow \mathfrak{c}$ in J, $\mathcal{M}(t) = \mathfrak{c}^{\mathcal{M}}$.*

For Boolean assignments, it means that formulae are interpreted with the correct truth values. Definition 6 uses $\mathcal{T}^+$-models, because assignments contain $\mathcal{T}^+$-values (e.g., $\sqrt{2}$), and therefore we need models that interpret $\mathcal{T}^+$-values, and interpret them consistently with the axioms (e.g., $\sqrt{2} \cdot \sqrt{2} = 2$).

Definition 7 (View endorsement). *A $\mathcal{T}^+[\mathcal{V}]$-model $\mathcal{M}$ view-endorses a $\mathcal{T}_\infty$-assignment H with $\mathsf{fv}_\Sigma(H) \subseteq \mathcal{V}$, if it endorses its $\mathcal{T}$-view $H_{\mathcal{T}}$.*

This definition combines endorsement and view (cf. Definition 2) because CDSAT works with $\mathcal{T}_\infty$-assignments, which mix $\mathcal{T}_k$-assignments for any k, $1 \leq k \leq n$. If H is Boolean, view endorsement collapses to endorsement.

6.1   Soundness

The sufficient condition for soundness is that for every theory module $\mathcal{I}_k$, for all $\mathcal{I}_k$-inferences $J \vdash_{\mathcal{I}_k} L$, and all $\mathcal{V}$ such that $\mathsf{fv}_{\Sigma_k}(J \cup \{L\}) \subseteq \mathcal{V}$, every $\mathcal{T}_k^+[\mathcal{V}]$-model that view-endorses J endorses L. Under this assumption, we prove that CDSAT is sound, by showing that each transition rule produces a trail whose restriction to level 0 is equisatisfiable to the input assignment.

Theorem 1 (Soundness). *For all input assignments H, if a CDSAT derivation from H reaches state* unsat, *no $T_\infty^+[\mathcal{V}]$-model with* $\mathsf{fv}_{\Sigma_\infty}(H) \subseteq \mathcal{V}$ *view-endorses H; if H is Boolean, no $T_\infty[\mathcal{V}]$-model with* $\mathsf{fv}_{\Sigma_\infty}(H) \subseteq \mathcal{V}$ *endorses H.*

All theory modules in Sect. 4 satisfy the soundness requirement.

6.2   Termination

As CDSAT allows the introduction of terms that are not in the input problem (cf. **Deduce**), termination is imperiled. For instance, applying the FM resolution rule of $\mathcal{I}_{\mathsf{LRA}}$ to problem R from Sect. 1, one can infer the formulae of Fig. 6. Such divergence is prevented by imposing finiteness of the global basis $\mathcal{B}$, that is the source of new terms in a CDSAT derivation.

$$
\begin{aligned}
l_0 &: -2\cdot x - y < 0 \\
l_1 &: \quad x + y < 0 \\
l_2 &: \quad x < -1 \\
l_3 &: \quad -y < -2 \quad (l_0 + 2l_2) \\
l_4 &: \quad x < -2 \quad (l_1 + l_3) \\
l_5 &: \quad -y < -4 \quad (l_0 + 2l_4) \\
l_6 &: \quad x < -4 \quad (l_1 + l_5) \\
l_7 &: \quad -y < -8 \quad (l_0 + 2l_6) \\
&\quad \cdots
\end{aligned}
$$

Theorem 2 (Termination). *If the global basis $\mathcal{B}$ is finite, every CDSAT derivation is guaranteed to terminate.*

Fig. 6. Divergence

Then the issue is to give sufficient conditions for the existence of a global basis $\mathcal{B}$, that is finite, and yet sufficiently rich for CDSAT to be *complete*. To address this question at the combination level we begin by imposing a similar requirement at the single theory level. We require that each theory module comes with a function basis_k, called *local basis*, that maps any finite set X of terms to a *finite* set of terms $\mathsf{basis}_k(X)$, and has the following properties: it is (i) *extensive* ($X \subseteq \mathsf{basis}_k(X)$), (ii) *monotone* ($X \subseteq Y$ implies $\mathsf{basis}_k(X) \subseteq \mathsf{basis}_k(Y)$), (iii) *idempotent* ($\mathsf{basis}_k(\mathsf{basis}_k(X)) = \mathsf{basis}_k(X)$), (iv) *downward-closed with respect to the subterm ordering* (if $t \lhd u$ and $u \in \mathsf{basis}_k(X)$ then $t \in \mathsf{basis}_k(X)$), (v) *closed with respect to equality* (if $t, u \in \mathsf{basis}_k(X)$, of a sort s different from prop, then $(t \simeq_s u) \in \mathsf{basis}_k(X)$), and (vi) *does not introduce foreign symbols* ($\mathsf{fv}_{\Sigma_k}(\mathsf{basis}_k(X)) \subseteq \mathsf{fv}_{\Sigma_k}(X) \cup \mathcal{V}_\infty$).

Intuitively, $\mathsf{basis}_k(X)$ is the supply of terms that $\mathcal{I}_k$ is allowed to introduce during a derivation from an input problem whose terms are in X. However, $\mathsf{basis}_k(X)$ is not pre-computed. Furthermore, basis_k should provide enough terms to make $\mathcal{I}_k$ complete, according to a notion of completeness of a theory module defined in the sequel in terms of both $\mathcal{I}_k$-inferences and basis_k.

The divergence in Fig. 6 involves only $\mathcal{I}_{\mathsf{LRA}}$. It can be avoided by assuming a fixed arbitrary order $\prec$ on Σ_{LRA}-variables [9], and defining $\mathsf{basis}_{\mathsf{LRA}}$ as the function that saturates its argument with the terms introduced by all positivization inferences and by the FM resolution inferences $(t_1 <_1 x), (x <_2 t_2) \vdash_{\mathsf{LRA}} (t_1 <_3 t_2)$ where x is the $\prec$-greatest Σ_{LRA}-variable in both $t_1 <_1 x$ and $x <_2 t_2$. For Fig. 6, assume that $y \prec x$. Then l_3, generated by $(-y < 2\cdot x), (2\cdot x < -2) \vdash_{\mathsf{LRA}} (-y < -2)$, is in the local basis, whereas l_4, generated by $(x < -y), (-y < -2) \vdash_{\mathsf{LRA}} (x < -2)$, is not, so that the series of inferences halts.

6.3 Completeness

As theory modules are used to extend the trail and reveal conflicts, the aim for completeness is that whenever no theory module can extend the trail, then the trail provides enough information to build a $\mathcal{T}_\infty^+$-model of the input problem. We begin by formalizing the concept that a theory module can extend an assignment.

Definition 8 (Assignment extension). *Module $\mathcal{I}_k$ with local basis basis_k can extend a $\mathcal{T}_k$-assignment J if*

- *Either there exists a $\mathcal{T}_k$-assignment $t \leftarrow \mathfrak{c}$, for a $\mathcal{T}_k$-relevant term t of J, that is acceptable for J and $\mathcal{I}_k$;*
- *Or there exist a $\mathcal{T}_k$-assignment $J' \subseteq J$, a formula $l \in \mathsf{basis}_k(J)$, and an $\mathcal{I}_k$-inference $J' \vdash_{\mathcal{I}_k} (l \leftarrow \mathfrak{b})$ such that $(l \leftarrow \mathfrak{b}) \notin J$.*

The first case is used for a Decide step and the second one for a Deduce, Fail, or ConflictSolve step. A module $\mathcal{I}_k$ is said to be *complete*, if for all plausible $\mathcal{T}_k$-assignments J that $\mathcal{I}_k$ cannot extend, there exists a $\mathcal{T}_k^+[\mathsf{fv}_{\Sigma_k}(J)]$-model $\mathcal{M}$ that view-endorses J. However, when no theory module can extend its view of a trail Γ, the existence of a theory-specific model for Γ for each theory does not imply the existence of a model for the combination of the theories. As in the equality-sharing method [16], these models need to agree on equalities between shared variables and on cardinalities of shared sorts. If all theories are *stably infinite*, the common cardinality is countably infinite. Nonetheless, there are interesting combinations that involve finite cardinalities, such as combining a theory with finite sorts and the theory of arrays with extensionality. CDSAT can handle such cases, if one of the combined theories, say $\mathcal{T}_1$, knows all the sorts (i.e., $S_1 = S_\infty$) and offers information about their cardinalities. A combination of stably infinite theories is the instance of this scheme where $\mathcal{T}_1$ is a theory $\mathcal{T}_\mathbb{N}$ whose models interpret every sort in $S_\infty \setminus \{\mathsf{prop}\}$ as a countably infinite set.

The *theory-specific requirements for completeness* of CDSAT are that $\mathcal{I}_1$ is complete, and all other modules are complete *relative* to $\mathcal{T}_1$. The latter notion, that we call $\mathcal{T}_1$-*completeness*, in turn relies on $\mathcal{T}_1$-*compatibility*, defined below.

Definition 9 ($\mathcal{T}_1$-compatibility). *A $\mathcal{T}_k$-assignment J is $\mathcal{T}_1$-compatible with $\mathcal{T}_k^+$, sharing a set of terms G, if for any $\mathcal{T}_1^+[\mathsf{fv}_{\Sigma_1}(J \cup G)]$-model $\mathcal{M}_1$ that view-endorses J, there exists a $\mathcal{T}_k^+[\mathsf{fv}_{\Sigma_k}(J \cup G)]$-model $\mathcal{M}$ that view-endorses J, such that for all sorts $s \in S_k$, $|s^{\mathcal{M}}| = |s^{\mathcal{M}_1}|$, and for all terms t and t' in G of sort s, $\mathcal{M}(t) = \mathcal{M}(t')$ if and only if $\mathcal{M}_1(t) = \mathcal{M}_1(t')$.*

A module $\mathcal{I}_k$ is $\mathcal{T}_1$-*complete*, if for all plausible $\mathcal{T}_k$-assignments J that $\mathcal{I}_k$ cannot extend, J is $\mathcal{T}_1$-compatible with $\mathcal{T}_k^+$, sharing all terms that occur in J. Then, the global basis $\mathcal{B}$ is *stable*, if $\mathsf{basis}_k(\mathcal{B}) \subseteq \mathcal{B}$ holds for all k, $1 \le k \le n$.

Theorem 3 (Completeness). *For all input assignments H, if the global basis $\mathcal{B}$ is stable and contains all terms that occur in H, whenever a CDSAT derivation from H reaches a state Γ other than* unsat *such that no CDSAT inference applies, there exists a $\mathcal{T}_\infty^+[\mathsf{fv}_{\Sigma_\infty}(\Gamma)]$-model that view-endorses Γ and H contained in Γ.*

The proof of this theorem [3] relies on the following:

Lemma 1 (Model glueing). *Let H be an assignment and G be the collection of shared terms inductively defined by:*

$$\frac{(t \leftarrow c) \in H}{t \in G} \qquad \frac{u, u' \in G \quad t \in \mathsf{fv}_{\Sigma_i}(u) \cap \mathsf{fv}_{\Sigma_j}(u') \quad i \neq j}{t \in G} \qquad \frac{u \in G \quad t \in \mathsf{fv}_{\Sigma_k}(u) \backslash \mathcal{V}_\infty}{t \in G}$$

If there exists a $\mathcal{T}_1^+[\mathsf{fv}_{\Sigma_1}(H)]$-model that view-endorses H, and such that for all k, $2 \leq k \leq n$, the $\mathcal{T}_k$-view $H_{\mathcal{T}_k}$ is $\mathcal{T}_1$-compatible with $\mathcal{T}_k^+$ sharing G, then there exists a $\mathcal{T}_\infty^+[\mathsf{fv}(H)]$-model that view-endorses H.

A derivation can reach a state satisfying the hypotheses of Lemma 1 long before it reaches a state that no module can extend. An implementation of a module could notify the main algorithm when the trail becomes $\mathcal{T}_1$-compatible with its theory. In this sense, Theorem 3 covers the worst-case scenario. A *stable* global basis can be obtained by taking $\mathcal{B} = \mathsf{basis}_{\pi(k)}(\ldots \mathsf{basis}_{\pi(1)}(X))$, where X is the set of terms occurring in the input assignment and π is a permutation of $\{1, \ldots, k\}$ that satisfies the following property: if $i < j$ then $\mathsf{basis}_{\pi(i)}(\mathsf{basis}_{\pi(j)}(X)) \subseteq \mathsf{basis}_{\pi(j)}(\mathsf{basis}_{\pi(i)}(X))$. A syntactic criterion on the local bases implies this permutability property [3].

For all theory modules of Sect. 4, except $\mathcal{I}_{\mathsf{LRA}}$, we can define a local basis that makes them $\mathcal{T}_{\mathbb{N}}$-complete (cf. [3] for stronger completeness properties). For $\mathcal{I}_{\mathsf{LRA}}$, the local basis $\mathsf{basis}_{\mathsf{LRA}}$ given above makes the module $\mathcal{T}_{\mathbb{N}}$-complete only under the strategy that assigns Σ_{LRA}-variables in $\prec$-increasing order. Otherwise, considering again problem R and the ordering $y \prec x$, the LRA-assignment $l_0, l_1, l_2, l_3, (x \leftarrow 0)$ cannot be extended by $\mathcal{I}_{\mathsf{LRA}}$ even though it is LRA-unsatisfiable. Indeed, the obvious FM resolution combining l_1 and l_3 would eliminate y, which is not maximal in l_1, as required by $\mathsf{basis}_{\mathsf{LRA}}$. An additional inference rule can be added to $\mathcal{I}_{\mathsf{LRA}}$ to make it complete regardless of strategy [3].

7 Discussion

In this paper we introduced CDSAT, a *conflict-driven* system for deciding the satisfiability of quantifier-free problems in the union of disjoint theories. CDSAT combines theory inference systems, termed *theory modules*. We presented several theory modules, including one for arrays which is the first integration of this theory in a conflict-driven combination. CDSAT lifts CDCL to SMT in the sense of *satisfiability modulo multiple theories*. Since it accepts input problems containing Boolean and first-order assignments, CDSAT solves a class of problems that extends SMT and that we call SMA for *Satisfiability Modulo Assignments*. For such problems, the input format presupposes the theory extensions (cf. Sect. 3).

CDSAT generalizes MCSAT [5,8,9,19] to theory combinations. Furthermore, CDSAT solves the hitherto open problem of integrating conflict-driven procedures and the black-box solvers used in the *equality sharing* method [16]. CDSAT generalizes equality sharing itself, which corresponds to the case where all theories are stably infinite, all theory modules are black-boxes (cf. Sect. 4.5), and CDSAT decisions are limited to equalities between shared variables.

Clause learning, including theory lemmas, can be easily added to the version of CDSAT presented here [3]. Directions for future work include: the generation of proofs, by composition of theory inferences; efficient techniques to detect the applicability of theory inference rules and determine whether an assignment is acceptable (e.g., watched variables [9]); and heuristic strategies to make decisions and prioritize theory inferences.

Acknowledgments. The authors thank Dejan Jovanović for fruitful discussions. Part of this research was conducted while the first author was an international fellow at the Computer Science Laboratory of SRI International, whose support is greatly appreciated. This research was funded in part by NSF grants 1528153 and CNS-0917375, by DARPA under agreement number FA8750-16-C-0043, and by grant "Ricerca di base 2015" of the Università degli Studi di Verona. The views and conclusions contained herein are those of the authors and should not be interpreted as necessarily representing the official policies or endorsements, either expressed or implied, of NSF, DARPA, or the U.S. Government.

References

1. Barrett, C., Nieuwenhuis, R., Oliveras, A., Tinelli, C.: Splitting on demand in SAT modulo theories. In: Hermann, M., Voronkov, A. (eds.) LPAR 2006. LNCS (LNAI), vol. 4246, pp. 512–526. Springer, Heidelberg (2006). doi:10.1007/11916277_35
2. Bonacina, M.P.: On conflict-driven reasoning. In: Dutertre, B., Shankar, N. (eds.) Proceedings of the Sixth Workshop on Automated Formal Methods (AFM), at the Ninth NASA Formal Methods Symposium (NFM), pp. 1–9 (2017, to appear). http://fm.csl.sri.com/AFM17/
3. Bonacina, M.P., Graham-Lengrand, S., Shankar, N.: A model-constructing framework for theory combination. Technical Report 99/2016, Dipartimento di Informatica, Università degli Studi di Verona, Verona, Italy, EU. https://hal.archives-ouvertes.fr/hal-01425305, also Technical report of SRI International and INRIA - CNRS - École Polytechnique; Revised April 2017
4. Cotton, S.: Natural domain SMT: a preliminary assessment. In: Chatterjee, K., Henzinger, T.A. (eds.) FORMATS 2010. LNCS, vol. 6246, pp. 77–91. Springer, Heidelberg (2010). doi:10.1007/978-3-642-15297-9_8
5. Moura, L., Jovanović, D.: A model-constructing satisfiability calculus. In: Giacobazzi, R., Berdine, J., Mastroeni, I. (eds.) VMCAI 2013. LNCS, vol. 7737, pp. 1–12. Springer, Heidelberg (2013). doi:10.1007/978-3-642-35873-9_1
6. Ganzinger, H., Rueß, H., Shankar, N.: Modularity and refinement in inference systems. Technical report CSL-SRI-04-02, Computer Science Laboratory, SRI International, Menlo Park, CA, USA (2004)
7. Haller, L., Griggio, A., Brain, M., Kroening, D.: Deciding floating-point logic with systematic abstraction. In: Cabodi, G., Singh, S. (eds.) Proceedings of the Twelfth International Conference on Formal Methods in Computer Aided Design (FMCAD). ACM and IEEE (2012)

8. Jovanović, D.: Solving nonlinear integer arithmetic with MCSAT. In: Bouajjani, A., Monniaux, D. (eds.) VMCAI 2017. LNCS, vol. 10145, pp. 330–346. Springer, Heidelberg (2017). doi:10.1007/978-3-319-52234-0_18

9. Jovanović, D., Barrett, C., de Moura, L.: The design and implementation of the model-constructing satisfiability calculus. In: Jobstman, B., Ray, S. (eds.) Proceedings of the Thirteenth Conference on Formal Methods in Computer Aided Design (FMCAD). ACM and IEEE (2013)

10. Jovanović, D., Moura, L.: Cutting to the chase: solving linear integer arithmetic. In: Bjørner, N., Sofronie-Stokkermans, V. (eds.) CADE 2011. LNCS, vol. 6803, pp. 338–353. Springer, Heidelberg (2011). doi:10.1007/978-3-642-22438-6_26

11. Jovanović, D., Moura, L.: Solving non-linear arithmetic. In: Gramlich, B., Miller, D., Sattler, U. (eds.) IJCAR 2012. LNCS (LNAI), vol. 7364, pp. 339–354. Springer, Heidelberg (2012). doi:10.1007/978-3-642-31365-3_27

12. Korovin, K., Tsiskaridze, N., Voronkov, A.: Conflict resolution. In: Gent, I.P. (ed.) CP 2009. LNCS, vol. 5732, pp. 509–523. Springer, Heidelberg (2009). doi:10.1007/978-3-642-04244-7_41

13. Krstić, S., Goel, A.: Architecting solvers for SAT modulo theories: Nelson-Oppen with DPLL. In: Konev, B., Wolter, F. (eds.) FroCoS 2007. LNCS (LNAI), vol. 4720, pp. 1–27. Springer, Heidelberg (2007). doi:10.1007/978-3-540-74621-8_1

14. Marques Silva, J., Lynce, I., Malik, S.: Conflict-driven clause learning SAT solvers. In: Biere, A., Heule, M., Van Maaren, H., Walsh, T. (eds.) Handbook of Satisfiability, Frontiers in Artificial Intelligence and Applications, vol. 185, pp. 131–153. IOS Press (2009)

15. McMillan, K.L., Kuehlmann, A., Sagiv, M.: Generalizing DPLL to richer Logics. In: Bouajjani, A., Maler, O. (eds.) CAV 2009. LNCS, vol. 5643, pp. 462–476. Springer, Heidelberg (2009). doi:10.1007/978-3-642-02658-4_35

16. Nelson, G., Oppen, D.C.: Simplification by cooperating decision procedures. ACM Trans. Prog. Lang. Syst. 1(2), 245–257 (1979)

17. Wang, C., Ivančić, F., Ganai, M., Gupta, A.: Deciding separation logic formulae by SAT and incremental negative cycle elimination. In: Sutcliffe, G., Voronkov, A. (eds.) LPAR 2005. LNCS (LNAI), vol. 3835, pp. 322–336. Springer, Heidelberg (2005). doi:10.1007/11591191_23

18. Wolfman, S.A., Weld, D.S.: The LPSAT engine and its application to resource planning. In: Dean, T. (ed.) Proceedings of the Sixteenth International Joint Conference on Artificial Intelligence (IJCAI), vol. 1, pp. 310–316. Morgan Kaufmann Publishers (1999)

19. Zeljić, A., Wintersteiger, C.M., Rümmer, P.: Deciding bit-vector formulas with mcSAT. In: Creignou, N., Le Berre, D. (eds.) SAT 2016. LNCS, vol. 9710, pp. 249–266. Springer, Heidelberg (2016). doi:10.1007/978-3-319-40970-2_16

Notions of Knowledge in Combinations of Theories Sharing Constructors

Serdar Erbatur[1], Andrew M. Marshall[2], and Christophe Ringeissen[3(✉)]

[1] Ludwig-Maximilians-Universität, München, Germany
[2] University of Mary Washington, Fredericksburg, USA
[3] LORIA – INRIA Nancy-Grand Est, Villers-lès-Nancy, France
Christophe.Ringeissen@loria.fr

Abstract. One of the most effective methods developed for the analysis of security protocols is an approach based on equational reasoning and unification. In this approach, it is important to have the capability to reason about the knowledge of an intruder. Two important measures of this knowledge, defined modulo equational theories, are deducibility and static equivalence. We present new combination techniques for the study of deducibility and static equivalence in unions of equational theories sharing constructors. Thanks to these techniques, we obtain new modularity results for the decidability of deducibility and static equivalence. In turn, this should allow for the analysis of protocols involving combined equational theories which previous disjoint combination methods could not address due to their non-disjoint axiomatization.

1 Introduction

The formal analysis of security protocols is a large area of research, with one of its primary starting points the paradigm developed by Dolev and Yao [16] in which equational theories play a central role. This field of research has resulted in the development of several automated tools for the analysis of security issues in protocols, including [3,8,14,19,21,23,26]. Unification procedures and their combinations are widely used in such tools, e.g., a disjoint combination procedure [5,24] is the basic engine of Cl-AtSe [26]. This disjoint combination procedure has been extended to solve satisfiability problems in non-disjoint hierarchical intruder theories [10]. Verifying the security of protocols requires the development of specific decision procedures to reason about the knowledge that an attacker may have. Two important measures of this knowledge, which are useful and widely used, are *deducibility* [20,22] and *static equivalence* [1]. Informally, deducibility is the question of whether an attacker, given their deductive capabilities and a set of messages representing their knowledge, can compute another message representing some secret. This is a critical measure of the capability

---

C. Ringeissen—This work has received funding from the European Research Council (ERC) under the H2020 research and innovation program (grant agreement No. 645865-SPOOC).

L. de Moura (Ed.): CADE 2017, LNAI 10395, pp. 60–76, 2017.
DOI: 10.1007/978-3-319-63046-5_5

of the protocol to maintain secrets. Deducibility is needed for many questions about the security of protocols. However, there are some questions for which we need to be able to decide more than deducibility. For some protocols, in addition to deducibility, we would like to know if an attacker can distinguish between different runs of the protocol. For example, in protocols which attempt to transmit encrypted votes we would like to know if, to the attacker, two different votes are indistinguishable. One measure of this is static equivalence, which is a critical measure of the capability of the protocol to maintain indistinguishability between different runs.

Much work has gone into investigating and developing decision procedures for the questions of deducibility and static equivalence [1,7,12,15]. The equational theories of interest are usually defined as unions of several simpler sub-theories. In these cases, it is quite natural to try to proceed in a modular way by combining the decision procedures already available for the sub-theories. This combination problem has been investigated in the analysis of sequent calculi [25] for deducibility, and saturation-based decision procedures [13] for both deducibility and static equivalence. However, these contributions [13,25] are restricted to the disjoint case, where sub-theories are signature-disjoint. Until now, the non-disjoint case remained unexplored. One difficulty in this study is that the sub-theories often share some axioms. For example, encryption and decryption axioms are often found in such equational theories. The approach of just removing the axioms from one theory can often lead to a dead end: it may no longer be possible to reuse any existing decision procedure for the theory if an axiom is removed. Furthermore, along with these shared axioms are often found function symbols, such as pairing, which are also shared between the combined theories. It is possible that the shared function symbol appear in some shared axioms and in some non-shared. Thus, the non-disjoint case offers more complexities.

The approach developed in [13] to solve the disjoint case for deducibility and static equivalence is based on locality principles, to restrict the application of saturation-based decision procedures to the finitely many terms occurring in the problem. Instead, we follow an approach based on the tuning of some combination techniques which are instrumental to prove the combination procedures for deducibility and static equivalence. From our point of view, this combination approach leads to simpler and shorter proofs.

Along the lines of previous works on non-disjoint combination [6,17,18], we focus on equational theories sharing *constructors*. An originality of our approach is the ability to consider both shared constructors and shared axioms as those defining the access to the components of a constructor. In the first portion of the paper, we clearly define the class of combined theories we consider. A combined term rewrite system is used to identify the constructors. This term rewrite system is useful to state results showing that some decision procedures known for sub-theories can be reused without loss of completeness for the combined theory. In particular, we are interested in solving some restricted context unification problems related to deducibility and static equivalence. The proposed combination procedures purify the problems by replacing, as usual, alien subterms with fresh names. This reduction by purification is correct if the problems are first transformed in an appropriate way: the knowledge specified by the problems must be completed before purification. These transformations are borrowed from the ones initiated in [13] for the disjoint case.

Outline. Section 2 presents the background information for this paper. Section 3 develops the new combination results for non-disjoint equational theories sharing constructors. In Sect. 4 we apply the results from Sect. 3 to the two knowledge questions from security protocols, deducibility in Sect. 4.1, and static equivalence in Sect. 4.2.

2   Preliminaries

We use the standard notation of equational logic and term rewriting [4]. As in [1] we use some concepts, such as names, borrowed from the applied pi calculus [2].

Given a first-order signature Σ, a set of *names* is a countable set of (free) constants N, such that $\Sigma \cap N = \emptyset$. Given a (countable) set of variables X, the set of $(\Sigma \cup N)$-terms over X is denoted by $T(\Sigma \cup N, X)$. The set of variables in a term t is denoted by $fv(t)$ and the set of names in t is denoted by $fn(t)$. A term t is *ground* if $fv(t) = \emptyset$. For any position p in a term t (including the root position ϵ), $t(p)$ denotes the symbol at position p, $t|_p$ denotes the subterm of t at position p, and $t[u]_p$ denotes the term t in which $t|_p$ is replaced by u. Given any $\Sigma' \subseteq \Sigma$, A term t is said to be Σ'-*rooted* if $t(\epsilon) \in \Sigma'$. A *context*, C, is a first-order term with "holes", or distinguished variable that occur only once. We may write $C[x_1, \ldots, x_n]$, to illustrate that the context C contains n distinguished variables.

Given a set E of Σ-axioms (i.e., pairs of Σ-terms, denoted by $l = r$), the *equational theory* $=_E$ is the congruence closure of E under the law of substitutivity. For any Σ-term t, the equivalence class of t with respect to $=_E$ is denoted by $[t]_E$. Since $\Sigma \cap N = \emptyset$, the Σ-equalities in E do not contain any names in N. A theory E is *trivial* if $x =_E y$, for two distinct variables x and y. In this paper, all the considered theories are assumed non-trivial.

A substitution σ is an endomorphism of $T(\Sigma \cup N, X)$ with only finitely many variables not mapped to themselves. Application of a substitution σ to a term t (resp. a substitution θ) is written $t\sigma$ (resp. $\theta\sigma$). The domain of σ is $Dom(\sigma) = \{x \in X \mid x\sigma \neq x\}$. The range of σ is $Ran(\sigma) = \{x\sigma \mid x \in Dom(\sigma)\}$. Given a substitution $\sigma = \{x_1 \mapsto t_1, \ldots, x_m \mapsto t_m\}$, we have $Dom(\sigma) = \{x_1, \ldots, x_m\}$ and $Ran(\sigma) = \{t_1, \ldots, t_m\}$. When θ and σ are two substitutions with disjoint domains and with only ground terms in their ranges, $\theta\sigma = \theta \cup \sigma$.

A *term rewrite system* (TRS) is a pair (Σ, R), where Σ is a signature and R is a set of rewrite rules of the form $l \rightarrow r$, such that l, r are Σ-terms, l is not a variable and $fv(r) \subseteq fv(l)$. When the signature is clear from the context, a TRS is simply denoted by R. A term s *rewrites* to a term t, denoted by $s \rightarrow_R t$ (or simply $s \rightarrow t$), if there exists a position p of s, a rule $l \rightarrow r \in R$, and a substitution σ such that $s|_p = l\sigma$ and $t = s[r\sigma]_p$. A term s is a *normal form with respect to the relation* $\to_R$ (or simply a normal form), if there is no term t such that $s \to_R t$. This notion is lifted to substitutions as follows: a substitution σ is *normalized* if, for every variable x in the domain of σ, $x\sigma$ is a normal form. A TRS R is *terminating* if there are no infinite reduction sequences with respect to $\to_R$. A TRS R is *confluent* if, whenever $t \to_R^* s_1$ and $t \to_R^* s_2$, there exists a term w such that $s_1 \to_R^* w$ and $s_2 \to_R^* w$. A confluent and terminating TRS is called *convergent*. In a convergent TRS R, any term t admits a unique R-normal form denoted by $t\downarrow_R$. A TRS is *finite* if its set of rules is finite. From now on, a finite TRS is denoted by a calligraphic letter, say $\mathcal{R}$. Given a finite TRS $(\Sigma, \mathcal{R})$, $\mathsf{D}(\mathcal{R}) = \{l(\epsilon) \mid l \to r \in \mathcal{R}\}$ and $\mathsf{C}(\mathcal{R}) = \Sigma \backslash \mathsf{D}(\mathcal{R})$. A finite convergent TRS $\mathcal{R}$ is said to be *subterm convergent* if for any $l \to r \in \mathcal{R}$, r is either a strict subterm of l or a constant. An equational theory is *subterm convergent* if it is presented by a subterm convergent TRS. Both deducibility and static equivalence are known to be decidable in subterm convergent theories [1].

3   Combination of Theories

In this section we begin with an example from security protocol analysis to help elucidate the new presentation of non-disjoint combination below.

Example 1. Consider the following equational theories:

$$T_1 = \left\{ \begin{array}{l} enc(\langle x, y\rangle, z) = \langle enc(x, z), enc(y, z)\rangle \\ dec(\langle x, y\rangle, z) = \langle dec(x, z), dec(y, z)\rangle, dec(enc(x, y), y) = x \end{array} \right\}$$

$T_2 = \{h(\langle x, y\rangle, z) = \langle h(x, z), h(y, z)\rangle\}$, $T_3 = \{fst(\langle x, y\rangle) = x, snd(\langle x, y\rangle) = y\}$. The theories $E_1 = T_1 \cup T_3$ and $E_2 = T_2 \cup T_3$ are two theories of homomorphism studied respectively in [1] and in [11].

In the above example, if one wishes to ask questions about the combined theory, $E = E_1 \cup E_2$, then there are several problems.

First, there is the shared symbol, $\langle\rangle$, which, if the equalities are oriented from left to right, is a shared constructor. In addition, there are two particular shared destructors, again via a left-to-right orientation, $fst(\langle x, y\rangle) = x$, and $snd(\langle x, y\rangle) = y$. This problem, having one or more axioms which are exactly the same but in two different presentations of two different equational theories, is common in theories arising from security protocols. For example, the axioms in T_3 are common, just like $dec(enc(x, y), y) = x$. To proceed by combination techniques we could try to consider E as the union of three theories T_1, T_2 and T_3. However, this union would still share the symbol $\langle\rangle$ and thus we couldn't rely on current combination methods. Furthermore, there is an additional problem of the availability of decision procedures for these *three* theories. Often, we are trying to combine two or more theories for which we have decision procedures available to obtain a decision procedure for the combined theory, E in our example. If we remove equalities from a presentation, we are not guaranteed to still have a decision procedure available. For example, deducibility has been studied for

E_1 and E_2, but has not been studied for $E_1 \backslash T_3$. Therefore, we consider a new method of non-disjoint combination which allows us to combine E_1 and E_2 and maintain decidability of such questions as deducibility and static equivalence.

Before continuing to the details let us briefly outline some of the key topics needed to achieve the combination results. In the following, the combined theory E is handled thanks to a combined convergent TRS R sharing constructors (cf. Definition 1). The purification of ground terms is processed by constant abstraction, which is formally defined via a bijection between R-normal forms and fresh names (cf. Definition 2). Fortunately, we can use layer-reduced forms as a computable alternative to R-normal forms (cf. Definition 3). The knowledge problems we focus on are expressed using the notion of frame defined as a ground substitution together with a set of restricted names. A completion mechanism is required to achieve all the knowledge encoded by a frame (cf. Definition 5). As shown in Sect. 4, our combination methods are based on the constant abstraction of completed frames.

3.1 Constructor-Sharing Theories

Let us formally describe the combined theories we are interested in. We focus on combinations of theories $T_1 \cup \cdots \cup T_n$ for which shared function symbols can be interpreted as *constructors*. To formalize the notion of constructor, it is convenient to rely on a term rewrite system. However, not every equational theory can be equivalently presented by a term rewrite system. Fortunately, it is always possible to rely on a ground term rewrite system that could be obtained by unfailing completion [5]. More directly, this term rewrite system and the related constructors are defined below with respect to a reduction ordering used to orient heterogeneous ground instances of T_i-equalities.

Definition 1. *Let T_i be an equational Ω_i-theory for $i = 1, \ldots, n$. Consider the signature $\Sigma = \Omega_1 \cup \cdots \cup \Omega_n$ and the equational Σ-theory $E = T_1 \cup \cdots \cup T_n$. Let $>$ be a Noetherian reduction ordering on $T(\Sigma \cup V)$ (i.e., stable by context) such that V denotes a (sufficiently large) finite set of free constants (including names) which are minimal w.r.t $>$. Consider a (possibly infinite) set of Ω_i-equalities A_i such that:*

- *For any $l = r \in A_i$ such that $l(\epsilon), r(\epsilon) \in \Omega_i$, and any substitution ψ such that $Ran(\psi) \subseteq T(\Sigma \cup V)$, we have $l\psi > r\psi$ or $r\psi > l\psi$.*
- *For any $l = x \in A_i$ such that $l(\epsilon) \in \Omega_i$, x is a variable, and any substitution ψ such that $Ran(\psi) \subseteq T(\Sigma \cup V)$, we have $l\psi > x\psi$.*
- *the TRS $R_i = \{l\psi \to r\psi \mid l = r \in A_i, l\psi > r\psi, Ran(\psi) \subseteq T(\Sigma \cup V)\}$ is convergent on $T(\Sigma \cup V)$ and $=_{R_i}$ is $=_{T_i}$ on $T(\Sigma \cup V)$.*

A function symbol $f \in \Sigma$ is a constructor *of R_i if for any terms $t_1, \ldots, t_m$ in $T(\Sigma \cup V)$, $f(t_1, \ldots, t_m) \downarrow_{R_i} = f(t_1 \downarrow_{R_i}, \ldots, t_m \downarrow_{R_i})$. E is said to be constructor-sharing (w.r.t $>$) if for any $i, j \in \{1, \ldots n\}$, $i \neq j$, function symbols in $\Omega_i \cap \Omega_j$ are constructors of both R_i and R_j. In that case, $R = R_1 \cup \cdots \cup R_n$ is the combined TRS of E and $SC = \bigcup_{i \neq j} \Omega_i \cap \Omega_j$ is the set of shared constructors of E.*

There are several ways to consider appropriate A_i's following Definition 1. In general, A_i can be chosen as the set of all Ω_i-equalities $l = r$ such that $l =_{T_i} r$. In the following example, we detail the prominent case of theories presented by finite convergent term rewrite systems.

Example 2. In Definition 1, consider T_i is presented by a finite convergent TRS $\mathcal{R}_i$ for $i = 1, \ldots, n$, such that $\mathcal{R}_1 \cup \cdots \cup \mathcal{R}_n$ is terminating for a reduction ordering on (the set of terms with variables) $T(\Sigma, X)$. Then, rules in $\mathcal{R}_i$ can be used to build A_i and R_i-normal forms are computable by $\mathcal{R}_i$-normalization. Assume that for any $i, j \in \{1, \ldots n\}$, $i \neq j$, we have $\Omega_i \cap \Omega_j \subseteq \mathsf{C}(\mathcal{R}_i) \cap \mathsf{C}(\mathcal{R}_j)$. Let $\mathcal{R} = \mathcal{R}_1 \cup \cdots \cup \mathcal{R}_n$. Then, the equational theory of $\mathcal{R}$ is constructor-sharing, where normal forms are computable by $\mathcal{R}$-normalization.

Proposition 1. *If E is a constructor-sharing Σ-theory, then its combined TRS R is a convergent TRS such that $=_R$ is $=_E$ on $T(\Sigma \cup V)$.*

In Definition 1, note that the constructors of any R_i remain constructors of R. If a term is R-reducible, then it is R-reducible by a rule whose left hand-side is $(\Sigma \setminus SC)$-rooted.

Assumption 1. Consider a constructor-sharing theory $E = T_1 \cup \cdots \cup T_n$ as in Definition 1, its combined TRS R, and its set of shared constructors SC. We assume E is split into two non-disjoint theories E_1 and E_2, defined as follows. Let $K_1, K_2 \subset \{1, \ldots, n\}$ such that $K_1 \cup K_2 = \{1, \ldots, n\}$. For $i = 1, 2$, consider the signature $\Sigma_i = \bigcup_{k \in K_i} \Omega_k$ and the Σ_i-theory $E_i = \bigcup_{k \in K_i} T_k$. So, $\Sigma = \Sigma_1 \cup \Sigma_2$, $E = E_1 \cup E_2$ and both E_1, E_2 include the equational theory $\bigcup_{k \in K_1 \cap K_2} T_k$. From now on, the R-normal form of any t is simply denoted by $t \downarrow$.

We illustrate the above notion of constructor-sharing theories with several examples. These examples originate from theories studied in the security protocol analysis literature.

Example 3 (Example 1 continued). Assumption 1 holds with $A_i = T_i$ for $i = 1, 2, 3$. Indeed, the left-to-right orientation of equalities in A_i leads to the TRS $\mathcal{R}_i$ for $i = 1, 2, 3$. The TRS $\mathcal{R} = \bigcup_{i=1}^{3} \mathcal{R}_i$ is convergent, where $\langle \rangle$ is a constructor of each TRS $\mathcal{R}_i$ for $i = 1, 2, 3$. Thus, E is a constructor-sharing theory.

Example 4. Consider the following equational theories:

$$T_1 = \left\{ \begin{array}{l} fst(\langle x, y \rangle) = x, snd(\langle x, y \rangle) = y \\ adec(aenc(x, pk(y), z), y) = x, dec(enc(x, y), y) = x \\ check_1(sign(x, y), pk(y)) = ok, msg(sign(x, y)) = x \end{array} \right\}$$

$$T_2 = \left\{ \begin{array}{l} open(commit(x, y), y) = x, getpk(host(x)) = x \\ unblind(blind(x, y), y) = x \\ unblind(sign(blind(x, y), z), y) = sign(x, z) \\ check_2(sign(x, y), pk(y)) = x \end{array} \right\}$$

The theories T_1 and T_2 are used for modeling respectively strong secrecy [9] and blind signatures in e-voting protocols [1]. Let $E_1 = T_1, E_2 = T_2$ and $E = E_1 \cup E_2$.

For the same reasons as in Example 1, E is a constructor-sharing theory, where *sign* and *pk* are the shared constructors. Alternatively, it is also possible to remove the axioms $check_i(sign(x,y), pk(y)) = \ldots$ from T_i ($i = 1,2$) and to consider a third theory, say $\{check(sign(x,y), pk(y)) = x\}$, that would be shared as the theory T_3 in Example 1.

3.2 Equational Proofs in Combined Theories

A modular approach is possible due to the close relationship between combined equational proofs (modulo E) and pure ones (modulo E_1 and E_2). To state this relationship, we use a well-known notion, called *abstraction* [5]. In our context, impure terms are abstracted by free constants, via a bijection denoted by π.

Definition 2 (Constant Abstraction). *Let $\mathcal{C}$ be a set of (free) constants such that V and $\mathcal{C}$ are disjoint. Let $\pi : \{t \downarrow \mid t \in T(\Sigma \cup V), t \downarrow \notin V\} \longrightarrow \mathcal{C}$ be a bijection called a* constant abstraction *with range $\mathcal{C}$. For $i = 1,2$, the i-abstraction of t is denoted by t^{π_i} and defined as follows:*

- *If $t \in V$, then $t^{\pi_i} = t$.*
- *If $t = f(t_1, \ldots, t_n)$ and $f \in \Sigma_i$, then $t^{\pi_i} = f(t_1^{\pi_i}, \ldots, t_n^{\pi_i})$.*
- *Otherwise (t is $\Sigma \backslash \Sigma_i$-rooted), $t^{\pi_i} = \pi(t \downarrow)$ if $t \downarrow \notin V$, else $t^{\pi_i} = t \downarrow$.*

An inverse mapping *of π is a mapping $\pi^{-1} : \mathcal{C} \longrightarrow (T(\Sigma \cup V) \backslash V)$ such that $\pi(\pi^{-1}(c) \downarrow) = c$ for any $c \in \mathcal{C}$.*

Given a signature Ω, $Alien_\Omega(t)$ denotes the set of maximal subterms of t rooted by a function symbol in $\Sigma \backslash \Omega$. $Alien_{\Sigma_i}(t)$ is abbreviated into $Alien_i(t)$. The terms in $Alien_i(t)$ are called the *i-alien subterms* of t. Given a substitution σ, $Alien_i(\sigma) = \bigcup_{x \in Dom(\sigma)} Alien_i(x\sigma)$. The set of *alien subterms* of t is $Alien(t) = Alien_1(t) \cup Alien_2(t) \backslash \{t\}$.

Lemma 1. *Let t be an arbitrary term such that its i-alien subterms are R-normalized. If t is R-reducible, then there exists a term t' such that $t \to_R t'$ and $(t)^{\pi_i} =_{E_i} (t')^{\pi_i}$ where the i-alien subterms of t' are R-normalized.*

Proof. Assume t is a term such that terms in $Alien_i(t)$ are R-normalized for some $i \in \{1,2\}$.

If t is variable, then t is R-irreducible. If t is $\Sigma \backslash \Sigma_i$-rooted, then $Alien_i(t) = \{t\}$, and so t is R-irreducible by assumption.

Let us now assume t is Σ_i-rooted. Then, the redex position, p, in t occurs necessarily above the i-alien subterms. Hence, without loss of generality, there is some $l\psi \to r\psi \in R$ such that $t|_p = l\psi$, $t' = t[r\psi]_p$, $Alien_i(t') \subseteq Alien_i(t)$ and $l =_{E_i} r$ where l, r are i-pure terms. On the one hand, we have $(t^{\pi_i})|_p = (t|_p)^{\pi_i} = l\psi^{\pi_i}$. On the other hand, $(t')^{\pi_i} = (t[r\psi]_p)^{\pi_i} = t^{\pi_i}[r\psi^{\pi_i}]_p$. Since $l =_{E_i} r$, we have $l\psi^{\pi_i} =_{E_i} r\psi^{\pi_i}$. Therefore, $t^{\pi_i} =_{E_i} t^{\pi_i}[r\psi^{\pi_i}]_p = (t')^{\pi_i}$. $\qquad\square$

Lemma 1 can be applied inductively to obtain the following result.

Lemma 2. *Let t be a term such that its i-alien subterms are normalized. Then $t^{\pi_i} =_{E_i} (t \downarrow)^{\pi_i}$.*

The notion of *layer-reduced form* [17] aims at providing a computable term with the same "theory shape" as the R-normal form.

Definition 3. *A term t is in layer-reduced form if*

- $t \in V$, *or*
- $t = f(t_1, \ldots, t_n)$, $f \in SC$ *and* $t_1, \ldots, t_n$ *are in layer-reduced form, or*
- $t(\epsilon), t \downarrow (\epsilon) \in \Omega_i \backslash SC$ *and the terms in $Alien_{\Omega_i}(t)$ are in layer-reduced form.*

A substitution σ is in layer-reduced form *if $x\sigma$ is in layer-reduced form for any $x \in Dom(\sigma)$.*

Example 5 (Example 1 continued). Consider $t = dec(\langle enc(x, y), enc(x, z) \rangle, y)$. The terms $\langle x, dec(enc(x, z), y) \rangle$, x, and $dec(enc(x, z), y)$ are layer-reduced forms of respectively t, $fst(t)$ and $snd(t)$.

As stated below, a layer-reduced form is computable provided that a particular case of match-equations is decidable for each Ω_i-theory T_i involved in the combined theory $E = E_1 \cup E_2 = \bigcup_{i=1}^n T_i$. A *$SC$-rooted pattern T_i-matching problem* is any match-equation $f(X_1, \ldots, X_m) =_{T_i}^? t$ where $f \in SC$, $X_1, \ldots, X_m$ are pairwise distinct variables, and t is a ground Ω_i-term. Of course, SC-rooted pattern T_i-matching is decidable if T_i-matching is decidable. To get the decidability of SC-rooted pattern T_i-matching, another sufficient condition is to assume that T_i is presented by a finite convergent TRS $\mathcal{R}_i$.

Proposition 2 *[17]. It is possible to compute an E-equal layer-reduced form of any term if SC-rooted pattern T_i-matching and T_i-equality is decidable for each $i = 1, \ldots, n$.*

In Example 2, layer-reduced forms are computable by $\mathcal{R}$-normalization. Lemma 1 can again be applied inductively to rephrase Lemma 2.

Lemma 3. *Let t be a term such that its i-alien subterms are in layer-reduced form. Then $t^{\pi_i} =_{E_i} (t \downarrow)^{\pi_i}$.*

3.3   Frames in Combined Theories

Along the lines of Lemma 3, we present a new result which will be instrumental in proving the correctness of combination methods for knowledge problems popular in protocol analysis, namely, the deduction and the static equivalence. These problems are defined using the notion of frame to express the intruder knowledge. A *frame*, $\phi = \nu\tilde{n}.\sigma$, consists of a finite set of restricted names, $\tilde{n}$, and a substitution σ such that $Ran(\sigma)$ contains only ground terms. This definition is borrowed from the applied pi-calculus [2] and more insight behind the definition is given is Sect. 4.

We say that a frame $\phi = \nu \tilde{n}.\sigma$ is in layer-reduced form if σ is in layer-reduced form. Given a term t, $St(t) = \{t\} \cup \bigcup_{a \in Alien(t)} St(a)$. For a set of terms T, $St(T) = \bigcup_{t \in T} St(t)$ and $fn(T) = \bigcup_{t \in T} fn(t)$. For a substitution σ, $St(\sigma) = St(Ran(\sigma))$. The set of terms $T \cup Ran(\sigma)$ is abbreviated into $T \sqcup \sigma$.

Definition 4. *Let* $\phi = \nu \tilde{n}.\sigma$ *be a frame, and* t *a ground term. We denote* $\phi \Vdash_E t$ *if there exists a term* s *such that* $s\sigma =_E t$ *and* $fn(s) \cap \tilde{n} = \emptyset$. *The term* s *is called a* recipe *of* t *in* ϕ *modulo* E.

Abstraction constants are particular restricted names. When a constant abstraction is performed to a get a pure problem, only finitely many terms are abstracted and only finitely many fresh names are introduced. For sake of simplicity, we assume that this finite set of abstraction constants is already included in the set of restricted names $(\tilde{n})$ of the considered frame. Thanks to this assumption, the i-abstraction of a frame can be defined without introducing new names to be restricted: they are already restricted. Also, we can assume without loss of generality that constants abstracting terms not in the knowledge problem are not restricted. All these assumptions can be formalized as follows.

Assumption 2. Consider a finite set F of frames in layer-reduced form and a finite set T of terms in layer-reduced form. Let $U_\sigma = St(T \sqcup \sigma) \backslash V$ for each $(\nu \tilde{n}.\sigma) \in F$ and a bijection ρ from $(\bigcup_{(\nu \tilde{n}.\sigma) \in F} U_\sigma)/=_E$ to a set of fresh constants. We assume that each frame $(\nu \tilde{n}.\sigma) \in F$ is equipped with a constant abstraction π with range $\mathcal{C}$ such that $\pi(t \downarrow) = \rho([t]_E)$ if $t \in U_\sigma$ and $\tilde{n} \cap \mathcal{C} = \{\rho([t]_E) \mid t \in U_\sigma\}$.

Assumption 2 is not restrictive. It clarifies the relationship between restricted names $\tilde{n}$ and constants $\mathcal{C}$ used by the constant abstraction.

Definition 5. *Under Assumption 2 introducing* F *and* T, *let* $\phi = \nu \tilde{n}.\sigma$ *be any frame in* F. *The* completion *of* ϕ *is the frame* $\phi_* = \nu \tilde{n}.\sigma_*$ *where*

$$\sigma_* = \sigma\{\chi_t \mapsto t \mid t \in St(T \sqcup \sigma) \cup \tilde{n}, \phi \Vdash_E t, t \notin Ran(\sigma)\}$$

such that the fresh variables χ_t *are bijectively mapped to the terms* t.
The i-abstraction *of* ϕ_* *is the frame* $\phi_*^{\pi i} = \nu \tilde{n}.\sigma_*^{\pi i}$ *where*

$$\sigma_*^{\pi i} = \{x \mapsto (x\sigma_*)^{\pi i} \mid x \in Dom(\sigma_*)\}.$$

The completion of a frame always exists. We will see in Sect. 4.1 how to compute it.

Example 6. Consider the theory E introduced in Example 1, $T = \emptyset$ and the frame $\phi = \nu \tilde{n}.\sigma$ where $\tilde{n} \backslash \mathcal{C} = \{s_1, k_1, k_2\}$ and $\sigma = \{x_1 \mapsto \langle s_2, k_1 \rangle, x_2 \mapsto enc(s_1, k_1), x_3 \mapsto h(s_2, k_2)\}$. Note that only the names s_1, k_1, and k_2 are restricted but not s_2. We have $St(\sigma) = \{\langle s_2, k_1 \rangle, enc(s_1, k_1), h(s_2, k_2)\}$ and $Ran(\sigma_*) \backslash Ran(\sigma)$ includes s_1 and k_1, since we have $dec(x_2, snd(x_1))\sigma =_E s_1$ and $snd(x_1)\sigma =_E k_1$. Later, we will be able to check that $\phi \nVdash_E k_2$.

Theorem 1. *Let $\phi_* = \nu\tilde{n}.\sigma_*$ be the completion of any frame $\phi = \nu\tilde{n}.\sigma$ following Assumption 2. For any term t such that $fn(t) \cap \tilde{n} = \emptyset$, there exists an i-pure term t_i such that $fn(t_i) \cap \tilde{n} = \emptyset$ and $((t\sigma_*) \downarrow)^{\pi_i} =_{E_i} t_i\sigma_*^{\pi_i}$.*

Proof. Proof by induction on the *theory height* of t, formally defined as follows:

- $ht(t) = 1 + \max_{a \in Alien_i(t)} ht(a)$ if t is Σ_i-rooted,
- $ht(t) = 1 + \max_{a \in Alien_j(t)} ht(a)$ if t is $\Sigma_j \backslash \Sigma_i$-rooted for $j \neq i$.

If t is i-pure, then $((t\sigma_*) \downarrow)^{\pi_i} =_{E_i} (t\sigma_*)^{\pi_i}$ by Lemma 2, where $(t\sigma_*)^{\pi_i} = t\sigma_*^{\pi_i}$. In that case, we can define $t_i = t$. Let us now assume that t is not i-pure.

(1) Consider the case t is a Σ_i-rooted term $C_i[a_1, \ldots, a_n]$ where $a_1, \ldots a_n$ are the i-aliens of t. Let $(t\sigma_*)_\downarrow$ be the term obtained from $t\sigma_*$ by replacing its i-alien subterms by their normal forms. We have:

$$
\begin{aligned}
((t\sigma_*) \downarrow)^{\pi_i} &=_{E_i} ((t\sigma_*)_\downarrow)^{\pi_i} \text{(by Lemma 2)} \\
&= C_i[((a_1\sigma_*) \downarrow)^{\pi_i}, \ldots, ((a_n\sigma_*) \downarrow)^{\pi_i}] \\
&=_{E_i} C_i[a_{1,i}\sigma_*^{\pi_i}, \ldots, a_{n,i}\sigma_*^{\pi_i}] \text{(by induction hypothesis)} \\
&= (C_i[a_{1,i}, \ldots, a_{n,i}])\sigma_*^{\pi_i}
\end{aligned}
$$

where $C_i[a_{1,i}, \ldots, a_{n,i}]$ is an i-pure term satisfying the name restriction.

(2) Consider the case t is $\Sigma_j \backslash \Sigma_i$-rooted for $j \neq i$.
- If $(t\sigma_*) \downarrow$ is Σ_i-rooted, then there exists some Σ_i-rooted term t' such that $(t\sigma_*) \downarrow$ is equal to $(t'\sigma_*) \downarrow$, $ht(t') \leq ht(t)$ and t' satisfies the name restriction. Then, the rest of the proof follows the case (1).
- If $(t\sigma_*) \downarrow$ is $\Sigma_j \backslash \Sigma_i$-rooted, then t_i is given as follows:
  (i) if $(t\sigma_*) \downarrow = s \downarrow$ with $s \in St(T \sqcup \sigma) \cup \tilde{n}$, then $\phi \vdash_E s$ and there exists some $x \in Dom(\sigma_*)$ such that $x\sigma_* = s$, and we define $t_i = x$;
  (ii) otherwise, t_i is defined as the abstraction constant $((t\sigma_*) \downarrow)^{\pi_i}$. This fresh constant cannot occur in $\tilde{n}$: otherwise, it would mean that (i) is satisfied. $\square$

4 Application to Two Notions of Knowledge in Protocols

We now apply the results from Sect. 3 to two questions on knowledge in protocol analysis; *deduction* and *static equivalence*. We begin by reviewing some background material on protocols and how knowledge can be represented in their analysis. As mentioned in Sect. 3, the applied pi calculus and frames are used to model attacker knowledge [2]. In this model, the set of messages or terms which the attacker knows, and which could have been obtained from observing one or more protocol sessions, are the set of terms in $Ran(\sigma)$ of the frame $\phi = \nu\tilde{n}.\sigma$. This allows us to not only keep the set of messages known by the attacker but also the variables in the domain of σ allow for the consideration of each term and the tracking of the order of transmission of each term. That is, it represents the order in which these messages/terms were obtained and transmitted.

We also need to model such cryptographic concepts as nonces, keys, and publicly known values. We do this by using names, which are essentially free constants. Here also, we need to track the names which the attacker knows, such as public values, and the names which the attacker does not know, such as freshly generated nonces. $\tilde{n}$ consists of a finite set of restricted names. The intuition is that these names represent freshly generated names which remain secret from the attacker.

4.1   Deduction Problem

The first combination problem we consider is the problem of deduction. That is, given a frame ϕ, representing the knowledge of the attacker, can a ground term M be deduced from ϕ? We denote the deduction of M from ϕ modulo E by $\phi \vdash_E M$. Deduction is axiomatized by the inference system given in Fig. 1.

$$\frac{}{\nu \tilde{n}.\sigma \vdash_E M} \quad \text{if } \exists x \in Dom(\sigma) \text{ s.t. } x\sigma = M$$

$$\frac{}{\nu \tilde{n}.\sigma \vdash_E s} \quad \text{if } s \notin \tilde{n}$$

$$\frac{\phi \vdash_E M_1, \ \ldots, \phi \vdash_E M_k}{\phi \ \vdash_E f(M_1, \ \ldots, \ M_k)} \quad \text{if } f \in \Sigma$$

$$\frac{\phi \vdash_E M}{\phi \ \vdash_E M'} \quad M =_E M'$$

Fig. 1. Deduction axioms

However, a useful characterization of deduction has been given in [1], relating $\vdash_E$ to $\Vdash_E$ (introduced in Definition 4).

Lemma 4 *[1]. $\phi \vdash_E M$ iff $\phi \Vdash_E M$.*

Lemma 5. *Under Assumption 2 introducing F and T, let $\phi = \nu\tilde{n}.\sigma$ be any frame in F. For any $M \in St(T \sqcup \sigma) \cup \tilde{n}$, we have $\phi \vdash_E M$ if and only if $(\phi_*)^{\pi_1} \vdash_{E_1} M^{\pi_1}$ or $(\phi_*)^{\pi_2} \vdash_{E_2} M^{\pi_2}$.*

Proof. The if-direction is simple. Let us focus on the only-if direction. By definition of ϕ_*, we have that $\phi \vdash_E M$ if and only if $\phi_* \vdash_E M$. Suppose t is a Σ_i-rooted term for some $i \in \{1, 2\}$ such that $t\sigma_* =_E M$ with $fn(t) \cap \tilde{n} = \emptyset$. By Lemma 3 and Theorem 1, we get an E_i-equality $t_i \sigma_*^{\pi_i} =_{E_i} ((t\sigma_*) \downarrow)^{\pi_i} = (M \downarrow)^{\pi_i} =_{E_i} M^{\pi_i}$ where $t_i \sigma_*^{\pi_i}$ is an i-pure term. By construction, the fresh constants introduced in t_i are not restricted, i.e. $fn(t_i) \cap \tilde{n} = \emptyset$.   □

Notice that Lemma 5 now provides a modular method for computing σ_*.

Corollary 1 *(Computing σ_*). Assume the deduction problem modulo E_i is decidable for each $i = 1, 2$. Under Assumption 2 introducing F and T, let $\phi = \nu\tilde{n}.\sigma$ be any frame in F. The completion ϕ_* is computable and the range of σ_* is the set S such that $Ran(\sigma) \subseteq S \subseteq St(T \sqcup \sigma) \cup \tilde{n}$ and $M \in S$ if and only if $(\nu\tilde{n}.S)^{\pi_1} \vdash_{E_1} M^{\pi_1}$ or $(\nu\tilde{n}.S)^{\pi_2} \vdash_{E_2} M^{\pi_2}$.*

Proof. If $M \in St(T \sqcup \sigma) \cup \tilde{n}$, then Lemma 5 applies: we have $M \in Ran(\sigma_*)$ iff $\phi \vdash_E M$ iff $(\phi_*)^{\pi_i} \vdash_{E_i} M^{\pi_i}$ for some $i = 1, 2$, where $\phi_* = \nu\tilde{n}.Ran(\sigma_*)$.   □

Example 7 (Example 1 continued). Assume $t_1 = \langle enc(h(a,b), c), enc(enc(c, d), c)\rangle$, $t_2 = \langle h(h(a, b), c), h(enc(c, d), c)\rangle$ and $t_3 = \langle enc(h(a, b), a), enc(enc(c, d), a)\rangle$. Let $T = \{t_1, t_2, t_3\}$ and the frame $\phi = \nu\tilde{n}.\sigma$ where $\tilde{n}\backslash\mathcal{C} = \{a, b, c\}$ and $\sigma = \{X \mapsto \langle h(a, b), enc(c, d)\rangle\}$. The completion ϕ_* is $\nu\tilde{n}.\sigma\{X_1 \mapsto c, X_2 \mapsto h(a, b), X_3 \mapsto enc(c, d), X_4 \mapsto t_1, X_5 \mapsto t_2\}$.

Directly from Lemma 5, we obtain our main result on the deduction problem.

Theorem 2. *Let $E = E_1 \cup E_2$ be a constructor-sharing theory following Assumption 1. The deduction problem modulo E is decidable if the deduction problem modulo E_i is decidable for each $i = 1, 2$.*

By applying Theorem 2, the deduction problem is decidable in a modular way for the combined theories given in Examples 1 and 4.

Example 8 (Example 7 continued). The following terms are deducible in ϕ modulo E since they occur in $Ran(\phi_*)$: c, with the recipe $dec(snd(X), d)$; t_1, with the recipe $enc(X, dec(snd(X), d))$; t_2, with the recipe $h(X, dec(snd(X), d))$. The term t_3 occurs in $T\backslash Ran(\phi_*)$ and so $\phi \nvdash_E t_3$.

4.2 Static Equivalence

Another form of knowledge is the ability to tell if two frames are *statically equivalent* modulo E, sometimes also called *indistiguishability*. Two terms s and t are *equal* in a frame $\phi = \nu\tilde{n}.\sigma$ modulo an equational theory E, denoted $(s =_E t)\phi$, iff $s\sigma =_E t\sigma$, and $\tilde{n} \cap (fn(s) \cup fn(t)) = \emptyset$. Two frames $\phi = \nu\tilde{n}.\sigma$ and $\psi = \nu\tilde{n}.\tau$ are *statically equivalent modulo E*, denoted as $\phi \approx_E \psi$, if $Dom(\sigma) = Dom(\tau)$ and for all terms s and t, we have $(s =_E t)\phi$ iff $(s =_E t)\psi$.

Given an equational Σ-theory E and a frame ϕ, $Eq_E(\phi)$ denotes the set of Σ-equalities $s = t$ such that $(s =_E t)\phi$. Thanks to the above notation, given $\phi = \nu\tilde{n}.\sigma$ and $\psi = \nu\tilde{n}.\tau$, we have $\phi \approx_E \psi$ if and only if $Dom(\sigma) = Dom(\tau)$ and $Eq_E(\phi) = Eq_E(\psi)$.

Definition 6. *Let $\phi = \nu\tilde{n}.\sigma$ be any frame following Assumption 2 (with $T = \emptyset$). A pair $(s = t, \phi)$ is an equality candidate of ϕ if $(fn(s) \cup fn(t)) \cap \tilde{n} = \emptyset$. An equality candidate $(s_i = t_i, \phi_i)$ is i-pure if s_i, t_i and ϕ_i are i-pure.*

Let $\phi_* = \nu\tilde{n}.\sigma_*$ be the completion of ϕ. An equality candidate $(s = t, \phi_*)$ is an E-instance of an i-pure equality candidate $(s_i = t_i, \phi_*^{\pi_i})$ if there exists some substitution μ such that $s\sigma_* =_E (s_i\sigma_*)\mu$ and $t\sigma_* =_E (t_i\sigma_*)\mu$.

We now state the relationship between $Eq_E(\phi_*)$ and $Eq_{E_i}(\phi_*^{\pi_i})$. First, any E-instance of any equality in $Eq_{E_i}(\phi_*^{\pi_i})$ leads to an equality in $Eq_E(\phi_*)$.

Lemma 6 (Soundness). *If $s_i = t_i \in Eq_{E_i}(\phi_*^{\pi_i})$, then for any E-instance $(s = t, \phi_*)$ of $(s_i = t_i, \phi_*^{\pi_i})$, we have $s = t \in Eq_E(\phi_*)$.*

Conversely, any equality in $Eq_E(\phi_*)$ is the E-instance of some equality in $Eq_{E_i}(\phi_*^{\pi_i})$:

Lemma 7 (Completeness). *If $s = t \in Eq_E(\phi_*)$, then there exists $s_i = t_i \in Eq_{E_i}(\phi_*^{\pi_i})$ such that $(s = t, \phi_*)$ is an E-instance of $(s_i = t_i, \phi_*^{\pi_i})$.*

Proof. if $s\sigma_* =_E t\sigma_*$, then $(s\sigma_*) \downarrow = (t\sigma_*) \downarrow$. By Theorem 1, we have for any $i = 1, 2$, $s_i(\sigma_*)^{\pi_i} =_{E_i} ((s\sigma_*) \downarrow)^{\pi_i} = ((t\sigma_*) \downarrow)^{\pi_i} =_{E_i} t_i(\sigma_*)^{\pi_i}$ where s_i and t_i are i-pure terms satisfying the name restriction. Moreover, we have $s_i(\sigma_*)^{\pi_i}\pi^{-1} =_E (s_i\sigma_*)\pi^{-1} =_E s\sigma_*$ and $t_i(\sigma_*)^{\pi_i}\pi^{-1} =_E (t_i\sigma_*)\pi^{-1} =_E t\sigma_*$. Consequently, $(s = t, \phi_*)$ is an E-instance of $(s_i = t_i, \phi_*^{\pi_i})$, where $s_i = t_i \in Eq_{E_i}(\phi_*^{\pi_i})$. $\square$

Lemma 8. *Let $\phi = \nu\tilde{n}.\sigma$ and $\psi = \nu\tilde{n}.\tau$ be any two frames following Assumption 2 (with $T = \emptyset$). We have $\phi_* \approx_E \psi_*$ iff $(\phi_*)^{\pi_1} \approx_{E_1} (\psi_*)^{\pi_1}$ and $(\phi_*)^{\pi_2} \approx_{E_2} (\psi_*)^{\pi_2}$.*

Proof. Follows from Lemmas 6 and 7. $\square$

To reduce any static equivalence problem $\phi \approx_E \psi$ into a static equivalence problem of completed frames $\phi_* \approx_E \psi_*$, we still need an additional form of frame extension introducing recipes [13].

Definition 7. *Let $\phi = \nu\tilde{n}.\sigma$ be a frame. A term t is compatible with ϕ if $fn(t) \cap \tilde{n} = \emptyset$ and $t\sigma$ is ground. Let Π be a set of terms compatible with ϕ. The Π-extension of ϕ is the frame $\Pi\phi = \nu\tilde{n}.\{\chi_t \mapsto t \mid t \in \Pi\}\sigma$.*

Given a term d E-deducible in ϕ, $rcp_\phi(d)$ denotes an admissible recipe of d in ϕ. By extension, given a set D of E-deducible terms in ϕ, $Rcp_\phi(D) = \{rcp_\phi(d) \mid d \in D\}$. If the deduction problem modulo E is decidable, then it is always possible to compute an admissible recipe of d. A brute force method consists in enumerating all possible admissible terms until a recipe r satisfying $r\sigma =_E d$ is found. It is also possible to proceed in a modular way. If the decision procedures known for the deduction problems modulo E_1 and E_2 are indeed "recipe-producing", then the combination method in Sect. 4.1 can easily be adapted to get a "recipe-producing" decision procedure for the deduction problem modulo $E = E_1 \cup E_2$.

In a way similar to [13], the recipes are used to define a set Π of admissible terms. Then, two new extended frames respectively E-equal to $\Pi\phi$ and $\Pi\psi$ are considered. Formally, two frames $\phi = \nu\tilde{n}.\sigma$ and $\phi' = \nu\tilde{n}.\sigma'$ are said to be E-equal, denoted by $\phi =_E \phi'$, if $Dom(\sigma) = Dom(\sigma')$ and $x\sigma =_E x\sigma'$ for any $x \in Dom(\sigma)$.

Lemma 9. *Let $\phi = \nu\tilde{n}.\sigma$, $\psi = \nu\tilde{n}.\tau$, $\bar{\phi} =_E \Pi\phi$, $\bar{\psi} =_E \Pi\psi$ be any frames following Assumption 2 (with $T = \emptyset$), where*

$$\Pi = St(Rcp_\phi(Ran(\sigma_*)\backslash Ran(\sigma)) \cup Rcp_\psi(Ran(\tau_*)\backslash Ran(\tau)))$$

Then, we have (i) $(\bar{\phi})_* = \bar{\phi}$ and $(\bar{\psi})_* = \bar{\psi}$; (ii) $\phi \approx_E \psi$ if and only if $\bar{\phi} \approx_E \bar{\psi}$.

Proof. Let us first prove that $(\bar{\phi})_* = \bar{\phi}$. The set of terms $St(\bar{\sigma}) \cup \tilde{n}$ is a superset of $St(\sigma) \cup \tilde{n}$:

- For any $t \in St(\sigma) \cup \tilde{n}$, we have $t \in Ran(\bar{\sigma}_*)$ implies $t \in Ran(\sigma_*)$ and then $t \in Ran(\bar{\sigma})$;
- For any other term $\bar{t} \in St(\bar{\sigma})$, $\bar{t} \in Ran(\bar{\sigma})$ since $St(\Pi) = \Pi$.

Hence, $Ran(\bar{\sigma}_*) \subseteq Ran(\bar{\sigma})$ and so $(\bar{\phi})_* = \bar{\phi}$. Similarly, we prove that $(\bar{\psi})_* = \bar{\psi}$. Let us now prove that $\phi \approx_E \psi$ if and only if $\bar{\phi} \approx_E \bar{\psi}$:

- (If direction) If $\phi \not\approx_E \psi$, then there exists $s = t$ such that $s = t \in Eq(\phi), s = t \notin Eq_E(\psi)$ or $s = t \notin Eq(\phi), s = t \in Eq_E(\psi)$, where $fv(s = t) \cap (Dom(\bar{\sigma})\backslash Dom(\sigma)) = \emptyset$.
- (Only-if direction) Assume $\phi \approx_E \psi$. For any $s = t \in Eq_E(\bar{\phi})$, there exist, by definition of $\bar{\phi}$, two terms s', t' such that $s'\sigma =_E s\bar{\sigma} =_E t\bar{\sigma} =_E t'\sigma$ and $(fn(s') \cup fn(t')) \cap \tilde{n} = \emptyset$. Hence $s' = t' \in Eq_E(\phi)$ and so, by assumption, $s' = t' \in Eq_E(\psi)$. Eventually, we have $s\bar{\tau} =_E s'\tau =_E t'\tau =_E t\bar{\tau}$, which means that $s = t \in Eq_E(\bar{\psi})$. □

Theorem 3. *Let $E = E_1 \cup E_2$ be a constructor-sharing theory following Assumption 1. The static equivalence modulo E and the deduction problem modulo E are both decidable if the static equivalence modulo E_i and the deduction problem modulo E_i are both decidable for each $i = 1, 2$.*

Proof. By Lemmas 8, 9 and Theorem 2. □

Example 9 (Example 1 continued). In [1], the authors introduce locally stable theories and locally finite theories, where respectively the deduction problem and the static equivalence are proven to be decidable. As an example, the theory E_1 is shown in [1] to be both locally stable and locally finite. By reusing the same proof technique as in [1], we can show in a similar way that E_2 is both locally stable and locally finite. Then Theorem 3 allows us to get the decidability of the static equivalence and the deduction problem modulo $E = E_1 \cup E_2$.

Example 10 (Example 4 continued). The decidability of the static equivalence and the deduction problem modulo $E = E_1 \cup E_2$ follows from Theorem 3, since the static equivalence and the deduction problem are decidable modulo E_1 (because E_1 is subterm convergent) and modulo E_2 [1].

Example 11 (Example 1 continued). Let $T = \emptyset$, $\phi = \nu\tilde{n}.\sigma$, $\psi = \nu\tilde{n}.\tau$ where $\tilde{n}\backslash\mathcal{C} = \{k_1, k_2\}$, $\sigma = \{x_1 \mapsto \langle enc(h(a, a), k_1), h(c, c)\rangle, x_2 \mapsto k_2\}$ and $\tau = \{x_1 \mapsto \langle enc(h(b, b), k_1), h(c, c)\rangle, x_2 \mapsto k_2\}$. By computing the completions, we have $\phi_* = \nu\tilde{n}.\sigma\{x_3 \mapsto enc(h(a,a), k_1), x_4 \mapsto h(c,c)\}$ and $\psi_* = \nu\tilde{n}.\tau\{x'_3 \mapsto enc(h(b,b), k_1), x_4 \mapsto h(c,c)\}$. Consider the set of admissible recipes $\Pi = \{fst(x_1), snd(x_1)\}$. By Definition 7, we use fresh variables, say x_3, x_4, to denote the respective instances of $fst(x_1), snd(x_1)$ in $\Pi\phi$ and in $\Pi\psi$. Thus, we have $\bar{\phi} = \nu\tilde{n}.\sigma\{x_3 \mapsto enc(h(a,a), k_1), x_4 \mapsto h(c,c)\} =_E \Pi\phi$ and $\bar{\psi} = \nu\tilde{n}.\tau\{x_3 \mapsto enc(h(b,b), k_1), x_4 \mapsto h(c,c)\} =_E \Pi\psi$. Notice that given $\bar{\phi}$ and $\bar{\psi}$ there is still no recipe for which subterms of $h(a,a)$ and $h(b,b)$ can be moved to the root of a term modulo E. Therefore, one would need to use the subterms $enc(h(a,a), k_1)$ and $enc(h(b,b), k_1)$ to distinguish two terms s and t such that $s = t \in Eq_E(\bar{\phi})$ but $s = t \notin Eq_E(\bar{\psi})$. However, this would violate the restriction that $\tilde{n} \cap (fn(t) \cup fn(s)) = \emptyset$. Hence, $\bar{\phi} \approx_E \bar{\psi}$, and by Lemma 9, $\phi \approx_E \psi$. One can verify that $(\bar{\phi})^{\pi_1} \approx_{E_1} (\bar{\psi})^{\pi_1}$ and $(\bar{\phi})^{\pi_2} \approx_{E_2} (\bar{\psi})^{\pi_2}$, where

$$(\bar{\phi})^{\pi_1} = \nu\tilde{n}.\{x_1 \mapsto \langle enc(a', k_1), c'\rangle, x_2 \mapsto k_2, x_3 \mapsto enc(a', k_1), x_4 \mapsto c'\}$$
$$(\bar{\psi})^{\pi_1} = \nu\tilde{n}.\{x_1 \mapsto \langle enc(b', k_1), c'\rangle, x_2 \mapsto k_2, x_3 \mapsto enc(b', k_1), x_4 \mapsto c'\}$$
$$(\bar{\phi})^{\pi_2} = \nu\tilde{n}.\{x_1 \mapsto \langle e_a, h(c,c)\rangle, x_2 \mapsto k_2, x_3 \mapsto e_a, x_4 \mapsto h(c,c)\}$$
$$(\bar{\psi})^{\pi_2} = \nu\tilde{n}.\{x_1 \mapsto \langle e_b, h(c,c)\rangle, x_2 \mapsto k_2, x_3 \mapsto e_b, x_4 \mapsto h(c,c)\}.$$

Now consider a small modification to the frames. Let $\phi = \nu\tilde{n}.\sigma$, $\psi = \nu\tilde{n}.\tau$ such that $\sigma = \{x_1 \mapsto \langle enc(h(a,a), k_1), h(c,c)\rangle, x_2 \mapsto k_1\}$ and $\tau = \{x_1 \mapsto \langle enc(h(b,b), k_1), h(c,c)\rangle, x_2 \mapsto k_1\}$. Now it seems to be the same situation as above. However, $\phi_* = \nu\tilde{n}.\sigma\{x_3 \mapsto enc(h(a,a), k_1), x_4 \mapsto h(c,c), x_5 \mapsto h(a,a)\}$ and $\psi_* = \nu\tilde{n}.\tau\{x'_3 \mapsto enc(h(b,b), k_1), x_4 \mapsto h(c,c), x'_5 \mapsto h(b,b)\}$. The set of admissible recipes is $\Pi = \{fst(x_1), snd(x_1), dec(fst(x_1), x_2)\}$. By Definition 7, we use fresh variables, say x_3, x_4, x_5, to denote the respective instances of $fst(x_1), snd(x_1), dec(fst(x_1), x_2)$ in $\Pi\phi$ and in $\Pi\psi$. Then, $\bar{\phi} = \nu\tilde{n}.\sigma_1\{x_3 \mapsto enc(h(a,a), k_1), x_4 \mapsto h(c,c), x_5 \mapsto h(a,a)\} =_E \Pi\phi$ and $\bar{\psi} = \nu\tilde{n}.\sigma_2\{x_3 \mapsto enc(h(b,b), k_1), x_4 \mapsto h(c,c), x_5 \mapsto h(b,b)\} =_E \Pi\psi$. Notice, if $s = x_5$ and $t = h(a,a)$, then $s = t \in Eq_E(\bar{\phi})$ and $s = t \notin Eq_E(\bar{\psi})$. Hence, $\bar{\phi} \not\approx_E \bar{\psi}$, and by Lemma 9, $\phi \not\approx_E \psi$. One can verify that $(\bar{\phi})^{\pi_2} \not\approx_{E_2} (\bar{\psi})^{\pi_2}$, where

$$(\bar{\phi})^{\pi_2} = \nu\tilde{n}.\{x_1 \mapsto \langle e_a, h(c,c)\rangle, x_2 \mapsto k_1, x_3 \mapsto e_a, x_4 \mapsto h(c,c), x_5 \mapsto h(a,a)\}$$
$$(\bar{\psi})^{\pi_2} = \nu\tilde{n}.\{x_1 \mapsto \langle e_b, h(c,c)\rangle, x_2 \mapsto k_1, x_3 \mapsto e_b, x_4 \mapsto h(c,c), x_5 \mapsto h(b,b)\}.$$

5   Conclusion

This paper presents new *non-disjoint* combination results for both deduction and static equivalence. That is, if the deduction and static equivalence problems are decidable for two *constructor sharing* theories E_1 and E_2 (following Assumption 1), then they are decidable for the theory $E_1 \cup E_2$. The procedure does not, however, require such properties as locally stable or locally finite [1]. While these are very useful for both obtaining decision procedures and combination (i.e., check for local stability in $E_1 \cup E_2$), our approach is applicable to theories which may not have such properties.

This new approach requires that the frames are extended with some finitely many deducible (sub)terms. For the deduction problem, the notion of completion is sufficient. For the static equivalence, another form of frame extension, introducing recipes, is required to get a modular decision procedure. Thus, it nicely illustrates some of the differences between the two problems.

A natural future work is to study how we could move beyond the sharing of absolutely free constructors, e.g., to allow Associative-Commutative constructors. One possible approach we are investigating is related to our work on hierarchical combination [18].

Acknowledgments. We would like to thank Véronique Cortier and Steve Kremer for the thoughtful comments and discussions.

References

1. Abadi, M., Cortier, V.: Deciding knowledge in security protocols under equational theories. Theoret. Comput. Sci. **367**(1–2), 2–32 (2006)
2. Abadi, M., Fournet, C.: Mobile values, new names, and secure communication. In: Proceedings of the 28th ACM SIGPLAN-SIGACT Symposium on Principles of Programming Languages, POPL 2001, pp. 104–115. ACM, New York (2001)
3. Armando, A., et al.: The AVISPA tool for the automated validation of internet security protocols and applications. In: Etessami, K., Rajamani, S.K. (eds.) CAV 2005. LNCS, vol. 3576, pp. 281–285. Springer, Heidelberg (2005). doi:10.1007/11513988_27
4. Baader, F., Nipkow, T.: Term Rewriting and All That. Cambridge University Press, New York (1998)
5. Baader, F., Schulz, K.U.: Unification in the union of disjoint equational theories: combining decision procedures. J. Symb. Comput. **21**(2), 211–243 (1996)
6. Baader, F., Tinelli, C.: Deciding the word problem in the union of equational theories. Inf. Comput. **178**(2), 346–390 (2002)
7. Baudet, M., Cortier, V., Delaune, S.: YAPA: a generic tool for computing intruder knowledge. ACM Trans. Comput. Log. **14**(1), 4 (2013)
8. Blanchet, B.: An efficient cryptographic protocol verifier based on prolog rules. In: 14th IEEE Computer Security Foundations Workshop (CSFW-14 2001), 11–13 June 2001, Cape Breton, Nova Scotia, Canada, pp. 82–96. IEEE Computer Society (2001)
9. Chadha, R., Cheval, V., Ciobâcă, Ş., Kremer, S.: Automated verification of equivalence properties of cryptographic protocols. ACM Trans. Comput. Log. **17**(4), 23:1–23:32 (2016). https://hal.inria.fr
10. Chevalier, Y., Rusinowitch, M.: Hierarchical combination of intruder theories. Inf. Comput. **206**(2–4), 352–377 (2008)
11. Comon-Lundh, H., Treinen, R.: Easy intruder deductions. In: Dershowitz, N. (ed.) Verification: Theory and Practice. LNCS, vol. 2772, pp. 225–242. Springer, Heidelberg (2003). doi:10.1007/978-3-540-39910-0_10
12. Conchinha, B., Basin, D.A., Caleiro, C.: FAST: an efficient decision procedure for deduction and static equivalence. In: Schmidt-Schauß, M. (ed.) Proceedings of RTA 2011, Novi Sad, Serbia. LIPIcs, vol. 10, pp. 11–20. Schloss Dagstuhl - Leibniz-Zentrum fuer Informatik (2011)
13. Cortier, V., Delaune, S.: Decidability and combination results for two notions of knowledge in security protocols. J. Autom. Reason. **48**(4), 441–487 (2010)

14. Cremers, C.J.F.: The scyther tool: verification, falsification, and analysis of security protocols. In: Gupta, A., Malik, S. (eds.) CAV 2008. LNCS, vol. 5123, pp. 414–418. Springer, Heidelberg (2008). doi:10.1007/978-3-540-70545-1_38
15. Ciobâcă, Ş., Delaune, S., Kremer, S.: Computing knowledge in security protocols under convergent equational theories. J. Autom. Reason. **48**(2), 219–262 (2012)
16. Dolev, D., Yao, A.C.: On the security of public key protocols (extended abstract). In: 22nd Annual Symposium on Foundations of Computer Science, 28–30 October 1981, Nashville, Tennessee, USA, pp. 350–357. IEEE Computer Society (1981)
17. Domenjoud, E., Klay, F., Ringeissen, C.: Combination techniques for non-disjoint equational theories. In: Bundy, A. (ed.) CADE 1994. LNCS, vol. 814, pp. 267–281. Springer, Heidelberg (1994). doi:10.1007/3-540-58156-1_19
18. Erbatur, S., Kapur, D., Marshall, A.M., Narendran, P., Ringeissen, C.: Hierarchical combination. In: Bonacina, M.P. (ed.) CADE 2013. LNCS (LNAI), vol. 7898, pp. 249–266. Springer, Heidelberg (2013). doi:10.1007/978-3-642-38574-2_17
19. Escobar, S., Meadows, C., Meseguer, J.: Maude-NPA: cryptographic protocol analysis modulo equational properties. In: Aldini, A., Barthe, G., Gorrieri, R. (eds.) FOSAD 2007–2009. LNCS, vol. 5705, pp. 1–50. Springer, Heidelberg (2009). doi:10.1007/978-3-642-03829-7_1
20. Millen, J., Shmatikov, V.: Constraint solving for bounded-process cryptographic protocol analysis. In: Proceedings of the 8th ACM Conference on Computer and Communications Security, CCS 2001, pp. 166–175. ACM, New York (2001)
21. Mödersheim, S., Viganò, L.: The open-source fixed-point model checker for symbolic analysis of security protocols. In: Aldini, A., Barthe, G., Gorrieri, R. (eds.) FOSAD 2007–2009. LNCS, vol. 5705, pp. 166–194. Springer, Heidelberg (2009). doi:10.1007/978-3-642-03829-7_6
22. Paulson, L.C.: The inductive approach to verifying cryptographic protocols. Comput. Secur. **6**, 85–128 (1998)
23. Schmidt, B., Meier, S., Cremers, C.J.F., Basin, D.A.: Automated analysis of Diffie-Hellman protocols and advanced security properties. In: Chong, S. (ed.) 25th IEEE Computer Security Foundations Symposium, CSF 2012, 25–27 June 2012, Cambridge, MA, USA, pp. 78–94. IEEE Computer Society (2012)
24. Schmidt-Schauß, M.: Unification in a combination of arbitrary disjoint equational theories. J. Symb. Comput. **8**, 51–99 (1989)
25. Tiu, A., Goré, R., Dawson, J.E.: A proof theoretic analysis of intruder theories. Log. Methods Comput. Sci. **6**(3:12), 1–37 (2010)
26. Turuani, M.: The CL-Atse protocol analyser. In: Pfenning, F. (ed.) RTA 2006. LNCS, vol. 4098, pp. 277–286. Springer, Heidelberg (2006). doi:10.1007/11805618_21

On the Combination
of the Bernays–Schönfinkel–Ramsey Fragment
with Simple Linear Integer Arithmetic

Matthias Horbach[1]([⊠]), Marco Voigt[1,2]([⊠]), and Christoph Weidenbach[1]([⊠])

[1] Max Planck Institute for Informatics,
Saarland Informatics Campus, Saarbrücken, Germany
matthiashorbach@gmx.de
[2] Saarbrücken Graduate School of Computer Science,
Saarland Informatics Campus, Saarbrücken, Germany
{mvoigt,weidenbach}@mpi-inf.mpg.de

Abstract. In general, first-order predicate logic extended with linear integer arithmetic is undecidable. We show that the Bernays-Schönfinkel-Ramsey fragment ($\exists^*\forall^*$-sentences) extended with a restricted form of linear integer arithmetic is decidable via finite ground instantiation. The identified ground instances can be employed to restrict the search space of existing automated reasoning procedures considerably, e.g., when reasoning about quantified properties of array data structures formalized in Bradley, Manna, and Sipma's *array property fragment*. Typically, decision procedures for the array property fragment are based on an exhaustive instantiation of universally quantified array indices with all the ground index terms that occur in the formula at hand. Our results reveal that one can get along with significantly fewer instances.

Keywords: Bernays–Schönfinkel–Ramsey fragment · Linear integer arithmetic · Complete instantiation

1 Introduction

The Bernays-Schönfinkel-Ramsey (BSR) fragment comprises exactly the first-order logic prenex sentences with the $\exists^*\forall^*$ quantifier prefix, resulting in a CNF where all occurring function symbols are constants. Formulas may contain equality. Satisfiability of the BSR fragment is decidable and NExpTime-complete [19]. Its extension with linear arithmetic is undecidable [10,11,13,23].

We prove decidability of the restriction to arithmetic constraints of the form $s \triangleleft t$, $x \triangleleft t$, where $\triangleleft$ is one of the standard relations $<, \leq, =, \neq, \geq, >$ and s, t are ground arithmetic terms, and $x \trianglelefteq y$, where $\trianglelefteq$ stands for $\leq$, $=$, or $\geq$. Underlying the result is the observation that similar to the finite model property of BSR, only finitely many instances of universally quantified clauses with arithmetic constraints need to be considered. Our construction is motivated by results from

© Springer International Publishing AG 2017
L. de Moura (Ed.): CADE 2017, LNAI 10395, pp. 77–94, 2017.
DOI: 10.1007/978-3-319-63046-5_6

quantifier elimination [20] and hierarchic superposition [3–5,11,18]. In particular, the insights gained from the quantifier elimination side lead to instantiation methods that can result in significantly fewer instances than known, more naive approaches for comparable logic fragments generate, such as the original instantiation approach for the *array property fragment* [6,8]. For example, consider the following two clauses (∧ and ∨ bind stronger than →)

$$x_2 \neq 5 \wedge R(x_1) \;\rightarrow\; Q(u_1, x_2)$$
$$y_1 < 7 \wedge y_2 \leq 2 \qquad\qquad \rightarrow\; Q(d, y_2) \vee R(y_1)$$

where the variable u_1 ranges over a freely selectable domain, x_i, y_i are variables over the integers, and the constant d addresses an element of the same domain that u_1 ranges over. All occurring variables are implicitly universally quantified. Our main result reveals that this clause set is satisfiable if and only if a finite set of ground instances is satisfiable in which (i) u_1 is being instantiated with the constant d, (ii) x_2 and y_2 are being instantiated with the (abstract) integer values $5 + 1$ and $-\infty$, and (iii) x_1 and y_1 are being instantiated with $-\infty$ only. The instantiation does not need to consider the constraints $y_1 < 7$, $y_2 \leq 2$, because it is sufficient to explore the integers either from $-\infty$ upwards—in this case upper bounds on integer variables can be ignored—or from $+\infty$ downwards—ignoring lower bounds—, as is similarly done in linear quantifier elimination over the reals [20]. Moreover, instantiation does not need to consider the value $5 + 1$ for x_1 and y_1, motivated by the fact that the argument x_1 of R is not affected by the constraint $x_2 \neq 5$.

The abstract values $-\infty$ and $+\infty$ are represented by Skolem constants over the integers, together with defining axioms. For the example, we introduce the fresh Skolem constant $c_{-\infty}$ to represent $-\infty$ (a "sufficiently small" value) together with the axiom $c_{-\infty} < 2$, where 2 is the smallest occurring constant. Eventually, we obtain the ground clause set

$$5 + 1 \neq 5 \wedge R(c_{-\infty}) \;\rightarrow\; Q(d, 5 + 1)$$
$$c_{-\infty} \neq 5 \wedge R(c_{-\infty}) \;\rightarrow\; Q(d, c_{-\infty})$$
$$c_{-\infty} < 7 \wedge 5 + 1 \leq 2 \qquad \rightarrow\; Q(d, 5 + 1) \vee R(c_{-\infty})$$
$$c_{-\infty} < 7 \wedge c_{-\infty} \leq 2 \qquad \rightarrow\; Q(d, c_{-\infty}) \vee R(c_{-\infty})$$
$$c_{-\infty} < 2$$

which has the model $\mathcal{A}$ with $c_{-\infty}^{\mathcal{A}} = 1$, $R^{\mathcal{A}} = \{1\}$, $Q^{\mathcal{A}} = \{(d,6), (d,1)\}$.

After developing our instantiation methodology in Sect. 3, we show in Sect. 4 that our instantiation methods are also compatible with uninterpreted functions and additional background theories under certain syntactic restrictions. These results are based on an (un)satifiability-preserving embedding of uninterpreted functions into BSR clauses. There are interesting known logic fragments that fall into this syntactic category: many-sorted clause sets over *stratified vocabularies* [1,16], the *array property fragment* [8], and the *finite essentially uninterpreted fragment*, possibly extended with simple integer arithmetic [12]. Consequently, reasoning procedures for these fragments that employ forms of instantiation may benefit from our findings. The paper ends with a discussion in Sect. 5, where we consider the impact of our results on automated reasoning procedures for our and similar logic fragments and outline possible further improvements.

Due to space limitations, we mostly resort to sketches of proofs. The interested reader is referred to the extended version of the present paper [14].

2   Preliminaries

Hierarchic combinations of first-order logic with background theories build upon sorted logic with equality [4,5]. We instantiate this framework with the BSR fragment and linear arithmetic over the integers as the *base theory*. The *base sort* $\mathcal{Z}$ shall always be interpreted by the integers $\mathbb{Z}$. For simplicity, we restrict our considerations to a single *free sort* $\mathcal{S}$, which may be freely interpreted as some nonempty domain, as usual.

We denote by $V_{\mathcal{Z}}$ a countably infinite set of base-sort variables. *Linear integer arithmetic (LIA) terms* are build from integer constants $0, 1, -1, 2, -2, \ldots$, the operators $+, -$, and the variables from $V_{\mathcal{Z}}$. We moreover allow base-sort constant symbols whose values have to be determined by an interpretation (*Skolem constants*). They can be conceived as existentially quantified. The LIA constraints we consider are of the form $s \lhd t$, where $\lhd \in \{<, \leq, =, \neq, \geq, >\}$ and s and t are either LIA variables or ground LIA terms.

In order to hierarchically extend the base theory by the BSR fragment, we introduce the free sort $\mathcal{S}$, a countably infinite set $V_{\mathcal{S}}$ of *free-sort variables*, a finite set Ω of *free (uninterpreted) constant symbols of sort* $\mathcal{S}$ and a finite set Π of *free predicate symbols* equipped with sort information. Note that every predicate symbol in Π has a finite, nonnegative arity and can have a mixed sort over the two sorts $\mathcal{Z}$ and $\mathcal{S}$, e.g. $P : \mathcal{Z} \times \mathcal{S} \times \mathcal{Z}$. We use the symbol $\approx$ to denote the built-in equality predicate on $\mathcal{S}$. To avoid confusion, we tacitly assume that no constant or predicate symbol is overloaded, i.e. they have a unique sort.

Definition 1 (BSR with Simple Linear Integer Constraints–BSR(SLI)).
A BSR(SLI) *clause has the form* $\Lambda \parallel \Gamma \to \Delta$, *where* Λ, Γ, Δ *are multisets of atoms satisfying the following conditions.*

(i) *Every atom in* Λ *is a LIA constraint of the form* $s \lhd t$ *or* $x \lhd t$ *or* $x \unlhd y$ *where* s, t *are ground,* $\lhd \in \{<, \leq, =, \neq, \geq, >\}$, *and* $\unlhd \in \{\leq, =, \geq\}$,

(ii) *Every atom in* Γ *and* Δ *is either an equation* $s \approx s'$ *with* $s, s' \in \Omega \cup V_{\mathcal{S}}$, *or a non-equational atom* $P(s_1, \ldots, s_m)$, *where every* s_i *of sort* $\mathcal{Z}$ *must be a variable* $x \in V_{\mathcal{Z}}$, *and every* s_i *of sort* $\mathcal{S}$ *may be a variable* $u \in V_{\mathcal{S}}$ *or a constant symbol* $c \in \Omega$.

We omit the empty multiset left of "$\to$" and denote it by $\square$ right of "$\to$" (where $\square$ at the same time stands for *falsity*). The clause notation separates arithmetic constraints from the *free* (also: *uninterpreted*) part. We use the vertical double bar "$\parallel$" to indicate this separation syntactically. Intuitively, clauses $\Lambda \parallel \Gamma \to \Delta$ can be read as $(\bigwedge \Lambda \wedge \bigwedge \Gamma) \to \bigvee \Delta$, i.e. the multisets Λ, Γ stand for conjunctions of atoms and Δ stands for a disjunction of atoms.

Requiring the free part $\Gamma \to \Delta$ of clauses to not contain any base-sort terms apart from variables does not limit expressiveness. Every base-sort term $t \notin V_{\mathcal{Z}}$ in the free part can safely be replaced by a fresh base-sort variable x_t when an atomic constraint $x_t = t$ is added to the constraint part of the clause (a process known as *purification* or *abstraction* [4,18]).

A *hierarchic interpretation* is an algebra $\mathcal{A}$ which interprets the base sort $\mathcal{Z}$ as $\mathcal{Z}^{\mathcal{A}} = \mathbb{Z}$, assigns integer values to all occurring base-sort Skolem constants, and interprets all LIA terms and constraints in the standard way. Moreover, $\mathcal{A}$ comprises a nonempty domain $\mathcal{S}^{\mathcal{A}}$, assigns to each free-sort constant symbol c in Ω a domain element $c^{\mathcal{A}} \in \mathcal{S}^{\mathcal{A}}$, and interprets every sorted predicate symbol $P{:}\xi_1 \times \ldots \times \xi_m$ in Π by a set $P^{\mathcal{A}} \subseteq \xi_1^{\mathcal{A}} \times \ldots \times \xi_m^{\mathcal{A}}$, as usual.

Given a hierarchic interpretation $\mathcal{A}$ and a sort-respecting *variable assignment* $\beta : V_{\mathcal{Z}} \cup V_{\mathcal{S}} \to \mathcal{Z}^{\mathcal{A}} \cup \mathcal{S}^{\mathcal{A}}$, we write $\mathcal{A}(\beta)(s)$ to address the *value of the term s under $\mathcal{A}$ with respect to the variable assignment β*. The variables occurring in clauses are implicitly universally quantified. Therefore, given a clause C, we call $\mathcal{A}$ a *hierarchic model of C*, denoted $\mathcal{A} \models C$, if and only if $\mathcal{A}, \beta \models C$ holds for every variable assignment β. For clause sets N, $\mathcal{A} \models N$ holds if and only if $\mathcal{A} \models C$ holds true for every clause $C \in N$. We call a clause C (a clause set N) *satisfiable* if and only if there exists a hierarchic model $\mathcal{A}$ of C (of N). Two clauses C, D (clause sets N, M) are *equisatisfiable* if and only if C (N) is satisfiable whenever D (M) is satisfiable and vice versa.

Given a BSR(SLI) clause C, consts(C) denotes the set of all constant symbols occurring in C. The set bconsts(N) (fconsts(N)) is the restriction of consts(N) to base-sort (free-sort) constant symbols. By vars(C) we denote the set of all variables occurring in C. Similar notation is used for other syntactic objects.

We define *substitutions* σ in the standard way as sort-respecting mappings from variables to terms. The *restriction of the domain of a substitution σ to a set V of variables* is denoted by $\sigma|_V$ and is defined such that $v\sigma|_V := v\sigma$ for every $v \in V$ and $v\sigma|_V = v$ for every $v \notin V$. While the application of a substitution σ to terms, atoms and multisets thereof is defined as usual, we need to be more specific for clauses. Consider a BSR(SLI) clause $C := \Lambda \,\|\, \Gamma \to \Delta$ and let $x_1, \ldots, x_k$ denote all base-sort variables occurring in C for which $x_i\sigma \neq x_i$. We then set $C\sigma := \Lambda\sigma, x_1 = x_1\sigma, \ldots, x_k = x_k\sigma \,\|\, \Gamma\sigma|_{V_S} \to \Delta\sigma|_{V_S}$.

A term, atom, etc. is called *ground*, if it does not contain any variables. A BSR(SLI) clause C is called *essentially ground* if it does not contain free-sort variables and for every base-sort variable x occurring in C there is a constraint $x = t$ in C for some ground LIA term t. A clause set N is *essentially ground* if all the clauses it contains are essentially ground.

Definition 2 (Normal Form of BSR(SLI) Clauses). *A BSR(SLI) clause $\Lambda \,\|\, \Gamma \to \Delta$ is in* normal form *if*

(1) all non-ground atoms in Λ have the form $x \trianglelefteq c$ or $x \leq y$ (or their symmetric variants) where c is an integer or Skolem constant and $\trianglelefteq \in \{\leq, =, \geq\}$,
(2) all base-sort variables that occur in Λ also occur in $\Gamma \to \Delta$, and
(3) Γ does not contain any equation of the form $u \approx t$.

A BSR(SLI) clause set N is in normal form *if all clauses in N are in normal form and pairwise variable disjoint. Moreover, we assume that N contains at least one free-sort constant symbol.*

For every BSR(SLI) clause set N there is an equisatisfiable BSR(SLI) clause set N' in normal form. It can be constructed from N by straightforward *purification/abstraction* methods [4,18] and a simple procedure for eliminating existentially quantified variables in LIA constraints (see [14] for details).

3   Instantiation for BSR(SLI)

In this section, we present and prove our main technical result:

Theorem 3. *Satisfiability of a finite BSR(SLI) clause set N is decidable.*

In essence, one can show that N is equisatisfiable to a finite set of essentially ground clauses (cf. Lemma 12). There are calculi, such as hierarchic superposition [3–5,11,18] or DPLL(T) [21], that can decide satisfiability of ground clause sets. Our decidability result for BSR(SLI) does not come as a surprise, given the similarity to other logic fragments that are known to be decidable, such as the *array property fragment* by Bradley, Manna, and Sipma [7,8] and Ge and de Moura's *finite essentially uninterpreted fragment* extended with simple integer arithmetic constraints [12].

More important than the obtained decidability result is the instantiation methodology that we employ, in particular for integer-sort variables. Typically, decision procedures for the integer-indexed array property fragment are based on an exhaustive instantiation of universally quantified array indices with all the ground index terms that occur in the formula at hand (cf. the original approach [6,8] and standard literature [7,17]). In more sophisticated approaches, only a *relevant portion* of the occurring arithmetic terms is singled out before instantiation [12].

Our methodology will also be based on a concept of relevant terms, determined by connections between the arguments of predicate symbols and instantiation points that are propagated along these connections. This part of our method is not specific for the integers but can be applied to the free part of our language as well. For integer variables, we investigate additional criteria to filter out unnecessary instances, inspired by the Loos–Weispfenning quantifier elimination procedure [20]. We elaborate on this in Sects. 3.1, 3.2, and 3.3.

3.1   Instantiation of Integer Variables

We first summarize the overall approach for the instantiation of integer variables in an intuitive way. To keep the informal exposition simple, we pretend that all LIA terms are constants from $\mathbb{Z}$. We even occasionally refer to the improper values $-\infty$ / $+\infty$ —"sufficiently small/large" integers. A formal treatment with proper definitions will follow.

Given a finite BSR(SLI) clause set N in normal form, we intend to partition $\mathbb{Z}$ into a set $\mathcal{P}$ of finitely many subsets $p \in \mathcal{P}$ such that satisfiability of N necessarily leads to the existence of a *uniform* hierarchic model.

Definition 4 (Uniform Interpretations). *A hierarchic interpretation $\mathcal{A}$ is uniform with respect to a partition $\mathcal{P}$ of the integers if and only if for every free predicate symbol Q occurring in N, every part $p \in \mathcal{P}$, and all integers $r_1, r_2 \in p$ we have $\langle \ldots, r_1, \ldots \rangle \in Q^{\mathcal{A}}$ if and only if $\langle \ldots, r_2, \ldots \rangle \in Q^{\mathcal{A}}$.*

As soon as we have found such a finite partition $\mathcal{P}$, we pick one integer value $r_p \in p$ as *representative* from each and every part $p \in \mathcal{P}$. Given a clause C that contains a base-sort variable x, and given constant symbols $d_1, \ldots, d_k$ whose values cover all these representatives, i.e. $\{d_1^{\mathcal{A}}, \ldots, d_k^{\mathcal{A}}\} = \{r_p \mid p \in \mathcal{P}\}$, we observe
$$\mathcal{A} \models C \text{ if and only if } \mathcal{A} \models \{C[x/d_i] \mid 1 \leq i \leq k\} \,.$$
This equivalence claims that we can transform universal quantification over the integer domain into finite conjunction over all representatives of subsets in $\mathcal{P}$. Formulated differently, we can extrapolate a model for a universally quantified clause set, if we can find a model of finitely many instances of this clause set. The formal version of this statement is given in Lemma 12. Uniform hierarchic models play a key role in its proof.

When we extract the partition $\mathcal{P}$ from the given clause set N, we exploit three aspects to increase efficiency:

(E-i) We group argument positions of free predicate symbols in such a way that the instantiation points relevant for these argument positions are identical. This means the variables that are associated to these argument positions, e.g. because they occur in such a place in some clause, need to be instantiated only with terms that are relevant for the respective group of argument positions. This is illustrated in Example 5.

(E-ii) Concerning the *relevant* integer constraints, i.e. the ones that produce instantiation points, one can choose to either stick to lower bounds exclusively, use $-\infty$ as a default (the lowest possible lower bound), and ignore upper bounds. Alternatively, one can focus on upper bounds, use $+\infty$ as default, and ignore lower bounds. This idea goes back to the Loos–Weispfenning quantifier elimination procedure over the reals [20]. Example 8 gives some intuition.

(E-iii) The choice described under (E-ii) can be made independently for every integer variable that is to be instantiated. See Examples 8 and 13.

Example 5. Consider the following clauses:
$$\begin{aligned} C_1 &:= & 1 \leq x_1, x_2 \leq 0 \parallel & \rightarrow T(x_1), \; Q(x_1, x_2) \,, \\ C_2 &:= & y_3 \leq 7, \; y_1 \leq y_3 \parallel Q(y_1, y_2) \rightarrow R(y_3) \,, \\ C_3 &:= & 6 \leq z_1 \parallel T(z_1) & \rightarrow \square \,. \end{aligned}$$
The variables x_1, x_2, y_1, y_2, y_3, and z_1 are affected by the constraints in which they occur explicitly. Technically, it is more suitable to speak of the *argument position* $\langle T, 1 \rangle$ instead of variables x_1 and z_1 that occur as the first argument of the predicate symbol T in C_1 and C_3, respectively. Speaking in such terms, argument position $\langle T, 1 \rangle$ is directly affected by the constraints $1 \leq x_1$ and $6 \leq z_1$, argument position $\langle Q, 1 \rangle$ is directly affected by $1 \leq x_1$ and $y_1 \leq y_3$, $\langle Q, 2 \rangle$ is affected by $x_2 \leq 0$, and, finally, $\langle R, 1 \rangle$ is affected by $y_3 \leq 7$ and $y_1 \leq y_3$. Besides such direct effects, there are also indirect effects that have to be taken into account. For example, the argument position $\langle Q, 1 \rangle$ is indirectly affected by the constraint $6 \leq z_1$, because C_1 establishes a connection between argument positions $\langle T, 1 \rangle$ and $\langle Q, 1 \rangle$ via the simultaneous occurrence of x_1 in both argument positions and $\langle T, 1 \rangle$ is affected by $6 \leq z_1$. This is witnessed by the fact that

C_1 and C_3 together logically entail the clause $D := 6 \leq x, y \leq 0 \,\|\, \rightarrow Q(x,y)$. D can be obtained by a hierarchic superposition step from C_1 and C_3, for instance. Another entailed clause is $6 \leq z, z \leq 7 \,\|\, \rightarrow R(z)$, the (simplified) result of hierarchically resolving D with C_2. Hence, $\langle R, 1 \rangle$ is affected by the constraints $6 \leq z$ and $z \leq 7$. Speaking in terms of argument positions, this effect can be described as propagation of the lower bound $6 \leq y_1$ from $\langle Q, 1 \rangle$ to $\langle R, 1 \rangle$ via the constraint $y_1 \leq y_3$ in C_2.   □

One lesson learned from the example is that argument positions can be connected by variable occurrences or constraints of the form $x \leq y$. Such links in a clause set N are expressed by the relation $\rightrightarrows_N$.

Definition 6 (Connections Between Argument Positions and Argument Position Closures). *Let N be a BSR(SLI) clause set in normal form. We define $\rightrightarrows_N$ to be the smallest preorder (i.e. a reflexive and transitive relation) over $\Pi \times \mathbb{N}$ such that $\langle Q, j \rangle \rightrightarrows_N \langle P, i \rangle$ whenever there is a clause $\Lambda \,\|\, \Gamma \rightarrow \Delta$ in N containing free atoms $Q(\ldots, u, \ldots)$ and $P(\ldots, v, \ldots)$ in which the variable u occurs at the j-th and the variable v occurs at the i-th argument position and*

(1) either $u = v$,
(2) or $u \neq v$, both are of sort $\mathcal{Z}$ and there are constraints $u = v$ or $u \leq v$ in Λ,
(3) or $u \neq v$, both are of sort $\mathcal{S}$ and there is an atom $u \approx v$ in Γ or in Δ.[1]

$\rightrightarrows_N$ induces downward closed sets $\Downarrow_N \langle P, i \rangle$ of argument positions, called argument position closures: $\Downarrow_N \langle P, i \rangle := \{ \langle Q, j \rangle \mid \langle Q, j \rangle \rightrightarrows_N \langle P, i \rangle \}$.

Consider a variable v that occurs at the i-th argument position of a free atom $P(\ldots, v, \ldots)$ in N. We denote the argument position closure related to v's argument position in N by $\Downarrow_N(v)$, i.e. $\Downarrow_N(v) := \Downarrow_N \langle P, i \rangle$. If v is a free-sort variable that exclusively occurs in equations, we set $\Downarrow_N(v) := \Downarrow \langle False_v, 1 \rangle$ (cf. Footnote [1]). To simplify notation a bit, we write $\rightrightarrows$, $\Downarrow \langle P, i \rangle$, and $\Downarrow(v)$ instead of $\rightrightarrows_N$, $\Downarrow_N \langle P, i \rangle$, and $\Downarrow_N(v)$, when the set N is clear from the context.

Notice that $\rightrightarrows$ confined to argument position pairs of the free sort is always symmetric. Asymmetry is only introduced by atomic constraints $x \leq y$.

While the relation $\rightrightarrows$ indicates how instantiation points are propagated between argument positions, the set $\Downarrow \langle P, i \rangle$ comprises all argument positions from which instantiation points are propagated to $\langle P, i \rangle$. For a variable v the set $\Downarrow(v)$ contains all argument positions that may produce instantiation points for v.

Next, we collect the instantiation points that are necessary to eliminate base-sort variables by means of finite instantiation.

Definition 7 (Instantiation Points for Base-Sort Argument Positions). *Let N be a BSR(SLI) clause set in normal form and let $P : \xi_1 \times \ldots \times \xi_m$ be*

---

[1] For any free-sort variable v that occurs in a clause $(\Lambda \,\|\, \Gamma \rightarrow \Delta) \in N$ exclusively in equations, we pretend that Δ contains an atom $False_v(v)$, for a fresh predicate symbol $False_v : \mathcal{S}$. This is merely a technical assumption. Without it, we would have to treat such variables v as a separate case in all definitions. The atom $False_v(v)$ is not added "physically" to any clause.

a free predicate symbol occurring in N. *For every* i *with* $\xi_i = \mathcal{Z}$ *we define* $\mathcal{I}_{P,i}$ *to be the smallest set satisfying the following condition. We have* $d \in \mathcal{I}_{P,i}$ *for any constant symbol* d *for which there exists a clause* C *in* N *that contains an atom* $P(\ldots, x, \ldots)$ *in which* x *occurs as the* i-*th argument and that contains a constraint* $x = d$ *or* $x \geq d$.

The most apparent peculiarity about this definition is that LIA constraints of the form $x \leq d$ are completely ignored when collecting instantiation points for x's argument position. This is one of the aspects that makes this definition interesting from the efficiency point of view, because the number of instances that we have to consider might decrease considerably in this way. The following example may help to develop an intuitive understanding.

Example 8. Consider two clauses $C := 3 \leq x, x \leq 5 \parallel \rightarrow T(x)$ and $D := x \leq 0 \parallel T(x) \rightarrow \square$. Recall that we are looking for a finite partition $\mathcal{P}$ of $\mathbb{Z}$ such that we can construct a uniform hierarchic model $\mathcal{A}$ of $\{C, D\}$, i.e. for every subset $p \in \mathcal{P}$ and all integers $r_1, r_2 \in p$ we want $r_1 \in T^{\mathcal{A}}$ to hold if and only if $r_2 \in T^{\mathcal{A}}$. A natural candidate for $\mathcal{P}$ is $\{(-\infty, 0], [1, 2], [3, 5], [6, +\infty)\}$, which takes every LIA constraint in C and D into account. Correspondingly, we find the candidate model $\mathcal{A}$ with $T^{\mathcal{A}} = [3, 5]$. Obviously, $\mathcal{A}$ is uniform with respect to $\mathcal{P}$.

But there are other interesting possibilities, for instance, the more coarse-grained partition $\{(-\infty, 2], [3, +\infty)\}$ together with the predicate $T^{\mathcal{A}} = [3, +\infty)$. This latter candidate partition completely ignores the constraints $x \leq 0$ and $x \leq 5$ that constitute upper bounds on x and in this way induces a simpler partition. Dually, we could have concentrated on the upper bounds instead (completely ignoring the lower bounds). This would have led to the partition $\{(-\infty, 0], [1, 5], [6, +\infty)\}$ and the candidate predicate $T^{\mathcal{A}} = [1, 5]$ (or $T^{\mathcal{A}} = [1, +\infty)$). Both ways are possible, but the former yields a coarser partition and is thus more attractive, as it will cause fewer instances in the end. $\square$

The example reveals quite some freedom in choosing an appropriate partition of the integers. A large number of parts directly corresponds to a large number of instantiation points—one for each interval—, and therefore leads to a large number of instances that need to be considered by a reasoning procedure. Hence, regarding efficiency, it is of great importance to keep the partition $\mathcal{P}$ of $\mathbb{Z}$ coarse.

It remains to address the question of why it is sufficient to consider lower bounds only. At this point, we content ourselves with an informal explanation.

Let $\varphi(x)$ be a satisfiable $\wedge$-$\vee$-combination of upper and lower bounds on some integer variable x. For the sake of simplicity, we assume that every atom in φ is of the form $c \leq x$ or $x \leq c$ with $c \in \mathbb{Z}$. When we look for some value of x that satisfies φ, we start from some "sufficiently small value" $-\infty$. If $-\infty$ yields a solution for φ, we are done. If $[x \mapsto -\infty] \not\models \varphi$, there must be some lower bound in φ that prevents $-\infty$ from being a solution. In order to find a solution, we successively increase the value of x until a solution is found. Interesting test points $r \in \mathbb{Z}$ for x are those where $r - 1$ violates some lower bound $c \leq x$ in φ and r satisfies the bound, i.e. $r = c$. Consider two lower bounds $c_1 \leq x$ and $c_2 \leq x$ in φ such that $c_1 < c_2$ and φ contains no further bound $d \leq x$ with

$c_1 < d < c_2$. Any assignment $[x \mapsto r]$ with $c_1 < r < c_2$ satisfies exactly the same lower bounds as the assignment $[x \mapsto c_1]$ does. Moreover, any such assignment satisfies *at most* the upper bounds that $[x \mapsto c_1]$ satisfies. In fact, it may violate some of them. Consequently, if neither $[x \mapsto c_1]$ nor $[x \mapsto c_2]$ satisfy φ, then $[x \mapsto r]$ with $c_1 < r < c_2$ cannot satisfy φ either. In other words, it suffices to test only values induced by lower bounds. The abstract value $-\infty$ serves as the default value, which corresponds to the implicit lower bound $-\infty < x$.

Definition 9 (Instantiation Points for Base-Sort Argument Position Closures and Induced Partition). *Let N be a BSR(SLI) clause set in normal form and let $\mathcal{A}$ be a hierarchic interpretation. For every base-sort argument position closure $\Downarrow\langle P, i\rangle$ induced by $\rightrightarrows$ we define the following:*

The set $\mathcal{I}_{\Downarrow\langle P,i\rangle}$ of instantiation points for $\Downarrow\langle P, i\rangle$ is defined by $\mathcal{I}_{\Downarrow\langle P,i\rangle} := \{c_{-\infty}\} \cup \bigcup_{\langle Q,j\rangle \in \Downarrow\langle P,i\rangle} \mathcal{I}_{Q,j}$, where we assume $c_{-\infty}$ to be a distinguished base-sort constant symbol that may occur in N.

Let the sequence $r_1, \ldots, r_k$ comprise all integers in the set $\{c^{\mathcal{A}} \mid c \in \mathcal{I}_{\Downarrow\langle P,i\rangle} \setminus \{c_{-\infty}\}\}$ ordered so that $r_1 < \ldots < r_k$. The partition $\mathcal{P}^{\mathcal{A}}_{\Downarrow\langle P,i\rangle}$ of the integers into finitely many intervals is defined by

$$\mathcal{P}^{\mathcal{A}}_{\Downarrow\langle P,i\rangle} := \{(-\infty, r_1 - 1], [r_1, r_2 - 1], \ldots, [r_{k-1}, r_k - 1], [r_k, +\infty)\}.$$

Please note that partitions as described in the definition do always exist, and do not contain empty parts.

Lemma 10. *Let N be a BSR(SLI) clause set in normal form and let $\mathcal{A}$ be a hierarchic interpretation. Consider two argument position pairs $\langle Q, j\rangle, \langle P, i\rangle$ for which $\langle Q, j\rangle \rightrightarrows \langle P, i\rangle$ holds in N. Then $\mathcal{I}_{\Downarrow\langle Q,j\rangle} \subseteq \mathcal{I}_{\Downarrow\langle P,i\rangle}$. Moreover, $\mathcal{P}^{\mathcal{A}}_{\Downarrow\langle P,i\rangle}$ is a refinement of $\mathcal{P}^{\mathcal{A}}_{\Downarrow\langle Q,j\rangle}$, i.e. for every $p \in \mathcal{P}^{\mathcal{A}}_{\Downarrow\langle P,i\rangle}$ there is some $p' \in \mathcal{P}^{\mathcal{A}}_{\Downarrow\langle Q,j\rangle}$ such that $p \subseteq p'$.*

Lemma 11. *Let N be a BSR(SLI) clause set in normal form and let $\mathcal{A}$ be a hierarchic interpretation. For every part $p \in \mathcal{P}^{\mathcal{A}}_{\Downarrow\langle P,i\rangle}$ of the form $p = [r_\ell, r_u]$ or $p = [r_\ell, +\infty)$ we find some constant symbol $c_{\Downarrow\langle P,i\rangle,p} \in \mathcal{I}_{\Downarrow\langle P,i\rangle}$ with $c^{\mathcal{A}}_{\Downarrow\langle P,i\rangle,p} = r_\ell$.*

Note that the lemma did not say anything about the part $(-\infty, r_u]$ which also belongs to every $\mathcal{P}^{\mathcal{A}}_{\Downarrow\langle P,i\rangle}$. Our intention is that the constant symbol $c_{-\infty}$ shall be interpreted by a value from this interval. Hence, we add the set of clauses $\Psi_N^{-\infty} := \{(c_{-\infty} \geq c \,\|\, \rightarrow \Box) \mid c \in \mathrm{bconsts}(N) \setminus \{c_{-\infty}\}\}$ whenever necessary. Note that if $\mathcal{A}$ is a hierarchic model of a given BSR(SLI) clause set N, then $\mathcal{A}$ can be turned into a model of $\Psi_N^{-\infty}$ just by changing the interpretation of $c_{-\infty}$. After this modification $\mathcal{A}$ is still a model of N, if $c_{-\infty}$ does not occur in N.

The next lemma shows that we can eliminate base-sort variables x from clauses C in a finite BSR(SLI) clause set N by replacing C with finitely many instances in which x is substituted with the instantiation points that we computed for x. In addition, the axioms that stipulate the meaning of $c_{-\infty}$ need to be added. Iterating this instantiation step for every base-sort variable in N eventually leads to a clause set that is essentially ground with respect to the constraint parts of the clauses it contains (free-sort variables need to be treated separately, of course, see Sect. 3.3).

Lemma 12 (Finite Integer-Variable Elimination). *Let N be a finite BSR(SLI) clause set in normal form such that, if the constant symbol $c_{-\infty}$ occurs in N, then $\Psi_N^{-\infty} \subseteq N$. Suppose there is a clause C in N which contains a base-sort variable x. Let $\widehat{N}_x$ be the clause set $\widehat{N}_x := (N \setminus \{C\}) \cup \{C[x/c] \mid c \in \mathcal{I}_{\Downarrow_N(x)}\} \cup \Psi_N^{-\infty}$. N is satisfiable if and only if $\widehat{N}_x$ is satisfiable.*

Proof sketch. The "only if"-part is trivial.

The "if"-part requires a more sophisticated argument. In what follows, the notations $\rightrightarrows$ and $\Downarrow$ always refer to the original clause set N. Let $\mathcal{A}$ be a hierarchic model of $\widehat{N}_x$. We use $\mathcal{A}$ to construct the hierarchic model $\mathcal{B} \models N$ as follows. For the domain $\mathcal{S}^{\mathcal{B}}$ we reuse $\mathcal{A}$'s free domain $\mathcal{S}^{\mathcal{A}}$. For every base-sort or free-sort constant symbol $c \in \text{consts}(N)$ we set $c^{\mathcal{B}} := c^{\mathcal{A}}$. For every predicate symbol $P : \xi_1 \times \ldots \times \xi_m$ that occurs in N, for every argument position i, $1 \leq i \leq m$, with $\xi_i = \mathcal{Z}$, and for every interval $p \in \mathcal{P}_{\Downarrow\langle P,i\rangle}^{\mathcal{A}}$ Lemma 11 and the extra clauses in $\Psi_N^{-\infty}$ guarantee the existence of a base-sort constant symbol $c_{\Downarrow\langle P,i\rangle,p} \in \mathcal{I}_{\Downarrow(x)}$, such that $c_{\Downarrow\langle P,i\rangle,p}^{\mathcal{A}} \in p$.

Based on this observation, we define the family of projection functions $\pi_{\Downarrow\langle P,i\rangle} : \mathbb{Z} \cup \mathcal{S}^{\mathcal{B}} \to \mathbb{Z} \cup \mathcal{S}^{\mathcal{A}}$ by

$$\pi_{\Downarrow\langle P,i\rangle}(\mathfrak{a}) := \begin{cases} c_{\Downarrow\langle P,i\rangle,p}^{\mathcal{A}} & \text{if } \xi_i = \mathcal{Z} \text{ and } p \in \mathcal{P}_{\Downarrow\langle P,i\rangle}^{\mathcal{A}} \\ & \text{is the interval } \mathfrak{a} \text{ lies in,} \\ \mathfrak{a} & \text{if } \xi_i = \mathcal{S}. \end{cases}$$

Using the projection functions $\pi_{\Downarrow\langle P,i\rangle}$, we define the sets $P^{\mathcal{B}}$ in such a way that for all domain elements $\mathfrak{a}_1, \ldots, \mathfrak{a}_m$ of appropriate sorts

$$\langle \mathfrak{a}_1, \ldots, \mathfrak{a}_m \rangle \in P^{\mathcal{B}} \text{ if and only if } \langle \pi_{\Downarrow\langle P,1\rangle}(\mathfrak{a}_1), \ldots, \pi_{\Downarrow\langle P,m\rangle}(\mathfrak{a}_m) \rangle \in P^{\mathcal{A}}.$$

We next show $\mathcal{B} \models N$. Consider any clause $C' := \Lambda' \,\|\, \Gamma' \to \Delta'$ in N and let $\beta : V_{\mathcal{Z}} \cup V_{\mathcal{S}} \to \mathbb{Z} \cup \mathcal{S}^{\mathcal{B}}$ be some variable assignment. From β we derive a special variable assignment β_π for which we shall infer $\mathcal{A}, \beta_\pi \models C'$ as an intermediate step: $\beta_\pi(v) := \pi_{\Downarrow(v)}(\beta(v))$ for every variable v. If $C' \neq C$, then $\widehat{N}_x$ already contains C', and thus $\mathcal{A}, \beta_\pi \models C'$ must hold. In case of $C' = C$, let p_* be the interval in $\mathcal{P}_{\Downarrow(x)}^{\mathcal{A}}$ containing the value $\beta(x)$, and let c_* be an abbreviation for $c_{\Downarrow(x),p_*}$. Due to $\beta_\pi(x) = c_*^{\mathcal{A}}$ and since $\mathcal{A}$ is a model of the clause $C[x/c_*]$ in $\widehat{N}_x$, we conclude $\mathcal{A}, \beta_\pi \models C$. Hence, in any case we can deduce $\mathcal{A}, \beta_\pi \models C'$. By case distinction on why $\mathcal{A}, \beta_\pi \models C'$ holds, we may use this result to infer $\mathcal{B}, \beta \models C'$. It follows that $\mathcal{B} \models N$. $\qquad\square$

3.2 Independent Bound Selection

By now we have mainly focused on lower bounds as sources for instantiation points. However, as we have already pointed out (cf. (E-ii) and (E-iii) in Sect. 3.1 and Example 8), there is also a dual approach in which upper bounds on integer variables play the central role. It turns out that the choice between the two approaches can be made independently for every variable that is to be instantiated. In the interest of efficiency, it makes sense to always choose the approach that results in fewer non-redundant instances or, more abstractly speaking, a set of instances whose satisfiability is easier to decide. Example 13 illustrates the overall approach.

Given a clause set N in normal form, the relation $\Rightarrow_N$ is defined as before. Dually to the sets $\Downarrow_N \langle P, i \rangle$, we define the sets $\Uparrow_N \langle P, i \rangle := \{ \langle Q, j \rangle \mid \langle P, i \rangle \Rightarrow_N \langle Q, j \rangle \}$, which constitute *upwards closed* sets with respect to $\Rightarrow_N$ rather than *downwards closed* sets. Regarding instantiation points, only LIA constraints $x = d$ and $x \leq d$ lead to $d \in \mathcal{I}_{\Uparrow_N(x)}$. In addition, $c_{+\infty}$ is by default added to every set $\mathcal{I}_{\Uparrow_N \langle P, i \rangle}$. In order to fix the meaning of $c_{+\infty}$, we introduce the set of axioms $\Psi_N^{+\infty} := \{ (c_{+\infty} \leq c \| \rightarrow \Box) \mid c \in \mathrm{bconsts}(N) \setminus \{c_{+\infty}\} \}$. The dual versions of Definitions 7 and 9 and Lemma 12 can be found in [14].

In both, Lemma 12 and its dual version, the equisatisfiable instantiation can be applied to the respective variable independently of the instantiation steps that have already been done or are still to be done in the future. This means, we can choose independently, whether to stick to the lower or upper bounds for instantiation. This choice can, for example, be made depending on the number of non-redundant instances that have to be generated.

Example 13. Consider the following BSR(SLI) clause set N:

$$1 \leq x_1, x_2 \leq 0 \| \qquad\qquad \rightarrow T(x_1),\ Q(x_1, x_2)\,,$$
$$y_3 \leq 7,\ y_1 \leq y_3 \| Q(y_1, y_2) \rightarrow R(y_3)\,,$$
$$6 \leq z_1,\ z_1 \leq 9 \| T(z_1) \qquad \rightarrow \Box\,.$$

We intend to instantiate the variables y_3, y_1, x_1, z_1 in this order. For y_3 we can choose between $\mathcal{I}_{\Downarrow_N(y_3)} = \{c_{-\infty}, 1, 6\}$ and $\mathcal{I}_{\Uparrow_N(y_3)} = \{7, c_{+\infty}\}$. Using the latter option, we obtain the instances

$$7 \leq 7,\ y_1 \leq 7,\ y_3 = 7 \| Q(y_1, y_2) \rightarrow R(y_3)$$
$$c_{+\infty} \leq 7,\ y_1 \leq c_{+\infty},\ y_3 = c_{+\infty} \| Q(y_1, y_2) \rightarrow R(y_3)$$

plus the clauses in $\Psi_N^{+\infty}$. The constraint $7 \leq 7$ can be removed, as it is redundant. The second instance can be dropped immediately, since the constraint $c_{+\infty} \leq 7$ is false in any model satisfying $\Psi_N^{+\infty}$. Dual simplifications can be applied to constraints with $c_{-\infty}$. Let N' contain the clauses in $\Psi_N^{+\infty}$ and the clauses

$$1 \leq x_1, x_2 \leq 0 \| \qquad\qquad \rightarrow T(x_1),\ Q(x_1, x_2)\,,$$
$$y_1 \leq 7,\ y_3 = 7 \| Q(y_1, y_2) \rightarrow R(y_3)\,,$$
$$6 \leq z_1,\ z_1 \leq 9 \| T(z_1) \qquad \rightarrow \Box\,.$$

For y_1 we use $\mathcal{I}_{\Downarrow_{N'}(y_1)} = \{c_{-\infty}, 1, 6\}$ rather than $\mathcal{I}_{\Uparrow_{N'}(y_1)} = \{7, 9, c_{+\infty}\}$ for instantiation and obtain N'' (after simplification):

$$1 \leq x_1, x_2 \leq 0 \| \qquad\qquad \rightarrow T(x_1),\ Q(x_1, x_2)\,,$$
$$y_3 = 7,\ y_1 = c_{-\infty} \| Q(y_1, y_2) \rightarrow R(y_3)\,,$$
$$y_3 = 7,\ y_1 = 1 \| Q(y_1, y_2) \rightarrow R(y_3)\,,$$
$$y_3 = 7,\ y_1 = 6 \| Q(y_1, y_2) \rightarrow R(y_3)\,,$$
$$6 \leq z_1,\ z_1 \leq 9 \| T(z_1) \qquad \rightarrow \Box\,,$$

plus the clauses in $\Psi_N^{-\infty}$ and $\Psi_N^{+\infty}$ and plus the clause $c_{-\infty} \geq c_{+\infty} \| \rightarrow \Box$. The sets of instantiation points for x_1 in N'' are $\mathcal{I}_{\Downarrow_{N''}(x_1)} = \{c_{-\infty}, 1, 6\}$ and $\mathcal{I}_{\Uparrow_{N''}(x_1)} = \{c_{-\infty}, 1, 6, 9, c_{+\infty}\}$. The latter set nicely illustrates how instantiation sets for particular variables can evolve during the incremental process of instantiation. We take the set with fewer instantiation points and obtain N''':

$$x_2 \leq 0, x_1 = 1 \parallel \qquad \rightarrow T(x_1), \ Q(x_1, x_2) \ ,$$
$$x_2 \leq 0, x_1 = 6 \parallel \qquad \rightarrow T(x_1), \ Q(x_1, x_2) \ ,$$
$$y_3 = 7, y_1 = c_{-\infty} \parallel Q(y_1, y_2) \rightarrow R(y_3) \ ,$$
$$y_3 = 7, y_1 = 1 \parallel Q(y_1, y_2) \rightarrow R(y_3) \ ,$$
$$y_3 = 7, y_1 = 6 \parallel Q(y_1, y_2) \rightarrow R(y_3) \ ,$$
$$6 \leq z_1, \ z_1 \leq 9 \parallel T(z_1) \qquad \rightarrow \square \ ,$$

plus $\Psi_N^{-\infty} \cup \Psi_N^{+\infty} \cup \{c_{-\infty} \geq c_{+\infty} \parallel \ \rightarrow \square\}$. We instantiate z_1 using the set $\mathcal{I}_{\Downarrow_{N'''}}(z_1) = \{c_{-\infty}, 1, 6\}$ and not $\mathcal{I}_{\Uparrow_{N'''}}(z_1) = \{c_{-\infty}, 1, 6, 9, c_{+\infty}\}$:

$$x_2 \leq 0, x_1 = 1 \parallel \ \rightarrow T(x_1), Q(x_1, x_2) \ ,$$
$$x_2 \leq 0, x_1 = 6 \parallel \ \rightarrow T(x_1), Q(x_1, x_2) \ ,$$

$$y_3 = 7, y_1 = c_{-\infty} \parallel Q(y_1, y_2) \rightarrow R(y_3) \ ,$$
$$y_3 = 7, y_1 = 1 \parallel Q(y_1, y_2) \rightarrow R(y_3) \ ,$$
$$y_3 = 7, y_1 = 6 \parallel Q(y_1, y_2) \rightarrow R(y_3) \ ,$$
$$z_1 = 6 \parallel T(z_1) \qquad \rightarrow \square \ ,$$

plus $\Psi_N^{-\infty} \cup \Psi_N^{+\infty} \cup \{c_{-\infty} \geq c_{+\infty} \parallel \ \rightarrow \square\}$. Until now, we have introduced 6 non-redundant instances. A completely naive instantiation approach where x_1, y_1, y_3, z_1 are instantiated with all occurring constant symbols $0, 1, 6, 7, 9$ leads to 17 non-redundant instances. This corresponds to the originally proposed method for the *array property fragment*, cf. [8]. A more sophisticated instantiation approach where x_1, y_1, y_3, z_1 are instantiated with $1, 6, 7, 9$ (as there is no connection from 0 to x_1, y_1, y_3, z_1) leads to 13 non-redundant instances. For instance, the methods described in [12] produce this set of instances. $\square$

3.3   Instantiation of Free-Sort Variables

We can also follow an instantiation approach for free-sort variables. In a nutshell, we collect only *relevant* instantiation points for a given argument position cf. (E-i) in Sect. 3.1. A similar approach is taken in [12]. Consult [14] for details.

4   Stratified Clause Sets

In this section we treat certain clause sets with uninterpreted non-constant function symbols. By a transformation into an equisatisfiable set of BSR clauses, we show that our instantiation methods are also applicable in such settings.

Definition 14. *Let N be a finite set of variable-disjoint first-order clauses in which also non-constant function symbols occur. By Π_N and Ω_N we denote the set of occurring predicate symbols and function symbols (including constants), respectively. N is considered to be* stratified *if we can define a mapping $lvl_N : (\Pi_N \cup \Omega_N) \times \mathbb{N} \rightarrow \mathbb{N}$ that maps argument position pairs (of predicate and function symbols) to nonnegative integers such that the following conditions are satisfied.*

(a) For every function symbol $f : \xi_1 \times \ldots \times \xi_m \rightarrow \xi_{m+1}$ and every $i \leq m$ we have $lvl_N\langle f, i \rangle > lvl_N\langle f, m+1 \rangle$.

(b) For every (sub)term $g(s_1, \ldots, s_{k-1}, f(t_1, \ldots, t_m), s_{k+1}, \ldots, s_{m'})$ occurring in N we have $lvl_N\langle f, m+1 \rangle = lvl_N\langle g, k \rangle$. This includes the case where f is a constant symbol and $m = 0$. Moreover, this also includes the case where g is replaced with a predicate symbol P.

(c) *For every variable v that occurs in two (sub)terms $f(s_1, \ldots, s_{k-1}, v, s_{k+1}, \ldots,$ $s_m)$ and $g(t_1, \ldots t_{k'-1}, v, t_{k'+1}, \ldots, t_{m'})$ in N we have $lvl_N\langle f, k \rangle = lvl_N\langle g, k' \rangle$. The same applies, if f or g or both are replaced with predicate symbols.*

(d) *For every equation $f(s_1, \ldots, s_m) \approx g(t_1, \ldots, t_{m'})$ we have $lvl_N\langle f, m+1 \rangle = lvl_N\langle g, m'+1 \rangle$. This includes the cases where f or g or both are constant symbols (with $m = 0$ or $m' = 0$ or both, respectively).*

Several known logic fragments fall into this syntactic category: many-sorted clauses over *stratified vocabularies* as described in [1,16], and clauses belonging to the *finite essentially uninterpreted fragment* (cf. Proposition 2 in [12]).

Lemma 15. *Let $C = \Gamma \to \Delta$ be a first-order clause and let $f_1, \ldots, f_n$ be a list of all uninterpreted non-constant function symbols occurring in C. Let $R_1, \ldots, R_n$ be distinct predicate symbols that do not occur in C and that have the sort $R_i :$ $\xi_1 \times \ldots \times \xi_m \times \xi_{m+1}$, if and only if f_i has the sort $\xi_1 \times \ldots \times \xi_m \to \xi_{m+1}$. Let Φ_1 and Φ_2 be the following sets of sentences:*
$\Phi_1 := \{\forall x_1 \ldots x_m uv.\ R_i(x_1, \ldots, x_m, u) \wedge R_i(x_1, \ldots, x_m, v) \to u \approx v \mid 1 \leq i \leq n\}$
and $\Phi_2 := \{\forall x_1 \ldots x_m \exists v.\ R_i(x_1, \ldots, x_m, v) \mid 1 \leq i \leq n\}$. There is a clause D that does not contain non-constant function symbols and for which the set $\{D\} \cup \Phi_1 \cup \Phi_2$ is equisatisfiable to C.

Proof sketch. We apply the following flattening rules. v stands for a fresh variable that has not occurred yet. P ranges over predicate symbols different from $\approx$. $\bar{s}$ and $\bar{t}$ stand for tuples of arguments.

$$\frac{\Gamma, f_i(\bar{s}) \approx f_j(\bar{t}) \to \Delta}{\Gamma, R_i(\bar{s}, v), R_j(\bar{t}, v) \to \Delta}\text{(fun-fun left)} \qquad \frac{\Gamma \to \Delta, f_i(\bar{s}) \approx f_j(\bar{t})}{\Gamma, R_i(\bar{s}, v) \to \Delta, R_j(\bar{t}, v)}\text{(fun-fun right)}$$

$$\frac{\Gamma, f_i(\bar{s}) \approx c \to \Delta}{\Gamma, R_i(\bar{s}, c) \to \Delta}\text{(fun-const left)} \qquad \frac{\Gamma \to \Delta, f_i(\bar{s}) \approx c}{\Gamma \to \Delta, R_i(\bar{s}, c)}\text{(fun-const right)}$$

$$\frac{\Gamma, f_i(\bar{s}) \approx x \to \Delta}{\Gamma, R_i(\bar{s}, x) \to \Delta}\text{(fun-var left)} \qquad \frac{\Gamma \to \Delta, f_i(\bar{s}) \approx x}{\Gamma \to \Delta, R_i(\bar{s}, x)}\text{(fun-var right)}$$

$$\frac{\Gamma, P(\ldots, f_i(\bar{s}), \ldots) \to \Delta}{\Gamma, R_i(\bar{s}, v), P(\ldots, v, \ldots) \to \Delta}\text{(fun left)} \qquad \frac{\Gamma \to \Delta, P(\ldots, f_i(\bar{s}), \ldots)}{\Gamma, R_i(\bar{s}, v) \to \Delta, P(\ldots, v, \ldots)}\text{(fun right)}$$

$\square$

Given a BSR clause $\Gamma \to \Delta$, we consider an atom $R_j(\bar{t}, v)$ in Δ to be *guarded*, if there is also an atom $R_i(\bar{s}, v)$ in Γ. With the exception of the rule (**fun-var right**) the flattening rules presented in the proof of Lemma 15 preserve guardedness of atoms in Δ and introduce atoms $R_j(\bar{t}, v)$ on the right-hand side of a clause only if at the same time a corresponding guard is introduced on the left-hand side of the clause.

Hence, if we are given a stratified clause set in which the atoms $x \approx t$ in the consequents of implications are subject to certain restrictions (e.g. $t \neq f(\ldots)$

and guardedness of atoms $u \approx c$ and $u \approx v$), then the above flattening rules yield clauses that belong to the following class of BSR(SLI) clauses—after necessary purification and normalization steps. In the definition we mark certain predicate symbols that are intended to represent uninterpreted functions. By adding suitable axioms later on, these will be equipped with the properties of function graphs.

Definition 16 (Stratified and Guarded BSR(SLI)). *Consider a BSR(SLI) clause set N in normal form. Let $R_1, \ldots, R_n$ be a list of predicate symbols that we consider to be* marked *in N. We call N* stratified and guarded *with respect to $R_1, \ldots, R_n$, if and only if the following conditions are met.*

(a) *There is some function $\mathrm{lvl}_N : \Pi \times \mathbb{N} \to \mathbb{N}$ that assigns to each argument position pair $\langle P, i \rangle$ a nonnegative integer $\mathrm{lvl}_N \langle P, i \rangle$ such that*

(a.1) *$\langle P, i \rangle \rightrightarrows_N \langle Q, j \rangle$ entails $\mathrm{lvl}_N \langle P, i \rangle = \mathrm{lvl}_N \langle Q, j \rangle$, and*

(a.2) *for every marked predicate symbol $R_j : \xi_1 \times \ldots \times \xi_m \times \xi_{m+1}$ we have $\mathrm{lvl}_N \langle R_j, i \rangle > \mathrm{lvl}_N \langle R_j, m+1 \rangle$ for every $i \leq m$.*

(b) *In every clause $\Lambda \,\|\, \Gamma \to \Delta$ in N any occurrence of an atom $R_j(s_1, \ldots, s_m, v)$ in Δ entails that Γ contains some atom $R_\ell(t_1, \ldots, t_{m'}, v)$.*

(c) *For every atom $u \approx t$ in N, where t is either a free-sort variable v or a free-sort constant symbol, at least one of two cases applies:*

(c.1) *$u \approx t$, which must occur in the consequent of a clause, is guarded by some atom $R_j(t_1, \ldots, t_m, u)$ occurring in the antecedent of the same clause.*

(c.2) *For every marked predicate symbol $R_j : \xi_1 \times \ldots \times \xi_m \times \xi_{m+1}$ and every argument position closure $\Downarrow_N \langle R_j, i \rangle$ with $1 \leq i \leq m$ we have $\Downarrow_N \langle R_j, i \rangle \cap \Downarrow_N(u) = \emptyset$. If $t = v$, we in addition have $\Downarrow_N \langle R_j, i \rangle \cap \Downarrow_N(v) = \emptyset$.*

Notice that any atom $u \approx v$ over distinct variables requires two guards $R(\bar{s}, u)$ and $R(\bar{t}, v)$ in order to be guarded in accordance with Condition (c.1).

Let N be a finite BSR(SLI) clause set in normal form that is stratified and guarded with respect to $R_1, \ldots, R_n$. Let $R_i : \xi_1 \times \ldots \times \xi_m \times \xi_{m+1}$ be marked in N and let $P : \zeta_1 \times \ldots \times \zeta_{m'}$ be any predicate symbol occurring in N (be it marked or not). We write $R_i \succeq P$ if and only if $\mathrm{lvl}_N \langle R_i, m+1 \rangle \geq \min_{1 \leq \ell \leq m'} (\mathrm{lvl}_N \langle P, \ell \rangle)$. Without loss of generality, we assume $R_1 \succeq_N \ldots \succeq_N R_n$. Let $\Phi_1 := \{ \forall x_1 \ldots x_m u u'.(R_i(x_1, \ldots, x_m, u) \wedge R_i(x_1, \ldots, x_m, u')) \to u \simeq u' \mid R_i \text{ has arity } m+1 \}$ and $\Phi_2 := \{ \forall x_1 \ldots x_m \exists u. R_i(x_1, \ldots, x_m, u) \mid R_i \text{ has arity } m+1 \}$, where "$\simeq$" is a placeholder for "$\approx$" in free-sort equations and for "$=$" in base-sort equations.

Given a set M of BSR(SLI) clauses and an $(m+1)$-ary predicate symbol R that is marked in M, we define the set $\Phi(R, M) :=$

$$\left\{ R(c_1, \ldots, c_m, d_{Rc_1 \ldots c_m}) \mid \langle c_1, \ldots, c_m \rangle \in \mathcal{I}_{\Downarrow_M \langle R, \cdot \rangle}^{[m]} \right\}$$

$$\cup \left\{ \forall x_1 \ldots x_m. \bigvee_{\langle c_1, \ldots, c_m \rangle \in \mathcal{I}_{\Downarrow_M \langle R, \cdot \rangle}^{[m]}} R(x_1, \ldots, x_m, d_{Rc_1 \ldots c_m}) \right\}$$

$$\cup \left\{ \forall x_1 \ldots x_m u. R(x_1, \ldots, x_m, u) \to \bigvee_{\langle c_1, \ldots, c_m \rangle \in \mathcal{I}_{\Downarrow_M \langle R, \cdot \rangle}^{[m]}} u \simeq d_{Rc_1 \ldots c_m} \right\}$$

$$\cup \left\{ \forall x_1 \ldots x_m. \ R(x_1, \ldots, x_m, d_{Rc_1\ldots c_m}), R(x_1, \ldots, x_m, d_{Rc'_1\ldots c'_m}) \right.$$
$$\left. \rightarrow d_{Rc_1\ldots c_m} \simeq d_{Rc'_1\ldots c'_m} \ \middle| \ \langle c_1, \ldots, c_m \rangle, \langle c'_1, \ldots, c'_m \rangle \in \mathcal{I}^{[m]}_{\Downarrow_M \langle R, \cdot \rangle} \right\}$$

where $\mathcal{I}^{[m]}_{\Downarrow_M \langle R, \cdot \rangle}$ is used as an abbreviation for $\mathcal{I}_{\Downarrow_M \langle R, 1 \rangle} \times \ldots \times \mathcal{I}_{\Downarrow_M \langle R, m \rangle}$ and the $d_{Rc_1\ldots c_m}$ are assumed to be fresh constant symbols. It is worth noticing that the clauses corresponding to $\Phi(R, M)$ are stratified and guarded BSR(SLI) clauses.

We construct the sequence $M_0, M_1, \ldots, M_n$ of finite clause sets as follows: $M_0 := N$, every $M_{\ell+1}$ with $\ell \geq 0$ is an extension of M_ℓ by the BSR(SLI) clauses that correspond to the sentences in $\Phi(R_{\ell+1}, M_\ell)$.

Lemma 17. *The set $N \cup \Phi_1 \cup \Phi_2$ is satisfiable if and only if M_n is satisfiable.*

This lemma entails that all the instantiation methods developed in Sect. 3 can be used to decide satisfiability of stratified and guarded BSR(SLI) clause sets.

We can add another background theory to the stratified and guarded fragment of BSR(SLI) while preserving compatibility with our instantiation approach. Let $\Pi_{\mathcal{T}}$ and $\Omega_{\mathcal{T}}$ be finite sets of sorted predicate symbols and sorted function symbols, respectively, and let $\mathcal{T}$ be some theory over $\Pi_{\mathcal{T}}$ and $\Omega_{\mathcal{T}}$. We assume that $\Pi_{\mathcal{T}}$ is disjoint from the set Π of uninterpreted predicate symbols. For any set X of variables, let $\mathbb{T}_{\mathcal{T}}(X)$ be the set of all well-sorted terms constructed from the variables in X and the function and constant symbols in $\Omega_{\mathcal{T}}$.

Definition 18 (BSR(SLI+$\mathcal{T}$)). *A clause set N belongs to BSR(SLI+$\mathcal{T}$) if it complies with the syntax of a BSR(SLI) clause set that is stratified and guarded with respect to certain predicate symbols $R_1, \ldots, R_n$ with the following exceptions. Let $C := \Lambda \| \Gamma \rightarrow \Delta$ be a clause in N. We allow atoms $P(s_1, \ldots, s_m)$ with $P \in \Pi_{\mathcal{T}}$ and $s_1, \ldots, s_m \in \mathbb{T}_{\mathcal{T}}(V_{\mathcal{Z}} \cup V_{\mathcal{S}})$—including equations $s_1 \approx s_2$—, if for every variable u occurring in any of the s_i there is either a LIA guard of the form $u = t$ in Λ with t being ground, or there is a guard $R_j(t_1, \ldots, t_{m'}, u)$ in Γ.*

The instantiation methods presented in Sect. 3 are also applicable to BSR(SLI+$\mathcal{T}$), since Lemma 17 can be extended to cover finite BSR(SLI+$\mathcal{T}$) clause sets. When computing instantiation points for BSR(SLI+$\mathcal{T}$) clause sets, we ignore $\mathcal{T}$-atoms. For example, a clause $\| R(t, u), P(s, c) \rightarrow P(s', u), Q(u)$ where $P(s, c)$ and $P(s', u)$ are $\mathcal{T}$-atoms, *does not* lead to an instantiation point c for $\Downarrow \langle Q, 1 \rangle$. If we stick to this approach, the proof of Lemma 17 can easily be adapted to handle additional $\mathcal{T}$-atoms. The involved model construction remains unchanged. $\mathcal{T}$-atoms are basically treated like guarded free-sort atoms $u \approx d$.

Proposition 19. *BSR(SLI+$\mathcal{T}$) allows an (un)satisfiability-preserving embedding of the array property fragment with integer-indexed arrays and element theory $\mathcal{T}$ (cf. [8]) and of the finite essentially uninterpreted fragment extended with simple integer arithmetic literals (cf. [12]) into BSR(SLI+$\mathcal{T}$).*

Example 20. The following formula φ belongs to the array property fragment with integer indices and the theory of bit vectors as the element theory $\mathcal{T}$. The operator $\sim$ stands for bitwise negation of bit vectors and the relations $\preceq$ and $\approx$

are used as the "at most" and the equality predicate on bit vectors, respectively. Moreover, $a[i]$ denotes a read operation on the array a at index i.

$$\varphi := \quad c \geq 1 \quad \wedge \quad \forall ij. \qquad 0 \leq i \leq j \;\rightarrow\; a[i] \preceq a[j]$$
$$\wedge \quad \forall i.\, 0 \leq i \leq c-1 \;\rightarrow\; a[i] \preceq {\sim} a[0]$$
$$\wedge \qquad\qquad\qquad\qquad \rightarrow\; a[c] \approx {\sim} a[0]$$
$$\wedge \quad \forall i. \qquad i \geq c+1 \;\rightarrow\; a[i] \succeq {\sim} a[0]$$

Translating φ into BSR(SLI+$\mathcal{T}$) yields the following clause set N, in which we consider P_a to be marked.

$$
\begin{array}{l|l}
\begin{array}{ll}
c < 1 \;\|\; & \rightarrow \square \\
e \neq c - 1 \;\|\; & \rightarrow \square \\
f \neq c + 1 \;\|\; & \rightarrow \square
\end{array}
&
\begin{array}{rll}
0 \leq i, i \leq j \;\| & P_a(i,u), P_a(j,v) \;\rightarrow\; u \preceq v \\
0 \leq i, i \leq e, y = 0 \;\| & P_a(i,u), P_a(y,v) \;\rightarrow\; u \preceq {\sim} v \\
x = c, y = 0 \;\| & P_a(x,u), P_a(y,v) \;\rightarrow\; u \approx {\sim} v \\
i \geq f, y = 0 \;\| & P_a(i,u), P_a(y,v) \;\rightarrow\; u \succeq {\sim} v
\end{array}
\end{array}
$$

In order to preserve (un)satisfiability, functional axioms have to be added for P_a (cf. the sets Φ_1 and Φ_2 that we used earlier). Doing so, we leave BSR(SLI+$\mathcal{T}$).

The clause set N induces the set $\mathcal{I}_{\Downarrow\langle P_a,1\rangle} = \{c_{-\infty}, 0, c, f\}$ of instantiation points for the index of the array. An adaptation of Lemma 17 for BSR(SLI+$\mathcal{T}$) entails that adding the clause set N' corresponding to the following set of sentences yields a BSR(SLI+$\mathcal{T}$) clause set $N \cup N'$ that is equisatisfiable to φ.

$$\{P_a(c', d_{P_a c'}) \mid c' \in \{c_{-\infty}, 0, c, f\}\}$$
$$\cup\; \{\forall i.\; \textstyle\bigvee_{c' \in \{c_{-\infty}, 0, c, f\}} P_a(i, d_{P_a c'})\}$$
$$\cup\; \{\forall iu.\; P_a(i, u) \rightarrow \textstyle\bigvee_{c' \in \{c_{-\infty}, 0, c, f\}} u \approx d_{P_a c'}\}$$
$$\cup\; \{\forall i.\; P_a(i, d_{P_a c'}), P_a(i, d_{P_a c''}) \rightarrow d_{P_a c'} \approx d_{P_a c''} \mid c', c'' \in \{c_{-\infty}, 0, c, f\}\}$$

Using the instantiation methods that we have developed in Sects. 3.1, 3.2, and 3.3, the set $N \cup N'$ can be turned into an equisatisfiable quantifier-free clause set. One possible (uniform) model $\mathcal{A} \models N \cup N'$ assigns $c_{-\infty}^{\mathcal{A}} = -1$, $e^{\mathcal{A}} = 2$, $c^{\mathcal{A}} = 3$, $f^{\mathcal{A}} = 4$, $d_{P_a c_{-\infty}}^{\mathcal{A}} = 00$, $d_{P_a 0}^{\mathcal{A}} = 01$, $d_{P_a e}^{\mathcal{A}} = 01$, $d_{P_a c}^{\mathcal{A}} = 10$, $d_{P_a f}^{\mathcal{A}} = 11$, and yields the array $\langle 01, 01, 01, 10, 11, 11, 11, \ldots \rangle$. $\square$

5   Discussion

We have demonstrated how universally quantified variables in BSR(SLI) clause sets can be instantiated economically. In certain cases our methods lead to exponentially fewer instances than a naive instantiation with all occurring integer terms would generate. Moreover, we have sketched how defining suitable finite-domain sort predicates instead of explicitly instantiating variables can avoid immediate blow-ups caused by explicit instantiation. It is then left to the theorem prover to actually instantiate variables as needed.

We have shown that our methods are compatible with uninterpreted, non-constant functions under certain restrictions. Even another background theory $\mathcal{T}$ may be added, leading to BSR(SLI+$\mathcal{T}$). This entails applicability of our instantiation approach to known logic fragments, such as the *array property fragment* [8], the *finite essentially uninterpreted fragment with arithmetic literals* [12], and many-sorted first-order formulas over *stratified vocabularies* [1,16].

The instantiation methodology that we have described specifically for integer variables can also be adapted to work for universally quantified variables ranging over the reals [24]. Our computation of instantiation points considers all argument positions in predicate atoms independently. This can be further refined by considering dependencies between argument positions and clauses. For example, this refinement idea was successfully applied in first-order logic [9,16].

Once all the integer variables are grounded by successive instantiation, we are left with a clause set where for every integer variable x in any clause there is a defining equation $x = c$ for some constant c. Thus, the clause set can actually be turned into a standard first-order BSR clause set by replacing the integer constants with respective fresh uninterpreted constants. Then, as an alternative to further grounding the free-sort variables, any state-of-the-art BSR decision procedure can be applied to test satisfiability [2,15,22]. It is even sufficient to know the instantiation sets for the base sort variables. Then, instead of explicit grounding, by defining respective finite-domain sort predicates for the sets, the worst-case exponential blow-up of grounding can be prevented.

References

1. Abadi, A., Rabinovich, A., Sagiv, M.: Decidable fragments of many-sorted logic. J. Symbolic Comput. **45**(2), 153–172 (2010)
2. Alagi, G., Weidenbach, C.: NRCL – A model building approach to the Bernays-Schönfinkel fragment. In: Lutz, C., Ranise, S. (eds.) FroCoS 2015. LNCS, vol. 9322, pp. 69–84. Springer, Cham (2015). doi:10.1007/978-3-319-24246-0_5
3. Althaus, E., Kruglov, E., Weidenbach, C.: Superposition modulo linear arithmetic SUP(LA). In: Ghilardi, S., Sebastiani, R. (eds.) FroCoS 2009. LNCS (LNAI), vol. 5749, pp. 84–99. Springer, Heidelberg (2009). doi:10.1007/978-3-642-04222-5_5
4. Bachmair, L., Ganzinger, H., Waldmann, U.: Refutational theorem proving for hierarchic first-order theories. Appl. Algebra Eng. Commun. Comput. **5**, 193–212 (1994)
5. Baumgartner, P., Waldmann, U.: Hierarchic superposition with weak abstraction. In: Bonacina, M.P. (ed.) CADE 2013. LNCS (LNAI), vol. 7898, pp. 39–57. Springer, Heidelberg (2013). doi:10.1007/978-3-642-38574-2_3
6. Bradley, A.R.: Safety Analysis of Systems. PhD thesis (2007)
7. Bradley, A.R., Manna, Z.: The Calculus of Computation – Decision Procedures with Applications to Verification. Springer, Heidelberg (2007)
8. Bradley, A.R., Manna, Z., Sipma, H.B.: What's decidable about arrays? In: Emerson, E.A., Namjoshi, K.S. (eds.) VMCAI 2006. LNCS, vol. 3855, pp. 427–442. Springer, Heidelberg (2005). doi:10.1007/11609773_28
9. Claessen, K., Lillieström, A., Smallbone, N.: Sort it out with monotonicity. In: Bjørner, N., Sofronie-Stokkermans, V. (eds.) CADE 2011. LNCS (LNAI), vol. 6803, pp. 207–221. Springer, Heidelberg (2011). doi:10.1007/978-3-642-22438-6_17
10. Downey, P.J.: Undecidability of Presburger Arithmetic with a Single Monadic Predicate Letter. Technical report, Center for Research in Computer Technology. Harvard University (1972)
11. Fietzke, A., Weidenbach, C.: Superposition as a decision procedure for timed automata. Math. Comput. Sci. **6**(4), 409–425 (2012)
12. Ge, Y., Moura, L.: Complete instantiation for quantified formulas in satisfiabiliby modulo theories. In: Bouajjani, A., Maler, O. (eds.) CAV 2009. LNCS, vol. 5643, pp. 306–320. Springer, Heidelberg (2009). doi:10.1007/978-3-642-02658-4_25

13. Halpern, J.Y.: Presburger arithmetic with unary predicates is Π_1^1 complete. J. Symbolic Logic **56**(2), 637–642 (1991)
14. Horbach, M., Voigt, M., Weidenbach, C.: On the combination of the Bernays-Schönfinkel-Ramsey fragment with simple linear integer arithmetic. ArXiv preprint, arXiv: 1705.08792 [cs.LO] (2017)
15. Korovin, K.: Inst–Gen – A modular approach to instantiation-based automated reasoning. In: Voronkov, A., Weidenbach, C. (eds.) Programming Logics. LNCS, vol. 7797, pp. 239–270. Springer, Heidelberg (2013). doi:10.1007/978-3-642-37651-1_10
16. Korovin, K.: Non-cyclic sorts for first-order satisfiability. In: Fontaine, P., Ringeissen, C., Schmidt, R.A. (eds.) FroCoS 2013. LNCS (LNAI), vol. 8152, pp. 214–228. Springer, Heidelberg (2013). doi:10.1007/978-3-642-40885-4_15
17. Kroening, D., Strichman, O.: Decision Procedures. Texts in Theoretical Computer Science. An EATCS Series, 2nd edn. Springer, Heidelberg (2016)
18. Kruglov, E., Weidenbach, C.: Superposition decides the first-order logic fragment over ground theories. Math. Comput. Sci. **6**(4), 427–456 (2012)
19. Lewis, H.R.: Complexity results for classes of quantificational formulas. J. Comput. Syst. Sci. **21**(3), 317–353 (1980)
20. Loos, R., Weispfenning, V.: Applying linear quantifier elimination. Comput. J. **36**(5), 450–462 (1993)
21. Nieuwenhuis, R., Oliveras, A., Tinelli, C.: Solving SAT and SAT modulo theories: from an abstract Davis-Putnam-Logemann-Loveland procedure to DPLL(T). J. ACM **53**, 937–977 (2006)
22. Piskac, R., de Moura, L.M., Bjørner, N.: Deciding effectively propositional logic using DPLL and substitution sets. J. Autom. Reasoning **44**(4), 401–424 (2010)
23. Putnam, H.: Decidability and essential undecidability. J. Symbolic Logic **22**(1), 39–54 (1957)
24. Voigt, M., Weidenbach, C.: Bernays-Schönfinkel-Ramsey with simple bounds is NEXPTIME-complete. ArXiv preprint, arXiv:1501.07209 [cs.LO] (2015)

Satisfiability Modulo Transcendental Functions via Incremental Linearization

Alessandro Cimatti[1], Alberto Griggio[1], Ahmed Irfan[1,2(✉)],
Marco Roveri[1], and Roberto Sebastiani[2]

[1] Fondazione Bruno Kessler, Trento, Italy
{cimatti,griggio,irfan,roveri}@fbk.eu
[2] DISI, University of Trento, Trento, Italy
roberto.sebastiani@unitn.it

Abstract. In this paper we present an abstraction-refinement approach
to Satisfiability Modulo the theory of transcendental functions, such as
exponentiation and trigonometric functions. The transcendental functions are represented as uninterpreted in the abstract space, which is
described in terms of the combined theory of linear arithmetic on the
rationals with uninterpreted functions, and are incrementally axiomatized by means of upper- and lower-bounding piecewise-linear functions.
Suitable numerical techniques are used to ensure that the abstractions
of the transcendental functions are sound even in presence of irrationals.
Our experimental evaluation on benchmarks from verification and mathematics demonstrates the potential of our approach, showing that it compares favorably with delta-satisfiability/interval propagation and methods based on theorem proving.

1 Introduction

Many applications require dealing with transcendental functions (e.g., exponential, logarithm, sine, cosine). Nevertheless, the problem of Satisfiability Modulo
the theory of transcendental functions comes with many difficulties. First, the
problem is in general undecidable [22]. Second, we may be forced to deal with
irrational numbers - in fact, differently from polynomial, transcendental functions most often have irrational values for rational arguments. (See, for example,
Hermite's proof that $\exp(x)$ is irrational for rational non-zero x.)

In this paper, we describe a novel approach to Satisfiability Modulo the
quantifier-free theory of (nonlinear arithmetic with) transcendental functions
over the reals - SMT(NTA). The approach is based on an abstraction-refinement
loop, using SMT(UFLRA) as abstract space, UFLRA being the combined theory of linear arithmetic on the rationals with uninterpreted functions. The Uninterpreted Functions are used to model nonlinear and transcendental functions.
Then, we iteratively incrementally axiomatize the transcendental functions with

This work was funded in part by the H2020-FETOPEN-2016-2017-CSA project SC²
(712689). We thank James Davenport and Erika Abraham for useful discussions.

© Springer International Publishing AG 2017
L. de Moura (Ed.): CADE 2017, LNAI 10395, pp. 95–113, 2017.
DOI: 10.1007/978-3-319-63046-5_7

a lemma-on-demand approach. Specifically, we eliminate spurious interpretations in SMT(UFLRA) by tightening the piecewise-linear envelope around the (uninterpreted counterpart of) the transcendental functions.

A key challenge is to compute provably correct approximations, also in presence of irrational numbers. We use Taylor series to exactly compute suitable accurate rational coefficients. We remark that nonlinear polynomials are only used to numerically compute the coefficients –i.e., no SMT solving in the theory of nonlinear arithmetic (SMT(NRA)) is needed– whereas the refinement is based on the addition, in the abstract space, of *piecewise-linear* axiom instantiations, which upper- and lower-bound the candidate solutions, ruling out spurious interpretations. To compute such piecewise-linear bounding functions, the concavity of the curve is taken into account. In order to deal with trigonometric functions, we take into account the periodicity, so that the axiomatization is only done in the interval between $-\pi$ and π. Interestingly, not only this is helpful for efficiency, but also it is required to ensure correctness.

Another distinguishing feature of our approach is a logical method to conclude the existence of a solution without explicitly constructing it. We use a sufficient criterion that consists in checking whether the formula is satisfiable under all possible interpretations of the uninterpreted functions (representing the transcendental functions) that are consistent with some rational interval bounds within which the correct values for the transcendental functions are guaranteed to exist. We encode the problem as a SMT(UFLRA) satisfiability check, such that an unsatisfiable result implies the satisfiability of the original SMT(NTA) formula.

We implemented the approach on top of the MATHSAT SMT solver [7], using the PYSMT library [14]. We experimented with benchmarks from SMT-based verification queries over nonlinear transition systems, including Bounded Model Checking of hybrid automata, as well as from several mathematical properties from the METITARSKI [1] suite and from other competitor solver distributions. We contrasted our approach with state-of-the-art approaches based on interval propagation (iSAT3 and DREAL), and with the deductive approach in METITARSKI. The results show that our solver compares favourably with the other solvers, being able to decide the highest number of benchmarks.

This paper is organized as follows. In Sect. 2 we describe some background. In Sect. 3 we overview the approach, defining the foundation for safe linear approximations. In Sect. 4 we describe the specific axiomatization for transcendental functions. In Sect. 5 we discuss the related literature, and in Sect. 6 we present the experimental evaluation. In Sect. 7 we draw some conclusions and outline directions for future work.

2 Background

We assume the standard first-order quantifier-free logical setting and standard notions of theory, satisfiability, and logical consequence. As usual in SMT, we denote with LRA the theory of linear real arithmetic, with NRA that of non-linear real arithmetic, with UF the theory of equality (with uninterpreted functions), and with UFLRA the combined theory of UF and LRA. Unless otherwise specified, we use the terms variable and free constant interchangeably. We denote formulas with φ, ψ, terms with t, variables with x, y, a, b, functions with f, tf, ftf, each possibly with subscripts. If x and y are two variables, we denote with $\varphi\{x \mapsto y\}$ the formula obtained by replacing all the occurrences of x in φ with y. We extend this notation to ordered sequences of variables in the natural way. If μ is a model and x is a variable, we write $\mu[x]$ to denote the value of x in μ, and we extend this notation to terms and formulas in the usual way. If Γ is a set of formulas, we write $\bigwedge \Gamma$ to denote the formula obtained by taking the conjunction of all its elements. We write $t_1 < t_2 < t_3$ for $t_1 < t_2 \wedge t_2 < t_3$.

A *transcendental function* is an analytic function that does not satisfy a polynomial equation (in contrast to an algebraic function [15, 26]). Within this paper we consider univariate exponential, logarithmic, and trigonometric functions. We denote with NTA the theory of (non-linear) real arithmetic extended with these transcendental functions.

A *tangent line* to a univariate function $f(x)$ at a point of interest $x = a$ is a straight line that "just touches" the function at the point, and represents the instantaneous rate of change of the function f at that one point. The tangent line $T_{f,a}(x)$ to the function f at point a is the straight line defined as follows:

$$T_{f,a}(x) \stackrel{\text{def}}{=} f(a) + \frac{d}{dx}f(a) * (x - a)$$

where $\frac{d}{dx}f$ is the first-order derivative of f wrt. x.

A *secant line* to a univariate function $f(x)$ is a straight line that connects two points on the function plot. The secant line $S_{f,a,b}(x)$ to a function f between points a and b is defined as follows:

$$S_{f,a,b}(x) \stackrel{\text{def}}{=} \frac{f(a) - f(b)}{a - b} * (x - a) + f(a).$$

For a function f that is twice differentiable at point c, the *concavity* of f at c is the sign of its second derivative evaluated at c. We denote open and closed intervals between two real numbers l and u as $]l, u[$ and $[l, u]$ respectively. Given a univariate function f over the reals, the *graph* of f is the set of pairs $\{\langle x, f(x)\rangle \mid x \in \mathbb{R}\}$. We might sometimes refer to an element $\langle x, f(x)\rangle$ of the graph as a point.

Taylor Series and Taylor's Theorem. Given a function $f(x)$ that has $n + 1$ continuous derivatives at $x = a$, the *Taylor series* of degree n centered around a is the polynomial:

$$P_{n,f(a)}(x) \stackrel{\text{def}}{=} \sum_{i=0}^{n} \frac{f^{(i)}(a)}{i!} * (x - a)^i$$

where $f^{(i)}(a)$ is the evaluation of i-th derivative of $f(x)$ at point $x = a$. The Taylor series centered around 0 is also called *Maclaurin series*.

```
bool SMT-NTA-check-abstract (φ):
  1.   φ̂ = initial-abstraction(φ)
  2.   Γ = ∅
  3.   precision := initial-precision ()
  4.   while true:
  5.       if budget-exhausted ():
  6.           abort
  7.       ⟨res, μ̂⟩ = SMT-UFLRA-check (φ̂ ∧ ⋀ Γ)
  8.       if not res:
  9.           return false
  10.      ⟨sat, Γ'⟩ := check-refine (φ, μ̂, precision)
  11.      if sat:
  12.          return true
  13.      else:
  14.          precision := maybe-increase-precision ()
  15.          Γ'' := refine-extra (φ, μ̂)
  16.      Γ := Γ ∪ Γ' ∪ Γ''
```

Fig. 1. Solving SMT(NTA) via abstraction to SMT(UFLRA).

According to *Taylor's theorem*, any continuous function $f(x)$ that is $n + 1$ differentiable can be written as the sum of the Taylor series and the remainder term:

$$f(x) = P_{n,f(a)}(x) + R_{n+1,f(a)}(x)$$

where $R_{n+1,f(a)}(x)$ is basically the Lagrange form of the remainder, and for some point b between x and a it is given by:

$$R_{n+1,f(a)}(x) \overset{\text{def}}{=} \frac{f^{(n+1)}(b)}{(n+1)!} * (x - a)^{n+1}.$$

The value of the point b is not known, but the upper bound on the size of the remainder $\overline{R_{n+1,f(a)}}^u(x)$ at a point x can be estimated by:

$$\overline{R_{n+1,f(a)}}^u(x) \overset{\text{def}}{=} \max_{c \in [\min(a,x), \max(a,x)]} (|f^{(n+1)}(c)|) * \frac{|(x - a)^{n+1}|}{(n+1)!}.$$

This allows to obtain two polynomials that are above and below the function at a given point x, by considering $P_{n,f(a)}(x) + \overline{R_{n+1,f(a)}}^u(x)$ and $P_{n,f(a)}(x) - \overline{R_{n+1,f(a)}}^u(x)$ respectively.

3   Overview of the Approach

Our procedure, which extends to SMT(NTA) and pushes further the approach presented in [5] for SMT(NRA), works by overapproximating the input formula with a formula over the combined theory of linear arithmetic and uninterpreted functions. The main algorithm is shown in Fig. 1. The solving procedure follows a classic abstraction-refinement loop, in which at each iteration, the current safe approximation $\widehat{\varphi}$ of the input SMT(NTA) formula φ is refined by adding new constraints Γ that rule out one (or possibly more) spurious solutions, until one of the following conditions occurs: (i) the resource budget (e.g. time, memory, number of iterations) is exhausted; or (ii) $\widehat{\varphi} \wedge \bigwedge \Gamma$ becomes unsatisfiable in SMT(UFLRA); or (iii) the SMT(UFLRA) satisfiability result for $\widehat{\varphi} \wedge \bigwedge \Gamma$ can be lifted to a satisfiability result for the original formula φ. An initial current precision is set (calling the function initial-precision), and this value is possibly increased at each iteration (calling maybe-increase-precision) according to the result of check-refine and some heuristic.

In Fig. 1 we distinguish between two different refinement procedures: (1) check-refine, which is described below; (2) refine-extra, which is described in Sect. 4, where we provide further details on the treatment of each specific transcendental function that we currently support.

Initial Abstraction. The function initial-abstraction takes in input an SMT(NTA) formula φ and returns a SMT(UFLRA) safe approximation $\widehat{\varphi}$ of it. First, we flatten each transcendental function application $tf(t)$ in φ in which t is not a variable by replacing t with a fresh variable y, and by conjoining $y = t$ to φ. Then, we replace each transcendental function $tf(x)$ in φ with a corresponding uninterpreted function $ftf(x)$, producing thus an SMT(UFLRA) formula $\widehat{\varphi}$. Finally, we add to $\widehat{\varphi}$ some simple initial axioms for the different transcendental functions, expressing general, simple mathematical properties about them. We shall describe such axioms in Sect. 4.

If φ contains also non-linear polynomials, we handle them as described in [5]: we replace each non-linear product $t_1 * t_2$ with an uninterpreted function application $fmul(t_1, t_2)$, and add to the input formula some initial axioms expressing general, simple mathematical properties of multiplications. (We refer the reader to [5] for details.)

$\langle$**bool**, axiom-set$\rangle$ check-refine $(\varphi, \widehat{\mu},$ precision$)$:

1. $\Gamma :=$ check-refine-NRA $(\varphi, \widehat{\mu})$ # *NRA refinement of [5]*
2. $\epsilon := 10^{-\text{precision}}$
3. **for all** $tf(x) \in \varphi$:
4. $c := \widehat{\mu}[x]$
5. $\langle P_l(x), P_u(x) \rangle :=$ poly-approx $(tf(x), c, \epsilon)$
6.   **if** $\widehat{\mu}[ftf(x)] \leq P_l(c)$ **or** $\widehat{\mu}[ftf(x)] \geq P_u(c)$:
7. $\Gamma := \Gamma \cup$ get-lemmas-point $(tf(x), \widehat{\mu}, P_l(x), P_u(x))$
8. **if** $\Gamma = \emptyset$:
9.   **if** check-model $(\varphi, \widehat{\mu})$:
10.   **return** $\langle$**true**, $\emptyset\rangle$
11.   **else**:
12.   **return** check-refine $(\varphi, \widehat{\mu},$ precision+1$)$
13. **else**:
14.   **return** $\langle$**false**, $\Gamma\rangle$

Fig. 2. The main refinement procedure.

Spuriousness Check and Abstraction Refinement. The core of our procedure is the check-refine function, shown in Fig. 2.

First, if the formula contains also some non-linear polynomials, check-refine performs the refinement of non-linear multiplications as described in [5]. In Fig. 2, this is represented by the call to the function check-refine-NRA at line 1, which may return some axioms to further constrain $fmul$ terms. If no non-linear polynomials occur in φ, then Γ is initialized as the empty set.

Then, the function iterates over all the transcendental function applications $tf(x)$ in φ (lines 3–7), and checks whether the SMT(UFLRA)-model $\widehat{\mu}$ is consistent with their semantics.

Intuitively, in principle, this amounts to check that $tf(\widehat{\mu}[x])$ is equal to $\widehat{\mu}[ftf(x)]$. In practice, however, the check cannot be exact, since transcendental functions at rational points typically have irrational values (see e.g. [21]), which cannot be represented in SMT(UFLRA). Therefore, for each $tf(x)$ in φ, we instead compute two polynomials, $P_l(x)$ and $P_u(x)$, with the property that $tf(\widehat{\mu}[x])$ belongs to the open interval $]P_l(\widehat{\mu}[x]), P_u(\widehat{\mu}[x])[$. The polynomials are computed using Taylor series, according to the given current precision, by the function poly-approx, which shall be described in Sect. 4.

If the model value $\widehat{\mu}[ftf(x)]$ for $tf(x)$ is outside the above interval, then the function get-lemmas-point is used to generate some linear lemmas that will remove the spurious point $\langle \widehat{\mu}[x], \widehat{\mu}[ftf(x)] \rangle$ from the graph of the current abstraction of $tf(x)$ (line 7).

If at least one point was refined in the loop of lines 3–7, the current set of lemmas Γ is returned (line 10). If instead none of the points was determined to be spurious, the function check-model is called (line 9). This function tries to determine whether the abstract model $\widehat{\mu}$ does indeed imply the existence of a model for the original formula φ (more details are given below). If the check fails, we repeat the check-refine call with an increased precision (line 12).

Refining a Spurious Point with Secant and Tangent Lines. Given a transcendental function application $tf(x)$, the get-lemmas-point function generates a set of lemmas for refining the interpretation of $ftf(x)$ by constructing a piecewise-linear approximation of $tf(x)$ around the point $\widehat{\mu}[x]$, using one of the polynomials $P_l(x)$ and $P_u(x)$ computed in check-refine. The kind of lemmas generated, and which of the two polynomials is used, depend on (i) the position of the spurious value $\widehat{\mu}[ftf(x)]$ relative to the correct value $tf(\widehat{\mu}[x])$, and (ii) the concavity of tf around the point $\widehat{\mu}[x]$. If the concavity is positive (resp. negative) or equal to zero, and the point lies below (resp. above) the function, then the linear approximation is given by a tangent to the lower (resp. upper) bound polynomial P_l (resp. P_u) at $\widehat{\mu}[x]$ (lines 4–9 of Fig. 3); otherwise, i.e. the concavity is negative (resp. positive) and the point is below (resp. above) the function, the linear approximation is given by a pair of secants to the lower (resp. upper) bound polynomial P_l (resp. P_u) around $\widehat{\mu}[x]$ (lines 10–22 of Fig. 3). The two situations are illustrated in Fig. 4.

axiom-set **get-lemmas-point** $(tf(x), \widehat{\mu}, P_l(x), P_u(x))$:

1. $c := \widehat{\mu}[x]$
2. $v := \widehat{\mu}[ftf(x)]$
3. $conc := $ **get-concavity** $(tf(x), c)$
4. **if** $(v \leq P_l(c)$ **and** $conc \geq 0)$ **or** $(v \geq P_u(c)$ **and** $conc \leq 0)$:
    # tangent refinement
5. $\quad P := (v \leq P_l(c))\ ?\ (P_l)\ :\ (P_u)$
6. $\quad T(x) := P(c) + \frac{d}{dx}P(c) \cdot (x - c)$ # tangent of P at c
7. $\quad \langle l, u \rangle := $ **get-tangent-bounds** $(tf(x), c, \frac{d}{dx}P(c))$
8. $\quad \psi := (conc < 0)\ ?\ (ftf(x) \leq T(x))\ :\ (ftf(x) \geq T(x))$
9. $\quad$ **return** $\{((x \geq l) \wedge (x \leq u)) \rightarrow \psi\}$
10. **else:** # $(v \leq P_l(c) \wedge conc < 0) \vee (v \geq P_u(c) \wedge conc > 0)$
    # secant refinement
11. $\quad prev := $ **get-previous-secant-points** $(tf(x))$
12. $\quad l := \max\{p \in prev \mid p < c\}$
13. $\quad u := \min\{p \in prev \mid p > c\}$
14. $\quad P := (v \leq P_l(c))\ ?\ (P_l)\ :\ (P_u)$
15. $\quad S_l(x) := \dfrac{P(l) - P(c)}{l - c} \cdot (x - l) + P(l)$ # secant of P between l and c
16. $\quad S_u(x) := \dfrac{P(u) - P(c)}{u - c} \cdot (x - u) + P(u)$
17. $\quad \psi_l := (conc < 0)\ ?\ (ftf(x) \geq S_l(x))\ :\ (ftf(x) \leq S_l(x))$
18. $\quad \psi_u := (conc < 0)\ ?\ (ftf(x) \geq S_u(x))\ :\ (ftf(x) \leq S_u(x))$
19. $\quad \phi_l := (x \geq l) \wedge (x \leq c)$
20. $\quad \phi_u := (x \geq c) \wedge (x \leq u)$
21. $\quad$ **store-secant-point** $(tf(x), c)$
22. $\quad$ **return** $\{(\phi_l \rightarrow \psi_l), (\phi_u \rightarrow \psi_u)\}$

Fig. 3. Piecewise-linear refinement for the transcendental function $tf(x)$ at point c.

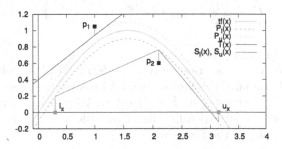

Fig. 4. Piecewise-linear refinement illustration.

In the case of tangent refinement, the function **get-tangent-bounds** (line 7) returns an interval $[l, u]$ such that the tangent line is guaranteed not to cross the transcendental function tf. In practice, this interval can be (under)approximated quickly by exploiting known properties of the specific function tf under consideration. For example, for the exponential function **get-tangent-bounds** always returns $[-\infty, +\infty]$; for other functions, the computation can be based e.g. on an analysis of the (known, precomputed) inflection points of tf around the point of interest $\widehat{\mu}[x]$ and the slope $\frac{d}{dx}P(c)$ of the tangent line.

In the case of secant refinement, a second value, different from $\widehat{\mu}[x]$, is required to draw a secant line. The function get-previous-secant-points returns the set of all the points at which a secant refinement was performed in the past for $tf(x)$. From this set, we take the two points closest to $\widehat{\mu}[x]$, such that $l < \widehat{\mu}[x] < u$ and that l, u do not cross any inflection point,[1] and use those points to generate two secant lines and their validity intervals. Before returning the set of the two corresponding lemmas, we also store the new secant refinement point $\widehat{\mu}[x]$ by calling store-secant-point.

Detecting Satisfiable Formulas. The function check-model tries to determine whether the UFLRA-model $\widehat{\mu}$ for $\widehat{\varphi} \wedge \bigwedge \Gamma$ implies the satisfiability of the original formula φ. If, for all $tf(x)$ in φ, tf has a rational value at the rational point $\widehat{\mu}[x]$,[2] and $\widehat{\mu}[ftf(x)]$ is equal to $tf(\widehat{\mu}[x])$, then $\widehat{\mu}$ can be directly lifted to a model μ for φ.

In the general case, we exploit this simple observation: we can still conclude that φ is satisfiable if we are able to show that $\widehat{\varphi}$ is satisfiable *under all possible interpretations of ftf* that are guaranteed to include also tf.

Using the model $\widehat{\mu}$, we compute safe lower and upper bounds $\underline{tf(\widehat{\mu}[x])}_l$ and $\overline{tf(\widehat{\mu}[x])}^u$ for the function tf at point $\widehat{\mu}[x]$ with the poly-approx function (see above). Let FTF be the set of all $ftf(x)$ terms occurring in $\widehat{\varphi}$. Let V be the set of variables x for $ftf(x) \in FTF$, and F be the set of all the function symbols in FTF. Intuitively, if we can prove the validity of the following formula:

$$\forall\, ftf \in F. \left(\bigwedge_{ftf(x) \in FTF} \underline{tf(\widehat{\mu}[x])}_l \leq ftf(\widehat{\mu}[x]) \leq \overline{tf(\widehat{\mu}[x])}^u \right) \rightarrow \widehat{\varphi}\{V \mapsto \widehat{\mu}[V]\}$$

then the original formula φ is satisfiable.

In order to be able to use a quantifier-free SMT(UFLRA)-solver, we reduce the problem to the validity check of a pure UFLRA formula. Let CT be the set of all terms $ftf(\widehat{\mu}[x])$ occurring in $\widehat{\varphi}\{V \mapsto \widehat{\mu}[V]\}$. We replace each occurrence of $ftf(\widehat{\mu}[x])$ in CT with a corresponding fresh variable $y_{ftf(\widehat{\mu}[x])}$ from a set Y. We then check the validity of the formula:

$$\varphi_{\widehat{\mu}}^{sat} \stackrel{def}{=} \forall Y. \left(\left(\bigwedge_{ftf(x) \in FTF} \underline{tf(\widehat{\mu}[x])}_l \leq ftf(\widehat{\mu}[x]) \leq \overline{tf(\widehat{\mu}[x])}^u \right) \rightarrow \widehat{\varphi}\{V \mapsto \widehat{\mu}[V]\} \right) \{CT \mapsto Y\}.$$

---

[1] For simplicity, we assume that this is always possible. If needed, this can be implemented e.g. by generating the two points at random while ensuring that $l < \widehat{\mu}[x] < u$ and that l, u do not cross any inflection point.

[2] Although, as mentioned above, this is not the case in general (see e.g. [21]), it is true for some special values, e.g. $\exp(0) = 1$, $\sin(0) = 0$.

If $\neg\varphi_{\bar\mu}^{\mathrm{sat}}$ is unsatisfiable, we conclude that φ is satisfiable. Clearly, this can be checked with a quantifier-free SMT(UFLRA)-solver, since $\neg\forall x.\phi$ is equivalent to $\exists x.\neg\phi$, and x can then be removed by Skolemization.

4   Abstraction Refinement for Transcendental Functions

In this section, we describe the implementation of the poly-approx and refine-extra for the transcendental functions that we currently support, namely exp and sin.[3]

The poly-approx($tf(x), c, \epsilon$) function uses the Maclaurin series of the corresponding transcendental function and Taylor's theorem to find the lower and upper polynomials. Essentially, this is done by expanding the series (and the remainder approximation) up to a certain n, until the desired precision ϵ (i.e. the difference between the upper and lower polynomials evaluated at c) is achieved. Notice that, since we can precisely evaluate the derivative of any order at 0 for both exp and sin,[4] the computation of both the Maclaurin series and the remainder polynomial is always exact.

4.1   Exponential Function

Piecewise-Linear Refinement. The polynomial $P_{n,\exp(0)}(x)$ given by the Maclaurin series behaves differently depending on the sign of x. For that reason, poly-approx distinguishes three cases for finding the polynomials $P_l(x)$ and $P_u(x)$:

Case $x = 0$: since $\exp(0) = 1$, we have $P_l(0) = P_u(0) = 1$;

Case $x < 0$: we have that $P_{n,\exp(0)}(x) < \exp(x)$ if n is odd, and $P_{n,\exp(0)}(x) > \exp(x)$ if n is even (where $P_{n,\exp(0)}(x) = \sum_{i=0}^{n} \frac{x^i}{i!}$); we therefore set $P_l(x) = P_{n,\exp(0)}(x)$ and $P_u(x) = P_{n+1,\exp(0)}(x)$ for a suitable n so that the required precision ϵ is met;

Case $x > 0$: we have that $P_{n,\exp(0)}(x) < \exp(x)$ and $P_{n,\exp(0)}(x) * (1 - \frac{x^{n+1}}{(n+1)!})^{-1} > \exp(x)$ when $(1 - \frac{x^{n+1}}{(n+1)!}) > 0$, therefore we set $P_l(x) = P_{n,\exp(0)}(x)$ and $P_u(x) = P_{n,\exp(0)}(x) * (1 - \frac{x^{n+1}}{(n+1)!})^{-1}$ for a suitable n.

Since the concavity of exp is always positive, the tangent refinement will always give lower bounds for $\exp(x)$, and the secant refinement will give upper bounds. Moreover, as exp has no inflection points, get-tangent-bounds always returns $[-\infty, +\infty]$.

---

[3] We remark that our tool (see Sect. 6) can handle also log, cos, tan, arcsin, arccos, arctan by means of rewriting. We leave as future work the possibility of handling such functions natively.

[4] Because (i) $\exp(0) = 1$, $\sin(0) = 0$, $\cos(0) = 1$, (ii) $\exp^{(i)}(x) = \exp(x)$ for all i, and (iii) $|\sin^{(i)}(x)|$ is $|\cos(x)|$ if i is odd and $|\sin(x)|$ otherwise.

Extra Refinement. The exponential function is monotonically increasing with a non-linear order. We check this property between two $fexp(x)$ and $fexp(y)$ terms in $\widehat{\varphi}$: if $\widehat{\mu}[x] < \widehat{\mu}[y]$, but $\widehat{\mu}[fexp(x)] \not< \widehat{\mu}[fexp(y)]$, then we add the following extra refinement lemma:

$$x < y \leftrightarrow fexp(x) < fexp(y)$$

Initial Axioms. We add the following initial axioms to $\widehat{\varphi}$.

$$\text{Lower Bound: } fexp(x) > 0$$
$$\text{Zero: } (x = 0 \leftrightarrow fexp(x) = 1) \wedge (x < 0 \leftrightarrow fexp(x) < 1) \wedge$$
$$(x > 0 \leftrightarrow fexp(x) > 1)$$
$$\text{Zero Tangent Line: } x = 0 \vee fexp(x) > x + 1$$

4.2   Sin Function

Piecewise-Linear Refinement. The correctness of our refinement procedure relies crucially on being able to compute the concavity of the transcendental function *tf* at a given point c. This is needed in order to know whether a computed tangent or secant line constitutes a valid upper or lower bound for *tf* around c (see Fig. 3). In the case of the sin function, computing the concavity at an arbitrary point c is problematic, since this essentially amounts to computing the remainder of c and π, which, being π a transcendental number, cannot be exactly computed.

In order to solve this problem, we exploit another property of sin, namely its periodicity (with period 2π). More precisely, we split the reasoning about sin depending on two kinds of periods: base period and extended period. A period is a *base period* for the sin function if it is from $-\pi$ to π, otherwise it is an *extended period*. In order to reason about periods, we first introduce a symbolic variable $\widehat{\pi}$, and add the constraint $l_\pi < \widehat{\pi} < u_\pi$ to $\widehat{\varphi}$, where l_π and u_π are valid rational lower and upper bounds for the actual value of π (in our current implementation, we have $l_\pi = \frac{333}{106}$ and $u_\pi = \frac{355}{113}$). Then, we introduce for each $fsin(x)$ term an "artificial" sin function application $fsin(y_x)$ (where y_x is a fresh variable), whose domain is the base period. This is done by adding the following constraints:

$$(-\widehat{\pi} \leq y_x \leq \widehat{\pi}) \wedge ((-\widehat{\pi} \leq x \leq \widehat{\pi}) \rightarrow y_x = x) \wedge fsin(x) = fsin(y_x).$$

We call these fresh variables *base variables*. Notice that the second and the third constraint are saying that $fsin(x)$ is the same as $fsin(y_y)$ in the base period.

Let $Fsin_{base}$ be the set of $fsin(y_x)$ terms that have base variables as arguments, $Fsin$ be the set of all $fsin(x)$ terms, and $Fsin_{ext} \overset{\text{def}}{=} Fsin - Fsin_{base}$. The tangent and secant refinement is performed for the terms in $Fsin_{base}$, while we add a *linear shift* lemma (described below) as refinement for the terms in $Fsin_{ext}$. Using this transformation, we can easily compute the concavity of sin at $\widehat{\mu}[y_x]$ by just looking at the sign of $\widehat{\mu}[y_x]$, *provided that* $-l_\pi \leq \widehat{\mu}[y_x] \leq l_\pi$, where l_π is the current lower bound for $\widehat{\pi}$.[5] In the case in which $-u_\pi < \widehat{\mu}[y_x] < -l_\pi$ or

---

[5] In the interval $[-\pi, \pi]$, the concavity of $sin(c)$ is the opposite of the sign of c.

$l_\pi < \widehat{\mu}[y_x] < u_\pi$, we do not perform the tangent/secant refinement, but instead we refine the precision of $\widehat{\pi}$. For each $fsin(y_x) \in FSin_{base}$, poly-approx tries to find the lower and upper polynomial using Taylor's theorem, which ensures that:

$$P_{n,\sin(0)}(y_x) - \overline{R_{n+1,\sin(0)}}^u(y_x) \le \sin(y_x) \le P_{n,\sin(0)}(y_x) + \overline{R_{n+1,\sin(0)}}^u(y_x)$$

where $P_{n,\sin(0)}(y_x) = \sum_{k=0}^n \frac{(-1)^k * y_x^{2k+1}}{(2k+1)!}$ and $\overline{R_{n+1,\sin(0)}}^u(y_x) = \frac{y_x^{2(n+1)}}{(2(n+1))!}$. Therefore, we can set $P_l(x) = P_{n,\sin(0)}(x) - \overline{R_{n+1,\sin(0)}}^u(x)$ and $P_u(x) = P_{n,\sin(0)}(x) + \overline{R_{n+1,\sin(0)}}^u(x)$.

Extra Refinement. For each $fsin(x) \in Fsin_{ext}$ with the corresponding base variable y_x, we check whether the value $\widehat{\mu}[x]$ after shifting to the base period is equal to the value of $\widehat{\mu}[y_x]$. We calculate the shift s of x as the rounding towards zero of $(\widehat{\mu}[x] + \widehat{\mu}[\widehat{\pi}])/(2 \cdot \widehat{\mu}[\widehat{\pi}])$, and we then compare $\widehat{\mu}[y_x]$ with $\widehat{\mu}[x] - 2s \cdot \widehat{\mu}[\widehat{\pi}]$. If the values are different, we add the following *shift lemma* for relating x with y_x in the extended period s:

$$(\widehat{\pi} * (2s - 1) \le x \le \widehat{\pi} * (2s + 1)) \to y_x = x - 2s * \widehat{\pi}.$$

In this way, we do not need the tangent and secant refinement for the extended period and we can reuse the refinements done in the base period. Note that even if the calculated shift value is wrong (due to the imprecision of $\widehat{\mu}[\widehat{\pi}]$ with respect to the real value π), we may generate something useless but never wrong.

We also check the monotonicity property of sin, which can be described for the base period as: (i) the sin is monotonically increasing in the interval $-\frac{\pi}{2}$ to $\frac{\pi}{2}$; (ii) the sin is monotonically decreasing in the intervals $-\pi$ to $-\frac{\pi}{2}$ and $\frac{\pi}{2}$ to π. We add one of the constraints below if it is in conflict according to the current abstract model for some $fsin(y_{x_1}), fsin(y_{x_2}) \in Fsin_{base}$.

$$(-\frac{\widehat{\pi}}{2} \le y_{x_1} < y_{x_2} \le \frac{\widehat{\pi}}{2}) \to fsin(y_{x_1}) < fsin(y_{x_2})$$

$$(-\widehat{\pi} \le y_{x_1} < y_{x_2} \le -\frac{\widehat{\pi}}{2}) \to fsin(y_{x_1}) > fsin(y_{x_2})$$

$$(\frac{\widehat{\pi}}{2} \le y_{x_1} < y_{x_2} \le \widehat{\pi}) \to fsin(y_{x_1}) > fsin(y_{x_2})$$

Initial Axioms. For each $fsin(z) \in Fsin$, we add the generic lower and upper bounds: $-1 \le fsin(z) \le 1$. For each $fsin(y_x) \in Fsin_{base}$, we add the following axioms.

$$\text{Symmetry: } fsin(y_x) = -fsin(-y_x)$$
$$\text{Phase: } (0 < y_x < \widehat{\pi} \leftrightarrow fsin(y_x) > 0) \wedge (-\widehat{\pi} < y_x < 0 \leftrightarrow fsin(y_x) < 0)$$
$$\text{Zero Tangent: } (y_x > 0 \to fsin(y_x) < y_x) \wedge (y_x < 0 \to fsin(y_x) > y_x)$$
$$\pi Tangent : (y_x < \widehat{\pi} \to fsin(y_x) < -y_x + \widehat{\pi}) \wedge$$
$$(y_x > -\widehat{\pi} \to fsin(y_x) > -y_x - \widehat{\pi})$$

Significant Values: $(fsin(y_x) = 0 \leftrightarrow (y_x = 0 \vee y_x = \widehat{\pi} \vee y_x = -\widehat{\pi})) \wedge$

$$(fsin(y_x) = 1 \leftrightarrow y_x = \frac{\widehat{\pi}}{2}) \wedge (fsin(y_x) = -1 \leftrightarrow y_x = -\frac{\widehat{\pi}}{2}) \wedge$$

$$(fsin(y_x) = \frac{1}{2} \leftrightarrow (y_x = \frac{\widehat{\pi}}{6} \vee y_x = \frac{5 * \widehat{\pi}}{6})) \wedge$$

$$(fsin(y_x) = -\frac{1}{2} \leftrightarrow (y_x = -\frac{\widehat{\pi}}{6} \vee y_x = -\frac{5 * \widehat{\pi}}{6}))$$

4.3   Optimization

We use infinite-precision to represent rational numbers. In our (model-driven) approach, we may have to deal with numbers with very large numerators and/or denominators. It may happen that we get such rational numbers from the bad model $\widehat{\mu}$ for the variables appearing as arguments of transcendental functions. As a result of the piecewise-linear refinement, we will feed to the SMT(UFLRA) solver numbers that have even (exponentially) larger numerators and/or denominators (due to the fact that poly-approx uses power series). This might significantly slow-down the performance of the solver. We address this issue by approximating "bad" values $\widehat{\mu}[x]$ with too large numerators and/or denominators by using continued fractions [20]. The precision of the rational approximation is increased periodically over the number of iterations. Thus we delay the use numbers with larger numerator and/or denominator, and eventually find those numbers if they are really needed.

5   Related Work

The approach proposed in this paper is an extension of the approach adopted in [5] for checking the invariants of transition systems over the theory of *polynomial* Nonlinear Real Arithmetic. In this paper we extend the approach to transcendental functions, with the critical issue of irrational valuations. Furthermore, we propose a way to prove SAT without being forced to construct the model.

In the following, we compare with related approaches found in the literature.

Interval Propagation and DELTASAT. The first approach to SMT(NTA) was pioneered by iSAT3 [11], that carries out interval propagation for nonlinear and transcendental functions. iSAT3 is both an SMT solver and bounded model checker for transition systems. A subsequent but very closely related approach is the DREAL solver, proposed in [12]. DREAL relies on the notion of delta-satisfiability [12], which basically guarantees that there exists a variant (within a user-specified δ "radius") of the original problem such that it is satisfiable. The approach cannot guarantee that the original problem is satisfiable, since it relies on numerical approximation techniques that only compute safe overapproximations of the solution space.

There are a few key insights that differentiate our approach. First, it is based on linearization, it relies on solvers for SMT(UFLRA), and it proceeds by incrementally axiomatizing transcendental functions. Compared to interval propagation, we avoid numerical approximation (even if within the bounds from DELTASAT). In a sense, the precision of the approximation is selectively detected at run time, while in iSAT3 and DREAL this is a user defined threshold that is uniformly adopted in the computations. Second, our method relies on piecewise linear approximations, which can provide substantial advantages when approximating a slope – intuitively, interval propagation ends up computing a piecewise-constant approximation. Third, a distinguishing feature of our approach is the ability to (sometimes) prove the existence of a solution even if the actual values are irrationals, by reduction to an SMT-based validity check.

Deductive Methods. The METITARSKI [1] theorem prover relies on resolution and on a decision procedure for NRA to prove quantified inequalities involving transcendental functions. It works by replacing transcendental functions with upper- or lower-bound functions specified by means of axioms (corresponding to either truncated Taylor series or rational functions derived from continued fraction approximations), and then using an external decision procedure for NRA for solving the resulting formulas. Differently from our approach, METITARSKI cannot prove the existence nor compute a satisfying assignment, while we are able to (sometimes) prove the existence of a solution even if the actual values are irrationals. Finally, we note that METITARSKI may require the user to manually write axioms if the ones automatically selected from a predefined library are not enough. Our approach is much simpler, and it is completely automatic.

The approach presented in [10], where the NTA theory is referred to as NLA, is similar in spirit to METITARSKI in that it combines the SPASS theorem prover [27] with the iSAT3 SMT solver. The approach relies on the SUP(NLA) calculus that combines superposition-based first-order logic reasoning with SMT(NTA). Similarly to our work, the authors also use a UFLRA approximation of the original problem. This is however done only as a first check before calling iSAT3. In contrast, we rely on solvers for SMT(UFLRA), and we proceed by incrementally axiomatizing transcendental functions instead of calling directly an NTA solver. Another similarity with our work is the possibility of finding solutions in some cases. This is done by post-processing an inconclusive iSAT3 answer, trying to compute a certificate for a (point) solution for the narrow intervals returned by the solver, using an iterative analysis of the formula and of the computed intervals. Although similar in spirit, our technique for detecting satisfiable instances is completely different, being based on a logical encoding of the existence of a solution as an SMT(UFLRA) problem.

Combination of Interval Propagation and Theorem Proving. GAPPA [9,18] is a standalone tool and a tactic for the COQ proof assistant, that can be used to prove properties about numeric programs (C-like) dealing with floating-point or fixed-point arithmetic. Another related COQ tactic is

COQ.INTERVAL [19]. Both GAPPA and COQ.INTERVAL combine interval propagation and Taylor approximations for handling transcendental functions. A
similar approach is followed also in [25], where a tool written in HOL-LIGHT to
handle conjunctions of non-linear equalities with transcendental functions is presented. The work uses Taylor polynomials up to degree two. NLCERTIFY [17] is
another related tool which uses interval propagation for handling transcendental
functions. It approximates polynomials with sums of squares and transcendental
functions with lower and upper bounds using some quadratic polynomials [2].
Internally, all these tools/tactics rely on multi-precision floating point libraries
for computing the interval bounds.

A similarity between these approaches and our approach is the use of the
Taylor polynomials. However, one distinguishing feature is that we use them to
find lower and upper linear constraints by computing tangent and secant lines.
Moreover, we do not rely on any floating point arithmetic library, and unlike
the mentioned approaches, we can also prove the existence of a solution. On
the other hand, some of the above tools employ more sophisticated/specialised
approximations for transcendental functions, which might allow them to succeed
in proving unsatisfiability of formulas for which our technique is not sufficiently
precise.

Finally, since we are in the context of SMT, our approach also has the benefits
of being: (i) fully automatic, unlike some of the above which are meant to be
used within interactive theorem provers; (ii) able to deal with formulas with an
arbitrary Boolean structure, and not just conjunctions of inequalities; and (iii)
capable of handling combinations of theories (including uninterpreted functions,
bit-vectors, arrays), which are beyond what the above, more specialised tools,
can handle.

6   Experimental Analysis

Implementation. The approach has been implemented on top of the MATH-
SAT SMT solver [7], using the PYSMT library [14]. We use the GMP infinite-
precision arithmetic library to deal with rational numbers. Our implementation and benchmarks are available at https://es.fbk.eu/people/irfan/papers/
cade17-smt-nta.tar.gz.

Setup. We have run our experiments on a cluster equipped with 2.6GHz Intel
Xeon X5650 machines, using a time limit of 1000 seconds and a memory limit
of 6 Gb.

We have run MATHSAT in two configurations: with and without universal
check for proving SAT (resp. called MATHSAT and MATHSAT-NOUNISAT).

The other systems used in the experimental evaluation are DREAL [13],
iSAT3 [24], and METITARSKI [1], in their default configurations (unless otherwise specified). Both iSAT3 and DREAL were also run with higher precision
than the default one. The difference between the two configurations is rather
modest and, when run with higher precision, they decrease the number of

MAYBESAT answers. METITARSKI can prove the validity of quantified formulae, answering either valid or unknown. As such, it is unfair to run it on satisfiable benchmarks. In general, we interpret the results of the comparison taking into account the features of the tools.

Benchmarks. We consider three classes of benchmarks. First, the *bounded model checking (BMC)* benchmarks are the results of unrolling transition systems with nonlinear and transcendental transition relations, obtained from the discretization of hybrid automata. We took benchmarks from the distributions of iSAT3, from the discretization (by way of HYCOMP [6] and NUXMV [4]) of benchmarks from [8] and from the hybrid model checkers HYST [3] and HARE [23]. Second, the *Mathematical* benchmarks are taken from the METITARSKI distribution. These are benchmarks containing quantified formulae over transcendental functions, and are all valid, most of them corresponding to known mathematical theorems. We selected the METITARSKI benchmarks without quantifier alternation and we translated them into quantifier-free SMT(NTA) problems. The third class of benchmarks consists of 944 instances from the DREAL distribution that contain transcendental functions.

Both the mathematical and the DREAL benchmarks contain several transcendental functions (log, cos, ...) that are not supported natively by our prototype. We have therefore applied a preprocessing step that rewrites those functions in terms of exp and sin.[6] iSAT3 requires bounds on the variables and it is unable to deal with the benchmarks above (that either do not specify any bound or specify too wide bounds for the used variables). Thus, we scaled down the benchmarks so that the variables are constrained in the $[-300, 300]$ interval since for higher bounds iSAT3 raises an exception due to reaching the machine precision limit. Finally, for the BMC benchmarks, we run iSAT3 in BMC mode, in order to ensure that its optimized unrolling is activated.

BMC and Mathematical Results. In Table 1, we present the results. The benchmarks are classified as either SAT or UNSAT when at least one of the solvers has been able to return a definite answer. If only MAYBESAT answers are returned, then the benchmark is classified as UNKNOWN. For each tool, we report the number of answers produced within the used resource limits. For the MAYBESAT benchmarks, the numbers in parentheses indicate the instances which have been classified as SAT/UNSAT by at least one other tool. For example, an entry "87 (32/7)" means that the tool returned MAYBESAT for 87 instances, of which 32 were classified as SAT and 7 UNSAT by some other tool.[7]

First, we notice that the universal SAT technique directly results in 72 benchmarks proved to be satisfiable by MATHSAT, without substantial degrade on

---

[6] Sometimes we used a relational encoding: e.g. if φ contains $\arcsin(x)$, we rewrite it as $\varphi\{\arcsin(x) \mapsto as_x\} \wedge \sin(as_x) = x \wedge -\frac{\pi}{2} \leq as_x \leq \frac{\pi}{2}$, where as_x is a fresh variable.

[7] There was no case in which two tools reported SAT and UNSAT for the same benchmark.

Table 1. Results on the BMC and Metitarski benchmarks.

Benchmarks	Bounded model checking (887)			Mathematical (681)		
Result	SAT	UNSAT	MaybeSAT	SAT	UNSAT	MaybeSAT
METITARSKI	N.A.	N.A.	N.A.	N.A.	**530**	N.A.
MATHSAT	**72**	553	N.A.	0	210	N.A.
MATHSAT-NOUNISAT	44	**554**	N.A.	0	221	N.A.
iSAT3	N.A.	N.A.	N.A.	N.A.	N.A.	N.A.
DREAL	N.A.	392	281 (67/23)	N.A.	285	316 (0/253)
Benchmarks	Scaled bounded model checking (887)			Scaled mathematical (681)		
Result	SAT	UNSAT	MaybeSAT	SAT	UNSAT	MaybeSAT
MATHSAT	**84**	**556**	N.A.	0	215	N.A.
MATHSAT-NOUNISAT	48	**556**	N.A.	0	229	N.A.
iSAT3	35	470	87 (32/7)	0	212	137 (0/115)
DREAL	N.A.	403	251 (77/23)	N.A.	**302**	245 (0/195)

the UNSAT benchmarks. Second, we notice that METITARSKI is very strong to deal with its own mathematical benchmarks, but is unable to deal with the BMC ones, which contain features that are beyond what it can handle (Boolean variables and tens of real variables).[8]

In the lower part of Table 1, we present the results on the scaled-down benchmarks, so that iSAT3 can be run. The results for DREAL and MATHSAT are consistent with the ones obtained on the original benchmarks – the benchmarks are slightly simplified for MATHSAT, that solves 12 more SAT instances and 2 more UNSAT ones, and for DREAL, that solves 11 more UNSAT instances. The performance of iSAT3 is quite good, halfway between DREAL and MATHSAT on the bounded model checking benchmarks, and slightly lower than MATHSAT on the mathematical ones. In the BMC benchmarks, iSAT3 is able to solve 35 SAT and 470 UNSAT instances, 102 more than DREAL and 135 less than MATHSAT.

The MAYBESAT results need further analysis. We notice that both iSAT3 and DREAL often return MAYBESAT on unsatisfiable benchmarks (e.g. all the mathematical ones are UNSAT). There are many cases where DREAL returns a DELTASAT result, but at the same time it prints an error message stating that the numerical precision limit has been reached. Thus, it is unlikely that the result is actually DELTASAT, but it should rather be interpreted as MAYBESAT in these cases.[9]

DREAL Benchmarks Results. The DREAL benchmarks turn out to be very hard. The results are reported in Table 2, where we show the performance of DREAL both on the original benchmarks and on the ones resulting from the removal via pre-processing of the transcendental functions not directly supported

---

[8] According to the documentation of METITARSKI, the tool is ineffective for problems with more than 10 real variables. Our experiments on a subset of the instances confirmed this.

[9] We contacted the authors of DREAL and they reported that this issue is currently under investigation.

Table 2. Results on the Dreal benchmarks.

Benchmarks	DREAL (all) (944)		
Status	SAT	UNSAT	MaybeSAT
DREAL (orig.)	N.A.	**102**	524(3/4)
MATHSAT	**3**	68	N.A.
DREAL	N.A.	44	57(3/4)
Benchmarks	DREAL (exp/sin only) (96)		
Status	SAT	UNSAT	MaybeSAT
DREAL (orig.)	N.A.	17	37 (3/3)
MATHSAT	**3**	39	N.A.

by MATHSAT. The results shows that in the original format DREAL solves many more instances, and this suggests that dealing with other transcendental functions in a native manner may lead to substantial improvement in MATHSAT too. Interestingly, if we focus on the subset of 96 benchmarks that only contain exp and sin (and are dealt by MATHSAT without the need of preprocessing), we see that MATHSAT is significantly more effective than DREAL in proving unsatisfiability, solving more than twice the number of instances (right part of Table 2).

We conclude by noticing that overall MATHSAT solves 906 benchmarks out of 2512, 127 more than DREAL, the best among the other systems. A deeper analysis of the results (not reported here for lack of space) shows that the performance of the solvers is complementary: the "virtual-best system" solves 1353 benchmarks. This suggests that the integration of interval propagation may yield further improvements.

7   Conclusion

We present a novel approach to Satisfiability Modulo the theory of transcendental functions. The approach is based on an abstraction-refinement loop, where transcendental functions are represented as uninterpreted ones in the abstract space SMT(UFLRA), and are incrementally axiomatized by means of piecewise-linear functions. We experimentally evaluated the approach on a large and heterogeneous benchmark set: the results demonstrates the potential of our approach, showing that it compares favorably with both delta-satisfiabily and interval propagation and with methods based on theorem proving.

In the future we plan to exploit the solver for the verification of infinite-state transition systems and hybrid automata with nonlinear dynamics, and for the analysis of resource consumption in temporal planning. Finally we would like to define a unifying framework to compare linearization and interval propagation, and to exploit the potential synergies.

References

1. Akbarpour, B., Paulson, L.C.: MetiTarski: an automatic theorem prover for real-valued special functions. JAR **44**(3), 175–205 (2010)
2. Allamigeon, X., Gaubert, S., Magron, V., Werner, B.: Certification of inequalities involving transcendental functions: combining SDP and max-plus approximation. In: 2013 European Control Conference (ECC), pp. 2244–2250. IEEE (2013)
3. Bak, S., Bogomolov, S., Johnson, T.T.: HYST: a source transformation and translation tool for hybrid automaton models. In: Proceedings of the 18th International Conference on Hybrid Systems: Computation and Control, pp. 128–133. ACM (2015)
4. Cavada, R., Cimatti, A., Dorigatti, M., Griggio, A., Mariotti, A., Micheli, A., Mover, S., Roveri, M., Tonetta, S.: The NUXMV symbolic model checker. In: Biere, A., Bloem, R. (eds.) CAV 2014. LNCS, vol. 8559, pp. 334–342. Springer, Cham (2014). doi:10.1007/978-3-319-08867-9_22
5. Cimatti, A., Griggio, A., Irfan, A., Roveri, M., Sebastiani, R.: Invariant checking of NRA transition systems via incremental reduction to LRA with EUF. In: Legay and Margaria [16], pp. 58–75. https://es-static.fbk.eu/people/griggio/papers/tacas17.pdf
6. Cimatti, A., Griggio, A., Mover, S., Tonetta, S.: HYCOMP: an SMT-Based model checker for hybrid systems. In: Baier, C., Tinelli, C. (eds.) TACAS 2015. LNCS, vol. 9035, pp. 52–67. Springer, Heidelberg (2015). doi:10.1007/978-3-662-46681-0_4
7. Cimatti, A., Griggio, A., Schaafsma, B.J., Sebastiani, R.: The MathSAT5 SMT solver. In: Piterman, N., Smolka, S.A. (eds.) TACAS 2013. LNCS, vol. 7795, pp. 93–107. Springer, Heidelberg (2013). doi:10.1007/978-3-642-36742-7_7
8. Cimatti, A., Mover, S., Sessa, M.: From electrical switched networks to hybrid automata. In: Fitzgerald, J., Heitmeyer, C., Gnesi, S., Philippou, A. (eds.) FM 2016. LNCS, vol. 9995, pp. 164–181. Springer, Cham (2016). doi:10.1007/978-3-319-48989-6_11
9. de Dinechin, F., Lauter, C., Melquiond, G.: Certifying the floating-point implementation of an elementary function using Gappa. IEEE Trans. Comput. **60**(2), 242–253 (2011)
10. Eggers, A., Kruglov, E., Kupferschmid, S., Scheibler, K., Teige, T., Weidenbach, C.: Superposition modulo non-linear arithmetic. In: Tinelli, C., Sofronie-Stokkermans, V. (eds.) FroCoS 2011. LNCS (LNAI), vol. 6989, pp. 119–134. Springer, Heidelberg (2011). doi:10.1007/978-3-642-24364-6_9
11. Fränzle, M., Herde, C., Teige, T., Ratschan, S., Schubert, T.: Efficient solving of large non-linear arithmetic constraint systems with complex boolean structure. JSAT **1**(3–4), 209–236 (2007)
12. Gao, S., Avigad, J., Clarke, E.M.: δ-Complete decision procedures for satisfiability over the reals. In: Gramlich, B., Miller, D., Sattler, U. (eds.) IJCAR 2012. LNCS, vol. 7364, pp. 286–300. Springer, Heidelberg (2012). doi:10.1007/978-3-642-31365-3_23
13. Gao, S., Kong, S., Clarke, E.M.: dReal: An SMT solver for nonlinear theories over the reals. In: Bonacina, M.P. (ed.) CADE 2013. LNCS (LNAI), vol. 7898, pp. 208–214. Springer, Heidelberg (2013). doi:10.1007/978-3-642-38574-2_14
14. Gario, M., Micheli, A.: PySMT: a solver-agnostic library for fast prototyping of SMT-based algorithms. In: SMT, pp. 373–384 (2015)
15. Hazewinkel, M.: Encyclopaedia of Mathematics: Stochastic Approximation Zygmund Class of Functions. Encyclopaedia of Mathematics. Springer, Netherlands (1993). https://books.google.it/books?id=1ttmCRCerVUC

16. Legay, A., Margaria, T. (eds.): TACAS 2017. LNCS, vol. 10205. Springer, Heidelberg (2017)
17. Magron, V.: NLCertify: a tool for formal nonlinear optimization. In: Hong, H., Yap, C. (eds.) ICMS 2014. LNCS, vol. 8592, pp. 315–320. Springer, Heidelberg (2014). doi:10.1007/978-3-662-44199-2_49
18. Martin-Dorel, É., Melquiond, G.: Proving tight bounds on univariate expressions with elementary functions in Coq. J. Autom. Reasoning **57**(3), 187–217 (2016)
19. Melquiond, G.: Coq-interval (2011)
20. Nemhauser, G.L., Wolsey, L.A.: Integer and Combinatorial Optimization. Wiley-Interscience, New York (1988)
21. Nieven, I.: Numbers: Rational and Irrational. Mathematical Association of America (1961)
22. Ratschan, S.: Efficient solving of quantified inequality constraints over the real numbers. TOCL **7**(4), 723–748 (2006)
23. Roohi, N., Prabhakar, P., Viswanathan, M.: HARE: A hybrid abstraction refinement engine for verifying non-linear hybrid automata. In: Legay and Margaria [16], pp. 573–588
24. Scheibler, K., Kupferschmid, S., Becker, B.: Recent improvements in the SMT solver iSAT. MBMV **13**, 231–241 (2013)
25. Solovyev, A., Hales, T.C.: Formal verification of nonlinear inequalities with taylor interval approximations. In: Brat, G., Rungta, N., Venet, A. (eds.) NFM 2013. LNCS, vol. 7871, pp. 383–397. Springer, Heidelberg (2013). doi:10.1007/978-3-642-38088-4_26
26. Townsend, E.: Functions of a Complex Variable. Read Books (2007)
27. Weidenbach, C., Dimova, D., Fietzke, A., Kumar, R., Suda, M., Wischnewski, P.: SPASS version 3.5. In: Schmidt, R.A. (ed.) CADE 2009. LNCS (LNAI), vol. 5663, pp. 140–145. Springer, Heidelberg (2009). doi:10.1007/978-3-642-02959-2_10

Satisfiability Modulo Bounded Checking

Simon Cruanes[✉]

University of Lorraine, CNRS, Inria, LORIA, 54000 Nancy, France
simon.cruanes@inria.fr

Abstract. We describe a new approach to find models for a computational higher-order logic with datatypes. The goal is to find counter-examples for conjectures stated in proof assistants. The technique builds on narrowing [14] but relies on a tight integration with a SAT solver to analyze conflicts precisely, eliminate sets of choices that lead to failures, and sometimes prove unsatisfiability. The architecture is reminiscent of that of an SMT solver. We present the rules of the calculus, an implementation, and some promising experimental results.

1 Introduction

Computational higher-order logics are widely used to reason about purely functional programs and form the basis of proof assistants such as ACL2 [12], Coq [8], and Isabelle [15]. Searching for models in such logics is useful both for refuting wrong conjectures and for testing — it is often faster and easier to test a property than to prove it. In this work we focus on a logic with algebraic datatypes and terminating recursive functions. Once proven terminating, these functions have a natural interpretation in any model as least fixpoints.

The typical use case is for the users to specify a property they believe to hold for the program they wrote and let a solver search for a (counter-)example until some resource is exhausted — time, patience, etc. Our goal is to build a tool that can be used for finding counter-examples in proof assistants. Figure 1 presents such a problem in TIP syntax [6] that defines natural numbers, lists, and operations on lists, where the (unsatisfiable) goal is to find a list of natural numbers that is a palindrome of length 2 with sum 3.

In the functional programming community, tools such as QuickCheck [5] and SmallCheck [18] have been used to test conjectures against random values or up to a certain depth. Feat [10] is similar to SmallCheck but enumerates inputs by increasing size, rather than depth. However, QuickCheck is limited when invariants have to be enforced (e.g. red-blackness of trees), forcing users to write custom random generators, and SmallCheck and Feat can get lost quickly in large search spaces. Lazy SmallCheck (LSC) is similar to SmallCheck but relies on the lazy semantics of Haskell to avoid enumerating inputs that are not needed to evaluate the property. LSC is close to narrowing [1,14], a symbolic approach that has ties to functional logic programming [11] and builds a model incrementally. Nevertheless, LSC and narrowing-based tools explore the space of

© Springer International Publishing AG 2017
L. de Moura (Ed.): CADE 2017, LNAI 10395, pp. 114–129, 2017.
DOI: 10.1007/978-3-319-63046-5_8

```
(declare−datatypes () ((Nat (Z) (S (prec Nat)))))
(declare−datatypes () ((List (Nil) (Cons (hd Nat) (tl List)))))
(define−fun−rec plus ((x Nat) (y Nat)) Nat
  (match x (case Z y) (case (S x2) (S (plus x2 y)))))
; some definitions omitted
(define−fun−rec rev ((l List)) List
  (match l (case Nil Nil) (case (Cons x l2) (append (rev l2) (Cons x Nil)))))
(assert−not (forall ((l List))
  (not (and (= l (rev l)) (= (length l) (S (S Z))) (= (sum l) (S (S (S Z))))))))
```

Fig. 1. Looking for impossible palindromes

possible inputs quite naively, making many counter-examples very hard to find. All these approaches lack a way of analyzing why a given search path failed.

Modern SMT solvers are often efficient in difficult combinatorial problems. They rely on a SAT solver to analyze conflicts and interleave theory reasoning with propositional choices. However, their focus is first-order classical logic, where symbols are neatly partitioned between theory symbols that have a precise definition and user-provided symbols that are axiomatized. When a user want to introduce their own parameterized operators, they must use quantifiers and full first order logic, where solvers are usually incomplete. Some work has been done on handling datatypes [4,16] and recursive functions in SMT solvers such as CVC4 [17] or calling an SMT solver repeatedly while expanding function definitions as in Leon [19], but each reduction step (e.g. function call) is very expensive.

Bridging the gap between QuickCheck and SMT solvers is HBMC [7] (Haskell Bounded Model Checker — not published yet). HBMC progressively encodes the evaluation graph into propositional constraints (effectively "bit-blasting" recursive functions and datatypes), leveraging the powerful constraint propagations of modern SAT solvers. However, it suffers from the same weakness as SMT-based techniques: every evaluation step has to be encoded, then performed, inside the SAT solver, making computations slow.

We present a new technique, *Satisfiability Modulo Bounded Checking* (SMBC) that occupies a middle ground between narrowing and HBMC. On the one hand, it can evaluate terms more efficiently than pure bit-blasting although not quite as fast as native code; on the other hand it benefits from propositional conflict-driven clause learning (CDCL) of modern SAT solvers to never make the same bad choice twice. Two main components are involved: (i) a symbolic evaluation engine (Sect. 3), and (ii) a SAT solver with incremental solving under assumptions (Sect. 4). Those two components communicate following lazy SMT techniques [3]. Inputs are lazily and symbolically enumerated using *iterative deepening* (Sect. 5) to ensure fairness, but we use the ability of the SAT solver to solve under assumptions to avoid the costly re-computations usually associated with that technique. In addition, building on CDCL allows SMBC to sometimes prove the unsatisfiability of the problem, something evaluation-based tools are incapable of.

We can extend SMBC to support uninterpreted types and unspecified functions (Sect. 6). After presenting refinements to the calculus (Sect. 7) and an implementation (Sect. 8), we run some experiments (Sect. 9) to compare SMBC with some of the previously mentioned tools on various families of problems. Detailed proofs and additional content can be found in our report.[1]

2   Logic

We consider a multi-sorted higher-order classical logic, without polymorphism. A finite set of mutually recursive *datatypes* $d_1, \ldots, d_k$ is defined by a system

$$\left(d_i \overset{\text{def}}{=} c_{i,1}(\overline{\alpha_{i,1}}) \mid \cdots \mid c_{i,n_i}(\overline{\alpha_{i,n_i}}) \right)_{i \in \{1,\ldots,k\}}$$

where the $\overline{\alpha_{i,j}}$ are tuples of type arguments. We consider only *standard models*, in which the domain of a datatype is the set of terms freely generated from its constructors. Similarly, mutually recursive *functions* $f_1, \ldots, f_k$ are defined by a set of equations $f_1(\overline{x_1}) \overset{\text{def}}{=} t_1, \ldots, f_k(\overline{x_k}) \overset{\text{def}}{=} t_k$ that we assume total and terminating. The term language comprises bound variables, datatype constructors, shallow pattern-matching over datatypes, λ-abstractions $\lambda x : \tau.\, t$, and applications $f\, t_1 \, \ldots \, t_n$. Constructors are always fully applied. $t\sigma$ is the application of a substitution over bound variables σ to t. $\mathsf{Bool} \overset{\text{def}}{=} \{\top, \bot\}$ is a special datatype, paired with tests if $a\, b\, c$ that are short for $\mathsf{case}\, a\, \mathsf{of}\, \top \to b \mid \bot \to c\, \mathsf{end}$. A *value* is a λ-abstraction or constructor application. The operators $\wedge : \mathsf{Bool} \to \mathsf{Bool} \to \mathsf{Bool}$ and $\neg : \mathsf{Bool} \to \mathsf{Bool}$ have the usual logical semantics; evaluation of $\wedge$ is parallel rather than the usual sequential semantics it has in most programming languages: $t \wedge \bot$ reduces to $\bot$ even if t is not a value. We will speak of *parallel conjunction*. Other boolean connectives are encoded in terms of $\wedge$ and $\neg$. We also define an ad hoc polymorphic equality operator $=$ that has the classic structural semantics on datatypes and booleans; comparison of functions is forbidden. An *unknown* is simply an uninterpreted constant which must be given a value in the model. This logic corresponds to the monomorphic fragment of TIP [6] or the extension of SMT-LIB [2] with recursive functions, with the additional assumption that they always terminate.

A *data value* is a term built only from constructor applications, bound variables, and λ-abstractions (without defined symbols, matching, or unknowns). The *depth* of a data value is recursively defined as 1 on constant constructors, $1 + \mathsf{depth}(t)$ for $\lambda x.\, t$, and $1 + \max_{i=1\ldots n} \mathsf{depth}(t_i)$ on constructor applications $c(t_1, \ldots, t_n)$.[2] A *goal set* G is a set of boolean terms. A *model* of G is a mapping

---

[1] https://cedeela.fr/~simon/files/cade_17_report.pdf.

[2] A more flexible definition $\mathsf{depth}(c(t_1, \ldots, t_n)) = \mathsf{cost}(c) + \max_{i=1\ldots n} \mathsf{depth}(t_i)$ can also be used to skew the search towards some constructors, as long as $\mathsf{cost}(c) > 0$ holds for all c.

from unknowns of G to data values, such that $\bigwedge_{t \in G} t$ evaluates to $\top$. The depth of a model is the maximal depth of the data values in it.

In the rest of this paper, t, u will represent terms, k will be unknowns, c, d will be constructors, and e will stand for explanations (conjunctions of literals). We will use an injective mapping to propositional variables denoted $\lVert \cdot \rVert$.

3 Evaluation with Explanations

The semantics of our logic relies on evaluating expressions that contain tests, pattern matching, and (recursive) functions. Because expressions can contain unknowns, their reduction is influenced by assignments to these unknowns. We need an evaluator that keeps track of which choices were used to reduce a term. In this way, when a goal term reduces to $\bot$, we know that this combination of choices is wrong.

In Fig. 2, we show the evaluation rules for terms, given a substitution ρ on unknowns. The notation $t \xrightarrow{\rho}_e u$ means that t reduces to u in one step, with explanations e (a set of boolean literals), under substitution ρ. We denote $t \xrightarrow{\rho}{}^*_e u$ for the transitive reflexive closure of the reduction. We write $t \downarrow_\rho$ (the *normal form* of t under ρ) for the unique term u such that $t \xrightarrow{\rho}{}^*_e u$ and no rule applies to u. In a first approximation, ignoring the explanations, the rules correspond to a normal call-by-need evaluation strategy for the typed λ-calculus. This matches the definition of values given earlier: a value is a weak head normal form. It is possible to use environments instead of substitutions, carrying bindings in every rule, but we chose this presentation for reasons related to hash-consing, as often used in SMT solvers. The choice of call-by-need rather than call-by-value is justified by the maximal amount of laziness it provides in presence of unknowns: instead of waiting for function call arguments, matched terms, or test conditions to be fully evaluated (and therefore, for their unknowns to be fully decided in the partial model), we can proceed with only a weak head normal form.

The rules **id** and **trans** specify how explanations are combined in the reflexive transitive closure; The rule **case** reduces a pattern matching once the matched term is a value (i.e. starts with a constructor, by typing). The rule **app** allows to reduce the function term in an application (until it becomes a value, that is, a λ-abstraction); rule β is the regular β-reduction; rule **def** unfolds definitions (in particular, recursive definitions are unfolded on demand). The rule **decision** replaces an unknown with its value in the current substitution ρ (i.e. the partial model). The other rules define the semantics of boolean operators and equality. We forbid checking equality of functions as is it not computable.

Whether to use small-step or big-step semantics (i.e. reducing a term by one step if a subterm reduces, or waiting for the subterm to become a value) is of little importance for most cases. The only exception is the rules for conjunction, in which big-step semantics is required (i.e. $a \wedge b$ does not always reduce when,

$$\frac{}{a \xrightarrow{\rho}{}^*_{\emptyset} a} \text{ id} \qquad \frac{a \xrightarrow{\rho}_{e_1} b \qquad b \xrightarrow{\rho}{}^*_{e_2} c}{a \xrightarrow{\rho}{}^*_{e_1 \cup e_2} c} \text{ trans}$$

$$\frac{c \text{ is a constructor} \qquad t \xrightarrow{\rho}{}^*_e c(t_1, \ldots, t_n)}{\text{case } t \text{ of } c(x_1, \ldots, x_n) \to u \mid \cdots \text{ end} \xrightarrow{\rho}_e u[t_1/x_1, \ldots, t_n/x_n]} \text{ case}$$

$$\frac{f \xrightarrow{\rho}_e g}{f\, t \xrightarrow{\rho}_e g\, t} \text{ app} \qquad \frac{}{(\lambda x.\, t)\, u \xrightarrow{\rho}_{\emptyset} t[u/x]} \beta \qquad \frac{x \overset{\text{def}}{=} t}{x \xrightarrow{\rho}_{\emptyset} t} \text{ def}$$

$$\frac{\rho(k) = t}{k \xrightarrow{\rho}_{\{\llbracket k := t \rrbracket\}} t} \text{ decision} \qquad \frac{a \xrightarrow{\rho}{}^*_e \bot}{a \wedge b \xrightarrow{\rho}_e \bot} \text{ and-left}$$

$$\frac{b \xrightarrow{\rho}{}^*_e \bot}{a \wedge b \xrightarrow{\rho}_e \bot} \text{ and-right} \qquad \frac{a \xrightarrow{\rho}{}^*_{e_a} \top \qquad b \xrightarrow{\rho}{}^*_{e_b} \top}{a \wedge b \xrightarrow{\rho}_{e_a \cup e_b} \top} \text{ and-true}$$

$$\frac{a \xrightarrow{\rho}{}^*_e \top}{\neg a \xrightarrow{\rho}_e \bot} \text{ not-true} \qquad \frac{a \xrightarrow{\rho}{}^*_e \bot}{\neg a \xrightarrow{\rho}_e \top} \text{ not-false}$$

$$\frac{a \xrightarrow{\rho}_e a'}{a = b \xrightarrow{\rho}_e a' = b} \text{ eq-left} \qquad \frac{b \xrightarrow{\rho}_e b'}{a = b \xrightarrow{\rho}_e a = b'} \text{ eq-right}$$

$$\frac{c, d \text{ are constructors} \qquad c \neq d}{c(\bar{t}) = d(\bar{u}) \xrightarrow{\rho}_{\emptyset} \bot} \text{ eq-conflict}$$

$$\frac{c \text{ is a constructor}}{c(t_1, \ldots, t_n) = c(u_1, \ldots, u_n) \xrightarrow{\rho}_{\emptyset} \bigwedge_{i=1}^n t_i = u_i} \text{ eq-sub}$$

Fig. 2. Evaluation rules under substitution ρ

e.g., a reduces). To see why, assume small-step semantics and consider $a \xrightarrow{\rho}{}^*_{e_1}$ $a' \xrightarrow{\rho}{}^*_{e_3} \bot$ and $b \xrightarrow{\rho}{}^*_{e_2} b'$ where a, b : Bool. The following reduction

$$a \wedge b \xrightarrow{\rho}{}^*_{e_1} a' \wedge b \xrightarrow{\rho}{}^*_{e_1 \cup e_2} a' \wedge b' \xrightarrow{\rho}{}^*_{e_1 \cup e_2 \cup e_3} \bot \wedge b' \xrightarrow{\rho}{}^*_{e_1 \cup e_2 \cup e_3} \bot$$

is imprecise because e_2 is not actually needed for $a \wedge b \xrightarrow{\rho}{}^* \bot$, $e_1 \cup e_3$ is sufficient. The resulting explanation is not as general as it could be, and a smaller part of the search space will be pruned as a result.

Evaluation of a normal form t that is not a value in a substitution ρ is *blocked* by a set of unknowns $\text{block}_\rho(t)$:

$$\text{block}_\rho(\lambda x.\ t) = \emptyset$$
$$\text{block}_\rho(c(u_1, \ldots, u_n)) = \emptyset \text{ if } c \text{ is a constructor}$$
$$\text{block}_\rho(f\ t) = \text{block}_\rho(f)$$
$$\text{block}_\rho(\text{case } t \text{ of } \ldots \text{ end}) = \text{block}_\rho(t\downarrow_\rho)$$
$$\text{block}_\rho(k) = \{k\} \text{ if } k \text{ is an unknown}$$
$$\text{block}_\rho(a = b) = \text{block}_\rho(a) \cup \text{block}_\rho(b)$$
$$\text{block}_\rho(\neg a) = \text{block}_\rho(a\downarrow_\rho)$$
$$\text{block}_\rho(a \wedge b) = \text{block}_\rho(a\downarrow_\rho) \cup \text{block}_\rho(b\downarrow_\rho)$$

In some cases, the blocking unknowns are found in the normal form of sub-terms of t. This corresponds to the evaluation rules that wait for the subterm to become a value before reducing.

Lemma 1 (Uniqueness of values for $\xrightarrow{\rho}{}^*$). *If* $t \xrightarrow{\rho}{}^*_{e_1} v_1$ *and* $t \xrightarrow{\rho}{}^*_{e_2} v_2$ *where* v_1 *and* v_2 *are values, then* $v_1 = v_2$.

Proof. The rules are deterministic, and values are always normal forms since no rule applies to them.   □

Lemma 2. *If* $t = t\downarrow_\rho$ *is a normal form, then* $\text{block}_\rho(t) = \emptyset$ *iff* t *is a value.*

Proof. By induction on the shape of t.   □

4   Delegating Choices and Conflict Analysis to SAT

We now have evaluation rules for reducing terms given a substitution on unknowns but have not yet explained how this substitution is built. As in narrowing [1,14], it is constructed by *refining* unknowns incrementally, choosing their head constructor (or boolean value) and applying it to new unknowns that might need to be refined in turn if they block evaluation.[3] However, in our case, the SAT solver will do the refinement of an unknown k once it has been *expanded*; the first time $k : \tau$ blocks the evaluation of a goal g (i.e., $k \in \text{block}_\rho(g)$), some clauses are added to the SAT solver, forcing it to satisfy exactly one of the literals $\llbracket k := c_i(k_{i,1}, \ldots, k_{i,n_i}) \rrbracket$, where c_i is a constructor of τ. Once one of the literals $\llbracket k := t_i \rrbracket$ is true in the SAT solver's partial model — implying that $\rho(k) = t_i$, as we will see next — evaluation of the goal g can resume using rule **decision** (in Fig. 2) and k is no longer blocking.

The state of the SAT solver is represented below as a pair $M \parallel F$ where M is the trail (a set of literals not containing both l and $\neg l$), and F is a set

---

[3] Our framework corresponds to the special case of needed narrowing when the only rewrite rules are those defining pattern matching.

of clauses. The operation $\mathsf{subst}(M)$ extracts a substitution on unknowns from positive literals in the trail:

$$\mathsf{subst}(M)(k) = t \quad \text{if} \quad \llbracket k := t \rrbracket \in M$$

The interactions between the SAT solver and the evaluation engine are bidirectional. When the SAT solver makes some decisions and propagations, yielding the new state $M \parallel F$, the substitution $\mathsf{subst}(M)$ is used to evaluate the goals in G. If all the goals evaluate to $\top$, we can report M as a model. Otherwise, if there is a goal $t \in G$ such that $t \xrightarrow{\mathsf{subst}(M)}{}^{*}_{e} \bot$, M must be discarded. This is done by adding to F a *conflict clause* $C \overset{\text{def}}{=} \bigvee_{a \in e} \neg a$ that blocks the set of choices in e. The SAT solver will *backjump* to explore models not containing e. Backjumping with clause C and state $M \parallel F$ returns to a state $M' \parallel F$ where M' is the longest prefix of M in which C is not absurd.

Lemma 3 (Monotonicity of Models). *A model of G, expressed as a trail M, satisfies $\bigwedge_{t \in G} t \xrightarrow{\mathsf{subst}(M)}{}^{*}_{e} \top$. No subset of M reduces $\bigwedge_{t \in G} t$ to $\bot$.*

5   Enumeration of Inputs and Iterative Deepening

We have not specified precisely how to enumerate possible models. This section presents a fair enumeration strategy based on Iterative Deepening [13].

A major issue with a straightforward combination of our evaluation function and SAT solver is that there is a risk of non-termination. Indeed, a wrong branch might never be totally closed. Consider the goal $p(b) \wedge a + b = Z$ with unknowns $\{a, b\}$, where $p(x) \overset{\text{def}}{=} \mathsf{case}\ x\ \mathsf{of}\ Z \to \top \mid S(\_) \to \top\ \mathsf{end}$ is trivial, and $+$ is defined on Peano numbers by recursion on its left argument. Then making the initial choice $b = S(b_2)$ (to unblock $p(b)$) and proceeding to refine a in order to unblock $a + b = Z$ will lead to an infinite number of failures related to a, none of which will backjump past $b = S(b_2)$.

To overcome this issue, we solve a series of problems where the *depth* of unknowns is limited to increasingly large values, a process inspired from iterative deepening. Because the SAT solver controls the shape of unknowns, we use special boolean literals $\llbracket \mathsf{depth} \leq n \rrbracket$ to forbid any choice that causes an unknown to be deeper than n; then we solve under assumption $\llbracket \mathsf{depth} \leq n \rrbracket$. If a model is found, it is also valid without the assumption and can be returned immediately to the user. Otherwise, we need the SAT solver to be able to provide *unsat cores* — the subset of its clauses responsible for the problem being unsatisfiable — to make the following distinction: if $\llbracket \mathsf{depth} \leq n \rrbracket$ contributed to the unsat core, it means that there is no solution within the depth limit, and we start again with $\llbracket \mathsf{depth} \leq n + \textsc{Step} \rrbracket$ (where $\textsc{Step} \geq 1$). The last case occurs when the conflict does not involve the assumption $\llbracket \mathsf{depth} \leq n \rrbracket$: then the problem is truly unsatisfiable (e.g., in Fig. 1).

The iterative deepening algorithm is detailed below, in three parts: (i) the main loop, in Algorithm 1; (ii) solving within a depth limit, in Algorithm 2; (iii) expanding unknowns, in Algorithm 3. These functions assume that the SAT solver provides functions for adding clauses dynamically (ADDSATCLAUSE), adding a conflict clause (CONFLICT), performing one round of decision then boolean propagation (MAKESATDECISION and BOOLPROPAGATE), and extracting unsat cores (UNSATCORE). These functions modify the SAT solver state $M \parallel F$. In practice, it is also possible to avoid computing unsat cores at line 7 in Algorithm 1, by checking for pure boolean satisfiability again, but without the depth-limit assumption. Most computations (including the current normal form of $\bigwedge_{t \in G} t$) can be done incrementally and are backtracked in case of conflict.

Algorithm 1. Main Loop Using Iterative Deepening

Require: STEP ≥ 1: depth increment, G: set of goals
 1: **function** MAINLOOP(G)
 2:     $d \leftarrow$ STEP   ▷ initial depth
 3:     **while** $d \leq$ MAXDEPTH **do**
 4:         res $\leftarrow$ SOLVEUPTO(G, d)
 5:         **if** res = SAT **then return** SAT
 6:         **else if** $\|$depth $\leq d\| \notin$ UNSATCORE(res) **then return** UNSAT
 7:         **else** $d \leftarrow d +$ STEP
 8:     **return** UNKNOWN

Algorithm 2. Solving Within a Depth Limit

Require: G: set of goal terms, d: depth limit
 1: **function** SOLVEUPTO(G, d)
 2:     ADDASSUMPTION($\|$depth $\leq d\|$)   ▷ local assumption
 3:     $M \parallel F \leftarrow \emptyset \parallel G$ ▷ initial model and clauses
 4:     **while** true **do**
 5:         $M \parallel F \leftarrow$ MAKESATDECISION($M \parallel F$)   ▷ model still partial
 6:         $M \parallel F \leftarrow$ BOOLPROPAGATE($M \parallel F$)
 7:         $G' \leftarrow \{(u,e) \mid t \in G, t \xrightarrow[e]{\text{subst}(M)}^* u\}$ ▷ current normal form of G
 8:         **if** $(\bot, e) \in G'$ **then**
 9:             $M \parallel F \leftarrow$ CONFLICT($M \parallel F \cup \{\bigvee_{a \in e} \neg a\}$)   ▷ backjump or UNSAT
10:         **else if** all terms in G' are $\top$ **then return** SAT
11:         **else**
12:             $B \leftarrow \bigcup_{(t,e) \in G'} \text{block}_{\text{subst}(M)}(t)$ ▷ blocking unknowns
13:             **for** $k \in B$, k not expanded **do**
14:                 $F \leftarrow F \cup$ EXPAND(k, d)   ▷ will add new literals and clauses

---

Theorem 1 (Termination). *The function* SOLVEUPTO *in Algorithm 2 terminates.*

Algorithm 3. Expansion of Unknowns

Require: k: unknown of type τ, d: depth limit

1: **function** EXPAND(k, d)
2:     **let** $\tau = c_1(\tau_{1,1}, \ldots, \tau_{1,n_1}) \mid \ldots \mid c_k(\tau_{k,1}, \ldots, \tau_{k,n_k})$
3:     $l \leftarrow \{c_i(k_{i,1}, \ldots, k_{i,n_i}) \mid i \in 1, \ldots, k\}$ ▷ each $k_{i,j:\tau_{i,j}}$ is a fresh unknown
4:     ADDSATCLAUSE($\bigvee_{t \in l} \llbracket k := t \rrbracket$)
5:     ADDSATCLAUSES($\{\neg \llbracket k := t_1 \rrbracket \vee \neg \llbracket k := t_2 \rrbracket \mid (t_1, t_2) \in l, t_1 \neq t_2\}$)
6:     **for** $t \in l$ **where** depth(t) $> d$ **do**
7:         ADDSATCLAUSE($\neg \llbracket \text{depth} \leq d \rrbracket \vee \neg \llbracket k := t \rrbracket$) ▷ block this choice at depth d

---

Theorem 2 (Soundness). *The function* SOLVEUPTO *in Algorithm 2 returns either* SAT *or* UNSAT. *If it returns* SAT, *then the substitution* subst(M) *from the boolean trail is a model. If it returns Unsat, then there are no solutions of depth smaller than* d.

Theorem 3 (Bounded Completeness). *If there exists a model of depth smaller at most* STEP $\lfloor$MAXDEPTH/STEP$\rfloor$, *then Algorithm 1 will return* SAT.

Proof. The depth d is always a multiple of STEP. Let $d_{\min} \leq$ MAXDEPTH be the smallest multiple of STEP such that there is a model of depth $\leq d_{\min}$. Iterations of the loop with $d < d_{\min}$ return UNSAT by soundness of SOLVEUPTO (Theorem 2); the iteration at depth $d_{\min}$ returns SAT.   □

5.1   Application to the Introductory Example

We illustrate our technique on an example.[4] Pick the same definitions as in Fig. 1, but with the goal set $G \overset{\text{def}}{=} \{\text{rev}(l) = l, \text{length}(l) = 2, \text{sum}(l) = 2\}$ where the unknown is a list l. Unlike in Fig. 1, this problem is satisfiable. Assuming STEP $= 1$, we start solving under constraint $\llbracket \text{depth} \leq 1 \rrbracket$. Under the empty substitution, G reduces to a set of terms all blocked by a pattern matching on l; expansion of l into $\{\text{Nil}, \text{Cons}(x_1, l_1)\}$ follows, where $x_1 :$ Nat and $l_1 :$ List are fresh unknowns. Suppose the SAT solver picks $\llbracket l := \text{Nil} \rrbracket$. G reduces to $\{\top, \bot, \bot\}$ with explanations $\{\llbracket l := \text{Nil} \rrbracket\}$, so the conflict clause $\neg \llbracket l := \text{Nil} \rrbracket$ is asserted, added to the partial model with no effect, and the solver backtracks.

The next boolean decision must be $\llbracket l := \text{Cons}(x_1, l_1) \rrbracket$. Subsequently, G reduces to

$$\{\text{append}(\text{rev}(l_1), \text{Cons}(x_1, \text{Nil})) = \text{Cons}(x_1, l_1), \text{length}(l_1) = 1, x_1 + \text{sum}(l_1) = 2\}$$

(more precisely, to a less readable version of these terms where function definitions are unfolded into some pattern matching). The resulting set is blocked both by l_1 (in the first two terms) and x_1 (in $x_1 + \text{sum}(l_1)$). Expansion of these

---

[4] The example is provided at https://cedeela.fr/~simon/files/cade_17.tar.gz along with other benchmarks.

terms yields $\{\text{Nil}, \text{Cons}(x_2, l_2)\}$ and $\{Z, S(y_1)\}$, but the choice $\text{Cons}(x_2, l_2)$ is blocked by $\lfloor \text{depth} \leq 1 \rfloor$. The solver must choose $\lfloor l_1 := \text{Nil} \rfloor$, which entails

$$\text{length}(l) = 2 \xrightarrow{\rho}{}^{*}_{\{\lfloor l:=\text{Cons}(x_1, l_1) \rfloor\}} \text{length}(l_1) = 1 \xrightarrow{\rho}{}^{*}_{\{\lfloor l_1:=\text{Nil} \rfloor\}} 0 = 1 \xrightarrow{\rho}{}^{*}_{\emptyset} \bot$$

The conflict clause $\neg \lfloor l := \text{Cons}(x_1, l_1) \rfloor \vee \neg \lfloor l_1 := \text{Nil} \rfloor$ triggers an UNSAT result, but only because of the assumption $\lfloor \text{depth} \leq 1 \rfloor$.

The main loop (Algorithm 1) then proceeds to depth 2, and tries to solve the problem again under the assumption $\lfloor \text{depth} \leq 2 \rfloor$. The SAT solver can now pick $\lfloor l_1 := \text{Cons}(x_2, l_2) \rfloor$. At some point, it will pick $\lfloor l_2 := \text{Nil} \rfloor$ (the other choice is too deep), $\lfloor x_1 := S(y_1) \rfloor$, $\lfloor y_1 := Z \rfloor$, $\lfloor x_2 := S(y_2) \rfloor$, and $\lfloor y_2 := Z \rfloor$. Other choices would reduce one of the goals to $\bot$: once the shape of l_1 is fixed by the length constraint, $\text{rev}(l) = l$ reduces to $x_1 = x_2$ and $\text{sum}(l) = 2$ becomes $x_1 + x_2 = 2$, and wrong choices quickly reduce those to $\bot$. At this point, $\bigwedge_{t \in G} t \xrightarrow{\rho}{}^{*} \top$ and we obtain the model $l = \text{Cons}(1, \text{Cons}(1, \text{Nil}))$.

6 Extensions of the Language

6.1 Uninterpreted Types

Finding counter-example for programs and formalizations that use only recursive function definitions might still involve uninterpreted types arising from type Skolemization or abstract types. To handle those in SMBC, e.g. for a type τ, which corresponds to a finite set of domain elements denoted $\text{elt}_0(\tau), \text{elt}_1(\tau), \ldots$ (domain elements behave like constructors for evaluation). We also introduce *type slices* $\tau_{[0\ldots]}, \tau_{[1\ldots]}, \ldots$ where $\tau \overset{\text{def}}{=} \tau_{[0\ldots]}$. Conceptually, a type slice $\tau_{[n\ldots]}$ corresponds to the subtype of τ that excludes its n first elements: $\tau_{[n\ldots]} \overset{\text{def}}{=} \{\text{elt}_n(\tau),$ $\ldots, \text{elt}_{\text{card}(\tau)-1}(\tau)\}$. Then, we introduce propositional literals $\lfloor \text{empty}(\cdot) \rfloor$ that will be given a truth value by the SAT solver; if $\lfloor \text{empty}(\tau_{[n\ldots]}) \rfloor$ is true, it means $\tau_{[n\ldots]} \equiv \emptyset$; otherwise, it means $\tau_{[n\ldots]} \equiv \{\text{elt}_n(\tau) \cup \tau_{[n+1\ldots]}\}$. We assume $\neg \lfloor \text{empty}(\tau_{[0\ldots]}) \rfloor$. Expansion of some unknown $k : \tau_{[n\ldots]}$ yields the following boolean constraints:

$$\lfloor \text{empty}(\tau_{[n-1\ldots]}) \rfloor \Rightarrow \lfloor \text{empty}(\tau_{[n\ldots]}) \rfloor$$
$$\lfloor \text{depth} \leq n \rfloor \Rightarrow \lfloor \text{empty}(\tau_{[n\ldots]}) \rfloor$$
$$\lfloor k = \text{elt}_n(\tau) \rfloor \vee \left(\neg \lfloor \text{empty}(\tau_{[n+1\ldots]}) \rfloor \wedge \lfloor k := k' \rfloor \right)$$

where $k' : \tau_{[n+1\ldots]}$ is a fresh unknown belonging in the next slice of τ. To express constraints on τ, the input language provides finite quantifiers $\forall x : \tau. \ F$ and $\exists x : \tau. \ F$ (which abbreviates $\neg(\forall x : \tau. \ \neg F)$). The quantifier is interpreted with the following rules:

$$\frac{\rho(\lfloor \text{empty}(\tau_{[n\ldots]}) \rfloor) = \top}{\forall x : \tau_{[n\ldots]}. \ F \xrightarrow{\rho}{}_{\{\lfloor \text{empty}(\tau_{[n\ldots]}) \rfloor\}} \top} \text{ forall-empty}$$

$$\frac{\rho(\lfloor \text{empty}(\tau_{[n\ldots]}) \rfloor) = \bot}{\forall x : \tau_{[n\ldots]}. \ F \xrightarrow{\rho}{}_{\{\neg \lfloor \text{empty}(\tau_{[n\ldots]}) \rfloor\}} F[\text{elt}_n(\tau)/x] \wedge \left(\forall x : \tau_{[n+1\ldots]}. \ F \right)} \text{ forall-pair}$$

6.2 Functional Unknowns

With uninterpreted types often come functions taking arguments of uninterpreted types. We can also wish to synthesize (simple) functions taking booleans
or datatypes as parameters. It is possible to build functions by *refinement*, using
currying (considering only one argument at a time) depending on its argument's
type. Expansion of a functional unknown $f : a \to b$ depends on a:

- If $a = \mathsf{Bool}$, $f \in \{\lambda x.\ \text{if } x\ t_1\ t_2\}$ where $t_1, t_2 : b$ are fresh unknowns of type b
  that are deeper than f.
- If a is uninterpreted, f is $\lambda x.\ \mathsf{switch}(x, m)$ where m is a table mapping
  $(\mathsf{elt}_i(a))_{i=0\dots}$ to fresh unknowns of type b (built lazily, in practice) and switch
  is otherwise similar to case.
- If a is a datatype, f is either a constant function $\lambda x.\ k_f$ where k_f is an
  unknown of type b or $\lambda x.\ \mathsf{case}\ x\ \text{of}\ c_i(\overline{y}) \to k_i\ \overline{y}\ |\ \cdots$ end where each k_i is a
  fresh unknown taking the corresponding constructor's arguments as parame-
  ters. The constant case is used to be able to build functions that only peek
  superficially at inputs — otherwise, all function descriptions would be infinite
  in the model. The choice between the two forms for f is performed by the
  SAT solver; the non-constant case might be blocked by depth constraints. If
  a is infinite, bounded completeness is lost immediately, as we cannot generate
  all functions $a \to b$.
- Otherwise, a is a function type and we should reject the initial problem.

7 Refinements to the Calculus

7.1 Multiple Conflict Clauses

Sometimes, a partial model causes a failure for several reasons: in the presence of
parallel conjunction, both formulas can reduce to $\bot$. It would be wasteful to keep
only one reason, because all of them might be useful to prune other branches.
In this case, instead of just picking one explanation and discard the others, as
suggested in Fig. 2, we add a new explanation constructor, $e_1 \oplus e_2$, that combines
two unrelated explanations, such that $\oplus$ is associative and commutative and
$(e_1 \oplus e_2) \cup e_3 \equiv (e_1 \cup e_3) \oplus (e_2 \cup e_3)$. Intuitively, $a \xrightarrow{\rho}_{e_1 \oplus e_2} b$ means that a
evaluates to b under substitution ρ assuming the choices in e_1 or in e_2 are made
— those choices are never incompatible, but they might not be the same subset
of $\mathsf{subst}(M)$. We add a new rule for $\wedge$:

$$\frac{a \xrightarrow{\rho}{}^{*}_{e_a} \bot \qquad b \xrightarrow{\rho}{}^{*}_{e_b} \bot}{a \wedge b \xrightarrow{\rho}_{e_a \oplus e_b} \bot} \textbf{ and-left-right}$$

In case of conflict $\bigwedge_{t \in G} \xrightarrow{\rho}{}^{*}_{\oplus_{i \in I} e_i} \bot$, we obtain a set of conflict clauses
$\{\bigvee_{a \in e_i} \neg a \mid i \in I\}$ that will prune distinct parts of the partial model.

7.2 Unification Rules

Equality already has many rules, but we can optimize it further. In our implementation, relying on hash-consing, we simplify $t = t$ into $\top$ in constant time, even when t contains unassigned unknowns. We can optimize equality further in the special case where reduction leads to a term $c(t_1, \ldots, t_n) = k$ or $k = c(t_1, \ldots, t_n)$ where k is an unknown and c a constructor or domain element. This term reduces with no explanation to if $\mathsf{check}_{\llbracket k \,:=\, c(u_1,\ldots,u_n)\rrbracket}\ (\bigwedge_{i=1}^{n} t_i = u_i)\ \bot$, where $\mathsf{check}_{\llbracket k \,:=\, c(u_1,\ldots,u_n)\rrbracket} : \mathsf{Bool}$ is a new term construct that requires $c(u_1, \ldots, u_n)$ to be one of the cases resulting from the expansion of k. In the $\bot$ case, the explanation forces the SAT solver to pick $c(u_1, \ldots, u_n)$ instead of ruling out the wrong choice $d(u_1, \ldots, u_m)$; if there are more than two constructors, this forces directly the right choice instead of trying every wrong choice.

$$\frac{c(u_1, \ldots, u_n) \text{ is a case of } k}{k = c(t_1, \ldots, t_n) \xrightarrow{\rho}_{\emptyset} \text{ if } \mathsf{check}_{\llbracket k \,:=\, c(u_1,\ldots,u_n)\rrbracket}\ (\bigwedge_{i=1}^{n} t_i = u_i)\ \bot} \ \text{unify}$$

$$\frac{\rho(k) = c(u_1, \ldots, u_n)}{\mathsf{check}_{\llbracket k \,:=\, c(u_1,\ldots,u_n)\rrbracket} \xrightarrow{\rho}_{\{k:=c(u_1,\ldots,u_n)\}} \top} \ \text{check-true}$$

$$\frac{\rho(k) = d(u_1, \ldots, u_m) \qquad d \neq c}{\mathsf{check}_{\llbracket k \,:=\, c(u_1,\ldots,u_n)\rrbracket} \xrightarrow{\rho}_{\{\neg(k:=c(u_1,\ldots,u_n))\}} \bot} \ \text{check-false}$$

8 Implementation

We implemented SMBC in OCaml[5] using a modular SAT solver[6] that is flexible enough that we can add clauses dynamically and parameterize it with a theory solver. It also supports incremental solving under assumptions, which is necessary for the efficiency of the iterative deepening exploration. The core solver is around 3,200 lines long, including the term data structures, the symbolic evaluation and the main loop. This implementation is a prototype that can be used, but we believe it could be made much faster with more work and perhaps by using a lower-level language. The code is free software, under a permissive license.

Our description of evaluation rules in Fig. 2 is quite high-level and can be implemented in various ways.[7] We chose to represent terms as perfectly shared directed acyclic graphs in which binders and bound variables rely on De Bruijn indices. The perfect sharing diminishes memory usage and makes let statements superfluous. We store in every term a pointer to a pair (explanation, term) that

---

[5] https://github.com/c-cube/smbc/.

[6] https://github.com/Gbury/mSAT.

[7] For example, it might be possible to write an efficient interpreter or compiler for use-cases where evaluation is the bottleneck, as long as explanations are tracked accurately and parallel conjunction is accounted for.

stores the current normal form of this term, effectively implementing a crude form of memoization. Any assignment of this pair must be undone upon backtracking — in a similar way as in congruence closure algorithms [3]. Similarly, unknowns are records with mutable pointers to a list of possible cases (once they have been expanded) and to their current assignment, which is reverted during backjumping thanks to a central backtracking stack that is controlled by the SAT solver. A good representation of explanations is required for efficiency, because union will be performed very often during the evaluation of terms and should be as fast as possible.

In addition, the evaluation function performs acyclicity checks to prune impossible branches early, and aggressively caches the normal forms of terms, stashing their old value on the central backtracking stack. Since we follow the architecture proposed by Barrett et al. [3], SMBC can delegate all branching to the SAT solver. Every time a boolean decision is made by the SAT solver (followed by propagation), the evaluation engine is called so as to prune bad models early. It does so by re-evaluating the set of goals G, which must contain at least one term not reduced yet, and cannot contain $\bot$ (see Algorithm 2). This re-evaluation is made faster by starting from the cached normal forms instead of the original goals. If all goals in G reduce to $\top$, the model is valid; if one of them reduces to $\bot$, the SAT solver immediately receives a conflict clause that will make it backtrack.

9   Experiments

We ran a few experiments to compare SMBC with other approaches, namely LSC, HBMC, CVC4 [17], and Inox, a standalone version of Leon [19]. We do not compare against QuickCheck, SmallCheck, or Feat, because they are not designed to solve such tightly constrained problems. All the data and the code of SMBC can be found at https://cedeela.fr/~simon/files/cade_17.tar.gz. For this experiment, we wrote some problems and borrowed some others from HBMC's test suite. We tried to pick diversified benchmarks so as to expose the strengths and weaknesses of each tool. TIP does not come yet with an exhaustive set of satisfiable benchmarks that would rely primarily on recursive functions. Benchmarks from our previous work on CVC4 [17] are expressed in SMT-LIB rather than TIP and use quantified axioms instead of recursive definitions, which makes them hard to use in our purely computational setting. The same holds of SMT-LIB and TPTP in general.

The solvers were run on a 4-cores Intel i5 CPU with 60 seconds timeout and a limit of 8 GB of RAM. Below, we give some numbers in Table 1 and then analyse the results on some categories of problems. The second column of the table is the number of satisfiable and unsatisfiable problems. Categories out of scope are marked with "–".

Table 1. Results of the Experiments

Problems	(SAT–UNSAT)	SMBC	HBMC	LSC	CVC4	Inox
Expr	(3–1)	2–0	**3–0**	2–0	0–0	**3–0**
Fold	(2–0)	**2–0**	–	–	–	–
Palindromes	(1–2)	**1–2**	1–1	0–0	0–0	0–1
Pigeon	(0–1)	**0–1**	–	–	**0–1**	0–0
Regex	(12–0)	7–0	2–0	**11–0**	–	0–0
Sorted	(2–2)	**2–2**	**2–2**	2–0	0–1	2–1
Sudoku	(1–0)	**1–0**	**1–0**	0–0	0–0	0–0
Type Checking	(2–0)	**2–0**	**2–0**	0–0	0–0	0–0

Expr. Given arithmetic expressions, an evaluation function and several flawed simplifications, the goal is to find an expression such that its simplification does not evaluate to the same term. Here HBMC and Inox shine, but SMBC and LSC have more trouble due to the large branching factor of the search tree.

Fold. Those examples are about synthesizing a function that distinguishes between lists by only looking at one element at a time (plus an accumulator). In other words, we fold a function f on all elements, and the goal is to pick f such that it can distinguish between close, but distinct, lists. This problem is outside the scope of all the tools the author knows about, simply because it combines an uninterpreted type with an unknown of function type, but SMBC has no problem synthesizing what is in essence a state machine transition function.

Palindromes. After defining unary natural numbers and lists, we look for lists that are palindromes (i.e., $rev(l) = l$) that have some additional constraint on their sum or length. Some of those problems are more difficult variations of the problem from Sect. 5.1. Some of the problems are satisfiable and some are unsatisfiable. For example, the goal in long_rev_sum2.smt2 is to disprove the existence of a palindrome of length 200 with sum 1; HBMC times out because there are too many computations, and LSC cannot detect unsatisfiability. Those problems are easy but the toplevel goal is a parallel conjunction that needs to be treated properly, which is why LSC fails to solve even the satisfiable instances.

Pigeon. A computational version of the classical pigeon hole problem, here with 4 holes for 5 pigeons. This requires handling uninterpreted types and unsatisfiable problems.

Regex. Basic regular expressions are represented by a datatype featuring constants, star, and disjunction. The goal is generally to find a regular expression that matches a given string. Here, LSC shines and HBMC is in trouble, because (comparatively) many computations are required to check each input. SMBC has a good success rate here, even though its relatively naive interpreter is much slower than LSC's native compiled code.

Sorted. Some problems about finding sorted lists of natural numbers that have additional properties (on their length, reverse, sum, etc.). The problems are fairly easy, but some of them are unsatisfiable.

Sudoku. A sudoku is represented as a list of lists of a datatype with 9 constructors. Some functions to check whether the sudoku is valid (no duplicate in any line, column or block) are defined, an initial state is given, and the goal is simply to solve the sudoku. This is also a combinatorial problem on which HBMC takes only 2 s, SMBC takes 12 s, and LSC times out. Here, it pays to bit-blast because the SAT solver can propagate constraints among the sudoku cells.

Type Checking. This example comes from the HBMC draft report [7]. Terms of the simply typed λ-calculus are defined by a datatype (variables being mapped to De Bruijn indices), along with a type-checking function that takes a term t, a type τ and an environment Γ (i.e. a list of types), and returns $\top$ iff $\Gamma \vdash t : \tau$ holds. The goal is to find a term that has type $(a \to b) \to (b \to c) \to (a \to c)$ in the empty environment: in other words, to synthesize the composition operator from its type. The task is difficult because of the fast growth of the search space, in which LSC drowns, but SMBC manages well.

Overall, SMBC appears to be well balanced and to have good results both on problems that require computations and on problems where pruning of impossible cases is critical. Given the simplicity of our implementation, we believe these results are promising, and that SMBC occupies a sweet spot between handling computations well and traversing the search space in a smart way.

10   Conclusion

After describing a new technique for finding models in a logic of computable functions and datatypes, we presented ways of extending the language and described a working implementation. By combining symbolic evaluation with SAT-based conflict analysis, the approach is aimed at difficult problems where the search space is large (e.g., because of parallel disjunction and independent sub-problems) and large amounts of computations must be performed before discovering failure. It can be described as a spiritual heir to evaluation-driven narrowing [14] that replaces traditional exploration of the space of possible inputs by conflict driven clause learning. We hope that this work will benefit model finders in proof assistants, in particular Nunchaku [9,17].

Acknowledgments. The author would like to thank Jasmin Blanchette, Martin Brain, Raphaël Cauderlier, Koen Claessen, Pascal Fontaine, Andrew Reynolds, and Martin Riener, and the anonymous reviewers, for discussing details of this work and suggesting textual improvements.

References

1. Antoy, S., Echahed, R., Hanus, M.: A needed narrowing strategy. J. ACM (JACM) **47**, 776–822 (2000)
2. Barrett, C., Fontaine, P., Tinelli, C.: The SMT-LIB Standard Version 2.6 (2016). http://www.SMT-LIB.org
3. Barrett, C., Nieuwenhuis, R., Oliveras, A., Tinelli, C.: Splitting on demand in SAT modulo theories. In: Hermann, M., Voronkov, A. (eds.) LPAR 2006. LNCS, vol. 4246, pp. 512–526. Springer, Heidelberg (2006). doi:10.1007/11916277_35
4. Barrett, C., Shikanian, I., Tinelli, C.: An abstract decision procedure for satisfiability in the theory of recursive data types. Electron. Notes Theor. Comput. Sci. **174**(8), 23–37 (2007)
5. Claessen, K., Hughes, J.: QuickCheck: a lightweight tool for random testing of Haskell programs. ACM Sigplan Not. **46**(4), 53–64 (2011)
6. Claessen, K., Johansson, M., Rosén, D., Smallbone, N.: TIP: tons of inductive problems. In: Kerber, M., Carette, J., Kaliszyk, C., Rabe, F., Sorge, V. (eds.) CICM 2015. LNCS, vol. 9150, pp. 333–337. Springer, Cham (2015). doi:10.1007/978-3-319-20615-8_23
7. Claessen, K., Rosén, D.: SAT-based bounded model checking for functional programs (2016) (unpublished). https://github.com/danr/hbmc
8. The Coq Development Team. The Coq Proof Assistant. http://coq.inria.fr/
9. Cruanes, S., Blanchette, J.C.: Extending Nunchaku to dependent type theory. In: Blanchette, J.C., Kaliszyk, C. (eds.) Proceedings First International Workshop on Hammers for Type Theories, HaTT@IJCAR 2016. EPTCS, vol. 210, Coimbra, Portugal, pp. 3–12, 1 July 2016
10. Duregård, J., Jansson, P., Wang, M.: Feat: functional enumeration of algebraic types. ACM SIGPLAN Not. **47**(12), 61–72 (2013)
11. Hanus, M.: A unified computation model for functional and logic programming. In: Proceedings of the 24th ACM SIGPLAN-SIGACT Symposium on Principles of Programming Languages. ACM (1997)
12. Kaufmann, M., Moore, S.J.: ACL2: an industrial strength version of Nqthm. In: Computer Assurance, COMPASS 1996, pp. 23–34. IEEE (1996)
13. Korf, R.E.: Depth-first iterative-deepening: an optimal admissible tree search. Artif. Intell. **27**(1), 97–109 (1985)
14. Lindblad, F.: Property directed generation of first-order test data. In: Trends in Functional Programming, pp. 105–123. Citeseer (2007)
15. Paulson, L.C.: Isabelle: A Generic Theorem Prover, vol. 828. Springer, Heidelberg (1994)
16. Reynolds, A., Blanchette, J.C.: A decision procedure for (Co)datatypes in SMT solvers. In: Felty, A.P., Middeldorp, A. (eds.) CADE 2015. LNCS, vol. 9195, pp. 197–213. Springer, Cham (2015). doi:10.1007/978-3-319-21401-6_13
17. Reynolds, A., Blanchette, J.C., Cruanes, S., Tinelli, C.: Model finding for recursive functions in SMT. In: Olivetti, N., Tiwari, A. (eds.) IJCAR 2016. LNCS (LNAI), vol. 9706, pp. 133–151. Springer, Cham (2016). doi:10.1007/978-3-319-40229-1_10
18. Runciman, C., Naylor, M., Lindblad, F.: Smallcheck and lazy smallcheck: automatic exhaustive testing for small values. ACM SIGPLAN Not. **44**, 37–48 (2008). ACM
19. Suter, P., Köksal, A.S., Kuncak, V.: Satisfiability modulo recursive programs. In: Yahav, E. (ed.) SAS 2011. LNCS, vol. 6887, pp. 298–315. Springer, Heidelberg (2011). doi:10.1007/978-3-642-23702-7_23

Short Proofs Without New Variables

Marijn J.H. Heule[1(✉)], Benjamin Kiesl[2], and Armin Biere[3]

[1] Department of Computer Science, The University of Texas at Austin, Austin, USA
marijn@cs.utexas.edu
[2] Institute of Information Systems, Vienna University of Technology, Vienna, Austria
[3] Institute for Formal Models and Verification, JKU Linz, Linz, Austria

Abstract. Adding and removing redundant clauses is at the core of state-of-the-art SAT solving. Crucial is the ability to add short clauses whose redundancy can be determined in polynomial time. We present a characterization of the strongest notion of clause redundancy (i.e., addition of the clause preserves satisfiability) in terms of an implication relationship. By using a polynomial-time decidable implication relation based on unit propagation, we thus obtain an efficiently checkable redundancy notion. A proof system based on this notion is surprisingly strong, even without the introduction of new variables—the key component of short proofs presented in the proof complexity literature. We demonstrate this strength on the famous pigeon hole formulas by providing short clausal proofs without new variables.

1 Introduction

Satisfiability (SAT) solvers are used for determining the correctness of hardware and software systems [1,2]. It is therefore crucial that these solvers justify their claims by providing proofs that can be independently verified. This holds also for various other applications that use SAT solvers. Just recently, long-standing mathematical problems were solved using SAT, including the Erdős Discrepancy Problem [3] and the Pythagorean Triples Problem [4]. Especially in such cases, proofs are at the center of attention, and without them, the result of a solver is almost worthless. What the mathematical problems and the industrial applications have in common, is that proofs are often of considerable size—in the case of the Pythagorean Triples Problem about 200 terabytes. As the size of proofs is influenced by the strength of the underlying proof system, the search for shorter proofs goes hand in hand with the search for stronger proof systems.

In this paper, we introduce highly expressive clausal proof systems that are closely related to state-of-the-art SAT solving. Informally, a clausal proof system allows the addition of redundant clauses to a formula in conjunctive normal form (CNF). Here, a clause is considered *redundant* if its addition preserves satisfiability. If the repeated addition of clauses allows us finally to add the

---

This work has been supported by the National Science Foundation under grant CCF-1526760 and the Austrian Science Fund (FWF) under project W1255-N23.

L. de Moura (Ed.): CADE 2017, LNAI 10395, pp. 130–147, 2017.
DOI: 10.1007/978-3-319-63046-5_9

empty clause—which is, by definition, unsatisfiable—the unsatisfiability of the original formula has been established.

Since satisfiability equivalence is not efficiently decidable, practical proof systems only allow the addition of a clause if it fulfills some efficiently decidable criterion that ensures redundancy. For instance, the popular DRAT proof system [5], which is the de-facto standard in practical SAT solving, only allows the addition of so-called *resolution asymmetric tautologies* [6]. Given a formula and a clause, one can decide in polynomial time whether the clause is a resolution asymmetric tautology with respect to the formula and therefore the soundness of DRAT proofs can be efficiently checked.

We present new redundancy criteria by introducing a characterization of clause redundancy based on a simple implication relationship between formulas. By replacing the logical implication relation in this characterization with stronger notions of implication that are computable in polynomial time, we then obtain powerful redundancy criteria that are still efficiently decidable. We show that these redundancy criteria not only generalize earlier ones like the above-mentioned resolution asymmetric tautologies or *set-blocked clauses* [7], but that they are also related to other concepts from the literature, namely *autarkies* [8], *safe assignments* [9], *variable instantiation* [10], and *symmetry breaking* [11].

Proof systems based on our new redundancy criteria turn out to be highly expressive, even without the introduction of new variables. This is in contrast to resolution, which is considered relatively weak as long as one does not allow the introduction of new variables via definitions as in the stronger proof system of *extended resolution* [12,13]. The introduction of new variables, however, has a major drawback: the search space of variables and clauses one could possibly add to a proof is infinite, even when bounding the size of clauses. Finding useful clauses with new variables is therefore hard in practice, although there have been a few successes in the past [14,15].

We illustrate the strength of our strongest proof system by providing short clausal proofs for the famous pigeon hole formulas without introducing new variables. The size of the proofs is linear in the size of the formulas and the longest clauses in the proofs have length two. In these proofs, we add redundant clauses that are similar in nature to symmetry-breaking predicates [11,16]. To verify the correctness of proofs in our new system, we implemented a proof checker. The checker is built on top of DRAT-trim [5], the checker used to validate the unsatisfiability results of the recent SAT competitions [17]. We compare our proofs with existing proofs of the pigeon hole formulas in other proof systems and show that our new proofs are much smaller and cheaper to validate.

2 Preliminaries

We consider propositional formulas in *conjunctive normal form* (CNF), which are defined as follows. A *literal* is either a variable x (a *positive literal*) or the negation $\overline{x}$ of a variable x (a *negative literal*). The *complementary literal* $\overline{l}$ of a literal l is defined as $\overline{l} = \overline{x}$ if $l = x$ and $\overline{l} = x$ if $l = \overline{x}$. Accordingly, for a set L

of literals, we define $\overline{L} = \{\overline{l} \mid l \in L\}$. A *clause* is a disjunction of literals. If not stated otherwise, we assume that clauses do not contain complementary literals. A *formula* is a conjunction of clauses. We view clauses as sets of literals and formulas as sets of clauses. For a set L of literals and a formula F, we define $F_L = \{C \in F \mid C \cap L \neq \emptyset\}$. We sometimes write F_l to denote $F_{\{l\}}$.

An *assignment* is a partial function from a set of variables to the truth values 1 (*true*) and 0 (*false*). An assignment is *total* w.r.t. a formula if it assigns a truth value to every variable occurring in the formula. A literal l is *satisfied* (*falsified*) by an assignment α if l is positive and $\alpha(var(l)) = 1$ ($\alpha(var(l)) = 0$, respectively) or if it is negative and $\alpha(var(l)) = 0$ ($\alpha(var(l)) = 1$, respectively). We often denote assignments by the sequences of literals they satisfy. For instance, $x\,\overline{y}$ denotes the assignment that assigns x to 1 and y to 0. A clause is satisfied by an assignment α if it contains a literal that is satisfied by α. Finally, a formula is satisfied by an assignment α if all its clauses are satisfied by α. A formula is *satisfiable* if there exists an assignment that satisfies it. Two formulas are *logically equivalent* if they are satisfied by the same assignments. Two formulas F and F' are *satisfiability equivalent* if F is satisfiable if and only if F' is satisfiable.

We denote the empty clause by $\bot$ and the satisfied clause by $\top$. Given an assignment α and a clause C, we define $C|_\alpha = \top$ if α satisfies C, otherwise $C|_\alpha$ denotes the result of removing from C all the literals falsified by α. Moreover, for a formula F, we define $F|_\alpha = \{C|_\alpha \mid C \in F \text{ and } C|_\alpha \neq \top\}$. We say that a clause C *blocks* an assignment α if $C = \{x \mid \alpha(x) = 0\} \cup \{\overline{x} \mid \alpha(x) = 1\}$. A *unit clause* is a clause that contains only one literal. The result of applying the *unit clause rule* to a formula F is the formula $F|_\alpha$ with α being the assignment that satisfies exactly the unit clauses in F. The iterated application of the unit clause rule to a formula, until no unit clauses are left, is called *unit propagation*. If unit propagation yields the empty clause $\bot$, we say that it derived a *conflict*.

By $F \vDash F'$, we denote that F implies F', i.e., all assignments satisfying F also satisfy F'. Furthermore, by $F \vdash_1 F'$ we denote that for every clause $C \in F'$, unit propagation of the negated literals of C on F derives a conflict (thereby, the negated literals of C are viewed as unit clauses). For example, $x \wedge y \vdash_1 (x \vee z) \wedge y$, since unit propagation of the unit clauses $\overline{x}$ and $\overline{z}$ derives a conflict with x, and propagation of $\overline{y}$ derives a conflict with y. Similarly, $F \vdash_0 F'$ denotes that every clause in F' is subsumed by (i.e., is a superset of) a clause in F. Observe that $F \supseteq F'$ implies $F \vdash_0 F'$, $F \vdash_0 F'$ implies $F \vdash_1 F'$, and $F \vdash_1 F'$ implies $F \vDash F'$.

3   Clause Redundancy and Clausal Proofs

In this section, we introduce a formal notion of clause redundancy and demonstrate how it provides the basis for clausal proof systems. We start by introducing clause redundancy [7]:

Definition 1. *A clause C is* redundant *w.r.t. a formula F if F and $F \cup \{C\}$ are satisfiability equivalent.*

For instance, the clause $C = x \vee y$ is redundant w.r.t. $F = \{\overline{x} \vee \overline{y}\}$ since F and $F \cup \{C\}$ are satisfiability equivalent (although they are not logically equivalent). Since this notion of redundancy allows us to add redundant clauses to a formula without affecting its satisfiability, it gives rise to clausal proof systems.

Definition 2. *A proof of a clause C_m from a formula F is a sequence of pairs $(C_1, \omega_1), \ldots, (C_m, \omega_m)$, where each C_i $(1 \leq i \leq m)$ is a clause that is redundant w.r.t. $F \cup \{C_j \mid 1 \leq j < i\}$, and this redundancy can be efficiently checked using the (arbitrary) witness ω_i. If $C_m = \bot$, the proof is a refutation of F.*

Clearly, since every clause-addition step preserves satisfiability, and since the empty clause is unsatisfiable, a refutation certifies the unsatisfiability of F due to transitivity. Note that the ω_i can be arbitrary witnesses (they can be assignments, or even left out if no explicit witness is needed) that certify the redundancy of C_i w.r.t. $F \cup \{C_j \mid 1 \leq j < i\}$, and by requiring that the redundancy can be *efficiently checked*, we mean that it can be checked in polynomial time w.r.t. the size of $F \cup \{C_j \mid 1 \leq j < i\}$.

By specifying in detail what kind of redundant clauses—and corresponding witnesses—one can add to a proof, we obtain concrete proof systems. This is usually done by defining an efficiently checkable syntactic criterion that guarantees that clauses fulfilling this criterion are redundant. A popular example for a clausal proof system is DRAT [5], the de-facto standard for unsatisfiability proofs in practical SAT solving. DRAT allows the addition of a clause if it is a so-called *resolution asymmetric tautology* [6] (RAT, defined in the next section). As it can be efficiently checked whether a clause is a RAT, and since RATs cover a large portion of redundant clauses, the DRAT proof system is very powerful.

The strength of a clausal proof system depends on the generality of the underlying redundancy criterion. We say that a redundancy criterion $\mathcal{R}_1$ is *more general* than a redundancy criterion $\mathcal{R}_2$ if, whenever $\mathcal{R}_2$ identifies a clause C as redundant w.r.t. a formula F, then $\mathcal{R}_1$ also identifies C as redundant w.r.t. F. For instance, whenever a clause is subsumed in some formula, it is a RAT w.r.t. that formula. Therefore, the RAT redundancy criterion is more general than the subsumption criterion. In the next section, we develop redundancy criteria that are even more general than RAT. This gives rise to proof systems that are stronger than DRAT but still closely related to practical SAT solving.

4   Clause Redundancy via Implication

In the following, we introduce a characterization of clause redundancy that reduces the question whether a clause is redundant w.r.t. a certain formula to a simple question of implication. The advantage of this is that we can replace the logical implication relation by stronger, polynomially decidable implication relations to derive powerful redundancy criteria that are still efficiently checkable. These redundancy criteria can then be used to obtain highly expressive clausal proof systems.

Our characterization is based on the observation that a clause in a CNF formula can be seen as a constraint that blocks those assignments falsifying the clause. Therefore, a clause can be safely added to a formula if it does not constrain the formula too much. What we mean by this, is that after adding the clause, there should still exist other assignments (i.e., assignments not blocked by the clause) under which the formula is at least as satisfiable as under the assignments blocked by the clause. Consider the following example:

Example 1. Let $F = \{x \vee y,\ x \vee z,\ \overline{x} \vee y \vee z\}$ and consider the (unit) clause $C = x$ which blocks all assignments that assign x to 0. The addition of C to F does not affect satisfiability: Let $\alpha = \overline{x}$ and $\omega = x$. Then, $F|\alpha = \{y,\ z\}$ while $F|\omega = \{y \vee z\}$. Clearly, every satisfying assignment of $F|\alpha$ is also a satisfying assignment of $F|\omega$ (i.e., $F|\alpha \vDash F|\omega$). Thus, F is at least as satisfiable under ω as it is under α. Moreover, ω satisfies C. The addition of C does therefore not affect the satisfiability of F. □

This motivates the characterization of clause redundancy we introduce next. Note that for a given clause C, "*the* assignment α blocked by C" can be a partial assignment, meaning that C actually rules out all assignments that extend α:

Theorem 1. *Let F be a formula, C a clause, and α the assignment blocked by C. Then, C is redundant w.r.t. F if and only if there exists an assignment ω such that ω satisfies C and $F|\alpha \vDash F|\omega$.*

Proof. For the "only if" direction, assume that F and $F \cup \{C\}$ are satisfiability equivalent. If $F|\alpha$ is unsatisfiable, then $F|\alpha \vDash F|\omega$ for every ω, hence the statement trivially holds. Assume now that $F|\alpha$ is satisfiable, implying that F is satisfiable. Then, since F and $F \cup \{C\}$ are satisfiability equivalent, there exists an assignment ω that satisfies both F and C. Since ω satisfies F, it holds that $F|\omega = \emptyset$ and so $F|\alpha \vDash F|\omega$.

For the "if" direction, assume that there exists an assignment ω such that ω satisfies C and $F|\alpha \vDash F|\omega$. Now, let γ be a (total) assignment that satisfies F and assume it falsifies C. As γ falsifies C, it coincides with α on $var(\alpha)$. Therefore, since γ satisfies F, it must satisfy $F|\alpha$ and since $F|\alpha \vDash F|\omega$ it must also satisfy $F|\omega$. Now, consider the following assignment γ':

$$\gamma'(x) = \begin{cases} \omega(x) & \text{if } x \in var(\omega), \\ \gamma(x) & \text{otherwise.} \end{cases}$$

Clearly, since ω satisfies C, γ' also satisfies C. Moreover, as γ satisfies $F|\omega$ and $var(F|\omega) \subseteq var(\gamma) \setminus var(\omega)$, γ' satisfies F. Hence, γ' satisfies $F \cup \{C\}$. □

This alternative characterization of redundancy allows us to replace the logical implication relation by stronger polynomially decidable relations. For instance, we can replace the condition $F|\alpha \vDash F|\omega$ by the stronger condition $F|\alpha \vdash_1 F|\omega$ (likewise, we could also use relations such as "$\vdash_0$" or "$\supseteq$" instead of "$\vdash_1$"). Now, if we are given a clause C—which implicitly gives us the blocked assignment α— and a *witnessing assignment* ω, then we can check in polynomial time whether

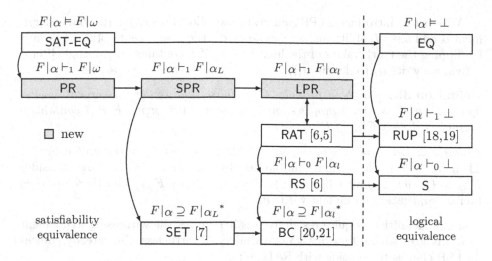

Fig. 1. Landscape of redundancy notions. SAT-EQ stands for all redundant clauses and EQ for implied clauses. A path from X to Y indicates that X is more general than Y. The asterisk (*) denotes that the exact characterization implies the shown one, e.g., for every set-blocked clause, the property $F|\alpha \supseteq F|\alpha_L$ holds, but not vice versa.

$F|\alpha \vdash_1 F|\omega$, implying that C is redundant w.r.t. F. We can therefore use this implication-based redundancy notion to define proof systems. A proof is then a sequence $(C_1, \omega_1), \dots, (C_m, \omega_m)$ where the ω_i are the witnessing assignments.

In the following, we use the propagation-implication relation "$\vdash_1$" to define the redundancy criteria of (1) *literal-propagation redundancy* (LPR), (2) *set-propagation redundancy* (SPR), and (3) *propagation redundancy* (PR). Basically, the three notions differ in the way we allow the witnessing assignment ω to differ from the assignment α blocked by a clause. The more freedom we give to ω, the more general the redundancy notion we obtain. We show that LPR clauses—the least general of the three—coincide with RAT. For the more general SPR clauses, we show that they generalize set-blocked clauses (SET) [7], which is not the case for LPR clauses. Finally, PR clauses are the most general ones. They give rise to an extremely powerful proof system that is still closely related to CDCL-based SAT solving. The new landscape of redundancy notions we thereby obtain is illustrated in Fig. 1. In the figure, RUP stands for the redundancy notion based on reverse unit propagation [18,19], S stands for subsumed clauses, RS for clauses with subsumed resolvents [6], and BC for blocked clauses [20,21].

As we will see, when defining proof systems based on LPR (e.g., the DRAT system) or SPR clauses, we do not need to add the explicit redundancy witnesses (i.e., the witnessing assignments ω) to a proof. In these two cases, a proof can thus just be seen as a sequence of clauses. A proof system based on SPR clauses can therefore have the same syntax as DRAT proofs, which makes it "downwards compatible". This is in contrast to a proof system based on PR clauses where, at least in general, we have to add the witnessing assignments to a proof, otherwise we cannot check the redundancy of a clause in polynomial time.

We start by introducing LPR clauses. In the following, given a (partial) assignment α and a set L of literals, we denote by α_L the assignment obtained from α by flipping the truth values of the literals in L. If L contains only a single literal l, then we write α_l to denote $\alpha_{\{l\}}$.

Definition 3. *Let F be a formula, C a clause, and α the assignment blocked by C. Then, C is literal-propagation redundant (LPR) w.r.t. F if it contains a literal l such that $F|\alpha \vdash_1 F|\alpha_l$.*

Example 2. Let $F = \{x \vee y,\ x \vee \overline{y} \vee z,\ \overline{x} \vee z\}$ and let C be the unit clause x. Then, $\alpha = \overline{x}$ is the assignment blocked by C, and $\alpha_x = x$. Now, consider $F|\alpha = \{y,\ \overline{y} \vee z\}$ and $F|\alpha_x = \{z\}$. Clearly, $F|\alpha \vdash_1 F|\alpha_x$ and therefore C is literal-propagation redundant w.r.t. F. □

The LPR definition is quite restrictive, as it requires the witnessing assignment α_l to disagree with α on exactly one variable. Nevertheless, this already suffices for LPR clauses to coincide with RATs [6]:

Definition 4. *Let F be a formula and C a clause. Then, C is a resolution asymmetric tautology (RAT) w.r.t. F if it contains a literal l such that, for every clause $D \in F_{\overline{l}}$, $F \vdash_1 C \cup (D \setminus \{\overline{l}\})$.*

Theorem 2. *A clause C is literal-propagation redundant w.r.t. a formula F if and only if it is a resolution asymmetric tautology w.r.t. F.*

Proof. For the "only if" direction, assume that C is LPR w.r.t. F, i.e., it contains a literal l such that $F|\alpha \vdash_1 F|\alpha_l$. Now, let $D \in F_{\overline{l}}$. We have to show that $F \vdash_1 C \cup (D \setminus \{\overline{l}\})$. First, note that $F|\alpha$ is exactly the result of propagating the negated literals of C on F (i.e., applying the unit clause rule with the negated literals of C but not performing further propagations). Moreover, since α_l falsifies $\overline{l}$, it follows that $D|\alpha_l \subseteq (D \setminus \{\overline{l}\})$. But then, since $F|\alpha \vdash_1 D|\alpha_l$, it must hold that $F \vdash_1 C \cup (D \setminus \{\overline{l}\})$, hence C is a RAT w.r.t. F.

For the "if" direction, assume that C is a RAT w.r.t. F, i.e., it contains a literal l such that, for every clause $D \in F_{\overline{l}}$, $F \vdash_1 C \cup (D \setminus \{\overline{l}\})$. Now, let $D|\alpha_l \in F|\alpha_l$ for $D \in F$. We have to show that $F|\alpha \vdash_1 D|\alpha_l$. Since α_l satisfies l and α falsifies C, D does neither contain l nor any negations of literals in C except for possibly $\overline{l}$. If D does not contain $\overline{l}$, then $D|\alpha = D|\alpha_l$ is contained in $F|\alpha$ and hence the claim immediately follows. Assume therefore that $\overline{l} \in D$.

As argued in the proof for the other direction, propagating the negated literals of C (and no other literals) on F yields $F|\alpha$. Therefore, since $F \vdash_1 C \cup (D \setminus \{\overline{l}\})$ and $D \setminus \{\overline{l}\}$ does not contain any negations of literals in C (which could otherwise be the reason for a unit propagation conflict that only happens because of C containing a literal whose negation is contained in $D \setminus \{\overline{l}\}$), it must be the case that $F|\alpha \vdash_1 D \setminus \{\overline{l}\}$. Now, the only literals of $D \setminus \{\overline{l}\}$ that are not contained in $D|\alpha_l$ are the ones falsified by α, but those are anyhow not contained in $F|\alpha$. It follows that $F|\alpha \vdash_1 D|\alpha_l$ and thus C is LPR w.r.t. F. □

By allowing the witnessing assignments to disagree with α on more than only one literal, we obtain the more general notion of set-propagation-redundant clauses:

Definition 5. *Let F be a formula, C a clause, and α the assignment blocked by C. Then, C is* set-propagation redundant (SPR) *w.r.t. F if it contains a non-empty set L of literals such that $F|\alpha \vdash_1 F|\alpha_L$.*

Example 3. Let $F = \{x \vee y,\; x \vee \overline{y} \vee z,\; \overline{x} \vee z,\; \overline{x} \vee u,\; \overline{u} \vee x\}$, $C = x \vee u$, and $L = \{x, u\}$. Then, $\alpha = \overline{x}\,\overline{u}$ is the assignment blocked by C, and $\alpha_L = x\,u$. Now, consider $F|\alpha = \{y,\; \overline{y} \vee z\}$ and $F|\alpha_L = \{z\}$. Clearly, $F|\alpha \vdash_1 F|\alpha_L$ and so C is set-propagation redundant w.r.t. F. Note also that C is not literal-propagation redundant w.r.t. F.   □

Since L is a subset of C, we do not need to add it (or the assignment α_L) explicitly to an SPR proof. By requiring that L must consist of the first literals of C when adding C to a proof (viewing a clause as a sequence of literals), we can ensure that the SPR property is efficiently decidable. For instance, when a proof contains the clause $l_1 \vee \cdots \vee l_n$, we first check whether the SPR property holds under the assumption that $L = \{l_1\}$. If not, we proceed by assuming that $L = \{l_1, l_2\}$, and so on until $L = \{l_1, \ldots, l_n\}$. Thereby, only linearly many candidates for L need to be checked. In contrast to LPR clauses and RATs, the notion of SPR clauses generalizes set-blocked clauses [7]:

Definition 6. *A clause C is* set-blocked (SET) *by a non-empty set $L \subseteq C$ in a formula F if, for every clause $D \in F_{\overline{L}}$, the clause $(C \setminus L) \cup \overline{L} \cup D$ contains two complementary literals.*

To show that set-propagation-redundant clauses generalize set-blocked clauses, we first characterize them as follows:

Lemma 3. *Let F be a clause, C a formula, $L \subseteq C$ a non-empty set of literals, and α the assignment blocked by C. Then, C is set-blocked by L in F if and only if, for every $D \in F$, $D|\alpha = \top$ implies $D|\alpha_L = \top$.*

Proof. For the "only if" direction, assume that there exists a clause $D \in F$ such that $D|\alpha = \top$ but $D|\alpha_L \neq \top$. Then, since α and α_L disagree only on literals in L, it follows that D contains a literal $l \in \overline{L}$ and therefore $D \in F_{\overline{L}}$. Now, α_L falsifies exactly the literals in $(C \setminus L) \cup \overline{L}$ and since it does not satisfy any of the literals in D, it follows that there exists no literal $l \in D$ such that its complement $\overline{l}$ is contained in $(C \setminus L) \cup \overline{L}$. Therefore, C is not set-blocked by L in F.

For the "if" direction, assume that C is not set-blocked by L in F, i.e., there exists a clause $D \in F_{\overline{L}}$ such that $(C \setminus L) \cup \overline{L} \cup D$ does not contain complementary literals. Clearly, $D|\alpha = \top$ since α falsifies L and $D \cap \overline{L} \neq \emptyset$. Now, since D contains no literal l such that $\overline{l} \in (C \setminus L) \cup \overline{L}$ and since α_L falsifies exactly the literals in $(C \setminus L) \cup \overline{L}$, it follows that α_L does not satisfy D, hence $D|\alpha_L \neq \top$.   □

Theorem 4. *If a clause C is set-blocked by a set L in a formula F, it is set-propagation redundant w.r.t. F.*

Proof. Assume that C is set-blocked by L in F. We show that $F|\alpha \supseteq F|\alpha_L$, which implies that $F|\alpha \vdash_1 F|\alpha_L$, and therefore that C is set-propagation redundant w.r.t. F. Let $D|\alpha_L \in F|\alpha_L$. First, note that D cannot be contained in F_L, for otherwise $D|\alpha_L = \top$ and thus $D|\alpha_L \notin F|\alpha_L$. Second, observe that D can also not be contained in $F_{\overline{L}}$, since that would imply that $D|\alpha = \top$ and thus, by Lemma 3, $D|\alpha_L = \top$. Therefore, $D \notin F_L \cup F_{\overline{L}}$ and so $D|\alpha = D|\alpha_L$. But then, $D|\alpha_L \in F|\alpha$. It follows that $F|\alpha \supseteq F|\alpha_L$. $\square$

We thus know that set-propagation-redundant clauses generalize both resolution asymmetric tautologies and set-blocked clauses. Since there exist resolution asymmetric tautologies that are not set-blocked (and vice versa) [7], it follows that set-propagation-redundant clauses are actually a *strict* generalization of these two kinds of clauses.

By giving practically full freedom to the witnessing assignments, i.e., by only requiring them to satisfy C, we finally arrive at propagation-redundant clauses, the most general of the three redundancy notions:

Definition 7. *Let F be a formula, C a clause, and α the assignment blocked by C. Then, C is* propagation redundant *(PR) w.r.t. F if there exists an assignment ω such that ω satisfies C and $F|\alpha \vdash_1 F|\omega$.*

Example 4. Let $F = \{x \vee y,\ \overline{x} \vee y,\ \overline{x} \vee z\}$, $C = x$, and let $\omega = x\,z$ be the witnessing assignment. Then, $\alpha = \overline{x}$ is the assignment blocked by C. Now, consider $F|\alpha = \{y\}$ and $F|\omega = \{y\}$. Clearly, unit propagation with the negated literal $\overline{y}$ of the unit clause $y \in F|\omega$ derives a conflict on $F|\alpha$. Therefore, $F|\alpha \vdash_1 F|\omega$ and so C is propagation redundant w.r.t. F. Note that C is not set-propagation redundant because for $L = \{x\}$, we have $\alpha_L = x$ and so $F|\alpha_L$ contains the two unit clauses y and z, but it does not hold that $F|\alpha \vdash_1 z$. The fact that ω satisfies z is crucial for ensuring propagation redundancy. $\square$

Since the witnessing assignments ω are allowed to assign variables that are not contained in C, we need—at least in general—to add them to a proof to guarantee that redundancy can be efficiently checked. In the next section, we illustrate the power of a proof system that is based on the addition of PR clauses.

5   Short Proofs of the Pigeon Hole Principle

In a landmark paper, Haken [13] showed that pigeon hole formulas cannot be refuted by resolution proofs that are of polynomial size w.r.t. the size of the formulas. In contrast, by using the stronger proof system of *extended resolution*, Cook [22] proved that one can actually refute pigeon hole formulas in polynomial size. What distinguishes extended resolution from general resolution is that it allows for the introduction of new variables via definitions. Cook showed how the introduction of such definitions helps to reduce a pigeon hole formula of size n to a pigeon hole formula of size $n - 1$ over new variables. The problem with the introduction of new variables, however, is that the search space of possible variables—and therefore clauses—that could be added to a proof is infinite.

In this section, we illustrate how a clausal proof system that allows the addition of PR clauses can yield short proofs of pigeon hole formulas without the need for introducing new variables. This shows that a proof system based on PR clauses is strictly stronger than the resolution calculus, even when we forbid the introduction of new variables. To recap, a pigeon hole formula PHP_n intuitively encodes that n pigeons have to be assigned to $n-1$ holes such that no hole contains more than one pigeon. In the encoding, a variable $x_{i,k}$ intuitively denotes that pigeon i is assigned to hole k:

$$PHP_n := \bigwedge_{1 \leq i \leq n} (x_{i,1} \vee \cdots \vee x_{i,n-1}) \wedge \bigwedge_{1 \leq i < j \leq n} \bigwedge_{1 \leq k \leq n-1} (\overline{x}_{i,k} \vee \overline{x}_{j,k})$$

Clearly, pigeon hole formulas are unsatisfiable. The main idea behind our approach is similar to that of Cook, namely to reduce a pigeon hole formula PHP_n to the smaller PHP_{n-1}. The difference is, that in our case, PHP_{n-1} is still defined on the same variables as PHP_n. Therefore, reducing PHP_n to PHP_{n-1} boils down to deriving the clauses $x_{i,1} \vee \cdots \vee x_{i,n-2}$ for $1 \leq i \leq n-1$.

Following Haken [13], we use array notation for clauses: Every clause is represented by an array of n columns and $n-1$ rows. An array contains a "+" ("−") in the i-th column and k-th row if and only if the variable $x_{i,k}$ occurs positively (negatively, respectively) in the corresponding clause. Representing PHP_n in array notation, we have for every clause $x_{i,1} \vee \cdots \vee x_{i,n-1}$, an array in which the i-th column is filled with "+". Moreover, for every clause $\overline{x}_{i,k} \vee \overline{x}_{j,k}$, we have an array that contains two "−" in row k—one in column i and the other in column j. For instance, PHP_4 is given in array notation as follows:

We illustrate the general idea for reducing a pigeon hole formula PHP_n to the smaller PHP_{n-1} on the concrete formula PHP_4. It should, however, become clear from our explanation that the procedure works for every $n > 1$. If we want to reduce PHP_4 to PHP_3, we have to obtain the following three clauses:

We can do so, by removing the "+" from the last row of every column full of "+", except for the last column, which can be ignored as it is not contained in PHP_3. The key observation is, that a "+" in the last row of the i-th column can be removed with the help of so-called "diagonal clauses" of the form $\overline{x}_{i,n-1} \vee \overline{x}_{n,k}$ ($1 \leq k \leq n-2$). We are allowed to add these diagonal clauses since they are, as we will show, propagation redundant w.r.t. PHP_n. The arrays below represent the diagonal clauses to remove the "+" from the last row of the first (left), second (middle), and third column (right):

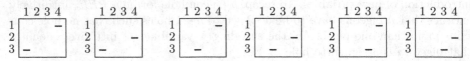

We next show how exactly these diagonal clauses allow us to remove the bottom "+" from a column full of "+", or, in other words, how they help us to remove the literal $x_{i,n-1}$ from a clause $x_{i,1} \lor \cdots \lor x_{i,n-1}$ $(1 \le i \le n-1)$. Consider, for instance, the clause $x_{2,1} \lor x_{2,2} \lor x_{2,3}$ in PHP_4. Our aim is to remove the literal $x_{2,3}$ from this clause. Before we explain the procedure, we like to remark that proof systems based on propagation redundancy can easily simulate resolution: Since every resolvent of clauses in a formula F is implied by F, the assignment α blocked by the resolvent must falsify F and thus $F|\alpha \vdash_1 \bot$. We explain our procedure textually before we illustrate it in array notation:

First, we add the diagonal clauses $D_1 = \overline{x}_{2,3} \lor \overline{x}_{4,1}$ and $D_2 = \overline{x}_{2,3} \lor \overline{x}_{4,2}$ to PHP_4. After this, we can derive the unit clause $\overline{x}_{2,3}$ by resolving the two diagonal clauses D_1 and D_2 with the original pigeon hole clauses $P_1 = \overline{x}_{2,3} \lor \overline{x}_{4,3}$ and $P_2 = x_{4,1} \lor x_{4,2} \lor x_{4,3}$ as follows: We resolve D_1 with P_2 to obtain $\overline{x}_{2,3} \lor x_{4,2} \lor x_{4,3}$. Then, we resolve this clause with D_2 to obtain $\overline{x}_{2,3} \lor x_{4,3}$, which we resolve with P_1 to obtain $\overline{x}_{2,3}$. Note that our proof system actually allows us to add $\overline{x}_{2,3}$ immediately without carrying out all the resolution steps explicitly. Finally, we resolve $\overline{x}_{2,3}$ with $x_{2,1} \lor x_{2,2} \lor x_{2,3}$ to obtain the desired clause $x_{2,1} \lor x_{2,2}$.

We next illustrate this procedure in array notation. We start by visualizing the clauses D_1, D_2, P_1, and P_2 that can be resolved to yield the clause $\overline{x}_{2,3}$. The clauses are given in array notation as follows:

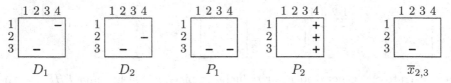

We can then resolve $\overline{x}_{2,3}$ with $x_{2,1} \lor x_{2,2} \lor x_{2,3}$ to obtain $x_{2,1} \lor x_{2,2}$:

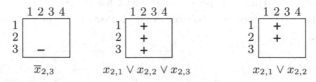

This should illustrate the general idea of how to reduce a clause of the form $x_{i,1} \lor \ldots x_{i,n-1}$ $(1 \le i \le n-1)$ to a clause $x_{i,1} \lor \ldots x_{i,n-2}$. By repeating this procedure for every column i with $1 \le i \le n-1$, we can thus reduce a pigeon hole formula PHP_n to a pigeon hole formula PHP_{n-1} without introducing new variables. Note that the last step, in which we resolve the derived unit clause $\overline{x}_{2,3}$ with the clause $x_{2,1} \lor x_{2,2} \lor x_{2,3}$, is actually not necessary for a valid PR proof of a pigeon hole formula, but we added it to simplify the presentation.

It remains to show that the diagonal clauses are indeed propagation redundant w.r.t. the pigeon hole formula. To do so, we show that for every assignment $\alpha = x_{i,n-1}\, x_{n,k}$ that is blocked by a diagonal clause $\overline{x}_{i,n-1} \vee \overline{x}_{n,k}$, it holds that for the assignment $\omega = \overline{x}_{i,n-1}\, \overline{x}_{n,k}\, x_{i,k}\, x_{n,n-1}$, $PHP_n\,|\alpha = PHP_n\,|\omega$, implying that $PHP_n\,|\alpha \vdash_1 PHP_n\,|\omega$. We also argue why other diagonal and unit clauses can be ignored when checking whether a new diagonal clause is propagation redundant.

We again illustrate the idea on PHP_4. From now on, we use array notation also for assignments, i.e., a "+" ("−") in column i and row k denotes that the assignment assigns 1 (0, respectively) to variable $x_{i,k}$. Consider, for instance, the diagonal clause $D_2 = \overline{x}_{2,3} \vee \overline{x}_{4,2}$ that blocks $\alpha = x_{2,3}\, x_{4,2}$. The corresponding witnessing assignment $\omega = \overline{x}_{2,3}\, \overline{x}_{4,2}\, x_{2,2}\, x_{4,3}$ can be seen as a "rectangle" with two "−" in the corners of one diagonal and two "+" in the other corners:

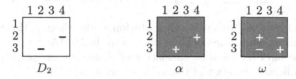

$$D_2 \qquad\qquad \alpha \qquad\qquad \omega$$

To see that $PHP_4\,|\alpha$ and $PHP_4\,|\omega$ coincide on clauses $x_{i,1} \vee \cdots \vee x_{i,n-1}$, consider that whenever α and ω assign a variable of such a clause, they both satisfy the clause (since they both have a "+" in every column in which they assign a variable) and so they both remove it from PHP_4. For instance, in the following example, both α and ω satisfy $x_{2,1} \vee x_{2,2} \vee x_{2,3}$ while both do not assign a variable of the clause $x_{3,1} \vee x_{3,2} \vee x_{3,3}$:

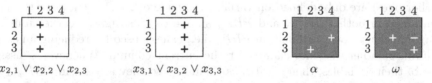

$$x_{2,1} \vee x_{2,2} \vee x_{2,3} \qquad x_{3,1} \vee x_{3,2} \vee x_{3,3} \qquad\qquad \alpha \qquad\qquad\qquad \omega$$

To see that $PHP_4\,|\alpha$ and $PHP_4\,|\omega$ coincide on clauses of the form $\overline{x}_{i,k} \vee \overline{x}_{j,k}$, consider the following: If α falsifies a literal of $\overline{x}_{i,k} \vee \overline{x}_{j,k}$, then the resulting clause is a unit clause for which one of the two literals is not assigned by α (since α does not assign two variables in the same row). Now, one can show that the same unit clause is also contained in $PHP_4\,|\omega$, where it is obtained from another clause: Consider, for example, again the assignment $\alpha = x_{2,3}\, x_{4,2}$ and the corresponding witnessing assignment $\omega = \overline{x}_{2,3}\, \overline{x}_{4,2}\, x_{2,2}\, x_{4,3}$ from above. The assignment α turns the clause $C = \overline{x}_{3,2} \vee \overline{x}_{4,2}$ into the unit clause $C\,|\alpha = \overline{x}_{3,2}$. The same clause is contained in $PHP_4\,|\omega$, as it is obtained from $C' = \overline{x}_{2,2} \vee \overline{x}_{3,2}$ since $C'\,|\omega = C\,|\alpha = \overline{x}_{3,2}$:

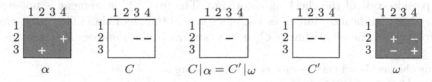

$$\alpha \qquad\qquad C \qquad\qquad C\,|\alpha = C'\,|\omega \qquad\qquad C' \qquad\qquad \omega$$

CNF Formula	DIMACS File	PR Proof File	Lemmas
	p cnf 12 22	**−3 −10** −3 −10 1 12 0	$\overline{x}_{1,3} \vee \overline{x}_{4,1}$
$x_{1,1} \vee x_{1,2} \vee x_{1,3}$	1 2 3 0	**−3 −11** −3 −11 2 12 0	$\overline{x}_{1,3} \vee \overline{x}_{4,2}$
$x_{2,1} \vee x_{2,2} \vee x_{2,3}$	4 5 6 0	**−3** 0	$\overline{x}_{1,3}$
$x_{3,1} \vee x_{3,2} \vee x_{3,3}$	7 8 9 0	**−6 −10** −6 −10 4 12 0	$\overline{x}_{2,3} \vee \overline{x}_{4,1}$
$x_{4,1} \vee x_{4,2} \vee x_{4,3}$	10 11 12 0	**−6 −11** −6 −11 5 12 0	$\overline{x}_{2,3} \vee \overline{x}_{4,2}$
$\overline{x}_{1,1} \vee \overline{x}_{2,1}$	−1 −4 0	**−6** 0	$\overline{x}_{2,3}$
$\overline{x}_{1,2} \vee \overline{x}_{2,2}$	−2 −5 0	**−9 −10** −9 −10 7 12 0	$\overline{x}_{3,3} \vee \overline{x}_{4,1}$
$\overline{x}_{1,3} \vee \overline{x}_{2,3}$	−3 −6 0	**−9 −11** −9 −11 8 12 0	$\overline{x}_{3,3} \vee \overline{x}_{4,2}$
$\overline{x}_{1,1} \vee \overline{x}_{3,1}$	−1 −7 0	**−9** 0	$\overline{x}_{3,3}$
$\overline{x}_{1,2} \vee \overline{x}_{3,2}$	−2 −8 0	**−2** 0	$\overline{x}_{1,2}$
$\overline{x}_{1,3} \vee \overline{x}_{3,3}$	−3 −9 0	**−5** 0	$\overline{x}_{2,2}$
...	...	0	⊥

Fig. 2. Left, ten clauses of PHP_4 using the notation as elsewhere in this paper and next to it the equivalent representation of these clauses in the DIMACS format used by SAT solvers. Right, the full PR refutation consisting of clause-witness pairs. A repetition of the first literal indicates the start of the optional witness.

Note that diagonal clauses and unit clauses that have been derived earlier can be ignored when checking whether the current one is propagation redundant. For instance, assume we are currently reducing PHP_n to PHP_{n-1}. Then, the assignments α and ω under consideration only assign variables in PHP_n. In contrast, the unit and diagonal clauses used for reducing PHP_{n+1} to PHP_n (or earlier ones) are only defined on variables outside of PHP_n. They are therefore contained in both $PHP_n|\alpha$ and $PHP_n|\omega$. We can also ignore earlier unit and diagonal clauses over variables in PHP_n, i.e., clauses used for reducing an earlier column or other diagonal clauses for the current column: Whenever α assigns one of their variables, then ω satisfies them and so they are not in $PHP_n|\omega$.

Finally, we want to mention that one can also construct short SPR proofs (without new variables) of the pigeon hole formulas by first adding SPR clauses of the form $\overline{x}_{i,n-1} \vee \overline{x}_{n,k} \vee x_{i,k} \vee x_{n,n-1}$ and then turning them into diagonal clauses using resolution. We left these proofs out since they are twice as large as the PR proofs and their explanation is less intuitive. For DRAT, we consider it unlikely that such proofs exist.

6   Evaluation

We implemented a PR proof checker[1] on top of DRAT-trim [5]. Figure 3 shows the pseudo code of the checking algorithm. The first "if" statement is not necessary but significantly improves the efficiency of the algorithm. The worst-case complexity of the algorithm is $\mathcal{O}(m^3)$, where m is the number of clauses in a

---

[1] The checker, benchmark formulas, and proofs are available at
http://www.cs.utexas.edu/~marijn/pr/.

proof. The reason for this is that there are m iterations of the outer for-loop and for each of these iterations, the inner for-loop is performed $|F|$ times (i.e., once for every clause in F). Given that F contains n clauses at the start of the algorithm, we know that the size of F is bounded by $m+n$ (the original n clauses of F plus the m clauses of the proof that are added to F by the algorithm). It follows that the inner for-loop is performed $m(m + n)$ times. Now, there is a unit propagation test in the inner if-statement: If k is the maximal clause size and $m + n$ is an upper bound for the size of the formula, then the complexity of unit propagation is known to be at most $k(m+n)$. Hence, the overall worst-case complexity of the algorithm is bounded by $m(m + n)k(m + n) = \mathcal{O}(m^3)$.

This complexity is the same as for RAT-proof checking. In fact, the pseudo-code for RAT-proof checking and PR-proof checking is the same apart from the first if-statement, which is always true in the worst case, both for RAT and PR. Although the theoretical worst-case complexity makes proof checking seem very expensive, it can be done quite efficiently in practice: For the RAT proofs produced by solvers in the SAT competitions, we observed that the runtime of proof checking is close to linear with respect to the sizes of the proofs.

Moreover, we want to highlight that verifying the PR property of a clause is relatively easy as long as a witnessing assignment is given. For an arbitrary clause *without* a witnessing assignment, however, we conjecture that it is an NP-complete problem to decide whether the clause is PR. We therefore believe that in general, the verification of PR proofs is simpler than the actual solving/proving.

The format of PR proofs is an extension of DRAT proofs: the first numbers of line i denote the literals in C_i. Positive numbers refer to positive literals, and negative numbers refer to negative literals. In case a witness ω_i is provided, the first literal in the clause is repeated to denote the start of the witness. Recall that the witness always has to satisfy the clause. It is therefore guaranteed that the witness and the clause have at least one literal in common. Our format requires that such a literal occurs at the first position of the clause and of the witness. Finally, 0 marks the end of a line. Figure 2 shows the formula and the PR proof of our running example PHP_4.

Table 1 compares our PR proofs with existing DRAT proofs of the pigeon hole formulas and of formulas from another challenging benchmark suite of the SAT competition that allow two pigeons per hole. For the latter suite, PR proofs

---

PRcheck (CNF formula F; PR proof $(C_1, \omega_1), \ldots, (C_m, \omega_m)$)

    for $i \in \{i, \ldots, m\}$ do

        for $D \in F$ do

            if $D|\omega_i \neq \top$ and $(D|\alpha_i = \top$ or $D|\omega_i \subset D|\alpha_i)$ then

                if $F|\alpha_i \nvdash_1 D|\omega_i$ then return *failure*

        $F := F \cup \{C_i\}$

    return *success*

Fig. 3. Pseudo code of the PR-Proof checking algorithm.

Table 1. The sizes (in terms of the number of variables and clauses) of pigeon hole formulas (top) and two-pigeons-per-hole formulas (bottom) as well as the sizes and validation times (in seconds) for their PR proofs (as described in Sect. 5) and their DRAT proofs (based on symmetry breaking [23]).

formula	input		PR proofs			DRAT proofs		
	#var	#cls	#var	#cls	time	#var	#cls	time
hole10.cnf	110	561	110	385	0.17	440	3,685	0.22
hole11.cnf	132	738	132	506	0.18	572	5,236	0.23
hole12.cnf	156	949	156	650	0.19	728	7,228	0.27
hole13.cnf	182	1,197	182	819	0.21	910	9,737	0.34
hole20.cnf	420	4,221	420	2,870	0.40	3,080	49,420	2.90
hole30.cnf	930	13,981	930	9,455	2.57	99,20	234,205	61.83
hole40.cnf	1,640	32,841	1,640	22,140	13.54	22,960	715,040	623.29
hole50.cnf	2,550	63,801	2,550	42,925	71.72	44,200	1,708,925	3,158.17
tph8.cnf	136	5,457	136	680	0.32	3,520	834,963	5.47
tph12.cnf	300	27,625	300	2,300	1.81	11,376	28,183,301	1,396.92
tph16.cnf	528	87,329	528	5,456	11.16	not available, too large		
tph20.cnf	820	213,241	820	10,660	61.69	not available, too large		

can be constructed in a similar way as those of the classical pigeon hole formulas. Notice that the PR proofs do not introduce new variables and that they contain fewer clauses than their corresponding formulas. The DRAT proof of PHP_n contains a copy of the formula PHP_k for each $k < n$. Checking PR proofs is also more efficient, as they are more compact.

7 Related Work

In this section, we shortly discuss how the concepts in this paper are related to *variable instantiation* [10], *autarkies* [8], *safe assignments* [9], and *symmetry breaking* [11]. If, for some literal l, it is possible to show $F|\bar{l} \vDash F|l$, then *variable instantiation*, as described by Andersson et al. [10], allows to assign the literal l in the formula F to 1. Analogously, we identify the unit clause l as redundant.

As presented by Kleine Büning and Kullmann [8], an assignment ω is an *autarky* for a formula F if it satisfies all clauses of F that contain a literal to which ω assigns a truth value. If an assignment ω is an autarky for a formula F, then F is satisfiability equivalent to $F|\omega$. Similarly, propagation redundancy PR allows us to add all the unit clauses falsified by an autarky, with the autarky serving as a witness: Let ω be an autarky for some formula F, $C = \bar{l}$ for a literal l falsified by ω, and α the assignment blocked by C. Notice that $F|\alpha \supseteq F|\omega$ and thus C is propagation redundant w.r.t. F.

According to Weaver and Franco [9], an assignment ω is considered *safe* if, for every assignment α with $var(\alpha) = var(\omega)$, it holds that $F|\alpha \vDash F|\omega$. If an assignment ω is safe, then $F|\omega$ is satisfiability equivalent to F. In a similar fashion, our approach allows us to block all the above-mentioned assignments $\alpha \neq \omega$. Through this, we obtain a formula that is logically equivalent to $F|\omega$.

Note that safe assignments generalize autarkies and variable instantiation. Moreover, while safe assignments only allow the application of an assignment ω to a formula F if $F|_\alpha \vDash F|_\omega$ holds for *all* assignments $\alpha \neq \omega$, our approach enables us to block an assignment α as soon as $F|_\alpha \vDash F|_\omega$.

Finally, symmetry breaking [11] can be expressed in the DRAT proof system [23] but existing methods introduce many new variables and duplicate the input formula multiple times. It might be possible to express symmetry breaking without new variables in the PR proof system. For one important symmetry, row-interchangeability [16], the symmetry breaking using PR without new variables appears similar to the method we presented for the pigeon hole formulas.

8   Conclusion

Based on an implication relation between a formula and itself under different partial assignments, we obtain a clean and simple characterization of the most general notion of clause redundancy considered in the literature so far. Replacing the implication relation by stronger notions of implication, e.g., the superset relation or implication through unit propagation, gives then rise to various polynomially checkable redundancy criteria. One variant yields a proof system that turns out to coincide with the well-known DRAT, while we conjecture the proof systems produced by the other two variants to be much more powerful. We showed that these more general variants admit short clausal proofs for the famous pigeon hole formulas, without the need to introduce new variables. Experiments show that our proofs are much more compact than existing clausal proofs and also much faster to check. Our new proof systems simulate many other concepts from the literature very concisely, including autarkies, variable instantiation, safe assignments, and certain kinds of symmetry reasoning.

Interesting future work includes the separation of our new proof systems from the DRAT proof system on the lower end and from extended resolution on the upper end, under the additional restriction that our proof systems and DRAT do not introduce new variables. The relation to extended resolution is a particularly interesting aspect from the proof complexity point of view. Other open questions are related to the space and width bounds of the smallest PR proofs, again without new variables, for well-known other hard problems such as Tseitin formulas [12,24] or pebbling games [25]. On the practical side, we want to implement a formally verified proof checker for PR proofs. Moreover, we want to pursue some preliminary ideas for automatically generating short PR proofs during actual SAT solving: Our initial plan is to enumerate unit and binary clauses and to add them to a formula if they are propagation redundant. We already have a prototype implementation which is able to find short proofs of pigeon hole formulas, but we are still searching for efficient heuristics that help solvers with finding short PR clauses in general formulas.

References

1. Clarke, E.M., Biere, A., Raimi, R., Zhu, Y.: Bounded model checking using satisfiability solving. Formal Meth. Syst. Des. **19**(1), 7–34 (2001)
2. Ivančić, F., Yang, Z., Ganai, M.K., Gupta, A., Ashar, P.: Efficient SAT-based bounded model checking for software verification. Theor. Comput. Sci. **404**(3), 256–274 (2008)
3. Konev, B., Lisitsa, A.: Computer-aided proof of Erdős discrepancy properties. Artif. Intell. **224**(C), 103–118 (2015)
4. Heule, M.J.H., Kullmann, O., Marek, V.W.: Solving and verifying the boolean pythagorean triples problem via cube-and-conquer. In: Creignou, N., Le Berre, D. (eds.) SAT 2016. LNCS, vol. 9710, pp. 228–245. Springer, Cham (2016). doi:10. 1007/978-3-319-40970-2_15
5. Wetzler, N.D., Heule, M.J.H., Hunt Jr., W.A.: DRAT-trim: efficient checking and trimming using expressive clausal proofs. In: Sinz, C., Egly, U. (eds.) SAT 2014. LNCS, vol. 8561, pp. 422–429. Springer, Cham (2014). doi:10.1007/ 978-3-319-09284-3_31
6. Järvisalo, M., Heule, M.J.H., Biere, A.: Inprocessing rules. In: Gramlich, B., Miller, D., Sattler, U. (eds.) IJCAR 2012. LNCS (LNAI), vol. 7364, pp. 355–370. Springer, Heidelberg (2012). doi:10.1007/978-3-642-31365-3_28
7. Kiesl, B., Seidl, M., Tompits, H., Biere, A.: Super-blocked clauses. In: Olivetti, N., Tiwari, A. (eds.) IJCAR 2016. LNCS (LNAI), vol. 9706, pp. 45–61. Springer, Cham (2016). doi:10.1007/978-3-319-40229-1_5
8. Kleine Büning, H., Kullmann, O.: Minimal unsatisfiability and autarkies. In: Biere, A., Heule, M.J.H., van Maaren, H., Walsh, T. (eds.) Handbook of Satisfiability. IOS Press, pp. 339–401 (2009)
9. Weaver, S., Franco, J.V., Schlipf, J.S.: Extending existential quantification in conjunctions of BDDs. JSAT **1**(2), 89–110 (2006)
10. Andersson, G., Bjesse, P., Cook, B., Hanna, Z.: A proof engine approach to solving combinational design automation problems. In: Proceedings of the 39th Annual Design Automation Conference (DAC 2002). ACM, pp. 725–730 (2002)
11. Crawford, J., Ginsberg, M., Luks, E., Roy, A.: Symmetry-breaking predicates for search problems. In: Proceedings of the 5th International Conference on Principles of Knowledge Representation and Reasoning (KR 1996). Morgan Kaufmann, pp. 148–159 (1996)
12. Tseitin, G.S.: On the complexity of derivation in propositional calculus. Stud. Math. Math. Logic **2**, 115–125 (1968)
13. Haken, A.: The intractability of resolution. Theor. Comput. Sci. **39**, 297–308 (1985)
14. Audemard, G., Katsirelos, G., Simon, L.: A restriction of extended resolution for clause learning sat solvers. In: Proceedings of the 24th AAAI Conference on Artificial Intelligence (AAAI 2010). AAAI Press (2010)
15. Manthey, N., Heule, M.J.H., Biere, A.: Automated reencoding of boolean formulas. In: Biere, A., Nahir, A., Vos, T. (eds.) HVC 2012. LNCS, vol. 7857, pp. 102–117. Springer, Heidelberg (2013). doi:10.1007/978-3-642-39611-3_14
16. Devriendt, J., Bogaerts, B., Bruynooghe, M., Denecker, M.: Improved static symmetry breaking for SAT. In: Creignou, N., Le Berre, D. (eds.) SAT 2016. LNCS, vol. 9710, pp. 104–122. Springer, Cham (2016). doi:10.1007/978-3-319-40970-2_8
17. Balyo, T., Heule, M.J.H., Järvisalo, M.: SAT competition 2016: recent developments. In: Proceedings of the 31st AAAI Conference on Artificial Intelligence (AAAI 2017). AAAI Press (2017, to appear)

18. Goldberg, E.I., Novikov, Y.: Verification of proofs of unsatisfiability for CNF formulas. In: Proceedings of the Conference on Design, Automation and Test in Europe (DATE 2003). IEEE Computer Society, pp. 10886–10891 (2003)
19. Van Gelder, A.: Producing and verifying extremely large propositional refutations. Ann. Math. Artif. Intell. **65**(4), 329–372 (2012)
20. Kullmann, O.: On a generalization of extended resolution. Discrete Appl. Math. **96–97**, 149–176 (1999)
21. Järvisalo, M., Biere, A., Heule, M.J.H.: Simulating circuit-level simplifications on CNF. J. Autom. Reasoning **49**(4), 583–619 (2012)
22. Cook, S.A.: A short proof of the pigeon hole principle using extended resolution. SIGACT News **8**(4), 28–32 (1976)
23. Heule, M.J.H., Hunt Jr., W.A., Wetzler, N.D.: Expressing symmetry breaking in DRAT proofs. In: Felty, A.P., Middeldorp, A. (eds.) CADE 2015. LNCS (LNAI), vol. 9195, pp. 591–606. Springer, Cham (2015). doi:10.1007/978-3-319-21401-6_40
24. Urquhart, A.: The complexity of propositional proofs. Bull. Symbolic Logic **1**(4), 425–467 (1995)
25. Nordström, J.: A simplified way of proving trade-off results for resolution. Inf. Process. Lett. **109**(18), 1030–1035 (2009)

Relational Constraint Solving in SMT

Baoluo Meng[1], Andrew Reynolds[1]([⊠]), Cesare Tinelli[1], and Clark Barrett[2]

[1] Department of Computer Science, The University of Iowa, Iowa City, USA
andrew.j.reynolds@gmail.com
[2] Department of Computer Science, Stanford University, Stanford, USA

Abstract. Relational logic is useful for reasoning about computational problems with relational structures, including high-level system design, architectural configurations of network systems, ontologies, and verification of programs with linked data structures. We present a modular extension of an earlier calculus for the theory of finite sets to a theory of finite relations with such operations as transpose, product, join, and transitive closure. We implement this extension as a theory solver of the SMT solver CVC4. Combining this new solver with the finite model finding features of CVC4 enables several compelling use cases. For instance, native support for relations enables a natural mapping from Alloy, a declarative modeling language based on first-order relational logic, to SMT constraints. It also enables a natural encoding of several description logics with concrete domains, allowing the use of an SMT solver to analyze, for instance, Web Ontology Language (OWL) models. We provide an initial evaluation of our solver on a number of Alloy and OWL models which shows promising results.

Keywords: Relational logic · SMT · Alloy · OWL

1 Introduction

Many computational problems require reasoning about relational structures. Examples include high-level system design, architectural configuration of network systems, reasoning about ontologies, and verification of programs with linked data structures. Relational logic is an appealing choice for reasoning about such problems. In this paper, we consider a many-sorted relational logic where relations of arity n are defined as sets of n-tuples with parametrized sorts for tuple elements. We define a version of this logic as a first-order theory of finite relations where relation terms are built from relation constants and variables, set operators, and relational operators such as join, transpose, product, and transitive closure.

In previous work [3], Bansal et al. developed a decision procedure for a theory of finite sets with cardinality constraints. The theory of finite relations presented here is an extension of that theory to relational constraints. We present a calculus for the satisfiability of quantifier-free formulas in this theory. Our calculus is in general refutation-sound and model-sound. It is also terminating

© Springer International Publishing AG 2017
L. de Moura (Ed.): CADE 2017, LNAI 10395, pp. 148–165, 2017.
DOI: 10.1007/978-3-319-63046-5_10

and refutation-complete for a restricted class of quantifier-free formulas that has useful applications.

The calculus is explicitly designed to be implementable as a theory solver in SMT solvers based on the DPLL(T) architecture [14]. We have implemented a modular component for it in our SMT solver CVC4 [4], allowing CVC4 to solve constraints on relations over elements from any of the theories it supports. This relational extension of CVC4's native input language enables natural mappings to SMT formulas from several modeling languages based on relations. This includes Alloy, a formal language based on first-order relational logic, as well as ontology languages such as OWL. A significant potential advantage of these mappings is that they bring to these languages the power of SMT solvers to reason natively about a variety of interpreted types, something that is challenging for existing reasoners for these languages.

1.1 Related Work

Alloy is a well-known declarative modeling language based on a relational logic with transitive closure, set cardinality, and integer arithmetic operators [13]. Alloy specifications, or *models*, can be analyzed for consistency or other entailment properties with the Alloy Analyzer, a static analyzer based on encoding models as propositional logic formulas, and passing them to an off-the-shelf propositional satisfiability (SAT) solver. This approach limits the analysis to models with explicit and concrete cardinality bounds on the relations involved; hence it is appropriate only for proving the consistency of a model or for disproving that a given property, encoded as a formula, holds for a model. Despite these limitations, Alloy and its analyzer have been quite useful for lightweight modeling and analysis of software systems. An earlier attempt to solve Alloy constraints without artificial cardinality bounds on relations was made by Ghazi and Taghdiri [8] using SMT solvers. They developed a translation from a subset of Alloy's language to the SMT-LIB language [5] and used the SMT solver Yices [7] to solve the resulting constraints. That approach can prove some properties of certain Alloy models, but it still requires explicitly *finitizing* relations when dealing with transitive closure, limiting the kind of properties that can be proven in models that contain applications of transitive closure. Later, the same authors introduced more general methods [9,10], implemented in the AlloyPE tool, to axiomatize relational operators as SMT formulas without finitization while covering the entire core language of Alloy. However, since quantified relational logic is in general undecidable and quantifiers are heavily used in the translation, the resulting SMT formulas translated from Alloy are often difficult or even impossible for SMT solvers to solve, especially when transitive closure is involved.

Description Logics (DLs) [1,2] are decidable fragments of relational logic explicitly developed for efficient knowledge representation and reasoning. They consider on purpose only unary and binary relations. The main building blocks of DLs are individuals, concepts, roles as well as operations over these, where concepts represent sets of individuals, roles represent binary relations between individuals, and operations include membership, subset, relational composition (join) and equality. Restricted use of quantifiers is allowed in DLs to encode more expressive constraints on roles and concepts. OWL [20], a standardized semantic web ontology language, represents an important application of DLs to ontological modeling. It consists of entities similar to those in DLs except for superficial differences in concrete syntax and for the inclusion of additional features that make reasoning about OWL models undecidable in general. Many efficient reasoners have been built for reasoning about OWL ontologies written in restricted fragments of OWL. These include Konclude [16], FaCT++ [18], and Chainsaw [19].

1.2   Formal Preliminaries

We define our theory of relations and our calculus in the context of many-sorted first-order logic with equality. We assume the reader is familiar with the following notions from that logic: signature, term, literal, formula, free variable, interpretation, and satisfiability of a formula in an interpretation (see, e.g., [6] for more details). Let Σ be a many-sorted signature. We will use $\approx$ as the (infix) logical symbol for equality—which has type $\sigma \times \sigma$ for all sorts σ in Σ and is always interpreted as the identity relation. We assume all signatures Σ contain the Boolean sort Bool, always interpreted as the binary set $\{true, false\}$, and a Boolean constant symbol true for $true$. Without loss of generality, we assume $\approx$ is the only predicate symbol in Σ, as all other predicates may be modeled as functions with return sort Bool. We will commonly write, e.g. $P(x)$, as shorthand for $P(x) \approx true$ where $P(x)$ has sort Bool. We write $s \not\approx t$ as an abbreviation of $\neg s \approx t$. If e is a term or a formula, we denote by $\mathrm{Vars}(e)$ the set of e's free variables, extending the notation to tuples and sets of terms or formulas as expected. We write $\varphi[\boldsymbol{x}]$ to indicate that all the free variables of a formula φ are from tuple $\boldsymbol{x}$.

   If φ is a Σ-formula and $\mathcal{I}$ a Σ-interpretation, we write $\mathcal{I} \models \varphi$ if $\mathcal{I}$ satisfies φ. If t is a term, we denote by $t^{\mathcal{I}}$ the value of t in $\mathcal{I}$. A *theory* is a pair $T = (\Sigma, \mathbf{I})$, where Σ is a signature and $\mathbf{I}$ is a class of Σ-interpretations that is closed under variable reassignment (i.e., every Σ-interpretation that differs from one in $\mathbf{I}$ only in how it interprets the variables is also in $\mathbf{I}$). $\mathbf{I}$ is also referred to as the *models* of T. A Σ-formula φ is *satisfiable* (resp., *unsatisfiable*) in T if it is satisfied by some (resp., no) interpretation in $\mathbf{I}$. A set Γ of Σ-formulas *entails in T* a Σ-formula φ, written $\Gamma \models_T \varphi$, if every interpretation in $\mathbf{I}$ that satisfies all formulas in Γ satisfies φ as well. We write $\models_T \varphi$ as an abbreviation for $\emptyset \models_T \varphi$. We write $\Gamma \models \varphi$ to denote that Γ entails φ in the class of all Σ-interpretations. Two Σ-formulas are *equisatisfiable in T* if for every model $\mathcal{A}$ of T that satisfies one, there is a model of T that satisfies the other and differs from $\mathcal{A}$ at most over the free variables not shared by the two formulas. When convenient, we will treat a finite set of formulas as the conjunction of its elements and vice versa.

2   A Relational Extension to a Theory of Finite Sets

A many-sorted theory of finite sets with cardinality T_S is described in detail in our previous work [3]. The theory T_S includes a set sort constructor $\mathsf{Set}(\alpha)$ parametrized by the sort of the set elements. The theory T_S can be combined with any other theory T Nelson-Oppen-style, by instantiating the parameter α with any sort in T. The signature of theory T_S includes function and predicate symbols for set union ($\sqcup$), intersection ($\sqcap$), difference ($\backslash$), the empty set ($[\,]$), singleton set construction ($[\_]$), set inclusion ($\sqsubseteq$), and membership ($\in$), all interpreted as expected. A sound, complete and terminating tableaux-style calculus for the theory T_S is implemented in the CVC4 SMT solver [4].

Set symbols:

$[\,] : \mathsf{Set}(\alpha)$ $\sqcup, \sqcap, \backslash : \mathsf{Set}(\alpha) \times \mathsf{Set}(\alpha) \to \mathsf{Set}(\alpha)$ $\in\, : \alpha \times \mathsf{Set}(\alpha) \to \mathsf{Bool}$

$[\_] : \alpha \to \mathsf{Set}(\alpha)$ $\sqsubseteq\, : \mathsf{Set}(\alpha) \times \mathsf{Set}(\alpha) \to \mathsf{Bool}$

Relation symbols:

$\langle \_, \ldots, \_ \rangle : \alpha_1 \times \cdots \times \alpha_n \to \mathsf{Tup}_n(\alpha_1, \ldots, \alpha_n)$

$* : \mathsf{Rel}_m(\boldsymbol{\alpha}) \times \mathsf{Rel}_n(\boldsymbol{\beta}) \to \mathsf{Rel}_{m+n}(\boldsymbol{\alpha}, \boldsymbol{\beta})$

$\bowtie \, : \mathsf{Rel}_{p+1}(\boldsymbol{\alpha}, \gamma) \times \mathsf{Rel}_{q+1}(\gamma, \boldsymbol{\beta}) \to \mathsf{Rel}_{p+q}(\boldsymbol{\alpha}, \boldsymbol{\beta})$ with $p + q > 0$

$\_^{-1} : \mathsf{Rel}_m(\alpha_1, \ldots, \alpha_m) \to \mathsf{Rel}_m(\alpha_m, \ldots, \alpha_1)$ $\_^+ : \mathsf{Rel}_2(\alpha, \alpha) \to \mathsf{Rel}_2(\alpha, \alpha)$

where $m, n > 0$, $\boldsymbol{\alpha} = (\alpha_1, \ldots, \alpha_m)$, $\boldsymbol{\beta} = (\beta_1, \ldots, \beta_n)$, and $\mathsf{Rel}_n(\boldsymbol{\gamma}) = \mathsf{Set}(\mathsf{Tup}_n(\boldsymbol{\gamma}))$.

Fig. 1. Signature Σ_R of our relational theory T_R.

In this section, we describe an extension T_R of this theory which, however, does not include a set cardinality operator or cardinality constraints.[1] The new theory T_R extends T_S with a parametric tuple sort $\mathsf{Tup}_n(\alpha_1, \ldots, \alpha_n)$ for every $n > 0$ and various relational operators defined over sets of tuples, that is, over values whose sort is an instance of $\mathsf{Set}(\mathsf{Tup}_n(\alpha_1, \ldots, \alpha_n))$. We call any sort σ of the form $\mathsf{Set}(\mathsf{Tup}_n(\sigma_1, \ldots, \sigma_n))$ a *relational sort (of arity n)* and abbreviate it as $\mathsf{Rel}_n(\sigma_1, \ldots, \sigma_n)$.

The full signature Σ_R of T_R is defined in Fig. 1. Note that the function symbols $*$, $\bowtie$, and $^{-1}$ are not only parametric but also overloaded, as they apply to relational sorts $\mathsf{Rel}_k(\boldsymbol{\sigma})$ of different arities k. The models of T_R are the expansions of the models of T_S that interpret $\langle \_, \ldots, \_ \rangle$ as the n-tuple constructor, $*$ as relational product, $\bowtie$ as relational join, $\_^{-1}$ as the transpose operator, and $\_^+$ as the transitive closure operator. A *relation term* is a Σ_R-term of some relational sort. A *tuple term* is a Σ_R-term of some tuple sort. A *T_R-constraint* is a (dis)equality of the form $(\neg)s \approx t$, where s and t are Σ_R-terms. We write

---

[1] A further extension of the theory to cardinality constraints is planned for future work.

$s \not\sqsubseteq t$ and $[t_1, \ldots, t_n]$ with $n > 1$ as an abbreviation of $\neg(s \sqsubseteq t \approx \text{true})$ and $[t_1] \sqcup \cdots \sqcup [t_n]$, respectively.

3 A Calculus for the Relational Extension

In this section, we describe a tableaux-style calculus for determining the satisfiability of finite sets of T_R-constraints. The calculus consists of a set of derivation rules similar to those in the calculus from [3] that deal with set constraints as well as new rules to process T_R-constraints. For simplicity, we will implicitly assume that the sort of any set or relation term is flat (i.e., set or relation elements are not themselves sets or relations) and allow only variables as terms of element sorts. Nested sets and relations and more complex element terms can be processed in a standard way by using a Nelson-Oppen-style approach which we will not discuss here.

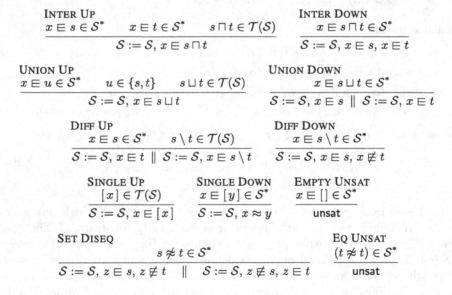

Fig. 2. Basic rules for set intersection, union, difference, singleton, disequality and contradiction. In SET DISEQ, z is a fresh variable.

The derivation rules modify a *state* data structure, where a state is either the distinguished state unsat or a set S of T_R-constraints. The rules are provided in Figs. 2 and 3 in *guarded assignment form*. In such form, the premises of a rule refer to the current state S and the conclusion describes how S is changed by the rule's application. Rules with two or more conclusions, separated by the symbol ∥, are non-deterministic branching rules. In the rules, we write S, c as an abbreviation of $S \cup \{c\}$, and denote by $T(S)$ the set of all terms and subterms occurring in $\mathcal{S}$. We define the following closure operator for $\mathcal{S}$ where $\models_{\text{tup}}$ denotes entailment in the Σ_R-theory of tuples:[2]

$$\mathcal{S}^* = \{s \approx t \mid s, t \in \mathcal{T}(\mathcal{S}), \mathcal{S} \models_{\text{tup}} s \approx t\} \cup$$
$$\{s \not\approx t \mid s, t \in \mathcal{T}(\mathcal{S}), \mathcal{S} \models_{\text{tup}} s \approx s' \wedge t \approx t' \text{ for some } s' \not\approx t' \in \mathcal{S}\} \cup$$
$$\{s \sqsubseteq t \mid s, t \in \mathcal{T}(\mathcal{S}), \mathcal{S} \models_{\text{tup}} s \approx s' \wedge t \approx t' \text{ for some } s' \sqsubseteq t' \in \mathcal{S}\}$$

The set $\mathcal{S}^*$ is computable by extending congruence closure procedures with a rule for deducing consequences of tuple equalities of the form $\langle s_1, \ldots, s_n \rangle \approx \langle t_1, \ldots, t_n \rangle$.

A derivation rule *applies* to a state $\mathcal{S}$ if all the conditions in the rule's premises hold for $\mathcal{S}$ *and* the rule application is not redundant. An application of a rule to a state $\mathcal{S}$ with a conclusion $\mathcal{S} \cup \{\varphi_1[\boldsymbol{x}_1, \boldsymbol{z}], \ldots, \varphi_n[\boldsymbol{x}_n, \boldsymbol{z}]\}$, where $\boldsymbol{z}$ are the fresh variables introduced by the rule's application (if any), is *redundant* if $\mathcal{S}$ already contains $\varphi_1[\boldsymbol{x}_1, \boldsymbol{t}], \ldots, \varphi_n[\boldsymbol{x}_n, \boldsymbol{t}]$ for some terms $\boldsymbol{t}$.

For simplicity and without loss of generality, we consider only initial states $\mathcal{S}_0$ that contain no variables of tuple sorts $\text{Tup}_n(\sigma_1, \ldots, \sigma_n)$, since such variables can be replaced by a tuple $\langle x_1, \ldots, x_n \rangle$ where each x_i is a variable of sort σ_i. We also assume that $\mathcal{S}_0$ contains no atoms of the form $s \sqsubseteq t$, since they can be replaced by $s \approx s \sqcap t$, or disequalities $\langle s_1, \ldots, s_n \rangle \not\approx \langle t_1, \ldots, t_n \rangle$ between tuple terms, since those can be treated by guessing a disequality $s_i \not\approx t_i$ between two of their respective components. All derivation rules preserve these restrictions.

Figure 2 presents the basic rules for the core set constraints in our theory. For each set operator, Fig. 2 contains a *downward* rule and an *upward* rule. Given a membership constraint $x \sqsubseteq s$, the downward rules infer either additional membership constraints over the immediate subterms of s, or an equality in the case where s is $\{y\}$. For example, rule INTER DOWN, infers the constraints $x \sqsubseteq s$ and $x \sqsubseteq t$ if $\mathcal{S}^*$ contains the constraint $x \sqsubseteq s \sqcap t$. The upward rules handle the case where some set s occurs in $\mathcal{S}$, and infer membership constraints of the form $x \sqsubseteq s$ based on other constraints from $\mathcal{S}$. Rule SET DISEQ introduces a witness for a disequality between two sets s and t by using a fresh variable z to assert that there is an element that is in s but not t, or in t but not in s. There are two rules for deriving unsat from trivially unsatisfiable constraints in $\mathcal{S}$: membership constraints of the form $x \sqsubseteq \emptyset$ (EMPTY UNSAT) and disequalities of the form $t \not\approx t$ (EQ UNSAT).

We supplement the set-specific rules with an additional set of rules for T_R-constraints, given in Fig. 3. From the membership of a tuple in the transpose of a relation R, rule TRANSP DOWN concludes that the reverse of the tuple is in R. Conversely, rule TRANSP UP ensures that the reverse of a tuple is in the transpose of a relation R if the tuple is in R and R^{-1} occurs in $\mathcal{S}$. From the constraint that a tuple t belongs to the join of two relations R_1 and R_2 with arities m and n respectively, rule JOIN DOWN infers that R_1 contains a tuple t_1 whose last element (named using a fresh Skolem variable z) is the first

---

[2] Note that this theory has all the function symbols of Σ_R, not just the tuple constructors $\langle \_, \ldots, \_ \rangle$. The extra symbols are treated as *uninterpreted*.

TRANSP UP

$$\frac{\langle x_1, \ldots, x_n \rangle \sqsubseteq R \in \mathcal{S}^* \quad R^{-1} \in \mathcal{T}(\mathcal{S})}{\mathcal{S} := \mathcal{S}, \langle x_n, \ldots, x_1 \rangle \sqsubseteq R^{-1}}$$

TRANSP DOWN

$$\frac{\langle x_1, \ldots, x_n \rangle \sqsubseteq R^{-1} \in \mathcal{S}^*}{\mathcal{S} := \mathcal{S}, \langle x_n, \ldots, x_1 \rangle \sqsubseteq R}$$

PROD UP

$$\frac{\langle x_1, \ldots, x_m \rangle \sqsubseteq R_1 \in \mathcal{S}^* \quad \langle y_1, \ldots, y_n \rangle \sqsubseteq R_2 \in \mathcal{S}^* \quad R_1 * R_2 \in \mathcal{T}(\mathcal{S})}{\mathcal{S} := \mathcal{S}, \langle x_1, \ldots, x_m, y_1, \ldots, y_n \rangle \sqsubseteq R_1 * R_2}$$

PROD DOWN

$$\frac{\langle x_1, \ldots, x_m, y_1, \ldots, y_n \rangle \sqsubseteq R_1 * R_2 \in \mathcal{S}^* \quad ar(R_1) = m}{\mathcal{S} := \mathcal{S}, \langle x_1, \ldots, x_m \rangle \sqsubseteq R_1, \langle y_1, \ldots, y_n \rangle \sqsubseteq R_2}$$

JOIN UP

$$\frac{\langle x_1, \ldots, x_m, z \rangle \sqsubseteq R_1, \langle z, y_1, \ldots, y_n \rangle \sqsubseteq R_2 \in \mathcal{S}^* \quad m + n > 0 \quad R_1 \bowtie R_2 \in \mathcal{T}(\mathcal{S})}{\mathcal{S} := \mathcal{S}, \langle x_1, \ldots, x_m, y_1, \ldots, y_n \rangle \sqsubseteq R_1 \bowtie R_2}$$

JOIN DOWN

$$\frac{\langle x_1, \ldots, x_m, y_1, \ldots, y_n \rangle \sqsubseteq R_1 \bowtie R_2 \in \mathcal{S}^* \quad ar(R_1) = m + 1}{\mathcal{S} := \mathcal{S}, \langle x_1, \ldots, x_m, z \rangle \sqsubseteq R_1, \langle z, y_1, \ldots, y_n \rangle \sqsubseteq R_2}$$

TCLOS UP I

$$\frac{\langle x_1, x_2 \rangle \sqsubseteq R \in \mathcal{S}^* \quad R^+ \in \mathcal{T}(\mathcal{S})}{\mathcal{S} := \mathcal{S}, \langle x_1, x_2 \rangle \sqsubseteq R^+}$$

TCLOS UP II

$$\frac{\langle x_1, x_2 \rangle \sqsubseteq R^+, \langle x_2, x_3 \rangle \sqsubseteq R^+ \in \mathcal{S}^*}{\mathcal{S} := \mathcal{S}, \langle x_1, x_3 \rangle \sqsubseteq R^+}$$

TCLOS DOWN

$$\frac{\langle x_1, x_2 \rangle \sqsubseteq R^+ \in \mathcal{S}^*}{\mathcal{S} := \mathcal{S}, \langle x_1, x_2 \rangle \sqsubseteq R \quad \| \quad \mathcal{S} := \mathcal{S}, \langle x_1, z \rangle \sqsubseteq R, \langle z, x_2 \rangle \sqsubseteq R}$$
$$\| \quad \mathcal{S} := \mathcal{S}, \langle x_1, z_1 \rangle \sqsubseteq R, \langle z_1, z_2 \rangle \sqsubseteq R^+, \langle z_2, x_2 \rangle \sqsubseteq R, z_1 \not\approx z_2$$

Fig. 3. Basic relational derivation rules. Letters z, z_1, z_2 denote fresh variables.

element of a tuple t_2 in R_2, where t is the join of t_1 and t_2. The JOIN UP rule computes the join of pairs of tuples explicitly asserted to belong to a relation R_1 and a relation R_2, respectively, provided that $R_1 \bowtie R_2$ is a term in $\mathcal{S}$. The PROD DOWN and PROD UP rules are defined similarly for the product of relations. The rules TCLOS UP I and TCLOS UP II compute members of the transitive closure of R based on the (currently asserted) members of R. When it can be inferreed that a tuple $\langle x_1, x_2 \rangle$ belongs to the transitive closure of a binary relation R, TCLOS DOWN can produce three alternative conclusions. In reachability terms, the first conclusion considers the case that x_2 is directly reachable from x_1 in the graph induced by R, the second that x_2 is reachable from x_1 in two steps, and the third that it is reachable in more steps. Note that the third case may lead to additional applications of TCLOS DOWN, possibly indefinitely, if the other constraints in $\mathcal{S}$ (implicitly) entail that $\langle x_1, x_2 \rangle$ does not in fact belong to R.

Example 1. Let $\mathcal{S} = \{\langle x, y \rangle \sqsubseteq R^{-1}, R \approx S, \langle y, x \rangle \not\sqsubseteq S\}$. By rule TRANSP DOWN, we can derive a constraint $\langle y, x \rangle \sqsubseteq R$, leading to a new $\mathcal{S}$:

$\{\langle x, y\rangle \in R^{-1}, R \approx S, \langle y, x\rangle \not\in S, \langle y, x\rangle \in R\}$. Then, $\langle y, x\rangle \in R$ is both equal and disequal to true in $\mathcal{S}^*$. Thus, we can derive unsat by EQ UNSAT, and conclude that $\mathcal{S}$ is T_R-unsatisfiable. $\qquad\square$

Example 2. Let $\mathcal{S}$ be $\{\langle x\rangle \in R, \langle y\rangle \in R, R * R \approx S \sqcap T, \langle y, x\rangle \not\in T\}$. By rule PROD UP, we derive constraints $\langle x, y\rangle \in R * R, \langle y, x\rangle \in R * R, \langle x, x\rangle \in R * R$ and $\langle y, y\rangle \in R * R$. By set reasoning rule INTER DOWN, we derive another four constraints $\langle x, y\rangle \in S, \langle y, x\rangle \in S, \langle x, y\rangle \in T$, and $\langle y, x\rangle \in T$, leading to a contradiction with $\langle y, x\rangle \not\in T$. Thus, we can derive unsat by rule EQ UNSAT. $\square$

Example 3. Let $\mathcal{S}$ be $\{\langle x, y\rangle \in R, \langle y, z\rangle \in R, \langle x, z\rangle \not\in R^+\}$. By rule TCLOS UP I, we derive two new constraints $\langle x, y\rangle \in R^+$ and $\langle y, z\rangle \in R^+$. Then, we can derive another constraint $\langle x, z\rangle \in R^+$, by rule TCLOS UP II, in contradiction with $\langle x, z\rangle \not\in R^+$. Thus, we can derive unsat by rule EQ UNSAT. $\square$

Example 4. Let $\mathcal{S}$ be $\{\langle x, y\rangle \in R^+, \langle x, y\rangle \not\in R\}$. By rule TCLOS DOWN, we construct a derivation tree with three child branches, which add to $\mathcal{S}$ the sets $\{\langle x, y\rangle \in R\}$, $\{\langle x, z\rangle \in R, \langle z, y\rangle \in R\}$, and $\{\langle x, z_1\rangle \in R, \langle z_1, z_2\rangle \in R^+, \langle z_2, y\rangle \in R, z_1 \not\approx z_2\}$ respectively, where z_1 and z_2 are fresh variables. By rule EQ UNSAT, we can derive unsat in the first branch. Since no rules apply to the second branch, we can conclude, as we will see, that $\mathcal{S}$ is T_R-satisfiable. $\square$

4   Calculus Correctness

In this section, we formalize the correctness properties satisfied by our calculus. These include refutation and model soundness in general and termination over a fragment of our language of constraints.[3] The rules of the calculus define a notion of *derivation trees*. These possibly infinite trees whose nodes are states where the children of each non-leaf node are the result of applying one of the derivation rules of the calculus to that node. A finite branch of a derivation tree is *closed* if it ends with unsat; it is *saturated* if no rules apply to its leaf. A derivation tree is *closed* if all of its branches are closed.

Proposition 1 (Refutation Soundness). *If there is a closed derivation tree with root node $\mathcal{S}$, then $\mathcal{S}$ is T_R-unsatisfiable.*

Proposition 2 (Model Soundness). *Let $\mathcal{S}$ be the leaf of a saturated branch in a derivation tree. There is a model $\mathcal{I}$ of T_R that satisfies $\mathcal{S}$ and is such that (i) for all $S \in \mathrm{Vars}(\mathcal{S})$ of set sort, $S^{\mathcal{I}} = \{x^{\mathcal{I}} \mid x \in S \in \mathcal{S}^*\}$, and (ii) for all other $x, y \in \mathrm{Vars}(\mathcal{S})$, $x^{\mathcal{I}} = y^{\mathcal{I}}$ if and only if $x \approx y \in \mathcal{S}^*$.*

Our calculus is terminating for a sublanguage of constraints involving only unary and binary relations and excluding transitive closure, product, or equality between relations. While this sublanguage, defined in Fig. 4, is quite restricted, it is useful in reductions of description logics to relational logic, which we discuss in Sect. 5.2.

---

[3] All proofs of the propositions below can be found in a longer version of this paper available at http://cvc4.cs.stanford.edu/papers/CADE2017-relations/.

(element)	$e := x$
(unary relation)	$u := x \mid [] \mid u_1 \sqcup u_2 \mid u_1 \sqcap u_2 \mid [\langle e \rangle] \mid b \bowtie u$
(binary relation)	$b := x \mid [] \mid b_1 \sqcup b_2 \mid b_1 \sqcap b_2 \mid [\langle e_1, e_2 \rangle] \mid b^{-1}$
(constraint)	$\varphi := e_1 \approx e_2 \mid \langle e \rangle \sqsubseteq u \mid \langle e_1, e_2 \rangle \sqsubseteq b \mid \neg \varphi_1$

Fig. 4. A restricted fragment of T_R-constraints. Letter x denotes variables.

Proposition 3 (Termination). *If S is a finite set of constraints generated by the grammar in* Fig. 4, *then all derivation trees with root node S are finite.*

Proof. Assume that S is a finite set containing only constraints φ from the grammar in Fig. 4. First, we construct the following mapping from relation terms to tuple terms. Let D_u (resp. D_b) be a mapping from unary (resp. binary) relation terms to sets of unary (resp. binary) tuple terms defined as the least solution to the following set of constraints, where the e's, the u's and the b's are implicitly universally quantified metavariables ranging over terms respectively of element, unary relation and binary relation sort:

$$\langle e \rangle \in D_u(u) \quad \text{if} \quad \langle e \rangle \sqsubseteq u \in S$$
$$\langle e \rangle \in D_u(u_1) \quad \text{if} \quad \langle e \rangle \in D_u(u_2) \text{ and } u_1 \in \mathcal{T}(u_2)$$
$$\langle z_{e,b,u} \rangle \in D_u(u) \quad \text{if} \quad \langle e \rangle \in D_u(b \bowtie u)$$
$$\langle e_1, e_2 \rangle \in D_b(b) \quad \text{if} \quad \langle e_1, e_2 \rangle \sqsubseteq b \in S$$
$$\langle e_1, e_2 \rangle \in D_b(b_1) \quad \text{if} \quad \langle e_i, e_j \rangle \in D_b(b_2) \text{ for } \{i,j\} = \{1,2\} \text{ and } b_1 \in \mathcal{T}(b_2)$$
$$\langle e, z_{e,b,u} \rangle \in D_b(b) \quad \text{if} \quad \langle e \rangle \in D_u(b \bowtie u)$$

where $z_{e,b,u}$ denotes a unique fresh variable for each value of e, b, and u. We require only one such variable for each triple (e, b, u) since our redundancy criteria for rule applications ensures that JOIN DOWN cannot be applied more than once for the same premise $\langle e \rangle \in D_u(b \bowtie u)$. Intuitively, D_u maps each relation term u in S to an overapproximation of the set of unary tuples $\langle e \rangle$ for which our calculus can infer the constraint $\langle e \rangle \sqsubseteq u$ using downward rules only, and similarly for the binary case D_b. The domain of D_u and that of D_b contain only relation terms occurring in S, and thus are finite. All sets in the ranges of D_u and D_b are also finite. To show this, we argue that only a finite number of fresh variables $z_{e,b,u}$ are introduced by this construction. We define a measure depth on element terms such that $\text{depth}(e) = 0$ for all $e \in \mathcal{T}(S)$, and $\text{depth}(z_{e,b,u}) = 1 + \text{depth}(e)$. For all variables $z_{e,b,u}$ in the range of D_u and D_b, we have that $b \bowtie u \in \mathcal{T}(S)$, and if e is a variable of the form $z_{e',b',u'}$, then $b \bowtie u$ is either a subterm of b' or u'. Thus, the depth of all element terms in the range of D_u and D_b is finite. Since there are finitely many element terms in $\mathcal{T}(S)$, and finitely many terms of the form $b \bowtie u$ in $\mathcal{T}(S)$, there are finitely many variables of the form $z_{e,b,u}$ and thus finitely many element terms occur in tuple terms in the range of D_u and D_b. Therefore, there are finitely many tuple terms in sets in the ranges of D_u and D_b.

Now, let U_u (resp. U_b) be a mapping from unary (resp. binary) relation terms to sets of unary (resp. binary) tuple terms, constructed to be the least solution to the following set of constraints (where again the e's, the u's and the b's are implicitly universally quantified metavariables as above):

$$\langle e \rangle \in U_u(u) \quad \text{if } \langle e \rangle \in D_u(u)$$
$$\langle e \rangle \in U_u(u_1) \quad \text{if } \langle e \rangle \in U_u(u_2), u_2 \in \mathcal{T}(u_1) \text{ and } u_1 \in \mathcal{T}(\mathcal{S})$$
$$\langle e \rangle \in U_u(u) \quad \text{if } u = [\,e\,] \text{ and } u \in \mathcal{T}(\mathcal{S})$$
$$\langle e_1 \rangle \in U_u(u_1) \quad \text{if } u_1 = b_1 \bowtie u_2 \text{ and } \langle e_1, e_2 \rangle \in U_b(b_1)$$
$$\langle e_1, e_2 \rangle \in U_b(b) \quad \text{if } \langle e_1, e_2 \rangle \in D_b(b)$$
$$\langle e_1, e_2 \rangle \in U_b(b_1) \quad \text{if } \langle e_i, e_j \rangle \in U_b(b_2) \text{ for } \{i, j\} = \{1, 2\}, b_2 \in \mathcal{T}(b_1), b_1 \in \mathcal{T}(\mathcal{S})$$
$$\langle e_1, e_2 \rangle \in U_b(b) \quad \text{if } b = [\,\langle e_1, e_2 \rangle\,] \text{ and } b \in \mathcal{T}(\mathcal{S})$$

Similar to the previous construction, U_u maps each relation term u in $\mathcal{S}$ to an over-approximation of the set of unary tuples $\langle e \rangle$ for which our calculus can infer the constraint $\langle e \rangle \sqsubseteq u$ using both downward and upward rules, and similarly for the binary case U_b. By construction, since the domains of D_u and D_b are subsets of $\mathcal{T}(\mathcal{S})$, the domains of U_u and U_b are also subsets of $\mathcal{T}(\mathcal{S})$, and thus are finite, hence their respective ranges R_u and R_b are finite too. Each set in R_u or R_b is finite as well, since the tuples in these ranges are built from element terms e that occur in the range of D_u and D_b or in singleton sets of the form $[\,\langle e \rangle\,]$, $[\,\langle e, e' \rangle\,]$ or $[\,\langle e', e \rangle\,]$ in $\mathcal{T}(\mathcal{S})$.

Now let $\widehat{\mathcal{S}}$ be the following set of constraints:

$$\widehat{\mathcal{S}} = \{(\neg)\langle e \rangle \sqsubseteq u \mid \langle e \rangle \in U_u(u), u \in \mathcal{T}(\mathcal{S})\} \cup$$
$$\{(\neg)\langle e_1, e_2 \rangle \sqsubseteq b \mid \langle e_1, e_2 \rangle \in U_b(b), b \in \mathcal{T}(\mathcal{S})\} \cup$$
$$\{(\neg)e_1 \approx e_2 \mid e_1, e_2 \in \mathcal{T}(R_u \cup R_b)\} \cup$$
$$\{\langle e_1 \rangle \approx \langle e_2 \rangle \mid e_1, e_2 \in \mathcal{T}(R_u \cup R_b)\} \cup$$
$$\{\langle e_1, e_2 \rangle \approx \langle e_3, e_4 \rangle \mid e_1, e_2, e_3, e_4 \in \mathcal{T}(R_u \cup R_b)\}$$

From the arguments above we can conclude that $\widehat{\mathcal{S}}$ is finite. By construction, $\mathcal{S} \subseteq \widehat{\mathcal{S}}$. One can show by structural induction on derivation trees that all descendants of $\mathcal{S}$ in a derivation tree are also subsets of $\widehat{\mathcal{S}}$. Since the size of a state strictly grows with each rule application not deriving unsat, we can conclude that no derivation tree can be grown indefinitely. Hence all derivation trees with root $\mathcal{S}$ are finite.   □

By Propositions 1, 2 and 3, we have that *any* rule application strategy for the calculus is a decision procedure for finite sets of constraints in the language generated by the grammar from Fig. 4.

5 Applications of T_R

Our main motivation for adding native support for relations in an SMT solver is that it enables more natural mappings from other logical formalisms ultimately based on relations. This opens the possibility of leveraging the power and flexibility of SMT to reason about problems expressed in those formalisms. We discuss here two potential applications: reasoning about Alloy specifications and reasoning about OWL ontologies. It should be clear to the knowledgeable reader though that the set of potential applications is much larger, encompassing description logics in general as well as various modal logics—via an encoding of their accessibility relation.

5.1 Alloy Specifications

Alloy is a formal specification language based on relational logic which is widely used for modeling structurally-rich problems [12]. Alloy specifications, called *models* in the Alloy literature, are built from relations and relational algebra operations in addition to the usual logical connectives and quantifiers. One can also specify expected properties of a specification as formulas, called *assertions* in Alloy, that should be entailed by the specification.

The analysis of Alloy specifications can be performed automatically by a tool called the Alloy Analyzer which uses as its reasoning engine Kodkod, a SAT-based finite model finder [17]. This requires the user to impose a (concrete, artificial) finite upper bound on the size of the domains of each relation, limiting the analyzer's ability to determine that a specification is consistent or has a given property. In the first case, the user has to manually increase the bounds until the Alloy Analyzer is able to find a satisfying interpretation for the specification; in the second case, until it can find a counter-example for the property. As a consequence, the analyzer cannot be used to prove that (*i*) a specification is inconsistent or (*ii*) it does have a certain property.

In contrast, thanks to its new theory solver for relational constraints based on the calculus described earlier, CVC4 is now able in many cases to do (*i*) and (*ii*) automatically, with no artificial upper bounds on domain sizes. Also, because of its own finite model finding capabilities [15], it can find minimal satisfying interpretations for consistent specifications or minimal counter-examples for properties without the need of user-provided artificial upper bounds on domain sizes. Finally, since its relational theory solver is fully integrated with its theory solvers for other theories (such as linear arithmetic, strings, arrays, and so on), CVC4 can natively support mixed constraints using relations over its various built-in types, something that is possible in the Alloy Analyzer only in rather limited form.[4] To evaluate CVC4's capabilities in solving Alloy problems, we have defined a translation from Alloy specifications to semantically equivalent SMT formulas that leverages our theory of relations. The translation focuses on Alloy's kernel language since non-kernel features can be rewritten to the kernel language by the Alloy Analyzer itself. We sketch our translation below.[5]

In Alloy, a *signature* is a set of uninterpreted atomic elements, called *atoms*. Signatures are defined with a syntax that is reminiscent of classes in object-oriented languages. A *relation (of arity n)* is a set of n-tuples of atoms and

---

[4] The Alloy Analyzer currently has built-in support for bounded integers. Any other data types need to be axiomatized in the specification.

[5] The translation is sound only if all Alloy signatures are assumed to be finite. A full account of the translation and a proof of its soundness are beyond the scope of this paper.

is declared as a *field* of some signature S, which acts as the domain of the elements in the first component. Multiplicity constraints on signatures and fields can be added with keywords such as some, no, lone, and one, which specify that a signature is non-empty, empty, has cardinality at most one, and is a singleton, respectively. Other keywords specify that a relation is one-to-one, one-to-many, and so on. One or more signatures can be declared to be subsets of another signature with extends or in. With extends, all specified signatures are additionally assumed to be mutually disjoint.

In the translation, we introduce an uninterpreted sort Atom for Alloy atoms. An Alloy signature sig S is translated as a constant[6] S of sort $\mathsf{Rel}_1(\mathsf{Atom})$, that is, a set of unary tuples. A field f:S_1 -> $\cdots$ -> S_n of a signature S is translated as a constant f of sort $\mathsf{Rel}_{n+1}(\mathsf{Atom}, \ldots, \mathsf{Atom})$ together with the additional constraint $f \sqsubseteq S * S_1 * \cdots * S_n$ to ensure that the components of f's tuples are from the intended signatures. The signature hierarchy is encoded using subset constraints. For example, the Alloy constraint sig S_1, ..., S_n extends S is translated as the set of constraints $\{S_1 \sqsubseteq S, \ldots, S_n \sqsubseteq S\} \cup \{S_i \sqcap S_j \approx [] \mid 1 \leq i < j \leq n\}$. If S above is also declared to be *abstract* (a notion similar to abstract classes in object-oriented languages), the additional constraint $S_1 \sqcup \cdots \sqcup S_n \approx S$ is added to enforce that. Similarly, signature declarations of the form sig S_1, $\cdots$, S_n in S, are translated just as $\{S_1 \sqsubseteq S, \ldots, S_n \sqsubseteq S\}$. Multiplicity constraints are translated as quantified formulas.

Since our theory supports all constructs and operators in Alloy's kernel language, Alloy expressions and formulas, which can include quantifiers ranging over atoms, can be more or less directly translated to their counterparts in CVC4's language. It is worth mentioning that our translation supports Alloy's set comprehension construct, by introducing a fresh relational constant for the set and adding definitional axioms for it. In addition, we partially support Alloy cardinality constraints of the form #$(r)\,op\;n$ where r is a relation term, $op \in \{<, >, =\}$, $n \in \mathbb{N}$, and # is the cardinality operator, by encoding them as subset constraints. For example, the Alloy constraint #(S) < 3 on a signature S is translated to $S \sqsubseteq [\langle k_1 \rangle, \langle k_2 \rangle]$ where S is the corresponding unary relation and k_1 and k_2 are two fresh constants of sort Atom.

5.2 OWL DL Ontologies

OWL is an ontology language whose current version, OWL 2, was adopted as a standard Semantic Web language by the W3 consortium. It includes a sublanguage, called OWL DL, that corresponds to the expressive, yet decidable, description logic $\mathcal{SHOIN}(\mathbf{D})$ [2]. We have defined an initial, partial translation from $\mathcal{SHOIN}(\mathbf{D})$ to SMT formulas that again leverages our theory of relations.

A mapping from salient $\mathcal{SHOIN}(\mathbf{D})$ constructs to their SMT counterparts is illustrated in Fig. 5. The figure shows only relations whose elements do not

---

[6] Free constants have the same effect as free variables for satisfiability purposes.

DL	CVC4
individual name: a	a : Atom
atomic concept C, role R	C : $\mathrm{Rel}_1(\mathsf{Atom})$, R : $\mathrm{Rel}_2(\mathsf{Atom}, \mathsf{Atom})$
intersection C ⊓ D, union C ⊔ D	C ⊓ D, C ⊔ D
inverse role R⁻, complement ¬C	R^{-1}, Univ \ C
top concept ⊤, bottom concept ⊥	Univ, []
existential restriction ∃R.C	R ⋈ C
universal restriction ∀R.C	$[\,x \mid x \in \mathsf{Univ} \wedge [x] \bowtie R \sqsubseteq C\,]$
at-least restriction $\geq_n$R.C	$[\,x \mid x \in \mathsf{Univ} \wedge \exists a_1,\dots,a_n : \mathsf{Atom}\,([x] \bowtie R) \sqcap C \sqsupseteq [\langle a_1\rangle,\dots,\langle a_n\rangle] \wedge \mathrm{dist}(a_1,\dots,a_n)\,]$
at-most restriction $\leq_n$R.C	$[\,x \mid x \in \mathsf{Univ} \wedge \exists a_1,\dots,a_n : \mathsf{Atom}\,([x] \bowtie R) \sqcap C) \sqsubseteq [\langle a_1\rangle,\dots,\langle a_n\rangle] \wedge [\langle a_1\rangle,\dots,\langle a_n\rangle] \sqsubseteq C\,]$
local reflexivity ∃R.Self	$[\,\langle x,y\rangle \mid \langle x,y\rangle \in R \wedge x \approx y\,]$
nominal {a}	$[\,\langle a\rangle\,]$
concept, role assertion C(a), R(a, b)	a ∈ C, ⟨a, b⟩ ∈ R
individual (dis)equality a ≈ b, a ≉ b	a ≈ b, a ≉ b
concept, role inclusion C ⊑ D, R ⊑ S	C ⊑ D, R ⊑ S
concept, role equiv. C ≡ D, R ≡ S	C ≈ D, R ≈ S
complex role inclusion $R_1 \circ R_2 \sqsubseteq S$	$R_1 \bowtie R_2 \sqsubseteq S$
role disjointness Disjoint(R, S)	R ⊓ S ≈ []

Fig. 5. A mapping from DL language to Σ_R-constraints.

belong to the so-called *concrete* domain(s) **D** of $\mathcal{SHOIN}(\mathbf{D})$.[7] As with the Alloy translation, we use the single sort Atom for all elements of non-concrete domains. The set comprehension notation is used here for brevity: for a set comprehension term of the form $[\,x \mid \varphi\,]$ where x has n-tuple sort, we introduce a fresh set constant S accompanied by the defining axiom $\forall x : \mathsf{Tup}_n(\mathsf{Atom})\ (x \in S \leftrightarrow \varphi)$. The constant Univ in the figure denotes the universal unary relation over Atom. Since this constant is currently not built-in as a symbol of T_R, it is accompanied by the defining axiom $\forall a : \mathsf{Atom}\ \langle a\rangle \in \mathsf{Univ}$. The expression $\mathrm{dist}(a_1,\dots,a_n)$ states that $a_1,\dots,a_n$ are pairwise different. We observe how the translation is immediate for most constructs, with the notable exception of universal and number restrictions, which require the use of complex quantified formulas.

6   Evaluation

To evaluate our theory solver for T_R in CVC4 we implemented translators from Alloy and from OWL based on the translations sketched in the previous section.

---

[7] Some of those domains in OWL correspond to built-in sorts in CVC4. A full translation from OWL concrete domains to CVC4 built-in sorts is beyond the scope of this work.

This section presents an initial evaluation on a selection of Alloy and OWL benchmarks.[8]

6.1 Experimental Evaluation on Alloy Models

We considered two sets of Alloy benchmarks; the first consists of 40 examples from the Alloy distribution and from a formal methods course taught by one of the authors; the second were used in [10] to evaluate AlloyPE. All benchmarks consist of an Alloy model together with a single property. We evaluated two configurations of CVC4. The first, denoted **CVC4**, enables full native support for relational operators via the calculus from Sect. 3. The second, denoted **CVC4+AX**, instead encodes all relational operators as uninterpreted functions and supplements the translation of benchmarks with additional axioms that specify their semantics. To compare CVC4 with other tools, we also evaluated the Alloy Analyzer, version 4.2, downloaded from the Alloy website, and El Ghazi et al.'s AlloyPE tool (kindly provided to us directly by its authors) using the SMT solver Z3 version 4.5.1 as a backend. All experiments were performed with a 300 s timeout on a machine with a 2.9 GHz Intel Core i7 CPU with 8 GB of memory.

Problem	Alloy Analyzer		CVC4		CVC4+AX		AlloyPE	
	Res.	Time/Scope	Res.	Time	Res.	Time	Res.	Time
academia_0	sat	0.60/3	sat	1.55	-	to	unk	84.76
academia_1	sat	0.53/2	sat	1.93	-	to	-	to
academia_2	sat	0.45/2	sat	0.49	-	to	unk	0.15
social_1	sat	0.52/3	sat	1.20	-	to	n/a	-
social_5	sat	1.56/2	sat	0.49	-	to	n/a	-
social_6	sat	0.49/2	sat	0.52	-	to	n/a	-
cf_0	sat	0.47/3	sat	0.51	-	to	n/a	-
cf_1	sat	0.49/3	sat	0.78	-	to	n/a	-
javatypes	sat	0.50/3	sat	0.42	-	to	uns	2.35
set	sat	0.45/2	sat	0.46	-	to	unk	0.92
loc_int	sat	0.57/1	sat	2.82	-	to	n/a	-
genealogy	sat	0.64/6	sat	89.20	-	to	n/a	-
number_1	sat	0.81/2	sat	8.65	-	to	n/a	-
railway	sat	0.67/4	sat	156.45	-	to	n/a	-
academia_3	b-uns	162.17/63	uns	0.49	uns	1.05	uns	0.28
academia_4	b-uns	246.92/162	uns	0.43	uns	0.54	uns	0.13
family_1	b-uns	146.62/68	uns	0.41	uns	0.44	uns	0.15
family_2	b-uns	279.77/30	uns	1.02	uns	48.78	uns	0.23
social_2	b-uns	256.98/56	uns	0.66	-	to	n/a	-
social_3	b-uns	191.45/57	uns	0.49	uns	35.91	n/a	-
social_4	b-uns	171.26/64	uns	0.46	uns	18.13	n/a	-
birthday	b-uns	156.08/53	uns	0.45	uns	0.61	uns	0.13
library	b-uns	259.54/119	uns	0.42	uns	0.40	uns	1.11
lights	b-uns	228.89/122	uns	32.69	-	to	n/a	-
INSLabel	b-uns	198.53/8	uns	1.46	-	to	n/a	-
farmers_1	sat	1.04/8	-	to	-	to	n/a	-
views	sat	9.91/9	-	to	-	to	n/a	-

Fig. 6. Evaluation on Alloy benchmarks.

---

[8] Detailed results and all benchmarks are available at http://cvc4.cs.stanford.edu/papers/CADE2017-relations/.

Problem	Alloy Analyzer		CVC4		CVC4+AX		AlloyPE	
	Res.	Time	Res.	Time	Res.	Time	Res.	Time
mem-wr	b-uns	195.98/35	uns	0.43	uns	0.48	uns	0.44
mem-wi	b-uns	260.66/29	uns	0.45	uns	0.50	uns	0.42
ab-ai	b-uns	185.06/28	uns	0.46	uns	0.79	uns	0.49
ab-dua	b-uns	193.33/27	uns	0.49	uns	0.48	uns	0.70
abt-dua	b-uns	137.87/14	uns	0.60	uns	0.81	uns	0.70
abt-ly-u	b-uns	261.23/9	uns	0.81	uns	28.26	uns	1.4
abt-ly-p	b-uns	277.86/8	uns	0.81	uns	1.77	uns	175.19
gp-nsf	b-uns	152.55/69	uns	0.41	uns	0.59	uns	0.43
gp-nsg	b-uns	166.75/66	uns	0.42	-	to	uns	0.44
com-1	b-uns	297.18/13	uns	2.95	-	to	uns	0.59
com-2	b-uns	295.73/13	-	to	-	to	uns	0.55
com-3	b-uns	295.33/14	uns	4.29	-	to	uns	0.64
com-4a	b-uns	301.57/13	uns	9.39	-	to	uns	0.99
com-4b	b-uns	299.77/13	uns	0.90	-	to	uns	0.61
fs-sd	b-uns	157.90/70	uns	0.42	-	to	uns	0.89
fs-nda	b-uns	271.38/44	uns	0.55	-	to	uns	0.83
gc-s1	b-uns	270.07/14	uns	4.92	uns	8.14	uns	14.27
gc-s2	b-uns	288.44/8	-	to	-	to	uns	10.66
gc-c	b-uns	287.73/8	-	to	-	to	uns	42.31
hr-l	b-uns	275.80/7	-	to	-	to	-	to

Fig. 7. Evaluation on AlloyPE benchmarks

Figures 6 and 7 show the results from running the Alloy Analyzer, CVC4 and AlloyPE on the two sets of Alloy benchmarks. We omit results for 13 of the benchmarks from the first set that no system solved. The second and third columns show the results of running the Alloy Analyzer. To evaluate the Alloy Analyzer on these benchmarks, we considered bounded scopes in an incremental fashion. Using a script, we set an initial upper bound, or *scope*, of 1 for the cardinality of all signatures in the problem, and kept increasing it by 1 if the Alloy Analyzer found the problem unsatisfiable (b-uns) in the current scope—meaning that it was not able to *disprove* the property in the problem. We terminated on time out (to), or when the analyzer was able to disprove the property (sat) or ran out of memory for a scope. We report the scope size for benchmarks where the tool returned an answer. The fourth and fifth columns show the results from CVC4 when invoked in finite model finding mode on the translated SMT problem. The last two columns are the results from AlloyPE, where n/a indicates that AlloyPE failed due either to the presence of unsupported Alloy constructs in the input problem or to internal errors during solving or translation.

As shown in the table, our approach is overall slower than the Alloy Analyzer for satisfiable benchmarks. For the unsatisfiable ones, CVC4 returns an answer within a reasonable time limit for most of the benchmarks and has advantages over the state of the art. It is important to note, however, that an unsat answer from CVC4 indicates that the property is valid as opposed to the b-uns answer from the Alloy Analyzer, which only means the property is valid within the given scope.

Compared to AlloyPE, we successfully solved all of their benchmarks but four, as indicated in Fig. 7. For these benchmarks, AlloyPE benefits from performing a static analysis of the problem that involves sophisticated heuristics to discover invariants. For our own set of benchmarks, in Fig. 6, AlloyPE failed on all sat benchmarks and was unable to solve many unsat ones due to failures during the translation or the solving phase. We observe that AlloyPE gives an unsound answer for the benchmark javatypes: it returns unsat, whereas both the Alloy Analyzer and CVC4 return sat.

Our results also indicate that native support for relational reasoning is important for reasoning efficiently for these benchmark sets. In fact, **CVC4+AX** is unable to report sat for any satisfiable benchmark due to its use of axioms for the relation operators, which quantify over set variables, where CVC4's finite model finding techniques are not applicable. More interestingly, **CVC4+AX** solves significantly fewer unsat benchmarks when compared to **CVC4**, indicating that using the calculus in Sect. 3 is superior to encoding the semantics of relational operators via an explicit axiomatization.

6.2   Experimental Evaluation on OWL Models

We built a preliminary translator from OWL to SMT, and we did a *consistency evaluation*, which checks whether or not an ontology is contradictory, for a set of OWL benchmarks in pure description logic from the 4th OWL Reasoner Evaluation competition.[9] Of the original 7,704 benchmarks, we considered only those whose size was under 1 MB, and further excluded benchmarks that involved some of the more sophisticated features of the OWL language that are currently not supported by our translator. We ran the experiments with a 30 s time out, on a machine with a 3.2 GHz Intel(R) Xeon CPU E5-2667 v3 and 20 GB of memory.

Among the selected 3,936 benchmarks, CVC4 found 3,639 consistent, found 7 inconsistent, and timed out on the remaining 290. By comparison, the state-of-the-art DL reasoner Konclude [16] gave an answer for all 3,936 benchmarks. However, Konclude and CVC4 disagreed on 9 benchmarks, all of which CVC4 found consistent. We determined that Konclude reports inconsistent for those 9 benchmarks possibly because the benchmarks are not syntactically compliant. For example, some include Boolean literals without a type declaration. In terms of performance, CVC4 takes on average 1.7 s per benchmark on the 3,646 it solves. This is significantly slower than Konclude, which takes on average 0.02 s per benchmark on the same set. We attribute this to the fact that CVC4 does not yet support the universal set and set complement natively, and has no specific quantifier instantiation heuristics for the quantified formulas generated by the translation of universal and number restrictions. Nevertheless, we find these results quite encouraging as they show that further investigation into efficient reasoning for OWL models in SMT solvers is an interesting direction of research.

7   Conclusion and Future Work

We presented a calculus for an extension to the theory of finite sets that includes support for relations and relational operators. We implemented the calculus as a modular extension to the set subsolver in our SMT solver CVC4. A preliminary evaluation has shown that our implementation is competitive with the

---

[9] See https://www.w3.org/community/owled/ore-2015-workshop/competition.

state of the art when used to prove properties or verify the consistency of Alloy specifications.

We are investigating more expressive fragments for which our calculus terminates, including those corresponding to fragments of description logic [11]. In future work, we would like to devise an approach for a theory that includes both relational constraints and cardinality constraints that is efficient in practice, together with specialized techniques geared toward reasoning about formulas resulting from the translation of description logic problems. In particular, we plan to extend our logic with the set complement operator and a constant for the universal set, and extend our calculus and its implementation to provide direct support for them.

Acknowledgements. This work was partially supported by NSF grant no. 1228765 and by a gift from GE Global Research. We are grateful to Jasmin Blanchette and the anonymous reviewers for their very detailed comments and questions which helped improve the presentation of the paper.

References

1. Baader, F.: The Description Logic Handbook: Theory, Implementation and Applications. Cambridge University Press, Cambridge (2003)
2. Baader, F., Horrocks, I., Sattler, U.: Description logics. In: Frank van Harmelen, V.L., Porter, B. (eds.) Handbook of Knowledge Representation, vol. 3. Foundations of Artificial Intelligence, pp. 135–179. Elsevier (2008)
3. Bansal, K., Reynolds, A., Barrett, C., Tinelli, C.: A new decision procedure for finite sets and cardinality constraints in SMT. In: Olivetti, N., Tiwari, A. (eds.) IJCAR 2016. LNCS (LNAI), vol. 9706, pp. 82–98. Springer, Cham (2016). doi:10. 1007/978-3-319-40229-1_7
4. Barrett, C., Conway, C.L., Deters, M., Hadarean, L., Jovanović, D., King, T., Reynolds, A., Tinelli, C.: CVC4. In: Gopalakrishnan, G., Qadeer, S. (eds.) CAV 2011. LNCS, vol. 6806, pp. 171–177. Springer, Heidelberg (2011). doi:10.1007/978-3-642-22110-1_14
5. Barrett, C., Fontaine, P., Tinelli, C.: The SMT-LIB standard–version 2.6. In: Gupta, A., Kroening, D. (eds.) SMT 2010 (2010)
6. Barrett, C., Sebastiani, R., Seshia, S., Tinelli, C.: Satisfiability modulo theories. In: Biere, A., Heule, M.J.H., van Maaren, H., Walsh, T. (eds.) Handbook of Satisfiability, vol. 185, chap. 26, pp. 825–885. IOS Press, February 2009
7. Dutertre, B., Moura, L.D.: The YICES SMT solver. Technical report, SRI International (2006)
8. Ghazi, A.A.E., Taghdiri, M.: Analyzing alloy constraints using an SMT solver: a case study. In: 5th International Workshop on Automated Formal Methods (AFM) (2010)
9. Ghazi, A.A., Taghdiri, M.: Relational reasoning via SMT solving. In: Butler, M., Schulte, W. (eds.) FM 2011. LNCS, vol. 6664, pp. 133–148. Springer, Heidelberg (2011). doi:10.1007/978-3-642-21437-0_12
10. El Ghazi, A.A., Taghdiri, M., Herda, M.: First-order transitive closure axiomatization via iterative invariant injections. In: Havelund, K., Holzmann, G., Joshi, R. (eds.) NFM 2015. LNCS, vol. 9058, pp. 143–157. Springer, Cham (2015). doi:10. 1007/978-3-319-17524-9_11

11. Horrocks, I., Sattler, U.: Decidability of SHIQ with complex role inclusion axioms. Artif. Intell. **160**(1–2), 79–104 (2004)
12. Jackson, D.: Alloy: a lightweight object modelling notation. ACM Trans. Softw. Eng. Methodol. **11**(2), 256–290 (2002)
13. Jackson, D.: Software Abstractions - Logic, Language, and Analysis. MIT Press (2006)
14. Nieuwenhuis, R., Oliveras, A., Tinelli, C.: Solving SAT and SAT modulo theories: from an abstract Davis-Putnam-Logemann-Loveland Procedure to DPLL(T). J. ACM **53**(6), 937–977 (2006)
15. Reynolds, A., Tinelli, C., Goel, A., Krstić, S.: Finite model finding in SMT. In: Sharygina, N., Veith, H. (eds.) CAV 2013. LNCS, vol. 8044, pp. 640–655. Springer, Heidelberg (2013). doi:10.1007/978-3-642-39799-8_42
16. Steigmiller, A., Liebig, T., Glimm, B.: Konclude: System description. Web Semant. Sci. Serv. Agents World Wide Web **27**(1), 1–86 (2014)
17. Torlak, E., Jackson, D.: Kodkod: a relational model finder. In: Grumberg, O., Huth, M. (eds.) TACAS 2007. LNCS, vol. 4424, pp. 632–647. Springer, Heidelberg (2007). doi:10.1007/978-3-540-71209-1_49
18. Tsarkov, D., Horrocks, I.: FaCT++ description logic reasoner: system description. In: Furbach, U., Shankar, N. (eds.) IJCAR 2006. LNCS (LNAI), vol. 4130, pp. 292–297. Springer, Heidelberg (2006). doi:10.1007/11814771_26
19. Tsarkov, D., Palmisano, I.: Chainsaw: a metareasoner for large ontologies. In: Horrocks, I., Yatskevich, M., Jiménez-Ruiz, E. (eds.) ORE (2012)
20. W3C. OWL 2 web ontology language. https://www.w3.org/2007/OWL/wiki/Syntax

Decision Procedures for Theories
of Sets with Measures

Markus Bender[✉] and Viorica Sofronie-Stokkermans

Universität Koblenz-Landau, Koblenz, Germany
{mbender,sofronie}@uni-koblenz.de

Abstract. In this paper we introduce a decision procedure for checking satisfiability of quantifier-free formulae in the combined theory of sets, measures and arithmetic. Such theories are important in mathematics (e.g. probability theory and measure theory) and in applications. We indicate how these ideas can be used for obtaining a decision procedure for a fragment of the duration calculus.

1 Introduction

For the verification of real world systems one often needs decision procedures for various, complex, data structures. One theory which was thoroughly investigated in the past is the theory of sets with cardinalities. Such data structures are important in mathematics, knowledge representation and verification, and have proven to be a useful abstraction in many verification areas. The decidability of this theory has been extensively studied. In addition to work by Ohlbach ([21]), by Kuncak and his collaborators ([19,20,24,25,27]) and the extension to the combined theory of sets, cardinalities, arithmetic and sums of sets ([3]), we mention work by Zarba ([26]), Chocron et al. ([12]), Alberti et al. ([1]) and Bansal et al. ([2]) in which the theory of sets and cardinalities – or fragments thereof – is considered and different decision procedures are proposed. However, so far we have not found any results on the more general case of reasoning with sets and arbitrary measures. The main idea of the approach proposed in [21] and later in [19] is to use an atomic decomposition of sets, using Venn diagrams, and use the additivity axioms for cardinalities for a reduction to checking the validity/satisfiability of formulae in Presburger arithmetic. This reduction method relies on the fact that sets with cardinality 0 are empty. This is not the case for more general theories of additive functions such as measures or probabilities on infinite sets: there can exist non-empty sets with measure 0.

In this paper we study theories of sets with measures, which are important in mathematics (e.g. probability theory and measure theory) and in applications, e.g. for the duration calculus (cf. e.g. [5]). The main contributions of this paper can be summarized as follows:

- We propose a method for checking satisfiability of quantifier-free formulae of theories of sets, measures and arithmetic by reduction to checking the

© Springer International Publishing AG 2017
L. de Moura (Ed.): CADE 2017, LNAI 10395, pp. 166–184, 2017.
DOI: 10.1007/978-3-319-63046-5_11

satisfiability of a formula in linear real arithmetic, and study its complexity. Our method relies – similarly to the approaches of Ohlbach [21] and Kuncak et al. [19] – on an atomic decomposition of sets.
- We prove a locality result for this theory and show that locality considerations allow us to identify tractable fragments of the theory.
- We indicate how these ideas can be used for obtaining a decision procedure for a fragment of the duration calculus [5] introduced in [13].

The locality properties we establish allow us to use results on preservation of locality properties for combinations of theories in [14] for proving – in a uniform way – locality properties for the combination of the theory of sets with measures with other local extensions of the theory of sets and provide an alternative to results obtained before in the context of combining reduction functions in [16], and for combinations of certain theories with shared set operations in [24].

Structure of the paper: In Sect. 2 we present the problems and the idea of our solutions on two examples. Section 3 introduces the definitions of the theories we consider. In Sects. 4 and 5 we present two versions of our approach; in Sect. 6 we show how it can be used for a fragment of the duration calculus.

2 Examples

We illustrate the idea of our method by two examples:

Example 1 (Probability theory). Consider two events e_1 and e_2. Assume that:

(i) e_1 implies e_2,
(ii) e_2 does not imply e_1 and
(iii) the probability that e_2 happens and e_1 does not happen is 0. Is it possible that the probability of e_1 and that of e_2 are different?

If we identify the events e_1, e_2 with subsets x_1, x_2 of a sample space $\mathcal{U}$, we can formulate the problem as checking the satisfiability of the following formula:

$$F = (x_1 \subseteq x_2) \ \wedge \ \neg(x_2 \subseteq x_1) \ \wedge \ P(x_2 \cap \overline{x_1}) \approx 0 \ \wedge \ P(x_1) \not\approx P(x_2)$$

in the combinations of the theory of sets and the theory of a measure function P, satisfying the following conditions

(P_1) $\qquad\qquad \forall X \ (0 \leq P(X))$

(P_2) $\qquad\qquad \forall X \ (X \approx \emptyset \rightarrow P(X) \approx 0)$

(P_3) $\qquad\qquad \forall X, Y \ (X \cap Y \approx \emptyset \rightarrow P(X \cup Y) \approx P(X) + P(Y))$

(P_4) $\qquad\qquad \forall X \ (P(X) \leq 1) \wedge P(\mathcal{U}) = 1$

We will show that in order to check the satisfiability of formula F we can proceed as follows: We generate all atomic sets corresponding to the Venn diagram associated with the sets occurring in the problem, in this case:

$$\mathcal{S}_{11} = x_1 \cap x_2, \quad \mathcal{S}_{10} = x_1 \cap \overline{x_2}, \quad \mathcal{S}_{01} = \overline{x_1} \cap x_2, \quad \mathcal{S}_{00} = \overline{x_1} \cap \overline{x_2},$$

and replace $x_1 \subseteq x_2$ with $\mathcal{S}_{10} \approx \emptyset$, and $x_2 \subseteq x_1$ with $\mathcal{S}_{01} \approx \emptyset$.

We then consider the following instances of the probability axioms (P_1)–(P_4): in (P_4) we replace X with the union of all atomic sets (all other instances are redundant); in (P_3) we instantiate X and Y with all possible disjoint unions of atomic sets. We use these instances to reduce the initial problem to the problem of checking the satisfiability of the following formula:

$$\mathcal{S}_{10} \approx \emptyset \;\wedge\; \mathcal{S}_{01} \not\approx \emptyset \;\wedge\; P(\mathcal{S}_{01}) \approx 0 \;\wedge\; P(\mathcal{S}_{11}) + P(\mathcal{S}_{10}) \not\approx P(\mathcal{S}_{01}) + P(\mathcal{S}_{11})$$

together with the corresponding instances of the axioms (P_1), and (P_2) in which the variable X is instantiated with $\mathcal{S}_{00}, \mathcal{S}_{01}, \mathcal{S}_{10}$ and $\mathcal{S}_{11}$. After purification by replacing $P(\mathcal{S}_{ij})$ with m_{ij}, and simplification we obtain the following constraints:

Def	Set	Num	Bridge
$m_{11} \approx P(\mathcal{S}_{11})$	$\mathcal{S}_{10} \approx \emptyset$	$m_{01} \approx 0,\;\; m_{11} + m_{10} \not\approx m_{01} + m_{11}$	$\mathcal{S}_{11} \approx \emptyset \to m_{11} \approx 0$
$m_{10} \approx P(\mathcal{S}_{10})$	$\mathcal{S}_{01} \not\approx \emptyset$	$0 \le m_{00}, 0 \le m_{10}, 0 \le m_{01}, 0 \le m_{11}$	$\mathcal{S}_{10} \approx \emptyset \to m_{10} \approx 0$
$m_{01} \approx P(\mathcal{S}_{01})$		$m_{11} + m_{01} + m_{10} + m_{11} = 1$	$\mathcal{S}_{01} \approx \emptyset \to m_{01} \approx 0$
$m_{00} \approx P(\mathcal{S}_{00})$			$\mathcal{S}_{00} \approx \emptyset \to m_{00} \approx 0$

We can check the satisfiability of the formula above as follows: We notice that the set constraints entail $\mathcal{S}_{10} \approx \emptyset$. Using $\mathcal{S}_{10} \approx \emptyset \to m_{10} \approx 0$, we obtain $m_{10} \approx 0$. This leads to a contradiction. In this paper we show that the instantiation procedure described above is sound, complete and terminating for the theory of sets with measures, and investigate two possibilities of propagating constraints of the form $\mathcal{S}_{ij} \approx \emptyset$ in order to entail $m_{ij} \approx 0$. We show that if the problems we consider do not contain unions or negation then we can replace axiom (P_3) with a monotonicity axiom for the measures and thus obtain a polynomial decision procedure for satisfiability of formulae in this fragment. ∎

Example 2 (Duration Calculus). Consider two "states" described by propositional variables x_1 and x_2 finitely varying on an interval $[b, e]$, where $b < e$. Assume that:

(i) at every moment of time t if a system is in state x_1, it is also in state x_2,
(ii) there are moments at which the system is in state x_2 but not in state x_1,
(iii) the "duration" in $[b, e]$ of the system being in state x_2 but not in x_1 is 0.

Can the durations in $[b, e]$ of x_1 and x_2 be different?

In the duration calculus, for a state described by a propositional variable x and an observation interval $[b, e]$, the duration of x in $[b, e]$ is $\int x = \int_b^e x(t)dt$. The problem above is that of checking the satisfiability of the formula:

$$(x_1 \subseteq x_2) \;\wedge\; \neg(x_2 \subseteq x_1) \;\wedge\; \int (x_2 \cap \overline{x_1}) \approx 0 \;\wedge\; \int x_1 \not\approx \int x_2$$

in the theory of sets with a measure function $\int$ satisfying axioms $(\int_1)$–$(\int_3)$ similar to (P_1)–(P_3); this is actually the problem in Example 2 without (P_4). ∎

3   Theories of Sets with Measures

In this section we define the theories considered in this paper.

Syntax. Let $S = \{\mathsf{num}, \mathsf{set}\}$ be a set of sorts, consisting of num (the *numerical sort*), set (the *sort of sets*). The following sets of function and predicate symbols:

$\Omega_{c_{\mathsf{num}}} = \{K \mid K \text{ a constant of sort } \mathsf{num} \text{ with fixed semantics}\}$

$\Omega_{c_{\mathsf{set}}} = \{\emptyset,\ \mathcal{U}\}$

$\Omega_{\mathsf{num}} = \Omega_{c_{\mathsf{num}}} \cup \{+, -, *\}$, where $a(+) = a(-) = a(*) = \mathsf{num} \times \mathsf{num} \to \mathsf{num}$

$\Omega_{\mathsf{set}} = \Omega_{c_{\mathsf{set}}} \cup \{\cup, \cap, \complement\}$, where $a(\cup) = a(\cap) = \mathsf{set} \times \mathsf{set} \to \mathsf{set}, a(\complement) = \mathsf{set} \to \mathsf{set}$

$\Pi_{\mathsf{num}} = \{\approx_{\mathsf{num}}, <\}$, where $a(\approx_{\mathsf{num}}) = a(<) = \mathsf{num} \times \mathsf{num}$

$\Pi_{\mathsf{set}} = \{\approx_{\mathsf{set}}, \subseteq\}$, where $a(\approx_{\mathsf{set}}) = a(\subseteq) = \mathsf{set} \times \mathsf{set}$

Ω_{m} consists of unary functions with $a(\mathsf{m}) = \mathsf{set} \to \mathsf{num}$ for all $\mathsf{m} \in \Omega_{\mathsf{m}}$

are used to define the following signatures that are used in this paper:

$$\Sigma_{\mathsf{arith}} = (\{\mathsf{num}\}, \Omega_{\mathsf{num}}, \Pi_{\mathsf{num}}), \quad \Sigma_{\mathsf{set}} = (\{\mathsf{set}\}, \Omega_{\mathsf{set}}, \Pi_{\mathsf{set}})$$
$$\Sigma_{\mathsf{set,m}} = (\{\mathsf{num}, \mathsf{set}\},\ \Omega_{\mathsf{num}} \cup \Omega_{\mathsf{set}} \cup \Omega_{\mathsf{m}},\ \Pi_{\mathsf{num}} \cup \Pi_{\mathsf{set}})$$

For all $f \in (\Omega_{\mathsf{num}} \cup \Omega_{\mathsf{set}} \cup \Omega_{\mathsf{m}})$, we refer to $a(f) = s_1 \times \ldots \times s_n \to s_0$ as the *sort* of f and n as the *arity* of f. Function symbols with arity 0 are called *constants*. The *measure functions* are the function symbols in Ω_{m} with sort $\mathsf{set} \to \mathsf{num}$. For clarity, functions with arity 2 are written in infix notation.

Let $\mathcal{X} = (\mathcal{X}_{\mathsf{num}}, \mathcal{X}_{\mathsf{set}})$ be a countably infinite two-sorted set of variables, where $\mathcal{X}_{\mathsf{num}}$ is a set of variables of sort num and $\mathcal{X}_{\mathsf{set}}$ is a set of variables of sort set.

Notation. If not stated otherwise, x, x_i, y denote variables of sort set, called *set variables*, k, k_i, m, m_i denote variables of sort num, called *arithmetical variables*, v, v_i denote set and arithmetical variables, and B, B_i denote arbitrary set expressions, where i is any index. We sometimes use $\overline{x}$ instead of $\complement x$ to denote the complement of a set and if the meaning is unambiguous, $\approx$ instead of $\approx_{\mathsf{num}}$, resp. $\approx_{\mathsf{set}}$. We use the symbols $\leq, \geq, >, \subset, \supseteq, \supset$ and $\not\approx$ with the usual definitions.

The language corresponding to $\Sigma_{\mathsf{set,m}}$ is described below:

$F ::= A \mid F \wedge F \mid F \vee F \mid \neg F$

$A ::= B \approx B \mid B \subseteq B \mid T \approx T \mid T < T$

$B ::= x \mid \emptyset \mid \mathcal{U} \mid B \cup B \mid B \cap B \mid \overline{B}$ where x is a variable of sort set

$T ::= k \mid K \mid T + T \mid T - T \mid K \cdot T \mid \mathsf{m}(B)$ where k is a variable of sort num

$K ::= $ a number, i.e. a constant of sort num with fixed semantics

Semantics. We consider the following theories:

- $\mathsf{LI}(\mathbb{R})$, the theory of linear arithmetic over $\mathbb{R}$.
- $\mathcal{T}_\mathsf{S}$, the theory of sets, having as models Σ_set-structures of the form $\mathcal{A} = (\mathcal{A}_\mathsf{sets}, \cup, \cap, \complement, \emptyset, \mathcal{U}_\mathcal{A}, \subseteq)$, where $\mathcal{A}_\mathsf{set}$ is a family of subsets of a set $\mathcal{U}_\mathcal{A}$, closed under $\cup$, $\cap$ and complementation w.r.t. $\mathcal{U}_\mathcal{A}$.
- $\mathcal{T}_\mathsf{S}{}^\mathsf{m}$, the theory of m-measurable sets, where m is a concrete measure function, having as models Σ_set-structures $\mathcal{A} = (\mathcal{A}_\mathsf{set}, \cup, \cap, \complement, \emptyset, \mathcal{U}_\mathcal{A}, \subseteq)$, where $\mathcal{U}_\mathcal{A}$ is a measurable set w.r.t. m with finite measure and $\mathcal{A}_\mathsf{set}$ is a family of measurable subsets (with finite measure) of $\mathcal{U}_\mathcal{A}$, closed under $\cup$, $\cap$ and complementation w.r.t. $\mathcal{U}_\mathcal{A}$.

The properties of the measure functions are described by the set $\mathcal{K}_\mathsf{M}$ consisting of the following axioms (the universally quantified variables are of sort set):

(M$_1$) $\forall x \; 0 \leq \mathsf{m}(x)$

(M$_2$) $\forall x \; x \approx \emptyset \rightarrow \mathsf{m}(x) \approx 0$

(M$_3$) $\forall x_1, \ldots, x_n \; \bigwedge_{i,j} x_i \cap x_j \approx \emptyset \wedge x \approx \bigcup_{i=1}^{n} x_i \rightarrow \mathsf{m}(x) \approx \sum_{i=1}^{n} \mathsf{m}(x_i).$

We consider two theories of sets and measures over $\mathbb{R}$, $\mathcal{T}_\mathsf{M}^u$ and $\mathcal{T}_\mathsf{M}^m$: In the models of $\mathcal{T}_\mathsf{M}^u$ the interpretation of m is free and in the models of $\mathcal{T}_\mathsf{M}^m$ the interpretation of m must follow the specific semantics of a given measure function. $\mathcal{T}_\mathsf{M}^u$ and $\mathcal{T}_\mathsf{M}^m$ have as models $\Sigma_{\mathsf{set},\mathsf{m}}$-structures $\mathcal{A} = (\mathcal{A}_\mathsf{num}, \mathcal{A}_\mathsf{set}, \Omega_\mathcal{A}, \Pi_\mathcal{A})$, where:

(1) For $\mathcal{T}_\mathsf{M}^u$: (i) $\mathcal{A}_\mathsf{num} = \mathbb{R}$, $\mathcal{A}_{|\Sigma_\mathsf{arith}}$ is a model of $\mathsf{LI}(\mathbb{R})$; (ii) $\mathcal{A}_{|\Sigma_\mathsf{set,m}}$ is a model of $\mathcal{T}_\mathsf{S}$; (iii) $\mathsf{m}_\mathcal{A} : \mathcal{A}_\mathsf{set} \rightarrow \mathcal{A}_\mathsf{num}$ is an arbitrary function satisfying the axioms $\mathcal{K}_\mathsf{M}$;
(2) For $\mathcal{T}_\mathsf{M}^m$, for a given measure function m: (i) $\mathcal{A}_\mathsf{num} = \mathbb{R}$, $\mathcal{A}_{|\Sigma_\mathsf{arith}}$ is a model of $\mathsf{LI}(\mathbb{R})$; (ii) $\mathcal{A}_{|\Sigma_\mathsf{set,m}}$ is a model of $\mathcal{T}_\mathsf{S}{}^\mathsf{m}$; (iii) $\mathsf{m}_\mathcal{A} = \mathsf{m}$, i.e. for every $S \in \mathcal{A}_\mathsf{set}$, $\mathsf{m}_\mathcal{A}(S) = \mathsf{m}(S)$. Every measure function satisfies axioms $\mathcal{K}_\mathsf{M}$. We assume that m also has the following property:

   (M$_\mathsf{m}$)   (a) For all finite families of numbers $c_1, \ldots, c_n \in \mathbb{R}; m_1, \ldots, m_n \in \mathbb{R}_+$ with the property that $c_i \approx 0 \rightarrow m_i \approx 0$ holds for $1 \leq i \leq n$ there exists a model $\mathcal{A}$ of $\mathcal{T}_\mathsf{S}{}^\mathsf{m}$ and there exist mutually disjoint sets $S_1, \ldots, S_n \in \mathcal{A}_\mathsf{set}$ such that $\mathsf{m}_\mathcal{A}(S_i) = m_i$ and such that $S_i = \emptyset$ iff $c_i = 0$.
   (b) For all Σ_set-formulae F_1, F_2, $F_1 \models_{\mathcal{T}_\mathsf{S}{}^\mathsf{m}} F_2$ iff $F_1 \models_{\mathcal{T}_\mathsf{S}} F_2$.

Property (M$_\mathsf{m}$) (a) expresses the fact that we can find disjoint sets with given cardinalities, and that we can encode $\mathcal{S}_i \approx \emptyset$ using a constraint $c_i \approx 0$. Condition (b) guarentees that properties of measures do not induce constraints on sets. We thus exclude pathologic situations such as "B is measurable iff B is empty".

In cases where we talk about a specific measure function, this will be denoted explicitly, e.g. with m_Les for the Lebesgue measure.

Task: We are interested in checking satisfiability of quantifier-free formulae w.r.t. $\mathcal{T}_M^u$ or $\mathcal{T}_M^m$. Since free variables can be seen as existentially quantified and replaced by constants by Skolemization, it does not make a difference if we talk about free variables or constants, so we treat both terms synonymously.

4 Reasoning About Sets and Measures

In this section we present a sound, complete and terminating method for checking the satisfiability of quantifier-free formulae in the theories of sets and measures introduced above. Since the method we propose relies on constructing atomic decompositions, we start by presenting the main ideas.

4.1 Atomic Decompositions

The concept of *atomic sets* and *atomic decompositions* was introduced by Ohlbach in [21] and used under the name of *cubes* by Kuncak et al. in [18]. They allow us to represent every set expression as union of disjoint sets. This representation makes it sufficient to only deal with instances of the bridging functions whose argument is a single atomic set.

For a formal definition, we refer to [3]; instead we just give a description with the help of Example 3. For n set variables, there are 2^n mutually disjoint regions in the Venn diagram that can be described as an intersection with n participating expressions, where each expression is either a set variable or the complement of a set variable. These regions are called *atomic sets*. Every set expression can be described as union of atomic sets (*atomic decomposition*). Due to the construction of the atomic sets, all $\mathcal{S}_i$ are disjoint, i.e.

$$\forall i, j \in \{0, \ldots, 2^n - 1\}(i \neq j \rightarrow (\mathcal{S}_i \cap \mathcal{S}_j) = \emptyset)$$

holds. If not stated otherwise, $\mathcal{S}, \mathcal{S}_i$ denote atomic sets, where i is any index.

Example 3. Let x_1, x_2 be two variables of sort set. The four atomic sets are: $\mathcal{S}_{00} = \overline{x_1} \cap \overline{x_2}$, $\mathcal{S}_{01} = \overline{x_1} \cap x_2$, $\mathcal{S}_{10} = x_1 \cap \overline{x_2}$, $\mathcal{S}_{11} = x_1 \cap x_2$. The atomic decompositions for the sets x_1 and x_2 are: $x_1 = \mathcal{S}_{10} \cup \mathcal{S}_{11} = (x_1 \cap \overline{x_2}) \cup (x_1 \cap x_2)$, and $x_2 = \mathcal{S}_{01} \cup \mathcal{S}_{11} = (\overline{x_1} \cap x_2) \cup (x_1 \cap x_2)$. ∎

4.2 Reasoning with Measures

We introduce a decision procedure for checking satisfiability of quantifier-free $\Sigma_{set,m}$ formulae w.r.t. $\mathcal{T}_M^u$ and w.r.t. $\mathcal{T}_M^m$, where m is a given measure function satisfying condition (M_m). The method relies on rewriting any ground $\Sigma_{set,m}$ formula F to an equisatisfiable formula F' in linear arithmetic and checking the satisfiability of F' with a decision procedure for $\mathsf{LI}(\mathbb{R})$. Before giving a detailed explanation of the procedure in Algorithm 1, we present the general idea:

(a) We use atomic decompositions followed by simplification to bring set expressions into a canonical form in which all atoms are of the form $\mathcal{S} \approx \emptyset$.

Algorithm 1. Rewrite a $\Sigma_{\text{set,m}}$ formula to an equisatisfiable Σ_{arith} formula.

1. Represent all set expressions as atomic decomposition.
2. Simplify set atoms by replacing all atoms of form

$$\bigcup_{i \in I} \mathcal{S}_i \cup \bigcup_{k \in K} \mathcal{S}_k \bowtie \bigcup_{j \in J} \mathcal{S}_j \cup \bigcup_{k \in K} \mathcal{S}_k \quad \text{with} \quad \bigcup_{i \in I} \mathcal{S}_i \bowtie \bigcup_{j \in J} \mathcal{S}_j$$

   where $\bowtie \in \{\approx, \supseteq, \supsetneq\}$ and $\mathcal{S}_i \neq \mathcal{S}_j$ for all $i \in I$ and for all $j \in J$.
3. Reduce set atoms to equalities with empty set by replacing all set atoms of form

$$\bigcup_{i \in I} \mathcal{S}_i \bowtie \bigcup_{j \in J} \mathcal{S}_j \text{ with } \begin{cases} \left(\bigwedge_{i \in I} \mathcal{S}_i \approx \emptyset \right) \wedge \left(\bigwedge_{j \in J} \mathcal{S}_j \approx \emptyset \right) & \text{if } \bowtie = \approx \\ \left(\bigwedge_{i \in I} \mathcal{S}_i \approx \emptyset \right) & \text{if } \bowtie = \subseteq \\ \left(\bigwedge_{i \in I} \mathcal{S}_i \approx \emptyset \right) \wedge \left(\bigvee_{j \in J} \mathcal{S}_j \not\approx \emptyset \right) & \text{if } \bowtie = \subsetneq \end{cases}$$

4. Replace all instances of m whose arguments are unions of atomic sets with the sum of the atomic instances by replacing terms of the form $\mathsf{m}(\mathcal{S}_1 \cup \ldots \cup \mathcal{S}_n)$ with $\mathsf{m}(\mathcal{S}_1) + \ldots + \mathsf{m}(\mathcal{S}_n)$.
5. Add the instances of (M$_1$) and (M$_2$) for all atomic sets $\mathcal{S}$ for which $\mathsf{m}(\mathcal{S})$ appears in the problem.
6. Purify by introducing new arithmetical variables for the instances of m.
7. Rewrite equalities of sets to equalities of arithmetic by replacing all atoms of form $\mathcal{S} \approx \emptyset$ with $c_{\mathcal{S}} \approx 0$.

(b) We then use (M$_3$) and the fact that the arguments of m are atomic decompositions to get a form where all arguments of m are atomic sets. Now, all literals that contain set terms are either of form $\mathcal{S} \approx \emptyset$ or of form $\mathcal{S} \not\approx \emptyset$.

(c) We replace all terms $\mathsf{m}(\mathcal{S}_i)$ in these instances of m with new free arithmetical variables m_i. The definitions, i.e. the connection between the instances of m and the new variables, are stored separately and not part of the formula.

(d) After this purification step, the only part that is not yet pure arithmetic are the set atoms. As last step of the transformation we replace set atoms $\mathcal{S}_i \approx \emptyset$ with arithmetical atoms $c_i \approx 0$ and thus obtain a pure arithmetical formula.

Examples 5 and 6 illustrate the approach on specific instances.

Theorem 4. *Let F be a $\Sigma_{\text{set,m}}$ formula and let F' be a formula that is built by applying the steps of Algorithm 1 to F. F is satisfiable w.r.t. T_M^u (resp. T_M^m for a given measure function m satisfying (M$_m$)) iff F' is satisfiable in $\mathsf{LI}(\mathbb{R})$.*

Proof (Idea). We show that for every step i of Algorithm 1, if F_{i-1} is the formula to which step i is applied and F_i is the formula obtained after that step then F_{i-1} and F_i are equisatisfiable. This is clearly the case for Steps 1, 2 and 3 due to the structure of the formulae. From (M$_3$) and the fact that the arguments of m are atomic decompositions, it follows F_3 and F_4 are equisatisfiable. This is clearly the case also for F_4 and F_5 if we consider satisfiability w.r.t. T_M^u. For T_M^m

we use the fact that by (M_m), for $m_i = m(S_i) \in \mathbb{R}_+, i = 1, \ldots, n$ we can find disjoint measurable subsets $S_i' \subseteq \mathcal{U}_\mathcal{A}$ with $m(S_i') = m_i$ and $S_i' = \emptyset$ iff $S_i = \emptyset$.

Step 6 (purification) leads to an equisatisfiable formula as well: F_5 is satisfiable modulo $\mathcal{T}_M^u$ iff F_6 is satisfiable modulo $\mathsf{LI}(\mathbb{R}) \cup \mathcal{T}_S$. This follows from the fact that, if $\mathsf{Def} = \{m_i \approx m(S_i) \mid S_i \text{ atomic set}\}$ and $\mathsf{Con}_0 = \{S_i \approx S_j \rightarrow m_i \approx m_j \mid m_i \approx m(S_i) \in \mathsf{Def}\}$, then F_5 is satisfiable w.r.t. $\mathcal{T}_M^u$ (resp. $\mathcal{T}_M^m$) iff $F_6 \cup \mathsf{Con}_0$ is satisfiable w.r.t. $\mathsf{LI}(\mathbb{R}) \cup \mathcal{T}_S$. Since two different atomic sets are equal only if they are both empty, the formulae in Con_0 are redundant in the presence of the purified instances of (M_1) and (M_2). Thus, $F_6 \cup \mathsf{Con}_0$ is satisfiable w.r.t. $\mathsf{LI}(\mathbb{R}) \cup \mathcal{T}_S$ iff F_6 is satisfiable w.r.t. $\mathsf{LI}(\mathbb{R}) \cup \mathcal{T}_S$.

To show that F_6 is satisfiable w.r.t. $(\mathsf{LI}(\mathbb{R}) \cup \mathcal{T}_S)$ iff F_7 is satisfiable w.r.t. $\mathsf{LI}(\mathbb{R})$ note that (i) if we have a model $\mathcal{A}, \beta$ of F_6, we can construct a model for F_7 by setting c_i to 0 if $\beta(S_i) \approx \emptyset$, and (ii) if we have a satisfying assignment β for F_7 we can construct a model $\mathcal{A}, \beta'$ of F_6 using condition (M_m). $\qquad\square$

Remark: Theorem 4 can be extended to a theory of measure functions $\mathcal{T}_M^m(D)$ having as models only algebras in which the interpretation of $\mathcal{U}_\mathcal{A}$ is fixed to be a measurable set D or a set with certain properties (for instance an interval $[b, e]$, where b and e are constants) if we replace condition (M_m) (a) with:

(M_m^D) (a) For every finite family of numbers $c_1, \ldots, c_n \in \mathbb{R}; m_1, \ldots, m_n \in \mathbb{R}_+$ with the property that $c_i \approx 0 \rightarrow m_i \approx 0$ holds for $1 \leq i \leq n$ there exists a model $\mathcal{A}$ of $\mathcal{T}_S^m$ with $\mathcal{U}_\mathcal{A} = D$, and there exist mutually disjoint sets $S_1, \ldots, S_n \in \mathcal{A}_{\mathsf{set}}$ such that $\bigcup_{i=1}^n S_i = D$, $m_\mathcal{A}(S_i) = m_i$ and $S_i = \emptyset$ iff $c_i = 0$.

Example 5. Let $F_0 = x_1 \subseteq x_2 \wedge m(x_1) \approx m(x_1 \cap \overline{x_2})$ We show how to check the satisfiability of F_0 w.r.t. $\mathcal{T}_M^u$ and $\mathcal{T}_M^m$ with our approach.

1. Represent all set expressions as atomic decomposition:
   $F_1 = S_{10} \cup S_{11} \subseteq S_{01} \cup S_{11} \wedge m(S_{10} \cup S_{11}) \approx m(S_{10})$
2. Simplify set atoms: $F_2 = S_{10} \subseteq S_{01} \wedge m(S_{10} \cup S_{11}) \approx m(S_{10})$
3. Reduce set atoms to equalities with empty set:
   $F_3 = S_{10} \approx \emptyset \wedge m(S_{10} \cup S_{11}) \approx m(S_{10})$
4. Use additivity of m: $F_4 = S_{10} \approx \emptyset \wedge m(S_{10}) + m(S_{11}) \approx m(S_{10})$
5. Instantiate axioms (M_1) and (M_2):
   $F_5 = F_4 \wedge 0 \leq m(S_{01}) \wedge (S_{01} \approx \emptyset \rightarrow m(S_{01}) \approx 0) \wedge$
   $\qquad\qquad 0 \leq m(S_{10}) \wedge (S_{10} \approx \emptyset \rightarrow m(S_{10}) \approx 0) \wedge$
   $\qquad\qquad 0 \leq m(S_{11}) \wedge (S_{11} \approx \emptyset \rightarrow m(S_{11}) \approx 0)$
6. Purify by introducing new arithmetical variables for the instances of m:

   $F_6 = S_{10} \approx \emptyset \wedge m_{10} + m_{11} \approx m_{10} \wedge 0 \leq m_{01} \wedge (S_{01} \approx \emptyset \rightarrow m_{01} \approx 0) \wedge$
   $\qquad\qquad\qquad 0 \leq m_{10} \wedge (S_{10} \approx \emptyset \rightarrow m_{10} \approx 0) \wedge$
   $\qquad\qquad\qquad 0 \leq m_{11} \wedge (S_{11} \approx \emptyset \rightarrow m_{11} \approx 0)$

   The definitions of m_{01}, m_{10}, m_{11} are kept outside of the formula.

7. Rewrite equalities of sets to equalities of arithmetic:

$$F_7 = c_{10} \approx 0 \wedge m_{10} + m_{11} \approx m_{10} \wedge 0 \leq m_{01} \wedge (c_{01} \approx 0 \rightarrow m_{01} \approx 0) \wedge$$
$$0 \leq m_{10} \wedge (c_{10} \approx 0 \rightarrow m_{10} \approx 0) \wedge$$
$$0 \leq m_{11} \wedge (c_{11} \approx 0 \rightarrow m_{11} \approx 0)$$

The definitions of c_{01}, c_{10}, c_{11} are kept outside of the formula.

We can check the satisfiability of F_7 with a prover for linear real arithmetic; a satisfying assignment is for instance $\beta(c_{10}) = \beta(m_{10}) = \beta(m_{11}) = 0$, $\beta(c_{11}) = \beta(c_{01}) = \beta(m_{01}) = \beta(c_{00}) = \beta(m_{00}) = 1$. We construct a satisfying assignment β' for F_0 as follows:

Satisfiability w.r.t. $\mathcal{T}_M^u$: We proceed as follows:

- As $\beta(c_{10}) = 0$, $\beta'(\mathcal{S}_{10}) = \emptyset$.
- As $\beta(c_{11}) = \beta(c_{00}) = \beta(c_{01}) = 1$, $\beta'(\mathcal{S}_{11}) \not\approx \emptyset$, $\beta'(\mathcal{S}_{00}) \not\approx \emptyset$, $\beta'(\mathcal{S}_{01}) \not\approx \emptyset$. We can choose $\beta'(\mathcal{S}_{11}) = \{a\}$, $\beta'(\mathcal{S}_{00}) = \{b\}$, $\beta'(\mathcal{S}_{01}) = \{c\}$.

We obtain a model with $\mathcal{A}_{\text{set}} = \mathcal{P}(\{a, b, c\})$, $\mathsf{m}_\mathcal{A}(A) = \mathsf{card}(A \cap \{b, c\})$ for every $A \subseteq \{a, b, c\}$, $\beta'(x_1) = \beta'(\mathcal{S}_{11}) \cup \beta'(\mathcal{S}_{10}) = \{a\}$, $\beta'(x_2) = \beta'(\mathcal{S}_{11}) \cup \beta'(\mathcal{S}_{01}) = \{a, c\}$.

Satisfiability w.r.t. $\mathcal{T}_M^m$: Assume that $\mathsf{m} = \mathsf{m}_{\text{Les}}$, the Lebesgue measure on $\mathbb{R}$. We construct a model for F_0 as follows:

- Since $\beta(m_{01}) = \beta(m_{00}) = 1$ we can choose $\beta'(\mathcal{S}_{01}), \beta'(\mathcal{S}_{00})$ to be disjoint subsets of $\mathbb{R}$ with Lebesgue measure 1, e.g. $\beta'(\mathcal{S}_{01}) = [0, 1], \beta'(\mathcal{S}_{00}) = [2, 3]$.
- Since $\beta(c_{10}) = 0$, we choose $\beta'(\mathcal{S}_{10}) = \emptyset$.
- Since $\beta(c_{11}) \not\approx 0$ and $\beta(m_{11}) = 0$, we choose $\beta'(\mathcal{S}_{11})$ to be a non-empty set (disjoint to the others) of Lebesgue measure 0, e.g. $\beta'(\mathcal{S}_{11}) = \{4\}$.

We obtain a model for F_0 in which $\mathcal{U}_\mathcal{A} = [0, 1] \cup [2, 3] \cup \{4\}$, $\mathcal{A}_{\text{set}}$ is the set of all measurable subsets of $\mathcal{U}_\mathcal{A}$, and $\beta'(x_1) = \beta'(\mathcal{S}_{11}) \cup \beta'(\mathcal{S}_{10}) = \{4\}$, $\beta'(x_2) = \beta'(\mathcal{S}_{11}) \cup \beta'(\mathcal{S}_{01}) = [0, 1] \cup \{4\}$.

Satisfiability w.r.t. $\mathcal{T}_M^m(D)$: Let $\mathsf{m} = \mathsf{m}_{\text{Les}}$, the Lebesgue measure on $\mathbb{R}$. Assume that D is the interval $[b, e]$ where b and e are constants. It can be seen that condition $(\mathsf{M}_m(D))$ holds and that F_0 is satisfiable w.r.t. $\mathcal{T}_M^m(D)$ if and only if $F_7' = F_7 \wedge m_{11} + m_{10} + m_{01} + m_{00} \approx e - b$ is satisfiable in $\mathsf{LI}(\mathbb{R})$. F_7' is satisfiable, a satisfying assignment is $\beta(c_{10}) = \beta(m_{10}) = \beta(m_{11}) = 0$, $\beta(c_{11}) = \beta(c_{01}) = \beta(m_{01}) = \beta(c_{00}) = \beta(m_{00}) = 1$, $\beta(e) = 2$, $\beta(b) = 0$. Using arguments similar to those used for $\mathcal{T}_M^m$ we can construct

$$\beta'(\mathcal{S}_{10}) = \emptyset, \beta'(\mathcal{S}_{01}) = [0, 1), \beta'(\mathcal{S}_{00}) = (1, 2] \text{ and } \beta'(\mathcal{S}_{11}) = \{1\}.$$

We obtain a model for F_0 in which $b_\mathcal{A} = 0, e_\mathcal{A} = 2, \mathcal{U}_\mathcal{A} = [0, 2]$, $\mathcal{A}_{\text{set}}$ is the set of all measurable subsets of $\mathcal{U}_\mathcal{A}$, and $\beta'(x_1) = \beta'(\mathcal{S}_{11}) \cup \beta'(\mathcal{S}_{10}) = \{1\}$, $\beta'(x_2) = \beta'(\mathcal{S}_{11}) \cup \beta'(\mathcal{S}_{01}) = \{1\} \cup [0, 1) = [0, 1]$. ∎

Example 6. We can use a similar approach for the formula:

$$F_0 = x_1 \subseteq x_2 \land \mathsf{m}(x_1) \approx \mathsf{m}(x_1 \cap \overline{x_2}) - 1$$

After Step 7 we obtain, as in Example 5, the formula:

$$F_7 = c_{10} \approx 0 \land m_{10} + m_{11} \approx m_{10} - 1 \land \ 0 \leq m_{01} \ \land \ (c_{01} \approx 0 \rightarrow m_{01} \approx 0) \ \land$$
$$0 \leq m_{10} \ \land \ (c_{10} \approx 0 \rightarrow m_{10} \approx 0) \ \land$$
$$0 \leq m_{11} \ \land \ (c_{11} \approx 0 \rightarrow m_{11} \approx 0)$$

which is unsatisfiable in $\mathsf{LI}(\mathbb{R})$. Thus, F_0 is unsatisfiable w.r.t. $\mathcal{T}^u_\mathsf{M}$, $\mathcal{T}^m_\mathsf{M}$ and $\mathcal{T}^m_\mathsf{M}(D)$ for every D. ∎

Theorem 7 (Complexity). *The satisfiability of a quantifier-free $\Sigma_{\mathsf{set},\mathsf{m}}$ formula F with n constants can be checked using Algorithm 1 in NPTIME$(2^n|F|)$.*

Proof (Idea). Let F be a ground $\Sigma_{\mathsf{set},\mathsf{m}}$ formula with size $|F|$ containing n set constants. Atomic decompositions introduce at most 2^n atomic sets; the length of the formula becomes at most $2^n|F|$. By adding instances of the measure function axioms (M_2) and (M_1) in which variables are instantiated with atomic sets, we add at most $2 \cdot 2^n$ new formulae of constant size. Thus, the size of the formula F' obtained using Algorithm 1 is of order $2^n|F|$. Satisfiability of conjunction literals in $\mathsf{LI}(\mathbb{R})$ can be checked in PTIME [17], so satisfiability of quantifier-free formulae in $\mathsf{LI}(\mathbb{R})$ is in NP. Therefore, checking satisfiability of the quantifier-free $\Sigma_{\mathsf{set},\mathsf{m}}$-formula F using Algorithm 1 is in NPTIME$(2^n|F|)$. □

5 Locality of Measure Axioms

We showed that the complexity of checking satisfiability of a quantifier-free formula F with n set variables using Algorithm 1 is in NPTIME$(2^n|F|)$. Since Step 3 in Algorithm 1 might introduce disjunctions, this creates the impression that the method is in NPTIME$(2^n|F|)$ even if the input formula F is a conjunction of literals. We propose an approach which allows us to obtain a better complexity for input formulae which are conjunctions of ground literals.

The instantiation scheme used in Sect. 4.2 indicates that the theories with sets and measures considered before satisfy a locality property (as defined in e.g. in [22] or [14]). Below we explain this in detail.

Let F be a $\Sigma_{\mathsf{set},\mathsf{m}}$ formula which is a conjunction of ground literals. Consider the atomic decomposition associated with the set expressions in F.

Notation: For every set expression B with the property that $\mathsf{m}(B)$ occurs in F let $At(B)$ be the family of all atomic sets in the atomic decomposition of B. Thus, $B = \bigcup_{\mathcal{S} \in At(B)} \mathcal{S}$. We use the following notation:

- $\mathsf{est}(F) = \{\mathsf{m}(B) \mid \mathsf{m}(B) \text{ occurs in } F\}$,
- $At(F) = \{\mathsf{m}(\mathcal{S}) \mid \exists B \text{ with } \mathsf{m}(B) \in \mathsf{est}(F) \text{ s.t. } \mathcal{S} \in At(B)\}$

Let $\Psi(F) = \mathrm{est}(F) \cup \mathrm{At}(F)$ be the set of all terms $\mathsf{m}(B)$ occurring in F together with all terms $\mathsf{m}(\mathcal{S})$, where $\mathcal{S}$ is an atomic set in $At(B)$.
We denote by $\mathcal{K}_{\mathsf{M}}[\Psi(F)]$ the following set of instances of the axioms in $\mathcal{K}_{\mathsf{M}}$:

$(\mathsf{M}_1)[\Psi(F)] \quad \{0 \le \mathsf{m}(B) \mid \mathsf{m}(B) \in \Psi(F)\}$

$(\mathsf{M}_2)[\Psi(F)] \quad \{B \approx \emptyset \to \mathsf{m}(B) \approx 0 \mid \mathsf{m}(B) \in \Psi(F)\}$

$(\mathsf{M}_3)[\Psi(F)] \quad \{\mathsf{m}(B) \approx \displaystyle\sum_{\mathcal{S} \in At(B)} \mathsf{m}(\mathcal{S}) \mid \mathsf{m}(B) \in \mathrm{est}(F)\}$

It can easily be seen that in the presence of $(\mathsf{M}_3)[\Psi(F)]$ the only non-redundant instances of (M_1) and (M_2) are:

$(\mathsf{M}_1)[\mathrm{At}(F)] \quad \{0 \le \mathsf{m}(\mathcal{S}) \mid \mathcal{S} \text{ atomic set}, \mathsf{m}(\mathcal{S}) \in \mathrm{At}(F)\}$

$(\mathsf{M}_2)[\mathrm{At}(F)] \quad \{\mathcal{S} \approx \emptyset \to \mathsf{m}(\mathcal{S}) \approx 0 \mid \mathcal{S} \text{ atomic set}, \mathsf{m}(\mathcal{S}) \in \mathrm{At}(F)\}$

Also, the instances in $(\mathsf{M}_3)[\Psi(F)]$ can be used to replace in F every occurrence of a term $\mathsf{m}(B)$ with the sum $\sum_{\mathcal{S} \in At(B)} \mathsf{m}(\mathcal{S})$. For any additional axioms, e.g. boundedness (cf. Axiom (P_4) in Sect. 2) we need to keep all instances.

We purify F and the clauses obtained this way by replacing every term of the form $\mathsf{m}(\mathcal{S}_i)$ with a new constant m_i. We keep all equalities $\mathsf{m}(\mathcal{S}_i) \approx m_i$ in a set Def. If $F = F_{\mathsf{set}} \wedge F_{\mathsf{num}}$, where F_{set} contains all set constraints in F and F_{num} all numerical constraints, including the constraints on measures on sets, then after purification we obtain a formula of the form:

$$F_{\mathsf{set}} \wedge F'_{\mathsf{num}} \wedge (\mathsf{M}_1)[\mathrm{At}(F)]' \wedge (\mathsf{M}_2)[\mathrm{At}(F)]' \wedge \mathrm{Def},$$

where F'_{num} is the purified version of F_{num} and $(\mathsf{M}_1)[\mathrm{At}(F)]'$ (resp. $(\mathsf{M}_2)[\mathrm{At}(F)]'$) the purified version of $(\mathsf{M}_1)[\mathrm{At}(F)]$ (resp. $(\mathsf{M}_2)[\mathrm{At}(F)]$).

Theorem 8. *Let F be a $\Sigma_{\mathsf{set},\mathsf{m}}$ formula which is a conjunction of ground literals. With the notations introduced above, the following hold:*

(A) The following are equivalent:
  (1) F is satisfiable w.r.t. $\mathcal{T}^u_{\mathsf{M}}$.
  (2) $F \wedge \mathcal{K}_{\mathsf{M}}[\Psi(F)]$ is satisfiable w.r.t. the combination of $\mathsf{LI}(\mathbb{R})$, $\mathcal{T}_{\mathsf{S}}$ and $\mathsf{UIF}_{\mathsf{m}}$ (the theory of a unary uninterpreted function m).
  (3) $F_{\mathsf{set}} \wedge F'_{\mathsf{num}} \wedge (\mathsf{M}_1)[\mathrm{At}(F)]' \wedge (\mathsf{M}_2)[\mathrm{At}(F)]' \wedge \mathrm{Def}$ is satisfiable w.r.t. the combination of $\mathsf{LI}(\mathbb{R})$, $\mathcal{T}_{\mathsf{S}}$ and $\mathsf{UIF}_{\mathsf{m}}$.
  (4) $F_{\mathsf{set}} \wedge F'_{\mathsf{num}} \wedge (\mathsf{M}_1)[\mathrm{At}(F)]' \wedge (\mathsf{M}_2)[\mathrm{At}(F)]'$ is satisfiable w.r.t. the combination of $\mathsf{LI}(\mathbb{R})$ and $\mathcal{T}_{\mathsf{S}}$.
(B) If m is a concrete measure function satisfying property $(\mathsf{M}_{\mathsf{m}})$ then the following are equivalent:
  (1) F is satisfiable w.r.t. the theory $\mathcal{T}^{\mathsf{m}}_{\mathsf{M}}$.
  (2) $F \wedge \mathcal{K}_{\mathsf{M}}[\Psi(F)]$ is satisfiable w.r.t. the combination of $\mathsf{LI}(\mathbb{R})$ and $\mathcal{T}_{\mathsf{S}}{}^{\mathsf{m}}$.
  (3) $F_{\mathsf{set}} \wedge F'_{\mathsf{num}} \wedge (\mathsf{M}_1)[\mathrm{At}(F)]' \wedge (\mathsf{M}_2)[\mathrm{At}(F)]' \wedge \mathrm{Def}$ is satisfiable w.r.t. the combination of $\mathsf{LI}(\mathbb{R})$ and $\mathcal{T}_{\mathsf{S}}{}^{\mathsf{m}}$.

(4) $F_{set} \wedge F'_{num} \wedge (M_1)[At(F)]' \wedge (M_2)[At(F)]'$ *is satisfiable w.r.t. the combination of* $LI(\mathbb{R})$ *and* $\mathcal{T}_S^m$.

Proof. Analogous to the proof of the similar results in Sect. 4.2, using also results on hierarchical reasoning in local theory extensions (cf. e.g. [22] or [14]) and the fact that all instances of the congruence axioms of the form $\mathcal{S}_i \approx \mathcal{S}_j \rightarrow m_i \approx m_j$ corresponding to the definitions in Def are redundant (because no two different atomic sets can be equal). $\qquad\square$

Theorem 9. *We can check the satisfiability in the combination of* $\mathcal{T}_S$ *and* $LI(\mathbb{R})$ *(resp.* $LI(\mathbb{R})$ *and* $\mathcal{T}_S^m$ *) of* $F' = F_{set} \wedge F'_{num} \wedge (M_1)[At(F)]' \wedge (M_2)[At(F)]'$ *as follows:*

1. *If* F_{set} *or* $F'_{num} \wedge (M_1)[At(F)]'$ *is unsatisfiable,* F' *is unsatisfiable.*
2. *If* $F_{set}, F'_{num} \wedge (M_1)[At(F)]'$ *are satisfiable, propagate to* F'_{num} *all conclusions* $m_i \approx 0$ *of instances in* $(M_2)[At(F)]'$ *whose premises* $\mathcal{S}_i \approx \emptyset$ *are entailed by* F_{set}.
3. *If after propagation the new set of numerical constraints is unsatisfiable, then* F' *is unsatisfiable, otherwise* F' *is satisfiable.*

Proof (Idea). In the case of the combination of $\mathcal{T}_S$ and $LI(\mathbb{R})$ we use the fact that checking entailment w.r.t. $\mathcal{T}_S$ can be reduced to checking entailment in the class of Boolean algebras (and, thus, $\mathcal{T}_S$ is convex). We show that the entailment test in Step 2 can be reduced to checking entailment in the two-element Boolean algebra. For the case of the combination $LI(\mathbb{R})$ and $\mathcal{T}_S^m$ we use the fact that $F_{set} \models_{\mathcal{T}_S^m} \mathcal{S}_i \approx \emptyset$ iff $F_{set} \models_{\mathcal{T}_S} \mathcal{S}_i \approx \emptyset$. $\qquad\square$

Example 10. We explain the ideas on the formula in Example 5:

$$F_0 = x_1 \subseteq x_2 \wedge m(x_1) \approx m(x_1 \cap \overline{x_2})$$

$F_{set} = x_1 \subseteq x_2$ and $F_{num} = m(x_1) \approx m(x_1 \cap \overline{x_2})$; $est(F_0) = \{m(x_1), m(x_1 \cap \overline{x_2})\}$, $At(x_1) = \{\mathcal{S}_{10}, \mathcal{S}_{11}\}$, $At(x_1 \cap \overline{x_2}) = \{\mathcal{S}_{10}\}$, where $\mathcal{S}_{10} = x_1 \cap \overline{x_2}, \mathcal{S}_{11} = x_1 \cap x_2$. Thus, $At(F_0) = \{\mathcal{S}_{10}, \mathcal{S}_{11}\}$. We instantiate the axioms (M_1) and (M_2) and obtain:

$(M_1)[At(F_0)]$ $0 \leq m(\mathcal{S}_{10}) \wedge 0 \leq m(\mathcal{S}_{11})$
$(M_2)[At(F_0)]$ $(\mathcal{S}_{10} \approx \emptyset \rightarrow m(\mathcal{S}_{10}) \approx 0) \wedge (\mathcal{S}_{11} \approx \emptyset \rightarrow m(\mathcal{S}_{11}) \approx 0)$

The instances in $(M_3)[\Psi(F_0)]$ are used to replace $m(x_1)$ with $m(\mathcal{S}_{10}) + m(\mathcal{S}_{11})$. After purification we obtain the following formulae:

Def	Set	Num		Bridge
$m_{10} \approx m(\mathcal{S}_{10})$	$x_1 \subseteq x_2$	$m_{11} + m_{10} \approx m_{10}$	$0 \leq m_{10}$	$\mathcal{S}_{10} \approx \emptyset \rightarrow m_{10} \approx 0$
$m_{11} \approx m(\mathcal{S}_{11})$			$0 \leq m_{10}$	$\mathcal{S}_{11} \approx \emptyset \rightarrow m_{11} \approx 0$

Both the set constraints and the numerical constraints are satisfiable. We test whether the premises of the $\mathcal{S}_i \approx \emptyset$ of $(M_2)[At(F)]'$ are entailed by F_{set}:

We first test whether $x_1 \subseteq x_2 \models_{\mathcal{T}_S} \mathcal{S}_{10} \approx 0$. As $\mathcal{S}_{10} = x_1 \cap \overline{x_2}$, this can be reduced to testing whether $B_2 \models x_1 \leq x_2 \rightarrow x_1 \wedge \overline{x_2} \approx 0$, where B_2 is the two-element Boolean algebra. As this is the case, we add the atom $m_{10} \approx 0$ to the set of numeric constraints.

The set of numerical constraints we obtain is satisfiable, thus F_0 is satisfiable w.r.t. $\mathcal{T}_M^u$ and also w.r.t. $\mathcal{T}_M^m$ for every measure function m satisfying (M_m). $\qquad\blacksquare$

Theorem 11 (Complexity). *Let F be a $\Sigma_{\text{set,m}}$ formula which is a conjunction of ground literals. The satisfiability of F w.r.t. $\mathcal{T}_{\mathsf{M}}^u$ or w.r.t. $\mathcal{T}_{\mathsf{M}}^m$ (where m is a concrete measure function satisfying property $(\mathsf{M_m})$) can be checked in exponential time in the number of set constants in F.*

Proof (Idea). Let n be the number of set constants occurring in $F = F_{\text{set}} \wedge F_{\text{num}}$. The number of atomic sets which need to be considered is at most 2^n, so the number of instances of $\mathcal{K}_{\mathsf{M}}$ is at most $2 \cdot 2^n$. We need to test the entailment from F_{set} for at most 2^n equations of the form $\mathcal{S} \approx \emptyset$; these can be expressed as entailment tests in the Boolean algebra B_2 with 2 elements (the problem is in NP). The complexity of each entailment test is at most $2^n|F|$, the propagation step has therefore complexity of order $4^n|F|$. Checking satisfiability of conjunctions of literals in $\mathsf{LI}(\mathbb{R})$ can be done in polynomial time [17]; the size of the numerical formula is exponential in n. This shows that the procedure we proposed has complexity at most $4^n|F_{\text{set}}| + p(2^n|F_{\text{num}}|)$, where p is a polynomial. $\square$

5.1   A Tractable Fragment of the Theory of Sets with Measures

We now consider the problem of checking satisfiability of $\Sigma_{\text{set,m}}$ formulae F which are conjunctions of ground literals which do not contain complements or unions and contain only the predicates $\approx$ and $\subseteq$. We show that in this case the additivity axiom for measures can be replaced with a monotonicity axiom:

(Mon) $\qquad\qquad\qquad \forall x_1, x_2 \ (x_1 \subseteq x_2 \to \mathsf{m}(x_1) \leq \mathsf{m}(x_2))$

We denote by $\mathcal{K}_{\mathsf{M}}{}^{\cap}$ the set of axioms consisting of $(\mathsf{M_1})$, $(\mathsf{M_2})$ and (Mon). In [23] we proved that monotonicity axioms define local theory extensions. Let $\mathcal{K}_{\mathsf{M}}{}^{\cap}[F]$ be the set consisting of the following instances:

$(\mathsf{M_1})[F] \qquad \{0 \leq \mathsf{m}(B) \mid \mathsf{m}(B) \in \text{est}(F)\}$

$(\mathsf{M_2})[F] \qquad \{B \approx \emptyset \to \mathsf{m}(B) \approx 0 \mid \mathsf{m}(B) \in \text{est}(F)\}$

$(\text{Mon})[F] \qquad \{B_1 \subseteq B_2 \to \mathsf{m}(B_1) \leq \mathsf{m}(B_2) \mid \mathsf{m}(B_1), \mathsf{m}(B_2) \in \text{est}(F)\}$

We can purify F and the clauses obtained this way by replacing every term of the form $\mathsf{m}(B)$ with a new constant m_B, and keeping the equations $\mathsf{m}(B) \approx m_B$ in a set Def of definitions. We obtain a formula of the form $F_{\text{set}} \wedge F_{\text{num}}' \wedge \mathcal{K}_{\mathsf{M}}{}^{\cap}[F]' \wedge \text{Def}$.

Theorem 12. *Assume that the $\Sigma_{\text{set,m}}$ formula F does not contain complements or unions. The following hold:*

(1) F is satisfiable w.r.t. $\mathcal{T}_{\mathsf{M}}^u$ iff $F \wedge \mathcal{K}_{\mathsf{M}}{}^{\cap}[F]$ is satisfiable w.r.t. the 2-sorted combination of the theories $\mathsf{LI}(\mathbb{R})$, $\mathcal{T}_{\mathsf{S}}$ and $\mathsf{UIF_m}$.

(2) If m is a measure function then F is satisfiable w.r.t. $\mathcal{T}_{\mathsf{M}}^m$ iff $F \wedge \mathcal{K}_{\mathsf{M}}{}^{\cap}[F]$ is satisfiable in the 2-sorted combination of $\mathsf{LI}(\mathbb{R})$ and $\mathcal{T}_{\mathsf{S}}^m$.

Proof. Follows from the locality results for monotone functions in [23] and the fact that satisfiability of conjunctions of set constraints without complements and unions can be reduced to checking satisfiability in the theory of semilattices. $\square$

Lemma 13. *With the notations introduced above, the following are equivalent:*

(1) $F = F_{\mathsf{set}} \wedge F_{\mathsf{num}}$ *is satisfiable in* T_M^u *or* T_M^m;
(2) $F_{\mathsf{set}} \wedge F'_{\mathsf{num}} \wedge \mathcal{K}_M{}^{\cap}[F]'$ *is satisfiable in the combination of* T_S *and* $\mathsf{LI}(\mathbb{R})$.

Proof. Consequence of results on hierarchical reasoning in local extensions [22].

Theorem 14 (Complexity). *Let* F *be a conjunction of ground literals of the form* $F = F_{\mathsf{set}} \wedge F_{\mathsf{num}}$ *which does not contain complements or unions and contain only the predicates* $\approx$ *and* $\subseteq$. *The procedure for checking the satisfiability of* F *we proposed above is polynomial in the size of the formula* F.

Proof (Idea). The proof relies on the convexity of the theory of sets and on the fact that checking entailment between formulae containing only conjunctions w.r.t. T_S can be reduced to checking entailment in the class of semilattices and ultimately to checking entailment in the semilattice with 2 elements, which can be done in PTIME. □

Example 15. Consider the formula: $F = x_1 \subseteq x_2 \cap x_3 \wedge \mathsf{m}(x_1 \cap x_3) \approx \mathsf{m}(x_3) + 1$. We have: $F_{\mathsf{set}} = x_1 \subseteq x_2 \cap x_3$; $F_{\mathsf{num}} = \mathsf{m}(x_1 \cap x_2) \approx \mathsf{m}(x_3) + 1$ and $\mathsf{est}(F) = \{\mathsf{m}(x_1 \cap x_2), \mathsf{m}(x_3)\}$. We instantiate (M_1) and (M_2) and (Mon) and obtain:

$(M_1)[F]$ $\quad 0 \leq \mathsf{m}(x_1 \cap x_2) \wedge 0 \leq \mathsf{m}(x_3)$	$(\mathsf{Mon})[F]$ $\quad x_1 \cap x_2 \subseteq x_3 \to \mathsf{m}(x_1 \cap x_2) \leq \mathsf{m}(x_3)$
$(M_2)[F]$ $\quad x_1 \cap x_2 \approx \emptyset \to \mathsf{m}(x_1 \cap x_2) \approx 0$	$\qquad\qquad x_3 \subseteq x_1 \cap x_2 \to \mathsf{m}(x_3) \leq \mathsf{m}(x_1 \cap x_2)$
$\qquad\qquad x_3 \approx \emptyset \to \mathsf{m}(x_3) \approx 0$	

After purification we obtain the following formulae:

Def	Set	Num	Bridge
$m_1 \approx \mathsf{m}(x_1 \cap x_2)$	$x_1 \subseteq x_2 \cap x_3$	$m_1 \approx m_2 + 1$	$x_1 \cap x_2 \approx \emptyset \to m_1 \approx 0$
$m_2 \approx \mathsf{m}(x_3)$		$0 \leq m_1$	$x_3 \approx \emptyset \to m_2 \approx 0$
		$0 \leq m_2$	$x_1 \cap x_2 \subseteq x_3 \to m_1 \leq m_2$
			$x_3 \subseteq x_1 \cap x_2 \to m_2 \leq m_1$

Both the set constraints and the numerical constraints are satisfiable. We prove that $F_{\mathsf{set}} \models x_1 \cap x_2 \subseteq x_3$ by showing that this holds in the two-element semilattice S_2. This can be reduced, using a structure-preserving translation to clause form, to checking the satisfiability of the following set of Horn clauses:

$(C1)$ $P_{x_1} \to P_{x_2 \cap x_3}$ $(C3)$ $P_{x_2 \cap x_3} \to P_{x_3}$ $(C5)$ $\neg P_{x_3}$ $\qquad$ $(C7)$ $P_{x_1 \cap x_2} \to P_{x_2}$
$(C2)$ $P_{x_2 \cap x_3} \to P_{x_2}$ $(C4)$ $P_{x_1 \cap x_2}$ $\qquad$ $(C6)$ $P_{x_1 \cap x_2} \to P_{x_1}$

We propagate $m_1 \leq m_2$ to the numerical constraints. It can be seen that $0 \leq m_1 \wedge 0 \leq m_2 \wedge m_1 \approx m_2 + 1 \wedge m_1 \leq m_2$ is unsatisfiable. Thus, F is unsatisfiable. ∎

6   Prospective Work: Duration Calculus

In this section we briefly indicate how the results established so far can be used for fragments of the duration calculus (abbreviated DC in the remainder) [7], a real-time logic developed for reasoning about durational constraints on time-dependent Boolean-valued states. We here present a fragment introduced in [13].

Syntax: We consider *state expressions* (described as Boolean combinations of state variables in a set V) and formulae. The syntax for state expressions and formulae is defined by:

$$S = 0 \mid 1 \mid P \mid \neg S \mid S_1 \vee S_2 \text{ where } P \in V$$
$$\varphi = l \bowtie k \mid \sum_{i=1}^{m} c_i \int S_i \bowtie k \mid \neg \varphi \mid \varphi \vee \psi \mid \varphi \wedge \psi \mid \varphi \frown \psi \text{ where } \bowtie \in \{<, \leq, >, \geq, \approx\}$$

Semantics: The semantics of a state expression S, given an interpretation $\mathcal{I}$, is a function: $\mathcal{I}_S : \mathbb{R}_{\geq 0} \to \{0, 1\}$, such that for every $t \geq 0$, $\mathcal{I}_S(t)$ is defined inductively in the usual way, using the semantics of the Boolean connectives. Satisfaction of formulae ϕ is defined over pairs $(\mathcal{I}, [a, b])$ (called observations) consisting of an interpretation $\mathcal{I}$ and a time interval $[a, b]$ with $b \geq a \geq 0$. The satisfaction relation $\mathcal{I}, [a, b] \models \varphi$ is defined inductively as follows:

$$\mathcal{I}, [a, b] \models l \bowtie k \qquad \text{iff } b - a \bowtie k$$
$$\mathcal{I}, [a, b] \models \sum_{i=1}^{m} c_i \int S_i \bowtie k \text{ iff } \sum_{i=1}^{m} c_i \int_a^b \mathcal{I}_{S_i}(t) dt \bowtie k$$
$$\mathcal{I}, [a, b] \models \neg \varphi \qquad \text{iff } \mathcal{I}, [a, b] \not\models \varphi$$
$$\mathcal{I}, [a, b] \models \varphi \wedge \psi \qquad \text{iff } \mathcal{I}, [a, b] \models \varphi \text{ and } \mathcal{I}, [a, b] \models \psi$$
$$\mathcal{I}, [a, b] \models \varphi \vee \psi \qquad \text{iff } \mathcal{I}, [a, b] \models \varphi \text{ or } \mathcal{I}, [a, b] \models \psi$$
$$\mathcal{I}, [a, b] \models \varphi \frown \psi \qquad \text{iff } \mathcal{I}, [a, m] \models \varphi \text{ and } \mathcal{I}, [m, b] \models \psi \text{ for some } m \in [a, b].$$

If $\mathcal{I}, [a, b] \models \varphi$ holds we say that φ is true in $[a, b]$ w.r.t. $\mathcal{I}$. A formula ϕ is satisfiable if it is true for some observation $(\mathcal{I}, [a, b])$.

Although satisfiability in the duration calculus (DC) is in general undecidable, various decidable fragments have been identified. As their exact definitions and the decision procedures are very different, these fragments are hard to compare. We here consider the language DC_{pos} that is defined in [13]. The syntax is defined as above, with the additional constraint that the chop operator occurs only under a positive number of negations. Every such formula is equivalent to a formula in which the chop operator does not occur below negations. We show that the decision procedures for sets with measures described in this paper yields a decision procedure for satisfiability of DC formulae of the form $F_{state} \wedge F_{DC}$, where F_{state} is a Boolean formula over the set V of state variables expressing hypotheses about the truth of state formulae, and F_{DC} is a formula in the duration calculus in which the chop operator does not occur below negations. Such chop operators can be eliminated at the price of introducing additional existentially quantified variables.

For a given interpretation $\mathcal{I}$ we can regard a state formula S as the set $A_S = \{t \geq 0 \mid \mathcal{I}_S(t) = 1\}$ of time points at which S is true. For any observation

$(\mathcal{I}, [a, b])$, $\int S$ is the measure of the set $A_S \cap [a, b]$. We therefore consider conjunctive formulae of the form $F = F_{state} \wedge F_{num}$, which are actually formulae in the language $\Sigma_{set,m}$ with the only difference that we talk about states instead of sets and the measure function is $\int$ rather than m.

Theorem 16. *The satisfiability of formulae of the form $F = F_{state} \wedge F_{num}$ – where F_{state} is a Boolean formula and F_{num} is a conjunction of linear inequalities involving terms of numeric sort built starting from constants l, k_i, a_i, b_i and from terms of the form $m(A_i \cap [a_i, b_i])$ – can be decided using a variant of the method described in this paper in at most $k! \cdot 2^n$ steps, where k is the number of bounds in the integrals – including those introduced by chops – and n is the number of state expressions.*

Proof. We can proceed as follows: We compute the atomic decomposition corresponding to the state expressions B_i. For the numeric constants a_i, b_i used as limits for the intervals some inequalities are included in F_{num}. This defines a partial ordering on these constants. We "guess" a total ordering extending this partial ordering, and consider all intervals of the form $[a_i, a_{i+1}]$, where a_{i+1} is the immediate successor of a_i in this total ordering. We now build as atomic sets the sets $S_{ij} = S_i \cap [a_j, a_{j+1}]$ and perform the instantiation of all axioms taking these atomic sets into account. We can then apply one of the methods proposed in this paper to check satisfiability of the resulting formula.   □

7   Conclusion and Outlook

In this paper we studied possibilities of checking satisfiability of quantifier-free formulae in the combined theory of sets, measures and arithmetic. Our approach relies – similarly to the approach by Ohlbach [21] and that of Kuncak et al. [19] – on an atomic decomposition of sets. We proposed two solution variants: The first variant performs a reduction to checking the satisfiability of constraints in $LI(\mathbb{R})$, the second uses locality properties in the theory of sets and measures and reduces the problems to entailment checking in the theory of sets followed by satisfiability checking in $LI(\mathbb{R})$. Both approaches have their own advantages.

- The first method can be used for arbitrary quantifier-free formulae and is easy to implement. We think that this method can be extended without major problems to a decision procedure for certain classes of formulae with arbitrary quantifier prefix. This is work in progress.
- The second method allowed us to recognize a tractable fragment of the theory of sets with measures and to make a finer complexity analysis for the conjunctive fragment. The locality properties we establish enable us to use locality properties for combinations of theories established in [14] to prove locality properties for theories with several measure functions or for the combination of the theory of sets with measures with other local extensions of real arithmetic or of the theory of sets.

Both methods can be improved by instantiation by demand, as in [15] or [2].

We indicated how the method can be adapted to situations in which we are interested in models in which the universe $\mathcal{U}_\mathcal{A}$ is given or has a given form (for instance must be an interval in all models). More generally, we might want to check whether a formula has a model in which the set variables are interpreted as intervals. Our methods can be used in this context if we introduce an additional step that checks the consistency of a computed model for the formula F w.r.t. the intended interpretations[1] and use conflict driven learning.

We showed how our method can be used for a fragment of the duration calculus [13]. While in general the duration calculus is undecidable, decidable fragments have been identified [4,6,8,10,11,13,28]. We hope that the ideas presented in this paper might help to obtain a uniform method that would yield decision procedures for several such fragments (for instance RDC ([5]), the fragments defined in [10] and [11] and the fragment studied in [9]) and would allow us to identify new decidable fragments.

Acknowledgments. We thank Ernst-Rüdiger Olderog, Martin Fränzle and Calogero Zarba for helpful discussions on the duration calculus. We also thank the anonymous reviewers for their constructive comments.

References

1. Alberti, F., Ghilardi, S., Pagani, E.: Counting constraints in flat array fragments. In: Olivetti, N., Tiwari, A. (eds.) IJCAR 2016. LNCS, vol. 9706, pp. 65–81. Springer, Cham (2016). doi:10.1007/978-3-319-40229-1_6
2. Bansal, K., Reynolds, A., Barrett, C., Tinelli, C.: A new decision procedure for finite sets and cardinality constraints in SMT. In: Olivetti, N., Tiwari, A. (eds.) IJCAR 2016. LNCS, vol. 9706, pp. 82–98. Springer, Cham (2016). doi:10.1007/978-3-319-40229-1_7
3. Bender, M.: Reasoning with sets and sums of sets. In: King, T., Piskac, R. (eds.) SMT@IJCAR 2016, Proceedings. CEUR Workshop Proceedings, vol. 1617, pp. 61–70. CEUR-WS.org (2016)
4. Bouajjani, A., Lakhnech, Y., Robbana, R.: From duration calculus to linear hybrid automata. In: Wolper, P. (ed.) CAV 1995. LNCS, vol. 939, pp. 196–210. Springer, Heidelberg (1995). doi:10.1007/3-540-60045-0_51
5. Chaochen, Z., Hansen, M.R.: Duration Calculus: A Formal Approach to Real-Time Systems. Springer, Berlin (2004)
6. Chaochen, Z., Hansen, M.R., Sestoft, P.: Decidability and undecidability results for duration calculus. In: Enjalbert, P., Finkel, A., Wagner, K.W. (eds.) STACS 1993. LNCS, vol. 665, pp. 58–68. Springer, Heidelberg (1993). doi:10.1007/3-540-56503-5_8

---

[1] For example, a model in which the set variables x_1, x_2, x_3 are interpreted as intervals I_1, I_2, I_3 and the atomic sets $\mathcal{S}_{001}, \mathcal{S}_{010}, \mathcal{S}_{100}, \mathcal{S}_{111}$ are assigned non-empty values and the other atomic intervals are empty, is inconsistent: There can be no section in which the intervals overlap ($\mathcal{S}_{111}$ not empty) that is joined by three sections where every set is disjoint from the other two ($\mathcal{S}_{001}, \mathcal{S}_{010}, \mathcal{S}_{100}$ are not empty).

7. Chaochen, Z., Hoare, C.A.R., Ravn, A.P.: A calculus of durations. Inf. Process. Lett. **40**(5), 269–276 (1991)
8. Chaochen, Z., Ravn, A.P., Hansen, M.R.: An extended duration calculus for hybrid real-time systems. In: Grossman, R.L., Nerode, A., Ravn, A.P., Rischel, H. (eds.) HS 1991-1992. LNCS, vol. 736, pp. 36–59. Springer, Heidelberg (1993). doi:10.1007/3-540-57318-6_23
9. Chetcuti-Sperandio, N.: Tableau-based automated deduction for duration calculus. In: Egly, U., Fermüller, C.G. (eds.) TABLEAUX 2002. LNCS, vol. 2381, pp. 53–69. Springer, Heidelberg (2002). doi:10.1007/3-540-45616-3_5
10. Chetcuti-Sperandio, N., del Cerro, L.F.: A decision method for duration calculus. J. UCS **5**(11), 743–764 (1999)
11. Chetcuti-Sperandio, N., del Cerro, L.F.: A mixed decision method for duration calculus. J. Log. Comput. **10**(6), 877–895 (2000)
12. Chocron, P., Fontaine, P., Ringeissen, C.: A gentle non-disjoint combination of satisfiability procedures. In: Demri, S., Kapur, D., Weidenbach, C. (eds.) IJCAR 2014. LNCS, vol. 8562, pp. 122–136. Springer, Cham (2014). doi:10.1007/978-3-319-08587-6_9
13. Fränzle, M., Hansen, M.R.: Deciding an interval logic with accumulated durations. In: Grumberg, O., Huth, M. (eds.) TACAS 2007. LNCS, vol. 4424, pp. 201–215. Springer, Heidelberg (2007). doi:10.1007/978-3-540-71209-1_17
14. Ihlemann, C., Sofronie-Stokkermans, V.: On hierarchical reasoning in combinations of theories. In: Giesl, J., Hähnle, R. (eds.) IJCAR 2010. LNCS, vol. 6173, pp. 30–45. Springer, Heidelberg (2010). doi:10.1007/978-3-642-14203-1_4
15. Jacobs, S.: Incremental instance generation in local reasoning. In: Bouajjani, A., Maler, O. (eds.) CAV 2009. LNCS, vol. 5643, pp. 368–382. Springer, Heidelberg (2009). doi:10.1007/978-3-642-02658-4_29
16. Kapur, D., Zarba, C.G.: A reduction approach to decision procedures (2005). https://www.cs.unm.edu/~kapur/mypapers/reduction.pdf,. Unpublished manuscript
17. Khachiyan, L.: A polynomial algorithm in linear programming. Soviet Math. Dokl. **20**(1), 191–194 (1979)
18. Kuncak, V., Nguyen, H.H., Rinard, M.: An algorithm for deciding BAPA: Boolean algebra with Presburger arithmetic. In: Nieuwenhuis, R. (ed.) CADE 2005. LNCS, vol. 3632, pp. 260–277. Springer, Heidelberg (2005). doi:10.1007/11532231_20
19. Kuncak, V., Nguyen, H.H., Rinard, M.C.: Deciding Boolean algebra with Presburger arithmetic. J. Autom. Reasoning **36**(3), 213–239 (2006)
20. Kuncak, V., Piskac, R., Suter, P.: Ordered sets in the calculus of data structures. In: Dawar, A., Veith, H. (eds.) CSL 2010. LNCS, vol. 6247, pp. 34–48. Springer, Heidelberg (2010). doi:10.1007/978-3-642-15205-4_5
21. Ohlbach, H.J.: Set description languages and reasoning about numerical features of sets. In: Lambrix, P., Borgida, A., Lenzerini, M., Möller, R., Patel-Schneider, P.F. (eds.) International Workshop on Description Logics (DL 1999), Proceedings. CEUR Workshop Proceedings, vol. 22. CEUR-WS.org (1999)
22. Sofronie-Stokkermans, V.: Hierarchic reasoning in local theory extensions. In: Nieuwenhuis, R. (ed.) CADE 2005. LNCS, vol. 3632, pp. 219–234. Springer, Heidelberg (2005). doi:10.1007/11532231_16
23. Sofronie-Stokkermans, V., Ihlemann, C.: Automated reasoning in some local extensions of ordered structures. Multiple-Valued Logic Soft Comput. **13**(4–6), 397–414 (2007)

24. Wies, T., Piskac, R., Kuncak, V.: Combining theories with shared set operations. In: Ghilardi, S., Sebastiani, R. (eds.) FroCoS 2009. LNCS, vol. 5749, pp. 366–382. Springer, Heidelberg (2009). doi:10.1007/978-3-642-04222-5_23

25. Yessenov, K., Piskac, R., Kuncak, V.: Collections, cardinalities, and relations. In: Barthe, G., Hermenegildo, M. (eds.) VMCAI 2010. LNCS, vol. 5944, pp. 380–395. Springer, Heidelberg (2010). doi:10.1007/978-3-642-11319-2_27

26. Zarba, C.G.: Combining sets with cardinals. J. Autom. Reasoning **34**(1), 1–29 (2005)

27. Zee, K., Kuncak, V., Rinard, M.C.: Full functional verification of linked data structures. In: Gupta, R., Amarasinghe, S.P. (eds.), Proceedings of the ACM SIGPLAN 2008 Conference on Programming Language Design and Implementation, Tucson, AZ, USA, 7–13 June 2008, pp. 349–361. ACM (2008)

28. Chaochen, Z., Jingzhong, Z., Lu, Y., Xiaoshan, L.: Linear duration invariants. In: Langmaack, H., Roever, W.-P., Vytopil, J. (eds.) FTRTFT 1994. LNCS, vol. 863, pp. 86–109. Springer, Heidelberg (1994). doi:10.1007/3-540-58468-4_161

A Decision Procedure for Restricted Intensional Sets

Maximiliano Cristiá[1]([⊠]) and Gianfranco Rossi[2]

[1] Universidad Nacional de Rosario and CIFASIS, Rosario, Argentina
cristia@cifasis-conicet.gov.ar
[2] Università di Parma, Parma, Italy
gianfranco.rossi@unipr.it

Abstract. In this paper we present a decision procedure for Restricted Intensional Sets (RIS), i.e. sets given by a property rather than by enumerating their elements, similar to set comprehensions available in specification languages such as B and Z. The proposed procedure is parametric with respect to a first-order language and theory $\mathcal{X}$, providing at least equality and a decision procedure to check for satisfiability of $\mathcal{X}$-formulas. We show how this framework can be applied when $\mathcal{X}$ is the theory of hereditarily finite sets as is supported by the language CLP($\mathcal{SET}$). We also present a working implementation of RIS as part of the {*log*} tool and we show how it compares with a mainstream solver and how it helps in the automatic verification of code fragments.

1 Introduction

Intensional sets, also called *set comprehensions*, are sets described by a property that the elements must satisfy, rather than by explicitly enumerating their elements. Intensional sets are widely recognized as a key feature to describe complex problems. Hence, having a decision procedure for an expressive class of intensional sets should be of interest to different communities, such as SMT solving, model finding and constraint programming.

In this paper we consider *Restricted Intensional Sets* (RIS). RIS are a subclass of the set comprehensions available in the formal specification languages Z [24] and B [20]. We say that this class of intensional sets is *restricted* because they denote *finite* sets, while in Z and B they can be infinite. In effect, given that the domain of a RIS fixes the maximum number of elements that the RIS can have and that the domain is necessarily a finite set, then RIS cannot have an infinite number of elements. Nonetheless, RIS can be not completely specified. In particular, as the domain can be a variable, RIS are finite but *unbounded*.

We define a constraint language, called $\mathcal{L}_{\mathcal{RIS}}$, which provides both RIS and extensional sets, along with basic operations on them, as primitive entities of the language. $\mathcal{L}_{\mathcal{RIS}}$ is *parametric* with respect to an arbitrary theory $\mathcal{X}$, for which we assume a decision procedure for any admissible $\mathcal{X}$-formula is available. Elements of $\mathcal{L}_{\mathcal{RIS}}$ sets are the objects provided by $\mathcal{X}$, which can be manipulated through the primitive operators that $\mathcal{X}$ offers (at least, $\mathcal{X}$-equality).

© Springer International Publishing AG 2017
L. de Moura (Ed.): CADE 2017, LNAI 10395, pp. 185–201, 2017.
DOI: 10.1007/978-3-319-63046-5_12

Hence, RIS in $\mathcal{L_{RIS}}$ represent *untyped unbounded finite hybrid sets*, i.e. unbounded finite sets whose elements are of any sort.

We provide a set of rewrite rules for rewriting $\mathcal{RIS}$-formulas that are proved to preserve satisfiability of the original formula. These rules are used to define a *decision procedure* for $\mathcal{L_{RIS}}$, called $SAT_{\mathcal{RIS}}$, which is proved to be correct, complete and terminating. $SAT_{\mathcal{RIS}}$ will be able to decide any propositional combination of the admissible $\mathcal{RIS}$-constraints and $\mathcal{X}$-formulas. Furthermore, for any satisfiable formula, $SAT_{\mathcal{RIS}}$ returns a finite representation of all its possible solutions.

$\mathcal{L_{RIS}}$ has been implemented in Prolog, and integrated with $\{log\}$ (pronounced 'setlog'), the freely available Prolog implementation of CLP($\mathcal{SET}$) [9]. This implementation is compared to ProB [16] w.r.t. intensional set manipulation and an example using $\{log\}$ to verify program correctness is also shown.

Section 2 introduces $\mathcal{L_{RIS}}$. Section 3 describes the solver which is proved to be a decision procedure for $\mathcal{L_{RIS}}$ in Sect. 4. A discussion of our approach is provided in Sect. 5. A working implementation of this solver is shown in Sect. 6. Section 7 compares our results with similar approaches.

2 $\mathcal{L_{RIS}}$: Syntax, Semantics and Applicability

$\mathcal{L_{RIS}}$ is parametric w.r.t. a first-order theory $\mathcal{X}$ which must include: a class of admissible $\mathcal{X}$-formulas based on a non-empty set of function symbols $\mathcal{F_X}$ and a set of predicate symbols $\Pi_{\mathcal{X}}$; an interpretation structure $\mathcal{I_X}$ with domain D_X and interpretation function $(\cdot)^{\mathcal{I_X}}$; and a decision procedure $SAT_{\mathcal{X}}$ for $\mathcal{X}$-formulas. We assume that $\Pi_{\mathcal{X}}$ contains at least the $=_{\mathcal{X}}$ operator, which is interpreted as the identity in D_X.

Definition 1. *The* signature Σ_{RIS} *of* $\mathcal{L_{RIS}}$ *is a triple* $\langle \mathcal{F}, \Pi, \mathcal{V} \rangle$ *where: (i)* $\mathcal{F}$ *is the set of function symbols, partitioned as* $\mathcal{F} \stackrel{\wedge}{=} \mathcal{F_S} \cup \mathcal{F_X}$, *where* $\mathcal{F_S} \stackrel{\wedge}{=} \{\emptyset, \{\cdot \sqcup \cdot\}, \{\cdot \mid \cdot \bullet \cdot\}\}$; *(ii)* Π *is the set of* primitive *predicate symbols, partitioned as* $\Pi \stackrel{\wedge}{=} \Pi_{\mathcal{S}} \cup \Pi_{\mathcal{X}}$ *where* $\Pi_{\mathcal{S}} \stackrel{\wedge}{=} \{=_{\mathcal{S}}, \in_{\mathcal{S}}, set, isX\}3$; *(iii)* $\mathcal{V}$ *is a denumerable set of variables, partitioned as* $\mathcal{V} \stackrel{\wedge}{=} \mathcal{V_S} \cup \mathcal{V_X}$.

$\mathcal{F_S}$-terms are called *set terms*. In particular: $\{t \sqcup A\}$ is an *extensional set term*, where t (*element part*) is a $\mathcal{X}$-term and A (*set part*) is a set term; $\{e[\boldsymbol{x}] : D \mid \Psi \bullet \tau[\boldsymbol{x}]\}$ is a *RIS term*, where e (*control term*) is a $\mathcal{X}$-term and $\boldsymbol{x} \stackrel{\wedge}{=} \langle x_1, \ldots, x_n \rangle$, $n > 0$, are all the variables occurring in it; D (*domain*) is a set term; Ψ (*filter*) is a $\mathcal{X}$-formula; and τ (*pattern*) is a $\mathcal{X}$-term containing $\boldsymbol{x}^1$. When useful, the domain D can be represented also as an interval $[m, n]$, m and n integer constants, which is intended as a shorthand for $\{m, m+1, \ldots, n\}$. Moreover, when the pattern is the control term and the filter is *true*, they can be omitted (as in Z), although one must be present. Both extensional set and RIS terms can be partially specified because elements and sets can be variables. A RIS term is a *variable-RIS* if its

---

^{1} The form of RIS terms is borrowed from the form of set comprehension expressions available in Z.

domain is a variable or (recursively) a variable-RIS; otherwise it is a *non-variable RIS*. As a notational convenience, we will write $\{t_1 \sqcup \{t_2 \sqcup \cdots \{t_n \sqcup A\} \cdots \}\}$ (resp., $\{t_1 \sqcup \{t_2 \sqcup \cdots \{t_n \sqcup \emptyset\} \cdots \}\}$) as $\{t_1, t_2, \ldots, t_n \sqcup A\}$ (resp., $\{t_1, t_2, \ldots, t_n\}$). $\mathcal{F}_S$-terms are of sort Set, while $\mathcal{F}_\mathcal{X}$-terms are of sort X.

Definition 2. *A $\mathcal{RIS}$-constraint is any atomic predicate of the form $A =_S B$, $u \in_S A$, $set(t)$ or $isX(t)$, where A and B are set terms, u is a $\mathcal{X}$-term, t is any term. The set $\Phi_{\mathcal{RIS}}$ of $\mathcal{RIS}$-formulas is given by the following grammar:*
$$\Phi_{\mathcal{RIS}} ::= true \mid \mathcal{C}_{\mathcal{RIS}} \mid \neg \mathcal{C}_{\mathcal{RIS}} \mid \Phi_{\mathcal{RIS}} \wedge \Phi_{\mathcal{RIS}} \mid \Phi_{\mathcal{RIS}} \vee \Phi_{\mathcal{RIS}} \mid \Phi_\mathcal{X}, \text{ where } \mathcal{C}_{\mathcal{RIS}}$$
represents any $\mathcal{RIS}$-constraint and $\Phi_\mathcal{X}$ represents any $\mathcal{X}$-formula.

If π is an infix predicate symbol, then $\neg \pi$ is written as $\not{\pi}$ (e.g. $\cdot \not\in \cdot$). For the sake of presentation, in coming examples, we will assume that the language of $\mathcal{X}$, $\mathcal{L}_\mathcal{X}$, provides the constant, function and predicate symbols of the theories of the integer numbers and ordered pairs. Moreover, we will write $=$ (resp. $\in$) in place of $=_\mathcal{X}$ and $=_S$ (resp. $\in_\mathcal{X}$ and $\in_S$) whenever is clear from context.

Example 1. The following are $\mathcal{RIS}$-formulas involving RIS terms.

- $\{x : [-2, 2] \mid x \bmod 2 = 0 \bullet x\} = \{-2, 0, 2\}$
- $(5, y) \in \{x : D \mid x > 0 \bullet (x, x * x)\}$, where D is a variable
- $(5, 0) \notin \{(x, y) : \{z \sqcup X\} \mid y \neq 0 \bullet (x, y)\}$, where z and X are variables.   □

Symbols in $\Sigma_{\mathcal{RIS}}$ are interpreted according to the structure $\mathcal{R} = \langle \mathcal{D}, (\cdot)^\mathcal{R} \rangle$, where $\mathcal{D}$ is the interpretation domain and $(\cdot)^\mathcal{R}$ is the corresponding interpretation function.

Definition 3. *The interpretation domain $\mathcal{D}$ is partitioned as $\mathcal{D} \triangleq D_{\mathsf{Set}} \cup D_\mathsf{X}$ where: (i) D_{Set} is the collection of all finite sets built from elements in D_X; and (ii) D_X is a collection of any other objects (not in D_{Set}).*

The *interpretation function* $(\cdot)^\mathcal{R}$ for symbols in $\mathcal{F}$ is informally defined as follows (see [4] for details): $\emptyset$ is interpreted as the empty set; $\{t \sqcup A\}$ is interpreted as the set $\{t\} \cup A$; $\{e[\boldsymbol{x}] : D \mid \Psi[\boldsymbol{x}, \boldsymbol{v}] \bullet \tau[\boldsymbol{x}, \boldsymbol{v}]\}$, where $\boldsymbol{v}$ is a vector of *free* variables, is interpreted as the set $\{y : \exists \boldsymbol{x}(e[\boldsymbol{x}] \in D \wedge \Psi[\boldsymbol{x}, \boldsymbol{v}] \wedge y =_\mathcal{X} \tau[\boldsymbol{x}, \boldsymbol{v}])\}$. As concerns predicate symbols in Π, $A =_S B$ is interpreted as the identity relation in D_{Set}, $u \in_S A$ as the set membership relation in D_{Set}, $isX(t)$ (resp. $set(t)$) as a predicate testing whether t belongs to the domain D_X (resp. D_{Set}) or not. Note that in RIS terms, $\boldsymbol{x}$ are bound variables whose scope is the RIS itself, while $\boldsymbol{v}$ are free variables possibly occurring in the formula where the RIS is participating in.

In order to precisely characterize the language for which we provide a decision procedure, the control term e and the pattern τ of a RIS term are restricted to be of specific forms. Namely, if x and y are variables ranging on D_X, then e can be either x or (x, y); while τ can be either e or (e, t) or (t, e), where t is any (uninterpreted/interpreted) $\mathcal{X}$-term, possibly involving the variables in e. As it will be evident from the various examples in this and in the next sections, in spite of these restrictions, $\mathcal{L}_{\mathcal{RIS}}$ is still a very expressive language. In particular, note that the restriction on patterns allows "plain" sets and partial functions (see examples below) to lay inside the decision procedure. Relaxing this assumption is feasible but it may compromise decidability (see Sect. 5).

One interesting application of RIS is to represent *restricted universal quantifiers*. That is, the formula $\forall x \in D : \Psi[x]$ can be easily represented by the $\mathcal{L_{RIS}}$ equality $D = \{x : D \mid \Psi[x]\}$ (see [4]). Then, as $\mathcal{L_{RIS}}$ is endowed with a decision procedure, it can decide a large fragment of quantified formulas.

Example 2. The minimum y of a set of integers S can be stated by means of the quantified formula $y \in S \wedge \forall x \in S : y \leq x$. This formula is encoded in $\mathcal{L_{RIS}}$ as follows: $y \in S \wedge S = \{x : S \mid y \leq x\}$. Hence, if $S = \{2, 4, 1, 6\}$, then y is bound to 1; and if S is a variable and $y = 5$, then one of the solutions is $S = \{5 \sqcup \{x : N \mid 5 \leq x\}\}$, where N is a new variable.   □

Another important application of RIS is to define *(partial) functions*. In general, a RIS of the form $\{x : D \mid \Psi \bullet (x, f(x))\}$, where f is any $\mathcal{L_X}$ function symbol, defines a partial function. Such a RIS contains ordered pairs whose first components belong to D, which cannot have duplicates (because it is a set). Given that RIS are sets, then, in $\mathcal{L_{RIS}}$, functions are sets of ordered pairs. Therefore, through standard set operators, functions can be evaluated, compared and point-wise composed; and by means of constraint solving, the inverse of a function can also be computed. The following examples illustrate these properties.

Example 3. The square of 5 can be calculated by: $(5, y) \in \{x : D \bullet (x, x * x)\}$, yielding $y = 25$. The same RIS calculates the square root of a given number: $(x, 36) \in \{x : D\bullet(x, x*x)\}$, returning $x = 6$ and $x = -6$. Set membership can also be used for the point-wise composition of functions. The function $f(x) = x^2 + 8$ can be evaluated on 5 as follows: $(5, y) \in \{x : D \bullet (x, x * x)\} \wedge (y, z) \in \{v : E \bullet (v, v + 8)\}$ returning $y = 25$ and $z = 33$.   □

Finally, note that we allow RIS terms to be the set part of extensional sets, e.g. $\{x \sqcup \{y : A \mid y \neq z\}\}$, as well as to be the domain of other RIS.

3   A Solver for $\mathcal{L_{RIS}}$

In this section we present a decision procedure for $\mathcal{L_{RIS}}$, called $SAT_{\mathcal{RIS}}$. Actually, $SAT_{\mathcal{RIS}}$ is a complete constraint solver which is able not only to decide satisfiability of $\mathcal{L_{RIS}}$ formulas, but also to compute a concise representation of all the concrete (or ground) solutions of the input formula. It is important to note that decidability of $\mathcal{RIS}$-formulas depends on the existence of a decision procedure for $\mathcal{X}$-formulas.

3.1   The Solver

$SAT_{\mathcal{RIS}}$ is a rewriting system whose global organization is shown in Algorithm 1, where STEP is the core of the algorithm. sort_infer is used to automatically add sort information to the input formula Φ to force arguments of $\mathcal{RIS}$-constraints to be of the proper sort (see Remark 1 below). sort_infer is called at the beginning of the Algorithm and within STEP for the constraints that are generated during constraint processing. sort_check checks sort constraints occurring in Φ: if they are satisfiable, then Φ is returned unchanged; otherwise, Φ is rewritten to *false*.

Algorithm 1. The $SAT_{\mathcal{RIS}}$ solver. Φ is the input formula.

procedure STEP(Φ)	**procedure** $SAT_{\mathcal{RIS}}(\Phi)$
$\quad \Phi \leftarrow \mathsf{rw}_\in(\mathsf{rw}_{\notin}(\mathsf{rw}_{\neq}(\mathsf{rw}_=(\Phi))))$	$\quad \Phi \leftarrow \mathsf{sort\_infer}(\Phi)$
$\quad \Phi \leftarrow \mathsf{sort\_check}(\mathsf{sort\_infer}(\Phi))$	$\quad$ **repeat**
$\quad$ **return** Φ	$\quad\quad \Phi' \leftarrow \Phi$
procedure $\mathsf{rw}_\pi(\Phi)$	$\quad\quad$ **repeat**
$\quad$ **if** *false* $\in \Phi$ **then**	$\quad\quad\quad \Phi'' \leftarrow \Phi$
$\quad\quad$ **return** *false*	$\quad\quad\quad \Phi \leftarrow$ STEP(Φ)
$\quad$ **else**	$\quad\quad$ **until** $\Phi = \Phi''$
$\quad\quad$ **repeat**	$\quad\quad \Phi \leftarrow \mathsf{remove\_neq}(\Phi)$
$\quad\quad\quad$ select any literal $t_1 \pi t_2$ in Φ	$\quad$ **until** $\Phi = \Phi'$
$\quad\quad\quad$ apply any applicable rule to $t_1 \pi t_2$	$\quad \Phi$ is $\Phi_{\mathcal{S}} \wedge \Phi_{\mathcal{X}}$
$\quad\quad$ **until** no rule applies to Φ	$\quad \Phi \leftarrow \Phi_{\mathcal{S}} \wedge SAT_{\mathcal{X}}(\Phi_{\mathcal{X}})$
$\quad$ **return** Φ	$\quad$ **return** Φ

---

remove_neq deals with the elimination of $\neq$-constraints involving RIS domains. For example, in $D \neq \emptyset \wedge \{x : D \,|\, \Psi \bullet \tau\} = \emptyset$, remove_neq rewrites $D \neq \emptyset$ as $y \in D$, where y is a new fresh variable. In turn, $y \in D$ is rewritten as $D = \{y \sqcup N\}$ for another new variable N. Finally, the whole formula is rewritten as $D = \{y \sqcup N\} \wedge \{x : \{y \sqcup N\} \,|\, \Psi \bullet \tau\} = \emptyset$, which fires one of the rules given in Sect. 3.2. This rewriting chain is fired only because D is the domain of a RIS; otherwise remove_neq does nothing with $D \neq \emptyset$. The complete definition of remove_neq is in [4].

STEP applies specialized rewriting procedures to the current formula Φ and returns the modified formula. Each rewriting procedure applies a few non-deterministic rewrite rules which reduce the syntactic complexity of $\mathcal{RIS}$-constraints of one kind. Procedure rw_π in Algorithm 1 represents the rewriting procedure for literals $t_1 \pi t_2$, π in $\{=, \neq, \in, \notin\}$. The execution of STEP is iterated until a fixpoint is reached—i.e. the formula cannot be simplified any further. STEP returns *false* whenever (at least) one of the procedures in it rewrites Φ to *false*. Some rewrite rules are described in detail in Sect. 3.2 and the rest in [4].

$SAT_{\mathcal{X}}$ is the constraint solver for $\mathcal{X}$-formulas. The formula Φ can be written as $\Phi_{\mathcal{S}} \wedge \Phi_{\mathcal{X}}$, where $\Phi_{\mathcal{S}}$ ($\Phi_{\mathcal{X}}$) is a conjunction of $\Pi_{\mathcal{S}}$- ($\Pi_{\mathcal{X}}$-)literals. $SAT_{\mathcal{X}}$ is applied only to the $\Phi_{\mathcal{X}}$ conjunct of Φ. Note that, conversely, STEP rewrites only $\Pi_{\mathcal{S}}$-literals, while it leaves all other literals unchanged. Nonetheless, as the rewrite rules show, $SAT_{\mathcal{RIS}}$ generates $\mathcal{X}$-formulas that are conjoined to $\Phi_{\mathcal{X}}$ so they are later solved by $SAT_{\mathcal{X}}$.

Remark 1. $\mathcal{L}_{\mathcal{RIS}}$ does not provide variable declarations. The sort of a variable is enforced by adding suitable *sort constraints* to the formula to be processed.

Sort constraints are automatically added by the solver. Specifically, a constraint $set(y)$ (resp., $isX(y)$) is added for each variable y which is required to be of sort Set (resp., X). For example, given $X = \{y \sqcup A\}$, sort_infer conjoins the sort constraints $set(X)$, $isX(y)$ and $set(A)$. If the set of function and predicate symbols of $\mathcal{L}_{\mathcal{RIS}}$ and $\mathcal{L}_{\mathcal{X}}$ are disjoint, each variable occurring in the formula has a unique sort constraint. □

3.2 Rewrite Rules

The rules are given as $\phi \longrightarrow \Phi_1 \vee \cdots \vee \Phi_n$, where ϕ is a $\Pi_{\mathcal{S}}$-literal and Φ_i, $i \geq 1$, are $\mathcal{RIS}$-formulas. Each $\Pi_{\mathcal{S}}$-literal matching ϕ is non-deterministically rewritten to one of the Φ_i. In all rules, variables appearing in the right-hand side but not in the left-hand side are assumed to be new, fresh variables, implicitly existentially quantified over each Φ_i. Moreover, A, B and D are extensional set terms, $\bar{X}$ and $\bar{D}$ are variables of sort Set, while t, t_i, u and d are any $\mathcal{X}$-terms.

Set equality between extensional sets implements set unification [11]. In turn, membership is strongly based on set equality. Some of the key rewrite rules for equality, membership and their negations dealing with extensional set terms (adapted from [9]) are shown in Fig. 1. In particular, rule $=_3$ deals with equality between two set terms: the second and third disjuncts take care of duplicates in the right-hand side and the left-hand side term, respectively, while the fourth disjunct takes care of permutativity of the set constructor $\{\cdot \sqcup \cdot\}$.

Basically, $\mathcal{L}_{\mathcal{RIS}}$ extends the rewrite rules for equality, membership and their negations to allow them to deal with RIS terms. Figure 2 lists all the rules applied by STEP to deal with constraints of the form $R = U$ and $R \neq U$, where either R

$$\bar{X} = A \longrightarrow \text{substitute } \bar{X} \text{ by } A \text{ in the rest of the formula} \qquad (=_1)$$

$$\bar{X} = \{t_0, \ldots, t_n \sqcup \bar{X}\} \longrightarrow \bar{X} = \{t_0, \ldots, t_n \sqcup N\} \qquad (=_2)$$

$$\{t \sqcup A\} = \{u \sqcup B\} \longrightarrow$$
$$t = u \wedge A = \{u \sqcup B\} \vee t = u \wedge \{u \sqcup A\} = B \qquad (=_3)$$
$$\vee\, t = u \wedge A = B \vee A = \{u \sqcup N\} \wedge \{t \sqcup N\} = B$$

$$\{t \sqcup A\} \neq \{u \sqcup B\} \longrightarrow$$
$$(y \in \{t \sqcup A\} \wedge y \notin \{u \sqcup B\}) \vee (y \notin \{t \sqcup A\} \wedge y \in \{u \sqcup B\}) \qquad (=_4)$$

$$t \in \{u \sqcup A\} \longrightarrow t = u \vee t \in A \qquad (\in_1)$$

$$t \in \bar{X} \longrightarrow \bar{X} = \{t \sqcup N\} \qquad (\in_2)$$

$$t \notin \{u \sqcup A\} \longrightarrow t \neq u \wedge t \notin A \qquad (\in_3)$$

Fig. 1. Rewrite rules dealing with extensional set terms

or U are RIS terms. In order to make the presentation more accessible: (a) the rules are given for RIS whose domain is not another RIS; (b) the control term of RIS is *variable* x in all cases and it is omitted to save space. Generalization to cases in which these restrictions are removed is discussed in [4].

Intuitively, the key idea behind the rules dealing with RIS terms is a sort of *lazy partial evaluation* of RIS. That is, a RIS term is treated as a block until it is necessary to identify one of its elements. When that happens, the RIS is transformed into an extensional set whose element part is the identified element and whose set part is the rest of the RIS. More formally, if y is known to be in $\{x : D \mid \Psi \bullet \tau\}$ then this RIS is rewritten as the extensional set $\{y \sqcup \{x : D' \mid \Psi \bullet \tau\}\}$, where $\{x : D' \mid \Psi \bullet \tau\}$ is semantically equal to $\{x : D \mid \Psi \bullet \tau\} \setminus \{y\}$.

Equality between a RIS and an extensional set is governed by rules $(=_5)$–$(=_8)$. In particular, rule $(=_6)$ deals with the case in which a RIS with a non-empty domain must be equal to the empty set. It turns out that to force a RIS $\{D \mid \Psi \bullet \tau\}$ to be empty it is enough that the filter Ψ is false for all elements in D, i.e. $\forall x \in D : \neg \Psi[x]$. This (restricted) universal quantification is conveniently implemented through recursion, by extracting one element d at a time from the RIS domain. Rule $(=_8)$ deals with equality between a variable-RIS and an extensional set. The intuition behind this rule is as follows. Given that $\{y \sqcup A\}$ is not empty, then $\bar{D}$ must be not empty in which case it is equal to $\{z \sqcup E\}$ for some z and E. Furthermore, z must satisfy Ψ and $\tau(z)$ must be equal to y. As the first element of $\{y \sqcup A\}$ belongs to the RIS, then the rest of the RIS must be equal to A. It is not necessary to consider the case where $\neg \Psi(z)$, as in rule $(=_7)$, because z is a new fresh variable.

$\{\emptyset \mid \Psi \bullet \tau\} = \emptyset \rightarrow true$ $\hspace{4cm}$ $(=_5)$

$\{\{d \sqcup D\} \mid \Psi \bullet \tau\} = \emptyset \rightarrow \neg \Psi(d) \wedge \{D \mid \Psi \bullet \tau\} = \emptyset$ $\hspace{1.5cm}$ $(=_6)$

If B is any set term except $\emptyset$:

$\{\{d \sqcup D\} \mid \Psi \bullet \tau\} = B \rightarrow$ $\hspace{5cm}$ $(=_7)$
$\Psi(d) \wedge \{\tau(d) \sqcup \{D \mid \Psi \bullet \tau\}\} = B \vee \neg \Psi(d) \wedge \{D \mid \Psi \bullet \tau\} = B$

$\{\bar{D} \mid \Psi \bullet \tau\} = \{y \sqcup A\} \rightarrow$ $\hspace{5.5cm}$ $(=_8)$
$\bar{D} = \{z \sqcup E\} \wedge \Psi(z) \wedge y =_{\mathcal{X}} \tau(z) \wedge \{E \mid \Psi \bullet \tau\} = A$

$\{D \mid \Psi \bullet \tau\} \neq A \rightarrow (y \in \{D \mid \Psi \bullet \tau\} \wedge y \notin A) \vee (y \notin \{D \mid \Psi \bullet \tau\} \wedge y \in A)$ $\hspace{0.5cm}$ $(=_9)$

Fig. 2. Rewrite rules for $R = U$ and $R \neq U$; R or U RIS terms

Rules of Fig. 2 exhaust all, but three, of the possible combinations of equality between a RIS and other $\mathcal{L}_{\mathcal{RIS}}$ set terms. The cases not considered (i.e. equality between a variable and a variable-RIS, between a variable-RIS and the empty set, and between two variable-RIS) are dealt with as irreducible (Sect. 4.1).

$$t \in \{\emptyset \mid \Psi \bullet \tau\} \longrightarrow false \tag{$\in_4$}$$

$$t \in \{\bar{D} \mid \Psi \bullet \tau\} \longrightarrow d \in \bar{D} \wedge \Psi(d) \wedge t =_X \tau(d) \tag{$\in_5$}$$

$$t \in \{\{d \sqcup D\} \mid \Psi \bullet \tau\} \longrightarrow \\ \Psi(d) \wedge t \in \{\tau(d) \sqcup \{D \mid \Psi \bullet \tau\}\} \vee \neg\Psi(d) \wedge t \in \{D \mid \Psi \bullet \tau\} \tag{$\in_6$}$$

$$t \notin \{\emptyset \mid \Psi \bullet \tau\} \longrightarrow true \tag{$\in_7$}$$

$$t \notin \{\{d \sqcup D\} \mid \Psi \bullet \tau\} \longrightarrow \\ \Psi(d) \wedge t \neq_X \tau(d) \wedge t \notin \{D \mid \Psi \bullet \tau\} \vee \neg\Psi(d) \wedge t \notin \{D \mid \Psi \bullet \tau\} \tag{$\in_8$}$$

Fig. 3. Rewrite rules for $t \in R$ and $t \notin R$; R RIS term

Rules dealing with constraints of the form $t \in R$ and $t \notin R$, where t is a $\mathcal{L}_X$ term and R is a RIS term, are listed in Fig. 3. The case $t \notin R$ where R is a variable-RIS is dealt with as irreducible (Sect. 4.1), while constraints of the form $t \in R$ are eliminated in all cases.

4   Decidability of $\mathcal{L}_{\mathcal{RIS}}$ Formulas

Decidability of the set theory fragment considered in this paper can be obtained by showing a reduction of $\mathcal{RIS}$-formulas to formulas of the $\forall^\pi_{0,2}$ language studied in [2]. $\forall^\pi_{0,2}$ is a two-sorted quantified fragment of set theory which allows restricted quantifiers of the forms $(\forall x \in A)$, $(\exists x \in A)$, $(\forall(x,y) \in R)$, $(\exists(x,y) \in R)$ and literals of the forms $x \in A$, $(x,y) \in R$, $A = B$, $R = S$, where A and B are set variables (i.e., variables ranging over sets) and R and S are relation variables (i.e., variables ranging over binary relations). Semantics of this language is based on the von Neumann standard cumulative hierarchy of sets, which is the class containing all the pure sets.

The extensional finite sets and the primitive set-theoretical operators provided by $\mathcal{L}_{\mathcal{RIS}}$ are easily mapped to the general sets and operators of $\forall^\pi_{0,2}$. The same mapping can be provided also for RIS as follows (for simplicity the control term is just a variable and the pattern is the control term itself—so it can be omitted). First, RIS are expressed in terms of a quantified formula:

$$S = \{x : D \mid \Psi[x])\} \equiv \\ \forall x(x \in S \implies x \in D \wedge \Psi[x]) \wedge \forall x(x \in D \wedge \Psi[x] \implies x \in S)$$

which then can be immediately written as the following $\forall^\pi_{0,2}$-formula:

$$(\forall x \in S)(x \in D \wedge \Psi[x]) \wedge (\forall x \in D)(\Psi[x] \implies x \in S)$$

Note that the fact that the control variable is restricted to range over a set (i.e. the RIS domain) is crucial to allow both implications to be written as restricted universal quantifiers, hence as $\forall^\pi_{0,2}$-formulas.

Since $\forall_{0,2}^\pi$ has been shown to be a decidable fragment of set theory, the availability of a complete mapping of $\mathcal{L}_{\mathcal{RIS}}$ to $\forall_{0,2}^\pi$ proves the decidability of $\mathcal{L}_{\mathcal{RIS}}$ as well. However, it is important to note that $\forall_{0,2}^\pi$ is mainly intended as a language to study decidability rather than as an effective tool to solve formulas of a constraint language, as $\mathcal{L}_{\mathcal{RIS}}$ is instead designed for.

In the rest of this section we show that $SAT_{\mathcal{RIS}}$ is indeed a decision procedure for $\mathcal{RIS}$-formulas. This is obtained by: (i) proving that formulas returned by $SAT_{\mathcal{RIS}}$, other than $false$, are trivially satisfiable; (ii) proving that $SAT_{\mathcal{RIS}}$ always terminates; and (iii) proving that the disjunction of the returned formulas is equisatisfiable to the input formula. Detailed proofs are given in [4].

4.1 Satisfiability of Solved Form

As stated in Sect. 3.1, the formula Φ handled by $SAT_{\mathcal{RIS}}$ can be written as $\Phi_S \wedge \Phi_X$ where all Π_S-literals are in Φ_S. Right before Algorithm 1 calls SAT_X, Φ_S is in a particular form referred to as *solved form*. This fact can be easily proved by analyzing the rewrite rules given in Sect. 3.2 and [4].

Definition 4 (Solved form). *Let Φ_S be a Π_S-formula; let X and x be variables of sort* Set *and* X, *respectively, and t any term of sort* X; *let S be any set term but not a RIS; and let $\bar{D}$ and $\bar{E}$ be either variables of sort* Set *or variable-RIS. A literal ϕ in Φ_S is in* solved form *if it has one of the following forms:*

1. *true*
2. $X = S$ *or* $X = \{\bar{D} \,|\, \Psi \bullet \tau\}$, *and X does not occur in S nor in $\Phi_S \setminus \{\phi\}$*
3. $X \neq S$, *and X does not occur in S nor as the domain of a RIS in Φ_S* [2]
4. $t \notin X$ *and X does not occur in t, or $t \notin \{\bar{D} \,|\, \Psi \bullet \tau\}$*
5. $set(X)$ *or* $isX(x)$
6. $\{\bar{D} \,|\, \Psi \bullet \tau\} = \emptyset$
7. $\{\bar{D} \,|\, \Psi_1 \bullet \tau_1\} = \{\bar{E} \,|\, \Psi_2 \bullet \tau_2\}$.

Φ_S is in solved form *if all its literals are simultaneously in solved form.*

Example 4. The following are $\mathcal{L}_{\mathcal{RIS}}$ literals in solved form (X, D and D_i variables; X does not occur elsewhere in the given $\mathcal{RIS}$-formula):

– $X = \{x : D \,|\, x \neq 0\}$ (X and D may be the same variable)
– $1 \notin \{x : D \,|\, x \neq 0\}$
– $\{x : D_1 \,|\, x \bmod 2 = 0 \bullet (x, x)\} = \{x : D_2 \,|\, x > 0 \bullet (x, x + 2)\}$ □

Right before Algorithm 1 calls SAT_X, Φ_S is either *false* or it is in solved form, but in this case it is satisfiable.

Theorem 1 (Satisfiability of solved form). *Any $\mathcal{RIS}$-formula in solved form is satisfiable w.r.t. the interpretation structure of $\mathcal{L}_{\mathcal{RIS}}$.*

Therefore, if Φ_S is not *false*, the satisfiability of Φ depends only on Φ_X.

Theorem 2 (Satisfiability of $\Phi_S \wedge \Phi_X$). *Let Φ be $\Phi_S \wedge \Phi_X$ right before Algorithm 1 calls SAT_X. Then either Φ_S is false or the satisfiability of Φ depends only on the satisfiability of Φ_X.*

---

[2] This is guaranteed by procedure remove_neq (see Sect. 3).

4.2   Termination and Equisatisfiability

Termination of $SAT_{\mathcal{RIS}}$ is stated by the following theorem.

Theorem 3 (Termination). *The $SAT_{\mathcal{RIS}}$ procedure can be implemented in such a way it terminates for every input $\mathcal{RIS}$-formula Φ.*

The termination of $SAT_{\mathcal{RIS}}$ and the finiteness of the number of non-deterministic choices generated during its computation guarantee the finiteness of the number of $\mathcal{RIS}$-formulas non-deterministically returned by $SAT_{\mathcal{RIS}}$. Therefore, $SAT_{\mathcal{RIS}}$ applied to a $\mathcal{RIS}$-formula Φ always terminates, returning either *false* or a finite collection of satisfiable $\mathcal{RIS}$-formulas in solved form.

In order to prove that Algorithm 1 is a decision procedure for $\mathcal{RIS}$-formulas, we still need to prove that it is correct and complete in the sense that it preserves the set of solutions of the input formula.

Theorem 4 (Equisatisfiability). *Let Φ be a $\mathcal{RIS}$-formula and $\{\phi_i\}_{i=1}^{n}$ be the collection of $\mathcal{RIS}$-formulas returned by $SAT_{\mathcal{RIS}}(\Phi)$. $\bigvee_{i=1}^{n} \phi_i$ is equisatisfiable to Φ, that is, every possible solution[3] of Φ is a solution of one of $\{\phi_i\}_{i=1}^{n}$ and, vice versa, every solution of one of these formulas is a solution for Φ.*

Thanks to Theorems 1–4 we can conclude that, given a $\mathcal{RIS}$-formula Φ, Φ is satisfiable with respect to the intended interpretation structure if and only if there is a non-deterministic choice in $SAT_{\mathcal{RIS}}(\Phi)$ that returns a $\mathcal{RIS}$-formula in solved form—i.e. different from *false*. Hence, $SAT_{\mathcal{RIS}}$ is a decision procedure for testing satisfiability of $\mathcal{RIS}$-formulas.

It is worth noting that the set of variables ranging on $\mathcal{RIS}$-terms and the set of variables ranging on $\mathcal{X}$-terms are assumed to be disjoint sets. This fact prevents us from creating *recursively defined* RIS, which could compromise the finiteness property of the sets we are dealing with. In fact, a formula such as $X = \{D \,|\, \Psi[X] \bullet \tau\}$ is not an admissible $\mathcal{RIS}$-constraint, since the outer and the inner X must be of different sorts according to the definition of RIS (recall that the filter is a $\mathcal{X}$-formula). Note that, on the contrary, a formula such as $X = \{D[X] \,|\, \Psi \bullet \tau\}$ is an admissible $\mathcal{RIS}$-constraint, and it is suitably handled by our decision procedure.

5   Discussion

The formula Φ of a (general) intensional set $\{x : \Phi[x]\}$ may depend on existentially quantified variables, declared inside the set. For example, if R is a set of ordered pairs and D is a set, then the subset of R where all the first components belong to D can be denoted by $\{p : \exists x, y (x \in D \wedge (x, y) \in R \wedge p = (x, y))\}$. We will refer to these existentially quantified variables as *parameters*.

---

[3] More precisely, each solution of Φ expanded to the variables occurring in ϕ_i but not in Φ, so to account for the possible fresh variables introduced into ϕ_i.

Allowing parameters in RIS rises major problems when RIS have to be manipulated through the rewrite rules considered in the previous section. In fact, if $\dot{p}$ is the vector of parameters possibly occurring in a RIS, then literals of the form $\neg\Psi(d)$, occurring in the rules (e.g. $(=_7)$), should be replaced with the more complex universally quantified formula $\forall\dot{p}(\neg\Psi[\dot{p}](d))$. This, in turn, would require that the theory $\mathcal{X}$ is equipped with a solver able to deal with such kind of formulas. To avoid relying on such a solver, RIS cannot depend on parameters.

Nevertheless, it can be observed that many uses of parameters can be avoided by a proper use of the control term and pattern of a RIS (see [4]). For example, the intensional set considered above can be expressed with a RIS (hence, without parameters) as follows: $\{(x,y) : R \mid x \in D\}$. Then, for instance, for $\{(x,y) : \{(a,1),(b,2),(a,2)\} \mid x \in D\} = \{(a,1),(a,2)\}$, $\mathcal{L}_{\mathcal{RIS}}$ returns $D = \{a \sqcup N\} \wedge b \notin N$ as the only solution; and for $\{(x,y) : \{(a,1),(b,2),(a,2)\} \mid x \in D\} = \{(a,1)\}$, it returns *false*.

Therefore, it would be interesting to extend RIS to allow more general forms of control expressions and patterns. Concerning patterns, from the proof of Theorem 4, it turns out that the necessary and sufficient condition for the equi-satisfiability result is that patterns adhere to the following definition.

Definition 5 (Bijective pattern). *Let $\{x : D \mid \Psi[x,v] \bullet \tau[x,v]\}$ be a RIS, then its pattern is* bijective *if* $\tau : \{(x,v) : (x,v) \in D \times V \wedge \Psi[x,v]\} \rightarrow Y$ *is a bijective function (where: Y images of τ; and V domain of variables v).*

Note that all the admissible patterns of $\mathcal{L}_{\mathcal{RIS}}$ are bijective patterns. Besides these, however, other terms can be bijective patterns. For example, $x + n$, n constant, is also a bijective pattern, though it is not allowed in $\mathcal{L}_{\mathcal{RIS}}$. Conversely, $x * x$ is not bijective as x and $-x$ have $x * x$ as image (note that, though, $(x, x * x)$ is a bijective pattern allowed in $\mathcal{L}_{\mathcal{RIS}}$).

The intuitive reason to ask for bijective patterns is that if y belongs to a RIS whose pattern, τ, is not bijective then there may be two or more elements in the RIS domain, say x_1 and x_2, such that $\tau(x_1) = \tau(x_2) = y$. If this is the case, then eliminating, say, x_1 from the domain is not enough to eliminate y from the RIS. And this makes it difficult, for instance, to prove the equality between a variable-RIS and a set (extensional or RIS) having at least one element.

Unfortunately, the property for a term to be a bijective pattern cannot be easily syntactically assessed. Thus we prefer to leave it out of the definition of $\mathcal{L}_{\mathcal{RIS}}$ and to adopt a more restrictive definition of admissible pattern. From a more practical point of view, however, we could admit also more general patterns, with the assumption that if they are bijective patterns the result is surely safe; while if they are not, it is not safe.

Finally, observe that if $\mathcal{L}_{\mathcal{X}}$ provides other function symbols, $\mathcal{L}_{\mathcal{RIS}}$ could allow other control terms and patterns which are (syntactically) guaranteed to be bijective patterns. All the extensions mentioned above for control terms and patterns are included in the implementation of $\mathcal{L}_{\mathcal{RIS}}$ within {log} (see Sect. 6).

Complexity. $SAT_{\mathcal{RIS}}$ strongly relies on set unification. Basically, rewrite rules dealing with RIS "extract" one element at a time from the domain of a RIS by means of set unification and construct the corresponding extensional set again through set unification. Hence, complexity of our decision procedure strongly depends on complexity of set unification. As observed in [11], the decision problem for set unification is NP-complete. A simple proof of the NP-hardness of this problem has been given in [8]. The proof is based on a reduction of 3-SAT to a set unification problem. Concerning NP-completeness, the algorithm presented here clearly does not belong to NP since it applies syntactic substitutions. Nevertheless, it is possible to encode this algorithm using well-known techniques that avoid explicit substitutions, maintaining a polynomial time complexity along each non-deterministic branch of the computation.

Besides, the detection of a solution of a unification problem (i.e. solving the function problem) clearly implies solving the related decision problem. Thus, the complexity of the function problem can be no better than the complexity of the decision problem. Finally, since $SAT_{\mathcal{RIS}}$ is parametric w.r.t. $SAT_{\mathcal{X}}$, its complexity is at least the maximum between the complexity of both.

6   RIS in Practice

RIS have been implemented in Prolog as an extension of $\{log\}$ [19], a freely available implementation of CLP($\mathcal{SET}$) [6,9]. In this case, the theory $\mathcal{X}$ is basically the theory of CLP($\mathcal{SET}$), that is the theory of *hereditarily finite hybrid sets*. This theory is endowed with a constraint solver which is proved to be a decision procedure for its formulas, provided each integer variable is associated to a finite domain. Syntactic differences between the abstract syntax used in this paper and the concrete syntax used in $\{log\}$ are made evident by the following examples.

Example 5. The $\mathcal{RIS}$-formula:

$$\{5\} \in \{x : \{y \sqcup D\} | x \neq \emptyset \wedge 5 \notin x \bullet x\}$$

is written in $\{log\}$ as:

$$\{5\} \text{ in ris}(X \text{ in } \{Y/D\}, X \text{ neq } \{\} \,\& \, 5 \text{ nin } X, X)$$

where ris is a function symbol whose arguments are: (i) a constraint of the form x in A where x is the control term and A the domain of the RIS; (ii) the filter given as a $\{log\}$ formula; and (iii) the pattern given as a $\{log\}$ term. Filters and patterns can be omitted as in $\mathcal{L}_{\mathcal{RIS}}$. Variables must start with an uppercase letter; the set constructor symbols for both $\mathcal{L}_{\mathcal{RIS}}$ and $\{log\}$ sets terms are written as $\{\cdot/\cdot\}$. If this formula is provided to $\{log\}$ it answers no because the formula is unsatisfiable.   □

The following are more examples of RIS that can be written in $\{log\}$.

Example 6.

- The multiples of N: ris$(X$ in $D, 0$ is X mod $N)$, where is is the Prolog predicate that forces the evaluation of the arithmetic expression in its right-hand side.
- The sets containing a given set A: ris$(S$ in $D, \mathsf{subset}(A, S))$.
- A function that maps integers to their squares: ris$([X, Y]$ in D, Y is $X * X)$, where ordered pairs are written using $[\cdot, \cdot]$. Note that the pattern can be omitted since it is the same as the control term, that is $[X, Y]$.   □

RIS patterns in {log} can be any term (including set terms). If they are bijective patterns, then the solver is guaranteed to be a decision procedure; otherwise this may be not the case. For example, the formula ris$(X$ in $\{2, 4/M\}$, $2 * X) = \{2, 4, 6, 8\}$ lies inside the decision procedure.

In {log} the language of the RIS and the language of the parameter theory $\mathcal{X}$ are completely amalgamated. Thus, it is possible for example to use predicates of the latter in formulas of the former, as well as to share variables of both. The following example uses this feature to prove a general property about sets.

Example 7. In *{log}* inters(A, B, C) means $C = A \cap B$. Then, if inters$(A, B, C) \wedge D = $ ris$(X$ in A, X in $B) \wedge C$ neq D is run on *{log}*, it (correctly) answers no.   □

The original version of *{log}* can deal with *general* intensional sets, which include our RIS as a special case. However, formulas involving such general intensional sets fall outside the scope of *{log}*'s decision procedure. For example, the same goal of Example 7 but written using general intensional sets is (wrongly) found to be satisfiable by *{log}*.

6.1   Using *{log}* for Program Verification

{log} can be used to automatically prove program properties, such as partial correctness. As an example consider program map_f (Fig. 4), written in an abstract programming language with an OO-like syntax and semantics. map_f applies function f to every element of (finite) set S outputting the result in set S_f. S is iterated by means of an iterator (S_i) which is emptied as elements are popped out of it (while S remains unchanged). At the right of Fig. 4 we see the pre- and post-condition and the loop invariant given as formulas over a suitable set theory. S_p is the subset of S which has already been processed inside the loop.

Then, to prove the partial correctness of map_f in a Hoare-like framework, it is necessary to prove that (among other conditions): (a) the invariant is preserved inside the loop while its condition is true; and (b) upon termination of the loop, the loop invariant implies the post-condition. Formally:

$$S_i = \{a \sqcup S_r\} \wedge S = S_i \cup S_p \wedge S_f = \{x : S_p \bullet f(x)\}$$
$$\implies S = S_r \cup \{a \sqcup S_p\} \wedge \{f(a) \sqcup S_f\} = \{x : \{a \sqcup S_p\} \bullet f(x)\} \tag{a}$$

$$S_i = \emptyset \wedge S = S_i \cup S_p \wedge S_f = \{x : S_p \bullet f(x)\}$$
$$\implies S_f = \{x : S \bullet f(x)\} \tag{b}$$

---

function Set map_f(Set S)   ▷ Pre-condition: *true*
  Set S_f = new Set
  Iterator S_i = S.iterator()
  while S_i.more() **do**   ▷ Invariant: $S = S_i \cup S_p \wedge S_f = \{x : S_p \bullet f(x)\}$
    S_f.add(f(S_i.next()))
  end while
  return S_f
end function   ▷ Post-condition: $S_f = \{x : S \bullet f(x)\}$

Fig. 4. map_f applies f to every element of set S and stores the results in set S_f

The negation of these verification conditions can be written in $\{log\}$ as:

$$S_i = \{A/S_r\} \wedge \mathsf{un}(S_i, S_p, S) \wedge S_f = \mathsf{ris}(X \text{ in } S_p, f(X))$$
$$\wedge \, (\mathsf{nun}(S_r, \{A/S_p\}, S) \vee \{f(A)/S_f\} \neq \mathsf{ris}(X \text{ in } \{A/S_p\}, f(X))) \tag{a'}$$

$$S_i = \emptyset \wedge \mathsf{un}(S_i, S_p, S) \wedge S_f = \mathsf{ris}(X \text{ in } S_p, f(X))$$
$$\wedge \, S_f \neq \mathsf{ris}(X \text{ in } S, f(X)) \tag{b'}$$

where un and nun means, respectively, set union and its negation.

When (a') and (b') are run on $\{log\}$ it answers no (i.e. (a) and (b) hold).

Observe that the set theory-based, human-oriented annotations can be easily translated into the set language provided by $\{log\}$ which then is used to discharge the proof obligations.

6.2   Comparison with ProB

In order to gain further confidence in that $\{log\}$ may be useful in practice, we compare it to ProB [16], a mainstream solver for sets supporting a very general notion of intensional sets. Thus, we defined a small benchmark consisting of 64 formulas involving RIS, and run them on $\{log\}$ and ProB. The benchmark covers the four operators supported by the decision procedure (i.e. =, ≠, ∈, ∉). A summary of the results is presented in Table 1; details are provided in [4], while the complete benchmark can be found at https://www.dropbox.com/s/vjsh91nym3g5tk2/experiments.tar.gz?dl=0. As can be seen, $\{log\}$ is able to solve RIS formulas that ProB does not solve, and in less time. This is an indication that $SAT_{\mathcal{RIS}}$ would also be of practical interest.

Table 1. Summary of the empirical evaluation (timeout 10s; AUTO = $100\frac{\text{SAT}+\text{UNSAT}}{\text{TOTAL}}$)

TOOL (VERSION)	SAT	UNSAT	TIMEOUT/WARNING	TOTAL	AUTO	TIME
$\{log\}$ (4.9.4)	30	34	0	64	100%	16s
ProB (1.6.0-SR1)	25	11	28	64	56%	103s

7   Related Work

Having intensional sets as first-class entities in programming and modeling languages is widely recognized as a valuable feature that makes programs and models potentially more readable and compact than those based on other data structures. Some form of intensional sets are offered for instance by modeling frameworks, such as Mini-Zinc [17], ProB [16] and Alloy [15]; general-purpose programming languages, such as SETL [21] and Python; and by (Constraint) Logic Programming languages, such as Gödel [14] and $\{log\}$ [8]. However, as far as we know, none of these proposals implements a decision procedure for intensional sets. For example, Alloy (even when using the Kodkod library) needs to set in advance the size of sets (or types). Such proposals lack, in general, the ability to perform high-level reasoning on general formulas involving intensional sets (e.g. the kind of reasoning shown in Example 7 and Sect. 6.1).

A very general proposal is CLP($\{\mathcal{D}\}$) [10], a CLP language offering arbitrarily nested extensional and intensional sets of elements over a generic constraint domain $\mathcal{D}$. However, no working implementation of this proposal has been developed. As observed in [10], the presence of undecidable constraints such as $\{x : p(x)\} = \{x : q(x)\}$ (where p and q can have an infinite number of solutions) "prevents us from developing a parametric and complete solver". Conversely, the same problem written using RIS, $\{x : D_1|p(x)\} = \{x : D_2|q(x)\}$, D_1, D_2 variables, always admits at least one solution, namely $D_1 = D_2 = \emptyset$. Generally speaking, finding a fragment of intensional sets that is both decidable and expressive is a key issue for the development of an effective tool for reasoning with intensional sets. RIS, as presented here, may be a first step toward this goal.

Several logics (e.g. [12,22,23]) provide some forms of intensional sets. However, in some cases, for the formula to be decidable, the intensional sets must have a ground domain; in others, set operators do not include set equality; and in others, they present a semi-decision procedure. Handling intensional sets can be related also to handling universal quantifiers in a logical setting, since intensional sets "hide" a universal quantifier. Tools such as SMT solvers deal with this kind of problems (see, e.g., [1,7]), although in general they are complete only in quite restricted cases [13].

Our decision procedure finds models for formulas with *finite* but *unbounded* domains, i.e. their cardinalities are not constrained by a fixed value. The field of finite model finding faces a similar problem but usually with *bounded* domains. There are two basic styles of model finding: the MACE-style in which the formula is transformed into a SAT problem [3]; and the SEM-style which uses constraint solving techniques [25]. Our approach is closer to the SEM-style as it is based on constraint programming. However, since both styles do not deal with quantified domains as sets, then they cannot reduce the domain every time an element is identified, as we do with RIS—for instance, in rule ($=_6$). Instead, they set a size for the domain and try to find a model at most as large as that.

Ideas from finite model finding were taken as inspiration by Reynolds et al. [18] for handling universal quantifiers in SMT. These authors propose to find finite models for infinite universally quantified formulas by considering finite domains. In particular, Reynolds et al. make use of the cardinality operator for the sorts of quantified variables and propose a solver for a theory based on this operator. Then, they make a guess of the cardinality for a quantified sort and use the solver to try to find a model there. In the default strategy, the initial guess is 1 and it is incremented in 1. Note that our approach does not need a cardinality operator because it operates directly over a theory of sets.

8   Concluding Remarks

We have shown a decision procedure for an expressive class of intensional sets, called Restricted Intensional Sets (RIS). Key features of this procedure are: it returns a finite representation of all possible solutions of the input formula; it allows set elements to be variables; it is parametric with respect to any first-order theory endowed with a decision procedure; and it is implemented as part of the {*log*} tool. On the other hand, we have shown through a number of simple examples that, although RIS are a subclass of general intensional sets, they are still sufficiently expressive as to encode and solve many interesting problems.

Nevertheless, it can be interesting trying to extend the language of RIS, for example, with rewrite rules for other set operators (e.g. union) because this would contribute to enlarge the class of problems that the decision procedure can deal with. Yet another line of investigation is to study the relation between RIS and the extension to binary relations recently added to {*log*} [5].

Acknowledgements. Part of the work of M. Cristiá is supported by ANPCyT's grant PICT-2014-2200.

References

1. Bjørner, N., McMillan, K., Rybalchenko, A.: On solving universally quantified horn clauses. In: Logozzo, F., Fähndrich, M. (eds.) SAS 2013. LNCS, vol. 7935, pp. 105–125. Springer, Heidelberg (2013). doi:10.1007/978-3-642-38856-9_8
2. Cantone, D., Longo, C.: A decidable two-sorted quantified fragment of set theory with ordered pairs and some undecidable extensions. Theor. Comput. Sci. **560**, 307–325 (2014). http://dx.doi.org/10.1016/j.tcs.2014.03.021
3. Claessen, K., Sörensson, N.: New techniques that improve MACE-style finite model building. In: CADE-19 Workshop: Model Computation - Principles, Algorithms, Applications, pp. 11–27 (2003)
4. Cristiá, M., Rossi, G.: Restricted insentional sets. http://people.dmi.unipr.it/gianfranco.rossi/SETLOG/risCADEonline.pdf
5. Cristiá, M., Rossi, G.: A decision procedure for sets, binary relations and partial functions. In: Chaudhuri, S., Farzan, A. (eds.) CAV 2016, Part I. LNCS, vol. 9779, pp. 179–198. Springer, Cham (2016). doi:10.1007/978-3-319-41528-4_10
6. Dal Palú, A., Dovier, A., Pontelli, E., Rossi, G.: Integrating finite domain constraints and CLP with sets. In: Proceedings of the 5th ACM SIGPLAN International Conference on Principles and Practice of Declaritive Programming, PPDP 2003, pp. 219–229. ACM, New York (2003). http://doi.acm.org/10.1145/888251.888272

7. Deharbe, D., Fontaine, P., Paleo, B.W.: Quantifier inference rules for SMT proofs. In: Workshop on Proof eXchange for Theorem Proving (2011)
8. Dovier, A., Omodeo, E.G., Pontelli, E., Rossi, G.: A language for programming in logic with finite sets. J. Log. Program. **28**(1), 1–44 (1996). http://dx.doi.org/10.1016/0743-1066(95)00147-6
9. Dovier, A., Piazza, C., Pontelli, E., Rossi, G.: Sets and constraint logic programming. ACM Trans. Program. Lang. Syst. **22**(5), 861–931 (2000)
10. Dovier, A., Pontelli, E., Rossi, G.: Intensional sets in *CLP*. In: Palamidessi, C. (ed.) ICLP 2003. LNCS, vol. 2916, pp. 284–299. Springer, Heidelberg (2003). doi:10.1007/978-3-540-24599-5_20
11. Dovier, A., Pontelli, E., Rossi, G.: Set unification. Theor. Pract. Log. Program. **6**(6), 645–701 (2006). http://dx.doi.org/10.1017/S1471068406002730
12. Drăgoi, C., Henzinger, T.A., Veith, H., Widder, J., Zufferey, D.: A logic-based framework for verifying consensus algorithms. In: McMillan, K.L., Rival, X. (eds.) VMCAI 2014. LNCS, vol. 8318, pp. 161–181. Springer, Heidelberg (2014). doi:10.1007/978-3-642-54013-4_10
13. Ge, Y., de Moura, L.: Complete instantiation for quantified formulas in satisfiabiliby modulo theories. In: Bouajjani, A., Maler, O. (eds.) CAV 2009. LNCS, vol. 5643, pp. 306–320. Springer, Heidelberg (2009). doi:10.1007/978-3-642-02658-4_25
14. Hill, P.M., Lloyd, J.W.: The Gödel Programming Language. MIT Press, Cambridge (1994)
15. Jackson, D.: Software Abstractions: Logic, Language, and Analysis. The MIT Press, Cambridge (2006)
16. Leuschel, M., Butler, M.: ProB: a model checker for B. In: Araki, K., Gnesi, S., Mandrioli, D. (eds.) FME 2003. LNCS, vol. 2805, pp. 855–874. Springer, Heidelberg (2003). doi:10.1007/978-3-540-45236-2_46
17. Nethercote, N., Stuckey, P.J., Becket, R., Brand, S., Duck, G.J., Tack, G.: MiniZinc: towards a standard CP modelling language. In: Bessière, C. (ed.) CP 2007. LNCS, vol. 4741, pp. 529–543. Springer, Heidelberg (2007). doi:10.1007/978-3-540-74970-7_38
18. Reynolds, A., Tinelli, C., Goel, A., Krstić, S.: Finite model finding in SMT. In: Sharygina, N., Veith, H. (eds.) CAV 2013. LNCS, vol. 8044, pp. 640–655. Springer, Heidelberg (2013). doi:10.1007/978-3-642-39799-8_42
19. Rossi, G.: {*log*} (2008). http://people.dmi.unipr.it/gianfranco.rossi/setlog.Home.html
20. Schneider, S.: The B-method: An Introduction. Cornerstones of Computing. Palgrave (2001). http://books.google.com.ar/books?id=Krs0OQAACAAJ
21. Schwartz, J.T., Dewar, R.B.K., Dubinsky, E., Schonberg, E.: Programming with Sets - An Introduction to SETL. Texts and Monographs in Computer Science. Springer, New York (1986). http://dx.doi.org/10.1007/978-1-4613-9575-1
22. Veanes, M., Saabas, A.: On bounded reachability of programs with set comprehensions. In: Cervesato, I., Veith, H., Voronkov, A. (eds.) LPAR 2008. LNCS, vol. 5330, pp. 305–317. Springer, Heidelberg (2008). doi:10.1007/978-3-540-89439-1_22
23. Wies, T., Piskac, R., Kuncak, V.: Combining theories with shared set operations. In: Ghilardi, S., Sebastiani, R. (eds.) FroCoS 2009. LNCS, vol. 5749, pp. 366–382. Springer, Heidelberg (2009). doi:10.1007/978-3-642-04222-5_23
24. Woodcock, J., Davies, J.: Using Z: Specification, Refinement, and Proof. Prentice-Hall, Inc., Upper Saddle River (1996)
25. Zhang, J., Zhang, H.: System description generating models by SEM. In: McRobbie, M.A., Slaney, J.K. (eds.) CADE 1996. LNCS, vol. 1104, pp. 308–312. Springer, Heidelberg (1996). doi:10.1007/3-540-61511-3_96

Decidability of the Monadic Shallow Linear First-Order Fragment with Straight Dismatching Constraints

Andreas Teucke[1,2]([✉]) and Christoph Weidenbach[1]

[1] Max-Planck Institut für Informatik, Saarland Informatics Campus,
66123 Saarbrücken, Germany
ateucke@mpi-inf.mpg.de
[2] Graduate School of Computer Science, Saarbrücken, Germany

Abstract. The monadic shallow linear Horn fragment is well-known to be decidable and has many application, e.g., in security protocol analysis, tree automata, or abstraction refinement. It was a long standing open problem how to extend the fragment to the non-Horn case, preserving decidability, that would, e.g., enable to express non-determinism in protocols. We prove decidability of the non-Horn monadic shallow linear fragment via ordered resolution further extended with dismatching constraints and discuss some applications of the new decidable fragment.

1 Introduction

Motivated by the automatic analysis of security protocols, the monadic shallow linear Horn (MSLH) fragment was shown to be decidable in [22]. In addition to the restriction to monadic Horn clauses, the main restriction of the fragment is positive literals of the form $S(f(x_1, \ldots, x_n))$ or $S(x)$ where all x_i are different, i.e., all terms are shallow and linear. The fragment can be finitely saturated by superposition (ordered resolution) where negative literals with non-variable arguments are always selected. As a result, productive clauses with respect to the superposition model operator $\mathcal{I}_N$ have the form $S_1(x_1), \ldots, S_n(x_n) \rightarrow S(f(x_1, \ldots, x_n))$. Therefore, the models of saturated MSLH clause sets can both be represented by tree automata [6] and shallow linear sort theories [8]. The models are typically infinite. The decidability result of MSLH clauses was rediscovered in the context of tree automata research [7] where in addition DEXPTIME-completeness of the MSLH fragment was shown. The fragment was further extended by disequality constraints [12,13] still motivated by security protocol analysis [14]. Although from a complexity point of view, the difference between Horn clause fragments and the respective non-Horn clause fragments is typically reflected by membership in the deterministic vs. the non-deterministic respective complexity fragment, for monadic shallow linear clauses so far there was no decidability result for the non-Horn case.

The results of this paper close this gap. We show the monadic shallow linear non-Horn (MSL) clause fragment to be decidable by superposition (ordered resolution). From a security protocol application point of view, non-Horn clauses

© Springer International Publishing AG 2017
L. de Moura (Ed.): CADE 2017, LNAI 10395, pp. 202–219, 2017.
DOI: 10.1007/978-3-319-63046-5_13

enable a natural representation of non-determinism. Our second extension to the fragment are unit clauses with disequations of the form $s \not\approx t$, where s and t are not unifiable. Due to the employed superposition calculus, such disequations do not influence saturation of an MSL clause set, but have an effect on potential models. They can rule out identification of syntactically different ground terms as it is, e.g., desired in the security protocol context for syntactically different messages or nonces. Our third extension to the fragment are straight dismatching constraints. These constraints are incomparable to the disequality constraints mentioned above [12, 13]. They do not strictly increase the expressiveness of the MSL theory, but enable up to exponentially more compact saturations. For example, the constrained clause

$$(S(x), T(y) \to S(f(x, y)); y \neq f(x', f(a, y')))$$

over constants a, b describes the same set of ground clauses as the six unconstrained clauses

$$S(x), T(a) \to S(f(x, a)) \qquad S(x), T(b) \to S(f(x, b)) \qquad \ldots$$

$$S(x), T(f(b, y')) \to S(f(x, f(b, y')))$$

$$S(x), T(f(f(x'', y''), y')) \to S(f(x, f(f(x'', y''), y'))).$$

Furthermore, for a satisfiability equivalent transformation into MSL clauses, the nested terms in the positive literals would have to be factored out by the introduction of further predicates and clauses. E.g., the first clause is replaced by the two MSL clauses $S(x), T(a), R(y) \to S(f(x, y))$ and $R(a)$ where R is a fresh monadic predicate. The constrained clause belongs to the MSL(SDC) fragment. Altogether, the resulting MSL(SDC) fragment is shown to be decidable in Sect. 3.

The introduction of straight dismatching constraints (SDCs) enables an improved refinement step of our approximation refinement calculus [18]. Before, several clauses were needed to rule out a specific instance of a clause in an unsatisfiable core. For example, if due to a linearity approximation from clause $S(x), T(x) \to S(f(x, x))$ to $S(x), T(x), S(y), T(y) \to S(f(x, y))$ an instance $\{x \mapsto f(a, x'),\ y \mapsto f(b, y')\}$ is used in the proof, before [18] several clauses were needed to replace $S(x), T(x) \to S(f(x, x))$ in a refinement step in order to rule out this instance. With straight dismatching constraints the clause $S(x), T(x) \to S(f(x, x))$ is replaced by the two clauses $S(f(a, x)), T(f(a, x)) \to S(f(f(a, x), f(a, x)))$ and $(S(x), T(x) \to S(f(x, x)); x \neq f(a, y))$. For the improved approximation refinement approach (FO-AR) presented in this paper, any refinement step results in just two clauses, see Sect. 4. The additional expressiveness of constraint clauses comes almost for free, because necessary computations, like, e.g., checking emptiness of SDCs, can all be done in polynomial time, see Sect. 2.

In addition to the extension of the known MSLH decidability result and the improved approximation refinement calculus FO-AR, we discuss in Sect. 5 the potential of the MSL(SDC) fragment in the context of FO-AR, Theorem 2, and its prototypical implementation in SPASS-AR (http://www.mpi-inf.mpg. de/fileadmin/inf/rg1/spass-ar.tgz). It turns out that for clause sets containing certain structures, FO-AR is superior to ordered resolution/superposition [1] and instance generating methods [10]. The paper ends with a discussion on challenges and future research directions, Sect. 6. In favor of many illustrating examples, most proofs and further technical details can be found in [20].

2   First-Order Clauses with Straight Dismatching Constraints: MSL(SDC)

We consider a standard first-order language where letters v, w, x, y, z denote variables, f, g, h functions, a, b, c constants, s, t terms, p, q, r positions and Greek letters $\sigma, \tau, \rho, \delta$ are used for substitutions. S, P, Q, R denote predicates, $\approx$ denotes equality, A, B atoms, E, L literals, C, D clauses, N clause sets and $\mathcal{V}$ sets of variables. $\overline{L}$ is the complement of L. The signature $\Sigma = (\mathcal{F}, \mathcal{P})$ consists of two disjoint, non-empty, in general infinite sets of function and predicate symbols $\mathcal{F}$ and $\mathcal{P}$, respectively. The set of all *terms* over variables $\mathcal{V}$ is $\mathcal{T}(\mathcal{F}, \mathcal{V})$. If there are no variables, then terms, literals and clauses are called *ground*, respectively. A *substitution* σ is denoted by pairs $\{x \mapsto t\}$ and its update at x by $\sigma[x \mapsto t]$. A substitution σ is a *grounding* substitution for $\mathcal{V}$ if $x\sigma$ is ground for every variable $x \in \mathcal{V}$.

The set of *free* variables of an atom A (term t) denoted by $\mathrm{vars}(A)$ ($\mathrm{vars}(t)$). A *position* is a sequence of positive integers, where ε denotes the empty position. As usual $t|_p = s$ denotes the subterm s of t at position p, which we also write as $t[s]_p$, and $t[p/s']$ then denotes the replacement of s with s' in t at position p. These notions are extended to literals and multiple positions.

A predicate with exactly one argument is called *monadic*. A term is *complex* if it is not a variable and *shallow* if it has at most depth one. It is called *linear* if there are no duplicate variable occurrences. A literal, where every argument term is shallow, is also called *shallow*. A variable and a constant are called *straight*. A term $f(s_1, \ldots, s_n)$ is called *straight*, if $s_1, \ldots, s_n$ are different variables except for at most one straight term s_i.

A *clause* is a multiset of literals which we write as an implication $\Gamma \rightarrow \Delta$ where the atoms in the multiset Δ (the *succedent*) denote the positive literals and the atoms in the multiset Γ (the *antecedent*) the negative literals. We write $\square$ for the empty clause. If Γ is empty we omit $\rightarrow$, e.g., we can write $P(x)$ as an alternative of $\rightarrow P(x)$. We abbreviate disjoint set union with sequencing, for example, we write $\Gamma, \Gamma' \rightarrow \Delta, L$ instead of $\Gamma \cup \Gamma' \rightarrow \Delta \cup \{L\}$. A clause $E, E, \Gamma \rightarrow \Delta$ is equivalent to $E, \Gamma \rightarrow \Delta$ and we call them equal *modulo duplicate literal elimination*. If every term in Δ is shallow, the clause is called *positive shallow*. If all atoms in Δ are linear and variable disjoint, the clause is called *positive linear*. A clause $\Gamma \rightarrow \Delta$ is called an *MSL clause*, if it is (i) positive shallow and linear, (ii) all occurring predicates are monadic, (iii) no equations occur in Δ, and (iv) no equations occur in Γ or $\Gamma = \{s \approx t\}$ and Δ is empty where s and t are not unifiable. *MSL* is the first-order clause fragment consisting of MSL clauses. Clauses $\Gamma, s \approx t \rightarrow \Delta$ where Γ, Δ are non-empty and s, t are not unifiable could be added to the MSL fragment without changing any of our results. Considering the superposition calculus, it will select $s \approx t$. Since the two terms are not unifiable, no inference will take place on such a clause and the clause will not contribute to the model operator. In this sense such clauses do not increase the expressiveness of the fragment.

An *atom ordering* $\prec$ is an irreflexive, well-founded, total ordering on ground atoms. It is lifted to literals by representing A and $\neg A$ as multisets $\{A\}$ and $\{A, A\}$, respectively. The multiset extension of the literal ordering induces an ordering on ground clauses. The clause ordering is compatible with the atom ordering; if the maximal atom in C is greater than the maximal atom in D then $D \prec C$. We use $\prec$ simultaneously to denote an atom ordering and its multiset, literal, and clause extensions. For a ground clause set N and clause C, the set $N^{\prec C} = \{D \in N \mid D \prec C\}$ denotes the clauses of N smaller than C.

A *Herbrand interpretation* $\mathcal{I}$ is a - possibly infinite - set of ground atoms. A ground atom A is called *true* in $\mathcal{I}$ if $A \in \mathcal{I}$ and *false*, otherwise. $\mathcal{I}$ is said to *satisfy* a ground clause $C = \Gamma \rightarrow \Delta$, denoted by $\mathcal{I} \vDash C$, if $\Delta \cap \mathcal{I} \neq \emptyset$ or $\Gamma \not\subseteq \mathcal{I}$. A non-ground clause C is satisfied by $\mathcal{I}$ if $\mathcal{I} \vDash C\sigma$ for every grounding substitution σ. An interpretation $\mathcal{I}$ is called a *model* of N, $\mathcal{I} \vDash N$, if $\mathcal{I} \vDash C$ for every $C \in N$. A model $\mathcal{I}$ of N is considered *minimal* with respect to set inclusion, i.e., if there is no model $\mathcal{I}'$ with $\mathcal{I}' \subset \mathcal{I}$ and $\mathcal{I}' \vDash N$. A set of clauses N is *satisfiable*, if there exists a model that satisfies N. Otherwise, the set is *unsatisfiable*.

A disequation $t \neq s$ is an *atomic straight dismatching constraint* if s and t are variable disjoint terms and s is straight. A straight dismatching constraint π is a conjunction of atomic straight dismatching constraints. Given a substitution σ, $\pi\sigma = \bigwedge_{i \in I} t_i\sigma \neq s_i$. $\mathrm{lvar}(\pi) := \bigcup_{i \in I} \mathrm{vars}(t_i)$ are the left-hand variables of π and the depth of π is the maximal term depth of the s_i. A *solution* of π is a grounding substitution δ such that for all $i \in I$, $t_i\delta$ is not an instance of s_i, i.e., there exists no σ such that $t_i\delta = s_i\sigma$. A dismatching constraint is solvable if it has a solution and unsolvable, otherwise. Whether a straight dismatching constraint is solvable, is decidable in linear-logarithmic time [19]. $\top$ and $\bot$ represent the true and false dismatching constraint, respectively.

We define constraint normalization $\pi\downarrow$ as the normal form of the following rewriting rules over straight dismatching constraints.

$$\pi \wedge f(t_1, \ldots, t_n) \neq y \qquad \Rightarrow \bot$$
$$\pi \wedge f(t_1, \ldots, t_n) \neq f(y_1, \ldots, y_n) \Rightarrow \bot$$
$$\pi \wedge f(t_1, \ldots, t_n) \neq f(s_1, \ldots, s_n) \Rightarrow \pi \wedge t_i \neq s_i \quad \text{if } s_i \text{ is complex}$$
$$\pi \wedge f(t_1, \ldots, t_n) \neq g(s_1, \ldots, s_m) \Rightarrow \pi$$
$$\pi \wedge x \neq s \wedge x \neq s\sigma \qquad \Rightarrow \pi \wedge x \neq s$$

Note that $f(t_1, \ldots, t_n) \neq f(s_1, \ldots, s_n)$ normalizes to $t_i \neq s_i$ for some i, where s_i is the one straight complex argument of $f(s_1, \ldots, s_n)$. Furthermore, the depth of $\pi\downarrow$ is less or equal to the depth of π and both have the same solutions.

A pair of a clause and a constraint $(C; \pi)$ is called a *constrained clause*. Given a substitution σ, $(C; \pi)\sigma = (C\sigma; \pi\sigma)$. $C\delta$ is called a ground clause of $(C; \pi)$ if δ is a solution of π. $\mathcal{G}((C; \pi))$ is the set of ground instances of $(C; \pi)$. If $\mathcal{G}((C; \pi)) \subseteq \mathcal{G}((C'; \pi'))$, then $(C; \pi)$ is an instance of $(C'; \pi')$. If $\mathcal{G}((C; \pi)) = \mathcal{G}((C'; \pi'))$, then $(C; \pi)$ and $(C'; \pi')$ are called variants. A Herbrand interpretation $\mathcal{I}$ satisfies $(C; \pi)$, if $\mathcal{I} \vDash \mathcal{G}((C; \pi))$. A constrained clause $(C; \pi)$ is called *redundant* in N if for every $D \in \mathcal{G}((C; \pi))$, there exist $D_1, \ldots, D_n$ in $\mathcal{G}(N)^{\prec D}$ such that $D_1, \ldots, D_n \vDash D$. A constrained clause $(C'; \pi')$ is called a *condensation* of $(C; \pi)$ if $C' \subset C$ and there exists a substitution σ such that, $\pi\sigma = \pi'$, $\pi' \subseteq \pi$, and for all $L \in C$ there is an $L' \in C'$ with $L\sigma = L'$. A finite unsatisfiable subset of $\mathcal{G}(N)$ is called an unsatisfiable core of N.

An MSL clause with straight dismatching constraints is called an *MSL(SDC)* clause with MSL(SDC) being the respective first-order fragment. Note that any clause set N can be transformed into an equivalent constrained clause set by changing each $C \in N$ to $(C; \top)$.

3 Decidability of the MSL(SDC) Fragment

In the following we will show that the satisfiability of the MSL(SDC) fragment is decidable. For this purpose we will define ordered resolution with selection on constrained clauses [19] and show that with an appropriate ordering and selection function, saturation of an MSL(SDC) clause set terminates.

For the rest of this section we assume an atom ordering $\prec$ such that a literal $\neg Q(s)$ is not greater than a literal $P(t[s]_p)$, where $p \neq \varepsilon$. For example, a KBO where all symbols have weight one has this property.

Definition 1 (sel). *Given an MSL(SDC) clause* $(C; \pi) = (S_1(t_1), \ldots, S_n(t_n) \rightarrow P_1(s_1), \ldots, P_m(s_m); \pi)$. *The Superposition Selection function* sel *is defined by* $S_i(t_i) \in \text{sel}(C)$ *if (1)* t_i *is not a variable or (2)* $t_1, \ldots, t_n$ *are variables and* $t_i \notin \text{vars}(s_1, \ldots, s_m)$ *or (3)* $\{t_1, \ldots, t_n\} \subseteq \text{vars}(s_1, \ldots, s_m)$ *and for some* $1 \leq j \leq m$, $s_j = t_i$.

The selection function sel (Definition 1) ensures that a clause $\Gamma \rightarrow \Delta$ can only be resolved on a positive literal if Γ contains only variables, which also appear in Δ at a non-top position. For example:

$$\text{sel}(P(f(x)), P(x), Q(z) \rightarrow Q(x), R(f(y)) = \{P(f(x))\}$$
$$\text{sel}(P(x), Q(z) \rightarrow Q(x), R(f(y))) = \{Q(z)\}$$
$$\text{sel}(P(x), Q(y) \rightarrow Q(x), R(f(y))) = \{P(x)\}$$
$$\text{sel}(P(x), Q(y) \rightarrow Q(f(x)), R(f(y))) = \emptyset.$$

Note that given an MSL(SDC) clause $(C; \pi) = (S_1(t_1), \ldots, S_n(t_n) \rightarrow P_1(s_1), \ldots P_m(s_m); \pi)$, if some $S_i(t_i)$ is maximal in C, then at least one literal is selected.

Definition 2. *A literal A is called* [strictly] *maximal in a constrained clause* $(C \vee A; \pi)$ *if and only if there exists a solution δ of π such that for all literals B in C, $B\delta \preceq A\delta$ [$B\delta \prec A\delta$].*

Definition 3 (SDC-Resolution).

$$\frac{(\Gamma_1 \rightarrow \Delta_1, A \; ; \; \pi_1) \qquad (\Gamma_2, B \rightarrow \Delta_2 \; ; \; \pi_2)}{((\Gamma_1, \Gamma_2 \rightarrow \Delta_1, \Delta_2)\sigma \; ; \; (\pi_1 \wedge \pi_2)\sigma\downarrow)}, \text{ if}$$

1. $\sigma = \text{mgu}(A, B)$ 2. $(\pi_1 \wedge \pi_2)\sigma\downarrow$ is solvable
3. $A\sigma$ is strictly maximal in $(\Gamma_1 \rightarrow \Delta_1, A; \pi_1)\sigma$ and $\text{sel}(\Gamma_1 \rightarrow \Delta_1, A) = \emptyset$
4. $B \in \text{sel}(\Gamma_2, B \rightarrow \Delta_2)$
5. $\text{sel}(\Gamma_2, B \rightarrow \Delta_2) = \emptyset$ and $\neg B\sigma$ maximal in $(\Gamma_2, B \rightarrow \Delta_2; \pi_2)\sigma$

Definition 4 (SDC-Factoring).

$$\frac{(\Gamma \rightarrow \Delta, A, B \; ; \; \pi)}{((\Gamma \rightarrow \Delta, A)\sigma; \pi\sigma\downarrow)}, \text{ if}$$

1. $\sigma = \text{mgu}(A, B)$ 2. $\text{sel}(\Gamma \rightarrow \Delta, A, B) = \emptyset$
3. $A\sigma$ is maximal in $(\Gamma \rightarrow \Delta, A, B; \pi)\sigma$ 4. $\pi\sigma\downarrow$ is solvable

Note that while the above rules do not operate on equations, we can actually allow unit clauses that consist of non-unifiable disequations, i.e., clauses $s \approx t \rightarrow$ where s and t are not unifiable. There are no potential superposition inferences on such clauses as long as there are no positive equations. So resolution and factoring suffice for completeness. Nevertheless, clauses such as $s \approx t \rightarrow$ affect the models of satisfiable problems. Constrained Resolution and Factoring are sound.

Definition 5 (Saturation). *A constrained clause set N is called saturated up to redundancy, if for every inference between clauses in N the result $(R; \pi)$ is either redundant in N or $\mathcal{G}((R; \pi)) \subseteq \mathcal{G}(N)$.*

Note that our redundancy notion includes condensation and the condition $\mathcal{G}((R; \pi)) \subseteq \mathcal{G}(N)$ allows ignoring variants of clauses.

Definition 6 (Partial Minimal Model Construction). *Given a constrained clause set N, an ordering $\prec$ and the selection function sel, we construct an interpretation $\mathcal{I}_N$ for N, called a partial model, inductively as follows:*

$$\mathcal{I}_C := \bigcup_{\substack{D \in \mathcal{G}(N) \\ D \prec C}} \delta_D, \text{ where } C \in \mathcal{G}(N)$$

$$\delta_D := \begin{cases} \{A\} & \text{if } D = \Gamma \rightarrow \Delta, A \\ & A \text{ strictly maximal, } \text{sel}(D) = \emptyset \text{ and } \mathcal{I}_D \not\models D \\ \emptyset & \text{otherwise} \end{cases}$$

$$\mathcal{I}_N := \bigcup_{C \in \mathcal{G}(N)} \delta_C$$

Clauses D with $\delta_D \neq \emptyset$ are called productive.

Lemma 1 (Ordered SDC Resolution Completeness). *Let N be a constrained clause set saturated up to redundancy by ordered SDC-resolution with selection. Then N is unsatisfiable, if and only if $\square \in \mathcal{G}(N)$. If $\square \notin \mathcal{G}(N)$ then $\mathcal{I}_N \models N$.*

Lemma 2. *Let N be a set of MSL(SDC) clauses without variants or uncondensed clauses over a finite signature Σ. N is finite if there exists an integer d such that for every $(C; \pi) \in N$, depth$(\pi) \leq d$ and*

(1) $C = S_1(x_1), \ldots, S_n(x_n), S_1'(t), \ldots, S_m'(t) \to \Delta$ or
(2) $C = S_1(x_1), \ldots, S_n(x_n), S_1'(t), \ldots, S_m'(t) \to S(t), \Delta$

with t shallow and linear, and vars$(t) \cap$ vars$(\Delta) = \emptyset$.

Lemma 3 (Finite Saturation). *Let N be an MSL(SDC) clause set. Then N can be finitely saturated up to redundancy by SDC-resolution with selection function sel.*

Theorem 1 (MSL(SDC) Decidability). *Satisfiability of the MSL(SDC) first-order fragment is decidable.*

4   Approximation and Refinement

In the following, we show how decidability of the MSL(SDC) fragment can be used to improve the approximation refinement calculus presented in [18].

Our approach is based on a counter-example guided abstraction refinement (CEGAR) idea. The procedure loops trough four steps: approximation, testing (un)satisfiability, lifting, and refinement. The approximation step transforms any first-order logic clause set into the decidable MSL(SDC) fragment while preserving unsatisfiability. The second step employs the decidability result for MSL(SDC), Sect. 3, to test satisfiability of the approximated clause set. If the approximation is satisfiable, the original problem is satisfiable as well and we are done. Otherwise, the third step, lifting, tests whether the proof of unsatisfiability found for the approximated clause set can be lifted to a proof of the original clause set. If so, the original clause set is unsatisfiable and we are again done. If not, we extract a cause for the lifting failure that always amounts to two different instantiations of the same variable in a clause from the original clause set. This is resolved by the fourth step, the refinement. The crucial clause in the original problem is replaced and instantiated in a satisfiability preserving way such that the different instantiations do not reoccur anymore in subsequent iterations of the loop.

As mentioned before, our motivation to use dismatching constraints is that for an unconstrained clause the refinement adds quadratically many new clauses to the clause set. In contrast, with constrained clauses the same can be accomplished with adding just a single new clause. This extension is rather simple as constraints are treated the same as the antecedent literals in the clause. Furthermore we present refinement as a separate transformation rule.

The second change compared to the previous version is the removal of the Horn approximation rule, where we have now shown in Sect. 3 that a restriction to Horn clauses is not required for decidability anymore. Instead, the linear and shallow approximations are extended to apply to non-Horn clauses instead.

The approximation consists of individual transformation rules $N \Rightarrow N'$ that are non-deterministically applied. They transform a clause that is not in the MSL(SDC) fragment in finite steps into MSL(SDC) clauses. Each specific property of MSL(SDC) clauses, i.e., monadic predicates, shallow and linear positive literals, is generated by a corresponding rule: the Monadic transformation encodes non-Monadic predicates as functions, the shallow transformation extracts non-shallow subterms by introducing fresh predicates and the linear transformation renames non-linear variable occurrences.

Starting from a constrained clause set N the transformation is parameterized by a single monadic projection predicate T, fresh to N and for each non-monadic predicate P a separate projection function f_P fresh to N. The clauses in N are called the original clauses while the clauses in N' are the approximated clauses. We assume all clauses in N to be variable disjoint.

Definition 7. *Given a predicate P, projection predicate T, and projection function f_P, define the injective function $\mu_P^T(P(\vec{t})) := T(f_p(\vec{t}))$ and $\mu_P^T(Q(\vec{s})) := Q(\vec{s})$ for $P \neq Q$. The function is extended to [constrained] clauses, clause sets and interpretations. Given a signature Σ with non-monadic predicates $P_1, \ldots, P_n$, define $\mu_\Sigma^T(N) = \mu_{P_1}^T(\ldots(\mu_{P_n}^T(N))\ldots)$ and $\mu_\Sigma^T(\mathcal{I}) = \mu_{P_1}^T(\ldots(\mu_{P_n}^T(\mathcal{I}))\ldots)$.*

Monadic $N \Rightarrow_{\mathrm{MO}} \mu_P^T(N)$

provided P is a non-monadic predicate in the signature of N.

Shallow $N \mathbin{\dot\cup} \{(\Gamma \to E[s]_p, \Delta; \pi)\} \Rightarrow_{\mathrm{SH}}$
$\qquad\qquad N \cup \{(S(x), \Gamma_l \to E[p/x], \Delta_l; \pi); (\Gamma_r \to S(s), \Delta_r; \pi)\}$

provided s is complex, $|p| = 2$, x and S fresh, $\Gamma_l\{x \mapsto s\} \cup \Gamma_r = \Gamma$, $\Delta_l \cup \Delta_r = \Delta$, $\{Q(y) \in \Gamma \mid y \in \mathrm{vars}(E[p/x], \Delta_l)\} \subseteq \Gamma_l$, $\{Q(y) \in \Gamma \mid y \in \mathrm{vars}(s, \Delta_r)\} \subseteq \Gamma_r$.

Linear 1 $N \mathbin{\dot\cup} \{(\Gamma \to \Delta, E'[x]_p, E[x]_q; \pi)\} \Rightarrow_{\mathrm{LI}}$
$\qquad\qquad N \cup \{(\Gamma\sigma, \Gamma \to \Delta, E'[x]_p, E[q/x']; \pi \wedge \pi\sigma)\}$

provided x' is fresh and $\sigma = \{x \mapsto x'\}$.

Linear 2 $N \mathbin{\dot\cup} \{(\Gamma \to \Delta, E[x]_{p,q}; \pi)\} \Rightarrow_{\mathrm{LI}}$
$\qquad\qquad N \cup \{(\Gamma\sigma, \Gamma \to \Delta, E[q/x']; \pi \wedge \pi\sigma)\}$

provided x' is fresh, $p \neq q$ and $\sigma = \{x \mapsto x'\}$.

Refinement $N \mathbin{\dot\cup} \{(C, \pi)\} \Rightarrow_{\mathrm{Ref}} N \cup \{(C; \pi \wedge x \neq t), (C; \pi)\{x \mapsto t\}\}$

provided $x \in \mathrm{vars}(C)$, t straight and $\mathrm{vars}(t) \cap \mathrm{vars}((C, \pi)) = \emptyset$.

Note that variables are not renamed unless explicitly stated in the rule. This means that original clauses and their approximated counterparts share variable names. We use this to trace the origin of variables in the approximation.

The refinement transformation $\Rightarrow_{\text{Ref}}$ is not needed to eventually generate MSL(SDC) clauses, but can be used to achieve a more fine-grained approximation of N, see below.

In the shallow transformation, Γ and Δ are separated into Γ_l, Γ_r, Δ_l, and Δ_r, respectively. The separation can be almost arbitrarily chosen as long as no atom from Γ, Δ is skipped. However, the goal is to minimize the set of shared variables, i.e., the variables of $(\Gamma \rightarrow E[s]_p, \Delta; \pi)$ that are inherited by both approximation clauses, $\text{vars}(\Gamma_r, s, \Delta_r) \cap \text{vars}(\Gamma_l, E[p/x], \Delta_l)$. If there are no shared variables, the shallow transformation is satisfiability equivalent. The conditions on Γ_l and Γ_r ensure that $S(x)$ atoms are not separated from the respective positive occurrence of x in subsequent shallow transformation applications.

Consider the clause $Q(f(x), y) \rightarrow P(g(f(x), y))$. The simple shallow transformation $S(x'), Q(f(x), y) \rightarrow P(g(x', y)); S(f(x))$ is not satisfiability equivalent – nor with any alternative partitioning of Γ. However, by replacing the occurrence of the extraction term $f(x)$ in $Q(f(x), y)$ with the fresh variable x', the approximation $S(x'), Q(x', y) \rightarrow P(g(x', y)); S(f(x))$ is satisfiability equivalent. Therefore, we allow the extraction of s from the terms in Γ_l and require $\Gamma_l\{x \mapsto s\} \cup \Gamma_r = \Gamma$.

We consider Linear 1 and Linear 2 as two cases of the same linear transformation rule. Their only difference is whether the two occurrences of x are in the same literal or not. The duplication of literals and constraints in Γ and π is not needed if x does not occur in Γ or π.

Further, consider a linear transformation $N \cup \{(C; \pi)\} \Rightarrow_{\text{LI}} N \cup \{(C_a; \pi_a)\}$, where a fresh variable x' replaces an occurrence of a non-linear variable x in $(C; \pi)$. Then, $(C_a; \pi_a)\{x' \mapsto x\}$ is equal to $(C; \pi)$ modulo duplicate literal elimination. A similar property can be observed of a resolvent of $(C_l; \pi)$ and $(C_r; \pi)$ resulting from a shallow transformation $N \cup \{(C; \pi)\} \Rightarrow_{\text{SH}} N \cup \{(C_l; \pi), (C_r; \pi)\}$. Note that by construction, $(C_l; \pi)$ and $(C_r; \pi)$ are not necessarily variable disjoint. To simulate standard resolution, we need to rename at least the shared variables in one of them.

Definition 8 ($\Rightarrow_{\text{AP}}$). *We define $\Rightarrow_{\text{AP}}$ as the priority rewrite system* [3] *consisting of $\Rightarrow_{\text{Ref}}$, $\Rightarrow_{\text{MO}}$, $\Rightarrow_{\text{SH}}$ and $\Rightarrow_{\text{LI}}$ with priority $\Rightarrow_{\text{Ref}} > \Rightarrow_{\text{MO}} > \Rightarrow_{\text{SH}} > \Rightarrow_{\text{LI}}$, where $\Rightarrow_{\text{Ref}}$ is only applied finitely many times.*

Lemma 4 ($\Rightarrow_{\text{AP}}$ is a Terminating Over-Approximation). *(i) $\Rightarrow_{\text{AP}}^*$ terminates, (ii) if $N \Rightarrow_{\text{AP}} N'$ and N' is satisfiable, then N is also satisfiable.*

Note that $\Rightarrow_{\text{Ref}}$ and $\Rightarrow_{\text{MO}}$ are also satisfiability preserving transformations.

Corollary 1. *If $N \Rightarrow_{\text{AP}}^* N'$ and N' is satisfied by a model $\mathcal{I}$, then $\mu_\Sigma^{-1}(\mathcal{I})$ is a model of N.*

On the basis of $\Rightarrow_{\text{AP}}$ we can define an ancestor relation $\Rightarrow_{\text{A}}$ that relates clauses, literal occurrences, and variables with respect to approximation.

This relation is needed in order to figure out the exact clause, literal, variable for refinement. The definition of $\Rightarrow_A$ itself is rather technical [20].

The over-approximation of a clause set N can introduce resolution refutations that have no corresponding equivalent in N which we consider a lifting failure. Compared to our previous calculus [18], the lifting process is identical with the exception that there is no case for the removed Horn transformation. We only update the definition of conflicting cores to consider constrained clauses.

Definition 9 (Conflicting Core). *A finite set of unconstrained clauses $N^\perp$ is a conflicting core of N if $N^\perp\sigma$ is an unsatisfiable core of N for all grounding substitutions σ. For a ground clause $D \in N^\perp\sigma$ and $(C;\pi) \in N$ such that $D \in \mathcal{G}((C;\pi))$, the clause $(C;\pi)$ is called the instantiated clause of D. We call $N^\perp$ complete if for every clause $C \in N^\perp$ and literal $L \in C$, there exists a clause $D \in N^\perp$ with $\overline{L} \in D$.*

A conflicting core is a generalization of a ground unsatisfiability core that allows global variables to act as parameters. This enables more efficient lifting and refinement compared to a simple ground unsatisfiable core. We show some examples at the end of this section.

We discuss the potential lifting failures and the corresponding refinements only for the linear and shallow case because lifting the satisfiability equivalent monadic and refinement transformations always succeeds. To reiterate from our previous work: in the linear case, there exists a clause in the conflicting core that is not an instance of the original clauses. In the shallow case, there exists a pair of clauses whose resolvent is not an instance of the original clauses. We combine these two cases by introducing the notion of a lift-conflict.

Definition 10 (Conflict). *Let $N \cup \{(C,\pi)\} \Rightarrow_{\text{LI}} N \cup \{(C_a, \pi_a)\}$ and $N^\perp$ be a complete ground conflicting core of $N \cup \{(C_a, \pi_a)\}$. We call a conflict clause $C_c \in N^\perp$ with the instantiated clause (C_a, π_a) a lift-conflict if C_c is not an instance of (C, π) modulo duplicate literal elimination. Then, C_c is an instance of (C_a, π_a), which we call the conflict clause of C_c.*

The goal of refinement is to instantiate the original parent clause in such a way that is both satisfiability equivalent and prevents the lift-conflict after approximation. Solving the refined approximation will then either necessarily produce a complete saturation or a new refutation proof, because its conflicting core has to be different. For this purpose, we use the refinement transformation to segment the original parent clause $(C;\pi)$ into two parts $(C;\pi \wedge x \neq t)$ and $(C;\pi)\{x \mapsto t\}$.

For example, consider N and its linear transformation N'.

$$\begin{array}{ccc} \rightarrow P(x,x) & \Rightarrow_{\text{LI}} & \rightarrow P(x,x') \\ P(a,b) \rightarrow & \Rightarrow^0_{\text{AP}} & P(a,b) \rightarrow \end{array}$$

The ground conflicting core of N' is

$$\begin{array}{c} \rightarrow P(a,b) \\ P(a,b) \rightarrow \end{array}$$

Because $P(a, b)$ is not an instance of $P(x, x)$, lifting fails. $P(a, b)$ is the lift-conflict. Specifically, $\{x \mapsto a\}$ and $\{x \mapsto b\}$ are conflicting substitutions for the parent variable x. We pick $\{x \mapsto a\}$ to segment $P(x, x)$ into $(P(x, x); x \neq a)$ and $P(x, x)\{x \mapsto a\}$. Now, any descendant of $(P(x, x); x \neq a)$ cannot have a at the position of the first x, and any descendant of $P(x, x)\{x \mapsto a\}$ must have an a at the position of the second x. Thus, $P(a, b)$ is excluded in both cases and no longer appears as a lift-conflict.

To show that the lift-conflict will not reappear in the general case, we use that the conflict clause and its ancestors have strong ties between their term structures and constraints.

Definition 11 (Constrained Term Skeleton). *The constrained term skeleton of a term t under constraint π, $skt(t, \pi)$, is defined as the normal form of the following transformation:*

$$(t[x]_{p,q}; \pi) \Rightarrow_{skt} (t[q/x']; \pi \wedge \pi\{x \mapsto x'\}), \text{ where } p \neq q \text{ and } x' \text{ is fresh.}$$

The constrained term skeleton of a term t is essentially a linear version of t where the restrictions on each variable position imposed by π are preserved. For (t, π) and a solution δ of π, $t\delta$ is called a ground instance of (t, π).

Lemma 5. *Let $N_0 \Rightarrow_{AP}^* N_k$, $(C_k; \pi_k)$ in N with the ancestor clause $(C_0; \pi_0) \in N_0$ and $N_k^{\perp}$ be a complete ground conflicting core of N_k. Let δ be a solution of π_k such that $C_k\delta$ is in $N_k^{\perp}$. If (L', q') is a literal position in $(C_k; \pi_k)$ with the ancestor (L, q) in (C_0, π_0), then (i) $L'\delta|_{q'}$ is an instance of $skt(L|_q, \pi_0)$, (ii) $q = q'$ if L and L' have the same predicate, and (iii) if $L'|_{q'} = x$ and there exists an ancestor variable y of x in (C_0, π_0), then $L|_q = y$.*

Proof. Idea. The proof is by induction on the length of the approximation $N_0 \Rightarrow_{AP}^* N_k$ and a case distinction of the first transformation $N_0 \Rightarrow_{AP} N_1$. Most cases are straightforward except for case (i) of the shallow transformation. Because $N_k^{\perp}$ is complete, any negative extraction literal $S(x)\delta$ matches some positive literal in $N_k^{\perp}$ which is necessarily an instance of $S(s)$, the extraction term. Therefore, the original term structure is preserved even after subterm extraction.

Next, we define the notion of descendants and descendant relations to connect lift-conflicts in ground conflicting cores with their corresponding ancestor clauses. The goal, hereby, is that if a ground clause D is not a descendant of a clause in N, then it can never appear in a conflicting core of an approximation of N.

Definition 12 (Descendants). *Let $N \Rightarrow_{AP}^* N'$, $[(C; \pi), N] \Rightarrow_A^* [(C'; \pi'), N']$ and D be a ground instance of $(C'; \pi')$. Then, we call D a descendant of $(C; \pi)$ and define the $[(C; \pi), N] \Rightarrow_A^* [(C'; \pi'), N']$-descendant relation $\Rightarrow_D$ that maps literals in D to literal positions in $(C; \pi)$ using the following rule:*

$$L'\delta \Rightarrow_D (L, r) \text{ if } L'\delta \in D \text{ and } [r, L, (C; \pi), N] \Rightarrow_A^* [\varepsilon, L', (C'; \pi'), N']$$

For the descendant relations it is of importance to note that while there are potentially infinite ways that a lift-conflict C_c can be a descendant of an original clause $(C; \pi)$, there are only finitely many distinct descendant relations over C_c and $(C; \pi)$. This means, if a refinement transformation can prevent one distinct descendant relation without generating new distinct descendant relations (Lemma 6), a finite number of refinement steps can remove the lift-conflict C_c from the descendants of $(C; \pi)$ (Lemma 7). Thereby, preventing any conflicting cores containing C_c from being found again.

A clause $(C; \pi)$ can have two descendants that are the same except for the names of the S-predicates introduced by shallow transformations. Because the used approximation $N \Rightarrow_{AP}^* N'$ is arbitrary and therefore also the choice of fresh S-predicates, if D is a descendant of $(C; \pi)$, then any clause D' equal to D up to a renaming of S-predicates is also a descendant of $(C; \pi)$. On the other hand, the actual important information about an S-predicate is which term it extracts. Two descendants of $(C; \pi)$ might be identical but their S-predicate extract different terms in $(C; \pi)$. For example, $P(a) \to S(f(a))$ is a descendant of $P(x), P(y) \to Q(f(x), g(f(x)))$ but might extract either occurrence of $f(x)$. These cases are distinguished by their respective descendant relations. In the example, we have either $S(f(a)) \Rightarrow_D (Q(f(x), g(f(x))), 1)$ or $S(f(a)) \Rightarrow_D (Q(f(x), g(f(x))), 2.1)$.

Lemma 6. *Let $N_0 = N \cup \{(C; \pi)\} \Rightarrow_{Ref} N \cup \{(C; \pi \wedge x \neq t), (C; \pi)\{x \mapsto t\}\} = N_1$ be a refinement transformation and D a ground clause. If there is a $[(C; \pi \wedge x \neq t), N_1] \Rightarrow_A^* [(C'; \pi'), N_2]$-or $[(C; \pi)\{x \mapsto t\}, N_1] \Rightarrow_A^* [(C'; \pi'), N_2]$-descendant relation $\Rightarrow_D^1$, then there is an equal $[(C; \pi), N_0] \Rightarrow_A^* [(C'; \pi'), N_2]$-descendant relation $\Rightarrow_D^0$.*

Proof. Let L_D be a literal of D and $L' \Rightarrow_D^1 (L, r)$. If D is a descendant of $(C; \pi \wedge x \neq t)$, then $[r, L, (C; \pi \wedge x \neq t), N_1] \Rightarrow_A^* [\varepsilon, L', (C'; \pi'), N_2]$. Because $[r, L, (C; \pi), N_0] \Rightarrow_A [r, L, (C; \pi \wedge x \neq t), N_1]$, $L' \Rightarrow_D^0 (L, r)$. If D is a descendant of $(C; \pi)\{x \mapsto t\}$, the proof is analogous. □

Lemma 7 (Refinement). *Let $N \Rightarrow_{AP} N'$ and $N^\perp$ be a complete ground conflicting core of N'. If $C_c \in N^\perp$ is a lift-conflict, then there exists a finite refinement $N \Rightarrow_{Ref}^* N_R$ such that for any approximation $N_R \Rightarrow_{AP}^* N_R'$ and ground conflicting core $N_R^\perp$ of N_R', C_c is not a lift-conflict in $N_R^\perp$ modulo duplicate literal elimination.*

Theorem 2 (Soundness and Completeness of FO-AR). *Let N be an unsatisfiable clause set and N' its MSL(SDC) approximation: (i) if N is unsatisfiable then there exists a conflicting core of N' that can be lifted to a refutation in N, (ii) if N' is satisfiable, then N is satisfiable too.*

Proof. (Idea) By Lemmas 4 and 7, where the latter can be used to show that a core of N' that cannot be lifted also excludes the respective instance for unsatisfiability of N.

Actually, Lemma 7 can be used to define a fair strategy on refutations in N' in order to receive also a dynamically complete FO-AR calculus, following the ideas presented in [18].

In Lemma 7, we segment the conflict clause's immediate parent clause. If the lifting later successfully passes this point, the refinement is lost and will be possibly repeated. Instead, we can refine any ancestor of the conflict clause as long as it contains the ancestor of the variable used in the refinement. By Lemma 5-(iii), such an ancestor will contain the ancestor variable at the same positions. If we refine the ancestor in the original clause set, the refinement is permanent because lifting the refinement steps always succeeds. Only variables introduced by shallow transformation cannot be traced to the original clause set. However, these shallow variables are already linear and the partitioning in the shallow transformation can be chosen such that they are not shared variables. Assume a shallow, shared variable y, that is used to extract the term t, in the shallow transformation of $\Gamma \to E[s]_p, \Delta$ into $S(x), \Gamma_l \to E[p/x], \Delta_l$ and $\Gamma_r \to S(s), \Delta_r$. Since $\Delta_l \cup \Delta_r = \Delta$ is a partitioning, y can only appear in either $E[p/x], \Delta_l$ or $S(s), \Delta_r$. If $y \in \text{vars}(E[p/x], \Delta_l)$ we instantiate Γ_r with $\{y \mapsto t\}$ and Γ_l, otherwise. Now, y is no longer a shared variable.

The refinement Lemmas only guarantee a refinement for a given ground conflicting core. In practice, however, conflicting cores contain free variables. We can always generate a ground conflicting core by instantiating the free variables with ground terms. However, if we only exclude a single ground case via refinement, next time the new conflicting core will likely have overlaps with the previous one. Instead, we can often remove all ground instances of a given conflict clause at once.

The simplest case is when unifying the conflict clause with the original clause fails because their instantiations differ at some equivalent positions. For example, consider $N = \{P(x, x); P(f(x, a), f(y, b)) \to\}$. N is satisfiable but the linear transformation is unsatisfiable with conflict clause $P(f(x, a), f(y, b))$ which is not unifiable with $P(x, x)$, because the two terms $f(x, a)$ and $f(y, b)$ have different constants at the second argument. A refinement of $P(x, x)$ is

$$(P(x, x) ; x \neq f(v, a))$$
$$(P(f(x, a), f(x, a)) ; \top)$$

$P(f(x, a), f(y, b))$ shares no ground instances with the approximations of the refined clauses.

Next, assume that again unification fails due to structural difference, but this time the differences lie at different positions. For example, consider $N = \{P(x, x); P(f(a, b), f(x, x)) \to\}$. N is satisfiable but the linear transformation of N is unsatisfiable with conflict clause $P(f(a, b), f(x, x))$ which is not unifiable with $P(x, x)$ because in $f(a, b)$ the first an second argument are different but the same in $f(x, x)$. A refinement of $P(x, x)$ is

$$(P(x,x)\,;x \neq f(a,v))$$
$$(P(f(a,x),f(a,x)))\,;x \neq a)$$
$$(P(f(a,a),f(a,a)))\,;\top)$$

$P(f(a,b),f(x,x))$ shares no ground instances with the approximations of the refined clauses.

It is also possible that the conflict clause and original clause are unifiable by themselves, but the resulting constraint has no solutions. For example, consider $N = \{P(x,x); (P(x,y) \rightarrow; x \neq a \wedge x \neq b \wedge y \neq c \wedge y \neq d)\}$ with signature $\Sigma = \{a,b,c,d\}$. N is satisfiable but the linear transformation of N is unsatisfiable with conflict clause $(\rightarrow P(x,y); x \neq a \wedge x \neq b \wedge y \neq c \wedge y \neq d)$. While $P(x,x)$ and $P(x,y)$ are unifiable, the resulting constraint $x \neq a \wedge x \neq b \wedge x \neq c \wedge x \neq d$ has no solutions. A refinement of $P(x,x)$ is

$$(P(x,x)\,;x \neq a \wedge x \neq b)$$
$$(P(a,a)\,;\top)$$
$$(P(b,b)\,;\top)$$

$(P(x,y); x \neq a \wedge x \neq b \wedge y \neq c \wedge y \neq d)$ shares no ground instances with the approximations of the refined clauses.

Lastly, we should mention that there are cases where the refinement process does not terminate. For example, consider the clause set $N = \{P(x,x); P(y,g(y)) \rightarrow\}$. N is satisfiable but the linear transformation of N is unsatisfiable with conflict clause $P(y,g(y))$, which is not unifiable with $P(x,x)$. A refinement of $P(x,x)$ based on the ground instance $P(a,g(a))$ is

$$(P(x,x)\,;x \neq g(v))$$
$$(P(g(x),g(x))\,;\top)$$

While $P(y,g(y))$ is not an instance of the refined approximation, it shares ground instances with $P(g(x),g(x'))$. The new conflict clause is $P(g(y),g(g(y)))$ and the refinement will continue to enumerate all $P(g^i(x),g^i(x))$ instances of $P(x,x)$ without ever reaching a satisfiable approximation. Satisfiability of first-order clause sets is undecidable, so termination cannot be expected by any calculus, in general.

5   Experiments

In the following we discuss several first-order clause classes for which FO-AR implemented in SPASS-AR immediately decides satisfiability but superposition and instantiation-based methods fail. We argue both according to the respective calculi and state-of-the-art implementations, in particular SPASS 3.9 [23], Vampire 4.1 [11,21], for ordered-resolution/superposition, iProver 2.5 [9] an implementation of Inst-Gen [10], and Darwin v1.4.5 [4] an implementation of the model evolution calculus [5]. All experiments were run on a 64-Bit Linux computer (Xeon(R) E5-2680, 2.70GHz, 256GB main memory). For Vampire and

Darwin we chose the CASC-sat and CASC settings, respectively. For iProver we set the schedule to "sat" and SPASS, SPASS-AR were used in default mode. Please note that Vampire and iProver are portfolio solvers including implementations of several different calculi including superposition (ordered resolution), instance generation, and finite model finding. SPASS, SPASS-AR, and Darwin only implement superposition, FO-AR, and model evolution, respectively.

For the first example

$$P(x, y) \rightarrow P(x, z), P(z, y); \quad P(a, a)$$

and second example,

$$Q(x, x); \quad Q(v, w), P(x, y) \rightarrow P(x, v), P(w, y); \quad P(a, a)$$

the superposition calculus produces independently of the selection strategy and ordering an infinite number of clauses of form

$$\rightarrow P(a, z_1), \ P(z_1, z_2), \ \ldots, \ P(z_n, a).$$

Using linear approximation, however, FO-AR replaces $P(x, y) \rightarrow P(x, z), P(z, y)$ and $\rightarrow Q(x, x)$ with $P(x, y) \rightarrow P(x, z), P(z', y)$ and $\rightarrow Q(x, x')$, respectively. Consequently, ordered resolution derives $\rightarrow P(a, z_1), P(z_2, a)$ which subsumes any further inferences $\rightarrow P(a, z_1), P(z_2, z_3), P(z_4, a)$. Hence, saturation of the approximation terminates immediately. Both examples belong to the Bernays-Schönfinkel fragment, so model evolution (Darwin) and Inst-Gen (iProver) can decide them as well. Note that the concrete behavior of superposition is not limited to the above examples but potentially occurs whenever there are variable chains in clauses.

On the third problem

$$P(x, y) \rightarrow P(g(x), z); \quad P(a, a)$$

superposition derives all clauses of the form $\rightarrow P(g(\ldots g(a) \ldots), z)$. With a shallow approximation of $P(x, y) \rightarrow P(g(x), z)$ into $S(v) \rightarrow P(v, z)$ and $P(x, y) \rightarrow S(g(x))$, FO-AR (SPASS-AR) terminates after deriving $\rightarrow S(g(a))$ and $S(x) \rightarrow S(g(x))$. Again, model evolution (Darwin) and Inst-Gen (iProver) can also solve this example.

The next example

$$P(a); \quad P(f(a)) \rightarrow; \quad P(f(f(x))) \rightarrow P(x); \quad P(x) \rightarrow P(f(f(x)))$$

is already saturated under superposition. For FO-AR, the clause $P(x) \rightarrow P(f(f(x)))$ is replaced by $S(x) \rightarrow P(f(x))$ and $P(x) \rightarrow S(f(x))$. Then ordered resolution terminates after inferring $S(a) \rightarrow$ and $S(f(x)) \rightarrow P(x)$.

The Inst-Gen and model evolution calculi, however, fail. In either, a satisfying model is represented by a finite set of literals, i.e., a model of the propositional approximation for Inst-Gen and the trail of literals in case of model evolution.

Therefore, there necessarily exists a literal $P(f^n(x))$ or $\neg P(f^n(x))$ with a maximal n in these models. This contradicts the actual model where either $P(f^n(a))$ or $P(f^n(f(a)))$ is true. However, iProver can solve this problem using its built-in ordered resolution solver whereas Darwin does not terminate on this problem.

Lastly consider an example of the form

$$f(x) \approx x \to; \ f(f(x)) \approx x \to; \ \ldots; f^n(x) \approx x \to$$

which is trivially satisfiable, e.g., saturated by superposition, but any model has at least $n+1$ domain elements. Therefore, adding these clauses to any satisfiable clause set containing f forces calculi that explicitly consider finite models to consider at least $n + 1$ elements. The performance of final model finders [15] typically degrades in the number of different domain elements to be considered.

Combining each of these examples into one problem is then solvable by neither superposition, Inst-Gen, or model evolution and not practically solvable with increasing n via testing finite models. For example, we tested

$$P(x,y) \to P(x,z), P(z,y); \quad P(a,a); \quad P(f(a),y) \to;$$
$$P(f(f(x)),y) \to P(x,y); \quad P(x,y) \to P(f(f(x)),y);$$
$$f(x) \approx x \to;, \ldots, f^n(x) \approx x \to;$$

for $n = 20$ against SPASS, Vampire, iProver, and Darwin for more than one hour each without success. Only SPASS-AR solved it in less than one second.

For iProver we added an artificial positive equation $b \approx c$. For otherwise, iProver throws away all disequations while preprocessing. This is a satisfiability preserving operation, however, the afterwards found (finite) models are not models of the above clause set due to the collapsing of ground terms.

6   Conclusion

The previous section showed FO-AR is superior to superposition, instantiation-based methods on certain classes of clause sets. Of course, there are also classes of clause sets where superposition and instantiation-based methods are superior to FO-AR, e.g., for unsatisfiable clause sets where the structure of the clause set forces FO-AR to enumerate failing ground instances due to the approximation in a bottom-up way.

Our prototypical implementation SPASS-AR cannot compete with systems such as iProver or Vampire on the respective CASC categories of the TPTP [17]. This is already due to the fact that they are all meanwhile portfolio solvers. For example, iProver contains an implementation of ordered resolution and Vampire an implementation of Inst-Gen. Our results, Sect. 5, however, show that these systems may benefit from FO-AR by adding it to their portfolio.

The DEXPTIME-completeness result for MSLH strongly suggest that both the MSLH and also our MSL(SDC) fragment have the finite model property. However, we are not aware of any proof. If MSL(DSC) has the finite model property, the finite model finding approaches are complete on MSL(SDC).

The models generated by FO-AR and superposition are typically infinite. It remains an open problem, even for fragments enjoying the finite model property, e.g., the first-order monadic fragment, to design a calculus that combines explicit finite model finding with a structural representation of infinite models. For classes that have no finite models this problem seems to become even more difficult. To the best of our knowledge, SPASS is currently the only prover that can show satisfiability of the clauses $R(x,x) \to$; $R(x,y), R(y,z) \to R(x,z)$; $R(x,g(x))$ due to an implementation of chaining [2,16]. Apart from the superposition calculus, it is unknown to us how the specific inferences for transitivity can be combined with any of the other discussed calculi, including the abstraction refinement calculus introduced in this paper.

Finally, there are not many results on calculi that operate with respect to models containing positive equations. Even for fragments that are decidable with equality, such as the Bernays-Schoenfinkel-Ramsey fragment or the monadic fragment with equality, there seem currently no convincing suggestions compared to the great amount of techniques for these fragments without equality. Adding positive equations to MSL(SDC) while keeping decidability is, to the best of our current knowledge, only possible for at most linear, shallow equations $f(x_1, \ldots, x_n) \approx h(y_1, \ldots, y_n)$ [8]. However, approximation into such equations from an equational theory with nested term occurrences typically results in an almost trivial equational theory. So this does not seem to be a very promising research direction.

Acknowledgements. We thank the reviewers as well as Konstantin Korovin and Giles Reger for a number of important remarks.

References

1. Bachmair, L., Ganzinger, H.: Rewrite-based equational theorem proving with selection and simplification. J. Logic Comput. **4**(3), 217–247 (1994). Revised version of Max-Planck-Institut für Informatik Technical report, MPI-I-91-208 (1991)
2. Bachmair, L., Ganzinger, H.: Ordered chaining calculi for first-order theories of transitive relations. J. ACM **45**(6), 1007–1049 (1998)
3. Baeten, J.C.M., Bergstra, J.A., Klop, J., Weijland, W.P.: Term-rewriting systems with rule priorities. Theor. Comput. Sci. **67**(2&3), 283–301 (1989)
4. Baumgartner, P., Fuchs, A., Tinelli, C.: Implementing the model evolution calculus. Int. J. Artif. Intell. Tools **15**(1), 21–52 (2006)
5. Baumgartner, P., Tinelli, C.: The model evolution calculus. In: Baader, F. (ed.) CADE 2003. LNCS (LNAI), vol. 2741, pp. 350–364. Springer, Heidelberg (2003). doi:10.1007/978-3-540-45085-6_32
6. Comon, H., Dauchet, M., Gilleron, R., Löding, C., Jacquemard, F., Lugiez, D., Tison, S., Tommasi, M.: Tree automata techniques and applications (2007). http://www.grappa.univ-lille3.fr/tata. Accessed 12 Oct 2007
7. Goubault-Larrecq, J.: Deciding $\mathcal{H}_1$ by resolution. Inf. Process. Lett. **95**(3), 401–408 (2005)
8. Jacquemard, F., Meyer, C., Weidenbach, C.: Unification in extensions of shallow equational theories. In: Nipkow, T. (ed.) RTA 1998. LNCS, vol. 1379, pp. 76–90. Springer, Heidelberg (1998). doi:10.1007/BFb0052362

9. Korovin, K.: iProver – an instantiation-based theorem prover for first-order logic (system description). In: Armando, A., Baumgartner, P., Dowek, G. (eds.) IJCAR 2008. LNCS, vol. 5195, pp. 292–298. Springer, Heidelberg (2008). doi:10.1007/978-3-540-71070-7_24

10. Korovin, K.: Inst-Gen – a modular approach to instantiation-based automated reasoning. In: Voronkov, A., Weidenbach, C. (eds.) Programming Logics. LNCS, vol. 7797, pp. 239–270. Springer, Heidelberg (2013). doi:10.1007/978-3-642-37651-1_10

11. Kovács, L., Voronkov, A.: First-order theorem proving and VAMPIRE. In: Sharygina, N., Veith, H. (eds.) CAV 2013. LNCS, vol. 8044, pp. 1–35. Springer, Heidelberg (2013). doi:10.1007/978-3-642-39799-8_1

12. Seidl, H., Reuß, A.: Extending H1-clauses with disequalities. Inf. Process. Lett. 111(20), 1007–1013 (2011)

13. Seidl, H., Reuß, A.: Extending $\mathcal{H}_1$-clauses with path disequalities. In: Birkedal, L. (ed.) FoSSaCS 2012. LNCS, vol. 7213, pp. 165–179. Springer, Heidelberg (2012). doi:10.1007/978-3-642-28729-9_11

14. Seidl, H., Verma, K.N.: Cryptographic protocol verification using tractable classes of horn clauses. In: Reps, T., Sagiv, M., Bauer, J. (eds.) Program Analysis and Compilation, Theory and Practice. LNCS, vol. 4444, pp. 97–119. Springer, Heidelberg (2007). doi:10.1007/978-3-540-71322-7_5

15. Slaney, J.K., Surendonk, T.: Combining finite model generation with theorem proving: problems and prospects. In: Baader, F., Schulz, K.U. (eds.), Frontiers of Combining Systems, First International Workshop FroCoS 1996, Munich, Germany, March 26-29, 1996, Proceedings, vol. 3. Applied Logic Series, pp. 141–155. Kluwer Academic Publishers (1996)

16. Suda, M., Weidenbach, C., Wischnewski, P.: On the saturation of YAGO. In: Giesl, J., Hähnle, R. (eds.) IJCAR 2010. LNCS (LNAI), vol. 6173, pp. 441–456. Springer, Heidelberg (2010). doi:10.1007/978-3-642-14203-1_38

17. Sutcliffe, G.: The TPTP problem library and associated infrastructure: the FOF and CNF Parts, v3.5.0. J. Autom. Reasoning 43(4), 337–362 (2009)

18. Teucke, A., Weidenbach, C.: First-order logic theorem proving and model building via approximation and instantiation. In: Lutz, C., Ranise, S. (eds.) FroCoS 2015. LNCS (LNAI), vol. 9322, pp. 85–100. Springer, Cham (2015). doi:10.1007/978-3-319-24246-0_6

19. Teucke, A., Weidenbach, C.: Ordered resolution with straight dismatching constraints. In: Fontaine, P., Schulz, S., Urban, J. (eds.) Proceedings of the 5th Workshop on Practical Aspects of Automated Reasoning Co-located with International Joint Conference on Automated Reasoning (IJCAR 2016), Coimbra, Portugal, 2 July 2016, vol. 1635. CEUR Workshop Proceedings, pp. 95–109 (2016). CEUR-WS.org

20. Teucke, A., Weidenbach, C.: Decidability of the monadic shallow linear first-order fragment with straight dismatching constraints (2017). http://arxiv.org/abs/1703.02837

21. Voronkov, A.: AVATAR: the architecture for first-order theorem provers. In: Biere, A., Bloem, R. (eds.) CAV 2014. LNCS, vol. 8559, pp. 696–710. Springer, Cham (2014). doi:10.1007/978-3-319-08867-9_46

22. Weidenbach, C.: Towards an automatic analysis of security protocols in first-order logic. CADE 1999. LNCS, vol. 1632, pp. 314–328. Springer, Heidelberg (1999). doi:10.1007/3-540-48660-7_29

23. Weidenbach, C., Dimova, D., Fietzke, A., Kumar, R., Suda, M., Wischnewski, P.: SPASS version 3.5. In: Schmidt, R.A. (ed.) CADE 2009. LNCS (LNAI), vol. 5663, pp. 140–145. Springer, Heidelberg (2009). doi:10.1007/978-3-642-02959-2_10

Efficient Certified RAT Verification

Luís Cruz-Filipe[1(✉)], Marijn J.H. Heule[2], Warren A. Hunt Jr.[2],
Matt Kaufmann[2], and Peter Schneider-Kamp[1]

[1] Department of Mathematics and Computer Science,
University of Southern Denmark, Odense, Denmark
{lcf,petersk}@imada.sdu.dk
[2] Department of Computer Science, The University of Texas at Austin, Austin, USA
{marijn,hunt,kaufmann}@cs.utexas.edu

Abstract. Clausal proofs have become a popular approach to validate the results of SAT solvers. However, validating clausal proofs in the most widely supported format (DRAT) is expensive even in highly optimized implementations. We present a new format, called LRAT, which extends the DRAT format with hints that facilitate a simple and fast validation algorithm. Checking validity of LRAT proofs can be implemented using trusted systems such as the languages supported by theorem provers. We demonstrate this by implementing two certified LRAT checkers, one in Coq and one in ACL2.

1 Introduction

Satisfiability (SAT) solvers are used in many applications in academia and industry, for example to check the correctness of hardware and software [5,8,9]. A bug in such a SAT solver could result in an invalid claim that some hardware or software model is correct. In order to deal with this trust issue, we believe a SAT solver should produce a proof of unsatisfiability [17]. In turn, this proof can and should be validated with a trusted checker. In this paper we will present a method and tools to do this efficiently.

Early work on proofs of unsatisfiability focused on resolution proofs [14,32]. In short, a resolution proof states how every new clause can be constructed using resolution steps. Resolution proofs are easy to validate, but difficult and costly to produce from today's SAT solvers [19]. Moreover, several state-of-the-art solvers use techniques, such as automated re-encoding [25] and symmetry breaking [11,20], that go beyond resolution, and therefore cannot be expressed using resolution proofs.

An alternative method is to produce *clausal proofs* [15,18,29], that is, sequences of steps that each modify the current formula by specifying the deletion of an existing clause or the addition of a new clause. Such proofs are supported by all state-of-the-art SAT solvers [6]. The most widely supported clausal proof

---

Supported by the National Science Foundation under grant CCF-1526760 and by the Danish Council for Independent Research, Natural Sciences, grant DFF-1323-00247.

L. de Moura (Ed.): CADE 2017, LNAI 10395, pp. 220–236, 2017.
DOI: 10.1007/978-3-319-63046-5_14

format is called DRAT [16], which is the format required by the recent SAT competitions[1]. The DRAT proof format was designed to make it as easy as possible to produce proofs, in order to make it easy for implementations to support it [31]. DRAT checkers increase the confidence in the correctness of unsatisfiability results, but there is still room for improvement, i.e., by checking the result using a highly-trusted system [10,22,28]. The only mechanically-verified checkers for DRAT [30] or RUP [14] are too slow for practical use. This holds for certified SAT solving [7,26,27] as well.

Our tool chain works as follows. When a SAT solver produces a clausal proof of unsatisfiability for a given formula, we validate this proof using a fast noncertified proof checker, which then produces an optimized proof with hints. Then, using a certified checker, we validate that the optimized proof is indeed a valid proof for the original formula. We do not need to trust whether the original proof is correct. In fact, the non-certified checker might even produce an optimized proof from an incorrect proof: since our non-certified checker trims the proof starting from the step that added the empty clause and chaining back through the steps that are necessary to support that step, if the proof contains incorrect steps that are not needed to support the addition of the empty clause, these will be ignored.

Validating clausal proofs is potentially expensive [31]. For each clause addition step in a proof of unsatisfiability, unit clause propagation (explained below) should result in a conflict when performed on the current formula, based on an assignment obtained by negating the clause to be added. Thus, we may need to propagate thousands of unit clauses to check the validity of a single clause addition step. Scanning over the formula thousands of times for a single check would be very expensive. This problem has been mitigated through the use of watch pointers. However, validating clausal proofs is often costly even with watch pointers.

In this paper we first present the new expressive proof format LRAT and afterwards show that this proof format enables the development of efficient certified proof checkers. This work builds upon previous work of some of the coauthors [12], as the LRAT format and the certified Coq checker presented here extend the GRIT format and the certified Coq checker presented there, respectively. Additionally, we implemented an efficient certified checker in the ACL2 theorem proving system, extending [30].

The LRAT format poses several restrictions on the syntax in order to make validation as fast as possible. Each clause in the proof must be suitably sorted. This allows a simple check that the clause does not contain duplicate or complementary literals. Hints are also sorted in such a way that they become unit from left to right. Finally, resolution candidates are sorted by increasing clause index; this allows scanning the formula once.

This paper is structured as follows. In Sect. 2 we briefly recapitulate the checking procedure for clausal proofs based on the DRAT format. The novel LRAT format is introduced in Sect. 3. Section 4 presents an algorithm for

---

[1] see http://satcompetition.org.

verifying LRAT proofs, and discusses its worst-case complexity. We demonstrate the benefits of LRAT by extracting two certified checkers for the format: one in Coq (Sect. 5) and one in ACL2 (Sect. 6). We evaluate the checkers and the potential of LRAT in Sect. 7. Finally, we draw some conclusions in Sect. 8.

Related Work. Independent of our work, Peter Lammich has developed a new format called GRAT and a certified checker based on Isabelle/HOL [23]. Both GRAT and LRAT build on the ideas from [12] and enrich DRAT proofs in the same way. As a consequence, there are now three different certified checkers for enriched DRAT proofs based on three major theorem provers. While equivalent from a theoretical standpoint, these checkers differ by tool chains, performance characteristics, and the extents and contents of the trusted base.

2   Background on Clausal Proof Checking

Consider a *formula*, or set of *clauses* implicitly conjoined, where each clause is a list of *literals* (Boolean proposition letters or their negations), implicitly disjoined. Satisfiability (SAT) solvers decide the question of whether a given formula is *satisfiable*, that is, true under some assignment of *true* and *false* values to the Boolean proposition letters of the formula. A formula is *unsatisfiable* if there is no assignment under which the formula is *true*.

Example 1. Consider the formula below, which we will use as a running example:

$$F = (x_1 \lor x_2 \lor \neg x_3) \land (\neg x_1 \lor \neg x_2 \lor x_3) \land (x_2 \lor x_3 \lor \neg x_4) \land (\neg x_2 \lor \neg x_3 \lor x_4) \land$$
$$(\neg x_1 \lor \neg x_3 \lor \neg x_4) \land (x_1 \lor x_3 \lor x_4) \land (\neg x_1 \lor x_2 \lor x_4) \land (x_1 \lor \neg x_2 \lor \neg x_4)$$

Each step in a clausal proof is either the addition or the deletion of a clause. Each clause addition step should preserve satisfiability; this should be checkable in polynomial time. The polynomial time checking procedure is described in detail below. Clause deletion steps need not be checked, because they trivially preserve satisfiability. The main reason to include clause deletion steps in proofs is to reduce the computational and memory costs to validate proofs.

A clause with only one literal is called a unit clause. Unit clauses are used to simplify CNF formulas via an algorithm called Unit Clause Propagation (UCP). UCP works as follows: for each unit clause (l), all other clauses containing l are removed from the formula, and all literal occurrences of $\bar{l}$ are removed from all clauses in the formula. Notice that this can result in new unit clauses. UCP terminates when either no literals can be removed, or when it results in a conflict, i.e., all literals in a clause have been removed.

If C is a clause, then $\overline{C}$ denotes its negation, which is a conjunction of all negated literals in C. A clause C has the property Asymmetric Tautology (AT) with respect to a CNF formula F iff UCP on $F \land (\overline{C})$ results in a conflict. This operational definition is also known as Reverse Unit Propagation (RUP). The core property used in the DRAT format is Resolution Asymmetric Tautology (RAT). A clause C has the RAT property with respect to a CNF formula F

if either it has the AT property, or there exists a literal $l \in C$ (the *pivot*) such that for all clauses D in F with $\neg l \in D$, the clause $C \vee (D \setminus \{\neg l\})$ has the property AT with respect to F. In this case, C can be added to F while preserving satisfiability. The proof of this last property is included in our formalization.

DRAT proof checking works as follows. Let F be the input formula and P be the clausal proof. At each step i, the formula is modified. The initial state is: $F_0 = F$. At step $i > 0$, the ith line of P is read. If the line has the prefix d, then the clause C described on that line is removed: $F_i = F_{i-1} \setminus \{C\}$. Otherwise, if there is no prefix, then C must have the RAT property with respect to formula F_{i-1}. This must be validated. If the RAT property can be validated, then the clause is added to the formula: $F_i = F_{i-1} \wedge C$. If the validation fails, then the proof is invalid.

The empty clause, typically at the end of the proof, should have the AT property, as it does not have a first literal.

3   Introducing the LRAT Format

The Linear RAT (LRAT) proof format is based on the RAT property, and it is designed to make proof checking as straightforward as possible. The purpose of LRAT proofs is to facilitate the implementation of proof validation software using highly trusted systems such as theorem provers. An LRAT proof can be produced when checking a DRAT proof with a non-certified checker (cf. the end of this section).[2]

The most costly operation during clausal proof validation is finding the unit clauses during unit propagation. The GRIT format [12] removes this problem by requiring proofs to include hints that list all unit clauses. This makes it much easier and faster to validate proofs, because the checker no longer needs to find the unit clauses. However, the GRIT format does not allow checking of all possible clauses that can be learned by today's SAT solvers and are expressible in the DRAT format.

The LRAT format extends the GRIT format to remove this limitation, by adding support for checking the addition of clauses justified by the non-trivial case of the RAT property. For efficiency, the LRAT format requires that all clauses containing the negated pivot be specified. Furthermore, for each resolvent it has to be specified how to perform UCP, as is done for AT in the GRIT approach. In addition, the pivot must be the first literal in the clause being added.

While the LRAT format is semantically an extension of the GRIT format, we updated two aspects. First, the clauses from the original CNF are *not* included, as this required verification that these clauses do indeed occur in the original

---

[2] DRAT proofs and LRAT proofs are syntactic objects that do not necessarily represent valid proofs. However, they are produced by tools that should only generate objects that correspond to semantically valid proofs, so we adopt this terminology. By "validating a DRAT/LRAT proof", we mean verifying by independent means that such an object indeed represents a valid proof.

224   L. Cruz-Filipe et al.

CNF formula	DRUP format	GRIT format	LRAT format
p cnf 4 8	<u>1</u> <u>2</u> 0	1 1 2 -3 0 0	9 <u>1 2</u> 0 <u>1</u> <u>6</u> <u>3</u> 0
1 2 -3 0	d 1 -3 2 0	2 -1 -2 3 0 0	9 d 1 0
-1 -2 3 0	<u>1</u> <u>3</u> 0	3 2 3 -4 0 0	10 <u>1 3</u> 0 <u>9</u> <u>8</u> <u>6</u> 0
2 3 -4 0	d 1 4 3 0	4 -2 -3 4 0 0	10 d 6 0
-2 -3 4 0	<u>1</u> 0	5 -1 -3 -4 0 0	11 <u>1 0</u> <u>10</u> <u>9</u> <u>4</u> <u>8</u> 0
-1 -3 -4 0	d 1 3 0	6 1 3 4 0 0	11 d 10 9 8 0
1 3 4 0	d 1 2 0	7 -1 2 4 0 0	12 <u>2 0</u> <u>11</u> <u>7</u> <u>5</u> <u>3</u> 0
-1 2 4 0	d 1 -4 -2 0	8 1 -2 -4 0 0	12 d 7 3 0
1 -2 -4 0	<u>2</u> 0	9 <u>1 2</u> 0 <u>1</u> <u>6</u> <u>3</u> 0	13 0 <u>11</u> <u>12</u> <u>2</u> <u>4</u> <u>5</u> 0
	d -1 4 2 0	0 1 0	
	d 2 -4 3 0	10 <u>1 3</u> 0 <u>9</u> <u>8</u> <u>6</u> 0	
	<u>0</u>	0 6 0	
		11 <u>1 0</u> <u>10</u> <u>9</u> <u>4</u> <u>8</u> 0	
		0 10 9 8 0	
		12 <u>2 0</u> <u>11</u> <u>7</u> <u>5</u> <u>3</u> 0	
		0 7 3 0	
		13 0 <u>11</u> <u>12</u> <u>2</u> <u>4</u> <u>5</u> 0	

Fig. 1. A CNF formula and three similar proofs of unsatisfiability in the DRUP, GRIT and LRAT format, respectively. Formula clauses are shown in normal font, deletion information in italic, learned clauses underlined, and unit propagation information doubly underlined. The proofs do not have clauses based on the RAT property. The spacing shown aims to improve readability, but extra spacing does not effect the meaning of a LRAT file.

CNF. The advantage of working only with a subset of clauses from the original CNF can be achieved by starting with a deletion step for clauses not relevant for the proof. Second, the syntax of the deletion information has been extended to include a clause identifier. To be recognized, deletion statements are now identified with lines that start with an index followed by "d". This change makes the format stable under permutations of lines. In practice, checkers expect proof statements in ascending order, which easily can be achieved by sorting the lines numerically. Stability under permutation is useful, as non-certified checkers performing backward analysis often output the steps in a different order than the one needed. This property ensures that e.g. deletions are performed at the right point of time.

To demonstrate these two changes, we first consider an example, which does *not* require the RAT property. Figure 1 shows an original CNF, the DRUP proof obtained by a SAT solver, the GRIT version of that proof, and, finally, the equivalent LRAT proof.

To specify the addition of a clause justified by the RAT property, we extend the format used for the AT property in GRIT. The line starts with the clause identifier of the new clause followed by the 0-terminated new clause. The first literal of the new clause is required to be the pivot literal. Next, for each clause with clause identifier i containing the negated pivot, we specify the (negative)

CNF formula	DRAT format	LRAT format
p cnf 4 8	<u>1 0</u>	9 <u>1 0</u> -2 <u>6 8</u> -5 <u>1 8</u> -7 <u>6 1</u> 0
1 2 -3 0	d *1 -4 -2 0*	9 d *8 6 1* 0
-1 -2 3 0	d *1 4 3 0*	10 <u>2 0</u> <u>9 7 5 3</u> 0
2 3 -4 0	d *1 2 -3 0*	10 d *7 3* 0
-2 -3 4 0	<u>2 0</u>	11 <u>0</u> <u>9 10 2 4 5</u> 0
-1 -3 -4 0	d *-1 2 4 0*	
1 3 4 0	d *2 -4 3 0*	
-1 2 4 0	<u>0</u>	
1 -2 -4 0		

Fig. 2. The LRAT format with the RAT property (with original clauses in normal font, deletion information in italic, learned clauses underlined, unit propagation information doubly underlined, and resolution clauses in bold).

integer $-i$ followed by a (possibly empty) list of (positive) clause identifiers used in UCP of the new clause with clause i.

For example, consider the first line of the LRAT proof in Fig. 2:

$$9 \ \underline{1 \ 0} \ \text{-2} \ \underline{6 \ 8} \ \text{-5} \ \underline{1 \ 8} \ \text{-7} \ \underline{6 \ 1} \ 0$$

The first number, 9 expresses that the new clause will get identifier 9. The numbers in between the identifier and the first 0 are the literals in the clause. In clause of clause 9 this is only literal 1. The first 0 is followed by the hints. All hints are clause identifiers or their negations. Positive hints express that the clause becomes unit or falsified. Negative hints express that the clause is a candidate for a RAT check, i.e., it contains the complement of the pivot. In the example line, there are three such negative hints: -2, -5, and -7. The LRAT format prescribes that negative literals are listed in increasing order of their absolute value.

After a negative hint, there may be positive hints that list the identifiers of clauses that become unit and eventually falsified. For example, assigning false to the literal in the new clause (1) and to the literals in the second clause apart from the negated pivot (2 and -3) causes the sixth clause to become unit (4), which in turn falsifies the eigth clause.

There are two extensions to this kind of simple RAT checking. (1) It is possible that there are no positive hints following a negative hint. In this case, the new clause and the candidate for a RAT check have two pairs of complementary literals. (2) It is also possible that some positive hints are listed before the first negative hint. In this case, these clauses (i.e., whose identifiers are listed) become unit after assigning the literals in the new clause to false.

The full syntax of the LRAT format is given by the grammar in Fig. 3, where, for the sake of sanity, whitespace (tabs and spaces) is ignored. Note that,

$$\begin{aligned}
\langle proof \rangle &= \{\langle line \rangle\} \\
\langle line \rangle &= (\langle rat \rangle \mid \langle delete \rangle), \text{``}\backslash n\text{''} \\
\langle rat \rangle &= \langle id \rangle, \langle clause \rangle, \text{``}0\text{''}, \langle idlist \rangle, \{\langle res \rangle\}, \text{``}0\text{''} \\
\langle delete \rangle &= \langle id \rangle, \text{``}d\text{''}, \langle idlist \rangle, \text{``}0\text{''} \\
\langle res \rangle &= \langle neg \rangle, \langle idlist \rangle \\
\langle idlist \rangle &= \{\langle id \rangle\} \\
\langle id \rangle &= \langle pos \rangle \\
\langle lit \rangle &= \langle pos \rangle \mid \langle neg \rangle \\
\langle pos \rangle &= \text{``}1\text{''} \mid \text{``}2\text{''} \mid \ldots \\
\langle neg \rangle &= \text{``-''}, \langle pos \rangle \\
\langle clause \rangle &= \{\langle lit \rangle\}, \text{``}0\text{''}
\end{aligned}$$

Fig. 3. EBNF grammar for the LRAT format.

syntactically, AT and RAT lines are both covered by RAT lines. AT is just the special case where there is a non-empty list of only positive hints.

Producing LRAT proofs directly from SAT solvers would add significant overhead both in runtime and memory usage, and it might require the addition of complicated code. Instead, we extended the DRAT-trim proof checker [16] to emit LRAT proofs. DRAT-trim already supported the emitting of optimized proofs in the DRAT and TraceCheck+ formats. DRAT-trim emits an LRAT proof after validation of a proof using the "-L proof.lrat" option.

We implemented an uncertified checker for LRAT in C that achieves runtimes comparable to the one from [12] on proofs without RAT lines.

4   Verifying LRAT Proofs

We now discuss how to check an LRAT proof. The algorithm we present takes as input a formula in CNF and an LRAT proof, and returns:

- YES, indicating that the proof has successfully been checked, and a new CNF, which is satisfiable if the input CNF was satisfiable;
- or NO, indicating that the proof could not be checked.

We are thus able both to check unsatisfiability (if the formula returned in the first case contains the empty clause) and addition of clauses preserving satisfiability.

The algorithm assumes a CNF to be a finite map from a set of positive integers to clauses. We write C_i for the clause with index i. The main step is checking individual RAT steps, which is done by Algorithm CHECK_RAT. We use the notation $\tilde{i}$ to denote a list $[i_1, \ldots, i_n]$.

Lines 4–10 perform UCP on $\varphi \wedge \overline{C_j}$ using the clauses referred to by $i_1^0, \ldots, i_n^0$. If the empty clause is derived at some stage, then C_j has the AT property w.r.t. φ. Otherwise, we store the extended clause C and let p be its first element (line 12). We then check that this clause has the RAT property: we go through all clauses in φ; lines 14 and 15 deal with the trivial cases, while lines 18–24 again perform UCP to show that C' has the AT property. If the algorithm terminates

---

Algorithm 1. Checking a single RAT step

1: **procedure** CHECK_RAT(φ, ℓ) $\triangleright$ $\varphi = \{C_i\}_{i \in \mathcal{I}}$ is a CNF, ℓ is a RAT step
2:   parse ℓ as $\left[j, C_j, 0, \widetilde{i^0}, \{-i^k, \widetilde{i^k}\}_{k=1}^n \right]$
3:           $\triangleright$ instantiate all variables as (vectors of) positive integers
4:   $C \leftarrow C_j$ $\triangleright$ recall that clauses are lists of literals
5:   **for all** $i \in \widetilde{i^0}$ **do**
6:    $C'_i \leftarrow C_i \setminus C$
7:    **if** $C'_i = \emptyset$ **then return** YES
8:    **if** $|C'_i| \geq 2$ **then return** NO
9:    $C \leftarrow C{+\!+}\bar{C}'_i$ $\triangleright$ we use $+\!+$ for append
10:   **end for**
11:   **if** $C = \emptyset$ **then return** NO
12:   $p \leftarrow (C)_1$
13:   **for all** $i \in \mathcal{I}$ **do**
14:    **if** C_i does not contain $\bar{p}$ **then skip**
15:    **if** C_i and C contain dual literals aside from p and $\bar{p}$ **then skip**
16:    find j such that $i^j = i$ (from ℓ)
17:    **if** no such j exists **then return** NO
18:    $C' \leftarrow C{+\!+}(C_i \setminus \{\bar{p}\})$
19:    **for all** $m \in \widetilde{i^j}$ **do**
20:     $C'_m \leftarrow C_m \setminus C'$
21:     **if** $C'_m = \emptyset$ **then skip** to next iteration of line 14
22:     **if** $|C'_m| \geq 2$ **then return** NO
23:     $C' \leftarrow C'{+\!+}\bar{C}'_m$
24:    **end for**
25:    **return** NO
26:   **end for**
27:   **return** YES
28: **end procedure**

Algorithm 2. Checking an LRAT proof

1: **procedure** CHECK_LRAT(φ, p) $\triangleright$ $\varphi = \{C_i\}_{i \in \mathcal{I}}$ is a CNF, p is an LRAT proof
2:   **for all** lines ℓ of p **do**
3:    **if** ℓ can be parsed as $\langle delete \rangle$ **then**
4:     remove all clauses C_i with $i \in \langle idlist \rangle$ from φ
5:    **end if**
6:    **if** ℓ can be parsed as $\langle rat \rangle$ **then** $\triangleright$ ℓ is $\left[j, C_j, 0, \widetilde{i^0}, \{-i^k, \widetilde{i^k}\}_{k=1}^n \right]$
7:     call CHECK_RAT(φ, ℓ)
8:     **if** the result is YES, **then** add C_j to φ
9:     **if** the result is NO, **then return** NO
10:    **else**
11:     **return** NO
12:    **end if**
13:   **end for**
14:   **return** YES and φ
15: **end procedure**

---

and returns YES, we have successfully verified that C_j satisfies the RAT property with respect to φ.

Algorithm CHECK_LRAT verifies an LRAT proof by giving each line denoting a RAT step to Algorithm CHECK_RAT.

Lemma 1 (Termination). *Algorithm* CHECK_LRAT *always terminates.*

Proof. Straightforward, as all cycles in both algorithms are **for** loops.

Theorem 1 (Soundness). *If the result of running* CHECK_LRAT *on* φ *and an LRAT proof is* YES *and* φ', *then: (i) all the steps in the LRAT proof are valid, and (ii) if* φ *is satisfiable, then* φ' *is also satisfiable.*

We skip the proof of this theorem, as this algorithm has been directly translated to ACL2 and proved sound therein (Sect. 6).

We now discuss the complexity of these algorithms. We assume efficient data structures, so that e.g. finding an element in a collection can be done in time logarithmic in the number of elements in the collection. In particular, literals in clauses are ordered, and we have constant-time access to any position in a clause. The main challenge is analysing the complexity of a single RAT check.

Lemma 2. *Algorithm* CHECK_RAT *runs in time*

$$\mathcal{O}\left(|\mathcal{I}| \cdot |\ell| \cdot (\log|\mathcal{I}| + c \cdot \log(\max(c, |\ell|)))\right),$$

where c *is the number of literals in the longest clause in* φ *and* $|\ell|$ *is the length of the input line.*

Proof. Lines 4, 11, 12 and 27 can obviously be done in constant time, while line 2 can be done in time linear in $|\ell|$. Furthermore, the loop in lines 5–10 is the same as that in lines 19–24 (starting with $|C| \leq |C'|$), so the worst-case asymptotic complexity of the whole algorithm is that of the loop in lines 13–26.

When reaching line 13, $|C| \leq |\ell|$: each literal in C comes either from C_j (which is part of ℓ) or from one iteration of the loop in lines 5–10, whose hint is obtained from ℓ. Similarly, $|C'| \leq c + |\ell|$ throughout the whole cycle: its literals come either from $C_i \in \varphi$, from C, or from an iteration of the loop in lines 19–24, whose hint is in a different part of ℓ than that used to build C.

Line 14 requires looking for a literal in C_i, which can be done in time $\mathcal{O}(\log c)$. Line 15 requires looking for $|C_i|$ literals in C, which can be done in time $\mathcal{O}(c \cdot \log(|\ell|))$. Line 16 requires finding an index in the data structure generated from ℓ in line 2, which can be done in time $\mathcal{O}(\log|\ell|)$. Lines 17, 18 and 25 can be done in constant time.

We now analyze the loop in lines 19–24, observing that it is executed at most $|\ell|$ times. The loop begins by retrieving C_m from φ, which can be done in time $\mathcal{O}(\log|\mathcal{I}|)$ if we assume CNFs to be stored e.g. in a binary tree. Line 20 then removes all elements of C' from C_m, which can be done efficiently by going through C_m and checking whether each element is in C'; this has a global complexity of $\mathcal{O}(c \cdot \log(c + |\ell|))$. (Note that, in the successful case – the one we are interested in – the result is always the empty clause or a single literal.) All the remaining lines can be done in constant time, so the total time required by the loop in lines 19–24 is $\mathcal{O}(|\ell|(\log|\mathcal{I}| + c \cdot \log(c + |\ell|)))$.

Since the loop in lines 13–26 is executed $|\mathcal{I}|$ times, the total time for the whole algorithm is thus

$$\mathcal{O}\left(|\mathcal{I}| \cdot (\log c + c \cdot \log|\ell| + \log|\ell| + |\ell|(\log|\mathcal{I}| + c \cdot \log(c + |\ell|)))\right).$$

Since both $\log c$ and $\log|\ell|$ are bounded by $\log(c + |\ell|)$, we can replace $\log c + c \cdot \log(c + |\ell|) + \log|\ell|$ by $(c + 2)\log(c + |\ell|)$, obtaining

$$\mathcal{O}\left(|\mathcal{I}| \cdot ((c + 2) \cdot \log(c + |\ell|) + |\ell|(\log|\mathcal{I}| + c \cdot \log(c + |\ell|)))\right)$$

which we can simplify to

$$\mathcal{O}\left(|\mathcal{I}| \cdot (|\ell| \log|\mathcal{I}| + (|\ell| + 2) \cdot c \cdot \log(c + |\ell|))\right)$$

or, equivalently,

$$\mathcal{O}\left(|\mathcal{I}| \cdot |\ell| \cdot (\log|\mathcal{I}| + c \cdot \log(c + |\ell|))\right)$$

since $|\ell|$ and $|\ell| + 2$ are asymptotically equivalent. Observing that $\log(c + |\ell|) \leq \log(2(\max(c, |\ell|))) = \log(2) + \log(\max(c, |\ell|))$ yields the bound in the lemma.

Theorem 2 (Complexity). *The complexity of checking an LRAT proof is*

$$\mathcal{O}\left(n \cdot (|\mathcal{I}| + n) \cdot l \left(\log(|\mathcal{I}| + n) + k \cdot \log k\right)\right)$$

where n is the number of lines in the DRAT proof, l is the length of the longest line in the proof, $\mathcal{I}$ and c are as before, and $k = \max(c, l)$.

Proof. The bound follows from observing that the loop in Algorithm CHECK_LRAT is executed n times (in case of success); in the worst case, all steps are RAT steps, adding one clause to φ (hence the increase in $|\mathcal{I}|$ to $|\mathcal{I}| + n$) and potentially making the size of the longest clause in φ increase to l (hence raising the multiplicative factor from c to k in the rightmost logarithmic term).

We make some observations. If we allow only the lengths of the proof n to grow while keeping all other parameters fixed, the asymptotic complexity of CHECK_LRAT is $\mathcal{O}(n^2 \log n)$. Similarly, if we compare proofs of the same length but consider variations of the length of the clauses in the original CNF, the asymptotic complexity is $O(c \log c)$. In practice, we observe that algorithm CHECK_RAT typically terminates in line 7; in these cases, the bound in Lemma 2 can be improved to $\mathcal{O}(|\ell| \cdot (\log|\mathcal{I}| + c \log c))$.

5   Checking LRAT Proofs in Coq

Our development of a verifier of LRAT proofs in Coq does not follow Algorithm CHECK_LRAT directly. This is due to the fact that we had previously developed a certified checker for GRIT proofs [12], by extracting an OCaml program from a Coq formalization, and we opted for extending this construction. In particular, the addition of clauses justified by AT (where CHECK_RAT returns YES in line 7) is verified using the original checker.

The complexity of checking the RAT property in our development is better than the theoretical upper bound, because we preprocess the LRAT proof and add additional information to bypass line 15 when it fails. (This preprocessing amounts to checking the proof with an untrusted verifier, so the overall complexity including this line is still that of Theorem 2.) The rationale for this preprocessing is that there is a big overhead in using extracted data structures (see [24]), which means that, even if the overall complexity of the extracted checker is optimal, there are large constants that slow down the checker's performance in practice. We work with a pure extracted program, where all data structures are extracted from their Coq formalizations.[3] This means, in particular, that we do not have lists with direct access. Thus, clauses are represented as binary search trees, which allows most of the operations to have optimal complexity; the exception is the addition in lines 9, 18 and 23, which takes time logarithmic in the size of the original clause, but which is dominated by other steps in the corresponding cycles.

Our experiments show that, with the optimizations enabled by preprocessing, this checker is fast enough to be used in the largest instances available.

The development of the checker in [12] is modular, with different functions that verify each type of line in a GRIT proof. We thus extended this set of functions with a function RAT_check that verifies RAT lines. This function implements a modified variant of Algorithm CHECK_RAT: the enriched proof indicates whether we should execute line 15 (and if so, it tells us which literal to look for). Its soundness theorem states that, if the check succeeds, then the clause given can be added to the CNF preserving satisfiability. The term c is the given CNF, while the clause C_j is pivot::cl (so the pivot is already singled out), and L contains the remaining information in the line justifying the RAT step.

Theorem RAT_theorem : $\forall$ c pivot cl L, RAT_check c pivot cl L = true $\rightarrow$
    $\forall$ V, satisfies V c $\rightarrow$
    $\exists$ V, satisfies V (CNF_add (pivot::cl) c).

(For readability, we omit type injections from the Coq listings.)

We then enrich the overall loop to include the case where the proof includes RAT lines, and reprove the correctness of the main function refute from [12], whose task it is to prove unsatisfiability of a given formula. Its arguments are only the CNF c (given as a list of pairs index/clause) and the preprocessed LRAT proof (whose type is formalized as Oracle).

Theorem refute_correct : $\forall$ (c:list (ad * Clause)) (O:Oracle),
    refute c O = true $\rightarrow$ unsat c.

---

[3] With the exception of integers, which are only used as labels and therefore can be extracted to a native type without compromising soundness of the extracted code.

By extracting `refute`, we again obtain a correct-by-construction checker for proofs of unsatisfiability using the full LRAT format. If this checker returns `true` when given a particular CNF and proof, this guarantees that the CNF is indeed unsatisfiable. The universal quantification over the oracle ensures that any errors in its implementation (and in particular in the interface connecting it to the checker) do not affect the correctness of this answer.

Satisfiability-preserving addition of clauses. Algorithm CHECK_LRAT is formulated not in terms of unsatisfiability, but of preservation of satisfiability – with unsatisfiability being a particular case where the empty clause is added. In order to provide this functionality, we tweaked our checker to return a pair consisting of a boolean value and a CNF. In the base case (when the input proof is empty), the checker now returns `true` (instead of `false`) together with the CNF currently stored. If the empty clause is derived at some point, the checker still returns `true` as before, but now together with a CNF containing only the empty clause. If any step fails, we return `false` and also provide the formula currently stored (which results from applying the longest initial segment of the LRAT proof that is verifiable); otherwise we proceed as before.

With these changes, we can still verify unsatisfiability as before, but we can also provide a target CNF and check that the oracle provides a correct reduction from the initial CNF to the target. Function `enrich` offers this new functionality.

```
Theorem enrich_correct : ∀ (c c':list (ad * Clause)) (O:Oracle),
   enrich c c' O = true → ICNF_reduces c c'.
```

(The predicate `ICNF_reduces` states that any valuation satisfying c can be used to construct a valuation satisfying c'.)

Results. After adapting the interface to be able to transform proofs in the full LRAT format into the oracle syntax defined above, we tested the extracted checker on 225 unsatisfiability proofs output by SAT solvers supporting RAT proofs. See Sect. 7 for further details.

We also used the possibility of adding new clauses to check the transformation proof from [21], the only SAT-related step in the original proof of the Boolean Pythagorean Triples problem that we were unable to verify in [12]. The certified LRAT checker in Coq was able to verify this proof in 8 minutes and 25 s, including approx. 15 s for checking that the formula generated by the proof coincides with the formula produced by the original SAT solver.

6   LRAT Checker in ACL2

In this section, in order to demonstrate the general applicability of our approach, we extended the original ACL2-based DRAT checker [30] to permit the checking of UNSAT proofs in the LRAT format. We have certified this extension using the ACL2 theorem-proving system.

We outline our formalization below using the Lisp-style ACL2 syntax, with comments to assist readers unfamiliar with Lisp syntax. Note that embedded comments begin with a ";" character and continue to the end of a line.

We omit the code here but note that it has been optimized for efficiency. In particular, applicative hash tables represent formulas, and are heuristically cleaned on occasion after deletion; and mutable objects [2] are used for assignments. These techniques reduce the complexity substantially. Of course, correctness of such optimizations was necessarily proved as part of the overall correctness proof. The code and top-level theorem are available from the top-level file `top.lisp` in the full proof development [4], included in the GitHub repository [3] that holds ACL2 and its libraries. Also see the `README` file in that directory. Here we focus primarily on the statement of correctness.

The top-level correctness theorem is as follows.

```
(defthm main-theorem
  (implies
    (and (formula-p formula)              ; Valid formula and
         (refutation-p proof formula))    ; Valid proof with empty clause
    (not (satisfiable formula))))         ; Imply unsatisfiable
```

The command `defthm` is an ACL2 system command that demands that the ACL2 theorem-proving system establish the validity of the claim that follows the name (in this case `main-theorem`) of the theorem to be checked.

The theorem above is expressed in terms of the three functions `formula-p`, `refutation-p`, and `satisfiable`. The first of these recognizes structures that represent sets of clauses; our particular representation uses applicative hash tables [1]. The function `refutation-p` recognizes valid proofs that yield a contradiction; thus, it calls other functions, including one that performs the necessary RAT checks. We verify an alleged proof by checking that each of its steps preserves satisfiability.

Finally, we define `satisfiable` to mean that there exists an assignment satisfying a given formula. The first definition says that the given assignment satisfies the given formula, while the second uses an existential quantifier to say that *some* assignment satisfies the given formula.

```
(defun solution-p (assignment formula)
  (and (clause-or-assignment-p assignment)
       (formula-truep formula assignment)))
```

```
(defun-sk satisfiable (formula)
  (exists assignment (solution-p assignment formula)))
```

Before our SAT proof checker can be called, an LRAT-style proof is read from a file, and during the reading process it is converted into an internal Lisp format that is used by our checker. Using the ACL2 theorem prover, we have verified the theorem `main-theorem` above, which states that our code correctly checks the validity of a proof of the empty clause.

Results. The ACL2 checker is able to check the validity of adding each of the 68,667 clauses in the transformation proof from [21] in less than 9 s. The certified checking of this LRAT proof is almost as fast as non-certified checking and conversion of the DRAT proof into the LRAT proof by DRAT-trim. This is a testament to the efficiency potential of the LRAT format in particular, and the approach taken in our work in general. At the moment of writing, the correspondence between the formula generated by the original SAT solver and by executing the proof has not been ported yet to the ACL2 checker, but this can easily be added in a similar way as we did for the Coq checker.

7   Experimental Evaluation

In order to evaluate the potential of the LRAT format, we performed extensive experiments on benchmarks from the 2016 SAT competition and the 2015 SAT race. The set of instances we considered consists of the 241 instances from the main and parallel tracks that could be shown to be UNSAT within 5,000 s using the 2016 competition version of CryptoMiniSat v5 [13]. (CryptoMiniSat was the only solver from this competition where we were able to obtain a non-trivial number of RAT lines in most proofs.) All experiments were performed on identical nodes equipped with dual Intel Xeon E5-2680v3 running at 2.50 GHz with 64 GByte RAM on CentOS with a 3.10.0 Linux kernel.

For each of these instances, the original CNF and proof were first trimmed and optimized and then output in LRAT using drat-trim in backward checking mode. A total of 225 out the 241 instances could be successfully processed by drat-trim within 20,000 s. Out of the remaining 16 instances, 12 timed out, 3 resulted in a segmentation fault and 1 proof could not be verified. In total there were 381,468,814 lines in the 225 proofs totalling 250 GByte, out of which 3,260,037 were non-trivial RAT lines.

The Coq checker verified 161 out of these 225 instances within a maximum runtime of 24 h. For the remaining 64 instances, it timed out (59), ran out of memory (1), or determined that the proof was invalid (4). The 161 verified proofs amount to a total of 88 GByte and were processed in just under 3 weeks of CPU time, or in other words at an average speed of 3 MByte per minute.

The ACL2 checker verified 212 out of the 225 instances within a maximum runtime of 6,708 s, typically being at least an order of magnitude faster than the Coq checker. For the remaining 13 instances, it ran out of memory (1), terminated unexpectedly[4] (1), or determined that the proofs were invalid (11). The 212 verified proofs amount to a total of 205 GByte and were processed in just under 17 h of CPU time, or in other words at an average speed of 207 MByte per minute.

The alleged LRAT proofs for the 11 instances where verification using the ACL2 checker failed range in size from 50 MByte to 6.4 GByte. The Coq checker

---

[4] Termination seems to occur due to an error condition of the underlying LISP runtime system (CCL) used, and could not be reproduced using another system (SBCL).

either agrees with the result (7) or times out (4). We then inspected the smallest alleged proofs by hand and found that they indeed are not valid LRAT proofs.

Given the size of the proofs involved, determining the reason for a failed verification is definitely a challenge. When the non-certified checker claims that it successfully verified the proof, but outputs an LRAT proof that cannot be verified by the certified checker, it seems reasonable to assume that at least the non-certified checker has bugs. This is because the non-certified checker does not only transform the proof from one format into another, but also checks the individual steps.

To summarize the experiments, both certified checkers have been found to be able to verify LRAT proofs of up to several GByte within reasonable computational resources. The input data, the executables, and instructions how to rerun the experiments are available from: http://imada.sdu.dk/~petersk/lrat/

8   Conclusions

We have introduced a novel format for clausal proof checking, *Linear RAT* (LRAT), which extends the GRIT format [12] to support checking all techniques used in state-of-the-art SAT solvers. We have shown that it allows for implementing efficient certified proof checkers for UNSAT proofs with the RAT property, both using Coq and using ACL2. The ACL2 LRAT checker is almost as fast as — and in some cases even faster than — non-certified checking by DRAT-trim of the corresponding DRAT proof. This suggests that certified checking can be achieved with a reasonable overhead.

Furthermore, we have shown that our Coq checker's ability to check transformation proofs has allowed us to check the transformation proof from [21], the only SAT-related step in the original proof of the Boolean Pythagorean Triples problem that we were unable to verify in [12].

References

1. ACL2 Community. ACL2 documentation topic: FAST-ALISTS. http://www.cs.utexas.edu/users/moore/acl2/current/manual/index.html?topic=ACL2____FAST-ALISTS
2. ACL2 Community. ACL2 documentation topic: STOBJ. http://www.cs.utexas.edu/users/moore/acl2/v7-2/manual/?topic=ACL2____STOBJ
3. ACL2 Community. ACL2 system and libraries on GitHub. https://github.com/acl2/acl2/
4. ACL2 LRAT checker. https://github.com/acl2/acl2/tree/master/books/projects/sat/lrat/
5. Ivančić, F., Yang, Z., Ganai, M.K., Gupta, A., Ashar, P.: Efficient SAT-based bounded model checking for software verification. Theoretical Computer Science **404**(3), 256–274 (2008)
6. Balyo, T., Heule, M.J.H., Järvisalo, M.: Sat competition 2016: Recent developments. In: AAAI 2017 (2017)

7. Blanchette, J.C., Fleury, M., Weidenbach, C.: A verified SAT solver framework with learn, forget, restart, and incrementality. In: Olivetti, N., Tiwari, A. (eds.) IJCAR 2016. LNCS (LNAI), vol. 9706, pp. 25–44. Springer, Cham (2016). doi:10.1007/978-3-319-40229-1_4

8. Clarke, E.M., Biere, A., Raimi, R., Zhu, Y.: Bounded model checking using satisfiability solving. Formal Methods Syst. Des. 19(1), 7–34 (2001)

9. Copty, F., Fix, L., Fraer, R., Giunchiglia, E., Kamhi, G., Tacchella, A., Vardi, M.Y.: Benefits of bounded model checking at an industrial setting. In: Berry, G., Comon, H., Finkel, A. (eds.) CAV 2001. LNCS, vol. 2102, pp. 436–453. Springer, Heidelberg (2001). doi:10.1007/3-540-44585-4_43

10. The Coq proof assistant. https://coq.inria.fr/

11. Crawford, J., Ginsberg, M., Luks, E., Roy, A.: Symmetry-breaking predicates for search problems. In: $KR\tilde{O}$ 1996, pp. 148–159. Morgan Kaufmann (1996)

12. Cruz-Filipe, L., Marques-Silva, J., Schneider-Kamp, P.: Efficient certified resolution proof checking. In: Legay, A., Margaria, T. (eds.) TACAS 2017. LNCS, vol. 10205, pp. 118–135. Springer, Heidelberg (2017). doi:10.1007/978-3-662-54577-5_7

13. Cryptominisat v5. http://baldur.iti.kit.edu/sat-competition-2016/solvers/main/cmsat5_main2.zip

14. Darbari, A., Fischer, B., Marques-Silva, J.: Industrial-strength certified SAT solving through verified SAT proof checking. In: Cavalcanti, A., Deharbe, D., Gaudel, M.-C., Woodcock, J. (eds.) ICTAC 2010. LNCS, vol. 6255, pp. 260–274. Springer, Heidelberg (2010). doi:10.1007/978-3-642-14808-8_18

15. Goldberg, E.I., Novikov, Y.: Verification of proofs of unsatisfiability for CNF formulas. In: DATE, pp. 10886–10891 (2003)

16. Heule, M.J.H.: The DRAT format and DRAT-trim checker. CoRR, abs/1610.06229 (2016). Source code, https://github.com/marijnheule/drat-trim

17. Heule, M.J.H., Biere, A.: Proofs for satisfiability problems. In: All about Proofs, Proofs for All (APPA), July 2014. http://www.easychair.org/smart-program/VSL2014/APPA-index.html

18. Heule, M.J.H., Hunt Jr., W.A., Wetzler, N.D.: Trimming while checking clausal proofs. In: FMCAD, pp. 181–188 (2013)

19. Heule, M.J.H., Hunt Jr., W.A., Wetzler, N.D.: Bridging the gap between easy generation and efficient verification of unsatisfiability proofs. Softw. Test., Verif. Reliab. 24(8), 593–607 (2014)

20. Heule, M.J.H., Hunt Jr., W.A., Wetzler, N.D.: Expressing symmetry breaking in DRAT proofs. In: Felty, A.P., Middeldorp, A. (eds.) CADE 2015. LNCS (LNAI), vol. 9195, pp. 591–606. Springer, Cham (2015). doi:10.1007/978-3-319-21401-6_40

21. Heule, M.J.H., Kullmann, O., Marek, V.W.: Solving and verifying the boolean pythagorean triples problem via cube-and-conquer. In: Creignou, N., Le Berre, D. (eds.) SAT 2016. LNCS, vol. 9710, pp. 228–245. Springer, Cham (2016). doi:10.1007/978-3-319-40970-2_15

22. Kaufmann, M., Moore, J S.: An industrial strength theorem prover for a logic based on common LISP. IEEE Trans. Softw. Eng. 23(4), 203–213 (1997)

23. Lammich, P.: Efficient verified (UN)SAT certificate checking. In: CADE-26. LNCS. Springer (to appear, 2017)

24. Letouzey, P.: Extraction in Coq: an overview. In: Beckmann, A., Dimitracopoulos, C., Löwe, B. (eds.) CiE 2008. LNCS, vol. 5028, pp. 359–369. Springer, Heidelberg (2008). doi:10.1007/978-3-540-69407-6_39

25. Manthey, N., Heule, M.J.H., Biere, A.: Automated reencoding of boolean formulas. In: Biere, A., Nahir, A., Vos, T. (eds.) HVC 2012. LNCS, vol. 7857, pp. 102–117. Springer, Heidelberg (2013). doi:10.1007/978-3-642-39611-3_14

26. Maric, F.: Formal verification of a modern SAT solver by shallow embedding into Isabelle/HOL. Theor. Comput. Sci. **411**(50), 4333–4356 (2010)
27. Maric, F., Janicic, P.: Formalization of abstract state transition systems for SAT. Logical Methods in Comput. Sci. **7**(3) (2011)
28. Nipkow, T., Paulson, L.C., Wenzel, M.: Isabelle/HOL - A Proof Assistant for Higher-Order Logic. Springer, Heidelberg (2002)
29. Van Gelder, A.: Producing and verifying extremely large propositional refutations - have your cake and eat it too. Ann. Math. Artif. Intell. **65**(4), 329–372 (2012)
30. Wetzler, N.D., Heule, M.J.H., Hunt Jr., W.A.: Mechanical verification of SAT refutations with extended resolution. In: Blazy, S., Paulin-Mohring, C., Pichardie, D. (eds.) ITP 2013. LNCS, vol. 7998, pp. 229–244. Springer, Heidelberg (2013). doi:10.1007/978-3-642-39634-2_18
31. Wetzler, N.D., Heule, M.J.H., Hunt Jr., W.A.: DRAT-trim: efficient checking and trimming using expressive clausal proofs. In: Sinz, C., Egly, U. (eds.) SAT 2014. LNCS, vol. 8561, pp. 422–429. Springer, Cham (2014). doi:10.1007/978-3-319-09284-3_31
32. Zhang, L., Malik, S.: Validating SAT solvers using an independent resolution-based checker: Practical implementations and other applications. In: DATE, pp. 10880–10885 (2003)

Efficient Verified (UN)SAT Certificate Checking

Peter Lammich[(✉)]

Technische Universität München, Munich, Germany
lammich@in.tum.de

Abstract. We present an efficient formally verified checker for satisfiability and unsatisfiability certificates for Boolean formulas in conjunctive normal form. It utilizes a two phase approach: Starting from a DRAT certificate, the unverified generator computes an enriched certificate, which is checked against the original formula by the verified checker.

Using the Isabelle/HOL Refinement Framework, we verify the actual implementation of the checker, specifying the semantics of the formula down to the integer sequence that represents it.

On a realistic benchmark suite drawn from the 2016 SAT competition, our approach is more than two times faster than the unverified standard tool drat-trim. Additionally, we implemented a multi-threaded version of the generator, which further reduces the runtime.

1   Introduction

Modern SAT solvers are highly optimized and use complex algorithms and heuristics. This makes them prone to bugs. Given that SAT solvers are used in software and hardware verification, a single bug in a SAT solver may invalidate the verification of many systems.

One measure to increase the trust in SAT solvers is to make them output a certificate, which is used to check the result of the solver by a simpler algorithm. Most SAT solvers support the output of a satisfying valuation of the variables as an easily checkable certificate for satisfiability. Certificates for unsatisfiability are more complicated, and different formats have been proposed (e. g. [39,41,42]). Since 2013, the SAT competition [35] requires solvers to output unsat certificates. Since 2014, only certificates in the DRAT format [42] are accepted [36].

The standard tool to check DRAT certificates is drat-trim [10,42]. It is a highly optimized C program with many features, including forward and backward checking mode, a satisfiability certificate checking mode, and a feature to output reduced (trimmed) certificates. However, the high degree of optimization and the wealth of features come at the price of code complexity, increasing the likelihood of bugs. And indeed, during our formalization of the RAT property, we realized that drat-trim was missing a crucial check, thus accepting (maliciously engineered) unsat certificates for satisfiable formulas. This bug has been confirmed by the authors, and is now fixed. Moreover, we discovered several numeric and buffer overflow issues in the parser [11], which could lead to misinterpretation of the formula. Thus, although being less complex than

© Springer International Publishing AG 2017
L. de Moura (Ed.): CADE 2017, LNAI 10395, pp. 237–254, 2017.
DOI: 10.1007/978-3-319-63046-5_15

SAT solvers, efficient DRAT checkers are still complex enough to easily overlook bugs.[1]

One method to eliminate bugs from software is to conduct a machine-checked correctness proof. A common approach is to prove correct a specification in the logic of an interactive theorem prover, and then generate executable code from the specification. Here, code generation is merely a syntax transformation from the executable fragment of the theorem prover's logic to the target language. Following the LCF approach [14], modern theorem provers like Isabelle [34] and Coq [3] are explicitly designed to maximize their trustworthiness. Unfortunately, the algorithms and low-level optimizations required for *efficient* unsat certificate checking are hard to verify and existing approaches (e. g. [8,41]) do not scale to large problems.

While working on the verification of an efficient DRAT checker, the author learned about GRIT, proposed by Cruz-Filipe et al. [7]: They use a modified version of drat-trim to generate an enriched certificate from the original DRAT certificate. The crucial idea is to record the required unit propagations, such that the checker of the enriched certificate only needs to implement a check whether a clause is unit, instead of a fully fledged unit propagation algorithm.

Cruz-Filipe et al. formalize a checker for their enriched certificates in the Coq theorem prover [3], and generate OCaml code from the formalization. However, their current approach still has some deficits: GRIT only supports the less powerful DRUP fragment [41] of DRAT, making it unsuitable for recent SAT solvers that output full DRAT (e. g. CryptoMiniSat, Riss6 [37]). Also, their checker does not consider the original formula, but assumes that the certificate correctly mirrors the formula. Moreover, they use unverified code to parse the certificate into the internal data structures of the checker. Finally, their verified checker is quite slow: Checking a certificate requires roughly the same time as generating it, which effectively doubles the verification time. However, an unverified implementation of their checker in C is two orders of magnitude faster.

In this paper, we present enriched certificates for full DRAT, along with a checker whose correctness is formally verified down to the integer sequence representing the formula. The simple unverified parser that reads a formula into an integer array is written in Standard ML [30], which guarantees that numeric and buffer overflows will not go unnoticed.

We use stepwise refinement techniques to obtain an efficient verified checker, and implement aggressive optimizations in the generator. As a result, our tool chain (generation plus checking) is more than two times faster than drat-trim, with the additional benefit of providing strong formal correctness guarantees. Another distinguishing is a multi-threaded mode for the generator, which allows us to trade hardware resources for additional speedup: With 8 threads, our tool chain verifies a DRAT-certificate seven times (on average) faster than drat-trim.

---

[1] Unfortunately, the available version history of drat-trim [9] only dates back to October 2016. We can only speculate whether the discovered bugs were present in the versions used for the 2014 and 2016 SAT competitions.

Building on the technology of our verified unsat certificate checker, we also provide a verified sat certificate checker, obtaining a complete, formally verified, and fast SAT solver certification tool chain. Our tools, formalizations, and benchmark results are available online [20].

Independently to us, Cruz-Filipe et al. also extended their work to DRAT [6]. Their certificate generator is still based on drat-trim, and first benchmarks indicate that our approach might be significantly faster.[2]

The rest of this paper is organized as follows: After briefly recalling the theory of DRAT certificates (Sect. 2), we introduce our enriched certificate format (Sect. 3). We then give a short overview of the Isabelle Refinement Framework (Sect. 4) and describe its application to verifying our certificate checker (Sect. 5). The paper ends with a brief description of our certificate generator (Sect. 6) and a report on the experimental evaluation of our tools (Sect. 7).

2   Unsatisfiability Certificates

We briefly recall the theory of DRAT unsatisfiability certificates. Let V be a set of variable names. The set of *literals* is defined as $L := V \dot{\cup} \{\neg v \mid v \in V\}$. We identify v and $\neg\neg v$. Let $F = C_1 \wedge \ldots \wedge C_n$ for $C_i \in 2^L$ be a formula in conjunctive normal form (CNF). F is *satisfied* by an *assignment* $A : V \Rightarrow$ bool iff instantiating the variables in F with A yields a true (ground) formula. We call F *satisfiable* iff there exists an assignment that satisfies F.

A clause C is called a *tautology* iff there is a variable v with $\{v, \neg v\} \subseteq C$. Removing a tautology from a formula yields an equivalent formula. In the following we assume that formulas do not contain tautologies. The empty clause is called a *conflict*. A formula that contains a conflict is unsatisfiable. A singleton clause $\{l\} \in F$ is called a *unit clause*. Removing all clauses that contain l, and all literals $\neg l$ from F yields an equisatisfiable formula. Repeating this exhaustively for all unit clauses is called *unit propagation*. When identifying formulas that contain a conflict, unit propagation is strongly normalizing. We name the result of unit propagation F^{u}, defining $F^{\mathrm{u}} = \{\emptyset\}$ if unit propagation yields a conflict.

A DRAT certificate $\chi = \chi_1 \ldots \chi_n$ with $\chi_i \in 2^L \dot{\cup} \{\mathrm{d}C \mid C \in 2^L\}$ is a list of clause addition and deletion items. The *effect* of a (prefix of) a DRAT certificate is to add/delete the specified clauses to/from the original formula F_0, and apply unit propagation:

$$\mathrm{eff}(\varepsilon) = (F_0)^{\mathrm{u}} \qquad \mathrm{eff}(\chi C) = (\mathrm{eff}(\chi) \wedge C)^{\mathrm{u}} \qquad \mathrm{eff}(\chi \mathrm{d}C) = \mathrm{eff}(\chi) \setminus C$$

where $F \setminus C$ removes one occurrence of clause C from F. We call the clause addition items of a DRAT certificate *lemmas*.

A DRAT certificate $\chi = \chi_1 \ldots \chi_n$ is *valid* iff $\mathrm{eff}(\chi) = \{\emptyset\}$ and each lemma has the RAT property wrt. the effect of the previous items:

$$\mathrm{valid}(\chi_1 \ldots \chi_n) := \forall 1 \leq i \leq n. \ \chi_i \in 2^L \implies \mathrm{RAT}(\mathrm{eff}(\chi_1 \ldots \chi_{i-1}), \chi_i)$$

---

[2] However, we expect that most of our optimizations can be transferred to their tools.

where a clause C has the *RAT* (*resolution asymmetric tautology*) property wrt. formula F (we write $\mathrm{RAT}(F, C)$) iff either C is empty and $F^{\mathrm{u}} = \{\emptyset\}$, or if there is a *pivot literal* $l \in C$, such that for all *RAT candidates* $D \in F$ with $\neg l \in D$, we have $(F \wedge \neg(C \cup D \setminus \{\neg l\}))^{\mathrm{u}} = \{\emptyset\}$. Adding a lemma with the RAT property to a formula preserves satisfiability, and so do unit propagation and deletion of clauses. Thus, existence of a valid DRAT certificate implies unsatisfiability of the original formula.

A strictly weaker property than RAT is *RUP* (*reverse unit propagation*): A lemma C has the RUP property wrt. formula F iff $(F \wedge \neg C)^{\mathrm{u}} = \{\emptyset\}$. Adding a lemma with the RUP property yields an equivalent formula. The predecessor of DRAT is DRUP [18], which admits only lemmas with the RUP property.

Checking a lemma for RAT is much more expensive than checking for RUP, as the clause database must be searched for candidate clauses, performing a unit propagation for each of them. Thus, practical DRAT certificate checkers first perform a RUP check on a lemma, and only if this fails they resort to a full RAT check. Exploiting that $(F \wedge \neg(C \cup D))^{\mathrm{u}}$ is equivalent to $((F \wedge \neg C)^{\mathrm{u}} \wedge \neg D)^{\mathrm{u}}$, the result of the initial unit propagation from the RUP check can even be reused. Another important optimization is *backward checking* [13,18]: The lemmas are processed in reverse order, marking the lemmas that are actually needed in unit propagations during RUP and RAT checks. Lemmas that remain unmarked need not be processed at all. To further reduce the number of marked lemmas, *core-first* unit propagation [42] prefers marked unit clauses over unmarked ones.

In practice, DRAT certificate checkers spend most time on unit propagation[3], for which highly optimized implementations of rather complex algorithms are used (e. g. drat-trim uses a two watched literals algorithm [32]). Unfortunately, verifying such highly optimized code in a proof assistant is a major endeavor. Thus, a crucial idea is to implement an unverified tool that enriches the certificate with additional information that can be used for simpler and more efficient verification. For DRUP, the GRIT format has been proposed recently [7]. It stores, for each lemma, a list of unit clauses in the order they become unit, followed by a conflict clause. Thus, unit propagation is replaced by simply checking whether a clause is unit or conflict. A modified version of drat-trim is used to generate a GRIT certificate from the original DRAT certificate.

3   The GRAT Format

The first contribution of this paper is to extend the ideas of GRIT from DRUP to DRAT. To this end, we define the GRAT format. Like for GRIT, each clause is identified by a unique positive ID. The clauses of the original formula implicitly get the IDs $1 \ldots N$. The lemma IDs explicitly occur in the certificate, and must be strictly ascending.

---

[3] Our profiling data indicates that, depending on the problem, up to 93% of the time is spent for unit propagation.

For memory efficiency reasons, we store the certificate in two parts: The lemma file contains the lemmas, and is stored in DIMACS format. During certificate checking, this part is entirely loaded into memory. The proof file contains the hints and instructions for the certificate checker. It is not completely loaded into memory, but only streamed during checking.

The proof file is a binary file, containing a sequence of 32 bit signed integers stored in 2's complement little endian format. The sequence is reversed (or the file is streamed backwards), and then interpreted according to the following grammar:

```
proof       ::= rat-counts item* conflict
literal     ::= int32 != 0
id          ::= int32 > 0
count       ::= int32 > 0
rat-counts  ::= 6 (literal count)* 0
item        ::= unit-prop | deletion | rup-lemma | rat-lemma
unit-prop   ::= 1 id* 0
deletion    ::= 2 id* 0
rup-lemma   ::= 3 id id* 0 id
rat-lemma   ::= 4 literal id id* 0 cand-prf* 0
cand-prf    ::= id id* 0 id
conflict    ::= 5 id
```

The checker maintains a *clause map* that maps IDs to clauses, and a *partial assignment* that maps variables to true, false, or undecided. Partial assignments are extended to literals in the natural way. Initially, the clause map contains the clauses of the original formula, and the partial assignment maps all variables to undecided. Then, the checker iterates over the items of the proof, processing each item as follows:

rat-counts. This item contains a list of pairs of literals and the number how often they are used in RAT proofs. This map allows the checker to maintain lists of RAT candidates for the relevant literals, instead of gathering the possible RAT candidates by iterating over the whole clause database for each RAT proof, which is expensive. Literals that are not used in RAT proofs at all do not occur in the list. This item is the first item of the proof.

unit-prop. For each listed clause ID, the corresponding clause is checked to be unit, and the unit literal is assigned to true. Here, a clause is unit if the unit literal is undecided, and all other literals are assigned to false.

deletion. The specified IDs are removed from the clause map.

rup-lemma. The item specifies the ID for the new lemma, which is the next unprocessed lemma from the lemma file, a list of unit clause IDs, and a conflict clause ID. First, the literals of the lemma are assigned to false. The lemma must not be blocked, i. e. none of its literals may be already assigned to true[4]. Note that assigning the literals of a clause C to false is equivalent to adding the conjunct $\neg C$ to the formula. Second, the unit clauses are checked and the

---

[4] Blocked lemmas are useless for unsat proofs, such that there is no point to include them into the certificate.

corresponding unit literals are assigned to true. Third, it is checked that the conflict clause ID actually identifies a conflict clause, i. e. that all its literals are assigned to false. Finally, the lemma is added to the clause-map and the assignment is rolled back to the state before checking of the item started.

rat-lemma. The item specifies a pivot literal l, an ID for the lemma, an initial list of unit clause IDs, and a list of candidate proofs. First, as for `rup-lemma`, the literals of the lemma are assigned to false and the initial unit propagations are performed. Second, it is checked that the provided RAT candidates are exhaustive, and the corresponding `cand-prf` items are processed: A `cand-prf` item consists of the ID of the candidate clause D, a list of unit clause IDs, and a conflict clause ID. To check a candidate proof, the literals of $D \setminus \{\neg l\}$ are assigned to false, the listed unit propagations are performed, and the conflict clause is checked to be actually conflict. Afterwards, the assignment is rolled back to the state before checking the candidate proof. Third, when all candidate proofs have been checked, the lemma is added to the clause map and the assignment is rolled back.

To simplify certificate generation in backward mode, we allow candidate proofs referring to arbitrary, even invalid, clause IDs. Those proofs must be ignored by the checker.

conflict. This is the last item of the certificate. It specifies the ID of the *root conflict* clause, i. e. the conflict found by unit propagation after adding the last lemma of the certificate. It is checked that the ID actually refers to a conflict clause.

4 Program Verification with Isabelle/HOL

Isabelle/HOL [34] is an interactive theorem prover for higher order logic. Its design features the LCF approach [14], where a small logical inference kernel is the only code that can produce theorems. Bugs in the non-kernel part may result in failure to prove a theorem, but never in a false proposition being accepted as a theorem. Isabelle/HOL includes a code generator [15–17] that translates the executable fragment of HOL to various functional programming languages, currently OCaml, Standard ML, Scala, and Haskell. Via Imperative HOL [5], the code generator also supports imperative code, modeled by a heap monad inside the logic.

A common problem when verifying efficient implementations of algorithms is that implementation details tend to obfuscate the proof and increase its complexity. Hence, efficiency of the implementation is often traded for simplicity of the proof. A well-known approach to this problem is stepwise refinement [1,2,43], where an abstract version of the algorithm is refined towards an efficient implementation in multiple correctness preserving steps. The abstract version focuses on the algorithmic ideas, leaving open the exact implementation, while the refinement steps focus on more and more concrete implementation aspects. This modularizes the correctness proof, and makes verification of complex algorithms manageable in the first place.

For Isabelle/HOL, the Isabelle Refinement Framework [22,24,25,29] provides a powerful stepwise refinement tool chain, featuring a nondeterministic shallowly embedded programming language [29], a library of efficient collection data structures and generic algorithms [24–26], and convenience tools to simplify canonical refinement steps [22,24]. It has been used for various software verification projects (e. g. [23,27,28]), including a fully fledged verified LTL model checker [4,12].

5   A Verified GRAT Certificate Checker

We give an overview of our Isabelle/HOL formalization of a GRAT certificate checker (cf. Sect. 3). We use the stepwise refinement techniques provided by the Isabelle Refinement Framework to verify an efficient implementation at manageable proof complexity.

Note that we display only slightly edited Isabelle source text, and try to explain its syntax as far as needed to get a basic understanding. Isabelle uses a mixture of common mathematical notations and Standard ML [30] syntax (e. g. there are algebraic data types, function application is written as f x, functions are usually curried, e. g. f x y, and abstraction is written as λx $y.$ t).

5.1   Syntax and Semantics of Formulas

The following Isabelle text specifies the abstract syntax of CNF formulas:

```
datatype'a literal = Pos'a | Neg'a
type_synonym'a clause ='a literal set
type_synonym 'a cnf = 'a clause set
```

We abstract over the type $'a$ of variables, use an algebraic data type to specify positive and negative literals, and model clauses as sets of literals, and a CNF formula as set of clauses.

A partial assignment has type $'a \Rightarrow bool$ $option$, which is abbreviated as $'a \rightharpoonup bool$ in Isabelle. It maps a variable to $None$ for undecided, or to $Some$ $True$ or $Some$ $False$. We specify the semantics of literals and clauses as follows:

```
primrec sem_lit' :: 'a literal ⇒ ('a⇀bool) ⇀bool where
   sem_lit' (Pos x) A = A x | sem_lit' (Neg x) A = map_option Not (A x)
definition sem_clause' C A ≡
   if (∃l∈C. sem_lit' l A = Some True) then Some True
   else if (∀l∈C. sem_lit' l A = Some False) then Some False
   else None
```

Note that we omitted the type specification for sem_clause', in which case Isabelle automatically infers the most general type.

For a fixed formula F, we define the *models* induced by a partial assignment to be all total extensions that satisfy the formula. We define two partial assignments to be *equivalent* if they induce the same models.

5.2   Unit Propagation and RAT

We define a predicate to state that, wrt. a partial assignment A, a clause C is unit, with unit literal l:

definition `is_unit_lit A C l`
  $\equiv$ `l∈C ∧ sem_lit' l A = None ∧ sem_clause' (C-{l}) A = Some False`

Assigning a unit literal to true yields an equivalent assignment:

lemma `unit_propagation`:
  assumes `C∈F` **and** `is_unit_lit A C l`
  shows `equiv' F A (assign_lit A l)`

In Isabelle, all variables that occur free in a lemma (here: `C,F,A,l`) are implicitly universally quantified.

Having formalized the basic concepts, we can show the essential lemma that justifies RAT (cf. Sect. 2):

lemma `abs_rat_criterion`:
  assumes `l∈C` **and** `sem_lit' l A` $\neq$ `Some False`
  assumes `∀D∈F. neg_lit l ∈ D` $\implies$ `implied_clause F A (C∪(D-{neg_lit l}))`
  shows `redundant_clause F A C`

Where a clause is *implied* if it can be added to the formula without changing the models, and it is *redundant* if adding the clause preserves satisfiability (but not necessarily the models).

5.3   Abstract Checker Algorithm

Having formalized the basic theory of CNF formulas wrt. partial assignments, we can specify an abstract version of the certificate checker algorithm. Our specifications live in an exception monad stacked onto the nondeterminism monad of the Isabelle Refinement Framework. Exceptions are used to indicate failure of the checker, and are never caught. We only prove soundness of our checker, i. e. that it does not accept satisfiable formulas. Our checker actually accepted all certificates in our benchmark set (cf. Sect. 7), yielding an empirical argument that it is sufficiently complete.

At the abstract level, we model the proof as a stream of integers. On this, we define functions **parse_id** and **parse_lit** that fetch an element from the stream, try to interpret it as ID or literal, and fail if this is not possible. The state of the checker is a tuple (`last_id,CM,A`). To check that the lemma IDs are strictly ascending, `last_id` stores the ID of the last processed lemma. The *clause map* `CM` contains the current formula as a mapping from IDs to clauses, and also maintains the RAT candidate lists. Finally, `A` is the current assignment.

As first example, we present the abstract algorithm that is invoked after reading the item-type of a `rup-lemma` item (cf. Sect. 3), i. e. we expect a sequence of the form `id id* "0" id`.

```
1   check_rup_proof ≡ λ(last_id,CM,A₀) it prf. do {
2     (i,prf) ← parse_id prf;
3     check (i>last_id);
4     (C,A',it) ← parse_check_blocked A₀ it;
5     (A',prf) ← apply_units CM A' prf;
6     (confl_id,prf) ← parse_id prf;
7     confl ← resolve_id CM confl_id;
8     check (sem_clause' confl A' = Some False);
9     CM ← add_clause i C CM;
10    return ((i,CM,A₀),it,prf)
11  }
```

We use do-notation to conveniently express monad operations. First, the lemma ID is pulled from the proof stream (line 2) and checked to be greater than `last_id` (3). The `check` function throws an exception unless the first argument evaluates to true. Next, `parse_check_blocked` (4) parses the next lemma from the lemma file, checks that it is not blocked, and assigns its literals to false. Then, the function `apply_units` (5) pulls the unit clause IDs from the proof stream, checks that they are actually unit, and assigns the unit literals to true. Finally, we pull the ID of the conflict clause (6), obtain the corresponding clause from the clause map (7), check that it is actually conflict (8), and add the lemma to the clause map (9). We return (10) the lemma ID as new last ID, the new clause map, and the *old* assignment, as the changes to the assignment are local and must be backtracked before checking the next clause. Additionally, we return the new position in the lemma file (`it`) and in the proof stream (`prf`). Note that this abstract specification contains non-algorithmic parts: For example, in line 8, we check for the semantics of the conflict clause to be *Some False*, without specifying how to implement this check. We prove the following lemma for `check_rup_proof`:

lemma `check_rup_proof_correct`:
  assumes `invar (last_id,CM,A)`
  shows `check_rup_proof (last_id,CM,A) it prf`
    $\leq$ `spec True (λ((last_id',CM',A'), it', prf').`
       `invar (last_id',CM',A') ∧ (sat' (cm_F CM) A ⟹ sat' (cm_F CM') A'))`

Here, **spec** Φ Ψ describes the postcondition Φ in case of an exception, and the postcondition Ψ for a normal result. As we only prove soundness of the checker, we use *True* as postcondition for exceptions. For normal results, we show that an invariant on the state is preserved, and that the resulting formula and partial assignment is satisfiable if the original formula and partial assignment was.

Finally, we present the specification of the checker's main function:

```
1   definition verify_unsat F_begin F_end it prf ≡ do {
2     let A = λ_. None;
3     (CM,prf) ← init_rat_counts prf;
4     (CM,last_id) ← read_cnf F_end F_begin CM;
5     let s = (last_id,CM,A);
6     (so,_) ← while (λ(so,it). so≠None) (λ(so,it).
7       do {
```

```
8        let (s,it,prf) = the so;
9        check_item s it
10    }) (Some (s,it,prf));
11 }
```

The parameters *F_begin* and *F_end* indicate the range that hold the representation of the formula, *it* points to the first lemma, and *prf* is the proof stream. After initializing the assignment (line 2, all variables undecided), the RAT literal counts are read (3), and the formula is parsed into the clause map (4). Then, the function iterates over the proof stream and checks each item (6–10), until the formula has been certified. (or an exception terminates the program) Here, the checker's state is wrapped into an option type, where *None* indicates that the formula has been certified. Correctness of the abstract checker is expressed by the following lemma:

lemma *verify_unsat_correct:*
  assumes *seg F_begin lst F_end*
  shows *verify_unsat F_begin F_end it prf*
    $\leq$ **spec** *True* $(\lambda\_.\ F\_invar\ lst \wedge \neg sat\ (F\_\alpha\ lst))$

Intuitively, if the range from *F_begin* to *F_end* is valid and contains the sequence *lst*, and if *verify_unsat* returns a normal value, then *lst* represents a valid CNF formula (*F_invar lst*) that is unsatisfiable ($\neg sat$ (*F_α lst*)). Note that the correctness statement does not depend on the lemmas (*it*) or the proof stream (*prf*). This will later allow us to use an optimized (unverified) implementation for streaming the proof, without impairing the formal correctness statement.

5.4   Refinement Towards an Efficient Implementation

The abstract checker algorithm that we described so far contains non-algorithmic parts and uses abstract types like sets. Even if we could extract executable code, its performance would be poor: For example, we model assignments as functions. Translating this directly to a functional language results in assignments to be stored as long chains of function updates with worst-case linear time lookup.

We now show how to refine the abstract checker to an efficient algorithm, replacing the specifications by actual algorithms, and the abstract types by efficient data structures. The refinement is done in multiple steps, where each step focuses on different aspects of the implementation. Formally, we use a *refinement relation* that relates objects of the refined type (e.g. a hash table) to objects of the abstract type (e.g. a set). In our framework, refinement is expressed by propositions of the form $(c,a) \in R \implies g\ c \leq \Downarrow S\ (f\ a)$: if the concrete argument *c* is related to the abstract argument *a* by *R*, then the result of the concrete algorithm *g c* is related to the result of the abstract algorithm *f a* by *S*. Moreover, if the concrete algorithm throws an exception, the abstract algorithm must also throw an exception.

In the first refinement step, we record the set of variables assigned during checking a lemma, and use this set to reconstruct the original assignment from the current assignment after the check. This saves us from copying the whole original assignment before each check. Formally, we define an A_0-*backtrackable* *assignment* to be an assignment A together with a set of assigned variables T, such that unassigning the variables in T yields A_0. The relation `bt_assign_rel` relates A_0-backtrackable assignments to plain assignments:

`bt_assign_rel` $A_0 \equiv \{ ((A,T),A) \mid A$ `T.` $T \subseteq$ `dom` $A \wedge A_0 = A\!\upharpoonright\!(-T) \}$

We define `apply_units_bt`, which operates on A_0-backtrackable assignments. If applied to assignments (A',T) and A related by `bt_assign_rel` A_0, and to the same proof stream position `prf`, then the results of `apply_units_bt` and `apply_units` are related by `bt_assign_rel` $A_0 \times$ `Id`, i.e. the returned assignments are again related by `bt_assign_rel` A_0, and the new proof stream positions are the same (related by `Id`):

lemma `apply_units_bt_refine`: assumes $((A',T),A) \in$`bt_assign_rel` A_0
  shows `apply_units_bt` CM A' T prf
    $\leq \Downarrow$(`bt_assign_rel` $A_0 \times$ `Id`) (`apply_units` CM A prf)

In the next refinement step, we implement clauses by iterators pointing to the start of a null-terminated sequence of integers. Thus, the clause map will only store iterators instead of (replicated) clauses. Now, we can specify algorithms for functions on clauses. For example, we define:

`check_conflict_clause1` A cref $\equiv$ `iterate_clause` cref $(\lambda l\ \_.$ do {
  check (`sem_lit'` l A = Some False)
}) ()

i.e. we iterate over the clause, checking each literal to be false. We show:

lemma `check_conflict_clause1_refine`: assumes CR: $(cref,C) \in$`cref_rel`
  shows `check_conflict_clause1` A cref
        $\leq \Downarrow$Id (check (`sem_clause'` C A = Some False))

where the relation `cref_rel` relates iterators to clauses.

In the next refinement step, we introduce efficient data structures. For example, we implement the iterators by indexes into an array of integers that stores both the formula and the lemmas. For many of the abstract types, we use general purpose data structures from the Isabelle Refinement Framework [24,25]. For example, we refine assignments to arrays, using the `array_map_default` data structure, which implements functions of type $nat \Rightarrow 'a$ `option` by arrays of type $'b$ `array`. It is parameterized by a relation $R :$ $('b \times 'a)$ `set` and a default concrete element d that does not correspond to any abstract element $(\nexists a.\ (d,a) \in R)$. The implementation uses d to represent the abstract value `None`. We define:

definition `vv_rel` $\equiv \{(1,$ False$), (2,$ True$)\}$
definition `assignment_assn` $\equiv$ `amd_assn` 0 `id_assn` (pure `vv_rel`)

i.e. we implement Some False by 1, Some True by 2, and None by 0. Here, `amd_assn` is the relation of the `array_map_default` data structure[5]. The refined

---

[5] The name suffix `_assn` instead of `_rel` indicates that the data structure may be stored on the heap.

programs and refinement theorems in this step are automatically generated by the Sepref tool [24]. For example, the command

sepref_definition `check_rup_proof3` is `check_rup_proof2`
 :: `cdb_assn`^{k} * `state_assn`^{d} * `it_assn`^{k} * `prf_assn`^{d}
    → `error_assn` + `state_assn` × `it_assn` × `prf_assn`

takes the definition of `check_rup_proof2`, generates a refined version, and proves the corresponding refinement theorem. The first parameter is refined wrt. `cdb_assn` (refining the set of clauses into an array), the second parameter is refined wrt. `state_assn` (refining the clause map and the assignment into arrays), the third parameter is refined wrt. `it_assn` (refining the iterator into an array index), and the fourth parameter is refined wrt. `prf_assn` (refining the stream position). Exception results are refined wrt. `error_assn` (basically the identity relation), and normal results are refined wrt. `state_assn`, `it_assn`, and `prf_assn`. The x^d and x^k annotations indicate whether the generated function may overwrite a parameter (d like *destroy*) or not (k like *keep*).

By combining all the refinement steps and unfolding some definitions, we prove the following correctness theorem for the implementation of our checker:

theorem `verify_unsat_impl_correct`:
  <`DBi` ↦$_a$ `DB`>
    `verify_unsat_impl DBi F_end it prf`
  <λ`result. DBi` ↦$_a$ `DB` * ↑(¬`isl result` ⟹ `formula_unsat_spec DB F_end`)>

This Hoare triple states that if `DBi` points to an array holding the elements `DB`, and we run `verify_unsat_impl`, the array will be unchanged, and if the return value is no exception, the formula represented by the range `1...F_end` in the array is unsatisfiable. We have experimented with many equivalent formulations of `formula_unsat_spec`, trying to reduce the *trusted base*, i. e. the concepts and definitions the specification depends on. A concise one is:

definition `assn_consistent` :: `(int ⇒ bool) ⇒ bool`
   where `assn_consistent` σ = (∀x. x≠0 ⟹ ¬ σ (-x) = σ x)
definition `formula_unsat_spec DB F_end` ≡ (
  let `lst = tl (take F_end DB)` **in**
    `1 < F_end` ∧ `F_end ≤ length DB` ∧ `last lst = 0`
  ∧ (∄σ. `assn_consistent` σ ∧ (∀`C`∈`set (tokenize 0 lst)`. ∃`l`∈`set C`. σ `l`)))

Here, a *consistent assignment* is a mapping from integers to Booleans, such that a negative value is mapped to the opposite as its absolute value. The specification then defines `lst` to be the elements `1,...,F_end` of the array[6], and states that `F_end` is in bounds, the last element of `lst` is a null, and that there is *no* assignment such that each clause contains a literal assigned to true. We define `tokenize 0 lst` to be the unique list of lists of non-null integers whose concatenation as null-terminated lists yields `lst`. This way, we specify an unsatisfiable formula down to the list of integers that represents it, only using basic list functions. The last section of the proof outline of our formalization [21] contains a detailed discussion of the correctness theorem.

---

[6] Element 0 is used as a guard in our implementation.

The final step to a verified efficient unsat checker is to use Isabelle/HOL's code generator to extract Standard ML code for `verify_unsat_impl` and to link this code with a small (40 LOC) parser to read the formula (and the lemmas) into an array. Moreover, we implement a buffered reader for the proof file. This, however, does not affect the correctness statement, which is valid for all proof stream implementations. The resulting program is compiled with MLton [31].

6 Multithreaded Generation of Enriched Certificates

In order to generate GRAT certificates, we extend a DRAT checker algorithm to record the unit clauses that lead to a conflict when checking each lemma.

Our certificate generator started as a reimplementation of the backward mode of drat-trim [10, 41] in C++, to which we then added GRAT certificate generation. As the certificate generator is not part of the trusted code base, we could afford to add aggressive novel optimizations: We maintain separate watchlists for marked and unmarked lemmas, which allows a more efficient implementation of core-first unit propagation. Moreover, we detect runs of lemmas with the same pivot element, which allows to reuse the results of (expensive) RAT candidate searches in certain cases. These optimizations alone make our generator more than two times faster than drat-trim.

Another common optimization is parallelization: If one has more DRAT certificates to check than processors available (e. g. when evaluating a SAT competition), one can simply run multiple instances of the certificate generator and checker in parallel. However, if one has only a few certificates to check (e. g. when using SAT solvers for checking a single model), a more fine grained parallelization is required to keep the available processors busy. To this end, our certificate generator provides a multi-threaded mode, which parallelizes the processing of lemmas, at the cost of using more memory. It uses all optimizations of the single-threaded mode, some of them slightly adjusted for multi-threading. For example, the lemmas of a run with the same pivot element are preferably scheduled to the same thread.

The basic idea is to let multiple threads run backwards over the certificate, verifying the lemmas in parallel. A thread tries to acquire a lemma before it starts verification. If the lemma is already acquired by another thread, this thread proceeds with the next lemma. This way, each lemma is only proved by one thread. For the marking of lemmas, the only required synchronization is that a thread sees its own markings: As every thread runs to the beginning, and on processing a lemma only earlier lemmas are marked, every thread will try to acquire at least the lemmas that it marked itself — and process them if no other thread was faster. However, in order to improve the effectiveness of core-first unit propagation, the threads periodically synchronize on their marking data.

7 Benchmarks

We present the experimental evaluation of our tools on a realistic set of benchmarks. We used CryptoMiniSat [37, 40] to generate DRAT certificates for the 110 unsatisfiable problems it solved at the 2016 SAT competition [38]. We ran the benchmarks on a standard server board with a 22 core Intel XEON Broadwell processor with 2.2 GHz and 128 GiB of RAM. To minimize interferences, we ran only one benchmark at a time, with no other load on the server. Due to the page limit of this paper, we only provide a short summary of our benchmark results. The complete results are available on the tool's homepage [20].

On each DRAT certificate, we ran drat-trim (version Nov 10 2016)[7] and our tool chain (version 1.2) with 1 and 8 threads. We measured the wall-clock time and memory consumption. First of all, our tools successfully checked all certificates, indicating that our approach is sufficiently complete. (Recall that only soundness is formally proved).

We start with comparing drat-trim to our tool in single-threaded mode: drat-trim timed out after 20.000 seconds on two certificates, and crashed on a third one. For checking the remaining 107 certificates, drat-trim required 42.3 hours, while our tool chain required only 17.3 hours. Out of the 17.3 hours, only 1.1 hours were required to run the verified certificate checker, i.e. its runtime is almost negligible compared to certificate generation time. Our tool-chain verified the three certificates for which drat-trim failed in 5.3 hours.

Our certificate generator requires roughly two times more memory than drat-trim. This is due to the generated certificate being stored in memory. We could not measure meaningful memory consumption values for our verified checker: The MLton garbage collector only gets active when memory falls short, resulting in unrealistic memory consumption values when being the only process running on a machine with 128 GiB of RAM.

Next, we report on running the certificate generator with 8 threads: The wall clock times required for generation and checking add up to only 8.3 hours. Excluding certificates that required less than one minute to check, the average speed up is 2.6 [min: 1.1, max: 4.9] compared to single-threaded mode, and 7.1 [min: 0.5, max: 36.0] compared to drat-trim. However, certificate generation requires significantly more memory, as the DRAT certificate is duplicated for each thread.

To complete the presentation, we briefly report on the results of our formally verified satisfiability checker: The certificates for the 64 satisfiable problems that CryptoMiniSat solved at the 2016 SAT competition [38] have a size of 229 MiB and could be verified in 40 seconds.

8   Conclusions

We have presented a formally verified tool chain to check DRAT unsatisfiability certificates. In single-threaded mode, our approach is more than two times faster than the (unverified) standard tool drat-trim, on a benchmark suite taken from the 2016 SAT competition. Additionally, we implemented a multi-threaded mode, which allows us to trade computing resources for significantly smaller

---

[7] The current version at the time of writing this paper.

response times. The formal proof covers the actual implementation of the checker and the semantics of the formula down to the sequence of integers that represents it.

Our approach involves two phases: The first phase generates an enriched certificate, which is then checked against the original formula by the second phase. While the main computational work is done by the first phase, soundness of the approach only depends on the second phase, which is also algorithmically less complex, making it more amenable to formal verification. Using stepwise refinement techniques, we were able to formally verify a rather efficient implementation of the second phase.

We conclude with some statistics: The formalization of the certificate checker is roughly 5k lines of code. In order to realize this formalization, several general purpose libraries (e.g. the exception monad and some imperative data structures) had to be developed. These sum up to additional 3.5k lines. The time spent on the formalization was roughly three man months. The multi-threaded certificate generator has roughly 3k lines of code, and took two man month to develop.

8.1   Future Work

Currently, the formal proof of our verified checker goes down to the representation of the formula as integer array, thus requiring a (small) unverified parser. A logical next step would be to verify the parser, too. Moreover, verification stops at the Isabelle code generator, whose correctness is only proved the classical way on paper [16,17]. There is work aiming at the mechanical verification of code generators [33], and even the subsequent compilers [19]. Unfortunately, this is not (yet) available for Isabelle/HOL.

We plan to attack the high memory consumption of our multi-threaded generator by trying to share more (read-only) data between the threads.

An interesting research topic would be to integrate enriched certificate generation directly into SAT solvers. The performance decrease in the solver could be weighed against the cost of generating an enriched certificate. However, such modifications are probably complex and SAT-solver specific, whereas DRAT certificates are designed to be easily integrated into virtually any CDCL based SAT solver.

Finally, we chose a benchmark set which is realistic, but can be run in a few days on the available hardware. We plan to run our tools on larger benchmark suites, once we have access to sufficient (supercomputing) hardware.

Acknowledgements. We thank Jasmin Blanchette and Mathias Fleury for very useful comments on the draft version of this paper, and Lars Hupel for instant help on any problems related to the benchmark server.

References

1. Back, R.-J.: On the correctness of refinement steps in program development. Ph.D. thesis, Department of Computer Science, University of Helsinki (1978)
2. Back, R.-J., von Wright, J.: Refinement Calculus - A Systematic Introduction. Springer, New York (1998)
3. Bertot, Y., Castran, P.: Interactive Theorem Proving and Program Development: Coq'Art the Calculus of Inductive Constructions, 1st edn. Springer, New York (2010)
4. Brunner, J., Lammich, P.: Formal verification of an executable LTL model checker with partial order reduction. In: Rayadurgam, S., Tkachuk, O. (eds.) NFM 2016. LNCS, vol. 9690, pp. 307–321. Springer, Cham (2016). doi:10.1007/978-3-319-40648-0_23
5. Bulwahn, L., Krauss, A., Haftmann, F., Erkök, L., Matthews, J.: Imperative functional programming with Isabelle/HOL. In: Mohamed, O.A., Muñoz, C., Tahar, S. (eds.) TPHOLs 2008. LNCS, vol. 5170, pp. 134–149. Springer, Heidelberg (2008). doi:10.1007/978-3-540-71067-7_14
6. Cruz-Filipe, L., Heule, M., Hunt, W., Matt, K., Schneider-Kamp, P.: Efficient certified RAT verification. In: de Moura, L. (ed.) CADE 2017. LNAI, vol. 10395, pp. 220–236. Springer, Cham (2017)
7. Cruz-Filipe, L., Marques-Silva, J., Schneider-Kamp, P.: Efficient certified resolution proof checking. In: Legay, A., Margaria, T. (eds.) TACAS 2017. LNCS, vol. 10205, pp. 118–135. Springer, Heidelberg (2017). doi:10.1007/978-3-662-54577-5_7
8. Darbari, A., Fischer, B., Marques-Silva, J.: Industrial-strength certified SAT solving through verified SAT proof checking. In: Cavalcanti, A., Deharbe, D., Gaudel, M.-C., Woodcock, J. (eds.) ICTAC 2010. LNCS, vol. 6255, pp. 260–274. Springer, Heidelberg (2010). doi:10.1007/978-3-642-14808-8_18
9. DRAT-TRIM GitHub repository. https://github.com/marijnheule/drat-trim
10. DRAT-TRIM homepage. https://www.cs.utexas.edu/~marijn/drat-trim/
11. DRAT-TRIM issue tracker. https://github.com/marijnheule/drat-trim/issues
12. Esparza, J., Lammich, P., Neumann, R., Nipkow, T., Schimpf, A., Smaus, J.-G.: A fully verified executable LTL model checker. In: Sharygina, N., Veith, H. (eds.) CAV 2013. LNCS, vol. 8044, pp. 463–478. Springer, Heidelberg (2013). doi:10.1007/978-3-642-39799-8_31
13. Goldberg, E., Novikov, Y.: Verification of proofs of unsatisfiability for CNF formulas. In: Proceedings of DATE. IEEE (2003)
14. Gordon, M.: From LCF to HOL: a short history. In: Proof, Language, and Interaction, pp. 169–185. MIT Press (2000)
15. Haftmann, F.: Code generation from specifications in higher order logic. Ph.D. thesis, Technische Universität München (2009)
16. Haftmann, F., Krauss, A., Kunčar, O., Nipkow, T.: Data refinement in Isabelle/HOL. In: Blazy, S., Paulin-Mohring, C., Pichardie, D. (eds.) ITP 2013. LNCS, vol. 7998, pp. 100–115. Springer, Heidelberg (2013). doi:10.1007/978-3-642-39634-2_10
17. Haftmann, F., Nipkow, T.: Code generation via higher-order rewrite systems. In: Blume, M., Kobayashi, N., Vidal, G. (eds.) FLOPS 2010. LNCS, vol. 6009, pp. 103–117. Springer, Heidelberg (2010). doi:10.1007/978-3-642-12251-4_9
18. Heule, M., Hunt, W., Wetzler, N.: Trimming while checking clausal proofs. In: 2013 Formal Methods in Computer-Aided Design, FMCAD 2013, pp. 181–188. IEEE (2013)

19. Kumar, R., Myreen, M.O., Norrish, M., Owens, S.: CakeML: a verified implementation of ML. In: Proceedings of POPL, pp. 179–192. ACM (2014)
20. Lammich, P.: Grat tool chain homepage. http://www21.in.tum.de/lammich/grat/
21. Lammich, P.: Gratchk proof outline. http://www21.in.tum.de/lammich/grat/outline.pdf
22. Lammich, P.: Automatic data refinement. In: Blazy, S., Paulin-Mohring, C., Pichardie, D. (eds.) ITP 2013. LNCS, vol. 7998, pp. 84–99. Springer, Heidelberg (2013). doi:10.1007/978-3-642-39634-2_9
23. Lammich, P.: Verified efficient implementation of gabow's strongly connected component algorithm. In: Klein, G., Gamboa, R. (eds.) ITP 2014. LNCS, vol. 8558, pp. 325–340. Springer, Cham (2014). doi:10.1007/978-3-319-08970-6_21
24. Lammich, P.: Refinement to Imperative/HOL. In: Urban, C., Zhang, X. (eds.) ITP 2015. LNCS, vol. 9236, pp. 253–269. Springer, Cham (2015). doi:10.1007/978-3-319-22102-1_17
25. Lammich, P.: Refinement based verification of imperative data structures. In: CPP, pp. 27–36. ACM (2016)
26. Lammich, P., Lochbihler, A.: The isabelle collections framework. In: Kaufmann, M., Paulson, L.C. (eds.) ITP 2010. LNCS, vol. 6172, pp. 339–354. Springer, Heidelberg (2010). doi:10.1007/978-3-642-14052-5_24
27. Lammich, P., Neumann, R.: A framework for verifying depth-first search algorithms. In: CPP 2015, pp. 137–146. ACM, New York (2015)
28. Lammich, P., Sefidgar, S.R.: Formalizing the Edmonds-Karp algorithm. In: Blanchette, J.C., Merz, S. (eds.) ITP 2016. LNCS, vol. 9807, pp. 219–234. Springer, Cham (2016). doi:10.1007/978-3-319-43144-4_14
29. Lammich, P., Tuerk, T.: Applying data refinement for monadic programs to Hopcroft's algorithm. In: Beringer, L., Felty, A. (eds.) ITP 2012. LNCS, vol. 7406, pp. 166–182. Springer, Heidelberg (2012). doi:10.1007/978-3-642-32347-8_12
30. Milner, R., Harper, R., MacQueen, D., Tofte, M.: The Definition of Standard ML. MIT Press, Cambridge (1997)
31. MLton Standard ML compiler. http://mlton.org/
32. Moskewicz, M.W., Madigan, C.F., Zhao, Y., Zhang, L., Malik, S.: Chaff: engineering an efficient SAT solver. In: Proceedings of DAC, pp. 530–535. ACM (2001)
33. Myreen, M.O., Owens, S.: Proof-producing translation of higher-order logic into pure and stateful ML. J. Funct. Program. 24(2–3), 284–315 (2014)
34. Nipkow, T., Wenzel, M., Paulson, L.C. (eds.): Isabelle/HOL — A Proof Assistant for Higher-Order Logic. LNCS, vol. 2283. Springer, Heidelberg (2002)
35. SAT competition (2013). http://satcompetition.org/2013/
36. SAT competition (2014). http://satcompetition.org/2014/
37. Proceedings of SAT Competition 2016: Solver and Benchmark Descriptions, vol. B-2016-1. University of Helsinki (2016)
38. SAT competition (2016). http://baldur.iti.kit.edu/sat-competition-2016/
39. Sinz, C., Biere, A.: Extended resolution proofs for conjoining BDDs. In: Grigoriev, D., Harrison, J., Hirsch, E.A. (eds.) CSR 2006. LNCS, vol. 3967, pp. 600–611. Springer, Heidelberg (2006). doi:10.1007/11753728_60
40. Soos, M., Nohl, K., Castelluccia, C.: Extending SAT solvers to cryptographic problems. In: Kullmann, O. (ed.) SAT 2009. LNCS, vol. 5584, pp. 244–257. Springer, Heidelberg (2009). doi:10.1007/978-3-642-02777-2_24
41. Wetzler, N., Heule, M.J.H., Hunt, W.A.: Mechanical verification of SAT refutations with extended resolution. In: Blazy, S., Paulin-Mohring, C., Pichardie, D. (eds.) ITP 2013. LNCS, vol. 7998, pp. 229–244. Springer, Heidelberg (2013). doi:10.1007/978-3-642-39634-2_18

42. Wetzler, N., Heule, M.J.H., Hunt, W.A.: DRAT-trim: efficient checking and trimming using expressive clausal proofs. In: Sinz, C., Egly, U. (eds.) SAT 2014. LNCS, vol. 8561, pp. 422–429. Springer, Cham (2014). doi:10.1007/978-3-319-09284-3_31
43. Wirth, N.: Program development by stepwise refinement. Commun. ACM **14**(4), 221–227 (1971)

Translating Between Implicit and Explicit Versions of Proof

Roberto Blanco[1]([⊠]), Zakaria Chihani[2], and Dale Miller[1]

[1] Inria & LIX/École Polytechnique, Palaiseau, France
{roberto.blanco,dale.miller}@inria.fr
[2] CEA-List, Gif-sur-Yvette, France
zakaria.chihani@cea.fr

Abstract. The Foundational Proof Certificate (FPC) framework can be used to define the semantics of a wide range of proof evidence. For example, such definitions exist for a number of textbook proof systems as well as for the proof evidence output from some existing theorem proving systems. An important decision in designing a proof certificate format is the choice of how many details are to be placed within certificates. Formats with fewer details are smaller and easier for theorem provers to output but they require more sophistication from checkers since checking will involve some proof reconstruction. Conversely, certificate formats containing many details are larger but are checkable by less sophisticated checkers. Since the FPC framework is based on well-established proof theory principles, proof certificates can be manipulated in meaningful ways. In this paper, we illustrate how it is possible to automate moving from implicit to explicit (*elaboration*) and from explicit to implicit (*distillation*) proof evidence via the proof checking of a *pair of proof certificates*. Performing elaboration makes it possible to transform a proof certificate with details missing into a certificate packed with enough details so that a simple kernel (without support for proof reconstruction) can check the elaborated certificate. We illustrate how trust in only a single, simple checker of explicitly described proofs can be used to provide trust in a range of theorem provers employing a range of proof structures.

1 Introduction

The study and development of programming languages have been aided by the use of (at least) two frameworks: context-free grammars (CFG) are used to define the structure of programs and structural operational semantics (SOS) [44] are used to define the evaluation and behavior of programming languages. Both of these frameworks make it possible to define the structure and meaning of a programming language in a way that is independent of a particular parser and particular compiler. Specifications in these frameworks are both mathematically rigorous and easily given prototype implementations using the logic programming paradigm [10,24,34,47].

The study and development of automated and interactive reasoning systems can similarly benefit from the introduction of frameworks that are capable of

© Springer International Publishing AG 2017
L. de Moura (Ed.): CADE 2017, LNAI 10395, pp. 255–273, 2017.
DOI: 10.1007/978-3-319-63046-5_16

defining the meaning of proof descriptions that are output by provers. Such formal semantics of proof languages make it possible to separate the production of proofs (via possibly untrusted and complex theorem provers) from the checking of proofs (via smaller and trusted checkers). In such a setting, the provenance of a proof should not be critical for checking a proof.

Separating theorem provers from proof checkers using a simple, declarative specification of proof certificates is not new: see [27] for a historical account. For example, the LF dependently typed λ-calculus [25] was originally proposed as a framework for specifying (natural deduction) proofs and the Elf system [41] provided both type checking and inference for LF: the proof-carrying code project of [40] used LF as a target proof language. The LFSC system is an extension of the dependently typed λ-calculus with side-conditions and an implementation of it has successfully been used to check proofs coming from the SMT solvers CLSAT and CVC4 [48]. Deduction modulo [18] is another extension to dependently typed λ-terms in which rewriting is available: the Dedukti checker, based on that extension, has been successfully used to check proofs from such systems as Coq [9] and HOL [4]. In the domain of higher-order classical logic, the GAPT system [22] can check proofs given by sequent calculus, resolution, and expansion trees and allows for checking and transforming among proofs in those formats.

Foundational Proof Certificates (FPC) is a recently proposed framework for defining the semantics of a wide range of proof languages for first-order classical and intuitionistic logic [13,16,17]. Instead of starting with dependently typed λ-calculus, the FPC framework is based on Gentzen's more low-level notion of sequent calculus proof. FPC definitions have been formulated for resolution refutations [46], expansion trees [38] (a generalization of Herbrand disjunctions), Frege proof systems, matings [2], simply typed and dependently typed λ-terms, equality reasoning [15], tableau proofs for some modal logics [30,31,37], and decision procedures based on conjunctive normal forms, truth table evaluation, and the G4ip calculus [21,50]. Additionally, FPCs have been used to formalize proof outlines [8] and have been applied to model checking [28]. As with other declarative and high-level frameworks, proof checkers for FPC specifications can be implemented using the logic programming model of computation [14,17,35].

A central issue in designing a proof certificate format involves choosing the level of proof detail that is stored within a certificate. If a lot of details (e.g., complete substitution instances and complete computation traces) are recorded within certificates, simple programs can be used to check certificates: of course, such certificates may also be large and impractical to communicate between prover and checker. On the other hand, if many details are left out, then proof checking would involve elements of *proof reconstruction* that can increase the time to perform proof checking (and reconstruction) as well as increase the sophistication of the proof checking mechanism.

One approach to this trade-off is to invoke the Poincaré principle [7] which states that computation traces (such as that for $2 + 2 = 4$) should be left out of a proof and reconstructed by the checker. This principle requires a checker to be complex enough to contain a (possibly small) programming language interpreter.

In LFSC and the Dedukti checker, such computations are performed using deterministic functional programs. The FPC framework goes a step beyond that by allowing nondeterministic computation as well. As is familiar from the study of finite state machines, nondeterministic specifications can be exponentially smaller than deterministic specifications: such a possibility for shortening specifications is an interesting option to exploit in specifying proof certificates. Of course, deterministic computations are instances of nondeterministic computations: similarly, FPCs can be restricted to deterministic computation when desired.

The following example illustrates a difference between requiring all details to be present in a certificate and allowing a certificate to drop some details. A proof checker for first-order classical logic could be asked to establish that a given disjunctive collection of literals, say, $L_1 \vee \ldots \vee L_n$ is provable. An explicit certificate of such a proof could be a (unordered) pair $\{i, j\} \subseteq \{1, \ldots, n\}$ such that L_i and L_j are complementary. If we allow nondeterminism, then the indexes i, j do not need to be provided: instead, we could simply confirm that there exist guesses for i and j such that literal L_i is the complement of L_j. (Of course, there may be more than one such pair of guesses.) The use of nondeterminism here is completely sensible since a systematic and naive procedure for attempting a proof of such a disjunction can reconstruct the missing details.

Since the sequent calculus can be used as the foundation for both logic programming and theorem proving, the nature and structure of nondeterministic choices in the search for sequent calculus proofs have received a lot of attention. For example, Gentzen's original LK and LJ sequent calculus proof systems [23] contained so many choices that it is hard to imagine performing meaningful proof search directly in those proof systems. Instead, those original proof systems can be replaced by *focused sequent calculus proof systems* in order to help structure nondeterminism. In particular, the common dichotomy between *don't-care* and *don't-know* nondeterminism gives rise to two different phases of focused proof construction. Don't-know nondeterminism is employed in the *positive* phase where significant choices (choices determined by, say, an oracle or a proof certificate) are chained together. Don't-care nondeterminism is employed in the *negative* phase and it is responsible for performing determinate (functional) computation. As we shall see, this second phase provides support for the Poincaré principle.

The next two sections describe and illustrate the main ideas behind focused proof systems and the FPC framework. Following that, we introduce the *pairing* FPC and illustrate how we can use it to elaborate proof certificates (introduce more details) and to distil proof certificates (remove some details). We then illustrate how such transformations of proof certificates can be used to provide trust in proof checking.

2   The Foundational Proof Certificates Framework

While we restrict our attention in this paper to first-order classical logic, much of what we develop here can also be applied to first-order intuitionistic logic and

$$\frac{true_c(\Xi)}{\Xi \vdash \Theta \Uparrow t^-, \Gamma} \qquad \frac{\Xi_1 \vdash \Theta \Uparrow A, \Gamma \quad \Xi_2 \vdash \Theta \Uparrow B, \Gamma \quad \wedge_c(\Xi, \Xi_1, \Xi_2)}{\Xi \vdash \Theta \Uparrow A \wedge^- B, \Gamma}$$

$$\frac{\Xi' \vdash \Theta \Uparrow \Gamma \quad f_c(\Xi, \Xi')}{\Xi \vdash \Theta \Uparrow f^-, \Gamma} \qquad \frac{\Xi' \vdash \Theta \Uparrow A, B, \Gamma \quad \vee_c(\Xi, \Xi')}{\Xi \vdash \Theta \Uparrow A \vee^- B, \Gamma}$$

$$\frac{\Xi' y \vdash \Theta \Uparrow [y/x]B, \Gamma \quad \forall_c(\Xi, \Xi')}{\Xi \vdash \Theta \Uparrow \forall x.B, \Gamma} \qquad \frac{\Xi_1 \vdash \Theta \Downarrow A \quad \Xi_2 \vdash \Theta \Downarrow B \quad \wedge_e(\Xi, \Xi_1, \Xi_2)}{\Xi \vdash \Theta \Downarrow A \wedge^+ B}$$

$$\frac{true_e(\Xi)}{\Xi \vdash \Theta \Downarrow t^+} \quad \frac{\Xi' \vdash \Theta \Downarrow B_i \quad i \in \{1,2\} \quad \vee_e(\Xi, \Xi', i)}{\Xi \vdash \Theta \Downarrow B_1 \vee^+ B_2} \quad \frac{\Xi' \vdash \Theta \Downarrow [t/x]B \quad \exists_e(\Xi, \Xi', t)}{\Xi \vdash \Theta \Downarrow \exists x.B}$$

$$\frac{\Xi_1 \vdash \Theta \Uparrow B \quad \Xi_2 \vdash \Theta \Uparrow \neg B \quad cut_e(\Xi, \Xi_1, \Xi_2, B)}{\Xi \vdash \Theta \Uparrow \cdot} cut \qquad \frac{init_e(\Xi, l) \quad \langle l, \neg P_a \rangle \in \Theta}{\Xi \vdash \Theta \Downarrow P_a} init$$

$$\frac{\Xi' \vdash \Theta, \langle l, C \rangle \Uparrow \Gamma \quad store_c(\Xi, \Xi', l)}{\Xi \vdash \Theta \Uparrow C, \Gamma} store \qquad \frac{\Xi' \vdash \Theta \Uparrow N \quad release_e(\Xi, \Xi')}{\Xi \vdash \Theta \Downarrow N} release$$

$$\frac{\Xi' \vdash \Theta \Downarrow P \quad decide_e(\Xi, \Xi', l) \quad \langle l, P \rangle \in \Theta \quad positive(P)}{\Xi \vdash \Theta \Uparrow \cdot} decide$$

Here, N is a negative formula, P is a positive formula, P_a is a positive literal, and C is a positive formula or a negative literal. The $\forall$-introduction rule has the proviso that the eigenvariable y is not free in the conclusion to that occurrence of the rule.

Fig. 1. The augmented LKF proof system LKF^a

to logics with higher-order quantification and fixed points. We assume that the reader is familiar with the one-sided version of Gentzen's LK calculus [23]. The FPC framework is layered on that sequent calculus by taking the following steps.

First, we employ the *LKF focused* sequent calculus of [29] in which proofs are divided into two alternating phases of inference rule applications. The *negative* phase uses sequents with an $\Uparrow$ and organizes the don't-care nondeterminism of rule application. Dually, the *positive* phase uses sequents with a $\Downarrow$ and is organized around don't-know nondeterminism. This proof system operates on *polarized* formulas, which differ from ordinary formulas in that there are positive and negative variants of the propositional constants t^-, $\wedge^-$, f^-, $\vee^-$, t^+, $\wedge^+$, f^+, $\vee^+$. A non-atomic formula is *positive* if its top-level connective is t^+, $\wedge^+$, f^+, $\vee^+$, or $\exists$, while a formula is *negative* if its top-level connective is t^-, $\wedge^-$, f^-, $\vee^-$, or $\forall$. (While the two variants of the propositional connectives have the same truth conditions, they behave differently in *LKF* proofs.) Literals can be given polarity arbitrarily: here we choose to fix the polarity of atoms to be positive and the polarity of negated atoms to be negative. The two kinds of sequents used in *LKF* are of the form $\vdash \Theta \Uparrow \Gamma$ and $\vdash \Theta \Downarrow B$ where Γ is a list of formulas, B is a formula, and Θ is a multiset of positive formulas or negative literals. We shall refer to the formulas in the Θ zone as *stored* formulas.

Second, the *LKF* proof system is *augmented* to get the LKF^a proof system displayed in Fig. 1. This augmentation consists of three kinds of items: *certificate terms* (the schematic variable Ξ), *indexes* (the schematic variable l), and *clerk and expert predicates*. Certificate terms are threaded through all inference rules by adding such a term to all LKF^a sequents. Every LKF inference rule is given an additional premise involving either a *clerk* predicate (identified by a subscripted c) or an *expert* predicate (identified by a subscripted e). These predicates are parameters to LKF^a: different ways to define these predicates will describe different styles of proof certificates that LKF^a can check. (In later sections, we shall present several different sets of definitions for these predicates.) Indexes are used to help manage the "storage and retrieval" of formulas. In particular, when in the part of the proof system used for performing all invertible rules (i.e., the don't-care nondeterminism phase), any formula whose introduction rule might not be invertible must be delayed: this is achieved by *storing* that formula. In LKF^a, when the store rule performs this duty, the formula is stored along with an *index*: subsequent references to stored formulas (in the decide and initial rules) make use of such indexes for accessing formulas. Thus, in the two kinds of sequents used by LKF^a, namely, $\Xi \vdash \Theta \Uparrow \Gamma$ and $\Xi \vdash \Theta \Downarrow B$, Ξ is a certificate term and Θ is a multiset of pairs $\langle l, C \rangle$ where l is an index and C is a positive formula or a negative literal. The clerk and expert premises are responsible for processing certificate terms and providing the continuation certificates (for any sequent premises) along with additional information that can be used to further instantiate the inference rule.

The soundness of LKF^a is immediate since an LKF^a proof contains a (one-sided) LK proof (which are known to be sound). More precisely: let B be an unpolarized formula and let $\hat{B}$ be some polarization of B (that is, the result of placing plus and minus signs on the propositional constants). If there is a proof of $\Xi \vdash \cdot \Uparrow \hat{B}$ then B is a first-order theorem since any proof of $\Xi \vdash \cdot \Uparrow \hat{B}$ can be made into an LK proof of B simply by deleting the clerk and expert premises and changing the up and down arrows into commas (as well as replacing pairs such as $\langle l, C \rangle$ in the storage context with simply C). Thus, soundness holds for this proof system *no matter how the clerks and experts are defined.*

The expert predicates used in the $\vee^+$ and $\exists$ introduction rules can examine the certificate Ξ and extract information (the value of i or the term t) and the continuation certificate Ξ'. There is no assumption that such an extraction is functional: indeed, the expert for the $\exists$ introduction might simply (nondeterministically) guess at some term. Similarly, we do not assume that there is a functional dependency between index and formulas: many formulas may be associated with the same index.

When examining proof construction in LKF^a, note that the negative ($\Uparrow$) phase is essentially *determinate*: in other words, clerks do routine computation and storage operations. On the other hand, experts can be nondeterministic: in particular, the certificate may lack specific information and the experts may simply guess at possible details. In this sense, the experts *consume* resources by either extracting information contained in a certificate term or by invoking nondeterminism.

The definition of a particular FPC is given by providing the constructors of proof certificate terms (Ξ) and of indexes (l) as well as the definition of the clerk and expert predicates. Figure 3 contains an example of a particular FPC.

While the FPC framework embraces a nondeterministic model of computation behind proof checking (and, hence, proof reconstruction), that framework obviously admits deterministic computation as well.

Proof checking a given certificate term will lead to the construction of a sequent calculus proof (in this case, in *LKF*): while the construction of such a proof helps us to trust the checking process, such a proof is *performed* and neither stored nor output. The FPC framework, however, is intended to make it possible to check many other forms of proof evidence: our clients will not need to understand sequent calculus in order to use our checker. By analogy, programmers in a high-level language such as, say, OCaml do not need to know about the many issues involved with compiling their code to bytecode or native code even though the execution of OCaml programs does generate a sequence of very low-level instructions.

3   Proof Checking Kernels as Logic Programs

Given that almost everything about the proof theory we described in the previous section is based on *relations*, the logic programming paradigm is, in principle, well suited to providing implementations of trusted proof checkers, also called *kernels*. (For an extended argument supporting this conclusion, see [35].) Many people may not wish to trust the implementations of such complex operations as unification and backtracking search, which would be inherent to a logic programming-based kernel. Also, implementations of logic programming, such as Prolog, have often supported unsound logical operations (for example, unification without the occurs-check). Fortunately, there have been many who have implemented logic programming languages that not only focus on sound deduction but also include a great deal more logic than, say, Prolog. Such systems include the Teyjus [39] and ELPI [20] implementations of λProlog [36] and the Twelf [42] and Beluga [43] implementations of LF [25].

The proof system in Fig. 1 can easily be seen as a program in λProlog, a language that supports hypothetical reasoning, variable bindings, (capture-avoiding) substitution, and unification that treats logic variables and eigenvariables soundly. To illustrate how inference rules can be specified in λProlog, the following four clauses specify the ∃-introduction rule, the ∀-introduction rule, the decide rule, and the store rule.

```
sync  Xi (some B)       :- someE Xi Xi' T, sync Xi' (B T).
async Xi [all B|Rest]   :- allC Xi Xi', pi w\ async (Xi' w) [B w|Rest].
async Xi nil            :- decideE Xi Xi' I, storage I P, isPos P, sync Xi' P.
async Xi [C|Rest]       :- (isPos C ; isNegAtm C),
                             storeC Xi Xi' I, storage I C => async Xi' Rest.
```

Here, provability of ⇑ and ⇓ sequents is encoded using the `async` and `sync` predicates, respectively. (Historically, the negative and positive phases have also been called *asynchronous* and *synchronous*, respectively [1].) The syntax `pi w\` denotes the universal quantification of the variable `w`: operationally, a λProlog interpreter instantiates the bound variable `w` with an eigenvariable (a new, scoped constant) when interpreting such a goal. Here, the hypothetical reasoning mechanism of λProlog (the symbol => denotes implication in a goal) is used to associate indexes with stored (positive or atomic) formulas (using the **storage** predicate): as a result, the Θ zone in Fig. 1 does not need to be an explicit argument in the specification of the kernel since it is encoded as hypothetical assumptions within λProlog.

The λProlog specification of LKF^a can be viewed as a trustworthy kernel. (Section 6 describes another trustworthy but more limited kernel written in OCaml.) Someone interested in having their proofs checked by this kernel must provide (in λProlog) the definition of certificate and index terms (of type **cert** and **index** respectively) and the definition of the clerk and expert predicates. The next section provides a few examples of such specifications.

4 Example FPCs

In this section, we provide the FPC definitions of three different proof formats.

4.1 Controlling the Decide Rule

The only place where Gentzen's structural rule of contraction is used within LKF^a is the decide rule. If contractions can be sufficiently controlled, naive search algorithms can often become decision procedures. To that end, it is easy to design a proof certificate that describes any LKF^a proof with an upper bound on its *decide depth* (that is, the maximum number of decide inference rules along any path in the proof). To convert this observation into an FPC, we need only one index, say, **indx** and we use just one form of certificate, namely, the term (dd D) where D is a natural number. Below is the specification of the clerk and expert predicates (here, s is the non-zero natural number constructor).

```
andNegC     (dd D) (dd D) (dd D).      orPosE      (dd D) (dd D) Choice.
andPosE     (dd D) (dd D) (dd D).      someE       (dd D) (dd D) T.
falseC      (dd D) (dd D).             storeC      (dd D) (dd D) indx.
releaseE    (dd D) (dd D).             initialE    (dd D) indx.
orNegC      (dd D) (dd D).             trueE       (dd D).
allC        (dd D) (x\ dd D).          decideE     (dd (s D)) (dd D) indx.
```

These clerks and experts leave the bound D untouched except for the **decideE** (the $decide_e$ predicate in Fig. 1) which decrements that bound. The experts for the positive disjunction and the existential quantifier are nondeterministic since, for example, every term T is a possible instantiation allowed by the **someE** expert specification. The two predicates that deal with indexes—**storeC** and **decideE**—always make use of the same index. Since the cut expert **cutE** is not defined, this FPC will only allow checking cut-free proofs. This FPC provides a high-level means of describing proofs in the sense that the goal formula (async (dd N) [B]) is provable from the kernel clauses and the clerk and expert clauses above if and only if B has an LKF proof of decide depth N or less.

Many other descriptions of proofs via FPCs are possible. For example, it is easy to design a certificate that is just a tree of nodes labeled with formulas that are used as cut formulas: all other details of the proof are unspecified. Another certificate design could be a tree of nodes labeled with indexes that record when an index is used during the decide inference rule. For now, we consider such certificates as descriptive and we make no assumption that checking that a given certificate holds for a given formula is decidable: with many high-level descriptions of proofs, such checking might indeed be undecidable.

4.2   Conjunctive Normal Form: A Decision Procedure as an FPC

Converting a propositional formula to conjunctive normal form provides an (expensive) decision procedure for determining whether or not a propositional formula is a tautology. The following FPC encodes this decision procedure. First, we choose to polarize all propositional connectives negatively. An *LKF* proof with only such a polarized formula in its conclusion consists of exactly one large negative phase that has, as premises, sequents containing only stored literals. Such a sequent is provable if and only if there is an index, say i, that labels a positive literal and the complement of that literal exists with the index j. We need only one certificate constructor, say cnf, and one index, say, lit. The clerk and expert predicates for this FPC can be defined as follows.

```
andNegC     cnf cnf cnf.        initialE            cnf lit.
orNegC          cnf cnf.        decideE         cnf cnf lit.
falseC          cnf cnf.        storeC          cnf cnf lit.
releaseE        cnf cnf.
```

In this case, the proof certificate size is constant (just the token cnf) while checking time can be exponential.

A simple variation of this FPC would be a certificate that stores every literal with different indexes and then accumulates all pairs $\langle i, j \rangle$ such that i and j are complementary literals within the same premise. Such an FPC essentially contains a *mating* [3]. Expansion trees [12,38] can also be accounted for by first admitting quantificational formulas and then storing in certificates the instantiations for the existential quantifiers.

4.3   Resolution Refutations

An FPC defining binary resolution refutations has been given in [16] and we describe it briefly here since the experimental results described in Sect. 7 build on this example. A *clause* is a formula of the form $\forall x_1 \ldots \forall x_p. [L_1 \vee \cdots \vee L_q]$, where $p, q \geq 0$ and $L_1, \ldots, L_q$ are all literals (i.e., atoms or negated atoms). As polarized formulas, disjunctions in clauses are polarized negatively. A resolution refutation is essentially two lists of clauses $C_1, \ldots, C_n$ and $C_{n+1}, \ldots, C_m$ where each element of the second list is also accompanied with a *justification* which is a triple of indexes $\langle i, j, k \rangle$ that carries the claim that C_k is the result of resolving C_i and C_j. We also assume that the last clause C_m is the empty clause, written as f^-. The first list of clauses is used to form the theorem to be proved, namely, $\vdash \neg C_1 \vee \cdots \vee \neg C_m$, where by $\neg C_i$ we mean the negation normal form of the negation of clause C_i.

The main element of a resolution proof is the claim that two clauses, say, C_i and C_j *resolve* to yield a third clause C_k: that is, that the triple $\langle i, j, k \rangle$ is the justification associated to C_k. If that claim is correct, then it is the case that the sequent $\vdash \neg C_i, \neg C_j \Uparrow C_k$ must be provable in *LKF* with a focused proof of decide depth three or less. Also, every resolution triple corresponds to a cut, as illustrated by the inference rule of *LKF*. In particular, this figure is part of the translation of the claim that C_i and C_j resolve to yield clause C_{n+1} where both i and j are members of $\{1, \ldots, n\}$.

$$
\cfrac{\vdash \neg C_i, \neg C_j \Uparrow C_{n+1} \qquad \cfrac{\vdash \neg C_1, \ldots, \neg C_n, \neg C_{n+1} \Uparrow \cdot}{\vdash \neg C_1, \ldots, \neg C_n \Uparrow \neg C_{n+1}} \; store}{\vdash \neg C_1, \ldots, \neg C_n \Uparrow \cdot} \; cut
$$

Here, the left premise is a small proof that involves at most three decide rules (one on both i and j and one on an unspecified literal): a certificate can easily be written that describes how such a proof might be constructed. The right premise leads to yet another use of cut in order to check the next claimed resolution triple. Such proof construction ends when $\neg C_m$ appears in the sequent on the extreme right branch of the proof: since that formula is t^+, that branch is finished.

We shall not present a formal definition of resolution refutations as an FPC here in order to save space: the interested reader can find such definitions in [13,16,17]. There are, of course, a lot of choices as to how much information is placed into a certificate for resolution. For example, the exact instantiations used to compute resolvents could be explicitly added or not. If the instantiations are not part of the certificate, then checking the certificate would require the checker to reconstruct those substitution terms: a kernel based on a logic programming engine (as described in Sect. 3) is capable of applying unification and backtracking search in order to produce such instantiations. If one is not willing to trust an implementation of unification and backtracking search, it is possible (as we describe later) to design a proof certificate format that includes such substitution information.

Another piece of information that is not explicitly captured in the usual definition of resolution is the order in which the clauses C_i and C_j are applied in order to build the subproof justifying the resolution triple $\langle C_i, C_j, C_m \rangle$. In this polarized setting, this order is important and certificates can be designed to attempt both orders or to use the explicit order given in the certificate. This difference in design will not affect the size of certificates but can affect the time required to check certificates (see Sect. 7).

5 Pairing Certificates

Because FPC definitions of proof evidence are declarative (in contrast to procedural), some formal manipulations of proof certificates are enabled easily. We illustrate how the formal *pairing* of two certificates can be used to transform proof certificates into either more or less explicit certificates.

```
cutE      (A <c> B) (C <c> D) (E <c> F) Cut :- cutE A C E Cut, cutE B D F Cut.
allC      (A <c> B) (x\ (C x) <c> (D x)) :- allC      A C,    allC      B D.
andNegC   (A <c> B) (C <c> D) (E <c> F)  :- andNegC   A C E,  andNegC   B D F.
andPosE   (A <c> B) (C <c> D) (E <c> F)  :- andPosE   A C E,  andPosE   B D F.
decideE   (A <c> B) (C <c> D) (I <i> J)  :- decideE   A C I,  decideE   B D J.
falseC    (A <c> B) (C <c> D)            :- falseC    A C,    falseC    B D.
initialE  (C <c> B) (I <i> J)            :- initialE  C I,    initialE  B J.
orNegC    (A <c> B) (C <c> D)            :- orNegC    A C,    orNegC    B D.
orPosE    (A <c> B) (C <c> D) E          :- orPosE    A C E,  orPosE    B D E.
releaseE  (A <c> B) (C <c> D)            :- releaseE  A C,    releaseE  B D.
someE     (A <c> B) (C <c> D) W          :- someE     A C W,  someE     B D W.
storeC    (A <c> B) (C <c> D) (I <i> J)  :- storeC    A C I,  storeC    B D J.
trueE     (A <c> B)                      :- trueE     A,      trueE     B.
```

Fig. 2. The pairing FPC

5.1   The Pairing FPC

Consider checking a proof certificate for a resolution refutation that does not contain the substitutions used to compute a resolvent. Since the checking process computes a detailed focused sequent in the background, that process must compute all the substitution terms required by sequent calculus proofs. If we could check *in parallel* a second certificate that allows for storing such substitution terms, then those instances could be inserted into the second, more explicit certificate. Fortunately, it is a simple matter to do just such parallel checking of two proof certificates.

Let `<c>` be an infix constructor of type `cert -> cert -> cert` and let `<i>` be an infix constructor of type `index -> index -> index`. The full specification (using λProlog syntax) of the FPC for pairing is given in Fig. 2. This pairing operation allows for the parallel checking of two certificates: clearly, both certificates must eventually expand into the same underlying sequent calculus proof but those certificates could retain different amounts of detail from each other. Note that the definition of pairing for the existential expert ensures that both certificates *agree* on the same information (here a witness *t*). Of course, one (or both) of those certificates do not need to actually contain the witness information. While paired certificates must be able to agree on substitution terms, choices for (positive) disjunctions, and cut formulas, they will not need to agree on the notion of index. Instead, we use the pairing constructor `<i>` to form an index out of two indexes.

While the transformations between proof certificates that can take place using this pairing FPC are useful (as we argue in the following sections), such transformations are also limited. For example, pairing cannot be used to transform a proof certificate based on, say conjunctive normal forms, into one based on resolutions, since the former makes no use of cut and the latter contains cuts. The pairing of two such certificates will (almost) always fail to succeed. Pairing is really limited to transforming within the spectrum of "many details, fewer details" and not between two different styles of proof. Thus, it is possible to transform a proof certificate encoding resolution that does not contain substitution terms to one that does contain substitution terms. The reverse is also possible.

```
kind max type.
type ix                      nat -> index.
type max           nat -> max -> cert.
type max0                          max.
type max1                   max -> max.
type max2           max -> max -> max.
type maxa                 index -> max.
type maxi        index -> max -> max.
type maxv        (tm -> max) -> max.
type maxt            tm -> max -> max.
type maxf   form -> max -> max -> max.
type maxc        choice -> max -> max.


allC      (max N (maxv C ))          (x\ max N (C x)).
andNegC   (max N (max2 A B))         (max N A) (max N B).
andPosE   (max N (max2 A B))         (max N A) (max N B).
cutE      (max N (maxf F A B))       (max N A) (max N B) F.
decideE   (max N (maxi I A))         (max N A) I.
storeC    (max N (maxi (ix N) A))  (max (s N) A) (ix N).
falseC    (max N (max1 A))           (max N A).
orNegC    (max N (max1 A))           (max N A).
releaseE  (max N (max1 A))           (max N A).
orPosE    (max N (maxc C A))         (max N A) C.
someE     (max N (maxt T A))         (max N A) T.
trueE     (max N  max0).
initialE  (max N (maxa I))  I.
```

Fig. 3. A certificate format including maximal details

5.2   A Maximally Explicit FPC

We can define a *maximally explicit* FPC that contains all the information that is explicitly needed to fill in all details in the augmented inference rules in Fig. 1. In principle, this certificate format records the full trace of the underlying sequent calculus proof computed during the execution of the kernel. The FPC in Fig. 3 is capable of storing all such details. Note that the natural number argument of max is used by the store clerk to choose a fresh index for every stored formula. The constructors of type max are different nodes of a symbolic proof tree, holding all information needed by the clerks and experts without recording the actual proof derivation. The constructors are as follows: max0 is a leaf node, max1 is a unary node, max2 is a binary node, maxv is used to bind an eigenvariable to the rest of the tree, maxt is annotated with a term, maxf with a cut formula, maxc with a (disjunctive) choice, and maxi with an index.

Such a proof certificate can be automatically obtained through elaboration of any other proof certificate and the use of the pairing of certificates. For example, if the sequent dd (s (s z)) ⊢ · ⇑ F is provable then calling the checker with the sequent dd (s (s z)) <c> (max z X) ⊢ · ⇑ F, where X is a logic variable of type max, will build a fully explicit proof object.

5.3   Elaboration and Distillation of Certificates

The kernel is building a formal sequent proof which is not explicitly stored but is, in a sense, performed by the kernel. It is the performance of such a sequent calculus proof that helps to provide trust in the kernel. If a certificate is lacking necessary details for building such a sequent calculus proof (such as substitution instances), a kernel could attempt to reconstruct those details. The formal pairing of certificates described above links two certificates that lead to the same performance of a sequent calculus proof: in the logic programming setting, it is completely possible to see such linking of certificates as a means to transform one certificate to another certificate. The term *elaboration* will be used to refer to the process of transforming an implicit proof certificate to a more explicit proof certificate. The converse operation, called *distillation*, can also be performed: during such distillation, certain proof details can be discarded.

Since a given proof certificate can be elaborated into a number of different sequent calculus proofs, certificates can be used to provide high-level descriptions of *classes* of proofs. For example, FPCs have been used to describe *proof outlines* [8]: using a logic programming based kernel to check such a proof outline means that the kernel will attempt to reconstruct a complete proof based on the information given in the outline. If such a reconstruction is possible, pairing the proof checking of a proof outline with an explicit form of FPC would mean that the missing proof details could be recorded. In a similar fashion, Martin Davis's notion of "obvious logical inference" [19] can be described easily as an FPC: here, an inference is "obvious" if all quantifiers are instantiated at most once. Thus, using a kernel to attempt to check such an FPC against a specific formula essentially implements the check of whether or not an "obvious inference" can complete the proof.

Since we shall focus on certificate elaboration in the rest of this paper, we conclude this section with a few comments about certificate distillation. Consider, for example, a proof certificate that contains substitution instances for all quantifiers that appear within a proof. In some situations, such terms might be large and their occurrences within a certificate could make a certificate large. In the first-order logic setting, however, if a certificate stores instead linkage or mating information between literals in a proof, then the implied unification problems can be used to infer the missing substitutions (assuming that the kernel contains a trusted implementation of unification). The resulting certificate could well be much smaller: checking them could, however, involve a possibly large unification problem to be performed. Besides such approaches to proof compression, distilling can provide an elegant way to answer questions such as: What lemmas have been used in this proof? How deep (counting decide rules) is a proof? What substitution terms were used in a certain subproof? Certificates that retain only some coarse information such as this could be used to provide some high-level insights into the structure of a given proof.

6   The Kernel as a Functional Program

Given that the maximally explicit certificate contains all the information needed to build a (focused) sequent calculus proof, a proof checker for only that FPC does not need to perform unification or backtracking search. Such a checker may be simple and easy to analyze and trust. To demonstrate this possibility, we have implemented in OCaml a proof checker for the maximal FPC in Fig. 3.

MaxChecker is an OCaml program of about 200 lines of code (available online at proofcert.github.io). Separate from the kernel is a parser that reads from an input that contains three items: (*i*) a collection of non-logical constants and their (simple) types; (*ii*) a polarized version of a formula (the proposed theorem); and (*iii*) a proof certificate in the maximal FPC format. The kernel is then asked to check whether or not the given certificate yields a proof of the proposed theorem. If this check is successful, the kernel prints out the (unpolarized) theorem as a means to confirm what formula it has actually checked.

As Pollack has argued in [45], the printer and parser of our system must be trusted to be faithfully representing the formulas that they input and output. Here, we assume that that concern is addressed in standard ways: in our particular tool, we have used standard parser generating tools in order to link trust in our tool with trust in a well engineered and frequently used tool.

It is now an easy matter to describe the architecture of a proof checker that we can use to check *any* FPC-defined proof certificate while only needing to trust MaxChecker. First, use the flexible λProlog based (or equivalent) interpreter to do the formal checking of any proof certificate accompanied by its FPC definition. If we do that checking using both the maximal and pairing FPCs then the maximal certificate (the most explicit form of the input certificate) can be extracted. Second, run MaxChecker on this final and explicit certificate.

We can push this issue of trust another step. Since the MaxChecker is a simple terminating functional program, it should be a simple matter to implement it within, say, the Coq proof assistant, and formally prove in Coq that a successful check leads to a formal proof in, say, Gentzen's LK and LJ proof systems. By reflecting [11,26] these weaker proof systems into Coq (including the axiom of excluded-middle for classical logic proofs), the chaining of a flexible certificate elaborator with the Coq based MaxChecker can then be used to get Coq to accept proofs from a range of other proof systems. The first author plans such a Coq implementation as part of his Ph.D. dissertation.

It is possible (at least in some logical settings) to leave out some details from a proof certificate while still providing for determinant proof checking. For example, consider the variant of the maximal FPC in which no substitution terms are stored: specifically, redefine the type as well as the clerk and expert predicates in Fig. 3 for the maxv and maxt constructors as follows.

```
type maxv        max -> max.
type maxt        max -> max.

allC    (max N (maxv C))    (max N C).
someE   (max N (maxt A))    (max N A) T.
```

Certificates of this modified format will not contain any reference to eigenvariables or to substitution terms (existential witnesses). A proof checker for such certificates can, however, use so-called *logic variables* instead of explicit witness terms and then perform unification during the implementation of the initial rule. Since the unification of first-order terms (even in the presence of eigenvariables and their associated constraints) is determinate, such proof checking will not involve the need to perform backtracking search. The main downside for this variant of the maximally explicit certificate is that checking will involve the somewhat more complex operation of unification. Of course, such unification must deal with either Skolem functions or eigenvariables in order to address quantifier alternation. (λProlog treats eigenvariables directly since it implements unification under a mixed quantifier prefix [33].)

7   Some Experiments with Certificate Elaboration

We have experimented with various uses of certificate pairing and we report briefly on some of those experiments here. The code, data, and results from these experiments are available at proofcert.github.io.

We have used pairing in our λProlog checker in order to distil and elaborate a number of matrix-style (cut-free) proofs: for example, we have elaborated the cnf proof certificates (Sect. 4.2) into matings [3] and elaborated the decide depth FPC into an FPC based on oracle strings (see [17, Sect. 7]). Furthermore, these various certificate formats can be elaborated to the maximally explicit certificate. Since these certificate formats are seldom used in actual theorem provers, we describe below our more extensive experiments with resolution refutations.

We have defined three variations on the FPC definition of resolution with factoring that is given in Sect. 4.3. Let us call the FPC given above in Sect. 4.3 unordered-without, meaning that that format does not store substitution information and that when the certificate contains the triple $\langle i, j, k \rangle$, the order in which one decides on i and j is unknown. (Existing resolution systems might not offer to order these indexes.) We also defined the ordered-without format: in that case, the triple $\langle i, j, k \rangle$ means that i must be decided on before j. This certificate format is a simple modification of the one in Sect. 4.3: just one line of the decide expert is deleted from the unordered-without FPC definition. Finally, a third variant ordered-with was also defined: this certificate retains substitution and eigenvariable information as well.

Our goal is to certify the output of a *bona fide*, complex proving tool, that is sufficiently powerful to provide us with reasonably sized and publicly available *proof corpora*. To that end, we have selected Prover9 [32], a legacy, automated theorem prover of modest capabilities: an important feature for our experiment is that Prover9's output exposes a relatively simple and well-documented resolution calculus. We have taken the full set of Prover9 refutations in the TPTP library [49]—a total of 2668 in version 6.4.0—and excluded 52 files with irregular formatting (the resulting set of examples is precisely that of version 6.3.0). Of these, 978 fall in the fragment supported by the resolution FPCs; 27 are empty proofs that refute false. The two largest problems are extreme outliers, also excluded since they would be of limited utility to establish or confirm trends. Each problem is expanded into a detailed proof with Prover9's Prooftrans tool. This proof is parsed and a proof certificate for the unordered FPC is extracted, along with type signatures for atoms and terms. The λProlog runtime uses pairing to elaborate and check the more explicit certificates, and it outputs the formula and the maximally explicit certificate to MaxChecker.

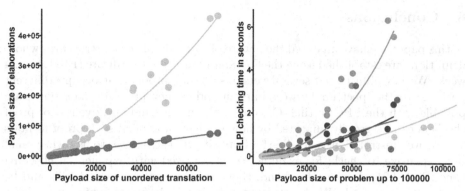

Data series: unordered-without, ordered-without, ordered-with, maximal.

Fig. 4. Complexity of certificate elaboration

Figure 4 shows a summary of our experiments with this output from Prover9. The size of a formula or term is simply a count of the number of constructors in that formula or term. The size of resolution certificates is defined here to be the sum of the sizes of the initial and derived clauses along with their justifications. The size of maximally explicit certificates is defined as the size of the actual certificate term plus the size of the original set of clauses. Certificate sizes grow as they are made more explicit, but the blowup here is bounded by small constants. Elaborating from unordered-without to ordered-without causes no change in size while elaborating further to ordered-with generally grows certificates by 16%. Finally, elaborating to the maximally explicit certificate causes an increase by an average factor of 2.8 (although that factor ranges from 1.02 to 6.54). Here, a natural number is counted as one symbol; the unary representation of numbers causes a blowup in size (the average factor being 5.8 with range from 1.2 to 361).

The second graph in Fig. 4 shows that the more detailed a certificate is, the faster it is to check. For example, a certificate in the unordered-without format of 75000 symbols can be checked in 6 or more seconds: a similarly sized certificate in the maximally explicit format can be checked in less than a second.

The choice of Teyjus [39] or ELPI [20] as λProlog runtime yields qualitatively similar results, but shows significant performance differences and asymmetries, especially in the substantial elaboration overhead; in general, ELPI is faster. The checking times for the MaxChecker on the large, maximally explicit certificates running in OCaml are negligible compared to elaboration times within λProlog: in particular, MaxChecker always ran in less than 0.01 seconds on each example displayed in Fig. 4.

We have successfully checked all resolution refutations produced by Prover9 that involved binary resolution and factoring. In order to capture all of Prover9's proofs in the TPTP repository we need to add support for paramodulation: the FPC for paramodulation given in [14] is a starting point.

8   Conclusions

In this paper, we have analyzed the nature of some simple proof structures whose definitions are established using the Foundational Proof Certificate (FPC) framework. We have illustrated several versions of such proofs that occupy different positions on the spectrum between implicit and explicit proof. Both extremes are possible with the FPC setting. Of course, the nature and effectiveness of proof checkers can be greatly impacted by how implicit or explicit such proof formats are. As we illustrated, it is possible for implicit proof structures to be rather small but expensive to check: for example, constant sized with exponential checking time (Sect. 4.2). On the other hand, they can also contain more details and be much easier to check. We have also noted that logic programming provides a simple, immediate, and sound proof checker for any formal FPC definition.

We then introduced the notion of formally pairing two certificates into one: when such a paired certificate is checked, it is possible for information to flow between proof certificates (which may store different aspects of a proof) with the implementation of the kernel (which must ultimately generate all details of a proof). In this way, checking an implicit certificate can lead to the construction of a more explicit certificate. In fact, we illustrated how it was possible to define a maximally explicit proof certificate in which enough details are present that a simple functional program (in our case, written in OCaml) is able to check the proof without needing backtracking search and unification. As such, if one is not willing to trust a logic programming checker, it is possible to use the logic programming checker to expand an implicit proof to a maximally explicit proof certificate and then certify the answer using the simpler (presumably) trusted functional program.

The pairing of proof certificates can be used with other tasks elaborating certificates. Distilling of proofs, the converse of elaboration, might also be useful in the analysis of proofs. For example, pairing can be used to extract from any certificate the tree of cut formulas used within it or to compute its decide depth.

While the discussion in this paper has been limited to treating classical first-order logic, focusing proof systems and the FPC framework have also been proposed for first-order intuitionistic logic [17,29] as well as logics extended with least and greatest fixed points [5,6]. As a result, most of the points described in this paper can also be applied to those settings as well.

Acknowledgement. We thank the anonymous reviewers for their comments on an earlier version of this paper. This work was funded, in part, by the ERC Advanced Grant ProofCert.

References

1. Andreoli, J.-M.: Logic programming with focusing proofs in linear logic. J. Logic Comput. **2**(3), 297–347 (1992)
2. Andrews, P.B.: Refutations by matings. IEEE Trans. Comput. **25**(8), 801–807 (1976)

3. Andrews, P.B.: Theorem proving via general matings. J. ACM **28**(2), 193–214 (1981)
4. Assaf, A., Burel, G.: Translating HOL to Dedukti. In: Kaliszyk, C., Paskevich, A. (eds.) Proceedings Fourth Workshop on Proof eXchange for Theorem Proving, PxTP 2015. EPTCS, vol. 186, Berlin, Germany, pp. 74–88, 2–3 August 2015
5. Baelde, D.: Least and greatest fixed points in linear logic. ACM Trans. Comput. Logic **13**(1), 2:1–2:44 (2012)
6. Baelde, D., Miller, D.: Least and greatest fixed points in linear logic. In: Dershowitz, N., Voronkov, A. (eds.) LPAR 2007. LNCS, vol. 4790, pp. 92–106. Springer, Heidelberg (2007). doi:10.1007/978-3-540-75560-9_9
7. Barendregt, H., Barendsen, E.: Autarkic computations in formal proofs. J. Autom. Reasoning **28**(3), 321–336 (2002)
8. Blanco, R., Miller, D.: Proof outlines as proof certificates: a system description. In: Cervesato, I., Schürmann, C. (eds.) Proceedings of the First International Workshop on Focusing. Electronic Proceedings in Theoretical Computer Science, vol. 197, pp. 7–14. Open Publishing Association, November 2015
9. Boespflug, M., Carbonneaux, Q., Hermant, O.: The λΠ-calculus modulo as a universal proof language. In: Pichardie, D., Weber, T. (eds.) Proceedings of PxTP 2012: Proof Exchange for Theorem Proving, pp. 28–43 (2012)
10. Borras, P., Clément, D., Despeyroux, T., Incerpi, J., Kahn, G., Lang, B., Pascual, V.: Centaur: the system. In: Third Annual Symposium on Software Development Environments (SDE3), Boston, pp. 14–24 (1988)
11. Boutin, S.: Using reflection to build efficient and certified decision procedures. In: Abadi, M., Ito, T. (eds.) TACS 1997. LNCS, vol. 1281, pp. 515–529. Springer, Heidelberg (1997). doi:10.1007/BFb0014565
12. Chaudhuri, K., Hetzl, S., Miller, D.: A multi-focused proof system isomorphic to expansion proofs. J. Logic Comput. **26**(2), 577–603 (2016)
13. Chihani, Z.: Certification of First-order proofs in classical and intuitionistic logics. Ph.D. thesis, Ecole Polytechnique, August 2015
14. Chihani, Z., Libal, T., Reis, G.: The proof certifier Checkers. In: Nivelle, H. (ed.) TABLEAUX 2015. LNCS, vol. 9323, pp. 201–210. Springer, Cham (2015). doi:10.1007/978-3-319-24312-2_14
15. Chihani, Z., Miller, D.: Proof certificates for equality reasoning. In: Benevides, M., Thiemann, R. (eds.) Post-proceedings of LSFA 2015: 10th Workshop on Logical and Semantic Frameworks, with Applications. ENTCS, vol. 323, Natal, Brazil (2016)
16. Chihani, Z., Miller, D., Renaud, F.: Foundational proof certificates in first-order logic. In: Bonacina, M.P. (ed.) CADE 2013. LNCS, vol. 7898, pp. 162–177. Springer, Heidelberg (2013). doi:10.1007/978-3-642-38574-2_11
17. Chihani, Z., Miller, D., Renaud, F.: A semantic framework for proof evidence. J. Autom. Reasoning. doi:10.1007/s10817-016-9380-6
18. Cousineau, D., Dowek, G.: Embedding pure type systems in the Lambda-Pi-Calculus modulo. In: Rocca, S.R. (ed.) TLCA 2007. LNCS, vol. 4583, pp. 102–117. Springer, Heidelberg (2007). doi:10.1007/978-3-540-73228-0_9
19. Davis, M.: Obvious logical inferences. In: Drinan, A. (ed.) Proceedings of the 7th International Joint Conference on Artificial Intelligence (IJCAI 1981), pp. 530–531. William Kaufmann, Los Altos, August 1991
20. Dunchev, C., Guidi, F., Sacerdoti Coen, C., Tassi, E.: ELPI: fast, embeddable, λProlog interpreter. In: Davis, M., Fehnker, A., McIver, A., Voronkov, A. (eds.) LPAR 2015. LNCS, vol. 9450, pp. 460–468. Springer, Heidelberg (2015). doi:10.1007/978-3-662-48899-7_32

21. Dyckhoff, R.: Contraction-free sequent calculi for intuitionistic logic. J. Symbolic Logic **57**(3), 795–807 (1992)
22. Ebner, G., Hetzl, S., Reis, G., Riener, M., Wolfsteiner, S., Zivota, S.: System description: GAPT 2.0. In: Olivetti, N., Tiwari, A. (eds.) IJCAR 2016. LNCS, vol. 9706, pp. 293–301. Springer, Cham (2016). doi:10.1007/978-3-319-40229-1_20
23. Gentzen, G.: Investigations into logical deduction. In: Szabo, M.E. (ed.) The Collected Papers of Gerhard Gentzen, pp. 68–131. North-Holland, Amsterdam (1935)
24. Hannan, J.: Extended natural semantics. J. Funct. Program. **3**(2), 123–152 (1993)
25. Harper, R., Honsell, F., Plotkin, G.: A framework for defining logics. J. ACM **40**(1), 143–184 (1993)
26. Harrison, J.: Metatheory and reflection in theorem proving: A survey and critique. Technical report, Citeseer (1995)
27. Harrison, J., Urban, J., Wiedijk, F.: History of interactive theorem proving. In: Siekmann, J. (ed.) Computational Logic. Handbook of the History of Logic, vol. 9, pp. 135–214. North Holland (2014)
28. Heath, Q., Miller, D.: A framework for proof certificates in finite state exploration. In: Kaliszyk, C., Paskevich, A. (eds.) Proceedings of the Fourth Workshop on Proof eXchange for Theorem Proving. Electronic Proceedings in Theoretical Computer Science, vol. 186, pp. 11–26. Open Publishing Association, August 2015
29. Liang, C., Miller, D.: Focusing and polarization in linear, intuitionistic, and classical logics. Theor. Comput. Sci. **410**(46), 4747–4768 (2009)
30. Libal, T., Volpe, M.: Certification of prefixed tableau proofs for modal logic. In: The Seventh International Symposium on Games, Automata, Logics and Formal Verification (GandALF 2016). EPTCS, vol. 226, Catania, Italy, pp. 257–271, September 2016
31. Marin, S., Miller, D., Volpe, M.: A focused framework for emulating modal proof systems. In: Beklemishev, L., Demri, S., Máté, A. (eds.) 11th Conference on Advances in Modal Logic. Advances in Modal Logic, vol. 11, Budapest, Hungary, pp. 469–488. College Publications, August 2016
32. McCune, W.: Prover9 and mace4 (2010). http://www.cs.unm.edu/~mccune/prover9/
33. Miller, D.: Unification under a mixed prefix. J. Symbolic Comput. **14**(4), 321–358 (1992)
34. Miller, D.: Formalizing operational semantic specifications in logic. In: Proceedings of the 17th International Workshop on Functional and (Constraint) Logic Programming (WFLP 2008), vol. 246, pp. 147–165, August 2009
35. Miller, D.: Proof checking and logic programming. Formal Aspects Comput. **29**(3), 383–399 (2017)
36. Miller, D., Nadathur, G.: Programming with Higher-Order Logic. Cambridge University Press, Cambridge (2012)
37. Miller, D., Volpe, M.: Focused labeled proof systems for modal logic. In: Davis, M., Fehnker, A., McIver, A., Voronkov, A. (eds.) Logic for Programming, Artificial Intelligence, and Reasoning (LPAR). LNCS, vol. 9450. Springer, Heidelberg (2015)
38. Miller, D.A.: Expansion tree proofs and their conversion to natural deduction proofs. In: Shostak, R.E. (ed.) CADE 1984. LNCS, vol. 170, pp. 375–393. Springer, New York (1984). doi:10.1007/978-0-387-34768-4_22
39. Nadathur, G., Mitchell, D.J.: System description: Teyjus—a compiler and abstract machine based implementation of λProlog. In: Ganzinger, H. (ed.) CADE 1999. LNCS, vol. 1632, pp. 287–291. Springer, Heidelberg (1999). doi:10.1007/3-540-48660-7_25

40. Necula, G.C.: Proof-carrying code. In: Conference Record of the 24th Symposium on Principles of Programming Languages 1997, Paris, France, pp. 106–119. ACM Press (1997)
41. Pfenning, F.: Elf: a language for logic definition and verified metaprogramming. In: 4th International Symposium on Logic in Computer Science, Monterey, CA, pp. 313–321, June 1989
42. Pfenning, F.: Logic programming in the LF logical framework. In: Huet, G., Plotkin, G.D. (eds.) Logical Frameworks, pp. 149–181. Cambridge University Press (1991)
43. Pientka, B., Dunfield, J.: Beluga: a framework for programming and reasoning with deductive systems (system description). In: Giesl, J., Hähnle, R. (eds.) IJCAR 2010. LNCS, vol. 6173, pp. 15–21. Springer, Heidelberg (2010). doi:10.1007/978-3-642-14203-1_2
44. Plotkin, G.D.: A structural approach to operational semantics. J. Logic Algebraic Program. **60–61**, 17–139 (2004)
45. Pollack, R.: How to believe a machine-checked proof. In: Sambin, G., Smith, J. (eds.) Twenty Five Years of Constructive Type Theory. Oxford University Press (1998)
46. Robinson, J.A.: A machine-oriented logic based on the resolution principle. J. ACM **12**, 23–41 (1965)
47. Shieber, S.M., Schabes, Y., Pereira, F.C.N.: Principles and implementation of deductive parsing. J. Logic Program. **24**(1–2), 3–36 (1995)
48. Stump, A., Oe, D., Reynolds, A., Hadarean, L., Tinelli, C.: SMT proof checking using a logical framework. Formal Methods Syst. Des. **42**(1), 91–118 (2013)
49. Sutcliffe, G.: The TPTP problem library and associated infrastructure. J. Autom. Reasoning **43**(4), 337–362 (2009)
50. Troelstra, A.S., Schwichtenberg, H.: Basic Proof Theory, 2nd edn. Cambridge University Press, Cambridge (2000)

A Unifying Principle for Clause Elimination in First-Order Logic

Benjamin Kiesl$^{(\boxtimes)}$ and Martin Suda$^{(\boxtimes)}$

Institute of Information Systems, Vienna University of Technology, Vienna, Austria
kiesl@kr.tuwien.ac.at, msuda@forsyte.at

Abstract. Preprocessing techniques for formulas in conjunctive normal form play an important role in first-order theorem proving. To speed up the proving process, these techniques simplify a formula without affecting its satisfiability or unsatisfiability. In this paper, we introduce the principle of implication modulo resolution, which allows us to lift several preprocessing techniques—in particular, several clause-elimination techniques—from the SAT-solving world to first-order logic. We analyze confluence properties of these new techniques and show how implication modulo resolution yields short soundness proofs for the existing first-order techniques of predicate elimination and blocked-clause elimination.

1 Introduction

Automatic theorem provers often have to deal with formulas that contain a considerable amount of redundant information. To speed up the proving process, they therefore usually employ dedicated preprocessing methods that aim at simplifying formulas as much as possible [1,2]. Since most provers are based on proof systems that require formulas to be in conjunctive normal form (CNF), preprocessing techniques operating on the clause level play a particularly important role. Research on SAT and on quantified Boolean formulas has given rise to a wide variety of CNF preprocessing techniques that significantly improve the performance of modern solvers [3], but for many of these techniques it was not clear whether they could be lifted to the level of first-order logic.

In this paper, we address this issue and introduce the principle of *implication modulo resolution*—a first-order generalization of *quantified implied outer resolvents* as introduced by Heule et al. [4] in the context of quantified Boolean formulas. Informally, a clause C is *implied modulo resolution* by a CNF formula F (which can be seen as a set of clauses) if C contains a literal such that all resolvents upon this literal are implied by $F \setminus \{C\}$. Here, by *all resolvents* we mean all resolvents with clauses in $F \setminus \{C\}$. In other words, although $F \setminus \{C\}$

This work has been supported by the Austrian Science Fund (FWF) under projects W1255-N23, S11403-N23, and S11409-N23, by the ERC Starting Grant 2014 SYM-CAR 639270, and by the National Science Foundation (NSF) under grant number CCF-1618574.

L. de Moura (Ed.): CADE 2017, LNAI 10395, pp. 274–290, 2017.
DOI: 10.1007/978-3-319-63046-5_17

might not necessarily *imply* the clause C, it implies all the conclusions that can be derived with C via resolution upon one of its literals. We show that this suffices to ensure that C can be removed from F without affecting the satisfiability or unsatisfiability of F.

The importance of implication modulo resolution lies in the fact that it allows us to construct soundness proofs for numerous preprocessing techniques. We therefore use the principle of implication modulo resolution to lift several SAT-preprocessing techniques to first-order logic without equality. These techniques, which have not been available in first-order logic so far, include clause-elimination procedures for *covered clauses* (CC) [5], *asymmetric tautologies* (AT) [6], *resolution asymmetric tautologies* (RAT) [7], and *resolution subsumed clauses* (RS) [7]. Moreover, we show how the use of implication modulo resolution yields short soundness proofs for the existing preprocessing techniques of *blocked-clause elimination* [8,9] and *predicate elimination* [2], again in the restricted case of first-order logic *without* equality.

Covered clauses are a generalization of the above-mentioned blocked clauses (which we discuss briefly in Sect. 4). To detect whether a clause is covered, one first adds a number of so-called *covered literals* to it and then checks whether the resulting clause is a blocked clause. Covered-clause elimination is more powerful than blocked-clause elimination in the sense that it implicitly removes all blocked clauses from a formula. As blocked-clause elimination leads to significant performance improvements of first-order theorem provers [8] and since the elimination of covered clauses has been shown to speed up modern SAT solvers [10], we expect covered-clause elimination to further boost prover performance.

Asymmetric tautologies and resolution asymmetric tautologies owe their popularity to the fact that their addition and elimination can simulate most of the reasoning techniques employed by state-of-the-art SAT solvers [7]. Because of this, they provide the basis for the well-known DRAT proof system [11], which is the de-facto standard for unsatisfiability proofs in practical SAT solving. Finally, the elimination of resolution subsumed clauses is another promising technique from the SAT world whose soundness on the first-order level can be easily shown using the principle of implication modulo resolution.

The main contributions of this paper are as follows: (1) We introduce the principle of implication modulo resolution. (2) We use implication modulo resolution to lift several clause-elimination techniques from the SAT world to first-order logic. (3) We show how implication modulo resolution yields short soundness proofs for existing preprocessing techniques from the literature. (4) We analyze confluence properties of the preprocessing techniques.

2   Preliminaries

We assume the reader to be familiar with the basics of first-order logic. As usual, formulas of a first-order language $\mathcal{L}$ are built using predicate symbols, function symbols, and constants from some given alphabet together with logical connectives, quantifiers, and variables. We use the letters $P, Q, R, S, \ldots$ as predicate symbols and the letters $f, g, h, \ldots$ as non-constant function symbols. Moreover, we use the letters $a, b, c, \ldots$ for constants and the letters $x, y, z, u, v, \ldots$ for variables (possibly with subscripts). An expression (i.e., a term, literal, formula, etc.) is *ground* if it contains no variables.

A *literal* is an atom or the negation of an atom, and a disjunction of literals is a *clause*. For a literal L, we define $\bar{L} = \neg P$ if $L = P$ and $\bar{L} = P$ if $L = \neg P$, where P is an atom. In the former case, L is of *positive polarity*; in the latter case, it is of *negative polarity*. If not stated otherwise, formulas are assumed to be in conjunctive normal form (CNF), i.e., a conjunction of clauses. Without loss of generality, clauses are assumed to be variable disjoint. Variables occurring in a CNF formula are implicitly universally quantified. We treat CNF formulas as sets of clauses and clauses as multisets of literals. A clause is a *tautology* if it contains both L and $\bar{L}$ for some literal L.

Regarding the semantics, we use the standard notions of *interpretation, model, validity, satisfiability,* and *logical equivalence*. We say that two formulas are *equisatisfiable* if they are either both satisfiable or both unsatisfiable. A *propositional assignment* is a mapping from ground atoms to the truth values 1 (*true*) and 0 (*false*). Accordingly, a set of ground clauses is *propositionally satisfiable* if there exists a propositional assignment that satisfies F under the usual semantics for the logical connectives. We sometimes write assignments as sequences of literals where a positive (negative) polarity of a literal indicates that the truth value 1 (0, respectively) is assigned to the literal's atom.

A *substitution* is a mapping from variables to terms that agrees with the identity function on all but finitely many variables. Let σ be a substitution. The domain, $dom(\sigma)$, of σ is the set of variables for which $\sigma(x) \neq x$. The range, $ran(\sigma)$, of σ is the set $\{\sigma(x) \mid x \in dom(\sigma)\}$. We denote the *inverse substitution* of σ, which is just the inverse function of σ, by σ^{-1}. A substitution is *ground* if its range consists only of ground terms. As common, $E\sigma$ denotes the result of applying σ to the expression E. If $E\sigma$ is ground, it is a *ground instance* of E. Juxtaposition of substitutions denotes their composition, i.e., $x\sigma\tau$ stands for $\tau(\sigma(x))$. The substitution σ is a *unifier* of the expressions $E_1, \ldots, E_n$ if $E_1\sigma = \cdots = E_n\sigma$. For substitutions σ and τ, we say that σ is *more general* than τ if there exists a substitution λ such that $\sigma\lambda = \tau$. Furthermore, σ is a *most general unifier* (*mgu*) of $E_1, \ldots, E_n$ if, for every unifier τ of $E_1, \ldots, E_n$, σ is more general than τ. It is well-known that whenever a set of expressions is unifiable, there exists an idempotent most general unifier of this set. In the rest of the paper, we use a popular variant of Herbrand's Theorem [12]:

Theorem 1. *A formula F is satisfiable if and only if every finite set of ground instances of clauses in F is propositionally satisfiable.*

Next, we introduce a formal notion of clause redundancy. Intuitively, a clause C is redundant w.r.t. a formula F if its removal from F does not affect the satisfiability or unsatisfiability of F [4]:

Definition 1. *A clause C is redundant w.r.t. a formula F if F and $F \setminus \{C\}$ are equisatisfiable.*

Note that this notion of redundancy does not require *logical* equivalence of F and $F \setminus \{C\}$, and that it differs from other well-known redundancy notions such as the one of Bachmair and Ganzinger that is usually employed within the context of ordered resolution [13]. It provides the basis for clause-elimination procedures. Note also that the redundancy of a clause C w.r.t. a formula F can be shown by proving that the satisfiability of $F \setminus \{C\}$ implies the satisfiability of F.

Finally, given two clauses $C = L_1 \vee \cdots \vee L_k \vee C'$ and $D = N_1 \vee \cdots \vee N_l \vee D'$ such that the literals $L_1, \ldots, L_k, \bar{N}_1, \ldots, \bar{N}_l$ are unifiable by an *mgu* σ, the clause $C'\sigma \vee D'\sigma$ is said to be a *resolvent* of C and D. If $k = l = 1$, it is a *binary resolvent* of C and D upon L_1.

3   Implication Modulo Resolution

In this section, we introduce the central concept of this paper—the principle of *implication modulo resolution* for first-order logic. We use the results of this section in subsequent sections to prove the soundness of various first-order pre-processing techniques. The definition of implication modulo resolution relies on the notion of L-resolvents:

Definition 2. Given two clauses $C = L \vee C'$ and $D = N_1 \vee \cdots \vee N_l \vee D'$ such that the literals $L, \bar{N}_1, \ldots, \bar{N}_l$ are unifiable by an *mgu* σ, the clause $C'\sigma \vee D'\sigma$ is called L-*resolvent* of C and D.

Example 1. Let $C = P(x) \vee Q(x)$, $D = \neg P(y) \vee \neg P(z) \vee R(y,z)$, and $L = P(x)$. Then, the substitution $\sigma = \{y \mapsto x, z \mapsto x\}$ is an *mgu* of $P(x)$, $P(y)$, and $P(z)$. Therefore, $Q(x) \vee R(x,x)$ is an L-resolvent of C and D. □

Before we next define the principle of implication modulo resolution, we want to highlight that whenever we say that a formula F *implies* a clause C, we mean that every model of F is a model of C, that is, $F \models C$.

Definition 3. A clause C is *implied modulo resolution upon* $L \in C$ by a formula F if all L-resolvents of C, with clauses in $F \setminus \{C\}$, are implied by $F \setminus \{C\}$.

We say that a clause C is implied modulo resolution by F if F implies C modulo resolution upon one of its literals. A simple example for clauses that are implied modulo resolution are clauses with *pure literals*. A pure literal is a literal whose predicate symbol occurs in only one polarity in the whole formula. Since there are no resolvents upon such a literal, the containing clause is trivially implied modulo resolution. The following example is a little more involved:

Example 2. Let $C = P(x) \vee Q(x)$ and

$$F = \{P(x) \vee Q(x),\ \neg P(y) \vee R(y),\ R(z) \vee S(z),\ \neg S(u) \vee Q(u)\}.$$

There is one $P(x)$-resolvent of C, namely $Q(x) \vee R(x)$, obtained by resolving C with $\neg P(y) \vee R(y)$. Clearly, this resolvent is implied by the clauses $R(z) \vee S(z)$ and $\neg S(u) \vee Q(u)$. Therefore, F implies C modulo resolution upon $P(x)$. □

B. Kiesl and M. Suda

In the following, we prove that implication modulo resolution ensures redundancy, i.e., if a clause C is implied modulo resolution by a formula F, then C is redundant w.r.t. F. The proof relies on Herbrand's Theorem (Theorem 1), which tells us that a formula F is satisfiable if and only if all finite sets of ground instances of clauses in F are propositionally satisfiable.

To prove that the satisfiability of $F \setminus \{C\}$ implies the satisfiability of F, we proceed as follows: Given a finite set of ground instances of clauses in F, we can obtain a satisfying propositional assignment of this set from an assignment that satisfies all the ground instances of clauses in $F \setminus \{C\}$. The latter assignment is guaranteed to exist because $F \setminus \{C\}$ is satisfiable. The key idea behind the modification of this assignment is to *flip* (interchange) the truth values of certain ground literals. We illustrate this on the following example:

Example 3. Consider C and F from Example 2, let $C' = P(a) \lor Q(a)$ be a ground instance of C, and $F' = \{P(a) \lor Q(a), \neg P(a) \lor R(a), \ R(a) \lor S(a), \ \neg S(a) \lor Q(a)\}$ a finite set of ground instances of F (in fact, F' is even a ground instance of F). Clearly, $F' \setminus \{C'\}$ is propositionally satisfied by the assignment $\alpha = \neg P(a) R(a) \neg S(a) \neg Q(a)$, but α falsifies C'. However, we can turn α into a satisfying assignment of C' by flipping the truth value of $P(a)$—the instance of the literal upon which C is implied modulo resolution. The resulting assignment $\alpha' = P(a) R(a) \neg S(a) \neg Q(a)$ could possibly falsify the clause $\neg P(a) \lor R(a)$ since it contains $\neg P(a)$ which is not satisfied anymore. But, the clause stays true since $R(a)$ is satisfied by α'. Therefore, α' satisfies F'.   □

In the above example, it is not a coincidence that $\neg P(a) \lor R(a)$ is still satisfied after flipping the truth value of $P(a)$. The intuitive explanation is as follows: The clause $Q(a) \lor R(a)$ is a ground instance of the $P(x)$-resolvent $Q(x) \lor R(x)$ (of C and $\neg P(y) \lor R(y)$) which is implied by $F \setminus \{C\}$. Therefore, since α satisfies all the ground instances of $F \setminus \{C\}$, it should also satisfy $Q(a) \lor R(a)$. But, since α does not satisfy $Q(a)$ (because α falsifies $C' = P(a) \lor Q(a)$), it must satisfy $R(a)$, and so it satisfies $\neg P(a) \lor R(a)$. Finally, since α' disagrees with α only on $P(a)$, it also satisifies $R(a)$. The following lemma formalizes this observation:

Lemma 2. *Let C be a clause that is implied modulo resolution upon L by F. Let furthermore α be an assignment that propositionally satisfies all ground instances of clauses in $F \setminus \{C\}$ but falsifies a ground instance $C\lambda$ of C. Then, the assignment α', obtained from α by flipping the truth value of $L\lambda$, still satisfies all ground instances of clauses in $F \setminus \{C\}$.*

Proof. Let $D\tau$ be a ground instance of a clause $D \in F \setminus \{C\}$ and suppose α satisfies $D\tau$. If $D\tau$ does not contain $\bar{L}\lambda$, it is trivially satisfied by α'. Assume therefore that $\bar{L}\lambda \in D\tau$ and let $N_1, \ldots, N_l$ be all the literals in D such that $N_i\tau = \bar{L}\lambda$ for $1 \le i \le l$. Then, the substitution $\lambda\tau = \lambda \cup \tau$ (note that C and D are variable disjoint by assumption) is a unifier of $L, \bar{N}_1, \ldots, \bar{N}_l$. Hence, $R = (C \setminus \{L\})\sigma \lor (D \setminus \{N_1, \ldots, N_l\})\sigma$, with σ being an *mgu* of $L, \bar{N}_1, \ldots, \bar{N}_l$, is an L-resolvent of C and thus implied by $F \setminus \{C\}$.

As σ is most general, it follows that there exists a substitution γ such that $\sigma\gamma = \lambda\tau$. Therefore,

$$(C \setminus \{L\})\sigma\gamma \vee (D \setminus \{N_1, \ldots, N_l\})\sigma\gamma$$
$$= (C \setminus \{L\})\lambda\tau \vee (D \setminus \{N_1, \ldots, N_l\})\lambda\tau$$
$$= (C \setminus \{L\})\lambda \quad \vee (D \setminus \{N_1, \ldots, N_l\})\tau$$

is a ground instance of R and so it must be satisfied by α. Thus, since α falsifies $C\lambda$, it must satisfy a literal $L'\tau \in (D \setminus \{N_1, \ldots, N_l\})\tau$. But, as all the literals in $(D \setminus \{N_1, \ldots, N_l\})\tau$ are different from $\bar{L}\lambda$, flipping the truth value of $L\lambda$ does not affect the truth value of $L'\tau$. It follows that α' satisfies $L'\tau$ and thus it satisfies $D\tau$. □

We can therefore satisfy a ground instance $C\lambda$ of C without falsifying ground instances of clauses in $F \setminus \{C\}$, by flipping the truth value of $L\lambda$—the ground instance of the literal L upon which C is implied modulo resolution. Still, as the following example shows, there could be other ground instances of C that contain the complement $\bar{L}\lambda$ of $L\lambda$:

Example 4. Suppose some formula F implies the clause $C = \neg P(x) \vee P(f(x))$ modulo resolution upon the literal $P(f(x))$ and consider two possible ground instances $C_1 = \neg P(a) \vee P(f(a))$ and $C_2 = \neg P(f(a)) \vee P(f(f(a)))$ of C. The assignment $P(a)\neg P(f(a))\neg P(f(f(a)))$ falsifies C_1, but we can satisfy C_1 by flipping the truth value of $P(f(a))$—the ground instance of $P(f(x))$—to obtain the assignment $P(a)P(f(a))\neg P(f(f(a)))$. However, by flipping the truth value of $P(f(a))$, we falsified the other ground instance C_2 of C. □

That this is not a serious problem is shown in the proof of our main result below. The key idea is to repeatedly satisfy ground instances of the literal upon which the clause is implied modulo resolution. In the above example, for instance, we can continue by also flipping the truth value of $P(f(f(a)))$ to obtain a satisfying assignment of both C_1 and C_2.

Theorem 3. *If a clause C is implied modulo resolution by a formula F, it is redundant w.r.t. F.*

Proof. Assume that F implies C modulo resolution upon $L \in C$ and that $F \setminus \{C\}$ is satisfiable. We show that F is satisfiable. By Herbrand's theorem (Theorem 1), it suffices to show that every finite set of ground instances of clauses in F is propositionally satisfiable. Let therefore F' and F_C be finite sets of ground instances of clauses in $F \setminus \{C\}$ and $\{C\}$, respectively. Since $F \setminus \{C\}$ is satisfiable, there exists an assignment α that propositionally satisfies all ground instances of clauses in $F \setminus \{C\}$ and thus it clearly satisfies F'. Assume now that α falsifies some ground instances of C that are contained in F_C.

By Lemma 2, for every falsified ground instance $C\lambda$ of C, we can turn α into a satisfying assignment of $C\lambda$ by flipping the truth value of $L\lambda$, and this flipping does not falsify any ground instances of clauses in $F \setminus \{C\}$. The only clauses that could possibly be falsified are other ground instances of C that contain the literal $\bar{L}\lambda$. But, once an instance $L\tau$ of L is true in a ground instance $C\tau$ of C, $L\tau$ cannot (later) be falsified by making other instances of L true. As there are only finitely many clauses in F_C, we can therefore turn α into a satisfying assignment of $F' \cup F_C$ by repeatedly making ground instances of C true by flipping the truth values of their instances of L. Hence, all finite sets of ground instances of clauses in F are propositionally satisfiable and so F is satisfiable. $\square$

For example, the clause C in Example 2 is redundant w.r.t. F since it is implied modulo resolution by F. In what follows, we use Theorem 3 to prove soundness of several first-order preprocessing techniques. We start with blocked-clause elimination, as both resolution asymmetric tautologies and covered clauses (which we introduce later) can be seen as generalizations of blocked clauses.

4   Blocked Clauses

Blocked clauses have been introduced by Kullmann [14], and their elimination significantly improves the performance of SAT [9] and QSAT solvers [15,16]. Also the first-order variant of blocked-clause elimination speeds up automatic theorem provers, especially on satisfiable formulas [8]. In propositional logic, a clause C is *blocked* in a formula F if it contains a literal L such that all binary resolvents of C upon L, with clauses in $F \setminus \{C\}$, are tautologies. In first-order logic, the notion of binary resolvents is replaced by L-resolvents [8]:

Definition 4. A clause C is *blocked* by a literal $L \in C$ in a formula F if all L-resolvents of C, with clauses in $F \setminus \{C\}$, are tautologies.

Example 5. Let $C = P(x) \vee \neg Q(x)$ and $F = \{P(x) \vee \neg Q(x), \neg P(y) \vee Q(y)\}$. There is only one $P(x)$-resolvent of C, namely the tautology $\neg Q(x) \vee Q(x)$, obtained by using the *mgu* $\sigma = \{y \mapsto x\}$. Therefore, C is blocked in F. $\square$

Since tautologies are trivially implied by every formula, blocked clauses are implied modulo resolution. The redundancy of blocked clauses, and therefore the soundness of blocked-clause elimination, is thus a consequence of the fact that implication modulo resolution ensures redundancy (Theorem 3):

Theorem 4. *If a clause is blocked in a formula F, it is redundant w.r.t. F.*

5   Asymmetric Tautologies and RATs

In this section, we first discuss the propositional notions of asymmetric tautologies and resolution asymmetric tautologies before lifting them to first-order logic. We start with asymmetric tautologies, which we use later to define resolution asymmetric tautologies. An asymmetric tautology is a clause that can be turned into a tautology by repeatedly adding so-called *asymmetric literals* to it. In propositional logic, a literal L is an *asymmetric literal* w.r.t. a clause C in a formula F if there exists a clause $D \vee \bar{L} \in F \setminus \{C\}$ such that D subsumes C, i.e., $D \subseteq C$. The addition of an asymmetric literal L to a clause C yields a clause that is logically equivalent in the sense that $F \setminus \{C\} \models (C \equiv C \vee L)$ [6]. Consider, for instance, the following example:

Example 6. Let $C = P \vee Q$ and $F = \{P \vee Q,\ Q \vee R,\ \neg R \vee S,\ P \vee \neg R \vee \neg S\}$. Since the subclause Q of $Q \vee R$ subsumes C, the literal $\neg R$ is an asymmetric literal w.r.t. C. We thus add it to C to obtain $C_1 = P \vee Q \vee \neg R$. We then use $\neg R \vee S$ to add $\neg S$ to C_1 and obtain $C_2 = P \vee Q \vee \neg R \vee \neg S$. Finally, we use $P \vee \neg R \vee \neg S$ to add $\neg P$ to C_2, and so we end up with $C_3 = P \vee Q \vee \neg R \vee \neg S \vee \neg P$, which is a tautology. It follows that C is an asymmetric tautology in F. Moreover, by transitivity, $F \setminus \{C\} \models (C \equiv C_3)$ and thus C is redundant w.r.t. F.   □

In first-order logic, a clause C *subsumes* a clause D if there exists a substitution λ such that $C\lambda \subseteq D$. This motivates the following first-order variants of asymmetric literals and asymmetric tautologies.

Definition 5. A literal L is an *asymmetric literal* w.r.t. a clause C in a formula F if there exist a clause $D \vee \bar{L}' \in F \setminus \{C\}$ and a substitution λ such that $D\lambda \subseteq C$ and $L = \bar{L}'\lambda$.

Example 7. Consider the clause $C = P(x) \vee Q(x) \vee R(x)$ and the formula $F = \{P(x) \vee Q(x) \vee R(x),\ P(y) \vee Q(y) \vee \neg S(y)\}$. Then, $S(x)$ is an asymmetric literal w.r.t. C in F since, for $\lambda = \{y \mapsto x\}$, $(P(y) \vee Q(y))\lambda \subseteq C$ and $S(x) = S(y)\lambda$.   □

First-order asymmetric-literal addition is harmless, because the original clause C can be obtained from $C \vee L$ and $D \vee \bar{L}'$ via resolution, as shown in the proof of the following lemma:

Lemma 5. *Let F be a formula, C a clause, and L an asymmetric literal w.r.t. C in F. Then, $F \setminus \{C\} \models (C \equiv C \vee L)$.*

Proof. Clearly, $C \rightarrow C \vee L$ is valid. It therefore suffices to prove that C is implied by $(F \setminus \{C\}) \cup \{C \vee L\}$. Since L is an asymmetric literal w.r.t. C in F, there exist a clause $D \vee L' \in F \setminus \{C\}$ and a substitution λ such that $D\lambda \subseteq C$ and $\bar{L}'\lambda = L$. But then C is a binary resolvent of $C \vee L$ and $D\lambda \vee L'\lambda$ upon L. It follows that C is implied by $(F \setminus \{C\}) \cup \{C \vee L\}$.   □

An asymmetric tautology is now a clause that can be turned into a tautology by repeatedly adding asymmetric literals (*asymmetric-literal addition*, ALA):

Definition 6. A clause C is an *asymmetric tautology* in a formula F if there exists a sequence $L_1, \ldots, L_n$ of literals such that each L_i is an asymmetric literal w.r.t. $C \vee L_1 \vee \cdots \vee L_{i-1}$ in $F \setminus \{C\}$ and $C \vee L_1 \vee \cdots \vee L_n$ is a tautology.

Example 8. Consider the clause $C = Q(x) \vee R(x)$ and the following formula $F = \{Q(x) \vee R(x),\ R(z) \vee S(z),\ \neg S(u) \vee Q(u)\}$. The subclause $R(z)$ of $R(z) \vee S(z)$ subsumes $R(x)$ via $\{z \mapsto x\}$ and so $\neg S(x)$ is an asymmetric literal w.r.t. C. We add it and obtain the clause $Q(x) \vee R(x) \vee \neg S(x)$. After this, $\neg S(u)$ subsumes $\neg S(x)$ via $\{u \mapsto x\}$ and thus $\neg Q(x)$ can be added to obtain the tautology $Q(x) \vee R(x) \vee \neg S(x) \vee \neg Q(x)$. Thus, C is an asymmetric tautology in F.   □

Note that in automatic theorem proving, we prefer short clauses over long ones, since the short clauses are usually stronger. Therefore, when performing asymmetric-tautology elimination, the asymmetric-literal additions are not meant to be permanent: We first add the literals and then test whether the resulting clause is a tautology. If so, we remove the clause; if not, we undo the asymmetric-literal additions to shrink the clause back to its original size. We next show that asymmetric tautologies are implied:

Theorem 6. *If C is an asymmetric tautology in F, it is implied by $F \setminus \{C\}$.*

Proof. Suppose C is an asymmetric tautology in F, i.e., there exists a sequence $L_1, \ldots, L_n$ of literals such that each L_i is an asymmetric literal w.r.t. the clause $C \vee L_1 \vee \cdots \vee L_{i-1}$ in $F \setminus \{C\}$ and $C \vee L_1 \vee \cdots \vee L_n$ is a tautology. By the repeated application of Lemma 5 (an easy induction argument), it follows that $F \setminus \{C\} \models (C \equiv C \vee L_1 \vee \cdots \vee L_n)$. But then, since $C \vee L_1 \vee \cdots \vee L_n$ is a tautology, it trivially holds that $F \setminus \{C\} \models C \vee L_1 \vee \cdots \vee L_n$. Therefore, $F \setminus \{C\} \models C$. □

Unlike in propositional logic, the first-order variant of asymmetric-literal addition is not guaranteed to terminate. Consider the following example:

Example 9. Let $C = P(a)$ and $F = \{P(x) \vee \neg P(f(x))\}$. Then, since $P(x)$ subsumes $P(a)$ via $\lambda = \{x \mapsto a\}$, we can add the asymmetric literal $P(f(a))$ to obtain $P(a) \vee P(f(a))$. After this, we can add $P(f(f(a)))$ via $\lambda = \{x \mapsto f(a)\}$, then $P(f(f(f(a))))$ and so on. This can be repeated infinitely many times. □

A resolution asymmetric tautology in first-order logic is then a clause C that contains a literal L such that all L-resolvents of C are asymmetric tautologies:

Definition 7. A clause C is a *resolution asymmetric tautology* (RAT) on a literal $L \in C$ w.r.t. a formula F if all L-resolvents of C, with clauses in $F \setminus \{C\}$, are asymmetric tautologies in $F \setminus \{C\}$.

Example 10. Consider the clause $C = P(x) \vee Q(x)$ and the following formula $F = \{P(x) \vee Q(x), \neg P(y) \vee R(y), R(z) \vee S(z), \neg S(u) \vee Q(u)\}$ (cf. Example 2). There is one $P(x)$-resolvent of C, namely $Q(x) \vee R(x)$. The formula $F \cup \{Q(x) \vee R(x)\}$ is a superset of the formula from Example 8 in which $Q(x) \vee R(x)$ is an asymmetric tautology. Thus, $Q(x) \vee R(x)$ is also an asymmetric tautology here: The literal $R(z)$ subsumes $R(x)$ via $\{z \mapsto x\}$ and so $\neg S(x)$ is an asymmetric literal w.r.t. $Q(x) \vee R(x)$. We add it to obtain $Q(x) \vee R(x) \vee \neg S(x)$. After this, $\neg S(u)$ subsumes $\neg S(x)$ via $\{u \mapsto x\}$ and so $\neg Q(x)$ can be added to obtain the tautology $Q(x) \vee R(x) \vee \neg S(x) \vee \neg Q(x)$. It follows that C is a RAT w.r.t. F. □

Theorem 7. *If a clause C is a RAT w.r.t. a formula F, then it is redundant w.r.t. F.*

Proof. Assume that C is a RAT w.r.t. F. Then, every L-resolvent of C with clauses in $F \setminus \{C\}$ is an asymmetric tautology in $F \setminus \{C\}$ and therefore, by Theorem 6, implied by $F \setminus \{C\}$. It follows that C is implied modulo resolution upon L by F and thus, by Theorem 3, C is redundant w.r.t. F. □

6   Covered Clauses

In this section, similar to the preceding one, we first recapitulate the notions of covered literals and covered clauses from propositional logic and then lift them to the first-order level. Informally, a clause C is *covered* in a propositional formula F, if the addition of so-called *covered literals* to C turns C into a blocked clause. A clause C *covers* a literal L' in F if C contains a literal L such that all non-tautological resolvents of C upon L contain L'. The crucial property of covered literals is, that they can be added to C without affecting satisfiability [5]. More precisely, given a formula F, a clause $C \in F$, and a literal L' that is covered by C in F, it holds that F and the formula F', obtained from F by replacing C with $C \vee L'$, are equisatisfiable.

Example 11. Consider the clause $C = P$ and the propositional formula $F = \{P,\ \neg P \vee \neg Q \vee R,\ \neg P \vee \neg Q \vee S\}$. There are two resolvents of C upon P, namely $\neg Q \vee R$ and $\neg Q \vee S$. As $\neg Q$ is contained in both resolvents, it is covered by C in F. Therefore, replacing C with $C \vee \neg Q$ in F does not affect satisfiability.   □

We next introduce a first-order variant of covered literals. Our definition guarantees that covered-literal addition (CLA) has no effect on satisfiability:

Definition 8. A clause C *covers* a literal L' in a formula F if C contains a literal L such that all non-tautological L-resolvents of C, with clauses in $F \cup \{C\}$, contain L'.

Note that resolvents of C with itself are required to contain the literal L'. Moreover, when talking about resolvents of C with itself, we mean resolvents of C with an instance $C\tau$ of C, where τ is a renaming that maps the variables in C to fresh variables that do not occur in F.

Example 12. Consider the clause $C = P(f(x))$ and the formula

$$F = \{\neg P(y) \vee Q(y) \vee R(y),\ \neg P(z) \vee Q(z) \vee S(z)\}.$$

There are two $P(f(x))$-resolvents of C: $Q(f(x)) \vee R(f(x))$, obtained by using the *mgu* $\{y \mapsto f(x)\}$, and $Q(f(x)) \vee S(f(x))$, obtained by using the *mgu* $\{z \mapsto f(x)\}$. Since $Q(f(x))$ is contained in both resolvents, it is covered by C in F.   □

As we will show below, the addition of a covered literal to the clause that covers it has no effect on satisfiability. The following example illustrates that this would not be the case if we did not require the covered literal to be contained in resolvents of the clause with itself:

Example 13. Consider the clause $C = \neg P(x) \vee P(f(x))$ and the formula $F = \{\neg P(x) \vee P(f(x)),\ \neg P(y) \vee Q(y),\ P(a),\ \neg Q(f(f(a)))\}$. The literal $Q(f(x))$ is contained in the (only) $P(f(x))$-resolvent $\neg P(x) \vee Q(f(x))$ of C with clauses in F *that are different from C itself*. However, F is unsatisfiable whereas the formula F', obtained from F by replacing C with $C \vee Q(f(x))$, is satisfiable.   □

Lemma 8. *If a clause C covers a literal L' in a formula F, then F and the formula F', obtained from F by replacing C with $C \vee L'$, are equisatisfiable.*

Proof. Assume that C covers L' in F, i.e., L' is contained in all non-tautological L-resolvents of C with clauses in F. First, we add $C\tau \vee L'\tau$ to F, with τ being a renaming that replaces the variables in $C \vee L'$ by fresh variables not occurring in F. Since $C\tau \vee L'\tau$ is subsumed by C, the formulas F and $F \cup \{C\tau \vee L'\tau\}$ are equisatisfiable. We next show that C is redundant w.r.t. $F \cup \{C\tau \vee L'\tau\}$ and that it can therefore by removed. To do so, we show that C is implied modulo resolution upon L by $F \cup \{C\tau \vee L'\tau\}$. As $F \cup \{C\tau \vee L'\tau\}$ and $F \cup \{C \vee L'\}$ are clearly equivalent, the claim then follows.

We show that all L-resolvents of C with clauses in F are implied by the formula $(F \setminus \{C\}) \cup \{C\tau \vee L'\tau\}$. Showing that the L-resolvents of C with $C\tau \vee L'\tau$ are also implied is done in a similar way. Since tautological L-resolvents are trivially implied, we consider only non-tautological ones. Let $C'\sigma \vee D'\sigma$ be a non-tautological L-resolvent of $C = C' \vee L$ with a clause $D = D' \vee N_1 \vee \cdots \vee N_k \in F$, where σ is an (idempotent) *mgu* of the literals $L, \bar{N}_1, \ldots, \bar{N}_k$. Since L' is covered by C in F, the resolvent $C'\sigma \vee D'\sigma$ contains L', and L' is of the form $P\sigma$ for some literal $P \in C' \vee D'$.

To prove that $C'\sigma \vee D'\sigma$ is implied by $(F \setminus \{C\}) \cup \{C\tau \vee L'\tau\}$, we show that it can be obtained from clauses in $(F \setminus \{C\}) \cup \{C\tau \vee L'\tau\}$ via resolution, instantiation, and factoring: Consider the clauses $C\tau \vee L'\tau = C'\tau \vee L\tau \vee L'\tau$ and $D = D' \vee N_1 \vee \cdots \vee N_k$. Since the literals $L, \bar{N}_1, \ldots, \bar{N}_k$ are unified by σ and since $dom(\tau^{-1}) \cap \mathrm{var}(D) = \emptyset$, it follows that $L\tau$ and $\bar{N}_1, \ldots, \bar{N}_k$ are unified by $\tau^{-1}\sigma$. Therefore, there exists an *mgu* σ' of $L\tau$ and $\bar{N}_1, \ldots, \bar{N}_k$. Hence, the clause $(C'\tau \vee L'\tau \vee D')\sigma'$ is an $L\tau$-resolvent. Now, since σ' is most general, there exists a substitution γ such that $\sigma'\gamma = \tau^{-1}\sigma$. But then,

$$
\begin{aligned}
(C'\tau \vee L'\tau \vee D')\sigma'\gamma \\
= (C'\tau \vee L'\tau \vee D')\tau^{-1}\sigma \\
= C'\sigma \vee L'\sigma \vee D'\sigma,
\end{aligned}
$$

from which we obtain $C'\sigma \vee D'\sigma$ by factoring, since $L' \in C'\sigma \vee D'\sigma$ and $L'\sigma = P\sigma\sigma = P\sigma = L'$. $\square$

Similar to asymmetric-literal addition, the addition of covered literals in first-order logic is also not guaranteed to terminate. Consider the following example:

Example 14. Let $C = P(a)$ and $F = \{P(a), \neg P(x) \vee P(f(x))\}$. Then, there exists one $P(a)$-resolvent of C, namely $P(f(a))$. Therefore, $P(f(a))$ is covered by C and thus it can be added to C to obtain $C' = P(a) \vee P(f(a))$. Now, there is one $P(f(a))$-resolvent of C', namely $P(f(f(a)))$, and thus $P(f(f(a)))$ can be added. This addition of covered literals can be repeated infinitely often. $\square$

Now, a clause C is covered in a formula F if the repeated addition of covered literals can turn it into a blocked clause. In the following, we denote by $F[C/D]$ the formula obtained from F by replacing the clause C with the clause D:

Definition 9. A clause C is *covered* in a formula F if there exists a sequence $L_1, \ldots, L_n$ of literals such that each L_i is covered by $C_{i-1} = C \vee L_1 \vee \cdots \vee L_{i-1}$ in $F[C/C_{i-1}]$ and C_n is blocked in $F[C/C_n]$.

Example 15. Consider the clause $C = P(a) \vee \neg Q(a)$ which is contained in the formula $F = \{P(a) \vee \neg Q(a), \neg P(y) \vee R(y), \neg R(z) \vee Q(z)\}$. Although C is not blocked in F, we can add the literal $R(a)$ since it is contained in its only $P(a)$-resolvent, obtained by resolving with $\neg P(y) \vee R(y)$. The resulting clause $P(a) \vee \neg Q(a) \vee R(a)$ is then blocked by $R(a)$ since there is only the tautological $R(a)$-resolvent $P(a) \vee \neg Q(a) \vee Q(a)$, obtained by resolving with $\neg R(z) \vee Q(z)$. Therefore, C is covered in F.   □

As in the case of asymmetric tautologies, the covered-literal additions used during covered-clause elimination are not meant to be permanent: We first add some covered literals and then test whether the resulting clause is blocked (and therefore covered). If so, we remove the clause; if not, we undo the literal additions.

Theorem 9. *If a clause C is covered in a formula F, it is redundant w.r.t. F.*

Proof. Assume that C is covered in F, i.e., we can add covered literals to C to obtain a clause C' that is blocked in F. Now, let F' be obtained from F by replacing C with C'. Then, by Lemma 8, F and F' are equisatisfiable. Moreover, since C' is blocked in F', it follows that $F' \setminus \{C'\}$ and F' are equisatisfiable. But then, as $F \setminus \{C\} = F' \setminus \{C'\}$, it follows that F and $F \setminus \{C\}$ are equisatisfiable and so C is redundant w.r.t. F.   □

7   Resolution Subsumption and More

The redundancy notion of *resolution subsumption* (RS) from SAT [7] can also be straightforwardly lifted to first-order logic, where redundancy is again an immediate consequence of Theorem 3 since subsumption ensures implication:

Definition 10. A clause C is *resolution subsumed* (RS) on a literal $L \in C$ in a formula F if all non-tautological L-resolvents of C, with clauses in $F \setminus \{C\}$, are subsumed in $F \setminus \{C\}$.

Theorem 10. *If a clause is resolution subsumed in a formula F, then it is redundant w.r.t. F.*

With the methods presented in this paper, we can define even more types of redundant clauses that have been considered in the SAT literature. We can do so by combining asymmetric-literal addition or covered-literal addition with tautology or subsumption checks. These checks can be performed either directly on the clause or for all resolvents of the clause upon one of its literals. The latter can be seen as some kind of "look-ahead" via resolution. Figure 1 illustrates possible combinations of techniques. Every path from the left to the right gives rise to a particular redundancy notion. We remark that ALA stands for asymmetric-literal addition and CLA stands for covered-literal addition.

Fig. 1. Combination of techniques to obtain redundancy notions.

For instance, to detect whether a clause is an asymmetric tautology, we first perform some asymmetric-literal additions and then check whether the resulting clause is a tautology. Another example are blocked clauses, where we ask whether all L-resolvents of the clause are tautologies. Similarly, we can obtain covered clauses, resolution subsumed clauses, and resolution asymmetric tautologies via such combinations. This gives rise to various other types of clauses like *asymmetric blocked clauses*, *asymmetric subsumed clauses* [7], or *asymmetric covered clauses* [3]. The redundancy of these clauses follows from the results in this paper, most importantly from the principle of implication modulo resolution.

8   Predicate Elimination

In this section, we show how the principle of implication modulo resolution allows us to construct a short soundness proof for the predicate elimination technique of Khasidashvili and Korovin [2]. Predicate elimination is a first-order variant of variable elimination, which is successfully used during preprocessing and inprocessing in SAT solving [17]. The elimination of a predicate P from a formula F is computed as follows: First, we add all the non-tautological binary resolvents upon literals with predicate symbol P to F. After this, all original clauses containing P are removed. To guarantee that this procedure does not affect satisfiability, the original definition requires P to be *non-recursive*, meaning that it must not occur more than once per clause.

Theorem 11. *If a formula F' is obtained from a formula F by eliminating a non-recursive predicate P, then F and F' are equisatisfiable.*

Proof. Let F_P be obtained from F by adding all non-tautological resolvents upon P. Clearly, F_P and F are equivalent. Now, let C be a clause that contains a literal L with predicate symbol P. Since all non-tautological L-resolvents of C with clauses in $F_P \setminus \{C\}$ are contained in $F_P \setminus \{C\}$, C is implied modulo resolution by F_P and so it is redundant w.r.t. F_P. Thus, after removing from F_P all clauses containing P, the resulting formula F' and F_P are equisatisfiable. Therefore, F' and F are equisatisfiable.   □

We want to highlight that Khasidashvili and Korovin [2] proved soundness of predicate elimination for first-order logic *with* equality while we restrict ourselves to first-order logic *without* equality.

9   Confluence Properties

In this section, we analyze confluence properties of the clause-elimination and literal-addition techniques discussed in this paper. Intuitively, confluence of a technique tells us that the order in which we perform the clause eliminations or the literal additions is not relevant to the final outcome of the technique.

To analyze confluence formally, we interpret our techniques as *abstract reduction systems* [18]. For instance, to analyze the confluence of a clause-elimination technique CE, we define the (reduction) relation $\rightarrow_{CE}$ over formulas as follows: $F_1 \rightarrow_{CE} F_2$ if and only if the technique CE allows us to obtain F_2 from F_1 by removing a clause. Likewise, for a literal-addition technique LA, we define the relation $\rightarrow_{LA}$ over clauses as $C_1 \rightarrow_{LA} C_2$ if and only if the technique LA allows us to obtain C_2 from C_1 by adding a literal. Hence, when we ask whether a certain preprocessing technique is confluent, what we actually want to know is whether its corresponding reduction relation is confluent [18]:

Definition 11. Let $\rightarrow$ be a relation and $\rightarrow_*$ its reflexive transitive closure. Then, $\rightarrow$ is *confluent* if, for all x, y_1, y_2 with $x \rightarrow_* y_1$ and $x \rightarrow_* y_2$, there exists an element z such that $y_1 \rightarrow_* z$ and $y_2 \rightarrow_* z$.

In our context, this means that whenever the elimination of certain clauses from a formula F yields a formula F_1, and the elimination of certain other clauses from F yields another formula F_2, then there is still a formula F_z that we can obtain from both F_1 and F_2. Likewise for the addition of literals to a clause. Therefore, we do not need to worry about "missed opportunities" caused by a bad choice of the elimination order. For some techniques in this paper, we can show the stronger *diamond property* which implies confluence [18]:

Definition 12. A relation $\rightarrow$ has the *diamond property* if, for all x, y_1, y_2 with $x \rightarrow y_1$ and $x \rightarrow y_2$, there exists a z such that $y_1 \rightarrow z$ and $y_2 \rightarrow z$.

Next, we present the confluence results. We start with blocked-clause elimination, for which confluence is easily shown. Define $F_1 \rightarrow_{BCE} F_2$ iff the formula F_2 can be obtained from the formula F_1 by removing a clause that is blocked in F_1.

Theorem 12. *Blocked-clause elimination is confluent, i.e., $\rightarrow_{BCE}$ is confluent.*

Proof. If a clause C is blocked in a formula F, it is also blocked in every subset F' of F, since the L-resolvents of C with clauses in $F' \setminus \{C\}$ are a subset of the L-resolvents with clauses in $F \setminus \{C\}$. Therefore, if all L-resolvents of C with clauses in $F \setminus \{C\}$ are tautologies, so are those with clauses in $F' \setminus \{C\}$. Hence, the relation $\rightarrow_{BCE}$ has the diamond property and thus it is confluent.   □

As in the propositional case, where covered-clause elimination is confluent [3], we can prove the confluence of its first-order variant. Define $F_1 \rightarrow_{CCE} F_2$ iff the formula F_2 can be obtained from F_1 by removing a clause that is covered in F_1.

Theorem 13. *Covered-clause elimination is confluent, i.e., $\rightarrow_{CCE}$ is confluent.*

Proof. We show that $\rightarrow_{CCE}$ has the diamond property. Let F be a formula and let $F \setminus \{C\}$ and $F \setminus \{D\}$ be obtained from F by respectively removing the covered clauses C and D. It suffices to prove that C is covered in $F \setminus \{D\}$ and D is covered in $F \setminus \{C\}$. We show that C is covered in $F \setminus \{D\}$. The other case is symmetric. Since C is covered in F, we can perform a sequence of covered-literal additions to turn C into a clause $C_n = C \vee L_1 \vee \cdots \vee L_n$ that is blocked in F_n, where by F_i we denote the formula obtained from F by replacing C with $C_i = C \vee L_1 \vee \cdots \vee L_i$ $(0 \le i \le n)$.

Now, if in $F \setminus \{D\}$, the clause C_n can be obtained from C by performing the same sequence of covered-literal additions, then C_n is also blocked in $F_n \setminus \{D\}$ and thus C is covered in $F \setminus \{D\}$. Assume now to the contrary that there exists a literal L_i that is not covered by C_{i-1} in $F_{i-1} \setminus \{D\}$ and suppose w.l.o.g. that L_i is the first such literal. It follows that there exists a non-tautological L-resolvent of C_{i-1} (with a clause in $F_{i-1} \setminus \{D\}$) that does not contain L_i. But then L_i is not covered by C_{i-1} in F_{i-1}, a contradiction. □

Covered-literal addition is confluent. Let F be a formula and define $C_1 \rightarrow_{\mathsf{CLA}} C_2$ iff C_2 can be obtained from C_1 by adding a literal L that is covered by C_1 in F.

Theorem 14. *Covered-literal addition is confluent, i.e., $\rightarrow_{\mathsf{CLA}}$ is confluent.*

Proof. We show that the relation $\rightarrow_{\mathsf{CLA}}$ has the diamond property. Let F be formula and C a clause. Let furthermore $C_1 = C \vee L_1$ and $C_2 = C \vee L_2$ be obtained from C by respectively adding literals L_1 and L_2 that are both covered by C in F. We have to show that C_1 covers L_2 and, analogously, that C_2 covers L_1. Since C covers L_2, it follows that C contains a literal L such that L_2 is contained in all non-tautological L-resolvents of C. But, as $L \in C_1$, every non-tautological L-resolvent of C_1 must also contain L_2. It follows that C_1 covers L_2. The argument for L_1 being covered by C_2 is symmetric. □

Asymmetric-literal addition is also confluent. Let F be a formula and define $C_1 \rightarrow_{\mathsf{ALA}} C_2$ iff C_2 can be obtained from C_1 by adding a literal L that is an asymmetric literal w.r.t. C_1 in F.

Theorem 15. *Asymmetric-literal addition is confluent, i.e., the relation $\rightarrow_{\mathsf{ALA}}$ is confluent.*

Proof. If L_1 is an asymmetric literal w.r.t. a clause C in a formula F, then there exists a clause $D \vee \bar{L} \in F \setminus \{C\}$ and a substitution λ such that $D\lambda \subseteq C$ and $L_1 = \bar{L}\lambda$. Thus, $D\lambda \subseteq C \vee L_2$ for each $C \vee L_2$ that was obtained from C by adding some asymmetric literal L_2, and so L_1 is an asymmetric literal w.r.t. every such clause. Hence, $\rightarrow_{\mathsf{ALA}}$ has the diamond property and so it is confluent. □

For asymmetric-tautology elimination, the non-confluence result from propositional logic [3] implies non-confluence of the first-order generalization. Finally, the following example shows that RS and RAT elimination are not confluent:

Example 16. Let $F = \{\neg Q \vee P, \neg R \vee Q, \neg P \vee R, \neg Q \vee R\}$. Then, $\neg Q \vee R$ is a RAT and RS on the literal R as there is only one R-resolvent, namely the tautology $\neg Q \vee Q$, obtained by resolving with $Q \vee \neg R$. If we remove $\neg Q \vee R$, none of the remaining clauses of F is a RAT or RS. In contrast, suppose we start

Table 1. Confluence properties of the first-order preprocessing techniques.

Technique	Confluent
Blocked-Clause Elimination	Yes
Covered-Clause Elimination	Yes
Asymmetric-Tautology Elimination	No
Resolution-Asymmetric-Tautology Elimination	No
Resolution-Subsumed-Clause Elimination	No
Covered-Literal Addition	Yes
Asymmetric-Literal Addition	Yes

by removing $\neg Q \vee P$, which is a RAT and RS on P, then all the other clauses can be removed, because they become RAT and RS: The clause $\neg R \vee Q$ becomes both RAT and RS on the literal Q as there is only a tautological resolvent upon Q, namely $\neg R \vee R$. For $\neg P \vee R$, there are no resolvents upon $\neg P$ and so it trivially becomes RAT and RS on $\neg P$. Finally, $\neg Q \vee R$ becomes RAT and RS on both R and $\neg Q$ as there are only tautological resolvents upon these two literals.   □

A summary of the confluence results is given in Table 1. Note that for all the confluent techniques, we could show that they also have the diamond property.

10 Conclusion

We introduced the principle of implication modulo resolution for first-order logic and showed that if a clause C is implied modulo resolution by a formula F, then C is redundant with respect to F. Using implication modulo resolution, we lifted several SAT-preprocessing techniques to first-order logic, proved their soundness, and analyzed their confluence properties. We furthermore demonstrated how implication modulo resolution yields short soundness proofs for the existing first-order techniques of predicate elimination and blocked-clause elimination.

For now, we have only considered first-order logic without equality. A variant of implication modulo resolution that guarantees redundancy in first-order logic with equality requires a refined notion of L-resolvents, possibly based on flat resolvents [2] as in the definition of equality-blocked clauses [8]. The focus of this paper is mainly theoretical, laying the groundwork for practical applications of the new first-order techniques. We plan to implement and empirically evaluate the preprocessing techniques proposed in this paper within the next year, since we expect them to improve the performance of first-order theorem provers.

References

1. Hoder, K., Khasidashvili, Z., Korovin, K., Voronkov, A.: Preprocessing techniques for first-order clausification. In: Proceedings of the 12th Conference on Formal Methods in Computer-Aided Design (FMCAD 2012). IEEE, pp. 44–51 (2012)

2. Khasidashvili, Z., Korovin, K.: Predicate elimination for preprocessing in first-order theorem proving. In: Creignou, N., Le Berre, D. (eds.) SAT 2016. LNCS, vol. 9710, pp. 361–372. Springer, Cham (2016). doi:10.1007/978-3-319-40970-2_22

3. Heule, M.J.H., Järvisalo, M., Lonsing, F., Seidl, M., Biere, A.: Clause elimination for SAT and QSAT. J. Artif. Intell. Res. **53**, 127–168 (2015)

4. Heule, M.J.H., Seidl, M., Biere, A.: Solution validation and extraction for QBF preprocessing. J. Autom. Reasoning **58**, 1–29 (2017)

5. Heule, M.J.H., Järvisalo, M., Biere, A.: Covered clause elimination. In: Short Papers for the 17th International Conference on Logic for Programming, Artificial intelligence, and Reasoning (LPAR-17-short), vol. 13. EPiC Series, EasyChair, pp. 41–46 (2010)

6. Heule, M.J.H., Järvisalo, M., Biere, A.: Clause elimination procedures for CNF formulas. In: Proceedings of the 17th International Conference on Logic for Programming, Artificial Intelligence, and Reasoning (LPAR-17), LNCS, vol. 6397, pp. 357–371. Springer, Heidelberg (2010)

7. Järvisalo, M., Heule, M.J.H., Biere, A.: Inprocessing rules. In: Gramlich, B., Miller, D., Sattler, U. (eds.) IJCAR 2012. LNCS (LNAI), vol. 7364, pp. 355–370. Springer, Heidelberg (2012). doi:10.1007/978-3-642-31365-3_28

8. Kiesl, B., Suda, M., Seidl, M., Tompits, H., Biere, A.: Blocked clauses in first-order logic. In: Proceedings of the 21st International Conference on Logic for Programming, Artificial Intelligence and Reasoning (LPAR-21), vol. 46. EPiC Series in Computing, EasyChair, pp. 31–48 (2017)

9. Järvisalo, M., Biere, A., Heule, M.: Blocked clause elimination. In: Esparza, J., Majumdar, R. (eds.) TACAS 2010. LNCS, vol. 6015, pp. 129–144. Springer, Heidelberg (2010). doi:10.1007/978-3-642-12002-2_10

10. Biere, A.: Splatz, Lingeling, Plingeling, Treengeling, YalSAT entering the SAT competition 2016. In: Proceedings of SAT Competition 2016 - Solver and Benchmark Descriptions, vol. B-2016-1 of Department of Computer Science Series of Publications B, University of Helsinki, pp. 44–45 (2016)

11. Wetzler, N., Heule, M.J.H., Hunt, W.A.: DRAT-trim: efficient checking and trimming using expressive clausal proofs. In: Sinz, C., Egly, U. (eds.) SAT 2014. LNCS, vol. 8561, pp. 422–429. Springer, Cham (2014). doi:10.1007/978-3-319-09284-3_31

12. Fitting, M.: First-Order Logic and Automated Theorem Proving, 2nd edn. Springer, New York (1996)

13. Bachmair, L., Ganzinger, H.: Resolution theorem proving. In: Robinson, J.A., Voronkov, A. (eds.) Handbook of Automated Reasoning (in 2 volumes). Elsevier and MIT Press, pp. 19–99 (2001)

14. Kullmann, O.: On a generalization of extended resolution. Discrete Appl. Math. **96–97**, 149–176 (1999)

15. Biere, A., Lonsing, F., Seidl, M.: Blocked clause elimination for QBF. In: Bjørner, N., Sofronie-Stokkermans, V. (eds.) CADE 2011. LNCS (LNAI), vol. 6803, pp. 101–115. Springer, Heidelberg (2011). doi:10.1007/978-3-642-22438-6_10

16. Lonsing, F., Bacchus, F., Biere, A., Egly, U., Seidl, M.: Enhancing search-based QBF solving by dynamic blocked clause elimination. In: Davis, M., Fehnker, A., McIver, A., Voronkov, A. (eds.) LPAR 2015. LNCS, vol. 9450, pp. 418–433. Springer, Heidelberg (2015). doi:10.1007/978-3-662-48899-7_29

17. Eén, N., Biere, A.: Effective preprocessing in SAT through variable and clause elimination. In: Bacchus, F., Walsh, T. (eds.) SAT 2005. LNCS, vol. 3569, pp. 61–75. Springer, Heidelberg (2005). doi:10.1007/11499107_5

18. Baader, F., Nipkow, T.: Term Rewriting and All That. Cambridge University Press, Cambridge (1998)

Splitting Proofs for Interpolation

Bernhard Gleiss[1], Laura Kovács[1,2], and Martin Suda[1(✉)]

[1] TU Wien, Vienna, Austria
{bgleiss,lkovacs,msuda}@forsyte.at
[2] Chalmers University of Technology, Gothenburg, Sweden

Abstract. We study interpolant extraction from local first-order refutations. We present a new theoretical perspective on interpolation based on clearly separating the condition on logical strength of the formula from the requirement on the common signature. This allows us to highlight the space of all interpolants that can be extracted from a refutation as a space of simple choices on how to split the refutation into two parts. We use this new insight to develop an algorithm for extracting interpolants which are linear in the size of the input refutation and can be further optimized using metrics such as number of non-logical symbols or quantifiers. We implemented the new algorithm in first-order theorem prover VAMPIRE and evaluated it on a large number of examples coming from the first-order proving community. Our experiments give practical evidence that our work improves the state-of-the-art in first-order interpolation.

1 Introduction

Starting with the pioneering work of McMillan [15], interpolation became a powerful approach in verification thanks to its use in predicate abstraction and model checking [1,16,19]. To prove program properties over a combination of data structures, such as integers, arrays and pointers, several approaches based on theory-specific reasoning have been proposed, see e.g. [4,5,14]. While powerful, these techniques are limited to quantifier-free fragments of first-order logic. Addressing reasoning in full first-order theories, quantified interpolants are computed in [3,11,17,23] and further optimized with respect to various measures in [9].

In this paper, we address interpolation in full first-order logic and introduce a novel approach to generate interpolants, possibly with quantifiers. Our approach improves and simplifies the aforementioned techniques, in particular [9,11]. In [9,11], the size of computed interpolants is in the worst case quadratic in the size of the proof and the generated interpolants may contain redundant subformulas. Our work addresses these issues and infers interpolants that are linear in

This work was supported by the ERC Starting Grant 2014 SYMCAR 639270, the Wallenberg Academy Fellowship 2014 TheProSE, the Swedish VR grant GenPro D0497701 and the FWF projects S11403-N23 and S11409-N23. We also acknowledge support from the FWF project W1255-N23.

L. de Moura (Ed.): CADE 2017, LNAI 10395, pp. 291–309, 2017.
DOI: 10.1007/978-3-319-63046-5_18

the size of the proof and are much simpler than in [9,11]. We proceed as follows. We separate the requirements on a formula being an interpolant into a part restricting the logical strength of an interpolant and a part restricting which symbols are allowed to be used in an interpolant. This way, we first handle formulas, called intermediants, satisfying the requirements on the logical strength of interpolants, and only then we restrict the generated space of intermediants to the ones that satisfy the restriction on the interpolants signature.

The work of [11] relies on so-called local proofs (or split proofs) and constructs interpolants by splitting local proofs into (maximal) subproofs. Splitting proofs is determined by the signature of formulas used in the proofs. We observed, however, that there are many ways to split a proof, resulting in interpolants that are different in size and strength. We therefore propose a general framework for splitting proofs and using the boundaries of the resulting sub-proofs to construct the intermediants. The key feature of our work is that the interpolants inferred from our various proof splits are linear in the size of the proof. When constructing interpolants from proof splits, we note that local proofs are exactly the ones that ensure that proof splits yield intermediants that satisfy the requirements of interpolants. Using local proofs and proof splits, we then describe a powerful heuristic and an optimality criterion how to choose the "best" proof split, and hence the resulting interpolant.

Contributions. The main contributions of this paper are as follows.

- We present a new algorithm for first-order-interpolation using local proofs in arbitrary sound inference systems. That is, our work can be used in any sound calculus and derives interpolants, possibly with quantifiers, in arbitrary first-order theories.
- Our interpolation algorithm is the first algorithm ensuring that the size of the interpolant is linear in the size of the proof while working with an arbitrary sound logical calculus. This result improves [11] and generalises the work of [17] to any sound inference system.
- We implemented our work in the VAMPIRE theorem prover [12] and evaluated our method on a large number of examples coming from the TPTP library [22]. Our experimental results confirm that our work improves the state-of-the-art in first-order interpolation.

The rest of this paper is structured as follows. The background notation on proofs and interpolation is covered in Sect. 2. We then show how to construct linear sized interpolants in Sect. 3 and present optimisations to the procedure in Sect. 4. We compare to related work in Sect. 5, describe our experimental results in Sect. 6, and conclude in Sect. 7.

2   Preliminaries

This section introduces the relevant theoretical notions to our work.

Formulas. We deal with standard first-order predicate logic with equality. We allow all standard logical connectives and quantifiers in the language and, in addition, assume that it contains the logical constants $\top$, $\bot$ for true and false, respectively. Without loss of generality, we restrict ourselves to closed formulas, i.e. we do not allow formulas to contain free variables. The non-logical symbols of a formula F, denoted by $\mathcal{N}(F)$, are all the predicate symbols and function symbols (including constants) occurring in F. Note that this excludes (quantified) variables and the equality symbol.

An *axiomatisable theory*, or simply a *theory* is any set of formulas. For example, we can use the theory of linear integer arithmetic or the theory of lists. We will from now on restrict ourself to a fixed theory $\mathcal{T}$ and give all definitions relative to $\mathcal{T}$. This includes that we write $F_1, \ldots, F_n \vDash F$ (instead of $F_1, \ldots, F_n \vDash_{\mathcal{T}} F$) to denote that every model of $\mathcal{T}$ which satisfies each $F_1, \ldots, F_n$ also satisfies F.

Definition 1. Let $F_1, \ldots, F_n, F$ be formulas, $n \geq 0$. An *inference rule* R is a tuple $(F_1, \ldots, F_n, F)$. An *inference system* $\mathfrak{S}$ is a set of inference rules.

An inference rule $R = (F_1, \ldots, F_n, F)$ is *sound*, if $F_1, \ldots, F_n \vDash F$. An inference system $\mathfrak{S}$ is called *sound*, if it only consists of *sound* inference rules.

From now on, we further restrict ourselves to a fixed inference system $\mathfrak{S}$ which is sound (relative to $\mathcal{T}$) and give all definitions relative to that system.

Derivations and proofs. We model logical proofs as directed hypergraphs in which vertices are associated with formulas and (hyper-)edges with inferences. Because an inference always has exactly one conclusion, we only need hypergraphs where each edge has exactly one end vertex. Moreover, because the order of premises of an inference may be important, we use tuples to model the edges. We will from now on refer to such (hyper-)edges simply as *inferences*.

Definition 2. Let G be a formula and $\mathcal{F}$ a set of formulas. A *proof of G from axioms $\mathcal{F}$* is a finite acyclic labeled directed hypergraph $P = (V, E, L)$, where V is a set of vertices, E a set of inferences, and L is a labelling function mapping each vertex $v \in V$ to a formula $L(v)$. For an inference $r \in E$ of the form $(v_1, \ldots, v_n, v)$, where $n \geq 0$, we call $v_1, \ldots, v_n$ the *premises of r* and v the *conclusion of r*.

Additionally, we require the following:

1. Each vertex $v \in V$ is a conclusion of exactly one inference $r \in E$.
2. There is exactly one vertex $v_0 \in V$ that is not a premise of any inference $r \in E$ and $L(v_0) = G$.
3. Each $r \in E$ is either (a) an inference of the form (v) and $L(v) \in \mathcal{F}$, or (b) an inference of the form $(v_1, \ldots, v_n, v)$ and $(L(v_1), \ldots, L(v_n), L(v)) \in \mathfrak{S}$. In the first case, we call r an *axiom inference*, in the second case, r is called a *proper inference*.

A *refutation from axioms $\mathcal{F}$* is a proof of the formula $\bot$ from $\mathcal{F}$.

Note that in order to support multiple occurrences of the same formula in a proof, one needs to distinguish between vertices and the formulas assigned to them via the labelling function L. However, because this generality is orthogonal to the ideas we want to present, we will from now on identify each node $v \in V$ with its formula $L(v)$ and stop referring to the labelling function explicitly.

In the above definition, condition 1 ensures that any formula of the proof is justified by exactly one inference. Later on we will look at subgraphs of a proof, which are not necessarily proofs themselves and in particular do not satisfy condition 1, since they contain formulas, which are not justified by any inference of the subgraph. We call such a subgraph a derivation and call the formulas which are not justified by any inference the premises of the derivation. We can see a proof as a derivation having no premises.

Definition 3. The definition of a *derivation of G from axioms $\mathcal{F}$* is the same as that of a proof $P = (V, E, L)$ of G from $\mathcal{F}$, except that condition 1 is generalised to:

1. Each formula $F \in V$ is a conclusion of *at most one* inference $r \in E$.

The *set of premises of a derivation* P, denoted by $\mathrm{Prem}(P)$, consists of all formulas $F \in V$, such that there exists no inference $r \in E$ with conclusion F.

The definition of a derivation is not natural as it distinguishes between axioms and premises. This distinction is, however, very important for us, as it enables a succinct presentation of the results in Sect. 3.

Lemma 4 (Soundness). Let P be a derivation of G from axioms $\mathcal{F}$. Then we have

$$\mathcal{F} \vDash \left(\bigwedge\nolimits_{F_k \in \mathrm{Prem}(P)} F_k \right) \to G.$$

To formalise the idea of a proof traversal in which the inferences are considered one by one from axioms to the final formula G, we make use of topological orderings.

Definition 5. Let $P = (V, E, L)$ be a derivation. A topological ordering $<^T$ for P is a linear ordering $<^T$ on E such that for any two inferences $r_1, r_2 \in E$ if the conclusion of r_1 is a premise of r_2 then $r_1 <^T r_2$.

A topological ordering exists for every derivation, because proofs, and thus also derivations, are required to be acyclic.

Interpolation. We now recall the notion of a logical interpolant.

Definition 6. Let A and B be formulas.

1. A non-logical symbol $s \in \mathcal{N}(A \to B)$ is called *A-local*, if $s \in \mathcal{N}(A) \setminus \mathcal{N}(B)$, *B-local*, if $s \in \mathcal{N}(B) \setminus \mathcal{N}(A)$, and *global* otherwise.
2. An *interpolant* for A, B is a formula I such that $\vDash A \to I$, $\vDash I \to B$ and all non-logical symbols of I are global.

Craig's interpolation theorem [6] guarantees the existence of an interpolant for any pair of formulas A, B for which $\vDash A \to B$. In the sequel, we assume A and B to be fixed and give all definitions relative to A and B.

Refutational theorem proving. To prove a first-order formula F in practice, a refutational theorem prover proceeds by negating the input formula, applying a normal form transformation, such as the Conjunctive Normal Form transformation, to the negation, and deriving a contradiction $\bot$ from the obtained set of formulas $\mathcal{C}_{\neg F} = CNF(\neg F)$. More specifically, in the case of proving the implication $A \to B$, the prover starts with axioms $CNF(A \wedge \neg B)$.

This is relevant for our work, because we rely on refutations as input for our method. However, a complication arises, because the normal form transformations CNF typically involves steps like sub-formula naming and Skolemisation [18,20], which (1) introduce new non-logical symbols, (2) in general do not preserve logical equivalence.

To deal with (1) we impose a restriction on CNF which dictates that the symbols newly introduced on behalf of A and $\neg B$ do not overlap. Formally, we require

$$\mathcal{N}(A) \cap \mathcal{N}(\neg B) = \mathcal{N}(CNF(A)) \cap \mathcal{N}(CNF(\neg B)), \tag{1}$$

which is a very natural condition, because the newly introduced symbols are invariably required to be fresh.[1]

To deal with (2), let us first recall that steps like sub-formula naming and Skolemisation, although they do not preserve logical equivalence, do preserve satisfiability. While this is sufficient to guarantee soundness of refutational theorem proving, it is not enough for the purposes of interpolation. Fortunately, a stronger property, which is rarely stated explicitly, usually holds for the normal form transformation, namely the *preservation of models over the common symbols*. Formally, we require for every formula F that

- every model $\mathcal{M}'$ of $CNF(F)$ is also a model of F, and
- every model $\mathcal{M}$ of F can be extended to $\mathcal{M}'$ which is a model of $CNF(F)$,

where extended means that $\mathcal{M}'$ restricted to $\mathcal{N}(F)$ equals $\mathcal{M}$.

Equipped with a transformation CNF satisfying the above requirements, the general approach to interpolation from refutations consists of the following steps:

1. Given formulas A and B, compute the respective normal forms $\mathcal{C}_A = CNF(A)$ and $\mathcal{C}_{\neg B} = CNF(\neg B)$.
2. Find a refutation P from axioms $\mathcal{C}_A \cup \mathcal{C}_{\neg B}$.
3. Extract from P a formula I such that $\mathcal{C}_A \vDash I$, $\mathcal{C}_{\neg B}, I \vDash \bot$, and all non-logical symbols of I are global.[2]

Lemma 7. The formula I obtained in the last step is an interpolant for A and B.

---

[1] This could potentially be violated by an advanced transformation based on formula sharing. In particular, the case would need to involve a common sub-formula of A and $\neg B$.

[2] Note that the symbols are global with respect to A and B if and only if they are global with respect to $\mathcal{C}_A$ and $\mathcal{C}_{\neg B}$ thanks to the requirement (1).

3   Interpolants from Refutations

We can separate the properties of an interpolant into two parts, the logical part and the restriction to the global symbols. Instead of considering only interpolants, we now want to look more generally at the formulas, which satisfy the logical part of the properties of interpolants, but not necessarily the restriction to the global symbols. We call such formulas intermediants.[3]

Definition 8. Let A, B be two formulas. An *intermediant* for A, B is a formula I such that we have both $\vDash A \to I$ and $\vDash I \to B$.

In the first part of this section, we want to investigate the space of intermediants, which is induced by a given refutation. In the second part, we look at the subspace of those intermediants which also respect the restriction on the global symbols, i.e. the formulas which are interpolants.

3.1   Splitting Refutations

Let us now show how to use a refutation of $A \to B$ to construct intermediants. Intuitively, we want to split the refutation into two parts and construct a formula which describes the boundaries between the parts.

In the light of the discussion at the end of the previous section, we assume the formulas A and $\neg B$ have been transformed to sets of axioms $\mathcal{C}_A$ and $\mathcal{C}_{\neg B}$. It is also natural to extend the notion of an intermediant to axiom sets:

Definition 9. Let $\mathcal{C}_A$ and $\mathcal{C}_{\neg B}$ be two sets of axioms. An *intermediant* for $\mathcal{C}_A, \mathcal{C}_{\neg B}$ is a formula I such that we have both $\mathcal{C}_A \vDash I$ and $\mathcal{C}_{\neg B}, I \vDash \bot$.

Splitting a proof into two parts for us means mapping each inference to one of the two parts. Formally, we introduce a two element set $\{\mathcal{A}, \mathcal{B}\}$ to serve as a co-domain of such mapping, where $\mathcal{A}$ denotes the A-part and $\mathcal{B}$ the B-part. It is natural to map the axioms from $\mathcal{C}_A$ to $\mathcal{A}$ and the axioms from $\mathcal{C}_{\neg B}$ to $\mathcal{B}$, therefore we only consider mappings of this form. All other inferences can be mapped to any part.

Definition 10. Let P be a refutation from axioms $\mathcal{C}_A \cup \mathcal{C}_{\neg B}$. A *splitting function* $\mathcal{S}$ is a function assigning each inference of P to either $\mathcal{A}$ or $\mathcal{B}$, such that for each axiom inference $r = (F)$, if $\mathcal{S}(r) = \mathcal{A}$ then $F \in \mathcal{C}_A$ and r is called an A-*axiom*, and if $\mathcal{S}(r) = \mathcal{B}$ then $F \in \mathcal{C}_{\neg B}$ and r is called a B-*axiom*.

A given splitting function $\mathcal{S}$ splits a proof into several maximal subderivations. We now want to capture this intuitive notion formally. We start with the concept of In-formulas (resp. Out-formulas) of P and $\mathcal{S}$. Intuitively, these are the formulas which occur at the boundary between the subderivations.

---

[3] Bonacina and Johansson [2] introduce the notion of a *provisional interpolant* with an analogous definition. However, the intended use of the notion is different. While provisional interpolants are meant to be modified to yield interpolants in a refinement stage, we give conditions under which intermediants are, in fact, interpolants.

Definition 11. Let $P = (V, E, L)$ be a refutation from axioms $\mathcal{C}_A \cup \mathcal{C}_{\neg B}$ and let $\mathcal{S}$ be a splitting function on P. The *set of in-formulas*, which is denoted $\text{In}(P, \mathcal{S})$, consists of those formulas $F \in V$, which has the following properties:

- There exists an inference $r_1 \in E$ with conclusion F and $\mathcal{S}(r_1) = \mathcal{B}$.
- There exists an inference $r_2 \in E$ with premise F and $\mathcal{S}(r_2) = \mathcal{A}$.

The *set of out-formulas*, denoted $\text{Out}(P, \mathcal{S})$, consists of formulas $F \in V$, such that

- There exists an inference $r_1 \in E$ with conclusion F and $\mathcal{S}(r_1) = \mathcal{A}$.
- Either there exists an inference $r_2 \in E$ with premise F and $\mathcal{S}(r_2) = \mathcal{B}$, or $F = \bot$.

Notice that the notions of in- and out-formulas are not entirely symmetrical. The reason for this will become clear later.

We are now able to formally introduce the maximal subderivations.

Definition 12. Let $P = (V, E, L)$ be a refutation from axioms $\mathcal{C}_A \cup \mathcal{C}_{\neg B}$ and let $\mathcal{S}$ be a splitting function on P. Let $r \in E$ be an inference and let $\{r_1, \ldots, r_l\}$ be the set of those inferences which derive a premise of r and are mapped by $\mathcal{S}$ to the same part as r, i.e. $\mathcal{S}(r) = \mathcal{S}(r_i)$ for $i = 1, \ldots l$. Then we define $\text{Sub}(r)$ recursively as

$$\text{Sub}(r) = \{r\} \cup \text{Sub}(r_1) \cup \cdots \cup \text{Sub}(r_l).$$

Now let $F \in \text{Out}(P, \mathcal{S})$ (resp. $F \in \text{In}(P, \mathcal{S})$) be a formula and r be the inference deriving F. We define the *maximal A-subderivation (resp. B-subderivation) of F*, denoted by $\text{Sub}(F)$, as the induced derivation $(V', \text{Sub}(r), L)$, where V' contains every vertex which is either a premise or a conclusion of an inference in $\text{Sub}(F)$. We call F the *conclusion* of $\text{Sub}(F)$.

The dependencies of F, written $\text{Dep}(F)$, are defined as the premises of $\text{Sub}(F)$.

We can observe that the In-formulas (resp. Out-formulas) are the premises (resp. conclusions) of all maximal A-subderivations. Dually, the In-formulas (resp. Out-formulas) are the conclusions (resp. premises) of all maximal B-subderivations. The use of the introduced concepts is demonstrated in Fig. 1.

Note that the A-subderivations contain all A-axioms, but no B-axiom. Therefore the A-axioms's contribution to the derivation is captured by the A-subderivations. The key idea of this subsection is that encoding the contribution of the A-subderivations as a formula therefore yields the intermediant I we are looking for. The following lemma tells us how to describe the contribution of an A-subderivation.

Lemma 13. Let P be a refutation from axioms $\mathcal{C}_A \cup \mathcal{C}_{\neg B}$ and let $\mathcal{S}$ be a splitting function on P.

1. Let $F \in \text{Out}(P, \mathcal{S})$. Then we have $\mathcal{C}_A \vDash (\bigwedge_{F_k \in \text{Dep}(F)} F_k) \rightarrow F$.
2. Let $F \in \text{In}(P, \mathcal{S})$. Then we have $\mathcal{C}_{\neg B} \vDash (\bigwedge_{F_k \in \text{Dep}(F)} F_k) \rightarrow F$.

$$
\begin{array}{cccc}
F_1 \quad F_2 & & F_6 \quad F_7 \\
\hline
F_3 \qquad F_4 & & F_8 \qquad\qquad F_9 \\
\hline
F_5 & & F_{10} \\
\hline
& \bot &
\end{array}
$$

Fig. 1. Consider the proof above along with the splitting function which is denoted by drawing the inferences assigned to $\mathcal{A}$ using solid red lines and the inferences assigned to $\mathcal{B}$ using dashed blue lines. The maximal A-subderivation of F_5 has premises F_1, F_2 (and conclusion F_5), the maximal A-subderivation of F_{10} has premise F_8. The maximal B-subderivation of F_1 has no premises, the maximal B-subderivation of $\bot$ has premises F_5 and F_{10}. The In-formulas are F_1, F_2 and F_8 and the Out-formulas are F_5 and F_{10}. The induced simple splitting formula is $((F_1 \wedge F_2) \to F_5) \wedge (F_8 \to F_{10})$.

We therefore arrive at the following definition.

Definition 14. Let P be a refutation from axioms $\mathcal{C}_A \cup \mathcal{C}_{\neg B}$ and let $\mathcal{S}$ be a splitting function on P. The formula

$$
I := \bigwedge_{F \in \mathrm{Out}(P,\mathcal{S})} ((\bigwedge_{F_k \in \mathrm{Dep}(F)} F_k) \to F)
$$

is called the *simple splitting formula* of P induced by $\mathcal{S}$.

Theorem 15. Let P be a refutation from axioms $\mathcal{C}_A \cup \mathcal{C}_{\neg B}$ and let $\mathcal{S}$ be a splitting function on P. Then the simple splitting formula I induced by $\mathcal{S}$ is an intermediant.

Proof.

1. For each $F \in \mathrm{Out}(P,\mathcal{S})$, we can use Lemma 13.1 to get $\mathcal{C}_A \vDash (\bigwedge_{F_k \in \mathrm{Dep}(F)} F_k) \to F$. Therefore we have $\mathcal{C}_A \vDash \bigwedge_{F \in \mathrm{Out}(P,\mathcal{S})}((\bigwedge_{F_k \in \mathrm{Dep}(F)} F_k) \to F)$.
2. Let $<^T$ be a topological ordering for P and let $F_1, \ldots, F_n$ denote the formulas of $\mathrm{In}(P) \cup \mathrm{Out}(P)$ in the order induced by $<^T$. We visit the formulas from F_1 to F_n and prove by complete induction that $I, \mathcal{C}_{\neg B} \vDash F_1, \ldots, F_i$. Since $F_n = \bot$, we afterwards are able to conclude $I, \mathcal{C}_{\neg B} \vDash \bot$.
   Inductive step: Let us assume, by the induction hypothesis, that $I, \mathcal{C}_{\neg B} \vDash F_1, \ldots, F_{i-1}$. We make a case distinction on $\mathcal{S}(r)$, where r is the inference which derived F_i:
   - Case $\mathcal{S}(r) = \mathcal{A}$: By the definition of I, we know that $I \vDash (\bigwedge_{F_k \in Dep(F_i)} F_k) \to F_i$. Using both the definition of topological orderings and the definition of Dep we know that $\mathrm{Dep}(F_i) \subseteq \{F_1, \ldots F_{i-1}\}$, so we can combine the previous facts to obtain $I, \mathcal{C}_{\neg B} \vDash F_1, \ldots, F_i$.
   - Case $\mathcal{S}(r) = \mathcal{B}$: We use Lemma 13.2 to conclude $\mathcal{C}_{\neg B} \vDash (\bigwedge_{F_k \in Dep(F_i)} F_k) \to F_i$. As in the previous case, we can use $\mathrm{Dep}(F_i) \subseteq \{F_1, \ldots F_{i-1}\}$ to conclude $I, \mathcal{C}_{\neg B} \vDash F_1, \ldots, F_i$.

We summarise the ideas of this subsection in Simple-splitting-formula (Algorithm 1).

Algorithm 1. Simple-splitting-formula

choose a splitting function on P.
compute $\mathrm{Out}(P)$ and $\mathrm{Dep}(F)$ for all F using depth first search
return I as defined in Definition 14

3.2 Intermediants of Linear Size

Simple-splitting-formula yields an intermediant of size which is in the worst case quadratic in the size of the proof. This may be prohibitively large for large proofs. In this subsection, we describe an algorithm which yields intermediants of size which is linear in the size of the proof. Modifying Algorithm 1 to generate such an intermediant is nontrivial: there are examples, where the simple splitting formula is provably logically stronger than any intermediant which uses every formula of the refutation only once, cf. Fig. 2. We therefore need to modify the algorithm such that it produces an intermediant which is logically weaker but still sufficiently strong to be inconsistent with C_B.

The key idea for the new algorithm is contained in the following definition.

$$
r_1 \frac{\overline{F_1} \qquad \overline{F_2}}{F_3 \quad F_5 \quad F_4} r_2
$$
$$
r_4 \frac{\qquad\qquad}{\bot}
$$

Fig. 2. Let $r_1 = (F_1, F_3)$, $r_2 = (F_2, F_4)$, $r_3 = (F_1, F_2, F_5)$, and $r_4 = (F_3, F_4, F_5, \bot)$. Let further $\mathcal{S}(r_1) = \mathcal{S}(r_2) = \mathcal{S}(r_3) = \mathcal{A}$ and $\mathcal{S}(r_4) = \mathcal{B}$. Then Algorithm 1 generates the simple splitting formula $I = (F_1 \to F_3) \wedge (F_2 \to F_4) \wedge ((F_1 \wedge F_2) \to F_5)$. There is no intermediant which is both logically equivalent to I and contains each formula of the given proof at most once.

Definition 16. Let P be a refutation from axioms $\mathcal{C}_A \cup \mathcal{C}_{\neg B}$, $\mathcal{S}$ a splitting function on P, and let $<^T$ be a topological ordering for P. Furthermore let $F_1, \ldots, F_n$ denote the formulas of $\mathrm{In}(P) \cup \mathrm{Out}(P)$ ordered by $<^T$. Now let

$$
I_i = \begin{cases} \top & \text{if } i = n+1 \\ F_i \to I_{i+1} & \text{if } F_i \in \mathrm{In}(P) \\ F_i \wedge I_{i+1} & \text{if } F_i \in \mathrm{Out}(P) \end{cases}
$$

Then I_1 is called *linear splitting formula of P induced by $\mathcal{S}$ and $<^T$*.

Note that the size of I_1 is linear in the size of P in Definition 16.

Theorem 17. Let P be a refutation from axioms $\mathcal{C}_A \cup \mathcal{C}_{\neg B}$, let $\mathcal{S}$ be a splitting function on P and let $<^T$ be a topological ordering for P. Then the linear splitting formula I induced by $\mathcal{S}$ and $<^T$ is an intermediant.

Proof. Let

$$I' = \bigwedge_{F_i \in \text{Out}(P)} ((\bigwedge_{F_k \in \text{In}(P), F_k <^T F_i} F_k) \rightarrow F_i).$$

First note that I' is logically equivalent to I: This can be proved by a simple induction using the two facts that conjunction on the right distributes over implication and that $A \rightarrow (B \rightarrow C)$ is equivalent to $(A \wedge B) \rightarrow C$.

Now we complete the proof by showing that I' is an intermediant:

1. Using both the definition of topological orderings and the definition of Dep we know that $\text{Dep}(F_i) \subseteq \{F_k \in \text{In}(P) \mid F_k <^T F_i\}$, so I' is logically weaker than the simple splitting formula. Therefore $\mathcal{C}_A \vDash I'$ follows from Theorem 15.1.
2. We can show $\mathcal{C}_{\neg B}, I' \vDash \bot$ by re-using the proof of Theorem 15.2 with $<^T$ as the topological ordering and by replacing $\text{Dep}(P)$ with $\{F_k \in \text{In}(P) \mid F_k <^T F_i\}$.

We summarise the presented ideas in Linear-splitting-formula (Algorithm 2) and conclude this subsection by pointing out the following basic lemma, which will become useful later in the paper.

Algorithm 2. Linear-splitting-formula

---
choose a splitting function and a topological ordering on P.
compute $\text{In}(P)$ and $\text{Out}(P)$
return I_1 as defined in Definition 16

Lemma 18. Let $P = (V, E, L)$ be a refutation from axioms $\mathcal{C}_A \cup \mathcal{C}_{\neg B}$ and let $\mathcal{S}$ be a splitting function on P. Let further I be the linear splitting formula induced by $\mathcal{S}$ and let $F \in V$ be an arbitrary formula different from $\bot$. Then F occurs in I if and only if there are two inferences r_1, r_2, where r_1 derives F, F is a premise of r_2 and $\mathcal{S}(r_1) \neq \mathcal{S}(r_2)$.

3.3   Interpolants as Special Intermediants

In the previous subsections, we discussed how to construct intermediants given a splitting function. We now look closer at the question which splitting function to choose. While studying the intermediants induced by different choices of a splitting function is an interesting topic in general, we turn our attention to the problem of choosing a splitting function such that the induced intermediant is an interpolant, i.e. we have the additional requirement that the intermediant contains no local symbols.

Let us recall the notion of local proofs—also called split proofs—introduced by Jhala and McMillan [10]:

Definition 19 (Local Proof). A proof $P = (V, E, L)$ from axioms $\mathcal{C}_A \cup \mathcal{C}_{\neg B}$ is *local* if for every inference $(F_1, \ldots, F_n, F) \in E$ we have either:

- $\mathcal{N}(F_1) \cup \ldots \cup \mathcal{N}(F_k) \cup \mathcal{N}(F) \subseteq \mathcal{N}(\mathcal{C}_A)$ or
- $\mathcal{N}(F_1) \cup \ldots \cup \mathcal{N}(F_k) \cup \mathcal{N}(F) \subseteq \mathcal{N}(\mathcal{C}_{\neg B})$.

The definition of local proofs ensures that we can define a splitting function $\mathcal{S}$ which maps all inferences with A-local symbols to $\mathcal{A}$ and those with B-local symbols to $\mathcal{B}$.

Definition 20. Let P be a local proof. A *local splitting function on* P is a splitting function $\mathcal{S}$ on P such that $\mathcal{S}(r) = \mathcal{A}$ (resp. $\mathcal{S}(r) = \mathcal{B}$) for all inferences r having as premise or conclusion a formula containing an A-local (resp. a B-local) symbol.

The corollary of the following lemma represents the central observation of this subsection: local proofs are exactly the proofs on which we can define a splitting function that induces an intermediant which is an interpolant.

Lemma 21. Let $P = (V, E, L)$ be a refutation from axioms $C_A \cup C_B$, $\mathcal{S}$ be a local splitting function on P, and I the corresponding simple (resp. linear) splitting formula.

(i) Then any formula $F \in \text{In}(P, \mathcal{S}) \cup \text{Out}(P, \mathcal{S})$ contains neither an A-local nor a B-local symbol.

(ii) I contains neither A-local nor B-local symbols.

Proof. (i) Consider any formula $F \in \text{Out}(P, \mathcal{S})$. If $F = \bot$ then F trivially contains neither an A-local nor a B-local symbol. Otherwise, we know that there exists an inference $r_1 \in E$ with premise F and $\mathcal{S}(r_1) = \mathcal{B}$. By the locality of $\mathcal{S}$ we get that F contains no A-local symbol. Furthermore, we know that there exists an inference $r_2 \in E$ with conclusion F and $\mathcal{S}(r_2) = \mathcal{A}$. By the locality of $\mathcal{S}$ we get that F contains no B-local symbol.
Now consider any formula $F \in \text{In}(P, \mathcal{S})$. We can use a similar argument to show that F contains neither an A-local nor a B-local symbol.

(ii) Follows immediately from (i) and the definition of the simple (resp. linear) splitting formula.

Corollary 22. Let P be a local refutation, let $\mathcal{S}$ be a local splitting function on P and let I be either the simple splitting formula or the linear splitting formula. Then I is an interpolant for A, B.

4   Implementing Local Splitting Functions

By the definition of a local splitting function we know that we need to assign axioms and inferences with local symbols to the corresponding part. All the other inferences— the inferences forming the so called *grey area* [9]— can be assigned freely to either part. Different choices on how to split the grey area result in different A-subproofs and therefore in different interpolants, which vary, e.g., in size, the number of contained quantifiers and in logical strength.

We want to minimize the interpolant with respect to a given weight function w, which maps each formula F to its weight $w(F)$. The task we want to solve in this section is, therefore, to be able to come up with a local splitting function which minimises the weight of the resulting interpolant.

We present two different solutions, a heuristical greedy approach and one of expressing the optimal splitting as a minimisation problem. Both solutions are based on the insight from Lemma 18 of Sect. 3: A conclusion F of an inference r_1 occurs in the linear splitting formula if and only if there is an inference r_2 with F as a premise such that the splitting function maps r_1 and r_2 to different parts.

4.1 Greedy Weighted Sum Heuristic

Consider an inference r of the grey area with premises $C_1, \ldots C_n, D_1, \ldots, D_m$ and assume that the inferences deriving $C_1, \ldots, C_n$ are already assigned to $\mathcal{A}$ and that the inferences deriving $D_1, \ldots, D_m$ are already assigned to $\mathcal{B}$. Using Lemma 18, we know that if we assign r to $\mathcal{A}$, then $D_1, \ldots, D_m$ will be added to the interpolant and if we assign r to $\mathcal{B}$, then $C_1, \ldots, C_n$ will be added to the interpolant.

We can therefore use the following greedy strategy to locally minimize the weight of the interpolant: for any inference r of the grey area, if $\sum_{k=1}^{n} w(C_k) > \sum_{k=1}^{m} w(D_k)$, map r to $\mathcal{A}$, otherwise to $\mathcal{B}$.

This results in Top-down-weighted-sum-heuristic (Algorithm 3):

Algorithm 3. Top-down-weighted-sum-heuristic

---

for each inference r of P (top-down) **do**
    if r is an A-axiom or r contains an A-local symbol **then**
        set $\mathcal{S}(r)$ to $\mathcal{A}$
    else if i is a B-axiom or r contains a B-local symbol **then**
        set $\mathcal{S}(r)$ to $\mathcal{B}$
    else
        if $\sum_{k=1}^{n} w(C_k) > \sum_{k=1}^{m} w(D_k)$ **then**
            set $\mathcal{S}(r)$ to $\mathcal{A}$
        else
            set $\mathcal{S}(r)$ to $\mathcal{B}$
return $\mathcal{S}$

The two reasons why a locally optimal choice is not a globally optimal choice can be seen in Figs. 3 and 4.

4.2 Encoding Optimal Splitting as a Minimisation Problem

Similar to the idea presented in [9], we can alternatively encode the problem of finding an optimal local splitting function as a minimisation problem and pass it to a pseudo-boolean constraint solver. This yields an optimal assignment, but is computationally more expensive.

$$\begin{array}{c} i_1 \dfrac{}{} \quad i_2 \dfrac{}{} \quad i_3 \dfrac{}{} \\[2pt] i_4 \dfrac{F_1 \qquad F_2 \qquad F_3}{} \, i_5 \\[2pt] i_6 \dfrac{F_4 \qquad\qquad F_5}{\bot} \end{array}$$

Fig. 3. Let $\mathcal{S}(i_1) = \mathcal{S}(i_3) = \mathcal{A}$ and $\mathcal{S}(i_2) = \mathcal{B}$. Let further $w(F_1) = w(F_3) = 2$ and $w(F_2) = 3$. For both inferences i_4 and i_5, the assignment of the inference to $\mathcal{B}$ is locally optimal, then causes the assignment of i_6 to $\mathcal{B}$ and finally yields an interpolant of weight 4. Note that F_2 is used as a premise of both i_4 and i_5, so due to the DAG-structure we would only include it once if we assigned both i_4 and i_5 to $\mathcal{A}$. This would then cause the assignment of i_6 to $\mathcal{A}$ and finally yield a smaller interpolant of weight 3.

$$\begin{array}{c} i_1 \dfrac{}{} \\[2pt] i_2 \dfrac{F_1}{} \\[2pt] i_3 \dfrac{F_2 \qquad F_3}{\bot} \end{array}$$

Fig. 4. Let $\mathcal{S}(i_1) = \mathcal{A}$ and $\mathcal{S}(i_3) = \mathcal{B}$. Let further $w(F_1) < w(F_2)$. Algorithm 3 would now assign i_2 to $\mathcal{A}$ and therefore include F_2 in the interpolant. It would be better to assign i_2 to $\mathcal{B}$ in order to include F_1 in the interpolant instead of F_2.

The encoding works as follows. We use propositional variables x_i to denote that inference i is assigned to $\mathcal{A}$ and use propositional variables L_i to denote that the conclusion of i occurs in the interpolant. We again predict the size of the resulting interpolant using Lemma 18, but this time use the optimisation procedure to make globally optimal choices instead of greedily making locally optimal ones. This leads to algorithm Weighted-sum-optimal (Algorithm 4).

Algorithm 4. Weighted-sum-optimal

---

    for each inference r of P **do**
        if r is an A-axiom or r contains an A-local symbol **then**
            assert x_r
        else if r is a B-axiom or r contains a B-local symbol **then**
            assert $\neg x_r$
        for each parent inference r' of r **do**
            assert $(\neg(x_r \leftrightarrow x_{r'})) \rightarrow L_{r'}$
    compute model M which minimises $\sum_{r \in P} w(concl(r)) \cdot L_r$
    for each inference r of P **do**
        if x_r evaluates to true in M **then**
            set $\mathcal{S}(r)$ to $\mathcal{A}$
        else
            set $\mathcal{S}(r)$ to $\mathcal{B}$
    return $\mathcal{S}$

---

5   Discussion and Related Work

There are two main existing approaches to constructing interpolants from arbitrary local proofs in arbitrary sound first-order proof systems with equality.

First, there is the work from Jhala and McMillan (Theorem 3 of [10]). They present an algorithm which consists of two main phases: A) Extract a propositionally unsatisfiable set of formulas F, B) obtain a propositional refutation of F using boolean constraint propagation and apply McMillan's interpolation algorithm for propositional logic [15] to the result in order to obtain an interpolant for the original local refutation.

One can easily see that the set F constructed in phase A consists of both the conjuncts of the splitting formula from Definition 14 and the conjuncts of the simple splitting formula obtained by swapping A and B in the proof. In contrast, Algorithm 1 only needs the former conjuncts. Furthermore we know from Corollary 22 that it is sufficient to conjoin all these conjuncts instead of unnecessarily constructing and interpolating from a propositional refutation. Besides conceptually simplifying the algorithm, this also enables the optimisations presented in Sect. 4.

More importantly, in [17], it is claimed that the complexity of the algorithm behind Theorem 3 of [10] is linear in the size of the proof. While phase B of the algorithm is clearly linear, we can see easily from Example 23 below that phase A is worst case quadratic in the size of the proof, making the whole algorithm quadratic, which is contrasts to out Algorithm 2, that is linear.

Example 23. Consider a split refutation with nodes $A_1, \ldots, A_n, B_1, \ldots, B_n, \perp$; edges $(A_i, A_{i+1}), (A_i, B_{i+1}), (B_i, A_{i+1}), (B_i, B_{i+1})$, for $1 \le i < n$ and $(A_n, \perp)$, $(B_n, \perp)$; and labeling $P(A_i) = A, P(B_i) = B, P(\perp) = $ arbitrary. Phase A) would construct a graph with edges $(A_i, B_j), (B_i, A_j)$ forall $0 < i < j \le n$, which is quadratic in n.

The second main approach to constructing interpolants in first-order logic with equality using an arbitrary sound inference system was introduced in [11] and later improved by an optimisation technique in [9]. Let us refer to the interpolation algorithm from [11] as $\mathcal{SE}$. In a nutshell, $\mathcal{SE}$ uses two main concepts:

As a first concept, it constructs the largest subderivations containing only symbols from one of the two partitions (cf. Lemma 8 of [11]). This construction corresponds to a commitment to a specific choice of local splitting function in our framework. In contrast, both Algorithms 1 and 2 are parametrized by an arbitrary local splitting function and different choices yield different interpolants.

As the main contribution of [9], the authors extend algorithm $\mathcal{SE}$ such that it also considers a space of different interpolants and optimise over this space. We can see that the extension simulates different choices of splitting function by merging proof steps. Both the algorithm from [9] and our Algorithm 4 encode the space of candidates and the minimisation objective as a pseudo-boolean constraint problem and then ask an optimising SMT-solver for an optimal solution. While encoding the space of splitting functions is trivial using Algorithm 4, encoding the space of local proofs, which are results from repeated pairwise merging of inferences, is much more involved. More critically, while we can make use of Lemma 18 to predict the size of the resulting interpolant, the approach from [9] uses a notion of so called digest to predict the size of the interpolant computed from the transformed proof. The authors claim that the interpolant is a boolean combination of formulas in the digest (Theorem 3.6, [9]). Unfortunately, this claim is wrong, which can be concluded from the counterexample presented in Fig. 5. Therefore the technique presented in [9] can potentially yield sub-optimal interpolants.

$$\frac{\displaystyle \frac{\displaystyle \frac{R_1 \quad G_1}{G_3} \quad \frac{B_1 \quad G_2}{}}{\displaystyle \frac{R_3 \qquad\qquad\qquad G_6}{R_4}}}{\bot}$$

Fig. 5. Consider the proof above, taken from Example 5.2 in [9]. Let R_1, R_3 and R_4 be formulas containing A-local symbols, B_1 a formula containing B-local symbols and let G_1, G_2, G_3 and G_6 be formulas containing no local symbols. Then the digest contains only G_6, but the algorithm from [11] would construct the interpolant $G_3 \wedge \neg G_6$, which also contains G_3.

As the second concept, the algorithm $\mathcal{SE}$ from [11] relies on a recursive construction to compute the interpolant: it computes for each largest subderivation a formula such that the formula of the outermost call yields an interpolant (cf. Lemma 10 of [11]). We now want to hint at the relation of algorithm $\mathcal{SE}$ and Algorithm 1. Consider a subderivation with premises $F_1, \ldots, F_k$ and conclusion F. Let further $I_1, \ldots, I_k$ denote the recursively computed formulas. Algorithm $\mathcal{SE}$ now constructs the following formulas:

- Case A: $I = ((I_1 \vee F_1) \wedge \cdots \wedge (I_k \vee F_k)) \wedge \neg(F_1 \wedge \cdots \wedge F_k)$.
- Case B: $I = ((I_1 \vee F_1) \wedge \cdots \wedge (I_k \vee F_k))$.

It is not difficult to see that one can reformulate the construction of $\mathcal{SE}$ as the following one, which we will refer to as $\mathcal{SE}'$:

- Case A: $I = ((I_1 \vee F_1) \wedge \cdots \wedge (I_k \vee F_k)) \vee F \wedge ((F_1 \wedge \cdots \wedge F_k) \rightarrow F)$.
- Case B: $I = (I_1 \wedge \cdots \wedge I_k)$.

Note that although the intermediate formulas of algorithm $\mathcal{SE}$ and $\mathcal{SE}'$ are potentially different, the result of the outermost call is the same for $\mathcal{SE}$ and $\mathcal{SE}'$.

We now state a recursive presentation of our Algorithm 1 in order to compare it to $\mathcal{SE}'$. The idea is to replace the global view on the refutation, i.e. the iteration over all elements of $\mathrm{Out}(P, \mathcal{S})$, by a recursive construction which collects all the formulas describing the boundaries of maximal A-subderivations.

Let P be a local proof of a formula F and let r be the inference which derives F. Let further $\mathcal{S}$ be a local splitting function on P. We compute a formula using the following recursive construction: Let $F_1, \ldots, F_k$ denote the elements of $\mathrm{Dep}(F)$ and let I_i denote the formula computed recursively from F_i.

- Case $\mathcal{S}(r) = \mathcal{A}$: $I = (I_1 \wedge \cdots \wedge I_n) \wedge ((F_1 \wedge \cdots \wedge F_n) \rightarrow F)$.
- Case $\mathcal{S}(e) = \mathcal{B}$: $I = (I_1 \wedge \cdots \wedge I_n)$.

If we now compare algorithm $\mathcal{SE}'$ and the recursive presentation of Algorithm 1 we see that they are the same with the exception that $\mathcal{SE}'$ contains redundant sub-formulas. More critically, since we know that Algorithm 1 yields an interpolant of size which is worst-case quadratic in the size of the proof, we know that the same holds for $\mathcal{SE}'$ and therefore for $\mathcal{SE}$, i.e. for the interpolation algorithm of [11]. This represents the most important downside of the approach of [11] and makes it inferior to Algorithm 2.

Finally, interpolation from first-order refutations is also studied in [2,13] where the authors present methods for computing interpolants from arbitrary proofs in first-order logic but either without equality or under the assumption that colored function symbols are only constants. While our proof splits are restricted to local proofs, in our approach we handle first-order theories with equality in full generality.

6   Experimental Results

We implemented Linear-splitting-formula (Algorithm 2, Sect. 3) in automated theorem prover VAMPIRE [12] and combined it with the two approaches for obtaining a local splitting function: the Top-down-weighted-sum-heuristic (Algorithm 3) and the Weighted-sum-optimal (Algorithm 4). We will from now on refer to the combinations as LinHeu and LinOpt, respectively. The aim of the experiment is to compare the performance of the new algorithms to algorithm from [11] combined with its optimising improvement from [9], which was already implemented in a previous version of VAMPIRE. We will from now on refer to this latter combination as SEOpt.[4]

To compensate for the lack of a representative set of benchmarks explicitly focusing on first-order interpolation, we made use of the first-order problems from the TPTP library [22] (version 6.4.0). We clausified each problem using VAMPIRE and split the obtained set of clauses into halves, treating the first half as $\mathcal{C}_A$ and the the second as $\mathcal{C}_{\neg B}$. We attempted to refute each of the obtained problems using VAMPIRE (which was instructed to generate only local proofs as described in [11]) and followed up by one of LinHeu, LinOpt, or SEOpt to compute an interpolant. We imposed a 60 s time limit on the proof search in VAMPIRE and a total limit of 100 s on each whole run. We ran the experiment on the StarExec compute cluster [21].

In total, we obtained 7442 local refutations. Out of these SEOpt failed to construct an interpolant in 723 cases. In contrast, LinOpt failed to construct an interpolant in only 16 cases and LinHeu always constructed an interpolant within the time limit. Furthermore, there were 353 cases in which SEOpt returned only an approximate result and 108 cases where optimisation failed and the

---

[4] The executables and connecting scripts used in the experiment are available at http://forsyte.at/static/people/suda/vampire_new_interpolation.zip.

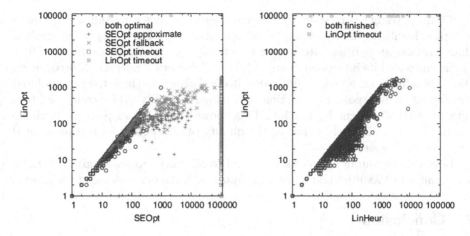

Fig. 6. Size comparison of interpolant produced by `SEOpt` and `LinOpt` (left), and `LinHeu` and `LinOpt` (right). Each point corresponds to a single refutation and its position to the sizes of the respective interpolants.

unoptimized version of [11] was used as a fallback instead. The observed higher computational demands of `SEOpt` can be mostly ascribed to the reliance on a different pseudo-boolean solver and different connecting technology.[5] These differences unfortunately exclude the possibility of a meaningful comparison of more detailed timing results. However, we would like to point out that the optimisation problem `SEOpt` constructs is arguably much more complex than the one stemming from Weighted-sum-optimal employed by `LinOpt`.

Figure 6 (left) contains a scatter plot comparison of the sizes of obtained interpolants for `LinOpt` and `SEOpt`. An artificial large value was substituted whenever a particular algorithm failed to provide an interpolant. This is reflected by the data points on the right and the upper border, respectively. The plot further separates the points to categories based on the optimality guarantee provided by `SEOpt`. We can see that `LinOpt` yields consistently better results. Moreover, the improvement tends to get more pronounced with the growing size of the instances. Finally, even when just focusing on instances where `SEOpt` finished optimising, there are numerous cases where the interpolant from `LinOpt` is several times smaller than that of `SEOpt`. This is because `SEOpt` cannot avoid repeating certain formulas from the refutation many times in the interpolant and corresponds to the worst case quadratic complexity discussed in Sect. 5.[6]

---

[5] `SEOpt` uses the SMT solver Yices [8] (version 1.0) and communicates via a file, while `LinOpt` one relies on Z3 [7] (version 4.5) and its API.

[6] An interesting side-effect is an ability of `SEOpt` to assign two different colors to a formula when considered from the perspective of two different sub-derivations. In rare cases, such formula does not need to appear at all, and the final interpolant may be smaller than what is achievable by `LinOpt`. An instance of this phenomenon occurred in our experiment on benchmark `SYN577-1`, which appears in Fig. 6 (left) slightly above the diagonal.

Figure 6 (right) correspondingly compares `LinOpt` with `LinHeu`. Although the plot highlights many examples where `LinHeu` yields a larger interpolant than `LinOpt`, an optimal interpolant is actually discovered by `LinHeu` in 79 % of the cases and its interpolants are only 11.6 % larger on average. Moreover, on the 7429 refutations on which both algorithms finished in time, the accumulated time spent on interpolant extraction by `LinHeu` was only 8.17 s compared to a total of 1901.03 s spent by `LinOpt`. This shows that `LinHeu` presents a viable alternative to `LinOpt` when trading the quality of interpolant for computational time becomes desirable.

Given the encouraging results we intend to officially replace `SEOpt` by `LinOpt` and `LinHeu` in Vampire and make it available with the next release of the prover.

7 Conclusion

We presented a new technique for constructing interpolants from first-order local refutations. The technique is based on an idea of proof splitting and on a novel non-inductive construction which arguably gives more insight than previous work and yields interpolants of linear size. This leads to a new interpolation algorithm which we implemented in the automated theorem prover Vampire. Finally, we confirmed in an extensive experiment that the algorithm also improves over the state-of-the-art in practice.

References

1. Alberti, F., Bruttomesso, R., Ghilardi, S., Ranise, S., Sharygina, N.: Lazy abstraction with interpolants for arrays. In: Bjørner, N., Voronkov, A. (eds.) LPAR 2012. LNCS, vol. 7180, pp. 46–61. Springer, Heidelberg (2012). doi:10.1007/978-3-642-28717-6_7
2. Bonacina, M.P., Johansson, M.: On interpolation in automated theorem proving. J. Autom. Reasoning **54**(1), 69–97 (2015)
3. Christ, J., Hoenicke, J.: Instantiation-based interpolation for quantified formulae. In: Decision Procedures in Software, Hardware and Bioware, April 18–23 April 2010, vol. 10161. Dagstuhl Seminar Proceedings. Schloss Dagstuhl - Leibniz-Zentrum für Informatik, Germany (2010)
4. Christ, J., Hoenicke, J.: Proof tree preserving tree interpolation. J. Autom. Reasoning **57**(1), 67–95 (2016)
5. Cimatti, A., Griggio, A., Sebastiani, R.: Efficient interpolant generation in satisfiability modulo theories. In: Ramakrishnan, C.R., Rehof, J. (eds.) TACAS 2008. LNCS, vol. 4963, pp. 397–412. Springer, Heidelberg (2008). doi:10.1007/978-3-540-78800-3_30
6. Craig, W.: Linear reasoning. a new form of the herbrand-gentzen theorem. J. Symb. Log. **22**(3), 250–268 (1957)
7. Moura, L., Bjørner, N.: Z3: an efficient SMT solver. In: Ramakrishnan, C.R., Rehof, J. (eds.) TACAS 2008. LNCS, vol. 4963, pp. 337–340. Springer, Heidelberg (2008). doi:10.1007/978-3-540-78800-3_24
8. Dutertre, B.: Yices 2.2. In: Biere, A., Bloem, R. (eds.) CAV 2014. LNCS, vol. 8559, pp. 737–744. Springer, Cham (2014). doi:10.1007/978-3-319-08867-9_49

9. Hoder, K., Kovács, L., Voronkov, A.: Playing in the grey area of proofs. In: Principles of Programming Languages, pp. 259–272. ACM (2012)
10. Jhala, R., McMillan, K.L.: A practical and complete approach to predicate refinement. In: Hermanns, H., Palsberg, J. (eds.) TACAS 2006. LNCS, vol. 3920, pp. 459–473. Springer, Heidelberg (2006). doi:10.1007/11691372_33
11. Kovács, L., Voronkov, A.: Interpolation and symbol elimination. In: Schmidt, R.A. (ed.) CADE 2009. LNCS (LNAI), vol. 5663, pp. 199–213. Springer, Heidelberg (2009). doi:10.1007/978-3-642-02959-2_17
12. Kovács, L., Voronkov, A.: First-order theorem proving and VAMPIRE. In: Sharygina, N., Veith, H. (eds.) CAV 2013. LNCS, vol. 8044, pp. 1–35. Springer, Heidelberg (2013). doi:10.1007/978-3-642-39799-8_1
13. Kovács, L., Voronkov, A.: First-order interpolation and interpolating proof systems. In: LPAR-21. 21st International Conference on Logic for Programming, Artificial Intelligence and Reasoning, vol. 46. EPiC Series in Computing, pp. 49–64. EasyChair (2017)
14. Lahiri, S.K., Mehra, K.K.: Interpolant based decision procedure for quantifier-free Presburger arithmetic. Technical Report MSR-TR-2005-121, Microsoft Research (2005)
15. McMillan, K.L.: Interpolation and SAT-based model checking. In: Hunt, W.A., Somenzi, F. (eds.) CAV 2003. LNCS, vol. 2725, pp. 1–13. Springer, Heidelberg (2003). doi:10.1007/978-3-540-45069-6_1
16. McMillan, K.L.: Lazy abstraction with interpolants. In: Ball, T., Jones, R.B. (eds.) CAV 2006. LNCS, vol. 4144, pp. 123–136. Springer, Heidelberg (2006). doi:10.1007/11817963_14
17. McMillan, K.L.: Quantified invariant generation using an interpolating saturation prover. In: Ramakrishnan, C.R., Rehof, J. (eds.) TACAS 2008. LNCS, vol. 4963, pp. 413–427. Springer, Heidelberg (2008). doi:10.1007/978-3-540-78800-3_31
18. Nonnengart, A., Weidenbach, C.: Computing small clause normal forms. In: Handbook of Automated Reasoning, vol. 2s, pp. 335–367. Elsevier and MIT Press (2001)
19. Podelski, A., Schäf, M., Wies, T.: Classifying bugs with interpolants. In: Aichernig, B.K.K., Furia, C.A.A. (eds.) TAP 2016. LNCS, vol. 9762, pp. 151–168. Springer, Cham (2016). doi:10.1007/978-3-319-41135-4_9
20. Reger, G., Suda, M., Voronkov, A.: New techniques in clausal form generation. In: GCAI 2016, 2nd Global Conference on Artificial Intelligence, vol. 41. EPiC Series in Computing, pp. 11–23. EasyChair (2016)
21. Stump, A., Sutcliffe, G., Tinelli, C.: StarExec, a cross community logic solving service (2012). https://www.starexec.org
22. Sutcliffe, G.: The TPTP problem library and associated infrastructure. J. Autom. Reasoning 43(4), 337–362 (2009)
23. Totla, N., Wies, T.: Complete instantiation-based interpolation. In: Principles of Programming Languages, pp. 537–548. ACM (2013)

Detecting Inconsistencies in Large First-Order Knowledge Bases

Stephan Schulz[1](✉), Geoff Sutcliffe[2](✉), Josef Urban[3](✉), and Adam Pease[4](✉)

[1] DHBW Stuttgart, Stuttgart, Germany
schulz@eprover.org
[2] University of Miami, Coral Gables, USA
geoff@cs.miami.edu
[3] Czech Technical University in Prague, Prague, Czech Republic
josef.urban@gmail.com
[4] Articulate Software, San Francisco, USA
apease@articulatesoftware.com

Abstract. Large formalizations carry the risk of inconsistency, and hence may lead to instances of spurious reasoning. This paper describes a new approach and tool that automatically probes large first-order axiomatizations for inconsistency, by selecting subsets of the axioms centered on certain function and predicate symbols, and handling the subsets to a first-order theorem prover to test for unsatisfiability. The tool has been applied to several large axiomatizations, inconsistencies have been found, inconsistent cores extracted, and semi-automatic analysis of the inconsistent cores has helped to pinpoint the axioms that appear to be the underlying cause of inconsistency.

1 Introduction

Automated Theorem Proving (ATP) is concerned with the development and use of computer programs that automate sound reasoning: the derivation of conclusions that follow inevitably from facts. The dual discipline, automated model finding, develops computer programs that establish that a set of statements is consistent. These capabilities lie at the heart of many important computational tasks, e.g., formal methods for software and hardware design and verification, [11,37], reasoning in meta-physics [4,46], solving hard problems in mathematics, [19,24], and inference for the semantic web [13]. The use of automated reasoning systems (theorem proving and model finding) requires a user to (rather precisely) describe the domain of application as a set of *axioms*. For theorem proving, an ATP system is then used to prove that a *conjecture* is a *theorem* of the axioms, and hopefully produce a proof. For model finding, a model finding system is used to demonstrate the *consistency* of the axioms, and hopefully produce a model of the axioms. Automated *theorem proving* in classical logic relies on the axioms being consistent, for otherwise all conjectures are theorems of the axiomatization.

J. Urban—Supported by the ERC Consolidator grant no. 649043 *AI4REASON*.

L. de Moura (Ed.): CADE 2017, LNAI 10395, pp. 310–325, 2017.
DOI: 10.1007/978-3-319-63046-5_19

The direct method of showing that a set of axioms is consistent is to use a model finder on the axioms. However, for large axiom sets this approach becomes rather difficult (or impossible), because most large axiomatizations have large or infinite models.

In the last 10 to 15 years there has been an increased, and increasingly successful, use of automated reasoning in "large theories", i.e., domain descriptions that have many symbols, and many axioms of which typically only a few are required for the proof of a theorem. Examples include commonsense and ontological knowledge bases such as Cyc [23,33] and the SUMO (Suggested Upper Merged Ontology) family of ontologies [26,29,31], large mathematical formalizations such as Mizar [42,44], Flyspeck [17] and Isabelle's *Archive of Formal Proofs* [20], and encodings of biological domains [10]. Such large axiomatizations always carry the risk of inconsistency - either because of mistakes in the original formulation, or because of errors encoding the original formulation into logic. Advances in ATP systems have revealed these inconsistencies while finding proofs of theorems [38], thus stimulating efforts to check such axiomatizations for consistency (for which model finding is largely unsuccessful, as noted above), and to pinpoint and fix inconsistencies.

This paper proposes a new approach and tool for automatically probing large first-order axiomatizations for inconsistencies. If inconsistencies are found, a small inconsistent core can typically be presented, which makes it easy to identify errors and to repair the axiomatization. This paper describes the idea and implementation of the method, and demonstrates how effective it can be on some existing large first-order axiomatizations.

2   Automated Reasoning in Large Theories

A common, almost necessary, part of reasoning over large axiomatizations is focussing on axioms that are likely to be relevant to proving a given conjecture. Typically, only a few axioms are needed for a proof. The irrelevant axioms increase the search space, often to the extent that it is impossible to find a proof. Axiom selection techniques address this problem [22,41]. A number of strong axiom selection methods for assisting formal mathematics [7] are based on various ways of learning from a large body of previous proofs [1,2,16,45]. In this work we are however to a large extent interested in common-sense knowledge bases, which mainly consist just of definitions and axioms. Below we therefore focus on *heuristic* rather than learning selection methods.

Relevance pruning tries to identify all formulae that are potentially relevant to proving a conjecture (or set of conjectures). Two formulae are relevant with respect to each other if they share a function or predicate symbol. Relevance pruning selects all formulae in the reflexive transitive closure of the conjecture with respect to the relevancy relation. Unrestricted relevance pruning maintains completeness in the non-equational case. A weakness is that the closure is often still very large.

A symbolic heuristic approach is the MePo families of filters [25] developed in the context of Sledgehammer [27], Isabelle's interface to ATP systems. The MePo filters represent formulae (and formula sets) as vectors of symbol occurrences, and iteratively select formulae with vectors similar to the vector of the already selected set. The process is again seeded with the conjecture.

Maybe the currently most widely used family of algorithms is derived from Hoder's SInE (SUMO Inference Engine) [15]). SInE can be seen as a heuristic variant of relevancy pruning. It is based on the idea of a "defines" relation between symbols and formulae. As for the previous approaches, SInE starts with a conjecture (and its symbols) and tries to add formulae until a fixpoint is reached in which all symbols in the set of selected formulae are defined. SInE assumes that rare symbols are typically defined in terms of more common symbols. Thus the "defines" relation associates a symbol with the formulae in which the symbol is the rarest symbol. Various implementations allow for slightly weaker constraints on this condition, or support early termination after a given number of formulae has been added or a maximum level of definitions has been followed. Variants of SInE have been implemented in, e.g., Vampire [21] and E [35,36], and are also the basis for this work.

3   Automatic Inconsistency Probing

In previous work, we have employed a method where we simply iterate through the set of axioms in the SUMO theory, testing them one at a time for inconsistency with the growing knowledge base [30]. The method starts from an empty knowledge base, and iteratively adds each axiom not proven to lead to a contradiction. However, this process can fail to find existing inconsistencies as soon as the knowledge base becomes complex enough that not every prover run terminates with a satisfiable/unsatisfiable result. Ideally, we would have a method fast enough to be run every time a new axiom is added to the theory.

The core idea of our new approach is to automatically extract subsets of an axiomatization, and test each for unsatisfiability. If any subset is unsatisfiable, so is the full axiomatization. The inconsistent core of such a subset can be extracted from the proof of unsatisfiability, and analyzed to pinpoint the cause of the inconsistency.

To extract a potentially unsatisfiable subset of axioms, a symbol is selected as the *seed symbol*. The seed symbol is used to select a set of seed formulae (possibly a single formula). The seed formulae are used as pseudo-goals for a SInE filter that recursively extracts definitions related to the seed formulae until the definitional closure is reached or one of the hard bounds (number of formulae or depth of definition chain) is reached. The resulting set of axioms is handed to a refutation-based ATP system that tries to show the set to be unsatisfiable. The overall architecture and data flow of the system is depicted in Fig. 1.

This general approach has a number of choice points: How to select the seed symbol, how to use the seed symbol to select seed formulae, which SInE filters to use, and how to parameterize the ATP system with respect to search strategy and resource limits.

The easiest way to select seed symbols is to try all the symbols in the axiomatization. For large axiomatizations with a big signature this leads to very many

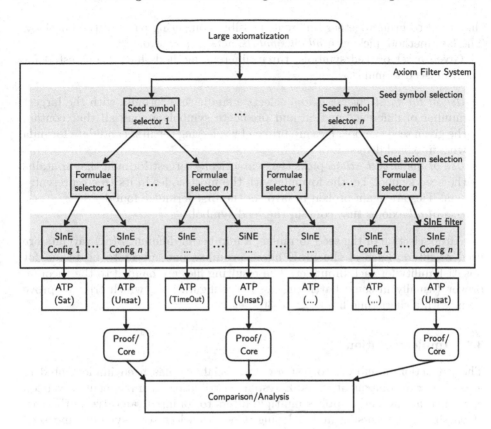

Fig. 1. Data flow and architecture

subsets to be tested for unsatisfiability, and hence is computationally challenging, although in many cases not prohibitively so. To limit the number of subsets, restrictions can be imposed on the type and number of seed symbols. First, the class of symbols considered as seeds can be restricted to predicate symbols only, proper function symbols (excluding constants) only, or constants only, or any combination of the three. At least in commonsense scenarios, a very large proportion of symbols are constants, and our experiments have shown that excluding constants does not seem to reduce the number of inconsistencies found.

Secondly, a subset of the eligible seed symbols can be selected, according to a desired number of seed symbols and a selection criterion. We implemented a variety of relatively simple methods to get an impression of the spectrum of behaviours. Here, the first approach is to pick *rare symbols*, i.e. symbols that do not occur in many axioms, as seed. This is based on the assumption that more specialized parts of the ontology will typically be less exercised than more general parts, and are hence more likely to contain hidden bugs. The opposite approach, picking the most *frequent symbols* as seeds, is based on the idea that they tend to bring together different, possibly conflicting parts of the ontology. The last method, picking *random symbols*, acts as a control.

Given a set of seed symbols, three different methods have been tested for selecting seed formulae:

- *Use of the most diverse axiom* selects a single seed formula with the largest number of different function and predicate symbols among all that contain the given seed symbol. Ties are broken by selecting the first candidate formula with maximal diversity.
- *Use of the largest axiom* picks the syntactically largest formula that contains the seed symbol, i.e. the formula with the most nodes in its tree representation. Ties are again broken in favor of the first formulae found.
- *Use of all* axioms that contain the seed symbol.

After selection of the seed formulae, a number of different SInE variants are used as filters. Each of the SInE filters produces one subset to be tested for unsatisfiability for each input set. The resulting files are handed to the theorem prover (usually in some batch processing configuration), which tries to prove them with a short time limit (3 s to 30 s).

3.1   Implementation

The extraction of subsets to test for unsatisfiability has been implemented in e_axfilter, a component of the E system distribution. It implements a version of SInE that efficiently applies multiple filters to its input, amortizing the cost of parsing, preprocessing and indexing. Code to select seed symbols and seed formulae was added, as described in the previous section.

In the experiments, SInE filters that have previously proven their worth with respect to conventional theorem proving were used. Of these, 9 different SInE configurations are applicable to this setting (which does not distinguish between the proper conjecture and additional local hypotheses, as there is no proper conjecture).

E 2.0pre12 was used as the default ATP system to check the extracted formula sets for unsatisfiability. The prover was configured to run in *automatic mode*, but without engaging its built-in SInE selection. Postprocessing and analysis of the unsatisfiable cores was done with simple shell scripts and some manual processing.

A cleaned up distribution of the current state of the system is available at http://eprover.eu/E-eu/AxProbing.html.

4   Experimental Results

4.1   SUMO Results

We have first applied our system to the TPTP v6.4.0 [39] axiom file CSR003+2.ax, which contains a first-order translation [28] of the 2010 release of SUMO, MILO (the *MId-Level Ontology*) and 30 domain ontologies. The file contains 55588 formulae, which use 1291 predicates, 291 non-constant function symbols, and 32838 constants. It was originally believed to be consistent, but results from the CASC-J6 ATP system competition revealed that the axioms were inconsistent [38], and further inconsistencies have been found since then. In each case corrections were made to make the theory consistent again, at least as far as was known at the time. The experiments for this paper revealed more inconsistencies. We explored the axiomatization, confirmed the inconsistency, and identified at least one common root cause.

The seed symbols were selected in each of the three ways ... randomly, the most frequently occurring, and the least frequently occurring. For each way, 600 symbols were selected ... 200 predicate symbols, 200 (non-constant) function symbols, and 200 constants. We ran E with a time limit of 3 seconds on current-generation hardware (2.6 GHz Intel Core processors, no memory limit, automatic mode) to determine the status of each probe.

Table 1 summarizes the properties of the generated files. At this stage, a number of interesting and maybe unintuitive observations can be made. First, we were surprised by the fact that less frequent symbols seem to generate larger probes - the naive assumption being that the larger set of seed axioms in the "use all applicable formulas" setting would bias the size up. However, the effect can be explained by looking at SInE's "defined" relation, which assumes that rare symbols are defined in terms of more common ones. Very specialized (rare) symbols have more levels of definitions to traverse until the fix-point is reached. The second observation is that success of the ATP - both for satisfiable and unsatisfiable probes - strongly correlates with the average size of the problem, with most successes for the smaller probes based on more common symbols.

Table 1. Properties of generated SUMO subsets

Seed symbols selection method	# formulae				ATP status		
	Min	Med	Avg	Max	SAT	UNS	TMO
Random	1	6855	1001	20001	1577	19	14604
Least frequent symbols	8	7963	3430	20001	965	11	15224
Most frequent symbols	1	5303	501	20001	4024	623	11553

Columns show the minimum number of axioms for probes in the corresponding category, the median size, the average size, the maximum size, and the number of probes shown satisfiable, unsatisfiable, or running into the time limit.

Table 2 provides an overview of the results. For each seed symbol selection method it provides the number of subsets that were found to be unsatisfiable, the number of distinct unsatisfiable cores, the number of distinct Predicate/Function/Constant seeds that led to an unsatisfiable subset, and the number of distinct seed symbols leading to the Diverse/Largest/All seed formula selection method producing an unsatisfiable probe.

Table 2. SUMO experimental results

Seed symbols selection method	# of UNS	# distinct	# by seed type			# by axiom select.		
	Subsets	UNS cores	P	F	C	D	L	A
Random	19	15	6	3	0	1	1	9
Least frequent symbols	11	9	2	4	0	1	1	6
Most frequent symbols	623	43	78	3	0	79	79	81
All together	653	67	86	9	0	81	81	95

The results indicate that (for at least this axiomatization) using the most frequently occurring predicate symbols as seed symbols is the most effective. We can also observe that the "Use all formulas with the seed symbol" method subsumes the other approaches - every symbol that was successful with one of the other seed axiom selection method also produced at least one unsatisfiable probe with that method.

Automated analysis of the unsatisfiable cores reveals that the following axiom is present in all of them:

```
fof(kb_SUMO_32603,axiom,(
    ! [V__C2,V__U,V__C1] :
     ( V__U = s__UnionFn(V__C1,V__C2)
   <=> ! [V__I1,V__I2,V__I3] :
         ( ( s__instance(V__C1,s__SetOrClass)
           & s__instance(V__U,s__SetOrClass)
           & s__instance(V__C2,s__SetOrClass) )
       => ( ( s__instance(V__I1,V__C1)
            & s__instance(V__I2,V__C2)
            & s__instance(V__I3,V__U) )
         => ( s__instance(V__I1,V__U)
            & s__instance(V__I2,V__U)
            & ( s__instance(V__I3,V__C1)
              | s__instance(V__I3,V__C2) ) ) ) ) ) )).
```

The axiom (incorrectly) defines the union function s__UnionFn, but mistakenly uses the s__instance predicate instead of the s__member predicate in the consequent of the outer implication on the right-hand side of the equivalence. If we remove the offending axiom, no more inconsistencies are found and SUMO is consistent to the best of our knowledge.

With this method for debugging SUMO we now have, for large logical theories, something approaching common practice in software engineering on nontrivial systems, of adding to a software system and then going through one or more cycles of validation and correction. Hopefully, further research will continue to yield methods that improve the completeness of the debugging process,

Table 3. Probe status by SInE configuration

SInE configuration	Min	Med	Avg	Max	SAT	UNS	TMO
gf120_h_gu_R02_F100_L20000	1	385	314	928	1109	241	4050
gf120_h_gu_RUU_F100_L00100	1	79	101	101	1258	0	4142
gf120_h_gu_RUU_F100_L00500	1	322	501	501	814	241	4345
gf120_h_gu_RUU_F100_L01000	1	601	978	1001	790	158	4452
gf150_h_gu_RUU_F100_L20000	8	6283	10075	10625	603	0	4797
gf200_h_gu_R03_F100_L20000	5	1590	1805	4003	833	13	4554
gf200_h_gu_RUU_F100_L20000	8	13211	17703	17966	516	0	4884
gf500_h_gu_R04_F100_L20000	15	11789	18156	20001	439	0	4961
gf600_h_gu_R05_F100_L20000	28	13472	20001	20001	204	0	5196

and improve its speed, so that it becomes possible to check every new axiom at the time it is authored for whether it introduces an inconsistency.

We can also analyze which of the 9 different SInE configurations have contributed most to finding inconsistent probes. Table 3 summarizes the result. We can see that only 4 of the 9 filter configurations generate at least one probe that is unsatisfiable. We can again confirm that the overall ATP success rate seems to strongly correspond to the median (and average) problem size, i.e. the larger the problems are, the more likely the ATP is to time out. On the other hand, for finding inconsistencies, we are only interested in UNS (unsatisfiable) results. There, over-pruning (as likely the case for gf120_h_gu_RUU_F100_L00100, which has a very small hard size limit and selects at most 100 formulae to complement the seed formulae) is also a risk.

4.2 OpenCyc Results

Experiments similar to those performed on the SUMO axiom set were performed on an export of a fragment of the OpenCyc knowledge base [33], in the TPTP v6.4.0 axiom file CSR002+4.ax. Two inconsistencies were found.

The first unsatisfiable subset was generated by selecting the 200 least frequently occurring predicate symbols as seed symbols, and selecting all axioms with those seed symbols as seed formulae. The offending unsatisfiable core of seven axioms contains the following two axioms, which confuse temporal objects with geographical subregions - clearly a mistake in the underlying Cyc axiomatization.

```
fof(ax4_357170,axiom,(
  ! [X] :
    ( temporalstufftype(X)
   => geographicalsubregiontypes(X,X) ) )).

fof(ax4_231810,axiom,(
  ! [ARG1,ARG2] :
```

```
( geographicalsubregiontypes(ARG1,ARG2)
=> temporalstufftype(ARG1) ) )).
```

The second unsatisfiable subset was generated by selecting 400 random predicate symbols as seed symbols, and selecting all axioms with those seed symbols as seed formulae. The offending unsatisfiable core of 20 axioms contains two axioms that mix temporal objects with physical parts, but in this case it is not obvious that they are the direct cause of the inconsistency.

4.3   Mizar Results

For the Mizar experiments the MPTP translation [42] of the Mizar Mathematical Library (MML) [12] to TPTP was used. More precisely, version $4.181.1147^1$ of the MML, which has been used for the so far most extensive ATP and premise-selection experiments over Mizar [18], was used. These previous experiments took several weeks of real-time computation on a 64-core AMD server. Several hundred combinations of premise selection methods and theorem provers were tried. Neither a contradiction, nor a proof that would be illegal with respect to the Mizar system was found. This makes it very unlikely to find a contradiction in our current experiments.

The axiomatization file statements[2] that was used for generating subtheories contains 146700 top-level Mizar lemmas, definitions, scheme instances, type-system formulae, and other formulae encoding the Mizar built-in knowledge. The formulae come from 1153 Mizar articles[3], containing 17355 function and constant symbols (including 3428 numbers), and 3689 predicate symbols[4].

Mizar Unsampled. Initially, all problems were generated using both predicate and function symbols and without subsampling. This takes about 15 hours using a single CPU and produces 286614 files taking up about 700GB. Then we run E in auto mode for 10 seconds on each problem. This takes 18 hours of real time using 50 CPUs in parallel. As expected, no problems are found to be Unsatisfiable.

Mizar Sampled. In the next version subsampling with m200 (picking the 200 most frequently occurring symbols as seeds) was used, limiting the seed symbols only to predicates (based on the SUMO experiments) and seed method dl (using the most diverse formula as a seed formula, and using the syntactically largest formula as a seed formula). This generates in 23 min 3600 problems taking up 11GB. Since this is much fewer problems, we can run E with higher time limit (30 seconds). This takes 45 min of real time when using 50 CPUs in parallel. Even with this higher time limit, no problems are found to be Unsatisfiable.

---

[1] http://grid01.ciirc.cvut.cz/~mptp/7.13.01_4.181.1147/.
[2] http://grid01.ciirc.cvut.cz/~mptp/7.13.01_4.181.1147/MPTP2/statements.
[3] http://grid01.ciirc.cvut.cz/~mptp/7.13.01_4.181.1147/html/.
[4] http://grid01.ciirc.cvut.cz/~mptp/7.13.01_4.181.1147/MPTP2/symbols.

Mizar Sampled with Some Omitted Type Guards. In the last Mizar experiment, a frequent error in formal mathematical developments was emulated by omitting an "obvious" assumption from a lemma. In particular, nonemptiness (and thus also non-zero) assumption was omitted from the toplevel Mizar statements. There are over 6000 affected statements.

Model finders such as Nitpick [8] and Nunchaku [34] can be tried in proof assistants to quickly find such errors. Such methods have however limited use when working over foundations such as set theory, where the underlying models (if any) are infinitary. Finding a contradiction caused by the too strongly stated lemma – using the methods developed here – is an interesting alternative.

Another scenario which actually occurred in various moments of the history of building translations between ITPs and ATPs is that such typing assumptions are sometimes omitted due to various corner cases in the ITP-ATP translation modules. The methods developed here can be used as a global debugging tool when creating such translations. Since it was known beforehand how to correct all the corrupted statements, it was also possible to fully automate and observe the process of gradually finding them with our tools, interleaved with (automated) correction and re-formulation. This provides an empirical evaluation of the strength of the tools.

To generate the problems, the corrupted `statements` file was used, and again subsampling was used to generate 3600 problems. As before, E was run with a 30 s time limit and 50-fold parallelization. E found 2312 of the 3600 problems to be unsatisfiable. E quickly finds very simple refutations (226 that use just three formulae), but also more complicated ones: 347 of the refutations use 10 or more formulae. All these 2312 refutations are due to only 8 corrupted formulae. The one that occurs most frequently (in 1227 of the refutations) is the corrupted Mizar typing statement `cc1_ami_3`:[5]

```
fof(cc1_ami_3,axiom,(
  ! [X1] :
    ( v7_ordinal1(X1)
  => ( ~ v1_xboole_0(X1)
     & v7_ordinal1(X1)
     & ~ v1_setfam_1(X1) ) ) )).
```

This claims that every natural number is non-empty and has an empty element. This is of course false for zero, which is modelled as the empty set in set theory.

After repairing the eight corrupted formulae that were found automatically in the 3600 generated problems, E was run again. This time 853 problems are found to be unsatisfiable, and 18 new corrupted formulae involved in the refutations were found. It is clear that the loop finds the most obvious offending formulae early, and proceeds to find more and more complicated proofs of the contradiction. After obtaining a fixpoint, the system becomes "effectively consistent" wrt. to our tool, however it is still possible to see if there are problematic formulae left.

---

[5] http://grid01.ciirc.cvut.cz/~mptp/7.13.01_4.181.1147/html/ami_3.html#CC1.

Table 4. 15 iterations of the contradiction-finding and axiom-correcting loop run on the 3600 problems constructed from the Mizar data with some type guards omitted.

Loop iteration	1	2	3	4	5	6	7	8	9	10	11	12	13	14	15
Bad formulae found	8	18	10	8	6	1	1	0	0	0	1	0	0	0	0
Unsat. problems found	2312	853	637	238	102	2	2	0	0	0	1	0	0	0	0
Average proof time	10.2	8.5	13.7	21.2	22.7	21.3	27.7				29.5				

This automated contradiction-finding and axiom-correcting loop is implemented in about 30 lines of Perl.[6] Note however that this can be easily automated only because the correct versions of all the intentionally modified facts are known beforehand. In general, the axiom-correcting step is nontrivial. The loop was run over the 3600 problems for 15 iterations, using a 30 s time limit for a problem and 50-fold parallelization. The 15 iterations thus took about 8 hours of real time and 400 hours of CPU time.

It takes 7 iterations to reach a state in which no more contradictions are found within the time limit. Many problematic formulae are however still left: 3590 of the 3600 problems still contain at least one of them after the 7th iteration. Letting the loop run further shows that adding more time will very likely discover further contradictions: in the 11th iteration, one more contradiction is found taking 29.5 s of CPU time. In total, the loop discovered 53 problematic formulae. The iterations are shown in Table 4.

A brief experiment was done with a different ATP system, thus offering a different notion of "effective consistency". Instead of E, Vampire 4.1 was used, again with a 30 s time limit on all the problems from the 15th iteration (none refutable by E). Vampire finds a contradiction in 297 of the problems, detecting 15 more problematic formulae. A fixpoint for Vampire is reached after 5 iterations and discovering in total 29 more problematic formulae.

The remaining number of problematic formulae in the 3600 repaired problems is however still high. 3590 of the repaired problems contain at least one of the formulae, 3188 different problematic formulae occur there, and the total number of occurrences of the formulae in all the problems is 1228432 (2.85% of all the 43049126 formulae there). For comparison, before starting the repairing loop, this number was 1378711 (3.2%), i.e., 11% of such occurrences were automatically removed.

5   Future Work

This paper has laid the groundwork to automatically search for inconsistencies in large knowledge bases. There is a number of possible extensions.

First, there are many ways to experiment with the filtering. We have so far only used E's existing SInE implementation and its existing filter configurations. One approach would be to try new filter configurations close to the parameter

---

[6] https://github.com/JUrban/MPTP2/blob/master/Ebot/loop.pl.

space demarcated by the so far most successful filters, using parameter-searching systems such as BliStr [43] on a large set of problems. This applies not just to the SInE filters, but to the whole interplay between seed symbol selection, seed axiom selection and SInE filtering. Again, we could try to narrow down the probes to a subset with a higher per-probe success rates, thus identifying a similar number of inconsistencies with less computational effort. In this context, we can also explore additional seed selection preferences (i.e. only use symbols with certain arities, or symbols with certain minimum frequency) and seed axiom selection methods (use the smallest axiom, use the least diverse axiom, etc.).

Second, we could add more axiom selection methods. For example, a very different *semantic* heuristic selection method is available in SRASS [40] and MaLARea [45]. It interleaves model finding for the axioms selected so far with adding a (most relevant) axiom that is false in the model found so far. When the loop stops (typically because no more models can be found), the axiom selection is given to an ATP. In situations when a large number of proofs is available (or generated e.g. by theory exploration), the current methods that produce the seeding formula could also be followed by axiom selection based on some of the many machine-learning methods developed recently.

Third, it would be instructive to apply our approach to additional large axiomatizations, both in mathematical domains (e.g. a first-order translation of the HOL Light Flyspeck corpus [14]), but also in more application-oriented domains, where an interesting example would be SnowMed CT [3]. There may be unsound-but-efficient encodings (historically used e.g. for Isabelle's first-order translation), that might keep most of their efficiency after automatically removing the worst sources of unsoundness using a similar process as described for Mizar in Sect. 4.3. This process – namely removal of type guards – will also apply to SUMO, since it uses a method for automatically adding explicit types to axioms that lack such expressions in their originally authored forms.

Finally, we could experiment with different sound encodings. In some early work, different methods for canonicalization of the knowledge base have lead to the surfacing of different possible inconsistencies. We expect to integrate these approaches and see if they yield more and different results. Our approach could be also extended to work directly with more expressive logics, e.g. the higher order logics used in systems like Isabelle, or the original higher order formulation of SUMO in SUO-KIF or its translation to THF [6], either by translation of higher-order theories to first order, or by direct use of higher-order provers like Leo-II [5] or Sattalax [9].

6   Conclusion

For any large theory under active development there is a process that combines the addition of new axioms to extend the coverage of the theory, with the use of tools that aim to ensure desired properties of the axiomatization. The tool presented here is one more in that armory, helping to ensure that the axiomatization is consistent. Both the SUMO and OpenCyc knowledge bases have, on-and-off, been considered to be consistent, particularly those parts that lie at their core. The discovery of inconsistencies might thus come as a surprise to users, particularly when the axiomatizations have been used productively in applications without revealing the contradictions. While the use of tools such as the one described in this paper can be very helpful in finding inconsistencies, it is important to note that such tools (including this one) are incomplete – they do not ensure that the axiomatization is consistent.

Therefore it remains important to guard against conclusions that have been derived because of inconsistency. Simply checking that the conjecture is part of its proof can guard against this. One can also employ more refined approaches based on paraconsistent logics [32].

As might be obvious from the differences in the experiments described in Sects. 4.1 to 4.3, the tool has been used independently, and successfully, in three quite distinct efforts. This shows the flexibility of the tool, and that different combinations of choices can be effective in different circumstances.

References

1. Alama, J., Heskes, T., Kühlwein, D., Tsivtsivadze, E., Urban, J.: Premise selection for mathematics by corpus analysis and kernel methods. J. Autom. Reasoning **52**(2), 191–213 (2014)
2. Alemi, A.A., Chollet, F., Eén, N., Irving, G., Szegedy, C., Urban, J.: DeepMath - deep sequence models for premise selection. In: Lee, D.D., Sugiyama, M., Luxburg, U.V., Guyon, I., Garnett, R. (eds.) Advances in Neural Information Processing Systems 29: Annual Conference on Neural Information Processing Systems 5–10, 2016, Barcelona, Spain, pp. 2235–2243 (2016). http://papers.nips.cc/paper/6280-deepmath-deep-sequence-models-for-premise-selection
3. Benson, T.: Principles of Health Interoperability: SNOMED CT, HL7 and FHIR (Health Information Technology Standards). Springer, London (2016)
4. Benzmüller, C., Woltzenlogel Paleo, B.: Automating gödel's ontological proof of god's existence with higher-order automated theorem provers. In: Schaub, T. (ed.) Proceedings of the 21st European Conference on Artificial Intelligence, pp. 93–98 (2014)
5. Benzmüller, C., Paulson, L.C., Theiss, F., Fietzke, A.: LEO-II - a cooperative automatic theorem prover for classical higher-order logic (System Description). In: Armando, A., Baumgartner, P., Dowek, G. (eds.) IJCAR 2008. LNCS (LNAI), vol. 5195, pp. 162–170. Springer, Heidelberg (2008). doi:10.1007/978-3-540-71070-7_14
6. Benzmller, C., Pease, A.: Higher-order aspects and context in SUMO. In: Jos Lehmann, I.J.V., Bundy, A. (eds.) Special issue on Reasoning with context in the Semantic Web, vol. 12–13. Science, Services and Agents on the World Wide Web (2012)
7. Blanchette, J.C., Kaliszyk, C., Paulson, L.C., Urban, J.: Hammering towards QED. J. Formalized Reasoning **9**(1), 101–148 (2016). http://dx.doi.org/10.6092/issn.1972-5787/4593
8. Blanchette, J.C., Nipkow, T.: Nitpick: a counterexample generator for higher-order logic based on a relational model finder. In: Kaufmann, M., Paulson, L.C. (eds.) ITP 2010. LNCS, vol. 6172, pp. 131–146. Springer, Heidelberg (2010). doi:10.1007/978-3-642-14052-5_11

9. Brown, C.E.: Reducing higher-order theorem proving to a sequence of SAT problems. In: Bjørner, N., Sofronie-Stokkermans, V. (eds.) CADE 2011. LNCS (LNAI), vol. 6803, pp. 147–161. Springer, Heidelberg (2011). doi:10.1007/978-3-642-22438-6_13

10. Chaudhri, V., Inclezan, D.: Representing states in a biology textbook. In: Leora Morgenstern, L., Patkos, T., Sloan, R. (eds.) Proceedings of 12th International Symposium on Logical Formalizations of Commonsense Reasoning. AAAI Press (2015)

11. Chaudhuri, S., Farzan, A. (eds.): Proceedings of the 28th International Conference on Computer Aided Verification. LNCS, vol. 9779–9780. Springer, Heidelberg (2016)

12. Grabowski, A., Korniłowicz, A., Naumowicz, A.: Mizar in a nutshell. J. Formalized Reasoning 3(2), 153–245 (2010)

13. Groth, P., Simperi, E., Gray, A., Sabou, M., Krötzsch, M., Lecue, F., Flöck, F., Gil, Y. (eds.): Proceedings of the 15th International Semantic Web Conference. LNCS, vol. 9981–9982. Springer, Heidelberg (2016)

14. Hales, T., Adams, M., Bauer, G., Dang, D.T., Harrison, J., Hoang, T.L., Kaliszyk, C., Magron, V., McLaughlin, S., Nguyen, T.T., et al.: A formal proof of the Kepler conjecture. arXiv preprint (2015). arXiv:1501.02155

15. Hoder, K., Voronkov, A.: Sine qua non for large theory reasoning. In: Bjørner, N., Sofronie-Stokkermans, V. (eds.) CADE 2011. LNCS (LNAI), vol. 6803, pp. 299–314. Springer, Heidelberg (2011). doi:10.1007/978-3-642-22438-6_23

16. Kaliszyk, C., Urban, J.: Stronger automation for Flyspeck by feature weighting and strategy evolution. In: Blanchette, J.C., Urban, J. (eds.) PxTP 2013. EPiC Series, vol. 14, pp. 87–95. EasyChair (2013)

17. Kaliszyk, C., Urban, J.: Learning-assisted automated reasoning with Flyspeck. J. Autom. Reasoning 53(2), 173–213 (2014)

18. Kaliszyk, C., Urban, J.: MizAR 40 for Mizar 40. J. Autom. Reasoning 55(3), 245–256 (2015). http://dx.doi.org/10.1007/s10817-015-9330-8

19. Kinyon, M., Veroff, R., Vojtěchovský, P.: Loops with abelian inner mapping groups: an application of automated deduction. In: Bonacina, M.P., Stickel, M.E. (eds.) Automated Reasoning and Mathematics. LNCS, vol. 7788, pp. 151–164. Springer, Heidelberg (2013). doi:10.1007/978-3-642-36675-8_8

20. Klein, G., Nipkow, T., Paulson, L.: The archive of formal proofs (2010). https://www.isa-afp.org/

21. Kovács, L., Voronkov, A.: First-order theorem proving and VAMPIRE. In: Sharygina, N., Veith, H. (eds.) CAV 2013. LNCS, vol. 8044, pp. 1–35. Springer, Heidelberg (2013). doi:10.1007/978-3-642-39799-8_1

22. Kühlwein, D., Laarhoven, T., Tsivtsivadze, E., Urban, J., Heskes, T.: Overview and evaluation of premise selection techniques for large theory mathematics. In: Gramlich, B., Miller, D., Sattler, U. (eds.) IJCAR 2012. LNCS (LNAI), vol. 7364, pp. 378–392. Springer, Heidelberg (2012). doi:10.1007/978-3-642-31365-3_30

23. Lenat, D.: CYC: a large-scale investment in knowledge infrastructure. Commun. ACM 38(11), 35–38 (1995)

24. McCune, W.: Solution of the robbins problem. J. Autom. Reasoning 19(3), 263–276 (1997)

25. Meng, J., Paulson, L.C.: Lightweight relevance filtering for machine-generated resolution problems. J. Appl. Logics 7(1), 41–57 (2009)

26. Niles, I., Pease, A.: Toward a standard upper ontology. In: Welty, C., Smith, B. (eds.) Proceedings of the 2nd International Conference on Formal Ontology in Information Systems (FOIS-2001) (2001)

27. Paulsson, L.C., Blanchette, J.C.: Three years of experience with Sledgehammer, a practical link between automatic and interactive theorem provers. In: Sutcliff, G., Ternovska, E., Schulz, S. (eds.) Proceedings of the 8th International Workshop on the Implementation of Logics (IWIL-2010), Yogyakarta, Indonesia. EPiC, vol. 2 (2012)

28. Pease, A., Sutcliffe, G.: First order reasoning on a large ontology. In: Urban, J., Sutcliffe, G., Schulz, S. (eds.) Proceedings of the CADE-21 Workshop on Empirically Successful Automated Reasoning in Large Theories, pp. 61–70. No. 257 in CEUR Workshop Proceedings (2007)

29. Pease, A.: Ontology: A Practical Guide. Articulate Software Press, Angwin (2011)

30. Pease, A., Benzmüller, C.: Sigma: an integrated development environment for logical theories. AI Commun. **26**, 9–97 (2013)

31. Pease, A., Niles, I., Li, J.: The suggested upper merged ontology: a large ontology for the semantic web and its applications. In: Working Notes of the AAAI-2002 Workshop on Ontologies and the Semantic Web (2002)

32. Priest, G.: Paraconsistent logic. In: Gabbay, D., Guenthner, F. (eds.) Handbook of Philosophical Logic, vol. 6, pp. 287–393. Kluwer Academic Publishers (2002)

33. Ramachandran, D., Reagan, P., Goolsbey, K.: First-orderized ResearchCyc: expressiveness and efficiency in a common sense knowledge base. In: Shvaiko, P. (ed.) Proceedings of the AAAI Workshop on Contexts and Ontologies: Theory, Practice and Applications (C&O-2005) (2005)

34. Reynolds, A., Blanchette, J.C., Cruanes, S., Tinelli, C.: Model finding for recursive functions in SMT. In: Olivetti, N., Tiwari, A. (eds.) IJCAR 2016. LNCS (LNAI), vol. 9706, pp. 133–151. Springer, Cham (2016). doi:10.1007/978-3-319-40229-1_10

35. Schulz, S.: E - A brainiac theorem prover. J. AI Commun. **15**(2/3), 111–126 (2002)

36. Schulz, S.: System description: E 1.8. In: McMillan, K., Middeldorp, A., Voronkov, A. (eds.) LPAR 2013. LNCS, vol. 8312, pp. 735–743. Springer, Heidelberg (2013). doi:10.1007/978-3-642-45221-5_49

37. Seligman, E., Schubert, T., Achutha Kiran Kumar, M.: Formal Verification: An Essential Toolkit for Modern VLSI Design. Morgan Kaufmann, San Francisco (2015)

38. Sutcliffe, G.: The CADE-23 automated theorem proving system competition - CASC-23. AI Commun. **25**(1), 49–63 (2012)

39. Sutcliffe, G.: The TPTP Problem Library and Associated Infrastructure. From CNF to TH0, TPTP v6.4.0. J. Autom. Reasoning. (2017, to appear)

40. Sutcliffe, G., Puzis, Y.: SRASS - a semantic relevance axiom selection system. In: Pfenning, F. (ed.) CADE 2007. LNCS (LNAI), vol. 4603, pp. 295–310. Springer, Heidelberg (2007). doi:10.1007/978-3-540-73595-3_20

41. Sutcliffe, G., Urban, J., Schulz, S. (eds.): Proceedings of the CADE-21 Workshop on Empirically Successful Automated Reasoning in Large Theories, CEUR Workshop Proceedings, vol. 257 (2007)

42. Urban, J.: MPTP 0.2: design, implementation, and initial experiments. J. Autom. Reasoning **37**(1), 21–43 (2006)

43. Urban, J.: BliStr: The blind strategymaker. In: Gottlob, G., Sutcliffe, G., Voronkov, A. (eds.) Proceedings of the Global Conference on Artificial Intelligence, Tibilisi, Georgia. EPiC, vol. 36, pp. 312–319. EasyChair (2015)

44. Urban, J., Rudnicki, P., Sutcliffe, G.: ATP and presentation service for Mizar formalizations. J. Autom. Reasoning **50**(2), 229–241 (2013)

45. Urban, J., Sutcliffe, G., Pudlák, P., Vyskočil, J.: MaLARea SG1 - machine learner for automated reasoning with semantic guidance. In: Armando, A., Baumgartner, P., Dowek, G. (eds.) IJCAR 2008. LNCS (LNAI), vol. 5195, pp. 441–456. Springer, Heidelberg (2008). doi:10.1007/978-3-540-71070-7_37

46. Zalta, E., Fitelson, B.: Steps toward a computational metaphysics. Australas. J. Philos. **36**(2), 227–247 (2007)

Theorem Proving for Metric Temporal Logic over the Naturals

Ullrich Hustadt[1]([⊠]), Ana Ozaki[2]([⊠]), and Clare Dixon[1]

[1] Department of Computer Science, University of Liverpool, Liverpool, UK
{uhustadt,cldixon}@liverpool.ac.uk
[2] Center for Advancing Electronics Dresden (cfaed), TU Dresden, Dresden, Germany
Ana.Ozaki@tu-dresden.de

Abstract. We study translations from Metric Temporal Logic (MTL) over the natural numbers to Linear Temporal Logic (LTL). In particular, we present two approaches for translating from MTL to LTL which preserve the ExpSpace complexity of the satisfiability problem for MTL. In each of these approaches we consider the case where the mapping between states and time points is given by (1) a strict monotonic function and by (2) a non-strict monotonic function (which allows multiple states to be mapped to the same time point). Our translations allow us to utilise LTL solvers to solve satisfiability and we empirically compare the translations, showing in which cases one performs better than the other.

1 Introduction

Linear and branching-time temporal logics have been used for the specification and verification of reactive systems. In linear-time temporal logic [11,22] we can, for example, express that a formula ψ holds now or at some point in the future using the formula $\Diamond\psi$ (ψ holds eventually). However, some applications require not just that a formula ψ will hold eventually but that it holds within a particular time-frame, for example, between 3 and 7 moments from now.

To express such constraints, a range of Metric Temporal Logics (MTL) have been proposed [3,4], considering different underlying models of time and operators allowed. MTL has been used to formalise vehicle routing problems [17], monitoring of algorithms [26] and cyber-physical systems [1], among others [15]. A survey about MTL and its fragments can be found in [20]. It is known that MTL over the reals is undecidable, though, decidable fragments have been investigated [2,5,6].

Here we consider MTL with pointwise semantics over the natural numbers, following [3], where each state in the sequence is mapped to a time point on a time line isomorphic to the natural numbers. In this instance of MTL, temporal operators are annotated with intervals, which can be finite or infinite. For example, $\Diamond_{[3,7]}$ means that p should hold in a state that occurs in the interval $[3, 7]$ of time, while $\Box_{[2,\infty)}p$ means that p should hold in all states that occur at least 2 moments from now. In contrast to LTL, where the time difference from one state to the next is always 1, in MTL, time is allowed to irregularly 'jump'

© Springer International Publishing AG 2017
L. de Moura (Ed.): CADE 2017, LNAI 10395, pp. 326–343, 2017.
DOI: 10.1007/978-3-319-63046-5_20

from one state to the next. For example, using $\bigcirc_{[2,2]}p$ we can state that the time difference from the current state to the next state is 2.

Furthermore, following Alur and Henzinger [3], the mapping between states and time points is given by a (weakly) monotonic function, which allows multiple states to be mapped to the same time point. Underlying this semantics is the so-called *digital-clock assumption*: Different states that are associated with the same discrete clock record events happening between successive clock ticks. Similarly, if no events occur over one or more successive clock ticks, no state will be associated with those clock ticks. In this work, we also consider the semantics where the mapping between states and time points is given by a strictly monotonic function, which forces time to progress from one state to another.

We provide two approaches for translating from MTL to LTL: in the first approach we introduce a fresh propositional variable that we call 'gap', which is used to encode the 'jumps' between states, as mentioned above; the second approach is inspired by [3], where fresh propositional variables encode time differences between states. In each approach we consider the case where the mapping between states and time points is given by

1. a strict monotonic function and by
2. a non-strict monotonic function (which allows multiple states to be mapped to the same time point).

All translations are polynomial w.r.t. the largest constant occurring in an interval (although exponential in the size of the MTL formula due to the binary encoding of the constants). Since the satisfiability problem for LTL is PSPACE-complete [24], our translations preserve the ExpSpace complexity of the MTL satisfiability problem over the natural numbers [3].

Using these translations from MTL to LTL, we apply four temporal solvers, one resolution based [16], one tableau based [13], one based on model checking [7], and the other based on labelled superposition with partial model guidance [18]; to investigate the properties of the resulting formulae experimentally. To the best of our knowledge, there are no implementations of solvers for MTL with pointwise discrete semantics. In particular, our contributions are:

- translations from MTL to LTL which preserve the ExpSpace complexity of the MTL satisfiability problem;
- an experimental analysis of the behaviour of LTL solvers on the resulting formulae;
- to exemplify which kind of problems can be solved using MTL we also provide encodings of the classical Multiprocessor Job-Shop Scheduling problem [8, 14] into MTL.

In the following we provide the syntax and semantics of LTL and MTL (Sect. 2), show our translations from MTL to LTL (Sects. 3 and 4) and experimental results (Sect. 5). We then show how one can encode the Multiprocessor Job-Shop Scheduling problem into MTL with strict and non-strict semantics (Sect. 6) and present experimental results (Sect. 7).

2   Preliminaries

We briefly state the syntax and semantics of LTL and MTL. Let $\mathcal{P}$ be a (count-ably infinite) set of propositional variables. Well formed formulae in LTL are formed according to the rule:

$$\varphi, \psi \quad := \quad p \mid \neg\varphi \mid (\varphi \wedge \psi) \mid \bigcirc\varphi \mid (\varphi\mathcal{U}\psi)$$

where $p \in \mathcal{P}$. We often omit parentheses if there is no ambiguity. We denote by $\bigcirc^c$ a sequence of c next operators, i.e., $\bigcirc^0\varphi = \varphi$ and $\bigcirc^{n+1}\varphi = \bigcirc\bigcirc^n\varphi$, for every $n \in \mathbb{N}$.

An *LTL model* or *state sequence* σ over $(\mathbb{N}, <)$ is an infinite sequence of states $\sigma_i \subseteq \mathcal{P}$, $i \in \mathbb{N}$. The semantics of LTL is defined as follows.

$$
\begin{aligned}
(\sigma, i) &\models p && \text{iff } p \in \sigma_i \\
(\sigma, i) &\models (\varphi \wedge \psi) && \text{iff } (\sigma, i) \models \varphi \text{ and } (\sigma, i) \models \psi \\
(\sigma, i) &\models \neg\varphi && \text{iff } (\sigma, i) \not\models \varphi \\
(\sigma, i) &\models \bigcirc\varphi && \text{iff } (\sigma, i+1) \models \varphi \\
(\sigma, i) &\models (\varphi\mathcal{U}\psi) && \text{iff } \exists k \geq i : (\sigma, k) \models \psi \text{ and } \forall j, \, i \leq j < k : (\sigma, j) \models \varphi
\end{aligned}
$$

Further connectives can be defined as usual: $\textbf{true} \equiv p \vee \neg p$, $\textbf{false} \equiv \neg(\textbf{true})$, $\Diamond\varphi \equiv \textbf{true}\mathcal{U}\varphi$ and $\Box\varphi \equiv \neg\Diamond\neg\varphi$. MTL formulae are constructed in a way similar to LTL, with the difference that temporal operators are now bounded by an interval I with natural numbers as end-points or ∞ on the right side. Note that since we work with natural numbers as end-points we can assume w.l.o.g that all our intervals are of the form $[c_1, c_2]$ or $[c_1, \infty)$, where $c_1, c_2 \in \mathbb{N}$. Well formed formulae in MTL are formed according to the rule:

$$\varphi, \psi \quad := \quad p \mid \neg\varphi \mid (\varphi \wedge \psi) \mid \bigcirc_I\varphi \mid (\varphi\mathcal{U}_I\psi)$$

where $p \in \mathcal{P}$. A *timed state sequence* $\rho = (\sigma, \tau)$ over $(\mathbb{N}, <)$ is a pair consisting of an infinite sequence σ of states $\sigma_i \subseteq \mathcal{P}$, $i \in \mathbb{N}$, and a function $\tau : \mathbb{N} \to \mathbb{N}$ that maps every i corresponding to the i-th state to a time point $\tau(i)$ such that $\tau(i) < \tau(i+1)$. A *non-strict* timed state sequence $\rho = (\sigma, \tau)$ over $(\mathbb{N}, <)$ is a pair consisting of an infinite sequence σ of states $\sigma_i \subseteq \mathcal{P}$, $i \in \mathbb{N}$, and a function $\tau : \mathbb{N} \to \mathbb{N}$ that maps every i corresponding to the i-th state to a time point $\tau(i)$ such that $\tau(i) \leq \tau(i+1)$. We assume w.l.o.g. that $\tau(0) = 0$. The semantics of MTL is defined as follows (we omit propositional cases, which are as in LTL).

$$
\begin{aligned}
(\rho, i) &\models p && \text{iff } p \in \sigma_i \\
(\rho, i) &\models (\varphi \wedge \psi) && \text{iff } (\rho, i) \models \varphi \text{ and } (\rho, i) \models \psi \\
(\rho, i) &\models \neg\varphi && \text{iff } (\rho, i) \not\models \varphi \\
(\rho, i) &\models \bigcirc_I\varphi && \text{iff } (\rho, i+1) \models \varphi \text{ and } \tau(i+1) - \tau(i) \in I \\
(\rho, i) &\models (\varphi\mathcal{U}_I\psi) && \text{iff } \exists k \geq i : \tau(k) - \tau(i) \in I \text{ and } (\rho, k) \models \psi \\
& && \quad \text{and } \forall j, \, i \leq j < k : (\rho, j) \models \varphi
\end{aligned}
$$

Further connectives can be defined as usual: $\Diamond_I\varphi \equiv \textbf{true}\mathcal{U}_I\varphi$ and $\Box_I\varphi \equiv \neg\Diamond_I\neg\varphi$. To transform an MTL formula into Negation Normal Form, one uses the constrained dual until $\tilde{\mathcal{U}}_I$ operator [20], defined as $(\varphi\tilde{\mathcal{U}}_I\psi) \equiv \neg(\neg\varphi\mathcal{U}_I\neg\psi)$.

Fig. 1. Example illustrating Definition 1

An MTL formula φ is in *Negation Normal Form (NNF)* iff the negation operator ($\neg$) occurs only in front of propositional variables. One of the differences between MTL and LTL is that in LTL we have the equivalence $\neg(\bigcirc p) \equiv \bigcirc \neg p$, whereas in MTL $\neg(\bigcirc_{[2,2]}p) \not\equiv \bigcirc_{[2,2]}\neg p$. If $\neg(\bigcirc_{[2,2]}p)$ then either p does not occur in the next state or the next state does not occur with time difference 2. We can express this as follows: $\neg(\bigcirc_{[2,2]}p) \equiv \bigcirc_{[2,2]}\neg p \vee \bigcirc_{[0,1]}\mathbf{true} \vee \bigcirc_{[3,\infty)}\mathbf{true}$.

An MTL formula φ is in *Flat Normal Form (FNF)* iff it is of the form $p_0 \wedge \bigwedge_i \square_{[0,\infty)}(p_i \rightarrow \psi_i)$ where p_0, p_i are propositional variables or $\mathbf{true}$ and ψ_i is either a formula of propositional logic or it is of the form $\bigcirc_I\psi_1$, $\psi_1\mathcal{U}_I\psi_2$ or $\psi_1\tilde{\mathcal{U}}_I\psi_2$ where ψ_1, ψ_2 are formulae of propositional logic.

One can transform an MTL formula into FNF by renaming subformulae with nested operators, as in [10,28]. For example, assume that we are given the following MTL formula: $\bigcirc_{[2,3]}(\neg\square_{[1,2]}q)$. We first transform our formula into NNF and obtain: $\bigcirc_{[2,3]}(\Diamond_{[1,2]}\neg q)$. We then transform it into FNF: $p_0 \wedge \square_{[0,\infty)}(p_0 \rightarrow \bigcirc_{[2,3]}p_1) \wedge \square_{[0,\infty)}(p_1 \rightarrow \Diamond_{[1,2]}\neg q)$. The transformations into NNF and FNF are satisfiability preserving and can be performed in polynomial time.

3   From MTL to LTL: Encoding 'gaps'

Assume that our MTL formulae are in NNF and FNF. The main idea for our proof is to map each timed state sequence $\rho = (\sigma, \tau)$ to a state sequence σ' such that $\rho = (\sigma, \tau)$ is a model of an MTL formula if, and only if, σ' is a model of our LTL translation. We first present our translation using the strict semantics and then show how to adapt it for the non-strict semantics, where multiple states are allowed to be mapped to the same time point.

Strict Semantics. We translate MTL formulae for discrete time models into LTL using a new propositional variable *gap*. $\neg gap$ is true in those states σ'_j of σ' such that there is $i \in \mathbb{N}$ with $\tau(i) = j$ and *gap* is true in all other states of σ'. We now define our mappings between MTL and LTL models.

Definition 1. *Given a timed state sequence $\rho = (\sigma, \tau)$, we define $\sigma' = \sigma'_0\sigma'_1\ldots$, where σ'_j is as follows:*

$$\sigma'_j = \begin{cases} \sigma_i & \text{if there is } i \in \mathbb{N} \text{ such that } \tau(i) = j; \\ \{gap\} & \text{otherwise.} \end{cases}$$

Figure 1 illustrates the mapping given by Definition 1. For instance, if $\rho = (\sigma, \tau)$ is the timed state sequence on the left side of Fig. 1 then $(\rho, 0) \models \bigcirc_{[2,3]}p$. As shown in Table 1, we translate $\bigcirc_{[2,3]}p$ into: $\bigvee_{2 \leq l \leq 3}(\bigcirc^l(\neg gap \wedge p) \wedge \bigwedge_{1 \leq k < l} \bigcirc^k gap)$.

Table 1. Strict gap translation from MTL to LTL, where α, β are propositional formulae and $c_1, c_2 > 0$.

MTL	Strict Gap Translation
$(\bigcirc_{[0,\infty)}\alpha)^{\sharp}$	$(\bigcirc_{[1,\infty)}\alpha)^{\sharp}$
$(\bigcirc_{[c_1,\infty)}\alpha)^{\sharp}$	$(\bigwedge_{1 \le k < c_1} \bigcirc^k gap) \wedge \bigcirc^{c_1}(gap\,\mathcal{U}(\alpha \wedge \neg gap))$
$(\bigcirc_{[c_1,c_2]}\alpha)^{\sharp}$	$\bigvee_{c_1 \le l \le c_2}(\bigcirc^l(\neg gap \wedge \alpha) \wedge \bigwedge_{1 \le k < l} \bigcirc^k gap)$
$(\bigcirc_{[0,0]}\alpha)^{\sharp}$	**false**
$(\bigcirc_{[0,c_2]}\alpha)^{\sharp}$	$(\bigcirc_{[1,c_2]}\alpha)^{\sharp}$
$(\alpha\mathcal{U}_{[0,\infty)}\beta)^{\sharp}$	$(gap \vee \alpha)\mathcal{U}(\neg gap \wedge \beta)$
$(\alpha\mathcal{U}_{[c_1,\infty)}\beta)^{\sharp}$	$(\bigwedge_{0 \le k < c_1} \bigcirc^k(gap \vee \alpha)) \wedge \bigcirc^{c_1}((gap \vee \alpha)\mathcal{U}(\neg gap \wedge \beta))$
$(\alpha\mathcal{U}_{[c_1,c_2]}\beta)^{\sharp}$	$\bigvee_{c_1 \le l \le c_2}(\bigcirc^l(\neg gap \wedge \beta) \wedge \bigwedge_{0 \le k < l} \bigcirc^k(gap \vee \alpha))$
$(\alpha\mathcal{U}_{[0,0]}\beta)^{\sharp}$	$\neg gap \wedge \beta$
$(\alpha\mathcal{U}_{[0,c_2]}\beta)^{\sharp}$	$(\neg gap \wedge \beta) \vee (\alpha\mathcal{U}_{[1,c_2]}\beta)^{\sharp}$

Note that the state sequence in Fig. 1 is a model of the translation. Since *gap* is a propositional variable not occurring in σ, the time points mapped by the image of τ do not contain *gap*.

Definition 2. *Given a state sequence σ' such that $(\sigma', 0) \models \neg gap \wedge \Box(\Diamond\neg gap)$, we inductively define $\rho = (\sigma_0, \tau(0))(\sigma_1, \tau(1))\ldots$, where $(\sigma_0, \tau(0)) = (\sigma'_0, 0)$ and, for $i, j, k \in \mathbb{N}$ and $i > 0$, $(\sigma_i, \tau(i))$ is as follows:*

$$\sigma_i = \sigma'_j \text{ and } \tau(i) = j \quad \text{if } j > \tau(i-1), \text{ gap} \notin \sigma'_j \text{ and for all } k,$$
$$\tau(i-1) < k < j, \text{ gap} \in \sigma'_k.$$

As σ' is such that $(\sigma', 0) \models \neg gap \wedge \Box(\Diamond\neg gap)$, for each $i \in \mathbb{N}$ we have $\tau(i) \in \mathbb{N}$. Also, for $i > 0$, $\tau(i) > \tau(i-1)$ and, so, $\tau : \mathbb{N} \to \mathbb{N}$ is well defined.

Example. Assume that we are given the following MTL formula in NNF and FNF: $\varphi = p_0 \wedge \Box_{[0,\infty)}(p_0 \to \bigcirc_{[2,3]}p_1) \wedge \Box_{[0,\infty)}(p_1 \to \Diamond_{[1,2]}\neg q)$. Using Table 1, we translate φ into LTL as follows (recall that $\Diamond_I\psi \equiv \mathbf{true}\mathcal{U}_I\psi$):

$$\varphi^{\sharp} = p_0 \wedge \Box_{[0,\infty)}(p_0 \to (\neg gap \wedge (\bigvee_{2 \le l \le 3}(\bigcirc^l(\neg gap \wedge p_1) \wedge \bigwedge_{1 \le k < l} \bigcirc^k gap))$$
$$\wedge \Box_{[0,\infty)}(p_1 \to (\neg gap \wedge (\bigvee_{1 \le l \le 2}(\bigcirc^l(\neg gap \wedge \neg q)))))$$

We are ready for Theorem 1, which states the correctness of our translation from MTL to LTL using 'gap's.

Theorem 1. *Let $\varphi = p_0 \wedge \bigwedge_i \Box_{[0,\infty)}(p_i \to \psi_i)$ be an MTL formula in NNF and FNF. Let $\varphi^{\sharp} = p_0 \wedge \bigwedge_i \Box(p_i \to (\neg gap \wedge \psi_i^{\sharp}))$ be the result of replacing each ψ_i in φ by $\psi_i^{\sharp}$ as in Table 1. Then, φ is satisfiable if, and only if, $\varphi^{\sharp} \wedge \neg gap \wedge \Box(\Diamond\neg gap)$ is satisfiable.*

Fig. 2. Example illustrating Definition 3

Proof (Sketch). Assume φ is satisfied by a timed state sequence $\rho = (\sigma, \tau)$. We then use Definition 1 to define a state sequence σ' and show with a structural inductive argument that σ' is a model of $\varphi^\sharp \wedge \neg gap \wedge \square(\lozenge \neg gap)$. For the other direction, we assume that $\varphi^\sharp \wedge \neg gap \wedge \square(\lozenge \neg gap)$ is satisfied by a state sequence σ' and use Definition 2 to define a timed state sequence ρ. We again use a structural inductive argument to show that ρ is a model of φ.   □

Non-strict Semantics. We now show how we modify the Gap translation for non-strict timed state sequences. We introduce a fresh propositional variable called 'same'. *same* is true exactly in those states σ'_j of σ' such that there is $i \in \mathbb{N}$ with $\tau(i) = j$ and, for $i > 0$, $\tau(i) = \tau(i-1)$. Note that *same* and *gap* cannot both be true in any state. We say that a state s is a *gap state* if $gap \in s$. We now define our mappings between MTL and LTL models.

Definition 3. *Let $\rho = (\sigma, \tau)$ be a non-strict timed state sequence. We define $\sigma' = \sigma'_0 \sigma'_1 \ldots$ by initially setting $\sigma' = \sigma$ and then modifying σ' with the two following steps:*

1. *For $i > 0$, if $\tau(i) - \tau(i-1) = 0$ then set $\sigma'_i := \sigma_i \cup \{same\}$;*
2. *For $i, j \geq 0$, if σ'_j is the i-th non-gap state in σ', σ'_{j+1} is a non-gap state and $\tau(i+1) - \tau(i) = k > 1$ then add $k-1$ states of the form $\{gap\}$ between σ'_j and σ'_{j+1}.*

Figure 2 illustrates the mapping given by Definition 3. For instance, if $\rho = (\sigma, \tau)$ is the non-strict timed state sequence in Fig. 2 then $(\rho, 0) \models \lozenge_{[2,2]} q$. As shown in Table 2, we translate $\lozenge_{[2,2]} q$ into: $same\mathcal{U}(\neg same \wedge \bigcirc(same\mathcal{U}(\neg same \wedge \bigcirc((q \wedge \neg gap) \vee \bigcirc(same\mathcal{U}(q \wedge same))))))$. The main distinction from the translation presented in Table 1 is that here we use nested until operators to make progress in our encoding of the time line whenever we find a state with $\neg same$. Note that the state sequence represented on the right side of Fig. 1 is a model of the translation (recall that $\lozenge_{[2,2]} q \equiv true\mathcal{U}_{[2,2]} q$).

Definition 4. *Let σ' be a state sequence such that $(\sigma', 0) \models \neg gap \wedge \neg same \wedge \square(\lozenge \neg gap) \wedge \square(\neg same \vee \neg gap) \wedge \square(gap \rightarrow \bigcirc \neg same)$. We first define $\tau : \mathbb{N} \rightarrow \mathbb{N}$ by setting $\tau(0) = 0$ and, for $i > 0$, $\tau(i)$ is as follows:*

$$\tau(i) = \begin{cases} \tau(i-1) & \text{if } \sigma'_j \text{ is the } i+1\text{-th non-gap state and } same \in \sigma'_j \\ \tau(i-1)+k+1 & \text{otherwise,} \end{cases}$$

where $k \geq 0$ is the number of gap states between the i-th and $i+1$-th non-gap states. We now define σ as follows:

Table 2. Non-strict gap translation from MTL to LTL, using *gap* and *same*, where α, β are propositional logic formulae, $c_1, c_2 > 0$ and $(\bigcirc_{[c_1,\infty)}\alpha)^\sharp$ and $(\bigcirc_{[c_1,c_2]}\alpha)^\sharp$ are as in Table 1.

MTL	Non-Strict Gap Translation
$(\bigcirc_{[0,\infty)}\alpha)^\sharp$	$(\bigcirc_{[0,0]}\alpha)^\sharp \vee (\bigcirc_{[1,\infty)}\alpha)^\sharp$
$(\bigcirc_{[0,c_2]}\alpha)^\sharp$	$(\bigcirc_{[0,0]}\alpha)^\sharp \vee (\bigcirc_{[1,c_2]}\alpha)^\sharp$
$(\bigcirc_{[0,0]}\alpha)^\sharp$	$\bigcirc(\alpha \wedge same)$
$(\alpha\mathcal{U}_{[c_1,\infty)}\beta)^\sharp$	$\alpha \wedge \bigcirc((\alpha \wedge same)\mathcal{U}(\neg same \wedge (\alpha\mathcal{U}_{[c_1-1,\infty)}\beta)^\sharp))$
$(\alpha\mathcal{U}_{[0,\infty)}\beta)^\sharp$	$(gap \vee \alpha)\mathcal{U}(\neg gap \wedge \beta)$
$(\alpha\mathcal{U}_{[c_1,c_2]}\beta)^\sharp$	$\alpha \wedge \bigcirc((\alpha \wedge same)\mathcal{U}(\neg same \wedge (\alpha\mathcal{U}_{[c_1-1,c_2-1]}\beta)^\sharp))$
$(\alpha\mathcal{U}_{[0,0]}\beta)^\sharp$	$(\beta \wedge \neg gap) \vee (\alpha \wedge \bigcirc((\alpha \wedge same)\mathcal{U}(\beta \wedge same)))$
$(\alpha\mathcal{U}_{[0,c_2]}\beta)^\sharp$	$(\alpha\mathcal{U}_{[0,0]}\beta)^\sharp \vee (\alpha\mathcal{U}_{[1,c_2]}\beta)^\sharp$

$$\sigma_i = \sigma'_j \setminus \{same\}, \text{ where } \sigma'_j \text{ is the } i+1\text{-th non-gap state.}$$

We are ready for Theorem 2, which states the correctness of our translation from MTL to LTL using the variables 'gap' and 'same'.

Theorem 2. *Let $\varphi = p_0 \wedge \bigwedge_i \square_{[0,\infty)}(p_i \rightarrow \psi_i)$ be an MTL formula in NNF and FNF. Let $\varphi^\sharp = p_0 \wedge \bigwedge_i \square(p_i \rightarrow (\neg gap \wedge \psi_i^\sharp))$ be the result of replacing each ψ_i in φ by $\psi_i^\sharp$ as in Table 2. Then, φ is satisfiable if, and only if, $\varphi^\sharp \wedge \neg gap \wedge \neg same \wedge \square(\Diamond \neg gap) \wedge \square(\neg same \vee \neg gap) \wedge \square(gap \rightarrow \bigcirc \neg same)$ is satisfiable.*

Proof (Sketch). We use Definitions 3 and 4 to map models of φ into models of $\varphi^\sharp \wedge \neg gap \wedge \square(\Diamond \neg gap)$ and vice versa. The correctness of our translation is again given by a structural inductive argument. As mentioned, the main difference w.r.t. to Theorem 1 is that here we use the propositional variable *same* to encode multiple states mapped to the same time point. □

4   From MTL to LTL: Encoding Time Differences

Assume that our MTL formulae are in NNF and FNF. Similar to the previous section our proof strategy relies on mapping each timed state sequence $\rho = (\sigma, \tau)$ to a state sequence σ' such that $\rho = (\sigma, \tau)$ is a model of an MTL formula if, and only if, σ' is a model of our LTL translation. We first show a translation under the strict semantics and then we show how to adapt it for the non-strict semantics.

Strict Semantics. Let $C - 1$ be the greatest number occurring in an interval in an MTL formula φ or 1, if none occur. We say that a timed state sequence $\rho = (\sigma, \tau)$ is *C-bounded*, for a constant $C \in \mathbb{N}$, if $\tau(0) \leq C$ and, for all $i \in \mathbb{N}$, $\tau(i+1) - \tau(i) \leq C$. To map a timed state sequence $\rho = (\sigma, \tau)$ to a state sequence σ' we employ the following result adapted from [4].

Theorem 3. *Let φ be an MTL formula. If there is a timed state sequence $\rho = (\sigma, \tau)$ such that $(\rho, 0) \models \varphi$ then there is a C-bounded timed state sequence ρ_C such that $(\rho_C, 0) \models \varphi$.*

By Theorem 3, w.l.o.g., we can consider only timed state sequences where the time difference from a state to its previous state is bounded by C. Then, we can encode time differences with a set $\Pi_\delta = \{\delta_i^- \mid 1 \leq i \leq C\}$ of propositional variables where each δ_i^- represents a time difference of i w.r.t. the previous state (one could also encode the time difference to the next state instead of the difference from the previous state). We also use propositional variables of the form s_m^n with the meaning that 'the sum of the time differences from the last n states to the current state is m'. For our translation, we only need to define these variables up to sums bounded by $2 \cdot C$. We can now define our mapping from an MTL model to an LTL model[1].

Definition 5. *Given a C-bounded timed state sequence $\rho = (\sigma, \tau)$, we define $\sigma' = \sigma_0' \sigma_1' \ldots$ by setting $\sigma_0' = \sigma_0$ and, for $i > 0$:*

$$\sigma_i' = \sigma_i \cup \{\delta_k^-, s_k^1 \mid \tau(i) - \tau(i-1) = k, 1 \leq k \leq C\}$$
$$\cup \; \{s_{\min(l+k, 2 \cdot C)}^{j+1} \mid s_k^1 \in \sigma_i' \text{ and } s_l^j \in \sigma_{i-1}'\}$$

where $1 \leq j < 2 \cdot C$, $1 \leq l \leq 2 \cdot C$ and $1 \leq k \leq C$ (assume variables of the form s_m^n and δ_n^- do not occur in σ).

In Definition 5, if, for example, $\tau(2) - \tau(0) = 4$ then $(\sigma', 2) \models s_4^2$. Intuitively, the variable s_4^2 allow us to group together all the cases where the sum of the time differences from the last 2 states to the current state is 4. This happens when: $\tau(2) - \tau(1) = 3$ and $\tau(1) - \tau(0) = 1$; or $\tau(2) - \tau(1) = 1$ and $\tau(1) - \tau(0) = 3$; or $\tau(2) - \tau(1) = 2$ and $\tau(1) - \tau(0) = 2$.

The next lemma gives the main properties of σ'. First, we need some notation. We use two additional n-ary boolean operators $\oplus_{=1}$ and $\oplus_{\leq 1}$. If $S = \{\varphi_1, \ldots, \varphi_n\}$ is a finite set of LTL formulae, then $\oplus_{=1}(\varphi_1, \ldots, \varphi_n)$, also written $\oplus_{=1}S$, is an LTL formula. Let σ' be a state sequence and $i \in \mathbb{N}$. Then $(\sigma', i) \models \oplus_{=1}S$ iff $(\sigma', i) \models \varphi_j$ for exactly one $\varphi_j \in S$, $1 \leq j \leq n$. Similarly, $(\sigma', i) \models \oplus_{\leq 1}S$ iff $(\sigma', i) \models \varphi_j$ for at most one $\varphi_j \in S$, $1 \leq j \leq n$. By definition of σ' the following lemma is immediate.

Lemma 1. *Let S_C be the conjunction of the following:*

1. $\bigcirc \square \oplus_{=1} \Pi_\delta$, *for* $\Pi_\delta = \{\delta_k^- \mid 1 \leq k \leq C\}$;
2. $\square(\delta_k^- \leftrightarrow s_k^1)$, *for* $1 \leq k \leq C$;
3. $\square \oplus_{\leq 1} \Pi^i$, *for* $1 \leq i \leq 2 \cdot C$ *and* $\Pi^i = \{s_j^i \mid i \leq j \leq 2 \cdot C\}$;
4. $\square((\bigcirc s_k^1 \wedge s_l^j) \rightarrow \bigcirc s_{\min(l+k, 2 \cdot C)}^{j+1})$, *for* $\{s_k^1, s_l^j, s_{\min(l+k, 2 \cdot C)}^{j+1}\} \subseteq \bigcup_{1 \leq i \leq 2 \cdot C} \Pi^i$.

Given a C-bounded timed state sequence $\rho = (\sigma, \tau)$, let $\sigma' = \sigma_0' \sigma_1' \ldots$ be as in Definition 5. Then, $(\sigma', 0) \models S_C$.

---

[1] We write $\min(l + k, 2 \cdot C)$ for the minimum between $l + k$ and $2 \cdot C$. If the minimum is $2 \cdot C$ then $s_{2 \cdot C}^{j+1}$ means that the sum of the last $j + 1$ variables is greater or equal to $2 \cdot C$.

Table 3. Strict time difference translation from MTL to LTL where α, β are propositional logic formulae and $c_1, c_2 > 0$.

MTL	Strict Time Difference Translation
$(\bigcirc_{[c_1,\infty)}\alpha)^\sharp$	$\bigcirc((\bigvee_{c_1 \leq i \leq C} \delta_i^-) \wedge \alpha)$
$(\bigcirc_{[0,\infty)}\alpha)^\sharp$	$\bigcirc\alpha$
$(\bigcirc_{[c_1,c_2]}\alpha)^\sharp$	$\bigcirc((\bigvee_{c_1 \leq i \leq c_2} \delta_i^-) \wedge \alpha)$
$(\bigcirc_{[0,c_2]}\alpha)^\sharp$	$(\bigcirc_{[1,c_2]}\alpha)^\sharp$
$(\bigcirc_{[0,0]}\alpha)^\sharp$	**false**
$(\alpha\mathcal{U}_{[c_1,\infty)}\beta)^\sharp$	$\bigvee_{1 \leq i \leq c_1}(\bigcirc^i((\bigvee_{c_1 \leq j \leq c_1+C} s_j^i) \wedge \alpha\mathcal{U}\beta) \wedge (\bigwedge_{0 \leq k < i} \bigcirc^k\alpha))$
$(\alpha\mathcal{U}_{[0,\infty)}\beta)^\sharp$	$\alpha\mathcal{U}\beta$
$(\alpha\mathcal{U}_{[c_1,c_2]}\beta)^\sharp$	$\bigvee_{1 \leq i \leq c_2}(\bigcirc^i((\bigvee_{c_1 \leq j \leq c_2} s_j^i) \wedge \beta) \wedge (\bigwedge_{0 \leq k < i} \bigcirc^k\alpha))$
$(\alpha\mathcal{U}_{[0,c_2]}\beta)^\sharp$	$\beta \vee (\alpha\mathcal{U}_{[1,c_2]}\beta)^\sharp$
$(\alpha\mathcal{U}_{[0,0]}\beta)^\sharp$	β

Point 1 ensures that at all times, the time difference k from the current state to the previous (if it exists) is uniquely encoded by the variable δ_k^-. In Point 2 we have that the sum of the difference of the last state to the current, encoded by s_k^1, is exactly δ_k^-. Point 3 ensures that at all times we cannot have more than one value for the sum of the time differences of the last i states. Finally, Point 4 has the propagation of sum variables: if the sum of the last j states is l and the time difference to the next is k then the next state should have that the sum of the last $j + 1$ states is $l + k$. We now define our mapping from an LTL model of S_C to an MTL model (for this mapping, we actually only need Point 1).

Definition 6. *Given a state sequence* $\sigma' = \sigma_0'\sigma_1' \ldots$ *such that* $(\sigma', 0) \models S_C$, *we define a* C-*bounded timed state sequence* $\rho = (\sigma, \tau)$ *by setting* $\sigma_i = \sigma_i' \setminus (\Pi_\delta \cup \bigcup_{1 \leq j \leq 2C} \Pi^j)$, *for* $i \in \mathbb{N}$, *and:*

$$\tau(i) = \begin{cases} 0 & \text{if } i = 0 \\ \tau(i-1) + k & \text{if } i > 0, \delta_k^- \in \sigma_i' \end{cases}$$

Note that ρ, in particular, τ, in Definition 6 is well-defined because for every $i \in \mathbb{N}$ there is exactly one k such that $\delta_k^- \in \sigma_i'$. As shown in Table 3, we translate, for example, $\bigcirc_{[2,3]}p$ into $\bigcirc((\delta_2^- \vee \delta_3^-) \wedge p)$. We are ready for Theorem 4, which states the correctness of our translation using time differences.

Theorem 4. *Let* $\varphi = p_0 \wedge \bigwedge_i \Box_{[0,\infty)}(p_i \rightarrow \psi_i)$ *be an MTL formula in NNF and FNF. Let* $\varphi^\sharp = p_0 \wedge \bigwedge_i \Box(p_i \rightarrow \psi_i^\sharp)$ *be the result of replacing each* ψ_i *in* φ *by* $\psi_i^\sharp$ *as in Table 3. Then,* φ *is satisfiable if, and only if,* $\varphi^\sharp \wedge S_C$ *is satisfiable.*

Proof (Sketch). Assume φ is satisfied by a timed state sequence $\rho = (\sigma, \tau)$. We then use Definition 5 to define a state sequence σ' and show with a structural

Table 4. Non-strict time difference translation from MTL to LTL where α, β are propositional logic formulae, $k_1, k_2 \geq 0$ and $c_1, c_2 > 0$.

MTL	Non-Strict Time Difference Translation
$(\bigcirc_{[k_1,\infty)}\alpha)^\sharp$	$\bigcirc((\bigvee_{k_1 \leq i \leq C} \delta_i^-) \wedge \alpha)$
$(\bigcirc_{[k_1,k_2]}\alpha)^\sharp$	$\bigcirc((\bigvee_{k_1 \leq i \leq k_2} \delta_i^-) \wedge \alpha)$
$(\alpha \mathcal{U}_{[c_1,\infty)}\beta)^\sharp$	$\alpha \wedge \bigcirc \bigvee_{1 \leq i \leq c_1}((\alpha \wedge \delta_0^-)\mathcal{U}^i(\neg\delta_0^- \wedge \alpha), (\neg\delta_0^- \wedge (\bigvee_{c_1 \leq j \leq c_1+C} s_j^i) \wedge \alpha\mathcal{U}\beta))$
$(\alpha \mathcal{U}_{[0,\infty)}\beta)^\sharp$	$\alpha \mathcal{U} \beta$
$(\alpha \mathcal{U}_{[c_1,c_2]}\beta)^\sharp$	$\alpha \wedge \bigcirc \bigvee_{1 \leq i \leq c_2}((\alpha\wedge\delta_0^-)\mathcal{U}^i(\neg\delta_0^-\wedge\alpha), (\neg\delta_0^-\wedge(\bigvee_{c_1 \leq j \leq c_2} s_j^i) \wedge (\alpha\mathcal{U}_{[0,0]}\beta)^\sharp))$
$(\alpha \mathcal{U}_{[0,c_2]}\beta)^\sharp$	$(\alpha\mathcal{U}_{[0,0]}\beta)^\sharp \vee (\alpha\mathcal{U}_{[1,c_2]}\beta)^\sharp$
$(\alpha \mathcal{U}_{[0,0]}\beta)^\sharp$	$\beta \vee (\alpha \wedge \bigcirc((\alpha \wedge \delta_0^-)\mathcal{U}(\beta \wedge \delta_0^-)))$

inductive argument that σ' is a model of $\varphi^\sharp \wedge S_C$. For the other direction, we assume that $\varphi^\sharp \wedge S_C$ is satisfied by a state sequence σ' and use Definition 6 to define a timed state sequence ρ. We again use a structural inductive argument to show that ρ is a model of φ.   □

Example. Assume that we are given the following MTL formula in NNF and FNF: $\varphi = p_0 \wedge \Box_{[0,\infty)}(p_0 \rightarrow \bigcirc_{[2,3]}p_1) \wedge \Box_{[0,\infty)}(p_1 \rightarrow \Diamond_{[1,2]}\neg q)$. Using Table 3, we translate φ into LTL as follows:

$$\varphi^\sharp = p_0 \wedge \Box_{[0,\infty)}(p_0 \rightarrow (\neg gap \wedge (\bigcirc_{[2,3]}p_1)^\sharp))$$
$$\wedge \Box_{[0,\infty)}(p_1 \rightarrow (\neg gap \wedge (\Diamond_{[1,2]}\neg q)^\sharp)),$$

where

$$(\bigcirc_{[2,3]}p_1)^\sharp = \bigcirc((\bigvee_{2 \leq i \leq 3}\delta_i^-) \wedge p_1)$$
$$(\Diamond_{[1,2]}\neg q)^\sharp = \bigvee_{1 \leq i \leq 2}(\bigcirc^i((\bigvee_{1 \leq j \leq 2}s_j^i) \wedge \neg q))$$

(recall that $\Diamond_I\psi \equiv \mathbf{true}\mathcal{U}_I\psi$). By Theorem 4, φ is satisfiable iff $\varphi^\sharp \wedge S_4$ is satisfiable, where S_4 is the conjunction of the following:

1. $\bigcirc\Box \oplus_{=1} \Pi_\delta$, for $\Pi_\delta = \{\delta_k^- \mid 1 \leq k \leq 4\}$;
2. $\Box(\delta_k^- \leftrightarrow s_k^1)$, for $1 \leq k \leq 4$;
3. $\Box \oplus_{\leq 1} \Pi^i$, for $1 \leq i \leq 8$ and $\Pi^i = \{s_j^i \mid i \leq j \leq 8\}$;
4. $\Box(\bigcirc s_k^1 \wedge s_l^j \rightarrow \bigcirc s_{\min(l+k,8)}^{j+1})$, for $\{s_k^1, s_l^j, s_{\min(l+k,8)}^{j+1}\} \subseteq \bigcup_{1 \leq i \leq 8} \Pi^i$.

Non-strict Semantics. We now show how we modify the Time Difference translation for non-strict timed state sequences. We extend the set $\Pi_\delta = \{\delta_i^- \mid 1 \leq i \leq C\}$ of propositional variables representing time differences with δ_0^-, which holds whenever the time difference to the previous state is 0. We say that a state is *non-zero* if the time difference to the previous state is non-zero. The meaning of the variables of the form s_m^n also needs to change, it now indicates that 'the sum of the time differences from the last n *non-zero* states to the current state is m'. As before, for our translation, we only need to define these variables up to sums bounded by $2 \cdot C$. We can now define our mapping from an MTL model to an LTL model.

Given a C-bounded non-strict timed state sequence (σ, τ), we define a state sequence σ' as in Definition 5, with the difference that, whenever $\tau(i) = \tau(i-1)$, we now make δ_0^- true in σ_i' and copy all variables of the form s_m^n in σ_{i-1}' to σ_i'. Let S_C' be the conjunction of the following:

1. $\bigcirc\Box \oplus_{=1} \Pi_\delta$, for $\Pi_\delta = \{\delta_k^- \mid 0 \leq k \leq C\}$;
2. $\Box(\delta_k^- \leftrightarrow s_k^1)$, for $1 \leq k \leq C$;
3. $\Box \oplus_{\leq 1} \Pi^i$, for $1 \leq i \leq 2 \cdot C$ and $\Pi^i = \{s_j^i \mid i \leq j \leq 2 \cdot C\}$;
4. $\Box((\bigcirc s_k^1 \wedge s_l^j) \to \bigcirc s_{\min(l+k, 2 \cdot C)}^{j+1})$, for $\{s_k^1, s_l^j, s_{\min(l+k, 2 \cdot C)}^{j+1}\} \subseteq \bigcup_{1 \leq i \leq 2 \cdot C} \Pi^i$;
5. $\Box((\bigcirc \delta_0^- \wedge s_l^j) \to \bigcirc s_l^j)$, for $s_l^j \in \bigcup_{1 \leq i \leq 2 \cdot C} \Pi^i$.

It is easy to see that $(\sigma', 0) \models S_C'$. Note that the only difference from S_C' to S_C, defined in Lemma 1, is Point 5 which propagates the variables of the form s_m^n to the next state if the time difference is zero. The mapping from an LTL model of S_C' to an MTL model is defined in the same way as in Definition 6 (but now k in δ_k^- can be zero). To simplify the notation, in Table 4 we write $\phi \mathcal{U}^n \gamma, \chi$ as a shorthand for $\phi \mathcal{U}(\gamma \wedge \bigcirc(\phi \mathcal{U}^{n-1}\gamma, \chi))$, where $\phi \mathcal{U}^1 \gamma, \chi = \phi \mathcal{U} \chi$. Theorem 5 states the correctness of our translation (Table 4) using non-strict time differences. It can be proved with ideas similar to those used in the proof of Theorem 4. The main distinction appears in the translation of the 'until' formulas, where we nest until operators so that we can count n non-zero states and then check whether a variable of the form s_m^n holds (in the strict case all states are non-zero, so in Table 3 we can count these states with next operators).

Theorem 5. *Let $\varphi = p_0 \wedge \bigwedge_i \Box_{[0,\infty)}(p_i \to \psi_i)$ be an MTL formula in NNF and FNF. Let $\varphi^\sharp = p_0 \wedge \bigwedge_i \Box(p_i \to \psi_i^\sharp)$ be the result of replacing each ψ_i in φ by $\psi_i^\sharp$ as in Table 4. Then, φ is satisfiable if, and only if, $\varphi^\sharp \wedge S_C'$ is satisfiable.*

Proof (Sketch). We use our modified versions of Definitions 5 and 6 for the non-strict semantics to map models of φ into models of $\varphi^\sharp \wedge S_C'$ and vice versa. The correctness of our translation is again given by a structural inductive argument. As mentioned, the main difference w.r.t. to Theorem 4 is that here we use the propositional variable δ_0^- to encode multiple states mapped to the same time point. $\Box$

5   Empirical Evaluation of the Translations

In order to empirically evaluate the translations, we have used them together with four LTL satisfiability solvers, LS4, NuSMV, pltl and TRP++. The last three performed well in the LTL solver comparison by Schuppan and Darmawan [23] while LS4 has been included because of its excellent performance in our experiments.

NuSMV 2.6.0 [19] uses a reduction of the LTL satisfiability problem to the LTL model checking problem [7]. It is then possible to decide the latter problem either

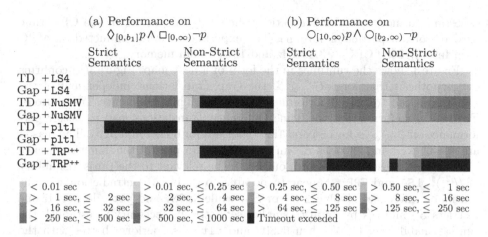

Fig. 3. Heat map for the performance of LTL provers on $\theta_{b_1}^1$ and $\theta_{b_2}^2$. Each rectangle represents the runtime of a prover on an encoding of a formula, with runtimes given in colours as indicated above.

using a BDD-based algorithm or a SAT-based algorithm. Here, we use the latter with completeness check enabled which turns NuSMV into a decision procedure for the LTL satisfiability problem. With the pltl [21] system we have used the **graph** method which is based on a one-pass and-or tree tableau calculus [13] and is time complexity optimal for LTL. TRP++ 2.2 [27] is based on an ordered resolution calculus that operates on LTL formulae in a clausal normal form [16]. LS4 [18] is an LTL prover based on labelled superposition with partial model guidance developed by Suda and Weidenbach [25]. It operates on LTL formulae in the same clausal normal form as TRP++.

We focus on formulae where differences between the two translations could lead to differences in the behaviour of solvers on these formulae. In particular, for $(\alpha \mathcal{U}_{[c_1,c_2]}\beta)$ the Strict and Non-Strict Time Difference Translations contain disjunctive subformulae of the form $\bigvee_{c_1 \leq j \leq c_2} s_j^i$ that have no equivalence in the Strict and Non-Strict Gap Translations of that formula. Each sum variable s_j^i is also subject to the constraints expressed by S_C. It is a reasonable hypothesis that this will have a detrimental effect on the performance of a solver. On the other hand, for $\bigcirc_{[c_1,\infty)}\alpha$ both Gap Translations contain an eventuality formula $gap\mathcal{U}(\alpha \wedge \neg gap)$ that is not present in the Time Difference Translations of this formula. Here, the hypothesis is that the Time Difference Translations lead to better behaviour of solvers.

To test our two hypotheses, we consider the unsatisfiable parameterised formulae $\theta_{b_1}^1 := \Diamond_{[0,b_1]}p \wedge \Box_{[0,\infty)}\neg p$ for values of b_1 between 0 and 10, and $\theta_{b_2}^2 := \bigcirc_{[10,\infty)}p \wedge \bigcirc_{[b_2,\infty)}\neg p$ for values of b_2 between 10 and 110 in steps of 10. After transformation to Flat Normal Form, we apply one of the four translations, and run a solver five times on the resulting LTL formula (with a timeout of 1000 CPU seconds), and then determine the median CPU time over those five runs. We refer to that median CPU time as the runtime. The repeated runs are necessary to moderate the fluctuations shown by all provers in the CPU time used to solve a particular formula. The experiments were conducted on a PC with Intel i7-2600 CPU @ 3.40GHz and 16GB main memory.

Figure 3 shows the runtimes in the form of a heat map. Figure 3(a) confirms our hypothesis that for $(\alpha \mathcal{U}_{[c_1,c_2]}\beta)$ the Gap Translations, independent of the semantics, lead to better performance than the Time Difference Translations. Figure 3(b) confirms that the Time Difference Translations lead to better performance on $\bigcirc_{[c_1,\infty)}\alpha$ for LS4 and TRP++, but not for NuSMV and pltl. The reason are the background theories S_C and S'_C that form part of the Time Difference Translations, most of which turn out not to be relevant to the (un)satisfiability of $(\theta^2_{b_2})^\sharp$. LS4 and TRP++ appear to be able to derive a contradiction without too many inferences involving S_C or S'_C, while NuSMV and pltl do not. If one restricts S_C and S'_C by hand to smaller sets strictly necessary to establish the (un)satisfiability of $(\theta^2_{b_2})^\sharp$, then NuSMV and pltl also perform better with the Time Difference Translations than with the Gap Translations.

6   An Example: Multiprocessor Job-Shop Scheduling

We consider a generalisation of the classic job-shop scheduling problem, called the Multiprocessor Job-shop Scheduling (MJS) problem [8,14]. The representation provided is based on that in [9]. Here a set of jobs have to be processed on a set of machines running in parallel. Each job requires a number of processor steps to complete (this number may also depend on the machine, i.e., job i may run faster in machine j than in machine l). The question is whether there is a scheduling such that after t time units all jobs will have been processed by the machines.

We first show how one can encode the problem in MTL with the strict semantics and then we show the encoding with the non-strict semantics. Our encodings have the property that: there is a scheduling if and only if there is a model for the resulting MTL formulae. One can use any model of the MTL formulae to create a scheduling satisfying the constraints of the problem.

Strict Semantics. Assume we have n jobs $j_1, j_2, \ldots, j_n$ and k machines $m_1, m_2, \ldots, m_k$. Let

- $start\_run_{j_i}$, run_{j_i} and $has\_run_{j_i}$ denote the start, the execution and the end of the execution of job j_i on some machine, respectively;
- $start\_run_{j_i m_l}$ and $run_{j_i m_l}$ denote the start and the execution of job j_i on machine m_l, respectively; and
- $t_{j_i m_l}$ to denote the time taken to run job j_i on machine m_l.

The following equations state that (1) once a job starts running it must start running on one of the machines and that (2) once a job starts running on a machine it must run on that machine (where $\bigwedge_{1 \le i \le n}$ and $\bigwedge_{1 \le i \le n, 1 \le l \le k}$ in front of the formulas is omitted for brevity)

$$\Box(start\_run_{j_i} \rightarrow \bigvee_{l=1}^{k} start\_run_{j_i m_l}) \tag{1}$$

$$\Box(start\_run_{j_i m_l} \rightarrow run_{j_i m_l}) \tag{2}$$

Equation (3) states that: if a job is running on one machine then it cannot be running on another (integrity of jobs); and another job cannot be running on the same machine (integrity of machines). By Eq. (4), once a job has started it cannot be started again.

$$\Box(run_{j_i m_l} \rightarrow (\textstyle\bigwedge_{p=1, p \neq l}^{k} \neg run_{j_i m_p} \wedge \bigwedge_{q=1, q \neq i}^{n} \neg run_{j_q m_l})) \tag{3}$$

$$\Box(start\_run_{j_i} \rightarrow \bigcirc\Box\neg start\_run_{j_i}) \tag{4}$$

We write $\neg run_{j_i}$ as a short hand for $\bigwedge_{l=1}^{k} \neg run_{j_i m_l}$. We can use (5) to denote that once job j_i is started to run on machine m_l it takes time $t_{j_i m_l}$ and (6) to denote that once job j_i has finished running on machine m_l it will not run again. Further, Eq. (7) denotes that job j_i cannot be run until it has started.

$$\Box(start\_run_{j_i m_l} \rightarrow \Box_{[0, t_{j_i m_l} - 1]} run_{j_i m_l} \wedge \neg has\_run_{j_i}) \tag{5}$$

$$\Box(start\_run_{j_i m_l} \rightarrow \Box_{[t_{j_i m_l}, \infty)} (\neg run_{j_i} \wedge has\_run_{j_i})) \tag{6}$$

$$\Box(\neg run_{j_i} \mathcal{U} start\_run_{j_i}) \tag{7}$$

We assume initially that no jobs have run, i.e., $\bigwedge_{i=1}^{n} \neg has\_run_{j_i}$; and that (8) if a job has not run and is currently not running then it has not run in the next moment.

$$\Box((\neg has\_run_{j_i} \wedge \neg run_{j_i}) \rightarrow \bigcirc\neg has\_run_{j_i}) \tag{8}$$

We can now check whether we can achieve a schedule after at most t time points by adding $\Diamond_{[0,t]} \bigwedge_{i=1}^{n} has\_run_{j_i}$. We can also specify constraints on jobs such as

- $\Box(run_{j_i} \leftrightarrow run_{j_i, m_l})$: job j_i must run on machine m_l;
- $\Diamond(start\_run_{j_i} \rightarrow \Diamond_{[1, \infty)} start\_run_{j_m})$: job j_i must start before job j_m;
- $\Diamond_{[c,d]} start\_run_{j_i}$: job j_i must start at a point within the interval $[c, d]$.

Non-strict Semantics. We again assume we have n jobs $j_1, j_2, \ldots, j_n$ and k machines $m_1, m_2, \ldots, m_k$. Let

- $start\_run_{j_i}$ and $has\_run_{j_i}$ denote the start and the end of job j_i on some machine, respectively;
- m_l denote a state of machine m_l;
- run_{j_i} denote that job j_i is running on some machine; and
- $t_{j_i m_l}$ denote the time taken to run job j_i on machine m_l.

In each state exactly one of the variables of the form m_l is true. Also, in each state at most one job is running, but now we may have multiple states at the same time. Let $\Pi_m = \{m_1, \ldots, m_k\}$ and $\Pi_j = \{run_{j_1}, \ldots, run_{j_n}\}$. The following states the constraints mentioned above (the meaning of $\oplus_{=1}$ and $\oplus_{\leq 1}$ is as described in Sect. 3):

$$\Box(\oplus_{=1} \Pi_m \wedge \oplus_{\leq 1} \Pi_j) \tag{9}$$

Equation (10) specifies that if a job is running on one machine then it cannot be running on another. Equation (11) states that once a job is started it cannot be started again (where $\bigwedge_{1 \leq i \leq n, 1 \leq l \leq k}$ and $\bigwedge_{1 \leq i \leq n}$ is again omitted).

$$\square((m_l \wedge run_{j_i}) \rightarrow \bigwedge_{l' \neq l} \square\neg(m_{l'} \wedge run_{j_i})) \tag{10}$$

$$\square(start\_run_{j_i} \rightarrow \bigcirc\square\neg start\_run_{j_i}) \tag{11}$$

We use the following

$$\square((start\_run_{j_i} \wedge m_l) \rightarrow (\square_{[0, t_{j_i m_l} - 1]}(\neg has\_run_{j_i} \wedge (m_l \rightarrow run_{j_i})) \tag{12}$$
$$\wedge \lozenge_{[0, t_{j_i m_l}]} has\_run_{j_i}))$$

to denote that once job j_i started to run on machine m_l it takes time $t_{j_i m_l}$ and (13) to denote that once job j_i has finished running on machine m_l it will not run again. Further, we use $\square(\neg run_{j_i} \mathcal{U} start\_run_{j_i})$ to state a job j_i cannot be run until it is started and $\square(\neg has\_run_{j_i} \mathcal{U} start\_run_{j_i})$ to state that a job cannot have run before it starts (another rule above will make sure that $has\_run_{j_i}$ will hold after the run has finished).

$$\square((start\_run_{j_i} \wedge m_l) \rightarrow \square_{[t_{j_i m_l} + 1, \infty)}(\neg run_{j_i} \wedge has\_run_{j_i})) \tag{13}$$

We assume initially that no jobs have run, i.e., $\bigwedge_{i=1}^{n} \neg has\_run_{j_i}$. We can now check whether we can achieve a schedule after at most t time points by adding $\lozenge_{[0,t]} \bigwedge_{i=1}^{n} has\_run_{j_i}$.

7   Experiments with MJS Problems

We have performed an experimental evaluation of the combination of our translations with LS4, NuSMV, pltl and TRP++. Regarding the MJS problems used in the evaluation we made the simplifying assumption that a job j_i, for each i, $1 \leq i \leq n$, takes the same amount of time t_i on whichever machine it is processed on. We can then characterise a MJS problem by stating (i) a *job list* J consisting of a list of durations $(t'_1, \ldots, t'_n)$, (ii) the number k of machines available, and (iii) the time bound t. In Eqs. 5, 6, 12 and 13, for every i, $1 \leq i \leq n$, and every l, $1 \leq l \leq k$, $t_{j_i m_l}$ will be given by t'_{j_i}. The time bound t is used in the formula $\lozenge_{[0,t]} \bigwedge_{i=1}^{n} has\_run_{j_i}$ that expresses the requirement for a schedule that completes all n jobs on k machines in at most t time points.

For our experiments we created 35 MJS problems with number n of jobs between 1 and 4, a duration t'_i of a job between 1 and 4, a number k of machines between 1 and 3 and finally a time bound t between 0 and 4. We then constructed corresponding MTL formulae for both the strict and the non-strict semantics. Each formula was transformed to FNF, translated to LTL using one of the encodings, and each solver run five times on the resulting LTL formula (with a timeout of 1000 CPU seconds), and the median CPU time over those five runs determined. We refer to that median CPU time as the runtime. Figure 4 shows the runtimes in the form of a heat map.

Regarding the formalisation of MJS problems in the strict semantics, we see in Fig. 4 that for every prover the Gap Translation results in equal or better

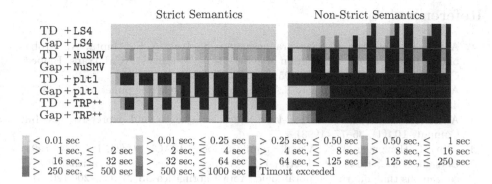

Fig. 4. Heat map for the performance of LTL provers on MJS problems. Each rectangle represents the runtime of a prover on an encoding of the MJS problem, with runtimes given in colours as indicated above.

performance than the Time Difference Translation on every single problem. The Gap Translation together with LS4 offers the best performance for every instance but does not provide models for satisfiable problems. NuSMV is the only prover that returns models of satisfiable problems and its combination with the Gap Translation provides the second best performance overall.

Regarding the formalisation of MJS problems in the non-strict semantics, the most striking observation we can make from Fig. 4 is how much more challenging the corresponding LTL satisfiability problems are for all the provers, as indicated by the very high number of timeouts. Overall, the Non-Strict Gap Translation still results in better performance than the Non-Strict Time Difference Translation. The combination of the Non-Strict Gap Translation and LS4 is again the best performing single approach, but exceeds the timeout for most of the unsatisfiable MJS problems. NuSMV is again the second best prover. It is able to solve and return a model for all satisfiable problems. With the Non-Strict Gap Translation it typically does so an order of magnitude faster than with the Non-Strict Time Difference Translation. On unsatisfiable problems, NuSMV with the Non-Strict Time Difference Translation exceeds the timeout on all unsatisfiable problems and with the Non-Strict Gap Translation it does so on 18 out of 20 unsatisfiable problems. In summary, the experimental results presented in this section provide further evidence of the significant performance improvements that can be gained from the use of the Gap over Time Difference Translations.

8   Conclusion

We presented and evaluated experimentally four translations from MTL to LTL. The translations using time difference are based on the MTL decision procedure presented in [3] and use the bounded model property. Note that the translations using 'gap' are proved independently of this property. Our translations provide a route to practical reasoning about MTL over the naturals via LTL solvers. As future work, we intend to investigate whether we can translate PDDL3.0 statements [12] into MTL and apply our translations to the planning domain.

References

1. Abbas, H., Fainekos, G., Sankaranarayanan, S., Ivančić, F., Gupta, A.: Probabilistic temporal logic falsification of cyber-physical systems. ACM Trans. Embed. Comput. Syst. (TECS) **12**(2s), 95: 1–95: 30 (2013)
2. Alur, R., Feder, T., Henzinger, T.A.: The benefits of relaxing punctuality. J. ACM **43**(1), 116–146 (1996)
3. Alur, R., Henzinger, T.A.: Real-time logics: complexity and expressiveness. Inf. Comput. **104**(1), 35–77 (1993)
4. Alur, R., Henzinger, T.A.: A really temporal logic. J. ACM **41**(1), 181–204 (1994)
5. Bersani, M.M., Rossi, M., Pietro, P.S.: A tool for deciding the satisfiability of continuous-time metric temporal logic. Acta Informatica **53**(2), 171–206 (2016)
6. Bouyer, P., Markey, N., Ouaknine, J., Worrell, J.: The cost of punctuality. In: Proceedings of LICS 2007, pp. 109–120. IEEE (2007)
7. Cimatti, A., Clarke, E., Giunchiglia, E., Giunchiglia, F., Pistore, M., Roveri, M., Sebastiani, R., Tacchella, A.: NuSMV 2: an opensource tool for symbolic model checking. In: Brinksma, E., Larsen, K.G. (eds.) CAV 2002. LNCS, vol. 2404, pp. 359–364. Springer, Heidelberg (2002). doi:10.1007/3-540-45657-0_29
8. Dauzère-Pérès, S., Paulli, J.: An integrated approach for modeling and solving the general multiprocessor job-shop scheduling problem using tabu search. Ann. Oper. Res. **70**, 281–306 (1997)
9. Dixon, C., Fisher, M., Konev, B.: Temporal logic with capacity constraints. In: Konev, B., Wolter, F. (eds.) FroCoS 2007. LNCS, vol. 4720, pp. 163–177. Springer, Heidelberg (2007). doi:10.1007/978-3-540-74621-8_11
10. Fisher, M.: A normal form for temporal logics and its applications in theorem-proving and execution. J. Logic Comput. **7**(4), 429–456 (1997)
11. Gabbay, D., Pnueli, A., Shelah, S., Stavi, J.: On the temporal analysis of fairness. In: Proceedings of POPL 1980, pp. 163–173. ACM (1980)
12. Gerevini, A., Haslum, P., Long, D., Saetti, A., Dimopoulos, Y.: Deterministic planning in the fifth international planning competition: PDDL3 and experimental evaluation of the planners. Artif. Intell. **173**(5—-6), 619–668 (2009)
13. Goré, R.: And-or tableaux for fixpoint logics with converse: LTL, CTL, PDL and CPDL. In: Demri, S., Kapur, D., Weidenbach, C. (eds.) IJCAR 2014. LNCS, vol. 8562, pp. 26–45. Springer, Cham (2014). doi:10.1007/978-3-319-08587-6_3
14. Graham, R.L.: Bounds for certain multiprocessing anomalies. Bell Labs Tech. J. **45**(9), 1563–1581 (1966)
15. Gunadi, H., Tiu, A.: Efficient runtime monitoring with metric temporal logic: a case study in the android operating system. In: Jones, C., Pihlajasaari, P., Sun, J. (eds.) FM 2014. LNCS, vol. 8442, pp. 296–311. Springer, Cham (2014). doi:10.1007/978-3-319-06410-9_21
16. Hustadt, U., Konev, B.: TRP++ 2.0: a temporal resolution prover. In: Baader, F. (ed.) CADE 2003. LNCS, vol. 2741, pp. 274–278. Springer, Heidelberg (2003). doi:10.1007/978-3-540-45085-6_21
17. Karaman, S., Frazzoli, E.: Vehicle routing problem with metric temporal logic specifications. In: Proceedings of CDC 2008, pp. 3953–3958. IEEE (2008)
18. LS4. https://github.com/quickbeam123/ls4
19. NuSMV. http://nusmv.fbk.eu/
20. Ouaknine, J., Worrell, J.: Some recent results in metric temporal logic. In: Cassez, F., Jard, C. (eds.) FORMATS 2008. LNCS, vol. 5215, pp. 1–13. Springer, Heidelberg (2008). doi:10.1007/978-3-540-85778-5_1

21. pltl. http://users.cecs.anu.edu.au/rpg/PLTLProvers/
22. Pnueli, A.: The temporal logic of programs. In: Proceedings of SFCS 1977, pp. 46–57. IEEE (1977)
23. Schuppan, V., Darmawan, L.: Evaluating LTL satisfiability solvers. In: Bultan, T., Hsiung, P.-A. (eds.) ATVA 2011. LNCS, vol. 6996, pp. 397–413. Springer, Heidelberg (2011). doi:10.1007/978-3-642-24372-1_28
24. Sistla, A.P., Clarke, E.M.: The complexity of propositional linear temporal logics. J. ACM **32**(3), 733–749 (1985)
25. Suda, M., Weidenbach, C.: A PLTL-prover based on labelled superposition with partial model guidance. In: Gramlich, B., Miller, D., Sattler, U. (eds.) IJCAR 2012. LNCS, vol. 7364, pp. 537–543. Springer, Heidelberg (2012). doi:10.1007/978-3-642-31365-3_42
26. Thati, P., Roşu, G.: Monitoring algorithms for metric temporal logic specifications. Electronic Notes Theoret. Comput. Sci. **113**, 145–162 (2005)
27. TRP++. http://cgi.csc.liv.ac.uk/konev/software/trp++/
28. Tseitin, G.S.: On the complexity of derivation in propositional calculus. In: Siekmann, J.H., et al. (eds.) Automation of Reasoning, pp. 466–483. Springer, Heidelberg (1983)

Scavenger 0.1: A Theorem Prover Based on Conflict Resolution

Daniyar Itegulov[1], John Slaney[2], and Bruno Woltzenlogel Paleo[2(✉)]

[1] ITMO University, St. Petersburg, Russia
ditegulov@gmail.com, bruno.wp@gmail.com
[2] Australian National University, Canberra, Australia
john.slaney@anu.edu.au

Abstract. This paper introduces Scavenger, the first theorem prover for pure first-order logic without equality based on the new conflict resolution calculus. Conflict resolution has a restricted resolution inference rule that resembles (a first-order generalization of) unit propagation as well as a rule for assuming decision literals and a rule for deriving new clauses by (a first-order generalization of) conflict-driven clause learning.

1 Introduction

The outstanding efficiency of current propositional SAT-solvers naturally raises the question of whether it would be possible to employ similar ideas for automating first-order logical reasoning. The recent *Conflict Resolution* calculus[1] (**CR**) [25] can be regarded as a crucial initial step to answer this question. From a proof-theoretical perspective, **CR** generalizes (to first-order logic) the two main mechanisms on which modern SAT-solvers are based: unit propagation and conflict-driven clause learning. The calculus is sound and refutationally complete, and **CR** derivations are isomorphic to implication graphs.

This paper goes one step further by defining proof search algorithms for **CR**. Familiarity with the propositional CDCL procedure [18] is assumed, even though it is briefly sketched in Sect. 2. The main challenge in lifting this procedure to first-order logic is that, unlike in propositional logic, first-order unit propagation does not always terminate and true clauses do not necessarily have uniformly true literals (cf. Sect. 4). Our solutions to these challenges are discussed in Sects. 5 and 6, and experimental results are presented in Sect. 7.

Related Work: **CR**'s unit-propagating resolution rule can be traced back to unit-resulting resolution [20]. Other attempts to lift DPLL [13,19] or CDCL [18] to first-order logic include *Model Evolution* [2–5], *Geometric Resolution* [24], *Non-Redundant Clause Learning* [1] and the *Semantically-Guided Goal Sensitive procedure* [6–9]. A brief summary of these approaches and a comparison with **CR** can be found in [25]. Furthermore, many architectures [11,12,15,16,29] for

---

Author order is alphabetical by surname.
[1] Not to be confused with the homonymous calculus for linear rational inequalities [17].

© Springer International Publishing AG 2017
L. de Moura (Ed.): CADE 2017, LNAI 10395, pp. 344–356, 2017.
DOI: 10.1007/978-3-319-63046-5_21

first-order and higher-order theorem proving use a SAT-solver as a black box for propositional reasoning, without attempting to lift it; and *Semantic Resolution* [14, 26] is yet another related approach that uses externally built first-order models to guide resolution.

2   Propositional CDCL

During search in the propositional case, a SAT-solver keeps a model (a.k.a. trail) consisting of a (conjunctive) list of decision literals and propagated literals. Literals of unit clauses are automatically added to the trail, and whenever a clause has only one literal that is not falsified by the current model, this literal is added to the model (thereby satisfying that clause). This process is known as *unit-propagation*. If unit propagation reaches a conflict (i.e. a situation where the dual of a literal already contained in the model would have to be added to it), the SAT-solver backtracks, removing from the model decision literals responsible for the conflict (as well as propagated literals entailed by the removed decision literals) and deriving, or learning, a conflict-driven clause consisting[2] of duals of the decision literals responsible for the conflict (or the empty clause, if there were no decision literals). If unit propagation terminates without reaching a conflict and all clauses are satisfied by the model, then the input clause set is satisfiable. If some clauses are still not satisfied, the SAT-solver chooses and assigns another decision literal, adding it to the trail, and satisfying the clauses that contain it.

3   Conflict Resolution

The inference rules of the conflict resolution calculus **CR** are shown in Fig. 1. The *unit propagating resolution* rule is a chain of restricted resolutions with unit clauses as left premises and a unit clause as final conclusion. *Decision literals* are denoted by square brackets, and the *conflict-driven clause learning* rule infers a new clause consisting of negations of instances of decision literals used to reach a conflict (a.k.a. the empty clause ⊥). A clause learning inference is said to discharge the decision literals that it uses. As in the resolution calculus, **CR** derivations are directed acyclic graphs that are not necessarily tree-like. A **CR** refutation is a **CR** derivation of ⊥ with no undischarged decision literals.

From a natural deduction point of view, a unit propagating resolution rule can be regarded as a chain of implication eliminations taking unification into account, whereas decision literals and conflict driven clause learning are reminiscent of, respectively, assumptions and chains of negation introductions, also generalized to first-order through unification. Therefore, **CR** can be considered a first-order hybrid of resolution and natural deduction.

---

[2] In practice, optimizations (e.g. 1UIP) are used, and more sophisticated clauses, which are not just disjunctions of duals of the decision literals involved in the conflict, can be derived. But these optimizations are inessential to the focus of this paper.

Unit-Propagating Resolution:

$$\frac{\ell_1 \quad \cdots \quad \ell_n \quad \overline{\ell_1'} \vee \ldots \vee \overline{\ell_n'} \vee \ell}{\ell \, \sigma} \; \mathbf{u}(\sigma)$$

where σ is a unifier of ℓ_k and ℓ_k', for all $k \in \{1, \ldots, n\}$.

Conflict:

$$\frac{\ell \quad \overline{\ell'}}{\bot} \; \mathbf{c}(\sigma)$$

where σ is a unifier of ℓ and ℓ'.

Conflict-Driven Clause Learning:

$$\frac{\begin{array}{ccc} [\ell_1]^i & & [\ell_n]^i \\ \vdots \; (\sigma_1^1, \ldots, \sigma_{m_1}^1) & & \vdots \; (\sigma_1^n, \ldots, \sigma_{m_n}^n) \\ & \vdots & \\ & \bot & \end{array}}{(\overline{\ell_1}\sigma_1^1 \vee \ldots \vee \overline{\ell_1}\sigma_{m_1}^1) \vee \ldots \vee (\overline{\ell_n}\sigma_1^n \vee \ldots \vee \overline{\ell_n}\sigma_{m_n}^n)} \; \mathbf{cl}^i$$

where σ_j^k (for $1 \leq k \leq n$ and $1 \leq j \leq m_k$) is the
composition of all substitutions used on the j-th path[a] from ℓ_k to $\bot$.

---

[a] Since a proof DAG is not necessarily tree-like, there may be more than one path connecting ℓ_k to $\bot$ in the DAG-like proof.

Fig. 1. The conflict resolution calculus **CR**

4 Lifting Challenges

First-order logic presents many new challenges for methods based on propagation and decisions, of which the following can be singled out:

(1) *non-termination of unit-propagation:* In first-order logic, unit propagation may never terminate. For example, the clause set $\{p(a), \neg p(X) \vee p(f(X)), q \vee r, \neg q \vee r, q \vee \neg r, \neg q \vee \neg r\}$ is clearly unsatisfiable, because there is no assignment of p and q to *true* or *false* that would satisfy all the last four clauses. However, unit propagation would derive the following infinite sequence of units, by successively resolving $\neg p(X) \vee p(f(X))$ with previously derived units, starting with $p(a)$: $\{p(f(a)), p(f(f(a))), \ldots, p(f(\ldots(f(a))\ldots)), \ldots\}$. Consequently, a proof search strategy that would wait for unit propagation to terminate before making decisions would never be able to conclude that the given clause set is unsatisfiable.

(2) *absence of uniformly true literals in satisfied clauses:* While in the propositional case, a clause that is true in a model always has at least one literal

that is true in that model, this is not so in first-order logic, because shared variables create dependencies between literals. For instance, the clause set $\{p(X) \lor q(X), \neg p(a), p(b), q(a), \neg q(b)\}$ is satisfiable, but there is no model where $p(X)$ is uniformly true (i.e. true for all instances of X) or $q(X)$ is uniformly true.

(3) *propagation without satisfaction:* In the propositional case, when only one literal of a clause is not false in the model, this literal is propagated and added to the model, and the clause necessarily becomes true in the model and does not need to be considered in propagation anymore, at least until backtracking. In the first-order case, on the other hand, a clause such as $p(X) \lor q(X)$ would propagate the literal $q(a)$ in a model containing $\neg p(a)$, but $p(X) \lor q(X)$ does not become true in a model where $q(a)$ is true. It must remain available for further propagations. If, for instance, the literal $\neg p(b)$ is added to the model, the clause will be used again to propagate $q(b)$.

(4) *quasi-falsification without propagation:* A clause is *quasi-falsified* by a model iff all but one of its literals are false in the model. In first-order logic, in contrast to propositional logic, it is not even the case that a clause will necessarily propagate a literal when only one of its literals is not false in the model. For instance, the clause $p(X) \lor q(X) \lor r(X)$ is quasi-falsified in a model containing $\neg p(a)$ and $\neg q(b)$, but no instance of $r(X)$ can be propagated.

The first two challenges affect search in a conceptual level, and solutions are discussed in Sect. 5. The last two prevent a direct first-order generalization of the data structures (e.g. *watched literals*) that make unit propagation so efficient in the propositional case. Partial solutions are discussed in Sect. 6.

5   First-Order Model Construction and Proof Search

Despite the fundamental differences between propositional and first-order logic described in the previous section, the first-order algorithms presented aim to adhere as much as possible to the propositional procedure sketched in the Sect. 2. As in the propositional case, the model under construction is a (conjunctive) list of literals, but literals may now contain (universal) variables. If a literal $\ell[X]$ is in a model M, then any instance $\ell[t]$ is said to be true in M. Note that checking that a literal ℓ is true in a model M is more expensive in first-order logic than in propositional logic: whereas in the latter it suffices to check that ℓ is in M, in the former it is necessary to find a literal ℓ' in M and a substitution σ such that $\ell = \ell'\sigma$. A literal ℓ is said to be *strongly true* in a model M iff ℓ is in M.

There is a straightforward solution for the second challenge (i.e. the absence of uniformly true literals in satisfied clauses): a clause is satisfied by a model M iff all its relevant instances have a literal that is true in M, where an instance is said to be relevant if it substitutes the clause's variables by terms that occur in M. Thus, for instance, the clause $p(X) \lor q(X)$ is satisfied by the model $[\neg p(a), p(b), q(a), \neg q(b)]$, because both relevant instances $p(a) \lor q(a)$ and $p(b) \lor q(b)$ have literals that are true in the model. However, this solution is costly, because it requires the generation of many instances. Fortunately, in many (though not all) cases, a satisfied clause will have a literal that is true in M, in which case the clause is said to be *uniformly satisfied*. Uniform satisfaction is cheaper to check than satisfaction. However, a drawback of uniform satisfaction is that the model construction algorithm may repeatedly attempt to satisfy a clause that is not uniformly satisfied, by choosing one of its literals as a decision literal. For example, the clause $p(X) \lor q(X)$ is not uniformly satisfied by the model $[\neg p(a), p(b), q(a), \neg q(b)]$. Without knowing that this clause is already satisfied by the model, the procedure would try to choose either $p(X)$ or $q(X)$ as decision literal. But both choices are *useless decisions*, because they would lead to conflicts with conflict-driven clauses equal to a previously derived clause or to a unit clause containing a literal that is part of the current model. A clause is said to be *weakly satisfied* by a model M if and only if all its literals are useless decisions.

Because of the first challenge (i.e. the non-termination of unit-propagation in the general first-order case), it is crucial to make decisions *during* unit propagation. In the example given in item 1 of Sect. 4, for instance, deciding q at any moment would allow the propagation of r and $\neg r$ (respectively due to the 4th and 6th clauses), triggering a conflict. The learned clause would be $\neg q$ and it would again trigger a conflict by the propagation of r and $\neg r$ (this time due to the 3rd and 5th clauses). As this last conflict does not depend on any decision literal, the empty clause is derived and thus the clause set is refuted. The question is how to interleave decisions and propagations. One straightforward approach is to keep track of the *propagation depth*[3] in the implication graph: any decision literal or literal propagated by a unit clause has propagation depth 0; any other literal has propagation depth $k + 1$, where k is the maximum propagation depth of its predecessors. Then propagation is performed exhaustively only up to a propagation depth threshold h. A decision literal is then chosen and the threshold is incremented. Such *eager decisions* guarantee that a decision will eventually be made, even if there is an infinite propagation path. However, eager decisions may also lead to spurious conflicts generating useless conflict-driven clauses. For instance, the clause set $\{1 : p(a), 2 : \neg p(X) \lor p(f(X)), 3 : \neg p(f(f(f(f(f(f(f(a))))))))), 4 : \neg r(X) \lor q(X), 5 : \neg q(g(X)) \lor \neg p(X), 6 : z(X) \lor r(X)\}$ (where clauses have been numbered for easier reference) is unsatisfiable, because a conflict with no decisions can be obtained by propagating $p(a)$ (by 1), and then $p(f(a))$, $p(f(f(a))), \ldots, p(f(f(f(f(f(f(f(a))))))))$, (by 2, repeatedly), which conflicts with $\neg p(f(f(f(f(f(f(f(a))))))))$ (by 3). But the former propagation has depth 6. If the propagation depth threshold is lower than 6, a decision literal is chosen before that conflict is reached. If $r(X)$ is chosen, for example, in an attempt to satisfy the sixth clause, there are propagations (using $r(X)$ and clauses 1, 4, 5 and 6)

---

[3] Because of the isomorphism between implication graphs and subderivations in Conflict Resolution [25], the propagation depth is equal to the corresponding subderivation's *height*, where initial axiom clauses and learned clauses have height 0 and the height of the conclusion of a unit-propagating resolution inference is $k + 1$ where k is the maximum height of its unit premises.

with depth lower than the threshold and reaching a conflict that generates the clause $\neg r(g(a))$, which is useless for showing unsatisfiability of the whole clause set. This is not a serious issue, because useless clauses are often generated in conflicts with non-eager decisions as well. Nevertheless, this example suggests that the starting threshold and the strategy for increasing the threshold have to be chosen wisely, since the performance may be sensitive to this choice.

Interestingly, the problem of non-terminating propagation does not manifest in fragments of first-order logic where infinite unit propagation paths are impossible. A well-known and large fragment is the *effectively propositional* (a.k.a. *Bernays-Schönfinkel*) class, consisting of sentences with prenex forms that have an $\exists^*\forall^*$ quantifier prefix and no function symbols. For this fragment, a simpler proof search strategy that only makes decisions when unit propagation terminates, as in the propositional case, suffices. Infinite unit propagation paths do not occur in the effectively propositional fragment because there are no function symbols and hence the term depth[4] does not increase arbitrarily. Whenever the term depth is bounded, infinite unit propagation paths cannot occur, because there are only finitely many literals with bounded term depth (given the finite set of constant, function and predicate symbols with finite arity occurring in the clause set).

The insight that term depth is important naturally suggests a different approach for the general first-order case: instead of limiting the propagation depth, limit the *term depth* instead, allowing arbitrarily long propagations as long as the term depth of the propagated literals are smaller than the current term depth threshold. A literal is propagated only if its term depth is smaller than the threshold. New decisions are chosen when the term-depth-bounded propagation terminates and there are still clauses that are not uniformly satisfied. As before, eager decisions may lead to spurious conflicts, but bounding propagation by term depth seems intuitively more sensible than bounding it by propagation depth.

6 Implementation Details

Scavenger is implemented in Scala and its source code and usage instructions are available in https://gitlab.com/aossie/Scavenger. Its packrat combinator parsers are able to parse TPTP CNF files [28]. Although Scavenger is a first-order prover, every logical expression is converted to a simply typed lambda expression, implemented by the abstract class E with concrete subclasses Sym, App and Abs for, respectively, *symbols*, *applications* and *abstractions*. A trait Var is used to distinguish *variables* from other symbols. Scala's *case classes* are used to make E behave like an algebraic datatype with (pattern-matchable) constructors. The choice of simply typed lambda expressions is motivated by the intention to generalize Scavenger to multi-sorted first-order logic and higher-order logic and support TPTP TFF and THF in the future. Every clause is internally represented as

---

[4] The depth of constants and variables is zero and the depth of a complex term is $k + 1$ when k is the maximum depth of its proper subterms.

an immutable two-sided sequent consisting of a set of positive literals (succedent) and a set of negative literals (antecedent).

When a problem is unsatisfiable, Scavenger can output a **CR** refutation internally represented as a collection of ProofNode objects, which can be instances of the following immutable classes: UnitPropagatingResolution, Conflict, ConflictDrivenClauseLearning, Axiom, Decision. The first three classes correspond directly to the rules shown in Fig. 1. Axiom is used for leaf nodes containing input clauses, and Decision represents a fictive rule holding decision literals. Each class is responsible for checking, typically through require statements, the soundness conditions of its corresponding inference rule. The Axiom, Decision and ConflictDrivenClauseLearning classes are less than 5 lines of code each. Conflict and UnitPropagatingResolution are respectively 15 and 35 lines of code. The code for analyzing conflicts, traversing the subderivations (conflict graphs) and finding decisions that contributed to the conflict, is implemented in a superclass, and is 17 lines long.

The following three variants of Scavenger were implemented:

– EP-Scavenger: aiming at the effectively propositional fragment, propagation is not bounded, and decisions are made only when propagation terminates.
– PD-Scavenger: Propagation is bounded by a propagation depth threshold starting at 0. Input clauses are assigned depth 0. Derived clauses and propagated literals obtained while the depth threshold is k are assigned depth $k + 1$. The threshold is incremented whenever every input clause that is neither uniformly satisfied nor weakly satisfied is used to derive a new clause or to propagate a new literal. If this is not the case, a decision literal is chosen (and assigned depth $k + 1$) to uniformly satisfy one of the clauses that is neither uniformly satisfied nor weakly satisfied.
– TD-Scavenger: Propagation is bounded by a term depth threshold starting at 0. When propagation terminates, a stochastic choice between either selecting a decision literal or incrementing the threshold is made with probability of 50% for each option. Only uniform satisfaction of clauses is checked.

The third and fourth challenges discussed in Sect. 4 are critical for performance, because they prevent a direct first-order generalization of data structures such as *watched literals*, which enables efficient detection of clauses that are ready to propagate literals. Without knowing exactly which clauses are ready to propagate, Scavenger (in its three variants) loops through all clauses with the goal of using them for propagation. However, actually trying to use a given clause for propagation is costly. In order to avoid this cost, Scavenger performs two quicker tests. Firstly, it checks whether the clause is uniformly satisfied (by checking whether one of its literals belongs to the model). If it is, then the clause is dismissed. This is an imperfect test, however. Occasionally, some satisfied clauses will not be dismissed, because (in first-order logic) not all satisfied clauses are uniformly satisfied. Secondly, for every literal ℓ of every clause, Scavenger keeps a set of decision literals and propagated literals that are unifiable with ℓ. A clause c is quasi-falsified when at most one literal of c has an empty set associated with it. This is a rough analogue of watched literals for detecting quasi-falsified clauses. Again, this is an imperfect test, because (in first-order logic) not all quasi-falsified clauses are ready to propagate. Despite the imperfections of these tests, they do reduce the number of clauses that need to be considered for propagation, and they are quick and simple to implement.

Overall, the three variants of Scavenger listed above have been implemented concisely. Their main classes are only 168, 342 and 176 lines long, respectively, and no attempt has been made to increase efficiency at the expense of the code's readability and pedagogical value. Premature optimization would be inappropriate for a first proof-of-concept.

Scavenger still has no sophisticated backtracking and restarting mechanism, as propositional SAT-solvers do. When Scavenger reaches a conflict, it restarts almost completely: all derived conflict-driven clauses are kept, but the model under construction is reset to the empty model.

7   Experiments

Experiments were conducted[5] in the StarExec cluster [27] to evaluate Scavenger's performance on TPTP v6.4.0 benchmarks in CNF form and without equality. For comparison, all other 21 provers available in StarExec's TPTP community and suitable for CNF problems without equality were evaluated as well. For each job pair, the timeouts were 300 CPU seconds and 600 Wallclock seconds.

Table 1. Number of problems solved by each prove.

Prover	Problems Solved		Prover	Problems Solved	
	EPR	All		EPR	All
PEPR-0.0ps	432	432	Bliksem-1.12	424	1107
GrAnDe-1.1	447	447	SOS-2.0	351	1129
Paradox-3.0	467	506	CVC4-FOF-1.5.1	452	1145
ZenonModulo-0.4.1	315	628	SNARK-20120808	417	1150
TD-Scavenger	*350*	*695*	Beagle-0.9.47	402	1153
PD-Scavenger	*252*	*782*	E-Darwin-1.5	453	1213
Geo-III-2016C	344	840	Prover9-1109a	403	1293
EP-Scavenger	*349*	*891*	Darwin-1.4.5	508	1357
Metis-2.3	404	950	iProver-2.5	551	1437
Z3-4.4.1	507	1027	ET-0.2	486	1455
Zipperpin-FOF-0.4	400	1029	E-2.0	489	1464
Otter-3.3	362	1068	Vampire-4.1	540	1524

Table 1 shows how many of the 1606 unsatisfiable CNF problems and 572 effectively propositional (EPR) unsatisfiable CNF problems each theorem prover solved; and Figs. 2 and 3 shows the performance in more detail. For a first implementation, the best variants of Scavenger show an acceptable performance.

---

[5] Raw experimental data are available at https://doi.org/10.5281/zenodo.293187.

All variants of Scavenger outperformed PEPR, GrAnDe, DarwinFM, Paradox and ZenonModulo; and EP-Scavenger additionally outperformed Geo-III. On the effectively propositional propblems, TD-Scavenger outperformed LEO-II, Zenon-Modulo and Geo-III, and solved only 1 problem less than SOS-2.0 and 12 less than Otter-3.3. Although Otter-3.3 has long ceased to be a state-of-the-art prover and has been replaced by Prover9, the fact that Scavenger solves almost as many problems as Otter-3.3 is encouraging, because Otter-3.3 is a mature prover with 15 years of development, implementing (in the C language) several refinements of proof search for resolution and paramodulation (e.g. orderings, set of support, splitting, demodulation, subsumption) [21, 22], whereas Scavenger is a yet unrefined and concise implementation (in Scala) of a comparatively straightforward search strategy for proofs in the Conflict Resolution calculus, completed in slightly more than 3 months. Conceptually, Geo-III (based on Geometric Resolution) and Darwin (based on Model Evolution) are the most similar to Scavenger. While Scavenger already outperforms Geo-III, it is still far from Darwin. This is most probably due to Scavenger's current eagerness to restart after every conflict, whereas Darwin backtracks more carefully (cf. Sects. 6 and 8). Scavenger and Darwin also treat variables in decision literals differently. Consequently, Scavenger detects more (and non-ground) conflicts, but learning conflict-driven clauses can be more expensive, because unifiers must be collected from the conflict graph and composed.

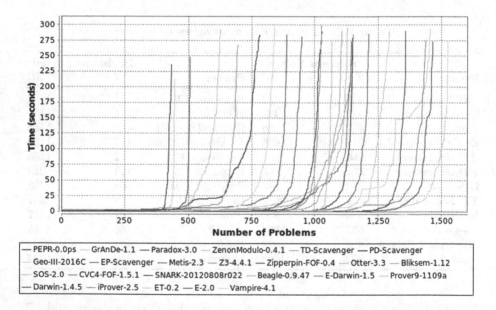

Fig. 2. Performance on all benchmarks (provers ordered by performance)

EP-Scavenger solved 28.2% more problems than TD-Scavenger and 13.9% more than PD-Scavenger. This suggests that non-termination of unit-

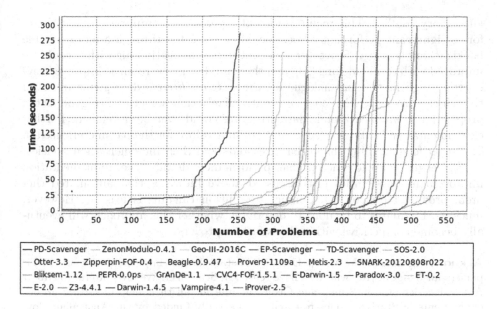

Fig. 3. Performance on EPR benchmarks only (provers ordered by performance)

propagation is an uncommon issue in practice: EP-Scavenger is still able to solve many problems, even though it does not care to bound propagation, whereas the other two variants solve fewer problems because of the overhead of bounding propagation even when it is not necessary. Nevertheless, there were 28 problems solved only by PD-Scavenger and 26 problems solved only by TD-Scavenger (among Scavenger's variants). EP-Scavenger and PD-Scavenger can solve 9 problems with TPTP difficulty rating 0.5, all from the SYN and FLD domains. 3 of the 9 problems were solved in less than 10 s.

8   Conclusions and Future Work

Scavenger is the first theorem prover based on the new Conflict Resolution calculus. The experiments show a promising, albeit not yet competitive, performance.

A comparison of the performance of the three variants of Scavenger shows that it is non-trivial to interleave decisions within possibly non-terminating unit-propagations, and further research is needed to determine (possibly in a problem dependent way) optimal initial depth thresholds and threshold incrementation strategies. Alternatively, entirely different criteria could be explored for deciding to make an eager decision before propagation is over. For instance, decisions could be made if a fixed or dynamically adjusted amount of time elapses.

The performance bottleneck that needs to be most urgently addressed in future work is backtracking and restarting. Currently, all variants of Scavenger restart after every conflict, keeping derived conflict-driven clauses but throwing away the model construct so far. They must reconstruct models from scratch after every conflict. This requires a lot of repeated re-computation, and therefore a significant performance boost could be expected through a more sensible backtracking strategy. Scavenger's current naive unification algorithm could be improved with term indexing [23], and there might also be room to improve Scavenger's rough first-order analogue for the *watched literals* data structure, even though the first-order challenges make it unlikely that something as good as the propositional watched literals data structure could ever be developed. Further experimentation is also needed to find optimal values for the parameters used in Scavenger for governing the initial thresholds and their incrementation policies.

Scavenger's already acceptable performance despite the implementation improvement possibilities just discussed above indicates that automated theorem proving based on the Conflict Resolution calculus is feasible. However, much work remains to be done to determine whether this approach will eventually become competitive with today's fastest provers.

Acknowledgments. We thank Ezequiel Postan for his implementation of TPTP parsers for Skeptik [10], which we have reused in Scavenger. We are grateful to Albert A.V. Giegerich, Aaron Stump and Geoff Sutcliffe for all their help in setting up our experiments in StarExec. This research was partially funded by the Australian Government through the Australian Research Council and by the Google Summer of Code 2016 program. Daniyar Itegulov was financially supported by the Russian Scientific Foundation (grant 15-14-00066).

References

1. Alagi, G., Weidenbach, C.: NRCL - a model building approach to the Bernays-Schönfinkel fragment. In: Lutz, C., Ranise, S. (eds.) FroCoS 2015. LNCS, vol. 9322, pp. 69–84. Springer, Cham (2015). doi:10.1007/978-3-319-24246-0_5
2. Baumgartner, P.: A first order Davis-Putnam-Longeman-Loveland procedure. In: Proceedings of the 17th International Conference on Automated Deduction (CADE), pp. 200–219 (2000)
3. Baumgartner, P.: Model evolution-based theorem proving. IEEE Intell. Syst. **29**(1), 4–10 (2014). http://dx.doi.org/10.1109/MIS.2013.124
4. Baumgartner, P., Fuchs, A., Tinelli, C.: Lemma learning in the model evolution calculus. In: Hermann, M., Voronkov, A. (eds.) LPAR 2006. LNCS, vol. 4246, pp. 572–586. Springer, Heidelberg (2006). doi:10.1007/11916277_39
5. Baumgartner, P., Tinelli, C.: The model evolution calculus. In: Baader, F. (ed.) CADE 2003. LNCS, vol. 2741, pp. 350–364. Springer, Heidelberg (2003). doi:10.1007/978-3-540-45085-6_32
6. Bonacina, M.P., Plaisted, D.A.: Constraint manipulation in SGGS. In: Kutsia, T., Ringeissen, C. (eds.) Proceedings of the Twenty-Eighth Workshop on Unification (UNIF), Seventh International Joint Conference on Automated Reasoning (IJCAR) and Sixth Federated Logic Conference (FLoC), pp. 47–54, Technical reports of the Research Institute for Symbolic Computation, Johannes Kepler Universität Linz (2014). http://vsl2014.at/meetings/UNIF-index.html

7. Bonacina, M.P., Plaisted, D.A.: SGGS theorem proving: an exposition. In: Schulz, S., Moura, L.D., Konev, B. (eds.) Proceedings of the Fourth Workshop on Practical Aspects in Automated Reasoning (PAAR), Seventh International Joint Conference on Automated Reasoning (IJCAR) and Sixth Federated Logic Conference (FLoC), July 2014. EasyChair Proceedings in Computing (EPiC), vol. 31, pp. 25–38, July 2015

8. Bonacina, M.P., Plaisted, D.A.: Semantically-guided goal-sensitive reasoning: model representation. J. Autom. Reasoning **56**(2), 113–141 (2016). http://dx.doi.org/10.1007/s10817-015-9334-4

9. Bonacina, M.P., Plaisted, D.A.: Semantically-guided goal-sensitive reasoning: Inference system and completeness. J. Autom. Reasoning, 1–54 (2017). http://dx.doi.org/10.1007/s10817-016-9384-2

10. Boudou, J., Fellner, A., Woltzenlogel Paleo, B.: Skeptik: a proof compression system. In: Demri, S., Kapur, D., Weidenbach, C. (eds.) IJCAR 2014. LNCS, vol. 8562, pp. 374–380. Springer, Cham (2014). doi:10.1007/978-3-319-08587-6_29

11. Brown, C.E.: Satallax: an automatic higher-order prover. In: Gramlich, B., Miller, D., Sattler, U. (eds.) IJCAR 2012. LNCS, vol. 7364, pp. 111–117. Springer, Heidelberg (2012). doi:10.1007/978-3-642-31365-3_11

12. Claessen, K.: The anatomy of Equinox - an extensible automated reasoning tool for first-order logic and beyond (talk abstract). In: Proceedings of the 23rd International Conference on Automated Deduction (CADE-23), pp. 1–3 (2011)

13. Davis, M., Putnam, H.: A computing procedure for quantification theory. J. ACM **7**, 201–215 (1960)

14. Hodgson, K., Slaney, J.K.: System description: SCOTT-5. In: Automated Reasoning, First International Joint Conference, IJCAR 2001, Siena, Italy, June 18–23, 2001, Proceedings, pp. 443–447 (2001). http://dx.doi.org/10.1007/3-540-45744-5_36

15. Korovin, K.: iProver – an instantiation-based theorem prover for first-order logic (system description). In: Armando, A., Baumgartner, P., Dowek, G. (eds.) IJCAR 2008. LNCS, vol. 5195, pp. 292–298. Springer, Heidelberg (2008). doi:10.1007/978-3-540-71070-7_24

16. Korovin, K.: Inst-Gen - a modular approach to instantiation-based automated reasoning. In: Programming Logics, pp. 239–270 (2013)

17. Korovin, K., Tsiskaridze, N., Voronkov, A.: Conflict resolution. In: Gent, I.P. (ed.) CP 2009. LNCS, vol. 5732, pp. 509–523. Springer, Heidelberg (2009). doi:10.1007/978-3-642-04244-7_41

18. João Marques-Silva, I.L., Malik, S.: Conflict-driven clause learning SAT solvers. In: Handbook of Satisfiability, pp. 127–149 (2008)

19. Martin Davis, G.L., Loveland, D.: A machine program for theorem proving. Commun. ACM **57**, 394–397 (1962)

20. McCharen, J., Overbeek, R., Wos, L.: Complexity and related enhancements for automated theorem-proving programs. Comput. Math. Appl. **2**, 1–16 (1976)

21. McCune, W.: Otter 2.0. In: Stickel, M.E. (ed.) CADE 1990. LNCS, vol. 449, pp. 663–664. Springer, Heidelberg (1990). doi:10.1007/3-540-52885-7_131

22. McCune, W.: OTTER 3.3 reference manual. CoRR cs.SC/0310056 (2003),. http://arxiv.org/abs/cs.SC/0310056

23. Nieuwenhuis, R., Hillenbrand, T., Riazanov, A., Voronkov, A.: On the evaluation of indexing techniques for theorem proving. In: Automated Reasoning, First International Joint Conference, IJCAR 2001, Siena, Italy, June 18–23, 2001, Proceedings, pp. 257–271 (2001). doi:http://dx.doi.org/10.1007/3-540-45744-5_19

24. Nivelle, H., Meng, J.: Geometric resolution: a proof procedure based on finite model search. In: Furbach, U., Shankar, N. (eds.) IJCAR 2006. LNCS, vol. 4130, pp. 303–317. Springer, Heidelberg (2006). doi:10.1007/11814771_28
25. Slaney, J., Woltzenlogel Paleo, B.: Conflict resolution: a first-order resolution calculus with decision literals and conflict-driven clause learning. J. Autom. Reasoning, 1–24 (2017). http://dx.doi.org/10.1007/s10817-017-9408-6
26. Slaney, J.K.: SCOTT: a model-guided theorem prover. In: Bajcsy, R. (ed.) Proceedings of the 13th International Joint Conference on Artificial Intelligence. Chambéry, France, August 28 - September 3, 1993, pp. 109–115. Morgan Kaufmann (1993). http://ijcai.org/Proceedings/93-1/Papers/016.pdf
27. Stump, A., Sutcliffe, G., Tinelli, C.: StarExec: a cross-community infrastructure for logic solving. In: Demri, S., Kapur, D., Weidenbach, C. (eds.) IJCAR 2014. LNCS, vol. 8562, pp. 367–373. Springer, Cham (2014). doi:10.1007/978-3-319-08587-6_28
28. Sutcliffe, G.: The TPTP problem library and associated infrastructure: the FOF and CNF parts, v3.5.0. J. Autom. Reasoning 43(4), 337–362 (2009)
29. Voronkov, A.: AVATAR: the architecture for first-order theorem provers. In: Biere, A., Bloem, R. (eds.) CAV 2014. LNCS, vol. 8559, pp. 696–710. Springer, Cham (2014). doi:10.1007/978-3-319-08867-9_46

WorkflowFM: A Logic-Based Framework for Formal Process Specification and Composition

Petros Papapanagiotou[(✉)] and Jacques Fleuriot

School of Informatics, University of Edinburgh, 10 Crichton Street,
Edinburgh EH8 9AB, UK
{ppapapan,jdf}@inf.ed.ac.uk

Abstract. We present a logic-based system for process specification and composition named WorkflowFM. It relies on an embedding of Classical Linear Logic and the so-called proofs-as-processes paradigm within the proof assistant HOL Light. This enables the specification of abstract processes as logical sequents and their composition via formal proof. The result is systematically translated to an executable workflow with formally verified consistency, rigorous resource accounting, and deadlock freedom. The 3-tiered server/client architecture of WorkflowFM allows multiple concurrent users to interact with the system through a purely diagrammatic interface, while the proof is performed automatically on the server.

Keywords: Process modelling · Workflows · Theorem proving · Classical linear logic

1 Introduction

Flowcharts, UML [19], and BPMN [16] are among the most commonly used languages to describe process workflows. These focus more on providing an expressive and intuitive representation for the user as opposed to an executable and verifiable output. In contrast, process calculi such as the π-calculus [15] have fully formal semantics, allowing an array of possibilities for further analysis and reasoning of the constructed models, but making it harder for non-expert users to model complex real-world systems effectively.

In this work, we introduce WorkflowFM as a tool for formal process modelling and composition. In this, processes are specified using Classical Linear Logic (CLL) [9], composed via formal proof, and then rigorously translated to executable process calculus terms. This is performed within the verified environment of the proof assistant HOL Light [11], thus enabling the development of correct-by-construction workflow models. In addition, WorkflowFM employs a client-server architecture, which enables remote access, and incorporates a fully diagrammatic user interface at the client side. These allow users to harness the reasoning power of WorkflowFM and its systematic approach to formal process

© Springer International Publishing AG 2017
L. de Moura (Ed.): CADE 2017, LNAI 10395, pp. 357–370, 2017.
DOI: 10.1007/978-3-319-63046-5_22

modelling in an inuitive way and without the need for expertise in logic or theorem proving. WorkflowFM is actively being used to model healthcare processes and patient pathways in collaboration with a number of clinical teams [2,17,18].

2 Logic-Based Process Modelling

We begin the description of WorkflowFM by breaking it down to its theoretical foundations, including the proofs-as-processes paradigm, CLL as a process specification language, logical inference for rigorous process composition, the automation required to facilitate workflow development, and the employed diagrammatic visualisation.

2.1 The Proofs-as-processes Paradigm

The proofs-as-processes paradigm [1,3] involves a mapping between CLL proofs and process calculus terms, similar to the Curry-Howard correspondence [12] between intuitionistic logic proofs and the λ-calculus. Bellin and Scott analyse this mapping by giving a corresponding π-calculus term for the conclusion of each of the CLL inference rules. As the inference rules are used in a CLL proof, a π-calculus term corresponding to that proof is built based on these mappings. At the end of the proof, it is guaranteed that applying the possible reductions in the resulting π-calculus term corresponds to the process of cut-elimination in the proof. This means that the cut-free version of the proof corresponds to an equivalent π-calculus term that cannot be reduced further. As a result, since π-calculus reductions correspond to process communications, any π-calculus process that corresponds to a CLL proof is inherently free of livelocks and deadlocks.

In this paper, we focus on the logical specification of processes and their compositions and do not examine the theory and mechanics of proofs-as-processes so that we can demonstrate the reasoning capabilities of WorkflowFM in a more easily understandable and succinct way. However, it is worth noting that the proofs-as-processes paradigm unlocks the potential for both rigorous and pragmatic process modelling. On the one hand, π-calculus workflows generated via CLL proofs are correct-by-construction with respect to type correctness, resource accounting, and deadlock freedom (see Sect. 2.3). On the other hand, the extracted π-calculus workflow is executable, which offers an array of possibilities for further qualitative and quantitative analysis, e.g. through simulation and model checking, and actual deployment. For example, we are developing a simulation engine for parallel π-calculus workflows, focusing on the management of persistent resources, such as measuring clinician and nurse workload, delays due to staff and equipment availability, among other metrics.

2.2 Process Specification Using Linear Logic

In Linear Logic, as proposed by Girard [9], the emphasis is not only on the truth of a statement, but also on formulas that represent resources. For example, in order to achieve a proof, formulas cannot be copied or deleted (no weakening or contraction), but rather must be *consumed* as resources.

The current work uses the multiplicative additive fragment of propositional CLL without units (MALL), which allows enough expressiveness for simple processes while keeping the reasoning complexity at a manageable level. More specifically, we use a one-sided sequent calculus version of MALL [21]. This simplifies the process specifications and reduces the number of inference rules, which can make automated proof search more efficient.

In this particular version of MALL, linear negation $(\cdot^{\perp})$ is defined as a syntactic operator, so that, for example, both A and $A^{\perp}$ are considered atomic formulas. In addition, de Morgan style equations (e.g. $(A \otimes B)^{\perp} \equiv A^{\perp} \,\mathbin{⅋}\, B^{\perp}$ and $(A \oplus B)^{\perp} \equiv A^{\perp} \& B^{\perp})$ are defined for linear negation (rather than inference rules). These equivalence equations demonstrate a symmetry in CLL where each operator has a dual. This duality can be exploited in order to represent the information flow of the corresponding resources [3]. We choose to treat negated literals, multiplicative disjunction $(⅋)$, and additive conjunction $(\&)$ as **inputs**, and positive literals, multiplicative conjunction $(\otimes)$, and additive disjunction $(\oplus)$ as **outputs**.

Based on this distinction, the semantics of the CLL operators can be given an intuitive interpretation where propositions correspond to resources:

- Multiplicative conjunction or the *tensor* operator $(A \otimes B)$ indicates a simultaneous or parallel output of A and B.
- Additive disjunction or the *plus* operator $(A \oplus B)$ indicates that either of A or B are produced but not both. When representing processes, additive disjunction can be used to indicate alternative outputs, including exceptions.
- Multiplicative disjunction or the *par* operator $(A \,⅋\, B)$ is the dual of multiplicative conjunction and represents simultaneous or parallel input.
- Additive conjunction or the *with* operator $(A \& B)$, can similarly be interpreted as the dual of additive disjunction, i.e. the representation of optional input.

As an example, based on this interpretation, a process with inputs A and B and outputs C and D can be specified by the CLL sequent $\vdash A^{\perp}, B^{\perp}, C \otimes D$.

In order for CLL sequents to represent meaningful specifications of processes, we impose some restrictions in their form. More specifically, each formula in the sequent can only consist of inputs (negative literals, $⅋$, and $\&$) or outputs (positive literals, $\otimes$, and $\oplus$). Moreover, we only allow a single (potentially composite) output formula[1]. We also remark that each CLL specification has a corresponding process-calculus specification based on the proofs-as-processes paradigm.

---

[1] The subtle reason for this restriction is that the cut rule (corresponding to a sequential composition of processes) allows only a single formula to be cut (connected) between 2 processes.

2.3 Composition via Proof

So far, we have described how CLL sequents (under some well-formedness limitations) correspond to specifications of processes. Naturally, the CLL inference rules can be applied to sequents in ways that correspond to rigorous transformation and composition of processes.

The inference rules of our selected version of CLL are presented in Fig. 1.

$$\frac{}{\vdash A,\, A^{\perp}}\; Id \qquad\qquad \frac{\vdash \Gamma,\, C \quad \vdash \Delta,\, C^{\perp}}{\vdash \Gamma,\, \Delta}\; Cut$$

$$\frac{\vdash \Gamma,\, A \quad \vdash \Delta,\, B}{\vdash \Gamma,\, \Delta,\, A \otimes B}\; \otimes \qquad\qquad \frac{\vdash \Gamma,\, A,\, B}{\vdash \Gamma,\, A \,⅋\, B}\; ⅋$$

$$\frac{\vdash \Gamma,\, A}{\vdash \Gamma,\, A \oplus B}\; \oplus_L \qquad \frac{\vdash \Gamma,\, B}{\vdash \Gamma,\, A \oplus B}\; \oplus_R \qquad \frac{\vdash \Gamma,\, A \quad \vdash \Gamma,\, B}{\vdash \Gamma,\, A \,\&\, B}\; \&$$

Fig. 1. The one-sided sequent calculus versions of the CLL inference rules.

Each rule has an intuitive correspondence to a process transformation (unary rules) or composition (binary rules) that we describe next.

- **Id** (Identity): This axiom introduces a process that receives some resource and immediately sends it forward. Such a process is known as an *axiom-buffer*.
- $\otimes$: This composes two processes *in parallel* (to yield a single composite, parallel output).
- $⅋$: This rule combines two inputs of a process into a single, parallel input.
- $\oplus$: This transforms the output of a process by adding an alternative output (which is never produced in practice).
- $\&$: This rule composes two processes *conditionally*. One input from each process becomes an option in a new, composite input. Either of the two original processes will be executed depending on which option is provided at runtime.
- **Cut**: The *Cut* rule composes two processes *sequentially*. The output of one process is connected to the matching input of another.

We can create complex process compositions in a rigorous way by applying combinations of these primitive rules. The properties of CLL and the proofs-as-processes paradigm provide the following key guarantees of correctness for any composite process we construct in this way:

1. Resources are consistently matched together. Processes that do not match are never connected.
2. Resources are always accounted for systematically, since no contraction or weakening is allowed.
3. The underlying *process-calculus* specification corresponding to the construction is free of deadlocks and livelocks.

2.4   Automation

Constructing meaningful process compositions usually requires the application of a large number of primitive steps using the CLL inference rules. This can be impractical, especially for a system that aspires to have users who may not be familiar with CLL or theorem proving more generally. For this reason, we developed 3 high-level automated procedures that perform the necessary proof steps to achieve basic compositions between 2 processes in an intuitive way. We call these procedures composition *actions*, and they are introduced as follows:

- The TENSOR action performs a *parallel* composition. Given 2 processes, it uses the $\otimes$ rule to compose them so that they are executed and provide their outputs in parallel.
- The WITH action performs a *conditional* composition. Given 2 processes P and Q, it requires a selected input $A^\perp$ from P and a selected input $B^\perp$ of Q. It then makes use of the & rule to construct a composite process with input $(A \oplus B)^\perp$. In this, if A is provided at runtime then P is executed, otherwise if B is provided then Q is executed.
- The JOIN action composes 2 given processes P and Q *sequentially*. It requires a selected subterm of the output of P and a *matching* subterm of an input of Q. For example, if P has output $A \otimes B$ and Q has an input $(C \oplus A)^\perp$ then the user can select the left branch A of the output and the matching right branch A of the input. It then makes use of the Cut rule to construct a composite process where P is executed first, its output A is fed to Q and then Q is executed.

These implemented actions go well-beyond the limited capabilities of their respective main inference rules ($\otimes$ rule, & rule, and Cut rule). In non-trivial cases, a number of inference rules is applied to first transform the processes into a form that is appropriate for use with the main composition rule. It is often the case, particularly in the JOIN action, that resources that cannot be handled directly by the involved processes (e.g. by the receiving process in a sequential composition) are automatically *buffered* with the use of axiom-buffers (introduced in Sect. 2.3).

In addition, we have implemented and integrated an automated CLL prover, based on proof strategies developed by Tammet [20], so that the system can handle cases where complex formulae need to be rearranged in particular ways. For example, the formula $A \otimes B$ can be rearranged to $B \otimes A$ by automatically proving the lemma $\vdash (A \otimes B)^\perp, B \otimes A$. Note that, from the process specification perspective, $A \otimes B$ and $B \otimes A$ have the equivalent intuitive interpretation of 2 parallel outputs A and B. However, at the rigorous level of the embedded logic, this reasoning needs to be performed explicitly (yet remain hidden from the user).

The resulting composite processes from each of the 3 actions have their own CLL and process calculus (corresponding to the CLL proof) specifications. These can be used as building blocks for further complex, action-based compositions.

2.5   Visualisation

Although the CLL and process specifications of a constructed composite process describe its structure in a complete and verified way, they may be difficult to grasp by the uninitiated. Their syntax can be difficult to follow, especially for large compositions, even for experts in logic and process algebras.

For this reason, we developed a visual representation and construction that aims to capture the intuitive interpretation of the logical specification and inference steps. The user can then develop correct-by-construction workflows by interacting with the system visually (see Sect. 4.3) without the need for expertise in CLL or theorem proving.

The representation involves a simple left-to-right, labelled box notation to represent processes. Dangling edges stand for the inputs and outputs of a process, with solid lines representing parallel resources (i.e.types connected by $\otimes$, $\bindnasrepma$, or separate inputs) while dashed lines represent optional resources (i.e.types connected by $\oplus$ or $\&$) as shown in the examples of Fig. 2.

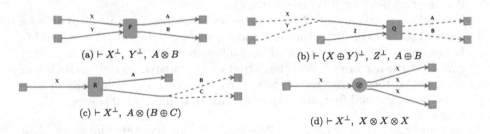

(a) $\vdash X^{\perp}, Y^{\perp}, A \otimes B$

(b) $\vdash (X \oplus Y)^{\perp}, Z^{\perp}, A \oplus B$

(c) $\vdash X^{\perp}, A \otimes (B \oplus C)$

(d) $\vdash X^{\perp}, X \otimes X \otimes X$

Fig. 2. Examples of specifications of atomic processes in CLL and their corresponding visualisations.

It is worth noting the special round node used for the representation of the so-called *copy nodes* (see Fig. 2d). These are processes that explicitly replicate a resource (assuming this is possible) since this is not allowed to happen within CLL but may be desirable in some scenarios (e.g.creating a copy of an electronic document).

As processes are composed by clicking on edges and boxes to form complex workflows, we adopt a couple of additional visual constructs. Firstly, some resources that are not explicitly handled by a particular process, but rather buffered through an axiom-buffer, are represented using grey edges. Secondly, the output of a composition, as constructed through rigorous CLL reasoning, may be a complex combination of the resources (inputs and outputs) of the component processes. In order to represent these combinations visually, we use triangular nodes that are similar to the decision/merge ones of UML and the gateways of BPMN (see Fig. 3 of Sect. 3 for an example).

Mapping logical composition steps to such a diagrammatic representation is non-trivial because of the complexity and size of the generated proofs and the particularities of CLL. In order to accurately represent the constructed workflow, the logical engine records important meta-data during each proof step (see Sect. 4.4 for more details).

3   Example

In order to demonstrate the capabilities of our system and the challenges faced, let us consider a hypothetical example from the healthcare domain. Assume a process `DeliverDrug` with 3 inputs: *Patient* (a resource containing the patient information), *Dosage* (a resource containing information about the drug dosage), and *NurseTime* (a number of allocated hours for a nurse to deliver the drug). Also assume this process can have 2 alternative outcomes: *Treated* in the case where the treatment was successful **or** *Failed* in the case where the drug delivery had no effect. Let us also introduce the process `Reassess`, during which a clinician reassesses the patient if the drug delivery failed. Its inputs are *Failed* and *ClinTime* (corresponding to the reserved clinical time for this task) and the output is *Reassessed*. In CLL, the 2 processes have the following specifications:

$$\vdash Patient^{\perp},\ Dosage^{\perp},\ NurseTime^{\perp},\ Treated \oplus Failed$$

$$\vdash Failed^{\perp},\ ClinTime^{\perp},\ Reassessed$$

We now want to compose the 2 processes into a composite one where the drug failure is handled by `Reassess`. We can use the `JOIN` action, selecting the optional output *Failed* of `DeliverDrug` and the matching input *Failed*$^{\perp}$ of `Reassess`. The reasoner will automatically connect the 2 processes in sequence by generating the following proof:

$$\cfrac{\cfrac{\cfrac{\vdash Treated^{\perp},\ Treated}{}\ Id \quad \cfrac{\vdash ClinTime^{\perp},\ ClinTime}{}\ Id}{\vdash Treated^{\perp},\ ClinTime^{\perp},\ Treated \otimes ClinTime}\ \otimes}{\vdash Treated^{\perp},\ ClinTime^{\perp},\ (Treated \otimes ClinTime) \oplus Reassessed}\ \oplus L \qquad (1)$$

$$\cfrac{\cfrac{\cfrac{\vdash Failed^{\perp},\ ClinTime^{\perp},\ Reassessed}{}\ Reassess}{(1)\quad \vdash Failed^{\perp},\ ClinTime^{\perp},\ (Treated \otimes ClinTime) \oplus Reassessed}\ \oplus R}{\vdash(Treated \oplus Failed)^{\perp},\ ClinTime^{\perp},\ (Treated \otimes ClinTime) \oplus Reassessed}\ \& \qquad (2)$$

$$\cfrac{\cfrac{\vdash Patient^{\perp},\ Dosage^{\perp},\ NurseTime^{\perp},\ Treated \oplus Failed}{}\ DeliverDrug \qquad (2)}{\vdash Patient^{\perp},\ Dosage^{\perp},\ NurseTime^{\perp},\ ClinTime^{\perp},\ (Treated \otimes ClinTime) \oplus Reassessed}\ Cut \qquad (3)$$

The result of this composition proof demonstrates the systematic resource tracking accomplished through the CLL rules. A human relying on the textual description of the processes might intuitively think that the composition of

DeliverDrug and Reassess can have 2 possible outcomes: either the patient was treated by the drug (*Treated*) or they were reassessed (*Reassessed*). However, the outcome of the formal composition tells a slightly different story. The output (*Treated*⊗*ClinTime*)⊕*Reassessed* indicates that, in the case where the patient was treated (*Treated*) there was also some unused clinical time (*ClinTime*) left over (which would have been used for reassessment in the case of failure).

Systematically accounting for such unused resources is non-trivial, especially considering larger workflows with tens or hundreds of processes and many different outcomes. The CLL inference rules enforce this by default and the proof reflects the level of reasoning required to achieve this. Part (1) in the proof is essentially dedicated to constructing a buffer for *Treated* and *ClinTime* as they remain unused in one of the 2 optional cases. The reasoner is capable of constructing such buffers automatically and infer which resources can be used directly or need to be buffered.

The effort to visualise such compositions adds another layer of complexity to the system. The visualisation of this particular example is shown in Fig. 3. In this case, the resources found in the output (*Treated*⊗*ClinTime*)⊕*Reassessed* come from 2 different sources: *Treated* is an output of DeliverDrug, whereas *ClinTime* and *Reassessed* are associated with Reassess. These resources are combined in the final output in a seemingly arbitrary way. Therefore, we are unable to directly connect each output edge to its original source, which is usually the case in other workflow languages. This is the reason behind the introduction of the triangle node as a "terminator" node that performs this combination of resources.

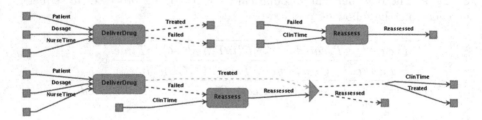

Fig. 3. The visualisation of the DeliverDrug and Reassess processes (top) and their sequential composition using JOIN (bottom).

In addition, *ClinTime* is *not* an output of Reassess, but an unused input that is buffered in one of the two cases. This makes it hard to track where *ClinTime* came from in the final output. One would be inclined to draw a grey *ClinTime* edge from Reassess to the triangle node, but this might give an erroneous impression that *ClinTime* is an output of Reassess (which could be the case in a different situation). For this reason, we have chosen not to display such an edge.

Our design decisions about the visualisation are still evolving as we carry out more case-studies and endeavour to make the interface as intuitive and straightforward as possible without compromising the correspondence with the logical underpinnings.

4   Architecture

WorkflowFM adopts a server-client architecture consisting of 3 tiers: the reasoner, the server, and the client. Each of the 3 components can be deployed separately and can be connected to each other remotely. More specifically, the reasoner connects to the server through a (local or remote) data pipe (e.g. via an SSH tunnel). A client can then connect to the server via a raw socket. The server effectively screens and relays JSON commands from the client to the reasoner and returns the response from the reasoner in the same way. Moreover, the server may connect with multiple, independent reasoners and distribute the commands between them. Multiple clients can also connect to the server and issue commands concurrently.

This architecture has several advantages over what would otherwise be a single user, stand-alone system (which is the case for most interactive theorem proving systems currently in existence), such as:

- It allows access through a lightweight, platform independent Java client. HOL Light has multiple system dependencies and can be difficult to install, setup, and run for a non-expert user. In contrast, WorkflowFM's HOL Light based reasoner can be installed and maintained by experts and can remain live and always online.
- Allowing multiple concurrent users on the server makes WorkflowFM potentially more scalable and accessible by a larger array of users.
- Having multiple connected reasoners allows us to process multiple tasks in parallel, thus improving responsiveness and efficiency.
- The reasoner can be upgraded without requiring a re-install at the client end. In this way, we can add new and improved functionality to the active reasoners incrementally, while the system remains online.

The overall system architecture coupled with the stacked architecture of the reasoner and the client are visualised in Fig. 4. We explain the structure and functionality of each component next.

4.1   The Reasoner

The reasoner is implemented on top of the interactive proof assistant HOL Light [11], which operates at the OCaml toplevel and provides a flexible, trustworthy environment that conveniently marries theorem proving and programming. Note that, although theorem proving systems for linear logic already exist (e.g. Forum [14] and LINK [10]), we aimed to implement WorkflowFM in a fully formal, trustworthy environment, with an expressive enough meta-logic to support the proofs-as-processes paradigm. HOL Light is a prime example of such an environment.

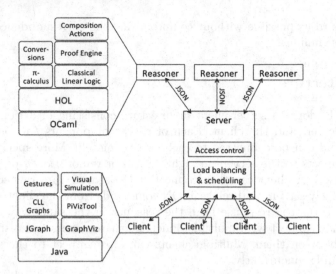

Fig. 4. The 3-tiered server-client architecture of WorkflowFM.

More specifically we have deeply embedded [5] the following within the Higher Order Logic setting of HOL Light:

1. The syntax (including primitive name binding and substitution) of the π-calculus.
2. The syntax of CLL formulae.
3. The CLL inference rules including their process calculus correspondences.

Given these embeddings, we developed the necessary proof infrastructure to apply the CLL inference rules for both forward and backward inference and the automated actions mentioned in Sect. 2.4.

The reasoner can be used at two levels. On the one hand, it is integrated in the HOL Light proof engine so that each composition action can be applied as a proof tactic. On the other hand, it has its own independent interface that relies on JSON data structures (see Sect. 4.4).

4.2   The Server

The server, currently written in Java, acts as an intermediate level between the reasoner and the client. Its primary function is to enable the management of multiple clients and multiple reasoners.

Firstly, it is able to connect to multiple instances of the reasoner, both locally and remotely. Thus, in cases where multiple users submit multiple commands at the same time, it can distribute the load among all connected reasoners. This is particularly important when considering that some reasoning tasks, especially for large or complex compositions, may take significant time (up to a few minutes). Moreover, this is facilitated by the fact that the reasoner is stateless, in the sense that it does not maintain any information about the state or context of the clients. In addition, it caches the results returned by the connected reasoners for each issued command.

Secondly, it manages multiple connections from clients. It exposes an open public socket that can receive connections and manages them, e.g. by mapping reasoner responses to the appropriate connection, handling timeouts and reconnections, and logging traffic and miscellaneous statistics.

4.3 The Client

The client is a Java-based graphical user interface, developed using the JGraph library [13], that renders the process specifications in the diagrammatic way described in Sect. 2.5.

Additionally, the client allows the construction of such process specifications and compositions via interactive gestures. Atomic process specifications are constructed in a visual way, starting from a process with one input and one output. The user augments this basic process specification e.g. by adding new resources, creating new types of branches (start an $\oplus$ branch in a $\otimes$ node and vice-versa), renaming resources and so on, via mouse-driven clicks.

Once the user is happy with the visual representation of the process they wish to construct, the specification is sent to the reasoner for verification. All such validated specifications (which include both the CLL and the process-calculus components) are stored in a list in the interface. From there they can be picked and composed in the current visual *workspace* using mouse gestures that implement the TENSOR, WITH and JOIN actions.

The composition results returned by the reasoner are stored as intermediate processes in their corresponding workspace. We note here that the WorkflowFM interface provides a multi-tabbed workspace environment that enables the user to develop different composition scenarios simultaneously without their respective intermediate steps interfering. Also note that in order to draw accurate and unambiguous representations of the composed workflow, the client expects some meta-data from the reasoner, as explained in more detail in Sect. 4.4.

Overall, the user-interface is driven by mouse gestures performed by the user and captured by handlers based on the principles of event-driven programming [8]. Through these, each gesture initiates a proof task in the reasoner resulting in a verified response. This can be thought of as *event-driven theorem proving*.

As previously mentioned, the reasoner itself is stateless and therefore the client is fully responsible for storing its state. More specifically, the client stores the atomic processes, stored composite processes and the composition actions required to construct them, and the workspaces with the intermediate compositions performed in each one.

Since the state is stored locally, it can potentially be modified to enable the maintenance of the constructed models. For example, the user can rename processes or resources, modify atomic process specifications, or reload the composition steps for a composite process in order to make alterations. However, such modifications may break the correctness of the corresponding process specification, as well as the specifications of all composite processes that use this process as a component. Thus, the client flags all possibly affected processes and forces the user to *verify* them again through the reasoner in order to maintain the various guarantees of correctness.

Finally, the client provides additional functionality, such as the creation of screenshots and the visual simulation of process calculus terms (as returned by the reasoner) using the PiVizTool [4] and GraphViz [7].

4.4 Data Structures

The 3 components of WorkflowFM communicate using JSON messages sharing a common schema. This allows them to be decoupled and thus developed and maintained independently. In a nutshell, the JSON data schema describes the following structures:

- Resources;
- Channels and process-calculus specifications;
- Composition actions with the process names and selected resources as arguments;
- Processes, each described as a record with fields describing (among other things) its name, input resources (paired with its process calculus channel), CLL specification, and so on;
- A composition state that records buffered resources, input and output provenance entries, etc. to ensure the appropriate visualisation of the connections between the processes;
- Commands that were issued to the reasoner along with their arguments;
- Responses from the reasoner to be interpreted by the client.

It is worth noting that the JSON data structures already provide a significant level of abstraction from the mechanics of the theorem proving backend. Our aim was to construct an API that incorporates all the necessary data (for both the reasoner and the client), but requires limited to no experience with logic or theorem proving.

5   Conclusion

In summary, WorkflowFM is a logic-based framework for workflow modelling. It employs an event-driven theorem proving approach where mouse gestures on graphs in the GUI trigger custom-built, automated proof procedures. This aims to alleviate much of the complexity inherent to interactive theorem proving in this domain. Its architecture consists of 3 distinct components. The reasoner, implemented within the proof assistant HOL Light, relies on the proofs-as-processes paradigm to allow formal process specification in CLL and correct-by-construction process composition through logical inference. The Java client visualises the CLL workflows and enables an intuitive user interaction. The server acts as a relay between multiple reasoners and multiple clients.

It is worth remarking that some of the other salient aspects of the system have not been covered in the current paper due to space limitations. These include the generation of executable code for the composed workflows and the ability to accommodate more advanced process calculus translations of CLL (e.g. with session types [6] or with the process calculus *CP* [22]).

Our plans for future work include efficiency optimisations for the reasoner, such as lemma caching for commonly proven lemmas, improved authentication, user identification, access control, and security for the server, and alternative implementations of the client, such as web or mobile applications. We are also planning to perform a more systematic evaluation of the usability and scalability of the system using both qualitative (such as demos and surveys involving real users) and quantitative (simulation and analysis of usage data) methods.

We believe WorkflowFM is a flexible system that successfully hides the complexity and formality of its theorem proving foundations. In so doing, it makes an inherently complicated process lightweight and approachable by non-expert users. As a result, WorkflowFM is proving to be an effective tool for general purpose process modelling, with guaranteed levels of consistency and resource accounting not currently achievable in other workflow tools.

Acknowledgements. This research is supported by the following EPSRC grants: The Integration and Interaction of Multiple Mathematical Reasoning Processes EP/N014758/1, SOCIAM: The Theory and Practice of Social Machines EP/J017728/1, and ProofPeer: Collaborative Theorem Proving EP/L011794/1.

References

1. Abramsky, S.: Proofs as processes. Theoret. Comput. Sci. **135**(1), 5–9 (1994)
2. Alexandru, C., Clutterbuck, D., Papapanagiotou, P., Fleuriot, J., Manataki, A.: A Step Towards the Standardisation of HIV Care Practices, November 2016
3. Bellin, G., Scott, P.: On the π-calculus and linear logic. TCS **135**(1), 11–65 (1994)
4. Bog, A., Puhlmann, F.: A tool for the simulation of π-calculus systems. Tech. rep., Open.BPM, Geschäftsprozessmanagement mit Open Source-Technologien, Hamburg, Germany (2006)
5. Boulton, R.J., Gordon, A.D., Gordon, M.J.C., Harrison, J., Herbert, J., Tassel, J.V.: Experience with embedding hardware description languages in HOL. In: Stavridou, V., Melham, T.F., Boute, R.T. (eds.) TPCD. IFIP Transactions, vol. A-10, pp. 129–156. North-Holland (1992)
6. Caires, L., Pfenning, F.: Session types as intuitionistic linear propositions. In: Gastin, P., Laroussinie, F. (eds.) CONCUR 2010. LNCS, vol. 6269, pp. 222–236. Springer, Heidelberg (2010). doi:10.1007/978-3-642-15375-4_16
7. Ellson, J., Gansner, E., Koutsofios, L., North, S.C., Woodhull, G.: Graphviz— open source graph drawing tools. In: Mutzel, P., Jünger, M., Leipert, S. (eds.) GD 2001. LNCS, vol. 2265, pp. 483–484. Springer, Heidelberg (2002). doi:10.1007/3-540-45848-4_57
8. Ferg, S.: Event-Driven Programming: Introduction, Tutorial, History (2016). http://eventdrivenpgm.sourceforge.net/

9. Girard, J.Y.: Linear logic: its syntax and semantics. In: Girard, J.Y., Lafont, Y., Regnier, L. (eds.) Advances in Linear Logic, vol. 222. London Mathematical Society Lecture Notes Series. Cambridge University Press (1995), http://iml.univ-mrs.fr/~girard/Synsem.pdf.gz

10. Habert, L., Notin, J.-M., Galmiche, D.: LINK: a proof environment based on proof nets. In: Egly, U., Fermüller, C.G. (eds.) TABLEAUX 2002. LNCS, vol. 2381, pp. 330–334. Springer, Heidelberg (2002). doi:10.1007/3-540-45616-3_23

11. Harrison, J.: HOL light: a tutorial introduction. In: Srivas, M., Camilleri, A. (eds.) FMCAD 1996. LNCS, vol. 1166, pp. 265–269. Springer, Heidelberg (1996). doi:10.1007/BFb0031814

12. Howard, W.A.: The formulas-as-types notion of construction. In: Seldin, J.P., Hindley, J.R. (eds.) To H. B. Curry: Essays on Combinatory Logic, Lambda Calculus, and Formalism, pp. 479–490. Academic Press (1980)

13. JGraph Ltd: The JGraph homepage (2013). http://www.jgraph.com/

14. Miller, D.: Forum: a multiple-conclusion specification logic. TCS **165**(1), 201–232 (1996)

15. Milner, R.: Communicating and Mobile Systems: The π-Calculus. Cambridge University Press, Cambridge (1999)

16. Object Management Group: Business Process Model and Notation (BPMN), version 2.0 (2011). http://www.omg.org/spec/BPMN/2.0/PDF

17. Papapanagiotou, P., Fleuriot, J.: Formal verification of collaboration patterns in healthcare. Behav. Inf. Technol. **33**(12), 1278–1293 (2014)

18. Papapanagiotou, P., Fleuriot, J.: Modelling and implementation of correct by construction healthcare workflows. In: Fournier, F., Mendling, J. (eds.) BPM 2014. LNBIP, vol. 202, pp. 28–39. Springer, Cham (2015). doi:10.1007/978-3-319-15895-2_3

19. Rumbaugh, J., Jacobson, I., Booch, G.: The Unified Modelling Language User Guide. Addison-Wesley (1999)

20. Tammet, T.: Proof strategies in linear logic. J. Autom. Reasoning **12**(3), 273–304 (1994)

21. Troelstra, A.S.: Lectures on Linear Logic. CSLI Lecture Notes, vol. 29, Stanford (1992)

22. Wadler, P.: Propositions as sessions. In: Proceedings of the 17th ACM SIGPLAN International Conference on Functional Programming, pp. 273–286. ACM (2012)

DepQBF 6.0: A Search-Based QBF Solver Beyond Traditional QCDCL

Florian Lonsing[(✉)] and Uwe Egly

Knowledge-Based Systems Group, Vienna University of Technology, Vienna, Austria
{florian.lonsing,uwe.egly}@tuwien.ac.at

Abstract. We present the latest major release version 6.0 of the *quantified Boolean formula (QBF)* solver DepQBF, which is based on *QCDCL*. QCDCL is an extension of the *conflict-driven clause learning (CDCL)* paradigm implemented in state of the art propositional satisfiability (SAT) solvers. The *Q-resolution calculus (QRES)* is a QBF proof system which underlies QCDCL. QCDCL solvers can produce QRES proofs of QBFs in *prenex conjunctive normal form (PCNF)* as a byproduct of the solving process. In contrast to traditional QCDCL based on QRES, DepQBF 6.0 implements a variant of QCDCL which is based on a generalization of QRES. This generalization is due to a set of additional axioms and leaves the original Q-resolution rules unchanged. The generalization of QRES enables QCDCL to potentially produce exponentially shorter proofs than the traditional variant. We present an overview of the features implemented in DepQBF and report on experimental results which demonstrate the effectiveness of generalized QRES in QCDCL.

1 Introduction

Propositional satisfiability (SAT) solvers based on *conflict-driven clause learning (CDCL)* [44] implement a combination of the DPLL algorithm [11] and propositional *resolution* [41] to derive *learned clauses* from a CNF to be solved.

CDCL has been extended to solve *quantified Boolean formulas (QBFs)* [20], resulting in the *QCDCL* approach [14,24,49]. The logic of QBFs allows for explicit universal and existential quantification of propositional variables. As a consequence, the satisfiability problem of QBFs is PSPACE-complete.

In contrast to SAT solving, where CDCL is the dominant solving paradigm in practice, QCDCL is complemented by *variable expansion* [1,6]. This approach successively eliminates variables from a QBF until it reduces to either true or false. Many modern solvers (e.g. [17,19,40]) implement expansion by *counterexample guided abstraction refinement (CEGAR)* [10].

The *Q-resolution calculus (QRES)* [14,21,24,49] is a QBF proof system that underlies QCDCL in a way that is analogous to propositional resolution in CDCL. The empty clause is derivable from a PCNF ψ by QRES iff ψ is unsatisfiable. According to QBF proof complexity, there is an exponential separation

---

Supported by the Austrian Science Fund (FWF) under grant S11409-N23.

L. de Moura (Ed.): CADE 2017, LNAI 10395, pp. 371–384, 2017.
DOI: 10.1007/978-3-319-63046-5_23

between the sizes of proofs that variable expansion and Q-resolution can produce for certain QBFs [5,18]. This theoretical result suggests to combine such orthogonal proof systems in QBF solvers to leverage their individual strengths.

As a first step towards a solver framework that allows for the combination of QBF proof systems in a systematic way, we present the latest major release version 6.0 of the QCDCL solver DepQBF.[1] In contrast to traditional QCDCL based on QRES [14,21,24,49], DepQBF 6.0 implements a variant of QCDCL that relies on a generalization of QRES. This generalization is due to a set of new axioms added to QRES [32]. In practice, derivations made by the added axioms in QCDCL are based on *arbitrary* QBF proof systems. As a consequence, when applying proof systems that are orthogonal to Q-resolution, the generalization of QRES via the new axioms enables QCDCL as implemented in DepQBF 6.0 to potentially produce exponentially shorter proofs than traditional QCDCL.

We report on experiments where we compare DepQBF 6.0 to state of the art QBF solvers. Experimental results demonstrate the effectiveness of generalized QRES in QCDCL. Additionally, we briefly summarize the evolution of DepQBF since the first version 0.1 [26]. We relate the features that were added to the different versions of DepQBF over time to the enhanced variant of QCDCL implemented in DepQBF 6.0.

2 Preliminaries

A QBF $\psi := \Pi.\phi$ in *prenex conjunctive normal form (PCNF)* consists of a *quantifier prefix* $\Pi := Q_1 X_1 \ldots Q_n X_n$ and a CNF ϕ not containing tautological clauses. The CNF ϕ is defined over the propositional variables $X_1 \cup \ldots \cup X_n$ that appear in Π. The variable sets X_i are pairwise disjoint and $Q_i \neq Q_{i+1}$ for $Q_i \in \{\forall, \exists\}$. QBFs $\psi := \Pi.\phi$ in *prenex disjunctive normal form (PDNF)* are defined analogously to PCNFs, where ϕ is a DNF consisting of *cubes*. A cube is a conjunction of literals. The *quantifier* $Q(\Pi, l)$ of a literal l is Q_i if the variable $\mathsf{var}(l)$ of l appears in X_i. If $Q(\Pi, l) = Q_i$ and $Q(\Pi, k) = Q_j$, then $l \leq_\Pi k$ iff $i \leq j$.

An *assignment* A maps variables of a QBF $\Pi.\phi$ to truth values *true* ($\top$) and *false* ($\bot$). We represent $A = \{l_1, \ldots, l_n\}$ as a set of literals such that if a variable x is assigned *true* (*false*) then $l_i \in A$ with $l_i = x$ ($l_i = \bar{x}$), where $\bar{x}$ is the negation of x. Further, $\mathsf{var}(l_i) \neq \mathsf{var}(l_j)$ for any $l_i, l_j \in A$ with $i \neq j$.

The PCNF ψ *under assignment* A, written as $\psi[A]$, is the PCNF obtained from ψ in which for all $l \in A$, all clauses containing l are removed, all occurrences of $\bar{l}$ are deleted, and $\mathsf{var}(l)$ is removed from the prefix. If the CNF of $\psi[A]$ is empty (respectively, contains the empty clause $\emptyset$), then it is satisfied (falsified) by A and A is a *satisfying (falsifying)* assignment, written as $\psi[A] = \top$ ($\psi[A] = \bot$). A *PDNF* ψ *under an assignment* A and an *empty cube* are defined in a way dual to PCNFs and empty clauses. A QBF $\Pi.\phi$ with $Q_1 = \exists$ ($Q_1 = \forall$) is satisfiable iff, for $x \in X_1$, $\Pi.\phi[\{x\}]$ or (and) $\Pi.\phi[\{\bar{x}\}]$ is satisfiable. Two QBFs ψ and ψ' are *satisfiability-equivalent* ($\psi \equiv_{sat} \psi'$), iff ψ is satisfiable whenever ψ' is satisfiable.

---

[1] DepQBF is licensed under GPLv3: http://lonsing.github.io/depqbf/.

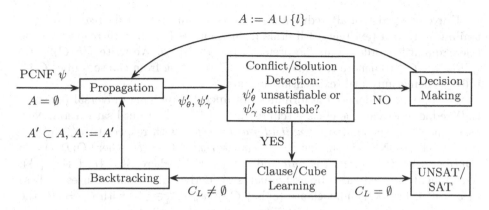

Fig. 1. Workflow of the variant of QCDCL implemented in DepQBF 6.0 that relies on a generalization of the Q-resolution calculus (QRES) (figure adapted from [32]).

3   QCDCL and the Generalized Q-Resolution Calculus

In the following, we present the variant of QCDCL implemented in DepQBF 6.0 that relies on a generalization of the Q-resolution calculus (QRES). We illustrate the workflow of that variant in Fig. 1.

In general, QCDCL is based on the successive generation of assignments that guide the application of the inference rules of QRES to derive *learned clauses* and *cubes* from a given input PCNF $\psi = \Pi.\phi$. Learned cubes are dual to clauses. While learned clauses represent assignments that falsify the CNF ϕ of ψ, learned cubes represent assignments that satisfy ϕ. The empty cube is derivable from a PCNF ψ by QRES iff ψ is satisfiable. Based on our presentation of the rules of QRES we illustrate the differences between traditional QCDCL and the variant implemented in DepQBF 6.0.

A QCDCL solver maintains a PCNF $\theta = \Pi.\theta'$ (PDNF $\gamma = \Pi.\gamma'$) consisting of a CNF θ' (DNF γ') of learned clauses (cubes). The clauses in θ are added conjunctively to ψ to obtain $\psi_\theta = \Pi.(\phi \wedge (\bigwedge_{C \in \theta'} C))$, and the cubes in γ are added disjunctively to ψ to obtain $\psi_\gamma = \Pi.(\phi \vee (\bigvee_{C \in \gamma'} C))$. It holds that $\psi \equiv_{sat} \psi_\theta$ and $\psi \equiv_{sat} \psi_\gamma$. Initially the current assignment A, the PCNF θ, and PDNF γ are empty. We use the notation C, C', and C_L for both clauses and cubes.

During *propagation*, the formulas ψ_θ and ψ_γ are first simplified under the current assignment A by computing $\psi_\theta[A]$ and $\psi_\gamma[A]$. Then *universal* and *existential* *reduction* is applied to $\psi_\theta[A]$ and to $\psi_\gamma[A]$ based on the following inference rule.

Definition 1 (Reduction [14,21,24,49]). Let $\psi = \Pi.\phi$ be a PCNF.

$$\frac{C \cup \{l\}}{C} \qquad \begin{array}{l} \textit{(1) } C \textit{ is a clause, } Q(\Pi, l) = \forall, \\ \quad l' <_\Pi l \textit{ for all } l' \in C \textit{ with } Q(\Pi, l') = \exists \textit{ or} \\ \textit{(2) } C \textit{ is a cube, } Q(\Pi, l) = \exists, \\ \quad l' <_\Pi l \textit{ for all } l' \in C \textit{ with } Q(\Pi, l') = \forall \end{array} \qquad (red)$$

Universal (existential) reduction of clauses (cubes) by rule *red* eliminates trailing universal (existential) literals from a clause (cube) with respect to the linear quantifier ordering in the prefix of the PCNF ψ. We write $UR(C) = C'$ ($ER(C) = C'$) to denote the clause (cube) C' resulting from clause (cube) C by fully reducing universal (existential) literals.

Let ψ'_θ and ψ'_γ denote the formulas obtained by applying universal (existential) reduction to all the clauses (cubes) in $\psi_\theta[A]$ ($\psi_\gamma[A]$) until saturation. New assignments are generated by *unit literal detection* with respect to ψ'_θ and ψ'_γ. If a PCNF (PDNF) ψ contains a *unit clause (cube)* $C = (l)$, where $Q(\Pi, l) = \exists$ ($Q(\Pi, l) = \forall$), then literal l is *unit* and $\psi \equiv_{sat} \psi[A']$ where $A' = \{l\}$ ($A' = \{\bar{l}\}$). Assignment A is extended by assignments A' derived from unit clauses (cubes) in ψ'_θ (ψ'_γ). For every unit clause (cube) $C' \in \psi'_\theta$ ($C' \in \psi'_\gamma$) with $C' = (l)$, the corresponding assignment $A' := \{l\}$ ($A' := \{\bar{l}\}$) is recorded.

After propagation, in *conflict/solution detection* it is checked whether ψ'_θ is unsatisfiable or whether ψ'_γ is satisfiable (only one of the two cases can occur). To this end, *incomplete* methods are applied. In traditional QCDCL, for example, it is *syntactically* checked if the current assignment A is falsifying or satisfying, i.e., whether ψ'_θ contains the empty clause (i.e., $\psi'_\theta = \bot$) or whether ψ'_γ contains the empty cube (i.e., $\psi'_\gamma = \top$). In DepQBF 6.0, we extend these incomplete syntactic checks to incomplete *semantic* checks based on *arbitrary* QBF decision procedures (proof systems) that are applied to ψ'_θ and ψ'_γ in a resource bounded way.

If neither ψ'_θ is found unsatisfiable nor ψ'_γ is found satisfiable by the incomplete satisfiability checks, then in *decision making* A is extended by heuristically assigning some *decision variable* x from the leftmost quantifier block of $\psi[A]$ ($A := A \cup \{l\}$ where $var(l) = x$), and propagation continues. Assignments by decision making must follow the prefix ordering of ψ, in contrast to assignments by propagation (unit literals), which results in assignments of the following kind.

Definition 2 (QCDCL assignment [25]**).** *Assignments generated by decision making and propagation in QCDCL are called* QCDCL assignments.

If ψ'_θ (ψ'_γ) is found unsatisfiable (satisfiable) in conflict/solution detection then a learned clause (cube) is derived using QRES depending on the incomplete satisfiability checks. In traditional QCDCL, conflict/solution detection relies only on falsifying or satisfying assignments. If $\psi'_\theta = \bot$ then ψ'_θ contains an empty clause $C' = \emptyset$ such that there is a clause $C \in \psi_\theta$ with $C' = UR(C[A])$. Clause C is the *falsified clause* with respect to assignment A. If C appears in the given PCNF ψ then in traditional QRES it is derived trivially by the following axiom.

Definition 3 (Clause Axiom [14,21,24,49]**).** *Let $\psi = \Pi.\phi$ be a PCNF.*

$$\frac{}{C} \quad C \text{ is a clause and } C \in \phi \qquad\qquad (cl\text{-}init)$$

If $\psi'_\theta \neq \bot$ but $\psi'_\gamma = \top$ then either (1) ψ'_γ contains an empty learned cube $C' = \emptyset$ such that there is a cube $C \in \psi_\gamma$ with $C' = ER(C[A])$, or (2) A is a satisfying assignment that satisfies all clauses in ψ'_γ. For case (2), a cube C is derived by the following axiom of traditional QRES (in either case (1) or (2) cube C is the *satisfied cube* with respect to A).

Definition 4 (Cube Axiom [14, 21, 24, 49]**).** *Let* $\psi = \Pi.\phi$ *be a PCNF.*

$$\frac{}{C} \quad A \text{ is an assignment, } \psi[A] = \top, \text{ and } C = (\bigwedge_{l \in A} l) \text{ is a cube} \qquad \text{(cu-init)}$$

DepQBF 6.0 supports the application of *arbitrary* (incomplete) QBF decision procedures (proof systems) in conflict/solution detection and thus generalizes the syntactic checks for falsifying and satisfying assignments in traditional QCDCL.

To check the satisfiability of ψ'_γ, in DepQBF 6.0 we apply a dynamic variant of *blocked clause elimination (QBCE)* [25]. This approach was introduced in version 5.0 of DepQBF. QBCE has been presented as a preprocessing technique to eliminate redundant *blocked clauses* [15, 23] from a PCNF. If all clauses in ψ'_γ are satisfied under A or identified as blocked, then ψ'_γ is determined satisfiable. In our implementation applications of QBCE are tightly integrated in the propagation phase via efficient data structures. Clauses that are blocked are temporarily considered as removed from the formula. Hence such clauses cannot be used to detect unit clauses or empty clauses during propagation.

In addition to dynamic QBCE, we implemented incomplete QBF satisfiability checks based on propositional abstractions of ψ'_θ and ψ'_γ [32], which are solved using an integrated SAT solver. These abstractions are constructed by treating universally quantified literals in the given PCNF ψ in a special way. Propositional abstractions and SAT solving leverage the benefits of techniques like *trivial truth* and *trivial falsity* presented already in early search-based QBF solvers [9]. Additionally, the power of *QU-resolution* [48], which is exponentially stronger than Q-resolution [21] but has not been applied systematically in QCDCL, is harnessed to a certain extent (cf. Example 3 in [32]).

As a simple way of applying a QBF decision procedure that is incomplete by its nature we integrated the preprocessor Bloqqer [15] in DepQBF 6.0. Preprocessing aims at simplifying a formula within a restricted amount of time but might already solve certain formulas (cf. [34]). Among several techniques, Bloqqer applies bounded expansion of universally quantified variables [6, 8]. Hence by integrating Bloqqer in QCDCL we in fact integrate expansion, a QBF proof system that is orthogonal to Q-resolution [5, 18]. Due to usability issues, in the follow-up release version 6.02 of DepQBF we replaced Bloqqer by the expansion based QBF solver Nenofex,[2] which is applied in a resource bounded way.

If ψ'_θ (ψ'_γ) is found unsatisfiable (satisfiable) by an incomplete decision procedure but, unlike above, A is neither falsifying nor satisfying, then a clause (cube) is derived by the following *generalized* axioms of QRES. These axioms are added to QRES and applied in addition to the traditional axioms *cl-init* and *cu-init*.

Definition 5 (Generalized Axioms [32]**).** *Let* $\psi = \Pi.\phi$ *be a PCNF.*

$$\frac{}{C} \quad \begin{array}{l} A \text{ is a QCDCL assignment, } \psi[A] \text{ is unsatisfiable,} \\ \text{and } C = (\bigvee_{l \in A} \bar{l}) \text{ is a clause} \end{array} \qquad \text{(gen-cl-init)}$$

---

[2] https://github.com/lonsing/nenofex.

$$\frac{}{C} \quad \begin{array}{l} A \text{ is a QCDCL assignment, } \psi[A] \text{ is satisfiable,} \\ \text{and } C = (\bigwedge_{l \in A} l) \text{ is a cube} \end{array} \qquad (gen\text{-}cu\text{-}init)$$

Note that the generalized axioms allow to derive clauses and cubes that cannot be derived by the traditional axioms *cl-init* and *cu-init* in general. This is due to the application of arbitrary QBF decision procedures (proof systems) for satisfiability checking in conflict/solution detection or in the side conditions of the axioms, respectively. In the side conditions the satisfiability of the PCNF $\psi[A]$ is checked, in contrast to formulas ψ'_θ and ψ'_γ as in conflict/solution detection. This is possible since $\psi'_\theta \equiv_{sat} \psi[A]$ and $\psi'_\gamma \equiv_{sat} \psi[A]$. The clause (cube) C derived by applying the generalized clause axiom *gen-cl-init* (*gen-cu-init*) is the *falsified clause (satisfied cube)* with respect to A.

During *clause (cube) learning*, a new *learned clause (cube)* C_L is derived by QRES. The falsified clause (satisfied cube) C is the start clause (cube) of a derivation of C_L. Given A, clauses (cubes) which became unit during propagation are systematically resolved based on the following *Q-resolution* rule.

Definition 6 (Q-Resolution [21]). *Let $\psi = \Pi.\phi$ be a PCNF.*

$$\frac{C_1 \cup \{p\} \qquad C_2 \cup \{\bar{p}\}}{C_1 \cup C_2} \quad \begin{array}{l} \text{For all } x \in \Pi : \{x, \bar{x}\} \not\subseteq (C_1 \cup C_2), \\ \bar{p} \notin C_1, \ p \notin C_2, \text{ and either} \\ \text{(1) } C_1, C_2 \text{ are clauses and } \mathsf{Q}(\Pi, p) = \exists \text{ or} \\ \text{(2) } C_1, C_2 \text{ are cubes and } \mathsf{Q}(\Pi, p) = \forall \end{array} \quad (res)$$

Rule *res* does not allow the resolvent $(C_1 \cup C_2)$ to be a tautological clause (contradictory cube) and requires existential (universal) variables as pivots p. In general, learning produces a nonempty clause (cube) $C_L \neq \emptyset$, which is added to the PCNF θ (PDNF γ) of learned clauses (cubes), and hence also to ψ_θ (ψ_γ).

In *backtracking*, a certain subassignment $A' \subset A$ is retracted such that C_L becomes unit in propagation. C_L is called an *asserting* clause (cube) [14]. Clauses (cubes) derived by rules *cl-init* and *gen-cl-init* (*cu-init* and *gen-cu-init*) are used in exactly the same way in learning to produce asserting clauses (cubes).

QCDCL terminates ("UNSAT" or "SAT" in Fig. 1) by deriving the empty learned clause (cube) $C_L = \emptyset$. A *clause (cube) resolution proof* of the unsatisfiability (satisfiability) of ψ can be obtained from the derivations of the learned clauses (cubes) up to the empty clause (cube).

By applying the generalized axioms using a complete QBF decision procedure, the empty assignment A, and an unlimited amount of time, the empty clause (cube) can be derived right away from any given unsatisfiable (satisfiable) PCNF ψ. *In practice* it is crucial to apply incomplete polynomial time procedures to limit the time spent on the satisfiability checks. However, the costs of frequent checks may outweigh the benefits. Hence in DepQBF 6.0, satisfiability checks for applications of the generalized axioms are dynamically disabled if they turn out to be too costly, and the traditional axioms are used instead. We refer to related work for implementation details [25, 32].

4   Features of DepQBF

We briefly summarize the general features of DepQBF that have been incorporated since its initial version 0.1 [26,27]. Most features were described in related publications. Additionally, we comment on the compatibility of the features with the implementation of QRES with generalized axioms (Fig. 1) in DepQBF 6.0.

Dependency Schemes. Since the initial version 0.1, DepQBF has been equipped with the *standard dependency scheme* [42] to relax the linear quantifier ordering in the prefix of a given PCNF ψ. In general, *dependency schemes* are used to compute *dependency relations* D, which are binary relations over the set of variables in ψ. If $(x,y) \notin D$ for two variables x and y then the ordering of x and y in ψ can safely be swapped. Otherwise, if $(x,y) \in D$ then y is considered to depend on x. The integration of dependency schemes in QCDCL results in the following reduction rule, which is added to QRES and implemented in DepQBF.

Definition 7 (Dependency-Aware Reduction [27]). *Let* $\psi = \Pi.\phi$ *be a PCNF and* D *be a dependency relation computed using a dependency scheme.*

$$\frac{C \cup \{l\}}{C} \quad \begin{array}{l} \text{(1) } C \text{ is a clause, } \mathsf{Q}(\Pi, l) = \forall, \\ \quad (l, l') \notin D \text{ for all } l' \in C \text{ with } \mathsf{Q}(\Pi, l') = \exists \text{ or} \\ \text{(2) } C \text{ is a cube, } \mathsf{Q}(\Pi, l) = \exists, \\ \quad (l, l') \notin D \text{ for all } l' \in C \text{ with } \mathsf{Q}(\Pi, l') = \forall \end{array} \quad (dep\text{-}red)$$

Rule *dep-red* generalizes the traditional reduction rule *red* by the use of dependency relation instead of the linear ordering of variables ($\leq_\Pi$) in the prefix of PCNF ψ. This way, it might be possible to reduce literals by rule *dep-red* which cannot be reduced by rule *red*. The soundness of QRES with rule *dep-red* has been proved for a dependency relation that is even more general (and thus allows for additional reductions) than the one implemented in DepQBF [45–47]. The generalized axioms *gen-cl-init* and *gen-cu-init* of QRES implemented in DepQBF 6.0 are naturally compatible with rule *dep-red*. Additionally, dependency schemes enable a relaxed variant of QCDCL assignments (Definition 2) based on the respective dependency relation rather than the prefix ordering of a PCNF ψ.

Long-Distance Resolution. The Q-resolution rule *res* [21] explicitly disallows to generate clauses (cubes) that are tautological (contradictory). This restriction is relaxed under certain side conditions in *long-distance (LD) Q-resolution* [2,49, 50]. LDQ-resolution was first implemented in the QCDCL solver Quaffle [49] and was incorporated in version 3.0 of DepQBF. Compared to QRES with traditional Q-resolution *res* [21], QRES with LDQ-resolution is exponentially more powerful in terms of proof sizes [13]. The generalized axioms *gen-cl-init* and *gen-cu-init* implemented in DepQBF 6.0 are not only compatible with the LDQ-resolution rule, but with *any* variants of Q-resolution (cf. [3]). Recently, the soundness of the combination of LDQ-resolution of clauses and dependency schemes in QRES has been proved [4,38], leaving the soundness of cube resolutions as an open problem. Therefore, the combination of LDQ-resolution and dependency schemes is not supported in DepQBF 6.0.

Incremental Solving. Since version 3.0, DepQBF has been equipped with an API in C and Java for incremental solving of sequences $S := \langle \psi_0, \ldots, \psi_n \rangle$ of syntactically related PCNFs ψ_i [28,35]. Incremental solving aims at reusing the clauses and cubes that were learned when solving PCNF ψ_i when it comes to solve the PCNFs ψ_j with $i < j$. The API of DepQBF allows to modify the PCNFs in S by manipulating the quantifier prefix and adding or removing sets of clauses in a stack-based way. Since version 4.0, it is possible to add or remove sets of clauses arbitrarily [29] and to extract *unsatisfiable cores*, i.e., unsatisfiable subformulas of the PCNF ψ_i. At any time when solving $\psi_i \in S$, the soundness property of QCDCL (Sect. 3) that $\psi \equiv_{sat} \psi_\theta$ and $\psi \equiv_{sat} \psi_\gamma$, where $\psi = \psi_i$, must hold. To guarantee that property when using the generalized axioms for incremental solving, DepQBF 6.0 currently only applies the generalized cube axiom *gen-cu-init* with dynamic QBCE used to check satisfiability of ψ'_γ in conflict/solution detection (Fig. 1). Although this configuration restricts the power of the generalized axioms, it has improved incremental solving in the context of QBF-based conformant planning [12]. As it is unclear how to use dependency schemes effectively in incremental solving, their application is disabled in DepQBF 6.0.

Generation of Proofs and Certificates. QCDCL solvers can produce *clause (cube) resolution proofs* of the unsatisfiability (satisfiability) of PCNFs as a byproduct of clause (cube) learning. Since version 1.0 [37], DepQBF is capable of producing proofs without employing dependency schemes by rule *dep-red*. Given a proof P of a PCNF ψ, a *certificate* of ψ can be extracted from P by inspecting the reduction steps by rule *red* in P [2]. A certificate of an unsatisfiable (satisfiable) PCNF ψ is given by a set of Herbrand (Skolem) functions which represent the universal (existential) variables in ψ. Applications of the generalized axioms in QCDCL in general impose considerable restrictions on the certificate extraction process. The workflow [2] to extract a certificate from P was originally presented for traditional QRES proofs. If proof P contains clauses (cubes) derived by rule *gen-cl-init* (rule *gen-cu-init*), then P may lack information needed to extract correct certificates. As a result, DepQBF 6.0 does not support cube resolution proof generation combined with the generalized cube axiom *gen-cu-init*. However, it supports clause resolution proof generation with the generalized clause axiom *gen-cl-init* provided that only propositional abstractions and SAT solving are used for satisfiability checking in the side condition of this axiom.

Advanced Generation of Learned Clauses and Cubes. The derivation of a single asserting clause (cube) starting from a falsified clause (satisfied cube) as implemented in traditional QCDCL [14,24,49] has an exponential worst case [48]. Since version 2.0 DepQBF comes with an approach that avoids this exponential case [33] by a revised selection of clauses (cubes) to be resolved in learning. This advanced approach is compatible with all the techniques presented above.

5   Experiments

We compare variants of DepQBF 6.02, which is the latest follow-up release of DepQBF 6.0, to top performing solvers of QBFEVAL'16 [39]. As benchmarks we consider all 825 instances from the PCNF track, both in original form (Table 1a) and preprocessed by Bloqqer version 37 (Table 1b). We take preprocessing into account as it might have a positive impact on certain solvers while a negative on others (cf. [34,36]). Experiments were run on an AMD Opteron 6238 processor (2.6 GHz) under 64-bit Ubuntu Linux 12.04 with time and memory limits of 1800 seconds and seven GB. Exceeding the memory limit is counted as a time out.[3]

Table 1. Solved instances (S), solved unsatisfiable $(\bot)$ and satisfiable ones $(\top)$, uniquely solved ones among all solvers (U), and total wall clock time including time outs on 825 PCNFs from QBFEVAL'16 without (1a) and with preprocessing by Bloqqer (1b).

(a) Original instances.

Solver	S	$\bot$	$\top$	U	Time
AIGSolve	603	301	302	34	440K
GhostQ	593	292	301	7	457K
QSTS	578	294	284	3	469K
DQ	458	255	203	0	682K
DQ-linldq	458	257	201	2	686K
DQ-lin	456	255	201	0	686K
DQ-ncl	448	246	202	0	703K
DQ-nq	397	228	169	0	788K
DQ-ncu	393	229	164	0	796K
DQ-n	383	221	162	0	814K
CAQE	378	202	176	9	831K
QESTO	369	210	159	0	864K
RAReQS	341	211	130	2	891K

(b) Preprocessed by Bloqqer.

Solver	S	$\bot$	$\top$	U	Time
QSTS	633	330	303	11	365K
RAReQS	633	334	299	8	375K
QESTO	620	321	299	0	395K
DQ-ncl	601	303	298	0	428K
DQ	601	301	300	0	429K
DQ-linldq	598	300	298	2	437K
DQ-lin	597	299	298	0	436K
CAQE	596	301	295	4	451K
DQ-n	593	296	297	0	444K
DQ-ncu	591	297	294	0	455K
DQ-nq	587	293	294	0	455K
GhostQ	570	282	288	0	485K
AIGSolve	567	286	281	14	481K

To assess the impact of the generalized axioms *gen-cl-init* and *gen-cu-init* on the performance, we consider DepQBF 6.02 using both *gen-cl-init* and *gen-cu-init* (variant DQ in the tables), without *gen-cl-init* (DQ-ncl), without *gen-cu-init* (DQ-ncu), and using no generalized axioms at all (DQ-n).

On original instances (Table 1a), DQ outperforms variants DQ-ncl, DQ-ncu, and DQ-n with restricted or without generalized axioms, respectively. Variant DQ-ncl without axiom *gen-cl-init* outperforms variant DQ-ncu without *gen-cu-init*. We attribute this effect to the use of dynamic QBCE (among other techniques) for applications of the cube axiom *gen-cu-init* in DQ-ncl. Compared to DQ, disabling only dynamic QBCE in variant DQ-nq severely impacts performance.

On preprocessed instances (Table 1b), we make similar observations regarding the impact of the generalized axioms like in Table 1a. However, variant DQ-ncl

---

[3] We refer to an appendix of this paper with additional experimental results [30].

Table 2. Related to Table 1a: solver performance on 402 filtered original (*not pre-processed*) instances partitioned into 261 instances with at most two (2a) and 141 with three or more quantifier alternations (2b).

(a) At most two quantifier alternations.

Solver	S	⊥	⊤	U	Time
GhostQ	176	75	101	5	171K
AIGSolve	138	66	72	14	250K
QSTS	136	58	78	0	232K
RAReQS	76	43	33	1	340K
DQ-lin	69	35	34	0	351K
DQ	69	35	34	0	351K
DQ-ncl	68	35	33	0	354K
DQ-linldq	67	34	33	0	354K
QESTO	66	37	29	0	359K
DQ-ncu	53	24	29	0	378K
DQ-n	52	24	28	0	378K
DQ-nq	52	23	29	0	379K
CAQE	43	17	26	3	397K

(b) Three or more quantifier alternations.

Solver	S	⊥	⊤	U	Time
DQ-linldq	81	50	31	2	120K
DQ	79	47	32	0	119K
DQ-ncl	79	47	32	0	120K
DQ-lin	78	47	31	0	123K
QSTS	72	44	28	3	132K
DQ-nq	56	37	19	0	159K
GhostQ	56	31	25	2	160K
DQ-n	55	36	19	0	159K
DQ-ncu	55	36	19	0	159K
AIGSolve	54	25	29	9	161K
QESTO	49	33	16	0	179K
CAQE	46	29	17	2	182K
RAReQS	43	33	10	0	180K

Table 3. Related to Table 1b: solver performance on 402 filtered and *preprocessed* instances partitioned into 270 instances with at most two (3a) and 132 with three or more quantifier alternations (3b).

(a) At most two quantifier alternations.

Solver	S	⊥	⊤	U	Time
RAReQS	157	79	78	8	227K
QESTO	138	66	72	0	255K
QSTS	136	62	74	2	255K
CAQE	118	49	69	2	298K
GhostQ	111	46	65	1	304K
DQ	107	43	64	1	311K
DQ-lin	106	42	64	0	311K
DQ-ncl	105	43	62	0	312K
DQ-n	105	41	64	0	313K
DQ-linldq	104	40	64	0	315K
AIGSolve	102	49	53	7	313K
DQ-nq	102	39	63	0	322K
DQ-ncu	102	40	62	0	323K

(b) Three or more quantifier alternations.

Solver	S	⊥	⊤	U	Time
DQ-ncl	83	51	32	0	96K
DQ	81	49	32	0	98K
DQ-linldq	81	51	30	2	102K
DQ-lin	78	48	30	0	105K
DQ-ncu	76	48	28	0	112K
QSTS	75	50	25	1	107K
DQ-n	75	46	29	0	112K
DQ-nq	72	45	27	0	113K
QESTO	69	45	24	0	120K
CAQE	64	42	22	0	136K
RAReQS	62	45	17	1	131K
AIGSolve	51	27	24	6	151K
GhostQ	46	26	20	0	162K

without the clause axiom *gen-cl-init* is on par with DQ. Preprocessing may blur the structure of an instance. We conjecture that this blurring hinders the success of the QBF decision procedures in DepQBF, on which applications of the generalized axioms are based. In general the performance difference between the variants of DepQBF is smaller than on original instances. The rankings of the solvers RAReQS [17], QESTO [19], and CAQE [40] are improved substantially by preprocessing, whereas those of AIGSolve [43] and GhostQ [17,22] become worse. The best variant DQ-ncl in Table 1b ranks fourth behind QSTS [7], RAReQS, and QESTO. However, the lag to the solver ranked third is 19 instances compared to 120 instances for the best variant DQ in Table 1a that also ranks fourth.

To analyze the effects of preprocessing in more detail, we filtered the 825 PCNFs from QBFEVAL'16 by discarding 354 PCNFs that are already solved by Bloqqer and 69 PCNFs where Bloqqer eliminated all universally quantified variables, resulting in a set of 402 PCNFs. Further, we considered the 402 PCNFs in their original form and preprocessed by Bloqqer and partitioned them into subsets containing PCNFs with at most two and with three or more quantifier alternations. Such partitioning is motivated by a related experimental study [31] where a large diversity of solver performance was observed on instance classes defined by alternations. Tables 2 and 3 show solver performance on these subsets without and with preprocessing, respectively. Notably, variants of DepQBF outperform the other solvers on the subsets with three or more alternations, both without and with preprocessing (Tables 2b and 3b).

All variants of DepQBF reported above apply dependency-aware reduction by rule *dep-red*. Variant DQ-lin is the same as DQ (including generalized axioms) but uses the traditional reduction rule *red* based on the linear quantifier ordering of PCNFs. Variant DQ outperforms DQ-lin in all tables except Table 2a, where DQ-lin is on par, which illustrates the benefits of dependency schemes in QCDCL. Variant DQ-linldq differs from DQ-lin in the use of LDQ-resolution in learning instead of traditional Q-resolution by rule *res*. The results with LDQ-resolution are mixed, despite being a stronger proof system than Q-resolution. Variant DQ-linldq outperforms DQ-lin in all tables except Tables 2a and 3a, i.e., on instances with at most two quantifier alternations.

6 Conclusion

We presented the latest major release version 6.0 of the QCDCL solver DepQBF. DepQBF 6.0 implements a variant of QCDCL that is based on a generalization of the Q-resolution calculus (QRES). The generalization is achieved by equipping QRES with generalized clause and cube axioms to be used in clause and cube learning [32]. The generalized axioms provide an extensible framework of interfaces for the integration of arbitrary QBF proof systems in QRES, and hence in QCDCL. The integration of proof systems orthogonal to Q-resolution, such as variable expansion, enables QCDCL to potentially produce proofs that are exponentially shorter than proofs produced by traditional QCDCL. This way, the state of the art of QCDCL solving can be further advanced. A related open problem is the inability of plain QCDCL to exploit the full power of Q-resolution [16].

The workflow of QCDCL with generalized axioms is not tailored towards DepQBF 6.0 but can be implemented in any QCDCL solver. Furthermore, it is compatible with dependency schemes [42,46] and any Q-resolution variant [3], which offers potential for further improvements.

Experiments with variants of DepQBF 6.0 showed considerable performance gains due to the application of generalized axioms. However, frequent applications are hindered by computationally expensive QBF satisfiability checks in the side conditions of the axioms. To limit the checking overhead, axiom applications must be carefully scheduled. In this respect, there is room for improvements in fine tuning DepQBF 6.0. Further, it may be beneficial to integrate the QBF decision procedures that are applied to satisfiability checking more tightly in the QCDCL workflow, like with dynamic blocked clause elimination (QBCE) [25].

References

1. Ayari, A., Basin, D.: QUBOS: Deciding quantified boolean logic using propositional satisfiability solvers. In: Aagaard, M.D., O'Leary, J.W. (eds.) FMCAD 2002. LNCS, vol. 2517, pp. 187–201. Springer, Heidelberg (2002). doi:10.1007/3-540-36126-X_12
2. Balabanov, V., Jiang, J.R.: Unified QBF certification and its applications. Formal Methods Syst. Des. **41**(1), 45–65 (2012)
3. Balabanov, V., Widl, M., Jiang, J.-H.R.: QBF resolution systems and their proof complexities. In: Sinz, C., Egly, U. (eds.) SAT 2014. LNCS, vol. 8561, pp. 154–169. Springer, Cham (2014). doi:10.1007/978-3-319-09284-3_12
4. Beyersdorff, O., Blinkhorn, J.: Dependency schemes in QBF calculi: semantics and soundness. In: Rueher, M. (ed.) CP 2016. LNCS, vol. 9892, pp. 96–112. Springer, Cham (2016). doi:10.1007/978-3-319-44953-1_7
5. Beyersdorff, O., Chew, L., Janota, M.: Proof complexity of resolution-based QBF calculi. In: STACS. LIPIcs, vol. 30, pp. 76–89. Schloss Dagstuhl-Leibniz-Zentrum fuer Informatik (2015)
6. Biere, A.: Resolve and expand. In: Hoos, H.H., Mitchell, D.G. (eds.) SAT 2004. LNCS, vol. 3542, pp. 59–70. Springer, Heidelberg (2005). doi:10.1007/11527695_5
7. Bogaerts, B., Janhunen, T., Tasharrofi, S.: SAT-to-SAT in QBFEval 2016. In: QBF Workshop. CEUR Workshop Proceedings, vol. 1719, pp. 63–70. CEUR-WS.org (2016)
8. Bubeck, U., Kleine Büning, H.: Bounded universal expansion for preprocessing QBF. In: Marques-Silva, J., Sakallah, K.A. (eds.) SAT 2007. LNCS, vol. 4501, pp. 244–257. Springer, Heidelberg (2007). doi:10.1007/978-3-540-72788-0_24
9. Cadoli, M., Giovanardi, A., Schaerf, M.: An algorithm to evaluate quantified boolean formulae. In: AAAI, pp. 262–267. AAAI Press/The MIT Press (1998)
10. Clarke, E.M., Grumberg, O., Jha, S., Lu, Y., Veith, H.: Counterexample-guided abstraction refinement for symbolic model checking. J. ACM **50**(5), 752–794 (2003)
11. Davis, M., Logemann, G., Loveland, D.W.: A machine program for theorem-proving. Commun. ACM **5**(7), 394–397 (1962)
12. Egly, U., Kronegger, M., Lonsing, F., Pfandler, A.: Conformant planning as a case study of incremental QBF solving. Ann. Math. Artif. Intell. **80**(1), 21–45 (2017)
13. Egly, U., Lonsing, F., Widl, M.: Long-distance resolution: proof generation and strategy extraction in search-based QBF solving. In: McMillan, K., Middeldorp, A., Voronkov, A. (eds.) LPAR 2013. LNCS, vol. 8312, pp. 291–308. Springer, Heidelberg (2013). doi:10.1007/978-3-642-45221-5_21
14. Giunchiglia, E., Narizzano, M., Tacchella, A.: Clause/Term resolution and learning in the evaluation of quantified boolean formulas. JAIR **26**, 371–416 (2006)
15. Heule, M., Järvisalo, M., Lonsing, F., Seidl, M., Biere, A.: Clause elimination for SAT and QSAT. JAIR **53**, 127–168 (2015)

16. Janota, M.: On Q-resolution and CDCL QBF solving. In: Creignou, N., Le Berre, D. (eds.) SAT 2016. LNCS, vol. 9710, pp. 402–418. Springer, Cham (2016). doi:10.1007/978-3-319-40970-2_25

17. Janota, M., Klieber, W., Marques-Silva, J., Clarke, E.: Solving QBF with counterexample guided refinement. Artif. Intell. **234**, 1–25 (2016)

18. Janota, M., Marques-Silva, J.: Expansion-based QBF solving versus Q-resolution. Theor. Comput. Sci. **577**, 25–42 (2015)

19. Janota, M., Marques-Silva, J.: Solving QBF by clause selection. In: IJCAI, pp. 325–331. AAAI Press (2015)

20. Kleine Büning, H., Bubeck, U.: Theory of quantified boolean formulas. In: Handbook of Satisfiability, FAIA, vol. 185, pp. 735–760. IOS Press (2009)

21. Kleine Büning, H., Karpinski, M., Flögel, A.: Resolution for quantified boolean formulas. Inf. Comput. **117**(1), 12–18 (1995)

22. Klieber, W., Sapra, S., Gao, S., Clarke, E.: A non-prenex, non-clausal QBF solver with game-state learning. In: Strichman, O., Szeider, S. (eds.) SAT 2010. LNCS, vol. 6175, pp. 128–142. Springer, Heidelberg (2010). doi:10.1007/978-3-642-14186-7_12

23. Kullmann, O.: On a generalization of extended resolution. Discrete Appl. Math. **96–97**, 149–176 (1999)

24. Letz, R.: Lemma and model caching in decision procedures for quantified boolean formulas. In: Egly, U., Fermüller, C.G. (eds.) TABLEAUX 2002. LNCS, vol. 2381, pp. 160–175. Springer, Heidelberg (2002). doi:10.1007/3-540-45616-3_12

25. Lonsing, F., Bacchus, F., Biere, A., Egly, U., Seidl, M.: Enhancing search-based QBF solving by dynamic blocked clause elimination. In: Davis, M., Fehnker, A., McIver, A., Voronkov, A. (eds.) LPAR 2015. LNCS, vol. 9450, pp. 418–433. Springer, Heidelberg (2015). doi:10.1007/978-3-662-48899-7_29

26. Lonsing, F., Biere, A.: DepQBF: a dependency-aware QBF solver. JSAT **7**(2–3), 71–76 (2010)

27. Lonsing, F., Biere, A.: Integrating dependency schemes in search-based QBF solvers. In: Strichman, O., Szeider, S. (eds.) SAT 2010. LNCS, vol. 6175, pp. 158–171. Springer, Heidelberg (2010). doi:10.1007/978-3-642-14186-7_14

28. Lonsing, F., Egly, U.: Incremental QBF solving. In: O'Sullivan, B. (ed.) CP 2014. LNCS, vol. 8656, pp. 514–530. Springer, Cham (2014). doi:10.1007/978-3-319-10428-7_38

29. Lonsing, F., Egly, U.: Incrementally computing minimal unsatisfiable cores of QBFs via a clause group solver API. In: Heule, M., Weaver, S. (eds.) SAT 2015. LNCS, vol. 9340, pp. 191–198. Springer, Cham (2015). doi:10.1007/978-3-319-24318-4_14

30. Lonsing, F., Egly, U.: DepQBF 6.0: A search-based QBF solver beyond traditional QCDCL. CoRR abs/1702.08256 (2017). http://arxiv.org/abs/1702.08256, CADE 2017 proceedings version with appendix

31. Lonsing, F., Egly, U.: Evaluating QBF solvers: quantifier alternations matter. CoRR abs/1701.06612 (2017). http://arxiv.org/abs/1701.06612, technical report

32. Lonsing, F., Egly, U., Seidl, M.: Q-resolution with generalized axioms. In: Creignou, N., Le Berre, D. (eds.) SAT 2016. LNCS, vol. 9710, pp. 435–452. Springer, Cham (2016). doi:10.1007/978-3-319-40970-2_27

33. Lonsing, F., Egly, U., Van Gelder, A.: Efficient clause learning for quantified boolean formulas via QBF pseudo unit propagation. In: Järvisalo, M., Van Gelder, A. (eds.) SAT 2013. LNCS, vol. 7962, pp. 100–115. Springer, Heidelberg (2013). doi:10.1007/978-3-642-39071-5_9

34. Lonsing, F., Seidl, M., Van Gelder, A.: The QBF gallery: behind the scenes. Artif. Intell. **237**, 92–114 (2016)

35. Marin, P., Miller, C., Lewis, M.D.T., Becker, B.: Verification of partial designs using incremental QBF solving. In: DATE, pp. 623–628. IEEE (2012)
36. Marin, P., Narizzano, M., Pulina, L., Tacchella, A., Giunchiglia, E.: Twelve years of QBF evaluations: QSAT is PSPACE-hard and it shows. Fundam. Inform. **149** (1–2), 133–158 (2016)
37. Niemetz, A., Preiner, M., Lonsing, F., Seidl, M., Biere, A.: Resolution-based certificate extraction for QBF. In: Cimatti, A., Sebastiani, R. (eds.) SAT 2012. LNCS, vol. 7317, pp. 430–435. Springer, Heidelberg (2012). doi:10.1007/978-3-642-31612-8_33
38. Peitl, T., Slivovsky, F., Szeider, S.: Long distance Q-resolution with dependency schemes. In: Creignou, N., Le Berre, D. (eds.) SAT 2016. LNCS, vol. 9710, pp. 500–518. Springer, Cham (2016). doi:10.1007/978-3-319-40970-2_31
39. Pulina, L.: The ninth QBF solvers evaluation - preliminary report. In: Proceedings of the 4th International Workshop on Quantified Boolean Formulas QBF 2016. CEUR Workshop Proceedings, vol. 1719, pp. 1–13. CEUR-WS.org (2016)
40. Rabe, M.N., Tentrup, L.: CAQE: a certifying QBF solver. In: FMCAD, pp. 136–143. IEEE (2015)
41. Robinson, J.A.: A machine-oriented logic based on the resolution principle. J. ACM **12**(1), 23–41 (1965)
42. Samer, M., Szeider, S.: Backdoor sets of quantified boolean formulas. JAR **42**(1), 77–97 (2009)
43. Scholl, C., Pigorsch, F.: The QBF solver AIGSolve. In: QBF Workshop. CEUR Workshop Proceedings, vol. 1719, pp. 55–62. CEUR-WS.org (2016)
44. Marques-Silva, J., Lynce, I., Malik, S.: Conflict-driven clause learning SAT solvers. In: Handbook of Satisfiability, FAIA, vol. 185, pp. 131–153. IOS Press (2009)
45. Slivovsky, F., Szeider, S.: Computing resolution-path dependencies in linear time. In: Cimatti, A., Sebastiani, R. (eds.) SAT 2012. LNCS, vol. 7317, pp. 58–71. Springer, Heidelberg (2012). doi:10.1007/978-3-642-31612-8_6
46. Slivovsky, F., Szeider, S.: Soundness of Q-resolution with dependency schemes. Theor. Comput. Sci. **612**, 83–101 (2016)
47. Van Gelder, A.: Variable independence and resolution paths for quantified boolean formulas. In: Lee, J. (ed.) CP 2011. LNCS, vol. 6876, pp. 789–803. Springer, Heidelberg (2011). doi:10.1007/978-3-642-23786-7_59
48. Van Gelder, A.: Contributions to the theory of practical quantified boolean formula solving. In: Milano, M. (ed.) CP 2012. LNCS, pp. 647–663. Springer, Heidelberg (2012). doi:10.1007/978-3-642-33558-7_47
49. Zhang, L., Malik, S.: Conflict driven learning in a quantified boolean satisfiability solver. In: ICCAD, pp. 442–449. ACM/IEEE Computer Society (2002)
50. Zhang, L., Malik, S.: Towards a symmetric treatment of satisfaction and conflicts in quantified boolean formula evaluation. In: Hentenryck, P. (ed.) CP 2002. LNCS, vol. 2470, pp. 200–215. Springer, Heidelberg (2002). doi:10.1007/3-540-46135-3_14

CSI: New Evidence – A Progress Report

Julian Nagele[✉], Bertram Felgenhauer, and Aart Middeldorp

Department of Computer Science, University of Innsbruck, Innsbruck, Austria
{julian.nagele,bertram.felgenhauer,aart.middeldorp}@uibk.ac.at

Abstract. CSI is a strong automated confluence prover for rewrite systems which has been in development since 2010. In this paper we report on recent extensions that make CSI more powerful, secure, and useful. These extensions include improved confluence criteria but also support for uniqueness of normal forms. Most of the implemented techniques produce machine-readable proof output that can be independently verified by an external tool, thus increasing the trust in CSI. We also report on CSI^oho, a tool built on the same framework and similar ideas as CSI that automatically checks confluence of higher-order rewrite systems.

1 Introduction

CSI [44] is an automatic confluence prover for rewrite systems, which participates in the annual confluence competition (CoCo) [1].

In this paper we report on recent additions to CSI, in particular support for higher-order rewrite systems, efficient decision procedures for the unique normal form properties for ground rewrite systems, support for first-order systems with associative and commutative symbols, and more refined non-confluence techniques. Several techniques have been formalized to enable certification of the output of CSI, making it the most trustworthy confluence tool.

We assume familiarity with rewriting [7]. Here we only recall notions that will be used in Sect. 2. We consider terms built from a signature $\mathcal{F}$ and a disjoint set of variables $\mathcal{V}$. Given a subset $\mathcal{F}_{AC} \subseteq \mathcal{F}$ of binary function symbols, the term rewrite system (TRS for short) AC consists of the AC rules $f(x, y) \to f(y, x)$ and $f(f(x, y), z) \to f(x, f(y, z))$ for every $f \in \mathcal{F}_{AC}$. We write $\sim_{AC}$ for the congruence induced by AC. Given a TRS $\mathcal{R}$ over the signature $\mathcal{F}$, we write $\mathcal{R}^e$ for the union of $\mathcal{R}$ and the extended rules $f(\ell, x) \to f(r, x)$ for all $\ell \to r \in \mathcal{R}$ such that $\mathsf{root}(\ell) = f \in \mathcal{F}_{AC}$. We write $\to_{\mathcal{R}/AC}$ for the relation $\sim_{AC} \cdot \to_{\mathcal{R}} \cdot \sim_{AC}$. The relation $\to_{\mathcal{R},AC}$ is defined as follows: $s \to_{\mathcal{R},AC} t$ if there exists a position p in s, a rewrite rule $\ell \to r$ in $\mathcal{R}$, and a substitution σ such that $s|p \sim_{AC} \ell\sigma$ and $t = s[r\sigma]_p$. The relations $\to_{\mathcal{R}/AC}$ and $\to_{\mathcal{R}^e,AC} \cdot \sim_{AC}$ coincide.

Consider two rewrite rules $\ell_1 \to r_1$ and $\ell_2 \to r_2$ without common variables and a function position p in ℓ_2 such that ℓ_1 and $\ell_2|p$ are unifiable modulo AC. Given a complete set S of AC unifiers of ℓ_1 and $\ell_2|p$, the pair $\ell_2[r_1]_p\sigma \approx r_2\sigma$ with $\sigma \in S$ is called an AC critical pair. The set of all AC critical pairs between rules of a TRS $\mathcal{R}$ and a TRS $\mathcal{S}$ is denoted by $\mathsf{CP}_{AC}(\mathcal{R}, \mathcal{S})$.

This research is supported by FWF (Austrian Science Fund) project P27528.

L. de Moura (Ed.): CADE 2017, LNAI 10395, pp. 385–397, 2017.
DOI: 10.1007/978-3-319-63046-5_24

The remainder of the paper is organized as follows. In the next section we report on the main extensions to CSI for (non-)confluence proving of TRSs. Section 3 is devoted to the support of CSI for the unique normal form properties. The extension to higher-order systems is covered in Sect. 4. An overview of the certified techniques in CSI is presented in Sect. 5. Some implementation details are given in Sect. 6 before we conclude in Sect. 7 with experimental data.

2   Extensions

In this section we describe the two features for (non-)confluence proving of TRSs that were added to CSI after CoCo 2016. Other extensions are briefly described in the one-page tool descriptions accompanying CoCo.[1]

TRSs that contain AC rules pose a challenge for confluence provers. The confluence problems database (Cops)[2] contains several such systems whose status is open. Aoto and Toyama [2] developed a special confluence technique for rewrite systems with AC rules and more general non-terminating rewrite systems, which is incorporated in the confluence prover ACP [5]. A key idea in [2] is that AC rules are *reversible*. This idea was combined with the extended critical pair lemma of Jouannaud and Kirchner [13] in Saigawa [15] and more recently in CoLL [38], where the technique is extended to handle associative rules in the absence of commutation rules.

Theorem 1 (Jouannaud and Kirchner [13], Shintani and Hirokawa [38]).
If $\mathcal{R} = \mathcal{S} \uplus \mathsf{AC}$ *such that* $s \to^*_{\mathcal{S},\mathsf{AC}} \cdot \sim_{\mathsf{AC}} \cdot {}_{\mathcal{S},\mathsf{AC}}{}^*\!\!\leftarrow t$ *for all* $s \approx t \in \mathsf{CP}_{\mathsf{AC}}(\mathcal{S}, \mathcal{S} \cup \mathsf{AC} \cup \mathsf{AC}^{-1})$ *and* $\mathcal{S}/\mathsf{AC}$ *is terminating then* $\mathcal{R}$ *is confluent.*

In CSI we incorporated the version of the AC critical pair lemma based on extended rules [32], which is used in the modern completion tool mkbtt.[3]

Theorem 2. *If* $\mathcal{R} = \mathcal{S} \uplus \mathsf{AC}$ *such that* $s \to^*_{\mathcal{S}/\mathsf{AC}} \cdot \sim_{\mathsf{AC}} \cdot {}_{\mathcal{S}/\mathsf{AC}}{}^*\!\!\leftarrow t$ *for all* $s \approx t \in \mathsf{CP}_{\mathsf{AC}}(\mathcal{S}^e, \mathcal{S}^e)$ *and* $\mathcal{S}/\mathsf{AC}$ *is terminating then* $\mathcal{R}$ *is confluent.*

We illustrate the use of Theorem 2 on two examples.

Example 3. The rewrite system (Cops 183)

$$+(0, x) \to x \qquad +(x, 0) \to x \qquad -(+(x, y)) \to +(-(x), -(y))$$
$$+(1, -(1)) \to 0 \qquad +(-(1), 1) \to 0 \qquad +(x, y) \to +(y, x)$$
$$-(0) \to 0 \qquad -(-(x)) \to x \qquad +(+(x, y), z) \to +(x, +(y, z))$$

cannot be handled by the recent *ground* confluence prover AGCP [3, Example 25]. After removing the AC rules $+(+(x, y), z) \to +(x, +(y, z))$ and $+(x, y) \to$

---

[1] Available from http://coco.nue.riec.tohoku.ac.jp/2013, http://coco.nue.riec.tohoku.ac.jp/2014, http://coco.nue.riec.tohoku.ac.jp/2015, http://coco.nue.riec.tohoku.ac.jp/2016, under Entrants.
[2] http://cops.uibk.ac.at.
[3] http://cl-informatik.uibk.ac.at/software/mkbtt.

CSI incorporates efficient decision procedures for both UNC and UNR for *ground* term rewrite systems, which are TRSs without variables. The former property can be decided in $O(n \log n)$ time, where n is the size of the input TRS, based on currying, the congruence closure algorithm by Nelson and Oppen [26], and an ad hoc enumeration of runs of a tree automaton that accepts convertible normal forms. The latter property is decided in $O(n^3)$ time, using currying and ground tree transducers that accept normal forms which are related by a peak. For details of these two algorithms, see [9]. Furthermore, CSI implements the following criterion for UNC for non-ground systems.

Theorem 8 (Kahrs and Smith [14]). *Every non-ω-overlapping TRS has unique normal forms with respect to conversions* (UNC).

A TRS is ω-*overlapping* if it has overlaps that may be infinite terms. In order to check for ω-overlaps, CSI implements a unification algorithm without occurs-check.

Example 9. The TRS consisting of the rules

$$f(x, x) \to a \qquad\qquad f(x, g(x)) \to b \qquad\qquad c \to g(c)$$

of [12] is not UNR because $a \leftarrow f(c, c) \to f(c, g(c)) \to b$ is a peak connecting two distinct normal forms. This TRS is non-overlapping but ω-overlapping because $f(g^\omega, g^\omega)$ is an instance of both $f(x, x)$ and $f(y, g(y))$ by substituting $\{x \mapsto g^\omega, y \mapsto g^\omega\}$. The TRS from Example 5 on the other hand is non-ω-overlapping and hence UNC by Theorem 8.

Finally, there is a simple check for non-UNR, where CSI attempts to find two distinct normal forms reachable from the same term by starting from critical peaks and overlaps at variables. Including variable overlaps enables CSI to find the peak in Example 9. Note that Lemma 7 also holds for UNR. This enables an alternative approach to finding a suitable peak for Example 9: There is an overlap between $f(c, c) \to b \in FC(\mathcal{R}^{-1})^{-1}$ and $f(x, x) \to a \in \mathcal{R}$, resulting in the critical pair $a \approx b$. Note that considering $FC(\mathcal{R})$ alone does not yield any progress in this example.

We aim for having a single tool that simultaneously attempts to prove and disprove all three properties UNR, UNC and CR, fully exploiting the chain of implications (1) for optimization. For example, if UNC has been established, any effort spent on proving UNR would be wasted, but the current implementation cannot use this information. For the time being, however, there are separate tool invocations for each of these properties.

4   Higher-Order Confluence

CSI^ho is an extension of CSI for proving confluence of higher-order rewrite systems. Higher-order rewriting combines first-order rewriting with notions and concepts from (typed) λ-calculus, resulting in rewriting systems with higher-order functions and bound variables. More precisely we consider pattern rewrite systems (PRSs) as introduced by Nipkow [20,27], i.e., terms are simply typed lambda terms with constants modulo $\lambda\beta\eta$ and rewriting uses higher-order matching. Additionally left-hand sides of rewrite rules are required to be patterns [21].[6] This restriction is essential for obtaining decidability of unification and thus makes it possible to compute critical pairs. To this end CSI^ho implements a version of Nipkow's algorithm for higher-order pattern unification [28].

Example 10. The untyped lambda calculus with β and η-reduction can be encoded as a PRS as follows:

$$\mathsf{abs}\colon (\mathsf{term} \to \mathsf{term}) \to \mathsf{term} \qquad\qquad \mathsf{app}\colon \mathsf{term} \to \mathsf{term} \to \mathsf{term}$$
$$\mathsf{app}(\mathsf{abs}(\lambda x.\, M(x)), N) \to M(N) \qquad\qquad \mathsf{abs}(\lambda x.\, \mathsf{app}(M, x)) \to M$$

Next we briefly explain the confluence criteria supported by CSI^ho. The first criterion is based on a higher-order version of the critical pair lemma.

Lemma 11 (Nipkow [27]). *A PRS $\mathcal{R}$ is locally confluent if and only if $s \downarrow t$ for all critical pairs $s \approx t$ of $\mathcal{R}$.*

The definition of critical pairs is essentially the same as in the first-order setting, with some additional technicalities to account for the presence of bound variables, see e.g. [20] for a formal definition. Together with Newman's Lemma this yields a confluence criterion for PRSs.

Corollary 12. *A terminating PRS $\mathcal{R}$ is confluent if and only if $s \downarrow t$ for all critical pairs $s \approx t$ of $\mathcal{R}$.*

For showing termination CSI^ho uses a basic higher-order recursive path ordering [33] and static dependency pairs with dependency graph decomposition and the subterm criterion [19]. Alternatively, one can also use an external termination tool like WANDA [18] as an oracle.

For potentially non-terminating systems CSI^ho supports two more classical criteria based on critical pairs. The first states that *weakly orthogonal* systems are confluent.

Theorem 13 (van Oostrom and van Raamsdonk [30]). *A left-linear PRS $\mathcal{R}$ is confluent if $s = t$ for all critical pairs $s \approx t$ of $\mathcal{R}$.*

The PRS from Example 10 has two trivial critical pairs and hence is confluent. This result was extended by van Oostrom to allow for non-trivial critical pairs that are connected by a development step.[7]

Theorem 14 (van Oostrom [29]). *A left-linear PRS $\mathcal{R}$ is confluent if $s \rightsquigarrow t$ for all critical pairs $s \approx t$ of $\mathcal{R}$.*

---

[6] A term is a pattern if free variables only have distinct bound variables as arguments.

[7] A development step $\rightsquigarrow$ contracts multiple, non-overlapping but possibly nested redexes at once.

As a divide-and-conquer technique CSI^ho implements modularity, i.e., decomposing a PRS into parts with disjoint signatures, for left-linear PRSs [6]. Note that the restriction to left-linear systems is essential—unlike for the first-order setting confluence is not modular in general. The following example illustrates the problem.

Example 15. Consider the PRS $\mathcal{R}$ from [6] consisting of the three rules

$$\mathsf{f}(x,x) \to \mathsf{a} \qquad \mathsf{f}(x,\mathsf{g}(x)) \to \mathsf{b} \qquad \mu(\lambda x.\, Z(x)) \to Z(\mu(\lambda x.\, Z(x)))$$

The first two rules and the third rule on their own are confluent, e.g. by Corollary 12 and Theorem 13 respectively. However, because of the peak

$$\mathsf{a} \leftarrow \mathsf{f}(\mu(\lambda x.\, \mathsf{g}(x)), \mu(\lambda x.\, \mathsf{g}(x))) \to \mathsf{f}(\mu(\lambda x.\, \mathsf{g}(x)), \mathsf{g}(\mu(\lambda x.\, \mathsf{g}(x)))) \to \mathsf{b}$$

$\mathcal{R}$ is not confluent. Note that $\mathcal{R}$ does not have critical pairs, making it non-trivial to find this peak.

As described in Sect. 2 redundant rules can used to find such peaks. Implementing transformations based on redundant rules for PRSs is straightforward, one just has to take care to only add rules that do not violate the pattern restriction.

Example 16. Consider the PRS from Example 15. After adding the redundant rule $\mathsf{f}(\mu(\lambda x.\, \mathsf{g}(x)), \mu(\lambda x.\, \mathsf{g}(x))) \to \mathsf{b}$ there is a critical pair $\mathsf{a} \approx \mathsf{b}$ and non-confluence is obvious.

To find new rules like the one above we again use narrowing, applying rules in both directions. In Example 16 unifying $Z(\mu(\lambda x.\, Z(x)))$ with $\mathsf{g}(x)$ and applying the reversed third rule to the left-hand side of the second rule yields the desired new rule. The following example illustrates removal of redundant rules.

Example 17. Consider the following encoding of lambda-calculus with Regnier's σ-reduction [34]:

$$\mathsf{app}(\mathsf{abs}(\lambda x.\, T(x)), S) \to T(S)$$
$$\mathsf{app}(\mathsf{abs}(\lambda y.\, \mathsf{abs}(\lambda x.\, M(y,x))), S) \to \mathsf{abs}(\lambda x.\, \mathsf{app}(\mathsf{abs}(\lambda y.\, M(y,x)), S))$$
$$\mathsf{app}(\mathsf{app}(\mathsf{abs}(\lambda x.\, T(x)), S), U) \to \mathsf{app}(\mathsf{abs}(\lambda x.\, \mathsf{app}(T(x), U)), S)$$

Since the left- and right-hand side of the second and third rule are convertible using the first rule, they can be removed and confluence of the first rule alone can be established by Theorem 13.

5   Certification

Due to the increasing interest in automatic analysis of rewrite systems in recent years, it is of great importance whether a proof, generated by an automatic tool, is indeed correct (cf. Example 4). Since the proofs produced by such tools are often complex and large, checking correctness is impractical for humans. Hence there is strong interest in verifying them using an independent certifier. A certifier is a tool that reads proof certificates, and either accepts them as correct or rejects them as erroneous. To ensure correctness of the certifier, the predominant solution is to use proof assistants like Coq or Isabelle to first formalize the underlying theory in the proof assistant and then use the formalization to obtain verified functions for inspecting the certificates.

As certifier we use CeTA [41], which reads certificates in CPF (certification problem format) [40]. Given a certificate CeTA will either answer CERTIFIED, or return a detailed error message why the proof was REJECTED. Its correctness is formally proved as part of IsaFoR, the Isabelle Formalization of Rewriting. IsaFoR contains executable check-functions for each formalized proof technique together with formal proofs that whenever such a check succeeds, the technique was indeed applied correctly. Isabelle's code-generation facility is used to obtain a trusted Haskell program from these check functions: the certifier CeTA.[8] Since 2012 CeTA supports checking (non-)confluence certificates. CSI supports certifiable output for the following criteria checkable by CeTA: Knuth and Bendix' criterion [17,39], (weak) orthogonality [25,35], Huet's results on strongly closed and parallel closed critical pairs and Toyama's extenson of the latter [12,24,42], the rule labeling heuristic for decreasing diagrams [23,45], and transformations based on redundant rules [22]. For non-confluence CeTA can check that, given derivations $s \to^* t_1$ and $s \to^* t_2$, t_1 and t_2 cannot be joined. Here the justifications used by CSI are: using tcap [44] (i.e., test that $\mathsf{tcap}(t_1\sigma)$ and $\mathsf{tcap}(t_2\sigma)$ are not unifiable), and reachability analysis using tree automata [11]. Experimental results for certified confluence analysis are presented in Sect. 7.

6   Implementation Details

CSI is open source and available as pre-compiled binary or via the web-interface shown in Fig. 1 from http://cl-informatik.uibk.ac.at/software/csi, CSI^ho can be obtained from http://cl-informatik.uibk.ac.at/software/csi/ho. Since its first release one of CSI's defining features has been its *strategy language*, which enables the combination techniques in a flexible manner and facilitates integration of new criteria. Some of the combinators provided to combine methods that we will use below are: sequential composition of strategies ;, alternative composition | (which executes its second argument if the first fails), parallel execution ||, and iteration *. A postfix n* executes a strategy at most n times while [n] executes its argument for at most n seconds. Finally ? applies a strategy optionally (i.e., only if it makes progress), and ! ensures that its argument only succeeds if confluence could be (dis)proved. For a full grammar of the strategy language pass the option -h to CSI. To illustrate its power we briefly compare the strategy used in CSI 0.1 with the one from CSI 1.0. The original strategy was

---

[8] IsaFoR/CeTA and CPF are available at http://cl-informatik.uibk.ac.at/software/ceta.

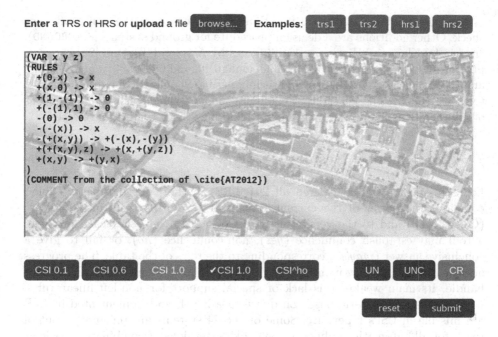

Enter a TRS or HRS or **upload** a file `browse...`   Examples: `trs1` `trs2` `hrs1` `hrs2`

```
(VAR x y z)
(RULES
  +(0,x) -> x
  +(x,0) -> x
  +(1,-(1)) -> 0
  +(-(1),1) -> 0
  -(0) -> 0
  -(-(x)) -> x
  -(+(x,y)) -> +(-(x),-(y))
  +(+(x,y),z) -> +(x,+(y,z))
  +(x,y) -> +(y,x)
)
(COMMENT from the collection of \cite{AT2012})
```

`CSI 0.1` `CSI 0.6` `CSI 1.0` `✓CSI 1.0` `CSI^ho`   `UN` `UNC` `CR`

`reset` `submit`

Fig. 1. The new web-interface of CSI.

```
(KB || NOTCR || (((CLOSED || DD) | add)2*)! || sorted -order)*
```

where `sorted -order` applies order-sorted decomposition and methods written in capitals are abbreviations for sub-strategies: `KB` applies Knuth-Bendix' criterion, `CLOSED` tests whether the critical pairs of a TRS are strongly or development closed, `DD` implements decreasing diagrams, and `NOTCR` tries to establish non-confluence. The current strategy is

```
(if trs then (sorted -order*;
(((GROUND || KB || AC || KH || AT || SIMPLE || CPCS2 ||
(REDUNDANT_DEL?; (CLOSED || DD || SIMPLE || KB || AC ||
GROUND))3*! || ((CLOSED || DD) | REDUNDANT_RHS)3*! ||
((CLOSED || DD) | REDUNDANT_JS)3*! || fail)[30] | CPCS[5]2*)2* ||
(NOTCR | REDUNDANT_FC)3*!)
) else fail)
```

which illustrates how to integrate new techniques independently or in combination with others, for instance the `REDUNDANT_X` strategies, which are different heuristics for finding redundant rules. The features described in Sect. 2 are reflected in `AC` and `REDUNDANT_FC`. The `AC` substrategy is simply tried in parallel to the existing methods for confluence and non-confluence. For the `REDUNDANT_FC` method, which *modifies* a problem, a different approach is used: first, a non-confluence proof (`NOTCR`) is attempted. If that fails, then rules from the forward closure are added, and the process is repeated, starting with another attempt at proving non-confluence. After 3 iterations, CSI gives up on the non-confluence check. Other additions are a decision procedure for ground systems [8] (GROUND), criteria by Klein and Hirokawa [15] (KH) and by Aoto and Toyama [2] (AT), simple to test syntactic criteria by Sakai, Oyamaguchi, and Ogawa [37], and Toyama and Oyamaguchi [43] (SIMPLE), and techniques based on critical pair closing systems [31] (CPCS). The full strategy configuration file (which consists of definitions of abbreviations like AC) grew from 76 to 233 lines since the initial release.

7   Experimental Results

For experiments[9] we considered all 291 TRSs in the Cops database. Table 1 compares the power of the current version of CSI (1.0) to its initial release (CSI 0.1 [44]) and to the version used in CoCo 2016 (0.6). For each problem, a tool may establish confluence (*yes*), non-confluence (*no*), or fail to give a conclusive answer (*maybe*), corresponding to the rows of the table. The progress achieved in the past few months is obvious. Of the 24 systems which CSI cannot handle, its main weakness is lack of special support for non-left-linear rules. Here for instance criteria based on quasi-linearity [4] and implemented in ACP are missing in CSI's repertoire. Some of the 24 systems are (currently) out of reach for all automatic confluence tools, like extensions of combinatory logic or self-distributivity.

The fourth column shows the results when using CSI's certifiable strategy, i.e., only criteria that can be checked by CeTA. Note that the *maybe* answers, in principle, include proofs produced by CSI that are not accepted by CeTA. However, because we also use Cops for testing the tools, this case does not occur for this set of problems. While all non-confluence proofs produced by CSI are certifiable there is still a gap in confluence analysis. The main missing techniques are a criterion to deal with AC rules, e.g. the ones from Sect. 2 or the one by Aoto and Toyama [2], advanced decomposition techniques based on layer systems [10], and techniques for dealing with non-left-linear systems, in particular the criteria by Klein and Hirokawa [15] and by Sakai, Oyamaguchi, and Ogawa [37]. The formalization and subsequent certification of most of these techniques requires serious effort, which we leave as future work.

Table 2 summarizes the results for UNR and UNC. We include CR in the table because proving confluence is a common way of establishing UNR or UNC.

Table 1. Confluence results.

	CSI 0.1	CSI 0.6	CSI 1.0	√CSI 1.0		CSI^ho
yes	115	179	206	116	yes	50
no	46	55	61	61	no	10
maybe	130	57	24	114	maybe	9

[9] Full details are available from CSI's website.

Table 2. Unique normal form results.

	T	UNR	UNC	CR
T	120	43	37	17
¬CR	81	20	14	–
¬UNC	33	6	–	–
¬UNR	27	–	–	–

The T row (where T stands for *true*) represents the positive (yes) results for the corresponding properties, whereas the T column represents the negative results. For these experiments we used 120 TRSs which are comprised of the 100 Cops that at most one of the tools ACP, CoLL-Saigawa, or CSI could show confluent in the respective version used in CoCo 2016, and an additional 20 TRSs that were used in the UNR demonstration category in CoCo 2016. Note that the table entries overlap. For example, there are 20 problems for which CR has been disproved and UNR has been established; these 20 problems include the 14 problems which have been shown to satisfy UNC but not CR. The number of problems for which none of the properties UNR, UNC, or CR was proved or disproved is $120 + 20 - 81 - 43 = 16$.

For experiments in the higher-order setting we again used Cops, which contains 69 PRSs. CSI^ho can show confluence of 50 and non-confluence of 10 of these. Solving the remaining 9 systems will require serious effort—they contain e.g. lambda calculus with surjective pairing and self-distributivity of explicit substitution.

Acknowledgments. We thank Sarah Winkler for contributing code and expertise related to AC termination and AC critical pairs.

References

1. Aoto, T., Hirokawa, N., Nagele, J., Nishida, N., Zankl, H.: Confluence competition 2015. In: Felty, A.P., Middeldorp, A. (eds.) CADE 2015. LNCS, vol. 9195, pp. 101–104. Springer, Cham (2015). doi:10.1007/978-3-319-21401-6_5
2. Aoto, T., Toyama, Y.: A reduction-preserving completion for proving confluence of non-terminating term rewriting systems. LMCS **8**(1: 31), 1–29 (2012). doi:10.2168/LMCS-8(1:31)2012
3. Aoto, T., Toyama, Y.: Ground confluence prover based on rewriting induction. In: Proceedings of 1st FSCD. LIPIcs, vol. 52, pp. 33: 1–33: 12 (2016). doi:10.4230/LIPIcs.FSCD.2016.33
4. Aoto, T., Toyama, Y., Uchida, K.: Proving confluence of term rewriting systems via persistency and decreasing diagrams. In: Dowek, G. (ed.) RTA 2014. LNCS, vol. 8560, pp. 46–60. Springer, Cham (2014). doi:10.1007/978-3-319-08918-8_4
5. Aoto, T., Yoshida, J., Toyama, Y.: Proving confluence of term rewriting systems automatically. In: Treinen, R. (ed.) RTA 2009. LNCS, vol. 5595, pp. 93–102. Springer, Heidelberg (2009). doi:10.1007/978-3-642-02348-4_7

6. Appel, C., van Oostrom, V., Simonsen, J.G.: Higher-order (non-)modularity. In: Proceedings of 21st RTA. LIPIcs, vol. 6, pp. 17–32 (2010). doi:10.4230/LIPIcs. RTA.2010.17
7. Baader, F., Nipkow, T.: Term Rewriting and All That. Cambridge University Press, New York (1998)
8. Felgenhauer, B.: Deciding confluence of ground term rewrite systems in cubic time. In: Proceedings of 23rd RTA. LIPIcs, vol. 15, pp. 165–175 (2012). doi:10.4230/ LIPIcs.RTA.2012.165
9. Felgenhauer, B.: Efficiently deciding uniqueness of normal forms and unique normalization for ground TRSs. In: Proceedings of 5th IWC, pp. 16–20 (2016)
10. Felgenhauer, B., Middeldorp, A., Zankl, H., Oostrom, V.O.: Layer systems for proving confluence. ACM TOCL 16(2: 14), 1–32 (2015). doi:10.1145/2710017
11. Felgenhauer, B., Thiemann, R.: Reachability analysis with state-compatible automata. In: Dediu, A.-H., Martín-Vide, C., Sierra-Rodríguez, J.-L., Truthe, B. (eds.) LATA 2014. LNCS, vol. 8370, pp. 347–359. Springer, Cham (2014). doi:10. 1007/978-3-319-04921-2_28
12. Huet, G.: Confluent reductions: Abstract properties and applications to term rewriting systems. JACM 27(4), 797–821 (1980). doi:10.23638/LMCS-13(2:4)2017
13. Jouannaud, J.P., Kirchner, H.: Completion of a set of rules modulo a set of equations. SIAM J. Comput. 15(4), 1155–1194 (1986). doi:10.1137/0215084
14. Kahrs, S., Smith, C.: Non-ω-overlapping TRSs are UN. In: Proceedings of 1st FSCD. LIPIcs, vol. 52, pp. 22: 1–22: 17 (2016). doi:10.4230/LIPIcs.FSCD.2016.22
15. Klein, D., Hirokawa, N.: Confluence of non-left-linear TRSs via relative termination. In: Bjørner, N., Voronkov, A. (eds.) LPAR 2012. LNCS, vol. 7180, pp. 258–273. Springer, Heidelberg (2012). doi:10.1007/978-3-642-28717-6_21
16. Klop, J.: Combinatory reduction systems. Ph.D. thesis, Utrecht University (1980)
17. Knuth, D., Bendix, P.: Simple word problems in universal algebras. In: Leech, J. (ed.) Computational Problems in Abstract Algebra, pp. 263–297. Pergamon Press, Oxford (1970)
18. Kop, C.: Higher order termination. Ph.D. thesis, Vrije Universiteit, Amsterdam (2012)
19. Kusakari, K., Isogai, Y., Sakai, M., Blanqui, F.: Static dependency pair method based on strong computability for higher-order rewrite systems. IEICE TIS 92– D(10), 2007–2015 (2009)
20. Mayr, R., Nipkow, T.: Higher-order rewrite systems and their confluence. TCS 192(1), 3–29 (1998). doi:10.1016/S0304-3975(97)00143--6
21. Miller, D.: A logic programming language with lambda-abstraction, function variables, and simple unification. JLP 1(4), 497–536 (1991). doi:10.1093/logcom/1.4. 497
22. Nagele, J., Felgenhauer, B., Middeldorp, A.: Improving automatic confluence analysis of rewrite systems by redundant rules. In: Proceedings of 26th RTA. LIPIcs, vol. 36, pp. 257–268 (2015). doi:10.4230/LIPIcs.RTA.2015.257
23. Nagele, J., Felgenhauer, B., Zankl, H.: Certifying confluence proofs via relative termination and rule labeling. LMCS (to appear) (2017)
24. Nagele, J., Middeldorp, A.: Certification of classical confluence results for left-linear term rewrite systems. In: Blanchette, J.C., Merz, S. (eds.) ITP 2016. LNCS, vol. 9807, pp. 290–306. Springer, Cham (2016). doi:10.1007/978-3-319-43144-4_18
25. Nagele, J., Thiemann, R.: Certification of confluence proofs using CeTA. In: Proceedings of 3rd IWC, pp. 19–23 (2014)
26. Nelson, G., Oppen, D.: Fast decision procedures based on congruence closure. JACM 27(2), 356–364 (1980). doi:10.1145/322186.322198

27. Nipkow, T.: Higher-order critical pairs. In: Proceedings of 6th LICS, pp. 342–349 (1991). doi:10.1109/LICS.1991.151658

28. Nipkow, T.: Functional unification of higher-order patterns. In: Proceedings of 8th LICS, pp. 64–74 (1993). doi:10.1109/LICS.1993.287599

29. van Oostrom, V.: Developing developments. TCS **175**(1), 159–181 (1997). doi:10.1016/S0304-3975(96)00173-9

30. van Oostrom, V., Raamsdonk, F.: Weak orthogonality implies confluence: the higher-order case. In: Nerode, A., Matiyasevich, Y.V. (eds.) LFCS 1994. LNCS, vol. 813, pp. 379–392. Springer, Heidelberg (1994). doi:10.1007/3-540-58140-5_35

31. Oyamaguchi, M., Hirokawa, N.: Confluence and critical-pair-closing systems. In: Proceedings of 3rd IWC, pp. 29–33 (2014)

32. Peterson, G.E., Stickel, M.E.: Complete sets of reductions for some equational theories. JACM **28**(2), 233–264 (1981). doi:10.1145/322248.322251

33. van Raamsdonk, F.: On termination of higher-order rewriting. In: Middeldorp, A. (ed.) RTA 2001. LNCS, vol. 2051, pp. 261–275. Springer, Heidelberg (2001). doi:10.1007/3-540-45127-7_20

34. Regnier, L.: Une équivalence sur les lambda-termes. TCS **126**(2), 281–292 (1994). doi:10.1016/0304-3975(94)90012--4

35. Rosen, B.: Tree-manipulating systems and Church-Rosser theorems. JACM **20**(1), 160–187 (1973). doi:10.1145/321738.321750

36. Rubio, A.: A fully syntactic AC-RPO. I&C **178**(2), 515–533 (2002). doi:10.1006/inco.2002.3158

37. Sakai, M., Oyamaguchi, M., Ogawa, M.: Non-E-overlapping, weakly shallow, and non-collapsing TRSs are confluent. In: Felty, A.P., Middeldorp, A. (eds.) CADE 2015. LNCS (LNAI), vol. 9195, pp. 111–126. Springer, Cham (2015). doi:10.1007/978-3-319-21401-6_7

38. Shintani, K., Hirokawa, N.: CoLL: A confluence tool for left-linear term rewrite systems. In: Felty, A.P., Middeldorp, A. (eds.) CADE 2015. LNCS (LNAI), vol. 9195, pp. 127–136. Springer, Cham (2015). doi:10.1007/978-3-319-21401-6_8

39. Sternagel, C., Thiemann, R.: Formalizing Knuth-Bendix orders and Knuth-Bendix completion. In: Proceedings of 24th RTA. LIPIcs, vol. 21, pp. 287–302 (2013).doi:10.4230/LIPIcs.RTA.2013.287

40. Sternagel, C., Thiemann, R.: The certification problem format. In: Proceedings of 11th UITP. EPTCS, vol. 167, pp. 61–72 (2014). doi:10.4204/EPTCS.167.8

41. Thiemann, R., Sternagel, C.: Certification of termination proofs using CeTA. In: Berghofer, S., Nipkow, T., Urban, C., Wenzel, M. (eds.) TPHOLs 2009. LNCS, vol. 5674, pp. 452–468. Springer, Heidelberg (2009). doi:10.1007/978-3-642-03359-9_31

42. Toyama, Y.: Commutativity of term rewriting systems. In: Fuchi, K., Kott, L. (eds.) Programming of Future Generation Computers II, pp. 393–407. North-Holland Publishing, North Holland (1988)

43. Toyama, Y., Oyamaguchi, M.: Church-Rosser property and unique normal form property of non-duplicating term rewriting systems. In: Proceedings of the 4th CTRS withDershowitz N., Lindenstrauss N. (eds.) CTRS 1994. LNCS, vol. 968 (1995). doi:10.1007/3-540-60381-6_19

44. Zankl, H., Felgenhauer, B., Middeldorp, A.: CSI – a confluence tool. In: Bjørner, N., Sofronie-Stokkermans, V. (eds.) CADE 2011. LNCS, vol. 6803, pp. 499–505. Springer, Heidelberg (2011). doi:10.1007/978-3-642-22438-6_38

45. Zankl, H., Felgenhauer, B., Middeldorp, A.: Labelings for decreasing diagrams. JAR **54**(2), 101–133 (2015). doi:10.1007/s10817-014-9316-y

Scalable Fine-Grained Proofs
for Formula Processing

Haniel Barbosa[1,2]([⊠]), Jasmin Christian Blanchette[1,3,4], and Pascal Fontaine[1]

[1] Université de Lorraine, CNRS, Inria, LORIA, Nancy, France
{haniel.barbosa,jasmin.blanchette,pascal.fontaine}@loria.fr
[2] Universidade Federal do Rio Grande do Norte, Natal, Brazil
[3] Vrije Universiteit Amsterdam, Amsterdam, The Netherlands
[4] Max-Planck-Institut für Informatik, Saarbrücken, Germany

Abstract. We present a framework for processing formulas in automatic theorem provers, with generation of detailed proofs. The main components are a generic contextual recursion algorithm and an extensible set of inference rules. Clausification, skolemization, theory-specific simplifications, and expansion of 'let' expressions are instances of this framework. With suitable data structures, proof generation adds only a linear-time overhead, and proofs can be checked in linear time. We implemented the approach in the SMT solver veriT. This allowed us to dramatically simplify the code base while increasing the number of problems for which detailed proofs can be produced, which is important for independent checking and reconstruction in proof assistants.

1 Introduction

An increasing number of automatic theorem provers can generate certificates, or proofs, that justify the formulas they derive. These proofs can be checked by other programs and shared across reasoning systems. Some users will also want to inspect this output to understand why a formula holds. Proof production is generally well understood for the core proving methods and for many theories commonly used in satisfiability modulo theories (SMT). But most automatic provers also perform some formula processing or preprocessing—such as clausification and rewriting with theory-specific lemmas—and proof production for this aspect is less mature.

For most provers, the code for processing formulas is lengthy and deals with a multitude of cases, some of which are rarely executed. Although it is crucial for efficiency, this code tends to be given much less attention than other aspects of provers. Developers are reluctant to invest effort in producing detailed proofs for such processing, since this requires adapting a lot of code. As a result, the granularity of inferences for formula processing is often coarse. Sometimes, processing features are even disabled to avoid gaps in proofs, at a high cost in proof search performance.

Fine-grained proofs are important for a variety of applications. We propose a framework to generate such proofs without slowing down proof search. Proofs

© Springer International Publishing AG 2017
L. de Moura (Ed.): CADE 2017, LNAI 10395, pp. 398–412, 2017.
DOI: 10.1007/978-3-319-63046-5_25

are expressed using an extensible set of inference rules (Sect. 2). The succedent of a rule is an equality between the original term and the translated term. (It is convenient to consider formulas a special case of terms.) The rules have a fine granularity, making it possible to cleanly separate theories. Clausification, theory-specific simplifications, and expansion of 'let' expressions are instances of this framework. Skolemization may seem problematic, but with the help of Hilbert's choice operator, it can also be integrated into the framework. Some provers provide very detailed proofs for parts of the solving, but we are not aware of any publications about practical attempts to provide easily reconstructible proofs for processing formulas containing quantifiers and 'let' expressions.

At the heart of the framework lies a generic contextual recursion algorithm that traverses the terms to translate (Sect. 3). The context fixes some variables, maintains a substitution, and keeps track of polarities or other data. The transformation-specific work, including the generation of proofs, is performed by plugin functions that are given as parameters to the framework. The recursion algorithm, which is critical for the performance and correctness of the generated proofs, needs to be implemented only once. Another benefit of the modular architecture is that we can easily combine several transformations in a single pass, without complicating the code unduly or compromising the level of detail of the proof output. For very large inputs, this can improve performance.

The inference rules and the contextual recursion algorithm enjoy many desirable properties (Sect. 4). The rules are sound, and the treatment of binders is correct even in the presence of name clashes. Moreover, with suitable data structures, proof generation adds an overhead that is proportional to the time spent processing the terms. Checking proofs represented as directed acyclic graphs (DAGs) can be performed with a time complexity that is linear in their size. Detailed proofs of the metatheory are included in a technical report [2], together with more explanations and examples.

We implemented the approach in veriT (Sect. 5), an SMT solver that is competitive on problems combining equality, linear arithmetic, and quantifiers [3]. Compared with other SMT solvers, veriT is known for its very detailed proofs [5], which are reconstructed in the proof assistants Coq [1] and Isabelle/HOL [6] and in the GAPT system [10]. As a proof of concept, we implemented a prototype checker in Isabelle/HOL.

By adopting the new framework, we were able to remove large amounts of complicated code in the solver, while enabling detailed proofs for more transformations than before. The contextual recursion algorithm had to be implemented only once and is more thoroughly tested than any of the monolithic transformations it subsumes. Our empirical evaluation reveals that veriT is as fast as before even though it now generates finer-grained proofs.

1.1 Conventions

Our setting is a many-sorted classical first-order logic as defined by the SMT-LIB standard [4]. A signature $\Sigma = (S, F)$ consists of a set S of sorts and a set F of function symbols. Nullary function symbols are called constants.

We assume that the signature contains a Bool sort and constants true, false : Bool, a family $(\simeq : \sigma \times \sigma \to \text{Bool})_{\sigma \in S}$ of function symbols interpreted as equality, and the connectives $\neg, \wedge, \vee,$ and $\longrightarrow$. Formulas are terms of type Bool, and equivalence is equality $(\simeq)$ on Bool. Terms are built over symbols from $\mathcal{F}$ and variables from a fixed family of infinite sets $(\mathcal{V}_\sigma)_{\sigma \in S}$. In addition to $\forall$ and $\exists$, we rely on two more binders: Hilbert's choice operator $\varepsilon x.\varphi$ and a 'let' construct, let $\bar{x}_n \simeq \bar{s}_n$ in t, which simultaneously assigns n variables.

We use the symbol $=$ for syntactic equality on terms. We reserve the names $\mathsf{a}, \mathsf{f}, \mathsf{p}, \mathsf{q}$ for function symbols; x, y for variables; r, s, t, u for terms (which may be formulas); φ, ψ for formulas; and Q for quantifiers ($\forall$ and $\exists$). We use the notations $\bar{a}_n$ and $(a_i)_{i=1}^n$ to denote the tuple, or vector, $(a_1, \ldots, a_n)$. We write $[n]$ for $\{1, \ldots, n\}$.

Given a term t, the set of its free variables is written $FV(t)$. The notation $t[\bar{x}_n]$ stands for a term that may depend on $\bar{x}_n$; $t[\bar{s}_n]$ is the corresponding term where the terms $\bar{s}_n$ are substituted for $\bar{x}_n$. Bound variables in t are renamed to avoid capture. Following these conventions, Hilbert choice and 'let' are characterized by

$$\models \exists x.\ \varphi[x] \longrightarrow \varphi[\varepsilon x.\varphi] \tag{ε_1}$$

$$\models (\forall x.\ \varphi \simeq \psi) \longrightarrow (\varepsilon x.\varphi) \simeq (\varepsilon x.\psi) \tag{ε_2}$$

$$\models (\text{let } \bar{x}_n \simeq \bar{s}_n \text{ in } t[\bar{x}_n]) \simeq t[\bar{s}_n] \tag{let}$$

Substitutions ρ are functions from variables to terms such that $\rho(x_i) \neq x_i$ for at most finitely many variables x_i. We write them as $\{\bar{x}_n \mapsto \bar{s}_n\}$. The substitution $\rho[\bar{x}_n \mapsto \bar{s}_n]$ maps each variable x_i to the term s_i and otherwise coincides with ρ. The application of a substitution ρ to a term t is denoted by $\rho(t)$. It is capture-avoiding; bound variables in t are renamed as necessary. Composition $\rho' \circ \rho$ is defined as for functions (i.e., ρ is applied first).

2 Inference System

The inference rules used by our framework depend on a notion of *context* defined by the grammar $\Gamma ::= \varnothing \mid \Gamma, x \mid \Gamma, \bar{x}_n \mapsto \bar{s}_n$. Each context entry either *fixes* a variable x or defines a *substitution* $\{\bar{x}_n \mapsto \bar{s}_n\}$. If a context introduces the same variable several times, the rightmost entry shadows the others. Abstractly, a context Γ fixes a set of variables and specifies a substitution $subst(\Gamma)$ defined by $subst(\varnothing) = \{\}$, $subst(\Gamma, x) = subst(\Gamma)[x \mapsto x]$, and $subst(\Gamma, \bar{x}_n \mapsto \bar{t}_n) = subst(\Gamma) \circ \{\bar{x}_n \mapsto \bar{t}_n\}$. In the second equation, the $[x \mapsto x]$ update shadows any replacement of x induced by Γ. We write $\Gamma(t)$ to abbreviate the capture-avoiding substitution $subst(\Gamma)(t)$.

Transformations of terms (and formulas) are justified by judgments of the form $\Gamma \triangleright t \simeq u$, where Γ is a context, t is an unprocessed term, and u is the corresponding processed term. The free variables in t and u must appear in the context Γ. Semantically, the judgment expresses the equality of the terms $\Gamma(t)$ and u for all variables fixed by Γ. Crucially, the substitution applies only on the left-hand side of the equality.

The inference rules for the transformations covered in this paper are presented below.

$$\frac{}{\Gamma \rhd t \simeq u} \ \text{Taut}\mathscr{T} \quad \text{if} \ \models_{\mathscr{T}} \Gamma(t) \simeq u$$

$$\frac{\Gamma \rhd s \simeq t \quad \Gamma \rhd t \simeq u}{\Gamma \rhd s \simeq u} \ \text{Trans} \quad \text{if} \ \Gamma(t) = t$$

$$\frac{(\Gamma \rhd t_i \simeq u_i)_{i=1}^{n}}{\Gamma \rhd \mathsf{f}(\bar{t}_n) \simeq \mathsf{f}(\bar{u}_n)} \ \text{Cong}$$

$$\frac{\Gamma, y, x \mapsto y \rhd \varphi \simeq \psi}{\Gamma \rhd (Qx.\, \varphi) \simeq (Qy.\, \psi)} \ \text{Bind} \quad \text{if} \ y \notin FV(Qx.\, \varphi)$$

$$\frac{\Gamma, x \mapsto (\varepsilon x.\varphi) \rhd \varphi \simeq \psi}{\Gamma \rhd (\exists x.\, \varphi) \simeq \psi} \ \text{Sko}_{\exists} \qquad \frac{\Gamma, x \mapsto (\varepsilon x.\neg \varphi) \rhd \varphi \simeq \psi}{\Gamma \rhd (\forall x.\, \varphi) \simeq \psi} \ \text{Sko}_{\forall}$$

$$\frac{(\Gamma \rhd r_i \simeq s_i)_{i=1}^{n} \quad \Gamma, \bar{x}_n \mapsto \bar{s}_n \rhd t \simeq u}{\Gamma \rhd (\text{let} \ \bar{x}_n \simeq \bar{r}_n \ \text{in} \ t) \simeq u} \ \text{Let} \quad \text{if} \ \Gamma(s_i) = s_i \ \text{for all} \ i \in [n]$$

- $\mathscr{T}$ relies on an oracle $\mathscr{T}$ to derive arbitrary lemmas in a theory $\mathscr{T}$. In practice, the oracle will produce some kind of certificate to justify the inference. An important special case, for which we use the name REFL, is syntactic equality.
- TRANS needs the side condition because the term t appears both on the left-hand side of $\simeq$ (where it is subject to Γ's substitution) and on the right-hand side.
- CONG can be used for any function symbol f, including the logical connectives.
- BIND is a congruence rule for quantifiers. The rule also justifies the renaming of the bound variable. The side condition prevents an unwarranted variable capture. In the antecedent, the renaming is expressed by a substitution in the context.
- SKO$_{\exists}$ and SKO$_{\forall}$ exploit (ε_1) to replace a quantified variable with a suitable witness, simulating skolemization. We can think of the ε expression in each rule abstractly as a fresh function symbol that takes any fixed variables it depends on as arguments.
- LET exploits (let) to expand a 'let' expression. The terms $\bar{r}_n$ assigned to the variables $\bar{x}_n$ can be transformed into terms $\bar{s}_n$.

The antecedents of all the rules inspect subterms structurally, without modifying them. Modifications to the term on the left-hand side are delayed; the substitution is applied only in TAUT. This is crucial to obtain compact proofs that can be checked efficiently. By systematically renaming variables in BIND, we can satisfy most side conditions trivially.

Judgments can be encoded into a well-understood theory of binders: the simply typed λ-calculus. This provides a solid basis to reason about them, and to reconstruct proofs expressed in the inference system. We refer to our technical report [2] for details.

The set of rules can be extended to cater for arbitrary transformations that can be expressed as equalities, using Hilbert choice to represent fresh symbols if necessary. The usefulness of Hilbert choice for proof reconstruction is well known [7,19,21], but we push the idea further and use it to simplify the inference system and make it more uniform.

Example 1. The following derivation tree justifies the expansion of a 'let' expression:

$$
\cfrac{
\cfrac{}{\rhd\, \mathsf{a} \simeq \mathsf{a}}\;\textsc{Cong}
\qquad
\cfrac{
\cfrac{}{x \mapsto \mathsf{a} \rhd x \simeq \mathsf{a}}\;\textsc{Refl}
\qquad
\cfrac{}{x \mapsto \mathsf{a} \rhd x \simeq \mathsf{a}}\;\textsc{Refl}
}{x \mapsto \mathsf{a} \rhd \mathsf{p}(x,x) \simeq \mathsf{p}(\mathsf{a},\mathsf{a})}\;\textsc{Cong}
}{\rhd\, (\text{let } x \simeq \mathsf{a} \text{ in } \mathsf{p}(x,x)) \simeq \mathsf{p}(\mathsf{a},\mathsf{a})}\;\textsc{Let}
$$

Skolemization can be applied regardless of polarity. Normally, we skolemize only positive existential quantifiers and negative universal quantifiers. However, skolemizing other quantifiers is sound in the context of proving. The trouble is that it is generally incomplete, if we introduce Skolem symbols and forget their definitions in terms of Hilbert choice. To paraphrase Orwell, all quantifiers are skolemizable, but some quantifiers are more skolemizable than others.

3   Contextual Recursion

We propose a generic algorithm for term transformations, based on structural recursion. The algorithm is parameterized by a few simple plugin functions embodying the essence of the transformation. By combining compatible plugin functions, we can perform several transformations in one traversal. Transformations can depend on some context that encapsulates relevant information, such as bound variables, variable substitutions, and polarity. Each transformation can define its own notion of context.

The output is generated by a proof module that maintains a stack of derivation trees. The procedure $apply(R, n, \Gamma, t, u)$ pops n derivation trees $\bar{\mathscr{D}}_n$ from the stack and pushes the tree of $\Gamma \rhd t \simeq u$ obtained by applying rule R to $\bar{\mathscr{D}}_n$. The plugin functions are responsible for invoking *apply* as appropriate.

3.1   The Generic Algorithm

The algorithm performs a depth-first postorder contextual recursion on the term to process. Subterms are processed first; then an intermediate term is built from the resulting subterms and is processed in turn. The context Δ is updated in a transformation-specific way with each recursive call. It is abstract from the point of view of the algorithm. The plugin functions are divided into two groups:

ctx_let, *ctx_quant*, and *ctx_app* update the context when entering the body of a binder or when moving from a function symbol to one of its arguments; *build_let*, *build_app*, *build_app*, and *build_var* return the processed term and produce the corresponding proof as a side effect.

> **function** *process*(Δ, t)
>   **match** t
>   **case** x:
>   **return** *build_var*(Δ, x)
>   **case** $f(\bar{t}_n)$:
> $\bar{\Delta}'_n \leftarrow (ctx\_app(\Delta, f, \bar{t}_n, i))_{i=1}^n$
>   **return** *build_app*$\big(\Delta, \bar{\Delta}'_n, f, \bar{t}_n, (process(\Delta'_i, t_i))_{i=1}^n\big)$
>   **case** $Qx.\,\varphi$:
> $\Delta' \leftarrow ctx\_quant(\Delta, Q, x, \varphi)$
>   **return** *build_quant*(Δ, Δ', Q, x, φ, $process(\Delta', \varphi)$)
>   **case let** $\bar{x}_n \simeq \bar{r}_n$ **in** t':
> $\Delta' \leftarrow ctx\_let(\Delta, \bar{x}_n, \bar{r}_n, t')$
>   **return** *build_let*(Δ, Δ', $\bar{x}_n$, $\bar{r}_n$, t', $process(\Delta', t')$)

3.2 'Let' Expansion

The first instance of the contextual recursion algorithm expands 'let' expressions and renames bound variables systematically to avoid capture. Skolemization and theory simplification, presented below, assume that this transformation has been performed. The context consists of a list of fixed variables and variable substitutions, as in Sect. 2. The plugin functions are as follows:

> **function** *ctx_let*(Γ, $\bar{x}_n$, $\bar{r}_n$, t)   **function** *ctx_app*(Γ, f, $\bar{t}_n$, i)
>   **return** $\Gamma, \bar{x}_n \mapsto (process(\Gamma, r_i))_{i=1}^n$ **return** Γ
>
> **function** *build_let*(Γ, Γ', $\bar{x}_n$, $\bar{r}_n$, t, u)   **function** *build_app*(Γ, $\bar{\Gamma}'_n$, f, $\bar{t}_n$, $\bar{u}_n$)
>   *apply*(LET, $n+1$, Γ, **let** $\bar{x}_n \simeq \bar{r}_n$ **in** t, u)   *apply*(CONG, n, Γ, $f(\bar{t}_n)$, $f(\bar{u}_n)$)
>   **return** u **return** $f(\bar{u}_n)$
>
> **function** *ctx_quant*(Γ, Q, x, φ)   **function** *build_var*(Γ, x)
> $y \leftarrow$ fresh variable   *apply*(REFL, 0, Γ, x, $\Gamma(x)$)
>   **return** $\Gamma, y, x \mapsto y$ **return** $\Gamma(x)$
>
> **function** *build_quant*(Γ, Γ', Q, x, φ, ψ)
> $y \leftarrow \Gamma'(x)$
>   *apply*(BIND, 1, Γ, $Qx.\,\varphi$, $Qy.\,\psi$)
>   **return** $Qy.\,\psi$

The *ctx_let* and *build_let* functions process 'let' expressions. In *ctx_let*, the substituted terms are processed further before they are added to a substitution entry in the context. In *build_let*, the LET rule is applied and the transformed term is returned. Analogously, the *ctx_quant* and *build_quant* functions rename quantified variables systematically. This ensures that any variables that arise in the range of the substitution specified by *ctx_let* will resist capture when the substitution is applied. Finally, the *ctx_app*, *build_app*, and *build_var* functions simply reproduce the term traversal in the generated proof; they perform no transformation-specific work.

Example 2. Following up on Example 1, assume $\varphi = $ let $x \simeq$ a in p(x, x). Given the above plugin functions, *process*$(\varnothing, \varphi)$ returns p(a, a). It is instructive to study the evolution of the stack during the execution of *process*. First, in *ctx_let*, the term a is processed recursively; the call to *build_app* pushes a nullary CONG step with succedent $\rhd$ a $\simeq$ a onto the stack. Then the term p(x, x) is processed. For each of the two occurrences of x, *build_var* pushes a REFL step onto the stack. Next, *build_app* applies a CONG step to justify rewriting under p: The two REFL steps are popped, and a binary CONG is pushed. Finally, *build_let* performs a LET inference with succedent $\rhd$ $\varphi \simeq$ p(a, a) to complete the proof: The two CONG steps on the stack are replaced by the LET step. The stack now consists of a single item: the derivation tree of Example 1.

3.3   Skolemization

Our second transformation, skolemization, assumes that 'let' expressions have been expanded and bound variables have been renamed apart. The context is a pair $\Delta = (\Gamma, p)$, where Γ is as defined in Sect. 2 and p is the polarity (+, −, or ?) of the term being processed. The main plugin functions are those that manipulate quantifiers:

> **function** *ctx_quant*$((\Gamma, p), Q, x, \varphi)$
>   **if** $(Q, p) \in \{(\exists, +), (\forall, -)\}$ **then**
> $\Gamma' \leftarrow \Gamma, x \mapsto sko\_term(\Gamma, Q, x, \varphi)$
>   **else**
> $\Gamma' \leftarrow \Gamma, x$
>   **return** (Γ', p)

The polarity is updated by *ctx_app*, which is not shown. For example, *ctx_app*$((\Gamma, -), \neg, \varphi, 1)$ returns $(\Gamma, +)$, because if $\neg\,\varphi$ occurs negatively in a larger formula, then φ occurs positively. The plugin functions *build_app* and *build_var* are as for 'let' expansion.

Positive occurrences of $\exists$ and negative occurrences of $\forall$ are skolemized. All other quantifiers are kept as they are. The *sko_term* function returns an applied Skolem function symbol following some reasonable scheme; for example, outer skolemization [20] creates an application of a fresh function symbol to all variables fixed in the context. To comply with the inference system, the application of SKO$_\exists$ or SKO$_\forall$ in *build_app* instructs the proof module to systematically replace the Skolem term with the corresponding ε term when outputting the proof.

3.4   Theory Simplification

All kinds of theory simplification can be performed on formulas. We restrict our focus to a simple yet quite characteristic instance: the simplification of $u + 0$ and $0 + u$ to u. We assume that 'let' expressions have been expanded. The context is a list of fixed variables. The plugin functions ctx_app and $build\_var$ are as for 'let' expansion; the remaining ones are presented below.

function $ctx\_quant(\Gamma, Q, x, \varphi)$
 return Γ, x

function $build\_quant(\Gamma, \Gamma', Q, x, \varphi, \psi)$
 $apply(\text{BIND}, 1, \Gamma, Qx.\, \varphi, Qx.\, \psi)$
 return $Qx.\, \psi$

function $build\_app(\Gamma, \bar{\Gamma}'_n, \mathsf{f}, \bar{t}_n, \bar{u}_n)$
 $apply(\text{CONG}, n, \Gamma, \mathsf{f}(\bar{t}_n), \mathsf{f}(\bar{u}_n))$
 if $\mathsf{f}(\bar{u}_n)$ has form $u + 0$ or $0 + u$
 then
  $apply(\text{TAUT}_+, 0, \Gamma, \mathsf{f}(\bar{u}_n), u)$
  $apply(\text{TRANS}, 2, \Gamma, \mathsf{f}(\bar{t}_n), u)$
  return u
 else
  return $\mathsf{f}(\bar{u}_n)$

The quantifier manipulation code, in ctx_quant and $build\_app$, is straightforward. The interesting function is $build\_app$. It first applies the CONG rule to justify rewriting the arguments. Then, if the resulting term $\mathsf{f}(\bar{u}_n)$ can be simplified further into a term u, it performs a transitive chain of reasoning: $\mathsf{f}(\bar{t}_n) \simeq \mathsf{f}(\bar{u}_n) \simeq u$.

3.5   Combinations of Transformations

Theory simplification can be implemented as a family of transformations, each member of which embodies its own set of theory-specific rewrite rules. If the union of the rewrite rule sets is confluent and terminating, a unifying implementation of $build\_app$ can apply the rules in any order until a fixpoint is reached. Moreover, since theory simplification modifies terms independently of the context, it is compatible with 'let' expansion and skolemization. This allows us to perform arithmetic simplification in the substituted terms of a 'let' expression in a single pass.

The combination of 'let' expansion and skolemization is less straightforward. Consider the formula $\varphi = \text{let } y \simeq \exists x.\, \mathsf{p}(x) \text{ in } y \to y$. When processing the subformula $\exists x.\, \mathsf{p}(x)$, we cannot (or at least should not) skolemize the quantifier, because it has no unambiguous polarity; indeed, the variable y occurs both positively and negatively in the 'let' expression's body. We can of course give up and perform two passes: The first pass expands 'let' expressions, and the second pass skolemizes and simplifies terms. There is also a way to perform all the transformations in a single instance of the framework, described in our report [2].

3.6   Scope and Limitations

Other possible instances of contextual recursion are the clause normal form (CNF) transformation and the elimination of quantifiers using one-point rules.

CNF transformation is an instance of rewriting of Boolean formulas and can be justified by a TAUT$_{Bool}$ rule. Tseytin transformation can be supported by representing the introduced constants by the formulas they represent, similarly to our treatment of Skolem terms. One-point rules—e.g., the transformation of $\forall x.\ x \simeq a \longrightarrow p(x)$ into $p(a)$—are similar to 'let' expansion and can be represented in much the same way in our framework.

Some transformations, such as symmetry breaking [9] and rewriting based on global assumptions, require a global analysis of the problem that cannot be captured by local substitution of equals for equals. They are beyond the scope of the framework. Other transformations, such as simplification based on associativity and commutativity of function symbols, require traversing the terms to be simplified when applying the rewriting. Since *process* visits terms in postorder, the complexity of the simplifications would be quadratic, while a processing that applies depth-first preorder traversal can perform the simplifications with a linear complexity. Hence, applying such transformations optimally is also outside the scope of the framework.

4   Theoretical Properties

The first two metatheoretical results below concern the soundness of the inference rules and the correctness of the recursion algorithm that generates proofs in that system. The other results have to do with the cost of proof generation and checking.

Theorem 1 (Soundness of Inferences). *If judgment $\Gamma \vartriangleright t \simeq u$ is derivable using the inference system with theories $\mathcal{T}_1, \ldots, \mathcal{T}_n$, then $\models_{\mathcal{T}_1 \cup \cdots \cup \mathcal{T}_n \cup \simeq \cup \varepsilon \cup \mathsf{let}}$ $\Gamma(t) \simeq u$.*

Theorem 2 (Total Correctness of Recursion). *For the instances presented in Sect. 3, the contextual recursion algorithm always produces correct proofs.*

Observation 3 (Complexity of Recursion). *For the instances presented in Sect. 3, the 'process' function is called at most once on every subterm of the input.*

As a corollary, if all the operations performed in *process* excluding the recursive calls can be accomplished in constant time, the algorithm has linear-time complexity with respect to the input. There exist data structures for which the following operations take constant time: extending the context with a fixed variable or a substitution, accessing direct subterms of a term, building a term from its direct subterms, choosing a fresh variable, applying a context to a variable, checking if a term matches a simple template, and associating the parameters of the template with the subterms. Thus, it is possible to have a linear-time algorithm for 'let' expansion and simplification. On the other hand, skolemization is at best quadratic in the worst case.

Observation 4 (Overhead of Proof Generation). *For the instances presented in Sect. 3, the number of 'apply' calls is proportional to the number of subterms in the input.*

Notice that all arguments to *apply* must be computed regardless of the *apply* calls. If an *apply* call takes constant time, the proof generation overhead is linear in the size of the input. To achieve this performance, it is necessary to use sharing to represent contexts and terms in the output.

Observation 5 (Cost of Proof Checking). *Checking an inference step can be performed in constant time if checking the side condition takes constant time.*

The above statement may appear weak, since checking the side conditions might itself be linear, leading to a cost of proof checking that can be at least quadratic in the size of the proof. Fortunately, most of the side conditions can be checked efficiently. For example, simplification proofs can be checked in linear time because $subst(\Gamma)$ is always the identity. Moreover, certifying a proof by checking each step locally is not the only possibility. An alternative is to use an algorithm similar to the *process* function to check a proof in the same way as it has been produced, exploiting sophisticated invariants.

5 Implementation

The ideas presented in this paper have been implemented in two tools. We implemented the contextual recursion algorithm and the transformations described in Sect. 3 in the SMT solver veriT [8], showing that replacing the previous ad hoc code with the generic proof-producing framework had no significant detrimental impact on the solving times. In addition, we developed a prototypical proof checker for the inference system described in Sect. 2 using Isabelle/HOL [18], to convince ourselves that veriT's output can easily be reconstructed.

5.1 Isabelle

The Isabelle/HOL proof assistant is based on classical higher-order logic (HOL), a variant of the simply typed λ-calculus. The proof checker is included in the development version of Isabelle.[1]

Derivations are represented by a recursive datatype in Standard ML, Isabelle's primary implementation language. A derivation is a tree whose nodes are labeled by rule names. Rule $\text{Taut}_{\mathcal{T}}$ also carries a theorem that represents the oracle $\models_{\mathcal{T}}$, and rules TRANS and LET are labeled with the terms that occur only in the antecedent (t and $\bar{s}_n$). Judgments $\Gamma \rhd t \simeq u$ are translated to HOL equalities $t' \simeq u'$, where t' and u' are HOL terms in which the context Γ is encoded using λ-abstractions and (for substitutions) applications. For example,

---

[1] http://isabelle.in.tum.de/repos/isabelle/file/00731700e54f/src/HOL/ex/
    veriT_Preprocessing.thy.

the judgment $x, y \mapsto \mathsf{g}(x) \rhd \mathsf{f}(y) \simeq \mathsf{f}(\mathsf{g}(x))$ is represented by the HOL equality $(\lambda x.\,(\lambda y.\,\mathsf{f}\,y)\,(\mathsf{g}\,x)) \simeq (\lambda x.\,\mathsf{f}\,(\mathsf{g}\,x))$.

Because reconstruction is not verified, there are no guarantees that it will always succeed, but when it does, the result is certified by Isabelle's LCF-style inference kernel [11]. We hard-coded a few dozen examples to test different cases, such as this one: Given the HOL terms

$$t = \neg\,\forall x.\,\mathsf{p} \wedge \exists x.\,\forall x.\,\mathsf{q}\,x\,x \quad u = \neg\,\forall x.\,\mathsf{p} \wedge \exists x.\,\mathsf{q}\,(\varepsilon x.\neg\,\mathsf{q}\,x\,x)\,(\varepsilon x.\neg\,\mathsf{q}\,x\,x)$$

and the ML tree

N (Cong, [N (Bind, [N (Cong, [N (Refl, []), N (Bind, [N (Sko_All, [N (Refl, [])])])])])])

the reconstruction function returns the HOL theorem $t \simeq u$.

5.2   veriT

We implemented the contextual recursion framework in the SMT solver veriT,[2] replacing large parts of the previous non-proof-producing, hard-to-maintain code. Even though it offers more functionality (proof generation), the preprocessing module is about 20% smaller than before and consists of about 3000 lines of code. There are now only two traversal functions instead of 10. This is, for us, a huge gain in maintainability.

We were able to reuse its existing proof module and proof format [5]. A proof is a list of inferences, each of which consists of an identifier, the name of the rule, the identifiers of the dependencies, and the derived clause. The use of identifiers makes it possible to represent proofs as DAGs. We extended the format with the inference rules of Sect. 2. The rules that augment the context take a sequence of inferences—a *subproof*—as a justification. The subproof occurs within the scope of the extended context.

In contrast with the abstract proof module described in Sect. 3, veriT leaves REFL steps implicit for judgments of the form $\Gamma \rhd t \simeq t$. The other inference rules are generalized to cope with missing REFL judgments. In addition, when printing proofs, the proof module can automatically replace terms in the inferences with some other terms. This is necessary for transformations such as skolemization and 'if–then–else' elimination. We must apply a substitution in the replaced term if the original term contains variables. In veriT, efficient data structures are available to perform this.

The implementation of contextual recursion uses a single global context, augmented before processing a subterm and restored afterwards. The context consists of a set of fixed variables, a substitution, and a polarity. In our setting, the substitution satisfies the side conditions by construction. If the context is empty, the result of processing a subterm is cached. For skolemization, a separate cache is used for each polarity. No caching is attempted under binders.

---

[2] http://matryoshka.gforge.inria.fr/pubs/processing/veriT.tar.gz.

Invoking *process* on a term returns the identifier of the inference at the root of its transformation proof in addition to the processed term. These identifiers are threaded through the recursion to connect the proof. The proofs produced by instances of contextual recursion are inserted into the larger resolution proof produced by veriT.

Transformations performing theory simplification were straightforward to port to the new framework: Their *build_app* functions simply apply rewrite rules until a fixpoint is reached. Porting transformations that interact with binders required special attention in handling the context and producing proofs. Fortunately, most of these aspects are captured by the inference system and the abstract contextual recursion framework, where they can be studied independently of the implementation.

Some transformations are performed outside of the framework. Proofs of CNF transformation are expressed using the inference rules of veriT's underlying SAT solver, so that any tool that can reconstruct SAT proofs can also reconstruct these proofs. Simplification based on associativity and commutativity of function symbols is implemented as a dedicated procedure, for efficiency reasons. It currently produces coarse-grained proofs.

To evaluate the impact of the new contextual recursion algorithm and of producing detailed proofs, we compare the performance of different configurations of veriT. Our experimental data is available online.[3] We distinguish three configurations. BASIC only applies transformations for which the old code provided some (coarse-grained) proofs. EXTENDED also applies transformations for which the old code did not provide any proofs, whereas the new code provides detailed proofs. COMPLETE applies all transformations available, regardless of whether they produce proofs.

More specifically, BASIC applies the transformations for 'let' expansion, skolemization, elimination of quantifiers based on one-point rules, elimination of 'if–then–else', theory simplification for rewriting n-ary symbols as binary, and elimination of equivalences and exclusive disjunctions with quantifiers in subterms. EXTENDED adds Boolean and arithmetic simplifications to the transformations performed by BASIC. COMPLETE performs global rewriting simplifications and symmetry breaking in addition to the transformations in EXTENDED.

The evaluation relies on two main sets of benchmarks from SMT-LIB [4] without bit vectors and nonlinear arithmetic (currently not supported by veriT): the 20 916 benchmarks in the quantifier-free (QF) categories, and the 30 250 benchmarks labeled as unsatisfiable in the non-QF categories. Our experiments were conducted on servers equipped with two Intel Xeon E5-2630 v3 processors, with eight cores per processor, and 126 GB of memory. Each run of the solver uses a single core. The time limit was set to 30 s, a reasonable value for interactive use within a proof assistant.

---

[3] http://matryoshka.gforge.inria.fr/pubs/processing/.

The table below shows the number of problems solved in total by each configuration.

| | Without proofs | | With proofs | |
	Old code	New code	Old code	New code
BASIC	42 235	42 258	42 104	42 118
EXTENDED	42 324	42 389	N/A	42 271
COMPLETE	42 585	42 613	N/A	N/A

These results indicate that the new generic contextual recursion algorithm and the production of detailed proofs do not impact performance negatively compared with the old code and coarse-grained proofs. Moreover, allowing Boolean and arithmetic simplifications leads to some improvements. We expect that generating proofs for the global transformations would lead to substantial improvements on quantifier-free problems.

6   Related Work

Most automatic provers that support the TPTP syntax for problems generate proofs in TSTP format [24]. Like a veriT proof, a TSTP proof consists of a list of inferences. TSTP does not mandate any inference system; the meaning of the rules and the granularity of inferences vary across systems. For example, the E prover [22] combines clausification, skolemization, and variable renaming into a single inference, whereas Vampire [15] appears to cleanly separate preprocessing transformations. SPASS's [25] custom proof format does not record preprocessing steps; reverse engineering is necessary to make sense of its output, and optimizations ought to be disabled [6, Sect. 7.3].

Most SMT solvers can parse the SMT-LIB [4] format, but each solver has its own output syntax. Z3's proofs can be quite detailed [17], but rewriting steps often combine many rewrites rules. CVC4's format is an instance of LF [13] with Side Conditions (LFSC) [23]; despite recent progress [12,14], neither skolemization nor quantifier instantiation are currently recorded in the proofs. Proof production in Fx7 [16] is based on an inference system whose formula processing fragment is subsumed by ours; for example, skolemization is more ad hoc, and there is no explicit support for rewriting.

7   Conclusion

We presented a framework to represent and generate proofs of formula processing and its implementation in veriT and Isabelle/HOL. The framework centralizes the delicate issue of manipulating bound variables and substitutions soundly and efficiently, and it is flexible enough to accommodate many interesting transformations. Although it was implemented in an SMT solver, there appears to be no intrinsic limitation that would prevent its use in other kinds of first-order, or even higher-order, automatic provers. The framework covers many preprocessing techniques and can be part of a larger toolbox.

Detailed proofs have been a defining feature of veriT for many years now. It now produces more detailed justifications than ever, but there are still some global transformations for which the proofs are nonexistent or leave much to be desired. In particular, supporting rewriting based on global assumptions would be essential for proof-producing inprocessing, and symmetry breaking would be interesting in its own right.

Acknowledgment. We thank Simon Cruanes for discussing many aspects of the framework with us as it was emerging, and we thank Robert Lewis, Stephan Merz, Lawrence Paulson, Anders Schlichtkrull, Mark Summerfield, Sophie Tourret, and the anonymous reviewers for suggesting many textual improvements. This research has been partially supported by the Agence nationale de la recherche/Deutsche Forschungsgemeinschaft project SMArT (ANR-13-IS02-0001, STU 483/2-1) and by the European Union project SC^2 (grant agreement No. 712689). The work has also received funding from the European Research Council under the European Union's Horizon 2020 research and innovation program (grant agreement No. 713999, Matryoshka). Experiments presented in this paper were carried out using the Grid'5000 testbed (https://www.grid5000.fr/), supported by a scientific interest group hosted by Inria and including CNRS, RENATER, and several universities as well as other organizations. A mirror of all the software and evaluation data described in this paper is hosted by Zenodo (https://doi.org/10.5281/zenodo.582482).

References

1. Armand, M., Faure, G., Grégoire, B., Keller, C., Théry, L., Werner, B.: A modular integration of SAT/SMT solvers to COQ through proof witnesses. In: Jouannaud, J.-P., Shao, Z. (eds.) CPP 2011. LNCS, vol. 7086, pp. 135–150. Springer, Heidelberg (2011). doi:10.1007/978-3-642-25379-9_12
2. Barbosa, H., Blanchette, J.C., Fontaine, P.: Technical report associated with this paper (2017). https://hal.inria.fr/hal-01526841
3. Barbosa, H., Fontaine, P., Reynolds, A.: Congruence closure with free variables. In: Legay, A., Margaria, T. (eds.) TACAS 2017. LNCS, vol. 10206, pp. 214–230. Springer, Heidelberg (2017). doi:10.1007/978-3-662-54580-5_13
4. Barrett, C., Fontaine, P., Tinelli, C.: The SMT-LIB standard: Version 2.5. Technical report, University of Iowa (2015). http://smt-lib.org/
5. Besson, F., Fontaine, P., Théry, L.: A flexible proof format for SMT: a proposal. In: Fontaine, P., Stump, A. (eds.) PxTP 2011, pp. 15–26 (2011)
6. Blanchette, J.C., Böhme, S., Fleury, M., Smolka, S.J., Steckermeier, A.: Semi-intelligible Isar proofs from machine-generated proofs. J. Autom. Reasoning **56**(2), 155–200 (2016). doi:10.1007/s10817-015-9335-3
7. Böhme, S., Weber, T.: Fast LCF-style proof reconstruction for Z3. In: Kaufmann, M., Paulson, L.C. (eds.) ITP 2010. LNCS, vol. 6172, pp. 179–194. Springer, Heidelberg (2010). doi:10.1007/978-3-642-14052-5_14
8. Bouton, T., de Oliveira, D.C.B., Déharbe, D., Fontaine, P.: veriT: an open, trustable and efficient SMT-solver. In: Schmidt, R.A. (ed.) CADE-22. LNCS, vol. 5663, pp. 151–156. Springer, Heidelberg (2009). doi:10.1007/978-3-642-02959-2_12

9. Déharbe, D., Fontaine, P., Merz, S., Woltzenlogel Paleo, B.: Exploiting symmetry in SMT problems. In: Bjørner, N., Sofronie-Stokkermans, V. (eds.) CADE 2011. LNCS, vol. 6803, pp. 222–236. Springer, Heidelberg (2011). doi:10.1007/978-3-642-22438-6_18

10. Ebner, G., Hetzl, S., Reis, G., Riener, M., Wolfsteiner, S., Zivota, S.: System description: GAPT 2.0. In: Olivetti, N., Tiwari, A. (eds.) IJCAR 2016. LNCS, vol. 9706, pp. 293–301. Springer, Cham (2016). doi:10.1007/978-3-319-40229-1_20

11. Gordon, M.J.C., Milner, R., Wadsworth, C.P.: CADE-23. LNCS, vol. 78. Springer, Heidelberg (1979). doi:10.1007/3-540-09724-4

12. Hadarean, L., Barrett, C., Reynolds, A., Tinelli, C., Deters, M.: Fine grained SMT proofs for the theory of fixed-width bit-vectors. In: Davis, M., Fehnker, A., McIver, A., Voronkov, A. (eds.) LPAR 2015. LNCS, vol. 9450, pp. 340–355. Springer, Heidelberg (2015). doi:10.1007/978-3-662-48899-7_24

13. Harper, R., Honsell, F., Plotkin, G.D.: A framework for defining logics. In: LICS 1987, pp. 194–204. IEEE Computer Society (1987)

14. Katz, G., Barrett, C.W., Tinelli, C., Reynolds, A., Hadarean, L.: Lazy proofs for DPLL(T)-based SMT solvers. In: Piskac, R., Talupur, M. (eds.) FMCAD 2016, pp. 93–100. IEEE Computer Society (2016). doi:10.1109/FMCAD.2016.7886666

15. Kovács, L., Voronkov, A.: First-order theorem proving and VAMPIRE. In: Sharygina, N., Veith, H. (eds.) CAV 2013. LNCS, vol. 8044, pp. 1–35. Springer, Heidelberg (2013). doi:10.1007/978-3-642-39799-8_1

16. Moskal, M.: Rocket-fast proof checking for SMT solvers. In: Ramakrishnan, C.R., Rehof, J. (eds.) TACAS 2008. LNCS, vol. 4963, pp. 486–500. Springer, Heidelberg (2008). doi:10.1007/978-3-540-78800-3_38

17. de Moura, L.M., Bjørner, N.: Proofs and refutations, and Z3. In: Rudnicki, P., Sutcliffe, G., Konev, B., Schmidt, R.A., Schulz, S. (eds.) LPAR 2008 Workshops. CEUR Workshop Proceedings, vol. 418 (2008). CEUR-WS.org

18. Nipkow, T., Paulson, L.C., Wenzel, M.: Isabelle/HOL: A Proof Assistant for Higher-Order Logic. LNCS, vol. 2283. Springer, Heidelberg (2002). doi:10.1007/3-540-45949-9

19. de Nivelle, H.: Translation of resolution proofs into short first-order proofs without choice axioms. Inf. Comput. 199(1–2), 24–54 (2005). doi:10.1016/j.ic.2004.10.011

20. Nonnengart, A., Weidenbach, C.: Computing small clause normal forms. In: Robinson, A., Voronkov, A. (eds.) Handbook of Automated Reasoning, vol. 1, pp. 335–367. Elsevier and MIT Press (2001)

21. Paulson, L.C., Susanto, K.W.: Source-level proof reconstruction for interactive theorem proving. In: Schneider, K., Brandt, J. (eds.) TPHOLs 2007. LNCS, vol. 4732, pp. 232–245. Springer, Heidelberg (2007). doi:10.1007/978-3-540-74591-4_18

22. Schulz, S.: System description: E 1.8. In: McMillan, K., Middeldorp, A., Voronkov, A. (eds.) LPAR 2013. LNCS, vol. 8312, pp. 735–743. Springer, Heidelberg (2013). doi:10.1007/978-3-642-45221-5_49

23. Stump, A.: Proof checking technology for satisfiability modulo theories. Electr. Notes Theor. Comput. Sci. 228, 121–133 (2009). doi:10.1016/j.entcs.2008.12.121

24. Sutcliffe, G., Zimmer, J., Schulz, S.: TSTP data-exchange formats for automated theorem proving tools. In: Zhang, W., Sorge, V. (eds.) Distributed Constraint Problem Solving and Reasoning in Multi-Agent Systems. Frontiers in Artificial Intelligence and Applications, vol. 112, pp. 201–215. IOS Press (2004)

25. Weidenbach, C., Dimova, D., Fietzke, A., Kumar, R., Suda, M., Wischnewski, P.: SPASS version 3.5. In: Schmidt, R.A. (ed.) CADE-22. LNCS, vol. 5663, pp. 140–145. Springer, Heidelberg (2009). doi:10.1007/978-3-642-02959-2_10

Certifying Confluence of Quasi-Decreasing Strongly Deterministic Conditional Term Rewrite Systems

Christian Sternagel$^{(\boxtimes)}$ and Thomas Sternagel$^{(\boxtimes)}$

University of Innsbruck, Innsbruck, Austria
{christian.sternagel,thomas.sternagel}@uibk.ac.at

Abstract. We formalize a confluence criterion for the class of quasi-decreasing strongly deterministic conditional term rewrite systems in Isabelle/HOL: confluence follows if all conditional critical pairs are joinable. However, quasi-decreasingness, strong determinism, and joinability of conditional critical pairs are all undecidable in general. Therefore, we also formalize sufficient criteria for those properties, which we incorporate into the general purpose certifier CeTA as well as the confluence checker ConCon for conditional term rewrite systems.

1 Introduction

In the area of equational reasoning *canonicity*—that is, termination together with confluence—plays an important role towards deciding equations with respect to equational theories and for avoiding redundant computations and nondeterminism. In the presence of powerful methods and tools for proving termination [1,11,17,18,31,33], the remaining issue is to also establish confluence.

For plain term rewrite systems (TRSs), this issue was settled early on by Newman's Lemma [22], stating that *any terminating relation is confluent iff it is locally confluent*. Then, by the Critical Pair Lemma [15,16], *local confluence reduces to joinability of all critical pairs*, which in turn, can be decided by exhaustive rewriting, due to termination.

However, for many applications plain TRSs are either inconvenient or not expressible enough, leading to several extensions of the base formalism. The one we are interested in here is *conditional term rewriting*. Two prominent areas where conditional rewriting is employed are the rewriting engines of modern proof assistants (like Isabelle's simplifier [23]) and functional(-logic) programming with where-clauses (like Haskell [21] and Curry [2]).

This work is supported by FWF (Austrian Science Fund) project P27502.

L. de Moura (Ed.): CADE 2017, LNAI 10395, pp. 413–431, 2017.
DOI: 10.1007/978-3-319-63046-5_26

Example 1. As a first example, consider the following Haskell program, which computes the minimum of a given list of natural numbers. Below, we give a straightforward translation into a conditional term rewrite system $\mathcal{R}_{\min}$ with six rules that serves as our running example.

```
min (x:[])          = x
min (x:xs)  | x < y  = x
            | otherwise = y
            where y = min xs
```

$$\min(\text{cons}(x, \text{nil})) \rightarrow x \tag{1}$$
$$\min(\text{cons}(x, xs)) \rightarrow x \Leftarrow \min(xs) \approx y, x < y \approx \text{true} \tag{2}$$
$$\min(\text{cons}(x, xs)) \rightarrow y \Leftarrow \min(xs) \approx y, x < y \approx \text{false} \tag{3}$$
$$x < 0 \rightarrow \text{false} \tag{4}$$
$$0 < \text{s}(y) \rightarrow \text{true} \tag{5}$$
$$\text{s}(x) < \text{s}(y) \rightarrow x < y \tag{6}$$

Issue. Alas, even in the presence of termination, confluence is in general still undecidable for conditional term rewrite systems (CTRSs). While Avenhaus and Loría-Sáenz [4] gave a critical pair criterion for quasi-reductive and strongly deterministic CTRSs: *joinability of all conditional critical pairs (CCPs) implies confluence*; joinability of CCPs is undecidable in general, due to the inherent complexities of conditional rewriting. This lead to the development of sufficient criteria that are implemented in confluence tools for CTRSs like ConCon [27].

Such tools ultimately aim at automatic (program) verification. But they are programs themselves, and rather complex ones at that. So why should we trust them? This consideration lead to the introduction of certification in the area of term rewriting [8, 9, 30]. Here, the output of an automated tool—the certificate—is checked by a formally verified certifier that is code generated from a formalization inside a proof assistant. This approach was already quite successful for termination and confluence of TRSs, where state-of-the-art certifiers cover more than 80% of all generated certificates in the respective tool competitions [3, 13].

For confluence of CTRSs, not so many techniques are known and even less are formalized and certifiable.

Contribution and Summary. In Sect. 3, we formalize the CCP criterion of Avenhaus and Loría-Sáenz [4, Theorem 4.2] (AL for short) and, based on our earlier work [28], strengthen it from quasi-reductivity to quasi-decreasingness.

Moreover, to certify confluence of quasi-decreasing and strongly deterministic CTRSs, we formalize the variant of AL replacing joinability of all CCPs by the requirement that every CCP is either unfeasible[1] or context-joinable (Sect. 4). Both unfeasibility and context-joinability rely on the notion of contextual rewriting, which we formalize together with the crucial lemma that *contextual rewriting implies conditional rewriting for satisfying substitutions*, a result that was stated without proof by Avenhaus and Loría-Sáenz [4, Lemma 4.2]. Unfeasibility further employs strong irreducibility, which like strong determinism is an undecidable property. Thus, we formalize these two properties together with the two sufficient and decidable criteria of absolute irreducibility and absolute determinism.

---

[1] This is a technical term (see Definition 3) introduced by Avenhaus and Loría-Sáenz [4] and should not be confused with *infeasibility*.

Along the way, we identify and fix some problems in proofs and definitions (of absolute irreducibility, contextual rewriting, and unfeasibility) and provide a (not entirely obvious) proof for [4, Lemma 4.2]. We further adapt the original proof of AL to the new definitions and extend it by infeasibility.

In Sect. 5, we point out some challenges concerning certification. Then, in Sect. 6, we give an overview of all the check functions that are new in CeTA. In Sect. 7, we evaluate our contribution through experiments on the confluence problems database (Cops) [10]. Finally, we conclude in Sect. 8.

This work substantially contributes to the greater effort of making ConCon 100% certifiable by formalizing all of its methods. Our formalization is part of the formal IsaFoR library and supported by version 2.29 of its accompanying certifier CeTA [30]. Both IsaFoR and CeTA are freely available online at

http://cl-informatik.uibk.ac.at/isafor/

2 Preliminaries

We assume familiarity with the basic notions of (conditional) term rewriting [5, 24], but shortly recapitulate terminology and notation that we use in the remainder. Given an arbitrary binary relation $\alpha_\rightarrow$, we write $\alpha_\leftarrow$, $\alpha^+_\rightarrow$, and $\alpha^*_\rightarrow$ for its *inverse*, its *transitive closure*, and its *reflexive transitive closure*, respectively. We use $\mathcal{V}(\cdot)$ to denote the set of variables occurring in a given list of syntactic objects, like terms, rules, etc. Given a term t, we write $\mathcal{P}os(t)$ for the *set of positions* in t and $t|_p$ with $p \in \mathcal{P}os(t)$ for the subterm of t at position p. We write $s[t]_p$ for the result of replacing $s|_p$ by t in s. We say that terms s and t *unify*, written $s \sim t$, if $s\sigma = t\sigma$ for some substitution σ. A substitution σ is $\mathcal{R}$-*normalized* if $\sigma(x)$ is an $\mathcal{R}$-normal form for all variables x. We call a bijective variable substitution π a *renaming* or *permutation*, and denote its inverse by π^-. For two substitutions σ, τ and a set of variables V we write $\sigma = \tau$ $[V]$ if $\sigma(x) = \tau(x)$ for all $x \in V$. We write $\sigma\tau$ for the composition of σ and τ where $(\sigma\tau)(x) = \sigma(x)\tau$. A term t is *strongly* $\mathcal{R}$-*irreducible* if $t\sigma$ is an $\mathcal{R}$-normal form for all $\mathcal{R}$-normalized substitutions σ. A *strongly deterministic oriented 3-CTRS (SDTRS)* $\mathcal{R}$ is a set of conditional rewrite rules of the shape $\ell \rightarrow r \Leftarrow c$ where ℓ and r are terms and c is a possibly empty sequence of pairs of terms (called *conditions*) $s_1 \approx t_1, \ldots, s_n \approx t_n$, satisfying: ℓ is not a variable (CTRS), $\mathcal{V}(r) \subseteq \mathcal{V}(\ell, c)$ (3-CTRS), $\mathcal{V}(s_i) \subseteq \mathcal{V}(\ell, t_1, \ldots, t_{i-1})$ for all $1 \leqslant i \leqslant n$ (DTRS), and t_i is strongly $\mathcal{R}$-irreducible for all $1 \leqslant i \leqslant n$ (SDTRS). We sometimes label rules like $\rho : \ell \rightarrow r \Leftarrow c$. For a rule $\rho : \ell \rightarrow r \Leftarrow c$ of an SDTRS $\mathcal{R}$ the set of *extra variables* is defined as $\mathcal{EV}(\rho) = \mathcal{V}(c) - \mathcal{V}(\ell)$. Given an SDTRS $\mathcal{R}$, extended TRSs $\mathcal{R}_n$ are inductively defined for each level $n \geqslant 0$

$$\mathcal{R}_0 = \varnothing$$

$$\mathcal{R}_{n+1} = \{\ell\sigma \rightarrow r\sigma \mid \ell \rightarrow r \Leftarrow c \in \mathcal{R} \text{ and } s\sigma \rightarrow^*_{\mathcal{R}_n} t\sigma \text{ for all } s \approx t \in c\}$$

where $\rightarrow_{\mathcal{R}_n}$ denotes the rewrite relation of the (unconditional) TRS $\mathcal{R}_n$, that is, the smallest relation $\rightarrow$ satisfying $t[\ell\sigma]_p \rightarrow t[r\sigma]_p$ whenever $\ell \rightarrow r$ is a rule in $\mathcal{R}_n$.

We write $s \to_{\mathcal{R},n} t$ if we have $s \to_{\mathcal{R}_n} t$ and $s \to_{\mathcal{R}} t$ whenever $s \to_{\mathcal{R}_n} t$ for some $n \geqslant 0$. We say that a substitution σ *satisfies* a sequence of conditions c if for all $s \approx t \in c$ we have $s\sigma \to_{\mathcal{R}}^* t\sigma$. Two variable-disjoint variants of rules $\ell_1 \to r_1 \Leftarrow c_1$ and $\ell_2 \to r_2 \Leftarrow c_2$ in $\mathcal{R}$ such that $\ell_1|_p$ is not a variable and $\ell_1|_p\mu = \ell_2\mu$ with most general unifier (mgu) μ, constitute a *conditional overlap*. A conditional overlap that does not result from overlapping two variants of the same rule at the root gives rise to a *conditional critical pair* (CCP) $r_1\mu \approx \ell_1[r_2]_p\mu \Leftarrow c_1\mu, c_2\mu$.

Example 2. The CTRS $\mathcal{R}_{\min}$ from Example 1 has 6 CCPs, 3 modulo symmetry:

$$x \approx x \Leftarrow \min(\mathsf{nil}) \approx y,\ x < y \approx \mathsf{true} \tag{1,2}$$

$$x \approx y \Leftarrow \min(\mathsf{nil}) \approx y,\ x < y \approx \mathsf{false} \tag{1,3}$$

$$x \approx y \Leftarrow \min(xs) \approx z,\ x < z \approx \mathsf{true},\ \min(xs) \approx y,\ x < y \approx \mathsf{false} \tag{2,3}$$

A CCP $u \approx v \Leftarrow c$ is said to be *infeasible* if its conditions are not satisfied by any substitution. Moreover, a CCP is *joinable* if $u\sigma \downarrow_{\mathcal{R}} v\sigma$ for all substitutions σ that satisfy c. The topmost part of a term that does not change under rewriting (sometimes called its "cap") can be approximated for example by the tcap function [12]. Informally, $\mathsf{tcap}(x)$ for a variable x results in a fresh variable, while $\mathsf{tcap}(t)$ for a non-variable term $t = f(t_1, \ldots, t_n)$ is obtained by recursively computing $u = f(\mathsf{tcap}(t_1), \ldots, \mathsf{tcap}(t_n))$ and then asserting $\mathsf{tcap}(t) = u$ in case u does not unify with any left-hand side of rules in $\mathcal{R}$, and a fresh variable, otherwise. It is well known that $\mathsf{tcap}(s) \not\sim t$ implies non-reachability of t from s. We denote the proper superterm relation by $\rhd$ and define $\succ_{\mathsf{st}} = (\succ \cup \rhd)^+$ for any order $\succ$. If $\succ$ is a reduction order, then an SDTRS $\mathcal{R}$ is *quasi-reductive* with respect to $\succ$ if for every substitution σ and every rule $\ell \to r \Leftarrow s_1 \approx t_1, \ldots, s_n \approx t_n$ in $\mathcal{R}$ we have that $s_j\sigma \succeq t_j\sigma$ for $1 \leqslant j < i$ implies $\ell\sigma \succ_{\mathsf{st}} s_i\sigma$ for all $1 \leqslant i \leqslant n$, and $s_j\sigma \succeq t_j\sigma$ for $1 \leqslant j \leqslant n$ implies $\ell\sigma \succ r\sigma$. An SDTRS $\mathcal{R}$ is *quasi-decreasing* if there exists a well-founded order $\succ$ such that $\succ = \succ_{\mathsf{st}}$, $\to_{\mathcal{R}} \subseteq \succ$, and for all rules $\ell \to r \Leftarrow s_1 \approx t_1, \ldots, s_n \approx t_n$ in $\mathcal{R}$, all substitutions σ, and $1 \leqslant i \leqslant n$, if $s_j\sigma \to_{\mathcal{R}}^* t_j\sigma$ for all $1 \leqslant j < i$ then $\ell\sigma \succ s_i\sigma$. Quasi-reductivity implies quasi-decreasingness—a fact that is available in IsaFoR.

3   Confluence of Quasi-Decreasing SDTRSs

The main result of Avenhaus and Loría-Sáenz is the following theorem:

Theorem 1 ([4, Theorem 4.1]). *Let the SDTRS $\mathcal{R}$ be quasi-reductive with respect to $\succ$. Then $\mathcal{R}$ is confluent iff all CCPs are joinable.*

That all CCPs of a CTRS $\mathcal{R}$ (no need for strong determinism or quasi-reductivity) are joinable if $\mathcal{R}$ is confluent is straightforward. Thus, we concentrate on the other direction. Our formalization is quite close to the original proof. The good news is: we could not find any errors (besides typos) in the original proof but as is often the case with formalizations there are places where the paper

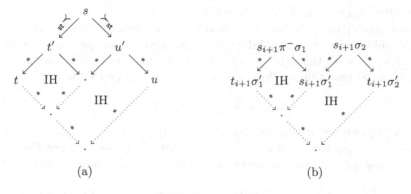

(a)   (b)

Fig. 1. Applying the induction hypothesis.

proof is vague or does not spell out the technical details in favor of readability. For example, we heavily rely on an earlier formalization of permutations [14] in order to formalize variants of rules up to renaming. In contrast, the change from quasi-reductivity to quasi-decreasingness was rather smooth.

Below, we give our main theorem and walk through the formalized proof.

Theorem 2. *Let the SDTRS $\mathcal{R}$ be quasi-decreasing with respect to $\succ$. Then $\mathcal{R}$ is confluent if all CCPs are joinable.*

Proof. Assume that all critical pairs are joinable. We consider an arbitrary peak $t \xleftarrow{*}_{\mathcal{R}} s \xrightarrow{*}_{\mathcal{R}} u$ and prove $t \downarrow_{\mathcal{R}} u$ by well-founded induction with respect to $\succ_{\mathrm{st}}$.

By induction hypothesis (IH) we have that for all terms t_0, t_1, t_2 such that $s \succ_{\mathrm{st}} t_0$ and $t_1 \xleftarrow{*}_{\mathcal{R}} t_0 \xrightarrow{*}_{\mathcal{R}} t_2$ there exists a join $t_1 \xrightarrow{*}_{\mathcal{R}} \cdot \xleftarrow{*}_{\mathcal{R}} t_2$.

If $s = t$ or $s = u$ then t and u are trivially joinable and we are done. So we may assume that the peak contains at least one step in each direction: $t \xleftarrow{*}_{\mathcal{R}} t' \xleftarrow{}_{\mathcal{R}} s \xrightarrow{}_{\mathcal{R}} u' \xrightarrow{*}_{\mathcal{R}} u$.

Let us show that $t' \downarrow_{\mathcal{R}} u'$ holds. Then $t \downarrow_{\mathcal{R}} u$ follows by two applications of the IH, as shown in Fig. 1a. Assume that $s = C[\ell_1\sigma_1]_p \xrightarrow{}_{\mathcal{R}} C[r_1\sigma_1]_p = t'$ and $s = D[\ell_2\sigma_2]_q \xrightarrow{}_{\mathcal{R}} D[r_2\sigma_2]_q = u'$ for rules $\rho_1 : \ell_1 \to r_1 \Leftarrow c_1$ and $\rho_2 : \ell_2 \to r_2 \Leftarrow c_2$ in $\mathcal{R}$, contexts C and D, positions p and q, and substitutions σ_1 and σ_2 such that $u\sigma_1 \xrightarrow{*}_{\mathcal{R}} v\sigma_1$ for all $u \approx v \in c_1$ and $u\sigma_2 \xrightarrow{*}_{\mathcal{R}} v\sigma_2$ for all $u \approx v \in c_2$. There are three possibilities: either the positions are parallel ($p \parallel q$), or p is above q ($p \leqslant q$), or q is above p ($q \leqslant p$). In the first case $t' \downarrow_{\mathcal{R}} u'$ holds because the two redexes do not interfere. The other two cases are symmetric and we only consider $p \leqslant q$ here. If $s \rhd s|_p = \ell_1\sigma_1$ then $s \succ_{\mathrm{st}} \ell_1\sigma_1$ (by definition of $\succ_{\mathrm{st}}$) and there exists a position r such that $q = pr$ and so we have the peak $r_1\sigma_1 \xleftarrow{*}_{\mathcal{R}} \ell_1\sigma_1 \xrightarrow{}_{\mathcal{R}} \ell_1\sigma_1[r_2\sigma_2]_r$ which is joinable by the IH. But then the peak $t' = s[r_1\sigma_1]_p \xleftarrow{*}_{\mathcal{R}} s[\ell_1\sigma_1]_p \xrightarrow{*}_{\mathcal{R}} s[\ell_1\sigma_1[r_2\sigma_2]_r]_q = u'$ is also joinable (by closure under contexts) and we are done. So we may assume that $p = \epsilon$ and thus $s = \ell_1\sigma_1$. Now, either q is a function position in ℓ_1 or there exists a variable position q' in ℓ_1 such that $q' \leqslant q$. In the first case we either have

1. a CCP which is joinable by assumption or we have
2. a root-overlap of variants of the same rule. Unlike in the unconditional case this could lead to non-joinability of the ensuing critical pair because of the extra-variables in the right-hand sides of conditional rules. We have $\rho_1\pi = \rho_2$ for some permutation π. Moreover, $s = \ell_1\sigma_1 = \ell_2\sigma_2$ and we have

$$\pi^-\sigma_1 = \sigma_2 \ [\mathcal{V}(\ell_2)] \tag{7}$$

We will prove $x\pi^-\sigma_1 \downarrow_{\mathcal{R}} x\sigma_2$ for all x in $\mathcal{V}(\rho_2)$. Since $t' = r_1\sigma_1 = r_2\pi^-\sigma_1$ and $u' = r_2\sigma_2$ this shows $t' \downarrow_{\mathcal{R}} u'$. Because $\mathcal{R}$ is terminating (by quasi-decreasingness) we may define two normalized substitutions σ_i' such that

$$x\pi^-\sigma_1 \xrightarrow[\mathcal{R}]{*} x\sigma_1' \text{ and } x\sigma_2 \xrightarrow[\mathcal{R}]{*} x\sigma_2' \text{ for all variables } x. \tag{8}$$

We prove $x\sigma_1' = x\sigma_2'$ for $x \in \mathcal{EV}(\rho_2)$ by an inner induction on the length of $c_2 = s_1 \approx t_1, \ldots, s_n \approx t_n$. If ρ_2 has no conditions this holds vacuously because there are no extra variables. In the step case the inner induction hypothesis (IH$_i$) is that $x\sigma_1' = x\sigma_2'$ for $x \in \mathcal{V}(s_1, t_1, \ldots, s_i, t_i) - \mathcal{V}(\ell_2)$ and we have to show that $x\sigma_1' = x\sigma_2'$ for $x \in \mathcal{V}(s_1, t_1, \ldots, s_{i+1}, t_{i+1}) - \mathcal{V}(\ell_2)$. If $x \in \mathcal{V}(s_1, t_1, \ldots, s_i, t_i, s_{i+1})$ we are done by the IH$_i$ and strong determinism of $\mathcal{R}$. So assume $x \in \mathcal{V}(t_{i+1})$. From strong determinism of $\mathcal{R}$, (7) and (8), and the IH$_i$ we have that $y\sigma_1' = y\sigma_2'$ for all $y \in \mathcal{V}(s_{i+1})$ and thus $s_{i+1}\sigma_1' = s_{i+1}\sigma_2'$. With this we can find a join between $t_{i+1}\sigma_1'$ and $t_{i+1}\sigma_2'$ by applying the IH twice as shown in Fig. 1b. Since t_{i+1} is strongly irreducible and σ_1' and σ_2' are normalized, this yields $t_{i+1}\sigma_1' = t_{i+1}\sigma_2'$ and thus $x\sigma_1' = x\sigma_2'$.
3. We are left with the case that there is a variable position q' in ℓ_1 such that $q = q'r'$ for some position r'. Let x be the variable $\ell_1|_{q'}$. Then $x\sigma_1|_{r'} = \ell_2\sigma_2$, which implies $x\sigma_1 \to_{\mathcal{R}}^* x\sigma_1[r_2\sigma_2]_{r'}$. Now let τ be the substitution such that $\tau(x) = x\sigma_1[r_2\sigma_2]_{r'}$ and $\tau(y) = \sigma_1(y)$ for all $y \neq x$, and τ' some normalization, that is, $y\tau \to_{\mathcal{R}}^* y\tau'$ for all y. Moreover, note that

$$y\sigma_1 \xrightarrow[\mathcal{R}]{*} y\tau \text{ for all } y. \tag{9}$$

We have $u' = \ell_1\sigma_1[r_2\sigma_2]_q = \ell_1\sigma_1[x\tau]_{q'} \to_{\mathcal{R}}^* \ell_1\tau$, and thus $u' \to_{\mathcal{R}}^* \ell_1\tau'$. From (9) we have $r_1\sigma_1 \to_{\mathcal{R}}^* r_1\tau$ and thus $t' = r_1\sigma_1 \to_{\mathcal{R}}^* r_1\tau'$. Finally, we will show that $\ell_1\tau' \to_{\mathcal{R}} r_1\tau'$, concluding the proof of $t' \downarrow_{\mathcal{R}} u'$. To this end, let $s_i \approx t_i \in c_1$. By (9) and the definition of τ' we obtain $s_i\sigma_1 \to_{\mathcal{R}}^* t_i\sigma_1 \to_{\mathcal{R}}^* t_i\tau'$ and $s_i\sigma_1 \to_{\mathcal{R}}^* s_i\tau'$. Then $s_i\tau' \downarrow_{\mathcal{R}} t_i\tau'$ by IH and also $s_i\tau' \to_{\mathcal{R}}^* t_i\tau'$, since t_i is strongly irreducible. $\square$

4   Certification

There are some complications for employing Theorem 2 in practice. Quasi-decreasingness, strong irreducibility, and joinability of CCPs are all undecidable in general. For quasi-decreasingness we fall back to the sufficient criterion that a deterministic 3-CTRS is quasi-decreasing if its unraveling (a transformation to an unconditional term rewrite system) is terminating. This result was formalized by Winkler and Thiemann [32] and is already available in IsaFoR. A sufficient condition for strong irreducibility is *absolute irreducibility*:

Definition 1. *A term t is* absolutely $\mathcal{R}$-irreducible *if none of its non-variable subterms unify with any variable-disjoint variant of left-hand sides of rules in the CTRS $\mathcal{R}$. A DTRS is called* absolutely deterministic *(or ADTRS for short) if for each rule all right-hand sides of conditions are absolutely $\mathcal{R}$-irreducible.*

The proof of the following lemma [4, Lemma 4.1(a,b)] is immediate.

Lemma 1. *For a term t and a CTRS $\mathcal{R}$:*

- *If t is absolutely $\mathcal{R}$-irreducible, then t is also strongly $\mathcal{R}$-irreducible.*
- *If $\mathcal{R}$ is absolutely deterministic, then $\mathcal{R}$ is also strongly deterministic.*   □

We replace joinability of CCPs by infeasibility [26] (already part of IsaFoR) together with two further criteria which rely on *contextual rewriting*.

Definition 2. *Consider a set C of equations between terms which we will call a* context. *First we define a function $\overline{\cdot}$ on terms such that $\bar{t}$ is the term t where each variable $x \in \mathcal{V}(C)$ is replaced by a fresh constant $\bar{x}$. Moreover, let $\overline{C}$ denote the set C where all variables have been replaced by fresh constants $\bar{x}$. For a CTRS $\mathcal{R}$ we can make a* contextual rewrite step, *denoted by $s \to_{\mathcal{R},C} t$, if we can make a conditional rewrite step with respect to the CTRS $\mathcal{R} \cup \overline{C}$ from $\bar{s}$ to $\bar{t}$.*

We formalized soundness of contextual rewriting [4, Lemma 4.2] as follows:

Lemma 2. *If $s \to^*_{\mathcal{R},C} t$ then $s\sigma \to^*_{\mathcal{R}} t\sigma$ for all substitutions σ satisfying C.*

This lemma is stated as obvious without proof by Avenhaus and Loría-Sáenz. However, we deem the strengthened statement $(\star)$ below intricate enough to warrant a full proof (since without this strengthening, as far as we can tell, the outermost induction fails).

Proof. Consider the auxiliary function $[t]_\sigma$, which substitutes each Skolem constant $\bar{x}$ in t by $\sigma(x)$, that is, it works like applying a substitution to a term, but to Skolem constants instead of variables. Note that $[\bar{t}]_\sigma = t\sigma$ whenever $\mathcal{V}(t) \subseteq \mathcal{V}(C)$. Now we show by induction on n that

$$s \to_{\mathcal{R} \cup \overline{C}, n} t \text{ implies } [s]_\sigma \to^*_{\mathcal{R},n} [t]_\sigma \tag{$\star$}$$

for any σ satisfying C. The base case is trivial. In the inductive step we have a rule $\ell \to r \Leftarrow c \in \mathcal{R} \cup \overline{C}$, a position p, and a substitution τ such that $s|_p = \ell\tau$, $t = s[r\tau]_p$, and $u\tau \to^*_{\mathcal{R} \cup \overline{C}, n} v\tau$ for all $u \approx v \in c$. If $\ell \to r \Leftarrow c \in \mathcal{R}$, then we obtain $[u\tau]_\sigma \to^*_{\mathcal{R} \cup \overline{C}, n} [v\tau]_\sigma$ for all $u \approx v \in c$ by IH. Then $s \to^*_{\mathcal{R} \cup \overline{C}, n+1} t$ can be shown by induction on the context $s[\cdot]_p$. Otherwise, $\ell \to r \Leftarrow c \in \overline{C}$ and thus c is empty, $\ell\tau = \ell$, and $r\tau = r$, since $\overline{C}$ is an unconditional ground TRS. Moreover, there is a rule $\ell' \to r' \in C$ (thus also $\mathcal{V}(\ell', r') \subseteq \mathcal{V}(C)$) such that $\overline{\ell'} = \ell$ and $\overline{r'} = r$. Again, the final result follows by induction on $s[\cdot]_p$.

Assume $s \to_{\mathcal{R},C} t$. Then $\overline{s} \to_{\mathcal{R}\cup\overline{C},n} \overline{t}$ for some level n. Let $\widetilde{t}$ denote the extension of $\overline{t}$ where all variables x in t (that is, not just those in $\mathcal{V}(C)$) are replaced by fresh constants $\overline{x}$. Note that $\widetilde{t} = (\overline{t})(\lambda x. \overline{x})$ for every term t. But then also $\widetilde{s} \to_{\mathcal{R}\cup\overline{C},n} \widetilde{t}$ since conditional rewriting is closed under substitutions. Further note that $[\widetilde{t}]_\sigma = t\sigma$ for all t. Thus taking $\widetilde{s}$ and $\widetilde{t}$ for s and t in ($\star$) we obtain $s\sigma \to_{\mathcal{R},n}^* t\sigma$. Since we just established the desired property for single contextual rewrite steps it is straightforward to extend it to rewrite sequences. $\square$

The above lemma is the key to overcome the undecidability issues of conditional rewriting. For example, for joinability of CCPs the problem is that a single joining sequence (as is usual in certificates for TRSs) does not prove joinability for all satisfying substitutions. However, contextual rewriting has this property.

Now we are able to define the two promised criteria for CCPs that employ contextual rewriting: *context-joinability* and *unfeasibility*.

Definition 3. *Let $s \approx t \Leftarrow c$ be a CCP induced by an overlap between variable-disjoint variants $\ell_1 \to r_1 \Leftarrow c_1$ and $\ell_2 \to r_2 \Leftarrow c_2$ of rules in $\mathcal{R}$ with mgu μ. We say that the CCP is* unfeasible *if we can find terms u, v, and w such that (1) for all σ that satisfy c we have $\ell_1\mu\sigma \succ u\sigma$, (2) $u \to_{\mathcal{R},c}^* v$, (3) $u \to_{\mathcal{R},c}^* w$, and (4) v and w are both strongly irreducible and $v \not\sim w$. Moreover, we call the CCP* context-joinable *if there exists some term u such that $s \to_{\mathcal{R},c}^* u$ and $t \to_{\mathcal{R},c}^* u$.*

Example 3. Consider the CTRS $\mathcal{R}_{\mathsf{last}}$ consisting of the two rules

$$\mathsf{last}(\mathsf{cons}(x,y)) \to x \Leftarrow y \approx \mathsf{nil} \quad \mathsf{last}(\mathsf{cons}(x,y)) \to \mathsf{last}(y) \Leftarrow y \approx \mathsf{cons}(z,v)$$

having the CCP $x \approx \mathsf{last}(y) \Leftarrow c$ with $c = \{y \approx \mathsf{nil}, y \approx \mathsf{cons}(z,v)\}$. This CCP is unfeasible because for all satisfying substitutions σ we have $\mathsf{last}(\mathsf{cons}(x,y))\sigma \succ y\sigma$, $y \to_{\mathcal{R}_{\mathsf{last}},c}^* \mathsf{cons}(z,v)$, $y \to_{\mathcal{R}_{\mathsf{last}},c}^* \mathsf{nil}$, and both $\mathsf{cons}(z,v)$ and nil are strongly irreducible and not unifiable. Now, look at the arbitrary CCP $x \approx \mathsf{min}(\mathsf{nil}) \Leftarrow c$ with $c = \{\mathsf{min}(\mathsf{nil}) \approx x\}$. Since $x \to_{\mathcal{R},c}^* x$ and $\mathsf{min}(\mathsf{nil}) \to_{\mathcal{R},c}^* x$ it is context-joinable (regardless of the actual CTRS $\mathcal{R}$).

Due to Lemma 2 above, context-joinability implies joinability of a CCP for arbitrary satisfying substitutions. The rationale for the definition of unfeasibility is a little bit more technical, since it only makes sense inside the proof (by induction) of the theorem below. Basically, unfeasibility is defined in such a way that unfeasible CCPs contradict the confluence of all $\succ$-smaller terms, which we obtain as induction hypothesis.

In the original paper the definition of quasi-reductivity requires its order to be closed under substitutions. This property is used in the proof of [4, Theorem 4.2]. By a small change to the definition of unfeasibility we avoid this requirement for our extension to quasi-decreasingness.

We are finally ready to state a concrete version of Theorem 2:

Theorem 3. *Let the ADTRS $\mathcal{R}$ be quasi-decreasing with respect to $\succ$. Then $\mathcal{R}$ is confluent if all CCPs are context-joinable, unfeasible, or infeasible.*

Proof. Unfortunately, we cannot directly reuse Theorem 2 and its proof, since we need our sufficient criteria in the induction hypothesis. However, the new proof is quite similar. It only differs in case (1), where we consider a CCP:

1. If the CCP is context-joinable, we obtain a join with respect to contextual rewriting which we can easily transform into a join with respect to $\mathcal{R}$ by an application of Lemma 2 because we have a substitution satisfying the conditions of the CCP.
2. If the CCP is unfeasible, we obtain two diverging contextual rewrite sequences. Again since there is a substitution satisfying the conditions of the CCP we may employ Lemma 2 to get two diverging conditional $\mathcal{R}$-rewrite sequences. Because $\ell_1\sigma \succ_{\mathsf{st}} t_0$ we can use the induction hypothesis to get a join between the two end terms. But from the definition of unfeasibility we also know that the end points are not unifiable (and hence are not the same) and cannot be rewritten (because of strong irreducibility), leading to a contradiction.
3. Finally, if the CCP is infeasible, then there is no substitution that satisfies its conditions, contradicting the fact that we already have such a substitution. $\square$

Example 4. The CTRS $\mathcal{R}_{\mathsf{min}}$ from Example 1 is actually an ADTRS and also quasi-decreasing. To conclude confluence of the system it remains to check its CCPs which are listed in Example 2. The first one, (1,2), is trivially context-joinable because the left- and right-hand sides coincide. Unfortunately, the methods used in ConCon are not able to handle either of the CCPs (1,3) and (2,3). So we are not able to conclude confluence of $\mathcal{R}_{\mathsf{min}}$ at this point.

We give a transformation on CTRSs which is often helpful in practice:

Definition 4 (Inlining of Conditions). *Given a conditional rewrite rule $\rho :$ $\ell \to r \Leftarrow s_1 \approx t_1, \ldots, s_n \approx t_n$ and an index $1 \leqslant i \leqslant n$ such that $t_i = x$ for some variable x, let $\mathsf{inl}_i(\rho)$ denote the rule resulting from inlining the ith condition of ρ, that is, $\ell \to r\sigma \Leftarrow s_1\sigma \approx t_1, \ldots, s_{i-1}\sigma \approx t_{i-1}, s_{i+1}\sigma \approx t_{i+1}, \ldots, s_n\sigma \approx t_n$ with $\sigma = \{x \mapsto s_i\}$.*

Lemma 3. *Let $\rho \in \mathcal{R}$ and $s \approx x$ be the ith condition of ρ. Whenever we have $x \notin \mathcal{V}(\ell, s, t_1, \ldots, t_{i-1}, t_{i+1}, \ldots, t_n)$, then the relations $\to_{\mathcal{R}}^*$ and $\to_{\mathcal{R}'}^*$, where $\mathcal{R}' = (\mathcal{R} \setminus \{\rho\}) \cup \{\mathsf{inl}_i(\rho)\}$, coincide.*

Proof. We show $\to_{\mathcal{R},n} \subseteq \to_{\mathcal{R},n}^*$ and $\to_{\mathcal{R}',n} \subseteq \to_{\mathcal{R},n}^*$ by induction on the level n. For $n = 0$ the result is immediate. Consider a step $s = C[\ell\sigma] \to_{\mathcal{R},n+1} C[r\sigma] = t$ employing rule ρ (for the other rules of $\mathcal{R}$ the result is trivial). Thus, $u\sigma \to_{\mathcal{R},n}^* v\sigma$ for all $u \approx v \in c$. In particular $s\sigma \to_{\mathcal{R},n}^* x\sigma$. Thus, using the IH, for each condition $u \approx v$ of $\mathsf{inl}_i(\rho)$ we have $1 \leqslant j \leqslant n$ such that $u\sigma = s_j\{x \mapsto s\}\sigma \to_{\mathcal{R}',n}^*$ $s_j\sigma \to_{\mathcal{R}',n}^* t_j\sigma = v\sigma$. Hence, $\ell\sigma \to_{\mathcal{R}',n+1} r\{x \mapsto s\}\sigma \to_{\mathcal{R}',n+1}^* r\sigma$ and thus $s \to_{\mathcal{R}',n+1}^* t$.

Now, consider a step $s = C[\ell\sigma] \to_{\mathcal{R}',n+1} C[r\{x \mapsto s\}\sigma]$ employing rule $\mathsf{inl}_i(\rho)$. Together with the IH this implies that $u\sigma \to_{\mathcal{R},n}^* v\sigma$ for all conditions $u \approx v$ in $\mathsf{inl}_i(\rho)$. Let τ be a substitution such that $\tau(x) = s\sigma$ and $\tau(y) = \sigma(y)$ for all $y \neq x$. We have $s_i\tau = s\tau = x\tau = t_i\tau$ and $s_j\tau = s_j\{x \mapsto s\}\sigma \to_{\mathcal{R},n}^* t_j\sigma = t_j\tau$ for all $1 \leqslant j \leqslant n$ with $i \neq j$, since x neither occurs in s nor the right-hand sides of conditions in $\mathsf{inl}_i(\rho)$. Therefore, $u \to_{\mathcal{R},n}^* v$ for all $u \approx v \in c$. In total, we have $s = C[\ell\sigma] = C[\ell\tau] \to_{\mathcal{R},n+1} C[r\tau] = C[r\{x \mapsto s\}\sigma]$, concluding the proof.   □

We are not aware of any mention of this simple method in the literature, but found that in practice, exhaustive application of inlining increases the applicability of other methods like infeasibility via tcap and non-confluence via plain rewriting: for the former inlining yields more term structure, which may prevent tcap from replacing a subterm by a fresh variable and thus makes non-unifiability more likely; while for the latter inlining may yield CCPs without conditions and thereby make them amenable to non-joinability techniques for plain term rewriting [34].

Example 5. Rules (2) and (3) of $\mathcal{R}_{\mathsf{min}}$ from Example 1 are both susceptible to inlining of conditions. For each of them, we may remove the first condition and replace y by $\mathsf{min}(xs)$ resulting in

$$\mathsf{min}(\mathsf{cons}(x, xs)) \to x \Leftarrow x < \mathsf{min}(xs) \approx \mathsf{true} \tag{2'}$$

$$\mathsf{min}(\mathsf{cons}(x, xs)) \to \mathsf{min}(xs) \Leftarrow x < \mathsf{min}(xs) \approx \mathsf{false} \tag{3'}$$

Now, instead of the CCPs from Example 2 we have the following CCPs (modulo symmetry as before):

$$x \approx x \Leftarrow x < \mathsf{min}(\mathsf{nil}) \approx \mathsf{true} \tag{1,2'}$$

$$x \approx \mathsf{min}(\mathsf{nil}) \Leftarrow x < \mathsf{min}(\mathsf{nil}) \approx \mathsf{false} \tag{1,3'}$$

$$x \approx \mathsf{min}(xs) \Leftarrow x < \mathsf{min}(xs) \approx \mathsf{true}, x < \mathsf{min}(xs) \approx \mathsf{false} \tag{2,3'}$$

Again, the first CCP $(1,2')$ is trivially context-joinable, $(1,3')$ is infeasible since $\mathsf{tcap}(x < \mathsf{min}(\mathsf{nil})) = x < \mathsf{min}(\mathsf{nil})$ and false are not unifiable, and $(2',3')$ is unfeasible because with contextual rewriting we can reach the two non-unifiable normal forms true and false starting from $x < \mathsf{min}(xs)$. Hence, we conclude confluence of the quasi-decreasing ADTRS $\mathcal{R}_{\mathsf{min}}$ by Theorem 3.

Inlining of conditions is implemented in ConCon 1.4.0 as a first preprocessing step and is certifiable by CeTA.

5   Certification Challenges

One of the main challenges towards actual certification is typically disregarded on paper: the definition of critical pairs may yield an infinite set of CCPs even for finite CTRSs. This is because we have to consider arbitrary variable-disjoint variants of rules. However, a hypothetical certificate would only contain those CCPs that were obtained from some specific variable-disjoint variants of rules. Now the argument typically goes as follows: *modulo variable renaming there are only finitely many CCPs. Done.*

However, this reasoning is valid only for properties that are either closed under substitution or at least invariant under renaming of variables. For joinability of plain critical pairs—arguably the most investigated case—this is indeed easy. But when it comes to contextual rewriting we spent a considerable amount of work on some results about permutations that were not available in IsaFoR.

To illustrate the issue, consider the abstract specification of the check function *check-CCPs*, such that *isOK* (*check-CCPs* $\mathcal{R}$) implies that each of the CCPs of $\mathcal{R}$ is either unfeasible, context-joinable, or infeasible. To this end we work modulo the assumption that we already have sound check functions for the latter three properties, which is nicely supported by Isabelle's locale mechanism:[2]

locale *al94-spec* =
    fixes v_x **and** v_y
        and *check-context-joinable*
        and *check-infeasible*
        and *check-unfeasible*
    assumes v_x **and** v_y are injective
        and $\operatorname{ran}(v_x) \cap \operatorname{ran}(v_y) = \varnothing$
        and *isOK* (*check-context-joinable* $\mathcal{R}\ s\ t\ C$) $\implies \exists u.\ s \to^*_{\mathcal{R},C} u \wedge t \to^*_{\mathcal{R},C} u$)
        ...

We just list the required properties of the renaming functions v_x and v_y and the soundness assumption for *check-context-joinable*.

Now what would a certificate contain and how would we have to check it? Amongst other things, the certificate would contain a finite set of CCPs $\mathcal{C}'$ that were computed by some automated tool. Internally, our certifier computes its own finite set of CCPs $\mathcal{C}$ where variable-disjoint variants of rules are created by fixed injective variable renaming functions v_x and v_y, whose ranges are guaranteed to be disjoint. The former prefixes the character "x" and the latter the character "y" to all variable names, hence the names. At this point we have to check that for each CCP in $\mathcal{C}$ there is one in $\mathcal{C}'$ that is its variant, which is not too difficult. More importantly, we have to prove that whenever some desired property P, say context-joinability, holds for any CCP, then P also holds for all of its variants (including the one that is part of $\mathcal{C}$).

To this end, assume that we have a CCP resulting from a critical overlap of the two rules $\ell_1 \to r_1 \Leftarrow c_1$ and $\ell_2 \to r_2 \Leftarrow c_2$ at position p with mgu μ. This means that there exist permutations π_1 and π_2 such that $(\ell_1 \to r_1 \Leftarrow c_1)\pi_1$ and $(\ell_2 \to r_2 \Leftarrow c_2)\pi_2$ are both in $\mathcal{R}$. In our certifier, mgus are computed by the function mgu(s,t) which either results in *None*, if $s \not\approx t$, or in *Some* μ such that μ is an mgu of s and t, otherwise. Moreover, variable-disjointness of rules is ensured

---

[2] For technical reasons, our formalization uses two locales (*al94-ops*, *al94-spec*) here.

by v_x and v_y, so that we actually call $\mathrm{mgu}(\ell_1|_p\pi_1 v_x, \ell_2\pi_2 v_x)$ for computing a concrete CCP corresponding to the one we assumed above. Thus, we need to show that $\mathrm{mgu}(\ell_1|_p, \ell_2) = \textit{Some } \mu$ also implies that $\mathrm{mgu}(\ell_1|_p\pi_1 v_x, \ell_2\pi_2 y_v) = \textit{Some } \mu'$ for some mgu μ'. Moreover, we are interested in the relationship between μ and μ' with respect to the variables in both rules. Previously—for an earlier formalization of infeasibility [25]—IsaFoR only contained a result that related both unifiers modulo some arbitrary substitution (that is, not necessarily a renaming).

Unfortunately, contextual rewriting is not closed under arbitrary substitutions. Nevertheless, contextual rewriting is closed under permutations, provided the permutation is also applied to C.

Lemma 4. *For every permutation π we have that $s\pi \to^*_{R,C\pi} t\pi$ iff $s \to^*_{R,C} t$.* $\square$

It remains to show that μ and μ' differ basically only by a renaming (at least on the variables of our two rules), which is covered by the following lemma.

Lemma 5. *Let $\mathrm{mgu}(s,t) = \textit{Some } \mu$ and $\mathcal{V}(s,t) \subseteq S \cup T$ for two finite sets of variables S and T with $S \cap T = \varnothing$. Then, there exist a substitution μ' and a permutation π such that for arbitrary permutations π_1 and π_2: $\mathrm{mgu}(s\pi_1 v_x, t\pi_2 v_y) = \textit{Some } \mu'$, $\mu = \pi_1\mu'v_x\pi$ $[S]$, and $\mu = \pi_2\mu'v_y\pi$ $[T]$.*

Proof. Let $h(x) = xv_x\pi_1$ if $x \in S$ and $h(x) = xv_y\pi_2$, otherwise. Then, since h is bijective between $S \cup T$ and $h(S \cup T)$ we can obtain a permutation π for which $\pi = h$ $[S \cup T]$. We define $\mu' =^- \pi\mu$ and abbreviate $s\pi_1 v_x$ and $t\pi_2 v_y$ to s' and t', respectively. Note that $s' = s\pi$ and $t' = t\pi$. Since μ is an mgu of s and t we have $s\mu = t\mu$, which further implies $s'\mu' = t'\mu'$. But then μ' is a unifier of s' and t' and thus there exists some μ'' for which $\mathrm{mgu}(s',t') = \textit{Some } \mu''$ and $s'\mu'' = t'\mu''$.

We now show that μ' is also most general. Assume $s'\tau = t'\tau$ for some τ. Then $s\pi\tau = t\pi\tau$ and thus there exists some δ such that $\pi\tau = \mu\delta$ (since μ is most general). But then $\pi^-\pi\tau = \pi^-\mu\delta$ and thus $\tau = \mu'\delta$. Hence, μ' is most general.

Since μ'' is most general too, it only differs by a renaming, say π', from μ', that is, $\mu'' = \pi'\mu'$. This yields $\mu = \pi_1\mu''v_x\pi'^-$ $[S]$ and $\mu = \pi_2\mu''v_y\pi'^-[T]$, and thus concludes the proof. $\square$

6   Available Check Functions

Before we can actually certify the output of CTRS confluence tools with CeTA, we have to provide an executable check function for each property that is required to apply Theorem 3 and prove its soundness. It is worth mentioning that the return type of these check functions is only "morally" bool. In order to have nice error messages we actually employ a monad. So whenever we need to handle the result of a check function as bool we encapsulate it in a call to *isOK* which results in *False* if there was an error and *True*, otherwise.

As mentioned earlier, the check functions for quasi-decreasingness and infeasibility are already in place. It remains to provide new check functions for absolute irreducibility, absolute determinism, contextual rewrite sequences, context-joinability, and unfeasibility together with their corresponding soundness proofs. For absolute irreducibility we provide the check function *check-airr*, employing existing machinery from IsaFoR for renaming and unification, and prove:

Lemma 6. *isOK* (*check-airr* $\mathcal{R}$ t) *iff the term t is absolutely $\mathcal{R}$-irreducible.* □

This, in turn, is used to define the check function *check-adtrs* and the accompanying lemma for ADTRSs.

Lemma 7. *isOK* (*check-adtrs* $\mathcal{R}$) *iff $\mathcal{R}$ is an ADTRS.* □

Concerning contextual rewriting, we provide the check function *check-csteps* for conditional rewrite sequences together with the following lemma:

Lemma 8. *Given a CTRS $\mathcal{R}$, a set of conditions C, two terms s and t, and a list of conditional rewrite proofs ps, we have that isOK* (*check-csteps* ($\mathcal{R} \cup \overline{C}$) $\overline{s}$ $\overline{t}$ $\overline{ps}$) *implies $s \rightarrow^*_{\mathcal{R},C} t$.* □

Although conditional rewriting is decidable in our setting (strong determinism and quasi-decreasingness), we require a *conditional rewrite proof* to provide all the necessary information for checking a single conditional rewrite step (the employed rule, position, and substitution; source and target terms; and recursively, a list of rewrite proofs for each condition of the applied rule). That way, we avoid having to formalize a rewriting engine for conditional rewriting in IsaFoR. With a check function for contextual rewrite sequences in place, we can easily give the check function *check-context-joinable* with the corresponding lemma:

Lemma 9. *Given a CTRS $\mathcal{R}$, three terms s, t, and u, a set of conditions C, and two lists of conditional rewrite proofs ps and qs, we have that isOK* (*check-context-joinable* u ps qs $\mathcal{R}$ s t C) *implies that there exists some term u' such that $s \rightarrow^*_{\mathcal{R},C} u' {}_{\mathcal{R},C}\!\!\leftarrow^* t$.* □

Here *check-context-joinable* is a concrete implementation of the homonymous function from the *al94-spec* locale. We further give the check function *check-unfeasible* and the accompanying soundness lemma:

Lemma 10. *Given a quasi-decreasing CTRS $\mathcal{R}$, two variable-disjoint variants of rules $\rho_1 : \ell_1 \rightarrow r_1 \Leftarrow c_1$ and $\rho_2 : \ell_2 \rightarrow r_2 \Leftarrow c_2$ in $\mathcal{R}$, an mgu μ of $\ell_1|_p$ and ℓ_2 for some position p, a set of conditions C such that $C = c_1\mu, c_2\mu$, three terms t, u, and v, and two lists of conditional rewrite proofs ps and qs, we have that isOK* (*check-unfeasible* t u v ps qs ρ_1 ρ_2 $\mathcal{R}$ ℓ_1 μ C) *implies that there exist three terms t', u', and v' such that for all σ we have $\ell_1\mu\sigma \succ t'\sigma$, whenever σ satisfies C, u' ${}_{\mathcal{R},C}\!\!\leftarrow^* t' \rightarrow^*_{\mathcal{R},C} v'$, u' and v' are both strongly irreducible, and $u' \not\sim v'$.* □

Again, *check-unfeasible* is a concrete implementation of the function of the same name from the *al94-spec* locale and it additionally performs various sanity checks.

At this point, interpreting the *al94-spec* locale using the three check functions *check-context-joinable*, *check-infeasible*, and *check-unfeasible* from above yields the concrete function *check-CCPs*, which is used in the final check *check-al94*.

Lemma 11. *Given a quasi-decreasing CTRS $\mathcal{R}$, a list of context-joinability certificates c, a list of infeasibility certificates i, and a list of unfeasibility certificates u. Then, isOK (check-al94 c i u $\mathcal{R}$) implies confluence of $\mathcal{R}$.*   □

7   Experiments

The largest available collection of CTRSs we are aware of is the confluence problems database (Cops) [10]. At the time of writing it contains a total of 152 CTRSs. Among these, there are 119 oriented 3-CTRSs from which exactly 100 are also ADTRSs. We compare ConCon 1.3.2, which participated in last years confluence competition (CoCo 2016) [3], to ConCon 1.4.0, the current version which implements the results of the paper at hand. Our experiments ran on the StarExec [29] platform with a timeout of 60 seconds per problem. The outcome is summarized in Table 1,[3] where columns labeled A, N, and T contain the results of applying Theorem 3, using non-confluence methods, and trying all methods implemented in ConCon concurrently, respectively. A suffix '+ i' indicates preprocessing by exhaustive inlining of conditions (Lemma 3). Results in parentheses are not just proved by ConCon but also certified by CeTA. For the two A-columns the numbers following the '/' indicate how many systems could only be solved by Theorem 3 but not by any other method.

In total, ConCon 1.3.2 can decide confluence of 82 systems. Of those, 56 are confluent and 26 are non-confluent. Using only Theorem 3, 42 systems can be shown confluent. For 7 of these, none of the other methods are successful. Neither Theorem 3 nor the non-confluence methods are certifiable in ConCon 1.3.2. However, in 38 cases (using other methods) the output of ConCon 1.3.2 is certifiable by CeTA. Also inlining of conditions is absent in ConCon 1.3.2.

The new version of ConCon can decide confluence of 86 systems. Of those, 57 are confluent and 29 are non-confluent. Seven of the generated confluence proofs cannot be certified by CeTA. This is due to an infeasibility method (using equational reasoning) that is not yet formalized. In contrast, all of the non-confluence proofs can be certified by CeTA. When we subtract the certifiably non-confluent systems we are left with 72 potentially confluent ADTRSs. From those 52 are certifiably quasi-decreasing. Theorem 3 succeeds on 46 of these quasi-decreasing ADTRSs (and can be certified for 43 of them). For three of these systems (288, 292, 326) testing for infeasibility is essential. When using inlining of conditions

Table 1. Comparison on 119 oriented 3-CTRSs from Cops.

ConCon	A	A + i	N	N + i	T	T + i
1.3.2	42 (0) / 7 (0)	-	26 (0)	-	82 (38)	-
1.4.0	46 (43) / 8 (11)	47(44) / 8 (11)	27 (27)	29 (29)	84 (77)	86 (79)

---

[3] Detailed results are available at http://cl-informatik.uibk.ac.at/experiments/2017/cade/.

we gain another (certifiably) confluent system (493). Finally, independent of inlining of conditions, there are 8 systems where only Theorem 3 is successful. In the certifiable case this number increases to 11 systems (because for 3 systems the other methods are not certifiable). The most important message of Table 1 is that with the new versions of ConCon and CeTA the number of certifiably (non-)confluent systems has more than doubled from 38 to 79, which means that more than 90% of the (non-)confluence proofs for CTRSs are certifiable.

8   Conclusion and Future Work

Even in the presence of a suitable notion of termination (like quasi-decreasingness), proving confluence of conditional term rewrite systems is still hard (unlike in the unconditional case, where confluence is decidable.)

We formalized a characterization of confluence of quasi-decreasing strongly deterministic CTRSs in Isabelle/HOL. It requires joinability of all conditional critical pairs, which is undecidable in general. Moreover, we formalized a more practical variant of the previous characterization for which each conditional critical pair must be either context-joinable, unfeasible, or infeasible. These properties, in turn, rely on strong irreducibility, which like strong determinism is undecidable in general. Thus, we further formalized decidable sufficient criteria.

In total, this paper constitutes the necessary work for the actual certification of confluence of quasi-decreasing SDTRSs, which complements our existing check functions for certifying confluence of CTRSs [26,32]. We have extended our confluence tool ConCon and the certifier CeTA accordingly.

Here is a rough impression of the involved effort: our formalization comprises 28 definitions, 14 recursive functions, and 83 lemmas with proofs, on approximately 2500 lines of Isabelle code (in addition to everything that we could reuse from the IsaFoR library). The whole development took about 6 person-months.

Future Work. Concerning certification, our extension from quasi-reductive to quasi-decreasing CTRSs is at the moment only of theoretical relevance, since the only way of certifying quasi-decreasingness with CeTA is via quasi-reductivity.

In principle it may be useful to use methods for proving operational termination [20]—a notation equivalent to quasi-decreasingness [19]—in order to increase the applicability of Theorem 3. However, IsaFoR is currently lacking the proof that operational termination and quasi-decreasingness coincide. Also, none of the methods for proving operational termination have been formalized so far. Moreover, when running AProVE [11] and MU-TERM [1] on the 72 ADTRSs of Cops which have not already been shown to be non-confluent, the former can show operational termination of the same 52 systems for which ConCon could show quasi-reductivity, and the latter can show two additional systems (266, 278), while losing another one (362). Of course, this insignificant difference could be due to our example database.

Open Problem. After having finished our formalization, we realized that it is not known whether quasi-decreasingness differs from quasi-reductivity at all, that is, the question whether there exists a quasi-decreasing CTRS that is not quasi-reductive, is still open. Regardless, we agree with Ohlebusch [24] that quasi-decreasingness has two advantages: (1) it does not depend on signature extensions and (2) $\ell\sigma \succ_{st} s_i\sigma$ is only required if $s_j\sigma \to_{\mathcal{R}}^* t_j\sigma$ instead of $s_j\sigma \succeq t_j\sigma$. Point (1) is illustrated by the quasi-decreasing CTRS $\mathcal{R}_{qd} = \{f(b) \to f(a), b \to c, a \to c \Leftarrow b \approx c\}$. Assume that $\mathcal{R}_{qd}$ is quasi-reductive with respect to $\succ$. Then, $f(b) \succ f(a)$ and $a \ (\succ \cup \rhd)^+ b$. If we are not allowed to introduce fresh function symbols, the latter implies $a \succ b$, for otherwise, we would have $a \succ f^k(b) \unrhd b$ for some $k \geqslant 0$, which together with closure under contexts and transitivity of $\succ$ contradicts the well-foundedness of $\succ$. But $a \succ b$ also contradicts the well-foundedness of $\succ$.

Proof Assistant. We found Sledgehammer [6,7] to be an indispensable tool for our development. On the one hand, to quickly discharge subgoals that seemed intuitively obvious but turned out tedious to prove, and on the other, as fast "fact finder" for the huge IsaFoR library (especially for the second author, who has not been involved in IsaFoR from the start).

Acknowledgments. We thank Bertram Felgenhauer and Julian Nagele for fruitful discussions on the subject matter. Moreover, we would like to thank the anonymous reviewers for their constructive and helpful comments.

A   Browsing Isabelle/HOL Theory Files

We provide the Isabelle/HOL theory files for the presented formalization (`AL94.thy`, `AL94_Impl.thy`, `Inline_Conditions.thy`, and `Inline_Conditions_Impl.thy` all in the subdirectory `thys/Conditional_Rewriting/`) as part of the formal IsaFoR library which depends on the Archive of Formal Proofs (AFP). First, get the AFP via

```
wget https://www.isa-afp.org/release/afp-current.tar.gz
```

and extract the archive. Then get IsaFoR via

```
hg clone \
    http://cl2-informatik.uibk.ac.at/rewriting/mercurial.cgi/IsaFoR
```

and from inside the `IsaFoR` directory update to tag `v2.29`:

```
hg update -r v2.29
```

For the remainder, you will need to have Isabelle2016-1 installed. Add the following lines to your `$HOME/.isabelle/Isabelle2016-1/etc/settings`

```
init_component "/path/to/afp/directory/"
init_component "/path/to/isafor/directory"
```

Finally—again from the `IsaFoR` directory—start Isabelle/jEdit in order to browse our formal development:

isabelle jedit -l TA thys/Conditional_Rewriting/AL94_Impl.thy

This will take some time, even on a (more than) decent machine, the first time around, but will be much faster thereafter.

References

1. Alarcón, B., Gutiérrez, R., Lucas, S., Navarro-Marset, R.: Proving termination properties with MU-TERM. In: Johnson, M., Pavlovic, D. (eds.) AMAST 2010. LNCS, vol. 6486, pp. 201–208. Springer, Heidelberg (2011). doi:10.1007/978-3-642-17796-5_12

2. Antoy, S., Hanus, M.: Functional logic programming. Commun. ACM **53**(4), 74–85 (2010). doi:10.1145/1721654.1721675

3. Aoto, T., Hirokawa, N., Nagele, J., Nishida, N., Zankl, H.: Confluence competition 2015. In: Felty, A.P., Middeldorp, A. (eds.) CADE 2015. LNCS (LNAI), vol. 9195, pp. 101–104. Springer, Cham (2015). doi:10.1007/978-3-319-21401-6_5

4. Avenhaus, J., Loría-Sáenz, C.: On conditional rewrite systems with extra variables and deterministic logic programs. In: Pfenning, F. (ed.) LPAR 1994. LNCS, vol. 822, pp. 215–229. Springer, Heidelberg (1994). doi:10.1007/3-540-58216-9_40

5. Baader, F., Nipkow, T.: Term Rewriting and All That. Cambridge University Press, Cambridge (1998)

6. Blanchette, J., Paulson, L.: Hammering away - a user's guide to sledgehammer for Isabelle/HOL (2010). https://isabelle.in.tum.de/dist/doc/sledgehammer.pdf

7. Blanchette, J.C., Kaliszyk, C., Paulson, L.C., Urban, J.: Hammering towards QED. J. Formalized Reasoning **9**(1), 101–148 (2016). doi:10.6092/issn.1972-5787/4593

8. Blanqui, F., Koprowski, A.: CoLoR: a Coq library on well-founded rewrite relations and its application to the automated verification of termination certificates. Math. Struct. Comput. Sci. **21**(4), 827–859 (2011). doi:10.1017/S0960129511000120

9. Contejean, É., Courtieu, P., Forest, J., Pons, O., Urbain, X.: Automated certified proofs with CiME 3 In: Proceedings of the 22nd International Conference on Rewriting Techniques and Applications (RTA). LIPIcs, vol. 10, pp. 21–30. Schloss Dagstuhl (2011), doi:10.4230/LIPIcs.RTA.2011.21

10. Cops: The confluence problems database. http://cops.uibk.ac.at/?q=ctrs

11. Giesl, J., Schneider-Kamp, P., Thiemann, R.: AProVE 1.2: automatic termination proofs in the dependency pair framework. In: Furbach, U., Shankar, N. (eds.) IJCAR 2006. LNCS, vol. 4130, pp. 281–286. Springer, Heidelberg (2006). doi:10.1007/11814771_24

12. Giesl, J., Thiemann, R., Schneider-Kamp, P.: Proving and disproving termination of higher-order functions. In: Gramlich, B. (ed.) FroCoS 2005. LNCS (LNAI), vol. 3717, pp. 216–231. Springer, Heidelberg (2005). doi:10.1007/11559306_12

13. Giesl, J., Mesnard, F., Rubio, A., Thiemann, R., Waldmann, J.: Termination competition (termCOMP 2015). In: Felty, A.P., Middeldorp, A. (eds.) CADE 2015. LNCS (LNAI), vol. 9195, pp. 105–108. Springer, Cham (2015). doi:10.1007/978-3-319-21401-6_6

14. Hirokawa, N., Middeldorp, A., Sternagel, C.: A new and formalized proof of abstract completion. In: Klein, G., Gamboa, R. (eds.) ITP 2014. LNCS, vol. 8558, pp. 292–307. Springer, Cham (2014). doi:10.1007/978-3-319-08970-6_19

15. Huet, G.: Confluent reductions: abstract properties and applications to term rewriting systems. J. ACM **27**(4), 797–821 (1980)
16. Knuth, D., Bendix, P.: Simple word problems in universal algebras. In: Leech, J. (ed.) Computational Problems in Abstract Algebra, pp. 263–297. Pergamon Press (1970)
17. Kop, C.: Higher-order termination: automatable techniques for proving termination of higher-order term rewriting systems. Ph.D. thesis, VU University Amsterdam (2012). http://hdl.handle.net/1871/39346
18. Korp, M., Sternagel, C., Zankl, H., Middeldorp, A.: Tyrolean Termination Tool 2. In: Treinen, R. (ed.) RTA 2009. LNCS, vol. 5595, pp. 295–304. Springer, Heidelberg (2009). doi:10.1007/978-3-642-02348-4_21
19. Lucas, S., Marché, C., Meseguer, J.: Operational termination of conditional term rewriting systems. Inf. Process. Lett. **95**(4), 446–453 (2005). doi:10.1016/j.ipl.2005.05.002
20. Lucas, S., Meseguer, J.: Dependency pairs for proving termination properties of conditional term rewriting systems. J. Logical Algebraic Methods Program. **86**(1), 236–268 (2017). doi:10.1016/j.jlamp.2016.03.003
21. Marlow, S.: Haskell 2010 language report. https://www.haskell.org/definition/haskell2010.pdf
22. Newman, M.: On theories with a combinatorial definition of equivalence. Ann. Math. **43**(2), 223–243 (1942)
23. Nipkow, T.: Equational reasoning in Isabelle. Sci. Comput. Program. **12**(2), 123–149 (1989). doi:10.1016/0167-6423(89)90038-5
24. Ohlebusch, E.: Advanced Topics in Term Rewriting. Springer, New York (2002)
25. Sternagel, C., Sternagel, T.: Level-confluence of 3-CTRSs in Isabelle/HOL. In: Proceedings of the 4th International Workshop on Confluence (IWC), arXiv:1602.07115 (2015)
26. Sternagel, C., Sternagel, T.: Certifying confluence of almost orthogonal CTRSs via exact tree automata completion. In: Proceedings of the 1st International Conference on Formal Structures for Computation and Deduction (FSCD). LIPIcs, vol. 51, pp. 29:1–29:16 (2016). doi:10.4230/LIPIcs.FSCD.2016.29
27. Sternagel, T., Middeldorp, A.: Conditional confluence (system description). In: Dowek, G. (ed.) RTA 2014. LNCS, vol. 8560, pp. 456–465. Springer, Cham (2014). doi:10.1007/978-3-319-08918-8_31
28. Sternagel, T., Sternagel, C.: Formalized confluence of quasi-decreasing, strongly deterministic conditional TRSs. In: Proceedings of the 5th International Workshop on Confluence (IWC), arXiv:1609.03341 (2016)
29. Stump, A., Sutcliffe, G., Tinelli, C.: StarExec: a cross-community infrastructure for logic solving. In: Demri, S., Kapur, D., Weidenbach, C. (eds.) IJCAR 2014. LNCS (LNAI), vol. 8562, pp. 367–373. Springer, Cham (2014). doi:10.1007/978-3-319-08587-6_28
30. Thiemann, R., Sternagel, C.: Certification of termination proofs using CeTA. In: Berghofer, S., Nipkow, T., Urban, C., Wenzel, M. (eds.) TPHOLs 2009. LNCS, vol. 5674, pp. 452–468. Springer, Heidelberg (2009). doi:10.1007/978-3-642-03359-9_31
31. Waldmann, J.: Matchbox: a tool for match-bounded string rewriting. In: Oostrom, V. (ed.) RTA 2004. LNCS, vol. 3091, pp. 85–94. Springer, Heidelberg (2004). doi:10.1007/978-3-540-25979-4_6
32. Winkler, S., Thiemann, R.: Formalizing soundness and completeness of unravelings. In: Lutz, C., Ranise, S. (eds.) FroCoS 2015. LNCS (LNAI), vol. 9322, pp. 239–255. Springer, Cham (2015). doi:10.1007/978-3-319-24246-0_15

33. Yamada, A., Kusakari, K., Sakabe, T.: Nagoya termination tool. In: Dowek, G. (ed.) RTA 2014. LNCS, vol. 8560, pp. 466–475. Springer, Cham (2014). doi:10. 1007/978-3-319-08918-8_32
34. Zankl, H., Felgenhauer, B., Middeldorp, A.: CSI – a confluence tool. In: Bjørner, N., Sofronie-Stokkermans, V. (eds.) CADE 2011. LNCS, vol. 6803, pp. 499–505. Springer, Heidelberg (2011). doi:10.1007/978-3-642-22438-6_38

A Transfinite Knuth–Bendix Order
for Lambda-Free Higher-Order Terms

Heiko Becker[1], Jasmin Christian Blanchette[2,3,4($\boxtimes$)], Uwe Waldmann[4],
and Daniel Wand[4,5]

[1] Max-Planck-Institut für Softwaresysteme, Saarbrücken, Germany
hbecker@mpi-sws.org
[2] Vrije Universiteit Amsterdam, Amsterdam, The Netherlands
j.c.blanchette@vu.nl
[3] Inria Nancy – Grand Est, Villers-lès-Nancy, France
jasmin.blanchette@inria.fr
[4] Max-Planck-Institut für Informatik, Saarbrücken, Germany
{jasmin.blanchette,uwe.waldmann,daniel.wand}@mpi-inf.mpg.de
[5] Technische Universität München, Munich, Germany
daniel.wand@in.tum.de

Abstract. We generalize the Knuth–Bendix order (KBO) to higher-order terms without λ-abstraction. The restriction of this new order to first-order terms coincides with the traditional KBO. The order has many useful properties, including transitivity, the subterm property, compatibility with contexts (monotonicity), stability under substitution, and well-foundedness. Transfinite weights and argument coefficients can also be supported. The order appears promising as the basis of a higher-order superposition calculus.

1 Introduction

Superposition [39] is one of the most successful proof calculi for first-order logic today, but in contrast to resolution [9,26], tableaux [4], and connections [1], it has not yet been generalized to higher-order logic (also called simple type theory). Yet, most proof assistants and many specification languages are based on some variant of higher-order logic. Tools such as HOLyHammer and Sledgehammer [13] encode higher-order constructs to bridge the gap, but their performance on higher-order problems is disappointing [45].

This motivates us to design a *graceful* generalization of superposition: a proof calculus that behaves like standard superposition on first-order problems and that smoothly scales up to arbitrary higher-order problems. The calculus should additionally be complete with respect to Henkin semantics [10,23]. A challenge is that superposition relies on a simplification order, which is fixed in advance of the proof attempt, to prune the search space. However, no simplification order > exists on higher-order terms viewed modulo β-equivalence; the cycle a $=_\beta$ ($\lambda x.$ a) (f a) > f a > a is a counterexample. (The two > steps follow from the subterm property—requirement that proper subterms of a term are smaller

© Springer International Publishing AG 2017
L. de Moura (Ed.): CADE 2017, LNAI 10395, pp. 432–453, 2017.
DOI: 10.1007/978-3-319-63046-5_27

than the term itself.) A solution is to give up interchangeability of β-equivalent terms, or even inclusion of β-reduction (i.e., $(\lambda x.\ s[x])\ t > s[t]$).

We start our investigations by focusing on a fragment devoid of λ-abstractions. A λ-free higher-order term is either a variable x, a symbol f, or an application $s\,t$. Application associates to the left. Functions take their arguments one at a time, in a curried style (e.g., f a b). Compared with first-order terms, the main differences are that variables may be applied (e.g., x a) and that functions may be supplied fewer arguments than they can take. Although λ-abstractions are widely perceived as the higher-order feature par excellence, they can be avoided by letting the proof calculus, and provers based on it, synthesize fresh symbols f and definitions f $x_1 \ldots x_m = t$ as needed, giving arbitrary names to otherwise nameless functions.

In recent work, we introduced a "graceful" λ-free higher-order recursive path order (RPO) [16]. We now contribute a corresponding Knuth–Bendix order (KBO) [30]. Leading superposition provers such as E [41], SPASS [48], and Vampire [34] implement both KBO and variants of RPO. To keep the presentation manageable, we introduce three KBO variants of increasing strength (Sect. 4): a basic KBO ($>_{hb}$); a KBO with support for function symbols of weight 0 ($>_{hz}$); and a KBO extended with coefficients for the arguments ($>_{hc}$). They all coincide with their first-order counterparts on terms that contain only fully applied function symbols and no applied variables. For all three variants, we allow different comparison methods for comparing the arguments of different symbols (Sect. 2). In addition, we allow ordinals for the weights and argument coefficients (Sect. 3), as in the transfinite first-order KBO [37].

Our KBO variants enjoy many useful properties, including transitivity, the subterm property, stability under substitution, well-foundedness, and totality on ground terms (Sect. 5). The orders with no argument coefficients also enjoy compatibility with contexts (sometimes called monotonicity), thereby qualifying as simplification orders. Even without this property, we expect the orders to be usable in a λ-free higher-order generalization of superposition, possibly at the cost of some complications [19]. Ground totality is used in the completeness proof of superposition. The proofs of the properties were formalized using the Isabelle/HOL proof assistant (Sect. 6). Proof sketches are included here; more complete justifications are included in a technical report [7].

Although this is not our primary focus, the new KBO can be used to establish termination of higher-order term rewriting systems (Sect. 7). However, more research will be necessary to combine the order with the dependency pair framework, implement them in a termination prover, and evaluate them on standard term-rewriting benchmarks.

To our knowledge, KBO has not been studied before in a higher-order setting. There are, however, a considerable number of higher-order variants of RPO [17,18,28,31,32,35] and many encodings of higher-order term rewriting systems into first-order systems [2,22,24,24,46]. The encoding approaches are more suitable to term rewriting systems than to superposition and similar proof calculi. We refer to our paper on the λ-free higher-order RPO for a discussion of such related work [16].

Conventions. We fix a set $\mathcal{V}$ of *variables* with typical elements x, y. A higher-order signature consists of a nonempty set Σ of (function) *symbols* a, b, c, f, g, h, ... Untyped λ-free higher-order (Σ-)*terms* $s, t, u \in \mathcal{T}_\Sigma$ $(= \mathcal{T})$ are defined inductively by the grammar $s ::= x \mid f \mid t\,u$. These terms are isomorphic to applicative terms [29], but we prefer the "higher-order" terminology. Symbols and variables are assigned an arity, $arity : \Sigma \uplus \mathcal{V} \to \mathbb{N} \cup \{\infty\}$, specifying their maximum number of arguments. Infinite arities are allowed for the sake of generality. Nullary symbols are called *constants*. A term of the form $t\,u$ is called an *application*. Non-application terms $\zeta, \xi, \chi \in \Sigma \uplus \mathcal{V}$ are called *heads*. A term s can be decomposed uniquely as a head with m arguments: $s = \zeta\,s_1 \dots s_m$. We define $hd(s) = \zeta$, $args(s) = (s_1, \dots, s_m)$, and $arity(s) = arity(\zeta) - m$.

The *size* $|s|$ of a term is the number of grammar rule applications needed to construct it. The set of *subterms* of a term consists of the term itself and, for applications $t\,u$, of the subterms of t and u. The multiset of variables occurring in a term s is written $vars_\#(s)$—e.g., $vars_\#(f\,x\,y\,x) = \{x, x, y\}$. We denote by $M(a)$ the multiplicity of an element a in a multiset M and write $M \subseteq N$ to mean $\forall a.\, M(a) \leq N(a)$.

We assume throughout that the arities of all symbols and variables occurring in terms are respected—in other words, all subterms of a term have nonnegative arities. A *first-order* signature is a higher-order signature with an arity function $arity : \Sigma \to \mathbb{N}$. A *first-order* term is a term in which variables are nullary and heads are applied to the number of arguments specified by their respective arities. Following the view that first-order logic is a fragment of higher-order logic, we will use a curried syntax for first-order terms. Accordingly, if $arity(a) = 0$ and $arity(f) = 2$, then $f\,a\,a$ is first-order, whereas f, $f\,a$, and $f\,f\,f$ are only higher-order.

Our focus on untyped terms is justified by a desire to keep the definitions simple and widely applicable to a variety of type systems (monomorphic, rank-1 polymorphic, dependent types, etc.). There are straightforward ways to extend the results presented in this paper to a typed setting: Types can be simply erased, they can be encoded in the terms, or they can be used to break ties when two terms are identical except for their types. Even in an untyped setting, the *arity* function makes some of the typing information visible. In Sect. 4.3, we will introduce a mapping, called ghd, that can be used to reveal more information about the typing discipline if desired.

2   Extension Orders

KBO relies on an extension operator to recurse through tuples of arguments—typically, the lexicographic order [3, 51]. We prefer an abstract treatment, in a style reminiscent of Ferreira and Zantema [21], which besides its generality has the advantage that it emphasizes the peculiarities of our higher-order setting.

Let $A^* = \bigcup_{i=0}^{\infty} A^i$ be the set of tuples (or finite lists) of arbitrary length whose components are drawn from a set A. We write its elements as $(a_1, \dots, a_m)$, where $m \geq 0$, or simply $\bar{a}$. The number of components of a tuple $\bar{a}$ is written $|\bar{a}|$. Given an m-tuple $\bar{a}$ and an n-tuple $\bar{b}$, we denote by $\bar{a} \cdot \bar{b}$ the $(m + n)$-tuple consisting of the concatenation of $\bar{a}$ and $\bar{b}$. Given a function $h : A \rightarrow A$, we let $h(\bar{a})$ stand for the componentwise application of h to $\bar{a}$. Abusing notation, we sometimes use a tuple where a set is expected. Moreover, since all our functions are curried, we write $\zeta\,\bar{s}$ for a curried application $\zeta\,s_1 \ldots s_m$.

Given a relation $>$, we write $<$ for its inverse and $\geq$ for its reflexive closure, unless $\geq$ is defined otherwise. A (strict) partial order is a relation that is irreflexive and transitive. A (strict) total order is a partial order that satisfies totality (i.e., $b \geq a \vee a > b$). A relation $>$ is well founded if and only if there exists no infinite chain of the form $a_0 > a_1 > \cdots$.

For any relation $> \subseteq A^2$, let $\gg \subseteq (A^*)^2$ be a relation on tuples over A. For example, $\gg$ could be the lexicographic or multiset extension of $>$. We assume throughout that if $B \subseteq A$, then the extension $\gg_B$ of the restriction $>_B$ of $>$ to elements from B coincides with $\gg$ on $(B^*)^2$. Moreover, the following properties are essential for all the orders defined later, whether first- or higher-order:

X1. *Monotonicity*: $\bar{b} \gg_1 \bar{a}$ implies $\bar{b} \gg_2 \bar{a}$ if $b >_1 a$ implies $b >_2 a$ for all a, b;

X2. *Preservation of stability*: $\bar{b} \gg \bar{a}$ implies $h(\bar{b}) \gg h(\bar{a})$ if
   (1) $b > a$ implies $h(b) > h(a)$ for all a, b, and
   (2) $>$ is a partial order on the range of h;

X3. *Preservation of irreflexivity*: $\gg$ is irreflexive if $>$ is irreflexive;

X4. *Preservation of transitivity*: $\gg$ is transitive if $>$ is irreflexive and transitive;

X5. *Modularity* ("head or tail"):
   if $>$ is transitive and total, $|\bar{a}| = |\bar{b}|$, and $b \cdot \bar{b} \gg a \cdot \bar{a}$, then $b > a$ or $\bar{b} \gg \bar{a}$;

X6. *Compatibility with tuple contexts*: $a \neq b$ and $b > a$ implies $\bar{c} \cdot b \cdot \bar{d} \gg \bar{c} \cdot a \cdot \bar{d}$.

Some of the conditions in X2, X4, X5, and X6 may seem gratuitous, but they are necessary for some extension operators if the relation $>$ is arbitrary. For KBO, $>$ will always be a partial order, but we cannot assume this until we have proved it.

It may seem as though X2 is a consequence of X1, by letting $>_1$ be $>$ and $b >_2 a \Leftrightarrow h(b) > h(a)$. However, $\bar{b} \gg_2 \bar{a}$ does not generally coincide with $h(\bar{b}) \gg h(\bar{a})$, even if $>$ satisfies X1. A counterexample follows: Let $\gg$ be the Huet–Oppen multiset extension as introduced below (Definition 6), and let $\bar{a} = \mathsf{d}$, $\bar{b} = (\mathsf{c}, \mathsf{c})$, $h(\mathsf{c}) = h(\mathsf{d}) = \mathsf{c}$, and $\mathsf{d} > \mathsf{c}$. Then $\bar{b} \gg_2 \bar{a}$ (i.e., $(\mathsf{c}, \mathsf{c}) \gg_2 \mathsf{d}$) is false, whereas $h(\bar{b}) \gg h(\bar{a})$ (i.e., $(\mathsf{c}, \mathsf{c}) \gg \mathsf{c}$) is true.

The remaining properties of $\gg$ will be required only by some of the orders or for some optional properties of $>$:

X7. *Preservation of totality*: $\gg$ is total if $>$ is total;

X8. *Compatibility with prepending*: $\bar{b} \gg \bar{a}$ implies $a \cdot \bar{b} \gg a \cdot \bar{a}$;

X9. *Compatibility with appending*: $\bar{b} \gg \bar{a}$ implies $\bar{b} \cdot a \gg \bar{a} \cdot a$;

X10. *Minimality of empty tuple*: $a \gg ()$.

Property X5, modularity, is useful to establish well-foundedness of $\gg$ from the well-foundedness of $>$. The argument is captured by Lemma 3.

Lemma 1. *For any well-founded total order $> \subseteq A^2$, let $\gg \subseteq (A^*)^2$ be a partial order that satisfies property X5. The restriction of $\gg$ to n-tuples is well founded.*

Proof. By induction on n. For the induction step, we assume that there exists an infinite descending chain of n-tuples $\bar{x}_0 \gg \bar{x}_1 \gg \cdots$ and show that this leads to a contradiction. Let $\bar{x}_i = x_i \cdot \bar{y}_i$. For each link $\bar{x}_i \gg \bar{x}_{i+1}$ in the chain, property X5 guarantees that (1) $x_i > x_{i+1}$ or (2) $\bar{y}_i \gg \bar{y}_{i+1}$. Since $>$ is well founded, there can be at most finitely many consecutive links of the first kind. Exploiting the transitivity of $\gg$, we can eliminate all such links, resulting in an infinite chain made up of links of the second kind. The existence of such a chain contradicts the induction hypothesis.   □

Lemma 2. *For any well-founded total order* $> \subseteq A^2$, *let* $\gg \subseteq (A^*)^2$ *be a partial order that satisfies property X5. The restriction of* $\gg$ *to tuples with at most n components is well founded.*

Lemma 3 (Bounded Preservation of Well-Foundedness). *For any well-founded partial order* $> \subseteq A^2$, *let* $\gg \subseteq (A^*)^2$ *be a partial order that satisfies properties X1 and X5. The restriction of* $\gg$ *to tuples with at most n components is well founded.*

Proof. By Zorn's lemma, let $>'$ be a well-founded total order that extends $>$. By property X1, $\gg \subseteq \gg'$. By Lemma 2, $\gg'$ is well founded; hence, $\gg$ is well founded.   □

Definition 4. The *lexicographic extension* $\gg^{\mathsf{lex}}$ of the relation $>$ is defined recursively by $() \not\gg^{\mathsf{lex}} \bar{a}$, $b \cdot \bar{b} \gg^{\mathsf{lex}} ()$, and $b \cdot \bar{b} \gg^{\mathsf{lex}} a \cdot \bar{a} \Leftrightarrow b > a \vee b = a \wedge \bar{b} \gg^{\mathsf{lex}} \bar{a}$.

The reverse, or right-to-left, lexicographic extension is defined analogously. The left-to-right operator lacks property X9; a counterexample is $\bar{b} = \mathsf{c}$, $\bar{a} = ()$, and $a = \mathsf{d}$, with $\mathsf{d} > \mathsf{c}$—we then have $\mathsf{c} \gg^{\mathsf{lex}} ()$ and $(\mathsf{c},\mathsf{d}) \not\gg^{\mathsf{lex}} \mathsf{d}$. Correspondingly, the right-to-left operator lacks X8. The other properties are straightforward to prove.

Definition 5. The *length-lexicographic extension* $\gg^{\mathsf{llex}}$ of the relation $>$ is defined by $\bar{b} \gg^{\mathsf{llex}} \bar{a} \Leftrightarrow |\bar{b}| > |\bar{a}| \vee |\bar{b}| = |\bar{a}| \wedge \bar{b} \gg^{\mathsf{lex}} \bar{a}$.

The length-lexicographic extension and its right-to-left counterpart satisfy all of the properties listed above, making them more interesting than the plain lexicographic extensions. We can also apply arbitrary permutations on same-length tuples before comparing them; however, the resulting operators fail to satisfy properties X8 and X9.

Definition 6. The *multiset extension* $\gg^{\mathsf{ms}}$ of the relation $>$ is defined by $\bar{b} \gg^{\mathsf{ms}} \bar{a} \Leftrightarrow A \neq B \wedge \forall x.\ A(x) > B(x) \Longrightarrow \exists y > x.\ B(y) > A(y)$, where A and B are the multisets corresponding to $\bar{a}$ and $\bar{b}$, respectively.

The above multiset extension, due to Huet and Oppen [25], satisfies all properties except X7. Dershowitz and Manna [20] give an alternative formulation that is equivalent for partial orders $>$ but exhibits subtle differences if $>$ is an arbitrary relation. In particular, the Dershowitz–Manna order does not satisfy property X3, making it unsuitable for establishing that KBO variants are partial orders. This, in conjunction with our desire to track requirements precisely, explains the many subtle differences between this section and the corresponding section of our paper about RPO [16]. One of the main differences is that instead of property X5, the definition of RPO requires preservation of well-foundedness, which unlike X5 is not satisfied by the lexicographic extension.

Finally, we consider the componentwise extension of relations to pairs of tuples of the same length. For partial orders >, this order underapproximates any extension that satisfies properties X4 and X6. It also satisfies all properties except X7.

Definition 7. The *componentwise extension* $\gg^{\mathrm{cw}}$ of the relation > is defined so that $(b_1, \ldots, b_n) \gg^{\mathrm{cw}} (a_1, \ldots, a_m)$ if and only if $m = n$, $b_1 \geq a_1$, $\ldots$, $b_m \geq a_m$, and $b_i > a_i$ for some $i \in \{1, \ldots, m\}$.

3   Ordinals

The transfinite KBO [37] allows weights and argument coefficients to be ordinals instead of natural numbers. We restrict our attention to the ordinals below ε_0. We call these the *syntactic ordinals* **O**. They are precisely the ordinals that can be expressed in Cantor normal form, corresponding to the grammar $\alpha ::= \sum_{i=1}^{m} \omega^{\alpha_i} k_i$, where $\alpha_1 > \cdots > \alpha_m$ and $k_i \in \mathbb{N}_{>0}$ for $i \in \{1, \ldots, m\}$. We refer to the literature for the precise definition [33,37].

The traditional sum and product operations are not commutative—e.g., $1 + \omega = \omega \neq \omega + 1$. For the transfinite KBO, the Hessenberg (or natural) sum and product are used instead. These operations are commutative and coincide with the sum and product operations on polynomials over ω. Somewhat nonstandardly, we let $+$ and $\cdot$ (or juxtaposition) denote these operators. It is sometimes convenient to use subtraction on ordinals and to allow polynomials over ω in which some of the coefficients may be negative (but all of the ω exponents are always plain ordinals). We call such polynomials *signed (syntactic) ordinals* **ZO**. One way to define $\alpha > \beta$ on signed ordinals is to look at the sign of the leading coefficient of $\alpha - \beta$. Which coefficient is leading depends recursively on >. The relation > is total for signed ordinals. Its restriction to plain ordinals is well founded.

4   Term Orders

This section presents five orders: the standard first-order KBO (Sect. 4.1), the applicative KBO (Sect. 4.2), and our three λ-free higher-order KBO variants (Sects. 4.3, 4.4, and 4.5). The orders are stated with ordinal weights for generality. The occurrences of **O** and $\mathbf{O}_{>0}$ below can be consistently replaced by $\mathbb{N}$ and $\mathbb{N}_{>0}$ if desired.

For finite signatures, we can restrict the weights to be ordinals below ω^{ω^ω} without loss of generality [33]. Indeed, for proving termination of term rewriting systems that are finite and known in advance, transfinite weights are not necessary at all [50]. In the context of superposition, though, the order must be chosen in advance, before the saturation process generates the terms to be compared, and moreover their number can be unbounded; therefore, the latter result does not apply.

4.1   The Standard First-Order KBO

What we call the "standard first-order KBO" is more precisely a transfinite KBO on first-order terms with different argument comparison methods (or "statuses") but without argument coefficients. Despite the generalizations, our formulation is similar to Zantema's [51] and Baader and Nipkow's [3].

Definition 8. Let $\succ$ be a well-founded total order, or *precedence*, on Σ, let $\varepsilon \in \mathbb{N}_{>0}$, let $w : \Sigma \to \mathbf{O}$, and for any $> \subseteq T^2$ and any $f \in \Sigma$, let $\gg^f \subseteq (T^*)^2$ be a relation that satisfies properties X1–X6. For each constant $c \in \Sigma$, assume $w(c) \geq \varepsilon$. If $w(\iota) = 0$ for some unary $\iota \in \Sigma$, assume $\iota \succeq f$ for all $f \in \Sigma$. Let $W : T \to \mathbf{O}_{>0}$ be defined recursively by

$$W(f(s_1, \ldots, s_m)) = w(f) + \sum_{i=1}^{m} W(s_i) \qquad W(x) = \varepsilon$$

The induced (*standard*) *Knuth–Bendix order* $>_{fo}$ on first-order Σ-terms is defined inductively so that $t >_{fo} s$ if $vars_\#(t) \supseteq vars_\#(s)$ and any of these conditions is met:

F1. $W(t) > W(s)$;
F2. $W(t) = W(s)$, $t \neq x$, and $s = x$;
F3. $W(t) = W(s)$, $t = g\,\bar{t}$, $s = f\,\bar{s}$, and $g \succ f$;
F4. $W(t) = W(s)$, $t = f\,\bar{t}$, $s = f\,\bar{s}$, and $\bar{t} \gg^f_{fo} \bar{s}$.

The inductive definition is legitimate by the Knaster–Tarski theorem owing to the monotonicity of $\gg^f$ (property X1).

Because the true weight of variables is not known until instantiation, KBO assigns them the minimum ε and ensures that there are at least as many occurrences of each variable on the greater side as on the smaller side. Constants must have a weight of at least ε. One *special* unary symbol, ι, is allowed to have a weight of 0 if it has the maximum precedence. Rule F2 can be used to compare variables x with terms $\iota^m x$.

The more recent literature defines KBO as a mutually recursive pair consisting of a strict order $>_{fo}$ and a quasiorder $\succsim_{fo}$ [44]. This approach yields a slight increase in precision, but that comes at the cost of substantial duplication in the proof development and appears to be largely orthogonal to the issues that interest us.

4.2   The Applicative KBO

One way to use standard first-order term orders on λ-free higher-order terms is to encode the latter using the *applicative encoding*: Make all symbols nullary and represent application by a distinguished binary symbol @. Because @ is the only symbol that is ever applied, $\gg^{@}$ is the only relevant member of the $\gg$ family. This means that it is impossible to use the lexicographic extension for some symbols and the multiset extension for others. Moreover, the applicative encoding is incompatible with refinements such as symbols of weight 0 (Sect. 4.4) and argument coefficients (Sect. 4.5).

Definition 9. Let Σ be a higher-order signature, and let $\Sigma' = \Sigma \uplus \{@\}$ be a first-order signature in which all symbols belonging to Σ are assigned arity 0 and @ is assigned arity 2. The *applicative encoding* $[\![\ ]\!] : \mathcal{T}_{\Sigma} \to \mathcal{T}_{\Sigma'}$ is defined recursively by the equations $[\![\zeta]\!] = \zeta$ and $[\![s\,t]\!] = @\,[\![s]\!]\,[\![t]\!]$. The *applicative Knuth–Bendix order* $>_{\mathsf{ap}}$ on higher-order Σ-terms is defined as the composition of the first-order KBO with the encoding $[\![\ ]\!]$, where @ is given the lowest precedence and weight 0.

The applicative KBO works quite differently from the standard KBO, even on first-order terms. Given $t = g\,t_1 t_2$ and $s = f\,s_1 s_2$, the order $>_{\mathsf{fo}}$ first compares the weights, then g and f, then t_1 and s_1, and finally t_2 and s_2; by contrast, $>_{\mathsf{ap}}$ compares the weights, then $g\,t_1$ and $f\,s_1$ (recursively starting with their weights), and finally t_2 and s_2.

Hybrid schemes have been proposed to strengthen the encoding: If a function f always occurs with at least k arguments, these can be passed directly in an uncurried style—e.g., @ $(f\,a\,b)\,x$. However, this relies on a closed-world assumption—namely, that all terms that will ever be compared arise in the input problem. This is at odds with the need for complete higher-order proof calculi to synthesize arbitrary terms during proof search [10], in which a symbol f may be applied to fewer arguments than anywhere in the problem. A scheme by Hirokawa et al. [24] circumvents this issue but requires additional symbols and rewrite rules.

4.3   The Graceful Higher-Order Basic KBO

Our "graceful" higher-order basic KBO exhibits strong similarities with the first-order KBO. It reintroduces the symbol-indexed family of extension operators. The adjective "basic" indicates that it does not allow symbols of weight 0, which complicate the picture because functions can occur unapplied in our setting. In Sect. 4.4, we will see how to support such symbols, and in Sect. 4.5, we will extend the order further with argument coefficients.

The basic KBO is parameterized by a mapping ghd from variables to nonempty sets of possible ground heads that may arise when instantiating the variables. This mapping is extended to symbols f by taking $ghd(f) = \{f\}$. The mapping is said to *respect arities* if, for all variables x, $f \in ghd(x)$ implies $arity(f) \geq arity(x)$. In particular, if $\iota \in ghd(\zeta)$, then $arity(\zeta) \leq 1$. A substitution $\sigma : \mathcal{V} \to \mathcal{T}$

respects the *ghd* mapping if for all variables x, we have $arity(x\sigma) \geq arity(x)$ and $ghd(hd(x\sigma)) \subseteq ghd(x)$. This mapping allows us to restrict instantiations, typically based on a typing discipline.

Convention 10. Precedences $\succ$ are extended to arbitrary heads by taking $\xi \succ \zeta \Leftrightarrow \forall g \in ghd(\xi), f \in ghd(\zeta). \ g \succ f$.

Definition 11. Let $\succ$ be a precedence following Convention 10, let $\varepsilon \in \mathbb{N}_{>0}$, let $w : \Sigma \to \mathbf{O}_{\geq \varepsilon}$, let $ghd : \mathcal{V} \to \mathcal{P}(\Sigma) - \{\emptyset\}$ be an arity-respecting mapping extended to symbols f by taking $ghd(f) = f$, and for any $> \subseteq \mathcal{T}^2$ and any $f \in \Sigma$, let $\gg^f \subseteq (\mathcal{T}^*)^2$ be a relation that satisfies properties X1–X6 and X8. Let $\mathcal{W} : \mathcal{T} \to \mathbf{O}_{>0}$ be defined by

$$\mathcal{W}(f) = w(f) \qquad \mathcal{W}(x) = \varepsilon \qquad \mathcal{W}(s\,t) = \mathcal{W}(s) + \mathcal{W}(t)$$

The induced *graceful basic Knuth–Bendix order* $>_{\mathsf{hb}}$ on higher-order Σ-terms is defined inductively so that $t >_{\mathsf{hb}} s$ if $vars_{\#}(t) \supseteq vars_{\#}(s)$ and any of these conditions is met, where $t = \xi\,\bar{t}$ and $s = \zeta\,\bar{s}$:

B1. $\mathcal{W}(t) > \mathcal{W}(s)$;
B2. $\mathcal{W}(t) = \mathcal{W}(s)$ and $\xi \succ \zeta$;
B3. $\mathcal{W}(t) = \mathcal{W}(s)$, $\xi = \zeta$, and $\bar{t} \gg^f_{\mathsf{hb}} \bar{s}$ for all symbols $f \in ghd(\zeta)$.

The main differences with the first-order KBO $>_{\mathsf{fo}}$ is that rules B2 and B3 also apply to terms with variable heads and that symbols with weight 0 are not allowed. Property X8, compatibility with prepending, is necessary to ensure stability under substitution: If $x\,b >_{\mathsf{hb}} x\,a$ and $x\sigma = f\,\bar{s}$, we also want $f\,\bar{s}\,b >_{\mathsf{hb}} f\,\bar{s}\,a$ to hold. Property X9, compatibility with appending, is not required by the definition, but it is necessary to ensure compatibility with a specific kind of higher-order context: If $f\,b >_{\mathsf{hb}} f\,a$, we often want $f\,b\,c >_{\mathsf{hb}} f\,a\,c$ to hold as well.

Example 12. It is instructive to contrast our new KBO with the applicative order on some examples. Let $h \succ g \succ f$, let $w(f) = w(g) = \varepsilon = 1$ and $w(h) = 2$, let $\gg$ be the length-lexicographic extension (which degenerates to plain lexicographic for $>_{\mathsf{ap}}$), and let $ghd(x) = \Sigma$ for all variables x. In all of the following cases, $>_{\mathsf{hb}}$ disagrees with $>_{\mathsf{ap}}$:

$$f\,f\,f\,(f\,f) >_{\mathsf{hb}} f\,(f\,f\,f)\,f \qquad g\,(f\,g) >_{\mathsf{hb}} f\,g\,f \qquad g\,(f\,(f\,f)) >_{\mathsf{hb}} f\,(f\,f)\,f$$

$$h\,h >_{\mathsf{hb}} f\,h\,f \qquad h\,(f\,f) >_{\mathsf{hb}} f\,(f\,f)\,f \qquad g\,(f\,x) >_{\mathsf{hb}} f\,x\,g$$

Rules B2 and B3 apply in a straightforward, "first-order" fashion, whereas $>_{\mathsf{ap}}$ analyses the terms one binary application at a time. For the first pair of terms, we have $f\,f\,f\,(f\,f) <_{\mathsf{ap}} f\,(f\,f\,f)\,f$ because $(f\,f\,f, f\,f) \ll^{\mathsf{lex}}_{\mathsf{ap}} (f\,(f\,f\,f), f)$. In the presence of variables, some terms are comparable only with $>_{\mathsf{hb}}$ or only with $>_{\mathsf{ap}}$:

$$g\,(g\,x) >_{\mathsf{hb}} f\,g\,g \qquad g\,(f\,x) >_{\mathsf{hb}} f\,x\,f \qquad h\,(x\,y) >_{\mathsf{hb}} f\,y\,(x\,f)$$

$$f\,f\,x >_{\mathsf{ap}} g\,(f\,f) \qquad x\,x\,g >_{\mathsf{ap}} g\,(g\,g) \qquad g\,x\,g >_{\mathsf{ap}} x\,(g\,g)$$

The applicative order tends to be stronger when either side is an applied variable.

The quantification over $f \in ghd(\zeta)$ in rule B3 can be inefficient in an implementation, when the symbols in $ghd(\zeta)$ disagree on which $\gg$ to use. We could generalize the definition of $>_{hb}$ further to allow underapproximation, but some care would be needed to ensure transitivity. As a simple alternative, we propose instead to enrich all sets $ghd(\zeta)$ that disagree with a distinguished symbol for which the componentwise extension $(\gg_{hb}^{cw})$ is used. Since this extension operator is more restrictive than any others, whenever it is present in a set $ghd(\zeta)$, there is no need to compute the others.

4.4 The Graceful Higher-Order KBO

The standard first-order KBO, as introduced by Knuth and Bendix, allows symbols of arity 2 or more to have weight 0. It also allows for a special unary symbol ι of weight 0. Rule F2 makes comparisons $\iota^m x >_{fo} x$ possible, for $m > 0$.

In a higher-order setting, symbols of weight 0 require special care. Functions can occur unapplied, which could give rise to terms of weight 0, violating the basic KBO assumption that all terms have at least weight $\varepsilon > 0$. Our solution is to add a penalty of δ for each missing argument to a function. Thus, even though a *symbol* f may be assigned a weight of 0, the *term* f ends up with a weight of at least $arity(f) \cdot \delta$. These two notions of weight are distinguished formally as w and $\mathcal{W}$. For the arithmetic to work out, the δ penalty must be added for all missing arguments to all symbols and variables. Symbols and variables must then have a finite arity. For the sake of generality, we allow δ to take any value between 0 and ε, but the special symbol ι is allowed only if $\delta = \varepsilon$, so that $\mathcal{W}(\iota\,s) = \mathcal{W}(s)$. The $\delta = 0$ case coincides with the basic KBO.

Let $mghd(\zeta)$ denote a symbol $f \in ghd(\zeta)$ such that $w(f) + \delta \cdot arity(f)$—its weight as a term—is minimal. Clearly, $mghd(f) = f$ for all $f \in \Sigma$, and $arity(mghd(\zeta)) \geq arity(\zeta)$ if ghd respects arities. The intuition is that any instance of the term ζ will have at least weight $w(f) + \delta \cdot arity(f)$. This property is important for stability under substitution.

Definition 13. Let $\succ$ be a precedence following Convention 10, let $\varepsilon \in \mathbb{N}_{>0}$, let $\delta \in \{0, \ldots, \varepsilon\}$, let $w : \Sigma \to \mathbf{O}$, let $ghd : \mathcal{V} \to \mathcal{P}(\Sigma) - \{\emptyset\}$ be an arity-respecting mapping extended to symbols f by taking $ghd(f) = f$, and for any $> \subseteq \mathcal{T}^2$ and any $f \in \Sigma$, let $\gg^f \subseteq (\mathcal{T}^*)^2$ be a relation that satisfies properties X1–X6, X8, and, if $\delta = \varepsilon$, X10. For each symbol $f \in \Sigma$, assume $w(f) \geq \varepsilon - \delta \cdot arity(f)$. If $w(\iota) = 0$ for some unary $\iota \in \Sigma$, assume $\iota \succeq f$ for all $f \in \Sigma$ and $\delta = \varepsilon$. Let $\mathcal{W} : \mathcal{T} \to \mathbf{O}_{>0}$ be defined by $\mathcal{W} : \mathcal{T} \to \mathbf{O}_{>0}$:

$$\mathcal{W}(\zeta) = w(mghd(\zeta)) + \delta \cdot arity(mghd(\zeta)) \qquad \mathcal{W}(s\,t) = \mathcal{W}(s) + \mathcal{W}(t) - \delta$$

If $\delta > 0$, assume $arity(\zeta) \neq \infty$ for all heads $\zeta \in \Sigma \uplus \mathcal{V}$. The induced *graceful (standard) Knuth–Bendix order* $>_{hz}$ on higher-order Σ-terms is defined inductively so that $t >_{hz} s$ if $vars_\#(t) \supseteq vars_\#(s)$ and any of these conditions is met, where $t = \xi\,\bar{t}$ and $s = \zeta\,\bar{s}$:

Z1. $\mathcal{W}(t) > \mathcal{W}(s)$;

Z2. $\mathcal{W}(t) = \mathcal{W}(s)$, $\bar{t} = t' \geq_{hz} s$, $\xi \not\succeq \zeta$, $\xi \not\preceq \zeta$, and $\iota \in ghd(\xi)$;

Z3. $\mathcal{W}(t) = \mathcal{W}(s)$ and $\xi \succ \zeta$;

Z4. $\mathcal{W}(t) = \mathcal{W}(s)$, $\xi = \zeta$, and $\bar{t} \gg_{hz}^{f} \bar{s}$ for all symbols $f \in ghd(\zeta)$.

The $>_{hz}$ order requires minimality of the empty tuple (property X10) if $\delta = \varepsilon$. This ensures that $\iota s >_{hz} \iota$, which is desirable to honor the subterm property. Even though $\mathcal{W}(s)$ is defined using subtraction, given an arity-respecting ghd mapping, the result is always a plain (unsigned) ordinal: Each penalty δ that is subtracted is accounted for in the weight of the head, since $\delta \cdot arity(mghd(\zeta)) \geq \delta \cdot arity(\zeta)$.

Rule Z2 is more complicated than its first-order counterpart F2, because it must cope with cases that cannot arise with first-order terms. The last three conditions of rule Z2 are redundant but make the calculus deterministic.

Example 14. The following examples illustrate how ι and variables that can be instantiated by ι behave with respect to $>_{hz}$. Let $arity(a) = arity(b) = 0$, $arity(f) = arity(\iota) = arity(x) = arity(y) = 1$, $\delta = \varepsilon$, $w(a) = w(b) = w(f) = \varepsilon$, $w(\iota) = 0$, $\iota \succ f \succ b \succ a$, and $ghd(x) = ghd(y) = \Sigma$. The following comparisons hold, where $m > 0$:

$$\iota^m\, f >_{hz} f \qquad \iota^m\, x >_{hz} x \qquad y^m\, f >_{hz} f \qquad y^m\, x >_{hz} x$$

$$\iota^m\,(f\,a) >_{hz} f\,a \quad \iota^m\,(x\,a) >_{hz} x\,a \quad y^m\,(f\,a) >_{hz} f\,a \quad y^m\,(x\,a) >_{hz} x\,a$$

$$\iota^m\,(f\,b) >_{hz} f\,a \quad \iota^m\,(x\,b) >_{hz} x\,a \quad y^m\,(f\,b) >_{hz} f\,a \quad y^m\,(x\,b) >_{hz} x\,a$$

The first column is justified by rule Z3. The remaining columns are justified by rule Z2.

4.5 The Graceful Higher-Order KBO with Argument Coefficients

The requirement that variables must occur at least as often in the greater term t than in the smaller term s—$vars_{\#}(t) \supseteq vars_{\#}(s)$—drastically restrains KBO. For example, there is no way to compare the terms $f\,x\,y\,y$ and $g\,x\,x\,y$, no matter which weights and precedences we assign to f and g.

The literature on transfinite KBO proposes argument (or subterm) coefficients to relax this limitation [33,37], but the idea is independent of the use of ordinals for weights; it has its origin in Otter's ad hoc term order [37,38]. With each m-ary symbol $f \in \Sigma$, we associate m positive coefficients: $coef_f : \{1, \ldots, arity(f)\} \to \mathbf{O}_{>0}$. We write $coef(f, i)$ for $coef_f(i)$. When computing the weight of $f\,s_1 \ldots s_m$, the weights of the arguments $s_1, \ldots, s_m$ are multiplied with $coef(f, 1), \ldots, coef(f, m)$, respectively. The coefficients also affect variable counts; for example, by taking 2 as the coefficient attached to g's third argument, we can make $g\,x\,x\,y$ larger than $f\,x\,y\,y$.

Argument coefficients are problematic for applied variables: When computing the weight of $x\,a$, what coefficient should be applied to a's weight? Our solution is to delay the decision by representing the coefficient as a fixed unknown. Similarly, we represent the weight of a term variable x by an unknown. Thus, given

$arity(x) = 1$, the weight of the term $x\,a$ is a polynomial $\mathbf{w}_x + \mathbf{k}_x W(\mathbf{a})$ over the unknowns $\mathbf{w}_x$ and $\mathbf{k}_x$. In general, with each variable $x \in \mathcal{V}$, we associate the unknown $\mathbf{w}_x \in \mathbf{O}_{>0}$ and the family of unknowns $\mathbf{k}_{x,i} \in \mathbf{O}_{>0}$ for $i \in \mathbb{N}_{>0}$, $i \le arity(x)$, corresponding to x's weight and argument coefficients, respectively. We let $\mathbf{P}$ denote the polynomials over these unknowns.

We extend w to variable heads, $w : \Sigma \uplus \mathcal{V} \to \mathbf{P}$, by letting $w(x) = \mathbf{w}_x$, and we extend $coef$ to arbitrary terms $s \in \mathcal{T}$, $coef_s : \{1, \ldots, arity(s)\} \to \mathbf{P}$, by having

$$coef(x, i) = \mathbf{k}_{x,i} \qquad\qquad coef(s\,t, i) = coef(s, i+1)$$

The second equation is justified by the observation that the ith argument of the term $s\,t$ is the $(i+1)$st argument of s. Thus, the coefficient that applies to b in $\mathsf{f}\,\mathsf{a}\,\mathsf{b}$ (i.e., the first argument to $\mathsf{f}\,\mathsf{a}$, or the second argument to f) is $coef(\mathsf{f}\,\mathsf{a}, 1) = coef(\mathsf{f}, 2) = \mathbf{k}_{\mathsf{f},2}$.

An assignment A is a mapping from the unknowns to the signed ordinals. (If $\delta = 0$, we can restrict the codomain to the plain ordinals.) The operator $p|_A$ evaluates a polynomial p under an assignment A. An assignment A is *admissible* if $\mathbf{w}_x|_A \ge w(mghd(x))$ and $\mathbf{k}_{x,i}|_A \ge 1$ for all variables x and indices $i \in \{1, \ldots, arity(x)\}$. If there exists an upper bound M on the coefficients $coef(s, i)$, we may also require $\mathbf{k}_{x,i}|_A \le M$. The $M = 1$ case coincides with the standard KBO without argument coefficients.

Given two polynomials p, q, we have $q > p$ if and only if $q|_A > p|_A$ for all admissible assignments A. Similarly, $q \ge p$ if and only if $q|_A \ge p|_A$ for all admissible A.

Definition 15. Let $\succ$ be a precedence following Convention 10, let $\varepsilon \in \mathbb{N}_{>0}$, let $\delta \in \{0, \ldots, \varepsilon\}$, let $w : \Sigma \to \mathbf{O}$, let $coef : \Sigma \times \mathbb{N}_{>0} \to \mathbf{O}_{>0}$, let $ghd : \mathcal{V} \to \mathcal{P}(\Sigma) - \{\emptyset\}$ be an arity-respecting mapping extended to symbols f by taking $ghd(\mathsf{f}) = \mathsf{f}$, and for any $> \subseteq \mathcal{T}^2$ and any $\mathsf{f} \in \Sigma$, let $\gg^{\mathsf{f}} \subseteq (\mathcal{T}^*)^2$ be a relation that satisfies properties X1–X6, X8, and, if $\delta = \varepsilon$, X10. For each symbol $\mathsf{f} \in \Sigma$, assume $w(\mathsf{f}) \ge \varepsilon - \delta \cdot arity(\mathsf{f})$. If $w(\iota) = 0$ for some unary $\iota \in \Sigma$, assume $\iota \succeq \mathsf{f}$ for all $\mathsf{f} \in \Sigma$ and $\delta = \varepsilon$. Let $W : \mathcal{T} \to \mathbf{P}$ be defined by

$$W(\zeta\,s_1 \ldots s_m) = w(\zeta) + \delta \cdot \big(arity(mghd(\zeta)) - m\big) + \sum_{i=1}^{m} coef(\zeta, i) \cdot W(s_i)$$

If $\delta > 0$, assume $arity(\zeta) \ne \infty$ for all heads $\zeta \in \Sigma \uplus \mathcal{V}$. The induced *graceful (standard) Knuth–Bendix order* $>_{\mathsf{hc}}$ *with argument coefficients* on higher-order Σ-terms is defined inductively so that $t >_{\mathsf{hc}} s$ if any of these conditions is met, where $t = \xi\,\bar{t}$ and $s = \zeta\,\bar{s}$:

C1. $W(t) > W(s)$;
C2. $W(t) \ge W(s)$, $\bar{t} = t' \ge_{\mathsf{hc}} s$, $\xi \not\succ \zeta$, $\xi \not\succeq \zeta$, and $\iota \in ghd(\xi)$;
C3. $W(t) \ge W(s)$ and $\xi \succ \zeta$;
C4. $W(t) \ge W(s)$, $\xi = \zeta$, and $\bar{t} \gg^{\mathsf{f}}_{\mathsf{hc}} \bar{s}$ for all symbols $\mathsf{f} \in ghd(\zeta)$.

The weight comparisons amount to nonlinear polynomial constraints over the unknowns, which are interpreted universally. Rules C2–C4 use $\ge$ instead of $=$ because $\mathcal{W}(s)$ and $\mathcal{W}(t)$ cannot always be compared precisely. For example, if $\mathcal{W}(s) = \varepsilon$ and $\mathcal{W}(t) = \mathbf{w}_y$, we might have $\mathcal{W}(t) \geq \mathcal{W}(s)$ but neither $\mathcal{W}(t) > \mathcal{W}(s)$ nor $\mathcal{W}(t) = \mathcal{W}(s)$.

Example 16. Let $ghd(x) = \Sigma$ for all variables x. Argument coefficients allow us to perform these comparisons: $\mathsf{g}\,x >_{\mathsf{hc}} \mathsf{f}\,x\,x$ and $\mathsf{g}\,x >_{\mathsf{hc}} \mathsf{f}\,x\,\mathsf{g}$. By taking $\delta = 0$, $coef(\mathsf{f}, i) = 1$ for $i \in \{1, 2\}$, $coef(\mathsf{g}, 1) = 3$, and $w(\mathsf{f}) = w(\mathsf{g}) = \varepsilon$, we have the constraints $\varepsilon + 3\mathbf{w}_x > \varepsilon + 2\mathbf{w}_x$ and $\varepsilon + 3\mathbf{w}_x > 2\varepsilon + \mathbf{w}_x$. Since $\mathbf{w}_x \geq \varepsilon$, we can apply rule C1 in both cases.

The constraints are in general undecidable, but they can be underapproximated in various ways. A simple approach is to associate a fresh unknown with each monomial and systematically replace the monomials by their unknowns.

Example 17. We want to derive $z\,(y\,(\mathsf{f}\,x)) >_{\mathsf{hc}} z\,(y\,x)$ using rule C1. For $\delta = 0$, the constraint is $w(\mathsf{f}) \cdot \mathbf{k}_{z,1}\mathbf{k}_{y,1} + coef(\mathsf{f}, 1) \cdot w(\mathsf{f}) \cdot \mathbf{k}_{z,1}\mathbf{k}_{y,1}\mathbf{w}_z > \mathbf{k}_{z,1}\mathbf{k}_{y,1}\mathbf{w}_z$. It can be underapproximated by the linear constraint $w(\mathsf{f}) \cdot \mathbf{a} + coef(\mathsf{f}, 1) \cdot w(\mathsf{f}) \cdot \mathbf{b} > \mathbf{b}$, which is true given the ranges of the coefficients and unknowns involved.

5 Properties

We now state and prove the main properties of our KBO with argument coefficients, $>_{\mathsf{hc}}$. The proofs carry over easily to the two simpler orders, $>_{\mathsf{hb}}$ and $>_{\mathsf{hz}}$. Many of the proofs are inspired by Baader and Nipkow [3] and Zantema [51].

Theorem 18 (Irreflexivity). $s \not>_{\mathsf{hc}} s$.

Proof. By strong induction on $|s|$. Assume $s >_{\mathsf{hc}} s$ and let $s = \zeta\,\bar{s}$. Clearly, due to the irreflexivity of $\succ$, the only rule that could possibly derive $s >_{\mathsf{hc}} s$ is C4. Hence, $\bar{s} \gg^{\mathsf{f}}_{\mathsf{hc}} \bar{s}$ for some $\mathsf{f} \in ghd(\zeta)$. On the other hand, by the induction hypothesis $>_{\mathsf{hc}}$ is irreflexive on the arguments $\bar{s}$ of f. Since $\gg^{\mathsf{f}}$ preserves irreflexivity (property X3), we must have $\bar{s} \not\gg^{\mathsf{f}}_{\mathsf{hc}} \bar{s}$, a contradiction. $\square$

Lemma 19. *If $t >_{\mathsf{hc}} s$, then $\mathcal{W}(t) \geq \mathcal{W}(s)$.*

Theorem 20. (Transitivity). *If $u >_{\mathsf{hc}} t$ and $t >_{\mathsf{hc}} s$, then $u >_{\mathsf{hc}} s$.*

Proof. By well-founded induction on the multiset $\{|s|, |t|, |u|\}$ with respect to the multiset extension of $>$ on $\mathbb{N}$. Let $u = \chi\,\bar{u}$, $t = \xi\,\bar{t}$, and $s = \zeta\,\bar{s}$. By Lemma 19, we have $\mathcal{W}(u) \geq \mathcal{W}(t) \geq \mathcal{W}(s)$. If either $u >_{\mathsf{hc}} t$ or $t >_{\mathsf{hc}} s$ was derived by rule C1, we get $u >_{\mathsf{hc}} s$ by rule C1. The remaining nine cases are quite tedious to prove, especially the case where both $u >_{\mathsf{hc}} t$ and $t >_{\mathsf{hc}} s$ are derived by rule C2. We refer to our report [7] and to the Isabelle formalization [6] for the full proof. $\square$

By Theorems 18 and 20, $>_{\mathsf{hc}}$ is a partial order. In the remaining proofs, we will often leave applications of these theorems (and of antisymmetry) implicit.

Lemma 21. $s\,t >_{\mathsf{hc}} t$.

Proof. By strong induction on $|t|$. First, we have $\mathcal{W}(s\,t) \geq \mathcal{W}(t)$, as required to apply rule C2 or C3. If $\mathcal{W}(s\,t) > \mathcal{W}(t)$, we derive $s\,t >_{\mathsf{hc}} t$ by rule C1. Otherwise, there must exist an assignment A such that $\mathcal{W}(s\,t)|_A = \mathcal{W}(t)|_A$. This can happen only if $\mathcal{W}(s)|_A = \delta = \varepsilon$, which in turns means that $\iota \in \mathit{ghd}(\mathit{hd}(s))$. Since ι is the maximal symbol for $\succ$, either $\mathit{hd}(s) = \mathit{hd}(t)$, $\mathit{hd}(s) \succ \mathit{hd}(t)$, or the two heads are incomparable. The last two possibilities are easily handled by appealing to rule C2 or C3. If $\mathit{hd}(s) = \mathit{hd}(t) = \zeta$, then t must be of the form ζ or $\zeta\,t'$, with $\iota \in \mathit{ghd}(\zeta)$. In the $t = \zeta$ case, we have $\zeta \gg_{\mathsf{hc}}^{\mathsf{f}} ()$ for all $\mathsf{f} \in \Sigma$ by minimality of the empty tuple (property X10). In the $t = \zeta\,t'$ case, we have $t >_{\mathsf{hc}} t'$ by the induction hypothesis and hence $t \gg_{\mathsf{hc}}^{\mathsf{f}} t'$ for any $\mathsf{f} \in \Sigma$ by compatibility with tuple contexts (property X6) together with irreflexibility (Theorem 18). In both cases, $\zeta\,t >_{\mathsf{hc}} \zeta\,t'$ by rule C4. □

Lemma 22. $s\,t >_{\mathsf{hc}} s$.

Proof. If $\mathcal{W}(s\,t) > \mathcal{W}(s)$, the desired result can be derived using C1. Otherwise, we have $\mathcal{W}(s\,t) \geq \mathcal{W}(s)$ and $\delta = \varepsilon$. The desired result follows from rule C4, compatibility with prepending (property X8), and minimality of the empty tuple (property X10). □

Theorem 23 (Subterm Property). *If s is a proper subterm of t, then $t >_{\mathsf{hc}} s$.*

Proof. By structural induction on t, exploiting Lemmas 21 and 22 and transitivity. □

The first-order KBO satisfies compatibility with Σ-operations. A slightly more general property holds for $>_{\mathsf{hc}}$:

Theorem 24 (Compatibility with Functions). *If $t' >_{\mathsf{hc}} t$, then $s\,t'\,\bar{u} >_{\mathsf{hc}} s\,t\,\bar{u}$.*

Proof. By induction on the length of $\bar{u}$. The base case, $\bar{u} = ()$, follows from rule C4, Lemma 19, compatibility of $\gg^{\mathsf{f}}$ with tuple contexts (property X6), and irreflexivity of $>_{\mathsf{hc}}$. In the step case, $\bar{u} = \bar{u}' \cdot u$, we have $\mathcal{W}(s\,t'\,\bar{u}') \geq \mathcal{W}(s\,t\,\bar{u}')$ from the induction hypothesis together with Lemma 19. Hence $\mathcal{W}(s\,t'\,\bar{u}) \geq \mathcal{W}(s\,t\,\bar{u})$ by the definition of $\mathcal{W}$. Thus, we can apply rule C4, again exploiting compatibility of $\gg^{\mathsf{f}}$ with contexts. □

To build arbitrary higher-order contexts, we also need compatibility with arguments. This property can be used to rewrite subterms such as $\mathsf{f}\,a$ in $\mathsf{f}\,a\,b$ using a rewrite rule $\mathsf{f}\,x \to t_x$. The property holds unconditionally for $>_{\mathsf{hb}}$ and $>_{\mathsf{hz}}$ but not for $>_{\mathsf{hc}}$: $s' >_{\mathsf{hc}} s$ does not imply $s'\,t >_{\mathsf{hc}} s\,t$, because the occurrence of t may weigh more as an argument to s than to s'. By restricting the coefficients of s and s', we get a weaker property:

Theorem 25. (Compatibility with Arguments). *Assume that $\gg^{\mathsf{f}}$ is compatible with appending (property X9) for every symbol $\mathsf{f} \in \Sigma$. If $s' >_{\mathsf{hc}} s$ and $\mathit{coef}(s', 1) \geq \mathit{coef}(s, 1)$, then $s'\,t >_{\mathsf{hc}} s\,t$.*

Proof. If $s' >_{hc} s$ was derived by rule C1, by exploiting $coef(s', 1) \geq coef(s, 1)$ and the definition of $\mathcal{W}$, we can apply rule C1 to get the desired result. Otherwise, we have $\mathcal{W}(s') \geq \mathcal{W}(s)$ by Lemma 19 and hence $\mathcal{W}(s' t) \geq \mathcal{W}(s t)$. Due to the assumption that $coef(s', 1)$ is defined, $s' >_{hc} s$ cannot have been derived by rule C2. If $s' >_{hc} s$ was derived by rule C3, we get the desired result by rule C3. If $s' >_{hc} s$ was derived by rule C4, we get the result by rule C4 together with property X9. □

The next theorem, stability under substitution, depends on a substitution lemma connecting term substitutions and polynomial unknown assignments.

Definition 26. The *composition* $A \circ \sigma$ of a substitution σ and an assignment A is defined by $(A \circ \sigma)(\mathbf{w}_x) = \mathcal{W}(x\sigma)|_A - \delta \cdot arity(mghd(x))$ and $(A \circ \sigma)(\mathbf{k}_{x,i}) = coef(x\sigma, i)|_A$.

Lemma 27 (Substitution). *Let σ be a substitution that respects the mapping ghd. Then $\mathcal{W}(s\sigma)|_A = \mathcal{W}(s)|_{A \circ \sigma}$.*

Theorem 28 (Stability under Substitution). *If $t >_{hc} s$, then $t\sigma >_{hc} s\sigma$ for any substitution σ that respects the mapping ghd.*

Proof. By well-founded induction on the multiset $\{|s|, |t|\}$ with respect to the multiset extension of $>$ on $\mathbb{N}$. We present only two of the four cases.

If $t >_{hc} s$ was derived by rule C1, $\mathcal{W}(t) > \mathcal{W}(s)$. Hence, $\mathcal{W}(t)|_{A \circ \sigma} > \mathcal{W}(s)|_{A \circ \sigma}$, and by the substitution lemma (Lemma 27), we get $\mathcal{W}(t\sigma) > \mathcal{W}(s\sigma)$. The desired result, $t\sigma >_{hc} s\sigma$, follows by rule C1.

If $t >_{hc} s$ was derived by rule C4, we have $\mathcal{W}(t) \geq \mathcal{W}(s)$, $hd(t) = hd(s) = \zeta$, and $args(t) \gg_{hc}^{f} args(s)$ for all $f \in ghd(\zeta)$. Since σ respects ghd, we have the inclusion $ghd(hd(s\sigma)) \subseteq ghd(\zeta)$. We apply preservation of stability of $\gg_{hc}^{f}$ (property X2) to derive $args(t)\sigma \gg_{hc}^{f} args(s)\sigma$ for all $f \in ghd(hd(s\sigma)) \subseteq ghd(\zeta)$. This step requires that $t' > s'$ implies $t'\sigma > s'\sigma$ for all $s', t' \in args(s) \cup args(t)$, which follows from the induction hypothesis. From $args(t)\sigma \gg_{hc}^{f} args(s)\sigma$, we get $args(t\sigma) = args(\zeta)\sigma \cdot args(t)\sigma \gg_{hc}^{f} args(\zeta)\sigma \cdot args(s)\sigma = args(s\sigma)$ by compatibility with prepending (property X8). Finally, we apply rule C4. □

The use of signed ordinals is crucial for Definition 26 and Lemma 27. Consider the signature $\Sigma = \{f, g\}$ where $arity(f) = 3$, $arity(g) = 0$, $w(f) = 1$, and $w(g) = \omega$. Assume $\delta = \varepsilon = 1$. Let $x \in \mathcal{V}$ be an arbitrary variable such that $ghd(x) = \Sigma$; clearly, $mghd(x) = f$. Let A be an assignment such that $A(x) = w(mghd(x)) = w(f) = 1$, and let σ be a substitution that maps x to g. A negative coefficient arises when we compose σ with A: $(A \circ \sigma)(x) = \mathcal{W}(g) - \delta \cdot arity(f) = w(g) + \delta \cdot arity(g) - \delta \cdot arity(f) = \omega - 3$. However, if we fix $\delta = 0$, we can use plain ordinals throughout.

Theorem 29 (Ground Totality). *Assume $\gg^{f}$ preserves totality (property X7) for every symbol $f \in \Sigma$, and let s, t be ground terms. Then either $t \geq_{hc} s$ or $t <_{hc} s$.*

Proof. By strong induction on $|s| + |t|$. Let $t = g\,\bar{t}$ and $s = f\,\bar{s}$. If $W(s) \neq W(t)$, then either $W(t) > W(s)$ or $W(t) < W(s)$, since the weights of ground terms contain no polynomial unknowns. Hence, we have $t >_{hc} s$ or $t <_{hc} s$ by rule C1. Otherwise, $W(s) = W(t)$. If $f \neq g$, then either $g \succ f$ or $g \prec f$, and we have $t >_{hc} s$ or $t <_{hc} s$ by rule C3. Otherwise, $g = f$. By preservation of totality (property X7), we have either $\bar{t} \gg_{hc}^t \bar{s}$, $\bar{t} \ll_{hc}^t \bar{s}$, or $\bar{s} = \bar{t}$. In the first two cases, we have $t >_{hc} s$ or $t <_{hc} s$ by rule C4. In the third case, we have $s = t$. ☐

Theorem 30 (Well-foundedness).   *There exists no infinite chain $s_0 >_{hc}$ $s_1 >_{hc} \cdots$.*

Proof. The proof largely follows Zantema [51]. We assume that there exists a chain $s_0 >_{hc} s_1 >_{hc} \cdots$ and show that this leads to a contradiction. Without loss of generality, we can assume that the chain has the form $f\,\bar{u}_0 >_{hc} f\,\bar{u}_1 >_{hc} \cdots$, where elements of the chain all have the same weight and the arguments in $\bar{u}_i$ are not part of any infinite descending chains of their own. From the weight, we derive an upper bound on the numbers of arguments $|\bar{u}_i|$. By bounded preservation of well-foundedness (Lemma 3), $\gg_{hc}^t$ is well founded. ☐

6   Formalization

The definitions and the proofs presented in this paper have been fully formalized in Isabelle/HOL [40] and are part of the *Archive of Formal Proofs* [6]. The formal development relies on no custom axioms; at most local assumptions such as "$\succ$ is a well-founded total order on Σ" are made. The development focuses on two KBO variants: the transfinite $>_{hc}$ with argument coefficients and the restriction of $>_{hz}$ to natural number weights. The use of Isabelle, including its model finder Nitpick [14] and a portfolio of automatic theorem provers [13], was invaluable for designing the orders, proving their properties, and carrying out various experiments.

The basic infrastructure for λ-free higher-order terms and extension orders is shared with our formalization of the λ-free higher-order RPO [15]. Beyond standard Isabelle libraries, the formal proof development also required polynomials and ordinals. For the polynomials, we used Sternagel and Thiemann's *Archive of Formal Proofs* entry [42]. For the ordinals, we developed our own library, with help from Mathias Fleury and Dmitriy Traytel [11]. Syntactic ordinals are isomorphic to the hereditarily finite multisets, which can be defined easily using Isabelle's (co)datatype definitional package [12]:

datatype *hmultiset* = HMSet (*hmultiset multiset*)

The above command introduces a type *hmultiset* generated freely by the constructor HMSet : *hmultiset multiset* → *hmultiset*, where *multiset* is Isabelle's unary (postfix) type constructor of finite multisets. A syntactic ordinal $\sum_{i=1}^{m} \omega^{\alpha_i} k_i$ is represented by the multiset consisting of k_1 copies of α_1, k_2 copies of α_2, ..., k_m copies of α_m. Accordingly, $0 = $ HMSet $\{\}$, $1 = $ HMSet $\{0\}$, $5 = $ HMSet $\{0,0,0,0,0\}$, and $2\omega = $ HMSet $\{1,1\}$. Signed syntactic ordinals are defined as finite signed multisets of *hmultiset* values. Signed (or hybrid) multisets generalize standard multisets by allowing negative multiplicities [5].

7 Examples

Notwithstanding our focus on superposition, we can use $>_{hc}$ or its special cases $>_{hb}$ and $>_{hz}$ to show the termination of λ-free higher-order term rewriting systems or, equivalently, applicative term rewriting systems [29]. To establish termination of a term rewriting system, it suffices to show that all of its rewrite rules $t \to s$ can be oriented as $t > s$ by a single *reduction order*: a well-founded partial order that is compatible with contexts and stable under substitutions. If the order additionally enjoys the subterm property, it is called a *simplification order*. Under the proviso that *ghd* honestly captures the set of ground heads that may arise when instantiating the variables, the order $>_{hz}$ is a simplification order. By contrast, $>_{hc}$ is not even a reduction order since it lacks compatibility with arguments. Nonetheless, the conditional Theorem 25 is sufficient if the outermost heads are fully applied or if their pending argument coefficients are known and suitable [16, Sect. 5].

In the examples below, unless specified otherwise, $\delta = 0$, $\varepsilon = 1$, $w(\mathsf{f}) = 1$, and $\gg^{\mathsf{f}}$ is the length-lexicographic order, for all symbols f.

Example 31. Consider the following system [16, Example 23], where f is a variable:

$$\mathsf{insert}\,(f\,n)\,(\mathsf{image}\,f\,A) \xrightarrow{1} \mathsf{image}\,f\,(\mathsf{insert}\,n\,A) \qquad \mathsf{square}\,n \xrightarrow{2} \mathsf{times}\,n\,n$$

Rule 1 captures a set-theoretic property: $\{f(n)\} \cup f[A] = f[\{n\} \cup A]$, where $f[A]$ denotes the image of set A under function f. We can prove this system terminating using $>_{hc}$: By letting $w(\mathsf{square}) = 2$ and $coef(\mathsf{square}, 1) = 2$, both rules can be oriented by C1. Rule 2 is beyond the reach of the orders $>_{ap}$, $>_{hb}$, and $>_{hz}$, because there are too many occurrences of n on the right-hand side. The system is also beyond the scope of the uncurrying approach of Hirokawa et al. [24], because of the applied variable f on the left-hand side of rule 1.

Example 32. The following system specifies map functions on ML-style option and list types, each equipped with two constructors:

$$\mathsf{omap}\,f\,\mathsf{None} \xrightarrow{1} \mathsf{None} \qquad \mathsf{omap}\,f\,(\mathsf{Some}\,n) \xrightarrow{2} \mathsf{Some}\,(f\,n)$$
$$\mathsf{map}\,f\,\mathsf{Nil} \xrightarrow{3} \mathsf{Nil} \qquad \mathsf{map}\,f\,(\mathsf{Cons}\,m\,ms) \xrightarrow{4} \mathsf{Cons}\,(f\,m)\,(\mathsf{map}\,f\,ms)$$

Rules 1–3 are easy to orient using C1, but rule 4 is beyond the reach of all KBO variants. To compensate for the two occurrences of the variable f on the right-hand side, we would need a coefficient of at least 2 on map's first argument, but the coefficient would also make the recursive call map f heavier on the right-hand side.

The limitation affecting the map function in Example 32 prevents us from using KBO to prove termination of most of the term rewriting systems we used to demonstrate our RPO [16]. Moreover, the above examples are easy for modern first-order termination provers, which use uncurrying techniques [24,43] to transform applicative rewrite systems into functional systems that can be analyzed by standard techniques. This is somewhat to be expected: Even with transfinite weights and argument coefficients, KBO tends to consider syntactically smaller terms smaller. However, for superposition, this limitation might be a strength. The calculus's inferences and simplifications rely on the term order to produce smaller and smaller terms (and literals and clauses). Using KBO, the terms will typically be syntactically smaller as well. This is desirable, because many algorithms and data structures do not scale well in term size.

Moreover, for superposition, the goal is not to orient a given set of equations in a particular way, but rather to obtain either $t > s$ or $t < s$ for a high percentage of terms s, t arising during proof search, quickly. The first-order KBO can be implemented so that it takes linear time to compute in the size of the terms [36]. The same techniques are easy to generalize to our KBO variants, if we use the approach discussed at the end of Sect. 4.3 to compare the arguments of variable heads.

8   Conclusion

When designing the KBO variants $>_{hb}$, $>_{hz}$, and $>_{hc}$ and the RPO variants that preceded them [16], we aimed at full coincidence with the first-order case. Our goal is to gradually transform existing first-order automatic provers into higher-order provers. By carefully generalizing the proof calculi and data structures, we aim at designing provers that behave exactly like first-order provers on first-order problems, perform mostly like first-order provers on higher-order problems that are mostly first-order, and scale up to arbitrary higher-order problems.

An open question is, *What is the best way to cope with λ-abstraction in a superposition prover?* The Leo-III prover [49] relies on the computability path order [17] to reduce the search space; however, the order lacks many of the properties needed for completeness. With its stratified architecture, Otter-λ [8] is closer to what we are aiming at, but it is limited to second-order logic and offers no completeness guarantees.

A simple approach to λ-abstractions is to encode them using SK combinators [47]. This puts a heavy burden on the superposition machinery (and is a reason why HOLyHammer and Sledgehammer are so weak on higher-order problems). We could alleviate some of this burden by making the prover aware of the combinators, implementing higher-order unification and other algorithms specialized for higher-order reasoning in terms of them. A more appealing approach may be to employ a lazy variant of λ-lifting [27], whereby fresh symbols f and definitions $f \bar{x} = t$ are introduced during proof search. Argument coefficients could be used to orient the definition as desired. For example, $\lambda x.\, x + x + x$ could be mapped to a symbol g with an argument coefficient of 3 and a sufficiently large weight to ensure that $g\, x \approx x + x + x$ is oriented from left to right. However, it is not even clear that a left-to-right orientation is suitable here. Since superposition provers generally work better on syntactically small terms, it might be preferable to fold the definition of g whenever possible rather than unfold it.

Acknowledgment. We are grateful to Stephan Merz, Tobias Nipkow, and Christoph Weidenbach for making this research possible; to Mathias Fleury and Dmitriy Traytel for helping us formalize the syntactic ordinals; to Andrei Popescu and Christian Sternagel for advice with extending a partial well-founded order to a total one in the mechanized proof of Lemma 3; to Andrei Voronkov for the enlightening discussion about KBO at the IJCAR 2016 banquet; and to Carsten Fuhs, Mark Summerfield, and the anonymous reviewers for suggesting many textual improvements.

Blanchette has received funding from the European Research Council (ERC) under the European Union's Horizon 2020 research and innovation program (grant agreement No. 713999, Matryoshka). Wand is supported by the Deutsche Forschungsgemeinschaft (DFG) grant Hardening the Hammer (NI 491/14-1).

References

1. Andrews, P.B., Cohen, E.L.: Theorem proving in type theory. In: Reddy, R. (ed.) IJCAI 1977, p. 566. William Kaufmann (1977)
2. Aoto, T., Yamada, T.: Termination of simply typed term rewriting by translation and labelling. In: Nieuwenhuis, R. (ed.) RTA 2003. LNCS, vol. 2706, pp. 380–394. Springer, Heidelberg (2003). doi:10.1007/3-540-44881-0_27
3. Baader, F., Nipkow, T.: Term Rewriting and All That. Cambridge University Press, Cambridge (1998)
4. Backes, J., Brown, C.E.: Analytic tableaux for higher-order logic with choice. J. Autom. Reasoning **47**(4), 451–479 (2011)
5. Banâtre, J.-P., Fradet, P., Radenac, Y.: Generalised multisets for chemical programming. Math. Struct. Comput. Sci. **16**(4), 557–580 (2006)
6. Becker, H., Blanchette, J.C., Waldmann, U., Wand, D.: Formalization of Knuth-Bendix orders for lambda-free higher-order terms. Archive of Formal Proofs (2016). Formal proof development, https://isa-afp.org/entries/Lambda_Free_KBOs.shtml
7. Becker, H., Blanchette, J.C., Waldmann, U., Wand, D.: Transfinite Knuth-Bendix orders for lambda-free higher-order terms. Tech. report (2017), http://cs.vu.nl/~jbe248/lambda_free_kbo_rep.pdf
8. Beeson, M.: Lambda logic. In: Basin, D., Rusinowitch, M. (eds.) IJCAR 2004. LNCS, vol. 3097, pp. 460–474. Springer, Heidelberg (2004). doi:10.1007/978-3-540-25984-8_34
9. Benzmüller, C., Kohlhase, M.: Extensional higher-order resolution. In: Kirchner, C., Kirchner, H. (eds.) CADE 1998. LNCS, vol. 1421, pp. 56–71. Springer, Heidelberg (1998). doi:10.1007/BFb0054248
10. Benzmüller, C., Miller, D.: Automation of higher-order logic. In: Siekmann, J.H. (ed.) Computational Logic. Handbook of the History of Logic, vol. 9, pp. 215–254. Elsevier (2014)
11. Blanchette, J.C., Fleury, M., Traytel, D.: Formalization of nested multisets, hereditary multisets, and syntactic ordinals. Archive of Formal Proofs (2016). Formal proof development, https://isa-afp.org/entries/Nested_Multisets_Ordinals.shtml
12. Blanchette, J.C., Hölzl, J., Lochbihler, A., Panny, L., Popescu, A., Traytel, D.: Truly modular (Co)datatypes for Isabelle/HOL. In: Klein, G., Gamboa, R. (eds.) ITP 2014. LNCS, vol. 8558, pp. 93–110. Springer, Cham (2014). doi:10.1007/978-3-319-08970-6_7
13. Blanchette, J.C., Kaliszyk, C., Paulson, L.C., Urban, J.: Hammering towards QED. J. Formalized Reasoning **9**(1), 101–148 (2016)

14. Blanchette, J.C., Nipkow, T.: Nitpick: a counterexample generator for higher-order logic based on a relational model finder. In: Kaufmann, M., Paulson, L.C. (eds.) ITP 2010. LNCS, vol. 6172, pp. 131–146. Springer, Heidelberg (2010). doi:10.1007/978-3-642-14052-5_11

15. Blanchette, J.C., Waldmann, U., Wand, D.: Formalization of recursive path orders for lambda-free higher-order terms. Archive of Formal Proofs (2016). Formal proof development, https://isa-afp.org/entries/Lambda_Free_RPOs.shtml

16. Blanchette, J.C., Waldmann, U., Wand, D.: A lambda-free higher-order recursive path order. In: Esparza, J., Murawski, A.S. (eds.) FoSSaCS 2017. LNCS, vol. 10203, pp. 461–479. Springer, Heidelberg (2017). doi:10.1007/978-3-662-54458-7_27

17. Blanqui, F., Jouannaud, J.-P., Rubio, A.: The computability path ordering. Log. Meth. Comput. Sci. **11**(4) (2015)

18. Bofill, M., Borralleras, C., Rodríguez-Carbonell, E., Rubio, A.: The recursive path and polynomial ordering for first-order and higher-order terms. J. Log. Comput. **23**(1), 263–305 (2013)

19. Bofill, M., Rubio, A.: Paramodulation with non-monotonic orderings and simplification. J. Autom. Reasoning **50**(1), 51–98 (2013)

20. Dershowitz, N., Manna, Z.: Proving termination with multiset orderings. Commun. ACM **22**(8), 465–476 (1979)

21. Ferreira, M.C.F., Zantema, H.: Well-foundedness of term orderings. In: Dershowitz, N., Lindenstrauss, N. (eds.) CTRS 1994. LNCS, vol. 968, pp. 106–123. Springer, Heidelberg (1995). doi:10.1007/3-540-60381-6_7

22. Giesl, J., Thiemann, R., Schneider-Kamp, P.: Proving and disproving termination of higher-order functions. In: Gramlich, B. (ed.) FroCoS 2005. LNCS, vol. 3717, pp. 216–231. Springer, Heidelberg (2005). doi:10.1007/11559306_12

23. Henkin, L.: Completeness in the theory of types. J. Symb. Log. **15**(2), 81–91 (1950)

24. Hirokawa, N., Middeldorp, A., Zankl, H.: Uncurrying for termination and complexity. J. Autom. Reasoning **50**(3), 279–315 (2013)

25. Huet, G., Oppen, D.C.: Equations and rewrite rules: a survey. In: Book, R.V. (ed.) Formal Language Theory: Perspectives and Open Problems, pp. 349–405. Academic Press (1980)

26. Huet, G.P.: A mechanization of type theory. In: Nilsson, N.J. (ed.) International Joint Conference on Artificial Intelligence (IJCAI 1973), pp. 139–146. William Kaufmann (1973)

27. Hughes, R.J.M.: Super-combinators: a new implementation method for applicative languages. In: LFP 1982, pp. 1–10. ACM Press (1982)

28. Jouannaud, J.-P., Rubio, A.: Polymorphic higher-order recursive path orderings. J. ACM **54**(1), 2:1–2:48 (2007)

29. Kennaway, R., Klop, J.W., Sleep, M.R., de Vries, F.: Comparing curried and uncurried rewriting. J. Symbolic Comput. **21**(1), 15–39 (1996)

30. Knuth, D.E., Bendix, P.B.: Simple word problems in universal algebras. In: Leech, J. (ed.) Computational Problems in Abstract Algebra, pp. 263–297. Pergamon Press (1970)

31. Kop, C.: Higher Order Termination. Ph.D. thesis, Vrije Universiteit Amsterdam (2012)

32. Kop, C., Raamsdonk, F.: A higher-order iterative path ordering. In: Cervesato, I., Veith, H., Voronkov, A. (eds.) LPAR 2008. LNCS, vol. 5330, pp. 697–711. Springer, Heidelberg (2008). doi:10.1007/978-3-540-89439-1_48

33. Kovács, L., Moser, G., Voronkov, A.: On transfinite Knuth-Bendix orders. In: Bjørner, N., Sofronie-Stokkermans, V. (eds.) CADE 2011. LNCS, vol. 6803, pp. 384–399. Springer, Heidelberg (2011). doi:10.1007/978-3-642-22438-6_29

34. Kovács, L., Voronkov, A.: First-order theorem proving and VAMPIRE. In: Sharygina, N., Veith, H. (eds.) CAV 2013. LNCS, vol. 8044, pp. 1–35. Springer, Heidelberg (2013). doi:10.1007/978-3-642-39799-8_1

35. Lifantsev, M., Bachmair, L.: An LPO-based termination ordering for higher-order terms without λ-abstraction. In: Grundy, J., Newey, M. (eds.) TPHOLs 1998. LNCS, vol. 1479, pp. 277–293. Springer, Heidelberg (1998). doi:10.1007/BFb0055142

36. Löchner, B.: Things to know when implementing KBO. J. Autom. Reasoning 36(4), 289–310 (2006)

37. Ludwig, M., Waldmann, U.: An extension of the Knuth-Bendix ordering with LPO-like properties. In: Dershowitz, N., Voronkov, A. (eds.) LPAR 2007. LNCS, vol. 4790, pp. 348–362. Springer, Heidelberg (2007). doi:10.1007/978-3-540-75560-9_26

38. McCune, W.: Otter 3.3 reference manual. Technical. Report 263 (2003)

39. Nieuwenhuis, R., Rubio, A.: Paramodulation-based theorem proving. In: Robinson, J.A., Voronkov, A. (eds.) Handbook of Automated Reasoning, vol. I, pp. 371–443. Elsevier and MIT Press (2001)

40. Nipkow, T., Wenzel, M., Paulson, L.C. (eds.): Isabelle/HOL: A Proof Assistant for Higher-Order Logic. LNCS, vol. 2283. Springer, Heidelberg (2002). doi:10.1007/3-540-45949-9

41. Schulz, S.: System description: E 1.8. In: McMillan, K., Middeldorp, A., Voronkov, A. (eds.) LPAR 2013. LNCS, vol. 8312, pp. 735–743. Springer, Heidelberg (2013). doi:10.1007/978-3-642-45221-5_49

42. Sternagel, C., Thiemann, R.: Executable multivariate polynomials. Archive of Formal Proofs (2010). Formal proof development, https://isa-afp.org/entries/Polynomials.shtml

43. Sternagel, C., Thiemann, R.: Generalized and formalized uncurrying. In: Tinelli, C., Sofronie-Stokkermans, V. (eds.) FroCoS 2011. LNCS, vol. 6989, pp. 243–258. Springer, Heidelberg (2011). doi:10.1007/978-3-642-24364-6_17

44. Sternagel, C., Thiemann, R.: Formalizing Knuth-Bendix orders and Knuth-Bendix completion. In: van Raamsdonk, F. (ed.) RTA 2013, vol. 21. LIPIcs, pp. 287–302. Schloss Dagstuhl (2013)

45. Sultana, N., Blanchette, J.C., Paulson, L.C.: LEO-II and Satallax on the Sledgehammer test bench. J. Applied Logic 11(1), 91–102 (2013)

46. Toyama, Y.: Termination of S-expression rewriting systems: lexicographic path ordering for higher-order terms. In: Oostrom, V. (ed.) RTA 2004. LNCS, vol. 3091, pp. 40–54. Springer, Heidelberg (2004). doi:10.1007/978-3-540-25979-4_3

47. Turner, D.A.: A new implementation technique for applicative languages. Softw. Pract. Experience 9(1), 31–49 (1979)

48. Weidenbach, C., Dimova, D., Fietzke, A., Kumar, R., Suda, M., Wischnewski, P.: SPASS version 3.5. In: Schmidt, R.A. (ed.) CADE 2009. LNCS, vol. 5663, pp. 140–145. Springer, Heidelberg (2009). doi:10.1007/978-3-642-02959-2_10

49. Wisniewski, M., Steen, A., Kern, K., Benzmüller, C.: Effective normalization techniques for HOL. In: Olivetti, N., Tiwari, A. (eds.) IJCAR 2016. LNCS, vol. 9706, pp. 362–370. Springer, Cham (2016). doi:10.1007/978-3-319-40229-1_25

50. Zankl, H., Winkler, S., Middeldorp, A.: Beyond polynomials and Peano arithmetic–automation of elementary and ordinal interpretations. J. Symb. Comput. **69**, 129–158 (2015)

51. Zantema, H.: Termination. In: Bezem, M., Klop, J.W., de Vrijer, R. (eds.) Term Rewriting Systems. Cambridge Tracts in Theoretical Computer Science, vol. 55, pp. 181–259. Cambridge University Press, Cambridge (2003)

Certifying Safety and Termination Proofs for Integer Transition Systems

Marc Brockschmidt[1], Sebastiaan J.C. Joosten[2], René Thiemann[2],
and Akihisa Yamada[2(✉)]

[1] Microsoft Research Cambridge, Cambridge, UK
[2] University of Innsbruck, Innsbruck, Austria
akihisa.yamada@uibk.ac.at

Abstract. Modern program analyzers translate imperative programs to
an intermediate formal language like integer transition systems (ITSs),
and then analyze properties of ITSs. Because of the high complexity of
the task, a number of incorrect proofs are revealed annually in the Software Verification Competitions.

In this paper, we establish the trustworthiness of termination and
safety proofs for ITSs. To this end we extend our Isabelle/HOL formalization IsaFoR by formalizing several verification techniques for ITSs, such as
invariant checking, ranking functions, etc. Consequently the extracted certifier CeTA can now (in)validate safety and termination proofs for ITSs. We
also adapted the program analyzers T2 and AProVE to produce machine-
readable proof certificates, and as a result, most termination proofs generated by these tools on a standard benchmark set are now certified.

1 Introduction

A number of recently introduced techniques for proving safety or termination of
imperative programs, such as Java [1,29,32] and C [6,16,34], rely on a two-step
process: the input program is abstracted into an intermediate formal language,
and then properties of the intermediate program are analyzed. These intermediate languages are usually variations of integer transition systems (ITSs), reflecting the pervasive use of built-in integer data types in programming languages,
as well as common abstractions like modeling algebraic datatypes by their size.
For example, the C program in Fig. 1 can be abstracted to the ITS in Fig. 2.

To establish the *trustworthiness* of such program analyzers, two problems
need to be tackled. First, the soundness of the translation from the source programming language to ITSs needs to be proven, requiring elaborate models that
capture the semantics of advanced programming languages [21,24,39]. Then, the
soundness of safety and termination proofs on ITSs needs to be validated.

This work was partially supported by FWF project Y757. The authors are listed in
alphabetical order regardless of individual contributions or seniority. We thank the
anonymous reviewers for their helpful comments.

L. de Moura (Ed.): CADE 2017, LNAI 10395, pp. 454–471, 2017.
DOI: 10.1007/978-3-319-63046-5_28

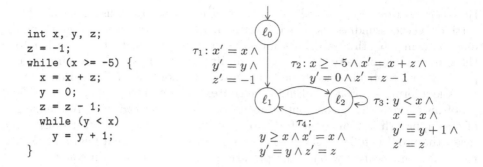

```
int x, y, z;
z = -1;
while (x >= -5) {
    x = x + z;
    y = 0;
    z = z - 1;
    while (y < x)
        y = y + 1;
}
```

Fig. 1. Input C program   **Fig. 2.** ITS $\mathcal{P}$ corresponding to Fig. 1

In this work, we tackle the second problem by extending IsaFoR [35], the Isabelle Formalization (originally) of Rewriting, by termination and safety proving techniques for ITSs. We then export verified code for the *certifier* CeTA, which validates proof *certificates* generated by untrusted program analyzers. In order for CeTA to read proofs for ITSs, we extend an XML certificate format [33] with syntax for ITS inputs and various proof techniques. Moreover, we adapt the program analyzers AProVE [18] and T2 [9] to produce certificates following the XML format.

The rest of the paper is organized as follows. In Sect. 2, we formalize *logic transition systems (LTSs)*, a generalization of ITSs. The termination and safety proofs are developed on LTSs, so that we can easily extend our results to bit vectors, arrays, etc. A number of approaches reduce the termination analysis problem to a sequence of program safety problems that derive suitable invariants [6,8,14,37]. Thus in Sect. 3, we formalize program invariant proofs as generated by the Impact algorithm [26], yielding a certifier for safety proofs. In Sect. 4 we consider certifying termination proofs. We recapitulate and formalize the concept of cooperation programs [8] and then present how to certify termination proofs. To instantiate the general results to ITSs, in Sect. 5 we discuss how to reason about linear integer arithmetic. In Sect. 6 we report on an experimental evaluation , showing that a large number of termination proofs can now be certified.

This paper describes what program analyzers need to provide in a proof certificate, and what CeTA has to check to certify them. As all proofs are checked by Isabelle [27], we have omitted them from this paper. The full formalization, consisting of around 10 000 lines of Isabelle code and an overview that links theorems as stated in this paper to the actual formalization is available at http://cl-informatik.uibk.ac.at/ceta/experiments/lts. The website further contains certificates for the two termination proofs of the ITS $\mathcal{P}$ in Fig. 2 that are developed in this paper.

Related Work: A range of methods has been explored to improve the trustworthiness of program analyzers. Most related to this work is the *certification* of termination and complexity proofs of term rewrite systems [5,12,35].

Here certification means to validate output of untrusted tools using a trustable certifier whose soundness is formally verified. Although our work is built upon one of them [35], the techniques for ITSs required a substantial addition to the library. SparrowBerry [11] follows a similar approach to validate numerical program invariants obtained by abstract interpretation [15] of C programs.

A less formal approach, taken in the context of complexity [2] and safety [3] proofs, is to cross-check a tool output using another (unverified) tool. A weakness of this approach is that, even if a "cross-checker" accepts a proof, it does not mean the proof is fully trustable. The cross-checker may have a bug, and both tools may be based on wrong (interpretations of) paper proofs. In contrast, we aim at termination, and we have formally proven in Isabelle that if our certifier accepts a proof, then the proof is indeed correct.

Another approach is to develop fully verified program analyzers, in which all intermediate steps in the proof search are formalized and verified, and not only the final proof as in our case. Examples of this approach have been used to develop a static analyzer for numerical domains [20] and to validate a Java Bytecode-like intermediate language in JINJA [21]. Compared to this approach, our certification approach demands much less work on the tool developers: they only have to output proofs that comply with the certificate format.

2   Logic Transition Systems

While our goal is specific to linear integer arithmetic, the used techniques apply to other logics as well. We separate the generic parts from the logic-specific parts. This clarifies the explanation of the generic parts, and makes it easier to extend our development to other logics in the future. We assume a sound validity checker for clauses (disjunctions of atoms) of the underlying logic. Linear integer arithmetic (i.e., Presburger arithmetic) can be considered as the canonical instance, but one may consider bit vectors, arrays, etc.

A logic describes how to interpret formulas of a certain shape. We first formalize the notion of *many-sorted algebras* [10,38] and formulas over them. We base our development on the (untyped) *term* datatype in IsaFoR.

Definition 1. *A many-sorted signature Σ consists of a set S of sorts and a disjoint family that assigns a set $\Sigma_{\sigma_1 \cdots \sigma_n \sigma}$ of function symbols to each list $\sigma_1, \ldots, \sigma_n, \sigma \in S$ of sorts. A sorted variable is a pair of a variable symbol v and a sort σ (written $v : \sigma$, or just v when the sort is clear from the context). Given a set V of sorted variables, the set $\mathcal{T}_\sigma(V)$ of expressions of sort σ is defined inductively as follows: $v : \sigma \in \mathcal{T}_\sigma(V)$, and $f(e_1, \ldots, e_n) \in \mathcal{T}_\sigma(V)$ if $f \in \Sigma_{\sigma_1 \cdots \sigma_n \sigma}$ and $e_i \in \mathcal{T}_{\sigma_i}(V)$ for each $i = 1, \ldots, n$.*

Definition 2. *A many-sorted Σ-algebra $\mathcal{A}$ specifies the domain A_σ of each sort $\sigma \in S$ and an interpretation $[\![f]\!] : A_{\sigma_1} \times \cdots \times A_{\sigma_n} \to A_\sigma$ of each $f \in \Sigma_{\sigma_1 \cdots \sigma_n \sigma}$.*

An assignment α on a set V of sorted variables assigns each variable $v : \sigma$ a value $\alpha(v) \in A_\sigma$. We define the interpretation $[\![e]\!]_\alpha$ of an expression e under α as usual: $[\![v]\!]_\alpha = \alpha(v)$ and $[\![f(e_1, \ldots, e_n)]\!]_\alpha = [\![f]\!]([\![e_1]\!]_\alpha, \ldots, [\![e_n]\!]_\alpha)$.

Definition 3. *We define a* many-sorted logic Λ *as a tuple consisting of a set of sorts $\mathcal{S}$, a many-sorted signature Σ on $\mathcal{S}$, and a Σ-algebra $\mathcal{A}$ such that* bool $\in \mathcal{S}$ *and* true, false $\in A_{\text{bool}}$. *Formulas $\Lambda(\mathcal{V})$ over typed variables from $\mathcal{V}$ are defined by the grammar $\phi :: = a \mid \phi \wedge \phi \mid \phi \vee \phi \mid \neg\phi,$[1] where an atom $a \in \mathcal{T}_{\text{bool}}(\mathcal{V})$ is an expression of sort* bool.

We say an assignment α satisfies a formula ϕ, written $\alpha \models \phi$, if ϕ evaluates to true *when every atom a in the formula is replaced by $[\![a]\!]_\alpha$. We write $\phi \models \psi$ iff $\alpha \models \phi$ implies $\alpha \models \psi$ for every assignment α.*

We define the notion of *logic transition systems (LTSs)* over a logic Λ. Note that an LTS can be seen as a labeled transition system, which also is commonly abbreviated to LTS.

In the following, we fix a set $\mathcal{L}$ of *locations* in a program and a set $\mathcal{V}$ of *variables* that may occur in the program.

Definition 4. *A* state *is a pair of $\ell \in \mathcal{L}$ and an assignment α on $\mathcal{V}$.*

To define state transitions, we introduce a fresh variable v' for each variable $v \in \mathcal{V}$. We write $\mathcal{V}'$ for the set $\{v' \mid v \in \mathcal{V}\}$, α' for the assignment on $\mathcal{V}'$ defined as $\alpha'(v') = \alpha(v)$, and e' (resp. ϕ') for the expression e (resp. formula ϕ) where all variables v are replaced by v'.

Definition 5. *A* transition rule *is a triple of $\ell, r \in \mathcal{L}$ and a transition formula $\phi \in \Lambda(\mathcal{V} \uplus \mathcal{V}'),$[2] written $\ell \xrightarrow{\phi} r$. A* logic transition system (LTS) *$\mathcal{P}$ is a set of transition rules, coupled with a special location $\ell_0 \in \mathcal{L}$ called the* initial *locations.*

In the rest of the paper, we always use ℓ_0 as the initial location. Hence we identify an LTS and the set of its transition rules.

For our formalization, we extend LTSs with *assertions*, i.e., a mapping Φ that assigns a formula describing all valid states to each location. We assume no assertions for an input LTS, i.e., $\Phi(\ell) = $ true for every $\ell \in \mathcal{L}$.

Definition 6. *The* transition step $\rightarrow_\tau$ *w.r.t. a transition rule $\tau : \ell \xrightarrow{\phi} r$ and an assertion Φ is defined by $(\ell, \alpha) \rightarrow_\tau (r, \beta)$ iff $\alpha \uplus \beta' \models \phi$, where $\alpha \models \Phi(\ell)$ and $\beta \models \Phi(r)$. For an LTS $\mathcal{P}$, we write $\rightarrow_\mathcal{P} = \bigcup_{\tau \in \mathcal{P}} \rightarrow_\tau$.*

Throughout the paper we establish methods that reduce a desired property of an LTS to zero or more subproblems of proving properties of refined LTSs. Hence the certificate forms a proof tree, where the root concludes the desired property of the input LTS, and all leafs are concluded by methods that yield no more subproblems.

In the formalization, corresponding theorems assume that LTSs are *well-typed*, i.e., atoms in transition formulas and assertions are of type bool. Well-typedness is checked only when an input LTS is given, and is statically proven for LTSs which are introduced as subproblems.

---

[1] In the Isabelle formalization and the certificate XML, formulas are represented in negation normal form and conjunction and disjunction are not necessarily binary.

[2] In the Isabelle formalization we admit *auxiliary* variables to appear in the transition formula. To ease readability we omit this ability in the paper.

3   Certifying Invariants and Safety Proofs

The safety of a program means that certain "bad" states cannot be reached, and is usually modeled by a set of *error locations* $\mathcal{L}_t \subseteq \mathcal{L}$ that are reached from such bad states. Safety then reduces to the unreachability of error locations.

Definition 7. *We say a state (ℓ_n, α_n) is reachable if there is a sequence of transition steps starting from the initial location: $(\ell_0, \alpha_0) \rightarrow_\mathcal{P} \cdots \rightarrow_\mathcal{P} (\ell_n, \alpha_n)$. A location ℓ_n is reachable if there is a reachable state (ℓ_n, α_n).*

A *program invariant* maps every $\ell \in \mathcal{L}$ to a formula ϕ such that $\alpha \models \phi$ for all reachable states (ℓ, α). Program safety can thus be proven by finding a program invariant that maps every error location to an unsatisfiable formula (e.g., false).

Definition 8. *We say a mapping $\mathcal{I} : \mathcal{L} \rightarrow \Lambda(V)$ is an invariant of an LTS $\mathcal{P}$ iff $\alpha \models \mathcal{I}(\ell)$ whenever (ℓ, α) is reachable in $\mathcal{P}$.*

One way to prove that a mapping is an invariant is to find an *unwinding* [26] of a program. We integrate support for invariant checking and safety proofs into CeTA by formalizing unwindings in Isabelle.

Definition 9. *An* unwinding *of LTS $\mathcal{P}$ under assertion Φ is a graph $\mathcal{G} = (N_t \cup N_c, \longrightarrow \cup \dashrightarrow)$ with $N_t \cup N_c \subseteq \mathcal{L} \times \Lambda(\mathcal{V})$, where nodes in N_t are called* transition *nodes, those in N_c are* covered *nodes, edges in $\longrightarrow$ are* transition *edges, those in $\dashrightarrow$ are* cover *edges, and the following conditions are satisfied:*

1. *$(\ell_0, \mathsf{true}) \in N_t \cup N_c$;*
2. *for every transition node $(\ell, \phi) \in N_t$, either ϕ is unsatisfiable or for every transition rule $\ell \xrightarrow{\chi} r \in \mathcal{P}$ there is a transition edge $(\ell, \phi) \longrightarrow (r, \psi)$ such that $\Phi(\ell) \wedge \phi \wedge \chi \models \psi'$;*
3. *for every covered node $(\ell, \phi) \in N_c$, there exists exactly one outgoing edge, which is a cover edge $(\ell, \phi) \dashrightarrow (\ell, \psi)$ with $(\ell, \psi) \in N_t$ and $\phi \models \psi$.*

Each node (ℓ, ϕ) in an unwinding represents the set of states $\{(\ell, \alpha) \mid \alpha \models \phi\}$. If ϕ is unsatisfiable then the node represents no state, and thus no successor of that node needs to be explored in condition 2. A location ℓ in the original program is represented by multiple transition nodes $(\ell, \phi_1), \ldots, (\ell, \phi_n)$, meaning that $\phi_1 \vee \ldots \vee \phi_n$ is a disjunctive invariant in ℓ.

Example 1. Consider the LTS $\mathcal{P}$ in Fig. 2 again. In order to prove the termination of the outer while loop, the invariant $z < 0$ in location ℓ_1 is essential. To prove this invariant, we use the graph $\mathcal{G}$ in Fig. 3, a simplified version of the unwinding constructed by the Impact algorithm [26].

Our definition of unwindings only roughly follows the original definition [26], in which nodes and transition edges are specified as a *tree* and cover edges are given as a separate set. This turned out to be unwieldy in the formalization; our definition is not restricted to trees, since being a tree or not is irrelevant

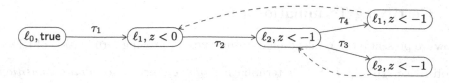

Fig. 3. An unwinding $\mathcal{G}$ of $\mathcal{P}$

for soundness. This flexibility gives some benefits. For instance, instead of introducing an additional node in Fig. 3 as the target of τ_4, the corresponding transition edge could just point back to the node $(\ell_1, z < 0)$. More significantly, we are able to certify invariants obtained by other means (e.g., abstract interpretation [15]). For this, an inductive invariant $\mathcal{I} : \mathcal{L} \to \Lambda(\mathcal{V})$ can be cast as an unwinding with transition nodes $\{(\ell, \mathcal{I}(\ell)) \mid \ell \in \mathcal{L}\}$ and transition edges $\{(\ell, \mathcal{I}(\ell)) \longrightarrow (r, \mathcal{I}(r)) \mid \ell \xrightarrow{\phi} r \in \mathcal{P}\}$, with no covered nodes.

Theorem 1 (Invariants via Unwindings). *Let $\mathcal{G}$ be an unwinding for an LTS $\mathcal{P}$. Then a mapping $\mathcal{I} : \mathcal{L} \to \Lambda(V)$ is an invariant of $\mathcal{P}$ if for every $l \in \mathcal{L}$,*

$$\left(\bigvee\nolimits_{(\ell,\phi)\in N_t} \phi \right) \models \mathcal{I}(\ell) \tag{1}$$

To verify that Theorem 1 is applied correctly, CeTA needs the invariant $\mathcal{I}$ and the unwinding $\mathcal{G}$ to be specified in the certificate. It checks conditions 1–3 of Definition 9, and then the entailment (1) for each location. For efficiency we further assume that each transition edge is annotated by the corresponding transition rule.

To use invariants in proofs for the desired properties (safety or termination), we turn invariants into *assertions*. As we have proven that the invariant formula is satisfied whenever a location is visited, "asserting" the formula merely makes implicit global information available at each location. This approach has the advantage that invariants become a part of input for the later proofs, and thus we do not have to prove that they are invariant repeatedly when we transform programs as required in Sect. 4.

Theorem 2 (Invariant Assertion for Safety Proofs). *Let $\mathcal{P}$ be an LTS, Φ an assertion on $\mathcal{P}$, and Ψ an invariant of $\mathcal{P}$. Then $\mathcal{P}$ under assertion Φ is safe if $\mathcal{P}$ under assertion Ψ is safe.*

Theorem 2 requires nothing to be checked, besides that the invariant is certified via Theorem 1. A typical application of Theorem 2 refines the current assertion Φ by a stronger one Ψ. When sufficiently strong assertions are made, one can conclude safety as follows.

Theorem 3 (Safety by Assertions). *Let $\mathcal{P}$ be an LTS, Φ an assertion on $\mathcal{P}$, and $\mathcal{L}_\sharp$ a set of error locations. If $\Phi(\ell)$ is unsatisfiable for every $\ell \in \mathcal{L}_\sharp$, then $\mathcal{P}$ under assertion Φ is safe.*

4 Certifying Termination Proofs

Now we present our formalization of techniques for proving termination of LTSs.

Definition 10. *An LTS $\mathcal{P}$ is terminating iff there exists no infinite transition sequence starting from the initial location:* $(\ell_0, \alpha_0) \to_{\mathcal{P}} (\ell_1, \alpha_1) \to_{\mathcal{P}} \cdots$.

We formalize a collection of transformation techniques for LTSs such that every transformation preserves nontermination, i.e., the termination of all resulting LTSs implies the termination of the original LTS. The *cooperation graph* method [8], the foundation of the termination tool T2, will be modeled by a combination of such transformations. The split into smaller techniques not only simplifies and modularizes the formalization task, but also provides a way to certify termination proofs of tools which use related methods. They can choose a subset of supported termination techniques that is sufficient to model their internally constructed termination proofs. For instance, we also integrate certificate export for LTSs in AProVE, which internally does *not* utilize cooperation graphs.

4.1 Initial Transformation

The key component of cooperation graphs is the use of two copies of the program: the original part is used to describe reachable program states, and a termination part is progressively modified during the termination proof. This approach makes it possible to apply transformations which would be unsound when performed on the original program; e.g., one can remove transitions from the termination part if they are proven to be usable only a finite number of times. This is unsound if it is performed on the original program; consider, e.g., a non-terminating LTS consisting of only the two transition rules $\ell_0 \xrightarrow{\text{true}} \ell_1$ and $\ell_1 \xrightarrow{\text{true}} \ell_1$. Clearly, the first transition rule can be applied only once. Nevertheless, if it is removed, ℓ_1 becomes unreachable, and the resulting LTS is terminating.

To describe the copies of programs, we introduce a fresh location $\ell^\sharp$ for each location $\ell \in \mathcal{L}$. We write $\mathcal{L}^\sharp$ for the set $\{\ell^\sharp \mid \ell \in \mathcal{L}\}$.

Definition 11. *A cooperation program $\mathcal{Q}$ is an LTS on locations $\mathcal{L} \cup \mathcal{L}^\sharp$ which is split into three parts:* $\mathcal{Q} = \mathcal{Q}^\natural \cup \mathcal{Q}^\sharp \cup \mathcal{Q}^{\sharp\sharp}$, *where* $\mathcal{Q}^\natural$, $\mathcal{Q}^\sharp$, $\mathcal{Q}^{\sharp\sharp}$ *consist of transitions of form* $\ell \xrightarrow{\phi} r$, $\ell \xrightarrow{\phi} r^\sharp$, $\ell^\sharp \xrightarrow{\phi} r^\sharp$, *respectively, where* $\ell, r \in \mathcal{L}$.

We say $\mathcal{Q}$ is CP-terminating if there exists no infinite sequence of form

$$(\ell_0, \alpha_0) \to_{\mathcal{Q}^\natural} \cdots \to_{\mathcal{Q}^\natural} (\ell_n, \alpha_n) \to_{\mathcal{Q}^\sharp} (\ell_n^\sharp, \alpha_n) \to_{\mathcal{Q}^{\sharp\sharp}} (\ell_{n+1}^\sharp, \alpha_{n+1}) \to_{\mathcal{Q}^{\sharp\sharp}} \cdots$$

where each transition rule used after the n-th step must be used infinitely often.

We call $\mathcal{Q}^\natural$ the *original part* and $\mathcal{Q}^{\sharp\sharp}$ the *termination part*. The termination of an LTS can be reduced to the CP-termination of a cooperation program which has the input LTS as the original part and its copy (where every location ℓ is renamed to $\ell^\sharp$) as the termination part, and additionally includes ϵ-*transitions* that allow to jump from locations ℓ to $\ell^\sharp$.

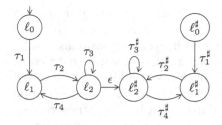

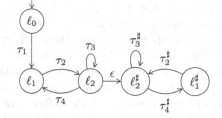

Fig. 4. Cooperation program Q constructed from P

Fig. 5. Cooperation program Q_1 resulting from SCC decomposition of Q

Definition 12. *We say a transition rule* $\tau : \ell \xrightarrow{\phi} r$ *is an* ϵ-*transition iff* $(\ell, \alpha) \rightarrow_\tau (r, \alpha)$ *for any assignment* α, *i.e.,* $\alpha \uplus \alpha' \models \phi$. *We write* $\ell \xrightarrow{\epsilon} r$ *to denote an* ϵ-*transition.*

Canonically, one can consider $\ell \xrightarrow{\epsilon} \ell^\sharp$ for *every* location ℓ, but we can also do a little better by employing the notion of *cutpoints*. For this, we view an LTS P as a *program graph* with nodes $\mathcal{L}$ and edges $\{(\ell, r) \mid \ell \xrightarrow{\phi} r \in P\}$.

Definition 13. *A set* $C \subseteq \mathcal{L}$ *of locations is a* cutpoint set *of an LTS* P *if the program graph of* $P \setminus C$ *is acyclic.*

Intuitively, if C is a cutpoint set of P, then any infinite execution of P must visit some *cutpoint* $\ell \in C$ infinitely often.

Theorem 4 (Initial Cooperation Program). *Let* P *be a finite LTS over* $\mathcal{L}$, Q *a cooperation program, and* $C \subseteq \mathcal{L}$ *such that*

1. *for each* $\ell \xrightarrow{\phi} r \in P$, *there exist* $\ell \xrightarrow{\phi} r \in Q$ *and* $\ell^\sharp \xrightarrow{\phi} r^\sharp \in Q$;
2. *for each* $\ell \in C$, *there exists* $\ell \xrightarrow{\epsilon} \ell^\sharp \in Q$; *and*
3. C *is a cutpoint set for* P.

Then P *is terminating if* Q *is CP-terminating.*

Example 2. In order to construct an initial cooperation program for P in Fig. 2, termination provers need to choose a cutpoint set. Let us consider a minimal one: $C = \{\ell_2\}$. We obtain the cooperation program Q in Fig. 4, where each transition $\tau_i^\sharp$ has the same transition formula as τ_i for $i = 1, \ldots, 4$ and ϵ has transition formula $x' = x \wedge y' = y \wedge z' = z$.

To check that Theorem 4 is applied correctly, we only require the added ϵ-transitions to be specified in the certificate. The other parts, e.g., the cutpoint set C, are automatically inferred by CeTA.

Condition 1 of Theorem 4 is always fulfilled, since these transitions are automatically generated by CeTA, and statically proven correct.

For condition 2, CeTA checks if the transition formula is of form $\bigwedge_{v \in W} v' = v$ for some set of variables $W \subseteq V$. Allowing $W \subset V$ can be useful: Consider a C fragment $x = x + 1$; $x = 2 * x$. This might be encoded into a single transition formula using an auxiliary variable, e.g., as $aux = x + 1 \wedge x' = 2 * aux$. It would make sense not to mention the auxiliary variables in epsilon transitions.

For condition 3, i.e., to check that C is indeed a cutpoint set, we must check acyclicity of graphs as required in Definition 13. Luckily we could reuse the certified implementation of Gabow's *strongly connected component (SCC)* decomposition algorithm [23] and check that after removing C from P, it has only trivial SCCs.

To reason about the termination of LTSs, we often require program invariants to allow us to reason about reachable program states. Thus, analogous to Theorem 2 for safety proofs, we provide a way to introduce program invariants in termination proofs. The following result is formalized both for normal LTSs w.r.t. Definition 10 as well for cooperation programs w.r.t. Definition 11.

Theorem 5 (Invariant Assertion for Termination). *Let P be an LTS, Φ an assertion on P, and Ψ an invariant of P. Then P under assertion Φ is (CP-)terminating if P under assertion Ψ is (CP-)terminating.*

4.2   SCC and Cutpoint Decompositions

In the setting of cooperation programs, it is sound to decompose the termination part into SCCs.

Theorem 6 (SCC Decomposition). *Given a cooperation program Q, if the cooperation program $Q^\natural \cup Q^\sharp \cup \{\ell^\sharp \xrightarrow{\phi} r^\sharp \in Q^{\sharp\sharp} \mid \ell^\sharp, r^\sharp \in S\}$ is CP-terminating for every non-trivial SCC S of the program graph of $Q^{\sharp\sharp}$, then Q is CP-terminating.*

To certify an application of Theorem 6, the certificate has to list the subproofs for each SCC. CeTA invokes the same certified SCC algorithm as in the cutpoint validation to check applications of the SCC decomposition.

Example 3. Using SCC decomposition, Q in Fig. 4 can be transformed into the new problem Q_1 in Fig. 5, where location $\ell_0^\sharp$ and transition $\tau_1^\sharp$ are removed.

We can also decompose a cooperation program by case distinction depending on which ϵ-transition for a cutpoint is taken. This can also be used to delete ϵ-transitions leading to locations whose outgoing transitions have already been removed by other means.

Theorem 7 (Cutpoint Decomposition). *Let P be a cooperation program with $P^\sharp = Q_0^\sharp \cup Q_1^\sharp \cup \ldots \cup Q_n^\sharp$, where for every $\ell \xrightarrow{\psi} \ell^\sharp \in Q_0^\sharp$ there is no transition rule of form $\ell^\sharp \xrightarrow{\phi} r^\sharp$ in $P^{\sharp\sharp}$. Then P is CP-terminating if $P^\natural \cup Q_i^\sharp \cup P^{\sharp\sharp}$ is CP-terminating for every $i = 1, \ldots, n$.*

A certificate for Theorem 7 needs to provide the considered partition $Q_1^\sharp \cup \ldots \cup Q_n^\sharp$ and a corresponding subproof for each of the newly created cooperation programs. CeTA determines $Q_0^\sharp$ and checks that it has no succeeding transitions in $P^{\sharp\sharp}$.

4.3 Transition Removal

A cooperation program is trivially CP-terminating if its termination part is empty. Hence we now formalize a way to remove transitions via rank functions, the core termination proving procedure for cooperation programs, and also for other termination methods as implemented by, e.g., AProVE or VeryMax [6].

Roughly speaking, a rank function is a mapping from program states to a mathematical domain on which a well-founded order exist (e.g., the natural numbers). We formalize such domains reusing a notion from term rewriting.

Definition 14. *We call a pair* $(\geq, >)$ *of relations a* (quasi-)order pair *if* $\geq$ *is reflexive, both are transitive, and they are "compatible", i.e.,* $(\geq \circ > \circ \geq) \subseteq >$. *We say that the order pair is* well-founded *if* $>$ *is well-founded.*

We model a rank function as a mapping that assigns an expression $f(\ell^\sharp) \in \mathcal{T}_\sigma(\mathcal{V})$ of sort σ to each location $\ell^\sharp$. Here we assume that the domain A_σ of σ has a well-founded order pair $(\geq, >)$. If some transitions in $\mathcal{Q}^{\sharp\sharp}$ strictly decrease a rank function and all other transitions "do not increase" this rank function, then the decreasing transitions can be used only finitely often, and thus can be removed from the termination part.

Theorem 8 (Transition Removal). *Let* $\mathcal{Q}$ *be a cooperation program with assertion* Φ, $(\geq, >)$ *a well-founded order pair[3] on* A_σ, $f : \mathcal{L}^\sharp \to \mathcal{T}_\sigma(\mathcal{V})$, *and* $\mathcal{D}^{\sharp\sharp} \subseteq \mathcal{Q}^{\sharp\sharp}$ *a set of transition rules such that for every* $\ell^\sharp \xrightarrow{\phi} r^\sharp \in \mathcal{Q}^{\sharp\sharp}$,

- $\Phi(\ell^\sharp) \wedge \Phi(r^\sharp)' \wedge \phi \models f(\ell^\sharp) > f(r^\sharp)'$ *if* $\ell^\sharp \xrightarrow{\phi} r^\sharp \in \mathcal{D}^{\sharp\sharp}$; *and*
- $\Phi(\ell^\sharp) \wedge \Phi(r^\sharp)' \wedge \phi \models f(\ell^\sharp) \geq f(r^\sharp)'$ *otherwise.*

Then $\mathcal{Q}$ *is CP-terminating if* $\mathcal{Q} \setminus \mathcal{D}^{\sharp\sharp}$ *is CP-terminating.*

To certify the correct application of Theorem 8, naturally the rank function and deleted transitions have to be specified in the certificate. For integer arithmetic σ is fixed to int, but one also needs to choose the well-founded order. Note that $>$ on integers is not well-founded, but its bounded variant $>_b$ is, where $s >_b t$ iff $s > t$ and $s \geq b$. Note also that $(\geq, >_b)$ forms an order pair.

Example 4. The program $\mathcal{P}$ from Fig. 2 can be shown terminating by repeatedly applying Theorem 8. Assume that we have applied Theorem 5 on $\mathcal{P}$ and established the assertion $z < -1$ on ℓ_2, based on the unwinding from Example 1, before transforming $\mathcal{P}$ into $\mathcal{Q}_1$ of Fig. 5. We then apply Theorem 8 with rank function x and bound -5 for all locations in $\mathcal{Q}_1^{\sharp\sharp}$. With the assertion $z < -1$, this allows us to remove $\tau_2^\sharp$. Then, using the constant rank functions 1 for $\ell_1^\sharp$ and 0 for $\ell_2^\sharp$, we can remove the transition $\tau_4^\sharp$ (alternatively, we could use SCC decomposition here). Finally, the rank function $x - y$ and bound 0 can be used to remove the last remaining transition $\tau_3^\sharp$.

---

[3] In the paper we use symbols $\geq$ and $>$ also for *formulas*. In the formalization we encode, e.g., by a formula $e_1 \geq_f e_2$ such that $\alpha \models e_1 \geq_f e_2$ iff $[\![e_1]\!]_\alpha \geq [\![e_2]\!]_\alpha$.

Simple rank functions on integers are sometimes too weak, so we also integrate *lexicographic* orderings.

Definition 15. *Given order pairs* $(\succsim_1, \succ_1), \ldots, (\succsim_n, \succ_n)$ *on* A, *their lexicographic composition is the order pair* $(\succsim^{lex}_{1,\ldots,n}, \succ^{lex}_{1,\ldots,n})$ *on length-n lists of* A *defined as follows:* $\langle x_1, \ldots, x_n \rangle \succ^{lex}_{1,\ldots,n} \langle y_1, \ldots, y_n \rangle$ *iff*

$$\exists i \leq n.\ x_1 \succsim_1 y_1 \wedge \cdots \wedge x_{i-1} \succsim_{i-1} y_{i-1} \wedge x_i \succ_i y_i \tag{2}$$

and $\langle x_1, \ldots, x_n \rangle \succsim^{lex}_{1,\ldots,n} \langle y_1, \ldots, y_n \rangle$ *iff* (2) *holds or* $x_1 \succsim_1 y_1 \wedge \cdots \wedge x_n \succsim_n y_n$.

The lexicographic composition of well-founded order pairs forms again a well-founded order pair. Hence, to conclude the correct application of Theorem 8, CeTA demands a list of bounds $b_1, \ldots, b_n$ to be given in the certificate, and then uses the lexicographic composition induced by bounded order pairs $(\geq, >_{b_1}), \ldots, (\geq, >_{b_n})$. An application is illustrated at the end of the next subsection in Example 6.

4.4   Variable and Location Additions

Transition removal is an efficient termination proving method, but relies on local syntactic structure of the program. Most significantly, it cannot find termination arguments that depend on interactions between succeeding transitions on a cycle. Safety-based termination proofs thus instead consider *evaluations* that represent a full cycle through a program SCC, from a cutpoint back to itself, and show that every such evaluation decreases some well-founded measure. In order to do this, a *snapshot variable* v_s is introduced for each program variable v and the program is extended to set v_s to the value of v on every transition leaving a cutpoint. Then, a rank function for the SCC satisfies $f(v_{1s}, \ldots, v_{ns}) > f(v_1, \ldots, v_n)$ whenever an evaluation reaches the cutpoint again. In our modified version of T2, we implement the setting of snapshot variables and checking of rank functions by adding dedicated fresh locations after and before a cutpoint.

Theorem 9 (Location Addition). *Let* $\mathcal{P}$ *be a cooperation program and* $\mathcal{Q}^{\sharp\sharp}$ *a set of transitions such that for every transition* $\ell^\sharp \xrightarrow{\phi} r^\sharp \in \mathcal{P}^{\sharp\sharp} \setminus \mathcal{Q}^{\sharp\sharp}$ *there exists a location* f *such that* $\ell^\sharp \xrightarrow{\phi} f, f \xrightarrow{\epsilon} r^\sharp \in \mathcal{Q}^{\sharp\sharp}$ *or* $\ell^\sharp \xrightarrow{\epsilon} f, f \xrightarrow{\phi} r^\sharp \in \mathcal{Q}^{\sharp\sharp}$. *Then* $\mathcal{P}$ *is CP-terminating if* $\mathcal{P}^\flat \cup \mathcal{P}^\sharp \cup \mathcal{Q}^{\sharp\sharp}$ *is CP-terminating.*

In certificates the new component $\mathcal{Q}^{\sharp\sharp}$ does not have to be provided. Instead it suffices to provide the new ϵ-transition $f \xrightarrow{\epsilon} r^\sharp$ (resp. $\ell^\sharp \xrightarrow{\epsilon} f$) with fresh location f. Then $\mathcal{Q}^{\sharp\sharp}$ is computed from $\mathcal{P}^{\sharp\sharp}$ by redirecting every transition with target $r^\sharp$ (resp. source $\ell^\sharp$) towards f.

Example 5. Here and in Example 6, we provide an alternative termination proof for the cooperation program $\mathcal{Q}_1$ of Fig. 5. We use the global reasoning that every cycle from $\ell^\sharp_2$ back to itself decreases the measure $\langle x, x - y \rangle$, bounded by -5 and 0 respectively. Note that x decreases in every iteration of the outer loop, and $x - y$ decreases in every iteration of the inner loop.

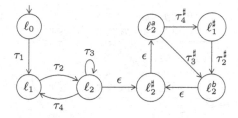

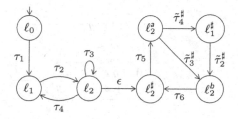

Fig. 6. Cooperation program Q_2 resulting from Q_1 by adding a location ℓ_2^a after $\ell_2^\sharp$ and a location ℓ_2^b before $\ell_2^\sharp$

Fig. 7. Cooperation program Q_3 resulting from Q_2 by adding snapshot variables

As a first step, we transform Q_1 into Q_2 of Fig. 6 by applying Theorem 9 twice, providing the transitions $\ell_2^b \xrightarrow{\epsilon} \ell_2^\sharp$ and $\ell_2^\sharp \xrightarrow{\epsilon} \ell_2^a$ to introduce fresh locations before and after the cutpoint $\ell_2^\sharp$.

The addition of snapshot variables is not trivially sound, as the operation involves *strengthening* transition formulas, e.g., from ϕ to $\phi \wedge x_s' = x$. Thus to ensure soundness, CeTA demands the new variable x_s and the formula added to each transition, and checks that no existing transition formula mentions x_s', and the added formulas do nothing more than giving a value to x_s'. The latter condition is more precisely formulated as follows.

Definition 16. *We say a variable x of sort σ is* definable *in a formula ψ iff for any assignment α, there exists $v \in A_\sigma$ such that $\alpha[x \mapsto v] \models \psi$, where $\alpha[x \mapsto v]$ maps x to v and $y \neq x$ to $\alpha(y)$.*

Theorem 10 (Variable Addition). *Let P and Q be cooperation programs, x a variable, and Ψ a mapping from transitions to formulas, such that for every transition $\tau : \ell \xrightarrow{\phi} r \in P$, x does not occur in ϕ and there exists $\ell \xrightarrow{\phi \wedge \Psi(\tau)} r \in Q$ where x is definable in $\Psi(\tau)$. Then P is CP-terminating if Q is CP-terminating.*

Example 6. We can transform Q_2 to Q_3 in Fig. 7. Here, each $\tilde{\tau}_i^\sharp$ extends $\tau_i^\sharp$ to keep the values of x_s, y_s, z_s unchanged; i.e., $x_s' = x_s \wedge y_s' = y_s \wedge z_s' = z_s$ is added to the transition formulas. The transition τ_6 keeps all variables unchanged, and τ_5 initializes the snapshot variables: $\ldots \wedge x_s' = x \wedge y_s' = y \wedge z_s' = z$. This transformation is achieved by repeatedly adding snapshot variables x_s, y_s, and z_s. To add x_s, for instance, we apply Theorem 10 on Q_2 with $\Psi(\ell_2^b \xrightarrow{\epsilon} \ell_2^a) = (x_s' = x)$ and $\Psi(\tau) = (x_s' = x_s)$ for all other transitions $\tau \in Q_2^{\sharp\sharp}$.

Every cycle from $\ell_2^\sharp$ back to itself decreases the bounded measure $\langle x, x - y \rangle$, so we are able to remove the transition τ_6 by Theorem 8, using the rank function f with $f(\ell_2^\sharp) = \langle x, x - y \rangle$ and $f(\ell^\sharp) = \langle x_s, x_s - y_s \rangle$ for all other locations $\ell^\sharp \neq \ell_2^\sharp$. To this end we need to be able to show $\langle x_s, x_s - y_s \rangle >_{-5,0}^{\text{lex}} \langle x, x - y \rangle$ for τ_6. Weak decreases required for other transitions are immediate from the transition formulas. So we need an invariant on ℓ_2^b that is strong enough to prove

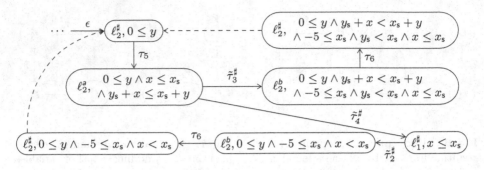

Fig. 8. Partial unwinding of $\mathcal{Q}_2$ from Fig. 6

$\langle x_\mathsf{s}, x_\mathsf{s} - y_\mathsf{s} \rangle >^{\mathsf{lex}}_{-5,0} \langle x, x - y \rangle$. To this end the following invariant works, and can be proven using the unwinding (partially) shown in Fig. 8.

$$(0 \leq y \wedge y_\mathsf{s} + x < x_\mathsf{s} + y \wedge -5 \leq x_\mathsf{s} \wedge y_\mathsf{s} < x_\mathsf{s} \wedge x \leq x_\mathsf{s})$$
$$\vee \, (0 \leq y \wedge -5 \leq x_\mathsf{s} \wedge x < x_\mathsf{s})$$

Having τ_6 removed, $\mathcal{Q}_3^{\sharp\sharp}$ contains no SCC anymore, and thus SCC decomposition (requiring no further subproofs) finishes the proof.

5   Linear Integer Arithmetic

In the preceding sections we have assumed that we can certify entailments $\psi \models \chi$, i.e., the validity of formulas $\neg\psi \vee \chi$. In this section, we provide such a validity checker when the underlying logic is linear integer arithmetic. Note that although Isabelle has already builtin support for reasoning about linear arithmetic, we cannot use these results: Isabelle *tactics* like `linarith` and `presburger` are not accessible to CeTA, since CeTA is a stand-alone Haskell program that has been constructed via code generation from Isabelle, and it has no access to Isabelle tactics at all.

5.1   Reduction to Linear Programming

As the initial step, CeTA converts the input formula (whose validity has to be verified) into conjunctive normal form (CNF). Note that here we cannot use the Tseitin transformation [36] since we are interested in checking validity, not satisfiability. By default, CeTA completely distributes disjunctions to obtain CNFs, but we also provide a "hint" format to indicate that some part of the formula should be erased or to explicitly apply distributivity rules at some position.

Next, we ensure the validity of a CNF by equivalently checking the validity of every clause. Hence, the underlying logic should provide at least a validity checker for disjunctions of literals, or equivalently an unsatisfiability checker for conjunctions of literals.

For linear integer arithmetic, all literals can be translated into inequalities of the form $e \geq 0$ by using straightforward rules such as $\neg(e_1 \leq e_2) \hookrightarrow e_1 - e_2 - 1 \geq 0$. Thus, we only need to prove unsatisfiability of a conjunction of linear inequalities, a question in the domain of integer linear programming (ILP).

Since the unsatisfiability of ILP instances is a coNP-complete problem [30, Chap. 18], there is little hope in getting small certificates which are easy to check. We provide two alternatives. Both interpret ILPs as linear programming problems (LPs) over $\mathbb{Q}$, not $\mathbb{Z}$, and thus are incomplete but sound, in the sense that the resulting LP might be satisfiable although the input ILP is unsatisfiable, but not vise versa. In our experiments the incompleteness was never encountered when certifying proofs generated by AProVE and T2.

Simplex Algorithm: The first alternative employs the existing Isabelle formalization of the simplex algorithm by Spasić and Marić [31]. We only had to manually rebase the formalization from Isabelle 2012 to Isabelle 2016-1, and then establish a connection between the linear rational inequalities as formalized by Spasić and Marić and our linear integer inequalities.

Farkas' Lemma: The second alternative demands the certificate to provide the coefficients as used in Farkas' Lemma [17]: Given an LP constraint $e_1 \geq 0 \wedge \ldots \wedge e_n \geq 0$ and a list of non-negative coefficients $\lambda_1, \ldots, \lambda_n$, we conclude $\sum_{i=1}^{n} \lambda_i e_i \geq 0$ and then check that this inequality is trivially unsatisfiable, i.e., that $\sum_{i=1}^{n} \lambda_i e_i$ is a negative constant. It is well known that this criterion is of the same power as the first alternative. The advantage of this alternative is that it is faster to validate—at the cost of more demanding certificates.

5.2 Executable Certifier for ITSs

To summarize, we developed a validity checker for formulas in linear integer arithmetic, whose correctness is formally proven. Hence we derive an executable checker for the correct application of Theorems 1–10 on linear ITSs. Thus CeTA is now able to certify safety and termination proofs for linear ITSs.

Corollary 1 (Safety and Termination Checker). *Let $\mathcal{P}$ be a linear ITS. If CeTA accepts a safety proof certificate (resp. termination proof certificate) for $\mathcal{P}$, then $\mathcal{P}$ is safe (resp. terminating).*

Our validity checker has exponential worst-case complexity and is incomplete, but the experimental results show that the current implementation of CeTA is good enough to validate all the proofs generated by AProVE and T2. A reason for this is that the transition formulas in the example ITSs are all conjunctions of atoms, and thus disjunctions are only due to invariants from the Impact algorithm and encoded lexicographic orderings. As a consequence, the CNF of formulas that have to be validated is at most quadratically larger than the original formula.

Table 1. Experimental results with AProVE, T2 and CeTA

Tool	# Yes	# No	# Certified	# Rejected	Average time tool	Average time CeTA
Certifiable T2	562	–	560	2	7.98 s	1.24 s
Certifiable T2 (w. hints)	540	–	539	1	8.35 s	0.54 s
Full T2	615	420	–	–	8.60 s	–
Certifiable AProVE	543	–	535	8	14.52 s	1.39 s
Full AProVE	512	369	–	–	21.19 s	–

6 Experiments

For our experiments, we used *full* (unmodified) versions of AProVE and T2 as well as *certifiable* versions, where the latter have to produce termination certificates in XML using only the techniques described in this work. Additionally, we also consider a version of T2 that provides "hints" to prove entailments of linear arithmetic formulas. These certificates will then be checked by CeTA version 2.30.

The modification to obtain the certifiable version of T2 consists of about 1 500 lines of additional code, mostly to produce the machine-readable certificates and to keep the required information about all proof steps. The certifiable version uses precisely the techniques presented without formalization in [8], and all of these techniques can be modeled by the formalized theorems of this paper. The difference between the certifiable and the full version of T2 is that the latter uses Spacer [22] instead of Impact, supports additional termination techniques [13], and searches for nontermination proofs, but does not produce certifiable output.

Although AProVE does not explicitly work on cooperation programs, its certifiable version inserts an application of Theorem 4 at the beginning of each certificate. Afterwards, SCC decompositions and ranking functions that AProVE internally computes are reformatted into the applications of Theorems 6 and 8, respectively. Ranking functions over rational numbers are converted into ones over the integers by multiplication with the common denominator. The difference between the certifiable and the full version of AProVE is that the latter tries more termination techniques like non-linear ranking functions and searches for nontermination proofs, but does not produce certifiable output.

We performed experiments of our implementation on an Intel Xeon E5-1620 (clocked at 3.6 GHz) with 16 GB RAM on the 1222 examples from the "Integer Transition System" category from the Termination Competition 2016. The source code of CeTA is exported in Haskell using Isabelle's code export function, and compiled by ghc. All tools were run with a timeout of 60 s.

Table 1 summarizes our experiments. The table contains five rows, one for each configuration. The column "# Yes" indicates the number of successful termination proofs, "# No" the number of successful nontermination proofs, "# Certified" the number of proofs that were validated by CeTA, and "# Rejected" the number of certificates that were not validated by CeTA. We note that for termination, the certifiable version of T2 already has 91 % of the power of the full version, even though many advanced techniques (e.g., polyranking rank functions [7]) are disabled. The certifiable version of AProVE was even more powerful than the full version w.r.t. termination proving, most likely since the full version also spends a significant amount of time to detect nontermination. Nearly all of the certificates were successfully validated by CeTA, except for two from AProVE where non-linear arithmetic reasoning is essential, and six which could not be certified in the given time. Currently, CeTA ignores all non-linear constraints when invoking the simplex algorithm. For T2, three certificates lead to CeTA parsing errors, caused by bugs in the certificate export.

Certification for T2 took in average about a sixth of the time T2 required to find a termination proof—the average time for successful runs of T2 (certifiable) is 7.98 s. Generating and exporting hints for entailments in T2 more than halves the time CeTA needs to check certificates.

All experimental details including links to AProVE, T2 and CeTA can be found on http://cl-informatik.uibk.ac.at/ceta/experiments/lts.

7   Conclusion and Future Work

We have presented a formalization of safety and termination proofs using the unwinding and cooperation graph techniques. Furthermore, we have implemented the certification of proof certificates in CeTA, and have extended T2 to produce such certificates. While we have focused on two specific techniques in this paper, our formalization is general enough to accommodate proofs produced by other safety and termination provers, witnessed by AProVE. It remains as future work to extend other tools to export proof certificates and support additional techniques they require.

Our experiments show that extending our formalization to also support *non-termination* proof certificates would be valuable. We are also interested in supporting other related program analyzes, such as inferring runtime complexity bounds or proving properties in temporal logics.

As the most part of our formalization is independent of the chosen logic, formalized decision procedures for other logics than linear integer arithmetic, such as non-linear arithmetic, bit-vectors, arrays, etc. will immediately extend our results to systems which cannot be expressed as linear ITSs. For example, the two rejected certificates from AProVE can be certified if non-linear arithmetic reasoning is supported. Incorporating the certified quantifier elimination algorithms by Nipkow [28] would not only lead to another alternative validity checker but also allow for quantified formulas appear in transition formulas and invariants.

Finally, we note that CeTA is usually an order of magnitude faster than the termination tools on term rewriting, a statement that is not yet true for ITSs. Here, profiling reveals that the validity checker for formulas over linear integer arithmetic is the bottleneck. Consequently, it seems to be fruitful to develop a formalized SMT solver by extending work on SAT solving [4,19,25].

References

1. Albert, E., Arenas, P., Codish, M., Genaim, S., Puebla, G., Zanardini, D.: Termination analysis of Java Bytecode. In: FMOODS 2008, pp. 2–18
2. Albert, E., Bubel, R., Genaim, S., Hähnle, R., Puebla, G., Román-Díez, G.: A formal verification framework for static analysis. Softw. Syst. Model. **15**(4), 987–1012 (2016)
3. Beyer, D., Dangl, M., Dietsch, D., Heizmann, M.: Correctness witnesses: exchanging verification results between verifiers. In: FSE 2016, pp. 326–337. ACM (2016)
4. Blanchette, J.C., Fleury, M., Weidenbach, C.: A verified SAT solver framework with learn, forget, restart, and incrementality. In: Olivetti, N., Tiwari, A. (eds.) IJCAR 2016. LNCS (LNAI), vol. 9706, pp. 25–44. Springer, Cham (2016). doi:10. 1007/978-3-319-40229-1_4
5. Blanqui, F., Koprowski, A.: CoLoR: a Coq library on well-founded rewrite relations and its application to the automated verification of termination certificates. Math. Struct. Comput. Sci. **21**(4), 827–859 (2011)
6. Borralleras, C., Brockschmidt, M., Larraz, D., Oliveras, A., Rodríguez-Carbonell, E., Rubio, A.: Proving termination through conditional termination. In: TACAS 2017 (to appear)
7. Bradley, A.R., Manna, Z., Sipma, H.B.: The polyranking principle. In: ICALP 2005, pp. 1349–1361
8. Brockschmidt, M., Cook, B., Fuhs, C.: Better termination proving through cooperation. In: CAV 2013, pp. 413–429
9. Brockschmidt, M., Cook, B., Ishtiaq, S., Khlaaf, H., Piterman, N.: T2: temporal property verification. In: TACAS 2016, pp. 387–393
10. Caleiro, C., Gonçalves, R.: On the algebraization of many-sorted logics. In: WADT 2006, pp. 21–36
11. Cho, S., Kang, J., Choi, J., Yi, K.: SparrowBerry: a verified validator for an industrial-strength static analyzer. http://ropas.snu.ac.kr/sparrowberry/
12. Contejean, E., Paskevich, A., Urbain, X., Courtieu, P., Pons, O., Forest, J.: A3PAT, an approach for certified automated termination proofs. In: PEPM 2010, pp. 63–72
13. Cook, B., See, A., Zuleger, F.: Ramsey vs. lexicographic termination proving. In: TACAS 2013, pp. 47–61
14. Cook, B., Podelski, A., Rybalchenko, A.: Termination proofs for systems code. In: PLDI 2006, pp. 415–426
15. Cousot, P., Cousot, R.: Abstract interpretation: A unified lattice model for static analysis of programs by construction or approximation of fixpoints. In: POPL 1977, pp. 238–252 (1977)
16. Falke, S., Kapur, D., Sinz, C.: Termination analysis of C programs using compiler intermediate languages. In: RTA 2011, pp. 41–50
17. Farkas, J.: Theorie der einfachen Ungleichungen. J. für die reine Angew. Math. **124**, 1–27 (1902)
18. Giesl, J., Aschermann, C., Brockschmidt, M., Emmes, F., Frohn, F., Fuhs, C., Hensel, J., Otto, C., Plücker, M., Schneider-Kamp, P., Ströder, T., Swiderski, S., Thiemann, R.: Analyzing program termination and complexity automatically with AProVE. J. Autom. Reason. **58**, 3–31 (2017)
19. Heule, M.J., Hunt, W.A., Wetzler, N.: Trimming while checking clausal proofs. In: FMCAD 2013, pp. 181–188. IEEE
20. Jourdan, J., Laporte, V., Blazy, S., Leroy, X., Pichardie, D.: A formally-verified C static analyzer. In: POPL 2015, pp. 247–259

21. Klein, G., Nipkow, T.: A machine-checked model for a java-like language, virtual machine and compiler. ACM Trans. Progr. Lang. Syst. **28**(4), 619–695 (2006)
22. Komuravelli, A., Gurfinkel, A., Chaki, S.: SMT-based model checking for recursive programs. In: CAV 2014, pp. 17–34
23. Lammich, P.: Verified efficient implementation of Gabow's strongly connected component algorithm. In: Klein, G., Gamboa, R. (eds.) ITP 2014, pp. 325–340
24. Leroy, X.: Formal verification of a realistic compiler. Commun. ACM **52**(7), 107–115 (2009)
25. Marić, F., Janičić, P.: Formal correctness proof for DPLL procedure. Informatica **21**(1), 57–78 (2010)
26. McMillan, K.: Lazy abstraction with interpolants. In: CAV 2006, pp. 123–136
27. Nipkow, T., Wenzel, M., Paulson, L.C. (eds.): Isabelle/HOL - A Proof Assistant for Higher-Order Logic. LNCS, vol. 2283. Springer, Heidelberg (2002)
28. Nipkow, T.: Linear quantifier elimination. J. Autom. Reason. **45**(2), 189–212 (2010)
29. Otto, C., Brockschmidt, M., von Essen, C., Giesl, J.: Automated termination analysis of Java Bytecode by term rewriting. In: RTA 2010, pp. 259–276
30. Schrijver, A.: Theory of Linear and Integer Programming. Wiley, Hoboken (1999)
31. Spasić, M., Marić, F.: Formalization of incremental simplex algorithm by stepwise refinement. In: Giannakopoulou, D., Méry, D. (eds.) FM 2012, pp. 434–449
32. Spoto, F., Mesnard, F., Payet, É.: A termination analyser for Java Bytecode based on path-length. ACM Trans. Progr. Lang. Syst. **32**(3), 8: 1–8: 70 (2010)
33. Sternagel, C., Thiemann, R.: The certification problem format. In: UITP 2014, EPTCS, vol. 167, pp. 61–72 (2014)
34. Ströder, T., Giesl, J., Brockschmidt, M., Frohn, F., Fuhs, C., Hensel, J., Schneider-Kamp, P., Aschermann, C.: Automatically proving termination and memory safety for programs with pointer arithmetic. J. Autom. Reason. **58**, 33–65 (2017)
35. Thiemann, R., Sternagel, C.: Certification of termination proofs using CeTA. In: TPHOLs 2009, pp. 452–468
36. Tseitin, G.S.: On the complexity of proof in prepositional calculus. Stud. Constr. Math. Math. Logic Part II **8**, 234–259 (1968)
37. Urban, C., Gurfinkel, A., Kahsai, T.: Synthesizing ranking functions from bits and pieces. In: TACAS 2016, pp. 54–70
38. Wang, H.: Logic of many-sorted theories. J. Symb. Logic **17**(2), 105–116 (1952)
39. Zhao, J., Nagarakatte, S., Martin, M.M., Zdancewic, S.: Formalizing the LLVM intermediate representation for verified program transformations. In: POPL 2012, pp. 427–440

Biabduction (and Related Problems) in Array Separation Logic

James Brotherston[1]([✉]), Nikos Gorogiannis[2], and Max Kanovich[1,3]

[1] University College London, London, UK
J.Brotherston@ucl.ac.uk
[2] Middlesex University, London, UK
[3] National Research University Higher School of Economics,
Moscow, Russian Federation

Abstract. We investigate *array separation logic* (ASL), a variant of symbolic-heap separation logic in which the data structures are either pointers or *arrays*, i.e., contiguous blocks of memory. This logic provides a language for compositional memory safety proofs of array programs. We focus on the *biabduction* problem for this logic, which has been established as the key to automatic specification inference at the industrial scale. We present an NP decision procedure for biabduction in ASL, and we also show that the problem of finding a consistent solution is NP-hard. Along the way, we study satisfiability and entailment in ASL, giving decision procedures and complexity bounds for both problems. We show satisfiability to be NP-complete, and entailment to be decidable with high complexity. The surprising fact that biabduction is simpler than entailment is due to the fact that, as we show, the element of choice over biabduction solutions enables us to dramatically reduce the search space.

Keywords: Separation logic · Arrays · Biabduction · Entailment · Complexity

1   Introduction

In the last 15 years, *separation logic* [34] has evolved from a novel way to reason about pointers to a mainstream technique for scalable program verification. Facebook's INFER [13] is perhaps the best known tool based on separation logic; other examples include SLAYER [5], VERIFAST [28] and HIP [15].

Separation logic is based upon *Hoare triples* of the form $\{A\}\,C\,\{B\}$, where C is a program and A, B are formulas in a logical language. Its compositional nature has two main pillars. The first pillar is the soundness of the *frame rule*:

$$\frac{\{A\}\,C\,\{B\}}{\{A * F\}\,C\,\{B * F\}}\text{ (Frame)}$$

where the *separating conjunction* $*$ is read as *"and separately in memory"*, and subject to the restriction that C does not modify any free variables in F [39].

© Springer International Publishing AG 2017
L. de Moura (Ed.): CADE 2017, LNAI 10395, pp. 472–490, 2017.
DOI: 10.1007/978-3-319-63046-5_29

The second pillar is a tractable algorithm for *biabduction* [14]: given formulas A and B, find formulas X, Y such that $A * X \models B * Y$, usually subject to the proviso that $A * X$ should be satisfiable. Solving this problem enables us to infer specifications for whole programs given specifications for their individual components [14]. E.g., if C_1 and C_2 have specifications $\{A'\} C_1 \{A\}$ and $\{B\} C_2 \{B'\}$, we can use a solution X, Y to the above biabduction problem to construct a specification for $C_1; C_2$ as follows, using the frame rule and the usual Hoare logic rules for consequence ($\models$) and sequencing (;):

$$\dfrac{\dfrac{\dfrac{\{A'\} C_1 \{A\}}{\{A' * X\} C_1 \{A * X\}} \text{ (Frame)}}{\{A' * X\} C_1 \{B * Y\}} (\models) \qquad \dfrac{\dfrac{\{B\} C_2 \{B'\}}{\{B * Y\} C_2 \{B' * Y\}} \text{ (Frame)}}{}}{\{A' * X\} C_1; C_2 \{B' * Y\}} (;)$$

Bottom-up interprocedural analyses based on separation logic, such as Facebook INFER, employ biabduction to infer program specifications from unannotated code. Typically, the underlying assertion language is the "symbolic heap" fragment of separation logic over linked lists [4], which is known to be tractable [16].

Here, we focus on a different, but ubiquitous data structure, namely *arrays*, which we view as contiguous blocks of memory. We propose an *array separation logic* (ASL) in which we replace the usual "list segment" predicate ls by an "array" predicate $\mathsf{array}(a, b)$, which denotes a contiguous block of allocated heap memory from address a to address b (inclusive), as was first proposed in [32]. In addition, since we wish to reason about array bounds, we allow assertions to contain linear arithmetic. Thus, for example, a pointer x to a memory block of length $n > 1$ starting at a can be represented in ASL by the assertion

$$n > 1 : x \mapsto a * \mathsf{array}(a, a + n - 1) .$$

The array predicate only records the bounds of memory blocks, not their contents; this is analogous to the abstraction from pointers to lists in standard separation logic. Similar to the situation for lists, memory safety of array-manipulating programs typically depends only on the memory footprint of the arrays.

Our focus is on the biabduction problem for ASL, the most critical step in building a bottom-up memory safety analysis à la INFER for array-manipulating programs. Our first main contribution is a decision procedure for the (quantifier-free) biabduction problem in ASL (Sect. 5). It relies on the idea that, given A and B, we can look for some consistent total ordering of all the array endpoints and pointers in both A and B, and impose this ordering, which we call a *solution seed*, as the arithmetical part of the solution X. Having done this, the computation of the "missing" arrays and pointers in X, Y is a polynomial-time process, and thus the entire algorithm runs in NP-time. We demonstrate that this algorithm is sound and complete, and that the biabduction problem itself is NP-hard, with further bounds for cases involving quantifiers.

We also study the *satisfiability* and *entailment* problems in ASL, and, as our second main contribution, we provide decision procedures and upper/lower complexity bounds for both problems. We find that satisfiability is NP-complete, while entailment is decidable with very high complexity: it can be encoded in Π_2^0 Presburger arithmetic, and is Π_2^P-hard. It may at first sight appear surprising that entailment is harder than biabduction, as biabduction also seems to involve solving an entailment problem. However, in biabduction, there is an element of *choice* over X, Y, and we exploit this to dramatically reduce the cost of checking these conditions. Namely, committing to a specific solution seed (see above) reduces biabduction to a simple computation rather than a search problem.

The remainder of this paper is structured as follows. Section 2 gives an example motivating the ASL biabduction problem in practice. The syntax and semantics of ASL is given formally in Sect. 3. We present algorithms and complexity bounds for satisfiability, biabduction and entailment for ASL in Sects. 4, 5 and 6 respectively. Section 7 surveys related work, and Sect. 8 concludes.

Due to space limitations, the proofs of the results in this paper are omitted or only sketched. They are, however, available in the long version of this article [11].

2   Motivating Example

Here, we give a simple example illustrating how the biabduction problem arises when verifying array programs, using ASL as our assertion language. Our example is deliberately high-level, in order to illustrate some key features of the general problem. However, more concrete examples, involving concrete array programs, can be found in Sect. 2 of [11].

Suppose we have a procedure foo that manipulates an array somehow, with specification $\{\mathsf{array}(c, d)\}\,\mathtt{foo}(\mathtt{c}, \mathtt{d})\,\{Q\}$ (supplied in advance, or computed at an earlier stage of the analysis). Now, consider a procedure including a call to foo, say $C; \mathtt{foo}(\mathtt{c}, \mathtt{d}); \dots$, and suppose that we have computed the specification $\{\mathsf{emp}\}\,C\,\{\mathsf{array}(a, b)\}$, say, for the code C prior to this call. As in the Introduction, this gives rise to the biabduction problem

$$\mathsf{array}(a, b) * X \models \mathsf{array}(c, d) * Y$$

with the effect that $\{X\}\,C; \mathtt{foo}(\mathtt{c}, \mathtt{d})\,\{Q * Y\}$ then becomes a valid specification for the initial code including the call to foo.

Solving this problem depends crucially on the position in memory of c and d relative to a and b; depending on *whether* and *how* the arrays $\mathsf{array}(a, b)$ and $\mathsf{array}(c, d)$ overlap, we have to add different arrays to X and Y so that the memory footprint of the two sides becomes the same. Such ordering information *might* be available as part of the postcondition computed for C; if not, then we have to guess it, as part of the "antiframe" X. The solutions include:

$X := a = c \wedge b = d : \mathsf{emp}$ and $Y := \mathsf{emp}$
$X := d < a : \mathsf{array}(c, d)$ and $Y := \mathsf{array}(a, b)$
$X := a < c \wedge d < b : \mathsf{emp}$ and $Y := \mathsf{array}(a, c - 1) * \mathsf{array}(b + 1, d)$
$X := a < c < b < d : \mathsf{array}(b + 1, d)$ and $Y := \mathsf{array}(a, c - 1)$

et cetera. Note that these solutions are all (a) spatially minimal, relative to the ordering constraints in X (i.e. the arrays are as small as possible), and (b) logically incomparable to one another. Thus, when dealing with arrays in separation logic, any complete biabduction algorithm *must* take into account the possible ways in which the arrays might be positioned relative to each other.

3   Array Separation Logic, ASL

Here, we present separation logic for arrays, ASL, which employs a similar *symbolic heap* formula structure to that in [4], but which treats contiguous *arrays* in memory rather than linked list segments; we additionally allow linear arithmetic.

Definition 3.1 (Symbolic heap). *Terms t, pure formulas Π, spatial formulas F and symbolic heaps SH are given by the following grammar:*

$$t:: = x \mid n \mid t + t \mid nt$$
$$\Pi:: = t = t \mid t \neq t \mid t \leq t \mid t < t \mid \Pi \wedge \Pi$$
$$F:: = \mathsf{emp} \mid t \mapsto t \mid \mathsf{array}(t,t) \mid F * F$$
$$SH:: = \exists \mathbf{z}.\ \Pi : F$$

where x ranges over an infinite set Var of variables, $\mathbf{z}$ over sets of variables, and n over $\mathbb{N}$. Whenever one of Π, F is empty in a symbolic heap, we omit the colon. We write $FV(A)$ for the set of free variables occurring in A. If $A = \exists \mathbf{z}.\ \Pi : F$ then we write $\mathsf{qf}(A)$ for $\Pi : F$, the quantifier-free part of A.

We interpret this language in a stack-and-heap model, where both locations and values are natural numbers. A *stack* is a function $s\colon \mathsf{Var} \to \mathbb{N}$. We extend stacks over terms as usual: $s(n) = n$, $s(t_1 + t_2) = s(t_1) + s(t_2)$ and $s(nt) = ns(t)$. If s is a stack, $z \in \mathsf{Var}$ and $m \in \mathbb{N}$, we write $s[z \mapsto v]$ for the stack defined as s except that $s[z \mapsto v](z) = v$. We extend stacks pointwise over term tuples.

A *heap* is a finite partial function $h\colon \mathbb{N} \to_{\mathsf{fin}} \mathbb{N}$ mapping finitely many locations to values; we write $\mathsf{dom}\,(h)$ for the domain of h, and e for the empty heap that is undefined on all locations. We write $\circ$ for *composition* of domain-disjoint heaps: if h_1 and h_2 are heaps, then $h_1 \circ h_2$ is the union of h_1 and h_2 when $\mathsf{dom}\,(h_1)$ and $\mathsf{dom}\,(h_2)$ are disjoint, and undefined otherwise.

Definition 3.2. *The satisfaction relation $s, h \models A$, where s is a stack, h a heap and A a symbolic heap, is defined by structural induction on A.*

$$
\begin{aligned}
s, h &\models t_1 \sim t_2 & &\Leftrightarrow s(t_1) \sim s(t_2)\ where \sim is\ =, \neq, <\ or \leq \\
s, h &\models \Pi_1 \wedge \Pi_2 & &\Leftrightarrow s, h \models \Pi_1\ and\ s, h \models \Pi_2 \\
s, h &\models \mathsf{emp} & &\Leftrightarrow h = e \\
s, h &\models t_1 \mapsto t_2 & &\Leftrightarrow \mathsf{dom}\,(h) = \{s(t_1)\}\ and\ h(s(t_1)) = s(t_2) \\
s, h &\models \mathsf{array}(t_1, t_2) & &\Leftrightarrow s(t_1) \leq s(t_2)\ and\ \mathsf{dom}\,(h) = \{s(t_1), \ldots, s(t_2)\} \\
s, h &\models F_1 * F_2 & &\Leftrightarrow \exists h_1, h_2.\ h = h_1 \circ h_2\ and\ s, h_1 \models F_1\ and\ s, h_2 \models F_2 \\
s, h &\models \exists \mathbf{z}.\ \Pi : F & &\Leftrightarrow \exists \mathbf{m} \in \mathbb{N}^{|\mathbf{z}|}.\ s[\mathbf{z} \mapsto \mathbf{m}], h \models \Pi\ and\ s[\mathbf{z} \mapsto \mathbf{m}], h \models F
\end{aligned}
$$

Satisfaction of pure formulas Π does not depend on the heap; we write $s \models \Pi$ to mean that $s, h \models \Pi$ (for any heap h). We write $A \models B$ to mean that A *entails* B, i.e. that $s, h \models A$ implies $s, h \models B$ for all stacks s and heaps h.

Remark 3.3. Our array predicate employs *absolute* addressing: $\mathsf{array}(k, \ell)$ denotes an array from k to ℓ. In practice, one often reasons about arrays using *base-offset* addressing, where $\mathsf{array}(b, i, j)$ denotes an array from $b + i$ to $b + j$. We can define such a ternary version of our array predicate, overloading notation, by $\mathsf{array}(b, i, j) =_{def} \mathsf{array}(b+i, b+j)$. Conversely, any $\mathsf{array}(k, \ell)$ can be represented in base-offset style as $\mathsf{array}(0, k, \ell)$. Thus, we may freely switch between absolute and base-offset addressing.

Satisfiability in the unrestricted pure part of our language is already NP-hard. Thus, in order to obtain sharper complexity results, we will sometimes confine our attention to symbolic heaps in the following special *two-variable form*.

Definition 3.4. *A symbolic heap* $\exists \mathbf{z}.\ \Pi : F$ *is said to be in* two-variable form *if*

(a) *its pure part* Π *is a conjunction of* 'difference constraints' *of the form* $x = k$, $x = y + k$, $x \leq y + k$, $x \geq y + k$, $x < y + k$, *and* $x > y + k$, *where* x *and* y *are variables, and* $k \in \mathbb{N}$; *(notice that* $x \neq y$ *is not here)*;
(b) *its spatial part* F *contains only formulas of the form* $k \mapsto v$, $\mathsf{array}(a, 0, j)$, $\mathsf{array}(a, 1, j)$, *and* $\mathsf{array}(k, j, j)$, *where* v, a, *and* j *are variables, and* $k \in \mathbb{N}$.

When pure formulas are conjunctions of 'difference constraints' as in Definition 3.4, their satisfiability becomes polynomial [17].

4   Satisfiability in ASL

Here, we show that *satisfiability* in ASL is NP-complete. This stands in contrast to the situation for symbolic-heaps over list segments, where satisfiability is polynomial [16], and over general inductive predicates, where it is EXP-complete [10].

Satisfiability Problem for ASL. *Given symbolic heap* A, *decide if there is a stack* s *and heap* h *with* $s, h \models A$.

First, we show that satisfiability of a symbolic heap can be encoded as a Σ_1^0 formula of *Presburger arithmetic* and can therefore be decided in NP time.

Definition 4.1. Presburger arithmetic (PbA) *is defined as the first-order theory (with equality) of the natural numbers* $\mathbb{N}$ *over the signature* $\langle 0, s, + \rangle$, *where* s *is the successor function, and* 0 *and* + *have their usual interpretations. It is immediate that the relations* $\neq$, $\leq$ *and* $<$ *can be encoded (possibly introducing an existential quantifier), as can the operation of multiplication by a constant.*

Note that a stack is just a standard first-order valuation, and that a pure formula in ASL is also a formula of PbA. Moreover, the satisfaction relations for

ASL and PbA coincide on such formulas. Thus, we overload $\models$ to include the standard first-order satisfaction relation of PbA.

The intuition behind our encoding of satisfiability is that a symbolic heap is satisfiable exactly when the pure part is satisfiable, each array is well-defined, and all pointers and arrays are non-overlapping with all of the others. For simplicity of exposition, we do this by abstracting away pointers with single-cell arrays.

Definition 4.2. *Let A be a quantifier-free symbolic heap, written (without loss of generality) in the form: $A = \Pi : \text{\Large$*$}_{i=1}^{n} \, \mathsf{array}(a_i, b_i) * \text{\Large$*$}_{i=1}^{m} \, c_i \mapsto d_i$. We define its* array abstraction *as*

$$\lfloor A \rfloor =_{def} \Pi : \text{\Large$*$}_{i=1}^{n} \, \mathsf{array}(a_i, b_i) * \text{\Large$*$}_{i=1}^{m} \, \mathsf{array}(c_i, c_i).$$

Lemma 4.3. *Let A be a quantifier-free symbolic heap and s a stack. Then, $\exists h. \, s, h \models A$ iff $\exists h'. \, s, h' \models \lfloor A \rfloor$.*

Definition 4.4. *Let A be a quantifier-free symbolic heap, and let $\lfloor A \rfloor$ be of the form $\Pi : \text{\Large$*$}_{i=1}^{n} \, \mathsf{array}(a_i, b_i)$. We define a corresponding formula $\gamma(A)$ of PbA as*

$$\gamma(A) =_{def} \Pi \wedge \bigwedge_{1 \le i \le n} a_i \le b_i \wedge \bigwedge_{1 \le i < j \le n} (b_i < a_j) \vee (b_j < a_i) \, .$$

Note that $\gamma(A)$ is defined in terms of the abstraction $\lfloor A \rfloor$.

Lemma 4.5. *For any stack s and any quantifier-free symbolic heap A, we have $s \models \gamma(A)$ iff $\exists h. \, s, h \models A$.*

Proposition 4.6. *Satisfiability for ASL is in NP.*

Proof. Follows from Lemma 4.5 and the fact that satisfiability for Σ_1^0 Presburger arithmetic is in NP [35]. $\qquad$ ∎

Proposition 4.6 may also be obtained by viewing ASL as a sub-fragment of the *array property fragment* [8]. However, we put forward Definition 4.4 and Lemma 4.5 as we make heavy use of them in Sect. 5.

Satisfiability is shown NP-hard by reduction from the 3-*partition problem* [21].

3-Partition Problem. *Given $B \in \mathbb{N}$ and a sequence of natural numbers $S = (k_1, k_2, \ldots, k_{3m})$ such that $\sum_{j=1}^{3m} k_j = mB$, and $B/4 < k_j < B/2$ for all $j \in [1, 3m]$, decide whether there is a partition of S into m groups of three, say $\{(k_{j_{i,1}}, k_{j_{i,2}}, k_{j_{i,3}}) \mid i \in [1, m]\}$, such that $k_{j_{i,1}} + k_{j_{i,2}} + k_{j_{i,3}} = B$ for all $i \in [1, m]$.*

Definition 4.7. *Given an instance (B, S) of the 3-partition problem, we define a symbolic heap $A_{B,S}$ as follows. First we introduce $m + 1$ numbers d_i acting as single-cell "delimiters" between chunks of memory of length B, (therefore, $d_{i+1} = d_i + B + 1$), and a_j to allocate arrays of length k_j in the space between some pair of delimiters d_i and d_{i+1}. Visually, the arrangement is as follows:*

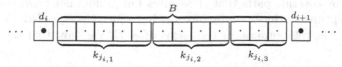

Concretely, $A_{B,S}$ is the following symbolic heap:

$$\bigwedge_{j=1}^{3m}(d_1 \le a_j) \wedge (a_j + k_j < d_{m+1}) : \mathop{\text{\Large *}}_{i=1}^{m+1} \text{array}(d_i, 0, 0) * \mathop{\text{\Large *}}_{j=1}^{3m} \text{array}(a_j, 1, k_j) \ .$$

Lemma 4.8. *Given a 3-partition problem (B, S), and letting $A_{B,S}$ be given by Definition 4.7, we have that $A_{B,S}$ is satisfiable iff there is a 3-partition of S (w.r.t. B).*

Theorem 4.9. *The satisfiability problem for* ASL *is* NP-*complete, even when symbolic heaps are restricted to be quantifier-free, and in two-variable form.*

Proof. Proposition 4.6 provides the upper bound. For the lower bound, Definition 4.7 and Lemma 4.8 establish a polynomial reduction from the 3-partition problem.   □

5 Biabduction

Here, we turn to the central focus of this paper, *biabduction* for ASL. In stating this problem, it is convenient to first lift the connective $*$ to symbolic heaps:

$$(\exists \mathbf{x}. \ \Pi : F) * (\exists \mathbf{y}. \ \Pi' : F') = \exists \mathbf{x} \cup \mathbf{y}. \ \Pi \wedge \Pi' : F * F' \ ,$$

where the existentially quantified variables $\mathbf{x}$ and $\mathbf{y}$ are assumed disjoint, and no free variable capture occurs (this can always be avoided by α-renaming).

Biabduction Problem for ASL. *Given satisfiable symbolic heaps A, B, find symbolic heaps X, Y such that $A * X$ is satisfiable and $A * X \models B * Y$.*

We first consider quantifier-free biabduction (Sect. 5.1), and investigate its complexity in Sect. 5.2. We then show that when quantifiers appear in B, Y which are appropriately restricted, existence of solutions can be decided using the machinery for the quantifier-free case (Sect. 5.3). In the same section we also characterise the complexity of biabduction in the presence of quantifiers.

5.1 An Algorithm for Quantifier-Free Biabduction

We give an algorithm for quantifier-free biabduction. Let (A, B) be a biabduction problem and (X, Y) a solution. The intuition is that a model s, h of both A and B induces a total order over the terms of A, B, dictating the form of X, Y.

Consider Fig. 1, which depicts a biabduction instance (A, B) and a solution (X, Y), where all array endpoints in A, B are totally ordered. Using this order, we can compute X, Y by covering parts that B requires but A does not provide (X) and by covering parts that A requires but B does not provide (Y).

We capture this intuition by introducing a formula Δ, called a *solution seed*, capturing the total order over the terms of A, B. We show that the existence of a solution seed Δ implies the existence of a solution (X, Y) for the biabduction problem (A, B), and is in turn implied by the satisfiability of a certain PbA formula $\beta(A, B)$. To complete the circle, we show that $\beta(A, B)$ is satisfiable whenever there is a biabduction solution for (A, B):

$$
\begin{array}{ccc}
\text{solution } (X, Y) & \xrightarrow{\text{Proposition 5.2}} & \beta(A, B) & \xrightarrow{\text{Theorem 5.5}} & \text{solution seed } \Delta \\
\text{for } (A, B) \text{ exists} & & \text{satisfiable} & & \text{for } (A, B) \text{ exists}
\end{array}
$$

$$\text{Theorem 5.11}$$

Finally, we show that the problem of finding a solution to a biabduction problem is in NP and that our algorithm is complexity-optimal (Proposition 5.13).

Definition 5.1 (The formula β). *Let (A, B) be an biabduction instance, where*

$$
A = \Pi : \underset{i=1}{\overset{n}{\ast}} \operatorname{array}(a_i, b_i) * \underset{i=1}{\overset{k}{\ast}} t_i \mapsto u_i \qquad B = \Pi' : \underset{i=1}{\overset{m}{\ast}} \operatorname{array}(c_i, d_i) * \underset{i=1}{\overset{\ell}{\ast}} v_i \mapsto w_i
$$

We define a formula $\beta(A, B)$ of PbA as follows:

$$
\beta(A, B) =_{def} \gamma(A) \wedge \gamma(B) \wedge \bigwedge_{j=1}^{\ell} \bigwedge_{i=1}^{n} (v_j < a_i \vee v_j > b_i) \wedge \bigwedge_{i=1}^{\ell} \bigwedge_{j=1}^{k} (t_i \neq v_j \vee u_i = w_j)
$$

Proposition 5.2. *If (A, B) has a solution, then $\beta(A, B)$ is satisfiable.*

Proof (Sketch). Letting X, Y be a solution for (A, B), there is a model s, h of $A * X$. We show that $s \models \beta(A, B)$, using Lemma 4.5 for the first conjunct of β, and the fact that $A * X \models B * Y$ for the other conjuncts. $\square$

Given an instance of the form in Definition 5.1, we define a set $T_{A,B}$ of terms by:

$$
T_{A,B} =_{def} T(A) \cup T(B) \cup \bigcup_{i=1}^{n} \{b_i + 1\} \cup \bigcup_{i=1}^{m} \{d_i + 1\} \cup \bigcup_{i=1}^{k} \{t_i + 1\} \cup \bigcup_{i=1}^{\ell} \{v_i + 1\}
$$

where $T(-)$ denotes the set of all terms in a symbolic heap.

Definition 5.3 (Solution seed). *A solution seed for a biabduction problem (A, B) in the form of Definition 5.1 is a pure formula $\Delta = \bigwedge_{i \in I} \delta_i$ such that:*

1. *Δ is satisfiable, and $\Delta \models \beta(A, B)$;*
2. *δ_i is of the form $(t < u)$ or $(t = u)$, where $t, u \in T_{A,B}$, for any $i \in I$;*
3. *for all $t, u \in T_{A,B}$, there is $i \in I$ such that δ_i is $(t < u)$ or $(u < t)$ or $(t = u)$.*

Lemma 5.4. *Let Δ be a solution seed for the problem (A, B). Δ induces a total order on $T_{A,B}$: for any $e, f \in T_{A,B}$, $\Delta \models e < f$ or $\Delta \models e = f$ or $\Delta \models f < e$.*

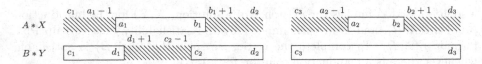

Fig. 1. Example showing solutions in Definition 5.6. Arrays of A, B are displayed as boxes and arrays in X, Y as hatched rectangles.

This lemma justifies abbreviating $\Delta \models e < f$ by $e <_\Delta f$; $\Delta \models e \leq f$ by $e \leq_\Delta f$; and, $\Delta \models e = f$ by $e =_\Delta f$.

Theorem 5.5. *If $\beta(A, B)$ is satisfiable, then there exists a solution seed Δ for the biabduction problem (A, B).*

Proof (Sketch). Given a stack s such that $s \models \beta(A, B)$, we define the formula

$$\Delta = \bigwedge\nolimits_{e,f \in T_{A,B}, \ s(e) < s(f)} e < f \ \wedge \ \bigwedge\nolimits_{e,f \in T_{A,B}, \ s(e) = s(f)} e = f$$

and show that it satisfies Definition 5.3.   □

We now present a way to compute a solution (X, Y) given a solution seed Δ. They key ingredient is the arrcov algorithm (Fig. 2). Intuitively, arrcov takes a solution seed Δ and the endpoints of an $\mathsf{array}(c_j, d_j)$ in B, and constructs arrays for X so that every model of $A * X$ includes a submodel that satisfies $\mathsf{array}(c_j, d_j)$. Arrays in A contribute to the coverage of $\mathsf{array}(c_j, d_j)$ and, in addition, the newly created arrays do not overlap with those of A (or themselves) for consistency.

Note that in arrcov we sometimes need to generate terms denoting the predecessor of the start of an array, even though there is no predecessor function in PbA. We do this by using primed terms a_i', and add constraints that induce this meaning $(a_i + 1 = a_1')$. This is done on demand in order to avoid the risk of trying to decrement a zero-valued term, thus obtaining an inconsistent formula.

Definition 5.6 (The formulas X, Y). *Let Δ be a solution seed for an instance (A, B) in the form given in Definition 5.1. The formulas X, Y are defined as follows:*

$$\Theta_X : F_X =_{def} \bigast\nolimits_{j=1}^{m} \mathsf{arrcov}_{A,\Delta}(c_j, d_j) * \bigast\nolimits_{j=1}^{\ell} \mathsf{ptocov}_{A,\Delta}(v_j, w_j)$$
$$\Theta_Y : F_Y =_{def} \bigast\nolimits_{i=1}^{n} \mathsf{arrcov}_{B,\Delta}(a_i, b_i) * \bigast\nolimits_{i=1}^{k} \mathsf{ptocov}_{B,\Delta}(t_i, u_i)$$
$$\hat{\Delta} =_{def} \Delta \wedge \Theta_X \wedge \Theta_Y \qquad X =_{def} \hat{\Delta} : F_X \qquad Y =_{def} \hat{\Delta} : F_Y$$

Every quantifier-free formula A of ASL is *precise* [33] (by structural induction): for any model s, h there exists *at most one* subheap h' of h such that $s, h' \models A$. This motivates the following notation: we will write $[\![A]\!]^{s,h}$ to denote the unique subheap $h' \subseteq h$ such that $s, h' \models A$, when it exists.

Proposition 5.7. *Let (A, B) be a biabduction problem of the form shown in Definition 5.1. Let Δ be a solution seed and let e, f be terms in $T_{A,B}$. Then, the call $\mathsf{arrcov}_{A,\Delta}(e, f)$:*

1 **Function** $\text{arrcov}_{A,\Delta}(e,f)$
  Data: a quantifier-free symbolic heap A;
        solution seed Δ; terms e, f in $\mathcal{T}_{A,B}$
  Result: quantifier-free symbolic heap
    // work with $\mapsto$-abstraction of A

2 **let** $\left(\Pi : \bigstar_{i=1}^{n+k} \text{array}(\hat{a}_i, \hat{b}_i) \right) = \lfloor A \rfloor$;

3 **if** $f <_\Delta e$ **then**
      // nothing to cover
4   **return** emp;
5 **end**

6 **if** $\exists i \in [1, n+k].\ \hat{a}_i \leq_\Delta e \leq_\Delta \hat{b}_i$ **then**
      // endpoint e covered by $\text{array}(\hat{a}_i, \hat{b}_i)$
7   **return** $\text{arrcov}_{A,\Delta}(\hat{b}_i + 1, f)$;
8 **end**

    // left endpoint e not covered

9 $E := \left\{ \hat{a}_j \ \middle| \ \begin{array}{l} e <_\Delta \hat{a}_j \leq_\Delta f \\ \text{for } j \in [1, n+k] \end{array} \right\}$;

10 **if** $E = \emptyset$ **then**
      // no part of $\text{array}(e,f)$ covered
11   **return** $\text{array}(e, f)$;
12 **end**

    // middle covered by $\text{array}(\hat{a}_i, \hat{b}_i)$
13 $\hat{a}_i := \min_\Delta(E)$;
14 **return** $(\hat{a}_i' + 1 = \hat{a}_i :$
    $\text{array}(e, \hat{a}_i')) * \text{arrcov}_{A,\Delta}(\hat{b}_i + 1, f)$;

1 **Function** $\text{ptocov}_{A,\Delta}(e,f)$
2 **let**

$$\left(\Pi : \bigstar_{i=1}^{n} \text{array}(a_i, b_i) * \bigstar_{i=1}^{k} t_i \mapsto u_i \right) = A;$$

3 **if** $\exists i \in [1, k].\ t_i =_\Delta e$ **then**
4   **return** emp;
5 **end**
6 **if** $\exists i \in [1, n].\ a_i \leq_\Delta e \leq_\Delta b_i$ **then**
7   **return** emp;
8 **end**
9 **return** $e \mapsto f$;

– **Arrays of** A / B appear as boxes with indicated bounds.
– **Arrays of** X appear in a hatched pattern.
– **Recursive calls** appear as dashed boxes with parameters.
– **Terms** a_i' are shown as $a_i - 1$ for readability.

Line 7:

Line 11:

Line 14:

Fig. 2. Left: the function $\text{arrcov}_{A,\Delta}(e, f)$. Top right: the function $\text{ptocov}_{A,\Delta}(e, f)$. Bottom right: arrays of A, B, X relevant to each **return** statement in the arrcov function.

1. *always terminates, issuing up to $n + k$ recursive calls;*
2. *returns a formula $\bigwedge_{i \in I}(a_i = a_i' + 1) \wedge \bigwedge_{i \in J}(t_i = t_i' + 1) : \bigstar_{i=1}^{q} \text{array}(l_i, r_i)$*
   for some $q \in \mathbb{N}$ and sets $I, J \subseteq \mathbb{N}$, where for all $i \in [1, q]$, $l_i \in \mathcal{T}_{A,B}$;
3. *for every $i \in [1, q]$, $\hat{\Delta} \models e \leq l_i \leq r_i \leq f$;*
4. *for every $i \in [1, q-1]$, $\hat{\Delta} \models r_i < l_{i+1}$.*

Lemma 5.8. *Let (A, B) be a biabduction instance, Δ a solution seed and X as in Definition 5.6. Then, $A * X$ is satisfiable.*

Definition 5.9 ($\mathcal{B}^{\text{arr}}, \mathcal{B}^{\text{pto}}, \mathcal{Y}^{\text{arr}}, \mathcal{Y}^{\text{pto}}$). *Let (A, B) be a biabduction problem, Δ a solution seed, X, Y as in Definition 5.6 and s, h a model such that $s, h \models A * X$. Then we define the following sequences $\mathcal{B}^{\text{arr}}, \mathcal{B}^{\text{pto}}, \mathcal{Y}^{\text{arr}}, \mathcal{Y}^{\text{pto}}$ of subheaps of h, such that:*

$\mathcal{B}_i^{\text{arr}} = [\![\text{array}(c_i, d_i)]\!]^{s,h} \ i \in [1, m]$ $\mathcal{Y}_i^{\text{arr}} = [\![\text{arrcov}_{B,\Delta}(a_i, b_i)]\!]^{s,h} \ i \in [1, n]$
$\mathcal{B}_i^{\text{pto}} = [\![v_i \mapsto w_i]\!]^{s,h} \qquad i \in [1, \ell]$ $\mathcal{Y}_i^{\text{pto}} = [\![\text{ptocov}_{B,\Delta}(t_i, u_i)]\!]^{s,h} \ i \in [1, k]$

Lemma 5.10. *All heaps in $\mathcal{B}^{\text{arr}}, \mathcal{B}^{\text{pto}}, \mathcal{Y}^{\text{arr}}, \mathcal{Y}^{\text{pto}}$ are well-defined. Also,*

1. *For any $\mathcal{S}$ of $\mathcal{B}^{\text{arr}}, \mathcal{B}^{\text{pto}}, \mathcal{Y}^{\text{arr}}, \mathcal{Y}^{\text{pto}}$, and any distinct $i, j \in [1, |\mathcal{S}|]$, $\mathcal{S}_i \mathbin{\#} \mathcal{S}_j$.*
2. *For any two distinct $\mathcal{S}, \mathcal{T}$ of $\mathcal{B}^{\text{arr}}, \mathcal{B}^{\text{pto}}, \mathcal{Y}^{\text{arr}}, \mathcal{Y}^{\text{pto}}$, and any i, j, $\mathcal{S}_i \mathbin{\#} \mathcal{T}_j$.*

3. $\text{dom}\,(h) \subseteq \bigcup_{i=1}^{m} \mathcal{B}_i^{\text{arr}} \cup \bigcup_{i=1}^{\ell} \mathcal{B}_i^{\text{pto}} \cup \bigcup_{i=1}^{n} \mathcal{Y}_i^{\text{arr}} \cup \bigcup_{i=1}^{k} \mathcal{Y}_i^{\text{pto}}$.

Theorem 5.11. *Given a solution seed Δ for the biabduction problem (A, B), the formulas X and Y, as computed by Definition 5.6, form a solution for that instance.*

Proof. That (X, Y) is a solution means that $A * X$ is satisfiable and that $A * X \models B * Y$. The first requirement is fulfilled by Lemma 5.8. Here, we show the second.

Let s, h be a model of $A * X$. We need to show that $s, h \models B * Y$. Using Definition 5.6, we have $A * X = \Pi \wedge \hat{\Delta} : F_{A*X}$ and $B * Y = \Pi' \wedge \hat{\Delta} : F_{B*Y}$. It is easy to see that $s \models \Pi' \wedge \hat{\Delta}$: by assumption, $s \models \hat{\Delta}$, and as $\hat{\Delta} \models \Delta$ (Definition 5.6) and $\Delta \models \gamma(B)$ (Definition 5.3), it follows that $s \models \Pi'$ as well (Definition 4.4).

It remains to show that $s, h \models F_{B*Y}$. We will do this by (a) defining a subheap $h' \subseteq h$ for each atomic formula σ in F_{B*Y}, such that $s, h' \models \sigma$. Having done this we will need (b) to show that all such subheaps are disjoint, and that (c) their disjoint union equals h.

The sequences $\mathcal{B}^{\text{arr}}, \mathcal{B}^{\text{pto}}, \mathcal{Y}^{\text{arr}}, \mathcal{Y}^{\text{pto}}$ from Definition 5.9, by construction, fulfil requirement (a) above, given they are well-defined as guaranteed by Lemma 5.10 (main statement). Requirement (b) is covered by items 1 and 2 of Lemma 5.10. Finally, requirement (c) is covered by item 3 of Lemma 5.10.

The solutions obtained via Definition 5.6 are constructed from terms in $\mathcal{T}_{A,B}$, so X, Y are as 'symbolic' as A, B are. However, our solutions are potentially stronger than required; our algorithm here always imposes a total order over all array endpoints in the antiframe X, even if only a *part* of this information is actually required in order to compute the spatial formulas in X and Y. We believe that our algorithm can be refined so as to avoid "over-committing".

Our method is, also, complete in the following sense. Suppose (X, Y) is a solution that does not impose a total order over $\mathcal{T}_{A,B}$. Then, there exists a solution (X', Y') computable by our method, such that $X' \models X$ and $Y' \models Y$.

5.2 Complexity of Quantifier-Free Biabduction in ASL

Lemma 5.12. *Let (A, B) be a biabduction instance and Δ a formula satisfying Conditions 2 and 3 of Definition 5.3. Let $\Gamma = \bigwedge \bigvee \pi$ be a formula where π is of the form $t < u$ or $t = u$ and $t, u \in \mathcal{T}_{A,B}$. Then, checking $\Delta \models \Gamma$ is in PTIME.*

Proposition 5.13. *Deciding if there is a solution for a biabduction problem (A, B), and constructing it if it exists, can be done in NP.*

Proof (Sketch). We guess a total order over $\mathcal{T}_{A,B}$ and a polynomially-sized assignment of values s ([35, Theorem 6]) to all terms in $\mathcal{T}_{A,B}$. We convert this order to a formula Δ and check if $s \models \Delta$ (thus showing the satisfiability of Δ) and whether $\Delta \models \beta(A, B)$. If all these conditions hold, we use Definition 5.6 and obtain formulas X, Y. By Proposition 5.7 and Lemma 5.12 this process runs in PTIME.

We establish NP-hardness of quantifier-free biabduction by reduction from the 3-partition problem, similarly to satisfiability in Sect. 4.

Definition 5.14. *Let (B, S) be an instance of the 3-partition problem. We define corresponding symbolic heaps $\widetilde{A}_{B,S}$ and $\widetilde{B}_{B,S}$. First, we define a satisfiable $\widetilde{A}_{B,S}$ as: $\bigwedge_{i=1}^{m}(d_{i+1} = d_i + B + 1)$: $*_{i=1}^{m+1}$ array$(d_i, 0, 0)$. The formula $\widetilde{B}_{B,S}$, a relaxed but satisfiable version of $A_{B,S}$ from Definition 4.7, is given by:*

$$\bigwedge_{i=1}^{m} d_{i+1} > d_i \wedge \bigwedge_{j=1}^{3m}(d_1 \leq a_j \wedge a_j + k_j < d_{m+1}):$$
$$\operatorname*{\LARGE *}_{i=1}^{m+1} \operatorname{array}(d_i, 0, 0) * \operatorname*{\LARGE *}_{j=1}^{3m} \operatorname{array}(a_j, 1, k_j)$$

Lemma 5.15. *Let $A_{B,S}$ be the symbolic heap given by Definition 4.7. Then we have the Presburger equivalence $\beta(\widetilde{A}_{B,S}, \widetilde{B}_{B,S}) \equiv \gamma(A_{B,S})$.*

Proof (Sketch). Follows from Definitions 4.4, 5.1 and 5.14.

Theorem 5.16. *The biabduction problem for* ASL *is NP-hard, even for (A, B) such that A, B are satisfiable, quantifier-free, and in two-variable form.*

Proof (Sketch). By reduction from the 3-partition problem (see Sect. 4). By Lemmas 4.5, 4.8 and 5.15, there is a complete 3-partition on S w.r.t. bound B iff $\beta(\widetilde{A}_{B,S}, \widetilde{B}_{B,S})$ is satisfiable. Using (Proposition 5.2/Theorem 5.5/Theorem 5.11), this is equivalent to the existence of a biabduction solution for $(\widetilde{A}_{B,S}, \widetilde{B}_{B,S})$.

5.3   Biabduction for ASL with Quantifiers

Here we show two complementary results about biabduction when B contains existential quantifiers. First, if the quantifiers are appropriately restricted, then the biabduction problem is equivalent to the quantifier-free case (thus in NP). If quantifiers are *not* restricted, then the problem becomes Π_2^P-hard [36].

Proposition 5.17. *Let A be quantifier-free, and let B be such that no variable appearing in the RHS of a $\mapsto$ formula is existentially bound. Then, a biabduction instance (A, B) has a solution if and only if $(A, \mathsf{qf}(B))$ has a solution.*

The construction of a suitable heap h in the proof of the nontrivial $(\Rightarrow)$ direction of Proposition 5.17 explains the reasons for our restrictions on quantifiers: the contents of the arrays in h must be chosen different to the data values occurring in the $\mapsto$-formulas in B. If any such values are quantified, this may be impossible. Indeed, $X = Y = \mathsf{emp}$ is a trivial biabduction solution for array$(x, x) * X \models (\exists y.\ x \mapsto y) * Y$, but no solution exists if we remove the quantifier.

In order to obtain the Π_2^P lower bound for biabduction with unrestricted quantifiers, we reduce from the following *colourability* problem, from [1].

2-Round 3-Colourability Problem. *Let $G = (V, E)$ be an undirected graph with n vertices $v_1, \ldots, v_k, v_{k+1}, \ldots v_n$, and let $v_1, v_2, \ldots, v_k$ be its* leaves. *The problem is to decide if every 3-colouring of the leaves can be extended to a 3-colouring of the graph, such that no two adjacent vertices share the same colour.*

Let $c_{i,1}$ denote the colour, 1, 2, or 3, the vertex v_i is marked by. We mark also each edge (v_i, v_j) by $\widetilde{c_{ij}}$, the colour "complementary" to $c_{i,1}$ and $c_{j,1}$.

As for the leaves v_i, we introduce k distinct locations $d_1, \ldots, d_k$ so that the value c_i stored in d_i can be used subsequently to identify the colour $c_{i,1}$ marking v_i, e.g., with the help of $(c_{i,1} - 1 \equiv c_i \pmod 3)$.

We encode the fact that $c_{i,1}$, $c_{j,1}$, and $\widetilde{c_{ij}}$ are distinct by taking $c_{i,1}$, $c_{j,1}$, and $\widetilde{c_{ij}}$ as the addresses, adjusted with a base-offset e_{ij}, for three consecutive cells within a memory chunk of length 3 given by $\mathsf{array}(e_{ij}, 1, 3)$, which forces these colours to form a *permutation* of $(1, 2, 3)$.

Definition 5.18. *An arbitrary 3-colouring of the leaves is encoded with a satisfiable A_G taken as*

$$A_G =_{def} (b = 3): \underset{i=1}{\overset{k}{\text{\Large *}}} \mathsf{array}(d_i, 1, 1) * \underset{(v_i, v_j) \in E}{\text{\Large *}} \mathsf{array}(e_{ij}, 1, 3) .$$

For a fixed b, a perfect b-colouring of the whole G is encoded with B_G taken as

$$\exists \mathbf{z}. \ (\bigwedge_{i=1}^{n} (1 \le c_{i,1} \le b) \wedge \bigwedge_{(v_i, v_j) \in E} (1 \le \widetilde{c_{ij}} \le b) \wedge \bigwedge_{i=1}^{k} (c_{i,1} - 1 \equiv c_i \pmod 3):$$

$$\underset{i=1}{\overset{k}{\text{\Large *}}} d_i \mapsto c_i * \underset{(v_i, v_j) \in E}{\text{\Large *}} \mathsf{array}(e_{ij}, c_{i,1}, c_{i,1}) * \mathsf{array}(e_{ij}, c_{j,1}, c_{j,1}) * \mathsf{array}(e_{ij}, \widetilde{c_{ij}}, \widetilde{c_{ij}})).$$

where the existentially quantified variables $\mathbf{z}$ are all variables occurring in B_G that are not mentioned explicitly in A_G.

B is *satisfiable*, e.g., for a large b, each vertex v_i can be marked by its own colour.

Lemma 5.19. *Let G be a 2-round 3-colouring instance. The biabduction problem (A_G, B_G) has a solution iff there is a winning strategy for the perfect 3-colouring G, where A_G and B_G are the symbolic heaps given by Definition 5.18.*

Theorem 5.20. *The biabduction problem (A, B) for ASL is Π_2^P-hard, even if A is quantifier-free and both A and B are satisfiable.*

Proof. Follows from Lemma 5.19.

6   Entailment

We now focus on *entailment* for ASL. We establish an upper bound of Π_1^{EXP} in the *weak* EXP *hierarchy* [26] via an encoding into Π_2^0 PbA, and a lower bound of Π_2^P [36]. Moreover, quantifier-free entailment is coNP-complete.

Entailment for ASL. *Given symbolic heaps A, B, decide if $A \models B$. A may be considered quantifier-free; similar to Proposition 5.17, the existential quantifiers in B may not mention variables appearing in the RHS of a $\mapsto$-formula.*

The intuition behind our encoding of entailment: There exists a counter-model for $A \models B$ iff there exists a stack s that induces a model for A (captured by $\gamma(A)$ from Sect. 4) and, for every instantiation of the existentially quantified variables in B (say $\mathbf{z}$), one of the following holds under s:

1. the quantifier-free body $\mathsf{qf}(B)$ of B becomes unsatisfiable; or
2. some heap location is covered by an array or pointer in A, but not by any array or pointer in B, or vice versa; or
3. the LHS of some pointer in B is covered by an array in A (thus we can choose the contents of the array different to the contents of the pointer); or
4. a pointer in B is covered by a pointer in A, but their data contents disagree.

Similar to Proposition 5.17, this intuition explains our restriction on quantification in the entailment problem: if we allow quantifiers over the RHS of $\mapsto$ formulas, then item 3 above might or might not be sufficient to construct a counter-model. For example, there is a countermodel for $\mathsf{array}(x, x) \models \exists y. \, y \leq 3 : x \mapsto y$, and for $\mathsf{array}(x, x) \models x \mapsto y$, but not for $\mathsf{array}(x, x) \models \exists y. \, x \mapsto y$.

Definition 6.1. *Let A and B be two $\mapsto$-free symbolic heaps such that*

$$A = \mathsf{array}(a_1, b_1) * \ldots * \mathsf{array}(a_n, b_n)$$
$$B = \mathsf{array}(c_1, d_1) * \ldots * \mathsf{array}(c_m, d_m)$$

Then we define the formula $\phi(A, B)$ of PbA to be

$$\phi(A, B) =_{def} \exists x. \bigvee_{i=1}^{n} a_i \leq x \leq b_i \wedge \bigwedge_{j=1}^{m} (x < c_j) \vee (x > d_j),$$

where x is fresh. We lift ϕ to arbitrary symbolic heaps by ignoring quantifiers and abstracting pointers to arrays using $\lfloor - \rfloor$, i.e., $\phi(A, B) = \phi(\lfloor \mathsf{qf}(A) \rfloor, \lfloor \mathsf{qf}(B) \rfloor)$.

Lemma 6.2. *We can rewrite $\phi(A, B)$ as a quantifier-free formula in polytime.*

Definition 6.3. *Let A and B be symbolic heaps with A quantifier-free:*

$$A = \Pi : \bigstar_{i=1}^{n} \mathsf{array}(a_i, b_i) * \bigstar_{i=1}^{k} t_i \mapsto u_i$$
$$B = \exists \mathbf{z}. \, \Pi' : \bigstar_{j=1}^{m} \mathsf{array}(c_j, d_j) * \bigstar_{j=1}^{\ell} v_j \mapsto w_j$$

where the existentially quantified variables $\mathbf{z}$ are disjoint from all variables in A. We define formulas $\psi_1(A, B)$, $\psi_2(A, B)$ and $\chi(A, B)$ of PbA as follows:

$\psi_1(A, B) = \bigvee_{i=1}^{n} \bigvee_{j=1}^{\ell} a_i \leq v_j \leq b_i$,
$\psi_2(A, B) = \bigvee_{i=1}^{k} \bigvee_{j=1}^{\ell} (t_i = v_j) \wedge (u_i \neq w_j)$, and
$\chi(A, B) = \gamma(A) \wedge \forall \mathbf{z}. (\neg \gamma(\mathsf{qf}(B)) \vee \phi(A, B) \vee \phi(B, A) \vee \psi_1(A, B) \vee \psi_2(A, B))$

where $\gamma(-)$ is given by Definition 4.4, and $\phi(-, -)$ by Definition 6.1.

Lemma 6.4. *For any instance (A, B) of the* ASL *entailment problem above, and for any stack s, we have $s \models \chi(A, B)$ iff $\exists h.\ s, h \models A$ and $s, h \not\models B$.*

Theorem 6.5. *Entailment is in Π_1^{EXP}. If the no. of variables in A, B is fixed, the problem is in Π_2^P, and if B is quantifier-free then the problem is in* coNP.

Proof. Follows from Lemmas 6.2 and 6.4, plus relevant complexity results for Presburger arithmetic [23, 25, 36]. □

In order to obtain the Π_2^P lower bound for entailment, we exhibit a reduction from the same colourability problem as in Sect. 5.3. See [11] for details.

Theorem 6.6. *The entailment problem $A \models B$ is Π_2^P-hard, even when A is quantifier-free, and A, B are satisfiable symbolic heaps in two-variable form. Moreover, the entailment problem is* coNP-*hard even for quantifier-free symbolic heaps in two-variable form.*

Proof. For the general case, we reduce from the 2-round 3-colourability problem, which is Π_2^P-hard [1]. For the quantifier-free case, the upper bound is immediate by Theorem 6.5. For the lower bound, consider the entailment $A_{B,\mathcal{S}} \models x < x :$ emp where $(B, \mathcal{S})$ is a 3-partition instance (see Sect. 4) and $A_{B,\mathcal{S}}$ is the symbolic heap in two-variable form given by Definition 4.7. Using Lemma 4.8, this entailment is valid iff there is *no* complete 3-partition on $\mathcal{S}$ w.r.t. B, a coNP-hard problem. □

In the general case, there is a gap between our upper and lower bounds for entailment: $\Pi_1^{\text{EXP}} = $ coNEXP versus $\Pi_2^P = $ coNP^{NP}, respectively. It is plausible that the lower bound is at least EXP: however, an encoding of, e.g., Π_0^2 PbA in ASL is not straightforward, because our pure formulas are conjunctions rather than arbitrary Boolean combinations of atomic Presburger formulas.

Nevertheless, we note the essential difference between the biabduction and entailment problems for ASL: by Theorem 6.6, entailment is still Π_2^P-hard whereas, by Propositions 5.13 and 5.17, biabduction is in NP.

7   Related Work

Here we briefly survey the literature most closely related to the present paper. A fuller discussion appears in [11].

First, symbolic-heap separation logic over linked lists [4], underpinning the INFER tool [13], has been extensively studied; its satisfiability and entailment problems have been shown to be in PTIME [16], and its abduction problem (where only an "antiframe" X is computed) is known NP-complete [22]. The biabduction problem is studied in [14]. However, this fragment and our ASL are largely disjoint: our arrays cannot be defined in terms of list segments or vice versa, while ASL also employs linear arithmetic rather than simple (dis)equalities. This is also reflected in the differences in their respective complexity bounds.

Moreover, even when arbitrary inductive definitions over symbolic heaps are permitted [9], an area that has received significant recent interest (see e.g. [3,10,12,27,38]) our ASL cannot be encoded in the absence of arithmetic. Very recently, in [24], decidability of satisfiability and entailment was obtained for a fragment of symbolic-heap separation logic with ("linearly compositional") inductive predicates *and* arithmetic. However, ASL cannot be encoded in this fragment, because pointers and data variables belong to disjoint sorts, effectively disallowing pointer arithmetic. A semidecision procedure for satisfiability in symbolic-heap separation logic with inductive definitions and Presburger arithmetic appears in [30]. ASL can be encoded in their logic, but, as far as we can tell, not into the subfragment for which they show satisfiability decidable.

The *iterated separating conjunction* (ISC) [34], a binding operator for expressing various unbounded data structures, was recognised early on as a way of reasoning about arrays. E.g., [31] uses the ISC to reasoning about memory permissions, with the aim of enabling symbolic execution of concurrent array-manipulating program. However, although our array predicate can be expressed using the ISC, we do not know of any existing decision procedures for biabduction, entailment or even satisfiability in such a logic, which may be of high complexity or become undecidable. We note for example that the analysis in [31] requires programs to be fully annotated.

Finally, a significant amount of research effort has previously focused on the verification of array-manipulating programs either via invariant inference and theorem proving, or via abstract interpretation (for instance [2,7,19,20,29,37]). These approaches differ from ours technically, but also in intention. First, the emphasis in these investigations is on data constraints and, thus, tends towards proving general safety properties of programs. Here, we intentionally restrict the language so that we can obtain sound and complete algorithms which can be used for establishing memory safety of programs but not for proving arbitrary safety properties. Second, such approaches are typically whole-program analyses that cannot be used bottom-up (with the possible exception of the non-SL-based [6,18]). In contrast, our focus is on biabduction, one of the key ingredients that makes such a compositional approach possible.

8   Conclusions and Future Work

In this paper, we investigate ASL, a separation logic aimed at compositional memory safety proofs for array-manipulating programs. We give a sound and complete NP algorithm for the crucial *biabduction* problem in this logic, and we show that the problem is NP-hard in the quantifier-free case. In addition, we show that the satisfiability problem for ASL is NP-complete, and entailment is decidable, being coNP-complete for quantifier-free formulas, and at least Π_2^P-hard (perhaps much harder) in general.

An obvious direction for future work is to build an abductive program analysis à la INFER [13] for array programs, using ASL as the assertion language. An outstanding issue is finding biabduction solutions that are as logically weak as possible; our algorithm currently commits to a total ordering of all arrays even if a partial ordering would be sufficient. We believe that, in practice, this could be resolved by refining the notion of a solution seed so that it carries *just* enough information for computing the spatial formulas. A more conceptually interesting problem is how we might assess the quality of logically incomparable solutions.

In addition, a program analysis for ASL will rely not just on biabduction but also on suitable *abstraction* heuristics for discovering loop invariants; this seems an interesting and non-trivial problem for the near future.

Another possible direction for future work is on combining ASL with other fragments of separation logic, such as the linked list fragment, for increased expressivity. We are uncertain whether our techniques would extend naturally to such logics, but we consider this a very interesting area for future study.

References

1. Ajtai, M., Fagin, R., Stockmeyer, L.J.: The closure of monadic NP. J. Comput. Syst. Sci. **60**(3), 660–716 (2000)
2. Alberti, F., Ghilardi, S., Sharygina, N.: Decision procedures for flat array properties. In: Ábrahám, E., Havelund, K. (eds.) TACAS 2014. LNCS, vol. 8413, pp. 15–30. Springer, Heidelberg (2014). doi:10.1007/978-3-642-54862-8_2
3. Antonopoulos, T., Gorogiannis, N., Haase, C., Kanovich, M., Ouaknine, J.: Foundations for decision problems in separation logic with general inductive predicates. In: Muscholl, A. (ed.) FoSSaCS 2014. LNCS, vol. 8412, pp. 411–425. Springer, Heidelberg (2014). doi:10.1007/978-3-642-54830-7_27
4. Berdine, J., Calcagno, C., O'Hearn, P.W.: A decidable fragment of separation logic. In: Lodaya, K., Mahajan, M. (eds.) FSTTCS 2004. LNCS, vol. 3328, pp. 97–109. Springer, Heidelberg (2004). doi:10.1007/978-3-540-30538-5_9
5. Berdine, J., Cook, B., Ishtiaq, S.: SLAYER: memory safety for systems-level code. In: Gopalakrishnan, G., Qadeer, S. (eds.) CAV 2011. LNCS, vol. 6806, pp. 178–183. Springer, Heidelberg (2011). doi:10.1007/978-3-642-22110-1_15
6. Bouajjani, A., Drăgoi, C., Enea, C., Sighireanu, M.: A logic-based framework for reasoning about composite data structures. In: Bravetti, M., Zavattaro, G. (eds.) CONCUR 2009. LNCS, vol. 5710, pp. 178–195. Springer, Heidelberg (2009). doi:10.1007/978-3-642-04081-8_13
7. Bouajjani, A., Drăgoi, C., Enea, C., Sighireanu, M.: Accurate invariant checking for programs manipulating lists and arrays with infinite data. In: Chakraborty, S., Mukund, M. (eds.) ATVA 2012. LNCS, pp. 167–182. Springer, Heidelberg (2012). doi:10.1007/978-3-642-33386-6_14
8. Bradley, A.R., Manna, Z., Sipma, H.B.: What's decidable about arrays? In: Emerson, E.A., Namjoshi, K.S. (eds.) VMCAI 2006. LNCS, vol. 3855, pp. 427–442. Springer, Heidelberg (2005). doi:10.1007/11609773_28
9. Brotherston, J.: Formalised inductive reasoning in the logic of bunched implications. In: Nielson, H.R., Filé, G. (eds.) SAS 2007. LNCS, vol. 4634, pp. 87–103. Springer, Heidelberg (2007). doi:10.1007/978-3-540-74061-2_6
10. Brotherston, J., Fuhs, C., Gorogiannis, N., Navarro Pérez, J.: A decision procedure for satisfiability in separation logic with inductive predicates. In: Proceedings of CSL-LICS, pp. 25:1–25:10. ACM (2014)

11. Brotherston, J., Gorogiannis, N., Kanovich, M.: Biabduction (and related problems) in array separation logic. CoRR abs/1607.01993 (2016). http://arxiv.org/abs/1607.01993

12. Brotherston, J., Gorogiannis, N., Kanovich, M., Rowe, R.: Model checking for symbolic-heap separation logic with inductive predicates. In: Proceedings of POPL-43, pp. 84–96. ACM (2016)

13. Calcagno, C., Distefano, D., Dubreil, J., Gabi, D., Hooimeijer, P., Luca, M., O'Hearn, P., Papakonstantinou, I., Purbrick, J., Rodriguez, D.: Moving fast with software verification. In: Havelund, K., Holzmann, G., Joshi, R. (eds.) NFM 2015. LNCS, vol. 9058, pp. 3–11. Springer, Cham (2015). doi:10.1007/978-3-319-17524-9_1

14. Calcagno, C., Distefano, D., O'Hearn, P.W., Yang, H.: Compositional shape analysis by means of bi-abduction. J. ACM 58(6) (2011)

15. Chin, W.N., David, C., Nguyen, H.H., Qin, S.: Automated verification of shape, size and bag properties via user-defined predicates in separation logic. Sci. Comp. Prog. 77(9), 1006–1036 (2012)

16. Cook, B., Haase, C., Ouaknine, J., Parkinson, M., Worrell, J.: Tractable reasoning in a fragment of separation logic. In: Katoen, J.-P., König, B. (eds.) CONCUR 2011. LNCS, vol. 6901, pp. 235–249. Springer, Heidelberg (2011). doi:10.1007/978-3-642-23217-6_16

17. Cormen, T.H., Leiserson, C.E., Rivest, R.L., Stein, C.: Introduction to Algorithms, 3rd edn. MIT Press, Cambridge (2009)

18. Cousot, P., Cousot, R., Fähndrich, M., Logozzo, F.: Automatic inference of necessary preconditions. In: Giacobazzi, R., Berdine, J., Mastroeni, I. (eds.) VMCAI 2013. LNCS, vol. 7737, pp. 128–148. Springer, Heidelberg (2013). doi:10.1007/978-3-642-35873-9_10

19. Cousot, P., Cousot, R., Logozzo, F.: A parametric segmentation functor for fully automatic and scalable array content analysis. In: Proceedings of POPL-38, pp. 105–118. ACM (2011)

20. Dillig, I., Dillig, T., Aiken, A.: Fluid updates: beyond strong vs. weak updates. In: Gordon, A.D. (ed.) ESOP 2010. LNCS, vol. 6012, pp. 246–266. Springer, Heidelberg (2010). doi:10.1007/978-3-642-11957-6_14

21. Garey, M.R., Johnson, D.S.: Computers and Intractability: A Guide to the Theory of NP-Completeness. W.H. Freeman, New York (1979)

22. Gorogiannis, N., Kanovich, M., O'Hearn, P.W.: The complexity of abduction for separated heap abstractions. In: Yahav, E. (ed.) SAS 2011. LNCS, vol. 6887, pp. 25–42. Springer, Heidelberg (2011). doi:10.1007/978-3-642-23702-7_7

23. Grädel, E.: Subclasses of Presburger arithmetic and the polynomial-time hierarchy. Theor. Comput. Sci. 56, 289–301 (1988)

24. Gu, X., Chen, T., Wu, Z.: A complete decision procedure for linearly compositional separation logic with data constraints. In: Olivetti, N., Tiwari, A. (eds.) IJCAR 2016. LNCS, vol. 9706, pp. 532–549. Springer, Cham (2016). doi:10.1007/978-3-319-40229-1_36

25. Haase, C.: Subclasses of Presburger arithmetic and the weak EXP hierarchy. In: Proceedings of CSL-LICS, pp. 47:1–47:10. ACM (2014)

26. Hartmanis, J., Immerman, N., Sewelson, V.: Sparse sets in NP-P: EXPTIME versus NEXPTIME. Inform. Control 65(2), 158–181 (1985)

27. Iosif, R., Rogalewicz, A., Simacek, J.: The tree width of separation logic with recursive definitions. In: Bonacina, M.P. (ed.) CADE 2013. LNCS, vol. 7898, pp. 21–38. Springer, Heidelberg (2013). doi:10.1007/978-3-642-38574-2_2

28. Jacobs, B., Smans, J., Philippaerts, P., Vogels, F., Penninckx, W., Piessens, F.: VeriFast: a powerful, sound, predictable, fast verifier for C and Java. In: Bobaru, M., Havelund, K., Holzmann, G.J., Joshi, R. (eds.) NFM 2011. LNCS, vol. 6617, pp. 41–55. Springer, Heidelberg (2011). doi:10.1007/978-3-642-20398-5_4

29. Kovács, L., Voronkov, A.: Finding loop invariants for programs over arrays using a theorem prover. In: Chechik, M., Wirsing, M. (eds.) FASE 2009. LNCS, vol. 5503, pp. 470–485. Springer, Heidelberg (2009). doi:10.1007/978-3-642-00593-0_33

30. Le, Q.L., Sun, J., Chin, W.-N.: Satisfiability modulo heap-based programs. In: Chaudhuri, S., Farzan, A. (eds.) CAV 2016. LNCS, vol. 9779, pp. 382–404. Springer, Cham (2016). doi:10.1007/978-3-319-41528-4_21

31. Müller, P., Schwerhoff, M., Summers., A.J.: Automatic verification of iterated separating conjunctions using symbolic execution. In: Proceedings of CAV-28 (2016, to appear)

32. O'Hearn, P.W.: Resources, concurrency and local reasoning. Theor. Comput. Sci. **375**(1–3), 271–307 (2007)

33. O'Hearn, P.W., Yang, H., Reynolds, J.C.: Separation and information hiding. In: Proceedings of POPL-31, pp. 268–280. ACM (2004)

34. Reynolds, J.C.: Separation logic: a logic for shared mutable data structures. In: Proceedings of LICS-17, pp. 55–74. IEEE (2002)

35. Scarpellini, B.: Complexity of subcases of Presburger arithmetic. Trans. Am. Math. Soc. **284**(1), 203–218 (1984)

36. Stockmeyer, L.J.: The polynomial-time hierarchy. Theor. Comput. Sci. **3**, 1–22 (1977)

37. Ströder, T., Giesl, J., Brockschmidt, M., Frohn, F., Fuhs, C., Hensel, J., Schneider-Kamp, P., Aschermann, C.: Automatically proving termination and memory safety for programs with pointer arithmetic. J. Autom. Reasoning **58**(1), 33–65 (2017)

38. Tatsuta, M., Kimura, D.: Separation logic with monadic inductive definitions and implicit existentials. In: Feng, X., Park, S. (eds.) APLAS 2015. LNCS, vol. 9458, pp. 69–89. Springer, Cham (2015). doi:10.1007/978-3-319-26529-2_5

39. Yang, H., O'Hearn, P.W.: A semantic basis for local reasoning. In: Nielsen, M., Engberg, U. (eds.) FoSSaCS 2002. LNCS, vol. 2303, pp. 402–416. Springer, Heidelberg (2002). doi:10.1007/3-540-45931-6_28

Automatically Verifying Temporal Properties of Pointer Programs with Cyclic Proof

Gadi Tellez$^{(\boxtimes)}$ and James Brotherston

Department of Computer Science, University College London, London, UK
`gadi.tellez.13@ucl.ac.uk`

Abstract. We propose a deductive reasoning approach to the automatic verification of temporal properties of pointer programs, based on *cyclic proof*. We present a proof system whose judgements express that a program has a certain temporal property over memory state assertions in *separation logic*, and whose rules operate directly on the temporal modalities as well as symbolically executing programs. Cyclic proofs in our system are, as usual, finite proof graphs subject to a natural, decidable soundness condition, encoding a form of proof by infinite descent.

We present a proof system tailored to proving CTL properties of nondeterministic pointer programs, and then adapt this system to handle *fair* execution conditions. We show both systems to be sound, and provide an implementation of each in the CYCLIST theorem prover, yielding an automated tool that is capable of automatically discovering proofs of (fair) temporal properties of heap-aware programs. Experimental evaluation of our tool indicates that our approach is viable, and offers an interesting alternative to traditional model checking techniques.

1 Introduction

Program verification can be described as the problem of deciding whether a given program exhibits a desired behaviour, often called its *specification*. Temporal logic, in its various flavours [24] is a very popular and widely studied specification formalism due to its relative simplicity and expressive power: a wide variety of *safety* ("something bad cannot happen") and *liveness* properties ("something good eventually happens") can be captured [20].

Historically, perhaps the most popular approach to verify temporal properties of programs has been *model checking*: one first builds an abstract model that overapproximates all possible executions of the program, and then checks that the desired temporal property holds for this model (see e.g. [10,12,15]). However, this approach has been applied mainly to integer programs; the situation for memory-aware programs over heap data structures becomes significantly more challenging, mainly because of the difficulties in constructing suitable abstract models. One possible approach is simply to translate such heap-aware programs into integer variables, in such a way that properties such as memory safety or termination of the original program follows from a corresponding property in

© Springer International Publishing AG 2017
L. de Moura (Ed.): CADE 2017, LNAI 10395, pp. 491–508, 2017.
DOI: 10.1007/978-3-319-63046-5_30

its integer translation [12,15,22]. However, for more general temporal properties, this technique might produce unsound results. In general, it is not clear whether it is feasible to provide suitable translations from heap to integer programs for any temporal property; in particular, numerical abstraction of heap programs often removes important information about the exact shape of heap data structures, which might be needed to prove some temporal properties.

Example 1. *Consider a "server" program that, given an acyclic linked list with head pointer x, nondeterministically alternates between adding an arbitrary number of "job requests" to the head of the list and removing all requests in the list:*

```
while(true){
  if(*) {
    while(x!=nil) { temp:=x.next; free(x); x:=temp; }
  } else {
    while(*) { y:=new(); y.next:=x; x:=y; }
  }
}
```

Memory safety of this program can be proven using a simple numeric abstraction recording emptiness/nonemptiness of the list. Proving instead that it is always possible for the heap to become empty, expressed in CTL as AGEF(emp), requires a finer abstraction, recording the length of the list. However, such an abstraction is still not sufficient to prove the property that the heap is always a nil-terminating acyclic list from x to nil, expressed in CTL as AG(ls(x, nil)) (where ls is the standard list segment predicate of separation logic [26]), because the information about acyclicity is lost.

Thus, although it is often possible to provide numeric abstractions to suit *specific* programs and temporal properties, it is not clear that this is so for *arbitrary* programs and properties.

In this paper, we instead approach the above problem via the main (perhaps less fashionable) alternative to model checking, namely the *direct deductive verification* of pointer programs. We formulate a *cyclic* proof system manipulating temporal judgements about programs, and employ automatic proof search in this system to verify that a program has a given temporal property. Given some fixed program, the judgements of our system express a temporal property of the program when started from any state satisfying a precondition written in a fragment of *separation logic*, a well-known language for describing heap memory [26]. The core of the proof system is a set of *symbolic execution* rules that simulate program execution steps. To handle the fact that symbolic execution can in general be applied *ad infinitum*, we employ *cyclic proof* [6,7,9,29], in which proofs are finite cyclic graphs subject to a global soundness condition. Using this approach, we are frequently able to verify temporal properties of heap programs in an automatic and sound way without the need of abstractions or program translations. Moreover, our analysis has the added benefit of producing independently checkable proof objects.

Our proof system is tailored to CTL program properties over separation logic assertions; subsequently, we show how to adapt this system to handle *fairness* constraints, where nondeterministic branching may not unfairly favour one branch over another. We have also adapted our system to (fair) LTL properties, though we do not present this adaptation in this paper due to space constraints.

We provide an implementation of our proof system as an automated verification tool within the CYCLIST theorem proving framework [9], and evaluate its performance on a range of examples. The source code, benchmark and executable binaries of the implementation are publicly available online [1]. Our tool is able to discover surprisingly complex cyclic proofs of temporal properties with times often in the millisecond range. Practically speaking, the advantages and disadvantages of our approach are entirely typical of deductive verification: on the one hand, we do not need to employ abstraction or program translation, and we guarantee soundness; on the other hand, our algorithms might fail to terminate, and (at least currently) we do not provide counterexamples in case of failure. Thus we believe our approach should be understood as a useful complement to, rather than a replacement for, model checking.

The remainder of this paper is structured as follows. Section 2 introduces our programming language, the memory state assertion language, and temporal (CTL) assertions over these. Section 3 introduces our proof system for verifying temporal properties of programs, and Sect. 4 modifies this system to account for fair program executions. Section 5 presents our implementation and experimental evaluation, Sect. 6 discusses related work and Sect. 7 concludes.

2 Programs and Assertions

In this section we introduce our programming language, our language of assertions about *memory states* (based on a fragment of separation logic) and our language for expressing *temporal properties* of programs, given by CTL over memory assertions.

Programming language. We use a simple language of while programs with pointers and (de)allocation, but without procedures. We assume a countably infinite set Var of *variables* and a first-order language of *expressions* over Var. *Branching conditions* B and *commands* C are given by the following grammar:

$$B ::= E = E \mid E \neq E \mid *$$
$$C ::= \mathrm{x} := [E] \mid [E] := E \mid \mathrm{x} := \mathbf{alloc}() \mid \mathbf{free}(E) \mid \mathrm{x} := E \mid$$
$$\quad \mathbf{skip} \mid \mathbf{if}\ B\ \mathbf{then}\ C\ \mathbf{else}\ C\ \mathbf{fi} \mid \mathbf{while}\ B\ \mathbf{do}\ C\ \mathbf{od} \mid C; C \mid \epsilon$$

where $x \in$ Var and E ranges over expressions. We write ϵ for the empty command, $*$ for a nondeterministic condition, and $[E]$ for dereferencing of expression E.

We define the semantics of the language in a *stack-and-heap model* employing heaps of records. We fix a set Val of *values*, and a set Loc $\subset$ Val of addressable memory *locations*. A *stack* is a map $s :$ Var $\rightarrow$ Val from variables to values. The semantics $[\![E]\!]s$ of expression E under stack s is standard; in particular, $[\![x]\!]s = s(x)$ for $x \in$ Var. We extend stacks pointwise to act on tuples of terms. A *heap* is a partial, finite-domain function $h :$ Loc $\rightharpoonup_{\mathrm{fin}}$ (Val List), mapping finitely many memory locations to *records*, i.e. arbitrary-length tuples of values; we write dom(h) for the set of locations on which h is defined. We write e for the *empty heap*, and $\uplus$ to denote composition of *domain-disjoint* heaps: $h_1 \uplus h_2$ is the union of h_1 and h_2 when dom(h_1) $\cap$ dom(h_2) $= \varnothing$ (and undefined otherwise). If f is a stack or a heap then we write $f[x \mapsto v]$ for the stack or heap defined as f except that $f[x \mapsto v](x) = v$. A paired stack and heap, (s, h), is called a *(memory) state*.

A *(program) configuration* γ is a triple $\langle C, s, h \rangle$ where C is a command, s a stack and h a heap. If γ is a configuration, we write γ_C, γ_s, and γ_h respectively for its first, second and third components. A configuration γ is called *final* if $\gamma_C = \epsilon$. The small-step operational semantics of programs is given by a binary relation $\rightsquigarrow$ on program configurations, where $\gamma \rightsquigarrow \gamma'$ holds if the execution of the command γ_C in the state (γ_s, γ_h) can result in the program configuration γ' in one step. We write $\rightsquigarrow^*$ for the reflexive-transitive closure of $\rightsquigarrow$. The special configuration fault is used to denote a memory fault, e.g., if a command tries to access non-allocated memory. For brevity, we omit the operational semantics here, since it is essentially standard.

An *execution path* is a (maximally finite or infinite) sequence $(\gamma_i)_{i \geq 0}$ of configurations such that $\gamma_i \rightsquigarrow \gamma_{i+1}$ for all $i \geq 0$. If π is a path, then we write π_i for the ith element of π. A path π *starts from* configuration γ if $\pi_0 = \gamma$.

Remark 1. In temporal program verification, it is relatively common to consider all program execution paths to be infinite, and all temporal properties to quantify over infinite paths. This can be achieved either (i) by modifying programs to contain an infinite loop at every exit point, or (ii) by modifying the operational semantics so that final configurations loop infinitely (i.e. $\langle \epsilon, s, h \rangle \rightsquigarrow \langle \epsilon, s, h \rangle$).

Here, instead, our temporal assertions quantify over paths that are either infinite or else maximally finite. This has the same effect as directly modifying programs or their operational semantics, but seems to us slightly cleaner.

Memory state assertions. We express properties of memory states (s, h) using a standard *symbolic-heap* fragment of separation logic (cf. [2]) extended with user-defined (inductive) predicates, typically needed to express data structures in the memory. We omit the schema for inductive predicates and their interpretations here, since they are identical to those used, e.g., in [7–9,27].

Definition 1. *A symbolic heap is given by a disjunction of assertions each of the form $\Pi : \Sigma$, where Π is a finite set of pure formulas of the form $E = E$ or $E \neq E$, and Σ is a spatial formula given by the following grammar:*

$$\Sigma ::= \mathsf{emp} \mid E \mapsto \mathbf{E} \mid \Sigma * \Sigma \mid \Psi(\mathbf{E}),$$

where E ranges over expressions, $\mathbf{E}$ over tuples of expressions and Ψ over predicate symbols (of arity matching the length of $\mathbf{E}$ in $\Psi(\mathbf{E})$).

Definition 2. *Given a state s, h and symbolic heap $\Pi : \Sigma$, we write $s, h \models \Pi : \Sigma$ if $s, h \models \varpi$ for all pure formulas $\varpi \in \Pi$, and $s, h \models \Sigma$, where the relation $s, h \models A$ between states and formulas is defined by*

$$s, h \models E_1 = E_2 \quad\Leftrightarrow\quad \llbracket E_1 \rrbracket s = \llbracket E_2 \rrbracket s$$
$$s, h \models E_1 \neq E_2 \quad\Leftrightarrow\quad \llbracket E_1 \rrbracket s \neq \llbracket E_2 \rrbracket s$$
$$s, h \models \mathsf{emp} \quad\Leftrightarrow\quad \mathrm{dom}(h) = \varnothing$$
$$s, h \models E \mapsto \mathbf{E} \quad\Leftrightarrow\quad \mathrm{dom}(h) = \{\llbracket E \rrbracket s\} \ and \ h(\llbracket E \rrbracket s) = \llbracket \mathbf{E} \rrbracket s$$
$$s, h \models \Psi(\mathbf{E}) \quad\Leftrightarrow\quad (\llbracket \mathbf{E} \rrbracket s, h) \in \llbracket \Psi \rrbracket$$
$$s, h \models \Sigma_1 * \Sigma_2 \quad\Leftrightarrow\quad h = h_1 \uplus h_2 \ and \ s, h_1 \models \Sigma_1 \ and \ s, h_2 \models \Sigma_2$$
$$s, h \models \Omega_1 \vee \Omega_2 \quad\Leftrightarrow\quad s, h \models \Omega_1 \ or \ s, h \models \Omega_2$$

Note that the semantics of a predicate symbol, $\llbracket \Psi \rrbracket \subseteq$ Val List $\times$ Heaps, is typically obtained from an inductive definition *of Ψ in a standard way (see e.g. [6]).*

Temporal assertions. We describe temporal properties of our programs using *temporal assertions*, built from the memory state assertions given above using standard operators of *computation tree logic* (CTL) [11], where the temporal operators quantify over execution paths from a given configuration.

Definition 3. *CTL assertions are described by the grammar:*

$$\varphi ::= P \mid \mathsf{error} \mid \mathsf{final} \mid \varphi \wedge \varphi \mid \varphi \vee \varphi \mid \Diamond \varphi \mid \Box \varphi$$
$$\mid EF\varphi \mid AF\varphi \mid EG\varphi \mid AG\varphi \mid E(\varphi U \varphi) \mid A(\varphi U \varphi)$$

where P ranges over memory state assertions (Definition 1).

Note that final and error denote final, respectively faulting configurations.

Definition 4. *A configuration γ is a* model *of the CTL assertion φ if the relation $\gamma \models \varphi$ holds, defined by structural induction as follows:*

$$\gamma \models P \quad\Leftrightarrow\quad \gamma_s, \gamma_h \models P$$
$$\gamma \models \mathsf{error} \quad\Leftrightarrow\quad \gamma = \mathsf{fault}$$
$$\gamma \models \mathsf{final} \quad\Leftrightarrow\quad \gamma_C = \epsilon$$
$$\gamma \models \varphi_1 \wedge \varphi_2 \quad\Leftrightarrow\quad \gamma \models \varphi_1 \ and \ \gamma \models \varphi_2$$
$$\gamma \models \varphi_1 \vee \varphi_2 \quad\Leftrightarrow\quad \gamma \models \varphi_1 \ or \ \gamma \models \varphi_2$$
$$\gamma \models \Diamond \varphi \quad\Leftrightarrow\quad \exists \gamma'. \ \gamma \rightsquigarrow \gamma' \ and \ \gamma' \models \varphi$$
$$\gamma \models \Box \varphi \quad\Leftrightarrow\quad \forall \gamma'. \ \gamma \rightsquigarrow \gamma' \ implies \ \gamma' \models \varphi$$
$$\gamma \models EF\varphi \quad\Leftrightarrow\quad \exists \gamma'. \ \gamma \rightsquigarrow^* \gamma' \ and \ \gamma' \models \varphi$$
$$\gamma \models AF\varphi \quad\Leftrightarrow\quad \forall \pi \ starting \ from \ \gamma. \ \exists \gamma' \in \pi. \gamma' \models \varphi$$
$$\gamma \models EG\varphi \quad\Leftrightarrow\quad \exists \pi \ starting \ from \ \gamma. \ \forall \gamma' \in \pi. \gamma' \models \varphi$$
$$\gamma \models AG\varphi \quad\Leftrightarrow\quad \forall \gamma'. \ if \ \gamma \rightsquigarrow^* \gamma' \ then \ \gamma' \models \varphi$$
$$\gamma \models E(\varphi_1 U \varphi_2) \quad\Leftrightarrow\quad \exists \pi \ starting \ from \ \gamma. \ \exists i \geq 0. \ \pi_i \models \varphi_2 \ and \ \forall j : 0 \leq j < i. \pi_j \models \varphi_1$$
$$\gamma \models A(\varphi_1 U \varphi_2) \quad\Leftrightarrow\quad \forall \pi \ starting \ from \ \gamma. \ \exists i \geq 0. \ \pi_i \models \varphi_2 \ and \ \forall j : 0 \leq j < i. \pi_j \models \varphi_1$$

Judgements in our system are given by $P \vdash C : \varphi$, where P is a symbolic heap, C is a command sequence and φ is a temporal assertion.

Definition 5 (Validity). *A CTL judgement $P \vdash C : \varphi$ is valid if and only if, for all memory states (s, h) such that $s, h \models P$, we have $\langle C, s, h \rangle \models \varphi$.*

3   A Cyclic Proof System for Verifying CTL Properties

In this section, we present a cyclic proof system for establishing the validity of our CTL judgements on programs, as described in the previous section.

Our proof rules for CTL judgements are shown in Fig. 1. The *symbolic execution* rules for commands are adapted from those in the proof system for program termination in [7], accounting for whether a diamond $\Diamond$ or box $\square$ property is being established. The dichotomy between $\Diamond$ and $\square$ is only visible for the non-deterministic components of a program. In the specific case of our language, the nondeterministic constructs are (i) nondeterministic while; (ii) nondetreministic if; and (iii) memory allocation; it is only for these constructs that we need a specific rule for each case, as shown in our symbolic execution rules. Incidentally, the difference between E properties and A properties is basically the same as the difference between $\Diamond$ and $\square$, but extended to execution paths rather than individual steps.

We also introduce *faulting execution rules* to allow us to prove that a program faults. The logical rules comprise standard rules for the logical connectives and standard unfolding rules for the temporal operators and inductive predicates in memory assertions. For brevity, we omit here the somewhat complex unfolding rule for inductive predicates, but similar rules can be found in, e.g., [7–9,27].

Proofs in our system are *cyclic proofs*: standard derivation trees in which open subgoals can be closed either by applying an axiom or by forming a *back-link* to an identical interior node. To ensure that such structures correspond to sound proofs, a global soundness condition is imposed. The following definitions, adaptations of similar notions in e.g. [6–9,27], formalise this notion.

Definition 6 (Pre-proof). *A leaf of a derivation tree is called* open *if it is not the conclusion of an axiom. A* pre-proof *is a pair* $\mathcal{P} = (\mathcal{D}, \mathcal{L})$*, where* $\mathcal{D}$ *is a finite derivation tree constructed according to the proof rules and* $\mathcal{L}$ *is a back-link function assigning to every open leaf of* $\mathcal{D}$ *a* companion: *an interior node of* $\mathcal{D}$ *labelled by an identical proof judgement.*

A pre-proof $\mathcal{P} = (\mathcal{D}, \mathcal{L})$ can be seen as a finite cyclic graph by identifying each open leaf of $\mathcal{D}$ with its companion. A *path in* $\mathcal{P}$ is then a path in this graph. It is easy to see that a path in a pre-proof corresponds to one or more paths in the execution of a program, interleaved with logical inferences.

To qualify as a proof, a cyclic pre-proof must satisfy a global soundness condition, defined using the notion of a *trace* along a path in a pre-proof.

Definition 7 (Trace). *Let* $(J_i = P_i \vdash C_i \colon \varphi_i)_{i \geq 0}$ *be a path in a pre-proof* $\mathcal{P}$*. The sequence of temporal formulas along the path,* $(\varphi_i)_{i \geq 0}$*, is a* $\square$*-trace (*$\Diamond$*-trace) following that path if there exists a formula* ψ *such that, for all* $i \geq 0$:

- *the formula* φ_i *is of the form* $AG\psi$ *(*$EG\psi$*) or* $\square AG\psi$ *(*$\Diamond EG\psi$*); and*
- $\varphi_i = \varphi_{i+1}$ *whenever* J_i *is the conclusion of the consequence rule (Cons).*

We say that a trace progresses *whenever a symbolic execution rule is applied. A trace is* infinitely progressing *if it progresses at infinitely many points.*

Symbolic execution rules:

$$\frac{P \vdash C : \varphi}{P \vdash (\mathbf{skip} \; ; \; C) : \bigcirc\varphi} \; \text{(Skip)} \qquad\qquad \frac{x = E[x'/x],\, P[x'/x] \vdash C : \varphi}{P \vdash (x := E \; ; \; C) : \bigcirc\varphi} \; \text{(Assign)}$$

$$\frac{x = E'[x'/x],\, (P * E \mapsto E')[x'/x] \vdash C : \varphi}{P * E \mapsto E' \vdash (x := [E] \; ; \; C) : \bigcirc\varphi} \; \text{(Read)} \qquad \frac{P * E \mapsto E' \vdash C : \varphi}{P * E \mapsto - \vdash ([E] := E' \; ; \; C) : \bigcirc\varphi} \; \text{(Write)}$$

$$\frac{P, B \vdash C_1 \; ; \; C_3 : \varphi \quad P, \neg B \vdash C_2 \; ; \; C_3 : \varphi}{P \vdash (\mathbf{if}\ B\ \mathbf{then}\ C_1\ \mathbf{else}\ C_2\ \mathbf{fi} \; ; \; C_3) : \bigcirc\varphi} \; \text{(If)} \qquad \frac{P \vdash C_1 \; ; \; C_3 : \varphi \quad P \vdash C_2 \; ; \; C_3 : \varphi}{P \vdash (\mathbf{if} * \mathbf{then}\ C_1\ \mathbf{else}\ C_2\ \mathbf{fi} \; ; \; C_3) : \Box\varphi} \; \text{(If*$\Box$)}$$

$$\frac{P \vdash C_1 \; ; \; C_3 : \varphi}{P \vdash (\mathbf{if} * \mathbf{then}\ C_1\ \mathbf{else}\ C_2\ \mathbf{fi} \; ; \; C_3) : \Diamond\varphi} \; \text{(If* $\Diamond$1)} \qquad \frac{P \vdash C_2 \; ; \; C_3 : \varphi}{P \vdash (\mathbf{if} * \mathbf{then}\ C_1\ \mathbf{else}\ C_2\ \mathbf{fi} \; ; \; C_3) : \Diamond\varphi} \; \text{(If* $\Diamond$2)}$$

$$\frac{P \vdash (C_1 \; ; \; \mathbf{while} * \mathbf{do}\ C_1\ \mathbf{od} \; ; \; C_2) : \varphi}{P \vdash (\mathbf{while} * \mathbf{do}\ C_1\ \mathbf{od} \; ; \; C_2) : \Diamond\varphi} \; \text{(Wh* $\Diamond$1)} \qquad \frac{P \vdash C_2 : \varphi}{P \vdash (\mathbf{while} * \mathbf{do}\ C_1\ \mathbf{od} \; ; \; C_2) : \Diamond\varphi} \; \text{(Wh* $\Diamond$2)}$$

$$\frac{P \vdash (C_1 \; ; \; \mathbf{while} * \mathbf{do}\ C_1\ \mathbf{od} \; ; \; C_2) : \varphi \quad P \vdash C_2 : \varphi}{P \vdash (\mathbf{while} * \mathbf{do}\ C_1\ \mathbf{od} \; ; \; C_2) : \Box\varphi} \; \text{(Wh*$\Box$)} \qquad \frac{P \vdash C : \varphi}{P * E \mapsto - \vdash (\mathbf{free}(E) \; ; \; C) : \bigcirc\varphi} \; \text{(Free)}$$

$$\frac{P[x'/x] * x \mapsto v \vdash C : \varphi}{P \vdash (x := alloc() \; ; \; C) : \Box\varphi} \; v\ \text{fresh (Alloc$\Box$)} \qquad \frac{P[x'/x] * x \mapsto v \vdash C : \varphi \quad v \in \mathrm{Val}}{P \vdash (x := alloc() \; ; \; C) : \Diamond\varphi} \; \text{(Alloc$\Diamond$)}$$

$$\frac{P, B \vdash (C_1 \; ; \; \mathbf{while}\ B\ \mathbf{do}\ C_1\ \mathbf{od} \; ; \; C_2) : \varphi \quad P, \neg B \vdash C_2 : \varphi}{P \vdash (\mathbf{while}\ B\ \mathbf{do}\ C_1\ \mathbf{od} \; ; \; C_2) : \bigcirc\varphi} \; \text{(Wh)} \qquad \frac{}{P \vdash \epsilon : \mathbf{final}} \; \text{(Final)}$$

Faulting execution rules:

$$\frac{P * E \mapsto \mathbf{nil} \not\models \bot}{P \vdash (x := [E] \; ; \; C) : \mathbf{error}} \; \text{(R$\bot$)} \qquad \frac{P * E \mapsto \mathbf{nil} \not\models \bot}{P \vdash ([E] := E' \; ; \; C) : \mathbf{error}} \; \text{(W$\bot$)} \qquad \frac{P * E \mapsto \mathbf{nil} \not\models \bot}{P \vdash (\mathbf{free}(E) \; ; \; C) : \mathbf{error}} \; \text{(Free$\bot$)}$$

Logical rules:

$$\frac{P \models Q}{P \vdash C : Q} \; \text{(Check)} \qquad \frac{}{\bot \vdash C : \varphi} \; \text{(Ex.Falso)} \qquad \frac{\Omega_1 \vdash C : \varphi \quad \Omega_2 \vdash C : \varphi}{\Omega_1 \vee \Omega_2 \vdash C : \varphi} \; \text{(Split)}$$

$$\frac{P \vdash C : \varphi \quad x \notin \mathrm{vars}(C)}{P[E/x] \vdash C : \varphi[E/x]} \; \text{(Subst)} \qquad \frac{P \vdash C : \varphi_1 \quad P \vdash C : \varphi_2}{P \vdash C : \varphi_1 \wedge \varphi_2} \; \text{(Conj)} \qquad \frac{P \vdash C : \varphi_i \quad i \in \{1,2\}}{P \vdash C : \varphi_1 \vee \varphi_2} \; \text{($\vee$)}$$

$$\frac{P \vdash C : \varphi \vee \Diamond EF\varphi}{P \vdash C : EF\varphi} \; \text{(EF)} \qquad \frac{P \vdash C : \varphi \quad P \vdash C : \Diamond EG\varphi}{P \vdash C : EG\varphi} \; \text{(EG)} \qquad \frac{P \vdash C : \psi \vee (\varphi \wedge \Diamond E(\varphi U \psi))}{P \vdash C : E(\varphi U \psi)} \; \text{(EU)}$$

$$\frac{P \vdash C : \varphi \vee \Box AF\varphi}{P \vdash C : AF\varphi} \; \text{(AF)} \qquad \frac{P \vdash C : \varphi \quad P \vdash C : \Box AG\varphi}{P \vdash C : AG\varphi} \; \text{(AG)} \qquad \frac{P \vdash C : \psi \vee (\varphi \wedge \Box A(\varphi U \psi))}{P \vdash C : A(\varphi U \psi)} \; \text{(AU)}$$

$$\frac{P \vdash \epsilon : \varphi}{P \vdash \epsilon : EG\varphi} \; \text{(EG-Finite)} \qquad \frac{P \vdash Q \quad Q \vdash C : \psi \quad \psi \vdash \varphi}{P \vdash C : \varphi} \; \text{(Cons)}$$

Fig. 1. Proof rules for CTL judgements. We write $\bigcirc\varphi$ to mean "either $\Box\varphi$ or $\Diamond\varphi$".

We also take account of precondition traces arising from inductive predicates in the precondition, as employed in [7]. Roughly speaking, a precondition trace tracks an occurrence of an inductive predicate in the preconditions of the judgements along the path, progressing whenever the predicate occurrence is unfolded. Again, see [7–9, 27] for similar notions.

Definition 8 (Proof). A pre-proof $\mathcal{P}$ is a proof if it satisfies the following global soundness condition: for every infinite path $(P_i \vdash C_i : \varphi_i)_{i \geq 0}$ in $\mathcal{P}$, there *is an infinitely progressing □-trace, ◇-trace or precondition trace following some tail $(P_i \vdash C_i : \varphi_i)_{i \geq n}$ of the path.*

Example 2. *Consider the server-like program in Example 1 in the Introduction. We can show that, given that the heap is initially a linked list from* x *to* nil, *it is always possible for the heap to become empty at any point during program execution. Writing* C *for our server program, this property is expressed as the judgement* $ls(x, nil) \vdash C : AGEF(\text{emp})$.

Figure 2 shows an outline cyclic proof of this judgement in our system (we suppress the internal judgements for space reasons, but show the cycle structure and rule applications). Note that the back-links depicted in blue do not form infinite loops as they all point to a companion that eventually leads to a (Check) axiom. The red back-links do give rise to infinite paths; one can see that the pre-proof qualifies as a valid cyclic proof since there is an infinitely progressing □-trace along every infinite path.

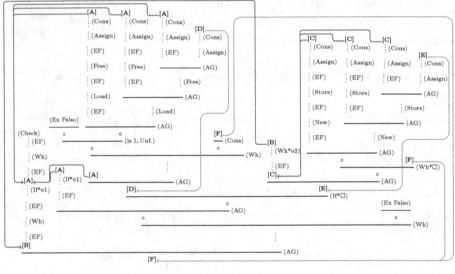

$[A] = ls(x, nil) \vdash \text{while}\, x \neq nil\, \text{do} \dots \text{od} : EF(\text{emp})$

$[B] = ls(x, nil) \vdash \text{while}\, x = x\, \text{do} \dots \text{od} : EF(\text{emp})$

$[C] = ls(x, nil) \vdash \text{while}\, *\, \text{do} \dots \text{od} : EF(\text{emp})$

$[D] = ls(x, nil) \vdash \text{while}\, x \neq nil\, \text{do} \dots \text{od} : AGEF(\text{emp})$

$[E] = ls(x, nil) \vdash \text{while}\, *\, \text{do} \dots \text{od} : AGEF(\text{emp})$

$[F] = ls(x, nil) \vdash \text{while}\, x = x\, \text{do} \dots \text{od} : AGEF(\text{emp})$

Fig. 2. Single threaded monolithic server example (Color figure online)

We now show that our proof system is sound.

Lemma 1. *Let* $J = (P \vdash C : \varphi)$ *be the conclusion of a proof rule R. If J is invalid under* (s, h), *then there exists a premise of the rule* $J' = P' \vdash C' : \varphi'$ *and a model* (s', h') *such that J' is not valid under* (s', h') *and, furthermore,*

1. *if there is a □-trace* (φ, φ') *following the edge* (J, J') *then, letting* ψ *be the unique subformula of* φ *given by Definition 7, there is a configuration* γ *such that* $\gamma \not\models \psi$, *and the finite execution path* $\pi' = \langle C', s', h' \rangle \ldots \gamma$ *is well-defined and a subpath of* $\pi = \langle C, s, h \rangle \ldots \gamma$. *Therefore* $\mathrm{length}(\pi') \leq \mathrm{length}(\pi)$. *Moreover,* $\mathrm{length}(\pi) < \mathrm{length}(\pi')$ *when* R *is a symbolic execution rule.*

2. *if there is a* $\Diamond$-trace (φ, φ') *following the edge* (J, J') *then, letting* ψ *be the unique subformula of* φ *given by Definition 7, there is a smallest finite execution tree* κ *with root* $\langle C, s, h \rangle$, *each of whose leaves* γ *satisfies* $\gamma \not\models \psi$. *Moreover,* κ *has a subtree* κ' *with root* $\langle C', s', h' \rangle$ *and whose leaves are all leaves of* κ. *Therefore* $\mathrm{height}(\kappa') \leq \mathrm{height}(\kappa)$. *Moreover,* $\mathrm{height}(\kappa') < \mathrm{height}(\kappa)$ *when* R *is a symbolic execution rule.*

Theorem 1 (Soundness). *If* $P \vdash C : \varphi$ *is provable, then it is valid.*

Proof. (Sketch) Suppose for contradiction that there is a cyclic proof $\mathcal{P}$ of $J = P \vdash C : \varphi$ but J is invalid. That is, for some stack s and heap h, we have $(s, h) \models P$ but $\langle C, s, h \rangle \not\models \varphi$. Then, by local soundness of the proof rules, we can construct an infinite path $(P_i \vdash C_i : \varphi_i)_{i \geq 0}$ in $\mathcal{P}$ of invalid judgements. Since $\mathcal{P}$ is a cyclic proof, by Definition 8 there exists an infinitely progressing trace following some tail $(P_i \vdash C_i : \varphi_i)_{i \geq n}$ of the path.

If this trace is a □-trace, using condition 1 of Lemma 1, we can construct an infinite sequence of finite paths to a *fixed* configuration γ of infinitely decreasing length, contradiction. A similar argument related to the height of computation trees applies in the case of a $\Diamond$-trace. A precondition trace yields an infinitely decreasing sequence of ordinal approximations of some inductive predicate, also a contradiction; see [7] for details.

The inductive-coinductive dichotomy shows nicely in our trace condition. Coinductive (G) properties need to show that something happens infinitely often whereas inductive (F) properties have to show that something *cannot* happen infinitely often. Both cases give us a progress condition: for coinductive properties, we essentially need program progress on the right of the judgements. For inductive properties, we need an infinite descent on the left of the judgements (or for the proof to be finite).

Readers familiar with Hoare-style proof systems might wonder about *relative completeness* of our system, i.e., whether all valid judgements are derivable if all valid entailments between formulas are derivable. Typically, such a result might be established by showing that for any program C and temporal property φ, we can (a) express the logically weakest precondition for C to satisfy φ, say $wp(C, \varphi)$, and (b) derive $wp(C, \varphi) \vdash C : \varphi$ in our system. Relative completeness then follows from the rule of consequence, (Cons). Unfortunately, it seems certain that such weakest preconditions are not expressible in our language. For example, in [7], the multiplicative implication of separation logic, $-\!\!*$, is needed to express weakest preconditions, whereas it is not present in our language due to the problems it poses for automation (a compromise typical of most separation logic analyses). Indeed, it seems likely that we would need to extend our precondition language well beyond this, since [7] only treats termination, whereas we treat arbitrary temporal properties. Since our focus in this paper is on automation, we leave such an analysis to future work.

4   Fairness

An important component in the verification of reactive systems is a set of *fairness requirements* to guarantee that no computation is neglected forever. These fairness constraints are usually categorised as *weak* and *strong* fairness [20]. However, since weak fairness requirements are usually restricted to the parallel composition of processes, a property that our programming language lacks, we limit ourselves to the treatment of strong fairness.

Definition 9 (Fair execution). *Let C be a program command and $\pi = (\pi_i)_{i \geq 0}$ a program execution. We say that π visits C infinitely often if there are infinitely many distinct $i \geq 0$ such that $\pi_i = \langle C, \_ , \_ \rangle$. A program execution π is fair for commands C_i, C_j if it is the case that π visits C_i infinitely often if and only if π visits C_j infinitely often. Furthermore, π is fair for a program C if it is fair for all pairs of commands C_i, C_j such that C contains a command of the form **if** $*$ **then** C_i **else** C_j **fi** or **while** $*$ **do** C_i **od** C_j.*

Note that every finite program execution is trivially fair. Also, for the purposes of fairness, we consider program commands to be uniquely labelled (to avoid confusion between different instances of the same command).

We now modify our cyclic CTL system to treat fairness constraints. First, we adjust the interpretation of judgements to account for fairness, then we lift the definition of fairness from program executions to paths in a pre-proof.

Definition 10 (Fair CTL judgement). *A fair CTL judgement $P \vdash_f C : \varphi$ is valid if and only if, for all memory states (s, h) such that $s, h \models P$, we have $\langle C, s, h \rangle \models_f \varphi$, where $\models_f$ is the satisfaction relation obtained from $\models$ in Definition 4 by interpreting the temporal operators as quantifying over fair paths, rather than all paths. For example, the clause for AG becomes*

$$\gamma \models_f AG\varphi \;\Leftrightarrow\; \forall \text{ fair } \pi \text{ starting from } \gamma.\; \forall \gamma' \in \pi.\; \gamma' \models_f \varphi.$$

Definition 11. *A path in a pre-proof $(J_i = P_i \vdash_f C_i : \varphi_i)_{i \geq 0}$ is said to visit C infinitely often if there are many distinct $i \geq 0$ such that $J_{i_C} = C$. A path in a pre-proof is fair for commands C_i, C_j if it is the case that $(J_i)_{i \geq 0}$ visits C_i infinitely often if and only if $(J_i)_{i \geq 0}$ visits C_j infinitely often. Finally, the path is fair for program C iff it is fair for all pairs of commands C_i, C_j such that C contains a command of the form **if** $*$ **then** C_i **else** C_j **fi** or **while** $*$ **do** C_i **od** C_j.*

Given these new definitions, the global soundness condition of our proofs is restricted to account only for fair paths in a pre-proof.

Definition 12 (Bad pre-proof). *A pre-proof $\mathcal{P}$ is* bad *if there is an infinite path in $\mathcal{P}$ such that the rule $(Wh^* \Diamond 1)/(If^* \Diamond 1)$ is applied infinitely often and $(Wh^* \Diamond 2)/(If^* \Diamond 2)$ is applied only finitely often, or vice versa.*

Definition 13 (Fair proof). *A pre-proof $\mathcal{P}$ is a* fair cyclic proof *if it is not bad, and for every infinite fair path $(P_i \vdash_f C_i : \varphi_i)_{i \geq 0}$ in $\mathcal{P}$, there is an infinitely progressing $\Box$-trace, $\Diamond$-trace or precondition trace following some tail $(P_i \vdash_f C_i : \varphi_i)_{i \geq n}$ of the path.*

Proposition 1 (Decidable soundness condition). *It is decidable whether a pre-proof is a valid fair cyclic proof.*

Proof. (Sketch) To check that a pre-proof $\mathcal{P}$ is not bad, we construct two Büchi automata; the first one $\mathcal{A}_{B_1}$ accepts all infinite paths in $\mathcal{P}$ such that the rule $((Wh^* \Diamond 1))/(If^* \Diamond 1)$ is applied infinitely often. The second Büchi automata $\mathcal{A}_{B_2}$ accepts all infinite paths such that the rule $(Wh^* \Diamond 2)/(If^* \Diamond 2)$ is applied infinitely often. We then check that the following relation holds of the languages accepted by each automata: $\mathcal{L}(\mathcal{A}_{B_1}) \subseteq \mathcal{L}(\mathcal{A}_{B_2})$ and $\mathcal{L}(\mathcal{A}_{B_2}) \subseteq \mathcal{L}(\mathcal{A}_{B_1})$, where language inclusion of Büchi automata is decidable.

Moreover, to check that there exists an infinitely progressing trace along every infinite path of $\mathcal{P}$ we construct two automata over strings of nodes of $\mathcal{P}$. The *fair automata* $\mathcal{A}_{Fair}$ that accepts all infinite fair paths in $\mathcal{P}$ is a Streett automata with acceptance condition formed of conjuncts of the form $(\text{Fin}(i) \vee \text{Inf}(j)) \wedge (\text{Fin}(j) \vee \text{Inf}(i))$ for each pair of fairness constraints (i, j). The *trace automata* $\mathcal{A}_{Trace}$ is a Büchi automata that accepts all infinite paths in $\mathcal{P}$ such that an infinitely progressing trace exists along the path (cf. [5]). $\mathcal{P}$ is then a valid cyclic proof if and only if $\mathcal{A}_{Trace}$ accepts all strings accepted by $\mathcal{A}_{Fair}$. We are then done since Streett automata can be transformed into Büchi automata [21] and inclusion between Büchi automata is decidable.

Example 3. *We return to our server program from Examples 1 and 2. Suppose we wish to prove, not that it is always possible for the heap to become empty, i.e. $AGEF(\mathsf{emp})$, but that the heap will* always eventually *become empty, i.e. $AGAF(\mathsf{emp})$. Our server program in fact does not satisfy this property, because the program can always choose to execute the second inner loop infinitely often, adding job requests to the list forever. However, it* does *satisfy this property under the assumption of fair execution, which prevents the second loop from being executed infinitely often without executing the first loop.*

Figure 3 shows the proof of this property in the adaptation of our system that is aware of fairness constraints as described above. Adding the fairness constraints relaxes the conditions under which back-links can be formed. This relaxed condition can be seen in back-links depicted in green as they cause an infinite path with no valid trace to be formed. Yet, because this infinite path is unfair, it is not considered in the global soundness condition. Our pre-proof qualifies as a valid cyclic proof since along every fair infinite path there is either a $\Box$-trace or a precondition trace progressing infinitely often.

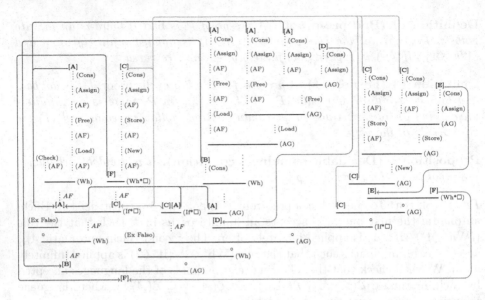

$[A] = ls(x, nil) \vdash \text{while } x \neq nil \text{ do} \ldots \text{od} : AF(\text{emp})$ $[D] = ls(x, nil) \vdash \text{while } x \neq nil \text{ do} \ldots \text{od} : AGAF(\text{emp})$

$[B] = ls(x, nil) \vdash \text{while } x = x \text{ do} \ldots \text{od} : AF(\text{emp})$ $[E] = ls(x, nil) \vdash \text{while } * \text{ do} \ldots \text{od} : AGAF(\text{emp})$

$[C] = ls(x, nil) \vdash \text{while } * \text{ do} \ldots \text{od} : AF(\text{emp})$ $[F] = ls(x, nil) \vdash \text{while } x = x \text{ do} \ldots \text{od} : AGAF(\text{emp})$

Fig. 3. Single threaded monolithic server example

Theorem 2 (Soundness). *If $P \vdash_f C : \varphi$ is provable, then it is valid.*

Proof. (Sketch) Suppose for contradiction that there is a fair cyclic proof $\mathcal{P}$ of $J = P \vdash_f C : \varphi$ but J is invalid. That is, for some stack s and heap h, we have $(s, h) \models P$ but $\langle C, s, h \rangle \not\models_f \varphi$. Then, by local soundness of the proof rules, we can construct an infinite path $(P_i \vdash_f C_i : \varphi_i)_{i \geq 0}$ in $\mathcal{P}$ of invalid sequents. By Definition 13 we know that said infinite path is a *fair* path (as any unfair path has been ruled out by requiring that $\mathcal{P}$ is not a *bad pre-proof* according to Definition 12). Since the path is an infinite fair path, by Definition 13 we also know that there is an infinitely progressing $\Box$-trace, $\Diamond$-trace or precondition trace following some tail of the path. Showing that the existence of an infinitely progressing trace along the path leads to a contradiction follows the same argument as in Sect. 3.

5   Implementation and Evaluation

We implement our proof systems on top of the CYCLIST theorem prover [9], a mechanised cyclic theorem proving framework. The implementation, source code and benchmarks are publicly available at [1] (under the subdirectory titled as the present paper).

Our implementation performs iterative depth-first search, aimed at closing open nodes in the proof by either applying an inference rule or forming a backlink. If an open node cannot be closed, we attempt to apply symbolic execution; if this is not possible, we try unfolding temporal operators and inductive predicates in the precondition to enable symbolic execution to proceed. Forming backlinks typically requires the use of the consequence rule (i.e. a lemma proven on demand) to re-establish preconditions altered by symbolic executions (as can be seen in Figs. 2 and 3). When all open nodes have been closed, a global soundness check of the cyclic proof is performed automatically. Entailment queries over symbolic heaps in separation logic, which arise at backlinks and when applying the (Check) axiom or checking rule side conditions, are handled by a separate instantiation of CYCLIST for separation logic entailments [9].

We evaluate the implementation on handcrafted nondeterministic and non-terminating programs similar to Example 1. Our test suite can be seen as an adaptation of the common model checking benchmarks presented in [14,15] for the verification of temporal properties of nondeterministic programs. Roughly speaking, operations/iterations on integer variables in the original benchmarks are replaced in favour of operations/iterations on heap data structures.

Our test suite comprises the following programs:

(i) Examples discussed in the paper are named EXMP;
(ii) FIN-LOCK - a finite program that acquires a lock and, once obtained, proceeds to free from memory the elements of a list and reset the lock;
(iii) INF-LOCK wraps the previous program inside an infinite loop;
(iv) ND-IN-LOCK is an infinite loop that nondeterministically acquires a lock, then proceeds to perform a nondeterministic number of operations before releasing the lock;
(v) INF-LIST is an infinite loop that nondeterministically adds a new element to the list or advances the head of the list by one element on each iteration;
(vi) INSERT-LIST has a nondeterministic if statement that either adds a single elements to the head of the list or deletes all elements but one, and is followed by an infinite loop;
(vii) APPEND-LIST appends the second argument to the end of the first argument;
(viii) CYCLIC-LIST is a nonterminating program that iterates through a non-empty cyclic list;
(ix) INF-BINTREE is an infinite loop that nondeterministically inserts nodes to a binary three or performs a random walk of the three;
(x) The programs named with BRANCH define a somewhat arbitrary nesting of nondeterministic if and while statements, aimed at testing the capability of the tool in terms of lines of code and nesting of cycles;
(xi) Finally we also cover sample programs taken from the Windows Update system (WIN UPDATE), the back-end infrastructure of the PostgreSQL database server (POSTGRESQL) and an implementation of the acquire-release algorithm taken from the aforementioned benchmarks (ACQ-REL).

We show the results of the evaluation of the CTL system and its extension to consider fairness constraints in Table 1. For each test, we report whether fairness constraints were needed to verify the desired property and the time taken in seconds. The tests were carried out on an Intel x-64 i5 system at 2.50 GHz.

Our experiments demonstrate the viability of our approach: our runtimes are mostly in the range of milliseconds and show similar performance to existing tools for the model checking benchmarks. Overall, the execution times in the evaluation are quite varied as they depend on a few factors such as the complexity of the program in question and temporal property to verify, but sources of potential slowdown can be witnessed by different test cases. Even at the level of pure memory assertions, the base case rule (Check) has to check entailments $P \models Q$ between symbolic heaps, which involves calling an inductive theorem prover; this is reasonably fast in some cases, but very costly in others (e.g. the APPEND-LIST example). Another source of slowdown is in attempting to form back-links too eagerly (e.g. when encountering the same command at two different program locations); since we check soundness when forming a back-link, which involves calling a model checker (cf. [9]), this too is an expensive operation, as can be seen in the runtimes of test cases with suffix BRANCH.

Note that despite the encouraging results, the implementation is not without limitations as it might, in some cases, fail to terminate and produce a valid proof. Generalising, our proof search tends to fail either when the temporal property in question does not hold, or when we fail to establish a sufficiently general "invariant" to form backlinks in the proof.

6   Related Work

Related work on the automated verification of temporal program properties can broadly be classified into two main schools, *model checking* and *deductive verification*. In recent years, model checking has been the more popular of these two. Although earlier work in model checking focused on finite-state transition systems (e.g. [11,25]), recent advances in areas such as state space restriction [3], precondition synthesis [12], CEGAR [15], bounded model checking [10] and automata theory [13] have enabled the treatment of infinite transition systems.

The present paper takes the deductive verification approach. A common limitation of early proof systems for various temporal logics is their restriction to finite state transition systems [4,18,19]. In the realm of infinite state systems, previous proof systems for verifying temporal properties of arbitrary transition systems [23,30] have shed some light on the soundness and relative completeness of deductive verification. However, these early systems have typically relied upon complex verification conditions that are seemingly difficult to fully automate, arguably the most cited argument against deductive verification. In contrast, our proof system can handle infinite state, non-terminating programs, even under fairness restrictions, and we provide an implementation and evaluation, showing that it can indeed work in practice.

Of particular relevance here are those proof systems for temporal properties based on cyclic proof. Our work can be seen as an extension of the cyclic termination proofs in [7] to arbitrary temporal properties. In [4], a procedure for the

Table 1. Experimental results.

Program	Precondition	Property	Fairness	Time (s)
EXMP	ls(x,nil)	AGEF emp	No	2.43
EXMP	ls(x,nil)	AGAF emp	Yes	4.29
EXMP	ls(x,nil)	AGAF (ls(x,nil))	No	0.26
EXMP	ls(x,nil)	AGEG (ls(x,nil))	No	0.44
EXMP	ls(x,nil)	AF emp	Yes	0.77
EXMP	ls(x,nil)	AFEG emp	Yes	0.86
FIN-LOCK	lock ↦ 0 * ls(x,nil)	AF (lock ↦ 1 * emp)	No	0.20
FIN-LOCK	lock ↦ 0 * ls(x,nil)	AGAF (lock ↦1 * emp)	No	0.62
FIN-LOCK	lock ↦ 0 * ls(x,nil)	AGAF (lock ↦ 1 * emp ∧ ◊lock ↦ 0)	No	0.24
INF-LOCK	lock ↦ 0 * ls(x,nil)	AGAF (lock ↦ 1 * emp)	No	1.52
INF-LOCK	lock ↦ 0 * ls(x,nil)	AGAF (lock ↦ 1 * emp ∧ ◊lock ↦ 0))	No	3.26
INF-LOCK	del = false : lock ↦ 0 * ls(x,nil)	AG (del != true ∨ AF (lock ↦ 1 * emp))	No	3.87
ND-INF-LOCK	lock ↦ 0	AF(lock ↦ 1)	Yes	0.15
ND-INF-LOCK	lock ↦ 0	AGAF (lock ↦ 1)	Yes	0.25
INF-LIST	ls(x,nil)	AG ls(x,nil)	No	0.21
INF-LIST	ls(x,nil)	AGEF x = nil	No	4.39
INF-LIST	ls(x,nil)	AGAF x = nil	Yes	8.10
INSERT-LIST	ls(three,zero)	EF ls(five,zero)	No	0.14
INSERT-LIST	ls(three,zero)	AF ls(five,zero)	Yes	0.26
INSERT-LIST	ls(n,zero)	AGAF n != zero	Yes	17.21
APPEND-LIST	ls(y,x) * ls(x,nil)	AF (ls(y,nil))	No	12.67
CYCLIC-LIST	cls(x,x)	AG cls(x,x)	No	0.88
CYCLIC-LIST	cls(x,x)	AGEG cls(x,x)	No	0.34
INF-BINTREE	x != nil : bintree(λ)	AGEG x != nil	No	0.72
AFAG BRANCH	x ↦ zero	AFAG x ↦ one	No	1.80
EGAG BRANCH	x ↦ zero	EGAG x ↦ one	No	0.23
EGAF BRANCH	x ↦ zero	EGAF x ↦ one	No	15.48
EG ⇒ EF BRANCH	p = zero ∧ q = zero : ls(zero,n)	EG(p != one ∨ EF q = one)	No	1.60
EG ⇒ AF BRANCH	p = zero ∧ q = zero : ls(zero,n)	EG(p != one ∨AF q = one)	Yes	5.33
AG ⇒ EG BRANCH	p = zero ∧ q = one : ls(zero,n)	AG(p != one ∨ EG q = one)	No	0.36
AG ⇒ EF BRANCH	p = zero ∧ q = one :u ls(zero,n)	AG(p != one ∨ EF q = one)	No	1.53
ACQ-REL	ls(zero,three)	AG(acq = 0 ∨ AF rel != 0)	No	1.25
ACQ-REL	ls(zero,three)	AG(acq = 0 ∨ EF rel != 0)	No	1.25
ACQ-REL	ls(zero,three)	EF acq != 0 ∧ EF AG rel = 0	No	0.33
ACQ-REL	ls(zero,three)	AF AG rel = 0	Yes	0.42
ACQ-REL	ls(zero,three)	EF acq != 0 ∧ EF EG rel = 0	No	0.25
ACQ-REL	ls(zero,three)	AF EG rel = 0	Yes	0.33
POSTGRESQL	w = true ∧ s = s' ∧ f = f' : emp	AGAF w = true ∧ s = s' ∧ flag = f' : emp	No	0.27
POSTGRESQL	w = true ∧ s = s' ∧ f = f' : emp	AGEF w = true ∧ s = s' ∧ flag = f' : emp	No	0.26
POSTGRESQL	w = true ∧ s = s' ∧ f = f' : emp	EFEG w = false ∧ s = s' ∧ flag = f'	No	0.44
POSTGRESQL	w = true ∧ s = s' ∧ f = f' : emp	EFAG w = false ∧ s = s' ∧ flag = f'	No	0.77
WIN UPDATE	W != nil : ls(W,nil)	AGAF W != nil : ls(W,nil)	No	1.50
WIN UPDATE	W != nil : ls(W,nil)	AGEF W != nil : ls(W,nil)	No	1.00
WIN UPDATE	W != nil : ls(W,nil)	EFEG W = nil : emp	No	3.60
WIN UPDATE	W != nil : ls(W,nil)	AFEG W = nil : emp	Yes	3.70
WIN UPDATE	W != nil : ls(W,nil)	EFAG W = nil : emp	No	3.15
WIN UPDATE	W != nil : ls(W,nil)	AFAG W = nil : emp	Yes	4.16

verification of CTL* properties is developed that employs a cyclic proof system for LTL as a sub-procedure. A subtle but important difference when compared to our work is the lack of cut/consequence rule (used e.g. to generalise precondition formulas or to apply intermediary lemmas). A side benefit of this restriction is a simplification of the soundness condition on cyclic proofs.

A cyclic proof system for the verification of CTL* properties of infinite-state transition systems is presented in [30]. Focusing on generality, this system avoids considering details of state formulas and their evolution throughout program execution by assuming an oracle for a general transition system. The system relies on a soundness condition that is similar to Definition 8, but does not track progress in the same way, imposing extra conditions on the order in which rules are applied. The success criterion for validity of a proof also presents some differences; it relies on finding ranking functions, intermediate assertions and checking for the validity of Hoare triples, and it is far from clear that such checks can be fully automated. In contrast, we rely on a relatively simple ω-regular condition, which is decidable and can be automatically checked by CYCLIST [5, 9, 29].

7   Conclusions and Future Work

Our main contribution in this paper is the formulation, implementation and evaluation of a deductive cyclic proof system for verifying temporal properties of pointer programs, building on previous systems for separation logic and for other temporal verification settings [4, 7, 30]. We present two variants of our system and prove both systems sound. We have implemented these proof systems, and proof search algorithms for them, in the CYCLIST theorem prover, and evaluated them on benchmarks drawn from the literature.

The main advantage of our approach is that we never obtain false positive results. This advantage is not in fact exclusive to deductive verification: some automata-theoretic model checking approaches are also proven to be sound [32]. Nonetheless, when compared to such approaches, our treatment of the temporal verification problem has the advantage of being direct. Owing to our use of separation logic and a deductive proof system, we do not need to apply approximation or transformations to the program as a first step; in particular, we avoid the translation of temporal formulas into complex automata [33] and the instrumentation of the original program with auxiliary constructs [13].

One natural direction for future work is to develop improved mechanised techniques, such as generalisation/abstraction, to enhance the performance of proof search in our system(s). Another possible direction is to consider larger classes of programs. In particular, concurrency is one very interesting such possibility, perhaps building on existing verification techniques for concurrency in separation logic (e.g. [31]). A different direction to explore is the enrichment of our assertion language, for example to CTL* [17] or μ-calculus [16]. The structure of CTL* formulas and their classification into path and state subformulas suggest a possible combination of our CTL system with an LTL system to produce a proof object composed of smaller proof structures (cf. [4, 30]). The encoding of CTL* into μ-calculus [16] and the applicability of cyclic proofs for the verification of μ-calculus properties (see e.g. [28]) hint at the feasibility of such an extension.

References

1. www.github.com/ngorogiannis/cyclist/releases
2. Berdine, J., Calcagno, C., O'Hearn, P.W.: A decidable fragment of separation logic. In: Lodaya, K., Mahajan, M. (eds.) FSTTCS 2004. LNCS, vol. 3328, pp. 97–109. Springer, Heidelberg (2004). doi:10.1007/978-3-540-30538-5_9
3. Beyer, D., Henzinger, T.A., Jhala, R., Majumdar, R.: The software model checker blast: applications to software engineering. Int. J. Softw. Tools Technol. Transf. **9**, 505–525 (2007)
4. Bhat, G., Cleaveland, R., Grumberg, O.: Efficient on-the-fly model checking for CTL*. In: Proceedings of LICS-10, pp. 388–397. IEEE (1995)
5. Brotherston, J.: Sequent calculus proof systems for inductive definitions. Ph.D. thesis, University of Edinburgh, November 2006
6. Brotherston, J.: Formalised inductive reasoning in the logic of bunched implications. In: Nielson, H.R., Filé, G. (eds.) SAS 2007. LNCS, vol. 4634, pp. 87–103. Springer, Heidelberg (2007). doi:10.1007/978-3-540-74061-2_6
7. Brotherston, J., Bornat, R., Calcagno, C.: Cyclic proofs of program termination in separation logic. In: Proceedings of POPL-35, pp. 101–112. ACM (2008)
8. Brotherston, J., Gorogiannis, N.: Cyclic abduction of inductively defined safety and termination preconditions. In: Müller-Olm, M., Seidl, H. (eds.) SAS 2014. LNCS, vol. 8723, pp. 68–84. Springer, Cham (2014). doi:10.1007/978-3-319-10936-7_5
9. Brotherston, J., Gorogiannis, N., Petersen, R.L.: A generic cyclic theorem prover. In: Jhala, R., Igarashi, A. (eds.) APLAS 2012. LNCS, vol. 7705, pp. 350–367. Springer, Heidelberg (2012). doi:10.1007/978-3-642-35182-2_25
10. Clarke, E., Kroening, D., Lerda, F.: A tool for checking ANSI-C programs. In: Jensen, K., Podelski, A. (eds.) TACAS 2004. LNCS, vol. 2988, pp. 168–176. Springer, Heidelberg (2004). doi:10.1007/978-3-540-24730-2_15
11. Clarke, E.M., Emerson, E.A.: Design and synthesis of synchronization skeletons using branching time temporal logic. In: Kozen, D. (ed.) Logic of Programs 1981. LNCS, vol. 131, pp. 52–71. Springer, Heidelberg (1982). doi:10.1007/BFb0025774
12. Cook, B., Khlaaf, H., Piterman, N.: On automation of CTL* verification for infinite-state systems. In: Kroening, D., Păsăreanu, C.S. (eds.) CAV 2015. LNCS, vol. 9206, pp. 13–29. Springer, Cham (2015). doi:10.1007/978-3-319-21690-4_2
13. Cook, B., Gotsman, A., Podelski, A., Rybalchenko, A., Vardi, M.Y.: Proving that programs eventually do something good. In: Proceedings of POPL-34, POPL 2007, pp. 265–276. ACM (2007)
14. Cook, B., Koskinen, E.: Making prophecies with decision predicates. In: Proceedings of POPL-38, vol. 46, pp. 399–410. ACM (2011)
15. Cook, B., Koskinen, E.: Reasoning about nondeterminism in programs. In: Proceedings of PLDI-34, pp. 219–230. ACM (2013)
16. Dam, M.: Translating CTL* into the modal μ-calculus. ECS-LFCS-, University of Edinburgh, Department of Computer Science, Laboratory for Foundations of Computer Science (1990)
17. Emerson, E.A., Halpern, J.Y.: "Sometimes" and "Not never" revisited: on branching versus linear time temporal logic. J. ACM **33**, 151–178 (1986)

18. Fix, L., Grumberg, O.: Verification of temporal properties. J. Log. Comput. **6**, 343–361 (1996)
19. Hungar, H., Grumberg, O., Damm, W.: What if model checking must be truly symbolic. In: Camurati, P.E., Eveking, H. (eds.) CHARME 1995. LNCS, vol. 987, pp. 1–20. Springer, Heidelberg (1995). doi:10.1007/3-540-60385-9_1
20. Lamport, L.: Proving the correctness of multiprocess programs. IEEE Trans. Software Eng. **3**, 125–143 (1977)
21. Löding, C., Thomas, W.: Methods for the transformation of ω-automata: complexity and connection to second order logic. Diploma thesis. University of Kiel (1998)
22. Magill, S., Tsai, M.H., Lee, P., Tsay, Y.K.: Automatic numeric abstractions for heap-manipulating programs. In: Proceedings of the 37th Annual Symposium on Principles of Programming Languages, POPL 2010, pp. 211–222. ACM (2010)
23. Manna, Z., Pnueli, A.: Completing the temporal picture (1991)
24. Pnueli, A.: The temporal logic of programs. In: 18th Annual Symposium on Foundations of Computer Science, pp. 46–57. IEEE (1977)
25. Queille, J.P., Sifakis, J.: Specification and verification of concurrent systems in CESAR. In: Dezani-Ciancaglini, M., Montanari, U. (eds.) Programming 1982. LNCS, vol. 137, pp. 337–351. Springer, Heidelberg (1982). doi:10.1007/3-540-11494-7_22
26. Reynolds, J.C.: Separation logic: a logic for shared mutable data structures. In: Proceedings of the LICS-17, pp. 55–74. IEEE (2002)
27. Rowe, R.N.S., Brotherston, J.: Automatic cyclic termination proofs for recursive procedures in separation logic. In: Proceedings of CPP-6. ACM (2016)
28. Schöpp, U., Simpson, A.: Verifying temporal properties using explicit approximants: completeness for context-free processes. In: Nielsen, M., Engberg, U. (eds.) FoSSaCS 2002. LNCS, vol. 2303, pp. 372–386. Springer, Heidelberg (2002). doi:10.1007/3-540-45931-6_26
29. Sprenger, C., Dam, M.: On the structure of inductive reasoning: circular and tree-shaped proofs in the μCalculus. In: Gordon, A.D. (ed.) FoSSaCS 2003. LNCS, vol. 2620, pp. 425–440. Springer, Heidelberg (2003). doi:10.1007/3-540-36576-1_27
30. Sprenger, C.: Deductive local model checking - on the verification of CTL* properties of infinite-state reactive systems. Ph.D. thesis, Swiss Federal Institute of Technology (2000)
31. Vafeiadis, V., Parkinson, M.: A marriage of rely/guarantee and separation logic. In: Caires, L., Vasconcelos, V.T. (eds.) CONCUR 2007. LNCS, vol. 4703, pp. 256–271. Springer, Heidelberg (2007). doi:10.1007/978-3-540-74407-8_18
32. Vardi, M.Y.: Verification of concurrent programs: the automata-theoretic framework*. Ann. Pure Appl. Logic **51**(1), 79–98 (1991)
33. Visser, W., Barringer, H.: Practical CTL* model checking: should spin be extended? Int. J. Softw. Tools Technol. Transfer **2**(4), 350–365 (2000)

Satisfiability of Compositional Separation Logic with Tree Predicates and Data Constraints

Zhaowei Xu[1,2], Taolue Chen[3,4], and Zhilin Wu[1(✉)]

[1] State Key Laboratory of Computer Science,
Institute of Software, Chinese Academy of Sciences, Beijing, China
wuzl@ios.ac.cn
[2] University of Chinese Academy of Sciences, Beijing, China
[3] Department of Computer Science, Middlesex University, London, UK
[4] State Key Laboratory of Novel Software Technology,
Nanjing University, Nanjing, China

Abstract. In this paper, we propose compositional separation logic with tree predicates (CSLTP), where properties such as sortedness and height-balancedness of complex data structures (for instance, AVL trees and red-black trees) can be fully specified. We show that the satisfiability problem of CSLTP is decidable. The main technical ingredient of the decision procedure is to compute the least fixed point of a class of inductively defined predicates that are non-linear and involve dense-order and difference-bound constraints, which are of independent interests.

1 Introduction

Program verification requires reasoning about complex, size-unbounded data structures that may carry data ranging over an infinite domain. Examples include multi-linked lists, nested lists, trees, etc. Programs manipulating these data structures may modify their shape as well as the data attached to their elements. *Separation Logic* (SL) is a well-established approach for deductive verification of programs that manipulate dynamic data structures [22,30]. Typically, SL is defined in combination with *inductive definitions* (SLID in short), which supports user-defined specifications of the data structures manipulated by a program.

Satisfiability is arguably one of the most fundamental questions for logic, and has certainly been a main focus in the study of SL. The satisfiability of SLID with data constraints is evidently undecidable in their most general forms. However, it is important—both in theory and practice—to identify subclasses which are sufficiently expressive while still being decidable. Within this context, our previous work [14] gave complete decision procedures for both the satisfiability and the entailment problem of *linearly* compositional SLID. This fragment is able

---

Taolue Chen is supported by UK EPSRC grant (EP/P00430X/1), European CHIST-ERA project SUCCESS, NSFC grant (61662035). He is also affiliated with Centre for Research and Innovation in Software Engineering, Southwest University. Zhilin Wu is supported by the NSFC grants (61572478, 61472474, 61100062, and 61272135).

© Springer International Publishing AG 2017
L. de Moura (Ed.): CADE 2017, LNAI 10395, pp. 509–527, 2017.
DOI: 10.1007/978-3-319-63046-5_31

to specify typical shape properties and data/size constraints of data structures, but is restricted to linear ones such as singly and doubly linked lists.

An obvious question left over is to handle non-linear structures such as trees. Notice that most tree-shaped data structures in programming require data/size constraints of one or another. They together, however, impose great challenges. For satisfiability, the main difficulty roots at the computation of the least fixed point of the inductively defined predicates derived from SL formulae. These predicates are *non-linear*, meaning that the defined predicate may occur more than once in the body of the inductive rule. They may also involve data/size constraints to capture, for instance, sortedness and height-balancedness of trees.

Contributions. We define CSLTP, a compositional fragment of SL with *tree predicates*, where typical tree structures involving data and size constraints (e.g., binary search trees, AVL trees, and red-black trees) can be expressed. The basic rationale of CSLTP is to focus on the compositional predicates introduced in [12,13] while restricting to dense-order data constraints and difference-bound size constraints. We remark that compositionality is vital for (deductive) program verification without which the entailment checking, an indispensable procedure for checking assertions in the style of Hoare logic, would otherwise be exceedingly difficult. (The price is that, instead of trees, one has to consider trees with *one hole* to guarantee the compositionality; cf. Sect. 3.) Our main contribution is summarised as follows:

(i) We provide algorithms to compute the least fixed point of the inductively defined predicates involving data/size constraints derived from CSLTP formulae (see Theorem 2). To this end, we employ a wide range of techniques from closed-form evaluation of Datalog programs with integer gap-order constraints [28], computation of reachability sets of alternating one-counter systems [4], and the decision procedure for the reachability problem of one-counter automata [15]. In addition, we show that computation of the least fixed point of the inductively defined predicates beyond CSLTP may be difficult in general. More specifically, we prove that, for the predicate corresponding to AVL trees with one hole where *all* parameters are of the *natural number* type, its least fixed point is *inexpressible* in Presburger arithmetic (see Theorem 1).

(ii) We propose a *complete* decision procedure for the satisfiability problem of CSLTP. Namely, from each CSLTP formula φ we define $\mathsf{Abs}(\varphi)$ as an abstraction of φ such that φ and $\mathsf{Abs}(\varphi)$ are equisatisfiable. Roughly speaking, $\mathsf{Abs}(\varphi)$ introduces Boolean variables to encode the spatial part of φ and encompasses computed least fixed points from (i) to address the data and size constraints. We then can resort to the state-of-the-art SMT solvers (e.g., Z3 [34]). We remark that most decision procedures for satisfiability of SL with inductive definitions *and* data/size constraints are incomplete (see the *related work* for more details).

Satisfiability checking serves as a cornerstone towards a complete procedure for entailment checking, which requires a separate paper to solve. It can also be widely used in, e.g., consistency checking of specifications written in SL, symbolic execution of programs manipulating dynamic data structures (see [2, 20]), etc. *Related work.* For SLID *without* data constraints, [6] provides a complete decision procedure, setting the satisfiability problem (almost) completely. We also mention some earlier results [2, 17] which focus on the symbolic heap fragments for list segments and binary trees, providing complete proof systems. [12] proposes a compositional fragment of SLID equipped with an incomplete decision procedure. In addition, [18, 19] provide complete decision procedures for the entailment problem of SLID (without data/size constraints) by reducing to the language inclusion problem of tree automata.

Towards adding data/size constraints, [29] presents a complete decision procedure for the quantifier-free fragment of SL (*without* inductive definitions) interpreted over heaplets with data elements ranging over a parametric multi-sorted (possibly infinite) domain. For SLID *with* data constraints, [8] provides an incomplete decision procedure based on invariants of inductive definitions. These invariants are essentially the fixed points of the inductively defined predicates involving data/size constraints, and are supposed to be provided by the users. [3] specifies the data/size constraints by universal quantifiers over the index variables (and thus is able to express set/multiset constraints), but restricts to the singly linked lists only. [23, 27] reduces the entailment problem of SLID with data/size constraints to the satisfiability problem in the theory of uninterpreted functions, though the procedure therein is *incomplete* and *not* fully automatic since it relies on the users to provide lemmas. [24–26] encode SLID into a fragment of first-order logic with reachability predicates (whose satisfiability is decidable in NP). However, this fragment cannot accommodate the size or multiset constraints. More recently, [20] considers the data constraints expressible in Presburger arithmetic. The decision procedure therein is based on cyclic proofs [5, 9] and is incomplete in general and is complete for a syntactic fragment defined with a specialized well-founded notion, which is incomparable to CSLTP.

With respect to data/size constraints, [33] is closest to our work, where the data/size constraints are expressed in Presburger arithmetic, and a complete decision procedure is given for the satisfiability problem. CSLTP differs from the fragment in [33] in both the shape properties and the data/size constraints: 1) For the shape properties, CSLTP addresses trees *with one hole* (which is crucial for the compositionality), while [33] does not. 2) For the data/size constraints, the class of data constraints in [33] is incomparable to that of CSLTP: On the one hand, CSLTP allows only one integer parameter, while [33] may have multiple ones, although there must be a dominating one. On the other hand, the order constraints (e.g. sortedness), which require comparing different data parameters and are covered by CSLTP, are inexpressible in [33]. In addition, even when restricted to size constraints, CSLTP goes beyond the fragment in [33]. For instance, the height-balancedness of red-black trees can be easily expressed in CSLTP, whereas it is inexpressible in [33]. This is because the inductive definition in [33] essentially allows only *one* inductive rule, with the aid of the max and min functions and (a form of) disjunctions in the data/size constraint.

Nevertheless, the height-balancedness of red-black trees requires multiple inductive rules to specify, even when max, min and disjunctions are present in the data/size constraint. Furthermore, we employ an automata-theoretic approach to compute the least fixed point of data predicates, which is quite different from the arguments ([33]) which are purely based on induction.

There are methods outside of the SL framework to tackle verification of tree structures and data constraints. Some of them are based on different extensions of tree automata, such as forest automata [1], tree automata with size constraints [16], ree automata with height constraints [11], and visibly tree automata with memory and constraints [10]. Interestingly, our approach to compute the least fixed point of data predicates is partially inspired by this line of work, especially [16]. Even further, [21] takes a logic-based approach to verify balanced trees. Finally, [31] proposes practical approaches for solving Horn-clause constraints, which are related to, albeit easier than, computing the least fixed point of data predicates in this paper. The method therein is based on the construction of disjunctive interpolants, which are used within an abstraction-refinement loop. The method therein is incomplete in general.

2   Preliminaries

Throughout the paper, $\mathbb{Z}$ and $\mathbb{N}$ denote the set of integers and natural numbers respectively. For each $n \in \mathbb{N}$, $[n] := \{1, \ldots, n\}$. For each vector $\boldsymbol{\alpha} = (a_1, \ldots, a_n)$, $|\boldsymbol{\alpha}|$ denotes the length of $\boldsymbol{\alpha}$ (i.e. n) and $\boldsymbol{\alpha}(i)$ denotes a_i for $i \in [n]$.

Definition 1 (A1CS and N1CS). *An* alternating one-counter system *(A1CS) is a pair* $\mathcal{A} = (Q, \Theta)$, *where* Q *is a finite set of* states, *and* $\Theta \subseteq Q \times 2^{(\mathsf{Inst} \times Q)}$ *is a finite set of transition rules, where* $\mathsf{Inst} = \{\circ\, n, +n, -n, \mathsf{reset}(n)\}$ *with* $\circ \in \{=, \leqslant, \geqslant\}$ *and* $n \in \mathbb{N}$. *A transition* $(p, \{(\ell_1, q_1), \cdots, (\ell_k, q_k)\}) \in \Theta$ *is usually written as* $p \hookrightarrow \{(\ell_1, q_1), \cdots, (\ell_k, q_k)\}$ *for readability. A* nondeterministic one-counter system *(N1CS) is an A1CS where for each* $p \hookrightarrow \{(\ell_1, q_1), \cdots, (\ell_k, q_k)\}$, $k = 1$.

A *configuration* of an A1CS $\mathcal{A}$ is (p, n) where $p \in Q$ and $n \in \mathbb{N}$ is the value of the counter. The transition rules induce a transition relation on configurations in an expected way: for $p \hookrightarrow \{(\ell_1, q_1), \cdots, (\ell_k, q_k)\} \in \Theta$, we have a *hyper-transition* $(p, n) \rightarrow \{(q_1, n_1), \cdots, (q_k, n_k)\}$ if for each $1 \leqslant i \leqslant k$, (1) $\ell_i = \circ\, n'$ implies that $n \circ n'$ and $n_i = n$, (2) $\ell_i = +n'$ implies that $n_i = n + n'$, (3) $\ell_i = -n'$ implies that $n - n' \geqslant 0$ and $n_i = n - n'$, and (4) $\ell_i = \mathsf{reset}(n')$ implies that $n_i = n'$. In this case, we say that (p, n) is the *immediate predecessor* of $\{(q_1, n_1), \cdots, (q_k, n_k)\}$.

A *computation tree* of $\mathcal{A}$ is a directed tree whose nodes are labelled by configurations, and where every node is either a leaf or an internal node which is labelled by a configuration c and has k children labelled by $c_1, \ldots, c_k$ respectively, satisfying that $c \rightarrow \{c_1, \ldots, c_k\}$ is a hyper-transition of $\mathcal{A}$. We define the reachability relation $\Rightarrow_{\mathcal{A}}$ as $c \Rightarrow_{\mathcal{A}} C$ if there exists a computation tree such that c labels the root and C is the set of labels of the leaves. If $c \Rightarrow_{\mathcal{A}} C$, then we say that C is reachable from c in $\mathcal{A}$. For $q \in Q$ and a set of configurations C, we use $\mathsf{Pre}^*_{\mathcal{A}}(q, C)$ to denote the set of $n \in \mathbb{N}$ such that $(q, n) \Rightarrow_{\mathcal{A}} C'$ for some $C' \subseteq C$.

The transition relation for an N1CS can be defined similarly, and is simpler in that the computation tree degenerates to a single path of configurations.

Proposition 1 ([4,7,15,32]). *The following facts hold for A1CS and N1CS.*

1. *Let $\mathcal{A} = (Q, \Theta)$ be an A1CS, $q \in Q$ be a state, C be a finite set of configurations of $\mathcal{A}$. Then a quantifier-free Presburger formula $\varphi_{q,C}(x)$ in disjunctive normal form can be computed in doubly exponential time to represent $\mathsf{Pre}^*_{\mathcal{A}}(q, C)$. In addition, if the constants in $\mathcal{A}$ and C are encoded in unary, then the computation is in exponential time.*
2. *Let $\mathcal{A} = (Q, \Theta)$ be an N1CS, and $p, q \in Q$. Then a quantifier-free Presburger formula $\varphi_{p,q}(x, y)$ can be computed in triply exponential time to represent the relation $\{(m, n) \in \mathbb{N}^2 \mid (p, m) \Rightarrow_{\mathcal{A}} (q, n)\}$. In addition, if the constants in $\mathcal{A}$ are encoded in unary, then the computation is in doubly exponential time.*

3   Compositional Separation Logic with Tree Predicates

In this section, we introduce the *compositional separation logic with tree predicates*, denoted by CSLTP[P], where P is an *inductive predicate*. We consider three data types, i.e., *location* type $\mathbb{L}$, *value* type $\mathbb{D}$, and *size* type $\mathbb{N}$. Intuitively, $\mathbb{D}$ represents the data values stored in the nodes of tree structures, and $\mathbb{N}$ represents the size of tree structures (e.g. height of trees), which we assume to be natural numbers. As a convention, we use $l, l', \cdots \in \mathbb{L}$ to denote locations, $d, d', \cdots \in \mathbb{D}$ to denote values, and $n, n', \cdots \in \mathbb{N}$ to denote sizes. Accordingly, variables in CSLTP[P] comprise *location variables* LVars ranged over by uppercase letters $E, F, X, Y, \cdots$, *value variables* DVars ranged over by $x, y, \cdots$, and *size variables* IVars ranged over by $h, i, j, \cdots$.

We consider two kinds of *fields*, i.e., location fields from $\mathcal{F}$ and data fields from $\mathcal{D}$. Each field $\mathfrak{f} \in \mathcal{F}$ (resp. $\mathfrak{d} \in \mathcal{D}$) is associated with $\mathbb{L}$ (resp. $\mathbb{D}$). We assume $\mathbb{D}$ is an *ordered, countably infinite, dense* set. That is, $\mathbb{D}$ is equipped with $<$ such that for each $d < d' \in \mathbb{D}$, $d'' \in \mathbb{D}$ exists with $d < d'' < d'$. Examples of $\mathbb{D}$ include the set of rationals with the natural order relation, and the set of strings with the lexicographical order relation. Note that any arithmetic over $\mathbb{D}$ is disregarded.

CSLTP[P] formulae may contain tree predicates, each of which is of the form $P(E, \boldsymbol{\alpha}; F, \boldsymbol{\beta})$ and has an associated inductive definition. The parameters of a tree predicate are classified into two groups: *source parameters* $E, \boldsymbol{\alpha}$ and *destination parameters* $F, \boldsymbol{\beta}$. We require that the source parameters $E, \boldsymbol{\alpha}$ and the destination parameters $F, \boldsymbol{\beta}$ are *matched* in types, namely, E and F are of the location type, and two tuples $\boldsymbol{\alpha}, \boldsymbol{\beta}$ have the same length $\ell > 0$ and for each $i : 1 \leqslant i \leqslant \ell$, both α_i and β_i have the natural number type or the value type. The parameters E, F are called the *location parameters* of P and $\boldsymbol{\alpha}, \boldsymbol{\beta}$ are called the *data parameters* of P. Intuitively, a tree predicate $P(E, \boldsymbol{\alpha}; F, \boldsymbol{\beta})$ defines binary trees with one hole and data constraints.

The CSLTP[P] formulae comprise three types of formulae: *pure formulae Π*, *data formulae Δ*, and *spatial formulae Σ*, which are defined as follows,

$$\Pi ::= E = F \mid E \neq F \mid \Pi \wedge \Pi \qquad \text{(pure formulae)}$$
$$\Delta ::= \Delta_{\mathbb{D}} \wedge \Delta_{\mathbb{N}} \qquad \text{(data formulae)}$$
$$\Delta_{\mathbb{D}} ::= \mathbf{true} \mid x \circ d \mid x \circ x' \mid \Delta_{\mathbb{D}} \wedge \Delta_{\mathbb{D}} \qquad \text{(value formulae)}$$
$$\Delta_{\mathbb{N}} ::= \mathbf{true} \mid h \circ n \mid h \circ h' + n \mid \Delta_{\mathbb{N}} \wedge \Delta_{\mathbb{N}} \qquad \text{(size formulae)}$$
$$\Sigma ::= \mathbf{emp} \mid E \mapsto \rho \mid P(E, \alpha; F, \beta) \mid \Sigma * \Sigma \qquad \text{(spatial formulae)}$$
$$\rho ::= \rho_{\mathsf{f}}, \rho_{\mathsf{d}} \qquad \text{(field-variable sequences)}$$
$$\rho_{\mathsf{f}} ::= (\mathsf{f}, X) \mid \rho_{\mathsf{f}}, \rho_{\mathsf{f}} \qquad \text{(location field-variable sequences)}$$
$$\rho_{\mathsf{d}} ::= (\mathfrak{d}, x) \mid \rho_{\mathsf{d}}, \rho_{\mathsf{d}} \qquad \text{(data field-variable sequences)}$$

where $\circ \in \{=, <, >, \leqslant, \geqslant\}$, $\mathsf{f} \in \mathcal{F}$, and $\mathfrak{d} \in \mathcal{D}$. For spatial formulae Σ, formulae of the form $\mathbf{emp}$, $E \mapsto \rho$, or $P(E, \alpha; F, \beta)$ are called *spatial atoms*. In particular, formulae of the form $E \mapsto \rho$ and $P(E, \alpha; F, \beta)$ are called *points-to atoms* and *predicate atoms* respectively.

A *tree predicate* P (with one hole) is defined by one base rule, and at least one inductive rule of the form R_1 or R_2:

– base rule R_0: $P(E, \alpha; F, \beta) ::= E = F \wedge \alpha = \beta \wedge \mathbf{emp}$,

– left-hole inductive rule R_1:
$$P(E, \alpha; F, \beta) ::= \exists X \exists Y \exists \boldsymbol{x} \exists \boldsymbol{h}. \ \Delta \wedge E \mapsto ((\mathtt{left}, X), (\mathtt{right}, Y), \rho_{\mathsf{d}}) *$$
$$P(X, \delta; F, \beta) * P(Y, \gamma; \mathsf{nil}, \epsilon),$$
where Δ is a data formula and ρ_{d} is a data field-variable sequence.

– right-hole inductive rule R_2:
$$P(E, \alpha; F, \beta) ::= \exists X \exists Y \exists \boldsymbol{x} \exists \boldsymbol{h}. \ \Delta \wedge E \mapsto ((\mathtt{left}, X), (\mathtt{right}, Y), \rho_{\mathsf{d}}) *$$
$$P(X, \gamma; \mathsf{nil}, \epsilon) * P(Y, \delta; F, \beta),$$
where Δ is a data formula and ρ_{d} is a data field-variable sequence.

The left-hand (resp. right-hand) side of a rule is called the *head* (resp. *body*) of the rule. We note that the bodies of R_1 and R_2 do not contain pure formulae.

In the sequel, we specify some constraints on the inductive rules.

The first constraint **C1** guarantees that $P(E, \alpha; F, \beta)$ enjoys the composition lemma $P(E_1, \alpha_1; E_2, \alpha_2) * P(E_2, \alpha_2; E_3, \alpha_3) \Rightarrow P(E_1, \alpha_1; E_3, \alpha_3)$, which is vital for compositionality (cf. [13]). Note that the destination parameter F does not occur elsewhere in the body of the inductive rules by definition, since X, Y are two existentially quantified location variables.

C1 Variables from β do *not* occur elsewhere in the body of the inductive rules.

The second constraint **C2** forbids the repeated occurrences of the variables in γ, δ and requires that no existentially quantified variables occur in the static parameters ϵ.

C2 $\gamma, \delta \subseteq \alpha \cup \boldsymbol{x} \cup \boldsymbol{h} \cup \mathbb{D} \cup \mathbb{N}$, each variable occurs at most once in γ (resp. δ), and $\epsilon \subseteq \alpha \cup \mathbb{D} \cup \mathbb{N}$.

The third constraint **C3** forbids the situation that an existentially quantified variable occurs only in Δ, but not in spatial atoms.

C3 All existentially quantified variables $\boldsymbol{x}, \boldsymbol{h}$ occur in some spatial atom.

The fourth constraint **C4** is to avoid the difficulty of dealing with inductive predicates with more than one size source parameter (cf. Theorem 1).

C4 α contains at most *one* parameter of the *size* type, in addition, if $\alpha(i)$ is of size type, then it must hold that, (i) $\delta(i), \gamma(i) \in h$ and $\epsilon(i) \in \mathbb{N}$, and (ii) the size-formula part of Δ is of the form $\alpha(i) = \delta(i) + n \wedge \Delta_{\mathbb{N}}$ or $\alpha(i) = \gamma(i) + n \wedge \Delta_{\mathbb{N}}$ such that $\alpha(i)$ does not occur in $\Delta_{\mathbb{N}}$.

For a tree predicate P, let $\mathrm{Flds}(P)$ (resp. $\mathrm{LFlds}(P)$) denote the set of fields (resp. location fields) occurring in the inductive rules of P. Evidently, $\mathrm{LFlds}(P) = \{\texttt{left}, \texttt{right}\}$. For a spatial atom a, let $\mathrm{Flds}(a)$ denote the set of fields that a refers to: if $a = E \mapsto \rho$, then $\mathrm{Flds}(a)$ is the set of fields occurring in ρ; if $a = P(-)$, then $\mathrm{Flds}(a) = \mathrm{Flds}(P)$.

We write $\mathsf{CSLTP}[P]$ for the collection of separation logic formulae $\varphi = \Pi \wedge \Delta \wedge \Sigma$ such that P is the only tree predicate allowed to appear in Σ, and for each points-to atom occurring in Σ, the set of fields of this atom is $\mathrm{Flds}(P)$. For a $\mathsf{CSLTP}[P]$ formula φ, let $\mathsf{Vars}(\varphi)$ (resp. $\mathsf{LVars}(\varphi)$, $\mathsf{DVars}(\varphi)$, $\mathsf{IVars}(\varphi)$) denote the set of (resp. location, value, size) variables occurring in φ. Moreover, we use $\varphi[\mu/\alpha]$ to denote the simultaneous replacement of the variables α_j by μ_j in φ.

For the semantics of $\mathsf{CSLTP}[P]$, each formula is interpreted on states. Formally, a *state* is a pair $(\mathfrak{s}, \mathfrak{h})$, where

- $\mathfrak{s}$ is an assignment function which is a partial function from $\mathsf{LVars} \cup \mathsf{DVars} \cup \mathsf{IVars}$ to $\mathbb{L} \cup \mathbb{D} \cup \mathbb{N}$ such that $dom(\mathfrak{s})$ is finite and $\mathfrak{s}$ respects the data type,
- $\mathfrak{h}$ is a *heap* which is a partial function from $\mathbb{L} \times (\mathcal{F} \cup \mathcal{D})$ to $\mathbb{L} \cup \mathbb{D}$ such that
  - $\mathfrak{h}$ respects the data type of fields, that is, for each $l \in \mathbb{L}$ and $\mathfrak{f} \in \mathcal{F}$ (resp. $l \in \mathbb{L}$ and $\mathfrak{d} \in \mathcal{D}$), if $\mathfrak{h}(l, \mathfrak{f})$ (resp. $\mathfrak{h}(l, \mathfrak{d})$) is defined, then $\mathfrak{h}(l, \mathfrak{f}) \in \mathbb{L}$ (resp. $\mathfrak{h}(l, \mathfrak{d}) \in \mathbb{D}$); and
  - $\mathfrak{h}$ is field-consistent, i.e. every location in $\mathfrak{h}$ possess the same set of fields.

For a heap $\mathfrak{h}$, we use $\mathsf{ldom}(\mathfrak{h})$ to denote the set of locations $l \in \mathbb{L}$ such that $\mathfrak{h}(l, \mathfrak{f})$ or $h(l, \mathfrak{d})$ is defined for some $\mathfrak{f} \in \mathcal{F}$ and $\mathfrak{d} \in \mathcal{D}$. Moreover, we use $\mathrm{Flds}(\mathfrak{h})$ to denote the set of fields $\mathfrak{f} \in \mathcal{F}$ or $\mathfrak{d} \in \mathcal{D}$ such that $\mathfrak{h}(l, \mathfrak{f})$ or $\mathfrak{h}(l, \mathfrak{d})$ is defined for some $l \in \mathbb{L}$.

Two heaps $\mathfrak{h}_1$ and $\mathfrak{h}_2$ are said to be *field-compatible* if $\mathrm{Flds}(\mathfrak{h}_1) = \mathrm{Flds}(\mathfrak{h}_2)$. We write $\mathfrak{h}_1 \# \mathfrak{h}_2$ if $\mathsf{ldom}(\mathfrak{h}_1) \cap \mathsf{ldom}(\mathfrak{h}_2) = \varnothing$. Moreover, we write $\mathfrak{h}_1 \uplus \mathfrak{h}_2$ for the disjoint union of two field-compatible fields $\mathfrak{h}_1$ and $\mathfrak{h}_2$ (this implies that $\mathfrak{h}_1 \# \mathfrak{h}_2$).

Let $(\mathfrak{s}, \mathfrak{h})$ be a state and φ be an $\mathsf{CSLTP}[P]$ formula. The semantics of $\mathsf{CSLTP}[P]$ formulae is defined as follows,

- $(\mathfrak{s}, \mathfrak{h}) \vDash E = F$ (resp. $(\mathfrak{s}, \mathfrak{h}) \vDash E \neq F$) if $\mathfrak{s}(E) = \mathfrak{s}(F)$ (resp. $\mathfrak{s}(E) \neq \mathfrak{s}(F)$),
- $(\mathfrak{s}, \mathfrak{h}) \vDash \Pi_1 \wedge \Pi_2$ if $(\mathfrak{s}, \mathfrak{h}) \vDash \Pi_1$ and $(\mathfrak{s}, \mathfrak{h}) \vDash \Pi_2$,
- $(\mathfrak{s}, \mathfrak{h}) \vDash x \circ c$ (resp. $(\mathfrak{s}, \mathfrak{h}) \vDash x \circ x'$) if $\mathfrak{s}(x) \circ c$ (resp. $\mathfrak{s}(x) \circ \mathfrak{s}(x')$),
- $(\mathfrak{s}, \mathfrak{h}) \vDash h \circ c$ (resp. $(\mathfrak{s}, \mathfrak{h}) \vDash h \circ h' + c$) if $\mathfrak{s}(h) \circ c$ (resp. $\mathfrak{s}(h) \circ \mathfrak{s}(h') + c$),
- $(\mathfrak{s}, \mathfrak{h}) \vDash \Delta_1 \wedge \Delta_2$ if $(\mathfrak{s}, \mathfrak{h}) \vDash \Delta_1$ and $(\mathfrak{s}, \mathfrak{h}) \vDash \Delta_2$,
- $(\mathfrak{s}, \mathfrak{h}) \vDash \mathsf{emp}$ if $\mathsf{ldom}(\mathfrak{h}) = \varnothing$,
- $(\mathfrak{s}, \mathfrak{h}) \vDash E \mapsto \rho$ if $\mathsf{ldom}(\mathfrak{h}) = \mathfrak{s}(E)$, and for each $(\mathfrak{f}, X) \in \rho$ (resp. $(\mathfrak{d}, x) \in \rho$), $\mathfrak{h}(\mathfrak{s}(E), \mathfrak{f}) = \mathfrak{s}(X)$ (resp. $\mathfrak{h}(\mathfrak{s}(E), \mathfrak{d}) = \mathfrak{s}(x)$),
- $(\mathfrak{s}, \mathfrak{h}) \vDash P(E, \alpha; F, \beta)$ if $(\mathfrak{s}, \mathfrak{h}) \in [\![P(E, \alpha; F, \beta)]\!]$,
- $(\mathfrak{s}, \mathfrak{h}) \vDash \Sigma_1 * \Sigma_2$ if there are $\mathfrak{h}_1, \mathfrak{h}_2$ such that $\mathfrak{h} = \mathfrak{h}_1 \uplus \mathfrak{h}_2$, $(\mathfrak{s}, \mathfrak{h}_1) \vDash \Sigma_1$ and $(\mathfrak{s}, \mathfrak{h}_2) \vDash \Sigma_2$.

where the semantics of predicates $[\![P(E, \boldsymbol{\alpha}; F, \boldsymbol{\beta})]\!]$ is given by the least fixed point of a monotone operator constructed from the body of rules for P in a standard way as in [6].

For a formula φ, let $[\![\varphi]\!]$ denote the set of states $(\mathfrak{s}, \mathfrak{h})$ such that $(\mathfrak{s}, \mathfrak{h}) \vDash \varphi$. We focus on the satisfiability problem, i.e., given a $\mathsf{CSLTP}[P]$ formula φ, decide whether $[\![\varphi]\!]$ is empty.

Example 1. The first example *bsth* specifies *binary search trees with one hole*, which exemplifies the usage of value variables for the sortedness constraints. Here x, y represent the lower and upper bounds of the data values from $\mathbb{D}$.

$$bsth(E, x, y; F, x', y'):: = E = F \wedge x = x' \wedge y = y' \wedge \mathsf{emp},$$
$$bsth(E, x, y; F, x', y'):: = \exists X, Y, z, x'', y''.\ y'' < z < x'' \wedge$$
$$E \mapsto ((\mathtt{left}, X), (\mathtt{right}, Y), (\mathtt{data}, z)) *$$
$$bsth(X, x, y''; F, x', y') * bsth(Y, x'', y; \mathsf{nil}, y, y),$$
$$bsth(E, x, y; F, x', y'):: = \exists X, Y, z, x'', y''.\ y'' < z < x'' \wedge$$
$$E \mapsto ((\mathtt{left}, X), (\mathtt{right}, Y), (\mathtt{data}, z)) *$$
$$bsth(X, x, y''; \mathsf{nil}, x, x) * bsth(Y, x'', y; F, x', y').$$

Note that a binary search tree can be simply defined as $bsth(E, x, y; \mathsf{nil}, x, x)$ or $bsth(E, x, y; \mathsf{nil}, y, y)$, where E is the root, and x, y are the lower respective upper bounds for the data values occurring in the tree nodes.

The second example *balthole* specifies *height-balancedness of AVL-trees with one hole*, which exemplifies the usage of size parameters. Here $h \in \mathbb{N}$ represents the height of the tree.

$$balthole(E, h; F, h'):: = E = F \wedge h = h' \wedge \mathsf{emp},$$
$$balthole(E, h; F, h'):: = \exists X, Y, h_1, h_2.\ h_1 \leqslant h_2 \leqslant h_1 + 1 \wedge h = h_2 + 1 \wedge$$
$$E \mapsto ((\mathtt{left}, X), (\mathtt{right}, Y)) * balthole(X, h_1; F, h') * balthole(Y, h_2; \mathsf{nil}, 0),$$
$$balthole(E, h; F, h'):: = \exists X, Y, h_1, h_2.\ h = h_1 + 1 \wedge h_1 = h_2 + 1 \wedge$$
$$E \mapsto ((\mathtt{left}, X), (\mathtt{right}, Y)) * balthole(X, h_1; F, h') * balthole(Y, h_2; \mathsf{nil}, 0),$$
$$balthole(E, h; F, h'):: = \exists X, Y, h_1, h_2.\ h_1 \leqslant h_2 \leqslant h_1 + 1 \wedge h = h_2 + 1 \wedge$$
$$E \mapsto ((\mathtt{left}, X), (\mathtt{right}, Y)) * balthole(X, h_1; \mathsf{nil}, 0) * balthole(Y, h_2; F, h'),$$
$$balthole(E, h; F, h'):: = \exists X, Y, h_1, h_2.\ h = h_1 + 1 \wedge h_1 = h_2 + 1 \wedge$$
$$E \mapsto ((\mathtt{left}, X), (\mathtt{right}, Y)) * balthole(X, h_1; \mathsf{nil}, 0) * balthole(Y, h_2; F, h').$$

The definitions of *bsth* and *balthole* can be combined to form a tree predicate $avlth(E, x, y, h; F, x', y', h')$, which specifies both the *sortedness* and the *height-balancedness* property of AVL-trees with one hole.

4   The Least Fixed Point of Data Predicates

Let $P(E, \boldsymbol{\alpha}; F, \boldsymbol{\beta})$ be a tree predicate. The *data predicate* induced by P, denoted by $P_D(\boldsymbol{\alpha}; \boldsymbol{\beta})$, is the predicate whose definition is obtained from the rules of P by ignoring the spatial variables and spatial atoms. Formally, $P_D(\boldsymbol{\alpha}; \boldsymbol{\beta})$ is defined by the rules of the following form,

– base rule: $P_D(\alpha; \beta):: = \alpha = \beta$,

– for each left-hole inductive rule
$$P(E, \alpha; F, \beta) :: = \exists X, Y \exists x \exists h.\ \Delta \wedge E \mapsto ((\texttt{left}, X), (\texttt{right}, Y), \rho_d) *$$
$$P(X, \delta; F, \beta) * P(Y, \gamma; \texttt{nil}, \epsilon),$$
there is an inductive rule for P_D of the form:

$$P_D(\alpha; \beta):: = \exists x \exists h.\ \Delta \wedge P_D(\delta; \beta) \wedge P_D(\gamma; \epsilon),$$

– similarly for the right-hole inductive rules.

Naturally, $P_D(\alpha; \beta)$ induces a monotonic function and we use $\mathsf{lfp}(P_D)$ to denote its least fixed point.

We start with a "negative" result stating that, if multiple size source parameters were allowed in the tree predicates then $\mathsf{lfp}(P_D)$ would be inexpressible in Presburger arithmetic in general. This result underpins the constraint **C4** which dictates that only one source parameter of type $\mathbb{N}$ is allowed.

Theorem 1. *If x, y, x', y' in $avlth(E, x, y, h; F, x', y', h')$ are assumed to be of the type $\mathbb{N}$, then $\mathsf{lfp}(avlth_D)$ is inexpressible in Presburger arithmetic.*

The intuition of Theorem 1 is explained as follows: If the data values in AVL-trees are assumed to be natural numbers, then in $avlth(E, x, y, h; \mathsf{nil}, x, x, 0)$, the predicate atom for AVL trees, $y - x$ correlates with h and is at least exponential in h. This relationship goes beyond Presburger arithmetic.

Next, for a tree predicate P in CSLTP, we show that a linear arithmetic formula can be computed to represent $\mathsf{lfp}(P_D)$.

Theorem 2. *A linear arithmetic formula can be computed in 5-fold exponential time to represent $\mathsf{lfp}(P_D)$. In addition, if the natural-number constants in the inductive definition of P_D are encoded in unary, then the complexity is reduced to 4-fold exponential time.*

The rest of this section is devoted to the proof of Theorem 2. We start with two simpler cases, i.e., **dense order constraints** and **single size parameter**.

4.1 Dense Order Constraints

In this subsection, we fix a tree predicate $P(E, \alpha; F, \beta)$ where all parameters in α and β are of the type $\mathbb{D}$. As a result, only value formulae $\Delta_{\mathbb{D}}$ are used in $P_D(\alpha; \beta)$. Let $\mathcal{C}(P_D)$ denote the set of constants occurring in the rules of P_D.

Definition 2 (Order graphs). *Let V be a finite subset of $\mathsf{DVars} \cup \mathbb{D}$. An order graph G on V is an edge-labelled graph (V, E), where $E \subseteq V \times \{\leqslant, <\} \times V$.*

It is evident that order graphs are simply another representation of value formulae, which are dense order constraints on $\mathbb{D}$. More specifically, from an order graph G on V, a dense order constraint $\Delta_{\mathbb{D}}(G)$ can be naturally defined. On the other hand, an order graph $G_{\Delta_{\mathbb{D}}}$ can be constructed from a value formula $\Delta_{\mathbb{D}}$. For two order graphs G_1, G_2, we will use $G_1 \models G_2$ to denote $\Delta_{\mathbb{D}}(G_1) \models \Delta_{\mathbb{D}}(G_2)$.

Definition 3 (Saturated order graphs). *Assume an order graph $G = (V, E)$. The saturated graph of G, denoted by $\mathsf{Sat}(G)$, is computed from G by the following procedure:*

1. *Initially, let $\mathsf{Sat}(G) := G$.*
2. *Repeat the following procedure until no more edges can be added to $\mathsf{Sat}(G)$.*
   - *If there are two edges (v_1, o_1, v_2) and (v_2, o_2, v_3) in $\mathsf{Sat}[G]$ such that o_1 and o_2 are both $\leqslant$ and $(v_1, \leqslant, v_3)$ is not an edge in $\mathsf{Sat}(G)$, then add $(v_1, \leqslant, v_3)$ into $\mathsf{Sat}(G)$.*
   - *If there are two edges (v_1, o_1, v_2) and (v_2, o_2, v_3) in $\mathsf{Sat}(G)$ such that at least one of o_1 and o_2 is $<$ and $(v_1, <, v_3)$ is not an edge in $\mathsf{Sat}(G)$, then add $(v_1, <, v_3)$ into $\mathsf{Sat}(G)$.*

$\mathsf{Sat}(G)$ *is said to be* consistent *if it does not contain edges of the form $(v, <, v)$ for $v \in V$. Otherwise, it is said to be* inconsistent.

Proposition 2. *Let $\Delta_{\mathbb{D}}$ be a value formula. Then $\Delta_{\mathbb{D}}$ is satisfiable iff $\mathsf{Sat}(G_{\Delta_{\mathbb{D}}})$ is consistent.*

For a finite set $V \subseteq \mathsf{DVars} \cup \mathbb{D}$, we use $\mathcal{G}_{\mathsf{ord}}(V)$ to denote the set of *consistent saturated* order graphs on V. Note that the cardinality of $\mathcal{G}_{\mathsf{ord}}(V)$ is exponential in the size of V.

To compute $\mathsf{lfp}(P_D)$, let $V = \boldsymbol{\alpha} \cup \boldsymbol{\beta} \cup \mathcal{C}(P_D)$. We define a monotone function $\mathcal{T}_{P_D} : 2^{\mathcal{G}_{\mathsf{ord}}(V)} \to 2^{\mathcal{G}_{\mathsf{ord}}(V)}$ to capture $P_D(\boldsymbol{\alpha}; \boldsymbol{\beta})$, and compute $\mathsf{lfp}(\mathcal{T}_{P_D})$ by a standard iteration: let $\mathcal{G}_0 = \varnothing$, and $\mathcal{G}_i := \mathcal{T}_{P_D}(\mathcal{G}_{i-1})$ until the iteration stabilises. The algorithm terminates in exponential time, since $\mathcal{T}_{P_D}$ is monotone and the cardinality of $\mathcal{G}_{\mathsf{ord}}(V)$ is exponential in the size of V.

Suppose $|\boldsymbol{\alpha}| = k$. For a vector $\boldsymbol{d}, \boldsymbol{d}' \in \mathbb{D}^k$, define an order graph $\mathcal{G}_{\boldsymbol{d},\boldsymbol{d}'} = (V, E_{\boldsymbol{d},\boldsymbol{d}'})$ as as follows: Let $\eta : V \to \boldsymbol{d} \cup \boldsymbol{d}' \cup \mathcal{C}(P_D)$ such that $\eta(\boldsymbol{\alpha}(i)) = \boldsymbol{d}(i)$ and $\eta(\boldsymbol{\beta}(i)) = \boldsymbol{d}'(i)$ for each $i \in [k]$, and $\eta(d'') = d''$ for each $d'' \in \mathcal{C}(P_D)$. Then for each $z, z' \in V$ and $\mathsf{o} \in \{<, \leqslant\}$, $(z, \mathsf{o}, z') \in E_{\boldsymbol{d},\boldsymbol{d}'}$ iff $\eta(z) \mathsf{o} \eta(z')$ holds in $\mathbb{D}$.

Proposition 3. *For any two vectors $\boldsymbol{d}, \boldsymbol{d}' \in \mathbb{D}^k$, $\mathsf{lfp}(P_D)(\boldsymbol{d}; \boldsymbol{d}')$ holds iff there exists $G \in \mathsf{lfp}(\mathcal{T}_{P_D})$ such that $\mathcal{G}_{\boldsymbol{d},\boldsymbol{d}'} \models G$.*

4.2   Single Size Parameter

In this subsection, we fix a tree predicate P where all (data) parameters are of type $\mathbb{N}$. Then according to **C4**, the parameters of P are of the form $(E, \alpha; F, \beta)$, where α, β are of type $\mathbb{N}$, in addition, each inductive rule of the associated data predicate $P_D(\alpha; \beta)$ is of the form

$$P_D(\alpha; \beta) ::= \exists \boldsymbol{h}. \; \Delta_{\mathbb{N}} \wedge P_D(\delta; \beta) \wedge P_D(\gamma; n). \tag{1}$$

Let $\mathcal{N}(P_D)$ denote the set of all constants n occurring in the predicate atom $P_D(\gamma; n)$ of the body $P_D(\alpha; \beta)$. By **C3** and **C4**, δ and γ are the *only* existentially quantified variables, that is, $\exists \boldsymbol{h} = \exists \delta \exists \gamma$. For each $n \in \mathcal{N}(P_D)$, we introduce a new predicate $P_{D,n}(\alpha)$, the definition of which is as follows:

- base rule: $P_{D,n}(\alpha):: = \alpha = n$,
- inductive rules: $P_{D,n}(\alpha):: = \exists\delta\exists\gamma.\ \Delta \wedge P_{D,n}(\delta) \wedge P_{D,n'}(\gamma)$, if there is an inductive rule $P_D(\alpha;\beta):: = \exists\delta\exists\gamma.\ \Delta \wedge P_D(\delta;\beta) \wedge P_D(\gamma;n')$.

The general strategy to solve (1) is to first compute $\mathsf{lfp}(P_{D,n})$ as a quantifier-free Presburger formula $\varphi_{P_{D,n}}(\alpha)$ for the predicates $P_{D,n}$ with $n \in \mathcal{N}(P_D)$. We then substitute $P_D(\gamma, n')$ in the body of the inductive rule of $P_D(\alpha;\beta)$ with $\varphi_{P_{D,n'}}(\gamma)$, resulting in a new collection of inductive rules for $P_D(\alpha;\beta)$. Finally, we compute the least fixed point of the function induced by this new collection of rules of $P_D(\alpha;\beta)$.

Computation of $\mathsf{lfp}(P_{D,n})$. We will reduce the problem to the computation of the reachability sets of an A1CS $\mathcal{A}_{P_D} = (Q, \Theta)$, where Q is the union of $\{P_{D,n} \mid n \in \mathcal{N}(P_D)\}$ and a set of auxiliary states (see below), and Θ is defined according to the inductive rules of the predicates $P_{D,n}$ for $n \in \mathcal{N}(P_D)$.

Let us fix a predicate $P_{D,n}$ and an inductive rule of $P_{D,n}$

$$P_{D,n}(\alpha):: = \exists\delta\exists\gamma.\ \Delta_{\mathbb{N}} \wedge P_{D,n}(\delta) \wedge P_{D,n'}(\gamma). \tag{2}$$

By **C4**, the size formula $\Delta_{\mathbb{N}}$ must be of the form $\alpha = \delta + m \wedge \Delta'$ or $\alpha = \gamma + m \wedge \Delta'$ such that α does not occur in Δ'. W.l.o.g., we assume that $\alpha = \delta + m$ holds. It follows that Δ' is a conjunction of difference bound constraints over δ and γ. Hence, we may constraint γ in terms of α (rather than δ; this is possible because $\alpha = \delta + m$). Namely, we may assume that $\Delta' = \Delta_1'(\alpha) \wedge \Delta_2'(\alpha, \gamma) \wedge \Delta_3'(\gamma)$, where $\Delta_1', \Delta_2', \Delta_3'$ are defined by the following rules,

1. $\Delta_1'(\alpha):: = \mathsf{true} \mid \alpha \geqslant l \mid \alpha \leqslant u \mid l \leqslant \alpha \leqslant u$, where $l, u \in \mathbb{N}$,
2. $\Delta_2'(\alpha, \gamma):: = \mathsf{true} \mid \gamma \geqslant \alpha + l \mid \gamma \leqslant \alpha + u \mid \alpha + l \leqslant \gamma \leqslant \alpha + u$, where $l, u \in \mathbb{Z}$,
3. $\Delta_3'(\gamma):: = \mathsf{true} \mid \gamma \geqslant l \mid \gamma \leqslant u \mid l \leqslant \gamma \leqslant u$, where $l, u \in \mathbb{N}$.

Θ comprises the transition rules for each predicate $P_{D,n}$ and each inductive rule of $P_{D,n}$ as in Eq. (2), defined as follows:

- the transition rules for $\Delta_1'(\alpha)$:
  - if $\Delta_1' = \mathsf{true}$, then $P_{D,n} \hookrightarrow \{(+0, q_1)\}$,
  - if $\Delta_1' = \alpha \geqslant l$, then $P_{D,n} \hookrightarrow \{(\geqslant l, q_1)\}$,
  - if $\Delta_1' = \alpha \leqslant u$, then $P_{D,n} \hookrightarrow \{(\leqslant u, q_1)\}$,
  - if $\Delta_1' = l \leqslant \alpha \leqslant u$, then $P_{D,n} \hookrightarrow \{(\geqslant l, q_1')\}$, $q_1' \hookrightarrow \{(\leqslant u, q_1)\}$;
- the transition rules for $\alpha = \delta + m \wedge \Delta_2'(\alpha, \gamma)$:
  - if $\Delta_2' = \mathsf{true}$, then $q_1 \hookrightarrow \{(-m, P_{D,n}), (\mathsf{reset}(0), q_2')\}$, $q_2' \hookrightarrow \{(+1, q_2')\}$, and $q_2' \hookrightarrow \{(+0, q_2)\}$,
  - if $\Delta_2' = \gamma \geqslant \alpha + l$, then $q_1 \hookrightarrow \{(-m, P_{D,n}), (l, q_2')\}$, $q_2' \hookrightarrow \{(+1, q_2')\}$, $q_2' \hookrightarrow \{(+0, q_2)\}$,
  - if $\Delta_2' = \gamma \leqslant \alpha + u$, then $q_1 \hookrightarrow \{(-m, P_{D,n}), (u, q_2')\}$, $q_2' \hookrightarrow \{(-1, q_2')\}$, $q_2' \hookrightarrow \{(+0, q_2)\}$,
  - if $\Delta_2' = \alpha + l \leqslant \gamma \leqslant \alpha + u$, then $q_1 \hookrightarrow \{(-m, P_{D,n}), (m', q_2)\}$ for each $l \leqslant m' \leqslant u$;

- the transition rules for $\Delta'_3(\gamma)$:
  - if $\Delta'_3 = \texttt{true}$, then $q_2 \hookrightarrow \{(+0, P_{D,n'})\}$,
  - if $\Delta'_3 = \gamma \geqslant l$, then $q_2 \hookrightarrow \{(\geqslant l, P_{D,n'})\}$,
  - if $\Delta'_3 = \gamma \leqslant u$, then $q_2 \hookrightarrow \{(\leqslant u, P_{D,n'})\}$,
  - if $\Delta'_3 = l \leqslant \gamma \leqslant u$, then $q_2 \hookrightarrow \{(\geqslant l, q'_3)\}$, $q'_3 \hookrightarrow \{(\leqslant u, P_{D,n'})\}$,

where $q_1, q_2, q'_1, q'_2, q'_3$ are the auxiliary (control) states.

For each predicate $P_{D,n}$, we use $\mathcal{P}(P_{D,n})$ to denote the set of predicates $P_{D,n'}$ such that $P_{D,n'}$ occurs in the body of some inductive rule of $P_{D,n}$. In particular, $P_{D,n} \in \mathcal{P}(P_{D,n})$. Then for each $P_{D,n}$, we define a set of *goal configurations* $\mathsf{GConf}(P_{D,n}) = \{(P_{D,n'}, n') \mid P_{D,n'} \in \mathcal{P}(P_{D,n})\}$.

Proposition 4. *For each predicate $P_{D,n}$ and $m \in \mathbb{N}$, $\mathsf{lfp}(P_{D,n})(m)$ holds iff $(P_{D,n}, m) \Rightarrow_{\mathcal{A}_{P_D}} \mathsf{GConf}(P_{D,n})$.*

Thanks to Proposition 4, we have $\mathsf{lfp}(P_{D,n}) = \mathsf{Pre}^*_{\mathcal{A}_{P_D}}(P_{D,n}, \mathsf{GConf}(P_{D,n}))$. According to Proposition 1, for each predicate $P_{D,n}$, a quantifier-free Presburger formula $\varphi_{P_{D,n}}(\alpha)$ in disjunctive normal form to represent $\mathsf{lfp}(P_{D,n})$, can be computed in doubly exponential time w.r.t. the size of $\mathcal{A}_{P_D}$ (thus in doubly exponential time w.r.t. the size of the inductive definition of P_D as well). In addition, if the constants in the inductive definition of P_D are encoded in unary, then the complexity is dropped to singly exponential time.

Computation of $\mathsf{lfp}(P_D)$. The main idea is to reduce the computation of $\mathsf{lfp}(P_D)$ to solving the reachability problem of an N1CS.

From the previous step, the solution of $P_{D,n}(\gamma)$ is expressed by the formula $\varphi_{P_{D,n}}(\gamma)$ in disjunctive normal form, say $\varphi_{P_{D,n}}(\gamma) = \bigvee\limits_{1 \leqslant i \leqslant \ell_n} \varphi^{(i)}_{P_{D,n}}(\gamma)$, where each $\varphi^{(i)}_{P_{D,n}}(\gamma)$ is of the form $\gamma = n_1$ or $\gamma \geqslant n_1 \wedge \gamma \equiv n_3 \bmod n_2$. Let $N \in \mathbb{N}$ be the least common multiplier of the divisors n_2 occurring in $\varphi_{P_{D,n}}(\alpha)$ for $n \in \mathcal{N}(P_D)$.

It follows that $P_D(\alpha; \beta):: = \exists \delta \exists \gamma. \; \Delta_{\mathbb{N}} \wedge P_D(\delta; \beta) \wedge P_D(\gamma; n) \equiv \bigvee\limits_{1 \leqslant i \leqslant \ell_n}$ $\exists \delta \exists \gamma. \; \Delta_{\mathbb{N}} \wedge \varphi^{(i)}_{P_{D,n}}(\gamma) \wedge P_D(\delta; \beta)$. Namely, it suffices to consider $P_D(\alpha; \beta)$ with multiple rules of the form

$$P_D(\alpha; \beta):: = \exists \delta \exists \gamma. \; (\Delta_{\mathbb{N}} \wedge \varphi^{(i)}_{P_{D,n}}(\gamma)) \wedge P_D(\delta; \beta), \tag{3}$$

for $1 \leqslant i \leqslant \ell_n$, where each $\varphi^{(i)}_{P_{D,n}}(\gamma)$ is of the form $\gamma = n_1$ or $\gamma \geqslant n_1 \wedge \gamma \equiv n_3 \bmod N$. This new collection of rules is *linear* in that the predicate P_D occurs at most once in the body of each rule, which is simpler than (2).

$\mathsf{lfp}(P_D)$ can now be computed by appealing to an N1CS $\mathcal{B}_{P_D} = (Q', \Theta')$. The N1CS $\mathcal{B}_{P_D}$ is constructed according to the new collection of rules of P_D. The states of $\mathcal{B}_{P_D}$ are of the form (q, r), where q is a location and $r \in \{0, \ldots, N-1\}$. In $\mathcal{B}_{P_D}$, a special location q_0 is used to represent the predicate P_D.

Let us fix an inductive rule of $P_D(\alpha; \beta)$, say

$$P_D(\alpha; \beta):: = \exists \delta \exists \gamma. \; (\Delta_{\mathbb{N}} \wedge \varphi^{(i)}_{P_{D,n}}(\gamma)) \wedge P_D(\delta; \beta). \tag{4}$$

We will demonstrate how to construct the transition rules of $\mathcal{B}_{P_D}$ according to this rule. We will only illustrate the construction for the case that each $\varphi_{P_D,n}^{(i)}(\gamma)$ is of the form $\gamma \geqslant n_1 \wedge \gamma \equiv n_3 \bmod N$. The construction for the case $\gamma = n_1$ is (much) simpler.

For (4), as before by **C4**, $\Delta_{\mathbb{N}}$ must be of the form $\alpha = \delta + m \wedge \Delta'$ or $\alpha = \gamma + m \wedge \Delta'$ such that α does *not* occur in Δ'. We will illustrate the construction by considering the former case, that is, $\alpha = \delta + m \wedge \Delta'$.

Since $\delta = \alpha - m$, we can assume that Δ' is a formula involving only α, γ (instead of δ, γ). As before, Δ' can be written as $\Delta_1'(\alpha) \wedge \Delta_2'(\alpha, \gamma) \wedge \Delta_3'(\gamma)$. Therefore,

$$\Delta' \wedge \varphi_{P_D,n}^{(i)}(\gamma) = \Delta_1'(\alpha) \wedge \Delta_2'(\alpha, \gamma) \wedge (\Delta_3'(\gamma) \wedge \gamma \geqslant n_1 \wedge \gamma \equiv n_3 \bmod N).$$

For each $r \in \{0, \ldots, N-1\}$, Θ' includes the transition rules defined below. Let us assume that the formula $\Delta_3'(\gamma) \wedge \gamma \geqslant n_1 \wedge \gamma \equiv n_3 \bmod N$ is satisfiable (since otherwise, no transition rules should be included into Θ' in this case).

– The transition rules for Δ_1':
  - if $\Delta_1' = \mathbf{true}$, then $(q_0, r) \hookrightarrow (+0, (q_1, r))$,
  - if $\Delta_1' = \alpha \geqslant l$, then $(q_0, r) \hookrightarrow (\geqslant l, (q_1, r))$,
  - if $\Delta_1' = \alpha \leqslant u$, then $(q_0, r) \hookrightarrow (\leqslant u, (q_1, r))$,
  - if $\Delta_1' = l \leqslant \alpha \leqslant u$, then $(q_0, r) \hookrightarrow (\geqslant l, (q_1', r))$, $(q_1', r) \hookrightarrow (\leqslant u, (q_1, r))$;
– the transition rules for

$$\Delta'' = \Delta_2'(\alpha, \gamma) \wedge (\Delta_3'(\gamma) \wedge \gamma \geqslant n_1 \wedge \gamma \equiv n_3 \bmod N) :$$

  - if $\Delta_2' = \mathbf{true}$, then $(q_1, r) \hookrightarrow (+0, (q_2, r))$, since $\Delta_3'(\gamma) \wedge \gamma \geqslant n_1 \wedge \gamma \equiv n_3 \bmod N$ is satisfiable (by assumption),
  - if $\Delta_2' = \gamma \geqslant \alpha + l$, then
    * if $\Delta_3' = \mathbf{true}$ or $\Delta_3' = \gamma \geqslant l'$, then

      $$\exists \gamma.\ \Delta'' = \exists \gamma.\ \gamma \geqslant \alpha + l \wedge \Delta_3' \wedge \gamma \geqslant n_1 \wedge \gamma \equiv n_3 \bmod N$$

      is satisfiable for every value of α, therefore, we have $(q_1, r) \hookrightarrow (+0, (q_2, r))$,
    * if $\Delta_3' = \gamma \leqslant u'$ or $\Delta_3' = l' \leqslant \gamma \leqslant u'$, let $l'' = n_1$ or $l'' = \max(l', n_1)$ respectively, then

      $$\exists \gamma.\ \Delta'' = \exists \gamma.\ \gamma \geqslant \alpha + l \wedge l'' \leqslant \gamma \leqslant u' \wedge \gamma \equiv n_3 \bmod N,$$

      from this, we have that for each $s \in \mathbb{N}$ such that $l'' \leqslant s \leqslant u'$ and $s \equiv n_3 \bmod N$, $(q_1, r) \hookrightarrow (\leqslant s - l, (q_2, r))$,
  - if $\Delta_2' = \gamma \leqslant \alpha + u$,
    * if $\Delta_3' = \mathbf{true}$ or $\Delta_3' = \gamma \geqslant l'$, let $l'' = n_1$ or $l'' = \max(l', n_1)$ respectively, then

      $$\exists \gamma.\ \Delta'' = \exists \gamma.\ \gamma \leqslant \alpha + u \wedge \gamma \geqslant l'' \wedge \gamma \equiv n_3 \bmod N,$$

      which is equivalent to $\alpha + u \geqslant l'' + s$, where s is the minimum natural number satisfying $0 \leqslant s < N$ and $l'' + s \equiv n_3 \bmod N$, therefore, we have $(q_1, r) \hookrightarrow (\geqslant l'' + s - u, (q_2, r))$,

* if $\Delta_3' = \gamma \leqslant u'$ or $\Delta_3' = l' \leqslant \gamma \leqslant u'$, let $l'' = n_1$ or $l'' = \max(l', n_1)$ respectively, then

$$\exists \gamma. \ \Delta'' = \exists \gamma. \ \gamma \leqslant \alpha + u \wedge l'' \leqslant \gamma \leqslant u' \wedge \gamma \equiv n_3 \bmod N,$$

from this, we have that for each $s \in \mathbb{N}$ such that $l'' \leqslant s \leqslant u'$ and $s \equiv n_3 \bmod N$, $(q_1, r) \hookrightarrow (\geqslant s - u, (q_2, r))$,

- if $\Delta_2' = \alpha + l \leqslant \gamma \leqslant \alpha + u$, then
  * if $\Delta_3' = \mathbf{true}$ or $\Delta_3' = \gamma \geqslant l'$, let $l'' = n_1$ or $l'' = \max(l', n_1)$ respectively, then

$$\exists \gamma. \ \Delta'' = \exists \gamma. \ \alpha + l \leqslant \gamma \leqslant \alpha + u \wedge \gamma \geqslant l'' \wedge \gamma \equiv n_3 \bmod N,$$

which is equivalent to $\alpha + s \geqslant l''$, provided that $\alpha \equiv r \bmod N$, where s is the maximum natural number such that $l \leqslant s \leqslant u$ and $r + s \equiv n_3 \bmod N$, therefore, we have $(q_1, r) \hookrightarrow (\geqslant l'' - s, (q_2, r))$,
  * if $\Delta_3' = \gamma \leqslant u'$ or $\Delta_3' = l' \leqslant \gamma \leqslant u'$, let $l'' = n_1$ or $l'' = \max(l', n_1)$ respectively, then

$$\exists \gamma. \ \Delta'' = \exists \gamma. \ \alpha + l \leqslant \gamma \leqslant \alpha + u \wedge l'' \leqslant \gamma \leqslant u' \wedge \gamma \equiv n_3 \bmod N,$$

from this, we have that for each $s \in \mathbb{N}$ such that $l'' \leqslant s \leqslant u'$ and $s \equiv n_3 \bmod N$, $(q_1, r) \hookrightarrow (\leqslant s - l, (q_2', r))$ and $(q_2', r) \hookrightarrow (\geqslant s - u, (q_2, r))$,
- the transition rule for $\alpha = \delta + m$: $(q_2, r) \hookrightarrow (-m, (q_0, (r - m) \bmod N))$,

where q_1, q_2, q_1', q_2' are the freshly introduced locations.

We have the following result:

Proposition 5. *For $m, n \in \mathbb{N}$, let $r = m \bmod N$ and $r' = n \bmod N$. Then $\mathsf{lfp}(P_D)(m, n)$ holds iff $((q_0, r), m) \Rightarrow_{\mathcal{B}_{P_D}} ((q_0, r'), n)$.*

From Proposition 1, for each $r, r' \in \{0, \ldots, N - 1\}$, a quantifier-free Presburger formula $\varphi_{(q_0, r), (q_0, r')}(\alpha, \beta)$ can be computed in triply exponential time w.r.t. the size of $\mathcal{B}_{P_D}$ to represent $\{(m, n) \in \mathbb{N}^2 \mid ((q_0, r), m) \Rightarrow_{\mathcal{B}_{P_D}} ((q_0, r'), n)\}$. Therefore, from Proposition 5, $\mathsf{lfp}(P_D)$ can be expressed with $\varphi_{P_D}(\alpha, \beta) \equiv \bigvee_{0 \leqslant r, r' < N} \varphi_{(q_0, r), (q_0, r')}(\alpha, \beta)$. Since the size of the new collection of inductive rules of P_D—thus the size of $\mathcal{B}_{P_D}$—is at most doubly exponential in the size of the (original) inductive definition of P_D, we conclude that the size of $\varphi_{P_D}(\alpha, \beta)$ is 5-fold exponential in the size of the (original) inductive definition of P_D. In addition, the size of $\varphi_{P_D}(\alpha, \beta)$ is 4-fold exponential if the constants in the inductive definition of P_D are encoded in unary.

4.3   The General Case

In the subsection, we show how to combine the techniques developed in the preceding sections to tackle the general case. Without loss of generality, we assume that the data predicate $P_D(\boldsymbol{\alpha}, \boldsymbol{\beta})$ satisfies that $|\boldsymbol{\alpha}| = k > 1$, $\boldsymbol{\alpha}(1), \cdots, \boldsymbol{\alpha}(k - 1)$

are of type $\mathbb{D}$, and $\alpha(k)$ is of type $\mathbb{N}$. For convenience, we write $\alpha = (\alpha', \alpha'')$ where $\alpha' = (\alpha(1), \ldots, \alpha(k-1))$ and $\alpha'' = \alpha(k)$. Similarly, $\beta = (\beta', \beta'')$. Then each inductive rule for P_D is of the form

$$P_D(\alpha', \alpha''; \beta', \beta''):: = \exists x \exists h. \ \Delta_\mathbb{D} \wedge \Delta_\mathbb{N} \wedge P_D(\delta', \delta''; \beta', \beta'') \wedge P_D(\gamma', \gamma''; \epsilon', n).$$

We split each inductive rule of P_D into two rules,

$$P_{D,\mathbb{D}}(\alpha'; \beta'):: = \exists x. \ \Delta_\mathbb{D} \wedge P_{D,\mathbb{D}}(\delta'; \beta') \wedge P_{D,\mathbb{D}}(\gamma'; \epsilon'),$$

$$P_{D,\mathbb{N}}(\alpha''; \beta''):: = \exists h. \ \Delta_\mathbb{N} \wedge P_{D,\mathbb{N}}(\delta''; \beta'') \wedge P_{D,\mathbb{N}}(\gamma''; n).$$

The computation of $\mathsf{lfp}(P_D)$ proceeds as follows. Intuitively, we first deal with $P_{D,\mathbb{D}}(\alpha'; \beta')$ and $P_{D,\mathbb{N}}(\alpha''; \beta'')$ separately by the constructions in Sects. 4.1 and 4.2. More specifically, $\mathsf{lfp}(\mathcal{T}_{P_{D,\mathbb{D}}})$, a set of order graphs on V, is computed, and the A1CS $\mathcal{A}_{P_{D,\mathbb{N}}}$ and the N1CS $\mathcal{B}_{P_{D,\mathbb{N}}}$ are constructed. We then integrate the order graphs from $\mathsf{lfp}(\mathcal{T}_{P_{D,\mathbb{D}}})$ into the states of $\mathcal{A}_{P_{D,\mathbb{N}}}$ and $\mathcal{B}_{P_{D,\mathbb{N}}}$.

As the first step, we use the algorithm in Sect. 4.1 to compute $\mathsf{lfp}(\mathcal{T}_{P_{D,\mathbb{D}}})$. As a result, we obtain a set of order graphs over $V = \alpha' \cup \beta' \cup \mathcal{C}(P_{D,\mathbb{D}})$, where $\mathcal{C}(P_{D,\mathbb{D}})$ is the set of constants occurring in the body of the rules of $P_{D,\mathbb{D}}(\alpha'; \beta')$.

Suppose $\mathcal{A}_{P_{D,\mathbb{N}}} = (Q, \Theta)$ is the A1CS constructed for $P_{D,\mathbb{N}}(\alpha''; \beta'')$ as in Sect. 4.2. Recall that Q is the union of $\{P_{D,\mathbb{N},n} \mid n \in \mathcal{N}(P_{D,\mathbb{N}})\}$ and a set of auxiliary states. We shall construct a new A1CS $\mathcal{A}'_{P_D}$. The state space of $\mathcal{A}'_{P_D}$ is $\mathsf{lfp}(\mathcal{T}_{P_{D,\mathbb{D}}}) \times Q$. As before, for each $n \in \mathcal{N}(P_{D,\mathbb{N}})$, we consider a predicate $P_{D,n}(\alpha', \alpha''; \beta')$ whose inductive definition is obtained from that of $P_D(\alpha', \alpha''; \beta', \beta'')$ by replacing β'' with n. Specifically, each inductive rule of $P_{D,n}$ is of the form,

$$P_{D,n}(\alpha', \alpha''; \beta'):: = \exists x \exists h. \ \Delta_\mathbb{D} \wedge \Delta_\mathbb{N} \wedge P_{D,n}(\delta', \delta''; \beta') \wedge P_{D,n'}(\gamma', \gamma''; \epsilon'). \quad (5)$$

Considering the inductive rule of $P_{D,\mathbb{N},n}(\alpha'')$ corresponding to (5),

$$P_{D,\mathbb{N},n}(\alpha''):: = \exists h. \ \Delta_\mathbb{N} \wedge P_{D,\mathbb{N},n}(\delta'') \wedge P_{D,\mathbb{N},n'}(\gamma''). \quad (6)$$

We lift the transition rules of $\mathcal{A}_{P_{D,\mathbb{N}}}$ for the inductive rule (6) of $P_{D,\mathbb{N},n}(\alpha'')$ to the ones of $\mathcal{A}'_{P_D}$ for the rule (5) of $P_{D,n}(\alpha', \alpha''; \beta')$ as follows: For every $G, G_1, G_2 \in \mathsf{lfp}(\mathcal{T}_{P_{D,\mathbb{D}}})$ satisfying the proper constraints induced by some inductive rule of $P_{D,\mathbb{D}}$, add G, G_1, G_2 as the first-component of states. For instance, the transitions $P_{D,\mathbb{N},n} \hookrightarrow (+0, q_1)$, $q_1 \hookrightarrow \{(-m, P_{D,\mathbb{N},n}), (\mathsf{reset}(0), q'_2)\}$, $q'_2 \hookrightarrow \{(+1, q'_2)\}$, $q'_2 \hookrightarrow \{(+0, q_2)\}$, and $q_2 \hookrightarrow \{(+0, P_{D,\mathbb{N},n'})\}$ in $\mathcal{A}_{P_{D,\mathbb{N}}}$ are changed to the following transitions in $\mathcal{A}'_{P_D}$ respectively: $(G, P_{D,\mathbb{N},n}) \hookrightarrow (+0, (G, q_1))$, $(G, q_1) \hookrightarrow \{(-m, (G_1, P_{D,\mathbb{N},n})), (\mathsf{reset}(0), (G, q'_2))\}$, $(G, q'_2) \hookrightarrow \{(+1, (G, q'_2))\}$, $(G, q'_2) \hookrightarrow \{(+0, (G, q_2))\}$, and $(G, q_2) \hookrightarrow \{(+0, (G_2, P_{D,\mathbb{N},n'}))\}$.

Recall that $\mathcal{P}(P_{D,\mathbb{N},n})$ is the set of predicates $P_{D,\mathbb{N},n'}$ occurring in the body of the inductive rules of $P_{D,\mathbb{N},n}$. Let $\mathsf{GConf}'(P_{D,n}) = \{((G_0, P_{D,\mathbb{N},n'}), n') \mid P_{D,\mathbb{N},n'} \in \mathcal{P}(P_{D,\mathbb{N},n})\}$, where G_0 is the order graph corresponding to the value formula $\alpha' = \beta'$. Again, from Proposition 1, for each state $(G, P_{D,\mathbb{N},n})$ of $\mathcal{A}'_{P_D}$, a quantifier-free Presburger formula $\varphi_{(G, P_{D,\mathbb{N},n})}$ can be computed to represent the set of natural numbers $\mathsf{Pre}^*_{\mathcal{A}'_{P_D}}((G, P_{D,\mathbb{N},n}), \mathsf{GConf}'(P_{D,n}))$. As a result, $\mathsf{lfp}(P_{D,n})$ is given by

$$\varphi_{P_{D,n}}(\alpha', \alpha''; \beta') = \bigvee_{G \in \mathsf{lfp}(\mathcal{T}_{P_{D,\mathbb{D}}})} (\Delta(G) \wedge \varphi_{(G, P_{D,\mathbb{N},n})}).$$

Next, we replace each predicate atom $P_D(\gamma', \gamma''; \epsilon', n)$ in the body of each inductive rule by the formula $\varphi_{P_{D,n}}(\gamma', \gamma''; \epsilon')$ and rewrite $\varphi_{P_{D,n}}(\gamma', \gamma''; \epsilon')$ into a disjunctive normal form, resulting into a new collection of *linear* inductive rules for $P_D(\alpha', \alpha''; \beta', \beta'')$.

We can then define the N1CS $\mathcal{B}'_{P_D}$ by adapting the construction of the N1CS $\mathcal{B}_{P_{D,\mathbb{N}}}$ for $P_{D,\mathbb{N}}$. Roughly speaking, this is done by adding the order graphs as components of the states of $\mathcal{B}_{P_{D,\mathbb{N}}}$. Finally, a linear arithmetic formula $\varphi_{P_D}(\alpha; \beta)$, which is a mixture of dense order constraints and quantifier-free Presburger formulae, is computed from $\mathcal{B}'_{P_D}$ to represent $\mathsf{lfp}(P_D)$, by using Proposition 1.

5   Satisfiability

Let $\varphi = \Pi \wedge \Delta \wedge \Sigma$ be a $\mathsf{CSLTP}[P]$ formula. Suppose $\Sigma = a_1 * \cdots * a_n$, where each a_i is either a points-to atom or a predicate atom. Let $P_D(\alpha; \beta)$ be the data predicate induced by P and $\varphi_{P_D}(\alpha, \beta)$ be the formula constructed in Sect. 4 to represent $\mathsf{lfp}(P_D)$. For each inductive rule R of $P(E, \alpha; F, \beta)$, we define $\Delta_R^{\geq 1}(\alpha; \beta)$ as follows.

– If R is a left-hole inductive rule

$$P(E, \alpha; F, \beta) :: = \exists X \exists Y \exists x \exists h.\ \Delta \wedge E \mapsto ((\mathtt{left}, X), (\mathtt{right}, Y), \rho_\mathsf{d}) * \\ P(X, \delta; F, \beta) * P(Y, \gamma; \mathsf{nil}, \epsilon),$$

then $\Delta_R^{\geq 1}(\alpha; \beta) := \exists x \exists h.\ \Delta \wedge \varphi_{P_D}[\delta/\alpha] \wedge \varphi_{P_D}[(\gamma, \epsilon)/(\alpha, \beta)]$.
– If R is a right-hole inductive rule, then $\Delta_R^{\geq 1}(\alpha; \beta)$ is defined similarly.

In addition, we define $\Delta_P^{\geq 1}(\alpha; \beta) := \bigvee_{R: \text{ inductive rule of } P} \Delta_R^{\geq 1}(\alpha; \beta).$

For each predicate atom $a_i = P(Z_1, \mu; Z_2, \nu)$, we define the formula $\mathsf{Ufld}^{\geq 1}(a_i)$ as $\Delta_P^{\geq 1}(\mu, \nu)$. Intuitively, $\mathsf{Ufld}^{\geq 1}(a_i)$ is the data constraint obtained by unfolding a_i at least once (with the inductive rules of P).

For each location variable E and atom a_i in Σ, we introduce a Boolean variable $[E, i]$ to represent whether E is allocated in a_i. Let $\mathsf{BVars}(\varphi)$ denote the set of introduced Boolean variables. We define *an abstraction of* φ [12,14] to be $\mathsf{Abs}(\varphi) :: = \Pi \wedge \Delta \wedge \phi_\Sigma \wedge \phi_*$ over $\mathsf{BVars}(\varphi) \cup \mathsf{Vars}(\varphi)$, where

– $\phi_\Sigma = \bigwedge_{1 \leqslant i \leqslant n} \mathsf{Abs}(a_i)$ is an abstraction of Σ where

  • if $a_i = E \mapsto \rho$, then $\mathsf{Abs}(a_i) = [E, i] \wedge E \neq \mathsf{nil}$,

  • if $a_i = P(Z_1, \mu; Z_2, \nu)$, then

    $$\mathsf{Abs}(a_i) = (\neg[Z_1, i] \wedge Z_1 = Z_2 \wedge \mu = \nu) \vee ([Z_1, i] \wedge Z_1 \neq \mathsf{nil} \wedge \mathsf{Ufld}^{\geq 1}(a_i)).$$

– ϕ_* states the separation constraint of spatial atoms,

$$\phi_* = \bigwedge_{[Z_1,i],[Z_1',j]\in\mathsf{BVars}(\varphi),i\neq j} (Z_1 = Z_1' \wedge [Z_1,i]) \rightarrow \neg[Z_1',j].$$

Proposition 6. *For* CSLTP$[P]$ *formula* φ, φ *and* Abs(φ) *are equisatisfiable.*

The formula Abs(φ) can be turned into a quantifier-free formula Abs$_{\mathsf{qf}}(\varphi)$ by removing all the existential quantifiers in Ufld$^{\geqslant 1}(a_i)$ and replace the existentially quantified variables with some freshly introduced variables. The formula Abs$_{\mathsf{qf}}(\varphi)$ can be seen as a mixed real and integer linear arithmetic constraint, thus its satisfiability can be decided in nondeterministic polynomial time in theory, and can be solved by using the state-of-the-art SMT solvers, e.g. Z3 [34], in practice.

Theorem 3. *The satisfiability of* CSLTP$[P]$ *formulae can be decided in 6-fold exponential time. In addition, if the natural-number constants in P are encoded in unary, the satisfiability can be decided in 5-fold exponential time.*

Remark 1. The decision procedure for the satisfiability problem can be easily generalised to n-ary trees, and to separation logic formulae where several inductive predicates, e.g., *lseg*$(E;F)$ and *bsth*$(E,x,y;F,x',y')$, occur simultaneously.

6   Conclusion

In this paper, we proposed CSLTP, the compositional separation logic with tree predicates. We gave a complete decision procedure for the satisfiability problem. To our best knowledge, this is one of the most expressive fragments of SLID with data/size constraints that is equipped with a *complete* decision procedure. The main ingredient of the decision procedure is to compute the least fixed point of data predicates involving dense order constraints and difference-bound size constraints, by utilising an automata-theoretical approach.

For the future work, the decision procedure for the satisfiability problem paves the way towards a compete decision procedure for the entailment problem of CSLTP. In addition, we plan to implement the decision procedure and apply it to the analysis and verification of programs manipulating tree data structures.

References

1. Abdulla, P.A., Holík, L., Jonsson, B., Lengál, O., Trinh, C.Q., Vojnar, T.: Verification of heap manipulating programs with ordered data by extended forest automata. In: Hung, D., Ogawa, M. (eds.) ATVA 2013. LNCS, vol. 8172, pp. 224–239. Springer, Cham (2013). doi:10.1007/978-3-319-02444-8_17
2. Berdine, J., Calcagno, C., O'Hearn, P.W.: Symbolic execution with separation logic. In: Yi, K. (ed.) APLAS 2005. LNCS, vol. 3780, pp. 52–68. Springer, Heidelberg (2005). doi:10.1007/11575467_5

3. Bouajjani, A., Drăgoi, C., Enea, C., Sighireanu, M.: Accurate invariant checking for programs manipulating lists and arrays with infinite data. In: Chakraborty, S., Mukund, M. (eds.) ATVA 2012. LNCS, pp. 167–182. Springer, Heidelberg (2012). doi:10.1007/978-3-642-33386-6_14

4. Bouajjani, A., Esparza, J., Maler, O.: Reachability analysis of pushdown automata: application to model-checking. In: Mazurkiewicz, A., Winkowski, J. (eds.) CONCUR 1997. LNCS, vol. 1243, pp. 135–150. Springer, Heidelberg (1997). doi:10.1007/3-540-63141-0_10

5. Brotherston, J., Distefano, D., Petersen, R.L.: Automated cyclic entailment proofs in separation logic. In: Bjørner, N., Sofronie-Stokkermans, V. (eds.) CADE 2011. LNCS, vol. 6803, pp. 131–146. Springer, Heidelberg (2011). doi:10.1007/978-3-642-22438-6_12

6. Brotherston, J., Fuhs, C., Perez, J.A.N., Gorogiannis, N.: A decision procedure for satisfiability in separation logic with inductive predicates. In: LICS, pp. 25:1–25:10 (2014)

7. Chandra, A.K., Kozen, D.C., Stockmeyer, L.J.: Alternation. J. ACM **28**(1), 114–133 (1981)

8. Chin, W.-N., David, C., Nguyen, H.H., Qin, S.: Automated verification of shape, size and bag properties via user-defined predicates in separation logic. Sci. Comput. Program. **77**(9), 1006–1036 (2012)

9. Chu, D.-H., Jaffar, J., Trinh, M.-T.: Automatic induction proofs of data-structures in imperative programs. In: PLDI, pp. 457–466 (2015)

10. Comon-Lundh, H., Jacquemard, F., Perrin, N.: Visibly tree automata with memory and constraints. Logical Methods Comput. Sci. **4**(2), 1–36 (2008)

11. Creus, C., Godoy, G.: Tree automata with height constraints between brothers. In: RTA-TLCA, pp. 149–163 (2014)

12. Enea, C., Lengál, O., Sighireanu, M., Vojnar, T.: Compositional entailment checking for a fragment of separation logic. In: Garrigue, J. (ed.) APLAS 2014. LNCS, vol. 8858, pp. 314–333. Springer, Cham (2014). doi:10.1007/978-3-319-12736-1_17

13. Enea, C., Sighireanu, M., Wu, Z.: On automated lemma generation for separation logic with inductive definitions. In: Finkbeiner, B., Pu, G., Zhang, L. (eds.) ATVA 2015. LNCS, vol. 9364, pp. 80–96. Springer, Cham (2015). doi:10.1007/978-3-319-24953-7_7

14. Gu, X., Chen, T., Wu, Z.: A complete decision procedure for linearly compositional separation logic with data constraints. In: IJCAR, pp. 532–549 (2016)

15. Haase, C., Kreutzer, S., Ouaknine, J., Worrell, J.: Reachability in succinct and parametric one-counter automata. In: Bravetti, M., Zavattaro, G. (eds.) CONCUR 2009. LNCS, vol. 5710, pp. 369–383. Springer, Heidelberg (2009). doi:10.1007/978-3-642-04081-8_25

16. Habermehl, P., Iosif, R., Vojnar, T.: Automata-based verification of programs with tree updates. Acta Inf. **47**(1), 1–31 (2010)

17. Hóu, Z., Goré, R., Tiu, A.: Automated theorem proving for assertions in separation logic with all connectives. In: Felty, A.P., Middeldorp, A. (eds.) CADE 2015. LNCS, vol. 9195, pp. 501–516. Springer, Cham (2015). doi:10.1007/978-3-319-21401-6_34

18. Iosif, R., Rogalewicz, A., Simacek, J.: The tree width of separation logic with recursive definitions. In: Bonacina, M.P. (ed.) CADE 2013. LNCS, vol. 7898, pp. 21–38. Springer, Heidelberg (2013). doi:10.1007/978-3-642-38574-2_2

19. Iosif, R., Rogalewicz, A., Vojnar, T.: Deciding entailments in inductive separation logic with tree automata. In: Cassez, F., Raskin, J.-F. (eds.) ATVA 2014. LNCS, vol. 8837, pp. 201–218. Springer, Cham (2014). doi:10.1007/978-3-319-11936-6_15

20. Le, Q.L., Sun, J., Chin, W.-N.: Satisfiability modulo heap-based programs. In: Chaudhuri, S., Farzan, A. (eds.) CAV 2016. LNCS, vol. 9779, pp. 382–404. Springer, Cham (2016). doi:10.1007/978-3-319-41528-4_21

21. Manna, Z., Sipma, H.B., Zhang, T.: Verifying balanced trees. In: Artemov, S.N., Nerode, A. (eds.) LFCS 2007. LNCS, vol. 4514, pp. 363–378. Springer, Heidelberg (2007). doi:10.1007/978-3-540-72734-7_26

22. O'Hearn, P., Reynolds, J., Yang, H.: Local reasoning about programs that alter data structures. In: Fribourg, L. (ed.) CSL 2001. LNCS, vol. 2142, pp. 1–19. Springer, Heidelberg (2001). doi:10.1007/3-540-44802-0_1

23. Pek, E., Qiu, X., Madhusudan, P.: Natural proofs for data structure manipulation in C using separation logic. In: PLDI, pp. 440–451 (2014)

24. Piskac, R., Wies, T., Zufferey, D.: Automating separation logic using SMT. In: Sharygina, N., Veith, H. (eds.) CAV 2013. LNCS, vol. 8044, pp. 773–789. Springer, Heidelberg (2013). doi:10.1007/978-3-642-39799-8_54

25. Piskac, R., Wies, T., Zufferey, D.: Automating separation logic with trees and data. In: Biere, A., Bloem, R. (eds.) CAV 2014. LNCS, vol. 8559, pp. 711–728. Springer, Cham (2014). doi:10.1007/978-3-319-08867-9_47

26. Piskac, R., Wies, T., Zufferey, D.: GRASShopper - complete heap verification with mixed specifications. In: TACAS, pp. 124–139 (2014)

27. Qiu, X., Garg, P., Stefănescu, A., Madhusudan, P.: Natural proofs for structure, data, and separation. In: PLDI, pp. 231–242 (2013)

28. Revesz, P.Z.: A closed-form evaluation for datalog queries with integer (gap)-order constraints. Theor. Comput. Sci. **116**(1), 117–149 (1993)

29. Reynolds, A., Iosif, R., Serban, C., King, T.: A decision procedure for separation logic in SMT. In: Artho, C., Legay, A., Peled, D. (eds.) ATVA 2016. LNCS, vol. 9938, pp. 244–261. Springer, Cham (2016). doi:10.1007/978-3-319-46520-3_16

30. Reynolds, J.C.: Separation logic: a logic for shared mutable data structures. In: LICS, pp. 55–74 (2002)

31. Rümmer, P., Hojjat, H., Kuncak, V.: Disjunctive interpolants for horn-clause verification. In: Sharygina, N., Veith, H. (eds.) CAV 2013. LNCS, vol. 8044, pp. 347–363. Springer, Heidelberg (2013). doi:10.1007/978-3-642-39799-8_24

32. Seidl, H., Schwentick, T., Muscholl, A., Habermehl, P.: Counting in trees for free. In: Díaz, J., Karhumäki, J., Lepistö, A., Sannella, D. (eds.) ICALP 2004. LNCS, vol. 3142, pp. 1136–1149. Springer, Heidelberg (2004). doi:10.1007/978-3-540-27836-8_94

33. Tatsuta, M., Le, Q.L., Chin, W.-N.: Decision procedure for separation logic with inductive definitions and presburger arithmetic. In: Igarashi, A. (ed.) APLAS 2016. LNCS, vol. 10017, pp. 423–443. Springer, Cham (2016). doi:10.1007/978-3-319-47958-3_22

34. Z3. http://rise4fun.com/z3

A Proof Strategy Language and Proof Script Generation for Isabelle/HOL

Yutaka Nagashima[1] and Ramana Kumar[1,2(✉)]

[1] Data61, CSIRO, Sydney, Australia
[2] Data61, CSIRO/UNSW, Sydney, Australia
ramana.kumar@data61.csiro.au

Abstract. We introduce a language, PSL, designed to capture high level proof strategies in Isabelle/HOL. Given a strategy and a proof obligation, PSL's runtime system generates and combines various tactics to explore a large search space with low memory usage. Upon success, PSL generates an efficient proof script, which bypasses a large part of the proof search. We also present PSL's monadic interpreter to show that the underlying idea of PSL is transferable to other ITPs.

1 Introduction

Currently, users of interactive theorem provers (ITPs) spend a lot of time iteratively interacting with their ITP to manually specialise and combine tactics. This time consuming process requires expertise in the ITP, making ITPs more esoteric than they should be. The integration of powerful automatic theorem provers (ATPs) into ITPs ameliorates this problem significantly; however, the exclusive reliance on general purpose ATPs makes it hard to exploit users' domain specific knowledge, leading to combinatorial explosion even for conceptually straightforward conjectures.

To address this problem, we introduce PSL, a programmable, extensible, meta-tool based framework, to Isabelle/HOL [22]. We provide PSL (available on GitHub [18]) as a language, so that its users can encode *proof strategies*, abstract descriptions of how to attack proof obligations, based on their intuitions about a conjecture. When applied to a proof obligation, PSL's runtime system creates and combines several tactics based on the given proof strategy. This makes it possible to explore a larger search space than has previously been possible with conventional tactic languages, while utilising users' intuitions on the conjecture.

We developed PSL to use engineers' downtime: with PSL, we can run an automatic proof search for hours while we are attending meetings, sleeping, or reviewing papers. PSL makes such expensive proof search possible on machines with limited memory: PSL's runtime system truncates failed proof attempts as soon as it backtracks to minimise its memory usage.

Furthermore, PSL's runtime system attempts to generate efficient proof scripts from a given strategy by searching for the appropriate specialisation and combination of tactics for a particular conjecture without direct user interaction.

© Springer International Publishing AG 2017
L. de Moura (Ed.): CADE 2017, LNAI 10395, pp. 528–545, 2017.
DOI: 10.1007/978-3-319-63046-5_32

Thus, PSL not only reduces the initial labour cost of theorem proving, but also keeps proof scripts interactive and maintainable by reducing the execution time of subsequent proof checking.

In Isabelle, `sledgehammer` adopts a similar approach [2]. It exports a proof goal to various external ATPs and waits for them to find a proof. If the external provers find a proof, `sledgehammer` tries to reconstruct an efficient proof script in Isabelle using hints from the ATPs. `sledgehammer` is often more capable than most tactics but suffers from discrepancies between the polymorphic higher-order logic of Isabelle and the monomorphic first-order logic of most backend provers. While we integrated `sledgehammer` as a sub-tool in PSL, PSL conducts a search using Isabelle tactics, thus avoiding the problems arising from the discrepancies and proof reconstruction.

The underlying implementation idea in PSL is the monadic interpretation of proof strategies, which we introduce in Sect. 6. We expect this prover-agnostic formalization brings the following strengths of PSL to other ITPs such as Lean [14] and Coq [28]:

- runtime tactic generation based on user-defined procedures,
- memory-efficient large-scale proof search, and
- generation of efficient proof scripts for proof maintenance.

2   Background

Interactive theorem proving can be seen as the exploration of a search tree. Nodes of the tree represent proof states. Edges represent applications of tactics, which transform the proof state. Tactics are context sensitive: they behave differently depending on information stored in background proof contexts. These proof contexts contain such information as the constants defined and auxiliary lemmas proved prior to the current step. Since tactic behaviour depends on the proof context, it is hard to predict the shape of the search tree in advance.

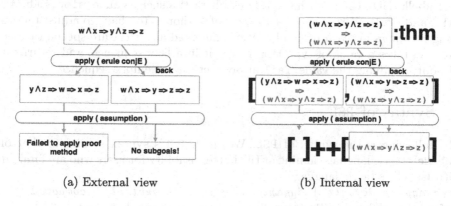

(a) External view   (b) Internal view

Fig. 1. External and internal view of proof search tree

The goal is to find a node representing a solved state: one in which the proof is complete. The search tree may be infinitely wide and deep, because there are endless variations of tactics that may be tried at any point. The goal for a PSL strategy is to direct an automated search of this tree to find a solved state; PSL will reconstruct an efficient path to this state as a human-readable proof script.

Figure 1 shows an example of proof search. At the top, the tactic `erule conjE` is applied to the proof obligation $w \wedge x \Rightarrow y \wedge z \Rightarrow z$. This tactic invocation produces two results, as there are two places to apply conjunction elimination. Applying conjunction elimination to $w \wedge x$ returns the first result, while doing so to $y \wedge z$ produces the second result. Subsequent application of proof by `assumption` can discharge the second result; however, `assumption` does not discharge the first one since the z in the assumptions is still hidden by the conjunction. Isabelle's proof language, *Isar*, returns the first result by default, but users can access the subsequent results using the keyword `back`.

Isabelle represents this non-deterministic behaviour of tactics using lazy sequences: tactics are functions of type `thm -> [thm]`, where [·] denotes a (possibly infinite) lazy sequence [25]. Figure 1b illustrates how Isabelle internally handles the above example where `++` stands for the concatenation of lazy sequences. Each proof state is expressed as a (possibly nested) implication which assumes proof obligations to conclude the conjecture. One may complete a proof by removing these assumptions using tactics. Tactic failure is represented as an empty sequence, which enables backtracking search by combining multiple tactics in a row [30]. For example, one can write `apply(erule conjE,assumption)` using the sequential combinator, (comma) in *Isar*; this tactic traverses the tree using backtracking and discharges the proof obligation without relying on the keyword `back`.

The search tree grows wider when choosing between multiple tactics, and it grows deeper when tactics are combined sequentially. In the implementation language level, the tactic combinators in Isabelle include `THEN` for sequential composition (corresponding to `,` in *Isar*), `APPEND` for non-deterministic choice, `ORELSE` for deterministic choice, and `REPEAT` for iteration.

Isabelle/HOL comes with several default tactics such as `auto`, `simp`, `induct`, `rule`, and `erule`. When using tactics, proof authors often have to adjust tactics using *modifiers* for each proof obligation. `succeed` and `fail` are special tactics: `succeed` takes a value of type `thm`, wraps it in a lazy sequence, and returns it without modifying the value. `fail` always returns an empty sequence.

3 Syntax of PSL

The following is the syntax of PSL. We made PSL's syntax similar to that of Isabelle's tactic language aiming at the better usability for users who are familiar with Isabelle's tactic language.

```
strategy := default | dynamic | special | subtool | compound
default  := Simp | Clarsimp | Fastforce | Auto | Induct
          | Rule | Erule | Cases | Coinduction | Blast
```

```
dynamic   := Dynamic (default)
special   := IsSolved | Defer | IntroClasses | Transfer
           | Normalization | Skip | Fail | User <string>
subtool   := Hammer | Nitpick | Quickcheck
compound  := Thens [strategy] | Ors [strategy] | Alts [strategy]
           | Repeat (strategy) | RepeatN (strategy)
           | POrs [strategy] | PAlts [strategy]
           | PThenOne [strategy] | PThenAll [strategy]
           | Cut int (strategy)
```

The *default* strategies correspond to Isabelle's default tactics without arguments, while *dynamic* strategies correspond to Isabelle's default tactics that are specialised for each conjecture. Given a *dynamic* strategy and conjecture, the runtime system generates variants of the corresponding Isabelle tactic. Each of these variants is specialised for the conjecture with a different combination of promising arguments found in the conjecture and its proof context. It is the purpose of the PSL runtime system to select the right combination automatically.

subtool represents Isabelle tools such as sledgehammer [2] and counterexample finders. The *compound* strategies capture the notion of tactic combinators: Thens corresponds to THEN, Ors to ORELSE, Alts to APPEND, and Repeat to REPEAT. POrs and PAlts are similar to Ors and Alts, respectively, but they admit parallel execution of sub-strategies. PThenOne and PThenAll take exactly two sub-strategies, combine them sequentially and apply the second sub-strategy to the results of the first sub-strategy in parallel in case the first sub-strategy returns multiple results. Contrary to PThenAll, PThenOne stops its execution as soon as it produces one result from the second sub-strategy. Users can integrate user-defined tactics, including those written in Eisbach [13], into PSL strategies using User. Cut limits the degree of non-determinism within a strategy.

In the following, we explain how to write strategies and how PSL's runtime system interprets strategies with examples.

4   PSL by Example

Example 1. For our first example, we take the following lemma from an entry [23] in the Archive of Formal Proofs (AFP):

```
lemma dfs_app: "dfs g (xs @ ys) zs = dfs g ys (dfs g xs zs)"
```

where dfs is a recursively defined function for depth-first search. As dfs is defined recursively, it is natural to expect that its proof involves some sort of mathematical induction. However, we do not know exactly how we should conduct mathematical induction here; therefore, we describe this rough idea as a proof strategy, DInductAuto, with the keyword strategy, and apply it to dfs_app with the keyword find_proof as depicted in Fig. 2. The find_proof command tells PSL's runtime system to interpret DInductAuto. For example, it interprets Auto as Isabelle's default tactic, auto.

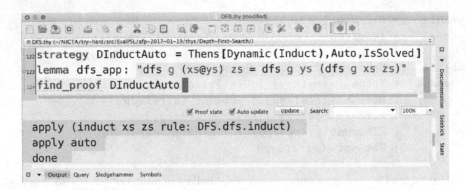

Fig. 2. Screenshot for Example 1.

The interpretation of `Dynamic(Induct)` is more involved: the runtime generates tactics using the information in `dfs_app` and its background context. First, PSL collects the free variables (noted in *italics* above) in `dfs_app` and applicable induction rules stored in the context. PSL uses the set of free variables to specify two things: on which variables instantiated tactics conduct mathematical induction, and which variables should be generalised in the induction scheme. The set of applicable rules are used to specify which rules to use. Second, PSL creates the powerset out of the set of all possible modifiers. Then, it attempts to instantiate a variant of the induct tactic for each subset of modifiers. Finally, it combines all the variants of `induct` with unique results using `APPEND`. In this case, PSL tries to generate 4160 induct tactics for `dfs_app` by passing several combinations of modifiers to Isabelle; however, Isabelle cannot produce valid induction schemes for some combinations, and some combinations lead to the same induction scheme. The runtime removes these, focusing on the 223 unique results. PSL's runtime combine these tactics with `auto` using `THEN`.

PSL's runtime interprets `IsSolved` as the `is_solved` tactic, which checks whether any proof obligations are left or not. If obligations are left, `is_solved` behaves as `fail`, triggering backtracking. If not, `is_solved` behaves as `succeed`, allowing the runtime to stop the search. This is how `DInductAuto` uses `IsSolved` to ensure that no sub-goals are left before returning an efficient proof script. For `dfs_app`, PSL interprets `DInductAuto` as the following tactic:

```
(induct1 APPEND induct2 APPEND...) THEN auto THEN is_solved
```

where `induct_ns` are variants of the induct tactic specialised with modifiers.

Within the runtime system, Isabelle first applies `induct1` to `dfs_app`, then `auto` to the resultant proof obligations. Note that each `induct` tactic and `auto` is deterministic: it either fails or returns a lazy sequence with a single element. However, combined together with `APPEND`, the numerous variations of `induct` tactics *en masse* are non-deterministic: if `is_solved` finds remaining proof obligations, Isabelle backtracks to the next `induct` tactic, `induct2` and repeats this process until either it discharges all proof obligations or runs out of the variations of `induct` tactics. The numerous variants of `induct` tactics from `DInductAuto` allow Isabelle to explore a larger search space than its naive alternative, `induct THEN auto`, does. Figure 3a illustrates this search procedure. Each edge and curved square represents a tactic application and a proof state, respectively, and edges leading to no object stand for tactic failures. The dashed objects represent possible future search space, which PSL avoids traversing by using lazy sequences.

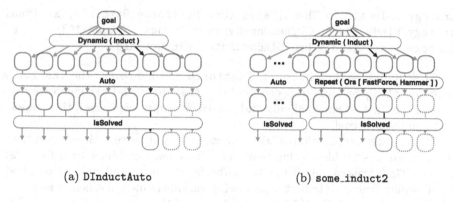

(a) `DInductAuto`   (b) `some_induct2`

Fig. 3. Proof search tree for `some_induct`

The larger search space specified by `DInductAuto` leads to a longer search time. PSL addresses this performance problem by tracing Isabelle's proof search: it keeps a log of successful proof attempts while removing backtracked proof attempts. The monadic interpretation discussed in Sect. 6 let PSL remove failed proof steps as soon as it backtracks. This minimises PSL memory usage, making it applicable to hours of expensive automatic proof search. Furthermore, since PSL follows Isabelle's execution model based on lazy sequences, it stops proof search as soon as it finds a specialisation and combination of tactics, with which Isabelle can pass the no-proof-obligation test imposed by `is_solved`.

We still need a longer search time with PSL, but only once: upon success, PSL converts the log of successful attempts into an efficient proof script, which bypasses a large part of proof search. For `dfs_app`, PSL generates the following proof script from `DInductAuto`.

```
apply (induct xs zs rule: DFS.dfs.induct) apply auto done
```

We implemented PSL as an Isabelle theory; to use it, PSL users only have to import the relevant theory files to use PSL to their files. Moreover, we have integrated PSL into Isabelle/Isar, Isabelle's proof language, and Isabelle/jEdit, its standard editor. This allows users to define and invoke their own proof strategies inside their ongoing proof attempts, as shown in Fig. 2; and if the proof search succeeds PSL presents a proof script in jEdit's output panel, which users can copy to the right location with one click. All generated proof scripts are independent of PSL, so users can maintain them without PSL.

Example 2. DInductAuto is able to pick up the right induction scheme for relatively simple proof obligations using backtracking search. However, in some cases even if PSL picks the right induction scheme, auto fails to discharge the emerging sub-goals. In the following, we define InductHard, a more powerful strategy based on mathematical induction, by combining Dynamic (Induct) with more involved sub-strategies to use external theorem provers.

```
strategy SolveAllG = Thens[Repeat(Ors[Fastforce,Hammer]),IsSolved]
strategy PInductHard = PThenOne[Dynamic(Induct),SolveAllG]
strategy InductHard = Ors[DInductAuto, PInductHard]
```

PSL's runtime system interprets Fastforce and Hammer as the fastforce tactic and sledgehammer, respectively. Both fastforce and sledgehammer try to discharge the first sub-goal only and return an empty sequence if they cannot discharge the sub-goal.

The repetitive application of sledgehammer would be very time consuming. We mitigate this problem using Ors and PThenOne. Combined with Ors, PSL executes PInductHard only if DInductAuto fails. When PInductHard is called, it first applies Dynamic(Induct), producing various induction schemes and multiple results. Then, SolveAllG tries to discharge these results in parallel. The runtime stops its execution when SolveAllG returns at least one result representing a solved state. We apply this strategy to the following conjecture, which states the two versions of depth-first search programs (dfs2 and dfs) return the same results given the same inputs.

```
lemma "dfs2 g xs ys = dfs g xs ys"
```

Then, our machine with 28 cores returns the following script within 3 minutes:

```
apply (induct xs ys rule: DFS.dfs2.induct)
apply fastforce
apply (simp add: dfs_app)
done
```

Figure 3b roughly shows how the runtime system found this proof script. The runtime first tried to find a complete proof as in Example 1, but without much success. Then, it interpreted PInductHard. While doing so, it found that induction on *xs* and *ys* using DFS.dfs2.induct leads to two sub-goals both of which can be discharged either by fastforce or sledgehammer. For the second sub-goal, sledgehammer found out that the result of *Example 1* can be used as an auxiliary lemma to prove this conjecture. Then, it returns an efficient proof script (simp add: dfs_app) to PSL, before PSL combines this with other parts and prints the complete proof script.

Example 3. In the previous examples, we used IsSolved to get a complete proof script from PSL. In Example 3, we show how to generate incomplete but useful proof scripts, using Defer. Incomplete proofs are specially useful when ITP users face numerous proof obligations, many of which are within the reach of high-level proof automation tools, such as sledgehammer, but a few of which are not.

Without PSL, Isabelle users had to manually invoke sledgehammer several times to find out which proof obligations sledgehammer can discharge. We developed a strategy, HamCheck, to automate this time-consuming process. The following shows its definition and a use case simplified for illustrative purposes.

```
strategy HamCheck = RepeatN(Ors[Hammer,Thens[Quickcheck,Defer]])
lemma safe_trans: shows
1:"ps_safe p s" and 2:"valid_tran p s s' c" and 3:"ps_safe p s'"
find_proof HamCheck
```

We made this example simple, so that two sub-goals, 1:"ps_safe p s" and 3:"ps_safe p s'", are not hard to prove; however, they are still beyond the scope of commonly used tactics, such as fastforce.

Generally, for a conjecture and a strategy of the form of RepeatN (strategy), PSL applies strategy to the conjecture as many times as the number of proof obligations in the conjecture. In this case, PSL applies Ors [Hammer, Thens [Quickcheck, Defer]] to safe_trans three times.

Note that we integrated quickcheck and nitpick into PSL as *assertion tactics*. Assertion tactics provide mechanisms for controlling proof search based on a condition: such a tactic takes a proof state, tests an assertion on it, then behaves as succeed or fail accordingly. We have already seen one of them in the previous examples: is_solved.

Ors [Hammer, Thens [Quickcheck, Defer]] first applies sledgehammer. If sledgehammer does not find a proof, it tries to find counter-examples for the sub-goal using quickcheck. If quickcheck finds no counter-examples, PSL interprets Defer as defer_tac 1, which postpones the current sub-goal to the end of the list of proof obligations.

In this example, sledgehammer fails to discharge 2:"valid_tran p s s' c". When sledgehammer fails, PSL passes 2 to Thens [Quickcheck, Defer], which finds no counter-example to 2 and sends 2 to the end of the list; then, PSL continues working on the sub-goal 3 with sledgehammer. The runtime stops its execution after applying Ors [Hammers,Thens [Quickcheck, Defer]] three times, generating the following proof script. This script discharges 1 and 3, but it leaves 2 as the meaningful task for human engineers, while assuring there is no obvious counter-examples for 2.

```
apply (simp add: state_safety ps_safe_def)
defer apply (simp add: state_safety ps_safe_def)
```

5   The Default Strategy: try_hard.

PSL comes with a default strategy, try_hard. Users can apply try_hard as a completely automatic tool: engineers need not provide their intuitions by writing strategies. Unlike other user-defined strategies, one can invoke this strategy by simply typing try_hard without find_proof inside a proof attempt. The lack of input from human engineers makes try_hard less specific to each conjecture; however, we made try_hard more powerful than existing proof automation tools for Isabelle by specifying larger search spaces presented.

We conducted a Judgement Day style evaluation [3] of try_hard against selected theory files from the AFP, coursework assignments and exercises [1], and Isabelle's standard library. Tables 1, 2 and 3 show that given 300 s for each proof goal try_hard solves 1115 proof goals out of 1526,while sledgehammer found proofs for 901 of themusing the same computational resources and reconstructed proofs in Isabelle for 866 of them. This is a 14% point improvement of proof search and a 16% point increase for proof reconstruction. Moreover, 299 goals (20% of all goals) were solved only by try_hard within 300 s. They also show that a longer time-out improves the success ratio of try_hard, which is desirable for utilising engineers' downtime.

Table 1. The number of automatically proved proof obligations from assignments. TH and SH stand for the number of obligations discharged by try_hard and sledgehammer, respectively. TH\SH represents the number of goals to which try_hard found proofs but sledgehammer did not. POs stands for the number of proof obligations in the theory file. $x(y)$ for SH means sledgehammer found proofs for x proof obligations, out of which it managed to reconstruct proof scripts in Isabelle for y goals. We omit these parentheses when these numbers coincide. Note that all proofs of PSL are checked by Isabelle/HOL. Besides, sledgehammer inside PSL avoids the smt proof method, as this method is not allowed in the Archive of Formal Proofs.

assignments [1]	POs	TH	SH	TH\SH	TH	SH	TH\SH
time out	-	30s	30s	30s	300s	300s	300s
assignment_1	19	17	14(13)	4	18	14(13)	5
assignment_2	22	21	5	16	22	5	17
assignment_3	52	30	27	8	35	27	10
assignment_4	82	66	61	10	71	61	10
assignment_5	64	36	41(39)	6	55	44(42)	17
assignment_6	26	11	12(11)	2	14	13(12)	3
assignment_8	52	36	45(39)	1	40	46(39)	0
assignment_9	61	31	32(30)	6	35	32(30)	6
assignment_11	26	14	15	1	20	17	3
sum	404	262	252(241)	54	310	259(246)	71

Table 2. The number of automatically proved proof obligations from exercises.

exercises [1]	POs	TH	SH	TH\SH	TH	SH	TH\SH
time out	-	30s	30s	30s	300s	300s	300s
exercise_1	15	12	8	4	12	8	4
exercise_2	7	4	3	2	5	3	2
exercise_3	42	27	26(25)	5	29	27(26)	5
exercise_4	23	11	15	0	17	15	2
exercise_5a	13	9	11	0	11	11	0
exercise_5b	83	65	74	1	74	74	1
exercise_6	4	1	2	0	1	3	0
exercise_7a	3	0	0	0	0	0	0
exercise_7b	9	5	6	1	8	6	2
exercise_8a	10	7	7	1	7	7	1
exercise_8b	26	11	9	4	12	12	2
exercise_9	31	14	17	3	19	17	3
exercise_10	15	5	5(4)	1	6	6(5)	1
exercise_11	10	4	6	0	9	6	3
exercise_12	30	8	10	1	12	10	3
sum	321	183	199(197)	23	222	205(203)	29

Table 3. The number of automatically proved proof goals from AFP entries and Isabelle's standard libraries.

theory name	POs	TH	SH	TH\SH	TH	SH	TH\SH
time out	-	30s	30s	30s	300s	300s	300s
DFS.thy [23]	51	24	28	6	34	29	7
Efficient_Sort.thy [27]	75	27	28(26)	8	33	31(28)	9
List_Index.thy [20]	105	48	72(70)	12	67	75(72)	14
Skew_Heap.thy [21]	16	8	6(5)	4	12	8(7)	5
Hash_Code.thy [10]	16	7	4	4	11	4	7
CoCallGraph.thy [4]	141	88	78(71)	29	104	79(73)	33
Coinductive_Language.thy [29]	139	57	69(68)	11	106	70(69)	43
Context_Free_Grammar.thy [29]	29	26	2	26	29	2	27
LTL.thy [26]	97	56	61	15	78	65(62)	15
HOL/Library/Tree.thy	124	93	70(68)	32	101	73(70)	32
HOL/Library/Tree_Multiset.thy	8	8	1	7	8	1	7
sum	801	442	419(404)	154	583	437(417)	199

try_hard is particularly more powerful than sledgehammer at discharging proof obligations that can be nicely handled by the following:

- mathematical induction or co-induction,
- type class mechanism,
- specific procedures implemented as specialised tactics (such as transfer and normalization), or
- general simplification rules (such as field_simps and algebra_simps).

Furthermore, careful observation of PSL indicates that PSL can handle the so-called "hidden fact" problem in relevance filtering. Hidden facts are auxiliary lemmas that are useful to discharge a given proof obligation but are not obviously relevant. For example, a hidden fact may share no constants with the proof obligation, because it is related only via an intermediate fact. With PSL, a user can write a strategy that applies rewriting before relevance filtering to reveal more information. This information allows the relevance filter to find useful facts that were previously hidden. For example, the following strategy "massages" the given proof obligation before invoking the relevance filter of sledgehammer: Thens [Auto, Repeat(Hammer),IsSolved].

For 3 theories out of 35, try_hard discharged fewer proof obligations, even given 300 seconds of time-out. This is due to the fact that PSL uses a slightly restricted version of sledgehammer internally for the sake of the integration with other tools and to avoid the smt method, which is not allowed in the AFP. In these files, sledgehammer can discharge many obligations and other obligations are not particularly suitable for other sub-tools in try_hard. Of course, given high-performance machines, users can run both try_hard and sledgehammer in parallel to maximise the chance of proving conjectures.

6   Monadic Interpretation of Strategy

The implementation of the tracing mechanism described in Sect. 4 is non-trivial: PSL's tracing mechanism has to support arbitrary strategies conforming to its syntax. What is worse, the runtime behaviour of backtracking search is not completely predictable statically since PSL generates tactics at runtime, using information that is not available statically. Moreover, the behaviour of each tactic varies depending on the proof context and proof obligation at hand.

It is likely to cause code clutter to specify where to backtrack explicitly with references or pointers, whereas explicit construction of search tree [17] consumes too much memory space when traversing a large search space. Furthermore, both of these approaches deviate from the standard execution model of Isabelle explained in Sect. 2. This deviation makes the proof search and the efficient proof script generation less reliable. In this section, we introduce our monadic interpreter for PSL, which yields a modular design and concise implementation of PSL's runtime system.

Program 1. Monad with zero and plus, and lazy sequence as its instance.

```
signature MONADOPLUS =
sig
  type 'a mOp;
  val return :   'a -> 'a mOp;
  val bind   :   'a mOp -> ('a -> 'b mOp) -> 'b mOp;
  val mzero  :   'a mOp;
  val ++     :   ('a mOp * 'a  mOp) -> 'a mOp;
end;
structure Nondet : MONADOPLUS =
struct
  type 'a mOp    = 'a Seq.seq;
  val return     = Seq.single;
  fun bind xs f  = Seq.flat (Seq.map f xs);
  val mzero      = Seq.empty;
  fun (xs ++ ys) = Seq.append xs ys;
end;
```

Monads in Standard ML. A monad with zero and plus is a constructor class[1] with four basic methods (**return, bind, mzero,** and **++**). As Isabelle's implementation language, Standard ML, does not natively support constructor classes, we emulated them using its module system [19]. Program 1 shows how we represent the type constructor, **seq**, as an instance of monad with zero and plus.

The body of **bind** for lazy sequences says that it applies f to all the elements of **xs** and concatenates all the results into one sequence. Attentive readers might notice that this is equivalent to the behaviour of **THEN** depicted in Fig. 1b and that of **Thens** shown in Fig. 3. In fact, we can define all of **THEN, succeed, fail,** and **APPEND**, using **bind, return, mzero,** and **++**, respectively.

Monadic Interpretation of Strategies. Based on this observation, we formalised PSL's search procedure as a monadic interpretation of strategies, as shown in Program 2, where the type **core_strategy** stands for the internal representation of strategies. Note that **Alt** and **Or** are binary versions of **Alts** and **Ors**, respectively; PSL desugars **Alts** and **Ors** into nested **Alts** and **Ors**. We could have defined **Or** as a syntactic sugar using **Alt, mzero, Fail,** and **Skip**, as explained by Martin *et al.* [11]; however, we prefer the less monadic formalisation in Program 2 for better time complexity.

eval deals with all the atomic strategies, which correspond to *default*, *dynamic*, and *special* in the surface language. For the *dynamic* strategies, **eval** expands them into dynamically generated tactics making use of contextual information from the current proof state. PSL combines these generated tactics

---

[1] Constructor classes are a class mechanism on type constructors such as **list** and **option**, whereas type classes are a class mechanism on types such as **int** and **double**. Commonly used constructor classes include functor, applicative, monoid, and arrow.

Program 2. The monadic interpretation of strategies.

```
interp :: core_strategy -> 'a -> 'a mOp
interp (Atom atom_str) n      = eval atom_str n
interp  Skip  n               = return n
interp  Fail  n               = mzero
interp (str1 Then str2) n     = bind (interp str1 n) (interp str2)
interp (str1 Alt  str2) n     = interp str1 n ++ interp str2 n
interp (str1 Or   str2) n     = let val result1 = interp str1 n
  in if (result1 != mzero) then result1 else interp str2 n end
interp (Rep str) n            = interp ((str THEN (Rep str)) Or Skip) n
interp (Comb (comb, strs)) n = eval_comb (comb, map interp strs) n
```

Program 3. The writer monad transformer as a ML functor.

```
functor writer_trans (structure Log:MONOID; structure Base:MONADOPLUS) =
struct
  type 'a mOp  = (Log.monoid * 'a) Base.mOp;
  fun return (m:'a) = Base.return (Log.mempty, m) : 'a mOp;
  fun bind (m:'a mOp) (func: 'a -> 'b mOp) : 'b mOp =
    Base.bind    m           (fn (log1, res1) =>
    Base.bind    (func res1) (fn (log2, res2) =>
    Base.return (Log.mappend log1 log2, res2)));
  val mzero = Base.mzero;
  val (xs ++ ys) = Base.++ (xs, ys);
end : MONADOPLUS;
```

either with APPEND or ORELSE, depending on the nature of each tactic. eval_comb handles non-monadic strategy combinators, such as Cut. We defined the body of eval and eval_comb for each atomic strategy and strategy combinator separately using pattern matching. As is obvious in Program 2, interp separates the complexity of compound strategies from that of runtime tactic generation.

Adding Tracing Modularly for Proof Script Generation. We defined interp at the constructor class level, abstracting it from the concrete type of proof state and even from the concrete type constructor. When instantiated with lazy sequence, interp tries to return the first element of the sequence, working as depth-first search. This abstraction provides a clear view of how compound strategies guide proof search while producing tactics at runtime; however, without tracing proof attempts, PSL has to traverse large search spaces every time it checks proofs.

We added the tracing mechanism to interp, combining the non-deterministic monad, Nondet, with the writer monad. To combine multiple monads, we emulate monad transformers using ML functors: Program 3 shows our ML functor, writer_trans, which takes a module of MONADOPLUS, adds the logging mechanism to it, and returns a module equipped with both the capability of the base monad and the logging mechanism of the writer monad. We pass `Nondet` to `writer_trans` as the base monad to combine the logging mechanism and the backtracking search based on non-deterministic choice. Observe Programs 1, 2 and 3 to see how `Alt` and `Or` truncate failed proof attempts while searching for a proof. The returned module is based on a new type constructor, but it is still a member of `MONADOPLUS`; therefore, we can re-use `interp` without changing it.

History-Sensitive Tactics using the State Monad Transformer. The flexible runtime interpretation might lead `PSL` into a non-terminating loop, such as `REPEAT succeed`. To handle such loops, `PSL` traverses a search space using iterative deepening depth-first search (IDDFS). However, passing around information about depth as an argument of `interp` as following quickly impairs its simplicity:

```
interp (t1 CSeq t2) level n = if level < 1 then return n else ...
interp (t1 COr  t2) level n = ...
```

where `level` stands for the remaining depth `interp` can proceed for the current iteration.

We implemented IDDFS without code clutter, introducing the idea of a *history-sensitive tactic*: a tactic that takes the log of proof attempts into account. Since the writer monad does not allow us to access the log during the search time, we replaced the writer monad transformer with the state monad transformer, with which the runtime keeps the log of proof attempt as the "state" of proof search and access it during search. By measuring the length of "state", `interp` computes the current depth of proof search at runtime.

The modular design and abstraction discussed above made this replacement possible with little change to the definition of `interp`: we only need to change the clause for `Atom`, providing a wrapper function, `iddfc`, for `eval`, while other clauses remain intact.

```
inter (CAtom atom_str) n = iddfc limit eval atom_str n
```

`iddfc limit` first reads the length of "state", which represents the number of edges to the node from the top of the implicit proof search tree. Then, it behaves as `fail` if the length exceeds `limit`; if not, it executes `eval atom_str n`.[2]

7   Related Work

ACL2 [9] is a functional programming language and mostly automated first-order theorem prover. ACL2 is known for the so-called waterfall model, which is essentially repeated application of various heuristics. Its users can guide proof search by supplying arguments called "hints", but the underlining operational procedure of the waterfall model itself is fixed. ACL2 does not produce efficient proof scripts after running the waterfall algorithm.

---

[2] In this sense, we implemented IDDFS as a tactic combinator.

PVS [24] provides a collection of commands called "strategies". Despite the similarity of the name to PSL, strategies in PVS correspond to tactics in Isabelle. The highest-level strategy in PVS, grind, can produce re-runnable proof scripts containing successful proof steps only. However, scripts returned by grind describe steps of much lower level than human engineers would write manually, while PSL's returned scripts are based on tactics engineers use. Furthermore, grind is known to be useful to complete a proof that does *not* require induction, while try_hard is good at finding proofs involving mathematical induction.

SEPIA [8] is an automated proof generation tool in Coq. Taking existing Coq theories as input, SEPIA first produces proof traces, from which it infers an extended finite state machine. Given a conjecture, SEPIA uses this model to search for its proof. The authors of SEPIA chose to use breadth-first search (BFS) to find shorter proofs. For PSL we could emulate the BFS strategy within the IDDFS framework. However, our experience tells us that the search tree tends to be very wide and some tactics, such as induct, need to be followed by other tactics to complete proofs. Therefore, we chose IDDFS for PSL. Both SEPIA and PSL off-load the construction of proof scripts to search and try to reconstruct efficient proof scripts. Compared to SEPIA, PSL allows users to specify their own search strategies to utilize the engineer's intuition, which enables PSL to return incomplete proof scripts, as discussed in Sect. 4.

Martin *et al.* first discussed a monadic interpretation of tactics for their language, *Angel*, in an unpublished draft [12]. We independently developed interp with the features discussed above, lifting the framework from the tactic level to the strategy level to traverse larger search spaces. The two interpreters for different ITPs turned out to be similar to each other, suggesting our approach is not specific to Isabelle but can be used for other ITPs.

Similar to Ltac [6] in Coq, Eisbach [13] is a framework to write *proof methods* in Isabelle. Proof methods are the *Isar* syntactic layer of tactics. Eisbach does not generate methods dynamically, trace proof attempts, nor support parallelism natively. Eisbach is good when engineers already know how to prove their conjecture, while try_hard is good when they want to find out how to prove it.

IsaPlanner [7] offers a framework for encoding and applying common patterns of reasoning in Isabelle, following the style of proof planning [5]. IsaPlanner addresses the performance issue by a memoization technique, on the other hand try_hard strips off backtracked steps while searching for a proof, which Isabelle can check later without try_hard. While IsaPlanner works on its own data structure *reasoning state*, try_hard managed to minimize the deviation from Isabelle's standard execution model using constructor classes.

8   Conclusions

PSL improves proof automation in higher-order logic, allowing us to exploit both the engineer's intuition and various automatic tools. The simplicity of the design is our intentional choice: we reduced the process of interactive proof development to the well-known dynamic tree search problem and added new features (efficient-proof script generation and IDDFS) by safely abstracting the original execution model and employing commonly used techniques (monad transformers).

We claim that our approach enjoys significant advantages. Despite the simplicity of the design, our evaluations indicate that PSL reduces the labour cost of ITP significantly. The conservative extension to the original model lowers the learning barrier of PSL and makes our proof script generation reliable by minimising the deviation. The meta-tool approach makes the generated proof script independent of PSL, separating the maintenance of proof scripts from that of PSL; furthermore, by providing a common framework for various tools we supplement one tool's weakness (e.g. induction for sledgehammer) with other tools' strength (e.g. the induct tactic), while enhancing their capabilities with runtime tactic generation. The parallel combinators reduce the labour-intensive process of interactive theorem proving to embarrassingly parallel problems. The abstraction to the constructor class and reduction to the tree search problem make our ideas transferable: other ITPs, such as Lean and Coq, handle inter-tactic backtracking, which is best represented in terms of MONADOPLUS.

Acknowledgements. We thank Jasmin C. Blanchette for his extensive comments that improved the evaluation of try_hard. Pang Luo helped us for the evaluation. Leonardo de Moura, Daniel Matichuk, Kai Engelhardt, and Gerwin Klein provided valuable comments on an early draft of this paper. We thank the anonymous reviewers for useful feedback, both at CADE-26 and for previous versions of this paper at other conferences. This work was partially funded by the ERC Consolidator grant 649043 - AI4REASON.

A   Appendix: Details of the Evaluation

All evaluations were conducted on a Linux machine with Intel (R) Core (TM) i7-600 @ 3.40 GHz and 32 GB memory. For both tools, we set the time-out of proof search to 30 and 300 s for each proof obligation.

Prior to the evaluation, the relevance filter of sledgehammer was trained on 27,041 facts and 18,695 non-trivial Isar proofs from the background libraries imported by theories under evaluation for both tools. Furthermore, we forbid sledgehammer inside PSL from using the smt method for proof reconstruction, since the AFP does not permit this method.

Note that try_hard does not use parallel strategy combinators which exploit parallelism. The evaluation tool does not allow try_hard to use multiple threads either. Therefore, given the same time-out, try_hard and sledgehammer enjoy the same amount of computational resources, assuring the fairness of the evaluation results.

The evaluation tool [16] and results [15] are available at our websites. We provide the evaluation tool and results in the following websites:

- http://ts.data61.csiro.au/Downloads/cade26_evaluation/
- http://ts.data61.csiro.au/Downloads/cade26_results/

References

1. Blanchette, J., Fleury, M., Wand, D.: Concrete Semantics with Isabelle/HOL (2015). http://people.mpi-inf.mpg.de/~jblanche/cswi/
2. Blanchette, J.C., Kaliszyk, C., Paulson, L.C., Urban, J.: Hammering towards QED. J. Formalized Reasoning **9**(1), 101–148 (2016). http://dx.doi.org/10.6092/issn.1972-5787/4593
3. Böhme, S., Nipkow, T.: Sledgehammer: Judgement day. In: Giesl, J., Hähnle, R. (eds.) IJCAR 2010. LNCS (LNAI), vol. 6173, pp. 107–121. Springer, Heidelberg (2010). doi:10.1007/978-3-642-14203-1_9
4. Breitner, J.: The safety of call arity. Archive of Formal Proofs, February 2015. http://isa-afp.org/entries/Call_Arity.shtml. Formal proof development
5. Bundy, A.: The use of explicit plans to guide inductive proofs. In: Lusk, E., Overbeek, R. (eds.) CADE 1988. LNCS, vol. 310, pp. 111–120. Springer, Heidelberg (1988). doi:10.1007/BFb0012826
6. Delahaye, D.: A tactic language for the system Coq. In: Parigot, M., Voronkov, A. (eds.) LPAR 2000. LNAI, vol. 1955, pp. 85–95. Springer, Heidelberg (2000). doi:10.1007/3-540-44404-1_7
7. Dixon, L., Fleuriot, J.: IsaPlanner: A prototype proof planner in isabelle. In: Baader, F. (ed.) CADE 2003. LNCS (LNAI), vol. 2741, pp. 279–283. Springer, Heidelberg (2003). doi:10.1007/978-3-540-45085-6_22
8. Gransden, T., Walkinshaw, N., Raman, R.: SEPIA: search for proofs using inferred automata. In: Felty, A.P., Middeldorp, A. (eds.) CADE 2003. LNCS, vol. 9195, pp. 246–255. Springer, Heidelberg (2015). http://dx.doi.org/10.1007/978-3-319-21401-6_16
9. Kaufmann, M., Moore, J.S., Manolios, P.: Computer-Aided Reasoning: An Approach. Kluwer Academic Publishers, Norwell (2000)
10. Lammich, P.: Collections framework. Archive of Formal Proofs, November 2009. http://isa-afp.org/entries/Collections.shtml. Formal proof development
11. Martin, A.P., Gardiner, P.H.B., Woodcock, J.: A tactic calculus-abridged version. Formal. Asp. Comput. **8**(4), 479–489 (1996). http://dx.doi.org/10.1007/BF01213535
12. Martin, A., Gibbons, J.: A monadic interpretation of tactics (2002)
13. Matichuk, D., Wenzel, M., Murray, T.: An isabelle proof method language. In: Klein, G., Gamboa, R. (eds.) ITP 2014. LNCS, vol. 8558, pp. 390–405. Springer, Cham (2014). doi:10.1007/978-3-319-08970-6_25
14. de Moura, L., Kong, S., Avigad, J., van Doorn, F., von Raumer, J.: The Lean theorem prover (system description). In: Felty, A.P., Middeldorp, A. (eds.) CADE 2003. LNCS, vol. 9195, pp. 378–388. Springer, Heidelberg (2015). http://dx.doi.org/10.1007/978-3-319-21401-6_26
15. Nagashima, Y.: Evaluation Results (2016). http://ts.data61.csiro.au/Downloads/cade26_results/
16. Nagashima, Y.: Evaluation Tool (2016). http://ts.data61.csiro.au/Downloads/cade26_evaluation/
17. Nagashima, Y.: Keep failed proof attempts in memory. In: Isabelle Workshop, Nancy, France, August 2016
18. Nagashima, Y.: PSL (2016). https://github.com/data61/PSL
19. Nagashima, Y., O'Connor, L.: Close encounters of the higher kind - emulating constructor classes in standard ML, September 2016

20. Nipkow, T.: List index. Archive of Formal Proofs, February 2010. http://isa-afp.org/entries/List-Index.shtml. Formal proof development

21. Nipkow, T.: Skew heap. Archive of Formal Proofs, August 2014. http://isa-afp.org/entries/Skew_Heap.shtml. Formal proof development

22. Nipkow, T., Paulson, L.C., Wenzel, M.: Isabelle/HOL - A Proof Assistant for Higher-Order Logic. LNCS, vol. 2283. Springer, Heidelberg (2002). http://dx.doi.org/10.1007/3-540-45949-9

23. Nishihara, T., Minamide, Y.: Depth first search. Archive of Formal Proofs, June 2004. http://isa-afp.org/entries/Depth-First-Search.shtml. Formal proof development

24. Owre, S., Rushby, J.M., Shankar, N.: PVS: A prototype verification system. In: Kapur, D. (ed.) CADE 1992. LNCS, vol. 607, pp. 748–752. Springer, Heidelberg (1992). doi:10.1007/3-540-55602-8_217

25. Paulson, L.C.: The foundation of a generic theorem prover. CoRR cs.LO/9301105 (1993). http://arxiv.org/abs/cs.LO/9301105

26. Sickert, S.: Linear temporal logic. Archive of Formal Proofs, March 2016. http://isa-afp.org/entries/LTL.shtml. Formal proof development

27. Sternagel, C.: Efficient mergesort. Archive of Formal Proofs, November 2011. http://isa-afp.org/entries/Efficient-Mergesort.shtml. Formal proof development

28. The Coq development team: The Coq proof assistant reference manual (2009)

29. Traytel, D.: A codatatype of formal languages. Archive of Formal Proofs, November 2013. http://isa-afp.org/entries/Coinductive_Languages.shtml. Formal proof development

30. Wadler, P.: How to replace failure by a list of successes a method for exception handling, backtracking, and pattern matching in lazy functional languages. In: Jouannaud, J.-P. (ed.) FPCA 1985. LNCS, vol. 201, pp. 113–128. Springer, Heidelberg (1985). doi:10.1007/3-540-15975-4_33

The Binomial Pricing Model in Finance: A Formalization in Isabelle

Mnacho Echenim[✉] and Nicolas Peltier

Univ. Grenoble Alpes, CNRS, LIG, 38000 Grenoble, France
{Mnacho.Echenim,Nicolas.Peltier}@univ-grenoble-alpes.fr

Abstract. The binomial pricing model is an option valuation method based on a discrete-time model of the evolution of an equity market. It allows one to determine the fair price of derivatives from the payoff they generate at their expiration date. A formalization of this model in the proof assistant Isabelle is provided. We formalize essential notions in finance such as the *no-arbitrage principle* and prove that, under the hypotheses of the model, the market is *complete*, meaning that any European derivative can be *replicated* by creating a portfolio that generates the same payoff regardless of the evolution of the market.

1 Introduction

There are several kinds of actors who trade on financial markets. The best-known actors are probably the speculators, who place bets on the markets by investing in assets with the hope of making a profit at a future time, and of course, risking to lose money if the price movements are not those they expected. Another category of actors consists of *hedgers*. Hedgers trade on financial markets in order to limit their exposure to price movements. They do not make any bets, but try to guarantee an outcome regardless of the market evolution.

All of these actors trade on different products, including risk-free assets such as sovereign bonds, stocks and *derivative securities*. Derivative securities are products whose values depend on that of underlying assets. Examples of derivative securities include contracts such as *forwards* on the equity market and *interest rate swaps* on the fixed income market; or options such as *calls* on the equity market and *swaptions* on the fixed income market. We provide an example illustrating the differences between some of these derivatives.

Consider a contractor who has just won a contract for a large construction due the following year. The price for the construction was determined in part by the price of cement, which was, at the time the proposal was written, 100€ per metric ton. The constructor will not want to buy the required quantity of cement right away, as this would incur storage costs and there is a risk of the contract being broken. But then, how can the unknown future price of cement be taken into account? The contractor is faced with three possibilities:

© Springer International Publishing AG 2017
L. de Moura (Ed.): CADE 2017, LNAI 10395, pp. 546–562, 2017.
DOI: 10.1007/978-3-319-63046-5_33

- Waiting for the entire year to pass and buying cement on the market at the new spot price. This is a speculative move: if this price is less than 100€, then the contractor will have made a profit; however, if the price is above 100€, then the unplanned extra cost can cause bankruptcy.
- Entering a *forward contract* with another financial actor, promising to buy the necessary quantity of cement at 100€ per metric ton in a year. If the metric ton of cement costs 120€ the following year, then the counterpart will pay the contractor 20€ per metric ton, thus in effect permitting the purchase of cement at the agreed upon price. If the metric ton costs 80€ however, then the contractor will have to pay 20€ per metric ton to the counterpart. Although the exposure to the cement price was hedged, the outcome may seem disappointing.
- Buying a *call option* from another financial actor, giving the contractor the right, *but not the obligation* to buy cement at 100€ per metric ton in a year. If the metric ton of cement costs 120€ the following year, then the counterpart will pay the contractor 20€ per metric ton, and if the metric ton costs 80€, then the option is considered to be void and the contractor will buy cement on the market at the spot price.

In general, the third solution is more appealing, and a natural question is: what is the minimal amount of money the seller should ask for to guarantee being able to pay what is needed one year later, *regardless of the price movement of cement*?

The contracts mentioned above for commodities also exist on the equity market, where the underlying product is a stock instead of cement. The call option is a particular kind of *European option*; these are options that can only be exercised at a precise agreed-upon date, the *maturity*. Such contracts are frequently traded by hedgers to reduce their risk exposure. One of the goals of mathematical finance is to answer the question: what is the *fair* price of a derivative security? In other words, how much should the derivative be sold to guarantee that neither the buyer nor the seller will have the opportunity to make a risk-free profit? Such risk-free profits are called *arbitrages*, and a standard assumption for reasoning in financial markets is that there is no arbitrage opportunity. A no-arbitrage argument shows that if it is possible to construct a *replicating portfolio* for a derivative, i.e., a portfolio whose value at maturity is exactly equal to the amount of money promised by the derivative (regardless of the market evolution), then the fair price of the derivative is the initial value of this replicating portfolio. The topic of this paper is the construction of replicating portfolios in a particular mathematical model of financial markets.

Mathematical finance is a domain that expanded extremely quickly after the proof by Black, Scholes and Merton in their seminal papers [1, 9] that it is possible to construct replicating portfolios for European options, under some assumptions on the evolution of the underlying assets. This domain is based on stochastic calculus and relies on deep theorems, but the resulting programs (commonly named *pricers*) which are used to, e.g., price derivatives have a relatively simple algorithmic structure, although numerical errors can be hard to detect. Another model for option valuation, using discrete time and called the *binomial model* or *CRR model*, was proposed by Cox, Ross and Rubinstein [3]. This approach can be viewed as a discrete version of the Black-Scholes model and in fact, as the length of the time steps decreases, the prices computed in this model converge on those computed in the Black-Scholes formula. The CRR model has the advantage of being easier to understand and much simpler from a mathematical point of view. As such, it is often used as an introductory example of financial mathematics at the late undergraduate or early graduate level (see, e.g., [11]). Its refinements are still used in financial institutions for pricing particular kinds of options, such as *American options*, which can be exercised by the owner at any time until the option maturity, or *Bermudan options*, which can be exercised at a set of predefined times until maturity.

In both the Black-Scholes and CRR models, the following additional assumptions are made:

- There are only two securities that can be traded: a risk-free asset and a stock. The risk-free asset grows at a constant rate, and can be viewed as a money market account where any amount of cash can be borrowed or lent at the same constant rate. Similarly, any fractional amount of the stock can be bought or sold (including short selling[1]) for the same price.
- The market allows instantaneous trading with no transaction fees.
- There is no risk-free way to make a profit on the market without investing any money. This *no-arbitrage principle* is an important condition in all financial models. In particular, this principle implies the *law of one price*, which states that two assets must have the same price today if they deliver the same cash-flow at the same time in the future regardless of the evolution of the market. For example, there cannot be two risk-free assets with distinct rates, because it would otherwise be possible to earn money without any risk by borrowing cash at the lower rate and lending it at the higher rate.

Under these assumptions, the authors prove that the market is *complete*, i.e., that every derivative admits a replicating portfolio. In this paper, we describe a formalization of the binomial model and of the construction of replicating portfolios for European derivatives. We also formalize financial notions such as the no-arbitrage principle which are sometimes left informal in textbooks, thus paving the way for the formal treatment of more elaborate models. All proofs are constructive, hence, from a practical point of view, our work can be used to construct certified pricers for *arbitrary* European derivatives in the binomial model. Certified pricers would be of interest to financial actors who could then benchmark their more efficient implementations against the former. All of our formalization is carried out in Isabelle (see https://isabelle.in.tum.de/ or [10]). This is a well-known and widely used proof assistant for higher order logic. It features both procedural and declarative languages for writing proofs, various automated proof procedures and a tool to invoke external provers and

---

[1] A short sale consists in borrowing an asset from actor A to sell it to actor B, and then buying the asset at a later point in time to return it to actor A.

automatically infer proof scripts. Our formalization uses the declarative language Isar [12] which allows to write human-readable structured proofs.

The rest of the paper is structured as follows. In Sect. 2, basic notions in finance are introduced along with elements of probability theory which have already been formalized in Isabelle. The enrichments to the formalization of probability theory in Isabelle which are necessary to define the CRR model are described in Sect. 3, and equity markets are formalized in Sect. 4. The formalization of the CRR model and the proof that the corresponding market is complete is the topic of Sect. 5. All the theory files in Isabelle can be downloaded at http:// crr-isabelle.forge.imag.fr.

2 Preliminary Notions

2.1 Some Notions in Finance

We begin by briefly reviewing some basic standard definitions about equity markets. This treatment is mainly based on Shreve [11], Vol. 1. An equity market contains a set of *assets* or *securities* that can be traded. An actor trading on a market has a *portfolio*, which contains different quantities of the traded assets. These quantities are real numbers that can be positive if the corresponding asset was bought, or negative if the asset was the object of a short sale. A portfolio can be *static* if its composition is fixed once and for all, and *dynamic* if its composition can evolve over time. Among dynamic portfolios, those of a particular interest are the *trading strategies*; these are the dynamic portfolios for which the composition at time t is a random variable that only depends on the available information up to time t. A portfolio in which all future trades are financed by buying or selling assets in the portfolio is a *self-financing portfolio*. An arbitrage represents a "free lunch": it is defined as a self-financing trading strategy with a 0 initial investment that offers a riskless possibility of making a profit. A market is *viable* if it offers no arbitrage opportunities.

Some of the securities that can be traded are basic securities, such as bonds, which are generally assumed to be risk-free assets, or stocks, which are risky assets. Others are *derivative* securities, whose payoffs (the amount of cash that should be exchanged at exercise time) depend on the evolution and values of basic securities. On the equity market, these derivative securities often have an expiry date, or maturity, after which they are no longer valid. An option, for instance, is a derivative that can be viewed as an insurance: when it is exercised, it gives the beholder the right—but not the obligation—to trade an instrument at a given price. In this paper we will focus on *European* options, which can only be exercised at the maturity, see, e.g., [8]. The best-known options are the call and the put options. A call (resp. put) option gives its beholder the right, at time T, to buy (resp. sell) the underlying security at the strike price K, thus guaranteeing that there is a cap (resp. floor) on the price that will be payed at a future time for the security. In practice, when at time T the price of the underlying security, denoted by S_T, is greater than the strike price K, the buyer of a call receives $S_T - K$ from the seller of the option, and buys the instrument on the market for S_T, in effect only spending K to obtain the instrument. When $S_T < K$, the seller of the call does not deliver any cash, as the buyer will directly buy the instrument on the market for a value that is less than K. Thus, a call option is a derivative that, at maturity T, delivers a payoff of $(S_T - K)^+ \overset{\text{def}}{=} \max(0, S_T - K)$. In a similar way, a put option delivers at time T a payoff of $(K - S_T)^+$. Options depart from *forwards*, for which both the buyer and seller are bound to perform the transaction at maturity; the payoff of these contracts is of the form $S_T - K$ or $K - S_T$.

Once a derivative is sold, the seller is meant to invest the cash by creating a trading strategy, in order to be able to pay the required amount of money when the derivative is exercised. A natural question is the following: how much should a buyer be expected to pay for a given derivative? Ideally, this price should not be so low that the buyer could make a riskless profit, and it should not be so high that the seller could make a riskless profit. The answer to this question is straightforward when the seller is capable of creating a trading strategy whose value at exercise time is exactly the payoff of the derivative, i.e., of creating a replicating portfolio. In this case, the fair price for the strategy is the initial value of the trading strategy. A market is *complete* if every derivative admits a replicating portfolio.

In some cases, replicating portfolios are simple to construct. Consider for example a forward contract for buying a given asset S at a price K at time T. This contract can be replicated by the seller, using a trading strategy with initial value $S_0 - \frac{K}{(1+r)^T}$, where S_0 is the current price of the asset and r is the risk-free rate. The seller borrows $\frac{K}{(1+r)^T}$ to buy the asset, and holds on to it until maturity. At time T, the seller has the asset and owes $\frac{K}{(1+r)^T}(1+r)^T = K$ to the bank. The asset is sold to the buyer for price K, which is used to reimburse the cash that is owed. The fair price for this contract is therefore $S_0 - \frac{K}{(1+r)^T}$, and any other price would lead to an arbitrage opportunity. For example, if the contract had been sold at a price $F > S_0 - \frac{K}{(1+r)^T}$, then the seller would only have to borrow $S_0 - F$ at time 0, and would make a riskless profit of $K - (S_0 - F)(1+r)^T > 0$ at time T.

The construction of replicating portfolios is not as straightforward for more complex derivatives, and it may not be clear whether such portfolios actually exist. An answer to the existence of replicating portfolios for European options was given by Fischer Black and Myron Scholes, and by Robert Merton in [1,9], in the so-called Black-Scholes-Merton model. They consider a risky asset, the stock, that pays no dividends and whose evolution is described by a *geometric Brownian motion* (see, e.g., [8]), and showed that, under some simple market hypotheses such as identical bidding and asking prices for the stock and the absence of arbitrage opportunities, a European option over a single stock can be replicated with a portfolio consisting of the stock and a cash account.

The Cox-Ross-Rubinstein model [3] that we consider in the present paper can be viewed as an approximation of the Black-Scholes-Merton model to the case where time is no longer continuous but discrete; i.e., to the case where securities are only traded at discrete times $1, 2, \ldots, n, \ldots$ In this setting, the evolution of the stock price is described by a geometric random walk, which can be viewed as a discrete version of the geometric Brownian motion: if the stock has a price s at time n, then at time $n + 1$, this price is either $u.s$ (upward movement) or $d.s$ (downward movement). The probability of the price going up is always $0 < p < 1$, and the probability of it going down is $1 - p$. The authors show that under these conditions, the market is complete: every derivative admits a replicating portfolio.

2.2 Probability Theory in Isabelle: Existing Notions

A large part of the formalization of measure and probability theory in Isabelle was carried out by Hölzl [5] and is now included in Isabelle's distribution. We briefly recap some of the notions that will be used throughout the paper and the way they are formalized in Isabelle. We assume the reader has knowledge of fundamental concepts of measure and probability theory; any missing notions can be found in Durrett [4] for example. For the sake of readability, in what follows, a term $F\,t$ will sometimes be written F_t.

Probability spaces are particular *measure spaces*. A measure space over a set Ω consists of a function μ that associates a nonnegative number or $+\infty$ to some subsets of Ω. The subsets of Ω that can be measured are closed under complement and countable unions and make up a σ-*algebra*. The σ-algebra *generated by a set* $\mathcal{C} \subseteq 2^\Omega$ is the smallest σ-algebra containing $\mathcal{C}$; it is denoted by $\overline{\sigma}(\mathcal{C})$.

The functions μ that measure the elements of a σ-algebra are positive and *countably additive*: if $\mathcal{A} \subseteq 2^\Omega$ is a σ-algebra and $\forall i \in \mathbb{N}$, $A_i \in \mathcal{A}$, then $\mu(\bigcup_{i\in\mathbb{N}} A_i) = \sum_{i\in\mathbb{N}} \mu(A_i)$. In Isabelle, measure spaces are defined as follows (where $\overline{\mathbb{R}}$ denotes $\mathbb{R} \cup \{-\infty, +\infty\}$ and $\mathbb{B} = \{\bot, \top\}$):

measure-space $\qquad\qquad :: \alpha\,\mathsf{set} \to \alpha\,\mathsf{set}\,\mathsf{set} \to (\alpha\,\mathsf{set} \to \overline{\mathbb{R}}) \to \mathbb{B}$
measure-space $\Omega\,\mathcal{A}\,\mu \Leftrightarrow$
$\quad$ σ-algebra $\Omega\,\mathcal{A}\,\wedge$ positive $\mathcal{A}\,\mu\,\wedge$ countably-additive $\mathcal{A}\,\mu$

A measure type is defined by fixing the measure of non-measurable sets to 0:

typedef $\alpha\,\mathsf{measure} = \{(\Omega, \mathcal{A}, \mu) \mid (\forall A \notin \mathcal{A}.\,\mu A = 0) \wedge \mathsf{measure\text{-}space}\ \Omega\,\mathcal{A}\,\mu\}$

If $\mathcal{M}$ is an element of type α **measure**, then the corresponding space, σ-algebra and measure are respectively denoted by $\Omega_\mathcal{M}$, $\mathcal{A}_\mathcal{M}$ and $\mu_\mathcal{M}$.

A function between two measurable spaces is *measurable* if the preimage of every measurable set is measurable. In Isabelle, sets of measurable functions are defined as follow:

measurable $\qquad\qquad :: \alpha\,\mathsf{measure} \to \beta\,\mathsf{measure} \to (\alpha \to \beta)\,\mathsf{set}$
measurable $\mathcal{M}\,\mathcal{N}\,\mu = \{f : \Omega_\mathcal{M} \to \Omega_\mathcal{N} \mid \forall A \in \mathcal{A}_\mathcal{N}.\,f^{-1}(A) \cap \Omega_\mathcal{M} \in \mathcal{A}_\mathcal{M}\}$

Probability measures are measure spaces on which the measure of Ω is finite and equal to 1. In Isabelle, they are defined by a *locale*; this allows one to delimit a range in which the existence of a measure satisfying the desired assumptions is assumed, instead of having to explicitly add the corresponding hypotheses in every theorem, which would be tedious.

locale prob-space = **finite-measure** + **assumes** $\mu_\mathcal{M}(\Omega_\mathcal{M}) = 1$

A *random variable* on a probability space $\mathcal{M}$ is a measurable function with domain $\Omega_\mathcal{M}$. In what follows, we will consider properties that hold *almost surely* (or *almost everywhere*), i.e., are such that the elements for which they do not hold reside within a set of measure 0:

lemma AE-IFF :
$$(\text{AE}_\mathcal{M}\, x.\ P\ x) \Leftrightarrow (\exists N \in \mathcal{A}_\mathcal{M}.\, \mu_\mathcal{M}(N) = 0 \wedge \{x \mid \neg P\ x\} \subseteq N).$$

3   Enriching the Probability Theory

In our context, asset prices and trading strategy values will be defined by sequences of random variables. These sequences cannot be arbitrary. For example, considering an asset price that depends on what happens at a future time is clearly irrelevant: this price should only depend on events that happened in the past. We introduce the additional notions from probability that we formalized to take these restrictions into account.

3.1   Modeling the Passage of Time

We defined several notions related to the passage of time. The first is the notion of a *filtration*, which is used to model the increasing amount of information that is available as time goes by. In general, a filtration is defined as an increasing collection of σ-algebras, and each element of the filtration is implicitly associated with a measure that is simply the restriction of the general measure to the considered algebra. In a formal setting it is more convenient to make this association explicit, thus we define a filtration as an increasing collection of measure spaces.

restr-measure   :: α **measure** $\to$ α **measure** $\to$ $\mathbb{B}$
restr-measure $\mathcal{M}\,\mathcal{N} \Leftrightarrow (\Omega_\mathcal{M} = \Omega_\mathcal{N}) \wedge (\mathcal{A}_\mathcal{N} \subseteq \mathcal{A}_\mathcal{M}) \wedge$
  $(\forall A \in \mathcal{A}_\mathcal{N}.\ \mu_\mathcal{N}(A) = \mu_\mathcal{M}(A))$

We will in particular make use of the restricted measure spaces generated by functions $f : \Omega_\mathcal{M} \to \Omega_\mathcal{N}$. These are measure spaces of the form $\mathcal{M}_f \overset{\text{def}}{=} (\Omega_\mathcal{M}, \mathcal{B}, \mu_\mathcal{M})$, where $\mathcal{B}$ is the σ-algebra generated by the set $\{f^{-1}(A) \cap \Omega_\mathcal{M} \mid A \in \mathcal{A}_\mathcal{N}\}$. When f is a measurable function, this is indeed a restricted measure space, and it is the smallest restricted measure space that makes f measurable relatively to $\mathcal{M}$.

lemma FCT-GEN-RESTR-IS-RESTR-MEASURE :
  $(f \in \text{measurable } \mathcal{M}\,\mathcal{N}) \Longrightarrow \text{restr-measure } \mathcal{M}\,\mathcal{M}_f$
lemma FCT-GEN-RESTR-MEASURE-MIN :
  $(\text{restr-measure } \mathcal{M}\,\mathcal{Q}) \Longrightarrow (f \in \text{measurable } \mathcal{Q}\,\mathcal{N})$
    $\Longrightarrow \text{restr-measure } \mathcal{Q}\,\mathcal{M}_f$

Restricted measures are used to define *filtrations*. Filtrations are meant to represent the accumulated information, and although the CRR model is restricted to a discrete setting, they are defined in a more general setting as a collection of increasing restricted measures over a totally ordered set. We also define a locale for probability spaces equipped with a filtration.

filtration   :: $((\iota :: \mathtt{linorder}) \to \alpha\,\mathtt{measure}) \to \mathbb{B}$
filtration $\mathcal{F} \Leftrightarrow (\forall t.\ \mathtt{restr\text{-}measure}\ \mathcal{M}\ \mathcal{F}_t) \land$
$\qquad\qquad\quad (\forall s\ t.\ s \le t \Rightarrow \mathtt{restr\text{-}measure}\ \mathcal{F}_t\ \mathcal{F}_s)$

locale filtrated-prob-space = prob-space +
  fixes $\mathcal{F}$ assumes filtration $\mathcal{F}$

In order to model quantities that evolve randomly with the passage of time, such as the price of a stock, we introduce *stochastic processes*, which are collections of random variables.

stoch-procs   :: $\alpha\,\mathtt{measure} \to \beta\,\mathtt{measure} \to (\iota \to (\alpha \to \beta))$ set
stoch-procs $\mathcal{M}\ \mathcal{N} = \{X \mid \forall t.\ X_t \in \mathtt{measurable}\ \mathcal{M}\ \mathcal{N}\}$

A particular class of stochastic processes of interest are those whose value at a given time depends only on the information contained in the corresponding filtration. Intuitively, this simply means that these processes cannot predict the future. These are *adapted* stochastic processes:

adapt-stoch-proc   :: $(\iota \to (\alpha \to \beta)) \to \beta\,\mathtt{measure} \to \mathbb{B}$
adapt-stoch-proc $X\ \mathcal{N} \Leftrightarrow \forall t.\ X_t \in \mathtt{measurable}\ \mathcal{F}_t\ \mathcal{N}$

When modeling equity markets, we will mainly be considering stochastic processes with real values. The natural σ-algebra on $\mathbb{R}$ is the *Borel σ-algebra*, which is the σ-algebra generated by the open sets of $\Omega = \mathbb{R}$.

abbreviation borel-adapt-stoch-proc $X \equiv$ adapt-stoch-proc X borel

3.2 The Infinite Coin Toss Space

As mentioned in the Introduction, in the CRR model, at every time n, the risky asset can only move upward or downward with respective probabilities p and $1 - p$. This means that the evolution of the risky asset price can be modeled by tossing at each time n a coin that lands on its head with a probability p, and having the price move upward at time $n + 1$ exactly when the coin lands on its head. The evolution of this price is thus controlled by sequences of coin tosses. In most introductory textbooks on the CRR model, these sequences are finite as the results are presented for a given derivative with a finite maturity. We choose to consider infinite sequences—or streams—of coin tosses for the sake of generality. Since at time n no event other than the outcome of the coin toss is required, this outcome can be represented by a Bernoulli distribution of parameter p. In Isabelle, because discrete probability distributions and probability mass functions are isomorphic, the type of probability mass functions are defined as a subtype of measures [7], along with an injective representation function measure-pmf :: α pmf $\rightarrow$ α measure. The Bernoulli distribution is thus defined as measure-pmf (bernoulli-pmf p). The measure space for infinite sequences of independent coin tosses is isomorphic to the infinite product of Bernoulli distributions with the same parameter. In Isabelle, this measure space is defined using the function stream-space :: α measure $\rightarrow$ (α stream) measure. The measure space thus defined is the smallest one in which the function nth :: α stream $\rightarrow$ $\mathbb{N} \rightarrow \alpha$ such that (nth s n) is the nth element of stream s is measurable [6]. The measure spaces we consider are defined as follows:

bernoulli-stream   :: $\mathbb{R} \rightarrow$ ($\mathbb{B}$ stream) measure
bernoulli-stream p = stream-space (measure-pmf (bernoulli-pmf p))

We define a locale in which we impose that $0 < p < 1$, and thus obtain a probability space:

locale infinite-coin-toss-space =
fixes p and M
assumes $0 < p < 1$ and M = bernoulli-stream p

The natural information that should be available at time n is the outcome of the first n coin tosses, and we define a filtration $\mathcal{F}^{\mathrm{nat}}$ accordingly: intuitively, in this filtration, two streams of coin tosses with the same first n outcomes cannot occur in distinct sets that are measurable in $\mathcal{F}^{\mathrm{nat}}$. In our setting, each restricted measure space $\mathcal{F}_n^{\mathrm{nat}}$ can be defined as generated by an arbitrary measurable function which maps all streams that agree on the first n coin tosses to the same element. We thus considered the sequence of so-called *pseudo-projection functions* $(\pi_n^\top)_{n \in \mathbb{N}}$, where:

$$\pi_n^\top : \qquad \Omega_\mathcal{M} \qquad\qquad \rightarrow \Omega_\mathcal{M}$$
$$(w_1, \cdots, w_n, w_{n+1}, \cdots) \mapsto (w_1, \cdots, w_n, \top, \top, \cdots)$$

These functions are measurable and permit to define a sequence of restricted measure spaces which is indeed a filtration:

$\mathcal{F}^{\mathrm{nat}}$ :: $\mathbb{N} \rightarrow$ ($\mathbb{B}$ stream) measure
$\mathcal{F}^{\mathrm{nat}}$ n = $\mathcal{M}_{(\pi^\top n)}$

We can thus define a locale for the infinite coin toss space along with this filtration:

locale infinite-cts-filtration = infinite-coin-toss-space +
fixes $\mathcal{F}$ assumes $\mathcal{F} = \mathcal{F}^{\mathrm{nat}}$

4 Modeling Equity Markets in Discrete Time

4.1 General Definitions

An equity market is characterized by the set of assets that can be traded. The locale for discrete equity markets is based on a *discrete* filtration and requires that the prices of the tradeable assets must be known at all times.

locale nat-filtrated-prob-space = prob-space +
  fixes $F :: \mathbb{N} \to (\alpha$ measure$)$
  assumes filtration F
locale disc-equity-market = nat-filtrated-prob-space +
  fixes market-assets $:: (\mathbb{N} \to \alpha \to \mathbb{R})$ set
  assumes $\forall X \in$ market-assets. borel-adapt-stoch-proc X

The two main notions that need to be modeled in an equity market are
derivatives and *portfolios*. A (European) derivative with maturity $T > 0$ is a
product defined by its *payoff*, i.e., by the amount of cash that its owner receives
at time T. The payoff depends only on the information available at time T, hence
must be Borel-measurable w.r.t. $\mathcal{F}_T$. The set of derivatives with maturity T is
thus defined as follows:

deriv-at $:: \mathbb{N} \to (\alpha \to \mathbb{R})$ set
deriv-at $T = \{f \mid f \in$ borel-measurable $\mathcal{F}_T\}$

A portfolio over n assets consists of two functions of domain $\{1,\ldots,n\}$, the
composition function and the *quantities* function, which respectively map each
$i \in \{1,\ldots,n\}$ to the price of the ith asset in the portfolio, and to the quantity of
the asset that is withheld. Because a portfolio can be dynamic, both functions are
time-dependent, and at any given time, they can be viewed as random variables.

func-seq $:: (\mathbb{N} \to \alpha \to \mathbb{R})$ set
func-seq = UNIV

disc-portfolio $:: \mathbb{N} \to (\mathbb{N} \to \mathbb{N} \to \alpha \to \mathbb{R}) \to$
                             $(\mathbb{N} \to \mathbb{N} \to \alpha \to \mathbb{R}) \to \mathbb{B}$
disc-portfolio n p q $\Leftrightarrow$
  $(p \in \{1..n\} \to$ func-seq$) \wedge (q \in \{1..n\} \to$ func-seq$)$

We define a discrete portfolio type:

typedef α disc-pf = $\{(n, p, q) \mid$ disc-portfolio n p q$\}$,
to which are associated three functions asset-nb, price and qty, that respectively permit to obtain the number of assets in the portfolio, their prices and
quantities in the portfolio. Associated to a portfolio is its value, which, at time
n, is obtained by multiplying each asset price by the withheld quantity:

val-process $:: \alpha$ disc-pf $\to \mathbb{N} \to \alpha \to \mathbb{R}$
val-process $p\ n\ \omega = \sum_{i=1}^{\text{asset-nb }p}($price $p\ i\ n\ \omega) \times ($qty $p\ i\ n\ \omega)$

The definition of a portfolio given above is very general and, in practice,
not of much use. It is at least necessary to consider portfolios that only contain
tradeable assets (that are available on the market), to have a constant initial
investment that docs not depend on any random event, and to know at all times
what quantities were traded for each asset. Portfolios satisfying this condition
are *trading strategies*:

```
trading-strat    :: α disc-pf → 𝔹
trading-strat p ⇔
```

$(\exists c. \forall \omega \in \Omega_{\mathcal{M}}.$ val-process $p\ 0\ \omega = c)\ \wedge$

$(\forall i \in \{1..(\text{asset-nb } p)\}.((\text{price } p)\ i) \in$ market-assets$)\ \wedge$

$(\forall i \in \{1..(\text{asset-nb } p)\}.$ borel-adapt-stoch-proc $((\text{qty } p)\ i)$

Self-financing portfolios are portfolios for which no cash is added or retrieved at any time other than 0, although the composition of the portfolio may change. In order to formalize this notion, we define the updated value of a portfolio, which reflects the evolution of the portfolio's value when the prices of the assets have changed but the quantities of each asset have not been updated. The updated value of a portfolio at time 0 is arbitrarily set to 0.

```
upd-val-process             :: α disc-pf → ℕ → α → ℝ
upd-val-process p 0 ω      = 0
upd-val-process p n+1 ω =
```

$$\sum_{i=1}^{\text{asset-nb } p} (\text{price } p\ i\ (n+1)\ \omega) \times (\text{qty } p\ i\ n\ \omega)$$

A portfolio is self-financing if its value at time $n+1$ is identical to its updated value at $n+1$; this means that the value of the portfolio may be affected by the evolution of the market but not by the changes in its composition.

```
self-financing    :: α disc-pf → 𝔹
self-financing p ⇔
```

$\forall n \in \mathbb{N}.$ val-process $p\ (n+1) =$ upd-val-process $p\ (n+1)$

A *replicating portfolio* for a derivative is a self-financing trading strategy which, at maturity, almost surely has a value exactly equal to the cash-flow of the considered derivative. If such a portfolio exists, then the derivative is *attainable*, and if every derivative available on a market is attainable, then the market is *complete*:

```
replic-pf        :: α disc-pf → (α → ℝ) → ℕ → 𝔹
replic-pf p V T ⇔ (trading-strat p) ∧
```

$(\text{self-financing } p) \wedge (\text{AE}_{\mathcal{M}}\ \omega.\ (\text{val-process } p)\ T\ \omega = V\ w)$

```
attainable      :: (α → ℝ) → ℕ → 𝔹
attainable V T ⇔ (∃p. replic-pf p V T)
```

```
complete-market :: 𝔹
complete-market ⇔ (∀T ∈ ℕ. ∀V ∈ (deriv-at T). attainable V T)
```

4.2   Arbitrage Processes and Viable Markets

We define the notion of arbitrage processes. Intuitively, an arbitrage is a trading strategy that offers the possibility of a riskless profit, e.g., by exploiting differences of prices between assets generating identical cash-flows. More formally, the investment and the probability of a loss should be null, and the probability of a gain should be strictly positive. Although such arbitrage opportunities do exist in real financial markets, they are quickly exploited and disappear. Most pricing results in financial mathematics are based on a no-arbitrage assumption.

$$\text{arbitrage-process} \quad :: \alpha \text{ disc-pf} \to \mathbb{B}$$
$$\text{arbitrage-process } p \Leftrightarrow$$

$$(\exists m \in \mathbb{N}.$$

$$(\text{trading-strat } p) \wedge (\text{self-financing } p) \wedge$$
$$(\text{AE}_{\mathcal{M}} \; \omega. \; (\text{val-process } p) \; 0 \; \omega = 0) \wedge$$
$$(\text{AE}_{\mathcal{M}} \; \omega. \; (\text{val-process } p) \; m \; \omega \geq 0) \wedge$$
$$(\mathcal{P}(\{\omega \in \Omega_{\mathcal{M}} \mid (\text{val-process } p) \; m \; \omega > 0\}) > 0)$$

We may then define a locale for *viable* markets, i.e., for markets in which there is no arbitrage process:

locale viable-market = filtrated-prob-space +
assumes $\forall p. \; \neg(\text{arbitrage-process } p)$

Models of equity markets generally assume the existence of an asset whose value is a deterministic process. It is thus a risk-free asset and acts as a money market account, into which cash can be deposited or from which cash can be borrowed at a same interest rate. In both the Black-Scholes-Merton and CRR models, the evolution of the price process of this asset is described by a constant *risk-free rate*.

$$\text{disc-rfr-proc} \qquad\qquad :: \mathbb{R} \to \mathbb{N} \to \alpha \to \mathbb{R}$$
$$(\text{disc-rfr-proc } r) \; 0 \; \omega \qquad = 1$$
$$(\text{disc-rfr-proc } r) \; (n+1) \; \omega = (1+r) \times ((\text{disc-rfr-proc } r) \; n \; \omega)$$

In other words, a quantity of cash S invested in the risk-free asset at time n amounts to obtaining $S.(1+r)^k$ at time $n+k$. We define a locale for a probability space in which there is a price process corresponding to a risk-free asset, with the additional assumption that the risk-free rate for this process is strictly greater than -1:

locale prob-space-risk-free = prob-space +
fixes r **and** riskless-asset
assumes $(-1 < r) \wedge (\text{riskless-asset} = \text{disc-rfr-proc } r)$

We define an operation in this locale to construct self-financing portfolios: it suffices to specify the quantity processes for the other assets in the portfolio, and a self-financing portfolio is constructed by investing the required quantity of cash in the risk-free asset. The function, named self-finance, takes two arguments, a number representing the initial value of the self-financing portfolio, and a portfolio that is potentially not self-financing.

lemma SELF-FINANCE-INITIAL-VALUE :
   $(\forall \omega.$ val-process (self-finance v p) 0 $\omega) = v$
lemma SELF-FINANCE-IS-SELF-FINANCING :
  (self-financing (self-finance v p))

By combining locales, we define a locale for a viable market in which there is a risk-free asset:

locale viable-market-risk-free =
  viable-market + prob-space-risk-free

5   The CRR Model

All the notions defined above are used to formalize the CRR model. It consists of a viable market in which there is one risk-free asset and one risky asset, the price of which evolves according to a sequence of coin tosses. More precisely, the price of the risky asset is modeled by a *geometric random walk* with parameters specifying the upward and downward movements as well as the price of the asset at time 0:

geom-rand-walk $:: \mathbb{R} \to \mathbb{R} \to \mathbb{R} \to$
                                     $(\mathbb{N} \to (\mathbb{B} \text{ stream}) \to \mathbb{R})$
(geom-rand-walk u d v) 0 ω $= v$
(geom-rand-walk u d v) $(n+1)$ $\omega =$ (**if** ω_n **then** u **else** d) $\times$
                                       $((\text{geom-rand-walk } u \ d \ v) \ n \ \omega)$

The geometric random walk process is an adapted process, in the infinite coin toss space equipped with its natural filtration, since its value at time n depends only on the outcome of the first n coin tosses:

lemma GEOM-RAND-WALK-BOREL-ADAPTED :
    borel-adapt-stoch-proc (geom-rand-walk u d v)

The locale for the market in the CRR model is defined as follows:

locale CRR-market = infinite-coin-toss-space+
    viable-market-risk-free +
fixes S **and** u **and** d **and** v_0
assumes $0 < d$ **and** $d < u$ **and** $0 < v_0$ **and**
    $S =$ geom-rand-walk u d v_0 **and** $S \in$ market-assets

A no-arbitrage reasoning provides an additional relationship between the risk-free rate and the upward and downward movements: we must have $d < 1 + r$ and $1 + r < u$. For example, if $1 + r \leq d$, then a risk-free profit can be made by borrowing enough money, say, v, at time 0 to buy the risky asset. At time 1, the amount $v \, . \, (1{+}r)$ is reimbursed and the risky asset is worth either $d \, . \, v \geq v \, . \, (1{+}r)$ or $u \, . \, v > v \, . \, (1 + r)$, thus it is impossible to lose any money and there is a probability p to win $(u - 1 - r) \, . \, v$.

We now informally describe how to construct a replicating portfolio for any derivative V of maturity T, and refer to [11] Vol. 1 for details. The construction is given by specifying the quantity that is invested in the risky asset and considering the corresponding self-financing portfolio, obtained by invoking the `self-finance` function with an initial value to be specified.

At a time n, the outcomes of the first n coin tosses are known, and we let $l \stackrel{\text{def}}{=} [\omega_1, \ldots, \omega_n]$ represent these outcomes. If we denote by $\lfloor \omega \rfloor_n$ the sequence made of the first n elements of ω, then the space of possible observable sequences at time n is $\{\omega \in \Omega_{\mathcal{M}} \mid \lfloor \omega \rfloor_n = l\}$. If X is a random variable that is $\mathcal{F}_n$-measurable, then by definition, $X(\omega)$ only depends on the value of $\lfloor \omega \rfloor_n$, and we may denote by X^l the value of $X(w)$ when $\lfloor \omega \rfloor_n = l$. Similarly, if Y is an $\mathcal{F}_{n+1}$-measurable random variable, then we denote by $Y^{l,\top}$ (resp. $Y^{l,\perp}$) the value of $Y(\omega)$, when $\lfloor \omega \rfloor_n = l$ and $\omega_{n+1} = \top$ (resp. $\omega_{n+1} = \perp$). Note that, in particular, since the risky asset is modeled by a geometric random walk, we have $S_{n+1}^{l,\top} = u.S_n^l$ and $S_{n+1}^{l,\perp} = d.S_n^l$. Finally, when Y is an $\mathcal{F}_{n+1}$-measurable random variable, we denote by Y^l the random variable that depends only on ω_{n+1}, and can take as values either $Y^{l,\top}$ or $Y^{l,\perp}$.

We now show that if V_{n+1} is a derivative[2] of maturity $n+1$, then it is possible to construct at time n a replicating portfolio for V_{n+1}. We define the numbers

$$\tilde{p} \stackrel{\text{def}}{=} \frac{1+r-d}{u-d} \quad \text{and} \quad \tilde{q} \stackrel{\text{def}}{=} \frac{u-1-r}{u-d}.$$

Their sum is equal to 1, which means that they can be interpreted as complementary probabilities, from which a corresponding Bernoulli space, of parameter $\tilde{p}$, can be constructed. We denote by $\tilde{\mathbb{E}}$ the expectation under this probability space. This probability space is called the *risk-neutral probability space*. The reason for this is that, in a standard financial market, the expected rate of growth of a risky asset should be strictly greater than the risk-free rate, since investors in the risky asset require a compensation for assuming this risk. In the risk-neutral probability space, the expected rate of growth of the risky asset is

$$\tilde{\mathbb{E}}[S_{n+1}^l] \stackrel{\text{def}}{=} \tilde{p} . S_{n+1}^{l,\top} + \tilde{q} . S_{n+1}^{l,\perp} = \tilde{p}.u.S_n^l + \tilde{q}.d.S_n^l = (1+r).S_n^l.$$

In other words, under the risk-neutral probability, the expected rate of growth of the risky asset is equal to the risk-free rate, meaning that investors are neutral to the fact that investing in the risky asset incurs a risk of losing money. Let V_n^l and Δ_n^l be defined as follows:

$$V_n^l \stackrel{\text{def}}{=} \frac{\tilde{\mathbb{E}}[V_{n+1}^l]}{1+r} = \frac{\tilde{p} . V_{n+1}^{l,\top} + \tilde{q} . V_{n+1}^{l,\perp}}{1+r}, \quad \text{and} \quad \Delta_n^l \stackrel{\text{def}}{=} \frac{V_{n+1}^{l,\top} - V_{n+1}^{l,\perp}}{S_{n+1}^{l,\top} - S_{n+1}^{l,\perp}}.$$

These are both real numbers; V_n^l is the discounted risk-neutral expectation of V_n^l, and Δ_n^l can be viewed as a discrete version of the first-order derivative of V_{n+1}^l w.r.t. S_{n+1}^l.

We claim that the self-financing portfolio starting at time $t = n$ with initial value V_n^l that at time n invests Δ_n^l in the risky asset is a replicating portfolio for V_{n+1}^l. The amount of cash invested in the risk-free asset is $V_n^l - \Delta_n^l . S_n^l$, and since the value of the risk-free asset at time n is $(1+r)^n$, the portfolio contains

---

[2] The subscript in V_{n+1} is unnecessary, since by definition, derivatives of maturity $n+1$ are $\mathcal{F}_{n+1}$-measurable random variables. It was added to make it easier to keep track of measurability properties of the objects that will be defined.

a quantity $\frac{V_n^l - \Delta_n^l \cdot S_n^l}{(1+r)^n}$ of the risk-free asset. Hence, if X^l represents the value process of this portfolio, then at time $n + 1$, when the outcome of the coin toss is a head, we have:

$$
\begin{aligned}
X^{l,\top} &= \Delta_n^l \cdot S_{n+1}^{l,\top} + \frac{V_n^l - \Delta_n^l \cdot S_n^l}{(1+r)^n} \cdot (1+r)^{n+1} \\
&= \Delta_n^l \cdot u \cdot S_n^l + (V_n^l - \Delta_n^l \cdot S_n^l) \cdot (1+r) \\
&= (1+r) \cdot V_n^l + \Delta_n^l \cdot S_n^l \cdot (u - 1 - r) \\
&= (1+r) \cdot V_n^l + \frac{V_{n+1}^{l,\top} - V_{n+1}^{l,\bot}}{S_n^l \cdot (u - d)} \cdot S_n^l \cdot (u - 1 - r) \\
&= \tilde{p} \cdot V_{n+1}^{l,\top} + \tilde{q} \cdot V_{n+1}^{l,\bot} + \tilde{q} \cdot V_{n+1}^{l,\top} - \tilde{q} \cdot V_{n+1}^{l,\bot} \\
&= V_{n+1}^{l,\top}.
\end{aligned}
$$

Similarly, $X^{l,\bot} = V_{n+1}^{l,\bot}$ and the portfolio is indeed a replicating portfolio.

Since the initial value V_n^l of this replicating portfolio is $\mathcal{F}_n$-measurable, it is possible to replicate its value by constructing a portfolio starting at time $n - 1$ (assuming $n > 0$). By backward induction, we define the adapted processes $(V_n)_{n \leq T}$ and $(\Delta_n)_{n \leq T}$, and show that the self-financing portfolio with initial value V_0, whose quantity process in the risky asset is $(\Delta_n)_{n \leq T}$ is a replicating portfolio for the derivative V with maturity T.

In our formalization, the adapted process $(V_n)_{n \leq T}$ is defined by a function `deriv-price`, that takes as parameters a random variable V and a number T such that V is $\mathcal{F}_T$-measurable. The adapted process $(\Delta_n)_{n \leq T}$ is defined by a function `delta-comp`, that also takes as parameters a random variable V and a number T such that V is $\mathcal{F}_T$-measurable. Using the second function we define the portfolio, named `delta-pf`, in which we only invest in the stock.

We then define the *delta-hedging* portfolio for the derivative, by considering the corresponding self-financing portfolio, and setting its initial value to the constant value $V_0 \overset{\text{def}}{=} (\text{deriv-price } V\ T)\ 0$:

```
delta-hedging      :: (𝔹 stream → ℝ) → ℕ → (𝔹 stream) disc-pf
delta-hedging V T = self-finance V₀ (delta-pf V T)
```

This portfolio is used to prove the two main results in the CRR model: that the delta-hedging portfolio is a replicating portfolio, which implies that every derivative is attainable; in other words, that the market is indeed complete.

lemma DELTA-NEUTRAL-PORTFOLIO-IS-REPLICATING :
$\quad (V \in \text{deriv-at } T) \implies (0 < T) \implies \text{replic-pf } (\text{delta-hedging } V\ T)$

lemma CRR-MARKET-COMPLETE :
`complete-market`

6 Discussion

The entire formalization of the Cox-Ross-Rubinstein model is a few thousand lines long, which is less than what was initially anticipated. This is due in a large part to Sledgehammer (a subsystem of Isabelle which allows one to invoke external provers, see for instance [2]); and it frequently turned out that parts of proofs that were expected to be cumbersome were carried out with one-liners thanks to this tool. The theories available in Isabelle keep expanding and the formalization would have required even less work if it had begun later. Indeed, this formalization was initially carried out in Isabelle 2016, and some of the notions that were formalized such as filtrations and conditional expectations (not presented in this paper) are now available in Isabelle 2016-1. The only proofs that required more work than expected are those that involved symbolic computations. These were carried out in Isabelle 2016, and we did not investigate whether they could be carried out more efficiently in Isabelle 2016-1; otherwise, it would be interesting to have more elaborate tactics supporting formal calculations, and more generally to have a tighter integration of theorem provers and formal computation tools.

Although the proof that every derivative is attainable in the Cox-Ross-Rubinstein model does not require a lot of mathematical background, its formalization was not straightforward, especially because some financial notions, such as that of an arbitrage, are not always defined formally in introductory pricing theory textbooks. It is straightforward to extract from the proof that every derivative is attainable in the CRR model, a program that generates the replicating portfolio of any European derivative. We did not work on this extraction here, because such a program would be of little practical use. However, obtaining similar results in refinements of the CRR model for American derivatives would allow us to construct a certified program that prices these, and such a program would actually be used by financial institutions, where these refinements are still frequently used for such derivatives. We are currently working on a generalization of the current results, to restate them in the context of *martingale pricing theory*, at which point we intend to generate the first completely certified pricer for American derivatives in the CRR model.

Acknowledgments. We thank Hervé Guiol for his valuable comments on this work.

References

1. Black, F., Scholes, M.: The pricing of options and corporate liabilities. J. Polit. Econ. **81**(3), 637–654 (1973)
2. Böhme, S., Nipkow, T.: Sledgehammer: judgement day. In: Giesl, J., Hähnle, R. (eds.) IJCAR 2010. LNCS (LNAI), vol. 6173, pp. 107–121. Springer, Heidelberg (2010). doi:10.1007/978-3-642-14203-1_9
3. Cox, J.C., Ross, S.A., Rubinstein, M.: Option pricing: a simplified approach. J. Financ. Econ. **7**(3), 229–263 (1979)

4. Durrett, R.: Probability: Theory and Examples. The Wadsworth & Brooks/Cole Statistics/Probability Series. Wadsworth Inc., Duxbury Press, Belmont (1991)
5. Hölzl, J.: Construction and stochastic applications of measure spaces in higher-order logic. Ph.D. thesis, Institut für Informatik, Technische Universität München, October 2012
6. Hölzl, J.: Markov chains and Markov decision processes in Isabelle/HOL. J. Autom. Reason., 1–43 (2016). doi:10.1007/s10817-016-9401-5
7. Hölzl, J., Lochbihler, A., Traytel, D.: A formalized hierarchy of probabilistic system types. In: Urban, C., Zhang, X. (eds.) ITP 2015. LNCS, vol. 9236, pp. 203–220. Springer, Cham (2015). doi:10.1007/978-3-319-22102-1_13
8. Hull, J.: Options, Futures and Other Derivatives. Pearson/Prentice Hall, Upper Saddle River (2009)
9. Merton, R.: The theory of rational option pricing. Bell J. Econ. Manag. Sci. **4**, 141–183 (1973)
10. Nipkow, T., Wenzel, M., Paulson, L.C.: Isabelle/HOL: A Proof Assistant for Higher-Order Logic. Springer, Heidelberg (2002)
11. Shreve, S.E.: Stochastic Calculus for Finance I: The Binomial Asset Pricing Model. Springer Finance. Springer, New York (2003)
12. Wenzel, M., Paulson, L.: Isabelle/Isar. In: Wiedijk, F. (ed.) The Seventeen Provers of the World. LNCS, vol. 3600, pp. 41–49. Springer, Heidelberg (2006). doi:10.1007/11542384_8

Monte Carlo Tableau Proof Search

Michael Färber[1]([⊠]), Cezary Kaliszyk[1], and Josef Urban[2]

[1] Universität Innsbruck, Innsbruck, Austria
{michael.faerber,cezary.kaliszyk}@uibk.ac.at
[2] Czech Technical University in Prague, Prague, Czech Republic
josef.urban@gmail.com

Abstract. We study Monte Carlo Tree Search to guide proof search in tableau calculi. This includes proposing a number of proof-state evaluation heuristics, some of which are learnt from previous proofs. We present an implementation based on the leanCoP prover. The system is trained and evaluated on a large suite of related problems coming from the Mizar proof assistant, showing that it is capable to find new and different proofs.

1 Introduction

Recent advances in Automated Reasoning include both theoretical improvements in the calculi, including combining superposition with SAT solving in recent versions of Vampire [4] and research on the InstGen calculus in iProver [16], but also more practical improvements, such as more efficient and precise term indexing techniques [24], efficient non-clausal tableau proof search [20], or the use of machine learning for problem size reduction [12]. Furthermore, many automated reasoning techniques have been extended to interesting theories beyond first-order logic, including the developments in SMT solving in CVC4 [3] or to higher-order logic [6,29]. Many of these developments have been of great value for interactive theorem provers, whose most powerful general purpose automation techniques today rely on automated reasoning tools [5].

However, current automated theorem provers are still quite weak in finding more complicated proofs, especially over large formal developments [27]. The search typically blows up after several seconds, making the chance of finding proofs in longer times exponentially decreasing [2]. This behaviour is reminiscent of poorly guided search in games such as chess and Go. The number of all possible variants there typically also grows exponentially, and intelligent guiding methods are needed to focus on exploring the most promising moves and positions.

The guiding method that has recently very significantly improved automatic game play is Monte Carlo Tree Search (MCTS), i.e., expanding the search based on its (variously guided) random sampling [7]. Recent developments in MCTS include combination of exploration and exploitation [15], combination of online and offline knowledge with the All-Moves-As-First (AMAF) heuristic [9], and adaptive tuning of rollout policies during search [21]. As shown for example in the AlphaGo system [25], machine learning can be used to train good

© Springer International Publishing AG 2017
L. de Moura (Ed.): CADE 2017, LNAI 10395, pp. 563–579, 2017.
DOI: 10.1007/978-3-319-63046-5_34

position evaluation heuristics even in very complicated domains that were previously thought to be solely in the realm of "human intuition". From the point of game theory, automated theorem proving is a combinatorial single-player game. For some games in this category, including SameGame [22] and the NP-hard Morpion Solitaire [21], MCTS has produced state-of-the-art players. [11] shows that proof search can be positively guided by one-step lookahead, and MCTS allows approximation of multi-step lookaheads by use of random sampling. While "finishing the randomly sampled game" – as used in the most straightforward MCTS for games – is not always possible in ATP (it would mean finishing the proof), there is a chance of learning good *proof state evaluation heuristics* that will guide MCTS for ATPs in a similar way as e.g. in AlphaGo.

In this work, we study MCTS methods that can guide the search in automated theorem provers, and evaluate their impact on interactive theorem proving problems in first-order logic. We focus on the tableau calculus and on the leanCoP prover [18], which has a compact implementation that is easy to experiment with. We can also build on previous machine learning extensions of lean-CoP [13,28]. To our knowledge, this is the first time MCTS has been applied to theorem proving.

Contributions

We introduce a set of MCTS heuristics tailored to proof search including two state transition probability heuristics, three state evaluation heuristics, and two tree expansion policies related to restricted backtracking (Sect. 4). Furthermore, we present an implementation interleaving a traditional proof search with MCTS (Sect. 5) and measure its performance on a set of Mizar Mathematical Library problems (Sect. 6).

2   Monte Carlo Tree Search

Monte Carlo Tree Search (MCTS) is a technique to guide search in a large decision space by taking random samples and evaluating their outcome. First, we will establish a format for problems tractable with MCTS. Then, we give a notation for Monte Carlo trees. Finally, we show how to create and evolve a Monte Carlo tree for given problems with problem-specific heuristics.

2.1   Problem Setting and Example

A tree search problem can be minimally characterised with:

- a set of states $\mathcal{S}$,
- an initial state $s_0 \in \mathcal{S}$, and
- a state transition function $\delta : \mathcal{S} \to 2^{\mathcal{S}}$.

As an example of a tree search problem, consider the travelling salesman problem: A salesman has to visit a set of cities C and wants to minimise the total distance travelled, where $d(c_1, c_2)$ is the distance between two cities.

A possible tree search characterisation of the travelling salesman problem is:

- The set of states S are the sequences of cities visited so far; for example [Prague], [Prague, Vienna, Bratislava], [Paris].
- The initial state s_0 is the empty sequence.
- The state transition function δ returns for a sequence of already visited cities the set of sequences where one previously unvisited city is added; i.e. $\delta(s) = \bigcup_{c \in C, c \notin s} [s, c]$. For example, $\delta([\text{Prague, Vienna}])$ could contain [Prague, Vienna, Budapest] and [Prague, Vienna, Bratislava].

The number of states of the travelling salesman problem is exponential in the number of cities, therefore constructing a whole tree to obtain an optimal solution is not feasible. To bias the tree search towards more promising regions, we define two types of heuristics:

- the probability $P : S \to [0, 1]$ of choosing a state and
- the reward $\rho : S \to [0, 1]$ for a state.

$P(s' \mid s)$ is the probability for choosing state s' when being in its predecessor state s, where $s' \in \delta(s)$. In the travelling salesman example,

$$P([\text{Prague, Vienna}] \mid [\text{Prague}]) > P([\text{Prague, Paris}] \mid [\text{Prague}])$$

means that when the salesman is in Prague, Vienna should be chosen as next city with a higher probability than Paris.

$\rho(s)$ is the overall quality of a (final) state s. Due to the MCTS flavour we use [15], it has to be normed between $[0, 1]$. In the travelling salesman example, a sensible ρ should yield larger values for city sequences with smaller overall distance.

2.2 Trees

A Monte Carlo tree stores the states that have been expanded during a tree search, and keeps statistics about the states. We define the set T of Monte Carlo tree nodes.

Definition 1 (Monte Carlo tree node). *A Monte Carlo tree node is a 5-tuple* $(n, r, s, S, T) \in T$, *where:*

- $n \in \mathbb{N}$ *is the number of times the node was visited,*
- $r \in \mathbb{R}$ *is the sum of the rewards of successors,*
- $s \in S$ *is the state of the node,*
- $S \in 2^S$ *are the unvisited successor states of s, and*
- $T \in 2^T$ *are the child tree nodes.*

Monte Carlo Tree Search evolves a tree by repeatedly applying a step function until a certain criterion is fulfilled, e.g. a certain number of steps is performed, time has elapsed etc. Ideally, every step should refine the quality estimate of the states in the Monte Carlo tree. We show the step function in the next section.

2.3   Monte Carlo Step Function

The Monte Carlo step function performs the following: First, it selects a *node* in the Monte Carlo tree. From the state of *node*, it randomly samples a sequence of successor states (called *simulation*). It then creates a new *node'* with some state from the simulation and makes it a child of the original *node*. Finally, a reward is calculated from the simulation and backpropagated to all ancestors of *node'*.

The idea is that rewards obtained from simulations starting from a certain node let us estimate the usefulness of the node itself. A description of the pseudocode in Algorithm 1 follows. For brevity, the pseudocode assumes that every state has at least one successor state (i.e., for every $s \in \mathcal{S}$, $|\delta(s)| > 0$).

Algorithm 1. Monte Carlo step function.

1: **procedure** STEP(*node*)
2:    **if** *node.S* = $\emptyset$ **then**
3:        *best* $\leftarrow$ arg max$_{t \in node.T}$ UCT(*node.n*, *t*)   ▷ selection
4:        *reward* $\leftarrow$ STEP(*best*)
5:    **else**
6:        s' $\leftarrow$ BIASEDDRAW(*P*, *node.s*, *node.S*)
7:        *sim* $\leftarrow$ SIMULATION(*D*, s')   ▷ simulation
8:        (*node'*, *reward*) $\leftarrow$ EXPANSION(*sim*)   ▷ expansion
9:        *node.S* $\leftarrow$ *node.S* \ {s'}
10:        *node.T* $\leftarrow$ *node.T* $\cup$ {*node'*}
11:    *node.n* $\leftarrow$ *node.n* + 1   ▷ backpropagation
12:    *node.r* $\leftarrow$ *node.r* + *reward*
13:    **return** reward

In l. 3, the step function recursively selects the child node with the highest UCT (Upper Confidence Bounds for Trees) value [15]. UCT establishes an order on nodes, combining *exploration* and *exploitation*: *exploration* prefers less frequently visited nodes, whereas *exploitation* prefers nodes with higher average reward. The ratio between these two goals is determined by the exploration constant C_p, where higher values give more emphasis to exploration. The average reward of a node (n_j, r_j, s, S, T) is $\frac{r_j}{n_j}$. The UCT function takes the number of times n that a parent node was visited, as well as a child node:

$$\mathrm{uct}(n, (n_j, r_j, s, S, T)) = \frac{r_j}{n_j} + C_p\sqrt{\frac{\ln n}{n_j}}.$$

As soon as a node with unvisited successor states is encountered (l. 5), an unvisited successor state s' is drawn (l. 6), where the probability of picking s' is proportional to $P(s' \mid s)$. From the chosen s', a simulation is performed up to a constant simulation depth D. A simulation starting from a state s_i draws a state s_{i+1} from $\delta(s_i)$, with probability $P(s_{i+1} \mid s_i)$. This is repeated for a certain number of times, yielding a simulation $[s_1, \ldots, s_D]$, where D is the simulation depth and for every i, $s_{i+1} \in \delta(s_i)$.

From the simulation, the expansion operation yields a new $node'$ and a $reward$. The default expansion policy creates $node'$ from the first state s_1 of the simulation and calculates the reward from the last state, i.e. $reward = \rho(s_D)$. Therefore, the new expansion node is $node' = (1, \rho(s_D), s_1, \delta(s_1), \emptyset)$.

The expansion node $node'$ is added to the child nodes (l. 10) and the $reward$ is propagated back until the root (l. 11–13).

3 Tableau

In this section, we shortly recall some basics of tableau [10] and introduce notions specific to representing tableau as MCTS.

Tableau calculi are methods to prove the inconsistency of formulae. A tableau is a tree with formulae as nodes. The root is the formula whose inconsistency one attempts to show. All other nodes are produced by application of tableau rules to nodes above them; such rules include α-rules to treat conjunctions and β-rules to treat disjunctions. For example, when a branch contains a disjunction (called β-formula), then an application of a β-rule (parametrised by the disjunction) adds the disjuncts as children to some leaf of the branch.

The choice of β-formulae in tableau proof search is one of the main sources of nondeterminism and has a considerable impact on the length of the proof search. It corresponds to the choice of given clauses in saturation-based provers and extension clauses in the connection calculus. Therefore, in this work, we focus on influencing the proof search mostly by influencing the choice of β-formulae. We will abstract from the actual tableau steps, only assuming that the considered tableau calculus that is sound and complete.

A branch of a tableau is closed iff it contains some formula and its negation. A tableau is closed iff all of its branches are closed. A formula is proven inconsistent when there is a closed tableau with the formula at the root. For the heuristics in Sect. 4, we define β-children, which correspond to open subgoals in interactive theorem provers and literals of open branches in the connection calculus.

Definition 2 (β-children). *Given a tableau t, we call direct children of branches β-children of t and denote them as $\beta(t)$.*

Open β-children (denoted $\beta_o(t)$) are all β-children on open branches not having any branch as descendant. Closed β-children (denoted $\beta_c(t)$) are all β-children that are not open, i.e. $\beta_c(t) = \beta(t) \setminus \beta_o(t)$.

Example 1. In state 4 in Fig. 1, closed β-children are p, $\neg p$, s, q, and $\neg q$. Open β-children are t and r.

The *successor tableaux* of a tableau are all tableaux that can be obtained from the original tableau by the application of some rule. We now give a description of tableau construction for a given formula f in the language of Sect. 2.1:

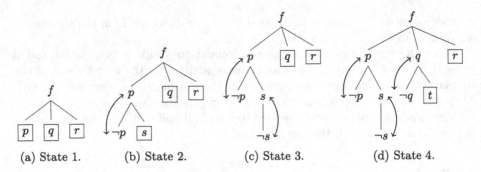

Fig. 1. Proof search for formula $f = (p\lor q\lor r)\land(\neg p\lor s)\land(\neg p\lor t\lor u)\land\neg s\land(\neg q\lor t)\land(\neg q\lor s)$. Open β-children are surrounded by boxes.

- The set of states S is the set of tableaux.
- The initial state s_0 is a tableau containing only the formula f as root.
- The transition function $\delta(s)$ obtains all successor tableaux of s produced by applications of tableaux rules.

This characterisation in conjunction with the default expansion policy from Sect. 2.3 has the downside that its Monte Carlo trees are approximately as deep as the number of proof *steps*, whereas the corresponding tableaux are as deep as the maximal proof *depth*. For example, the TPTP [26] problem PUZ035-1 permits a proof consisting of about 40 proof steps in a tableau of depth 6. The Monte Carlo tableau characterisation, however, requires building a Monte Carlo search tree with a depth close to 40, which is challenging even when using a good state reward ρ. The required tree depth can be often decreased with the tableau-specific expansion policies described in Sect. 4.3, but finding a characterisation that reliably reduces the depth of the search tree remains future work.

4   Tableau Heuristics

In Sect. 2.1, we defined two kinds of heuristics to guide Monte Carlo Tree Search, namely transition probability and state reward. In this section, we propose such heuristics, as well as a set of incomplete expansion policies.

4.1   Transition Probability

The transition probability $P(s' \mid s)$ is the probability of choosing state s' as successor state when in state s, where $s' \in \delta(s)$. P is used to bias the selection of a successor state in random simulations, as well as to determine the order of visiting previously unvisited successor states; see Algorithm 1.

When in some state s, different kinds of tableau rules might be applicable; for example α-rules and β-rules (similarly to extension and reduction rules in the connection calculus). In this work, we focus on influencing the probability of

β-rules depending on their used β-formulae, which corresponds to earlier work about choosing good extension clauses in the connection calculus [28]. Therefore, we only vary the probabilities of β-rules and attribute to all non-β-rules the same probabilities.

As transition probabilities are among of the most frequently calculated values in Monte Carlo Tree Search, the speed of this heuristic is important. The baseline heuristic is to give the same probability to all transitions, i.e. $P_1(s' \mid s) \propto 1$.

4.1.1 β-size

The β-size heuristic attributes a probability to a β-rule that is inversely proportional to the number of newly opened β-children:

$$P_\beta(s' \mid s) \propto (|\beta_o(s')| - |\beta_o(s)|)^{-1}.$$

Example 2. In state 1 of Fig. 1, it is possible to apply the β-rule to the leftmost branch with either $\neg p \vee s$ or $\neg p \vee t \vee u$. The first formula consists of two disjuncts and the second of three disjuncts, so the β-size heuristic attributes a probability proportional to $\frac{1}{2}$ to the first and $\frac{1}{3}$ to the second formula. The probabilities are normalized to sum to 1, obtaining the actual values $\frac{3}{5}$ and $\frac{2}{5}$ respectively.

4.1.2   Naive Bayesian Probability

Given the information about the formulae that were used in previous successful proofs at particular proof states, it is possible to calculate the likelihood that a given formula contributes to the current proof attempt in the current proof state. Naive Bayesian probability is used in [13] to order formulae by

$$P(l_i \mid \boldsymbol{f}) = \frac{P(l_i) P(\boldsymbol{f} \mid l_i)}{P(\boldsymbol{f})} \propto P(l_i) \prod_j P(f_j \mid l_i),$$

where l_i is a β-formula from a set $\boldsymbol{l}$ of applicable β-formulae, and $\boldsymbol{f}$ is a set of features that characterises the current tableau, such as its formulae symbols.

$P(l_i)$ and $P(f_j \mid l_i)$ as in [13] frequently yield values such that the probability of applying β-rules is magnitudes smaller than for non-β-rules, slowing down proof search. For that reason, we introduce normed probability estimates.

First, let us denote the knowledge about the usage of β-formulae in previous proofs by $F(l_i)$, which is the multiset of sets of features having occurred in conjunction with l_i when l_i was used in a proof. $|F(l_i)|$ is the total number of times that l_i was used in previous proofs.

Example 3. $F(l_1) = \{\{f_1, f_2\}, \{f_2, f_3\}\}$ means that the formula l_1 was used twice in previous proofs; once in a situation characterised by the features f_1 and f_2, and once when features f_2 and f_3 were present.

This allows us to write the normed formula probability as

$$P(l_i) = \frac{|F(l_i)|}{\max_{l_j \in l} |F(l_j)|}.$$

Using max instead of $\sum$ yields larger probabilities, while still ensuring that the probabilities do not exceed 1.

To obtain the normed conditional feature probability, we distinguish whether the feature already appeared in conjunction with the formula. In case it did, its probability is

$$P(f_j \mid l_i, \exists \boldsymbol{f}' \in F(l_i).f_j \in \boldsymbol{f}') = \frac{\sum_{\boldsymbol{f}' \in F(l_i)} 1_{\boldsymbol{f}'}(f_j)}{|F(l_i)|},$$

where $1_A(x)$ denotes the indicator function that returns 1 if $x \in A$ and 0 otherwise. In case the feature f_j has never appeared with the rule l_i before, we attribute it some minimal probability with respect to all current features $\boldsymbol{f}$ and all currently applicable rules $\boldsymbol{l}$:

$$P(f_j \mid l_i, \neg\exists \boldsymbol{f}' \in F(l_i).f_j \in \boldsymbol{f}') = \min_{f_j \in \boldsymbol{f}, l_i \in \boldsymbol{l}, \exists \boldsymbol{f}' \in F(l_i).f_j \in \boldsymbol{f}'} P(f_j \mid l_i)$$

The two definitions form a complete description of the normed feature probability $P(f_j \mid l_i)$.

4.2 State Reward

The state reward $\rho(s)$ is evaluated for the final state s of a random simulation. It estimates the likelihood of finding a proof from any ancestor of the starting node of the random simulation. Therefore, the state reward influences which regions of the Monte Carlo tree are explored.

As the state reward is only calculated once per random simulation, it can in practice be a function that is more expensive to calculate than, say, the transition probability. A baseline state reward function ρ_r returns random values between 0 and 1.

To estimate the *discrimination* of a heuristic, i.e. its ability to distinguish nodes that lead to proofs from nodes that do not, we take the ratio of the average rewards on the Monte Carlo tree branch leading to a proof and the average rewards of all Monte Carlo tree nodes.

4.2.1 β-ratio

The β-ratio reward function considers the ratio of closed β-children and all β-children in the tableau:

$$\rho_\beta(s) = \frac{|\beta_c(s)|}{|\beta(s)|}.$$

This heuristic guarantees that for a closed tableau s, the reward $\rho_\beta(s)$ is 1.

Example 4. For state 4 in Fig. 1, there are five closed β-children and seven β-children in total. Therefore, the reward ρ_β is $\frac{5}{7}$.

4.2.2   Formula Weight Reward

The formula weight reward heuristic calculates the average inverse weight (i.e. formula size) of all open β-children, encouraging tableaux with smaller formulae. Furthermore, the heuristic gives higher impact to formulae closer to the root, because the closer to the root a formula is in the tableau, the more likely it is to be chosen in other random simulations from the same starting node, therefore it is more characteristic for the starting node. For that reason, the heuristic weighs every inverse formula weight with the *depth* of the formula in the tableau, where the depth of a formula f in a tableau is expressed as $d(f)$. However, because rewards need to be normed between 0 and 1, the depth needs to be normalised. For that purpose, we introduce the concept of a *normalisation function*.

Definition 3 (Normalisation function). *A normalisation function* N_l^u : $[0, \infty) \to [u, l)$ *with* $l < u$ *is strictly increasing and fulfils* $\lim_{x \to \infty} N_l^u(x) = u$ *and* $N_l^u(0) = l$.

We choose the normalisation function $N_l^u(x) = u - \left(x + (u - l)^{-1}\right)^{-1}$. This allows us to write the final formula weight function:

$$\rho_w(s) = \frac{1}{|\beta_o(s)|} \sum_{c \in \beta_o(s)} \frac{1}{|c|} N_l^1(d(c)),$$

where $l > 0$ is a constant that determines the impact of formula depth. For example, when $l = 1$, then depth has no influence whatsoever, whereas $l \approx 0$ gives hardly any weight to formulae close to the root. In this particular ρ_w, we use the arithmetic mean, but we have also experimented with geometric and harmonic means as well as the minimum.

Example 5. The open β-children r and t in state 4 of Fig. 1 are at depth 1 and 2, respectively. Therefore, the formula weight reward of the tableau is the mean of $\frac{1}{|r|} N_l^1(1)$ and $\frac{1}{|t|} N_l^1(2)$.

This heuristic is based on similar ideas as the *pick-given ratio* popularised by Otter [23].

4.2.3   Machine-Learnt Refutability Estimate

The *refutability* of a tableau s can be estimated with knowledge how often open β-children of s were successfully refuted in previous proofs.

We call a formula refuted when all branches on which it lies are closed. A formula is unsuccessfully refuted if it is present in the tableau, but lies on at least one open branch. Note that refuted β-children are always closed (as defined in Sect. 3), but closed β-children are not necessarily refuted.

Example 6. The β-child q in state 4 of Fig. 1 is closed, but not refuted.

When statistics about previous refutations of formulae are available, we use them to estimate the refutability of formulae in the current proof search, similarly to [8]. Let $p(f)$ be the number of successful and $n(f)$ the number of unsuccessful refutations of a formula f. Then the irrefutability ratio of f is $\frac{n(f)}{p(f)+n(f)}$.

We want the irrefutability ratio to have an effect proportional to the amount of information available about previous refutation attempts. Consider the case for a formula f where $p(f) = 0$ and $n(f) = 1$. The irrefutability ratio of f then is 100%, but because we have information about only a single refutation attempt, we want to attribute less meaning to it compared to, say, a formula where $p(f) = 0$ and $n(f) = 1000$. To achieve this, we weigh the irrefutability with $N_u^l(v(p(f)+n(f)))$, where $v \geq 0$, $u \geq 0$ and $l \leq 1$ are constants. This term reflects the *confidence* in the irrefutability ratio. v determines how fast we gain confidence, u is the minimal and l is the maximal confidence.

The estimated refutability of the formula f then is the opposite of its confidence-weighted irrefutability:

$$1 - N_u^l(v(p(f) + n(f)))\frac{n(f)}{p(f) + n(f)}$$

The machine-learnt refutability estimate of a whole tableau is the mean of estimated refutabilities of the tableau's open β-children.

Example 7. The open β-children in state 4 of Fig. 1 are t and r. Assume that $p(t) = 222$, $n(t) = 115$, $p(r) = 62$, and $n(r) = 553$. Then the machine-learnt refutability estimate of the tableau is the mean of $1 - N_u^l(v \cdot 337)\frac{115}{337}$ and $1 - N_u^l(v \cdot 615)\frac{553}{615}$. In case we have total confidence in the statistics (e.g. by setting $u = l = 1$) and use the arithmetic mean, the resulting refutability estimate is 0.38.

4.3 β-minimal Expansion Policies

The default expansion policy in Sect. 2.3 creates new nodes in the Monte Carlo tree from the first state s_1 of a random simulation $[s_1, \ldots, s_D]$. This can be counterproductive in cases where the random simulation closes a subtree, but fails to find a proof in the end. In that case, keeping the successful part of the proof attempt, i.e. the closed subtree, can accelerate proof search.

This motivates β-minimal expansion policies, where new nodes are created not from the first state of a simulation, but from some state minimising a function related to β-children.

The first policy is the β-child expansion policy, which chooses the state with fewest open β-children, i.e., $\min_i |\beta_o(s_i)|$.

The second policy is the β-parent expansion policy, which chooses the state with fewest parents of open β-children, i.e. $\min_i \left| \bigcup_{o \in \beta_o(s_i)} p(o) \right|$, where $p(s)$ denotes the parent of a node s.

Similarly to restricted backtracking [19], the β-minimal expansion policies lose completeness, but can in practice perform significantly better than complete strategies.

Example 8. In the proof search in Fig. 1, the proof attempt failed. We assume that the proof search started from a Monte Carlo node n containing state 1. The default expansion policy would add a new node corresponding to state 2 as child tree node of n to the Monte Carlo tree. However, this would discard the closed subtree found in state 3. In contrast, the β-child expansion policy compares the open β-children in all successor states of state 1: State 2 has three open β-children (s, q, and r), state 3 has two (q and r) and state 4 has two as well (t and r). State 3 and 4 are therefore minimal, in which case the first of them (i.e. state 3) is used as state for a new Monte Carlo leaf node that is added as child tree node of n to the Monte Carlo tree.

5   Implementation

We implemented the proposed Monte Carlo Tableau calculus in the OCaml version [14] of leanCoP [18]. The implementation and experimental data are available at: http://cl-informatik.uibk.ac.at/users/mfaerber/cade-26.html. In the rest of this paper, we refer to the OCaml version of leanCoP as leanCoP.

Monte Carlo proof search can be used to *advise* a *base prover*: The proof search is conducted by a base prover such as leanCoP. When the base prover has a choice between different applicable proof rules, it starts the advisor, i.e. Monte Carlo proof search, which returns after a certain number of iterations an order on the proof rules to be tried by the base prover. This order is based on the average Monte Carlo rewards achieved for each rule. Furthermore, when Monte Carlo proof search finds proofs while establishing the proof rule order, the proofs are used directly by the base prover. In the extreme case, when setting the number of Monte Carlo iterations to ∞, the whole proof search is done by Monte Carlo proof search and the base prover is only responsible for starting it and printing the proof. We refer to our implementation of Monte Carlo proof search as advisor for leanCoP as *Monte Carlo Prover*.

In contrast to leanCoP, Monte Carlo proof search does not require iterative deepening. Instead, an important parameter is the simulation depth D as shown in Sect. 2.3, which determines the length of random simulations.

leanCoP is equipped with a set of strategies, where each strategy consists of a set of options, such as whether to use definitional clausal normal form. A strategy schedule tries different strategies for a defined amount of time until a strategy succeeds. One of the most influential developments in leanCoP was restricted backtracking [19], which discards other possibilities to close a subtree once it has been closed. See Fig. 2 for a comparison of the complete strategy with the restricted backtracking strategy, as well as an illustration of a Monte Carlo search.

In the next section, we evaluate how well our Monte Carlo prover performs in comparison to single leanCoP strategies.

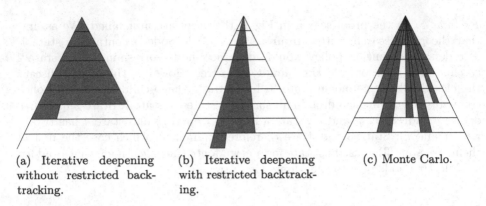

(a) Iterative deepening without restricted backtracking.

(b) Iterative deepening with restricted backtracking.

(c) Monte Carlo.

Fig. 2. The two main leanCoP strategies compared with Monte Carlo proof search.

6 Evaluation

In this section, we evaluate the Monte Carlo prover described in Sect. 5. We first describe the dataset and the evaluation parameters. Then we evaluate the different heuristics given in Sect. 4, as well as the influence of several numeric parameters. Finally, we show our best obtained Monte Carlo configuration and compare it to leanCoP.

Experimental Setup. We used the bushy version of the MPTP2078 dataset [1], which is particularly valuable for our machine learning algorithms as it provides consistent symbols over all problems. To generate training data for the machine learning heuristics, we ran leanCoP for 60 s on all the MPTP2078 problems, using a strategy schedule with three strategies, including a restricted backtracking and a complete strategy. The outcome of the training runs were formula usability data for the Naive Bayes heuristic in Sect. 4.1.2 as well as formula refutability data for the heuristic in Sect. 4.2.3.

For the main evaluation, we used definitional classification and a timeout of 10 s per problem for both leanCoP and the Monte Carlo prover, where the 10 s timeout is also used for the MPTP2078 evaluation in [14]. In that setting, leanCoP solves 509 problems with restricted backtracking and 388 without, the union being 562 problems. In the remainder of this paper, leanCoP refers to the restricted backtracking strategy of leanCoP.

For the Monte Carlo prover, we used the following initial parameters:

- Maximal simulation depth D: 50
- Exploration constant C_p: 1 (see Sect. 2.3)
- Transition probability: β-size (see Sect. 4.1.1)
- State reward: β-ratio (see Sect. 4.2.1)
- Depth attenuation for formula weight reward: 0 (see Sect. 4.2.2)
- Refutability mean: min (see Sect. 4.2.3)
- Refutability confidence velocity: 1 (see Sect. 4.2.3)

- Minimal/maximal refutability confidence: 0/1 (see Sect. 4.2.3)
- Expansion policy: β-child expansion policy (see Sect. 4.3)

Heuristics Influence. We evaluated the Monte Carlo prover with a set of configurations where each configuration deviates by one heuristic from the initial parameters. For every configuration, we collected the set of solved problems. Furthermore, we collected the problems solved by all Monte Carlo configurations, amounting to 196 problems. On these problems, for all Monte Carlo configurations, we evaluated the average number of MCTS iterations and MCTS simulation steps, as well as the average reward discrimination; see Table 1.

The machine-learnt reward heuristic performs best, with a very good discrimination rate of 2.30. Surprisingly, the random reward heuristic solves only three problems less, despite its worse discrimination.

The Bayesian transition probability shows very poor performance. The β-size heuristic is the winner for transition probability.

The β-parent expansion policy outperforms the default expansion policy by 20 problems, i.e. 6%.

Table 1. Comparison of Monte Carlo heuristics. Iterations, simulation steps and discrimination ratio are averages on the 196 problems solved by all configurations.

Configuration	Iterations	Sim. steps	Discr.	Solved
Base	116.46	1389.82	1.37	332
Random reward	104.88	1167.98	1.19	364
Formula weight reward	108.13	1268.88	1.12	334
ML reward	108.52	1151.61	**2.30**	**367**
Bayes P	528.39	8014.03	1.35	248
Constant P	949.62	17539.59	1.31	237
β-parent exp.	224.72	2769.12	1.40	348
Default exp.	371.81	4793.58	1.38	328

Parameter Influence. We identified three numeric parameters to be highly influential for proof search; namely the simulation depth D, the exploration constant C_p, and the maximal number of MCTS iterations per base prover step. We evaluated a large range of values for these parameters, keeping the remaining parameters fixed to the standard values. The results are shown in Fig. 3.

We achieve the highest performance of the Monte Carlo prover when using it as an advisor for a base prover. From Fig. 3a, it becomes clear that the Monte Carlo prover is most useful when given between 20 and 40 iterations per base prover step. Below that mark, the reward estimates are too imprecise, and above that mark, the reward precision increases only marginally, compared to the time spent in the MCTS prover.

The higher the maximal simulation depth D (see Fig. 3b), the more time the prover spends looking for proofs at less promising higher depths. Figure 3c shows that the average number of simulation steps decreases with increasing D. This indicates that at higher simulation depths, the computational effort to calculate the set of possible steps increases.

Figure 3d shows the number of solved problems for the β-ratio and the machine-learnt state evaluation heuristics as function of the exploration constant C_p. For a good state reward heuristic, one expects in such a graph a local optimum, where exploration and exploitation combine each other best. As one can see, this is given for the machine-learnt heuristic at $C_p \approx 0.75$, whereas the curve for the β-ratio heuristic does not expose such an optimum.

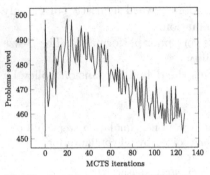

(a) Maximal number of MCTS iterations.

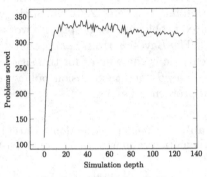

(b) Simulation depth D.

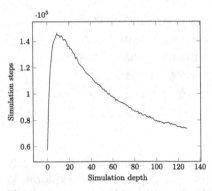

(c) Simulation steps / Simulation depth.

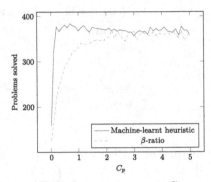

(d) Exploration constant C_p.

Fig. 3. Parameter influence.

Best Found Monte Carlo Configuration. Our best found configuration MC^+ for the Monte Carlo prover uses the arithmetic mean for the ML reward, a maximal number of 27 MCTS iterations and a simulation depth of 20. Interestingly, is has a discrimination ratio of only 1.07, which suggests that a high discrimination ratio indicates good performance, but is not absolutely necessary to achieve it.

MC$^+$ performs on average 902 times more inferences in MCTS than in the base prover. Furthermore, for the problems solved both by leanCoP and by MC$^+$, leanCoP takes on average 21698 inferences, while MC$^+$ takes 20243 inferences (sum of base prover + MCTS inferences).

MC$^+$ solves 538 problems, compared to 509 by leanCoP. Of the 538 problems, 90 problems were previously not solved by leanCoP. The union of MC$^+$ and leanCoP solves 599 problems, compared to 531 problems solved by leanCoP with a timeout of 20 s. That means that we solve 12.8% more problems. Furthermore, MC$^+$ proves more problems than leanCoP when given only half the time.

Prover	Timeout [s]	Solved problems
leanCoP	10	509
MC$^+$	10	538
leanCoP + MC$^+$	10 + 10	599
leanCoP	20	531

7 Conclusion

We have proposed a combination of Monte Carlo Tree Search and tableau automated theorem proving. MCTS provides a theoretically founded fine-grained mechanism to control the search space of tableau-based theorem provers based on random sampling and state evaluation heuristics, which might eventually even replace iterative deepening. We have shown that a fast rollout policy combined with a machine-learnt state evaluation heuristic and a custom expansion policy produce the best results. The strength of the current system has turned out to be its function as advisor for existing provers, demonstrated by our integration into leanCoP. This opens a wide space of future work, profiting from the ongoing research in MCTS; examples include self-updating reward heuristics, adaptive simulation depths, automatic parameter tuning, and different characterisations of tableau search or expansion policies such as AMAF to produce more shallow Monte Carlo trees. Furthermore, identifying controversial choices in the base prover would allow using the Monte Carlo prover as advisor more efficiently. Finally, neural networks could be used as state reward heuristics.

Acknowledgements. We thank the anonymous CPP and CADE referees for their valuable comments on previous versions of this paper. This work has been supported by the Austrian Science Fund (FWF) grant P26201 and the European Research Council (ERC) grants no. 649043 *AI4REASON* and no. 714034 *SMART*.

References

1. Alama, J., Heskes, T., Kühlwein, D., Tsivtsivadze, E., Urban, J.: Premise selection for mathematics by corpus analysis and kernel methods. J. Autom. Reasoning **52**(2), 191–213 (2014)
2. Alama, J., Kühlwein, D., Urban, J.: Automated and human proofs in general mathematics: an initial comparison. In: Bjørner, N., Voronkov, A. (eds.) LPAR 2012. LNCS, vol. 7180, pp. 37–45. Springer, Heidelberg (2012). doi:10.1007/978-3-642-28717-6_6
3. Barrett, C., Conway, C.L., Deters, M., Hadarean, L., Jovanović, D., King, T., Reynolds, A., Tinelli, C.: CVC4. In: Gopalakrishnan, G., Qadeer, S. (eds.) CAV 2011. LNCS, vol. 6806, pp. 171–177. Springer, Heidelberg (2011). doi:10.1007/978-3-642-22110-1_14
4. Biere, A., Dragan, I., Kovács, L., Voronkov, A.: Experimenting with SAT solvers in Vampire. In: Gelbukh, A., Espinoza, F.C., Galicia-Haro, S.N. (eds.) MICAI 2014. LNCS, vol. 8856, pp. 431–442. Springer, Cham (2014). doi:10.1007/978-3-319-13647-9_39
5. Blanchette, J.C., Kaliszyk, C., Paulson, L.C., Urban, J.: Hammering towards QED. J. Formaliz. Reasoning **9**(1), 101–148 (2016)
6. Brown, C.E.: Satallax: an automatic higher-order prover. In: Gramlich, B., Miller, D., Sattler, U. (eds.) IJCAR 2012. LNCS (LNAI), vol. 7364, pp. 111–117. Springer, Heidelberg (2012). doi:10.1007/978-3-642-31365-3_11
7. Browne, C., Powley, E.J., Whitehouse, D., Lucas, S.M., Cowling, P.I., Rohlfshagen, P., Tavener, S., Liebana, D.P., Samothrakis, S., Colton, S.: A survey of Monte Carlo tree search methods. IEEE Trans. Comput. Intell. AI Games **4**(1), 1–43 (2012)
8. Färber, M., Brown, C.E.: Internal guidance for Satallax. In: Olivetti and Tiwari [17], pp. 349–361
9. Gelly, S., Silver, D.: Combining online and offline knowledge in UCT. In: Ghahramani, Z. (ed.) ICML, vol. 227, pp. 273–280. ACM, New York (2007)
10. Hähnle, R.: Tableaux and related methods. In: Robinson, J.A., Voronkov, A. (eds.) Handbook of Automated Reasoning, vol. 2, pp. 100–178. Elsevier and MIT Press, New York (2001)
11. Hoder, K., Reger, G., Suda, M., Voronkov, A.: Selecting the selection. In: Olivetti and Tiwari [17], pp. 313–329
12. Kaliszyk, C., Schulz, S., Urban, J., Vyskočil, J.: System description: E.T. 0.1. In: Felty, A.P., Middeldorp, A. (eds.) CADE 2015. LNCS (LNAI), vol. 9195, pp. 389–398. Springer, Cham (2015). doi:10.1007/978-3-319-21401-6_27
13. Kaliszyk, C., Urban, J.: FEMaLeCoP: fairly efficient machine learning connection prover. In: Davis, M., Fehnker, A., McIver, A., Voronkov, A. (eds.) LPAR 2015. LNCS, vol. 9450, pp. 88–96. Springer, Heidelberg (2015). doi:10.1007/978-3-662-48899-7_7
14. Kaliszyk, C., Urban, J., Vyskocil, J.: Certified connection tableaux proofs for HOL Light and TPTP. In: Leroy, X., Tiu, A. (eds.) CPP, pp. 59–66. ACM, New York (2015)
15. Kocsis, L., Szepesvári, C.: Bandit based Monte-Carlo planning. In: Fürnkranz, J., Scheffer, T., Spiliopoulou, M. (eds.) ECML 2006. LNCS (LNAI), vol. 4212, pp. 282–293. Springer, Heidelberg (2006). doi:10.1007/11871842_29
16. Korovin, K.: Inst-Gen – a modular approach to instantiation-based automated reasoning. In: Voronkov, A., Weidenbach, C. (eds.) Ganzinger Festschrift. LNCS, vol. 7797, pp. 239–270. Springer, Heidelberg (2013). doi:10.1007/978-3-642-37651-1_10

17. Olivetti, N., Tiwari, A. (eds.): IJCAR 2016. LNCS (LNAI), vol. 9706. Springer, Cham (2016). doi:10.1007/978-3-319-40229-1
18. Otten, J.: leanCoP 2.0 and ileanCoP 1.2: high performance lean theorem proving in classical and intuitionistic logic (system descriptions). In: Armando, A., Baumgartner, P., Dowek, G. (eds.) IJCAR 2008. LNCS (LNAI), vol. 5195, pp. 283–291. Springer, Heidelberg (2008). doi:10.1007/978-3-540-71070-7_23
19. Otten, J.: Restricting backtracking in connection calculi. AI Commun. 23(2–3), 159–182 (2010)
20. Otten, J.: nanoCoP: a non-clausal connection prover. In: Olivetti and Tiwari [17], pp. 302–312
21. Rosin, C.D.: Nested rollout policy adaptation for Monte Carlo tree search. In: Walsh, T. (ed.) IJCAI, pp. 649–654. IJCAI/AAAI, New York (2011)
22. Schadd, M.P.D., Winands, M.H.M., Tak, M.J.W., Uiterwijk, J.W.H.M.: Single-player Monte-Carlo tree search for SameGame. Knowl.-Based Syst. 34, 3–11 (2012)
23. Schulz, S.: E - a brainiac theorem prover. AI Commun. 15(2–3), 111–126 (2002)
24. Schulz, S.: System description: E 1.8. In: McMillan, K., Middeldorp, A., Voronkov, A. (eds.) LPAR 2013. LNCS, vol. 8312, pp. 735–743. Springer, Heidelberg (2013). doi:10.1007/978-3-642-45221-5_49
25. Silver, D., Huang, A., Maddison, C.J., Guez, A., Sifre, L., van den Driessche, G., Schrittwieser, J., Antonoglou, I., Panneershelvam, V., Lanctot, M., Dieleman, S., Grewe, D., Nham, J., Kalchbrenner, N., Sutskever, I., Lillicrap, T., Leach, M., Kavukcuoglu, K., Graepel, T., Hassabis, D.: Mastering the game of Go with deep neural networks and tree search. Nature 529, 484–503 (2016)
26. Sutcliffe, G.: The 6th IJCAR automated theorem proving system competition - CASC-J6. AI Commun. 26(2), 211–223 (2013)
27. Urban, J., Hoder, K., Voronkov, A.: Evaluation of automated theorem proving on the Mizar Mathematical Library. In: Fukuda, K., van der Hoeven, J., Joswig, M., Takayama, N. (eds.) ICMS 2010. LNCS, vol. 6327, pp. 155–166. Springer, Heidelberg (2010). doi:10.1007/978-3-642-15582-6_30
28. Urban, J., Vyskočil, J., Štěpánek, P.: MaLeCoP machine learning connection prover. In: Brünnler, K., Metcalfe, G. (eds.) TABLEAUX 2011. LNCS (LNAI), vol. 6793, pp. 263–277. Springer, Heidelberg (2011). doi:10.1007/978-3-642-22119-4_21
29. Wisniewski, M., Steen, A., Benzmüller, C.: LEOPARD — a generic platform for the implementation of higher-order reasoners. In: Kerber, M., Carette, J., Kaliszyk, C., Rabe, F., Sorge, V. (eds.) CICM 2015. LNCS, vol. 9150, pp. 325–330. Springer, Cham (2015). doi:10.1007/978-3-319-20615-8_22

Author Index